# SAT®
# Prep Plus
# 2020

**Editor-in-Chief**
Alexandra Strelka, MA

**Contributing Editors**
Dr. Brandon Deason, MD; M. Dominic Eggert; Kathryn Sollenberger, MEd; Glen Stohr, JD

**Special thanks to our faculty authors and reviewers**
Michael Cook; Christopher Cosci; Boris Dvorkin; John Evans; Jack Hayes; Rebecca Knauer; Jo L'Abbate; Bird Marathe; Karen McCulloch; Melissa McLaughlin; Gail Rivers; Anne Marie Salloum; Jason Selzer; Gordon Spector; Caroline Sykes; Bob Verini, MFA; Bonnie Wang; and Ethan Weber

**Additional special thanks to**
Laura Aitcheson; Matthew Callan; Paula L. Fleming, MA, MBA; Joanna Graham; Adam Grey; Rebekah Hawthorne; Rebecca Knauer; Abnia Loriston, MEd; Mandy Luk; Kristin Murner, PhD and the countless others who made this project possible.

SAT® is a trademark registered and/or owned by the College Board, which was not involved in the production of, and does not endorse, this product.

This publication is designed to provide accurate information in regard to the subject matter covered as of its publication date, with the understanding that knowledge and best practice constantly evolve. The publisher is not engaged in rendering medical, legal, accounting, or other professional service. If medical or legal advice or other expert assistance is required, the services of a competent professional should be sought. This publication is not intended for use in clinical practice or the delivery of medical care. To the fullest extent of the law, neither the Publisher nor the Editors assume any liability for any injury and/or damage to persons or property arising out of or related to any use of the material contained in this book.

# TABLE OF CONTENTS

GO ONLINE

*www.kaptest.com/ moreonline*

# How to Use This Book

Congratulations on taking this important step in your college admissions process! By studying with Kaplan, you'll maximize your score on the SAT, a major factor in your overall college application.

Our experience shows that the greatest SAT score increases result from active engagement in the preparation process. Kaplan will give you direction, focus your preparation, and teach you the specific skills and effective test-taking strategies you need to know for the SAT. We will help you achieve your top performance on test day, but your effort is crucial. The more you invest in preparing for the SAT, the greater your chances of achieving your target score and getting into your top-choice college.

**Are you registered for the SAT?** Kaplan cannot register you for the official SAT. If you have not already registered for the upcoming SAT, talk to your high school guidance counselor or visit the College Board's website at www.collegeboard.org to register online and for information on registration deadlines, test sites, accommodations for students with disabilities, and fees.

## Practice Tests

Kaplan's practice tests are just like the actual SAT. By taking a practice exam you will prepare yourself for the actual test day experience. Two of your practice tests are included in this book and three more can be accessed online. See the "Digital Resources" section below to learn how to access your online practice tests.

## Chapter Organization

The chapters in this book follow a standard format to make this book as easy to use as possible. Most chapters in this book start with a section called "How Much Do You Know?" that allows you to get a sense of how comfortable you already are with the material in the chapter. Answers and explanations follow immediately in the "Check Your Work" section. Each lesson in a chapter starts with a question typical of the way the SAT tests a given topic and ends with a set of practice questions called "Try on Your Own." There is yet another practice set at the end of each chapter called "How Much Have You Learned?" to reinforce the concepts explained in the chapter. Answers and Explanations for the "Try on Your Own" and "How Much Have You Learned?" sections are provided at the end of each chapter for easy reference.

## Smartpoints®

Different topics are worth different numbers of points on the SAT because they show up more or less frequently in questions. By studying the information released by the College Board, Kaplan has been able to determine how often certain topics are likely to appear on the SAT, and therefore how many points these topics are worth on test day. If you master a given topic, you can expect to earn the corresponding number of SmartPoints® on test day.

We have used a 600-point scale for Smartpoints® because that's the number of points you can earn within the Math and Verbal subscores: the SAT scoring scale is 200–800, so there are $800 - 200 = 600$ points to be earned within each major section of the test. The breakdown of SmartPoints® for Math, Reading, and Writing & Language are summarized in the following tables. Keep in mind that these values are approximate because testing administrations differ.

| Math | | |
|---|---|---|
| **SmartPoints® Category** | **# of Points** | **Sub-Categories** |
| Linear Equations | 110 | Linear equations, linear graphs, word problems |
| Functions | 105 | Functions, graphs of functions, functions in word problems |
| Ratios, Proportions, and Percents | 70 | Setting up a proportion to solve for an unknown, unit conversion, calculating percent and percent change |
| Geometry | 65 | Triangles, circles, 3-dimensional figures |
| Quadratics | 60 | Quadratic equations, parabolas, modeling data, mixed systems of equations |
| Statistics and Probability | 50 | Descriptive statistics, probability, tables and charts, data samples |
| Systems of Linear Equations | 45 | Systems of equations, number of possible solutions |
| Inequalities | 35 | Inequalities, graphical representations of inequalities |
| Scatterplots | 25 | Scatterplots, lines of best fit, modeling data |
| Exponents, Radicals, Polynomials, and Radical Expressions | 25 | Exponents, radicals, polynomial operations, graphs of polynomials, modeling growth and decay, rational expressions/equations |
| Imaginary Numbers | 5 | Adding, subtracting, multiplying, and dividing complex numbers |
| Trigonometry | 5 | Sine, cosine, tangent |
| **TOTAL** | **600** | |

| Reading | | |
|---|---|---|
| **SmartPoints® Category** | **# of Points** | **Sub-Categories** |
| Inference questions | 90 | Making deductions |
| Command of Evidence questions | 60 | Citing evidence |
| Detail questions | 45 | Finding details in the text |
| Vocab-in-Context questions | 45 | Determining the meaning of a word as it is used in the passage |
| Function questions | 40 | Explaining *why* the author included a certain detail |
| Global questions | 20 | Determining Central Ideas and Themes, Summarizing |
| **TOTAL** | **300** | |

| Writing & Language | | |
|---|---|---|
| SmartPoints® Category | # of Points | Sub-Categories |
| Sentence Structure | 85 | Correcting run-ons and fragments, using correct conjunctions, punctuation |
| Development | 85 | Precision, relevance, revising text |
| Agreement | 60 | Subject-verb agreement, verb tense, pronoun agreement, modifiers, idioms |
| Organization | 40 | Transitions, sentence placement |
| Conciseness | 20 | Avoiding wordiness and redundancy |
| Graphs | 10 | Drawing inferences from a graph included with a passage |
| **TOTAL** | **300** | |

## Digital Resources

To access the online resources that accompany this book, which include three full-length practice tests, extra practice questions, and study planning guidance, follow the steps below:

GO ONLINE

*www.kaptest.com/ moreonline*

1. Go to: kaptest.com/moreonline

2. Have this book available as you complete the on-screen instructions.

PART 1

# The SAT and You

# CHAPTER 1

# Inside the SAT

## SAT Structure

The SAT, like any standardized test, is predictable. The more comfortable you are with the test structure, the more confidently you will approach each question type, thus maximizing your score.

The SAT is 3 hours long, or 3 hours and 50 minutes long if you choose to complete the optional Essay Test. The SAT is made up of mostly multiple-choice questions that test two subject areas: Evidence-Based Reading and Writing, and Math. The former is broken into a Reading Test and a Writing and Language Test.

| Test | Allotted Time (minutes) | Question Count |
|------|------------------------|----------------|
| Reading | 65 | 52 |
| Writing and Language | 35 | 44 |
| Math | 80 | 58 |
| Essay (optional) | 50 | 1 |
| Total | 180 OR 230 (w/Essay) | 154 OR 155 (w/Essay) |

If you choose not to write the essay, you may also see an additional 20-minute multiple-choice section, but this is fairly rare.

## SAT Scoring

SAT scoring can be pretty complex. You will receive one score ranging from 200–800 for Evidence-Based Reading and Writing and another for Math. Your overall SAT score will range from 400–1600 and is calculated by adding these two scores together. You will receive a separate score for the Essay Test, if you choose to take it.

In addition to your overall scores, you will receive subscores that provide a deeper analysis of your SAT performance. The SAT also gives you a percentile ranking, which allows you to compare your scores with those of other test takers. For example, a student who scored in the 63rd percentile did better than 63 percent of all others who took that test.

The scores you need depend primarily on which colleges you are planning to apply to. For example, if you want to attend an engineering school, you'll typically need a higher math score than if you want to attend a liberal arts college. Research the colleges you are interested in, find out what scores they require, and structure your SAT studying accordingly.

## How to Maximize Your Score

What is most important to remember while taking the test is that maximizing all the various scores and subscores depends on getting the most points you can out of every section. You'll find advice on test-taking strategies below and in the section management chapters at the end of the Math, Reading, and Writing and Language sections of this book. However, if you still have a meaningful amount of time to prepare for the SAT, the best advice we can give you is to improve the skills you need to answer Math and Verbal questions correctly and efficiently. That's what this book is for. Use it in any order you like; you don't need to start with Math. But do use it. Read the instructional text for those topics you feel weak in and work your way through the practice questions. There are hundreds of them in this book, and they are very similar to those that you will see on test day. Practice will not only improve your skills; it will also raise your confidence, and that's very important to test-day success.

## Where and When to Take the SAT

The SAT is offered every year on multiple Saturday test dates. Typically, exams are offered in August, October, November, December, March, May, and June. You can take the SAT multiple times. Some states offer special administrations of the SAT on different dates. Sunday tests are available by request for students requiring religious or other exemptions. The SAT is administered at high schools around the country that serve as testing centers. Your high school may or may not be a testing center. Check www.collegeboard.org for a list of testing centers near you. Note that you must register for the SAT approximately one month in advance to avoid paying a late fee. Some SAT test dates also offer SAT Subject Tests. You may not take both the SAT and the Subject Tests in a single sitting.

## The SAT Math Test

The SAT Math Test is broken down into a calculator section and a no-calculator section. Questions across the sections consist of multiple-choice, student-produced response (Grid-in), and more comprehensive multi-part question sets.

|  | No-Calculator Section | Calculator Section | Total |
|---|---|---|---|
| **Duration (minutes)** | 25 | 55 | 80 |
| **Multiple-choice** | 15 | 30 | 45 |
| **Grid-in** | 5 | 8 | 13 |
| **Total Questions** | 20 | 38 | 58 |

The SAT Math Test is divided into four content areas: Heart of Algebra, Problem Solving and Data Analysis, Passport to Advanced Math, and Additional Topics in Math.

| SAT Math Test Content Area Distribution | |
| --- | --- |
| **Heart of Algebra** (19 questions) | Analyzing and solving equations and systems of equations; creating expressions, equations, and inequalities to represent relationships between quantities and to solve problems; rearranging and interpreting formulas |
| **Problem Solving and Data Analysis** (17 questions) | Creating and analyzing relationships using ratios, proportions, percentages, and units; describing relationships shown graphically; summarizing qualitative and quantitative data |
| **Passport to Advanced Math** (16 questions) | Using function notation; creating, analyzing, and solving quadratic and higher-order equations; manipulating polynomials to solve problems |
| **Additional Topics in Math** (6 questions) | Making area and volume calculations in context; investigating lines, angles, triangles, and circles using theorems; working with trigonometric functions and complex numbers |

A few math questions might look like something you'd expect to see on a science or history test. These "crossover" questions are designed to test your ability to use math in real-world scenarios. There are a total of 18 "crossover" questions that will contribute to subscores that span multiple tests. Nine of the questions will contribute to the Analysis in Science subscore, and 9 will contribute to the Analysis in History/Social Studies subscore.

## The SAT Reading Test

The SAT Reading Test will focus on your comprehension and reasoning skills when you are presented with challenging extended prose passages taken from a variety of content areas.

| SAT Reading Test Overview | |
| --- | --- |
| **Timing** | 65 minutes |
| **Questions** | 52 passage-based multiple-choice questions |
| **Passages** | 4 single passages; 1 set of paired passages |
| **Passage Length** | 500–750 words per passage or passage set |

Passages will draw from U.S. and World Literature, History/Social Studies, and Science. One set of History/Social Studies or Science passages will be paired. History/Social Studies and Science passages can also be accompanied by graphical representations of data such as charts, graphs, tables, and so on.

| Reading Test Passage Types | |
| --- | --- |
| **U.S. and World Literature** | 1 passage with 10 questions |
| **History/Social Studies** | 2 passages or 1 passage and 1 paired-passage set with 10–11 questions each |
| **Science** | 2 passages or 1 passage and 1 paired-passage set with 10–11 questions each |

The multiple-choice questions for each passage will be arranged with main idea questions at the beginning of the set so that you can consider the entire passage before answering questions about details.

| Skills Tested by Reading Test Questions | |
|---|---|
| **Reading for Detail** | Finding details in the passage, citing textual evidence |
| **Summarizing** | Determining central ideas and themes, understanding how a passage is structured, understanding relationships |
| **Drawing Inferences** | Understanding relationships, drawing conclusions from facts stated in a passage, interpreting words and phrases in context |
| **Rhetorical Analysis** | Analyzing word choice, analyzing point of view, determining why a fact is included, analyzing arguments |
| **Synthesis** | Analyzing multiple texts, analyzing quantitative information |

## The SAT Writing and Language Test

The SAT Writing and Language Test will focus on your ability to revise and edit text from a range of content areas.

| SAT Writing and Language Test Overview | |
|---|---|
| **Timing** | 35 minutes |
| **Questions** | 44 passage-based, multiple-choice questions |
| **Passages** | 4 single passages with 11 questions each |
| **Passage Length** | 400–450 words per passage |

The SAT Writing and Language Test will contain four single passages, one from each of the following subject areas: Careers, Humanities, History/Social Studies, and Science.

| Writing and Language Passage Types | |
|---|---|
| **Careers** | Hot topics in "major fields of work" such as information technology and health care |
| **Humanities** | Texts about literature, art, history, music, and philosophy pertaining to human culture |
| **History/ Social Studies** | Discussion of historical or social sciences topics such as anthropology, communication studies, economics, education, human geography, law, linguistics, political science, psychology, and sociology |
| **Science** | Exploration of concepts, findings, and discoveries in the natural sciences including Earth science, biology, chemistry, and physics |

Passages will also vary in the "type" of text. A passage can be an argument, an informative or explanatory text, or a nonfiction narrative.

| Writing and Language Passage Text Type Distribution | |
|---|---|
| **Argument** | 1–2 passages |
| **Informative/Explanatory Text** | 1–2 passages |
| **Nonfiction Narrative** | 1 passage |

Some passages and/or questions will refer to one or more data tables or charts. Questions associated with these graphics will ask you to revise and edit the passage based on the data presented in the graphic.

The most prevalent question format on the SAT Writing and Language Test will ask you to choose the best of three alternatives to an underlined portion of the passage or to decide that the current version is the best option. You will be asked to improve the development, organization, and diction in the passages to ensure they conform to conventional standards of English grammar, usage, and style.

| Skills Tested by Writing and Language Test Questions | |
| --- | --- |
| **Expression of Ideas** (24 questions) | Organization and development of ideas |
| **Standard English Conventions** (20 questions) | Sentence structure, conventions of usage, and conventions of punctuation |

## The SAT Essay Test (Optional)

The SAT Essay Test assesses your college and career readiness. The essay tests your ability to read and analyze a high-quality source document. Your goal is to write a coherent analysis for the source supported with critical reasoning and evidence from the given text.

The SAT Essay Test features an argumentative source text of 650–750 words aimed toward a large audience. Passages will examine ideas, debates, and shifts in the arts and sciences as well as civic, cultural, and political life. Rather than having a simple for/against structure, these passages will be nuanced and will relate views on complex subjects. These passages will also be logical in their structure and reasoning.

It is important to note that prior knowledge is not required.

The SAT Essay Test prompt will ask you to explain how the presented passage's author builds an argument to convince an audience. In writing your essay, you may analyze elements such as the author's use of evidence, reasoning, style, and persuasion; you will not be limited to those elements listed, however.

Rather than writing about whether you agree or disagree with the presented argument, you will write an essay in which you analyze *how* the author makes an argument.

The SAT Essay Test will be broken down into three categories for scoring: Reading, Analysis, and Writing. Each of these elements will be scored on a scale of 1–4 by two graders, for a total score of 2–8 for each category.

## Test-Taking Strategies

You have already learned about the overall structure of the SAT as well as the structure of the three main areas it entails: Reading, Writing and Language, and Math. The strategies outlined in this section can be applied to any of these tests.

The SAT is different from the tests you are used to taking in school. The good news is that you can use the SAT's particular structure to your advantage.

For example, on a test given in school, you probably go through the questions in order. You spend more time on the harder questions than on the easier ones because harder questions are usually worth more points. You also probably show your work because your teacher tells you that how you approach a question is as important as getting the correct answer.

This approach is not optimal for the SAT. On the SAT, you benefit from moving around within a section if you come across tough questions, because the harder questions are worth the same number of points as the easier questions. Similarly, showing your work is unimportant. It doesn't matter how you arrive at the correct answer—only that you bubble in the correct answer choice.

## Strategy #1: Triaging the Test

You do not need to complete questions on the SAT in order. Every student has different strengths and should attack the test with those strengths in mind. Your main objective on the SAT should be to score as many points as you can. While approaching questions out of order may seem counterintuitive, it is a surefire way to achieve your best score.

Just remember, you can skip around within each section, but you cannot work on a section other than the one you've been instructed to work on.

To triage a section effectively, do the following:

- First, work through all the easy questions that you can do quickly. Skip questions that are hard or time-consuming. For the Reading Test, start with the passage you find most manageable and work toward the one you find most challenging. You do not need to go in order.
- Second, work through the questions that are doable but time-consuming.
- Third, work through the hard questions.

A Letter of the Day is an answer choice letter (A, B, C, or D) that you choose before test day to select for questions you guess on.

## Strategy #2: Elimination

Even though there is no wrong-answer penalty on the SAT, Elimination is still a crucial strategy. If you can determine that one or more answer choices are definitely incorrect, you can increase your chances of getting the right answer by paring the selection down.

To eliminate answer choices, do the following:

- Read each answer choice.
- Cross out the answer choices that are incorrect.
- There is no wrong-answer penalty, so take your best guess.

## Strategy #3: Strategic Guessing

Each multiple-choice question on the SAT has four answer choices and no wrong-answer penalty. That means if you have no idea how to approach a question, you have a 25 percent chance of randomly choosing the correct answer. Even though there's a 75 percent chance of selecting the incorrect answer, you won't lose any points for doing so. The worst that can happen on the SAT is that you'll earn zero points on a question, which means you should *always* at least take a guess, even when you have no idea what to do.

When guessing on a question, do the following:

- Try to strategically eliminate answer choices before guessing.
- If you run out of time, or have no idea what a question is asking, pick a Letter of the Day.
- If a question is taking too long, skip it and guess. Spend your time on those questions that you know how to do; don't allow yourself to get bogged down in fighting it out with a question that is too time-consuming.

# PART 2

# SAT Math

# CHAPTER 2

# Prerequisite Skills and Calculator Use

**LEARNING OBJECTIVES**

After completing this chapter, you will be able to:

- Identify skills necessary to obtain the full benefits of the Math sections of this book
- Use efficiency tips to boost your test-day speed
- Distinguish between questions that need a calculator and questions in which manual calculations are more efficient

## Math Fundamentals

**LEARNING OBJECTIVES**

After this lesson, you will be able to:

- Identify skills necessary to obtain the full benefits of the Math sections of this book
- Use efficiency tips to boost your test-day speed

### Prerequisites

This book focuses on the skills that are tested on the SAT. It assumes a working knowledge of arithmetic, algebra, and geometry. Before you dive into the subsequent chapters where you'll try testlike questions, there are a number of concepts—ranging from basic arithmetic to geometry—that you should master. The following sections contain a brief review of these concepts.

## Algebra and Arithmetic

**Order of operations** is one of the most fundamental of all arithmetic rules. A well-known mnemonic device for remembering this order is PEMDAS: Please Excuse My Dear Aunt Sally. This translates to Parentheses, Exponents, Multiplication/Division, Addition/Subtraction. Perform multiplication and division from left to right (even if it means division before multiplication) and treat addition and subtraction the same way:

$$(14 - 4 \div 2)^2 - 3 + (2 - 1)$$
$$= (14 - 2)^2 - 3 + (1)$$
$$= 12^2 - 3 + 1$$
$$= 144 - 3 + 1$$
$$= 141 + 1$$
$$= 142$$

Three basic properties of number (and variable) manipulation—commutative, associative, and distributive—will assist you with algebra on test day:

- **Commutative:** Numbers can swap places and still provide the same mathematical result. This is valid only for addition and multiplication:

$$a + b = b + a \rightarrow 3 + 4 = 4 + 3$$
$$a \times b = b \times a \rightarrow 3 \times 4 = 4 \times 3$$

  BUT: $3 - 4 \neq 4 - 3$ and $3 \div 4 \neq 4 \div 3$

- **Associative:** Different number groupings will provide the same mathematical result. This is valid only for addition and multiplication:

$$(a + b) + c = a + (b + c) \rightarrow (4 + 5) + 6 = 4 + (5 + 6)$$
$$(a \times b) \times c = a \times (b \times c) \rightarrow (4 \times 5) \times 6 = 4 \times (5 \times 6)$$

  BUT: $(4 - 5) - 6 \neq 4 - (5 - 6)$ and $(4 \div 5) \div 6 \neq 4 \div (5 \div 6)$

- **Distributive:** A number that is multiplied by the sum or difference of two other numbers can be rewritten as the first number multiplied by the two others individually. This does *not* work with division:

$$a(b + c) = ab + ac \rightarrow 6(x + 3) = 6x + 6(3)$$
$$a(b - c) = ab - ac \rightarrow 3(y - 2) = 3y + 3(-2)$$

  BUT: $12 \div (6 + 2) \neq 12 \div 6 + 12 \div 2$

  Note: When subtracting an expression in parentheses, such as in $4 - (x + 3)$, distribute the negative sign outside the parentheses first: $4 + (-x - 3) \rightarrow 1 - x$.

Subtracting a positive number is the same as adding its negative. Likewise, subtracting a negative number is the same as adding its positive:

$$r - s = r + (-s) \rightarrow 22 - 15 = 7 \text{ and } 22 + (-15) = 7$$
$$r - (-s) = r + s \rightarrow 22 - (-15) = 37 \text{ and } 22 + 15 = 37$$

You should be comfortable manipulating both proper and improper fractions.

- To add and subtract fractions, first find a common denominator, then add the numerators together:

$$\frac{2}{3} + \frac{5}{4} \rightarrow \left(\frac{2}{3} \times \frac{4}{4}\right) + \left(\frac{5}{4} \times \frac{3}{3}\right) = \frac{8}{12} + \frac{15}{12} = \frac{23}{12}$$

- Multiplying fractions is straightforward: multiply the numerators together, then repeat for the denominators. Cancel when possible to simplify the answer:

$$\frac{5}{8} \times \frac{8}{3} = \frac{5}{\cancel{8}_1} \times \frac{\cancel{8}^1}{3} = \frac{5 \times 1}{1 \times 3} = \frac{5}{3}$$

- Dividing by a fraction is the same as multiplying by its reciprocal. Once you've rewritten a division problem as multiplication, follow the rules for fraction multiplication to simplify:

$$\frac{3}{4} \div \frac{3}{2} = \frac{\cancel{3}^1}{\cancel{4}_2} \times \frac{\cancel{2}^1}{\cancel{3}_1} = \frac{1 \times 1}{2 \times 1} = \frac{1}{2}$$

**Absolute value** means the distance a number is from 0 on a number line. Because absolute value is a distance, it is always positive or 0. Absolute value can *never* be negative:

$$|-17| = 17, |21| = 21, |0| = 0$$

Whatever you do to one side of an equation, you must do to the other. For instance, if you multiply one side by 3, you must multiply the other side by 3 as well.

The ability to solve straightforward, one-variable equations is critical on the SAT. For example:

$$\frac{4x}{5} - 2 = 10$$
$$\frac{4x}{5} = 12$$
$$\frac{5}{4} \times \frac{4x}{5} = 12 \times \frac{5}{4}$$
$$x = 15$$

Note: $\frac{4x}{5}$ is the same as $\frac{4}{5}x$. You could see either form on the SAT.

You will encounter **irrational numbers**, such as common radicals and $\pi$, on test day. You can carry an irrational number through your calculations as you would a variable (e.g., $4 \times \sqrt{2} = 4\sqrt{2}$). Only convert to a decimal when you have finished any intermediate steps and when the question asks you to provide an *approximate* value.

## Mental Math

Even if you're a math whiz, you need to adjust your thought process in terms of the SAT to give yourself the biggest advantage you can. Knowing a few extra things will boost your speed on test day.

- Don't abuse your calculator by using it to determine something as simple as $15 \div 3$ (we've seen it many times). Besides, what if you're in the middle of the no-calculator section? Save time on test day by reviewing multiplication tables. At a bare minimum, work up through the 10s. If you know them through 12 or 15, that's even better!
- You can save a few seconds of number crunching by memorizing **perfect squares**. Knowing perfect squares through 10 is a good start; go for 15 or even 20 if you can.
- **Percent** means "out of a hundred." For example, $27\% = \frac{27}{100}$. You can write percents as decimals, for example, $27\% = 0.27$.

- The ability to recognize a few simple fractions masquerading in decimal or percent form will save you time on test day, as you won't have to turn to your calculator to convert them. Memorize the content of the following table.

| Fraction | Decimal | Percent |
|----------|---------|---------|
| $\frac{1}{10}$ | 0.1 | 10% |
| $\frac{1}{5}$ | 0.2 | 20% |
| $\frac{1}{4}$ | 0.25 | 25% |
| $\frac{1}{3}$ | $0.33\overline{3}$ | $33.3\overline{3}\%$ |
| $\frac{1}{2}$ | 0.5 | 50% |
| $\frac{3}{4}$ | 0.75 | 75% |

Tip: If you don't have the decimal (or percent) form of a multiple of one of the fractions shown in the table memorized, such as $\frac{2}{5}$, just take the fraction with the corresponding denominator ($\frac{1}{5}$ in this case), convert to a decimal (0.2), and multiply by the numerator of the desired fraction to get its decimal equivalent:

$$\frac{2}{5} = \frac{1}{5} \times 2 = 0.2 \times 2 = 0.4 = 40\%$$

## Graphing

- Basic two-dimensional graphing is performed on a **coordinate plane**. There are two **axes**, $x$ and $y$, that meet at a central point called the **origin**. Each axis has both positive and negative values that extend outward from the origin at evenly spaced intervals. The axes divide the space into four sections called **quadrants**, which are labeled I, II, III, and IV. Quadrant I is always the upper-right section and the rest follow counterclockwise, as shown below:

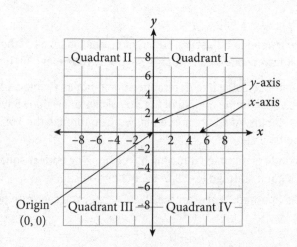

- To plot points on the coordinate plane, you need their coordinates. The **x-coordinate** is where the point falls along the *x*-axis, and the **y-coordinate** is where the point falls along the *y*-axis. The two coordinates together make an **ordered pair** written as (*x*, *y*). When writing ordered pairs, the *x*-coordinate is always listed first (think alphabetical order). Four points are plotted in the following figure as examples:

- When two points are vertically or horizontally aligned, calculating the distance between them is easy. For a horizontal distance, only the *x*-value changes; for a vertical distance, only the *y*-value changes. Take the positive difference of the *x*-coordinates (or *y*-coordinates) to determine the distance—that is, subtract the smaller number from the larger number so that the difference is positive. Two examples are presented here:

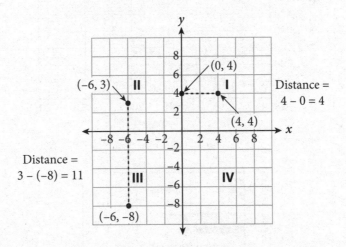

- Two-variable equations have an **independent variable** (input) and a **dependent variable** (output). The dependent variable (often *y*), depends on the independent variable (often *x*). For example, in the equation $y = 3x + 4$, *x* is the independent variable; any *y*-value depends on what you plug in for *x*. You can construct a table of values for the equation, which can then be plotted as shown on the next page.

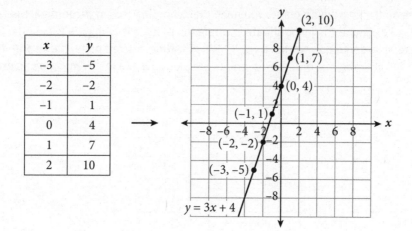

| x | y |
|----|----|
| −3 | −5 |
| −2 | −2 |
| −1 | 1 |
| 0 | 4 |
| 1 | 7 |
| 2 | 10 |

$y = 3x + 4$

- You may be asked to infer relationships from graphs. In the first of the following graphs, the two variables are year and population. Clearly, the year does not depend on how many people live in the town; rather, the population increases over time and thus depends on the year. In the second graph, you can infer that plant height depends on the amount of rain; thus, rainfall is the independent variable. Note that the independent variable for the second graph is the vertical axis; this can happen with certain nonstandard graphs. On the standard coordinate plane, however, the independent variable is always plotted on the horizontal axis as shown below:

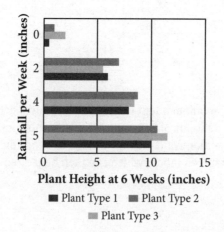

- When two straight lines are graphed simultaneously, one of three possible scenarios will occur:
  - The lines will not intersect at all (no solution).
  - The lines will intersect at one point (one solution).
  - The lines will lie on top of each other (infinitely many solutions).

## Geometry

- **Adjacent angles** can be added to find the measure of a larger angle. The following diagram demonstrates this:

- Two angles that sum to 90° are called **complementary angles**. Two angles that sum to 180° are called **supplementary angles**.

- Two distinct lines in a plane will either intersect at one point or extend indefinitely without intersecting. If two lines intersect at a right angle (90°), they are **perpendicular** and are denoted with ⊥. If the lines never intersect, they are **parallel** and are denoted with ||:

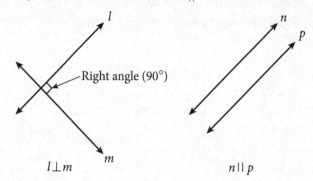

- **Perimeter** and **area** are basic properties that all two-dimensional shapes have. The perimeter of a polygon can easily be calculated by adding the lengths of all its sides. Area is the amount of two-dimensional space a shape occupies. The most common shapes for which you'll need these two properties on test day are triangles, parallelograms, and circles.

- The **area (A) of a triangle** is given by $A = \frac{1}{2}bh$, where $b$ is the base of the triangle and $h$ is its height. The base and height are always perpendicular. Any side of a triangle can be used as the base; just make sure you use its corresponding height (a line segment perpendicular to the base, terminating in the opposite vertex). You can use a right triangle's two legs as the base and height, but in non-right triangles, if the height is not given, you'll need to draw it in (from the vertex of the angle opposite the base down to the base itself at a right angle) and compute it.

- The **interior angles** of a triangle sum to 180°. If you know any two interior angles, you can calculate the third.

- **Parallelograms** are quadrilaterals with two pairs of parallel sides. Rectangles and squares are subsets of parallelograms. You can find the **area of a parallelogram** using $A = bh$. As with triangles, you can use any side of a parallelogram as the base, and again, the height is perpendicular to the base. For a rectangle or square, use the side perpendicular to the base as the height. For any other parallelogram, the height (or enough information to find it) will be given.

- A circle's perimeter is known as its **circumference (C)** and is found using $C = 2\pi r$, where $r$ is the **radius** (distance from the center of the circle to its edge). The **area of a circle** is given by $A = \pi r^2$. The strange symbol is the lowercase Greek letter pi ($\pi$, pronounced "pie"), which is approximately 3.14. As mentioned in the algebra section, you should carry $\pi$ throughout your calculations without rounding unless instructed otherwise.

- A **tangent line,** shown below, touches a circle at exactly one point and is perpendicular to a circle's radius at the point of contact:

The presence of a right angle opens up the opportunity to draw otherwise hidden shapes, so pay special attention to tangents when they're mentioned.

- A shape is said to have **symmetry** when it can be split by a line (called an **axis of symmetry**) into two identical parts. Consider folding a shape along a line: if all sides and vertices align once the shape is folded in half, the shape is symmetrical about that line. Some shapes have no axis of symmetry, some have one, some have multiple axes, and still others can have infinite axes of symmetry (e.g., a circle):

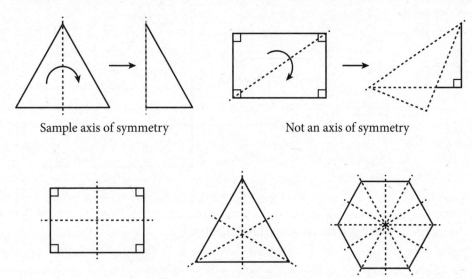

Sample axis of symmetry         Not an axis of symmetry

Sample shapes with corresponding axes of symmetry

- **Congruence** is simply a geometry term that means identical. Angles, lines, and shapes can be congruent. Congruence is indicated by using hash marks: everything with the same number of hash marks is congruent:

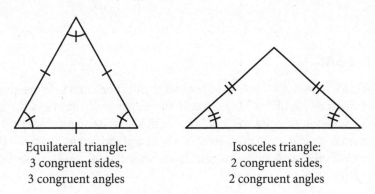

Equilateral triangle:
3 congruent sides,
3 congruent angles

Isosceles triangle:
2 congruent sides,
2 congruent angles

- **Similarity** between shapes indicates that they have identical angles and proportional sides. Think of taking a shape and stretching or shrinking each side by the same ratio. The resulting shape will have the same angles as the original. While the sides will not be identical, they will be proportional:

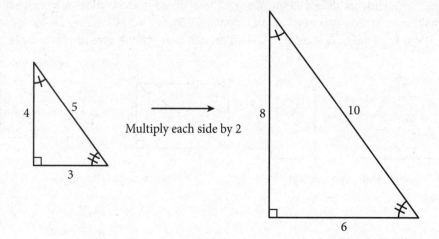

Multiply each side by 2

If you're comfortable with these concepts, read on for tips on calculator use. If not, review this lesson and remember to refer to it for help if you get stuck in a later chapter.

# Calculator Use

## LEARNING OBJECTIVE

After this lesson, you will be able to:

- Distinguish between questions that need a calculator and questions in which manual calculations are more efficient

## Calculators and the SAT

Educators believe that calculators serve a role in solving Math questions, but they are sometimes concerned that students rely too heavily on calculators. They believe this dependence weakens students' overall ability to think mathematically. Therefore, the SAT has a policy on calculator use to promote the idea that students need to be able to analyze and solve math problems both with and without a calculator. The first Math section you see will require you to work without a calculator, while the second Math section will allow you to use one.

Many students never stop to ask whether using a calculator is the most efficient way to solve a problem. This chapter will show you how the strongest test takers use their calculators strategically; that is, they carefully evaluate when to use the calculator and when to skip it in favor of a more streamlined approach. As you will see, even though you can use a calculator, sometimes it's more beneficial to save your energy by approaching a question more strategically. Work smarter, not harder.

## Which Calculator Should You Use?

The SAT allows four-function, scientific, and graphing calculators. No matter which calculator you choose, start practicing with it now. You don't want to waste valuable time on test day looking for the exponent button or figuring out how to correctly graph equations. Due to the wide range of mathematics topics you'll encounter on test day, **we recommend using a graphing calculator,** such as the TI-83/84. If you don't already own one, see if you can borrow one from your school's math department or a local library.

A graphing calculator's capabilities extend well beyond what you'll need for the test, so don't worry about memorizing every function. The next few pages will cover which calculator functions you'll want to know how to use for the SAT. If you're not already familiar with your graphing calculator, you'll want to get the user manual; you can find this on the Internet by searching for your calculator's model number. Identify the calculator functions necessary to answer various SAT Math questions, then write down the directions for each to make a handy study sheet.

## When Should You Use a Calculator?

Some SAT question types are designed based on the idea that students will do some or all of the work using a calculator. As a master test taker, you want to know what to look for so you can identify when calculator use is advantageous. Questions involving statistics, determining roots of complicated quadratic equations, and other topics are generally designed with calculator use in mind.

Other questions aren't intentionally designed to involve calculator use. Solving some with a calculator can save you time and energy, but you'll waste both if you go for the calculator on others. You will have to decide which method is best when you encounter the following topics:

- Long division and other extensive calculations
- Graphing quadratics
- Simplifying radicals and calculating roots
- Plane and coordinate geometry

Practicing **long computations** by hand and with the calculator will not only boost your focus and mental math prowess, but it will also help you determine whether it's faster to do the work for a given question by hand or reach for the calculator on test day.

**Graphing quadratic equations** may be a big reason you got that fancy calculator in the first place; it makes answering these questions a snap! This is definitely an area where you need to have an in-depth knowledge of your calculator's functions. The key to making these questions easy with the calculator is being meticulous when entering the equation.

Another stressful area for many students is **radicals**, especially when the answer choices are written as decimals. Those two elements are big red flags that trigger a reach for the calculator. Beware: not all graphing calculators have a built-in radical simplification function, so consider familiarizing yourself with this process.

**Geometry** can be a gray area for students when it comes to calculator use. Consider working by hand when dealing with angles and lines, specifically when filling in information on complementary, supplementary, and congruent angles. You should be able to work fluidly through those questions without using your calculator.

If you choose to use **trigonometric functions** to get to the answer on triangle questions, make sure you have your calculator set to degrees or radians as required by the question.

## To Use or Not to Use?

A calculator is a double-edged sword on the SAT: using one can be an asset for verifying work if you struggle when doing math by hand, but turning to it for the simplest computations will cost you time that you could devote to more complex questions. Practice solving questions with and without a calculator to get a sense of your personal style as well as your strengths and weaknesses. Think critically about when a calculator saves you time and when mental math is faster. Use the exercises in this book to practice your calculations so that by the time test day arrives, you'll be in the habit of using your calculator as effectively as possible!

# The Method for SAT Math Questions

## How to Do SAT Math

SAT Math questions can seem more difficult than they actually are, especially when you are working under time pressure. The method we are about to describe will help you answer SAT questions, whether you are comfortable with the math content or not. This method is designed to give you the confidence you need to get the right answers on the SAT by helping you think through a question logically, one piece at a time.

Take a look at this question and take a minute to think about how you would attack it if you saw it on test day:

> Building M is an apartment building in city Z. According to data kept by the housing commission in city Z, 24% of the 150 apartments in building M have at least 3 bedrooms. There are 1,350 apartment buildings in city Z and the average number of apartments in those buildings is 150. If building M is representative of the apartment buildings in city Z, then which of the following is the best estimate of how many apartments in city Z have fewer than 3 bedrooms?

- A)  48,600
- B)  67,500
- C)  153,900
- D)  202,500

Many test takers will see a question like this and panic. Others will waste a great deal of time reading and rereading without a clear goal. You want to avoid both of those outcomes.

Start by defining clearly for yourself **what the question is actually asking**. What do the answer choices represent? In this question, they represent *the number of apartments in city Z that have fewer than 3 bedrooms*.

Next, **examine the information** that you have and organize it logically. The question asks about the number of apartments with fewer than 3 bedrooms. Okay, then what information do you have about number of bedrooms? You know that 24% of the 150 building M apartments have *at least 3* bedrooms. That's the opposite of *fewer than 3*. You can deduce that $100\% - 24\% = 76\%$ of the 150 apartments in building M have *fewer than 3* bedrooms.

Now **make a strategic decision** about how to proceed. The answer choices are far apart, so you might consider rounding 76% to $\frac{3}{4}$ and estimating. However, this question appears on the calculator section, and it's a quick calculation. Let's say that you decide to use your calculator. Plug the numbers into your calculator and jot down what you know so far:

$$\text{Fewer than 3 in building M:} \quad 0.76 \times 150 = 114$$

The question asks for the number of apartments *in city Z* with fewer than 3 bedrooms, so hunt for information tying building M to city Z. You're told that the average number of apartments in city Z buildings is 150, which is identical to the number of apartments in building M, and that building M is "representative" of the apartment buildings in city Z. Translation: what is true for building M is also true for all apartment buildings in city Z. You also know that there are 1,350 apartment buildings in city Z. You can deduce that the number of apartments with fewer than 3 bedrooms in building M (114) times the total number of apartment buildings in city Z (1,350) will give you the number of apartments with fewer than 3 bedrooms in all of city Z. Plug that into your calculator:

$$114 \times 1{,}350 = 153{,}900$$

Finally, **confirm** that you answered the right question: you want the number of apartments in city Z with fewer than 3 bedrooms. Great! You're done; the correct answer is **(C)**.

Here are the steps of the method we just used:

| Method for SAT Math Questions | |
| --- | --- |
| Step 1. | State what the question is asking |
| Step 2. | Examine the given information |
| Step 3. | Choose your approach |
| Step 4. | Confirm that you answered the right question |

You can think of these steps as a series of questions to ask yourself: What do they want? What are they giving me to work with? How should I approach this? Did I answer the right question?

Not all SAT Math questions will require time spent on all the steps. The question above, because it is a word problem, required a fair amount of analysis in steps 1 and 2, but choosing an approach (step 3) was straightforward; the calculations were quick to do on a calculator, so there was no need to estimate. Other questions will require very little thought in steps 1 and 2 but will benefit from a careful strategy decision in step 3. Step 4 is always quick, but you should always do it: just make sure you answered the question that was actually asked before you bubble in your response. Doing so will save you from speed mistakes on questions that you know how to do and should be getting credit for.

There are several approaches you can choose from in step 3: doing the traditional math, as we did in the question above; Picking Numbers; Backsolving; estimating; or taking a strategic guess. In the next two examples, you'll see Picking Numbers and Backsolving in action.

Here's another example. This one is not a word problem, so steps 1 and 2 require negligible mental energy, but pay attention when you get to step 3.

Which of the following is equivalent to the expression $\frac{8x-2}{x+1}$ ?

A) $8 - \dfrac{10}{x+1}$

B) $8 - \dfrac{2}{x+1}$

C) $8 + \dfrac{2}{x+1}$

D) $\dfrac{8-2}{1}$

**Step 1:** What do they want? An answer choice that is equal to $\frac{8x-2}{x+1}$.

**Step 2:** What do they give you? Only the expression $\frac{8x-2}{x+1}$.

**Step 3:** What approach will you use?

Here's where it gets interesting. The creator of this question may be expecting you to use polynomial long division to solve, and we'll cover that technique in chapter 11 because you may want to have it in your arsenal. But if you don't know how to do polynomial long division, there's no need to panic. You could use an alternate approach called **Picking Numbers** that will work just as well: choose a number to substitute for $x$ in the question, then substitute the same number for $x$ in the choices and see which one matches. Like this:

Pick a small number for $x$, say 2. When $x = 2$, the original expression becomes:

$$\frac{8x-2}{x+1} = \frac{8(2)-2}{2+1} = \frac{14}{3}$$

Now plug $x = 2$ into the choices:

(A) $8 - \dfrac{10}{x+1} = 8 - \dfrac{10}{3} = \dfrac{24}{3} - \dfrac{10}{3} = \dfrac{14}{3}$

This is a match. It is always possible that another answer choice can produce the same result, so check the rest to be sure there isn't another match when $x = 2$. (If there is, go back and pick another number to distinguish between the choices that match.)

(B) $8 - \dfrac{2}{x+1} = 8 - \dfrac{2}{3} = \dfrac{24}{3} - \dfrac{2}{3} = \dfrac{22}{3}$

Eliminate (B).

(C) $8 + \dfrac{2}{x+1} = 8 + \dfrac{2}{3} = \dfrac{24}{3} + \dfrac{2}{3} = \dfrac{26}{3}$

Eliminate (C).

(D) $\dfrac{8-2}{1} = 6$

Eliminate (D).

**Step 4:** Did you solve for the right thing? You found the equivalent expression, so yes. Only **(A)** is a match, so it is the correct answer.

When picking numbers, use numbers that are **permissible** and **manageable**. That is, use numbers that are allowed by the stipulations of the question and that are easy to work with. In this question, you could have picked any real number because *x* was not defined as positive, negative, odd, even, a fraction, etc. A small positive integer is usually the best choice in this situation. In other questions, other kinds of numbers may be more manageable. For example, in percents questions, 100 is typically a smart number to pick.

Try one more:

> Mr. Dvorkin is distributing colored markers to a group of children. If he gives each child 4 markers, he will have 3 markers left over. In order to give each child 5 markers, with no markers left over, he will need 17 additional markers. How many markers does Mr. Dvorkin have?
>
> A)  55
> B)  68
> C)  83
> D)  101

**Step 1:** What do they want? The number of markers.

**Step 2:** What do they give you? Two unknowns (the number of children and the number of markers) and sufficient information to set up a system of equations.

**Step 3:** What approach will you use? You could set up the system of equations, but it might be faster to use a technique called **Backsolving**: plug the choices in for the unknown and see which one works. Here, you need an answer choice that will leave a remainder of 3 when divided by 4. Choices (B) and (D) don't meet this condition, so the answer must be (A) or (C).

(A) If Mr. Dvorkin has 55 markers, and gives each child 4 markers, he will indeed have 3 markers left over, since $55 \div 4 = 13 \, R3$. Now, what happens in the other situation? With an extra 17 markers, Mr. Dvorkin should be able to give each child exactly 5 markers. But $55 + 17 = 72$, which is not evenly divisible by 5. Eliminate (A).

You've now eliminated every choice but **(C)**, so it must be correct—you don't even need to test it! For the record:

(C) If Mr. Dvorkin has 83 markers and gives each child 4 markers, he will indeed have 3 left over, since $83 \div 4 = 20 \, R3$. With an extra 17 markers, Mr. Dvorkin should be able to give each child exactly 5 markers, and this is in fact what happens: $83 + 17 = 100$, which is evenly divisible by 5.

**Step 4:** Did you solve for the right thing? The question asked for the number of markers. You found that 83 markers satisfies all conditions of the problem. Choose **(C)** and move on.

Although it wasn't the case in this question, when backsolving it often makes sense to start with (B) or (C) in case you can tell from the context whether you'll need a larger or smaller answer choice if the one you're testing fails.

Now, it's your turn. Be deliberate with these questions. If there is analysis to do up front, do it. If there is more than one way to do a question, consider carefully before choosing your approach. And be sure to check whether you answered the right question. Forming good habits now, in slow and careful practice, will build your confidence for test day.

## Try on Your Own

**Directions:** Take as much time as you need on these questions. Work carefully and methodically. There will be opportunities for timed practice in future chapters.

1.  A cargo airplane has a maximum takeoff weight of 19,000 kilograms. The airplane, crew, and fuel have a combined weight of 14,750 kilograms. The airplane will be loaded with $n$ identical cargo containers, each of which has a weight of 125 kilograms. What is the greatest value of $n$ such that the airplane does not exceed its maximum takeoff weight?

    A)  28
    B)  34
    C)  118
    D)  152

2.  A certain model of laptop computer is priced at $550 at a local electronics store. The same model laptop at an online retailer sells for $\frac{9}{10}$ of the electronics store's price. At a luxury department store, the same model laptop sells for $\frac{7}{5}$ of the electronics store's price. How many dollars more is the cost of the laptop at the luxury department store than at the online retailer?

    A)  198
    B)  220
    C)  275
    D)  495

3.  A stack of 75 identical plastic plates forms a column approximately $9\frac{7}{8}$ inches tall. At this rate, which of the following is closest to the number of plates that would be needed to form a column 20 inches tall?

    A)  125
    B)  150
    C)  185
    D)  220

4.  Last month, Kiera ran 22 more miles than Bianca did. If they ran a combined total of 86 miles, how many miles did Bianca run?

    A)  27
    B)  32
    C)  43
    D)  54

5.  If $\frac{4x}{2y} = 4$, what is the value of $\frac{3y}{x}$ ?

    A)  $\frac{3}{4}$
    B)  $\frac{4}{3}$
    C)  $\frac{3}{2}$
    D)  2

6.

| $x$ | 2 | 4 | 6 | 8 | 10 |
|-----|---|---|---|---|----|
| $y$ | $\frac{7}{5}$ | $\frac{11}{5}$ | $\frac{15}{5}$ | $\frac{19}{5}$ | $\frac{23}{5}$ |

Which of the following equations relates $y$ to $x$ according to the values shown in the table above?

    A)  $y = \left(\frac{2}{5}\right)^x - \frac{7}{5}$
    B)  $y = \left(\frac{3x}{5}\right)^2 - 2$
    C)  $y = \frac{5}{2}x - \frac{3}{5}$
    D)  $y = \frac{2}{5}x + \frac{3}{5}$

7. $n - \sqrt{c + 5} = 1$

In the equation above, $c$ is a constant. If $n = 5$, what is the value of $c$?

A) $-1$

B) 0

C) 3

D) 11

8. At a child's lemonade stand, $p$ pitchers of lemonade are made by adding $m$ packets of lemonade mix to cold water. If $m = 2p + 4$, how many more packets of lemonade mix are needed to make each additional pitcher of lemonade?

A) 0

B) 1

C) 2

D) 4

9. A health club charges a one-time membership fee of $125 plus $n$ dollars for each month. If a member pays $515 dollars for the first six months, including the membership fee, what is the value of $n$?

A) 55

B) 65

C) 75

D) 85

10. If $x > 0$, which of the following is equivalent to $\dfrac{2}{\dfrac{1}{x+6} + \dfrac{1}{x+2}}$ ?

A) $x^2 + 8x + 12$

B) $\dfrac{x+4}{x^2 + 8x + 12}$

C) $2x + 8$

D) $\dfrac{x^2 + 8x + 12}{x+4}$

# A Note About Grid-ins

You will see an occasional question without answer choices throughout the Math chapters of this book, starting in the next chapter. On the SAT, several of these Grid-in questions appear at the end of each Math section. Instead of bubbling in a letter, you'll enter your responses to these questions into a grid that looks like this:

If you are gridding a value that doesn't take up the whole grid, such as 50, you can enter it anywhere in the grid as long as the digits are consecutive; it doesn't matter which column you start in. Gridding mixed numbers and decimals requires some care. Anything to the left of the fraction bar will be read as the numerator of a fraction, so you must grid mixed numbers as improper fractions. For instance, say you want to grid the mixed fraction $5\frac{1}{2}$. If you enter 5 1/2 into the grid, your answer will be read as $\frac{51}{2}$. Instead, enter your response as 1 1/2, which will be read (correctly) as $\frac{11}{2}$. Alternatively, you could grid this answer as 5.5.

A repeating decimal can either be rounded or truncated, but it must be entered to as many decimal places as possible. This means it must fill the entire grid. For example, you can grid $\frac{1}{6}$ as .166 or .167 but not as .16 or .17.

Note that you cannot grid a minus sign or any value larger than 9,999, so if you get an answer that is negative or larger than 9,999 to a grid-in question, you've made a mistake and should check your work.

# Reflect

**Directions:** Take a few minutes to recall what you've learned and what you've been practicing in this chapter. Consider the following questions, jot down your best answer for each one, and then compare your reflections to the expert responses on the following page. Use your level of confidence to to determine what to do next.

Think about your current habits when attacking SAT questions. Are you a strategic test taker? Do you take the time to think through what would be the fastest way to the answer?

_____

_____

_____

Do word problems give you trouble?

_____

_____

_____

What are the steps of the Method for SAT Math, and why is each step important?

_____

_____

_____

## Expert Responses

Think about your current habits when attacking SAT questions. Are you a strategic test taker? Do you take the time to think through what would be the fastest way to the answer?

*If yes, good for you! If not, we recommend doing questions more than one way whenever possible as part of your SAT prep. If you can discover now, while you're still practicing, that Picking Numbers is faster for you on certain types of questions but not on others, you'll be that much more efficient on test day.*

Do word problems give you trouble?

*If word problems are difficult for you, get into the habit of taking an inventory, before you do any math, of what the question is asking for and what information you have.*

What are the steps of the Method for SAT Math, and why is each step important?

*Here are the steps:*

**Step 1.** *State what the question is asking*

**Step 2.** *Examine the given information*

*(Taking an inventory is especially important in word problems.)*

**Step 3.** *Choose your approach*

*(Taking a moment to decide what approach will be the fastest way to the answer will ultimately save you time.)*

**Step 4.** *Confirm that you answered the right question*

*(Making sure you solved for the right thing will save you from losing points to speed mistakes on questions that you know how to do and should be getting credit for.)*

## Next Steps

If you answered most questions correctly in the "How Much Have You Learned?" section, and if your responses to the Reflect questions were similar to those of the SAT expert, then consider the Method for SAT Math Questions an area of strength and move on to the next chapter. Do keep using the method as you work on the questions in future chapters.

If you don't yet feel confident, review those parts of this chapter that you have not yet mastered and try the questions you missed again. As always, be sure to review the explanations closely.

# Answers and Explanations

## 1.   B

**Difficulty:** Medium

**Category:** Solving Equations

**Strategic Advice:** Break apart the question into its mathematical parts; determine what information you have and what value you need to find and then determine how you'll find that value.

**Getting to the Answer:** You're given the weight of everything on the airplane except the combined weight of the cargo containers and you're given the maximum takeoff weight of the plane. Therefore, the difference between the maximum takeoff weight and the weight of the plane, crew, and fuel must be the maximum combined weight of the cargo containers.

You're also told that $n$ represents the number of cargo containers that will be loaded on the plane and that each container weighs 125 kilograms. You need to find the number of containers, $n$, that make up the difference in weights.

The maximum takeoff weight of the plane is 19,000 kilograms and the weight of the plane, crew, and fuel is 14,750 kilograms. Hence, the maximum number of cargo containers can have a combined weight no greater than $19,000 - 14,750 = 4,250$ kilograms. That means that the maximum number of containers, $n$, must be 4,250 kilograms $\div$ 125 kilograms = 34 containers. Thus, **(B)** is correct.

## 2.   C

**Difficulty:** Medium

**Category:** Solving Equations

**Strategic Advice:** Think about what you're being asked to find—the difference between the price of the laptop at the luxury department store and at the online retailer—and what information you're given—the actual price at a local electronics store and two fractions of that price that represent the prices at the online retailer and at the luxury department store.

**Getting to the Answer:** The price of the laptop at the electronics store is $550. You also know that the price at the online retailer is $\frac{9}{10}$ of this, so that price is $\frac{9}{10} \times \$550 = \$495$. The question also states that the price at the luxury store is $\frac{7}{5}$ of the price at the

electronics store, so that's $\frac{7}{5} \times \$550 = \$770$. Therefore, the difference between the price at the luxury department store and the price at the online retailer is $\$770 - \$495 = \$275$. Choice **(C)** is correct.

## 3.   B

**Difficulty:** Easy

**Category:** Proportions

**Strategic Advice:** Because the answer choices are widely spaced apart, and the question asks for the answer that is "closest to the number," estimation will be a better approach than wading into unnecessarily detailed and tedious calculations.

**Getting to the Answer:** Notice the relationship between the height of the stack of 75 plates and the height of the unknown number of plates: $9\frac{7}{8}$ inches is *about half* of 20 inches. Put another way, a 20-inch stack of plates will be about twice as tall as a stack of 75 plates. Therefore, it's logical to deduce that approximately twice as many plates, or about $2 \times 75 = 150$, will be needed to form a stack 20 inches tall. Hence, **(B)** is correct.

## 4.   B

**Difficulty:** Medium

**Category:** Heart of Algebra/Systems of Linear Equations

**Strategic Advice:** Use the answer choices to your advantage to quickly find Bianca's distance.

**Getting to the Answer:** The question gives two unknowns and enough information to create a system of equations; therefore, it could be solved with a traditional algebraic approach.

There is, however, a more efficient way: assess the answer choices to see which makes sense for Bianca's distance. Since Kiera ran 22 miles farther than Bianca, and the combined distance they ran is 86 miles, Bianca must have run less than half of 86 miles. Since one-half of 86 is 43, you can quickly eliminate (C) and (D), which are both too big.

Now check (B) against the known information. If Bianca ran 32 miles, then Kiera ran $32 + 22 = 54$ miles. Check if Bianca's distance and Kiera's distance add up to 86: $32 + 54 = 86$; thus, **(B)** is correct.

If you're curious about the algebraic approach, here it is: let $b$ stand for the number of miles Bianca ran and $k$ stand for the number of miles Kiera ran. Then $b + k = 86$, and $k = b + 22$. Now, substitute the value of $k$ in terms of $b$ into the first equation:

$$b + (b + 22) = 86$$
$$2b + 22 = 86$$
$$2b = 64$$
$$b = 32$$

Again, Bianca ran 32 miles, and **(B)** is correct.

### 5.   C

**Difficulty:** Medium

**Category:** Solving Equations

**Strategic Advice:** You have two variables, but only one equation, so solving for each variable will not be possible. Instead, pick numbers for $x$ and $y$ that will make the equation true.

**Getting to the Answer:** Pick a simple number for $x$, solve for $y$, and if $y$ is also easy to work with, plug them into the expression you're trying to find. Say $x = 2$; then you have $\frac{4(2)}{2y} = 4$, which simplifies to $\frac{8}{2y} = 4$. Solving for $y$, you multiply both sides by $2y$ and get $8 = 8y$, so $y = 1$, another manageable number.

Now, plug these same values of $x$ and $y$ into $\frac{3y}{x}$ to get $\frac{3(1)}{(2)} = \frac{3}{2}$. Thus, **(C)** is correct.

### 6.   D

**Difficulty:** Medium

**Category:** Heart of Algebra/Linear Equations

**Strategic Advice:** The answer choices are split into two types: the first two are exponential and the second two are linear. Therefore, to quickly narrow down the answers, examine the table to determine whether the change in $x$-values versus $y$-values is exponential or linear.

**Getting to the Answer:** Notice that, for every increase of 2 in the $x$-value, the $y$-value increases by $\frac{4}{5}$. Therefore, you have a linear relationship, so you can eliminate (A) and (B), which are both exponential functions.

Now, plug values from the table into the remaining answers to see whether the math works out. Try the first column in the table and plug in 2 for $x$ and $\frac{7}{5}$ for $y$:

(C): $\frac{7}{5} = \frac{5}{2} \times 2 - \frac{3}{5} = 5 - \frac{3}{5} = \frac{25}{5} - \frac{3}{5} = \frac{22}{5}$. This doesn't work out, so **(D)** must be correct. No need to check it. For the record:

**(D):** $\frac{7}{5} = \frac{2}{5} \times 2 + \frac{3}{5} = \frac{4}{5} + \frac{3}{5} = \frac{7}{5}$

### 7.   D

**Difficulty:** Medium

**Category:** Heart of Algebra/Linear Equations

**Strategic Advice:** Backsolve by plugging the answer choices in for $c$ to determine which one makes the given equation true.

**Getting to the Answer:** The question provides a linear equation and the value of one of the variables.

Since you're told that $n = 5$, fill this value into the equation, and then simplify to find the root:

$$5 - \sqrt{c + 5} = 1$$
$$4 - \sqrt{c + 5} = 0$$
$$4 = \sqrt{c + 5}$$

Simplifying to this point makes it easier to see if the value of $c$ you plug in works. Now check the answer choices, starting with (B) or (C). If the answer you choose is too large or too small, you'll know which direction to go when testing the next choice.

(B): $4 \neq \sqrt{0 + 5}$. This answer is too small, so try (C) next.

(C): $4 \neq \sqrt{3 + 5}$. This choice is still too small, so the correct choice must be **(D)**. No need to check it. For the record:

(D): $4 = \sqrt{11 + 5} = \sqrt{16} = 4$.

If you prefer the algebraic approach, here it is:

$$5 - \sqrt{c + 5} = 1$$
$$4 - \sqrt{c + 5} = 0$$
$$4 = \sqrt{c + 5}$$
$$4^2 = c + 5$$
$$16 = c + 5$$
$$11 = c$$

Again, **(D)** is correct.

## 8.  C

**Difficulty:** Medium

**Category:** Heart of Algebra/Linear Equations

**Strategic Advice:** Pick a number for $p$ to determine how many packets of mix will be needed, and then pick another number for $p$ to see how the number of packets changes.

**Getting to the Answer:** Say $p = 2$, then $m = 2(2) + 4 = 8$, so there are 8 packets of mix needed to make 2 pitchers of lemonade. Now try $p = 3$: $m = 2(3) + 4 = 10$. For one additional pitcher, the packets needed increased from 8 to 10, which is a change of 2. Therefore, **(C)** is correct. You can confirm by trying $p = 4$, then $m = 2(4) + 4 = 12$.

## 9.  B

**Difficulty:** Medium

**Category:** Heart of Algebra/Linear Equations

**Strategic Advice:** Backsolve by plugging the answer choices in for $n$ to determine which one matches the given price of six months of membership.

**Getting to the Answer:** Check the answer choices, starting with (B) or (C). If the answer you choose is too large or too small, you'll know which direction to go when testing the next choice. Multiply the value in the answer choice by the six months and then add the $125 membership fee.

(B): $65 \times 6 = \$390$. $\$390 + \$125 = \$515$. This is a match, so **(B)** is correct. Since there can be only one correct answer, you're finished.

Alternatively, you can solve algebraically:

$$\$125 + 6n = \$515$$
$$6n = \$390$$
$$\frac{6n}{6} = \frac{\$390}{6}$$
$$n = \$65$$

**(B)** is correct.

## 10.  D

**Difficulty:** Medium

**Category:** Heart of Algebra/Linear Equations

**Strategic Advice:** Pick a number for $x$ to determine the numerical value of the given expression, then plug the same number into the answer choices to find the one that matches.

**Getting to the Answer:** To make calculations easy, say $x = 1$; then the given expression becomes $\dfrac{2}{\dfrac{1}{1+6} + \dfrac{1}{1+2}}$. Now, simplify this expression:

$$\frac{2}{\frac{1}{7} + \frac{1}{3}}$$
$$= \frac{2}{\frac{3}{21} + \frac{7}{21}}$$
$$= \frac{2}{\left(\frac{10}{21}\right)}$$
$$= 2 \times \frac{21}{10}$$
$$= \frac{21}{5}$$

Next, plug 1 in for $x$ in the answer choices to see which yields the same value:

(A): $1^2 + 8 \times 1 + 12 = 21$. Eliminate.

(B): $\dfrac{1+4}{1^2 + 8 \times 1 + 12} = \dfrac{5}{21}$. Eliminate.

(C): $2 \times 1 + 8 = 10$. Eliminate. You have eliminated three answer choices so the one left is correct; **(D)** is correct.

For the record: (D): $\dfrac{1^2 + 8 \times 1 + 12}{1 + 4} = \dfrac{21}{5}$. This is a match, which confirms that **(D)** is correct.

You might also have noticed that (B) gave you the reciprocal of the value you were looking for; therefore, the reciprocal of the expression in (B) must give you the correct answer, and that is **(D)**.

# The Heart of Algebra

# CHAPTER 4

# Linear Equations and Graphs

## LEARNING OBJECTIVES

After completing this chapter, you will be able to:

- Isolate a variable
- Translate word problems into equations
- Calculate the slope of a line given two points
- Write the equation of a line in slope-intercept form
- Discern whether the slope of a line is positive, negative, zero, or undefined based on its graph
- Describe the slopes of parallel and perpendicular lines

110/600 SmartPoints®

# How Much Do You Know?

**Directions:** Try the questions that follow. Show your work so that you can compare your solutions to the ones found in the Check Your Work section immediately after this question set. The "Category" heading in the explanation for each question gives the title of the lesson that covers how to solve it. If you answered the question(s) for a given lesson correctly, and if your scratch-work looks like ours, you may be able to move quickly through that lesson. If you answered incorrectly or used a different approach, you may want to take your time on that lesson.

$$v = \frac{2\pi r}{T}$$

1. Uniform circular motion is used in physics to describe the motion of an object traveling at a constant speed in a circle. The speed of the object is called tangential velocity and it can be calculated using the formula above, where $r$ is the radius of the circle and $T$ is the time is takes for the object to make one complete circle, called a period. Which of the following formulas could be used to find the length of one period if you know the tangential velocity and the radius of the circle?

   A)  $T = \dfrac{v}{2\pi r}$

   B)  $T = \dfrac{2\pi r}{v}$

   C)  $T = 2\pi rv$

   D)  $T = \dfrac{1}{2\pi rv}$

$$F = \gamma \frac{m_1 m_2}{r^2}$$

2. The formula above is Newton's law of universal gravitation, where $F$ is the attractive force, $\gamma$ is the gravitational constant, $m_1$ and $m_2$ are the masses of the particles, and $r$ is the distance between their centers of mass. Which of the following gives $r$ in terms of $F$, $\gamma$, $m_1$, and $m_2$?

   A)  $r = \sqrt{\dfrac{(m_1)(m_2)}{F(\gamma)}}$

   B)  $r = \sqrt{\dfrac{F(m_2)}{\gamma(m_1)}}$

   C)  $r = \sqrt{\dfrac{\gamma(m_1)}{F(m_2)}}$

   D)  $r = \sqrt{\dfrac{\gamma(m_1)(m_2)}{F}}$

3. Andrew works at a travel agency. He gets paid $120 for a day's work, plus a bonus of $25 for each cruise he books. Which of the following equations represents the relationship between the total Andrew earns in a day, $d$, and the number of cruises he books, $c$?

   A)  $c = 25d + 120$

   B)  $c = 120d + 25$

   C)  $d = 25c + 120$

   D)  $d = 120c + 25$

4. Vera is on her school's track and field team. In a practice long-jump competition against her teammates, she gets 5 points for landing over the nearer line and 10 points for landing over the more distant line. She gets a total of 7 jumps and lands $x$ times over the more distant line and the rest of the times over the nearer line. Which of the following equations represents the relationship between Vera's total score, $y$, and the number of times she lands over the more distant line, $x$?

A) $y = 10x$

B) $y = 5x + 35$

C) $y = 10x + 5$

D) $y = 70 - 5x$

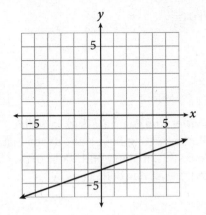

6. The graph shown represents which of the following equations?

A) $y = -3x + 4$

B) $y = -\frac{1}{3}x + 4$

C) $y = \frac{1}{3}x - 4$

D) $y = 3x - 4$

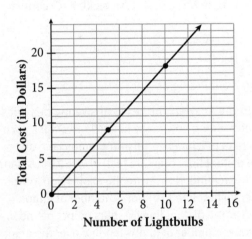

**Number of Lightbulbs**

5. A hardware store sells light bulbs in different quantities. The graph shows the cost of various quantities. According to the graph, what is the cost of a single light bulb?

A) $0.56

B) $1.80

C) $2.50

D) $3.60

# Check Your Work

**1. B**

**Difficulty:** Easy

**Category:** Solving Equations

**Getting to the Answer:** The goal here is to solve the equation for $T$. Start by getting $T$ out of the denominator of the fraction. To do this, multiply both sides of the equation by $T$, and then divide both sides by $v$:

$$v = \frac{2\pi r}{T}$$

$$T \times v = \left(\frac{2\pi r}{T}\right) \times T$$

$$Tv = 2\pi r$$

$$T = \frac{2\pi r}{v}$$

Choice **(B)** is the correct answer.

**2. D**

**Difficulty:** Medium

**Category:** Solving Equations

**Strategic Advice:** Even when the equation is entirely made up of variables, the process for isolating one variable is still the same.

**Getting to the Answer:** This equation needs to be rearranged to solve for $r$, so start by multiplying both sides by $r^2$ to get that expression out of the denominator:

$$(r^2)(F) = \gamma(m_1)(m_2)$$

Next, divide both sides by $F$:

$$r^2 = \frac{\gamma(m_1)(m_2)}{F}$$

Finally, take the square root of both sides to get $r$ by itself:

$$r = \sqrt{\frac{\gamma(m_1)(m_2)}{F}}$$

**(D)** is correct.

**3. C**

**Difficulty:** Easy

**Category:** Word Problems

**Getting to the Answer:** When writing a linear equation to represent a real-world scenario, a flat rate is a constant while a unit rate is always multiplied by the independent variable. You can identify the unit rate by looking for words like *per* or *for each*.

Because the amount Andrew gets paid daily, $120, is a flat rate that doesn't depend on the number of cruises he books, 120 should be the constant in the equation. This means you can eliminate (B) and (D). The question tells you to multiply $25 by the number of cruises he books, $c$, so the equation is *total pay* $= 25 \times$ *number of cruises* $+ 120$, or $d = 25c + 120$, making **(C)** correct.

**4. B**

**Difficulty:** Hard

**Category:** Word Problems

**Getting to the Answer:** The key to answering this question is determining how many jumps land across each line. If Vera gets 7 jumps total and $x$ jumps land over the more distant line, then the rest, or $7 - x$, must land over the nearer line. Now, write the expression in words: points per distant line (10) times number of jumps landing over the distant line ($x$), plus points per near line (5) times number of jumps landing over the near line ($7 - x$). Next, translate the words into numbers, variables, and operations: $10x + 5(7 - x)$. This is not one of the answer choices, so simplify the expression by distributing the 5 and combining like terms: $10x + 5(7 - x) = 10x + 35 - 5x = 5x + 35$, so the equation is $y = 5x + 35$. **(B)** is correct.

**5.  B**

**Difficulty:** Easy

**Category:** Linear Graphs

**Getting to the Answer:** The *x*-axis represents the number of light bulbs, so find 1 on the *x*-axis and trace up to where it meets the graph of the line. The *y*-value is somewhere between $1 and $2, so the only possible correct answer choice is $1.80. **(B)** is correct.

You could also find the unit rate by calculating the slope of the line using two of the points shown on the graph: the graph rises 9 units and runs 5 units from one point to the next, so the slope is $\frac{9}{5}$, or 1.8, which confirms that **(B)** is correct.

**6.  C**

**Difficulty:** Medium

**Category:** Linear Graphs

**Getting to the Answer:** Use the graph to identify the *y*-intercept and the slope of the line and then write an equation in slope-intercept form, $y = mx + b$. Once you have your equation, look for the answer choice that matches. The line crosses the *y*-axis at $(0, -4)$ so the *y*-intercept, *b*, is $-4$. The line rises 1 unit for every 3 units that it runs to the right, so the slope, *m*, is $\frac{1}{3}$. The equation of the line is $y = \frac{1}{3}x - 4$, which matches **(C)**.

You could also graph each of the answer choices in your calculator to see which one matches the given graph, but this is not the most time-efficient strategy. You also have to be very careful when entering fractions—to graph **(C)**, for example, you would enter $(1/3)x - 4$.

## Solving Equations

**LEARNING OBJECTIVE**

After this lesson, you will be able to:

- Isolate a variable

### To answer a question like this:

$$\frac{1}{2}(3x + 14) = \frac{1}{6}(7x - 10)$$

Which value of $x$ satisfies the equation above?

A)  $-26$

B)  $2$

C)  $8$

D)  $16$

### You need to know this:

**Isolating a variable** means getting that variable by itself on one side of the equation. To do this, use inverse operations to manipulate the equation, remembering that whatever you do to one side of the equation, you must do to *both* sides.

### You need to do this:

It usually makes sense to proceed in this order:

- Eliminate any fractions
- Collect and combine like terms
- Divide to leave the desired variable by itself

### Explanation:

Eliminate the fractions by multiplying both sides of the equation by 6:

$$\left(\frac{6}{1}\right)\frac{1}{2}(3x + 14) = \left(\frac{6}{1}\right)\frac{1}{6}(7x - 10)$$
$$3(3x + 14) = (7x - 10)$$

In order to collect all the $x$ terms on one side, you'll first need to distribute the 3 on the left side of the equation:

$$9x + 42 = 7x - 10$$

Next, subtract $7x$ from both sides:

$$2x + 42 = -10$$

Now, subtract 42 from both sides:

$$2x = -52$$

Finally, divide both sides by 2 to leave $x$ by itself:

$$x = -26$$

Choice **(A)** is correct.

If you find isolating a variable to be challenging, try these Drill questions before proceeding to the Try on Your Own set. Isolate the variable in each equation. Turn the page and look at the bottom of the page to see the answers.

## Drill

a. $3(x + 2) = 14 - 2(3 - 2x)$

b. $5(6 - 3b) = 3b + 3$

c. $\dfrac{r}{6} - \dfrac{3r}{5} = \dfrac{1}{2}$

d. Isolate $F$: $C = \dfrac{5}{9}(F - 32)$

e. Isolate $b$: $A = \dfrac{1}{2}(a + b)h$

## Try on Your Own

**Directions:** Take as much time as you need on these questions. Work carefully and methodically. There will be an opportunity for timed practice at the end of the chapter.

---

HINT: For Q1, what do you need to do before you can collect all the y terms on one side?

---

$$3y + 2(y - 2) = \frac{3y}{2} + 1$$

1.  What value of $y$ satisfies the equation above?

    A)  $-\frac{10}{7}$

    B)  $-\frac{6}{13}$

    C)  $\frac{7}{9}$

    D)  $\frac{10}{7}$

$$S = \frac{C - \frac{1}{4}I}{C + I}$$

2.  A teacher uses the formula above to calculate her students' scores, $S$, by subtracting $\frac{1}{4}$ of the number of questions the students answered incorrectly, $I$, from the number of questions they answered correctly, $C$, and dividing by the total number of questions. Which of the following expresses the number of questions answered incorrectly in terms of the other variables?

    A)  $\frac{C(1 - 4S)}{4S + 1}$

    B)  $\frac{C(1 + 4S)}{4S - 1}$

    C)  $\frac{4C(1 - S)}{4S + 1}$

    D)  $\frac{4C(1 + S)}{4S - 1}$

Drill answers from previous page:

a. $3x + 6 = 14 - 6 + 4x$
   $3x = 2 + 4x$
   $x = -2$

b. $30 - 15b = 3b + 3$
   $-18b = -27$
   $\frac{-18b}{-18} = \frac{-27}{-18}$
   $b = \frac{3}{2}$

c. $30 \times \left(\frac{r}{6} - \frac{3r}{5}\right) = \left(\frac{1}{2}\right) \times 30$
   $5r - 6(3r) = 15$
   $-13r = 15$
   $r = -\frac{15}{13}$

d. $\frac{9}{5} \times C = \frac{9}{5} \times \frac{5}{9}(F - 32)$
   $\frac{9}{5}C = F - 32$
   $\frac{9}{5}C + 32 = F$

e. $A = \frac{1}{2}(a + b)h$
   $2A = (a + b)h$
   $\frac{2A}{h} = a + b$
   $\frac{2A}{h} - a = b$

3. What value of $n$ satisfies the equation $\frac{7}{8}(n-6) = \frac{21}{2}$ ?

HINT: For Q5, simplify the numerators before clearing
the equation of fractions.

$$\frac{4 + z - (3 + 2z)}{6} = \frac{-z - 3(5-2)}{7}$$

5. What is the value of $z$ in the equation above?

A) $-61$

B) $-\dfrac{61}{27}$

C) $\dfrac{61}{27}$

D) $61$

HINT: For Q4, use $\frac{a}{b}$ as your target and solve for that expression
rather than solving for $a$ and $b$ separately.

4. If $b \neq 0$ and $\dfrac{3a+b}{b} = \dfrac{11}{2}$, which of the following
could be the value of $\dfrac{a}{b}$ ?

A) $\dfrac{3}{2}$

B) $\dfrac{7}{2}$

C) $\dfrac{9}{2}$

D) It is not possible to determine a value of $\dfrac{a}{b}$.

# Word Problems

> **LEARNING OBJECTIVE**
>
> After this lesson, you will be able to:
>
> - Translate word problems into equations

## To answer a question like this:

A laser tag arena sells two types of memberships. One package costs $325 for one year of membership with an unlimited number of visits. The second package has a $125 enrollment fee, includes five free visits, and costs an additional $8 per visit after the first five. How many visits over a one-year period would a person who purchases the second package need to use for the cost to equal that of the one-year membership?

A) 20

B) 25

C) 30

D) 40

## You need to know this:

The SAT likes to test your understanding of how to describe real-world situations using math equations. For some questions, it will be up to you to extract and solve an equation; for others, you'll have to interpret an equation in a real-life context. The following table shows some of the most common phrases and mathematical equivalents you're likely to see on the SAT.

| Word Problems Translation Table | |
| --- | :---: |
| **English** | **Math** |
| *equals, is, equivalent to, was, will be, has, costs, adds up to, the same as, as much as* | $=$ |
| *times, of, multiplied by, product of, twice, double* | $\times$ |
| *divided by, out of, ratio* | $\div$ |
| *plus, added to, sum, combined, increased by* | $+$ |
| *minus, subtracted from, smaller than, less than, fewer, decreased by, difference between* | $-$ |
| *a number, how much, how many, what* | $x, n,$ etc. |

## You need to do this:

When translating from English to math, *start by defining the variables,* choosing letters that make sense. Then, *break down the question into small pieces*, writing down the translation for one phrase at a time.

## Explanation:

The phrase "how many visits" indicates an unknown, so you need a variable. Use an intuitive letter to represent the number of visits; call it $v$. The question asks when the two memberships will cost the "same amount," so write an equation that sets the total membership costs equal to each other.

The first membership type costs $325 for unlimited visits, so write 325 on one side of the equal sign. The second type costs $8 per visit (not including, or *except*, the first 5 visits), or $8(v-5)$, plus a flat $125 enrollment fee, so write $8(v-5) + 125$ on the other side of the equal sign. That's it! Now solve for $v$:

$$325 = 8(v-5) + 125$$
$$200 = 8v - 40$$
$$240 = 8v$$
$$30 = v$$

The answer is **(C)**.

## Try on Your Own

**Directions:** Take as much time as you need on these questions. Work carefully and methodically. There will be an opportunity for timed practice at the end of the chapter.

6.  A local restaurant is hosting a dance-a-thon for charity. Each couple must dance a minimum of three hours before earning any money for the charity. After the first three hours, couples earn $50 per half-hour of continuous dancing. Which expression represents the total amount earned by a couple who dance $h$ hours, assuming they dance at least three hours?

    A)  $25h$

    B)  $100h$

    C)  $50(h-3)$

    D)  $100h - 300$

---

HINT: For Q7, start with the most concrete information:
1 is the second value.

---

7.  The final value, $v$, in a four-digit lock code is determined by multiplying the second value by two, subtracting that expression from the first value, and dividing the resulting expression by half of the third value. The first value is $f$, the second value is 1, and the third value is $t$. What is the final value, $v$, in terms of $f$ and $t$?

    A)  $\dfrac{f-2}{t}$

    B)  $\dfrac{2f-4}{t}$

    C)  $\dfrac{t}{2f-4}$

    D)  $\dfrac{2t-4}{f}$

---

HINT: For Q8, profit = sales − expenses

---

8.  A pizzeria's top-selling pizzas are The Works and The Hawaiian. The Works sells for $17, and The Hawaiian sells for $13. Ingredient costs for The Works are $450 per week, and ingredient costs for The Hawaiian are $310 per week. If $x$ represents the number of each type of pizza sold in one week, and the weekly profit from the sale of each type of pizza is the same, what is the value of $x$ ?

    A)  30

    B)  35

    C)  140

    D)  145

9.  A student opens a checking account when she starts a new job so that her paychecks can be directly deposited into the account. Her balance can be computed using the expression $10nw + 50$, where $n$ is the number of hours she works every week and $w$ is the number of weeks that she has worked so far. Assuming she does not withdraw any money from her account, which of the terms in the expression most logically will change if the student gets a raise?

    A)  10

    B)  $n$

    C)  $w$

    D)  The expression will not change if the student gets a raise.

10. Malik starts a job at which his starting salary is $25,500 per year. He expects that his salary will increase by a constant dollar amount annually. In 12 years, his salary will be double his starting salary. Assuming salary increases take place only at the end of a full year, how many years must Malik wait until his salary is at least $40,000 annually?

# Linear Graphs

## LEARNING OBJECTIVES

After this lesson, you will be able to:

- Calculate the slope of a line given two points
- Write the equation of a line in slope-intercept form
- Discern whether the slope of a line is positive, negative, zero, or undefined based on its graph
- Describe the slopes of parallel and perpendicular lines

## To answer a question like this:

What is the equation of the line that passes through the points $(-3, -1)$ and $(1, 3)$ ?

A) $y = -x + 2$

B) $y = -x - 2$

C) $y = x - 2$

D) $y = x + 2$

## You need to know this:

The answer choices in this question are written in slope-intercept form: $y = mx + b$. In this form of a linear equation, $m$ represents the **slope** of the line and $b$ represents the **y-intercept**. You can think of the slope of a line as how steep it is. The $y$-intercept is the point at which the line crosses the $y$-axis and can be written as the ordered pair $(0, y)$.

You can calculate the slope of a line if you know any two points on the line. The formula is $m = \frac{y_2 - y_1}{x_2 - x_1}$, where $(x_1, y_1)$ and $(x_2, y_2)$ are the coordinates of the two points on the line.

A line that moves from the bottom left to the top right has a positive slope. A line that moves from the top left to the bottom right has a negative slope. A horizontal line has a slope of 0 and a vertical line has an undefined slope.

Some SAT questions ask about parallel or perpendicular lines. Parallel lines have the same slope, while perpendicular lines have negative reciprocal slopes.

## You need to do this:

- Find the slope of the line
- Write the equation in slope-intercept form, substituting the value of the slope you found and one of the known points for $x$ and $y$
- Solve for the $y$-intercept

## Explanation:

In this question, $m = \dfrac{3-(-1)}{1-(-3)} = \dfrac{4}{4} = 1$. Of the answer choices, only (C) and (D) have a slope of 1, so rule out (A) and (B), which both have a slope of $-1$.

To find the $y$-intercept of the line, write the equation for the line in slope-intercept form and plug in one of the known points for $x$ and $y$:

$$y = 1x + b$$
$$3 = 1(1) + b$$
$$2 = b$$

The correct answer is **(D)**. For the record, here is the graph of the line. Note that as you would expect from the fact that $m$ is positive, the line moves from the lower left to upper right, and it crosses the $y$-axis at the $y$-intercept of $b = 2$.

## Try on Your Own

**Directions:** Take as much time as you need on these questions. Work carefully and methodically. There will be an opportunity for timed practice at the end of the chapter.

---

HINT: For Q11, what do you know about lines that never intersect?

---

11. Line A passes through the coordinate points $\left(-\frac{2}{5}, 0\right)$ and $(0, 1)$. Which of the following lines will line A never intersect?

    A)

    B)

    C)

    D)

12. In the $xy$-plane, the point $(4, 7)$ lies on the line $t$, which is perpendicular to the line $y = -\frac{4}{3}x + 6$. What is the equation of line $t$?

    A) $y = \frac{3}{4}x + 4$

    B) $y = -\frac{4}{3}x + 4$

    C) $y = \frac{3}{4}x + 7$

    D) $y = -\frac{3}{4}x + 4$

---

HINT: For Q13, remember that at the $y$-intercept, $x = 0$.

---

13. The graph shows the correlation between ambient air temperature, $t$, in degrees Fahrenheit and the number of chirps, $c$, per minute that a snowy tree cricket makes at that temperature. Which of the following equations represents the line shown in the graph?

    A) $c = 4t - 160$

    B) $c = \frac{1}{4}t - 160$

    C) $c = \frac{1}{2}t - 40$

    D) $c = 4t + 160$

| Minutes Charging | 10 | 15 | 30 |
|---|---|---|---|
| Percent Charged | 34 | 41.5 | 64 |

HINT: For Q14, the starting point (flat fee) is the *y*-intercept.
The rate of change (price per pound) is the slope.

**Box Airmail**

15. Xia is charging her laptop. She records the battery charge for the first 30 minutes after she plugs it in to get an idea of when it will be completely charged. The table above shows the results. If *y* is the percent battery charge on Xia's laptop, which linear equation represents the correct relationship between *y* and *x*?

A) $y = 1.5x + 19$

B) $y = 2x + 14$

C) $y = 2.5x + 9$

D) $y = 10x + 34$

14. A freight airline charges a flat fee to airmail a box, plus an additional charge for each pound the box weighs. The graph above shows the relationship between the weight of the box and the total cost to airmail it. Based on the graph, how much would it cost in dollars to airmail a 40-pound box?

## On Test Day

Remember that the SAT doesn't ask you to show your work. If you find the algebra in a question challenging, there is often another way to get to the answer.

Try this question first using algebra and then using the Picking Numbers strategy you learned in chapter 3. Time yourself. Which approach do you find easier? Which one was faster? Did you get the correct answer both times? Remember your preferred approach and try it first if you see a question like this on test day.

$$\frac{2(a-3)}{b} = \frac{4}{7}$$

16. If the equation above is true, which of the following must NOT be true?

A) $\dfrac{b}{a-3} = \dfrac{7}{2}$

B) $\dfrac{2a}{b} = -\dfrac{10}{7}$

C) $14a - 4b = 42$

D) $\dfrac{a-3}{b} = \dfrac{2}{7}$

The correct answer and both ways of solving can be found at the end of this chapter.

# How Much Have You Learned?

**Directions:** For testlike practice, give yourself 15 minutes to complete this question set. Be sure to study the explanations, even for questions you got right. They can be found at the end of this chapter.

17. Which value of $x$ makes the equation

$\frac{8}{5}\left(x + \frac{33}{12}\right) = 16$ true?

    A) 7.25

    B) 8.75

    C) 12.75

    D) 13.25

**Number of Songs Purchased**

18. The graph above shows the cost of joining and buying music from a music subscription service. What does the $y$-intercept of the line most likely represent?

    A) The cost per song

    B) The cost to join the service

    C) The cost of buying 20 songs

    D) The cost of 20 subscriptions to the service

19. If $\frac{3}{4}y = 6 - \frac{1}{3}c$, then what is the value of $2c + \frac{9}{2}y$ ?

20. Three years ago, Madison High School started charging an admission fee for basketball games to raise money for new bleachers. The initial price was $2 per person; the school raised the price of admission to $2.50 this year. Assuming this trend continues, which of the following equations can be used to describe $c$, the cost of admission, $y$ years after the school began charging for admission to games?

    A) $c = 6y + 2$

    B) $c = \frac{y}{6} + 2.5$

    C) $c = \frac{y}{6} + 2$

    D) $c = \frac{y}{2} + 2$

| Price of One Pound | Projected Number of Pounds Sold |
|---|---|
| $1.20 | 15,000 |
| $1.40 | 12,500 |
| $1.60 | 10,000 |
| $1.80 | 7,500 |
| $2.00 | 5,000 |
| $2.20 | 2,500 |

21. Which of the following equations best describes the linear relationship shown in the table, where $g$ represents the number of pounds of grain sold and $d$ represents the price in dollars of one pound of grain?

    A) $g = 1.2d + 12,500$

    B) $g = 12,500d + 15,000$

    C) $g = -12,500d + 17,500$

    D) $g = -12,500d + 30,000$

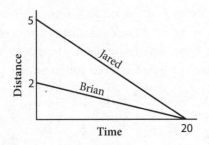

22. Brian and Jared live in the same apartment complex and both bike to and from work every day. The figure above shows a typical commute home for each of them. Based on the figure, which of the following statements is true?

    A) It takes Brian longer to bike home because his work is farther away.

    B) It takes Jared longer to bike home because his work is farther away.

    C) Jared and Brian arrive home at the same time, so they must bike at about the same rate.

    D) Jared bikes a longer distance than Brian in the same amount of time, so Jared must bike at a faster rate.

23. When graphing a linear equation that is written in the form $y = mx + b$, the variable $m$ represents the slope of the line and $b$ represents the $y$-intercept. Assuming that $b > 0$, which of the following best describes how reversing the sign of $b$ will affect the graph?

    A) The new line will be shifted down $b$ units.

    B) The new line will be shifted down $2b$ units.

    C) The new line will be a perfect reflection across the $x$-axis.

    D) The new line will be a perfect reflection across the $y$-axis.

24. The graph of a line in the $xy$-plane passes through the points $(5, 4)$ and $\left(3, \frac{1}{2}\right)$. Which of the following equations describes the line?

    A) $y = \frac{7}{4}x + \frac{19}{4}$

    B) $y = -\frac{7}{4}x - \frac{19}{4}$

    C) $y = \frac{7}{4}x - \frac{19}{4}$

    D) $y = \frac{4}{7}x + \frac{8}{7}$

25. Line $f$ in the $xy$-plane passes through the origin and has a slope of $-\frac{2}{5}$. Line $z$ is perpendicular to line $f$ and passes through the point $(6, 2)$. Which of the following is the equation of line $z$?

A) $y = -\frac{2}{5}x$

B) $y = -\frac{2}{5}x - 13$

C) $y = \frac{5}{2}x$

D) $y = \frac{5}{2}x - 13$

$$V = \frac{1}{3}\pi\left(\frac{d}{2}\right)^2 h$$

26. A circle of rubber with a constant diameter $d$ is placed on a table; its perimeter is anchored to the table and a string is attached to its center. When the string is pulled upwards, a cone is formed with height $h$ and volume $V$. The relationship between $d$, $h$, and $V$ is represented above. Which of the following statements must be true?

   I. As the volume of the cone decreases, the height also decreases.
   II. If the diameter of the base of the cone is 6 centimeters, the height can be determined by dividing the volume by $3\pi$.
   III. If the height of the cone triples, the volume must also triple.

A) I only

B) I and II only

C) II and III only

D) I, II, and III

# Reflect

**Directions:** Take a few minutes to recall what you've learned and what you've been practicing in this chapter. Consider the following questions, jot down your best answer for each one, and then compare your reflections to the expert responses on the following page. Use your level of confidence to to determine what to do next.

What should you do to isolate a particular variable in an equation?

_____

_____

_____

What types of key words should you look for when translating English into math?

_____

_____

_____

What is the most useful equation for a line in the coordinate plane? Why?

_____

_____

_____

When the SAT gives you two points on a line, what can you figure out?

_____

_____

_____

How are parallel and perpendicular lines related to each other?

_____

_____

_____

## Expert Responses

What should you do to isolate a particular variable in an equation?

*Perform inverse operations until the variable is by itself on one side of the equal sign. If the equation has fractions, make them disappear by multiplying both sides of the equation by the denominator(s). If like terms appear on different sides of the equation, collect them on the same side so that you can combine them.*

What types of key words should you look for when translating English into math?

*Look for key words that signal equality ("is," "has," "was"), variable names ("Marina's age," "the cost of one bathtub"), or one of the four arithmetic operations (addition, subtraction, multiplication, and division).*

What is the most useful equation for a line in the coordinate plane? Why?

*The best equation is slope-intercept form, $y = mx + b$, because it tells you the slope ($m$) and the y-intercept ($b$). Conversely, if you need to derive an equation yourself, you can plug the slope and y-intercept into slope-intercept form and you're done.*

When the SAT gives you two points on a line, what can you figure out?

*If you know two points, you can figure out the slope of the line with the equation $m = \dfrac{y_2 - y_1}{x_2 - x_1}$. From there, you can plug one of the points and the slope into slope-intercept form and find the y-intercept.*

How are parallel and perpendicular lines related to each other?

*Parallel lines never intersect and they have equal slopes. Perpendicular lines intersect at a 90° angle and they have negative reciprocal slopes.*

## Next Steps

If you answered most questions correctly in the "How Much Have You Learned?" section, and if your responses to the Reflect questions were similar to those of the SAT expert, then consider linear equations and graphs an area of strength and move on to the next chapter. Come back to this topic periodically to prevent yourself from getting rusty.

If you don't yet feel confident, review those parts of this chapter that you have not yet mastered. In particular, review the variable isolation drills in the Solving Equations lesson and the definition of slope-intercept form in the Linear Graphs lesson. Then try the questions you missed again. As always, be sure to review the explanations closely.

# Answers and Explanations

## 1. D

**Difficulty:** Easy

**Getting to the Answer:** Distribute the factor of 2, combine like terms, multiply both sides of the equation by 2 to clear the fraction, and then solve for $y$:

$$3y + 2y - 4 = \frac{3y}{2} + 1$$

$$5y - 4 = \frac{3y}{2} + 1$$

$$10y - 8 = 3y + 2$$

$$7y = 10$$

$$y = \frac{10}{7}$$

Choice **(D)** is correct.

## 2. C

**Difficulty:** Hard

**Strategic Advice:** Complicated-looking equations appear difficult, but they always succumb to the steps of solving an equation. First, clear the equation of fractions, then collect like terms, and solve for the desired variable.

**Getting to the Answer:** Clear the equation of the fraction in the numerator by multiplying both sides by 4 to yield:

$$4S = \frac{4C - I}{C + I}$$

Now, multiply both sides by the denominator $C + I$ to clear the equation of fractions:

$$4S(C + I) = 4C - I$$

Distribute the $4S$:

$$4SC + 4SI = 4C - I$$

To solve for $I$, collect all the terms that include $I$ on one side of the equation:

$$4SI + I = 4C - 4SC$$

Factor out the $I$:

$$I(4S + 1) = 4C - 4SC$$

Divide to isolate $I$, and factor out $4C$ from the numerator:

$$I = \frac{4C - 4SC}{4S + 1} = \frac{4C(1 - S)}{4S + 1}$$

**(C)** is correct.

## 3. 18

**Difficulty:** Easy

**Getting to the Answer:** First, clear the fractions by multiplying both sides of the equation by 8. Then solve for $x$ using inverse operations:

$$\frac{7}{8}(n - 6) = \frac{21}{2}$$

$$8\left[\frac{7}{8}(n - 6)\right] = 8\left[\frac{21}{2}\right]$$

$$7(n - 6) = 4(21)$$

$$7n - 42 = 84$$

$$7n = 126$$

$$n = 18$$

Grid in **18**.

## 4. A

**Difficulty:** Medium

**Strategic Advice:** Noticing key information about the answer choices and using that information to pick numbers saves time by eliminating algebra.

**Getting to the Answer:** Rearranging the terms of the equation such that $\frac{a}{b}$ is on one side and the constants are all on the other will work for this problem. First, cross-multiply to get rid of the fractions. Then, use inverse operations to isolate $\frac{a}{b}$:

$$\frac{3a + b}{b} \times \frac{11}{2}$$

$$2(3a + b) = 11b$$

$$6a + 2b = 11b$$

$$6a = 9b$$

$$a = \frac{9}{6}b$$

$$\frac{a}{b} = \frac{3}{2}$$

The answer is **(A)**.

There is a faster approach. Notice that 2 shows up in the denominator in most of the choices, indicating that it is likely that $b$ equals 2. If $b = 2$, then $a$ must be 3 for the numerator to equal 11. Test this by plugging the numbers into the equation:

$$\frac{3(3) + 2}{2} = \frac{11}{2}$$

Thus, $\frac{a}{b} = \frac{3}{2}$, confirming **(A)** as the answer. You can avoid a lot of work by using key information in the answer choices to pick numbers.

### 5.  D

**Difficulty:** Medium

**Getting to the Answer:** Simplify the numerators as much as possible, then isolate the variable. Begin by combining like terms on both sides of the equation. Then cross-multiply and solve for $z$:

$$\frac{4 + z - (3 + 2z)}{6} = \frac{-z - 3(5 - 2)}{7}$$
$$\frac{1 - z}{6} = \frac{-z - 9}{7}$$
$$7 - 7z = -6z - 54$$
$$-z = -61$$
$$z = 61$$

Choice **(D)** is correct.

### 6.  D

**Difficulty:** Medium

**Getting to the Answer:** Use the information in the question to write your own expression, then look for the answer choice that matches. Simplify your expression only if you don't find a match. If a couple earns $50 *per half-hour* that they dance, then they earn $50 \times 2 = \$100$ *per hour*. Multiply this amount by the number of hours (not including the first 3 hours). This can be expressed as $100(h - 3)$. This is not one of the answer choices, so simplify by distributing the 100 to get $100h - 300$, which is **(D)**.

If you're struggling with the algebra, try Picking Numbers. Pick a number of hours a couple might dance, like 5. They don't earn anything for the first 3 hours, but they earn $50 per half-hour for the last 2 hours, which is 50 times 4 half-hours, or $200. Now, find the expression that gives you an answer of $200 when $h = 5$ hours: $100(5) - 300 = 500 - 300 = 200$. If you use Picking Numbers, remember that it is possible that the number

you choose satisfies more than one answer choice, so plug it in to the other three choices. In this case, $h = 5$ does not give a value of 200 in any other equation, which confirms that **(D)** is correct.

### 7.  B

**Difficulty:** Medium

**Getting to the Answer:** Translate piece by piece to get a final expression for the final value, $v$. Multiply the second value by 2 to get $2(1) = 2$. Subtract that from the first value to get $f - 2$. Divide this expression by half of the third value to get $\dfrac{f - 2}{\frac{t}{2}}$, which you can simplify by multiplying by the reciprocal: $\left(\dfrac{f - 2}{1}\right)\left(\dfrac{2}{t}\right) = \left(\dfrac{2f - 4}{t}\right)$.

Choice **(B)** matches the final expression. Watch out for (D), the trap answer choice that switches the variables.

### 8.  B

**Difficulty:** Medium

**Getting to the Answer:** Write expressions to represent the profit generated by selling each type of pizza. You're told The Works sells for $17 each and that its ingredients cost the pizzeria $450 per week. This means the weekly profit generated by this pizza's sales can be represented by the expression $17x - 450$. Do the same for The Hawaiian: Each one sells for $13, but the pizzeria loses $310 to pay for ingredients each week. Therefore, the weekly profit from this pizza can be represented by $13x - 310$. To determine the value of $x$ at which the profit from the sale of each type of pizza is the same, set the two profit expressions equal to each other and solve:

$$17x - 450 = 13x - 310$$
$$4x = 140$$
$$x = 35$$

Thus, **(B)** is correct. Always be sure you're answering the right question; choice (D), 145, is the profit when $x = 35$.

## 9.  A

**Difficulty:** Easy

**Getting to the Answer:** When faced with a question that includes abstract expressions, it is helpful to pick concrete numbers to work with. These numbers don't have to be realistic; just choose numbers that are easy to work with. Suppose the student checks her balance after 2 weeks working 3 hours each week. She would have worked a total of 6 hours, which would have to be multiplied by the amount she is paid per hour to get her total pay. In the expression, plugging in $w = 3$ and $n = 2$ demonstrates that the number 10 in the expression must be the amount that she is paid per hour, and thus is the term that would change if the student got a raise. **(A)** is correct. Although 50 is not an answer choice, you can deduce that it must have been her checking account's original balance because it is a constant.

## 10.  7

**Difficulty:** Medium

**Getting to the Answer:** First, notice that the actual dollar amount of the increase each year is unknown, so assign a variable like $d$. After 12 increases, his salary will rise by $25,500, so write a formula $12d = 25,500$. Solve for $d$ to find that Malik will receive an increase of $2,125 per year.

The question asks how many years must go by until Malik's salary is at least $40,000; the number of years is another unknown, so assign it a variable like $n$. Multiplying $n$ by the amount of each increase will give you the total increase of dollars over $n$ years, but don't forget to add in the starting salary to reflect his total salary amount:

$$25,500 + 2,125n = 40,000$$
$$2,125n = 14,500$$
$$n \approx 6.8$$

The question asks you to assume that salary increases only take place at the end of a full year. If you are unsure and want to prove that the answer is not 6, check by using $n = 6$ to calculate the total dollar amount: $25,500 + 2,125(6) = 38,250$. Six years is not long enough; grid in **7**.

## 11.  B

**Difficulty:** Easy

**Getting to the Answer:** You're asked to identify the line that the one described in the question stem will never intersect. Lines that never intersect are parallel and therefore have identical slopes, so start by finding the slope of the line whose two coordinate pairs are given. You'll find:

$$m = \frac{1-0}{0-\left(-\frac{2}{5}\right)} = \frac{1}{\frac{2}{5}} = \frac{5}{2}$$

Choices (C) and (D) have negative slopes, so eliminate them. Next, find the slopes of (A) and (B). No need to use the slope formula; counting units on the graphs will be faster. The slope of (A) is $\frac{2}{5}$ because for every 2 units the line rises, it runs 5 units to the right. The slope of (B) is $\frac{5}{2}$ because when the line goes up 5 units, it goes 2 units to the right. Therefore, **(B)** is correct.

## 12.  A

**Difficulty:** Medium

**Strategic Advice:** Remember that parallel lines have the same slope and perpendicular lines have opposite sign reciprocal slopes.

**Getting to the Answer:** The first useful piece of information is that the slope of the line perpendicular to line $t$ is $-\frac{4}{3}$. Perpendicular lines have negative reciprocal slopes, so the slope of line $t$ is $\frac{3}{4}$. Eliminate (B) and (D) because they have the incorrect slopes.

Plug the values for the slope and the coordinate point $(4, 7)$ into the slope-intercept equation to solve for $b$:

$$7 = \frac{3}{4}(4) + b$$
$$7 = 3 + b$$
$$7 - 3 = b$$
$$b = 4$$

Eliminate (C) because it does not have the correct $y$-intercept. Choice **(A)** is correct.

## 13. A

**Difficulty:** Medium

**Getting to the Answer:** Start by finding the slope of the line by picking a pair of points, such as $(40, 0)$ and $(65, 100)$: $m = \frac{100 - 0}{65 - 40} = \frac{100}{25} = 4$. Choices (B) and (C) have slopes other than 4, so eliminate them. Choices (A) and (D) have $y$-intercepts of $-160$ and 40, respectively. Now, read the axis labels carefully: the horizontal axis begins at 40 (not 0). The line is trending downward as $x$-values get smaller, so the $y$-intercept (when $x = 0$) must be well below 0 on the vertical axis. Therefore, the answer must be **(A)**.

## 14. 70

**Difficulty:** Hard

**Getting to the Answer:** Because 40 pounds is not shown on the graph, you need more information. In a real-world scenario, the $y$-intercept of a graph usually represents a flat fee or a starting amount. The slope of the line represents a unit rate, such as the cost per pound to airmail the box.

The $y$-intercept of the graph is 10, so the flat fee is $10. To find the cost per pound (the unit rate), substitute two points from the graph into the slope formula. Using the points $(0, 10)$ and $(4, 16)$, the cost per pound is $\frac{16 - 10}{4 - 0} = \frac{6}{4} = 1.5$, which means it costs $1.50 per pound to airmail a box. The total cost to airmail a 40-pound box is $\$10 + 1.50(40) = \$10 + \$60 = \$70$. Grid in **70**.

## 15. A

**Difficulty:** Hard

**Getting to the Answer:** The question tells you that the relationship is linear, so start by finding the rate of change (the slope, $m$) using any two pairs of values from the table and the slope formula. Next, substitute the slope and any pair of values from the table, such as $(10, 34)$, into the equation $y = mx + b$ and solve for $b$. Finally, use the values of $m$ and $b$ to write the function.

$$m = \frac{y_2 - y_1}{x_2 - x_1} = \frac{64 - 34}{30 - 10} = \frac{30}{20} = 1.5$$

You can stop right there! Only **(A)** has a slope of 1.5, so it must be the correct answer. For the record:

$$34 = 10(1.5) + b$$
$$34 = 15 + b$$
$$19 = b$$

## 16. B

**Difficulty:** Hard

**Strategic Advice:** Watch out for the "NOT" keyword in the question stem. Picking numbers based on clues in the equation is faster than doing the algebra.

**Getting to the Answer:** To find the answer using Picking Numbers, take advantage of the fact that the equation is a proportion (that is, two fractions equal to each other). If $b = 7$ and $2(a - 3) = 4$, then both fractions will be the same and the numbers you've picked will be valid. Solve for $a$: $a - 3 = 2$, and $a = 5$. Now plug $b = 7$ and $a = 5$ into the choices, looking for the one that ISN'T true:

(A) $\frac{b}{a - 3} = \frac{7}{5 - 3} = \frac{7}{2}$, eliminate.

(B) $\frac{2a}{b} = \frac{2(5)}{7} = \frac{10}{7} \neq -\frac{10}{7}$

You're done; pick **(B)** and move on. For the record:

(C) $14a - 4b = 14(5) - 4(7) = 70 - 28 = 42$, eliminate.

(D) $\frac{a - 3}{b} = \frac{5 - 3}{7} = \frac{2}{7}$, eliminate.

To solve this question using algebra, first cross-multiply and simplify the original equation:

$$\frac{2(a - 3)}{b} = \frac{4}{7}$$
$$14(a - 3) = 4b$$
$$7(a - 3) = 2b$$
$$7a - 21 = 2b$$
$$7a - 2b = 21$$

Then, repeat this entire process for each answer choice, looking for the one that *doesn't* yield the same equation:

(A) $\frac{b}{a - 3} = \frac{7}{2}$, $2b = 7a - 21$, $21 = 7a - 2b$, eliminate.

(B) $\frac{2a}{b} = -\frac{10}{7}$, $14a = -10b$, $7a = -5b$, $7a + 5b = 0$

This equation is different from the one in the question, so **(B)** is correct. For the record:

(C) $14a - 4b = 42$, $7a - 2b = 21$, eliminate.

(D) $\frac{a - 3}{b} = \frac{2}{7}$, $7a - 21 = 2b$, $7a - 2b = 21$, eliminate.

## 17. A

**Difficulty:** Medium

**Category:** Solving Equations

**Getting to the Answer:** This question has multiple fractions, so clear the $\frac{8}{5}$ by multiplying both sides of the equation by its reciprocal, $\frac{5}{8}$. Then, because the answers are given in decimal form, change the other fraction to a decimal by dividing the numerator by the denominator.

$$\frac{8}{5}\left(x + \frac{33}{12}\right) = 16$$

$$\frac{\cancel{5}}{\cancel{8}} \times \left[\frac{\cancel{8}}{\cancel{5}}\left(x + \frac{33}{12}\right)\right] = \frac{5}{8} \times 16$$

$$x + 2.75 = 10$$

$$x = 7.25$$

**(A)** is correct.

## 18. B

**Difficulty:** Easy

**Category:** Linear Graphs

**Getting to the Answer:** Read the axis labels carefully. The $y$-intercept is the point at which $x = 0$, which means the number of songs purchased is 0. The $y$-intercept is (0, 20), so the cost is $20 before buying any songs and therefore most likely represents a flat membership fee for joining the service. **(B)** is correct.

## 19. 36

**Difficulty:** Medium

**Category:** Solving Equations

**Getting to the Answer:** When you're asked to find an expression rather than a variable value, it means there's likely a shortcut: try to make the expression you have look like the expression you want. Start by eliminating the fractions. A common multiple of 4 and 3 is 12, so multiply both sides of the equation by that. Once the fractions are gone, move both variable terms to the same side:

$$12\left(\frac{3}{4}y = 6 - \frac{1}{3}c\right)$$

$$9y = 72 - 4c$$

$$4c + 9y = 72$$

$$2c + \frac{9}{2}y = 36$$

The expression on the left side is precisely what you're looking for, so grid in **36**.

## 20. C

**Difficulty:** Medium

**Category:** Word Problems

**Getting to the Answer:** Look closely; buried in the text are two sets of coordinates you can use. The question states that admission was $2 when the admission charge was first implemented and increased to $2.50 after 3 years, making your coordinates (0, 2) and (3, 2.5). The slope of the line passing through these is $m = \frac{2.5 - 2}{3 - 0} = \frac{0.5}{3} = \frac{1}{6}$. Eliminate (A) and (D). Because the admission fee started at $2, 2 is the $y$-intercept, so the full equation is $y = \frac{c}{6} + 2$. **(C)** is correct.

Because the question says "three years ago," it may be tempting to use (−3, 2) and (0, 2.5) as your coordinates. Think about what that would mean: the first admission charge would be $2.50, as it's impossible to have a negative year. This contradicts the question stem, so (B) is incorrect.

## 21. D

**Difficulty:** Medium

**Category:** Word Problems

**Getting to the Answer:** Take a quick peek at the answer choices. The equations are given in slope-intercept form, so start by finding the slope. Substitute two pairs of values from the table (try to pick easy ones, if possible) into the slope formula, $m = \frac{y_2 - y_1}{x_2 - x_1}$. Keep in mind that the projected number of pounds sold *depends* on the price, so the price is the independent variable ($x$) and the projected number is the dependent variable ($y$). Using the points (1.2, 15,000) and (2.2, 2,500), you can find the slope:

$$m = \frac{2,500 - 15,000}{2.2 - 1.2}$$

$$m = \frac{-12,500}{1}$$

$$m = -12,500$$

This means you can eliminate (A) and (B) because the slope is not correct. Don't let (B) fool you—the projected number of pounds sold goes *down* as the price goes *up*, so there is an inverse relationship, which means the slope must be negative. To choose between (C) and (D), you could find the $y$-intercept of the line. Pick a point with easy values, such as (2, 5,000), and plug in 5,000 for $y$ and 2 for $x$:

$$y = mx + b$$
$$5,000 = -12,500(2) + b$$
$$5,000 = -25,000 + b$$
$$30,000 = b$$

**(D)** is correct. Another option is to substitute (2, 5,000) into (C) and (D) only. Again, **(D)** is correct because $5,000 = -12,500(2) + 30,000$ is a true statement.

## 22. D

**Difficulty:** Medium

**Category:** Word Problems

**Getting to the Answer:** Consider each choice systematically, using the numbers on the figure to help you evaluate each statement.

It takes Brian and Jared each 20 minutes to bike home, so (A) and (B) are false. Jared bikes 5 miles in 20 minutes, while Brian only bikes 2 miles in 20 minutes; their rates are not the same, so (C) is false. This means **(D)** must be true. Jared starts out farther away than Brian, so Jared must bike at a faster rate to arrive home in the same amount of time.

## 23. B

**Difficulty:** Hard

**Category:** Linear Graphs

**Getting to the Answer:** You aren't given any numbers in this question, so make some up. Sketch a quick graph of any simple linear equation that has a positive $y$-intercept (because it is given that $b > 0$). Then, change the sign of the $y$-intercept and sketch the new graph on the same coordinate plane. Pick a simple equation that you can sketch quickly, such as $y = x + 3$, and then change the sign of $b$. The new equation is $y = x - 3$. Sketch both graphs. The second line is shifted down 6 units, and because $b = 3$, 6 is $2b$ units. **(B)** is correct. The graph that follows illustrates this. If you're still unsure, try another pair of equations.

## 24. C

**Difficulty:** Medium

**Category:** Linear Graphs

**Strategic Advice:** Be careful when the answer choices look very similar to each other. Eliminating incorrect answers during intermediate steps lowers your odds of making a careless mistake.

**Getting to the Answer:** The question provides two coordinate points, which means that the best approach is to find the slope using the formula $m = \dfrac{y_2 - y_1}{x_2 - x_1}$, then use the slope-intercept equation for a line to find $b$, the $y$-intercept. Plugging the results into the slope formula results in:

$$\frac{\frac{1}{2} - 4}{3 - 5} = \frac{\frac{1}{2} - \frac{8}{2}}{-2} = \frac{-\frac{7}{2}}{-2} = -\frac{7}{2} \times -\frac{1}{2} = \frac{7}{4}$$

Eliminate (B) and (D) because they do not have the slope $\frac{7}{4}$. Plug the slope and one of the given points (5, 4) into the slope-intercept equation to solve for $b$:

$$4 = \frac{7}{4}(5) + b$$
$$4 = \frac{35}{4} + b$$
$$\frac{16}{4} - \frac{35}{4} = b$$
$$b = -\frac{19}{4}$$

Eliminate (A) because it does not have the correct $y$-intercept; therefore only **(C)** is left and is correct. Plugging the calculated values for the slope and the $y$-intercept into the slope-intercept equation indeed gives you choice **(C)**: $y = \frac{7}{4}x - \frac{19}{4}$.

After eliminating (B) and (D), you can save time by noticing that the two possible y-intercepts are $\frac{19}{4}$ and $-\frac{19}{4}$. You really only need to determine if $b$ is positive or negative.

## 25.  D

**Difficulty:** Easy

**Category:** Linear Graphs

**Getting to the Answer:** This question provides an equation for a line perpendicular to line z and a coordinate point for line z, (6, 2). The opposite sign reciprocal of the slope of the perpendicular line, $\frac{5}{2}$, is the slope of line z. Eliminate (A) and (B) because they have the incorrect slope.

Plug the values for the slope and the coordinate point (6, 2) into the slope-intercept equation to solve for b:

$$2 = \frac{5}{2}(6) + b$$
$$2 = 15 + b$$
$$2 - 15 = b$$
$$b = -13$$

Plug the values for the slope and the y-intercept into the slope-intercept equation to get $y = \frac{5}{2}x - 13$. **(D)** is correct.

You can save a little time if you eliminate (C) as soon as you see that $b \neq 0$, which you should be able to tell as soon as you see that $2 = 15 + b$.

## 26.  D

**Difficulty:** Hard

**Category:** Word Problems

**Strategic Advice:** In problems that include verifying statements marked with roman numerals, start with the easiest statement to verify and work to the hardest, eliminating answer choices along the way. This may save you time on test day.

**Getting to the Answer:** The key to this problem is to see that because the question stem states that d is constant, the cumbersome expression $\frac{1}{3}\pi\left(\frac{d}{2}\right)^2$ is just a constant that is the coefficient of the variable h. The formula is really $V = $ (some constant) $\times h$. In any formula written such that $y = ax$, where a is a constant, as one amount increases (or decreases), the other amount must increase (or decrease) at the same rate. So if V decreases, h must have decreased. Statement I is true; eliminate (C).

Pick the next easiest statement to verify; in this case, statement III. If h increases by tripling, V must also increase by the same rate; it must triple, too. Test this statement if you like by picking a number for h and solving for V, then tripling h and solving for V again. Statement III is true; eliminate (A) and (B). That leaves **(D)** as the correct answer.

On test day, you'd stop here. For the sake of learning, though, you can verify whether statement II is true. Plug $d = 6$ into the formula and solve for h in terms of V:

$$V = \frac{1}{3}\pi\left(\frac{6}{2}\right)^2 h$$
$$V = \frac{(3)^2}{3}\pi h$$
$$\frac{V}{3\pi} = \frac{3\cancel{\pi} h}{3\cancel{\pi}}$$
$$h = \frac{V}{3\pi}$$

Thus, statement II is indeed true.

# CHAPTER 5

# Systems of Linear Equations

## LEARNING OBJECTIVES

After completing this chapter, you will be able to:

- Solve systems of linear equations by substitution
- Solve systems of linear equations by combination
- Determine the number of possible solutions for a system of linear equations, if any

45/600 SmartPoints®

# How Much Do You Know?

**Directions:** Try the questions that follow. Show your work so that you can compare your solutions to the ones found in the Check Your Work section immediately after this question set. The "Category" heading in the explanation for each question gives the title of the lesson that covers how to solve it. If you answered the question(s) for a given lesson correctly, and if your scratchwork looks like ours, you may be able to move quickly through that lesson. If you answered incorrectly or used a different approach, you may want to take your time on that lesson.

$$-7x + 2y = 18$$
$$x + y = 0$$

1. In the system of equations above, what is the value of $x$?

   A) $-2$

   B) $0$

   C) $2$

   D) $4$

2. At a certain movie theater, there are 16 rows and each row has either 20 or 24 seats. If the total number of seats in all 16 rows is 348, how many rows have 24 seats?

   A) $7$

   B) $9$

   C) $11$

   D) $13$

3. If $17x - 5y = 8$ and $14x - 7y = -7$, what is the value of $3x + 2y$?

   A) $-15$

   B) $-5$

   C) $5$

   D) $15$

4. If $0.2x = 10 - 0.5y$, then $10y + 4x =$

$$\frac{1}{2}x - \frac{2}{3}y = 7$$
$$ax - 8y = -1$$

5. If the system of linear equations above has no solution, and $a$ is a constant, then what is the value of $a$?

   A) $-2$

   B) $-\frac{1}{2}$

   C) $2$

   D) $6$

Answers and explanations are on the next page.  ▶ ▶ ▶

**Math**

## Check Your Work

**1.  A**

**Difficulty:** Easy

**Category:** Substitution

**Getting to the Answer:** Solve the second equation for $y$ in terms of $x$, then substitute into the first equation and solve:

$$y = -x$$
$$-7x - 2x = 18$$
$$-9x = 18$$
$$x = -2$$

**(A)** is correct.

**2.  A**

**Difficulty:** Hard

**Category:** Substitution

**Getting to the Answer:** Create a system of equations in which $x$ represents the number of rows with 20 seats and $y$ represents the number of rows with 24 seats. The first equation should represent the total *number of rows*, each with 20 or 24 seats, or $x + y = 16$. The second equation should represent the total *number of seats*. Because $x$ represents rows with 20 seats and $y$ represents rows with 24 seats, the second equation should be $20x + 24y = 348$. Now solve the system using substitution. Solve the first equation for either variable and substitute the result into the second equation:

$$x + y = 16$$
$$x = 16 - y$$
$$20(16 - y) + 24y = 348$$
$$320 - 20y + 24y = 348$$
$$320 + 4y = 348$$
$$4y = 28$$
$$y = 7$$

So 7 rows have 24 seats, which means **(A)** is correct. This is all the question asks for, so you don't need to find the value of $x$.

**3.  D**

**Difficulty:** Medium

**Category:** Combination

**Getting to the Answer:** Subtract the second equation from the first to find that $3x + 2y = 15$, making **(D)** the correct answer.

**4.  200**

**Difficulty:** Medium

**Category:** Number of Possible Solutions

**Getting to the Answer:** Rearrange the equation so that the $y$ and $x$ terms appear, in that order, on the left side: $0.5y + 0.2x = 10$. What number do you need to multiply $0.5y$ by to get $10y$? Twenty. Notice that $10y + 4x$ is 20 times $0.5y + 0.2x$. Multiply both sides of the equation by 20 to find that $10y + 4x = $ **200**. Note that both of these equations describe the same line.

**5.  D**

**Difficulty:** Hard

**Category:** Number of Possible Solutions

**Getting to the Answer:** Graphically, a system of linear equations that has no solution indicates two parallel lines—that is, two lines that have the same slope but different $y$-intercepts. To have the same slope, the $x$- and $y$-coefficients must be the same. To get from $-\frac{2}{3}$ to $-8$, you multiply by 12, so multiply $-\frac{1}{2}x$ by 12 as well to yield $6x$. Because the other $x$-coefficient is $a$, it must be that $a = 6$, and **(D)** is correct. Note that, even though it is more work, you could also write each equation in slope-intercept form and set the slopes equal to each other to solve for $a$.

# Substitution

## LEARNING OBJECTIVE

After this lesson, you will be able to:

- Solve systems of linear equations by substitution

## To answer a question like this:

If $3x + 2y = 15$ and $x + y = 10$, what is the value of $y$?

A)  $-15$

B)  $-5$

C)  $5$

D)  $15$

## You need to know this:

A **system** of two linear equations simply refers to the equations of two lines. "Solving" a system of two linear equations usually means finding the point where the two lines intersect. (However, see the lesson titled "Number of Possible Solutions" later in this chapter for exceptions.)

There are two ways to solve a system of linear equations: substitution and combination. For some SAT questions, substitution is faster; for others, combination is faster. We'll cover combination in the next lesson.

## You need to do this:

To solve a system of two linear equations by substitution:

- Isolate a variable (ideally, one whose coefficient is 1) in one of the equations
- Substitute the result into the other equation

## Explanation:

Isolate $x$ in the second equation, then substitute the result into the first equation:

$$x = 10 - y$$
$$3(10 - y) + 2y = 15$$
$$30 - 3y + 2y = 15$$
$$-y = -15$$
$$y = 15$$

If you needed to know the value of $x$ as well, you could now substitute 15 for $y$ into either equation to find that $x = -5$. The correct answer is **(D)**.

## Try on Your Own

**Directions:** Solve these questions by substitution. Take as much time as you need on these questions. Work carefully and methodically. There will be an opportunity for timed practice at the end of the chapter.

---

HINT: For Q1, which equation is the easier one to solve for one variable in terms of the other?

---

1. If $7c + 8b = 15$ and $3b - c = 2$, what is the value of $b$?

---

HINT: For Q2, the second equation is in a convenient form for substitution. But look at the first equation: what can you learn quickly about $x$ and $y$?

---

$$\begin{cases} 3x - 3y = 0 \\ y = 2x + 5 \end{cases}$$

2. Given the system of equations above, what is the sum of $x$ and $y$?

A) $-10$

B) $-5$

C) $0$

D) $5$

$$\begin{cases} 4x + 3y = 14 - y \\ x - 5y = 2 \end{cases}$$

3. If $(x, y)$ is a solution to the system of equations above, then what is the value of $x - y$?

A) $\dfrac{1}{4}$

B) $1$

C) $3$

D) $18$

4. If $5a = 6b + 7$ and $a - b = 3$, what is the value of $\dfrac{b}{2}$?

A) $2$

B) $4$

C) $5.5$

D) $11$

5. Marisol is selling snacks at her school's soccer games to raise money for a service project. She buys nuts in cases that contain 24 bags and granola bars in cases that contain 20 packages. She sells the nuts for $1.25 a bag and the granola bars for $1.75 a package. If she raised $160 and sold 112 items, how many cases of granola bars did Marisol buy?

A) $2$

B) $3$

C) $40$

D) $72$

# Combination

## To answer a question like this:

$$\begin{cases} 4x - 5y = 10 \\ 2x + 3y = -6 \end{cases}$$

If the solution to the system of equations above is $(x, y)$, what is the value of $y$ ?

A) $-2$

B) $-1$

C) $1$

D) $2$

## You need to know this:

Combining two equations means adding or subtracting them, usually with the goal of either eliminating one of the variables or solving for a combination of variables (e.g., $5n + 5m$).

## You need to do this:

To solve a system of two linear equations by combination:

- Make sure that the coefficients for one variable have the same absolute value. (If they don't, multiply one equation by an appropriate constant. Sometimes, you'll have to multiply both equations by constants.)
- Either add or subtract the equations to eliminate one variable
- Solve for the remaining variable, then substitute its value into either equation to solve for the variable you eliminated in the preceding step

### Explanation:

Both variables have different coefficients in the two equations, but you can convert the $2x$ in the second equation to $4x$ by multiplying the entire second equation by 2:

$$2(2x + 3y = -6)$$
$$4x + 6y = -12$$

Now that the coefficients for one variable are the same, subtract the second equation from the first to eliminate the $x$ variable. (Note that if the $x$-coefficients were 4 and $-4$, you would add the equations instead of subtracting.)

$$4x - 5y = 10$$
$$\underline{-(4x + 6y = -12)}$$
$$0x - 11y = 22$$

Solve this equation for $y$:

$$-11y = 22$$
$$y = -2$$

**(A)** is the correct answer. If the question asked for $x$ instead of $y$, you would now substitute $-2$ into either of the original equations and solve for $x$. (For the record, $x = 0$.)

## Try on Your Own

**Directions:** Solve these questions using combination. Take as much time as you need on these questions. Work carefully and methodically. There will be an opportunity for timed practice at the end of the chapter.

---

HINT: For Q6, there's no need to solve for $x$ and $y$ separately.

---

$$\begin{cases} 3x + 2y = 15 \\ 2x + 3y = 10 \end{cases}$$

6.  Given the system of equations above, what is the value of $5x + 5y$?

---

HINT: For Q7, should you add or subtract these equations to eliminate a variable?

---

7.  If $2x - 3y = 14$ and $5x + 3y = 21$, what is the value of $x$?

    A)   $-1$

    B)   $0$

    C)   $\dfrac{7}{3}$

    D)   $5$

8.  If $7c - 2b = 15$ and $3b - 6c = 2$, what is the value of $b + c$?

    A)   $-27$

    B)   $-3$

    C)   $8$

    D)   $17$

9.  If $y = -x - 15$ and $\dfrac{5y}{2} - 37 = -\dfrac{x}{2}$, then what is the value of $2x + 6y$?

10. If $2x + 2y = 22$ and $3x - 4y = 12$, what is the value of $\dfrac{y}{x}$?

# Number of Possible Solutions

**LEARNING OBJECTIVE**

After this lesson, you will be able to:

- Determine the number of possible solutions for a system of linear equations, if any

## To answer a question like this:

$$\begin{cases} 5x - 3y = 10 \\ 6y = kx - 42 \end{cases}$$

In the system of linear equations above, $k$ represents a constant. If the system of equations has no solution, what is the value of $2k$?

A) $\dfrac{5}{2}$

B) $5$

C) $10$

D) $20$

## You need to know this:

The solution to a system of linear equations consists of the values of the variables that make both equations true.

A system of linear equations may have one solution, infinitely many solutions, or no solution.

If a system of equations represents two lines that intersect, then the system will have exactly **one solution** (in which the $x$- and $y$-values correspond to the point of intersection).

If a system of equations has **infinitely many solutions**, the two equations actually represent the same line. For example, $2x + y = 15$ and $4x + 2y = 30$ represent the same line. If you divide the second equation by 2, you arrive at the first equation. Every point along this line is a solution.

If a system of equations has **no solution**, as in the question above, the lines are parallel: there is no point of intersection.

No Solution          One Solution          Infinitely Many Solutions

## You need to do this:

- If the question states that the system has no solution, manipulate the equations to make the $x$-coefficients equal to each other and the $y$-coefficients equal to each other, but be sure that the $y$-intercepts (or constant terms, if the equations are in $ax + by + c$ form) are different.

- If the question states that the system has infinitely many solutions, make the $x$-coefficients equal to each other, the $y$-coefficients equal to each other, and the $y$-intercepts (or constant terms) equal to each other.

- If the question states that the system has one solution and provides the point of intersection, substitute the values at that point of intersection for $x$ and $y$ in the equations.

## Explanation:

Start by recognizing that for two lines to be parallel, the coefficients for $x$ must be identical in the two equations; ditto for the coefficients for $y$. Manipulate the second equation so that it is in the same format as the first one:

$$kx - 6y = 42$$

The $y$-coefficient in the first equation, $5x - 3y = 10$, is 3. Divide the second equation by 2 in order to make the $y$-coefficients in both equations equal:

$$\frac{k}{2}x - 3y = 21$$

Now set the $x$-coefficient equal to the $x$-coefficient in the first equation:

$$\frac{k}{2} = 5$$
$$k = 10$$

Note that the question asks for the value of $2k$, so the correct answer is **(D)**, 20.

## Try on Your Own

**Directions:** Take as much time as you need on these questions. Work carefully and methodically. There will be an opportunity for timed practice at the end of the chapter.

$$\begin{cases} 21x - 6y = 54 \\ 9 + y = 3.5x \end{cases}$$

11. The system of equations shown above has how many solutions?

    A) Zero

    B) One

    C) Two

    D) Infinitely many

---

HINT: For Q12, if a system of equations has infinitely many solutions, what do you know about the two equations?

---

$$\begin{cases} 6x + 3y = 18 \\ qx - \dfrac{y}{3} = -2 \end{cases}$$

12. In the system of linear equations above, $q$ is a constant. If the system has infinitely many solutions, what is the value of $q$?

    A) $-9$

    B) $-\dfrac{2}{3}$

    C) $\dfrac{2}{3}$

    D) $9$

---

HINT: For Q13, the point of intersection is the solution to the system of equations. Use those concrete $x$- and $y$-values.

---

$$\begin{cases} hx - 4y = -10 \\ kx + 3y = -15 \end{cases}$$

13. If the graphs of the lines in the system of equations above intersect at $(-3, 1)$, what is the value of $\dfrac{k}{h}$?

    A) $\dfrac{1}{3}$

    B) $2$

    C) $3$

    D) $6$

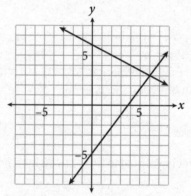

14. What is the $y$-coordinate of the solution to the system shown above?

    A) $-5$

    B) $3$

    C) $5$

    D) $6$

$$\begin{cases} 3x - 9y = -6 \\ \dfrac{1}{2}x - \dfrac{3}{2}y = c \end{cases}$$

15. If the system of linear equations above has infinitely many solutions, and $c$ is a constant, what is the value of $c$?

    A) $-6$

    B) $-3$

    C) $-2$

    D) $-1$

## On Test Day

Many SAT Math questions can be solved in more than one way. A little efficiency goes a long way in helping you get through the Math sections on time, so it's useful to try solving problems more than one way to learn which way is fastest.

Try this question using two approaches: both substitution and combination. Time yourself on each attempt. Which approach allowed you to get to the answer faster?

16. If $28x - 5y = 36$ and $15x + 5y + 18 = 68$, what is the value of $x$ ?

    A)  1
    B)  2
    C)  3
    D)  4

The answer and both ways of solving can be found at the end of this chapter.

# How Much Have You Learned?

**Directions:** For testlike practice, give yourself 15 minutes to complete this question set. Be sure to study the explanations, even for questions you got right. They can be found at the end of this chapter.

17. If $8x - 2y = 10$ and $3y - 9x = 12$, then what is the value of $y - x$?

    A)  −8

    B)  2

    C)  12

    D)  22

18. A state college has separate fee rates for resident students and nonresident students. Resident students are charged $421 per semester and nonresident students are charged $879 per semester. The college's sophomore class of 1,980 students paid a total of $1,170,210 in fees for the most recent semester. Which of the following systems of equations represents the number of resident ($r$) and nonresident ($n$) sophomores and the amount of fees the two groups paid?

    A)  $r + n = 1{,}170{,}210$
        $421r + 879n = 1{,}980$

    B)  $r + n = 1{,}980$
        $879r + 421n = 1{,}170{,}210$

    C)  $r + n = 1{,}980$
        $421r + 879n = 1{,}170{,}210$

    D)  $r + n = 1{,}170{,}210$
        $879r + 421n = 1{,}980$

19. A sofa costs $50 less than three times the cost of a chair. If the sofa and chair together cost $650, how much more does the sofa cost than the chair?

    A)  $175

    B)  $225

    C)  $300

    D)  $475

| Equation 1 | |
|---|---|
| $x$ | $y$ |
| −2 | 6 |
| 0 | 4 |
| 2 | 2 |
| 4 | 0 |

| Equation 2 | |
|---|---|
| $x$ | $y$ |
| −8 | −8 |
| −4 | −7 |
| 0 | −6 |
| 4 | −5 |

20. The tables above represent data points for two linear equations. If the two equations form a system, what is the $x$-coordinate of the solution to that system?

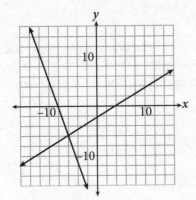

21. If $(A, B)$ is the solution to the system of equations shown above, and $A$ and $B$ are integers, then what is the value of $A + B$?

A)  $-12$

B)  $-6$

C)  $0$

D)  $6$

$$\begin{cases} -16 = 7y + 4x \\ k = \dfrac{7}{8}y + \dfrac{1}{2}x \end{cases}$$

22. If the system of linear equations above has infinitely many solutions, and $k$ is a constant, what is the value of $k$?

A)  $-8$

B)  $-4$

C)  $-2$

D)  $-1$

$$\begin{cases} -13 = ay + 24x \\ 9 + 6bx = 5y \end{cases}$$

23. If the system of equations above has no solution, and $a$ and $b$ are constants, then what is the value of $|a + b|$?

A)  $0$

B)  $1$

C)  $4$

D)  $9$

24. If $\dfrac{1}{4}x + 2y = \dfrac{11}{4}$ and $-6y - x = 7$, what is half of $y$?

25. At a certain toy store, tiny stuffed pandas cost \$3.50 and giant stuffed pandas cost \$14. If the store sold 29 panda toys and made \$217 in revenue in one week, how many tiny stuffed pandas and giant stuffed pandas were sold?

A)  18 tiny stuffed pandas, 11 giant stuffed pandas

B)  11 tiny stuffed pandas, 18 giant stuffed pandas

C)  12 tiny stuffed pandas, 17 giant stuffed pandas

D)  18 tiny stuffed pandas, 13 giant stuffed pandas

26. A bead shop sells wooden beads for \$0.20 each and crystal beads for \$0.50 each. If a jewelry artist buys 127 beads total and pays \$41 for them, how much more did she spend on crystal beads than wooden beads?

A)  \$11

B)  \$15

C)  \$23

D)  \$26

# Reflect

**Directions:** Take a few minutes to recall what you've learned and what you've been practicing in this chapter. Consider the following questions, jot down your best answer for each one, and then compare your reflections to the expert responses on the following page. Use your level of confidence to determine what to do next.

When is substitution a good choice for solving a system of equations?

_____

_____

_____

When is combination a good choice for solving a system of equations?

_____

_____

_____

What does it mean if a system of equations has no solution? Infinitely many solutions?

_____

_____

_____

## Expert Responses

When is substitution a good choice for solving a system of equations?

*Substitution works best when at least one of the variables has a coefficient of 1, making the variable easy to isolate. This system, for example, is well suited for substitution:*

$$a + 3b = 5$$
$$4a - 6b = 21$$

*That's because in the first equation, you can easily isolate a as a = 5 − 3b and plug that in for a in the other equation. By contrast, substitution would not be a great choice for solving this system:*

$$2a + 3b = 5$$
$$4a - 6b = 21$$

*If you used substitution now, you'd have to work with fractions, which is messy.*

When is combination a good choice for solving a system of equations?

*Combination is always a good choice. It is at its worst in systems such as this one:*

$$2a + 3b = 5$$
$$3a + 5b = 7$$

*Neither a coefficient is a multiple of the other, and neither b coefficient is a multiple of the other, so to solve this system with combination you'd have to multiply both equations by a constant (for example, multiply the first equation by 3 and the second equation by 2 to create a 6a term in both equations). But substitution wouldn't be stellar in this situation, either.*

*Note that combination may be particularly effective when the SAT asks for a variable expression. For example, if a question based on the previous system of equations asked for the value of 5a + 8b, then you could find the answer instantly by adding the equations together.*

What does it mean if a system of equations has no solution? Infinitely many solutions?

*A system of equations with no solution represents two parallel lines, which never cross. The coefficient of a variable in one equation will match the coefficient of the same variable in the other equation, but the constants will be different. For example, this system has no solution:*

$$2x + 3y = 4$$
$$2x + 3y = 5$$

*Subtracting one equation from the other yields the equation 0 = −1, which makes no sense.*

*If a system of equations has infinitely many solutions, then the two equations represent the same line. For example, this system has infinitely many solutions:*

$$2x + 3y = 4$$
$$4x + 6y = 8$$

*Dividing the second equation by 2 yields 2x + 3y = 4, so although the two equations look different, they are actually the same.*

## Next Steps

If you answered most questions correctly in the "How Much Have You Learned?" section, and if your responses to the Reflect questions were similar to those of the SAT expert, then consider Systems of Equations an area of strength and move on to the next chapter. Come back to this topic periodically to prevent yourself from getting rusty.

If you don't yet feel confident, review those parts of this chapter that you have not yet mastered. In particular, review the mechanics for solving a system of equations by substitution and by combination. Then try the questions you missed again. As always, be sure to review the explanations closely.

# Answers and Explanations

**1.  1**

**Difficulty:** Medium

**Getting to the Answer:** Start by isolating $c$ in the second equation: $c = 3b - 2$. Then substitute into the first equation and solve:

$$7(3b - 2) + 8b = 15$$
$$21b - 14 + 8b = 15$$
$$29b - 14 = 15$$
$$29b = 29$$
$$b = 1$$

Grid in **1**.

**2.  A**

**Difficulty:** Easy

**Getting to the Answer:** The quickest way to solve is to realize that you can rearrange the first equation to find that $x = y$. Then substitute $y$ in for $x$ in the second equation: $y = 2y + 5$. Solve to find that $y = -5$. Because $x = y$, $x$ also equals $-5$, and $x + y = -10$. **(A)** is correct.

**3.  C**

**Difficulty:** Medium

**Getting to the Answer:** Because $x$ has a coefficient of 1 in the second equation, solve the system using substitution. Before you select your answer, make sure you found the right quantity (the difference between $x$ and $y$).

First, solve the second equation for $x$ and substitute:

$$x - 5y = 2$$
$$x = 2 + 5y$$
$$4(2 + 5y) + 3y = 14 - y$$
$$8 + 20y + 3y = 14 - y$$
$$8 + 23y = 14 - y$$
$$24y = 6$$
$$y = \frac{6}{24} = \frac{1}{4}$$

Next, substitute this value back into $x = 2 + 5y$ and simplify:

$$x = 2 + 5\left(\frac{1}{4}\right)$$
$$x = \frac{8}{4} + \frac{5}{4}$$
$$x = \frac{13}{4}$$

Finally, subtract $x - y$ to find the difference:

$$\frac{13}{4} - \frac{1}{4} = \frac{12}{4} = 3$$

**(C)** is correct.

**4.  B**

**Difficulty:** Medium

**Getting to the Answer:** It's equally easy to solve the second equation for either variable. The question asks for $\frac{b}{2}$, so solve for $a$ and substitute to create an equation in only one variable:

$$a = b + 3$$
$$5(b + 3) = 6b + 7$$
$$5b + 15 = 6b + 7$$
$$8 = b$$

So $\frac{b}{2} = 4$, and **(B)** is correct.

**5.  A**

**Difficulty:** Medium

**Getting to the Answer:** Set up two equations: one for the number of items sold and one for the money collected. Let $N$ = the number of bags of nuts sold and $G$ = the number of packages of granola bars sold.

The equation for the total items is $N + G = 112$.

The equation for the money collected is $1.25N + 1.75G = 160$.

Even though this is a calculator question, quickly converting the second equation to fractions is an efficient way to save time and prevent an entry mistake: $\frac{5}{4}N + \frac{7}{4}G = 160$.

Multiply by 4 to clear the equation of fractions to get $5N + 7G = 640$.

At this point, you could solve by either combination or substitution. If you use substitution, solve the first equation for $N$, the number of bags of nuts, because the question asks for $G$, the number of packages of granola bars. Solving the first equation for $N$ yields $N = 112 - G$.

Substituting that equation into the second equation gives:

$$5(112 - G) + 7G = 640$$
$$560 - 5G + 7G = 640$$
$$560 + 2G = 640$$
$$2G = 80$$
$$G = 40$$

Remember the question asks for the number of *cases* of granola bars Marisol purchased, so divide 40 by 20, the number of packages of granola bars per case. **(A)** is correct.

As an alternative approach, if you read the question carefully and recognized you're solving for the number of *cases*, not packages, the correct answer would have to be either (A) or (B), since (C) and (D) are way too big. You could then test one of those choices, say (A) 2, by multiplying by 20 packages of granola bars per case: $2 \times 20 = 40$. Subtract that number from 112 to get the number of bags of nuts: $112 - 40 = 72$. Multiply each quantity by the price per package: $72 \times 1.25 = 90$ and $40 \times 1.75 = 70$. Then add the sales of the two items together: $90 + 70 = 160$. You've now confirmed the correct answer because $160 is how much Marisol raised. If you had tested (B) instead, then you could have eliminated it and still arrived at the correct answer with no more work because you eliminated all choices except **(A)**.

If you chose any of the other options, you likely answered the wrong question. (B) is the number of cases of nuts Marisol purchased, (C) is the number of packages of granola bars sold, and (D) is the number of bags of nuts sold.

**6. 25**

**Difficulty:** Easy

**Getting to the Answer:** Often, when the SAT asks for a sum or difference of variables, solving by combination yields the answer very quickly. Add the equations:

$$\begin{array}{r} 2x + 3y = 15 \\ +\ 3x + 2y = 10 \\ \hline 5x + 5y = 25 \end{array}$$

Grid in **25** and move on.

**7. D**

**Difficulty:** Easy

**Getting to the Answer:** This system is already set up perfectly to solve using combination because the $y$ terms ($-3y$ and $3y$) are opposites. Add the two equations to cancel $-3y$ and $3y$. Then solve the resulting equation for $x$:

$$\begin{array}{r} 2x - 3y = 14 \\ +\ 5x + 3y = 21 \\ \hline 7x \quad\quad = 35 \\ x \quad\quad = 5 \end{array}$$

Choice **(D)** is correct. The question asks only for the value of $x$, so you don't need to substitute $x$ back into either equation to find the value of $y$.

**8. D**

**Difficulty:** Easy

**Getting to the Answer:** If you're not asked to find the value of an individual variable, the question may lend itself to combination. This question asks for $b + c$, so don't waste your time finding the variables individually if you can avoid it. After rearranging the equations so that variables and constants are aligned, you can add the equations together:

$$\begin{array}{r} -2b + 7c = 15 \\ +3b - 6c = 2 \\ \hline b + c = 17 \end{array}$$

This matches **(D)**.

**9.  59**

**Difficulty:** Hard

**Getting to the Answer:** You're asked for the value of an expression rather than the value of one of the variables, so try combination. Start by rearranging the two equations so that variables and constants are aligned:

$$x + y = -15$$
$$\frac{x}{2} + \frac{5y}{2} = 37$$

Clear the fractions in the second equation and then add the equations:

$$2\left(\frac{x}{2} + \frac{5y}{2} = 37\right) \rightarrow x + 5y = 74$$

$$\begin{array}{r} x + y = -15 \\ +\ \ x + 5y = 74 \\ \hline 2x + 6y = 59 \end{array}$$

This is precisely what the question asks for, so you're done. Grid in **59**.

**10.  $\frac{3}{8}$**

**Difficulty:** Medium

**Getting to the Answer:** None of the coefficients in either equation is 1, so using combination is a better strategy than substitution here. Examine the coefficients of $x$: they don't share any factors, so multiply each equation by the coefficient from the other equation:

$$3(2x + 2y = 22) \rightarrow 6x + 6y = 66$$
$$2(3x - 4y = 12) \rightarrow 6x - 8y = 24$$

Subtract the second equation from the first:

$$\begin{array}{r} 6x + 6y = 66 \\ -\ (6x - 8y = 24) \\ \hline 14y = 42 \\ y = 3 \end{array}$$

Next, you need $x$ so you can determine the value of $\frac{y}{x}$. Substitute 3 for $y$ in one of the original equations:

$$2x + 2(3) = 22$$
$$2x + 6 = 22$$
$$2x = 16$$
$$x = 8$$

Plug your $x$- and $y$-values into $\frac{y}{x}$ to get $\frac{3}{8}$. Grid in $\frac{3}{8}$.

**11.  D**

**Difficulty:** Medium

**Strategic Advice:** Note that (C) is impossible. There are only three possibilities: the lines intersect, in which case there is one solution; the lines are parallel, in which case there are no solutions; or the equations describe the same line, in which case there are infinitely many solutions.

**Getting to the Answer:** Get the two equations into the same format so that you can distinguish among these possibilities:

$$21x - 6y = 54$$
$$3.5x - y = 9$$

Now it's easier to see that the first equation is equivalent to multiplying every term in the second equation by 6. Both equations describe the same line, so there are infinitely many solutions; **(D)** is correct.

**12.  B**

**Difficulty:** Hard

**Getting to the Answer:** A system of equations that has infinitely many solutions describes a single line. Therefore, manipulation of one equation will yield the other. Look at the constant terms: to turn the 18 into a $-2$, divide the first equation by $-9$:

$$\frac{(6x + 3y = 18)}{-9} \rightarrow -\frac{6}{9}x - \frac{3}{9}y = -2$$

$$\rightarrow -\frac{2}{3}x - \frac{1}{3}y = -2$$

The $y$ terms and constants in the second equation now match those in the first; all that's left is to set the coefficients of $x$ equal to each other: $q = -\frac{2}{3}$. Choice **(B)** is correct.

Note that you could also write each equation in slope-intercept form and set the slopes equal to each other to solve for $q$.

## 13. C

**Difficulty:** Medium

**Getting to the Answer:** If the graphs intersect at $(-3, 1)$, then the solution to the system is $x = -3$ and $y = 1$. Substitute these values into both equations and go from there:

$$hx - 4y = -10 \qquad kx + 3y = -15$$
$$h(-3) - 4(1) = -10 \quad k(-3) + 3(1) = -15$$
$$-3h - 4 = -10 \qquad -3k + 3 = -15$$
$$-3h = -6 \qquad -3k = -18$$
$$h = 2 \qquad k = 6$$

So, $\frac{k}{h} = \frac{6}{2} = 3$, making **(C)** correct.

## 14. B

**Difficulty:** Easy

**Getting to the Answer:** The solution to a system of linear equations represented graphically is the point of intersection. If the lines do not intersect, the system has no solution.

According to the graph, the lines intersect, or cross each other, at (6, 3). The question asks for the $y$-coordinate of the solution, which is 3, so **(B)** is correct.

## 15. D

**Difficulty:** Hard

**Getting to the Answer:** A system of linear equations has infinitely many solutions if both lines in the system have the same slope and the same $y$-intercept (in other words, they are the same line).

To have the same slope, the $x$- and $y$-coefficients of the two equations must be the same. Use the $x$-coefficients here: to turn $\frac{1}{2}$ into 3, multiply by 6. So $c$ becomes $6c$, and $6c = -6$, or $c = -1$, which is **(D)**.

Note that you could also write each equation in slope-intercept form and set the $y$-intercepts equal to each other to solve for $c$.

## 16. B

**Difficulty:** Medium

**Strategic Advice:** The numbers here are fairly large, so substitution is not likely to be convenient. Moreover, the $y$-coefficients have the same absolute value, so combination will probably be the faster way to solve.

**Getting to the Answer:** Start by writing the second equation in the same form as the first, then use combination to solve for $x$:

$$\begin{array}{r} 28x - 5y = 36 \\ + 15x + 5y = 50 \\ \hline 43x \qquad = 86 \\ x \qquad = 2 \end{array}$$

Choice **(B)** is correct.

If you feel more comfortable using substitution, you can maximize efficiency by solving one equation for $5y$ and substituting that value into the other equation:

$$15x + 5y = 50$$
$$5y = 50 - 15x$$
$$28x - (50 - 15x) = 36$$
$$43x - 50 = 36$$
$$43x = 86$$
$$x = 2$$

Note that the arithmetic is fundamentally the same, but the setup using combination is quicker and visually easier to follow.

## 17. D

**Difficulty:** Medium

**Category:** Combination

**Strategic Advice:** When a question asks for a sum or difference of variables, consider solving by combination.

**Getting to the Answer:** Rearrange the equations to be in the same form, with the $y$ terms before the $x$ terms, and then add:

$$\begin{array}{r} -2y + 8x = 10 \\ +(3y - 9x = 12) \\ \hline y - x = 22 \end{array}$$

The correct answer is **(D)**.

**18. C**

**Difficulty:** Medium

**Category:** Substitution/Combination

**Getting to the Answer:** Because you're given the variables ($r$ for resident and $n$ for nonresident), the only thing left for you to do is to break the wording apart into phrases and translate into math. Add together both student types to get the first equation: $r + n = 1,980$. This eliminates (A) and (D). Residents pay $421 in fees ($421r$), which eliminates (B). Only **(C)** is left, so it has to be the answer.

**19. C**

**Difficulty:** Medium

**Category:** Substitution

**Getting to the Answer:** Write a system of equations where $c =$ the cost of the chair in dollars and $s =$ the cost of the sofa in dollars. A sofa costs $50 less than three times the cost of the chair, or $s = 3c - 50$; together, a sofa and a chair cost $650, so $s + c = 650$.

The system is:

$$\begin{cases} s = 3c - 50 \\ s + c = 650 \end{cases}$$

The top equation is already solved for $s$, so substitute $3c - 50$ into the bottom equation for $s$ and solve for $c$:

$$3c - 50 + c = 650$$
$$4c - 50 = 650$$
$$4c = 700$$
$$c = 175$$

Remember to check if you solved for the right thing! The chair costs $175, so the sofa costs $3(175) - 50 = 525 - 50 = \$475$. This means the sofa costs $\$475 - \$175 = \$300$ more than the chair. Therefore, **(C)** is correct.

**20. 8**

**Difficulty:** Medium

**Category:** Number of Possible Solutions

**Strategic Advice:** The solution to the system is the point that both tables will have in common, but the tables, as given, do not share any points. You could use the data to write the equation of each line and then solve the system, but this will use up valuable time on test day. Instead, look for patterns that can be extended.

**Getting to the Answer:** In the table for Equation 1, the $x$-values increase by 2 each time and the $y$-values decrease by 2. In the table for Equation 2, the $x$-values increase by 4 each time and the $y$-values increase by 1. Use these patterns to continue the tables.

| Equation 1 | |
|:---:|:---:|
| $x$ | $y$ |
| −2 | 6 |
| 0 | 4 |
| 2 | 2 |
| 4 | 0 |
| 6 | −2 |
| **8** | **−4** |

| Equation 2 | |
|:---:|:---:|
| $x$ | $y$ |
| −8 | −8 |
| −4 | −7 |
| 0 | −6 |
| 4 | −5 |
| **8** | **−4** |
| 12 | −3 |

The point $(8, -4)$ satisfies both equations, so the $x$-coordinate of the solution to the system is **8**.

## 21. A

**Difficulty:** Easy

**Category:** Number of Possible Solutions

**Getting to the Answer:** The solution to a system of equations shown graphically is the point of intersection. Read the axis labels carefully. Each grid line represents 2 units. The two lines intersect at the point $(-6, -6)$, so $A + B = -6 + (-6) = -12$, which means **(A)** is correct.

## 22. C

**Difficulty:** Hard

**Category:** Number of Possible Solutions

**Getting to the Answer:** The system has infinitely many solutions, so both equations must describe the same line. Notice that if you multiply the $x$- and $y$-coefficients in the second equation by 8, you arrive at the $x$- and $y$-coefficients in the first equation. The constant $k$ times 8 must then equal the constant in the first equation, or $-16$:

$$8k = -16$$
$$k = -2$$

The correct answer is **(C)**.

## 23. B

**Difficulty:** Hard

**Category:** Number of Possible Solutions

**Getting to the Answer:** Rearrange the equations and write them on top of each other so that the $x$ and $y$ variables line up:

$$\begin{cases} 24x + ay = -13 \\ 6bx - 5y = -9 \end{cases}$$

In a system of equations that has no solution, the $x$-coefficients must equal each other and the $y$-coefficients must equal each other. Thus, for the $x$-coefficients, $24 = 6b$, which means that $b = 4$. For the $y$-coefficients, $a = -5$. The question asks for the value of $|a + b|$, which is $|-5 + 4| = |-1| = 1$, choice **(B)**. (Note that if you used the equation $-6bx + 5y = 9$, you would get $a = 5$ and $b = -4$, which would still result in the correct answer.)

## 24. $\frac{9}{2}$ or 4.5

**Difficulty:** Medium

**Category:** Substitution/Combination

**Getting to the Answer:** Start by clearing the fractions from the first equation (by multiplying by 4) to make the numbers easier to work with. Then use combination to solve for $y$:

$$\begin{array}{r} x + 8y = 11 \\ + \quad -x - 6y = 7 \\ \hline 2y = 18 \\ y = 9 \end{array}$$

Take half of 9 to get $\frac{9}{2}$, then grid in $\frac{9}{2}$ or **4.5**.

## 25. A

**Difficulty:** Medium

**Category:** Substitution/Combination

**Getting to the Answer:** Choose intuitive letters for the variables: $t$ for tiny pandas, $g$ for giant pandas. You're given the cost of each as well as the number of each sold and the total revenue generated. Then write the system of equations that represents the information given:

$$t + g = 29$$
$$3.5t + 14g = 217$$

Multiplying the top equation by $-14$ allows you to solve for $t$ using combination:

$$\begin{array}{r} -14t - 14g = -406 \\ + \quad 3.5t + 14g = 217 \\ \hline -10.5t \qquad = -189 \\ t \qquad = 18 \end{array}$$

Solving for $t$ gives 18, which eliminates (B) and (C). Plugging 18 into $t$ in the first equation allows you to find $g$, which is 11. Choice **(A)** is correct.

**26. A**

**Difficulty:** Hard

**Category:** Substitution/Combination

**Getting to the Answer:** Choose letters that make sense for the variables: $w$ for wooden and $c$ for crystal. You know the jewelry artist bought 127 beads total. You're also told each wooden bead costs \$0.20 ($0.2w$) and each crystal bead costs \$0.50 ($0.5c$), as well as the fact that she spent \$41 total. You'll have two equations: one relating the number of wooden beads and crystal beads and a second relating the costs associated with each:

$$w + c = 127$$
$$0.2w + 0.5c = 41$$

Either combination or substitution is a good choice for solving this system. Both are shown here:

Combination:

$$2(0.2w + 0.5c = 41) \rightarrow 0.4w + c = 82$$
$$w + \cancel{c} = 127$$
$$-\ \underline{0.4w + \cancel{c} = 82}$$
$$0.6w\ \ \ \ \ = 45$$
$$w\ \ \ \ \ = 75$$

Substitution:

$$w + c = 127 \rightarrow c = 127 - w$$
$$0.2w + 0.5(127 - w) = 41$$
$$0.2w + 63.5 - 0.5w = 41$$
$$-0.3w = -22.5$$
$$w = 75$$
$$75 + c = 127 \rightarrow c = 52$$

The question asks for the difference in the amount spent on each type of bead, not the difference in the quantity of each type. Multiply the bead counts by the correct pricing to get $75 \times \$0.2 = \$15$ for the wooden beads and $52 \times \$0.5 = \$26$ for the crystal beads. Take the difference to get $\$26 - \$15 = \$11$, which is **(A)**.

# CHAPTER 6

# Inequalities

**LEARNING OBJECTIVES**

After completing this chapter, you will be able to:

- Solve an inequality for a range of values
- Identify the graph of an inequality or a system of inequalities
- Solve for the point of intersection of the boundary lines of a system of inequalities
- Solve algebraically a system of one inequality with two variables and another inequality with one variable
- Identify one or more inequalities that match a real-life situation

35/600 SmartPoints®

# How Much Do You Know?

**Directions:** Try the questions that follow. Show your work so that you can compare your solutions to the ones found in the Check Your Work section immediately after this question set. The "Category" heading in the explanation for each question gives the title of the lesson that covers how to solve it. If you answered the question(s) for a given lesson correctly, and if your scratchwork looks like ours, you may be able to move quickly through that lesson. If you answered incorrectly or used a different approach, you may want to take your time on that lesson.

1.  If $\frac{3}{5}p - 2 \geq 5$, what is the least possible value of $\frac{6}{5}p + 2$?

    A)  7

    B)  10

    C)  16

    D)  18

2.  If $-3 < \frac{4}{3}h + \frac{1}{6} < 1$, then what is one possible value of $12h - 4$?

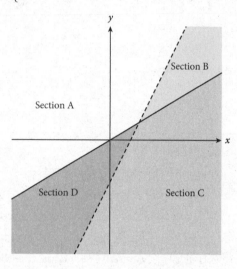

$$\begin{cases} y > 2x - 3 \\ 5y \leq 3x \end{cases}$$

3.  The graph above depicts the system of inequalities shown. Which of the labeled section or sections of the graph could represent all of the solutions of the system?

    A)  Sections A and D

    B)  Section B

    C)  Sections C and D

    D)  Section D

4.  A bowling alley charges a flat $6.50 fee for shoe and ball rental plus $3.75 per game and 6.325 percent sales tax. If each person in a group of seven people has $20 to spend on a bowling outing, and at least some members of the group must rent shoes and a ball, which inequality best describes this situation, given that the number of shoe and ball rentals is represented by $r$ and the number of games is represented by $g$?

    A)  $1.06325(6.5r + 3.75g) \leq 140$

    B)  $1.06325(6.5r + 3.75g) \leq 20$

    C)  $1.06325\left(\dfrac{6.5}{r} + \dfrac{3.75}{g}\right) \leq 140$

    D)  $0.06325(6.5r + 3.75g) \leq 20$

5. Marco is paid $80 per day plus $15 per hour for overtime. If he works five days per week and wants to make a minimum of $520 this week, what is the fewest number of hours of overtime he must work?

6. An architect in an arid region determines that a building's current landscaping uses $1,640 worth of water monthly. The architect plans to replace the current landscaping with arid-zone landscaping at a cost of $15,900, which will reduce the monthly watering cost to $770. Which of the following inequalities can be used to find $m$, the number of months after replacement that the savings in water costs will be at least as much as the cost of replacing the landscaping?

A) $15,900 \geq (1,640 - 770)m$

B) $15,900 > 770m$

C) $15,900 \leq (1,640 - 770)m$

D) $15,900 \leq 770m$

## Check Your Work

**1. C**

**Difficulty:** Medium

**Category:** Linear Inequalities

**Getting to the Answer:** You might be tempted to solve for $p$, but some critical thinking and algebra make that unnecessary. First, get $\frac{3}{5}p$ by itself by adding 2 to both sides: $\frac{3}{5}p \geq 7$. Next, multiply both sides by 2 to get the value range of $\frac{6}{5}p \geq 14$. Finally, add 2 to both sides to get $\frac{6}{5}p + 2 \geq 14 + 2$. Thus, $\frac{6}{5}p + 2 \geq 16$, so **(C)** is correct.

**2. Any value greater than or equal to 0 and less than 3.5**

**Difficulty:** Hard

**Category:** Linear Inequalities

**Getting to the Answer:** Don't automatically start solving the two inequalities separately. Instead, look for a series of quick manipulations to convert $\frac{4}{3}h + \frac{1}{6}$ to $12h - 4$. Start by multiplying the entire inequality by 9 to yield $-27 < 12h + \frac{3}{2} < 9$. Next, subtract $\frac{3}{2}$ and then 4 more (to get the desired $-4$) from all parts of the inequality (converting the fraction component to a decimal will make this step easier), which will become $-32.5 < 12h - 4 < 3.5$. Because grid-in answers cannot be negative, pick any value that is **greater than or equal to 0 but less than 3.5**.

**3. D**

**Difficulty:** Medium

**Category:** Systems of Inequalities

**Getting to the Answer:** Sections A and D are all the $y$ values greater than $2x - 3$, so those sections are the solution set for the inequality $y > 2x - 3$. Similarly, Sections C and D are the solution set for $5y \leq 3x$. The solutions for a system of inequalities are all the points that satisfy all (both, in this case) of the inequalities. The points in Section D are in the solution set for both inequalities, so **(D)** is correct.

**4. A**

**Difficulty:** Medium

**Category:** Modeling Real-Life Situations with Inequalities

**Getting to the Answer:** The question has defined the variables for you ($r$ and $g$). The bowling alley charges $6.50 for shoe and ball rental and $3.75 per game. Sales tax is 6.325% (0.06325 in decimal form). Rental and game costs are given by $6.5r$ and $3.75g$, respectively. To incorporate sales tax into the total cost, multiply the sum of $6.5r$ and $3.75g$ by 1.06325 (not 0.06325, which gives the cost of sales tax only). The question asks for an inequality that represents the amount that the group can spend, which can be no more than $7 \times 20 = 140$; therefore, the correct inequality is $1.06325(6.5r + 3.75g) \leq 140$. This matches **(A)**.

**5. 8**

**Difficulty:** Medium

**Category:** Modeling Real-Life Situations with Inequalities

**Getting to the Answer:** Translate from English into math to create an inequality in which $h$ represents the number of hours of overtime Marco must work. Marco gets paid a daily wage plus an hourly rate for overtime, so his weekly pay is his daily rate ($80) times 5 days, plus the number of hours of overtime he works ($h$) times his overtime rate ($15). If he wants to make *at least* $520, which means that much or more, the inequality is $(80 \times 5) + 15h \geq 520$. Solve for $h$:

$$400 + 15h \geq 520$$
$$15h \geq 120$$
$$h \geq 8$$

Marco must work at least 8 hours of overtime to make $520 or more this week. Grid in **8**.

**6.   C**

**Difficulty:** Medium

**Category:** Modeling Real-Life Situations with Inequalities

**Getting to the Answer:** The question asks for the point at which the savings will be *at least as much* as the cost of replacing the landscaping, so the value range could include a value equal to the exact cost of replacement; eliminate the strict inequality in (B). Because you need a value range that is at least as much as the cost of landscaping, you need the cost of landscaping, $15,900, to be *less than* or equal to the value range. Eliminate (A).

The value range will be the value of the monthly savings times the number of months, which will be $m$ times the difference between the old monthly water cost and the new monthly water cost: $(1,640 - 770)m$. Therefore, the entire inequality expression is $15,900 \leq (1,640 - 770)m$, so **(C)** is correct.

# Linear Inequalities

**LEARNING OBJECTIVES**

After this lesson, you will be able to:

● Solve an inequality for a range of values

● Identify the graph of an inequality

## To answer a question like this:

Which of the following graphs represents the solution set for $5x - 10y > 6$ ?

A)

B)

C)

D)

## You need to know this:

Linear inequalities are similar to linear equations but have two differences:

- You are solving for a **range of values** rather than a single value.
- If you multiply or divide both sides of the inequality by a negative, you must **reverse the inequality sign**.

While linear equations graph as simple lines, inequalities graph as shaded regions. Use solid lines for inequalities with $\leq$ or $\geq$ signs because the line itself is included in the solution set. Use dashed lines for inequalities with $<$ or $>$ signs because, in these cases, the line itself is not included in the solution set. The shaded region represents all points that make up the solution set for the inequality.

## You need to do this:

To graph an inequality, start by writing the inequality in slope-intercept form, then graph the solid or dashed line. Finally, add shading:

- For $y > mx + b$ and $y \geq mx + b$, shade the region *above* the line.
- For $y < mx + b$ and $y \leq mx + b$, shade the region *below* the line.

If it's hard to tell which region is above/below the line (which can happen when the line is steep), compare the $y$-values on both sides of the line.

## Explanation:

Rewrite the inequality in slope-intercept form and then identify which half-plane should be shaded. Subtract $5x$ from both sides of the inequality, divide both sides by $-10$, and flip the inequality symbol to yield $y < \frac{1}{2}x - \frac{3}{5}$. Eliminate (A) and (D) because they have positive $y$-intercepts. The "less than" symbol indicates that the half-plane below the line should be shaded, making **(C)** the correct answer.

## Try on Your Own

**Directions:** Take as much time as you need on these questions. Work carefully and methodically. There will be an opportunity for timed practice at the end of the chapter.

$$-\frac{a}{6} - a > -\frac{4}{3}$$

1. Which of the following is equivalent to the inequality above?

   A)  $a < \frac{7}{8}$

   B)  $a > \frac{7}{8}$

   C)  $a < \frac{8}{7}$

   D)  $a > \frac{8}{7}$

---

HINT: For Q2, save time by solving for the entire expression, not *c*.

---

2. If $-5c - 7 \le 8$, what is the least possible value of $15c + 7$?

   A)  $-38$

   B)  $-4$

   C)  $15$

   D)  $22$

---

HINT: For Q3, be careful not to "lose" a negative sign.

---

$$-\frac{1}{8}(8 - 10x) > 3x - 2$$

3. Which of the following describes all possible values of $x$?

   A)  $x < -\frac{12}{7}$

   B)  $x > -\frac{4}{7}$

   C)  $x < \frac{4}{7}$

   D)  $x > \frac{4}{7}$

$$\frac{1}{4}a - \frac{1}{16}b + 3 < 5$$

4. Which of the following is equivalent to the inequality above?

   A)  $4a - b < 8$

   B)  $4a - b < 32$

   C)  $a - 4b < 32$

   D)  $4b - a < 4$

5. If $4c + 20 \ge 31$, what is the least possible value of $12c + 7$?

   A)  18

   B)  40

   C)  51

   D)  58

# Systems of Inequalities

**To answer a question like this:**

If $12x - 4y > 8$ and $\frac{2}{3}x + 6y \geq 14$ form a system of inequalities, which of the following graphs shows the solution set for the system?

A)

B)

C)

D)

## You need to know this:

The solution set for a system of inequalities is not a single point (a single x-value and y-value) but a region of overlap between the two inequalities: that is, a range of x-values and y-values. It is easiest to see this graphically.

Systems of inequalities can be presented graphically with multiple boundary lines and multiple shaded regions. Follow the same rules as for graphing single inequalities, but keep in mind that **the solution set is the region where the shading overlaps**.

Note that you generally cannot use substitution or combination to solve a system of two inequalities where both have two variables. That said, the SAT may ask for the maximum or minimum x- or y-value of a system of inequalities. These questions are actually asking about the intersection of the **boundary lines** of the system. If you see one of these questions, use substitution or combination to solve for the point of intersection, as you learned to do in chapter 5. For an example of this type of question (which is rare on the SAT), see question number 8 in the Try on Your Own set for this lesson.

You may also see an occasional question without a graph asking you to solve a system of one inequality in two variables and another inequality in one variable. As long as both inequalities have the same symbol, you can do this by substitution. Question number 6 in this lesson's Try on Your Own set is an example of this rare question type.

## You need to do this:

- To identify the graph of a system of inequalities, follow the same rules as for single inequalities. The solution set is the region where the shading overlaps.
- For a question asking for a maximum or minimum, solve for the intersection point of the boundary lines.
- For a question asking for the range of values that satisfies a system of one inequality in two variables and one inequality in one variable (both with the same sign), solve by substitution.

## Explanation:

Rewrite the inequalities in slope-intercept form. Once complete, determine whether each line should be solid or dashed and which half of the plane (above or below the line) should be shaded for each. The correct graph should have a dashed line with a positive slope ($y < 3x - 2$) and a solid line with a negative slope $\left(y \geq -\frac{1}{9}x + \frac{7}{3}\right)$; eliminate (C) because the dashed and solid lines are incorrect. According to the inequality symbols, the half-plane above the solid line and the half-plane below the dashed line should be shaded; the only match is **(B)**.

## Try on Your Own

**Directions:** Take as much time as you need on these questions. Work carefully and methodically. There will be an opportunity for timed practice at the end of the chapter.

$$a < 6b + 4$$
$$3b < 8$$

6. Which of the following consists of all the $a$-values that satisfy the system of inequalities above?

A)  $a < 20$

B)  $a < 16$

C)  $a < 12$

D)  $a < \dfrac{8}{3}$

---

HINT: For Q7, remember that the solution set is the overlap between both inequalities. Make a sketch or use a graphing calculator.

---

7. If the system of inequalities $y \le -x + 1$ and $y < \dfrac{1}{2}x$ is graphed on the above plane, which of the quadrants contain(s) no solutions to the system?

A)  Quadrant I

B)  Quadrant II

C)  Quadrant III

D)  Quadrants I and II

$$-y \le 6x - 2200$$
$$3y \ge 9x - 1500$$

8. Given the system of inequalities above, if point $(a, b)$ lies within the solution set, what is the minimum possible value of $b$?

$$x < 4 - 2y$$
$$y \le -2x + 1$$

9. Which of the following ordered pairs satisfies both of the inequalities above?

A)  $(-1, 3)$

B)  $(1, 1)$

C)  $(2, -3)$

D)  $(4, 4)$

HINT: For Q10, remember that *solution* means "an $(x, y)$ pair
that is true for both inequalities."

$$y > x + r$$
$$y < s - x$$

10. If $x = y = 1$ is a solution to the system of inequalities above, which of the following ordered pairs could correspond to $(r, s)$ ?

A)  $(-1, 1)$

B)  $\left(-\dfrac{1}{2}, 2\right)$

C)  $\left(-\dfrac{1}{10}, 3\right)$

D)  $(3, -1)$

# Modeling Real-Life Situations with Inequalities

**LEARNING OBJECTIVE**

After this lesson, you will be able to:

- Identify one or more inequalities that match a real-life situation

## To answer a question like this:

To make its sales goals for the month, a toy manufacturer must sell at least $10,400 of toy hoops and basketballs. Toy hoops sell for $8 and basketballs sell for $25. The company hopes to sell more than three times as many basketballs as toy hoops. If $h$ represents the number of toy hoops and $b$ represents the number of basketballs, where $h$ and $b$ are positive integers, which of the following systems of inequalities best describes this situation?

A) $8h + 25b \geq 10$

$400b > 3h$

B) $8h + 25b \geq 10$

$400h > 3b$

C) $25h + 8b \geq 10$

$400b > 3h$

D) $25h + 8b \geq 10$

$400h > 3b$

## You need to know this:

Word problems involving inequalities require you to do the same sort of translation that you learned in chapter 4. They also require you to get the direction of the inequality sign right. The following table shows which symbols correspond to which words.

| English | Symbol |
|---|---|
| more, greater, longer, heavier | > |
| less, fewer, shorter, lighter | < |
| no less than, no fewer than, at least | ≥ |
| no more than, no greater than, at most | ≤ |

## You need to do this:

Break down the word problem one inequality at a time. For each one:

- Identify the correct symbol based on the table above
- Put the value that follows the word "than" or "as" on the right and the other value on the left
- If the sentence does not use the words "than" or "as," use logic to determine the relationship between the values

### Explanation:

"At least $10,400" means $\geq 10,400$. It's the money from the sales of toy hoops and basketballs that has to be greater than or equal to $10,400, so that's what needs to go on the left of the $\geq$ sign. Each toy hoop costs $8, so the cash generated by sales of toy hoops will be $8h$. Each basketball costs $25, so basketballs will generate $25b$. Add them: $8h + 25b \geq 10,400$. Eliminate (C) and (D).

The company wants to sell "*more than* three times as many basketballs as toy hoops," so write down $>$ and work out what needs to go on each side. The company wants to sell more basketballs than toy hoops, so $b$ should go on the left. Specifically, they want basketball sales to be more than 3 times toy hoop sales, so the final statement is $b > 3h$. **(A)** is correct.

## Try on Your Own

**Directions:** Take as much time as you need on these questions. Work carefully and methodically. There will be an opportunity for timed practice at the end of the chapter.

---

HINT: For Q11, set up one inequality for the number of ads and a second inequality for the money the ads bring in.

---

11. Ariel enters a contest to sell advertisements in her school's yearbook. To qualify for a prize, she has to sell at least $1,500 worth of advertisements consisting of no fewer than 15 individual ads. Each full-page ad costs $110, each half-page ad costs $70, and each quarter-page ad costs $50. Which of the following systems of inequalities represents this situation, where $x$ is the number of full-page ads she sells, $y$ is the number of half-page ads she sells, and $z$ is the number of quarter-page ads she sells?

    A)  $110x + 70y + 50z \geq 1{,}500$
        $x + y + z \leq 15$

    B)  $110x + 70y + 50z \leq 1{,}500$
        $x + y + z \leq 15$

    C)  $110x + 70y + 50z \geq 1{,}500$
        $x + y + z \geq 15$

    D)  $110x + 70y + 50z \leq 1{,}500$
        $x + y + z \geq 15$

12. A farmer sells watermelons, cantaloupes, and tomatoes from a small cart at a county fair. He needs to sell at least $200 of produce each day. His watermelons are priced at $0.50 per pound, his cantaloupes at $1 per pound, and his tomatoes at $2.50 per pound. His cart can hold no more than 250 pounds. Which of the following inequalities represents this scenario, if $w$ is the number of pounds of watermelons, $c$ is the number of pounds of cantaloupes, and $t$ is the number of pounds of tomatoes?

    A)  $0.5w + 1c + 2.5t \geq 200$
        $w + c + t \leq 250$

    B)  $0.5w + 1c + 2.5t \leq 200$
        $w + c + t \leq 250$

    C)  $0.5w + 1c + 2.5t \geq 200$
        $w + c + t \geq 250$

    D)  $0.5w + 1c + 2.5t \leq 200$
        $w + c + t \geq 250$

13. Allison is planting a garden with at least 15 trees. There will be a combination of apple trees, which cost $120 each, and pear trees, which cost $145 each. Allison's budget for purchasing the trees is no more than $2,050. She must plant at least 5 apple trees and at least 3 pear trees. Which of the following systems of inequalities represents the situation described if $x$ is the number of apple trees and $y$ is the number of pear trees?

A) $120x + 145y \geq 2,050$
$x + y \leq 15$
$x \geq 5$
$y \geq 3$

B) $120x + 145y \geq 2,050$
$x + y \geq 15$
$x \leq 5$
$y \leq 3$

C) $120x + 145y \leq 2,050$
$x + y \geq 15$
$x \leq 5$
$y \leq 3$

D) $120x + 145y \leq 2,050$
$x + y \geq 15$
$x \geq 5$
$y \geq 3$

14. A utility shelf in a warehouse is used to store containers of paint and containers of varnish. Containers of paint weigh 50 pounds each and containers of varnish weigh 35 pounds each. The shelf can hold up to 32 containers, the combined weight of which must not exceed 1,450 pounds. Let $x$ be the number of containers of paint and $y$ be the number of containers of varnish. Which of the following systems of inequalities represents this relationship?

A) $50x + 35y \leq 32$
$x + y \leq 1,450$

B) $50x + 35y \leq 1,450$
$x + y \leq 32$

C) $85(x + y) \leq 1,450$
$x + y \leq 32$

D) $50x + 35y \leq 1,450$
$x + y \leq 85$

---

HINT: For Q15, read carefully. *At least* is a minimum, so which way should the inequality sign point?

---

15. A bakery is buying flour and sugar from its supplier. The supplier will deliver no more than 750 pounds in a shipment. Each bag of flour weighs 50 pounds and each bag of sugar weighs 20 pounds. The bakery wants to buy at least three times as many bags of sugar as bags of flour. If $f$ represents the number of bags of flour and $s$ represents the number of bags of sugar, where $f$ and $s$ are nonnegative integers, which of the following systems of inequalities represents this situation?

A) $50f + 60s \leq 750$
$f \leq 3s$

B) $50f + 20s \leq 750$
$f \leq 3s$

C) $50f + 20s \leq 750$
$3f \leq s$

D) $150f + 20s \leq 750$
$3f \leq s$

## On Test Day

Modeling real life situations with inequalities can be tricky, especially when there are multiple inequalities involved or when a question doesn't state the information in the most straightforward way. The good news is that you can often make use of the answer choices to get to the answer quickly.

Try the question below. If you use the choices, you shouldn't have to do any calculations. Just pay close attention to the direction of the inequality signs.

16. A florist is organizing a sale that offers carnations at a price of $4 for 10 and daisies at a price of $7 for 5. The florist plans to order a maximum of 500 flowers for the sale and wants the revenue from the sale to be at least $400. If $x$ is the number of carnations and $y$ is the number of daisies, and the florist sells all the flowers ordered, which system of inequalities best describes this situation?

A) $0.4x + 1.4y \geq 400$

$x + y \leq 500$

B) $0.4x + 1.4y \leq 400$

$x + y \leq 500$

C) $0.4x + 1.4y \geq 400$

$x + y \geq 500$

D) $0.4x + 1.4y \leq 400$

$x + y \geq 500$

The answer and explanation can be found at the end of this chapter.

Math

# How Much Have You Learned?

**Directions:** For testlike practice, give yourself 15 minutes to complete this question set. Be sure to study the explanations, even for questions you got right. They can be found at the end of this chapter.

17. The figure above shows the solution set for this system of inequalities:

$$\begin{cases} y < \dfrac{3}{5}x - 2 \\ y \le -\dfrac{4}{3}x + 5 \end{cases}$$

Which of the following is NOT a solution to this system?

A) $(-1, -4)$

B) $(1, -1)$

C) $(4, -1)$

D) $(6, -3)$

18. Ezekiel has $5.00 to spend on snacks. Candy bars cost $0.60 each, gum costs $0.50 per pack, and nuts are priced at $1.29 per small bag. If $c$ represents the number of candy bars, $g$ represents the number of packs of gum, and $n$ represents the number of bags of nuts, which of the following inequalities correctly describes Ezekiel's choices?

A) $\dfrac{c}{0.60} + \dfrac{g}{0.50} + \dfrac{n}{1.29} \le \dfrac{1}{5}$

B) $c + g + n \le 5$

C) $0.60c + 0.50g + 1.29n \le 5.00$

D) $0.60c + 0.50g + 1.29n \ge 5.00$

19. A shipping company employee is in charge of packing cargo containers for shipment. He knows a certain cargo container can hold a maximum of 50 microwaves or a maximum of 15 refrigerators. Each microwave takes up 6 cubic feet of space, and each refrigerator takes up 20 cubic feet. The cargo container can hold a maximum of 300 cubic feet. The employee is trying to figure out how to pack a container containing both microwaves and refrigerators. Which of the following systems of inequalities can the employee use to determine how many of each item (microwaves, $m$, and refrigerators, $r$) he can pack into one cargo container?

A) $m \le 6$
   $r \le 20$
   $50m + 15r \le 300$

B) $m \le 50$
   $r \le 15$
   $m + r \le 300$

C) $m \le 50$
   $r \le 15$
   $6m + 20r \le 300$

D) $m \le 50$
   $r \le 15$
   $50m + 15r \le 300$

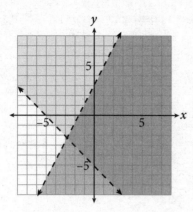

$$\begin{cases} y > -x - 5 \\ y < 2x + 3 \end{cases}$$

20. The figure above shows the solution for the system of inequalities shown. Suppose $(a, b)$ is a solution to the system. If $a = 0$, what is the greatest possible integer value of $b$ ?

$$3x + 2 > 5$$
$$-2x + 8 > -10$$

21. Which of the following describes the range of $x$ ?

   A) $x > 1$

   B) $x > 9$

   C) $-1 < x < 9$

   D) $9 > x > 1$

$$y \geq -3x + 18$$
$$y \geq 9x$$

22. In the $xy$ plane, the point $(a, b)$ lies in the solution set of the system of inequalities above. What is the minimum possible value of $b$ ?

   A) $1\frac{1}{2}$

   B) $3$

   C) $7\frac{1}{2}$

   D) $13\frac{1}{2}$

23. Francine sells advertising time packages for a local television station. She is able to make up to 15 sales calls per week offering potential advertisers either a prime time package for \$12,000 or a non prime time package for \$8,000. Her weekly sales goal is to sell more than \$20,000 worth of advertising. Which of the following systems of inequalities represents this situation in terms of $p$, the number of prime time packages Francine sells in a week, $n$, the number of non prime time packages, and $u$, the number of unsuccessful sales calls for which she sells neither offering?

   A) $p + n + u \leq 15$
      $12,000p + 8,000n > 20,000$

   B) $p + n + u \geq 15$
      $12,000p + 8,000n > 20,000$

   C) $p + n + u \leq 15$
      $12,000p + 8,000(n + u) > 20,000$

   D) $p + n + u \leq 15$
      $12,000p + 8,000n < 20,000$

Math

24. Luis has $25 to spend on school supplies. Pencils
(*p*) cost $1.25 per package, notebooks (*n*) are priced
at $2.50 each, and markers (*m*) sell for $4 per pack.
He must buy exactly one calendar/planner for
$5.75. Which of the following describes how many
markers Luis can buy?

A) $m \le \dfrac{1.25p + 2.5n + 5.75}{25}$

B) $m \le \dfrac{19.25 - 1.25p - 2.5n}{4}$

C) $m \le \dfrac{25 - 1.25p - 2.5n}{4} - 5.75$

D) $m \le 19.25 - 1.25p - 2.5n$

25. Let *a* and *b* be numbers such that $-a < b + 1 < a$.

Which of the following must be true?

I. $a > 0$

II. $|b| < a$

III. $b > a + 1$

A) I only

B) I and II

C) II only

D) I, II, and III

26. The variable *x* is a positive integer. If
$3(x - 1) + 5 > 11$ and $-5x + 18 \ge -12$,
how many possible values are there for *x* ?

# Reflect

**Directions:** Take a few minutes to recall what you've learned and what you've been practicing in this chapter. Consider the following questions, jot down your best answer for each one, and then compare your reflections to the expert responses on the following page. Use your level of confidence to determine what to do next.

What is the difference between a linear inequality and a linear equation?

_____

_____

_____

The rules for manipulating an inequality are very similar to those for manipulating an equation. What is the major difference?

_____

_____

_____

When two lines cross in the coordinate plane, they create four regions. How many regions will be shaded if the system of inequalities uses the word "and"? The word "or"?

_____

_____

_____

## Expert Responses

What is the difference between a linear inequality and a linear equation?

*A linear equation is solved for a single value, whereas a linear inequality is solved for a range of values.*

The rules for manipulating an inequality are very similar to those for manipulating an equation. What is the major difference?

*When solving an inequality, you can do the same thing to both sides, just as you could for an equation. The big difference is that if you divide or multiply both sides of an inequality by a negative number, you have to flip the inequality sign.*

When two lines cross in the coordinate plane, they create four regions. How many regions will be shaded if the system of inequalities uses the word "and"? The word "or"?

*Of the four regions, one represents values that satisfy neither inequality. One represents values that satisfy both inequalities. The other two regions represent values that satisfy one inequality but not the other. For an "and" inequality, only the region of values that satisfy both inequalities will be shaded. For an "or" inequality, the only region not shaded will be the one that satisfies neither inequality; the other three regions will be shaded.*

## Next Steps

If you answered most questions correctly in the "How Much Have You Learned?" section, and if your responses to the Reflect questions were similar to those of the SAT expert, then consider inequalities an area of strength and move on to the next chapter. Come back to this topic periodically to prevent yourself from getting rusty.

If you don't yet feel confident, review those parts of this chapter that you have not yet mastered and try the questions you missed again. As always, be sure to review the explanations closely.

# Answers and Explanations

**1. C**

**Difficulty:** Easy

**Getting to the Answer:** Begin by multiplying all parts of the inequality by 6 to clear the fractions: $-a - 6a > -\frac{24}{3}$, which, when simplified, is $-7a > -8$. Divide both sides by $-7$, remembering to switch the direction of the sign: $a < \frac{8}{7}$. Therefore, **(C)** is correct.

**2. A**

**Difficulty:** Medium

**Getting to the Answer:** Don't solve for $c$ on autopilot. Instead, solve for $15c$, then add 7 to both sides. To do this, first multiply both sides of the inequality by $-1$ to get $5c + 7 \geq -8$. (Notice that the inequality sign had to be flipped due to multiplication by a negative number.) Then subtract 7 from both sides to yield $5c \geq -15$. Multiply both sides by 3: $15c \geq -45$. Finally, add 7 to both sides: $15c + 7 \geq -38$. Choice **(A)** is correct.

**3. C**

**Difficulty:** Medium

**Getting to the Answer:** First, to clear the fraction, multiply both sides of the inequality by $-8$, remembering to flip the direction of the inequality sign: $8 - 10x < -24x + 16$.

Next, subtract 8 from both sides, and then add $24x$ to both sides. Divide both sides by 14, and then simplify the fraction.

$$-10x < -24x + 8$$
$$14x < 8$$
$$x < \frac{8}{14}$$
$$x < \frac{4}{7}$$

Thus, **(C)** is correct.

**4. B**

**Difficulty:** Medium

**Getting to the Answer:** Begin by subtracting 3 from both sides of the inequality to get $\frac{1}{4}a - \frac{1}{16}b < 2$. Next, clear the fractions in that inequality by multiplying all terms by 16: $16 \times \left(\frac{1}{4}a - \frac{1}{16}b < 2\right) = 4a - b < 32$. **(B)** is correct.

**5. B**

**Difficulty:** Medium

**Strategic Advice:** Because the given inequality contains $4c$ and the value you're solving for has $12c$ (a multiple of $4c$), solve for $4c$ and then multiply by 3 to find $12c$.

**Getting to the Answer:** Subtract 20 from both sides of the inequality to find that $4c \geq 11$. Multiply by 3: $12c \geq 33$. Finally, add 7 to both sides: $12c + 7 \geq 40$. So the least permissible value for $12c + 7$ is 40. **(B)** is correct.

**6. A**

**Difficulty:** Easy

**Getting to the Answer:** The question offers a value range of $a$ in terms of $6b$ and a value range for $3b$. Therefore, use the known value range of $3b$ to find the value range of $6b$.

Since $6b$ is two times $3b$, multiply both sides of the second inequality by 2 to find the value range of $6b$: $2 \times 3b < 2 \times 8$, so $6b < 16$.

Because the signs are the same in the two inequalities (both are less-than signs), you can plug 16 in for $b$ in the first inequality: $a < 16 + 4$, or $a < 20$. Hence, **(A)** is correct.

**7. B**

**Difficulty:** Medium

**Getting to the Answer:** Draw a sketch of the two lines to help visualize the system of inequalities.

Clearly, quadrants III and IV contain solutions to the system. Eliminate (C). Quadrant II contains no solutions, so you can also eliminate (A). Look closely at quadrant I. The line for $y \leq -x + 1$ intersects both the $x$ and $y$ axes at $+1$. The line for $y < \frac{1}{2}x$ passes through the origin and upward into quadrant I. Thus, there is a very small triangle of solutions to both inequalities that lies in quadrant I. Therefore, **(B)** is correct.

**8.  400**

**Difficulty:** Medium

**Getting to the Answer:** The first task is to express both inequalities in terms of $y$. Multiply $-y \leq 6x - 2200$ by $-1$ to get $y \geq -6x + 2200$; don't forget to flip the sign since you are multiplying by a negative number. Divide $3y \geq 9x - 1500$ by 3 to get $y \geq 3x - 500$.

The solution set for these inequalities is the area of the coordinate plane on or above both lines. Thus, the minimum $y$-value will occur at the intersection of the two lines, whose equations are $y = -6x + 2200$ and $y = 3x - 500$. To find the point of intersection, set these two equations equal to each other: $-6x + 2200 = 3x - 500$. Isolate the $x$-values on one side to yield $-9x = -2700$ and $x = 300$. Plug this value into one of the equations (it doesn't matter which one because $x = 300$ is where they intersect) to obtain the $y$-coordinate at the point of intersection: $3(300) - 500 = 400$. The $y$-coordinate at the point of intersection is the minimum possible value of $b$ that the question was asking for, so grid in **400**.

**9.  C**

**Difficulty:** Medium

**Getting to the Answer:** You could plot the two lines and identify the solution set on a graph, but testing the choices to see if they satisfy both inequalities is a more efficient approach, particularly since one inequality is "less than" and the other is "less than or equal to." If you take this approach, you don't even need to rearrange the inequalities to isolate $y$ on one side.

(A): Substituting these values for $x$ and $y$ in $x < 4 - 2y$ gives you $(-1) < 4 - 2(3)$, which is $-1 < -2$ (not a true statement). You don't need to evaluate the other inequality since this ordered pair is not in the solution set for $x < 4 - 2y$. Eliminate (A).

(B): Substituting these values for $x$ and $y$ in $x < 4 - 2y$ gives you $(1) < 4 - 2(1)$, which is $1 < 2$. The ordered pair is in the solution set for this inequality, so plug the values into $y \leq -2x + 1$ to get $(1) \leq -2(1) + 1$, which simplifies to $1 \leq -1$. Thus, this ordered pair is not in the solution set for the second inequality. Eliminate (B).

(C): Substituting these values for $x$ and $y$ in $x < 4 - 2y$ gives you $(2) < 4 - 2(-3)$, which is $2 < 10$. The ordered pair is in the solution set for this inequality, so plug the values into $y \leq -2x + 1$ to get $(-3) \leq -2(2) + 1$, which

simplifies to $-3 \leq -3$. Since the sign for this inequality is "less than or equal to," this ordered pair is in the solution set. **(C)** is correct.

(D): Since you already identified the correct choice, you do not need to check this pair.

**10.  C**

**Difficulty:** Hard

**Getting to the Answer:** Since the question states that $x = y = 1$ is a solution to the system, plug those values in to get $1 > 1 + r$ and $1 < s - 1$. These inequalities further simplify to $r < 0$ and $s > 2$. Check each pair of values in the answer choices to see which complies with these limitations. Only **(C)** has both $r < 0$ and $s > 2$, and is correct. (B) is incorrect because $s$ must be greater than 2, and (D) reverses $r$ and $s$.

**11.  C**

**Difficulty:** Medium

**Getting to the Answer:** Translate each part of the word problem into its mathematical equivalent. Because $x$, $y$, and $z$ represent the numbers of each of the three ad sizes, the total number of ads will be $x + y + z$. "No fewer than 15 ads" means $x + y + z \geq 15$, so eliminate (A) and (B).

The total cost of the ads Ariel sells will be represented by the number of each size ad sold times the respective cost of each size ad. Thus, $110x + 70y + 50z$ represents the total cost of all of the ads; "at least 1,500" means that $110x + 70y + 50z \geq 1,500$. Therefore, **(C)** is correct.

**12.  A**

**Difficulty:** Medium

**Getting to the Answer:** Translate each part of the word problem into its mathematical equivalent. The total weight of produce will be represented by the combined pounds of watermelons, $w$, cantaloupes, $c$, and tomatoes, $t$. This combined weight cannot exceed 250 pounds, so the inequality is $w + c + t \leq 250$. Eliminate (C) and (D).

The total money for the produce sold is represented by the price per pound of each type of produce times the number of pounds of that type. This must be at least (greater than or equal to) \$200, so the inequality is $0.5w + 1c + 2.5t \geq 200$. **(A)** is correct.

### 13. D

**Difficulty:** Medium

**Getting to the Answer:** Translate each part of the word problem into its mathematical equivalent, beginning with the easiest-to-translate components. Allison needs at least 5 apple trees and at least 3 pear trees, so the correct inequalities are $x \geq 5$ and $y \geq 3$. Eliminate (B) and (C). The total number of apple and pear trees combined that Allison purchases must be at least 15, so the correct inequality is $x + y \geq 15$. Eliminate (A). Only **(D)** is left and is correct.

Note that, by being strategic, you never even have to determine the first, most complicated inequality in each of the answer choices. For the record: apple trees cost $120 and pear trees cost $145, so the total amount Allison will spend on trees is $120x + 145y$. This total amount cannot go above $2,050, which means it must be less than or equal to $2,050. Therefore: $120x + 145y \leq 2,050$.

### 14. B

**Difficulty:** Medium

**Getting to the Answer:** First, define the relationship between the weight of each kind of container and the weight the shelf can hold. Since $x$ is the number of 50-pound containers of paint and $y$ is the number of 35-pound containers of varnish, the combined weight of the containers will be represented by $50x + 35y$. This needs to be no more than 1,450 pounds, so the inequality that represents this is $50x + 35y \leq 1,450$. Eliminate (A) and (C).

The question also states that the total number of containers the shelf can hold is no more than 32, so the combined number of containers of paint and containers of varnish must be no more than 32. This is represented by the inequality $x + y \leq 32$. Thus, **(B)** is correct.

### 15. C

**Difficulty:** Hard

**Getting to the Answer:** Begin by translating the weight of the combined bags of flour and sugar. The weight of each bag of flour times the number of bags of flour—plus the weight of each bag of sugar times the number of bags of sugar—will yield the total. Thus, $50f + 20s$ will describe the weight of all of the bags combined. Since

the weight that the supplier can deliver is no more than 750 pounds, the inequality that describes this situation is $50f + 20y \leq 750$. Eliminate (A) and (D).

The question also specifies that the bakery needs to buy at least three times as many bags of sugar as bags of flour. In other words, the number of bags of sugar must be equal to or greater than three times the number of bags of flour. This is represented by $s \geq 3f$, which can be rewritten as $3f \leq s$. **(C)** is correct.

### 16. A

**Difficulty:** Hard

**Strategic Advice:** All the numbers in the answer choices are the same, so you don't actually have to calculate the cost of one carnation or one daisy. The answer choices have done that for you.

**Getting to the Answer:** Focus on the keywords that tell you the direction of the inequality signs. The florist plans to order a "maximum" of 500 flowers, so that's $\leq 500$. Eliminate (C) and (D). The florist wants to earn "at least" $400, or $\geq 400$. The correct answer is **(A)**.

### 17. B

**Difficulty:** Medium

**Category:** Systems of Inequalities

**Getting to the Answer:** The intersection (overlap) of the two shaded regions is the solution to the system of inequalities. Check each point to see whether it lies in the region where the shading overlaps. Be careful—you are looking for the point that is *not* a solution to the system. Choices (A) and (C) lie in the overlap, so you can eliminate them. Choice (D), which is the point $(6, -3)$, lies on a boundary line, and because the line is solid, the point *is* included in the solution region. The only point that does not lie within the overlap must be (B). To check this, plug $(1, -1)$ into the first inequality:

$$y < \frac{3}{5}x - 2$$

$$-1 < \frac{3}{5}(1) - 2$$

$$-1 \not< -\frac{7}{5}$$

Because $-1$ is not less than $-\frac{7}{5}$, **(B)** is correct.

## 18. C

**Difficulty:** Easy

**Category:** Modeling Real-Life Situations with Inequalities

**Getting to the Answer:** The fact that Ezekiel has exactly $5.00 means that he can spend up to and including $5.00, so use the less than or equal symbol ($\leq$) for the limit on how much he can spend. For that reason alone you can eliminate (D). The amount of money Ezekiel spends on each type of snack is the number of units of that snack times its price. So, $0.60c + 0.50g + 1.29n \leq 5.00$. **(C)** is correct.

## 19. C

**Difficulty:** Medium

**Category:** Modeling Real-Life Situations with Inequalities

**Getting to the Answer:** The clue "holds a maximum" means the container can hold exactly that much or less, so use the less than or equal to symbol ($\leq$) throughout. The cargo container can hold a maximum of 50 microwaves, so the first inequality is $m \leq 50$. Eliminate (A). The container can hold a maximum of 15 refrigerators, so the second inequality is $r \leq 15$. The third inequality deals with the size of each appliance. The cargo container can hold $m$ microwaves multiplied by the size of the microwave, which is 6 cubic feet; it can hold $r$ refrigerators multiplied by the size of the refrigerator, which is 20 cubic feet; and it can hold a maximum of 300 cubic feet total. Put these together to write the final inequality: $6m + 20r \leq 300$, which is **(C)**.

## 20. 2

**Difficulty:** Hard

**Category:** Systems of Inequalities

**Getting to the Answer:** If $(a, b)$ is a solution to the system, then $a$ is the $x$-coordinate of any point in the region where the shading overlaps, and $b$ is the corresponding $y$-coordinate. When $a = 0$ (or $x = 0$), the maximum possible value for $b$ lies on the upper boundary line, $y < 2x + 3$. It looks like the $y$-coordinate is 3, but to be sure, substitute $x = 0$ into the equation and simplify. You can replace the inequality symbol with an equal sign to make it an equation because you are finding a point on the boundary line, not a range:

$$y = 2(0) + 3$$
$$y = 3$$

The point on the boundary line is $(0, 3)$. The boundary line is dashed (because the inequality is strictly less than), so $(0, 3)$ is *not* a solution to the system. This means 2 is the greatest possible *integer* value for $b$ when $a = 0$. Grid in **2**.

## 21. D

**Difficulty:** Medium

**Category:** Linear Inequalities

**Getting to the Answer:** Isolate $x$ in each of the given inequalities, then consider the results in combination. For $3x + 2 > 5$, subtract 2 from each side to get $3x > 3$, which means that $x > 1$. For $-2x + 8 > -10$, subtract 8 from each side to get $-2x > -18$. Divide each side by $-2$, which means that you have to flip the inequality sign to get $x < 9$. Taking the two inequalities together, $x$ must be greater than 1 but less than 9. This can be expressed as $1 < x < 9$ or, alternatively, $9 > x > 1$. **(D)** is correct.

## 22. D

**Difficulty:** Medium

**Category:** Systems of Inequalities

**Strategic Advice:** If the given inequalities are graphed in the $xy$-plane, the solution set is the portion of the plane on or above both lines. Since the value of $y$ for both lines increases moving away from the point where they intersect, the minimum value of $y$ will occur at the intersection of these lines, which is the point $(a, b)$.

**Getting to the Answer:** The boundary lines of this system of inequalities are $y = -3x + 18$ and $y = 9x$. To find their intersection point, set them equal to each other to get $9x = -3x + 18$. So, $12x = 18$ and $x = 1\frac{1}{2}$. That represents $a$, but the question asks for the value of $b$. Substitute $1\frac{1}{2}$ for $x$ in either equation, preferably the simpler one: use $y = 9x$ to get $y = 9\left(1\frac{1}{2}\right) = 13\frac{1}{2}$. Therefore, **(D)** is correct.

### 23. A

**Difficulty:** Medium

**Category:** Modeling Real-Life Situations with Inequalities

**Strategic Advice:** Translating English into math, set up one inequality for Francine's number of sales calls and another for the dollar amount of sales in terms of her goal.

**Getting to the Answer:** Since Francine can make *up to* 15 sales calls per week and there are three categories of the results of her efforts, you can write the inequality $p + n + u \leq 15$. Eliminate (B). For the monetary goal, that is *more than* \$20,000, so this inequality is $12,000p + 8,000n > 20,000$. Note that the unsuccessful sales calls are not included in this inequality since they do not generate any revenue. **(A)** is correct.

### 24. B

**Difficulty:** Medium

**Category:** Modeling Real-Life Situations with Inequalities

**Getting to the Answer:** The amount Luis spends on each item is that item's price times the quantity he buys. The total amount must be less than or equal to \$25. Thus, you can write the inequality $1.25p + 2.50n + 4.00m + 1(5.75) \leq 25.00$. Since the question asks for the number of markers, isolate $m$ on one side of the inequality: $4m \leq 25 - 1.25p - 2.5n - 5.75$. Therefore, $m \leq \dfrac{19.25 - 1.25p - 2.5n}{4}$. **(B)** is correct.

### 25. B

**Difficulty:** Hard

**Category:** Linear Inequalities

**Getting to the Answer:** Examine each of the roman numeral choices individually, determine which one or ones must be true, then select the correct choice. Subtract 1 from all terms in the given inequality to get $-a - 1 < b < a - 1$, so that $b$ stands alone.

I. Ignoring the middle term, $b$, the given inequality tells you that $-a < a$. The only way this can be true is if $a$ is a positive number, so statement I must be true. If you have a hard time seeing this, pick a negative number for $a$. For example, if $a = -1$, then the inequality would say $-(-1) < -1$, which is $1 < -1$, which is false. Note that if $a = 0$, then the inequality becomes $0 < 0$, which is also false. Because statement I must be true, you can eliminate (C).

II. Recall that the absolute value of any number is its distance from 0 on the number line, which is its value without a sign. If $b$ is positive or 0, then, since $b < a - 1$, the value of $b$, which is the same as $|b|$, must also be less than $a$. However, if $b$ is negative, the relationship is not directly clear. Pick some numbers that satisfy the original inequality, such as $a = 4$ and $b = -2$. For these numbers, $-a - 1 = -5$, $|b| = 2$, $a - 1 = 3$. Thus, $-5 < 2 < 3$, so $-a - 1 < |b| < a - 1$, which means that $a$ must be more than 1 greater than $|b|$. Because $a$ must be positive (as determined by statement I) and because $a$ must be more than 1 greater than $b$ (from the original inequality), the value of $-a - 1$ must be less than $b$. Thus, statement II must be true. Eliminate (A). If the logic here is difficult, plug in more numbers for $a$ and $b$ to find a pattern.

III. Since $a$ must be positive and any positive value of $b$ is less than $a - 1$, there is no way that $b > a + 1$. Statement III is not true, so eliminate (D).

Because I and II must be true, and III cannot be true, **(B)** is correct.

### 26. 3

**Difficulty:** Medium

**Category:** Linear Inequalities

**Strategic Advice:** Isolate $x$ in each of the two inequalities to determine a range for $x$.

**Getting to the Answer:** Expand the first inequality to get $3x - 3 + 5 > 11$, so $3x > 9$ and $x > 3$. Multiply the second inequality by $-1$, so that $5x - 18 \leq 12$. This simplifies to $x \leq 6$. Combine the two results: $3 < x \leq 6$. There are 3 allowable integer values for $x$: 4, 5, and 6. Grid in **3**.

# Data Analysis

# CHAPTER 7

# Ratios, Proportions, and Percents

## LEARNING OBJECTIVES

After completing this chapter, you will be able to:

- Set up and solve a proportion for a missing value
- Use proportions to perform unit conversions
- Calculate percents and percent change

70/600 SmartPoints®

# How Much Do You Know?

**Directions:** Try the questions that follow. Show your work so that you can compare your solutions to the ones found in the Check Your Work section immediately after this question set. The "Category" heading in the explanation for each question gives the title of the lesson that covers how to solve it. If you answered the question(s) for a given lesson correctly, and if your scratchwork looks like ours, you may be able to move quickly through that lesson. If you answered incorrectly or used a different approach, you may want to take your time on that lesson.

1. Leonardo da Vinci asserted that a person's height is proportional to the length of the person's palm. Don's palm is 5 centimeters in length and he is 120 centimeters tall. Mateo's palm is 7.5 centimeters in length. Assuming that da Vinci's theory is correct, how tall, in centimeters, is Mateo?

   A) 60 centimeters

   B) 80 centimeters

   C) 160 centimeters

   D) 180 centimeters

2. As of 2009, there were about 225 quarters for every 2 fifty-cent coins in circulation. If there were 380 million quarters in circulation that year, approximately how many total quarters and fifty-cent coins, in millions, were there in circulation?

   A) 383

   B) 415

   C) 493

   D) 605

3. If $\dfrac{5}{7a} = \dfrac{1}{b-a}$, which of the following proportions is equivalent?

   A) $\dfrac{a}{b} = \dfrac{5}{12}$

   B) $\dfrac{a}{b} = \dfrac{5}{2}$

   C) $\dfrac{b-a}{a} = \dfrac{5}{7}$

   D) $\dfrac{b-a}{a} = -\dfrac{7}{5}$

4. British Thermal Units (BTUs) and calories are two measures of heat energy. If there are 2,016 calories in 8 British Thermal Units, how many calories are in 3 British Thermal Units?

5. Sai's car is leaking engine oil at a rate of 2.5 milliliters per hour. If his car's engine contains 6 liters of oil, what will be the amount of oil, in milliliters, remaining in Sai's engine after 24 hours? (Note: There are 1,000 milliliters in 1 liter.)

6.

| Category | Percentage |
|---|---|
| Completely satisfied | |
| Somewhat satisfied | |
| Somewhat dissatisfied | 15% |
| Completely dissatisfied | 25% |

A company conducts a customer satisfaction survey. The results are partly summarized in the table. If 240 customers responded to the survey, how many customers were either completely or somewhat satisfied?

A) 60

B) 96

C) 144

D) 204

7. In a week, a light bulb factory produces 12,500 light bulbs. The ratio of light emitting diodes (LED bulbs) to compact fluorescent lamps (CFL bulbs) is 2:3. Of the LED bulbs produced, 3 percent were defective. If the factory produces no other kind of bulbs, how many LED bulbs were NOT defective?

A) 2,425

B) 4,850

C) 7,275

D) 8,083

8. In 1950, scientists estimated a certain animal population in a particular geographical area to be 6,400. In 2000, the population had risen to 7,200. If this animal population experiences the same percent increase over the next 50 years, what will the approximate population be?

A) 8,000

B) 8,100

C) 8,400

D) 8,600

Math

# Check Your Work

**1.    D**

**Difficulty:** Easy

**Category:** Proportions

**Getting to the Answer:** Since you are given the palm-to-height ratio for Don's as well as Mateo's palm length, set up a proportion using $M$ to represent Mateo's height:

$$\frac{5\,cm}{120\,cm} = \frac{7.5\,cm}{M}$$

Cross-multiply to solve for $M$:

$$5M = 7.5(120)$$
$$M = \frac{7.5(120)}{5}$$
$$M = 180$$

The correct answer is **(D)**.

**2.    A**

**Difficulty:** Easy

**Category:** Proportions

**Getting to the Answer:** Notice that the question asks you for the total number of coins in millions, but the ratio given specifies only the parts. Set up a proportion using the given ratio:

$$\frac{225 \text{ quarters}}{2 \text{ fifty-cent coins}} = \frac{380 \text{ million quarters}}{x \text{ fifty-cent coins}}$$

Cross-multiply: $225x = 2 \times 380$ million. Solve for $x$ to find that $x = 3.3\overline{7}$ million fifty-cent coins in circulation. To calculate the total number of fifty-cent coins and quarters in circulation in millions in 2009, add the number of fifty-cent coins to the number of quarters: $3.3\overline{7}$ million $+ 380$ million $\approx 383$ million. Choice **(A)** is correct.

**3.    A**

**Difficulty:** Medium

**Category:** Proportions

**Getting to the Answer:** Since the answer choices are expressed as $\frac{a}{b} =$ and $\frac{b-a}{a} =$, cross-multiply the proportion and rewrite it to get an expression that matches one of the answer choices. Solving for $\frac{b-a}{a}$, you get the following:

$$\frac{5}{7a} = \frac{1}{b-a}$$
$$5(b-a) = 7a$$
$$\frac{b-a}{a} = \frac{7}{5}$$

This does not match (C) or (D), so eliminate them. Now solve for $\frac{a}{b}$:

$$5(b-a) = 7a$$
$$5b - 5a = 7a$$
$$5b = 12a$$
$$\frac{5}{12} = \frac{a}{b}$$

This matches **(A)**.

**4.    756**

**Difficulty:** Easy

**Category:** Unit Conversion

**Getting to the Answer:** Let $x$ represent the number of calories in 3 BTUs, and set up a proportion equating the ratio of 8 BTUs to 2,016 calories to the ratio of 3 BTUs to $x$ calories: $\frac{8\,BTU}{2,016\,CAL} = \frac{3\,BTU}{x\,CAL}$. Solving for $x$ gives 756 calories. Grid in **756**.

**5.   5940**

**Difficulty:** Medium

**Category:** Unit Conversion

**Getting to the Answer:** First, determine the amount of oil that will leak out of Sai's engine after 24 hours: $\frac{2.5 \text{ mL}}{1 \text{ hr}} \times 24 \text{ hr} = 60 \text{ mL}$. Then, use the conversion to determine the amount of oil, in milliliters, initially in the engine: $6 \text{ L} \times \frac{1,000 \text{ mL}}{1 \text{ L}} = 6,000 \text{ mL}$. Calculate the difference between the two to find the amount of oil remaining in the engine after 24 hours: $6,000 \text{ mL} - 60 \text{ mL} = \textbf{5,940}$ mL. Grid in **5940**.

**6.   C**

**Difficulty:** Easy

**Category:** Percents

**Getting to the Answer:** According to the table, 25% of the customers are completely dissatisfied and 15% are somewhat dissatisfied. So, $100\% - 25\% - 15\% = 60\%$ of the customers are completely or somewhat satisfied. Thus, the number of customers who are completely or somewhat satisfied is 60% of 240, or $0.6 \times 240 = 144$ customers, making **(C)** correct.

**7.   B**

**Difficulty:** Hard

**Category:** Percents

**Getting to the Answer:** Approach the question as a series of steps. Before you bubble in your answer, check that you answered the right question (the number of LED bulbs that were *not* defective).

First, find the total number of LED bulbs produced. Since the ratio of LED to CFL is 2:3 and a total of 12,500 of both kinds of bulbs were produced, two parts LED plus three parts CFL equals 12,500. Let $x$ be the number of LED bulbs produced and use the part to whole ratio to set up a proportion:

$$\frac{2}{5} = \frac{x}{12,500}$$

Solve for $x$ by cross-multiplying:

$$2(12,500) = 5x$$
$$25,000 = 5x$$
$$5,000 = x$$

Now find the number of LED bulbs that were not defective: $5,000 \times 97\% = 5,000 \times 0.97 = 4,850$. Choice **(B)** is correct.

**8.   B**

**Difficulty:** Medium

**Category:** Percent Change

**Getting to the Answer:** Find the percent increase in the population from 1950 to 2000 using this formula: $\% \text{ increase} = \frac{\text{amount of increase}}{\text{original amount}} \times 100\%$. Then apply the same percent increase to the animal population in 2000.

The amount of increase is $7,200 - 6,400 = 800$, so the percent increase is $\frac{800}{6,400} \times 100\% = 0.125 \times 100\% = 12.5\%$ between 1950 and 2000. If the total percent increase over the next 50 years is the same, the animal population should be about

$$7,200 \times (100\% + 12.5\%) = 7,200 \times (112.5\%) =$$
$$7,200 \times 1.125 = 8,100.$$

**(B)** is correct.

# Ratios and Proportions

## LEARNING OBJECTIVE

After this lesson, you will be able to:

- Set up and solve a proportion for a missing value

## To answer a question like this:

The World War II aircraft carrier *Essex* was 872 feet long with a beam (width) of 147 feet. A museum wishes to build an exact replica scale model of the Essex that is 8 feet long. Approximately how many <u>inches</u> wide will the scale model's beam be? (1 foot = 12 inches)

A) 13

B) 16

C) 26

D) 109

## You need to know this:

A **ratio** is a comparison of one quantity to another. When writing ratios, you can compare one part of a group to another part of that group or you can compare a part of the group to the whole group. Suppose you have a bowl of apples and oranges: you can write ratios that compare apples to oranges (part to part), apples to total fruit (part to whole), and oranges to total fruit (part to whole).

Keep in mind that ratios convey *relative* amounts, not necessarily actual amounts, and that they are typically expressed in lowest terms. For example, if there are 10 apples and 6 oranges in a bowl, the ratio of apples to oranges would likely be expressed as $\frac{5}{3}$ on the SAT rather than as $\frac{10}{6}$. However, if you know the ratio of apples to oranges and either the actual number of apples or the total number of pieces of fruit, you can find the actual number of oranges by setting up a proportion (see below).

---

Note that the SAT may occasionally use the word "proportion" to mean "ratio."

---

A **proportion** is simply two ratios set equal to each other, such as, $\frac{a}{b} = \frac{c}{d}$. Proportions are an efficient way to solve certain problems, but you must exercise caution when setting them up. Noting the units of each piece of the proportion will help you put each piece of the proportion in the right place. Sometimes the SAT may ask you to determine whether certain proportions are equivalent—check this by cross-multiplying. You'll get results that are much easier to compare.

$$\text{If } \frac{a}{b} = \frac{c}{d}, \text{ then: } ad = bc, \frac{a}{c} = \frac{b}{d}, \frac{d}{b} = \frac{c}{a}, \frac{b}{a} = \frac{d}{c}, \text{ BUT } \frac{a}{d} \neq \frac{c}{b}$$

Each derived ratio shown except the last one is simply a manipulation of the first, so all except the last are correct. You can verify this via cross-multiplication ($ad = bc$ in each case except the last).

Alternatively, you can pick equivalent fractions $\frac{2}{3}$ and $\frac{6}{9}$ ($a = 2$, $b = 3$, $c = 6$, $d = 9$). Cross-multiplication gives $2 \times 9 = 3 \times 6$, which is a true statement. Dividing 2 and 3 by 6 and 9 gives $\frac{2}{6} = \frac{3}{9}$, which is also true, and so on. However, attempting to equate $\frac{2}{9}$ and $\frac{3}{6}$ will not work.

If you know any three numerical values in a proportion, you can solve for the fourth. For example, say a fruit stand sells 3 peaches for every 5 apricots, and you are supposed to calculate the number of peaches sold on a day when 20 apricots were sold. You would use the given information to set up a proportion and solve for the unknown:

$$\frac{3}{5} = \frac{p}{20}$$

You can now solve for the number of peaches sold, $p$, by cross-multiplying:

$$60 = 5p$$
$$p = 12$$

Alternatively, you could use the common multiplier to solve for $p$: the numerator and denominator in the original ratio must be multiplied by the same value to arrive at their respective terms in the new ratio. To get from 5 to 20 in the denominator, you multiply by 4, so you also have to multiply the 3 in the numerator by 4 to arrive at the actual number of peaches sold: $4(3) = 12$.

## You need to do this:

- Set up a proportion and solve for the unknown, either by cross-multiplying or by using the common multiplier

## Explanation:

The ratio of the length of the real Essex to that of the scale model is $\frac{872 \text{ ft}}{8 \text{ ft}}$. You know the actual beam width (147 feet), so set up a proportion and solve for the scale model's beam width:

$$\frac{872 \text{ ft}}{8 \text{ ft}} = \frac{147 \text{ ft}}{x \text{ ft}}$$
$$872x = 1{,}176 \text{ ft}$$
$$x \approx 1.349 \text{ ft}$$

The question asks for the answer in inches, not feet, so multiply by 12 inches per foot: $1.349 \text{ ft} \times 12 \text{ in/ft} = 16.188$ inches. The correct answer is **(B)**.

Math

## Try on Your Own

**Directions:** Take as much time as you need on these questions. Work carefully and methodically. There will be an opportunity for timed practice at the end of the chapter.

1.  Teachers at a certain school know that, when reviewing for exams, the number of topics they can cover is directly proportional to the length of time they have to review. If teachers can cover 9 topics in a single 45-minute period, how many topics can they cover in a 1-hour period?

    A)   5
    B)   7
    C)   10
    D)   12

2.  Objects weigh less on the Moon because the Moon's gravitational pull is less than Earth's. In general, 1 pound on Earth is equal to approximately 0.166 pounds on the Moon. If a person weighs 29 pounds on the Moon, approximately how much, in pounds, does the person weigh on Earth?

    A)   21
    B)   48
    C)   175
    D)   196

3.  A machine produces 6 defective parts out of every 3,500 it makes. How many total parts were made during the time the machine produced 27 defective parts?

    A)   14,000
    B)   15,750
    C)   17,500
    D)   21,000

4.  The ratio of freshmen to sophomores in an auditorium was 3 to 10. After an additional 270 freshmen and 120 sophomores entered the auditorium, the ratio of freshmen to sophomores was 6 to 5. No other students entered or left the auditorium. How many freshmen were in the auditorium before the additional students entered?

    A)   15
    B)   42
    C)   140
    D)   182

---

HINT: For Q5, which conversion will be easier? Minutes to hours or hours to minutes?

---

5. Riding her bicycle, Reyna can travel 1 mile in 5.5 minutes. If she rides at a constant rate, which of the following is closest to the distance she will travel in 1.5 hours?

    A) 9 miles

    B) 11 miles

    C) 13 miles

    D) 16 miles

6. If $\dfrac{x + y}{x} = \dfrac{4}{9}$, which of the following proportions is equivalent?

    A) $\dfrac{y}{x} = -\dfrac{5}{9}$

    B) $\dfrac{y}{x} = \dfrac{13}{9}$

    C) $\dfrac{y - x}{x} = -\dfrac{4}{9}$

    D) $\dfrac{y - x}{x} = -\dfrac{9}{4}$

---

HINT: For Q7, start with the proportion $\dfrac{physicists}{total} = \dfrac{2}{5}$, then think about what to substitute for "physicists" and "total."

---

7. All of the attendees at a symposium are either physicists or biologists. If there are 123 physicists and 270 biologists, then how many additional physicists must arrive at the symposium in order for the ratio of physicists to total attendees to become 2 to 5 ?

    A) 25

    B) 50

    C) 57

    D) 114

# Unit Conversion

**LEARNING OBJECTIVE**

After this lesson, you will be able to:

- Use proportions to perform unit conversions

## To answer a question like this:

The nearest star to the Sun, Proxima Centauri, is approximately 4.3 light years away. Another star, Sirius A, is twice that distance from the Sun. If one light year equals 63,000 astronomical units (AU), and 1 AU equals 150 million kilometers, approximately how far is Sirius A from the Sun in trillions of kilometers? (1 trillion = 1,000,000,000,000)

A)  2.2

B)  20

C)  41

D)  81

## You need to know this:

You can set up a proportion to perform unit conversions. This is especially useful when there are multiple conversions or when the units are unfamiliar.

For example, though these units of measurement are no longer commonly used, there are 8 furlongs in a mile and 3 miles in a league. Say you're asked to convert 4 leagues to furlongs. A convenient way to do this is to set up a proportion so that equivalent units cancel:

$$4 \text{ leagues} \times \frac{3 \text{ miles}}{1 \text{ league}} \times \frac{8 \text{ furlongs}}{1 \text{ mile}} = 4 \times 3 \times 8 = 96 \text{ furlongs}$$

Notice that all the units cancel out except the furlongs, which is the one you want.

## You need to do this:

Set up a proportion to make equivalent units cancel. (Keep track of the units by writing them down next to the numbers in the proportion.) You should be left with the units you're converting into.

## Explanation:

Sirius A is twice as far from the Sun as Proxima Centauri, so it is $2(4.3) = 8.6$ light years away from the Sun. Set up a proportion to convert to trillion kilometers:

$$8.6 \ \cancel{\text{light years}} \times \frac{63,000 \ \cancel{\text{AU}}}{1 \ \cancel{\text{light year}}} \times \frac{150 \ \text{million km}}{1 \ \cancel{\text{AU}}} = 8.6 \times 63,000 \times 150 \ \text{million km}$$

$$= 81,270,000 \ \text{million km}$$

$$= 81.27 \ \text{trillion km}$$

Because there are 6 zeroes in a million, 81,270,000 million is 81,270,000,000,000. There are 12 zeroes in a trillion, so this number equals 81.27 trillion. The correct answer is **(D)**.

## Try on Your Own

**Directions:** Take as much time as you need on these questions. Work carefully and methodically. There will be an opportunity for timed practice at the end of the chapter.

---

HINT: For Q8, *cubic feet* means ft³ or ft × ft × ft.

---

8. Quinn wants to rent a self-storage unit for her college dorm room furniture for the summer. She estimates that she will need 700 cubic feet of storage space, but the self-storage provider measures its units in cubic meters. If 1 meter is approximately 3.28 feet, about how many cubic meters of space will Quinn need?

    A)  19.84

    B)  25.93

    C)  65.07

    D)  213.41

9. Because court reporters must type every word at a trial or hearing, they must be able to type at a minimum rate of 3.75 words per second in order to be certified. Suppose a trial transcript contains 25 pages with an average of 675 words per page. Assuming the court reporter typed the transcript at the minimum rate, how long was he actively typing?

    A)  1 hour, 15 minutes

    B)  1 hour, 45 minutes

    C)  2 hours, 30 minutes

    D)  3 hours

---

HINT: For Q10, *how many more* means you're solving for a difference. Subtract, then convert pounds/hour to ounces/minute.

---

10. At 350°F, an oven can cook approximately 3 pounds of turkey per hour. At 450°F, it can cook approximately 4.5 pounds per hour. How many more ounces of turkey can the oven cook at 450°F than at 350°F in 10 minutes? (1 pound = 16 ounces)

    A)  4

    B)  6

    C)  8

    D)  12

11. An emergency room doctor prescribes a certain pain medication to be delivered through an IV drip. She prescribes 800 milliliters of the medication to be delivered over the course of 8 hours. The IV delivers 1 milliliter of medication over the course of 30 drips. How many drips per minute are needed to deliver the prescribed dosage?

12. Botanists studying a particular coastal redwood tree determined that the tree grew 46 meters in the first 50 years of its life. On average, how many centimeters per day did it grow during this period? Assume that there are 365 days in a year and round your answer to the nearest hundredth of a centimeter.

# Percents

**LEARNING OBJECTIVE**

After this lesson, you will be able to:

● Calculate percents

## To answer a question like this:

Political canvassers polled voters in two locations on whether they viewed a particular candidate for governor favorably. At the first location, they asked 125 people and of those, 22.4 percent responded favorably. At the second location, 37.5 percent of 272 people responded favorably. Approximately what percent of all the people surveyed responded favorably?

A) 25.7%

B) 30.0%

C) 31.5%

D) 32.7%

## You need to know this:

To calculate percents, use this basic equation:

$$\text{Percent} = \frac{\text{part}}{\text{whole}} \times 100\%$$

Alternatively, use this statement: [blank] percent of [blank] is [blank]. Translating from English into math, you get [blank]% × [blank] = [blank].

## You need to do this:

- Plug in the values for any two parts of the formula and solve for the third
- In some calculations, you may find it convenient to express percents as decimals. To do this, use the formula above but stop before you multiply by 100% at the end.

### Explanation:

Use a variation of the three-part percent formula to answer this question: whole × percent = part, where the percent is expressed as a decimal.

First, find the number of people at each location who responded favorably using the formula. Start with the first location: $125 \times 0.224 = 28$. Move on to the second location: $272 \times 0.375 = 102$. Next, find the total number of people who were surveyed at both locations, which is $125 + 272 = 397$, and the total number who responded favorably, $28 + 102 = 130$. Finally, find the percent of people who responded favorably by using the formula one more time:

$$397 \times \text{percent} = 130 \times 100\%$$
$$\text{percent} = \frac{130}{397} \times 100\%$$
$$\approx 0.327 \times 100\%$$
$$= 32.7\%$$

Of all the people surveyed, about 32.7% responded favorably, making **(D)** the correct answer.

## Try on Your Own

**Directions:** Take as much time as you need on these questions. Work carefully and methodically. There will be an opportunity for timed practice at the end of the chapter.

13. A college athletics program found that approximately 3 percent of 308 runners were injured during workouts and that approximately 6 percent of 237 weightlifters were injured during workouts. Which of the following is the closest to the total number of runners and weightlifters who were injured?

A) 50

B) 39

C) 26

D) 23

---

HINT: For Q14, what percent of the attendees are teachers?

---

14. At a high school conference, 15 percent of the attendees are sophomores, 30 percent are juniors, 25 percent are seniors, and the remaining 18 attendees are teachers. How many more juniors are there than seniors?

---

HINT: For Q15, how many gallons of *pigment* is the painter starting with? How many gallons of *pigment* are needed for the final mix? How many gallons of the final paint will it take to provide the needed pigment?

---

15. A painter has 20 gallons of a paint mixture that is 15 percent blue pigment. How many gallons of a mixture that is 40 percent blue pigment would the painter need to add to achieve a mixture that is 20 percent blue pigment?

A) 4

B) 5

C) 8

D) 12

16. On August 1, the price of one share of a company's stock was $75. On September 1, the price of one share was $10 more than it was on August 1 and 80 percent of the price of one share on October 1. To the nearest dollar, what was the price of one share on October 1?

A) $68

B) $99

C) $102

D) $106

# Percent Change

---

**LEARNING OBJECTIVE**

After this lesson, you will be able to:

- Calculate percent change

---

**To answer a question like this:**

On a particular day, a power company makes several changes in the power allocated to a neighborhood. First, it increases the power by 20 percent. Then, it decreases the power by 10 percent. Finally, it increases the power by 30 percent. What is the net percent increase in this neighborhood's power allocation, to the nearest tenth of a percent? (The percent sign is understood after your answer. For example, if the answer is 15.1%, grid in 15.1.)

**You need to know this:**

You can determine the **percent change** in a given situation by applying this formula:

$$\text{Percent increase or decrease} = \frac{\text{amount of increase or decrease}}{\text{original amount}} \times 100\%$$

Sometimes, more than one change will occur. Be careful here, as it can be tempting to take a "shortcut" by just adding two percent changes together (which will almost always lead to an incorrect answer). Instead, you'll need to find the total amount of the increase or decrease and then apply the formula.

**You need to do this:**

- Calculate the actual increase or decrease
- Divide by the *original* amount (not the new amount!)
- Multiply by 100%

## Explanation:

The question does not give an initial value for power allocation, so pick 100 (often the best number to use when picking numbers for questions involving percents) and then calculate the actual change. A 20% increase from 100 is $100 + 100 \times 0.2$ and brings the power allocation to $100 + 20 = 120$. A 10% decrease from 120 is $120 - 120 \times 0.1$ and brings the power allocation to $120 - 12 = 108$. Lastly, an increase of 30% puts the final power allocation at $108 + 0.3 \times 108 = 108 + 32.4 = 140.4$. The actual increase, then, is $140.4 - 100 = 40.4$. (Again, note that simply combining the percents would get you the wrong answer: $10\% - 20\% + 30\% = 40\%$.)

Plugging this increase into the percent change formula yields the following (remember to divide by the *original* amount, 100, rather than by the new amount, 140.4):

$$\text{Percent change} = \frac{40.4}{100} \times 100\% = 40.4\%$$

Grid in **40.4**.

## Try on Your Own

**Directions:** Take as much time as you need on these questions. Work carefully and methodically. There will be an opportunity for timed practice at the end of the chapter.

HINT: For Q17, remember to divide by the *original* value.

17. A homeowner's annual property tax payment was $1,494. Due to a property value reassessment, the tax payment was increased to $1,572. To the nearest tenth of a percent, by what percent was the home-owner's property tax payment increased?

A) 0.1%

B) 5.0%

C) 5.2%

D) 7.9%

18. The price of a single share of a certain corporation's stock was $35. Six months later, the price of a single share of the corporation's stock had risen to $49. To the nearest percent, what was the percent increase in the price per share?

A) 14%

B) 29%

C) 40%

D) 48%

HINT: For Q19, how does the wording of the question help you determine which container of coins is the original amount?

19. The number of coins in jar $X$ is 75. The number of coins in jar $Y$ is 54. By what percent is the number of coins in jar $Y$ less than the number of coins in jar $X$?

A) 21%

B) 28%

C) 39%

D) 72%

HINT: For Q20, if you have 75% more senior than juniors, you have all the juniors (100%) plus 75%, or 175%. Adding the percents at the start saves a calculation step.

20. At a school rally, there are 50 sophomores, 80 juniors, and 75 percent more seniors than juniors. By what percent is the number of seniors greater than the number of sophomores?

A) 80%

B) 140%

C) 150%

D) 180%

HINT: For Q21, the final 25% discount is applied to an already reduced price. You *cannot* add the percent discounts together.

21. The original price of a newly released smart phone was $y$ dollars. A year later, the original price of the phone was discounted by 36 percent. After another six months, an online retailer was selling the phone at a price that was 25 percent less than the previously discounted price. By what percent was the online retailer's price less than $y$?

A) 27%

B) 48%

C) 52%

D) 61%

## On Test Day

When a question features multiple percentages, you have to make a key strategic decision: can I do the arithmetic on the percentages themselves and get the answer right away, or do I have to calculate each percentage individually and do the arithmetic on the actual values?

For example, suppose a car traveling 50 miles per hour increases its speed by 20 percent and then decreases its speed by 20 percent. Can you just say that its final speed is 50 miles per hour since $+20\% - 20\% = 0$? No, because after a 20% increase, the car's speed becomes 120% of the original: $1.2(50) = 60$. When the car "decreases its speed by 20 percent," that 20 percent is calculated based on the new speed, 60, not the original speed, and 20 percent of 60 is greater than 20 percent of 50. Thus, the car's final speed is lower than its starting speed: $50(1.2)(0.8) = 48$ miles per hour.

By contrast, suppose you have to find how many more non-smokers than occasional smokers live in a certain region where there are 13,450 residents, given that 62 percent of them don't smoke, and 8 percent of them do smoke occasionally. It may be tempting to find 62 percent of 13,450 ($0.62 \times 13,450 = 8,339$), then find 8 percent of 13,450 ($0.08 \times 13,450 = 1,076$), and finally subtract those two numbers to get the answer ($8,339 - 1,076 = 7,263$). This is a waste of time, though. Instead, you can quickly find the difference between the two percentages ($62 - 8 = 54$) and take 54 percent of the total to get the answer in one step: $13,450 \times 0.54 = 7,263$, the same answer.

If you *can* do arithmetic using the percentages but choose to do arithmetic on the raw numbers instead, you'll waste time doing unnecessary work. But if you *can't* do arithmetic on the percentages (as in the first example) but do anyway, then you'll get the wrong answer. So, being able to tell whether you can or can't do the arithmetic on the percentages is a useful skill.

Luckily, the fundamental principle is simple: you can always do arithmetic on the percentages as long as the percentages are out of the same total. If the totals are different, then you must convert the percentages into actual values. Practice applying this principle on the following question.

22. Flanders Corporation has 250 full-time and 250 part-time employees. If 92 percent of the full-time employees qualify for health insurance benefits, and 74 percent of the part-time employees do not qualify for health insurance benefits, then how many more full-time than part-time employees at Flanders Corporation qualify for health insurance benefits?

    A)    45

    B)    90

    C)    165

    D)    330

The answer and explanation can be found at the end of this chapter.

# How Much Have You Learned?

**Directions:** For testlike practice, give yourself 15 minutes to complete this question set. Be sure to study the explanations, even for questions you got right. They can be found at the end of this chapter.

**Undergraduate Costs at a State University**

| 2014–15 | 2015–16 | 2016–17 | 2017–18 | 2018–19 | 2019–20 |
|---------|---------|---------|---------|---------|---------|
| $12,192 | $12,804 | $13,446 | $14,118 | $14,820 | $15,564 |

23. The table above summarizes the total cost per undergraduate student per year at a state university for each academic year from 2014–15 to 2019–20.

    If fees account for 8.75 percent of one year's total costs, what is the average fee increase per academic year? Round your answer to the nearest dollar.

24. A gardener planted a 20-inch tall sapling in his yard. Four months later, the sapling was 27 inches tall. By what percent did the height of the sapling increase over the four months?

    A)  7%

    B)  26%

    C)  35%

    D)  74%

25. From 1997 to 1998, company T's profits increased by 25 percent. From 1998 to 1999, company T's profits rose from $375 million to $483 million. By what percent did company T's profits increase from 1997 to 1999?

    A)  38%

    B)  49%

    C)  54%

    D)  61%

26. At a certain store, the price of a calculator is $150, the price of a radio is $75, and the price of a printer is 16 percent less than the price of a radio. By what percent is the price of a printer less than the price of a calculator?

    A)  39%

    B)  58%

    C)  63%

    D)  87%

27. A car that is traveling at a constant speed of 9 miles per hour is traveling at a constant speed of how many feet per second? (1 mile = 5,280 feet)

    A)  1.5

    B)  6.1

    C)  13.2

    D)  79.2

28. In a certain music store, every guitar is either a dreadnought or a parlor guitar. The ratio of dreadnoughts to parlor guitars in the music store is 4 to 15, and there is a total of 114 guitars in the music store. How many guitars in the music store are dreadnoughts?

    A) 24

    B) 29

    C) 34

    D) 46

29. The population of a town was 84,600 on January 1, 2016, and 74,025 on January 1, 2017. By what percent did the population of the town decrease from January 1, 2016, to January 1, 2017?

    A) 10.5%

    B) 12.5%

    C) 14.5%

    D) 17%

30. The perimeter of regular pentagon *P* is half the perimeter of regular hexagon *H*. What is the ratio of the length of a side of the pentagon to a side of the hexagon?

    A) 1:2

    B) 3:5

    C) 5:6

    D) 5:3

31. A jar contains red, white, and yellow candy pieces in the ratio of 9:5:4, respectively. When 7 pieces of red candy and 5 pieces of white candy are removed from the jar and 3 pieces of yellow candy are added, the ratio of red to white to yellow becomes 4:2:3. If the jar contains only these three colors of candy, how many pieces were originally in the jar?

32. Juan's air mattress deflates at a constant rate of 100 milliliters per minute. If Juan's air mattress contains 300 liters of air, how long will it take, in hours, for the air mattress to completely deflate? (Note: there are 1,000 milliliters in 1 liter).

# Reflect

**Directions:** Take a few minutes to recall what you've learned and what you've been practicing in this chapter. Consider the following questions, jot down your best answer for each one, and then compare your reflections to the expert responses on the following page. Use your level of confidence to determine what to do next.

What is a ratio and how is it different from a proportion?

If you're given a ratio of one quantity to another, what can you say about the total number of quantities?

When doing unit conversions, how can you make sure you're doing them correctly?

Suppose the value of something increases by 20 percent. How can you calculate the final value in the fewest number of steps? What if the value decreases by 20 percent?

What is the percent change formula and what is the biggest pitfall to avoid when using it?

## Expert Responses

What is a ratio and how is it different from a proportion?

*A ratio is the relative comparison of one quantity to another. For example, if the ratio of dogs to cats in an animal shelter is 3 to 5, then there are 3 dogs for every 5 cats. A proportion is two ratios set equal to each other.*

If you're given a ratio of one quantity to another, what can you say about the total number of quantities?

*Given a ratio, you know that the total must be a multiple of the sum of the ratio's parts. For example, if the ratio of dogs to cats is 3 to 5, then the total number of dogs and cats must be a multiple of 3 + 5, or 8. This means that when the SAT gives you one ratio, it's actually giving you several. If you're told that dogs:cats = 3:5, then you also know that dogs:total = 3:8 and cats:total = 5:8. You can use this "hidden" knowledge to your advantage.*

When doing unit conversions, how can you make sure you're doing them correctly?

*To do unit conversions correctly, set up the conversion in whichever way makes units cancel. For example, to convert 3 feet into inches, you multiply 3 feet by 12 inches per foot, because it cancels out the feet unit. If instead you multiplied 3 feet by 1 foot per 12 inches, then the resulting units would be "feet squared per inch," which makes no sense.*

Suppose the value of something increases by 20 percent. How can you calculate the final value in the fewest number of steps? What if the value decreases by 20 percent?

*The fastest way to increase a value by 20 percent is to multiply it by 1.2, which is 100% + 20% = 120%. Similarly, to decrease something by 20 percent, you multiply it by 0.8, as that is 100% − 20% = 80%.*

What is the percent change formula and what is the biggest pitfall to avoid when using it?

*The percent change formula is as follows:*

$$\text{Percent change} = \frac{\text{amount of increase or decrease}}{\text{original amount}} \times 100\%$$

*A common mistake is to put the new amount on the bottom of the fraction rather than the original amount.*

## Next Steps

If you answered most questions correctly in the "How Much Have You Learned?" section, and if your responses to the Reflect questions were similar to those of the SAT expert, then consider ratios and the related topics in this chapter to be an area of strength and move on to the next chapter. Come back to this topic periodically to prevent yourself from getting rusty.

If you don't yet feel confident, review those parts of this chapter that you have not yet mastered and try the questions you missed again. As always, be sure to review the explanations closely.

**Math**

# Answers and Explanations

## 1. D

**Difficulty:** Easy

**Getting to the Answer:** To answer a question that says "directly proportional," set two ratios equal to each other and solve for the missing amount. Be sure to match the units in the numerators and in the denominators on both sides of the proportion.

Because the first rate is given in minutes, write 1 hour as 60 minutes. Let $t$ equal the number of topics the teachers can cover in a 60-minute period. Set up a proportion and solve for $t$:

$$\frac{9 \text{ topics}}{45 \text{ minutes}} = \frac{t \text{ topics}}{60 \text{ minutes}}$$
$$9(60) = 45(t)$$
$$540 = 45t$$
$$12 = t$$

Choice **(D)** is correct.

## 2. C

**Difficulty:** Easy

**Getting to the Answer:** Think about how your answer should look. A person weighs *less* on the Moon, so that person should weigh *more* on Earth. This means your answer must be greater than 29, so you can eliminate (A) right away.

Now, set up a proportion:

$$\frac{0.166 \text{ lb on Moon}}{1 \text{ lb on Earth}} = \frac{29 \text{ lb on Moon}}{p \text{ lb on Earth}}$$
$$0.166p = 29(1)$$
$$p \approx 174.7$$

The person weighs about 175 pounds on Earth. Choice **(C)** is correct.

## 3. B

**Difficulty:** Easy

**Getting to the Answer:** This is a typical proportion question. Use words first to write the proportion. Then translate from English into math. Let $n$ equal the total number of parts made. Set up a proportion and solve for $n$. Be sure to match the units in the numerators and in the denominators on both sides of the proportion:

$$\frac{\text{defective parts}}{\text{number made}} = \frac{\text{defective parts}}{\text{number made}}$$
$$\frac{6}{3,500} = \frac{27}{n}$$
$$6n = 27(3,500)$$
$$6n = 94,500$$
$$n = 15,750$$

This means **(B)** is correct.

## 4. B

**Difficulty:** Hard

**Getting to the Answer:** This question has two unknowns: you don't know the starting number of either freshmen or sophomores. To solve for two unknowns, you need two equations. Let $f$ represent the original number of freshmen in the auditorium and $s$ represent the original number of sophomores. The starting ratio is $\frac{f}{s} = \frac{3}{10}$. Cross-multiplying yields $10f = 3s$. This is your first equation.

Set up a second equation to represent the adjusted number of freshmen and sophomores:

$$\frac{f + 270}{s + 120} = \frac{6}{5}$$
$$5(f + 270) = 6(s + 120)$$
$$5f + 1,350 = 6s + 720$$

You've determined from the first ratio that $10f = 3s$, and if you multiply this equation by 2, you get $20f = 6s$. Now substitute $20f$ for $6s$ in the above equation:

$$5f + 1,350 = 20f + 720$$
$$630 = 15f$$
$$42 = f$$

There were 42 freshmen in the auditorium to start, so **(B)** is correct.

**5. D**

**Difficulty:** Medium

**Getting to the Answer:** Use the known time of 5.5 minutes it takes Reyna to travel 1 mile to calculate the distance she can cover in 1.5 hours. So that you're working with the same units, first convert 1.5 hours to minutes: $1.5 \times 60 = 90$ minutes. Let $d$ be the unknown distance and then set up a proportion to solve for $d$:

$$\frac{1}{5.5} = \frac{d}{90}$$
$$90 = 5.5d$$
$$\frac{90}{5.5} = d$$
$$d \cong 16$$

Therefore, **(D)** is correct.

**6. A**

**Difficulty:** Medium

**Getting to the Answer:** Since the answer choices are expressed as $\frac{y}{x} =$ and $\frac{y-x}{x} =$, cross-multiply the proportion and rewrite it to get an expression that matches the form of one of the answer choices. Solve for $\frac{y}{x}$:

$$\frac{x+y}{x} = \frac{4}{9}$$
$$9(x+y) = 4x$$
$$9x + 9y = 4x$$
$$9y = -5x$$
$$\frac{y}{x} = -\frac{5}{9}$$

This matches **(A)**.

Alternatively, you could rewrite the proportion as follows:

$$\frac{x}{x} + \frac{y}{x} = \frac{4}{9}$$
$$1 + \frac{y}{x} = \frac{4}{9}$$
$$\frac{y}{x} = \frac{4}{9} - 1$$
$$\frac{y}{x} = -\frac{5}{9}$$

Note that multiplying both sides of the proportion by $-1$ would give $-\frac{(x+y)}{x} = -\frac{4}{9}$ or $\frac{-x-y}{x} = -\frac{4}{9}$, which does not match (C) or (D).

**7. C**

**Difficulty:** Hard

**Getting to the Answer:** The ratio of physicists to total attendees is the number of physicists divided by the number of all attendees. Suppose $x$ new physicists arrive at the symposium. The new number of physicists will be $123 + x$, and the new number of all attendees will be the original physicists (123) + biologists (270) + the newcomer physicists ($x$). The ratio of the first number over the second equals 2 to 5, so set up a proportion and solve for $x$:

$$\frac{123 + x}{123 + 270 + x} = \frac{2}{5}$$
$$\frac{123 + x}{393 + x} = \frac{2}{5}$$
$$5(123 + x) = 2(393 + x)$$
$$615 + 5x = 786 + 2x$$
$$3x = 171$$
$$x = 57$$

Therefore, **(C)** is correct.

**8. A**

**Difficulty:** Medium

**Getting to the Answer:** Map out your route from starting units to ending units, being mindful of the fact that the question deals with units of volume (cubic units). The starting quantity is in $\text{ft}^3$, and the desired quantity is in $\text{m}^3$. The only conversion factor you need is $1 \text{ m} \approx 3.28 \text{ ft}$, but you'll need to use it three times. Setting up your route to $\text{m}^3$, you get:

$$\frac{700 \text{ ft}^3}{1} \times \frac{1 \text{ m}}{3.28 \text{ ft}} \times \frac{1 \text{ m}}{3.28 \text{ ft}} \times \frac{1 \text{ m}}{3.28 \text{ ft}} = \frac{700}{(3.28)^3} \text{m}^3$$
$$\approx 19.84 \text{ m}^3$$

This matches **(A)**.

## 9. A

**Difficulty:** Hard

**Getting to the Answer:** Whenever multiple rates are given, pay very careful attention to the units. Starting with the number of pages the reporter typed, set up your proportion so that equivalent units cancel. Be sure your units match those in the answer choices:

$$25 \text{ pages} \times \frac{675 \text{ words}}{1 \text{ page}} \times \frac{1 \text{ second}}{3.75 \text{ words}}$$

$$\times \frac{1 \text{ minute}}{60 \text{ seconds}} \times \frac{1 \text{ hour}}{60 \text{ minutes}} = 1.25 \text{ hours}$$

Because 1.25 hours is not an answer choice, convert 0.25 to minutes: $0.25 \times 60$ minutes $= 15$ minutes, making **(A)** the correct answer.

## 10. A

**Difficulty:** Medium

**Getting to the Answer:** The 450° oven cooks $4.5 - 3 = 1.5$ more pounds per hour than the 350° oven. However, the question asks for the answer in ounces per 10 minutes, so convert from pounds per hour to ounces per minute, then multiply by 10 minutes:

$$\frac{1.5 \text{ lb}}{1 \text{ hr}} \times \frac{16 \text{ oz}}{1 \text{ lb}} \times \frac{1 \text{ hr}}{60 \text{ min}} \times 10 \text{ min} = 4 \text{ oz}$$

In 10 minutes, the oven at 450° can cook 4 ounces more than the oven at 350°, making **(A)** the correct answer.

## 11. 50

**Difficulty:** Medium

**Getting to the Answer:** Starting with the prescribed dosage, set up your proportion so that equivalent units cancel and you get drips per minute:

$$\frac{800 \text{ mL}}{8 \text{ hours}} \times \frac{30 \text{ drips}}{1 \text{ mL}} \times \frac{1 \text{ hour}}{60 \text{ minutes}} = 50 \frac{\text{drips}}{\text{minute}}$$

Grid in **50**.

## 12. 0.25

**Difficulty:** Easy

**Getting to the Answer:** The question provides the growth rate, in meters, over a 50-year period. You need to convert this to a rate of centimeters per day. Set up a proportion so that the units cancel:

$$\frac{46 \text{ meters}}{50 \text{ years}} \times \frac{100 \text{ centimeters}}{1 \text{ meter}} \times \frac{1 \text{ year}}{365 \text{ days}}$$

$$\cong 0.252 \frac{\text{centimeters}}{\text{day}}$$

You're told to round to the nearest hundredth of a centimeter, so grid in **.25**.

## 13. D

**Difficulty:** Easy

**Getting to the Answer:** The question asks for the approximate combined number of runners and weightlifters who were injured. Calculate the approximate number from each group who were injured and then add the numbers together:

$$3\% \times 308 = 0.03 \times 308 \cong 9$$
$$6\% \times 237 = 0.06 \times 237 \cong 14$$
$$9 + 4 = 23$$

Therefore, **(D)** is correct.

## 14. 3

**Difficulty:** Medium

**Strategic Advice:** First find the total number of attendees; then calculate the difference in the actual number of juniors and seniors.

**Getting to the Answer:** The question gives you the percents of sophomores, juniors, and seniors attending the conference, as well as the actual number of teachers. Add up all of the percents to find the total percent of the attendees who are *not* teachers: $15\% + 25\% + 30\% = 70\%$. Therefore, the 18 teachers account for $100\% - 70\% = 30\%$ of the attendees.

You can solve for the total number of attendees (the whole) by plugging in the corresponding values for percent and part into the equation part = percent × whole. Say the total number of attendees is $t$:

$$18 = 0.30t$$
$$\frac{18}{0.30} = t$$
$$t = 60$$

So the total number of attendees is 60. Juniors are 30% of this number and seniors are 25%, so the difference between juniors and seniors is 30% − 25% = 5%. Now calculate 5% of the total: 60 × 0.05 = 3. Thus, there are 3 more juniors than seniors. Grid in **3**.

**15. B**

**Difficulty:** Hard

**Getting to the Answer:** The question gives you the amount of 15% mixture and the desired concentration (20%) that the painter wants to achieve by adding an unknown quantity of 40% mixture. In effect, the question is asking you to calculate a weighted average where the desired average is known.

Let $x$ represent the unknown number of gallons of the 40% mixture that the painter needs to add. Set up a weighted average equation using the known amount (20 gallons) of the 15% mixture and the unknown amount of the 40% mixture to equal the desired mixture concentration of 20%:

$$\frac{0.15(20) + 0.40(x)}{20 + x} = 0.20$$

Next, multiply both sides of the equation by the denominator and then solve for $x$:

$$0.15(20) + 0.40x = 0.20(20 + x)$$
$$3 + 0.40x = 4 + 0.20x$$
$$0.20x = 1$$
$$x = 5$$

Thus, the painter needs to add 5 gallons of the 40% mixture to achieve the desired 20% concentration of blue pigment. **(B)** is correct.

**16. D**

**Difficulty:** Medium

**Getting to the Answer:** You need to find the price of a share of the stock on October 1. You know that the price of a share was $75 on August 1 and that on September 1 the price was $10 higher than it was on August 1. Thus, on September 1, it was $75 + $10 = $85.

The question also states that the September 1 price is 80% of the October 1 price. Set up an equation where $p$ represents the October 1 price:

$$0.8p = \$85$$
$$p = \frac{\$85}{0.8}$$
$$p = \$106.25$$

The question asks for the price to the nearest dollar, so **(D)** is correct.

**17. C**

**Difficulty:** Easy

**Getting to the Answer:** The formula for percent increase or decrease is $\frac{\text{actual change}}{\text{original amount}} \times 100\%$. In this case, that's $\frac{1,572 - 1,494}{1,494} \times 100\% \cong 5.2\%$. Therefore, **(C)** is correct.

If you chose (B), you likely divided by the new amount, $1,572, instead of the original amount, $1,494.

**18. C**

**Difficulty:** Easy

**Getting to the Answer:** The formula for percent increase or decrease is $\frac{\text{actual change}}{\text{original amount}} \times 100\%$. Since the price per share of stock started at $35 and ended up at $49, that's $\frac{49 - 35}{35} \times 100\% = 40\%$.

Therefore, **(C)** is correct.

### 19. B

**Difficulty:** Medium

**Getting to the Answer:** The question asks for a percent decrease in the number of coins from the larger jar to the smaller one. The formula for percent decrease is $\frac{\text{actual change}}{\text{original amount}} \times 100\%$. Jar $X$ has 75 coins and jar $Y$ has 54 coins. The phrase "less than" means that you're calculating percent decrease from a starting value of 75 coins (the "original amount"); the calculation is $\frac{75-54}{75} \times 100\% = \frac{21}{75} \times 100\% = 28\%$. Therefore, **(B)** is correct.

### 20. D

**Difficulty:** Medium

**Strategic Advice:** Begin by calculating the number of seniors and then figure out what percent greater this number is than the number of sophomores.

**Getting to the Answer:** The number of seniors is 75% greater than the number of juniors, so that is $80 + (0.75 \times 80)$, or $1.75 \times 80 = 140$.

The formula for percent increase is $\frac{\text{actual change}}{\text{original amount}} \times 100\%$. In this case, the actual change is the number of seniors minus the number of sophomores, $140 - 50$. The original amount is the number of sophomores because the question asks for a percent "greater than"—greater than the original amount, which is sophomores, or 50: $\frac{140-50}{50} \times 100\% = \frac{90}{50} \times 100\% = 180\%$. Thus, **(D)** is correct.

### 21. C

**Difficulty:** Hard

**Strategic Advice:** When presented with a two-part percent change scenario, you cannot simply add the two percents; you have to calculate the second percent change on the adjusted value that results from the first percent change.

**Getting to the Answer:** The price of the phone goes through two different changes: an initial discount of 36% and a second reduction of 25% from that discounted price. Because you don't know $y$, the original price of the phone, you can pick a number to make calculations easier.

Usually, the best number to pick when calculating the percent change of an unknown value is 100, so assume that the initial price of the phone was $100 (the numbers don't have to be realistic, just easy to work with). Now, calculate the resulting price after the first discount: 36% of $100 is $0.36 \times \$100 = \$36$, so the new price of the phone will be $\$100 - \$36 = \$64$.

Next, calculate the change in price after an additional 25% off of the current price of $64: 25% of $64 is $0.25 \times \$64 = \$16$, so the final price will be $\$64 - \$16 = \$48$. (Note you could have also calculated the new price by subtracting the percent discount from 100 percent: $100\% - 25\% = 75\%$, so $0.75 \times \$64 = \$48$.)

The formula for percent change is $\frac{\text{actual change}}{\text{original amount}} \times 100\%$.

Use the starting price of $100 and the final price of $48: $\frac{100-48}{100} \times 100\% = \frac{52}{100} \times 100\% = 52\%$.

Thus, **(C)** is correct.

### 22. C

**Difficulty:** Hard

**Getting to the Answer:** Although the full-time and part-time employees are separate groups, the total number of employees in each group is the same. Thus, you don't need to calculate the individual number of full- and part-time employees who have benefits. Instead, find the difference as a percent, then find that percent of 250 to get the answer in one step.

Be careful: 74 percent of part-time employees *don't* qualify for benefits. This means that $100\% - 74\% = 26\%$ of them do qualify. Since 92 percent of full-time employees qualify for benefits, the percent difference is $92 - 26 = 66$. Find 66 percent of 250: $250 \times 0.66 = 165$. **(C)** is correct.

**23. 59**

**Difficulty:** Hard

**Category:** Percents

**Getting to the Answer:** Don't switch on autopilot and do five separate cost increase calculations because you can do just one and save time. First, determine the total increase from 2014−15 through 2019−20: $15,564 − $12,192 = $3,372. Dividing $3,372 by 5 (the number of increases) gives $674.40, the average increase per year. To determine what portion of this amount is fees, find 8.75% of $674.40: 0.0875 × $674.40 = $59.01. Rounded to the nearest dollar, the correct answer is 59. Grid in **59**.

**24. C**

**Difficulty:** Easy

**Category:** Percent Change

**Getting to the Answer:** The formula for percent increase or decrease is $\frac{\text{actual change}}{\text{original amount}} \times 100\%$. In this case, that works out to

$$\frac{27-20}{20} \times 100\% = \frac{7}{20} \times 100\% = 0.35 \times 100\% = 35\%.$$

Hence, **(C)** is correct.

**25. D**

**Difficulty:** Hard

**Category:** Percent Change

**Strategic Advice:** Begin by determining how much profit company T made in 1997 so that you can calculate the percent increase in profit from 1997 to 1999.

**Getting to the Answer:** The question indicates that the 1998 profit of $375 million was 25% greater than the 1997 profit. Therefore, you can set up this equation: 125% × 1997 profit = $375 million. This can be written as $1.25p = \$375$ million, where $p$ represents the 1997 profit. Divide both sides by 1.25 to find that $p = \$300$ million. Thus, the actual change in profit from 1997 to 1999 was $483 million − $300 million = $183 million. The formula for percent increase or decrease is $\frac{\text{actual change}}{\text{original amount}} \times 100\%$. In this scenario, that's $\frac{183}{300} \times 100\% = 61\%$. **(D)** is correct.

**26. B**

**Difficulty:** Medium

**Category:** Percent Change

**Strategic Advice:** Before you can calculate the percent difference between the price of a printer and the price of a calculator, you need to determine the price of the printer.

**Getting to the Answer:** The question indicates that the price of the printer is 16% less than the price of the radio, or 16% less than $75. Therefore, the price of the printer is $(100 − 16)\% \times \$75 = 0.84 \times \$75 = \$63$. Thus, the difference in price between the calculator and the printer is $150 − $63 = $87. With this value, you can determine what percent less this is than $150.

The formula for percent increase or decrease is $\frac{\text{actual change}}{\text{original amount}} \times 100\%$. Hence, the price of the printer is $\frac{87}{150} \times 100\% = 58\%$ less than the price of the calculator, so **(B)** is correct.

**27. C**

**Difficulty:** Easy

**Category:** Unit Conversions

**Getting to the Answer:** The question provides the speed of a car in miles per hour and asks for the speed in feet per second. Set up a proportion so that the units cancel:

$$\frac{9 \text{ miles}}{1 \text{ hour}} \times \frac{5{,}280 \text{ feet}}{1 \text{ mile}} \times \frac{1 \text{ hour}}{60 \text{ minutes}} \times \frac{1 \text{ minute}}{60 \text{ seconds}}$$

$$= 13.2 \frac{\text{feet}}{\text{second}}$$

Hence, **(C)** is correct.

**28. A**

**Difficulty:** Medium

**Category:** Proportions

**Getting to the Answer:** This is a proportions question that requires you to relate the total known number of guitars to the given ratio in order to find the unknown number of dreadnoughts, a type of guitar. First, define the relationship in the proportion with words. Then, translate from English into math. Let $d$ equal the unknown number of dreadnoughts. Set up a proportion and cross-multiply to solve for $d$:

$$\frac{\text{number of dreadnoughts in the ratio}}{\text{total number of guitars in the ratio}}$$
$$= \frac{\text{actual number of dreadnoughts}}{\text{actual number of guitars}}$$
$$\frac{4}{4+15} = \frac{d}{114}$$
$$4 \times 114 = (4+15)d$$
$$456 = 19d$$
$$24 = d$$

Thus, **(A)** is correct.

Here's another way to approach this question. The total of the two values in the ratio 4:15 is 19. The total number of guitars is 114, which is $6 \times 19$. Thus, the number of dreadnoughts is $6 \times 4 = 24$.

**29. B**

**Difficulty:** Easy

**Category:** Percent Change

**Getting to the Answer:** The formula for percent increase or decrease is $\frac{\text{actual change}}{\text{original amount}} \times 100\%$.

In this case, that works out to

$$\frac{84,600 - 74,025}{84,600} \times 100\% = \frac{10,575}{84,600} \times 100\% = 12.5\%.$$

Choice **(B)** is correct.

**30. B**

**Difficulty:** Medium

**Category:** Proportions

**Getting to the Answer:** Call the length of each side of the pentagon $p$ and the length of each side of the hexagon $h$. The perimeter of the pentagon is $5 \times p$ and the perimeter of the hexagon is $6 \times h$, so you can write

the proportion $\frac{5p}{6h} = \frac{1}{2}$. Rather than cross-multiplying, multiply both sides by $\frac{6}{5}$ which is $\frac{6}{5} \times \frac{5p}{6h} = \frac{6}{5} \times \frac{1}{2}$. This simplifies to $\frac{p}{h} = \frac{6}{10} = \frac{3}{5}$. This is another way of expressing 3:5, so **(B)** is correct.

**31. 54**

**Difficulty:** Hard

**Category:** Proportions

**Getting to the Answer:** Since you are given both the initial values of the different-colored candies and their values after additions and deletions in terms of ratios, you can express these as amounts relative to each other. There are the least amount of yellow candies, so you can write that the initial number of yellow candies is $y$, the number of white candies is $\frac{5}{4}y$, and the number of red ones is $\frac{9}{4}y$.

Now you can compare the "before and after" quantities of the red or white candies in terms of $y$. If you choose to look at the red candies, after the deletions and additions, the number of red candies is $\frac{4}{3}(y+3)$ because 3 yellow candies were added. But, 7 reds were removed, so the equation is $\frac{9}{4}y - 7 = \frac{4}{3}(y+3)$. Multiply both sides by 12 to clear the fractions: $27y - 84 = 16y + 48$. So, $11y = 132$, and $y = 12$.

The original number of white candies is $\frac{5}{4}(12) = 15$, and the original number of red is $\frac{9}{4}(12) = 27$. So, the total number of all three colors before the changes is $12 + 15 + 27 = 54$. Grid in **54**.

Another way to solve this question is by picking numbers, making sure they are permissible according to the ratios. You know that the ratio of red to white is 9 to 5, and that after 7 red and 5 white are removed, the ratio will be 4 to 2—in other words, there will be twice as many red as white. Start with 9 red and 5 white candies and work up from there until you find a multiple that works:

9 red, 5 white
2 red, 0 white: doesn't work

18 red, 10 white
11 red, 5 white: doesn't work

27 red, 15 white
20 red, 10 white: this works!

The common multiplier is 3, and there are
$4 \times 3 = 12$ yellow candies. The total is
$27 + 15 + 12 = $ **54** candies.

## 32.  50

**Difficulty:** Medium

**Category:** Unit Conversion

**Getting to the Answer:** Since the rate of deflation is

$100\frac{mL}{min}$, convert the initial volume of 300 liters of air to
milliliters: $300 \, \cancel{L} \times \frac{1,000 \, mL}{1 \, \cancel{L}} = 300,000 \, mL$.

Then, to determine the number of hours it will take
for the air mattress to completely deflate, set up
the calculation so that equivalent units cancel:

$300,000 \, \cancel{mL} \times \frac{1 \, \cancel{min}}{100 \, \cancel{mL}} \times \frac{1 \, hr}{60 \, \cancel{min}} = 50 \, hr$

Grid in **50**.

# CHAPTER 8

# Tables, Statistics, and Probability

**LEARNING OBJECTIVES**

After completing this chapter, you will be able to:

- Draw inferences about data presented in a variety of graphical formats
- Find an unknown value given the average
- Calculate mean, median, mode, and range
- Describe standard deviation and margin of error
- Determine whether a survey is valid or biased
- Draw inferences about surveys and data samples
- Calculate probabilities based on data sets

50/600 SmartPoints®

# How Much Do You Know?

**Directions:** Try the questions that follow. Show your work so that you can compare your solutions to the ones found in the Check Your Work section immediately after this question set. The "Category" heading in the explanation for each question gives the title of the lesson that covers how to solve it. If you answered the question(s) for a given lesson correctly, and if your scratchwork looks like ours, you may be able to move quickly through that lesson. If you answered incorrectly or used a different approach, you may want to take your time on that lesson.

**Questions 1 and 2 refer to the following information.**

The amount of glucose, or sugar, in a person's blood is the primary indicator of diabetes. When a person without diabetes fasts (doesn't eat) for eight hours prior to taking a blood sugar test, that person's glucose level will be below 100 milligrams per deciliter. An individual is considered at risk for diabetes, but is not diagnosed as diabetic, when fasting glucose levels are between 100 and 125. If the level is above 125, the person is considered to have diabetes. The following table shows the ages and glucose levels of a group of study participants.

| Study Results | | | | |
|---|---|---|---|---|
| **Age Group** | **<100 mg/dL** | **100–125 mg/dL** | **>125 mg/dL** | **Total** |
| **18–25** | 9 | 22 | 17 | 48 |
| **26–35** | 16 | 48 | 34 | 98 |
| **36–45** | 19 | 35 | 40 | 94 |
| **Older than 45** | 12 | 27 | 21 | 60 |
| **Total** | 56 | 132 | 112 | 300 |

1. According to the data, which age group had the smallest percentage of people with a healthy blood sugar level?

   A) 18–25

   B) 26–35

   C) 36–45

   D) Older than 45

2. Based on the table, if a single participant is selected at random from all the participants, what is the probability that he or she will be at risk for diabetes and be at least 36 years old?

   A) $\dfrac{7}{60}$

   B) $\dfrac{11}{25}$

   C) $\dfrac{31}{77}$

   D) $\dfrac{31}{150}$

**History Majors Declared at College X**

| Year | Number of History Majors |
|------|--------------------------|
| 2010 | 225 |
| 2011 | 287 |
| 2012 | 162 |
| 2013 | 240 |
| 2014 | $s$ |

3. The table above shows the number of history majors declared each year at a certain college from 2010 to 2014. If the median number of history majors declared for the five years was 225, what is the greatest possible value of $s$ ?

A) 161

B) 225

C) 239

D) 288

4. A writers association sponsored a nationwide convention attended by 1,650 nonfiction writers. Before the convention, the association surveyed 150 of the writers who were planning to attend (chosen at random) about their lunch preferences. Thirty-eight said they preferred salads, 23 preferred pizza, 59 preferred sandwiches, and 30 preferred grilled chicken. Based on the results of this survey, how many of the writers attending the convention can be expected to want sandwiches for lunch?

5. A researcher conducted a poll to determine how many people in a city of 100,000 residents enjoy the taste of non-dairy milks such as coconut milk or almond milk. The researcher polled 800 city residents who are allergic to dairy. Of those polled, 72 percent responded that they enjoyed the taste of non-dairy milks.

Which of the following indicates why the survey results would not allow for a reliable conclusion about the taste preferences of the city's residents?

A) The researcher did not ask people if they prefer the taste of dairy milk to non-dairy milks.

B) The survey sample is not representative of the city's residents.

C) The population of the city is too large to get a reliable survey sample.

D) The survey sample likely consisted of only adults and did not consider the opinion of children.

**Cookies Baked**

| | Chocolate Chip | Oatmeal Raisin | Total |
|---|---|---|---|
| **With Nuts** | | 40 | |
| **Without Nuts** | | | 104 |
| **Total** | | | 186 |

6. A baker makes 186 cookies. Some are chocolate chip and some are oatmeal raisin, and both kinds are made with and without nuts, as shown in the table above. Because they are more popular, the baker makes $\frac{2}{3}$ of the cookies chocolate chip. If a chocolate chip cookie is chosen at random, what is the probability that it will have nuts?

A) $\frac{21}{93}$

B) $\frac{21}{62}$

C) $\frac{41}{93}$

D) $\frac{21}{41}$

## Check Your Work

**1.  B**

**Difficulty:** Medium

**Category:** Tables and Graphs

**Getting to the Answer:** To calculate the percentage of people in each age group with a healthy blood sugar level ($<$100 mg/dL), divide the number of people in that age group with a healthy blood sugar level by the total number of participants in that same age group and multiply by 100%. Choice **(B)** is correct because $\frac{16}{98} \times 100\% \approx 0.1633 \times 100\% = 16.33\%$, which is a lower percentage than in the other age groups (18.75% for 18–25; 20.21% for 36–45; and 20% for Older than 45).

**2.  D**

**Difficulty:** Medium

**Category:** Probability

**Getting to the Answer:** This question requires careful reading of the table. The first criterion is fairly straightforward—you're looking for a participant with a blood sugar level in the 100–125 mg/dL range, so focus on that column in the table. The second criterion is a bit trickier—*at least 36 years old* means you'll need to use the values in both the row for 36–45 and the row for Older than 45. Within the 100–125 mg/dL range, there are 35 in the 36–45 age group and 27 in the Older than 45 age group, resulting in a total of $35 + 27 = 62$ out of 300 total participants overall. The probability of randomly selecting one participant who fits the criteria, therefore, is $\frac{62}{300}$, which reduces to $\frac{31}{150}$, or **(D)**.

**3.  B**

**Difficulty:** Medium

**Category:** Statistics

**Getting to the Answer:** The median is the middle number in a series of numbers. Arrange the number of history majors from least to greatest, making sure that 225 is in the middle. Use $s$ to balance out the number of history majors on either side of 225. Because there are already two numbers above the median (240 and 287), there must be two numbers below the median, 162 and $s$:

$s$, 162, 225, 240, 287

or

162, $s$, 225, 240, 287

Because $s$ could be on either side of 162, it could be anything less than or equal to 225. Its greatest possible value is therefore 225, which is **(B)**.

**4.  649**

**Difficulty:** Medium

**Category:** Surveys and Data Samples

**Getting to the Answer:** The question indicates that of the 150 survey respondents, 59 wanted sandwiches. To find the number of the writers attending the convention who can be expected to want sandwiches for lunch, set up a proportion using the number of survey respondents who want sandwiches, the total number of survey respondents, and the total number of writers attending the convention: $\frac{59}{150} = \frac{x}{1,650}$. Cross-multiply to find that $x = 649$. Grid in **649**.

**5. B**

**Difficulty:** Medium

**Category:** Surveys and Data Samples

**Getting to the Answer:** Determine who is being surveyed and what results are intended. In this question, the intended result is to determine whether people in a large city like non-dairy milks. To obtain a representative sample of the population, the survey should randomly select individuals from the population. However, the researcher polled only people who have a dairy allergy. Those people may have acquired tastes and may not be representative of the general population of the city, making **(B)** the correct answer.

**6. B**

**Difficulty:** Medium

**Category:** Probability

**Getting to the Answer:** The table is not complete, so your first step is to fill in the missing values. Start with what you know and work from there. It may not be necessary to complete the entire table, so stop when you have enough information to answer the question.

There are 186 cookies total and 104 are without nuts, which means $186 - 104 = 82$ have nuts. Because the table already indicates that 40 of those cookies are oatmeal raisin, $82 - 40 = 42$ are chocolate chip. Recall that $\frac{2}{3}$ of the total number of cookies are chocolate chip, which means there are $\frac{2}{3} \times 186 = 124$ chocolate chip cookies, so you can fill this number in the "Total" row of the chocolate chip column. You do not need to fill in any more of the table because the question asks only about chocolate chips cookies with nuts. There are 124 chocolate chip cookies total and 42 of them have nuts, so the probability of randomly choosing one with nuts is $\frac{42}{124}$, or $\frac{21}{62}$, which is **(B)**.

Each "X" represents one instance in the data set of each "number sold." So, for example, there were two different days on which this person sold 3 appliances, three different days on which this person sold 4 appliances, and so on. The data could just as easily be written as a data set: {3, 3, 4, 4, 4, 5, 6, 6, 6, 7, 8, 10, 10}, or placed in a frequency table:

| Number Sold | Frequency |
|:---:|:---:|
| 1 | 0 |
| 2 | 0 |
| 3 | 2 |
| 4 | 3 |
| 5 | 1 |
| 6 | 3 |
| 7 | 1 |
| 8 | 1 |
| 9 | 0 |
| 10 | 2 |

- **Histograms** look a lot like bar charts and can be read in the same way, but they are similar to frequency tables and dot plots in that they show how many times a certain value shows up in a data set for a variable. The histogram for the appliances data set would look like this:

Notice that the histogram is basically the same as the dot plot for this data set. Histograms are better for representing larger data sets for which individual dots would be difficult to count.

## You need to do this:

- When presented with a question that uses a graph or table to present information, first inspect the format of the graph or table. What kind of graph or table is it? What information is presented on each axis? What information do you need to find in order to answer the question?

- Find the information you need from the table or graph and then use the information for any calculation the question might require, such as taking the average, finding the median, or thinking about standard deviation.

- Use the average formula, $\text{average} = \dfrac{\text{sum}}{\text{number of items}}$, to find unknowns. For example, if you know that the average of 5 terms is 7, and you know that 4 of the terms are 3, 6, 8, and 9, you can call the last term $x$ and plug into the equation, then solve for $x$:

$$7 = \frac{3+6+8+9+x}{5}.$$
$$35 = 26 + x$$
$$x = 9$$

## Explanation

This question gives you an average and asks for a missing value, which is a kind of calculation that shows up in word problems all the time. First, set up a general equation for the average:

$$\text{Average} = \frac{\text{sum}}{\text{number of items}}$$

The scenario takes place over 14 days, and the average is given as 6 items per day. Let $a$ represent the unknown number of appliances sold on the 14th day and then fill in the number of appliances sold the previous days from the dot plot:

$$6 = \frac{3+3+4+4+4+5+6+6+6+7+8+10+10+a}{14}$$

Multiply both sides by 14 to get rid of the fraction and simplify the addition on the right before isolating $a$:

$$84 = 3+3+4+4+4+5+6+6+6+7+8+10+10+a$$
$$84 = 76 + a$$
$$a = 8$$

Choice **(D)** is correct.

## Try on Your Own

**Directions:** Take as much time as you need on these questions. Work carefully and methodically. There will be an opportunity for timed practice at the end of the chapter.

### Questions 1 and 2 refer to the following information.

| | Bob's Bookshop | Clara's Bookshop | Derek's Bookshop | Evelyn's Bookshop | Total |
|---|---|---|---|---|---|
| Monday | 14 | 7 | 15 | 12 | 48 |
| Tuesday | 8 | 13 | 15 | 13 | 49 |
| Wednesday | 10 | 13 | 12 | 14 | 49 |
| Thursday | 8 | 15 | 14 | 10 | 47 |
| Friday | 13 | 7 | 10 | 9 | 39 |
| Total | 53 | 55 | 66 | 58 | 232 |

---

HINT: For Q1, fraction $= \dfrac{\text{part}}{\text{whole}}$. Which *part* is the question asking for? Out of which *whole*?

---

1. Which of the four bookshops made the greatest fraction of its total sales on Tuesday?

   A) Bob's Bookshop

   B) Clara's Bookshop

   C) Derek's Bookshop

   D) Evelyn's Bookshop

2. What fraction of all the books sold on Monday, Wednesday, and Friday were sold at Derek's Bookshop and Evelyn's Bookshop?

   A) $\dfrac{9}{29}$

   B) $\dfrac{11}{32}$

   C) $\dfrac{9}{17}$

   D) $\dfrac{18}{31}$

### Questions 3 and 4 refer to the following information.

Numerous health studies have found that people who eat breakfast are generally healthier and weigh less than people who skip this meal. The following table shows the results of a study related to this topic.

**Breakfast Study Results**

| | Breakfast ≤1 Time per Week | Breakfast 2–4 Times per Week | Breakfast 5–7 Times per Week | Total |
|---|---|---|---|---|
| Within Healthy Weight Range | 6 | 15 | 36 | 57 |
| Outside Healthy Weight Range | 38 | 27 | 9 | 74 |
| Total | 44 | 42 | 45 | 131 |

3. What percent of the participants who were outside a healthy weight range ate breakfast one or fewer times per week?

   A) 29.01%

   B) 51.35%

   C) 56.49%

   D) 86.36%

---

HINT: For Q4, which group in the study is of interest to this company?

---

4. A large company that provides breakfast for all its employees wants to determine how many of them are likely to be within a healthy weight range, given that all the employees take advantage of the free breakfast all five weekdays. If the company has 3,000 employees, and assuming the participants in the study are a good representative sample, about how many of the employees are likely to be within a healthy weight range?

   A) 825

   B) 1,030

   C) 1,900

   D) 2,400

**Questions 5 and 6 refer to the following information.**

When people sleep, they experience various types of brain activity. Scientists have classified these types of activity into four sleep stages: 1, 2, 3, and 4 (also known as REM). Stage 3 is the only stage considered to be deep sleep. Suppose a person went to a sleep clinic to have his or her sleeping brainwaves analyzed. A technician monitored the person's brainwaves in 15-minute intervals, for 8 continuous hours, and categorized them into one of the four stages. The bar graph below shows the results of the one-night study.

**8-Hour Sleep Study Results**

**Each Bar = 15 Minutes**

5.  Based on the graph, how many minutes did the patient spend in non-deep sleep over the course of the entire night?

6.  After the completion of the one-night study, the patient was monitored an additional four nights. Over the total number of nights that the patient spent at the clinic, he spent an average of 180 minutes in stage 3 sleep per night. If the patient spent an average of 175 minutes in stage 3 sleep on the second, third, and fourth nights, how many minutes did he spend in stage 3 sleep on the last night?

7. A microbiologist is comparing the growth rates of two different yeast strains. She indirectly measures the number of yeast cells by recording the optical density (OD600) of each strain every 10 hours. The measurements are presented in the graph above. Based on the data, which of the following is NOT a true statement?

A) Between hours 30 and 80, Strain 1 had a higher OD600 reading than Strain 2.

B) The growth rate of Strain 2 was less than the growth rate of Strain 1 until hour 50, at which point Strain 1's growth rate became the lesser one.

C) Between hours 50 and 70, Strain 2's OD600 reading increased by approximately 0.03 every hour.

D) The growth rate of Strain 1 was greater than the growth rate of Strain 2 throughout the monitored period.

# Statistics

**LEARNING OBJECTIVES**

After this lesson, you will be able to:

• Calculate mean, median, mode, and range

• Describe standard deviation and margin of error

## To answer a question like this:

Two classes of 25 students each took an identical exam. Their percent correct scores are shown in the dot plots above. If $M_A$ and $S_A$ are the median and standard deviation, respectively, of class A, and $M_B$ and $S_B$ are the median and standard deviation, respectively, of class B, then which of the following statements is true?

A) $M_A < M_B$ and $S_A < S_B$

B) $M_A > M_B$ and $S_A < S_B$

C) $M_A > M_B$ and $S_A > S_B$

D) $M_A < M_B$ and $S_A > S_B$

## You need to know this:

Suppose a nurse took a patient's pulse at different times of day and found it to be 75, 78, 71, 71, and 68. Here are six fundamental statistics figures you can determine for this data set:

- **Mean (also called arithmetic mean or average):** The sum of the values divided by the number of values. For this data set, the mean pulse is $\dfrac{75+78+71+71+68}{5} = \dfrac{363}{5} = 72.6$.

- **Median:** The value that is in the middle of the set *when the values are arranged in ascending order*. The pulse values in ascending order are 68, 71, 71, 75, and 78. The middle term is the third term, making the median 71. (If the list consists of an even number of values, the median is the average of the middle two values.)

- **Mode:** The value that occurs most frequently. The value that appears more than any other is 71, which appears twice (while all other numbers appear only once), so it is the mode. If more than one value appears the most often, that's okay; a set of data can have multiple modes. For example, if the nurse took the patient's pulse a sixth time and it was 68, then both 71 and 68 would be modes for this data set.

- **Range:** The difference between the highest and lowest values. In this data set, the lowest and highest values are 68 and 78, respectively, so the range is $78 - 68 = 10$.

- **Standard deviation:** A measure of how far a typical data point is from the mean. A low standard deviation means most values in the set are fairly close to the mean; a high standard deviation means there is much more spread in the data set. On the SAT, *you will need to know what standard deviation is and what it tells you about a set of data, but you won't have to calculate it.*

- **Margin of error:** A description of the maximum expected difference between a true statistics measure (for example, the mean or median) for a data pool and that same statistics measure for a random sample from the data pool. A lower margin of error is achieved by increasing the size of the random sample. As with standard deviation, *you will need to know what a margin of error is on the SAT, but you won't be asked to calculate one.*

## You need to do this:

- To compare two standard deviations, look at how spread out the data set is. The more clustered the data, the lower the standard deviation.

- To find the median, arrange *all* values in order. In a dot plot or frequency distribution table, that means finding the group with the middle value.

## Explanation:

Start with the standard deviation. The scores in class A are more clustered around the mean, so the standard deviation for class A will be smaller than that for class B, where the scores are more spread out. Eliminate (B) and (C).

To calculate the medians of the two classes, you need to find the middle value in each data set. Each class has 25 students, so the middle score will be the 13th term. Count from the left of each dot plot to find that the 13th score for class A is 85 and for class B is 86. So the median for class B is greater. **(A)** is correct.

## Try on Your Own

**Directions:** Take as much time as you need on these questions. Work carefully and methodically. There will be an opportunity for timed practice at the end of the chapter.

**Questions 8 and 9 refer to the following information.**

An anthropologist chose 250 citizens at random from each of two European countries and separated them into groups based on how many languages they spoke. The results are shown in the table below.

| Number of Languages | Country A | Country B |
|---|---|---|
| 1 | 55 | 70 |
| 2 | 80 | 30 |
| 3 | 50 | 20 |
| 4 | 40 | 70 |
| 5 | 25 | 60 |

There are a total of 550,000 citizens in country A and 1.3 million citizens in country B.

8. What is the median number of languages spoken by the sample of citizens from country B?

A) 1

B) 2

C) 3

D) 4

9. Based on the data in the table, which of the following statements most accurately reflects the estimated total number of citizens who speak multiple languages in both countries?

A) Half as many citizens in both countries combined speak exactly five languages as citizens who speak exactly four languages.

B) Twice as many citizens in both countries combined speak exactly five languages as citizens who speak exactly four languages.

C) The number of citizens in both countries combined who speak exactly two languages is less than the number of citizens who speak exactly four languages.

D) The number of citizens in both countries combined who speak exactly two languages is greater than the number of citizens who speak exactly four languages.

HINT: For Q10, when you see the word *consistent,* think "standard deviation."

|  | Charles | Gautam | Brin |
|---|---|---|---|
| **Run 1** | 8.3 | 8.5 | 8.4 |
| **Run 2** | 7.7 | 8.0 | 8.0 |
| **Run 3** | 7.1 | 8.5 | 7.5 |
| **Run 4** | 6.6 | 7.8 | 9.0 |
| **Run 5** | 8.0 | 8.1 | 7.5 |
| **Run 6** | 6.6 | 7.5 | 7.2 |
| **Mean Score** | 7.38 | 8.07 | 7.93 |
| **Standard Deviation** | 0.73 | 0.39 | 0.67 |

10. Charles, Gautam, and Brin participated in a snowboarding competition. The scores for each of their six qualifying runs are shown in the table above. According to the data, which of the following is a valid conclusion?

    A) Charles had the smallest mean score, so his performance was the least consistent.

    B) Gautam had the smallest standard deviation, so his performance was the most consistent.

    C) Charles had the largest standard deviation, so his performance was the most consistent.

    D) Brin had the highest score on any one run, so her performance was the most consistent.

**Ages of Used Cars in Dealer Inventory**

| Age (Model Years) | Number of Cars |
|---|---|
| 1 | 3 |
| 2 | 5 |
| 3 | 18 |
| 4 | 17 |
| 5 | 11 |
| 6 | 6 |
| 7 | 2 |

11. The table above shows the distribution of the ages (in model years) of the cars in a certain dealer's inventory. Which of the following correctly lists the mean, median, and mode of the ages of the cars in ascending order?

    A) Mean, Median, Mode

    B) Median, Mode, Mean

    C) Mode, Mean, Median

    D) Mode, Median, Mean

HINT: For Q12, start with the most definite information. What
do you know, given the average of the first 12 days?

12. A company produces an equal number of a certain
product each working day in the month. The daily
reject rates for the first 12 days of this month
ranged from 0.0 percent to 1.5 percent with an
average of 0.4 percent. If there are 22 working
days this month and the company's monthly reject
goal is 0.5 percent or less, what is the maximum
reject rate, as a percent, for the 13th day that would
still enable the company to attain its goal for the
month? (Round your answer to the nearest tenth
and ignore the percent sign when gridding your
response.)

# Surveys and Data Samples

## LEARNING OBJECTIVES

After this lesson, you will be able to:

- Determine whether a survey is valid or biased
- Draw inferences about surveys and data samples

## To answer a question like this:

A book club wanted to determine the average number of books read each year by residents of a certain town, so it conducted a survey of 100 patrons of the town's public library. The average number of books read per year by these 100 patrons was 51.5. Which of the following statements must be true based on this information?

A) The survey is biased due to a poor choice of sampling method.

B) The survey is not biased and will likely produce a correct estimate of the number of books read annually by the town's residents.

C) The average number of books read annually by all the town's residents is 51.5.

D) The average number of books read per town resident per year cannot be determined from such a small sample.

## You need to know this:

You will see occasional questions on the SAT Math sections that do not test any calculation or even your ability to interpret numerical data. Instead, these questions test your ability to draw logical conclusions about surveys and data sampling methods.

Answering these questions correctly hinges on your ability to tell whether a data sample is **representative** of the larger population. A representative sample is a small group that shares key characteristics with a larger group you are trying to draw conclusions about.

A sample that is selected truly at random is generally representative of the larger group. For example, a scientist who wants to learn the average height of the penguins in a colony of 200 might measure the heights of a random sample of only 20 penguins. As long as the 20 penguins are selected at random, their average height will approximate the average height of the birds in the entire colony.

On the other hand, a sample that is not selected at random may not be representative and may lead to a biased conclusion. For instance, imagine that a small town uses volunteer firefighters and that a stipulation for becoming a volunteer firefighter is living within a mile of the fire station. If you wanted to know what percent of households in the town include at least one volunteer firefighter, you would need to survey a random sample of households from the entire town, not just a sample of households within a mile of the fire station. A sample of households within a mile of the fire station would be a biased sample and would lead to an erroneous conclusion (namely, that the percent of households in the town that include at least one volunteer firefighter is higher than it actually is).

## You need to do this:

- Check whether the data sample represents the larger population. If it doesn't, the survey is biased.
- In questions that ask you to draw a conclusion from a random (unbiased) sample, look for the answer choice for which the representative sample accurately reflects the larger population. For example, in a question asking for a conclusion based on a sample of librarians, the correct answer will match the sample to a larger population of librarians, not to a population of, say, accountants.

## Explanation:

The sample in this question includes 100 public library patrons. This is not a randomly selected sample. It's a good bet that frequent readers of books will be overrepresented at a public library. Thus, the survey is biased, so **(A)** is correct.

## Try on Your Own

**Directions:** Take as much time as you need on these questions. Work carefully and methodically. There will be an opportunity for timed practice at the end of the chapter.

---

HINT: For Q13, who is in the survey group? Who is in the larger population? Are these groups different?
If so, the survey is likely biased.

---

13. A railroad company is planning to build a new station along one of its busiest lines into the downtown area where many commuters work. The company chooses a town where it plans to build the new station. To assess the opinion of the town's residents, the company surveys a sample of 200 residents who commute to the downtown area for work. Over 80 percent of those surveyed are in favor of building the new station.

    Which of the following is true about the survey's reliability?

    A)  It is unreliable because the survey sample is not representative of the entire town.

    B)  It is unreliable because the survey sample is too small.

    C)  It is reliable because nobody in the survey sample works for the railroad company.

    D)  It is reliable because the survey sample excludes people who do not ride the train.

14. A bottled water company conducts a survey to find out how many bottles of water people consume per day. If a representative and random sample of 500 people is chosen from a population estimated to be 50,000, which of the following accurately describes how the mean of the sample data relates to the estimated mean of the entire population?

    A)  The mean of the sample data is equal to the estimated mean of the population.

    B)  The mean of the sample data cannot be used to estimate the mean of the much larger population.

    C)  The mean of the sample data should be multiplied by 100 to get the estimated mean of the population.

    D)  The mean of the sample data should be multiplied by 1,000 to get the estimated mean of the population.

15. A department store manager wants to determine why customers return the products they buy. The manager surveyed randomly selected customers and asked them to explain why they were returning their products. This sample included 70 customers who were returning dinnerware, of whom 80 percent indicated that at least one piece of dinnerware was chipped or broken.

    Which of the following conclusions is best supported by the sample data?

    A)  Most of the products returned to the store contain chipped or broken pieces.

    B)  Dinnerware products are more likely to contain chipped or broken pieces than other products.

    C)  Most customers returning dinnerware returned products containing chipped or broken pieces.

    D)  At least 80 percent of the products sold at the store contain chipped or broken pieces.

16. The owner of a miniature golf course wants to determine what color golf ball is most popular at the course. The owner asked 150 randomly surveyed children what color they prefer. Approximately 60 percent of them said they prefer red, while approximately 30 percent of them said blue.

This data best supports which of the following conclusions?

A)  Most people prefer a red golf ball when playing miniature golf.

B)  Red golf balls are used twice as often for miniature golf as blue golf balls.

C)  Most children at the miniature golf course prefer a red golf ball.

D)  Approximately 10 percent of miniature golf players prefer a white golf ball.

HINT: For Q17, find the result of the sample in the chart, and then apply that result to the larger group.

17. A candy company sells jelly beans in five colors: black, green, orange, red, and yellow. The company sells boxes of jelly beans, each of which contains 20 individual bags. Each individual bag contains 75 jelly beans. A customer purchased 5 boxes of jelly beans and selected one bag at random from each box. The customer counted the number of each color in each bag. The results are shown in the chart below.

| Color | Bag 1 | Bag 2 | Bag 3 | Bag 4 | Bag 5 |
|-------|-------|-------|-------|-------|-------|
| Black | 10 | 12 | 8 | 11 | 9 |
| Green | 13 | 11 | 13 | 12 | 12 |
| Orange | 22 | 20 | 21 | 21 | 21 |
| Red | 20 | 21 | 23 | 21 | 22 |
| Yellow | 10 | 11 | 10 | 10 | 11 |

Which of the following is the closest approximation of the total number of green jelly beans in the customer's purchase?

A)      60

B)     240

C)   1,200

D)   4,500

# Probability

## To answer a question like this:

**Number of Cyclists in Regional Race, by Age and Town**

| Town | Age (years) | | | | | Total |
|---|---|---|---|---|---|---|
| | **15 to 18** | **19 to 25** | **26 to 34** | **35 to 46** | **47 and Older** | |
| Pine Falls | 9 | 52 | 31 | 26 | 29 | 147 |
| Greenville | 14 | 38 | 42 | 53 | 30 | 177 |
| Salem | 5 | 17 | 18 | 13 | 10 | 63 |
| Fairview | 19 | 41 | 32 | 34 | 27 | 153 |
| Total | 47 | 148 | 123 | 126 | 96 | 540 |

The table above shows the number of participants in a regional bicycle race, categorized by town and age group. Based on the table, if a cyclist from Fairview is chosen at random, which of the following is closest to the probability that the cyclist was 35 or older at the time of the race?

A) 0.40

B) 0.18

C) 0.11

D) 0.05

## You need to know this:

**Probability** is a fraction or decimal between 0 and 1 comparing the number of desired outcomes to the number of total possible outcomes. A probability of 0 means that an event will not occur; a probability of 1 means that it definitely will occur. The formula is as follows:

$$\text{Probability} = \frac{\text{number of desired outcomes}}{\text{number of total possible outcomes}}$$

For instance, if you roll a six-sided die, each side showing a different number from 1 to 6, the probability of rolling a number higher than 4 is $\frac{2}{6} = \frac{1}{3}$, because there are two numbers higher than 4 (5 and 6) and six numbers total (1, 2, 3, 4, 5, and 6).

To find the probability that an event will *not* happen, subtract the probability that the event will happen from 1. Continuing the previous example, the probability of *not* rolling a number higher than 4 would be:

$$1 - \frac{1}{3} = \frac{2}{3}$$

The SAT tends to test probability in the context of data tables. Using a table, you can find the probability that a randomly selected data value (be it a person, object, etc.) will fit a certain profile. For example, the following table summarizing a survey on water preference might be followed by a question asking for the probability that a person randomly selected for a follow-up survey falls into a given category.

| | Tap | Carbonated | Bottled | Total |
|---|---|---|---|---|
| **Female** | 325 | 267 | 295 | 887 |
| **Male** | 304 | 210 | 289 | 803 |
| **Total** | 629 | 477 | 584 | 1,690 |

If the question asked for the probability of randomly selecting a female who prefers tap water from all the participants of the original survey, you would calculate it using the same general formula as before:

$$\frac{\# \text{ female, tap}}{\# \text{ total}} = \frac{325}{1,690} = \frac{5}{26} \approx 0.192.$$

If the question asked for the probability of randomly selecting a female for the follow-up survey, given that the chosen participant prefers tap water, the setup is a little different. This time, the number of possible outcomes is the total participants *who prefer tap water*, which is 629, not the grand total of 1,690. The calculation is now $\frac{\# \text{ female, tap}}{\# \text{ total, tap}} = \frac{325}{629} \approx 0.517.$

Conversely, if you needed to find the probability of selecting someone who prefers tap water for the follow-up survey, given that the chosen participant is female, the new number of possible outcomes would be the female participant total (887). The calculation becomes $\frac{\# \text{ female, tap}}{\# \text{ total, females}} = \frac{325}{887} \approx 0.366.$

## You need to do this:

- Determine the number of desired and total possible outcomes by looking at the table.
- Read the question carefully when determining the number of possible outcomes: do you need the entire set or a subset?

## Explanation:

The number of desired outcomes is the number of cyclists from Fairview who are 35 or older. That means you need to add the "35 to 46" and "47 and Older" categories: $34 + 27 = 61$. The number of possible outcomes is the total number of cyclists from Fairview. The number is given in the totals column: 153. Plug these numbers into the probability formula and divide:

$$\text{Probability} = \frac{\# \text{ Fairview, 35 and Older}}{\# \text{ Fairview, Total}} = \frac{61}{153} \approx 0.40$$

The correct answer is **(A)**.

## Try on Your Own

**Directions:** Take as much time as you need on these questions. Work carefully and methodically. There will be an opportunity for timed practice at the end of the chapter.

|  | Marked Defective | Not Marked Defective | Total |
|---|---|---|---|
| Defective Bearing | 392 | 57 | 449 |
| Non-defective Bearing | 168 | 49,383 | 49,551 |
| Total | 560 | 49,440 | 50,000 |

18. A manufacturing plant produces 50,000 bearings per week. Of these, 449 will be defective. The manager of the plant installs a new quality control device that is designed to detect defective bearings and mark them with a laser. The device is allowed to run for a week and the results are tallied as shown in the table above. According to these results, to the nearest percent, what is the probability that a part that is marked defective will actually be defective?

A) 30%

B) 43%

C) 70%

D) 87%

HINT: For Q19, what percentage of the fish at the hatchery are salmon? How many salmon are there? How many of those were tested?

19. The table below shows the distribution of four species of fish at a hatchery that has approximately 6,000 fish.

| Species | Percent of Total |
|---|---|
| Carp | 50 |
| Salmon | 25 |
| Tilapia | 15 |
| Tuna | 10 |

A biologist randomly tests 5 percent of each species of fish for mercury content. Her findings are shown in the following table.

**Mercury Content Test Results**

| Species | Number of Fish with Dangerous Mercury Levels |
|---|---|
| Carp | 11 |
| Salmon | 6 |
| Tilapia | 5 |
| Tuna | 8 |

Based on the biologist's findings, if a single salmon is randomly selected from those that were tested, what is the probability that this particular fish would have a dangerous mercury level?

A) 0.001

B) 0.004

C) 0.02

D) 0.08

| Type of Engineer | Specialization | | Total |
|---|---|---|---|
| | Robotics | AV | |
| Mechanical | 198 | 245 | 443 |
| Electrical | 149 | 176 | 325 |
| Total | 347 | 421 | 768 |

20. In a research study, a group of mechanical and electrical engineers indicated their specialization preference between robotics and autonomous vehicles (AV). The results are shown in the table above. What is the probability that a randomly selected engineer will be a mechanical engineer specializing in autonomous vehicles?

A) 0.229

B) 0.319

C) 0.553

D) 0.582

HINT: For Q21, how many groups have *at least* 8 days vacation?

21. **Yearly Paid Vacation Days at Excor Manufacturing**

| | 0–7 | 8–14 | 14–30 | Total |
|---|---|---|---|---|
| **Hourly** | 79 | 183 | 38 | 300 |
| **Salaried** | 8 | 27 | 65 | 100 |
| **Total** | 87 | 210 | 103 | 400 |

The human resources department at Excor Manufacturing decided to collect data on the paid vacation days accrued by hourly and salaried employees. The table above shows the results of the data collection. If an employee has at least 8 paid vacation days, what is the probability that the person is a salaried employee?

A) $\dfrac{92}{313}$

B) $\dfrac{221}{300}$

C) $\dfrac{313}{400}$

D) $\dfrac{92}{100}$

| Engine Type | Fuel Economy (miles per gallon) | |
|---|---|---|
| | 0–45 mpg | 45+ mpg |
| Hybrid | | |
| Internal Combustion (IC) | | |
| Total | 53 | 258 |

22. The daily engine production goals of an automobile manufacturer are summarized in the incomplete table above. The factory produced six times as many hybrid engines that achieve 45+ miles per gallon as it did hybrid engines that achieve 0–45 miles per gallon, and the factory produced four times as many internal combustion (IC) engines that achieve 45+ miles per gallon as it did IC engines that achieve 0–45 miles per gallon. If the factory produced 53 engines that achieve 0–45 miles per gallon and 258 engines that achieve 45+ miles per gallon, which of the following is the approximate probability that a 45+ miles per gallon engine selected at random is IC?

A) 0.566

B) 0.535

C) 0.465

D) 0.386

# On Test Day

The SAT tests the concept of average fairly heavily. The average formula will serve you well on questions that ask about a sum of values or the average of a set of values, but for questions that give you the average and ask for a missing value in the data set, there is an alternative that can be faster: the balance approach.

The balance approach is based on the the idea that if you know what the average is, you can find the totals on both sides of the average and then add the missing value that makes both sides balance out. This approach is especially helpful if the values are large and closely spaced. Imagine that a question gives you the set $\{976, 980, 964, 987, x\}$ and tells you that the average is 970. You would reason as follows: 976 is 6 over the average, 980 is 10 over, 964 is 6 under, and 987 is 17 over. That's a total of $6 + 10 - 6 + 17 = 27$ over, so $x$ needs to be 27 under the average, or $970 - 27 = 943$.

Try solving the question below both ways, using first the average formula and then the balance approach. If you find the latter to be fast and intuitive, add it to your test-day arsenal.

| Height Change in Inches | | | | | | | |
|---|---|---|---|---|---|---|---|
| Plant Type | Week 3 | Week 4 | Week 5 | Week 6 | Week 7 | Week 8 | Week 9 |
| Zinnia | 3 | 2 | 1 | 4 | 2 | 1 | 1 |
| Sunflower | 3 | | 8 | 6 | 7 | 2 | 5 |
| Marigold | 1 | 1 | 3 | 2 | 4 | 4 | 3 |

23. The table above summarizes the height change (inches) over a seven-week period of three different plants grown by Ms. Walker's biology class. If the mean height change for the sunflower plant over the seven-week period is 5 inches, what was the height change in week 4?

The correct answer and both ways of solving can be found at the end of the chapter.

# How Much Have You Learned?

**Directions:** For testlike practice, give yourself 15 minutes to complete this question set. Be sure to study the explanations, even for questions you got right. They can be found at the end of this chapter.

**Question 24 refers to the following information.**

The table below summarizes the results of a survey about favorite leisure activities for a group of high school students. Assume that every student has a favorite leisure activity and that each student could select only one favorite.

|              | Freshmen | Sophomores | Juniors | Seniors | Total |
|--------------|----------|------------|---------|---------|-------|
| Sports       | 144      | 122        | 134     | 115     | 515   |
| Video Games  | 126      | 140        | 152     | 148     | 566   |
| Music        | 120      | 117        | 153     | 148     | 538   |
| Reading      | 110      | 114        | 63      | 98      | 385   |
| Total        | 500      | 493        | 502     | 509     | 2,004 |

24. The research group that conducted the survey wants to select one sophomore at random for a follow-up survey. What is the probability that the student selected will prefer a type of leisure activity other than video games?

A) $\dfrac{140}{493}$

B) $\dfrac{140}{2,004}$

C) $\dfrac{353}{493}$

D) $\dfrac{353}{2,004}$

**Questions 25 and 26 refer to the following information.**

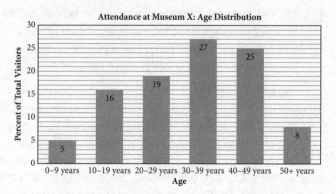

The bar graph above shows the age distribution of visitors to museum X in 2014. Visitors aged 0–9 years get into museum X for free, visitors aged 50 and older pay $5 for admission and everyone else pays $10.

25. If 553 people aged 20 years and older visited museum X in 2014, then approximately how many people visited museum X in 2014?

26. Assuming, as before, that 553 people aged 20 years and older visited museum X in 2014, how much revenue did museum X collect from tickets sold to people aged 40 and older in 2014? (Ignore the dollar sign when gridding your response.)

27. According to the table, what percent of all the board games sold by the boutique have a "bad" average customer rating? Round to the nearest tenth of a percent and ignore the percent sign when entering your answer.

**Questions 27 and 28 refer to the following information.**

|  | 1 | 2 | 3 | 4 | 5 | Total |
|---|---|---|---|---|---|---|
| **Strategy** | 5 | 17 | 24 | 10 | 5 | 61 |
| **Trivia** | 3 | 12 | 28 | 8 | 3 | 54 |
| **Role-playing** | 3 | 10 | 30 | 14 | 2 | 59 |

A small boutique sells board games online. The boutique specializes in strategy, trivia, and role-playing games. Any customer who purchases a game is invited to rate the game on a scale of 1 to 5. A rating of 1 or 2 is considered "bad," a rating of 3 is considered "average," and a rating of 4 or 5 is considered "good." The table above shows the distribution of average customer ratings of the games sold. For example, 24 of the strategy games sold have an average customer rating of 3.

28. The boutique decides to stop selling 50 percent of the games that have a "bad" average customer rating to make room for promising new stock. Assuming no significant changes in ratings in the foreseeable future, what should the difference be between the percentages of games with a "bad" average customer rating before and after the games are removed? Round to the nearest tenth of a percent and ignore the percent sign when entering your answer.

29. Fit and Fab, a membership-only gym, is hoping to open a new branch in a small city in Pennsylvania that currently has no fitness centers. According to the gym management's research, approximately 12,600 residents live within driving distance of the gym. Fit and Fab sends out surveys to a sample of 300 randomly selected residents in this area (all of whom respond) and finds that 40 residents say they would visit a gym if one were located in their area. Based on past survey research, Fit and Fab estimates that approximately 30 percent of these respondents would actually join the gym if one were opened in the area. Based on this information and the results of the sample survey, about how many residents should Fit and Fab expect to join its new branch?

A) 134

B) 504

C) 1,680

D) 3,780

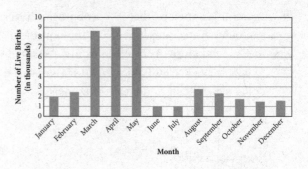

30. Most animals give birth during a general time of year. This is because animals naturally breed so that their young will be born at the time of year when there will be an adequate food supply. The bar graph shows the number of live births in California of a particular jackrabbit species, the black-tailed jackrabbit, over the course of year X. Based on the data, which of the following would be an appropriate conclusion?

A) In general, rabbits give birth during March, April, and May.

B) In general, rabbits give birth during June, July, and August.

C) In general, black-tailed jackrabbits in California give birth during March, April, and May.

D) In general, black-tailed jackrabbits in California give birth during June, July, and August.

31. Soil contains a wide variety of nutrients, including nitrogen, phosphorous, potassium, magnesium, sulfur, and iron. A fertilizer company conducted an experimental study to determine which of five additives is most effective in helping soil retain nutrients. If, after application of the additives, the fertilizer company tested only for the soil nutrients nitrogen and potassium, which of the following is a valid conclusion?

    A) The additive that is found to be the most effective will work for all nutrients in the soil.

    B) The additive that is found to be the most effective will work only for nitrogen and potassium.

    C) The study is biased and therefore not significantly relevant to determining which additive is most effective.

    D) The study will be able to produce results concerning only the effects of the additives on nitrogen and potassium.

32. As part of its market research, a company sent out a survey to see how much consumers would be willing to pay for a certain product. The survey distinguished between a store brand version of the product and a brand name version, and people participating in the survey received questions about only one of the versions. A summary of the survey results is shown in the following bar graph.

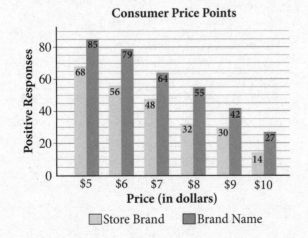

**Consumer Price Points**

If a consumer is chosen at random from the 600 respondents, what is the probability that the consumer is willing to pay at least $8 for the product?

33. The average (arithmetic mean) of $p + 12t - 5$, $q + 16t + 4$, and $r - 7t + 25$ is $10t + 34$. In terms of $t$, what is the average of $p$, $q$, and $r$?

    A) $3t + 26$

    B) $4t + 16$

    C) $6t + 16$

    D) $8t - 37$

# Reflect

**Directions:** Take a few minutes to recall what you've learned and what you've been practicing in this chapter. Consider the following questions, jot down your best answer for each one, and then compare your reflections to the expert responses on the following page. Use your level of confidence to determine what to do next.

What are some common ways the SAT may present data?

_____

_____

_____

What is the difference between median, mode, and range?

_____

_____

_____

What does the standard deviation of a data set tell you?

_____

_____

_____

When can you generalize the results of a survey of a small group to a larger group?

_____

_____

_____

What are two ways to calculate the probability of a single event?

_____

_____

_____

## Expert Responses

What are some common ways the SAT may present data?

*The SAT may present data in tables, bar charts, line graphs, dot plots, and histograms.*

What is the difference between median, mode, and range?

*The median of a set is the middle value, whereas the mode is the most common value. The range of a set is the distance between the smallest value and the largest one.*

What does the standard deviation of a data set tell you?

*A data set's standard deviation reflects how far apart the numbers are from each other. The standard deviation of a set whose numbers are all the same—for example, {5, 5, 5, 5}—is 0. The greater the distance between the numbers, the greater the standard deviation.*

When can you generalize the results of a survey of a small group to a larger group?

*A survey can be generalized to a larger population if the data sample is representative. To be representative, the data sample needs to be drawn at random from the larger population.*

What are two ways to calculate the probability of a single event?

*One way is to use the basic probability formula:*

$$\text{Probability} = \frac{\text{number of desired outcomes}}{\text{number of total outcomes}}$$

*Alternatively, the probability that an event happens is 1 minus the probability that it doesn't happen.*

## Next Steps

If you answered most questions correctly in the "How Much Have You Learned?" section, and if your responses to the Reflect questions were similar to those of the SAT expert, then consider tables, statistics, and probability an area of strength and move on to the next chapter. Come back to this topic periodically to prevent yourself from getting rusty.

If you don't yet feel confident, review those parts of this chapter that you have not yet mastered, then try the questions you missed again. In particular, make sure that you understand the six terms explained in the Statistics lesson and the probability formulas explained in the Probability lesson. As always, be sure to review the explanations closely.

# Answers and Explanations

**1. B**

**Difficulty:** Easy

**Getting to the Answer:** The trickiest part of this question is understanding what is being asked. You need to find the shop that had the most Tuesday sales *as a fraction of its total sales*, so focus only on those rows in the table. For each shop, divide the number of books it sold on Tuesday by the number of books it sold all week. Use your calculator to speed up this step.

Bob's Bookshop: $\dfrac{\text{Tuesday total}}{\text{weekly total}} = \dfrac{8}{53} \approx 0.1509$

Clara's Bookshop: $\dfrac{\text{Tuesday total}}{\text{weekly total}} = \dfrac{13}{55} \approx 0.2364$

Derek's Bookshop: $\dfrac{\text{Tuesday total}}{\text{weekly total}} = \dfrac{15}{66} \approx 0.2273$

Evelyn's Bookshop: $\dfrac{\text{Tuesday total}}{\text{weekly total}} = \dfrac{13}{58} \approx 0.2241$

The greatest portion of Tuesday sales belongs to Clara's Bookshop, so **(B)** is correct.

**2. C**

**Difficulty:** Medium

**Getting to the Answer:** Add the number of books sold by Derek and Evelyn on Monday, Wednesday, and Friday; then divide the result by the total number of books sold on those days.

Derek's and Evelyn's M/W/F sales:
$(15 + 12) + (12 + 14) + (10 + 9) = 72$

Total M/W/F sales: $48 + 49 + 39 = 136$

Divide Derek's and Evelyn's M/W/F sales by total M/W/F sales to get $\dfrac{72}{136}$, which simplifies to $\dfrac{9}{17}$. Choice **(C)** is correct.

**3. B**

**Difficulty:** Easy

**Getting to the Answer:** The question asks only about participants who were outside a healthy weight range, so focus on this row: 38 out of the 74 participants who were outside a healthy weight range ate breakfast one or fewer times per week. This expressed as a percent is $\dfrac{38}{74} \times 100\% = 0.51351 \times 100\% = 51.35\%$, which matches **(B)**.

**4. D**

**Difficulty:** Medium

**Getting to the Answer:** The question asks about employees who eat breakfast every weekday, so focus on the "5–7 times per week" column in the table. Assuming the participants in the study were a good representative sample, 36 out of 45, or 80%, of the 3,000 employees are likely to be within a healthy weight range. Multiply $0.8 \times 3,000$ to arrive at 2,400, which is **(D)**.

**5. 300**

**Difficulty:** Easy

**Getting to the Answer:** Read the graph carefully, including the key at the bottom indicating that each bar represents 15 minutes. The question states that only stage 3 is considered deep sleep, and the question asks how much time was spent in non-deep sleep. You could count all of the bars that don't represent stage 3, but it would be faster to count the bars that do and then subtract that number from the total. There are 12 bars that represent stage 3, which means the person spent $12 \times 15 = 180$ minutes in deep sleep. The study was for 8 hours, or 480 minutes, so the person spent $480 - 180 = \textbf{300}$ minutes in non-deep sleep.

**6. 195**

**Difficulty:** Medium

**Strategic Advice:** In multi-part Math question sets, the second question often uses information that you had to calculate in the first question. Keep track of your computations and reuse information so that you don't waste time repeating calculations.

**Getting to the Answer:** Set up the average formula and start filling in the values to find the missing night's stage 3 sleep. You're given two of the three quantities needed for the average formula: the total number of nights is 5 and the average over all the nights is 180 minutes. You know from your work in the previous question that the patient spent 180 minutes in stage 3 sleep on the first night. The following 3 nights, as given in the questions stem, average out to 175 minutes each, so even though you don't know their precise values, you can represent them as 175 three times. Use a variable, $x$, for the unknown number of minutes in stage 3 sleep on the fifth night and solve:

$$180 = \frac{180 + 175 + 175 + 175 + x}{5}$$

$$900 = 705 + x$$

$$x = 195$$

Grid in **195**.

**7.   D**

**Difficulty:** Medium

**Getting to the Answer:** Compare each statement to the line graph one at a time, eliminating true statements as you work. Start with (A): at every reading after 20 hours, Strain 1 has a higher OD600 level than Strain 2, so this statement is true. Eliminate (A). Choice (B) states that Strain 2's growth rate (slope) overtook Strain 1's at hour 50, which is consistent with the line graph; eliminate it. It looks as though (C) requires time-consuming calculations, so skip it for now. Choice (D) states that Strain 1's growth rate was greater than Strain 2's over the entire period. This statement contradicts what you already confirmed in (B), which makes **(D)** false and, therefore, correct. There's no need to check (C).

**8.   D**

**Difficulty:** Medium

**Strategic Advice:** The median is the middle value when all of the values are in numerical order, so you'll need to find the total number of values in the set and figure out which one is the middle value.

**Getting to the Answer:** The note above the chart says that the total number of people who were surveyed in country B is 250. Since it is an even set of values, the median will be the average of the 125th and 126th values. To get to those values, add the number of citizens who speak one or two languages: $70 + 30 = 100$. The hundredth value falls within the group that speaks two languages. Keep going because this group does not include the 125th and 126th values. Add the citizens who speak three languages: $100 + 20 = 120$. Still not quite there, so add the citizens who speak four languages: $120 + 70 = 190$. This means that the 125th and 126th values are both 4, so the median is 4. **(D)** is correct.

**9.   C**

**Difficulty:** Hard

**Getting to the Answer:** The answer choices compare the number of citizens who speak different numbers of languages. (A) and (B) compare the number of

citizens who speak exactly five languages to the number of citizens who speak exactly four languages. Notice that in both countries, the fraction that speaks exactly five languages is smaller than the fraction that speaks exactly four languages, so (B) can be eliminated.

To evaluate (A), you need to calculate the number of citizens who speak five languages and the number of citizens who speak four languages. Take the population in each country and multiply it by the fraction of citizens surveyed who speak the specified number of languages (the denominator of the fraction will be the total number surveyed, 250):

Country A: $(550,000)\left(\frac{25}{250}\right) = (550,000)\left(\frac{1}{10}\right) = 55,000$

Country B: $(1,300,000)\left(\frac{60}{250}\right) = (1,300,000)\left(\frac{6}{25}\right) = 312,000$

This means that $55,000 + 312,000 = 367,000$ citizens speak five languages. Next, calculate how many citizens speak exactly four languages:

Country A: $(550,000)\left(\frac{40}{250}\right) = (550,000)\left(\frac{4}{25}\right) = 88,000$

Country B: $(1,300,000)\left(\frac{70}{250}\right) = (1,300,000)\left(\frac{7}{25}\right) = 364,000$

This means that $88,000 + 364,000$, or $452,000$, citizens speak exactly four languages. Because 312,000 is not half of 364,000, eliminate (A).

Use logic to decide between (C) and (D). Notice that the fraction of citizens who speak four languages in country B, which has a larger population, is more than twice the fraction of citizens in country B who speak two languages—while in country A, which has a smaller population, the fraction of citizens who speak two languages is exactly twice the fraction of citizens who speak four languages. Country B's larger population means that overall, more citizens of both countries combined will speak four languages than two languages. Choice **(C)** is correct.

For the record, here are the calculations for **(C)** and (D):

Country A: $(550,000)\left(\frac{80}{250}\right) = (550,000)\left(\frac{8}{25}\right) = 176,000$

Country B: $(1,300,000)\left(\frac{30}{250}\right) = (1,300,000)\left(\frac{3}{25}\right) = 156,000$

The number of citizens who speak two languages in both countries is $176,000 + 156,000$, or $332,000$, which is fewer than the 452,000 who speak four languages.

## 10. B
**Difficulty:** Easy

**Getting to the Answer:** Consider the definitions of mean and standard deviation: mean is a measure of center, while standard deviation is a measure of spread. The closer the data points for a given snowboarder are to the mean, the more consistent that snowboarder's performance, so the explanation should involve standard deviation. Based on this, you can eliminate (A) and (D). Greater consistency means lower standard deviation (and vice versa); the only choice that reflects this—and correctly represents the data in the table—is **(B)**.

## 11. C
**Difficulty:** Medium

**Getting to the Answer:** You'll have to determine the values of all three measurements so that you can place them in ascending order. Start with the easiest, the mode. That is 3 because there are 18 cars of that age, which is the most of any age. Next, calculate the total number of cars, since you'll need that to compute both the mean and median. Adding the total in the right-hand column gives you $3 + 5 + 18 + 17 + 11 + 6 + 2 = 62$ cars in inventory. Since this is an even number, the median age will be the average of the 31st and 32nd values. The are $3 + 5 + 18 = 26$ cars that are 1, 2, and 3 years old and 17 that are 4 years old. Thus, the 27th through 43rd ($26 + 17 = 43$) values are 4, and that is the median.

Calculating the mean is more complex since it is a weighted average. Multiply each value by its frequency, total those values, and divide by 62. So, $1 \times 3 = 3$, $2 \times 5 = 10$, $3 \times 18 = 54$, $4 \times 17 = 68$, $5 \times 11 = 55$, $6 \times 6 = 36$, and $7 \times 2 = 14$, and $3 + 10 + 54 + 68 + 55 + 36 + 14 = 240$. You could divide 240 by 62 to get approximately 3.87, or you could recognize that 240 divided by 60 is 4, so the result when divided by 62 is just less than 4, which is all you need to know to answer this question. The ascending order of the three values is mode (3), mean (3.87), and median (4), so **(C)** is correct.

## 12. 6.2
**Difficulty:** Hard

**Getting to the Answer:** Read this question carefully, since it is rather unusual. In order to meet a goal of a 0.5% reject rate for the month, use the average formula,
$$0.5\% = \frac{\text{maximum allowable sum of the daily reject rates}}{22}.$$
Thus, the sum of the daily reject rates for a 0.5% average is $22 \times 0.5\% = 11.0\%$. Since 12 days have already passed with an average reject rate of 0.4%, the sum of the daily rates so far is $12 \times 0.4\% = 4.8\%$. So, the sum of the daily rates for the next 10 days cannot exceed $11.0\% - 4.8\% = 6.2\%$ if the monthly average is to be 0.5% or less.

The question doesn't ask for the total or average of the next 10 days, however. Instead, it asks for the maximum reject rate on the next single day that could still conceivably allow the company to meet its monthly goal. If the other 9 remaining days all had a 0.0% reject rate, then the 10-day total would be the reject rate for that 13th day. This is 6.2%, so grid in **6.2**.

## 13. A
**Difficulty:** Easy

**Getting to the Answer:** Any sample used to determine a general opinion needs to be representative and unbiased. The railroad company fails to meet that requirement, surveying only people who commute to work and who would probably benefit from the station. This potentially leaves out a large portion of the population who may not share the commuters' favorable opinion. The use of a biased sample group makes the survey unreliable and not representative, which makes **(A)** the correct answer.

## 14. A
**Difficulty:** Medium

**Getting to the Answer:** As long as a sample is representative, without bias, and relatively large, inferences can be drawn from the sample data about the population from which the sample was taken. The sample here meets all of these requirements. If the mean number of bottles of water consumed per person each day were 2.5, then it could be assumed that the average number consumed in the general population would also be approximately 2.5. The mean of the sample equals the estimated mean of the general population, and **(A)** is the correct answer.

**15. C**

**Difficulty:** Medium

**Getting to the Answer:** As the customers were selected at random, it is reasonable to assume that the survey results will be representative of what is true for customers in general. However, the data provided refers only to people who bought dinnerware. So, an inference can be drawn only about dinnerware returns. Based on the 80% of surveyed customers who returned dinnerware items because of damage, it is reasonable to infer that this statistic will be similar for all customers who return dinnerware. That makes **(C)** the correct answer. Choices (A), (B), and (D) are incorrect because they are not confined to dinnerware.

**16. C**

**Difficulty:** Medium

**Getting to the Answer:** To make a reliable inference from a survey, the survey sample needs to be representative, unbiased, and relatively large. In this case, the miniature golf course owner surveyed only children who played at that course. Thus, any inference drawn from the data must be about such children. Since 60% of the surveyed children prefer a red golf ball, it is reasonable to infer that a similar percentage of total children at that golf course would prefer red golf balls. Thus, **(C)** is the correct answer.

**17. C**

**Difficulty:** Hard

**Getting to the Answer:** The customer purchased 5 boxes, each of which contains 20 bags, which means the customer bought a total of $5 \times 20 = 100$ bags. In each bag tested, there were between 11 and 13 green jelly beans. As the bags were chosen at random, it's reasonable to expect that the results will be consistent for all 100 bags. With 11–13 beans per bag, the total number of green jelly beans will likely be between $11 \times 100 = 1,100$ and $13 \times 100 = 1,300$. Right in the middle of that range is 1,200, making **(C)** the correct answer.

Note that if you chose (A) 60, you might have been thinking of the total green jelly beans in just the five randomly selected bags. Similarly, if you chose (B) 240, you calculated the approximate number in just one box of 20 bags. Incorrect answer choices often try to anticipate minor mistakes you might make in your calculations. Be sure to confirm that you answered the question being asked.

**18. C**

**Difficulty:** Medium

**Getting to the Answer:** The number of desired outcomes is 392 (marked bearings that are defective). The number of total possible outcomes is 560 (all the bearings that are marked defective). Thus, the probability that a bearing marked defective is in fact defective is $\frac{392}{560} \times 100\% = 0.70 \times 100\% = 70\%$. **(C)** is correct.

**19. D**

**Difficulty:** Hard

**Getting to the Answer:** The probability that one randomly selected salmon from those that were tested would have a dangerous level of mercury is equal to the number of salmon that had dangerous mercury levels divided by the total number of salmon that were tested. This means you need only two numbers to answer this question. One of those numbers is in the second table—6 salmon had dangerous mercury levels. Finding the other number is the tricky part. Use information from the question stem and the first table. The biologist tested 5% of the total number of each species of fish, and 25% of the 6,000 fish are salmon. So the biologist tested 5% of 25% of 6,000 fish. Multiply to find that $0.05 \times 0.25 \times 6,000 = 75$ salmon were tested. This means the probability is $\frac{6}{75} = 0.08$, which matches **(D)**.

**20. B**

**Difficulty:** Medium

**Strategic Advice:** Recognizing which value goes in the denominator, whether it is the entire total or the total of a subgroup, is essential for probability questions that are based on data in a table.

**Getting to the Answer:** The question indicates that the random selection is from all the engineers, or the entire total of 768. The specific engineer to be selected is a mechanical engineer who specializes in autonomous vehicles, and the table indicates that there are 245 such engineers. Therefore, the probability of selecting a mechanical engineer specializing in autonomous vehicles from all the engineers is $\frac{245}{768}$, which is $\approx 0.319$. **(B)** is correct.

Note that the incorrect answer choices often reflect common misunderstandings and simple table-reading errors. For example, (C) and (D) both use the wrong total and (A) is the probability of choosing an electrical engineer specializing in autonomous vehicles.

**21. A**

**Difficulty:** Medium

**Strategic Advice:** Be on the lookout for "at least" language. It will usually require adding data from multiple rows or columns.

**Getting to the Answer:** The probability of choosing an employee with "at least" 8 paid vacation days who is salaried is the number of salaried employees with 8 or more paid vacation days divided by the total number of employees with 8 or more paid vacation days. Find the number of salaried employees with 8 or more paid vacation by adding the salaried employees with 8–14 paid vacation days, 27, and the salaried employees with 15–30 paid vacation days, 65. That means there are 27 + 65, or 92, salaried employees with 8 or more paid vacation days. The total number of employees with 8 or more paid vacation days is 210 (the total number of employees with 8–14 paid vacation days) plus 103 (the total number of employees with 15–30 paid vacation days), or 313. The probability is $\frac{92}{313}$. **(A)** is correct.

**22. C**

**Difficulty:** Hard

**Strategic Advice:** If totals and the relationships between the data are the only information provided, write out a system of equations.

**Getting to the Answer:** The question gives the relationships between unknown values in the table, so fill them in accordingly. For hybrid engines, let $h$ be the number that are rated 0–45 miles per gallon. There are 6 times as many hybrid engines that achieve 45+ miles per gallon, so that is $6h$. Similarly, for IC, let $c$ be the number of IC engines that are 0–45 miles per gallon. Because the factory produced four times as many IC engines that achieve 45+ miles per gallon, fill in that blank with $4c$:

| | Fuel Economy (miles per gallon) | |
| --- | --- | --- |
| **Engine Type** | **0–45 mpg** | **45+ mpg** |
| Hybrid | $h$ | $6h$ |
| Internal Combustion (IC) | $c$ | $4c$ |
| Total | 53 | 258 |

Write a system of equations based on the two miles per gallon columns:

$$h + c = 53$$
$$6h + 4c = 258$$

Solve the first equation for $h$ and substitute the result into the second equation to solve for $c$:

$$h = 53 - c$$
$$6(53 - c) + 4c = 258$$
$$318 - 6c + 4c = 258$$
$$-2c = -60$$
$$c = 30$$

If $c$ is 30, then there are $4 \times 30$, or 120, IC engines that achieve 45+ miles per gallon. The probability of choosing one of those 120 engines out all 258 engines that achieve 45+ miles per gallon is $\frac{120}{258}$, or 0.465. **(C)** is correct. Notice that there is no need to actually calculate $h$ to answer this question.

**23. 4**

**Difficulty:** Medium

**Category:** Statistics

**Strategic Advice:** When the goal is to find a missing value in a set of data and the average is given, consider using the balance approach. We'll demonstrate both approaches starting with the average formula.

**Getting to the Answer:** The question is about the height change for the sunflower plant, so ignore the data for the other plants. The given height changes for the other six weeks are: 3, 8, 6, 7, 2, and 5. The average change in height for the sunflower plant is given as 5. If you call the missing value $x$, plugging the known values into the average formula results in the following:

$$\frac{3 + x + 8 + 6 + 7 + 2 + 5}{7} = 5$$

$$\frac{3 + x + 8 + 6 + 7 + 2 + 5}{7} = 5$$

$$\frac{31 + x}{7} = 5$$

$$31 + x = 35$$

$$x = 4$$

Grid in **4** as the correct answer.

Alternatively, to use the balance approach, write down how much each value is above or below the average of 5. For example, the Week 3 value of 3 is 2 below the average: $3 - 5 = -2$.

| Week 3 | Week 5 | Week 6 | Week 7 | Week 8 | Week 9 |
|--------|--------|--------|--------|--------|--------|
| 3: −2 | 8: +3 | 6: +1 | 7: +2 | 2: −3 | 5: +0 |

Now observe that, excluding Week 4, the values are $-2 + 3 + 1 + 2 - 3 = 1$. Without Week 4, the total is 1 more than what you'd expect based on the average. So for the values to balance out to the average, the Week 4 value must be one less than the average of 5, or $5 - 1 = 4$. Grid in **4**.

### 24. C

**Difficulty:** Medium

**Category:** Probability

**Getting to the Answer:** The research firm is choosing one student from among the sophomores, so you need the total number of sophomores, 493, in the denominator of the probability formula, not the total number of students. There are $493 - 140 = 353$ sophomores who prefer activities other than video games, so the probability of choosing a sophomore who doesn't prefer video games is $\frac{353}{493}$. Choice **(C)** is correct.

### 25. 700

**Difficulty:** Medium

**Category:** Tables and Graphs

**Getting to the Answer:** Identify the pieces of the graph you need and then convert from the percent to the total. You know from the graph that 21% (5% + 16%) of the visitors are *not* aged 20 or older. This means that $100\% - 21\% = 79\%$ were aged 20+. Given that the number of visitors aged 20+ is 553, use the three-part percent formula to calculate the total:

$$\text{total} \times 79\% = 553$$
$$\text{total} = \frac{553}{0.79} = 700$$

### 26. 2030

**Difficulty:** Medium

**Category:** Tables and Graphs

**Getting to the Answer:** From the previous question, you know that the total number of visitors in 2014 was 700. According to the bar graph, 25% of all the visitors were aged 40–49, and 8% were aged 50+. This means that $0.25 \times 700 = 175$ attendees were aged 40–49, and $0.08 \times 700 = 56$ were aged 50+. The visitors aged 40–49 paid $175 \times \$10 = \$1,750$ for their tickets, and the visitors aged 50+ paid $56 \times \$5 = \$280$ for their tickets. The total revenue for the two groups was therefore $\$1,750 + \$280 = \$2,030$. Grid in **2030**.

### 27. 28.7

**Difficulty:** Medium

**Category:** Tables and Graphs

**Getting to the Answer:** To be considered "bad," a game must have a rating of 1 or 2. Begin by counting the number of "bad" games. There are $5 + 3 + 3 = 11$ games with a rating of 1 and $17 + 12 + 10 = 39$ games with a rating of 2. That's a total of $11 + 39 = 50$ games. Divide this by the total number of games and multiply by 100%: $\frac{50}{61 + 54 + 59} \times 100\% \approx 28.7\%$. Grid in **28.7**.

### 28. 12

**Difficulty:** Medium

**Category:** Tables and Graphs

**Getting to the Answer:** You know from the previous question that 50 games are "bad." Reducing this number by 50% is the same as halving it, meaning there will be 25 remaining "bad" games after the removal. Subtract this from the original total game count ($61 + 54 + 59 = 174$) to get the new total, $174 - 25 = 149$. Divide the new "bad" count by this total, and then multiply by 100% as you did before: $\frac{25}{149} \times 100\% \approx 16.7785\%$. Subtracting the new percentage from the old one (rounded to a minimum of 4 decimal places just to be safe) gives $28.7356\% - 16.7785\% = 11.9571\%$. This rounds to 12.0%. Grid in **12**.

## 29. B

**Difficulty:** Medium

**Category:** Surveys and Data Samples

**Getting to the Answer:** According to the sample survey, $\frac{40}{300}$ *say* they would join the gym. But the gym estimates that only 30% of these respondents would *actually* join, so multiply 40 by 30% to find that the gym can expect $\frac{12}{300} = 0.04 = 4\%$ of the respondents to join. Multiply this by the total number of residents: $12,600 \times 0.04 = 504$ residents, so **(B)** is correct.

## 30. C

**Difficulty:** Easy

**Category:** Tables and Graphs

**Getting to the Answer:** The question states that the data collected was about black-tailed jackrabbits in California, so any conclusion drawn can be generalized only to that particular species of rabbit in California, not to all rabbits generally. According to the data, the California jackrabbit gives birth mostly during March, April, and May, so **(C)** is correct.

## 31. D

**Difficulty:** Medium

**Category:** Surveys and Data Samples

**Getting to the Answer:** The question indicates that there are a wide variety of nutrients in the soil, but the study only tests for nitrogen and potassium, so the sample is limited. You can eliminate (A) and (B) because all nutrients were not included in the sample, so you can't say anything about them one way or the other. The additives may or may not help the soil retain other types of nutrients, and you certainly don't know which of the five additives would produce the best results. You can eliminate (C) because the question doesn't tell you anything about the data collection methods, so you can't determine whether the study was biased. This means that the study will only be able to produce results concerning the effects of the additives on soil retention of nitrogen and potassium. Thus, **(D)** is correct.

## 32. 1/3 or .333

**Difficulty:** Medium

**Category:** Probability

**Getting to the Answer:** First, find the number of respondents willing to pay at least $8 (which means $8 or more). Be careful—the question doesn't specify store brand or brand name, so use both versions of the product:

$$32 + 55 + 30 + 42 + 14 + 27 = 200$$

Now, find the total number of people in the survey. Again, the question doesn't specify store brand or brand name. The question stem states that there is a total of 600 respondents. This means the probability that a randomly chosen respondent is willing to pay at least $8 is $\frac{200}{600}$, or $\frac{1}{3}$. Grid in **1/3** or **.333**.

## 33. A

**Difficulty:** Hard

**Category:** Statistics

**Getting to the Answer:** The number of variables may look daunting, but the question is just asking you to find an average. The average of a set of terms is equal to the sum of the terms divided by the number of terms; thus, the average of $p$, $q$, and $r$ is $\frac{p+q+r}{3}$.

Use the average formula to set up an equation using the rest of the information in the problem. Even though you are given expressions with lots of variables, the average formula is still the sum of the terms divided by the number of terms. Notice that the question states that the average of these expressions is $10t + 34$, which translates to "$= 10t + 34$." So you can set up an equation like this:

$$\frac{(p + 12t - 5) + (q + 16t + 4) + (r - 7t + 25)}{3} = 10t + 34$$

Because the question asks for the average of $p$, $q$, and $r$ in terms of $t$, solve the equation above for $\frac{p+q+r}{3}$:

$$\frac{p + 12t - 5 + q + 16t + 4 + r - 7t + 25}{3} = 10t + 34$$

$$\frac{p + q + r + 21t + 24}{3} = 10t + 34$$

$$\frac{p+q+r}{3} + \frac{21t}{3} + \frac{24}{3} = 10t + 34$$

$$\frac{p+q+r}{3} = 10t + 34 - 7t - 8$$

$$\frac{p+q+r}{3} = 3t + 26$$

**(A)** is correct.

# CHAPTER 9

# Scatterplots

## LEARNING OBJECTIVES

After completing this chapter, you will be able to:

- Determine the average rate of change
- Write an equation for a line of best fit
- Extrapolate values from the line of best fit
- Determine whether a linear, a quadratic, or an exponential model describes the data presented in a scatterplot

25/600 SmartPoints®

K    193

Math

# How Much Do You Know?

**Directions:** Try the questions that follow. Show your work so that you can compare your solutions to the ones found in the Check Your Work section immediately after this question set. The "Category" heading in the explanation for each question gives the title of the lesson that covers how to solve it. If you answered the question(s) for a given lesson correctly, and if your scratchwork looks like ours, you may be able to move quickly through that lesson. If you answered incorrectly or used a different approach, you may want to take your time on that lesson.

Source: CDC

1. The scatterplot shows the prevalence of obesity plotted against the prevalence of diabetes in various areas of the United States. Which of the following best estimates the average rate of change in the prevalence of diabetes as compared to the prevalence of obesity?

   A) 0.3

   B) 0.9

   C) 1.1

   D) 3

**Questions 2 and 3 refer to the following stimulus.**

2. Wind chill, a measurement that reflects the temperature that one feels when outside based on the actual temperature and the wind speed, was first introduced in 1939, and the formula was revised in 2001. If the outside temperature is 0°F, what is the approximate wind chill at 40 miles per hour based on the 2001 formula?

   A) −20°F

   B) −30°F

   C) −40°F

   D) −50°F

3. What wind speed would produce the same wind chill using the 1939 formula as the wind chill produced using the 2001 formula when the outside temperature is 0°F and the wind speed is 40 miles per hour?

   A) 10 miles per hour

   B) 15 miles per hour

   C) 20 miles per hour

   D) 40 miles per hour

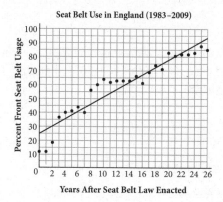

Seat Belt Use in England (1983–2009)

4. The scatterplot above shows data collected each year after the British Parliament enacted a mandatory seat belt law and the line of best fit to the data. Which of the following equations best represents the trend of the data shown in the figure?

A) $y = 0.4x + 25$

B) $y = 1.8x + 15$

C) $y = 2.1x + 35$

D) $y = 2.6x + 25$

6. Scientists measured the concentration of an experimental medication in blood samples over time. If a quadratic function is used to model the data, which of the following best explains the meaning of the vertex?

A) The average maximum medicine concentration in the blood sample is 7.5 units.

B) The average maximum medicine concentration is more than 20 units.

C) The average maximum medicine concentration in the blood samples occurs around 2.5 minutes.

D) The average maximum medicine concentration in the blood sample occurs between 5 and 10 minutes.

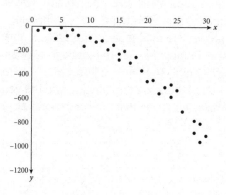

5. The scatterplot above shows the average therms of natural gas used by residential customers over a 12-month period. Of the following equations, which best models the data in the scatterplot?

A) $y = 1.061^x + 312.9$

B) $y = -1.061^x - 312.9$

C) $y = 6.1x^2 - 85.1x + 312.9$

D) $y = -6.1x^2 + 85.1x - 312.9$

7. For which of the following values of $a$ and $b$ does the equation $y = ax^b$ model the data in the scatterplot above?

A) $a < 0, b < 0$

B) $a < 0, b > 0$

C) $a > 0, b < 0$

D) $a > 0, b > 0$

## Check Your Work

**1. A**

**Difficulty:** Easy

**Category:** Line of Best Fit

**Getting to the Answer:** The scatterplot shows obesity prevalence plotted against diabetes prevalence, and because the line goes up as it moves to the right, there is a positive linear correlation between the two. The phrase "rate of change" is the same as the slope of the line of best fit, so pick two points to plug into the slope formula. Estimating, the endpoints appear to be $(14, 7)$ and $(44, 17)$. (If your estimate is different, that's okay—whenever the SAT requires you to make an estimate, the answer choices will be spread far enough apart that you'll get the right answer as long as you're looking in the right place and thinking the right way.) Calculate the slope, $m$:

$$m = \frac{y_2 - y_1}{x_2 - x_1} = \frac{17 - 7}{44 - 14} = \frac{10}{30} = 0.3$$

This matches **(A)**.

**2. B**

**Difficulty:** Medium

**Category:** Line of Best Fit

**Getting to the Answer:** The 2001 formula plot has a slight curve that straightens as wind speed increases. Extend the line to reflect this trend; once complete, draw a straight line from 40 mph on the x-axis to the extended 2001 formula plot (a straight edge such as an extra pencil will help). Then draw a horizontal line from the intersection of the 2001 formula line and the vertical line to the y-axis; you'll see that the corresponding wind chill is $-30°F$. **(B)** is correct.

**3. B**

**Difficulty:** Medium

**Category:** Line of Best Fit

**Getting to the Answer:** Since the conditions mentioned are the same as those in the previous question, start with the wind chill calculated using the 2001 formula for that question, $-30°F$.

Draw a horizontal line from $-30°F$ on the y-axis until it intersects a data point on the 1939 formula plot. Draw a vertical line from that point down to the x-axis;

you'll find that in 1939, a wind speed of approximately 15 mph would yield a wind chill of $-30°F$. Therefore, the correct answer is **(B)**.

**4. D**

**Difficulty:** Medium

**Category:** Line of Best Fit

**Getting to the Answer:** A line that "represents the trend of the data" is another way of referring to the line of best fit, which is linear in this diagram. Use the y-intercept and slope of the line of best fit to eliminate the choices.

Start by finding the y-intercept. For this graph, it's about 25, so eliminate (B) and (C). To choose between (A) and (D), find the approximate slope using two points that lie on (or very close to) the line of best fit. Use the y-intercept, $(0, 25)$, as one of the points to save time (it's easy to subtract 0) and estimate the second, such as $(21, 80)$. Then, use the slope formula to find the slope:

$$m = \frac{y_2 - y_1}{x_2 - x_1} = \frac{80 - 25}{21 - 0} = \frac{55}{21} = 2.62$$

The result is very close to the slope in **(D)**, making it the correct answer.

**5. C**

**Difficulty:** Medium

**Category:** Scatterplot Modeling

**Getting to the Answer:** The data in the scatterplot can be modeled by a parabola opening upward. (A) is an exponential growth equation, and (B) is an exponential decay equation. Neither will graph as a parabola, so eliminate both. Recall that a parabola is the graph of a quadratic. For a quadratic equation in the form $ax^2 + bx + c$, $a$ determines whether the parabola opens upward or downward and $c$ is the y-intercept. When $a > 0$, the parabola opens upward, so **(C)** is correct. (D) is a quadratic equation, but $a < 0$, so this equation would graph as a parabola that opens downward.

**6.  D**

**Difficulty:** Medium

**Category:** Scatterplot Modeling

**Getting to the Answer:** The vertex of a parabola opening downward, like this one, is at the maximum. For this scatterplot, the medicine concentration is measured on the $y$-axis, and the maximum value (the vertex) is about 2.6 units, so the average maximum medicine concentration cannot be above 2.6 units. Eliminate (A) and (B). The $x$-value of the vertex occurs between 5 and 10 minutes; therefore, **(D)** is correct.

**7.  B**

**Difficulty:** Hard

**Category:** Scatterplot Modeling

**Getting to the Answer:** The shape of the data is concave down with an increasingly negative slope as $x$ increases. The $y$-values of the data are negative, which indicates $a < 0$. Eliminate (C) and (D). As $x$ increases, the magnitude of the $y$-values increases. This indicates $b > 0$. Note that If $b < 0$, the $y$-values would approach 0 as $x$ increases. Thus, **(B)** is correct.

Math

# Line of Best Fit

### LEARNING OBJECTIVES

After this lesson, you will be able to:

● Determine the average rate of change

● Write an equation for a line of best fit

● Extrapolate values from the line of best fit

## To answer a question like this:

Which of the following equations corresponds to the line of best fit for the data set shown above?

A) $y = 0.4x - 1$

B) $y = 0.4x + 1$

C) $y = 2.5x + 1$

D) $y = 2.5x - 1$

## You need to know this:

A **scatterplot** is a visual representation of a set of data points. The data points are plotted on the *x*- and *y*-axes such that each axis represents a different characteristic of the data set. For example, in the scatterplot below, each data point represents a dachshund. The *x*-axis represents the dog's length and the *y*-axis represents its height.

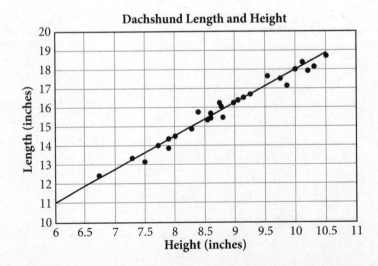

The **line of best fit**, or trend line, is drawn through the **data points** to describe the relationship between the two variables as an equation. This line does not necessarily go through any single data point, but it does accurately reflect the trend shown by the data with about half the points above the line and half below.

The **equation of the line of best fit** is the equation that describes the line of best fit algebraically. On test day, you'll most likely encounter this equation as linear, quadratic, or exponential, though it can also be other types of equations. The next lesson will cover these various forms.

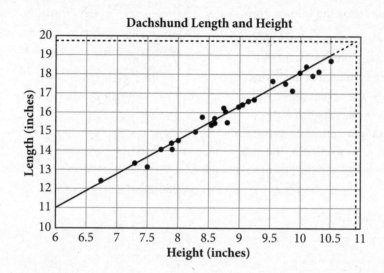

Some SAT questions will require you to extrapolate from the line of best fit. (Question 1 in the Try on Your Own set is an example of this type of question.) For example, you might be asked to predict the length of a dachshund that is 10.9 inches in height. Trace your way up to the line of best fit from the given x-value and trace over to find the corresponding y-value, in this case about 19.75 inches.

## You need to do this:

To determine the equation of the line of best fit for a linear equation, like the one in the dachshund scatterplot, start by finding the slope, also called the **average rate of change**. Watch out for the units when you do this. In the dachshund example, using the points (6, 11) and (10, 18), the slope is $\frac{y_2 - y_1}{x_2 - x_1} = \frac{18 - 11}{10 - 6} = \frac{7}{4} = 1.75$. Next, find the y-intercept. Using the point (10, 18) and plugging those values into slope-intercept form yields $18 = 1.75(10) + b$. Thus, $b = 0.5$ in the dachshund example. So the equation in slope-intercept form is length $= (1.75 \times \text{height}) + 0.5$.

You can also extrapolate using the equation for the line of best fit. For a dachshund that is 11 inches tall, the calculation would be: length $= 1.75(11) + 0.5 = 19.75$.

## Explanation:

Knowing where the y-intercept of the line of best fit falls will help you eliminate answer choices. Because the line of best fit intersects the y-axis below the x-axis, you know that the y-intercept is negative, so eliminate (B) and (C) (the y-intercept is $+1$ for each of those lines). Now, look at the slope. The line rises along the y-axis much faster than it runs along the x-axis, so the slope must be greater than 1, making **(D)** correct.

## Try on Your Own

**Directions:** Take as much time as you need on these questions. Work carefully and methodically. There will be an opportunity for timed practice at the end of the chapter.

**Questions 1 and 2 refer to the following information.**

Most chickens reach maturity and begin laying eggs at around 20 weeks of age. From this point forward, however, as the chicken ages, its egg production decreases. A farmer was given a flock of 100 chickens (all of which were the same age) and asked to measure daily egg output for the entire flock at random intervals starting at maturity until the chickens were 70 weeks old. The data are recorded in the scatterplot below and the line of best fit has been drawn.

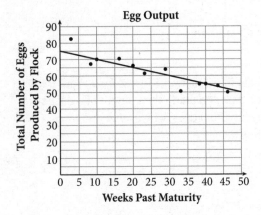

1. Based on the line of best fit, what is the predicted number of eggs that will be produced by the flock when it is 33 weeks past maturity?

   A) 33

   B) 50

   C) 58

   D) 64

---

HINT: For Q2, how many tick marks on the y-axis represent 5 eggs?

---

2. How many times did the farmer's data differ by more than 5 eggs from the number of eggs predicted by the line of best fit?

HINT: For Q3, look at the slope. Which two choices can you eliminate immediately?

HINT: For Q4, rate of change, increase or decrease, means slope.

3. The scatterplot above shows the number of minor muscle strain injuries sustained in a year by athletes, plotted against their self-reported amount of time spent stretching and doing other "warm up" activities before engaging in rigorous physical activity. Which of the following best estimates the average rate of change in the number of injuries compared with the number of minutes spent warming up?

A)  −1.2

B)  −0.8

C)  2

D)  20

4. The graph above shows the percent of school-age children in the United States who received immunizations for various illnesses between 1996 and 2012. What was the average rate of increase in the percent of children immunized per year over the given time period?

A)  5 percent per year

B)  10 percent per year

C)  25 percent per year

D)  70 percent per year

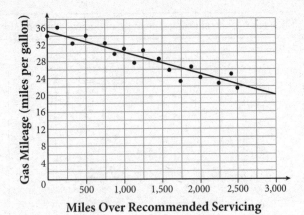

5. A car manufacturer compiled data that indicated gas mileage decreased as the number of miles driven between recommended servicing increased. The manufacturer used the equation $y = -\frac{1}{200}x + 35$ to model the data. Based on the information, how many miles per gallon could be expected if this particular car is driven 3,400 miles over the recommended miles between servicing?

# Scatterplot Modeling

> **LEARNING OBJECTIVE**
>
> After this lesson, you will be able to:
>
> • Determine whether a linear, quadratic, or exponential model describes the data presented in a scatterplot

## To solve a question like this:

Given that *a*, *b*, and *c* are constants and that $a > 0$, which of the following is the equation for the line of best fit for the above scatterplot?

A)  $y = ax + b$

B)  $y = a^{bx}$

C)  $y = -ax^2 + bx + c$

D)  $y = ax^2 + bx + c$

## You need to know this:

There are several patterns that are common forms for the line of best fit. Scatterplots are typically constructed so that the variable on the *x*-axis is the independent variable (input) and the variable on the *y*-axis is the dependent variable (output). The equation for the line of best fit quantifies the relationship between the variables represented by the two axes. The patterns that you are most likely to encounter on the SAT are shown in the table below.

| Best Fit Description | Relationship Between Variables |
|---|---|
| Upward-sloping straight line | Linear and positive |
| Downward-sloping straight line | Linear and negative |
| Upward-opening parabola | Quadratic with a positive coefficient in front of the squared term |
| Downward-opening parabola | Quadratic with a negative coefficient in front of the squared term |
| Upward-sloping curve with an increasing slope | Exponential and positive (e.g., compound interest) |
| Downward-sloping curve with a flattening slope | Exponential and negative (e.g., radioactive decay) |

Here are visual representations of linear, quadratic, and exponential models:

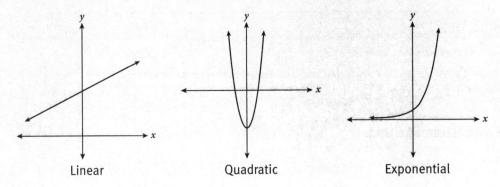

Linear          Quadratic          Exponential

## You need to do this:

- Examine the line of best fit (draw it in, if necessary) and determine its curvature.
- If the line of best fit is straight, the scatterplot represents a linear relationship and the correct answer choice will not contain any exponents. It will likely be in slope-intercept form, $y = mx + b$.
- If the line of best fit is a parabola, the correct answer will be in the form of a quadratic equation, $y = ax^2 + bx + c$. If the parabola opens downward, $a$ will be negative; if upward, $a$ will be positive. (Chapter 12 presents more detailed information about parabolas, but this will suffice for now.)
- If the line of best fit starts with a gradual rate of change that steepens over time, the correct answer will represent an exponential relationship in the form $y = ab^x + c$.

## Explanation:

The line of best fit for this scatterplot is curved, so it is not a straight line as would be created by the linear equation $y = ax + b$. Eliminate (A).

The exponential equation $y = a^{bx}$ would result in a curve that opens upward in one direction. The line of best fit of the scatterplot opens upward in two directions, so (B) is incorrect.

Quadratic equations create parabolas when graphed, but the negative coefficient of the $x^2$ term means that (C) would be a downward-opening parabola rather than the upward-opening parabola of the scatterplot. Thus, **(D)** is correct since that equation would be graphed as an upward-opening parabola.

## Try on Your Own

**Directions:** Take as much time as you need on these questions. Work carefully and methodically. There will be an opportunity for timed practice at the end of the chapter.

6. Which of the following is best modeled using a linear regression equation, $y = ax + b$, where $a < 0$ ?

A)

B)

C)

D)

HINT: For Q7, in an exponential equation, you're taking a starting value and multiplying repeatedly by some other value.

7. Adriana used the data from a scatterplot she found on the U.S. Census Bureau's website to determine a regression model showing the relationship between the population in the area where she lived and the number of years, $x$, after she was born. The result was an exponential growth equation of the form $y = x_0(1 + r)^x$. Which of the following does $x_0$ most likely represent in the equation?

A) The population in the year that she was born

B) The rate of change of the population over time

C) The maximum population reached during her lifetime

D) The number of years after her birth when the population reached its maximum

8. Suppose a scatterplot shows a weak negative linear correlation. Which of the following statements is true?

A) The slope of the line of best fit will be a number less than $-1$.

B) The slope of the line of best fit will be a number between $-1$ and $0$.

C) The data points will follow, but not closely, the line of best fit, which has a negative slope.

D) The data points will be closely gathered around the line of best fit, which has a negative slope.

9.  A drain at the bottom of a cylindrical water tank is opened and the height of the water is measured at regular time intervals. The tank is refilled and the process is then repeated. The scatterplot above shows the measured height on the *y*-axis and time on the *x*-axis for the two trials. Which of the following conclusions can be drawn from the observations in the scatterplot?

    A)  Water flows out of the drain at a constant rate.
    B)  The flow rate from the tank decreases as the height of the water in the tank decreases.
    C)  The drain is inefficiently designed.
    D)  The is no relationship between the height of the water in the tank and time.

# On Test Day

The SAT often tests your understanding of the real-world implications of the *y*-intercept of the line of best fit. The *y*-intercept indicates the starting value of the item measured on the *y*-axis before any time has passed. Scatterplots will test your ability to recognize the meaning of the *y*-intercept in various ways:

- For linear lines of best fit, common examples include the flat fee for renting an item before the hourly rate begins or the down payment on an item before the monthly payments begin.
- For quadratic lines of best fit, the most common example is the path of a projectile where the *y*-intercept is the starting height of the projectile.
- For exponential lines of best fit, common examples include the principal when calculating compound interest, the starting amount of an isotope with a specific half-life (radioactive decay), or the initial population when calculating population growth over time.

Keep in mind that lines of best fit are only approximate based on the given data, but the logic is straightforward: the *y*-intercept is directly related to the approximate initial amount of what is measured on the *y*-axis. Try the following question to see if you can recognize the real-world implication of the *y*-intercept of the line of best fit.

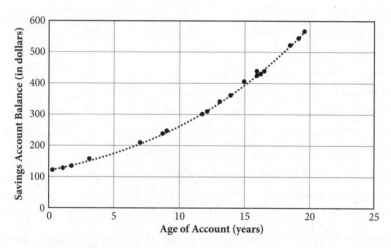

10. Students in a finance class surveyed 20 percent of the account holders at Docen Bank to determine whether the bank's "Stock Market Special" savings account actually paid account holders the promised 10 percent annual interest rate. The scatterplot above shows the data the students collected from account holders about how long ago they opened their accounts and their current balances. The students calculated a line of best fit with the equation $y = 120\left(1 + \frac{.08}{12}\right)^{12x}$, which means that the bank was actually paying account holders only an 8 percent annual interest rate. Which of the following best explains how the number 120 in the equation relates to the scatterplot?

A) A "Stock Market Special" account with $120 initially will likely have less than $350 after 15 years.

B) All "Stock Market Special" accounts started with a $120 initial investment.

C) The difference between the promised 10 percent annual interest rate and the actual 8 percent rate is $120 a year.

D) A "Stock Market Special" account with $120 initially will likely have more than $350 after 15 years.

# How Much Have You Learned?

**Directions:** For testlike practice, give yourself 15 minutes to complete this question set. Be sure to study the explanations, even for questions you got right. They can be found at the end of this chapter.

**Employee Sick Day Usage**

Outside Temperature

**Number of Sick Days Used**

11. The Human Resources department of a company tracks employee sick day usage to see if there are patterns. One of the HR representatives decides to check employee sick day usage against outside temperature. He compiles the information for the employees' sick day usage and temperature in the scatterplot above. Which of the following conclusions can he draw based on this data?

A) There is no relationship between the number of sick days used by employees in general and outside temperature.

B) There is no relationship between the number of sick days used by this company's employees and outside temperature.

C) No conclusions can be drawn about the number of sick days used by this company's employees and outside temperature.

D) There is a relationship, but not a causal link, between the number of sick days used by this company's employees and outside temperature.

12. Scientists plotted data for two animal populations on a scatterplot: population A, which they graphed along the $x$-axis, and population B, which they graphed along the $y$-axis. The data showed a strong negative correlation. Which of the following statements is justified?

A) The rise in population A caused the decline in population B.

B) The decline in population B caused the rise in population A.

C) Because the correlation is negative, there cannot be causation between the two populations.

D) The rise in population A is correlated to the decline in population B, but causation is unknown.

13. By what percent does the $y$-coordinate of the data point $(12, 12)$ deviate from the $y$-value predicted by the line of best fit for an $x$-value of 12 ? (Ignore the percent sign and grid your response to the nearest percent.)

14. The scatterplot below compares the average gasoline prices in Boston, per gallon, to the average gasoline prices across the United States, per gallon, during a one-year period from 2017 to 2018.

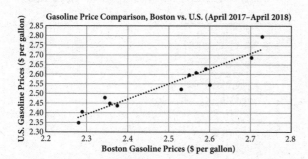

Of the following equations, which best models the data in the scatterplot?

A)  $y = -1.7848x + 0.5842$

B)  $y = 1.7848x + 1.5842$

C)  $y = 0.7848x + 0.5842$

D)  $y = -0.7848x + 0.5842$

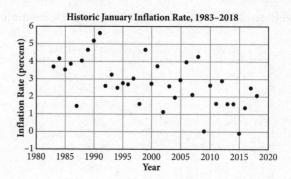

16. Which of the following is the most accurate statement about the scatterplot above?

A)  The data in the scatterplot has a weak positive correlation.

B)  The data in the scatterplot has a strong positive correlation.

C)  The data in the scatterplot has a negative correlation.

D)  There is no correlation in the data set.

15. A physics professor presented the scatterplot above to her first-year students. What is the significance of the slope of the line of best fit?

A)  The slope represents the rate at which time spent on an exam increases based on a student's exam performance.

B)  The slope represents the average grade on the exam.

C)  The slope represents the rate at which a student's exam grade increases based on time spent on the exam.

D)  The slope has no significance.

**Questions 17 and 18 refer to the following information.**

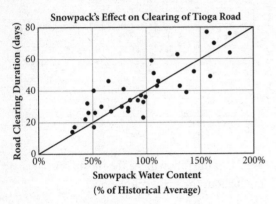

Snowpack's Effect on Clearing of Tioga Road

(Data source: www.nps.gov/yose/planyourvisit/tiogaopen.htm)

Tioga Road is a mountain pass that crosses the Sierra Nevada through northern Yosemite National Park. The road is closed from about November through late May. This time period can change depending on the quantity and nature of the season's snowfall, as well as unforeseen obstacles such as fallen trees or rocks. The scatterplot above compares the snowpack water content on April 1 (for years 1981–2014) as a percent of the historical average to the time it takes the National Park Service to fully clear the road and open it to traffic.

17. For every 5 percent increase in snowpack water content, how many more days does it take the National Park Service to clear Tioga Road?

18. Assuming no unforeseen obstacles or machinery issues, if the road's snowpack water content on April 1 is 248 percent of the historical average, based on the prior experience shown on the graph, how many days will it take to fully clear Tioga Road?

19. Which of the following scatterplots shows a relationship that is appropriately modeled with the equation $y = -ax^2 + bx - c$, where $a$ and $c$ are negative and $b$ is positive?

A)

B)

C)

D)

20. The scatterplot above shows the actual and estimated number of customers visiting a new shopping plaza within the first hour of opening. Which of the following statements correctly compares the rates of increase for the actual and estimated numbers of customers?

A) The rate of increase for the actual number of customers is greater than that of the estimated number in every 20-minute interval.

B) The rate of increase for the actual number of customers is less than that of the estimated number in every 20-minute interval.

C) The rate of increase for the actual number of customers is greater than that of the estimated number in the interval from 20 to 40 minutes and less in the interval 40 to 60 minutes.

D) The rate of increase for the actual number of customers is less than that of the estimated number in the interval from 20 to 40 minutes and greater in the interval 40 to 60 minutes.

# Reflect

**Directions:** Take a few minutes to recall what you've learned and what you've been practicing in this chapter. Consider the following questions, jot down your best answer for each one, and then compare your reflections to the expert responses on the following page. Use your level of confidence to determine what to do next.

What is the significance of a scatterplot's line of best fit?

_____

_____

_____

Given a scatterplot and a line of best fit, how can you tell whether the line of best fit is an accurate one?

_____

_____

_____

What are the three most common patterns for modeling scatterplots that you'll see on test day?

_____

_____

_____

## Expert Responses

What is the significance of a scatterplot's line of best fit?

*The line of best fit describes the relationship between the two variables of the scatterplot. For example, if the line of best fit is linear and has a positive slope, then the two variables have a linear and positive relationship: as one variable increases, the other one also increases and at a constant rate.*

Given a scatterplot and a line of best fit, how can you tell whether the line of best fit is an accurate one?

*A line of best fit should be drawn such that approximately half the points are above it and half are below it.*

What are the three most common patterns for modeling scatterplots that you'll see on test day?

*Most test day scatterplots can be modeled by a linear ($y = mx + b$), quadratic ($y = ax^2 + bx + c$), or exponential ($y = ab^x + c$) relationship.*

## Next Steps

If you answered most questions correctly in the "How Much Have You Learned?" section, and if your responses to the Reflect questions were similar to those of the SAT expert, then consider scatterplots an area of strength and move on to the next chapter. Come back to this topic periodically to prevent yourself from getting rusty.

If you don't yet feel confident, review those parts of this chapter that you have not yet mastered, then try the questions you missed again. In particular, make sure that you feel comfortable extrapolating data from a line of best fit. As always, be sure to review the explanations closely.

# Answers and Explanations

**1. C**

**Difficulty:** Easy

**Getting to the Answer:** In this case, you merely need to match the $y$-value on the line of best fit with the $x$-value of 33, since the $x$-axis of the graph represents the number of weeks after maturity. Take care to use the line of best fit rather than an individual point on the graph; (B) is a trap answer. At $x = 33$, the $y$-value of the line of best fit seems to be just shy of 60. Thus, **(C)** is correct.

**2. 2**

**Difficulty:** Easy

**Getting to the Answer:** Examine the graph, including the axis labels and numbering. Each vertical grid line represents 5 eggs, so look to see how many data points are more than a complete grid space away from the line of best fit. Only 2 data points meet this requirement—the first data point at about 3 weeks and the one between 30 and 35 weeks, making **2** the correct answer.

**3. A**

**Difficulty:** Medium

**Getting to the Answer:** Examine the graph, paying careful attention to units and labels. The average rate of change is the same as the slope of the line of best fit. The data is decreasing (going down from left to right), so eliminate (C) and (D). To choose between (A) and (B), find the slope of the line of best fit using the slope formula, $m = \dfrac{y_2 - y_1}{x_2 - x_1}$, and any two points that lie on (or very close to) the line. Using the two points $(5, 14)$ and $(10, 8)$, the average rate of change is about $\dfrac{8 - 14}{10 - 5} = \dfrac{-6}{5} = -1.2$, which matches **(A)**.

**4. A**

**Difficulty:** Easy

**Getting to the Answer:** The question asks for a rate of change, which means you'll need the slope of the line of best fit. Pick a pair of points to use in the slope formula, such as $(1998, 20)$ and $(2012, 90)$:

$$m = \frac{y_2 - y_1}{x_2 - x_1} = \frac{90 - 20}{2012 - 1998} = \frac{70}{14} = 5$$

Choice **(A)** is correct.

**5. 18**

**Difficulty:** Medium

**Getting to the Answer:** Because the $y$-value of the graph when $x = 3{,}400$ is not shown, this question requires a mathematical solution; extending the line of best fit will not provide an accurate enough answer. The equation of the model is given as $y = -\dfrac{1}{200}x + 35$. Miles over recommended servicing are graphed along the $x$-axis, so substitute 3,400 for $x$ to find the answer:

$$y = -\frac{1}{200}(3{,}400) + 35 = -17 + 35 = 18$$

Grid in **18**.

**6. C**

**Difficulty:** Easy

**Getting to the Answer:** A regression equation is the equation of the line (or curve) that best fits the data. A *linear* regression is used to model data that follows the path of a straight line. In the equation given, $a$ represents the slope of the linear regression (the line of best fit), so you are looking for data that is linear and is decreasing, or falling from left to right, which happens with $a$ is negative, or as the question states, when $a < 0$. You can eliminate (A), which is a quadratic curve, and (D), an exponential curve. You can also eliminate (B) because it is increasing (rising from left to right) instead of decreasing (falling from left to right). **(C)** is correct.

**7. A**

**Difficulty:** Easy

**Getting to the Answer:** When an exponential equation is written in the form $y = x_0(1 + r)^x$, the value of $x_0$ gives the $y$-intercept of the equation's graph. To answer this question, you need to think about what the $y$-intercept would represent in the context described.

Whenever time is involved in a relationship that is modeled by an equation or a graph, it is almost always the independent variable and therefore graphed on the $x$-axis. Therefore, for this question, population would be graphed on the $y$-axis, so $x_0$ most likely represents the population when the time elapsed was zero, or in other words, in the year that Adriana was born, making **(A)** correct.

**8. C**

**Difficulty:** Medium

**Getting to the Answer:** "Correlation" simply means relationship. The word "weak" refers to the strength of the relationship (how close the data lies to the line of best fit), which has no effect on slope. Be careful not to confuse slope and strength. The fact that a data set shows a weak correlation does not give you any information about the magnitude of the slope. This means you can eliminate (A) and (B). Also, keep in mind that the terms "weak" and "negative" are not related, but rather are two independent descriptors of the correlation. So the fact that the rate of change is negative has nothing to do with the strength of the correlation. In a weak correlation, the data points will loosely follow the line of best fit, which makes **(C)** the correct answer.

**9. B**

**Difficulty:** Easy

**Getting to the Answer:** A line of best fit for the scatterplot would show that the measured height of the water decreases over time, but the slope becomes less steep over time, too. The slope, change in height divided by change in time, represents the flow rate of water out of the tank. Since the flow changes as the height of the water changes, (A) is incorrect. Because the slope of the line of best fit becomes less steep as the height of the water decreases, it follows that the flow rate decreases as the height of the water decreases. **(B)** is correct. (D) is incorrect because the height of the water decreases (though at an ever slower rate) as time progresses, so there is a relationship between the height of the water and time. (C) is incorrect because the data presented doesn't imply anything about the efficiency of the drain design.

**10. D**

**Difficulty:** Medium

**Strategic Advice:** Lines of best fit only approximate trends based on a given data set.

**Getting to the Answer:** In the line of best fit equation that the students calculated, the initial principal is $120, but that does not necessarily mean that *all* of the account holders had that much in the account initially. Eliminate (B).

To test (A) and (D), sketch in the line of best fit:

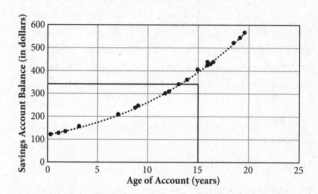

Notice that the line of best fit, which is based on an initial principal of $120, is definitely above $350 at the 15 year mark, so **(D)** is correct. Since the line of best fit is exponential, not linear, there will not be a consistent difference between the 10 percent annual rate and 8 percent annual rate, which makes (C) incorrect.

**11. B**

**Difficulty:** Medium

**Category:** Scatterplot Modeling

**Getting to the Answer:** There are two things to keep in mind for a question like this: correlation does not prove causation, and as a general rule, conclusions can be drawn only about the population studied, not about all populations. The population in the study is only the employees at the company, not all employees in general, so eliminate (A). The data points are scattered and do not form any discernible pattern. This means there is no correlation, which is another way of saying the two variables aren't related, so you can eliminate (D). You can also eliminate (C) because the HR representative *is* able to draw a conclusion—that there is no relationship. Therefore, **(B)** is correct.

**12. D**

**Difficulty:** Medium

**Category:** Scatterplot Modeling

**Getting to the Answer:** The fact that the two variables are strongly correlated, whether it be negatively or positively, shows only that there is a relationship between the variables. It does not indicate whether the change in one variable caused the change in the other. For example, population A might thrive in wet climates, while population B does not, and in the years studied, rainfall may have increased, which caused the changes in the populations. Eliminate (A) and (B). Conversely, the negative correlation does not discount the possibility of causation; rather, the data does not allow you to draw a conclusion about causation, so eliminate (C). This means **(D)** is the correct answer.

**13. 33**

**Difficulty:** Medium

**Category:** Line of Best Fit

**Getting to the Answer:** The point $(12, 12)$ is 3 full grid lines away from the line of best fit, which goes through $(12, 9)$. To find the percent difference between the expected and actual $y$-values, use the percent change formula. Note that the phrasing of the question indicates that the original value to use is 9, the $y$-value on the line of best fit: $\frac{12-9}{9} \times 100\% = \frac{3}{9} \times 100\% = 33.3\%$. Grid in **33**.

**14. C**

**Difficulty:** Medium

**Category:** Scatterplot Modeling

**Strategic Advice:** For scatterplot questions, it is important to determine whether using logic or plugging in values is more efficient.

**Getting to the Answer:** Notice that the answer choices involve very precise coefficients, which is a good indicator that logic is the best way to get to the correct answer. The slope of the line of best fit is positive, so eliminate (A) and (D), which have negative slopes. It is also important to note that the lower-left corner of the graph is not the origin, which means that the $y$-intercept needs to be extrapolated. With only two choices left, you can test only one of them. If the equation you test works, then it is correct. If the equation you test does not work, the other is correct. To test (B), choose one of the values

from the scatterplot that is close to the line of best fit, for example $(2.7, 2.7)$. Plugging 2.7 in for $x$ should mean that $y = 2.7$, but with the equation in choice (B) you get:

$$y = 1.7848(2.7) + 1.5842$$
$$y = 4.81896 + 1.5842$$
$$y = 6.40316$$

This does not match the coordinate point, so **(C)** is correct.

**15. C**

**Difficulty:** Medium

**Category:** Line of Best Fit

**Getting to the Answer:** The slope of a line is always a rate of change of some sort, so you can eliminate (B) and (D). The graph indicates that time spent on the exam is the independent variable, so exam performance depends on it. The choice that correctly describes this relationship is **(C)**.

**16. C**

**Difficulty:** Medium

**Category:** Scatterplot Modeling

**Strategic Advice:** Correlation refers to how closely the values on the scatterplot match the line of best fit.

**Getting to the Answer:** Since correlation is related to the best-fit line, it is important to sketch one on the graph. Here's a rough approximation:

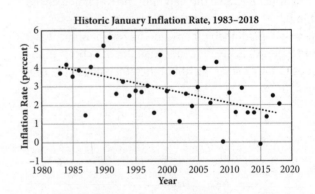

A strong correlation means that the data points are closely gathered around the line of best fit; a weak correlation means that the data points are farther from the line of best fit. The line of best fit has a definite negative slope, so eliminate (A) and (B). When there is no correlation, the data set is distributed evenly over the entire graph, but that is not the case here, so (D) can be eliminated as well. **(C)** is correct.

### 17. 2

**Difficulty:** Medium

**Category:** Line of Best Fit

**Getting to the Answer:** You're asked for a rate; this means finding the slope of the line of best fit. Start by picking a pair of points, preferably where the line of best fit passes through a grid line intersection to minimize error. The points (0, 0) and (50, 20) are good choices to make the calculation easy. Determine the slope:

$$m = \frac{y_2 - y_1}{x_2 - x_1} = \frac{20 - 0}{50 - 0} = \frac{20}{50} = \frac{2}{5}$$

Don't grid in $\frac{2}{5}$, though. Remember what you're being asked: you need the road clearing duration increase for a 5% increase in snowpack water content, not a 1% increase. Therefore, multiply $\frac{2}{5}$ by 5, which yields 2. Grid in **2**.

### 18. 99.2

**Difficulty:** Medium

**Category:** Line of Best Fit

**Getting to the Answer:** The slope you found in the previous question will save you some time here. The line of best fit on the scatterplot intersects the $y$-axis at (0, 0). Therefore, the equation of the line of best fit is $y = \frac{2}{5}x$. Plug 248 in for $x$ and simplify:

$$y = \frac{2}{5}(248) = \frac{496}{5} = 99.2$$

The road clearing time at 248% snowpack water content will take **99.2** days.

### 19. D

**Difficulty:** Medium

**Category:** Line of Best Fit

**Strategic Advice:** Think about how the graphs of different equations look and eliminate the choices that don't match.

**Getting to the Answer:** Sketch in the lines of best fit for the answer choices. (A) and (D) are parabolas that open up, (B) is a parabola that opens down, and (C) is an exponential curve. The equation that needs to be modeled is $y = -ax^2 + bx - c$, which is quadratic and graphs as a parabola. Eliminate (C). Pay careful attention to the details "$a$ and $c$ are negative and $b$ is positive." The coefficient in front of the $x^2$ term determines whether the parabola opens up or down. The negative sign in front of the $a$ multiplies by the negative value for $a$ to create a positive coefficient in front of the $x^2$ term, which means that the parabola opens up. Eliminate (B). Finally, the $c$ coefficient in the equation determines the $y$-intercept for the graph. Again, the negative sign in front of $c$ multiplies by the negative value for $c$ to create a positive $y$-intercept. Eliminate (A) because the best-fit parabola has a negative $y$-intercept. **(D)** is correct.

### 20. C

**Difficulty:** Hard

**Category:** Scatterplot Modeling

**Getting to the Answer:** For every 20-minute interval, draw a line of best fit through the data for the actual number of customers and similarly for the estimated number of customers. Then compare the slopes of the lines of best fit for actual and estimated for each 20-minute interval to compare the rates of increase.

In the interval from 0 to 20 minutes, the slope of the line of best fit for the actual number of customers is slightly greater (steeper) than that of the estimated model. In the interval from 20 to 40 minutes, the slope of the line of best fit for the actual data is greater than that of the estimated data. In the interval from 40 to 60 minutes, the slope of the line of best fit for the actual data is less than that of the estimated data. Thus, **(C)** is correct.

# Passport to Advanced Math

# CHAPTER 10

# Functions

---

**LEARNING OBJECTIVES**

After completing this chapter, you will be able to:

- Apply function notation
- Define the domain and range of a function
- Evaluate the output of a function for a given input
- Interpret the graph of a function
- Write a function to describe a rule or data set

---

105/600 SmartPoints®

---

# How Much Do You Know?

**Directions:** Try the questions that follow. Show your work so that you can compare your solutions to the ones found in the Check Your Work section immediately after this question set. The "Category" heading in the explanation for each question gives the title of the lesson that covers how to solve it. If you answered the question(s) for a given lesson correctly, and if your scratchwork looks like ours, you may be able to move quickly through that lesson. If you answered incorrectly or used a different approach, you may want to take your time on that lesson.

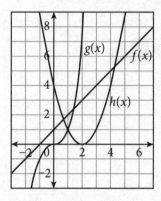

3. In the figure above, what is the value of $h(0) - 3(g(1) - f(2))$ ?

   A)  $-2$

   B)   5

   C)  10

   D)  12

$$p(x) = 7x + 4$$
$$s(x) = 7 - p(x)$$

1. What is the value of $s(-1)$ ?

   A)  $-3$

   B)   4

   C)  10

   D)  17

| $x$ | 2 | 3 | 4 | 5 |
|---|---|---|---|---|
| $f(x)$ | 7 | 13 | 19 | 25 |

4. Some values of the function $f$ are shown in the table above. Which of the following defines $f$ ?

   A)  $f(x) = 7x - 1$

   B)  $f(x) = 6x - 5$

   C)  $f(x) = 5x + 1$

   D)  $f(x) = 4x + 5$

2. A function is defined by the equation $f(x) = \dfrac{x^2}{4} - 11$. For this function, which of the following domain values corresponds to a range value of 14 ?

   A)  $-4$

   B)   10

   C)   38

   D)   100

5.   Briana is writing a 60-page paper for a law school class. She estimates that she will average 45 words per minute while typing. If one page contains approximately 500 words, which of the following correctly estimates the number of pages, $p$, remaining as a function of the number of minutes, $m$, that Briana types?

A)   $p(m) = 60 - \dfrac{9m}{100}$

B)   $p(m) = \dfrac{60 - 100}{9m}$

C)   $p(m) = 60 - \dfrac{100}{9m}$

D)   $p(m) = \dfrac{60 - 9m}{100}$

# Check Your Work

**1.   C**

**Difficulty:** Medium

**Category:** Function Notation

**Getting to the Answer:** To evaluate a function at any value, substitute that value for the variable in the function definition. The question asks for the value of $s(-1)$, so replace the $x$ in the $s$ function with $-1$: $s(-1) = 7 - p(-1)$. To find the value of $p(-1)$, replace the $x$ in the $p$ function with $-1$: $p(-1) = 7(-1) + 4 = -3$. Replace $p(-1)$ with its value, $-3$, in the $s$ function: $s(-1) = 7 - (-3) = 10$. **(C)** is correct.

**2.   B**

**Difficulty:** Medium

**Category:** Function Notation

**Getting to the Answer:** In this question, you are given a range value (14), which means $f(x) = 14$, and you are asked for the corresponding domain value ($x$-value). This means you are solving for $x$, not substituting for $x$. Set the function equal to 14 and solve using inverse operations:

$$14 = \frac{x^2}{4} - 11$$
$$25 = \frac{x^2}{4}$$
$$100 = x^2$$
$$\pm 10 = x$$

Because $-10$ is not one of the answer choices, you know the answer is 10. **(B)** is correct.

**3.   C**

**Difficulty:** Medium

**Category:** Graphs of Functions

**Getting to the Answer:** Start with $h(0)$, which means the $y$-value when $x = 0$. Based on the graph of the $h$ function, $h(0) = 4$. Repeat with $g(1)$, which is 1, and $f(2)$, which is 3. Manipulate these values as instructed: $4 - 3(1 - 3) = 4 + 6 = 10$. Choice **(C)** is correct.

**4.   B**

**Difficulty:** Easy

**Category:** Graphs of Functions

**Getting to the Answer:** Use one of the given points to test the functions. Choose the point that is easiest for you to test. When $x = 2$, $y = 7$, so plug $x = 2$ into the choices and find the one that yields $y = 7$.

Test (A): $f(2) = 7(2) - 1 = 13$. Eliminate (A).

Test (B): $f(2) = 6(2) - 5 = 7$. Keep (B).

Test (C): $f(2) = 5(2) + 1 = 11$. Eliminate (C).

Test (D): $f(2) = 4(2) + 5 = 13$. Eliminate (D).

Only **(B)** remains, and it is correct.

Since all the choices have different slopes, an alternative approach would be to find the slope of the line by using two points.

Use the formula Slope $= \dfrac{\text{rise}}{\text{run}}$ to get $\dfrac{13 - 7}{3 - 2} = 6$. **(B)** is correct.

**5.   A**

**Difficulty:** Hard

**Category:** Describing Real-Life Situations with Functions

**Getting to the Answer:** Use the two given rates to determine Briana's typing rate in pages per minute. She types 45 words per minute, which becomes:

$$\frac{45 \text{ words}}{1 \text{ minute}} \times \frac{1 \text{ page}}{500 \text{ words}} = \frac{45 \text{ pages}}{500 \text{ minutes}} = \frac{9 \text{ pages}}{100 \text{ minutes}}$$

Multiplying this rate by $m$ gets you the number of pages typed after $m$ minutes, which can then be subtracted from the starting page count, 60, to get the number of pages Briana has left to type. The function should read $p(m) = 60 - \dfrac{9m}{100}$, which matches **(A)**.

# Function Notation

### LEARNING OBJECTIVES

After this lesson, you will be able to:

- Apply function notation
- Define the domain and range of a function
- Evaluate the output of a function for a given input

## To answer a question like this:

$$h(x) = \frac{2x + 7}{x - 4}$$

Which of the following must be true about $h(x)$?

I. $h(14) = 3.5$

II. The domain of $h(x)$ is all real numbers

III. $h(x)$ may be positive or negative

A) I and II only

B) I and III only

C) II and III only

D) I, II, and III

## You need to know this:

A **function** is a rule that generates one unique output for a given input. In function notation, the $x$-value is the input and the $y$-value, designated by $f(x)$, is the output. (Note that other letters besides $x$ and $f$ may be used.)

For example, a linear function has the same form as the slope-intercept form of a line; $f(x)$ is equivalent to $y$:

$$f(x) = mx + b$$

In questions that describe real-life situations, the $y$-intercept will often be the starting point for the function. You can think of it as $f(0)$, or that value of the function where $x = 0$.

The set of all possible $x$-values is called the **domain** of the function, while the set of all possible $y$-values is called the **range**.

## You need to do this:

- To find $f(x)$ for some value of $x$, substitute the concrete value in for the variable and do the arithmetic.
- For questions that ask about the domain of a function, check whether any inputs are not allowed, for example, because they cause division by 0.
- For questions that ask about a function of a function, for example, $g(f(x))$, start on the inside and work your way out.

## Explanation:

Check each statement. For the first statement, plug in 14 for $x$:

$$\frac{2(14)+7}{14-4} = \frac{28+7}{10} = \frac{35}{10} = 3.5$$

So the first statement is true. Eliminate choice (C).

For the second statement, you need to determine the set of all permitted $x$-values for this function. Note that the function will be undefined at $x = 4$ (because at $x = 4$, the denominator would be 0.) Thus, 4 is not a permitted $x$-value, and the domain is not all real numbers. The second statement is false. Eliminate (A) and (D).

By process of elimination, the answer is **(B)**, and on test day, you would stop here. For the record, here's why the third statement is true: you've already established that $h(x) = 3.5$ is a permitted value. If you plug in a smaller value, such as 0, you get: $h(0) = \frac{2(0)+7}{0-4} = \frac{7}{-4} = -\frac{7}{4}$, so $f(x)$ can be negative as well.

## Try on Your Own

**Directions:** Take as much time as you need on these questions. Work carefully and methodically. There will be an opportunity for timed practice at the end of the chapter.

---

HINT: For Q1, replace every $x$ in the function definition with $-2$.

---

1. If $g(x) = -2x^2 + 7x - 3$, what is the value of $g(-2)$ ?

   A)  $-25$

   B)  $-9$

   C)  $-1$

   D)  $3$

2. If $k(x) = 5x + 2$, what is the value of $k(4) - k(1)$ ?

   A)  15

   B)  17

   C)  19

   D)  21

---

HINT: For Q3, work from the inside parentheses out.

---

| $x$ | $g(x)$ |
|-----|--------|
| $-6$ | $-3$ |
| $-3$ | $-2$ |
| $0$ | $-1$ |
| $3$ | $0$ |
| $6$ | $1$ |

| $x$ | $h(x)$ |
|-----|--------|
| $0$ | $6$ |
| $1$ | $-4$ |
| $2$ | $2$ |
| $3$ | $0$ |
| $4$ | $-2$ |

3. Several values for the functions $g(x)$ and $h(x)$ are shown in the tables above. What is the value of $g(h(3))$ ?

   A)  $-1$

   B)  $0$

   C)  $3$

   D)  $6$

4. If $p(x) = x^2 - 4x + 8$ and $q(x) = x - 3$, what is the value of $\dfrac{q(p(5))}{p(q(5))}$ ?

   A)  0

   B)  0.4

   C)  1

   D)  2.5

| $n$ | $f(n)$ | $g(n)$ |
|-----|--------|--------|
| 2 | 11.6 | 1.5 |
| 3 | 13.9 | 1 |
| 4 | 16.2 | 0.5 |

5. The table above shows some values of the linear functions $f$ and $g$. If $h(n) = 2 \times f(n) - g(n)$, what is the value of $h(6)$ ?

   A)  21.3

   B)  35.0

   C)  41.1

   D)  42.1

Math

# Graphs of Functions

## To answer a question like this:

| $x$ | $h(x)$ |
|-----|--------|
| 0 | −3 |
| 1 | −2 |
| 2 | 1 |
| 3 | 6 |
| 4 | 13 |
| 5 | 22 |
| 6 | 33 |

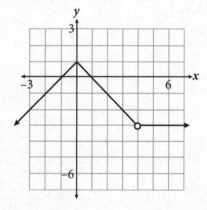

The maximum value of function $g$, whose graph is shown above, is $m$. Values for the function $h$ are shown in the table. What is the value of $h(m)$ ?

A)  −3

B)  −2

C)   2

D)   4

## You need to know this:

Interpreting graphs of functions is similar to interpreting graphs of equations. For example:

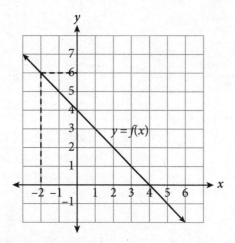

Say the graph above represents the function $f(x)$ and you're asked to find the value of $x$ for which $f(x) = 6$. Because $f(x)$ represents the output value, or range, you can translate this to, "When does the $y$ value equal 6?" To answer the question, find 6 on the $y$-axis, then trace over to the function (the line). Read the corresponding $x$-value: it's $-2$, so when $f(x) = 6$, $x$ must be $-2$.

The SAT may sometimes ask about a function's **maximum** or **minimum**. These terms mean the greatest and least value of the function, respectively. This graph of $f(x)$ does not have a maximum or minimum, as the arrows on the line indicate that it continues infinitely in both directions. The question above, however, does show a function with a maximum.

## You need to do this:

- Treat $f(x)$ as the $y$-coordinate on a graph.
- The maximum and minimum refer to a function's greatest and least $y$-coordinates, respectively.

## Explanation

Start by identifying $m$, which occurs at the apex of the function at $(0, 1)$. The "maximum value of function $g$" means the greatest $y$-value, so $m = 1$. Next, use the table to find $h(1)$, which is the $y$-value when $x = 1$. According to the table, when $x = 1$, $h(x) = -2$. **(B)** is correct.

## Try on Your Own

**Directions:** Take as much time as you need on these questions. Work carefully and methodically. There will be an opportunity for timed practice at the end of the chapter.

HINT: For Q6, $p(x)$ means the $y$-value of the function at $x$.

6.  The above figure shows the function $p(x) = |x|$. Which statement about the function is NOT true?

    A)  $p(0) = 0$

    B)  $p(-4) = 4$

    C)  $p(4) = -4$

    D)  The domain of $p(x)$ is all real numbers.

7.  The graph of $f(x)$ is shown above. Which of the following represents the domain and range of the function?

    A)  Domain: $f(x) \geq 4$; range: all real numbers

    B)  Domain: $f(x) \leq 4$; range: all real numbers

    C)  Domain: all real numbers; range: $f(x) \geq 4$

    D)  Domain: all real numbers; range: $f(x) \leq 4$

8.  Based on the above graph, if the coordinates of the maximum of $f(x)$ are $(a, b)$ and the coordinates of the minimum of $f(x)$ are $(c, d)$, what is the value of $a + b + c + d$?

9. The graph of the linear function $f$ has intercepts at $(c, 0)$ and $(0, d)$ in the $xy$-plane. If $2c = d$ and $d \neq 0$, which of the following is true about the slope of the graph of $f$?

A) It is positive.

B) It is negative.

C) It equals zero.

D) It is undefined.

HINT: For Q10, which roman numeral statement appears the most often in the answer choices? What advantage would you have if you knew that statement was not part of the correct answer?

10. The complete graph of the function $f$ is shown in the figure above. Which of the following is equal to $-1$?

I. $f(-4)$

II. $f(0)$

III. $f(3)$

A) I and II

B) II only

C) I, II, and III

D) III only

# Describing Real-Life Situations with Functions

> ### LEARNING OBJECTIVE
>
> After this lesson, you will be able to:
>
> - Write a function to describe a rule or data set

## To answer a question like this:

| Type of Ingredient | Number of Cookies per Box | Profit per Box (dollars) |
|---|---|---|
| Walnuts | 22 | 1.26 |
| Pecans | 20 | 1.10 |
| Butterscotch | 24 | 1.42 |
| Mint | 18 | 0.94 |
| Macadamias | 12 | 0.46 |
| Hazelnuts | 16 | 0.78 |

A certain cookie company sells several varieties of chocolate cookies, each with an added ingredient. The company sells the different varieties in differently sized boxes. The number of cookies per box and the profit per box for the different varieties is shown in the table above. The relationship between the number of cookies per box and the profit, in dollars, that the company makes per box can be represented by a linear function. Which of the following functions correctly represents the relationship?

A) $p(n) = 0.11n - 0.25$

B) $p(n) = 0.1n - 0.35$

C) $p(n) = 0.09n - 0.45$

D) $p(n) = 0.08n - 0.5$

## You need to know this:

Modeling real-life situations using functions is the same as modeling them using equations; the only difference is the function notation and the rule that each input has only one output.

For example, suppose a homeowner wants to determine the cost of installing a certain amount of carpet in her living room. Say that the carpet costs \$0.86 per square foot, the installer charges a \$29 installation fee, and sales tax on the total cost is 7%. Using your algebra and function knowledge, you can describe this situation in which the cost, $c$, is a function of square footage, $f$. The equation would be $c = 1.07(0.86f + 29)$. In function notation, this becomes $c(f) = 1.07(0.86f + 29)$, where $c(f)$ is shorthand for "cost as a function of square footage." The following table summarizes what each piece of the function represents in the scenario.

| English | Overall cost | Square footage | Material cost | Installation fee | Sales tax |
|---|---|---|---|---|---|
| **Math** | $c$ | $f$ | $0.86f$ | 29 | 1.07 |

## You need to do this:

In word problems involving function notation, translate the math equations exactly as you learned in chapter 4 in the Word Problems lesson, but substitute $f(x)$ for $y$.

## Explanation:

Note that the question asks for the relationship between the number of cookies per box and the profit per box and that the answer choices all start with $p(n)$. Given the context, this translates to the relationship "profit as a function of the number of cookies." All the choices express a linear relationship, so you can't rule out any of them on that basis.

There are several approaches you could take to find the correct answer. One would be to recognize that all the choices are in the form $p(n) = kn + b$ (a variation of the slope-intercept form $y = mx + b$) and that you can set up a system of linear equations using the data from any two rows of the table to solve for $k$ and $b$. That approach would look like this:

$$1.26 = 22k + b$$
$$- \quad (1.10 = 20k + b)$$
$$\overline{0.16 = 2k}$$
$$0.08 = k$$

$$1.10 = 20(.08) + b$$
$$1.10 = 1.60 + b$$
$$b = -0.5$$

Because $k = 0.08$ and $b = -0.5$, the correct function is $p(n) = 0.08k - 0.5$, so **(D)** is correct.

Another approach would be to use two of the pairs of data points from the table to calculate a slope; for example, using the "pecans" and "macadamias" rows would yield $\frac{1.10 - 0.46}{20 - 12} = \frac{0.64}{8} = 0.08$. Because only one answer has a slope of 0.08, you can pick **(D)**.

Finally, you could backsolve. Plug any one of the rows of data from the table into all four answer choices. The second row has the easiest numbers to work with, so use those. You are checking which equation will produce a profit of \$1.10 per box given 20 cookies per box:

A)  $0.11(20) - 0.25 = 1.95 \neq 1.10$

B)  $0.1(20) - 0.35 = 1.65 \neq 1.10$

C)  $0.09(20) - 0.45 = 1.35 \neq 1.10$

D)  $0.08(20) - 0.5 = 1.10$

Again, **(D)** is correct.

## Try on Your Own

**Directions:** Take as much time as you need on these questions. Work carefully and methodically. There will be an opportunity for timed practice at the end of the chapter.

---

HINT: For Q11, pick the easiest number of days from the chart, plug that into the choices, and eliminate any that don't give you the correct vote count. Repeat if necessary until only one choice is left.

---

| Day | Vote Count |
|-----|------------|
| 3 | 21 |
| 4 | 35 |
| 5 | 53 |
| 6 | 75 |
| 7 | 101 |

11. Paulo is one of five contest finalists in the running for a year's worth of college book expenses. The winner is the finalist with the highest number of votes on the contest host's website. Paulo recorded his vote total each day of the contest; data for five days are in the table above. Which of the following represents Paulo's vote count, $v$, as a function of time, $t$, in days?

   A) $v(t) = 2t^2 + 3$

   B) $v(t) = \dfrac{t^2}{2} + 3$

   C) $v(t) = 2t^2 + 21$

   D) $v(t) = \dfrac{t^2}{2} + 21$

---

HINT: For Q12, the faster the rate of change, the steeper the slope.

---

Speed vs. Fuel Economy

12. The graph above shows a compact car's fuel economy as a function of speed. Which of the following is true?

   A) The rate of increase in fuel economy below 50 miles per hour is greater than the rate of decrease in fuel economy above 50 miles per hour.

   B) The rate of increase in fuel economy below 50 miles per hour is equal to the rate of decrease in fuel economy above 50 miles per hour.

   C) The rate of increase in fuel economy below 50 miles per hour is less than the rate of decrease in fuel economy above 50 miles per hour.

   D) Fuel economy peaks at 50 miles per hour, but nothing can be said about the rates of change in fuel economy above and below 50 miles per hour.

13. The graph above shows Carmel's distance from home over a one-hour period, during which time she first went to the library, then went to the grocery store, and then returned home. Which of the following statements must be true?

A) The grocery store is about 5 miles from Carmel's house.

B) Carmel traveled a total of 7 miles from the time she left home until she returned.

C) The grocery store is 7 miles farther from Carmel's house than the library is.

D) Carmel spent 10 minutes at the library and 15 minutes at the grocery store.

HINT: For Q14, which two readings will be easiest to use to find the number of visitors admitted every 15 minutes?

| Time | Total Number of Visitors for the Day |
|---|---|
| 10:10 am | 140 |
| 12:30 pm | 420 |
| 2:00 pm | 600 |
| 2:50 pm | 700 |

14. The entrance gates at a museum allow a constant number of visitors to enter every 15 minutes. A supervisor records the cumulative number of visitors for the day at various times as shown in the table above. The museum does not admit any visitors after 4:45 pm. What is the projected total number of visitors for the day, assuming that the same number of visitors are granted entrance each 15-minute period throughout the day?

A) 810

B) 895

C) 930

D) 960

## On Test Day

The SAT likes to test the modeling of real-life situations. Get comfortable with function notation in these questions. Remember that you can write the equation of a line as $y = mx + b$ or as $f(x) = mx + b$, where $m$ is the slope and $b$ is the $y$-intercept. Both mean the same thing. In the formula using function notation, the slope indicates rate of change. Often, in questions asking about real-life situations, the $x$-variable indicates time. In that case, the $y$-intercept (that is, the value of the function at $x = 0$, or $f(0)$) indicates the starting point.

15. An environmental agency is working to reduce the amount of plastic that a community discards in the ocean. Currently, the community discards 6.2 million pounds of plastic annually, and the agency's goal is to eliminate that amount by collecting and recycling the plastic. If the agency increases its collection and recycling capacity at a constant rate, and meets its goal at the end of the eighth year, which of the following linear functions, $f$, could the agency use to model the amount of plastic being added to the ocean $t$ years into the program?

A) $f(t) = -\dfrac{62}{40}t + 6.2$

B) $f(t) = -\dfrac{31}{40}t + 6.2$

C) $f(t) = \dfrac{31}{40}t + 6.2$

D) $f(t) = \dfrac{62}{40}t + 6.2$

The correct answer and explanation can be found at the end of the chapter.

# How Much Have You Learned?

**Directions:** For testlike practice, give yourself 15 minutes to complete this question set. Be sure to study the explanations, even for questions you got right. They can be found at the end of this chapter.

16. Based on the figure above, what is the value of $f(-2) + g(2)$ ?

    A) $-3$

    B) $0$

    C) $3$

    D) $6$

17. A company uses the function $P(x) = 150x - x^2$ to determine how much profit the company will make when it sells 150 units of a certain product that sells for $x$ dollars per unit. How much more profit per unit, in dollars, will the company make if it charges \$25 for the product than if it charges \$20? (Ignore the dollar sign when gridding your response.)

18. The customer service department of a wireless cellular provider has found that on Wednesdays, the polynomial function $C(t) = -0.0815t^4 + t^3 + 12t$ approximates the number of calls received by any given time, where $t$ represents the number of hours that have passed during the workday. Based on this function, how many calls can be expected by the end of one 10-hour workday?

19. A biologist is studying the effect of pollution on the reproduction of a specific plant. She uses the function $n(p)$ to represent these effects, where $p$ is the number of seeds germinated by the test group of the plant over a given period of time. Which of the following lists could represent a portion of the domain for the biologist's function?

    A) $\{\ldots -150, -100, -50, 0, 50, 100, 150 \ldots\}$

    B) $\{-150, -100, -50, 0, 50, 100, 150\}$

    C) $\{0, 0.25, 0.5, 0.75, 1, 1.25, 1.5 \ldots\}$

    D) $\{0, 20, 40, 60, 80 \ldots\}$

20. If $f(x) = 3 - x$ and $g(x) = \dfrac{x^2}{2}$, which of the following is NOT in the range of $f(g(x))$ ?

   A)  $-3$

   B)  $0$

   C)  $2$

   D)  $4$

$g(x) = -3x - 5$

21. The function $g$ is defined above. What is the value of $g(-4x)$ ?

   A)  $7$

   B)  $-12x - 5$

   C)  $12x - 5$

   D)  $12x^2 - 20x$

$r(x) = 3x - 7$

$t(x) = 3x + r(x)$

22. The functions $r$ and $t$ are defined above. What is the value of $t(2)$ ?

   A)  $-3$

   B)  $-1$

   C)  $0$

   D)  $5$

$f(x) = ax^2 + 3x + 5$

23. The function $f$ is defined above, and $f(3) = -4$. If $a$ is a constant, what is the value of $f(2)$ ?

   A)  $-2$

   B)  $3$

   C)  $5$

   D)  $19$

24. A function $a$ satisfies $a(-2) = 3$ and $a(3) = 8$. A function $b$ satisfies $b(3) = 4$ and $b(7) = -2$. What is the value of $a(b(7))$ ?

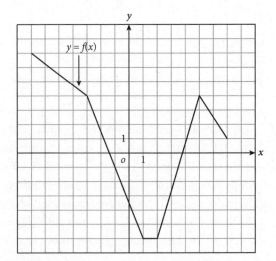

25. The function $f$, shown in the graph above, is defined for $-7 \le x \le 7$. For which of the following values of $x$ does $f(x) = 4$ ?

   I.  $-4$

   II.  $-3$

   III.  $5$

   A)  III only

   B)  I and II only

   C)  II and III only

   D)  I, II, and III

# Reflect

**Directions:** Take a few minutes to recall what you've learned and what you've been practicing in this chapter. Consider the following questions, jot down your best answer for each one, and then compare your reflections to the expert responses on the following page. Use your level of confidence to determine what to do next.

What are the domain and range of a function?

_____

_____

_____

What is another way to write the function $f(x) = x + 4$?

_____

_____

_____

In the function in question 2, what does $x$ represent? What does $f(x)$ represent?

_____

_____

_____

What will the function in question 2 look like when graphed?

_____

_____

_____

In a function whose $x$-value represents time, what does the $y$-intercept represent?

_____

_____

_____

Math

## Expert Responses

What are the domain and range of a function?

*The domain of a function indicates the possible x-values and the range of a function indicates the possible y-values. For example, in the function $f(x) = x^2$, the domain is all real numbers because any number can be squared, and the range is any number greater than or equal to 0, because $x^2$ can't be negative.*

What is another way to write the function $f(x) = x + 4$?

*When you graph the function on the xy-coordinate plane, you can replace $f(x)$ with y. This function is equivalent to $y = x + 4$.*

In the function in question 2, what does $x$ represent? What does $f(x)$ represent?

*In this function, x is the input and $f(x)$ is the output.*

What will the function in question 2 look like when graphed?

*The slope of the line is 1 and its y-intercept is 4, so it will move from the lower left to the upper right and cross the y-axis at $y = 4$.*

In a function whose $x$-value represents time, what does the $y$-intercept represent?

*The y-intercept represents the initial quantity when $t = 0$. Say a function represents the progress of a machine manufacturing widgets at a rate of 6 widgets per hour. The machine adds the widgets it makes to a growing pile that consisted of 12 widgets when the machine started working. If this function were graphed as a function of time, the y-intercept would be 12—the pile of 12 widgets that were there when the machine started its task.*

## Next Steps

If you answered most questions correctly in the "How Much Have You Learned?" section, and if your responses to the Reflect questions were similar to those of the SAT expert, then consider functions an area of strength and move on to the next chapter. Come back to this topic periodically to prevent yourself from getting rusty.

If you don't yet feel confident, review those parts of this chapter that you have not yet mastered. All three lessons in this chapter cover question types that are fairly common on the SAT, and it is to your advantage to have a firm grasp on this material, so go back over it until you feel more confident. Then try the questions you missed again. As always, be sure to review the explanations closely.

# Answers and Explanations

## 1.  A

**Difficulty:** Easy

**Getting to the Answer:** The notation $g(-2)$ is asking for the value of $g(x)$ when $x$ is $-2$, so substitute $-2$ for $x$ and simplify. Don't forget to use the correct order of operations as you work:

$$g(-2) = -2(-2)^2 + 7(-2) - 3$$
$$= -2(4) + (-14) - 3$$
$$= -8 - 14 - 3$$
$$= -25$$

**(A)** is correct.

## 2.  A

**Difficulty:** Easy

**Getting to the Answer:** The notation $k(4)$ is equivalent to the output value of the function when 4 is substituted for the input $x$, and $k(1)$ is the output value of the function when 1 is substituted for the input $x$. Substitute 4 and 1 into the function, one at a time, and then subtract the results:

$$k(4) = 5(4) + 2 = 20 + 2 = 22$$
$$k(1) = 5(1) + 2 = 5 + 2 = 7$$
$$k(4) - k(1) = 22 - 7 = 15$$

Choice **(A)** is correct. Caution—subtracting 1 from 4 and then substituting 3 into the function will give a different and incorrect result.

## 3.  A

**Difficulty:** Medium

**Getting to the Answer:** The notation $g(h(x))$ can be read "g of h of x." It means that the output when $x$ is substituted in $h(x)$ becomes the input for $g(x)$. First, use the table on the right to find that $h(3)$ is 0. This is your new input. Now, use the table on the left to find $g(0)$, which is $-1$, making **(A)** the correct answer.

## 4.  D

**Difficulty:** Medium

**Getting to the Answer:** Evaluate the numerator and denominator separately:

$$p(5) = 5^2 - 4(5) + 8 = 13$$
$$q(p(5)) = q(13) = 13 - 3 = 10$$
$$q(5) = 5 - 3 = 2$$
$$p(q(5)) = p(2) = 2^2 - 4(2) + 8 = 4$$

Then combine to get $\dfrac{q(p(5))}{p(q(5))} = \dfrac{10}{4} = 2.5$. The correct answer is **(D)**.

## 5.  D

**Difficulty:** Hard

**Getting to the Answer:** Determine the linear change of the functions relative to the change in $n$, then extrapolate to get the values of $f(6)$ and $g(6)$. You don't need to determine the actual expressions for the functions. As a shortcut, find the changes per 2 unit increase of $n$ and apply that to the values of the functions when $n = 4$. For $f(n)$, the increase from $n = 2$ to $n = 4$ is $16.2 - 11.6 = 4.6$. Thus, the value of $f(6)$ is $f(4) + 4.6 = 16.2 + 4.6 = 20.8$. The change in $g(n)$ for $n = 2$ to $n = 4$ is $0.5 - 1.5 = -1$. So the value of $g(6)$ is $g(4) + (-1) = 0.5 - 1 = -0.5$. Now, calculate $h(6)$: $h(6) = 2 \times f(6) - g(6) = 2(20.8) - (-0.5) = 41.6 + 0.5 = 42.1$. **(D)** is correct.

## 6.  C

**Difficulty:** Easy

**Getting to the Answer:** The function graphed is the absolute value function, and all of the values in its range (the $y$-values) are positive. That makes any negative value as an output impossible. Because you're looking for the statement that is *not* true, **(C)** is correct.

**7.   D**

**Difficulty:** Easy

**Getting to the Answer:** To determine the domain, look at the *x*-values. To determine the range, look at the *y*-values. For the domain, the graph is continuous (no holes or gaps in the graph) and has arrows on both sides, so the domain is all real numbers. This means you can eliminate (A) and (B). For the range, the function's maximum (the vertex) is located at $(-3, 4)$, which means that the greatest possible *y*-value of $f(x)$ is 4. The graph is continuous and opens downward, so the range of the function is $y \leq 4$, which is the same as $f(x) \leq 4$, making **(D)** correct.

**8.   8**

**Difficulty:** Medium

**Getting to the Answer:** The maximum of $f(x)$ occurs at the point where the *y*-value is the greatest, which in this case is $(2, 4)$. So, $a = 2$ and $b = 4$. The point with the smallest *y*-value is $(4, -2)$. Thus, $c = 4$ and $d = -2$. The total of the four values is $2 + 4 + 4 + (-2) = 8$. Grid in **8**.

**9.   B**

**Difficulty:** Medium

**Strategic Advice:** Quickly sketching the different possibilities can be helpful.

**Getting to the Answer:** Because $2c = d$, both the *x*-intercept, *c*, and the *y*-intercept, *d*, must have the same sign. If both are positive, then *d* would be greater than *c*, and the graph of *f* would look something like this:

This is all you need to do to solve the problem. According to the choices, the slope is always the same regardless of the sign of *c* and *d*. In other words, if the slope is negative at one point, then it must be negative all the time. Therefore, **(B)** is correct. On test day, you would move on to the next question without needing to

check what the line looks like when *c* and *d* are negative. For the record, if *c* and *d* are negative, then *d* will be less than *c*, and the graph would look like this:

If you're curious to see the algebra, plug $(0, d)$ and $(c, 0)$ into the slope formula:

$$m = \frac{y_2 - y_1}{x_2 - x_1} = \frac{d - 0}{0 - c} = -\frac{d}{c}$$

The question states that $d = 2c$, so sub in 2*c* for *d*:

$$-\frac{d}{c} = -\frac{(2c)}{c} = -2$$

Therefore, the slope is $-2$, and the answer is indeed **(B)**.

**10.   D**

**Difficulty:** Easy

**Strategic Advice:** Save time on questions with roman numerals in the choices by testing the roman numeral that appears most often in the choices first. Here, check statement II first because it appears in three of the four choices.

**Getting to the Answer:** Plug each of the *x*-values into the function and see which produces a *y*-value of $-1$. Statement II is $f(0)$. When $x = 0$, the function's *y*-value is 2. Statement II is not equal to $-1$, so any answer choices that include statement II are incorrect. Eliminate (A), (B), and (C). Only **(D)** is left and is correct. On test day, you would stop here and move on to the next question. For the record, statement I is $f(-4) = 0$ and statement III is $f(3) = -1$. Also note that there are two other places where the function's output is $-1$: $f(-3)$ and $f(-1.5)$, neither of which is an answer choice.

**11. A**

**Difficulty:** Medium

**Getting to the Answer:** Thinking about the *y*-intercept (the starting amount) for the function will reduce the amount of work you need to do. The table indicates that Paulo had 21 votes on day 3, when $t = 3$, not at the start of the contest, when $t = 0$. This means that (C) and (D) are incorrect. To evaluate the remaining answer choices, pick a point, try it in a function, and if it works, then you've found the correct answer. If it doesn't work, then you can confidently select the other answer choice without any further work:

$$(A): 35 = 2(4)^2 + 3$$
$$35 = 2(16) + 3$$
$$35 = 32 + 3$$
$$35 = 35$$

**(A)** is correct. On test day, you would stop here. For the record, here is the reason (B) is incorrect:

$$(B): 35 = \frac{1}{2}(4)^2 + 3$$
$$35 = \frac{1}{2}(16) + 3$$
$$35 = 8 + 3$$
$$35 \neq 11$$

**12. C**

**Difficulty:** Medium

**Getting to the Answer:** Examine the graph and look for trends in the rate of increase and decrease of fuel economy before and after 50 mph. Note the increase below 50 mph (to the left of 50 on the horizontal axis) and the decrease above 50 mph (to the right of 50): the decreasing part of the graph is steeper than the increasing part. In other words, the rate of increase below 50 mph is less than the rate of increase above 50 mph. Choice **(C)** is correct.

**13. D**

**Difficulty:** Medium

**Getting to the Answer:** Compare each answer choice to the graph, eliminating false statements as you go.

(A): Carmel went to the library first, so the library (not the grocery store) is about 5 miles from her home. Eliminate (A).

(B): Carmel traveled 7 miles away from her home (between $t = 0$ minutes and $t = 30$ minutes), but then also traveled 7 miles back (between $t = 45$ minutes and $t = 60$ minutes), so she traveled a total of 14 miles. Eliminate (B).

(C): When Carmel reached the library, she was 5 miles from home; when she reached the grocery store, she was 7 miles from home. This means the grocery store must be $7 - 5 = 2$ miles farther away. Eliminate (C).

**(D)** must be correct. Carmel is the same distance from home (5 miles) between $t = 15$ minutes and $t = 25$ minutes, so she spent 10 minutes at the library. She is stopped once again (at the grocery store) between $t = 30$ minutes and $t = 45$ minutes, so she spent 15 minutes at the grocery store.

**14. C**

**Difficulty:** Medium

**Strategic Advice:** The fact that the number of visitors each 15 minutes is constant means that the cumulative number of visitors is a linear function.

**Getting to the Answer:** Because the time between the numbers of cumulative visitors in the table varies, pick an interval that is easy to work with to determine the number of visitors who enter every 15 minutes. Next, use that value to find how many entered by 4:45 p.m. There are six 15-minute periods between 12:30 p.m. and 2:00 p.m. The number of visitors admitted during that time was $600 - 420 = 180$. So, $\frac{180}{6} = 30$ visitors enter every 15 minutes.

In order to project the cumulative, or total, number of visitors for a specific time, set up a function, $f(v)$. Pick a time that is convenient, such as 2:00 pm. Since you know that there were 600 visitors by 2:00 pm, you can write $f(v) = 600 + 30v$, where $v$ is the number of 15-minute periods after 2:00 pm. The question asks for the cumulative visitors admitted by 4:45 pm. Thus, $v$ is the number of 15-minute periods between 2:00 and 4:45, which is 11. So, $f(11) = 600 + 30(11) = 930$. **(C)** is correct.

## 15. B

**Difficulty:** Medium

**Strategic Advice:** When modeling a real-life situation with a linear function, the starting point in the description is the $y$-intercept of the equation and the rate of change is the slope. Eliminate choices as you go; you may find that you are able to answer the question after only one or two steps. Never do more math than necessary to answer the question.

**Getting to the Answer:** In this question, the agency is reducing the amount of plastic disposed annually, so the slope must be negative. Eliminate (C) and (D) because their positive slopes indicate an *increasing* function.

The starting point, or $y$-intercept, is the amount of plastic the community is now discarding, or 6.2 million pounds. Unfortunately, this value is the same in (A) and (B), so you will need to find the slope.

The agency wants to eliminate the total amount of plastic in 8 years, so to find the amount of reduction per year, divide 6.2 by 8.

Because $-\frac{6.2}{8}$ does not appear in the choices, and the slopes in the choices do not have decimal points, multiply the fraction by 1 in the form of $\frac{10}{10}$ to get $-\frac{6.2}{8} \times \frac{10}{10} = -\frac{62}{80} = -\frac{31}{40}$. Choice **(B)** is correct.

## 16. C

**Difficulty:** Medium

**Category:** Graphs of Functions

**Getting to the Answer:** Graphically, the notation $f(-2)$ means the $y$-value when $x$ is $-2$. Pay careful attention to which graph is which. It may help to draw dots on the graph. Find $x = -2$ along the horizontal axis, trace up to the graph of $f(x)$, and draw a dot on the graph. Do the same for $g(2)$, as shown here:

Now, read the $y$-coordinates from the graph and add: $f(-2)$ is 6 and $g(2)$ is $-3$, so $f(-2) + g(2) = 6 + (-3) = 3$, which is **(C)**.

## 17. 3.5 or 3.50

**Difficulty:** Medium

**Category:** Describing Real-Life Situations with Functions

**Getting to the Answer:** Start by evaluating the function at $x = 25$ and at $x = 20$. Make sure you follow the correct order of operations as you simplify:

$$P(25) = 150(25) - (25)^2$$
$$= 3,750 - 625$$
$$= 3,125$$
$$P(20) = 150(20) - (20)^2$$
$$= 3,000 - 400$$
$$= 2,600$$

The question asks how much more profit *per unit* the company makes, so find the difference in the amounts of profit and divide by the number of units (150) to get $\frac{3,125 - 2,600}{150} = \frac{525}{150} = \$3.50$. Grid in **3.5**.

**18. 305**

**Difficulty:** Easy

**Category:** Describing Real-Life Situations with Functions

**Getting to the Answer:** At the end of one workday, 10 hours have passed, so evaluate the function at $t = 10$. Make sure you follow the correct order of operations as you simplify:

$$C(t) = -0.0815t^4 + t^3 + 12t$$
$$C(10) = -0.0815(10)^4 + 10^3 + 12(10)$$
$$= -0.0815(10,000) + 1,000 + 120$$
$$= -815 + 1,000 + 120$$
$$= 305$$

Grid in **305**.

**19. D**

**Difficulty:** Easy

**Category:** Describing Real-Life Situations with Functions

**Getting to the Answer:** The domain of a function includes every possible input value, which is usually represented by $x$. In this function, instead of $x$, the input is represented by $p$, which is the number of seeds germinated by the plants over a given period of time. Because there cannot be a negative number of seeds germinated or a fraction of a seed germinated, the list in **(D)** is the only one that could represent a portion of the function's domain.

**20. D**

**Difficulty:** Hard

**Category:** Graphs of Functions

**Getting to the Answer:** When working with a composition (also called nested functions), the range of the inner function becomes the domain of the outer function, which in turn produces the range of the composition. In the composition $f(g(x))$, the function $g(x) = \frac{x^2}{2}$ is the inner function. Every value of $x$, when substituted into this function, will result in a non-negative value because the result of squaring a number is always a positive number. This means the smallest possible range value of $g(x)$ is 0. If you don't see this relationship, try plugging in various values for $x$ and look for a pattern. Now look at $f(x)$. Substituting large positive values of $x$ in the function will result in

large negative numbers. Consequently, substituting the smallest value from the range of $g$, which is 0, results in the largest range value for the composition, which is $3 - 0 = 3$. Therefore, 4 is not in the range of $f(g(x))$. **(D)** is correct.

**21. C**

**Difficulty:** Medium

**Category:** Function Notation

**Getting to the Answer:** To evaluate a function at a particular value, replace the variable in the function with the value. In this question, replace $x$ in the function definition with $-4x$ to get $g(-4x) = -3(-4x) - 5 = 12x - 5$. **(C)** is correct.

Note that you can replace one variable with another. In this question, $-4x$ replaces $x$. If you chose (A), you likely replaced $x$ in the function definition with $-4$. If you chose (B), you may have "lost" a negative sign. Finally, (D) results if you multiply each term in the definition by $-4x$ instead of replacing $x$ with $-4x$.

**22. D**

**Difficulty:** Medium

**Category:** Function Notation

**Getting to the Answer:** To evaluate the value of a function, replace the variable in the definition with the given value. Since the question asks for $t(2)$, and the definition of the $t$ function includes the $r$ function, evaluate $r(2)$ first, then use that result to evaluate $t(2)$:

$$r(2) = 3(2) - 7 = 6 - 7 = -1$$

Because $t(2) = 3(2) + r(2) = 6 - 1 = 5$, **(D)** is correct.

### 23. B

**Difficulty:** Medium

**Category:** Function Notation

**Getting to the Answer:** To evaluate a function for a particular value, substitute the value for the variable in the function. In this case, substitute 3 for $x$ and then use the given value for $f(3)$ to solve for the value of $a$:

$$f(3) = a(3)^2 + 3(3) + 5$$
$$-4 = 9a + 9 + 5$$
$$-4 = 9a + 14$$
$$-18 = 9a$$
$$-2 = a$$

Next, use the known value of $a$ to find $f(2)$:

$$f(2) = -2(2)^2 + 3(2) + 5$$
$$f(2) = -2(4) + 6 + 5$$
$$f(2) = -8 + 11$$
$$f(2) = 3$$

**(B)** is correct.

### 24. 3

**Difficulty:** Medium

**Category:** Function Notation

**Getting to the Answer:** To evaluate a composite function (a set of nested functions), start with the innermost function and work outward. For this question, begin by evaluating $b(7)$. Because $b(7) = -2$, you know that $a(b(7)) = a(-2)$, so next, evaluate $a(-2)$. The question tells you that $a(-2) = 3$, which makes **(B)** correct.

### 25. C

**Difficulty:** Easy

**Category:** Graphs of Functions

**Getting to the Answer:** The term $f(x)$ is equivalent to the $y$-value of the function at $x$. So this question is asking, "Which values of $x$ produce a $y$-value of 4?" Draw a horizontal line at the point $y = 4$ and identify where that line intercepts the function. The two points of intersection are $-3$ and $5$. **(C)** is correct.

# CHAPTER 11

# Exponents, Radicals, Polynomials, and Rational Expressions

## LEARNING OBJECTIVES

After completing this chapter, you will be able to:

- Apply exponent rules
- Apply radical rules
- Add, subtract, multiply, and factor polynomials
- Divide polynomials
- Define root, solution, zero, and *x*-intercept and identify them on the graph of a nonlinear function
- Determine whether the growth or decay described in a question is linear or exponential
- Apply the linear and exponential equations to answer growth and decay questions
- Simplify rational expressions
- Isolate a variable in a rational equation

25/600 SmartPoints®

Math

# How Much Do You Know?

**Directions:** Try the questions that follow. Show your work so that you can compare your solutions to the ones found in the Check Your Work section immediately after this question set. The "Category" heading in the explanation for each question gives the title of the lesson that covers how to solve it. If you answered the question(s) for a given lesson correctly, and if your scratchwork looks like ours, you may be able to move quickly through that lesson. If you answered incorrectly or used a different approach, you may want to take your time on that lesson.

1. Which expression is equivalent to $2(-4\,j^3k^{-4})^{-3}$?

   A) $-\dfrac{k^{12}}{512\,j^9}$

   B) $-\dfrac{k^{12}}{32\,j^9}$

   C) $-\dfrac{j^9}{32k^{12}}$

   D) $-\dfrac{k^{12}}{128\,j^9}$

$$T = 2\pi\sqrt{\dfrac{L}{g}}$$

2. The formula above was created by Italian scientist Galileo Galilei in the early 1600s to demonstrate that the time it takes for a pendulum to complete a swing—called its period, $T$—can be found using only the length of the pendulum, $L$, and the force of gravity, $g$. He proved that the mass of the pendulum did not affect its period. Based on the equation above, which of the following equations could be used to find the length of the pendulum given its period?

   A) $L = \dfrac{gT}{2\pi}$

   B) $L = \dfrac{gT^2}{4\pi^2}$

   C) $L = \dfrac{T^2}{4\pi^2 g}$

   D) $L = \dfrac{g}{4\pi^2 T^2}$

3. Which of the following represents $\dfrac{\sqrt[6]{x^{10}y^{12}}}{\sqrt[3]{x^5y^6}}$ written in simplest form, given that $x > 0$ and $y > 0$?

   A) 1

   B) 2

   C) $x^2y^3\sqrt{x}$

   D) $xy^2\sqrt[3]{x^2}$

4. What is the result when $4x^3 - 5x^2 + x - 3$ is divided by $x - 2$?

   A) $4x + 3 + \dfrac{11}{x-2}$

   B) $4x^2 + 3x - 6$

   C) $4x^2 + 3x + 18$

   D) $4x^2 + 3x + 7 + \dfrac{11}{x-2}$

5. The function $f$ is a parabolic function that intersects the $x$-axis. Which of the following statements must be true?

   A) The function has at least one real root.

   B) The function has no real roots.

   C) The function intersects the positive $y$ axis.

   D) The function has two zeros.

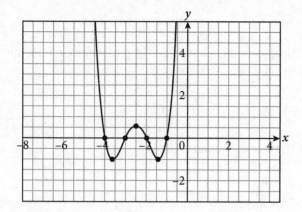

| Age (months) | Height (centimeters) |
|---|---|
| 15 | 80 |
| 18 | 82.5 |
| 21 | 85 |
| 24 | 87.5 |
| 27 | 90 |

6. The function $f(x) = (x+1)(x+2)(x+3)(x+4)$ is graphed above. If $k$ is a constant such that $g(x) = k$ and the system of functions $f$ and $g$ have exactly two real solutions, which of the following could be a value of $k$?

A) $-2$

B) $0$

C) $0.5$

D) $1$

8. The growth of a young child is given in the chart above. If $t$ represents the number of months after 15 and $f(t)$ represents the child's height, which of the following equations is the best model for the data in the age range shown?

A) $f(t) = 80t + 3$

B) $f(t) = \frac{5}{6}t + 80$

C) $f(t) = 80\left(\frac{5}{6}\right)^t$

D) $f(t) = \frac{5}{6}(80)^t$

7. In the equation $ax^4 + bx^3 + cx^2 - dx = 0$, $a$, $b$, $c$, and $d$ are constants. If the equation crosses the $x$-axis at 0, $-2$, 3, and 5, which of the following is a factor of $ax^4 + bx^3 + cx^2 - dx$?

A) $x - 2$

B) $x + 3$

C) $x - 5$

D) $x + 5$

$$\frac{8x}{3(x-5)} + \frac{2x}{3x-15} = \frac{50}{3(x-5)}$$

9. What value(s) of $x$ satisfy the equation above?

A) $0$

B) $5$

C) No solution

D) Any value such that $x \neq 5$

10. If $\frac{6}{2x-3} + 6a = \frac{10}{2x-3} + 4b$ and $3a - 2b = 2$, what is the value of $x$?

A) $\frac{1}{2}$

B) $2$

C) No solution

D) The value cannot be determined from the information given.

## Check Your Work

**1.  B**

**Difficulty:** Easy

**Category:** Exponents

**Getting to the Answer:** Move the expression in parentheses to the denominator to make the sign of the exponent outside positive; do not change the signs of the exponents inside the parentheses. Next, distribute the exponent as usual. Divide the 2 into $-64$, and move $k^{-12}$ back to the numerator and change the sign of its exponent. Work for these steps is shown below:

$$2\left(-4j^3k^{-4}\right)^{-3} = \frac{2}{\left(-4j^3k^{-4}\right)^3}$$

$$= \frac{2}{(-4)^3\left(j^3\right)^3\left(k^{-4}\right)^3}$$

$$= \frac{2}{-64\,j^9k^{-12}}$$

$$= -\frac{k^{12}}{32j^9}$$

Choice **(B)** is the correct answer.

**2.  B**

**Difficulty:** Medium

**Category:** Radicals

**Getting to the Answer:** The question asks you to solve the equation for $L$. Use inverse operations to accomplish the task. Divide both sides of the equation by $2\pi$ and then square both sides. You'll need to apply the exponent to all the terms on the left side of the equation, including the $\pi$:

$$T = 2\pi\sqrt{\frac{L}{g}}$$

$$\frac{T}{2\pi} = \sqrt{\frac{L}{g}}$$

$$\left(\frac{T}{2\pi}\right)^2 = \left(\sqrt{\frac{L}{g}}\right)^2$$

$$\frac{T^2}{4\pi^2} = \frac{L}{g}$$

Finally, multiply both sides by $g$ to remove $g$ from the denominator and isolate $L$:

$$L = \frac{gT^2}{4\pi^2}$$

The correct answer is **(B)**.

**3.  A**

**Difficulty:** Hard

**Category:** Radicals

**Getting to the Answer:** You can't simplify an expression that has different roots (in this case, sixth and third), so rewrite the expression with fraction exponents first, and then use exponent rules to simplify it. The rule for fraction exponents is "power over root"; use this to rewrite the expression:

$$\frac{\sqrt[6]{x^{10}y^{12}}}{\sqrt[3]{x^5y^6}} = \frac{x^{\frac{10}{6}}y^{\frac{12}{6}}}{x^{\frac{5}{3}}y^{\frac{6}{3}}}$$

When dividing like bases, subtract the exponents. Find common denominators as needed:

$$x^{\frac{10}{6}-\frac{5}{3}}y^{\frac{12}{6}-\frac{6}{3}} = x^{\frac{10}{6}-\frac{10}{6}}y^{\frac{12}{6}-\frac{12}{6}} = x^0y^0$$

Any number raised to the zero power becomes 1, so the expression becomes $1 \times 1 = 1$. Choice **(A)** is correct.

**4. D**

**Difficulty:** Medium

**Category:** Polynomial Division

**Getting to the Answer:** Since factoring the numerator does not appear to be practical, use polynomial division to find the result:

$$x - 2 \overline{)\, 4x^3 - 5x^2 + x - 3\,}$$

The first number in this process will be $4x^2$ since $4x^2 \cdot x = 4x^3$:

$$
\begin{array}{r}
4x^2 \phantom{+3x+7} \\
x - 2 \overline{)\, 4x^3 - 5x^2 + x - 3\,} \\
\underline{-\left(4x^3 - 8x^2\right)} \\
3x^2 \phantom{+x}
\end{array}
$$

Next, complete the rest of the polynomial division process:

$$
\begin{array}{r}
4x^2 + 3x + 7 \\
x - 2 \overline{)\, 4x^3 - 5x^2 + x - 3\,} \\
\underline{-\left(4x^3 - 8x^2\right)} \\
3x^2 + x \\
\underline{-\left(3x^2 - 6x\right)} \\
7x - 3 \\
\underline{-(7x - 14)} \\
11
\end{array}
$$

Remember that you are dividing by $x - 2$, so the remainder of 11 is actually $\dfrac{11}{x - 2}$. **(D)** is correct.

**5. A**

**Difficulty:** Easy

**Category:** Graphs of Polynomial Functions

**Getting to the Answer:** The key to this question is knowing that an $x$-intercept is another word for root, or zero; those three terms are synonyms. Even though the question stem does not say how many roots $f$ has, you know it must have at least one if it intersects the $x$-axis. **(A)** is correct. Watch out for trap answer (D), which does not consider the case when a parabola touches the $x$-axis at one point but does not cross it.

**6. D**

**Difficulty:** Medium

**Category:** Graphs of Polynomial Functions

**Strategic Advice:** Working backward from the answer choices saves time.

**Getting to the Answer:** The solution or solutions of a system of functions, like a system of equations, can be found at the points of intersection. Because the function $g(x)$ is equal to a constant, all $x$-values produce the same output—it must represent a horizontal line. A horizontal line and a 4th degree function could intersect 0, 1, 2, 3, or 4 times. Set each of the answer choices equal to $k$ and sketch the resulting functions on the graph. You'll see that only $g(x) = 1$ intersects $f$ exactly twice, so **(D)** is correct. Pay special attention to the scale of the axes to avoid trap answers like (A).

**7. C**

**Difficulty:** Medium

**Category:** Graphs of Polynomial Functions

**Getting to the Answer:** The question is asking for a factor of the function and tells you where the function crosses the $x$-axis. The roots are the $y$-values where the graph crosses the $x$-axis. To find the factors from the roots, consider what expressions would produce a value of zero. Thus, if the roots are at 0, $-2$, 3, and 5, then the factored form of this equation must be $x(x + 2)(x - 3)(x - 5)$ because plugging in any one of the four roots will equal zero. The only factor that appears in the answer choices is $x - 5$, so **(C)** is correct.

## 8. B

**Difficulty:** Easy

**Category:** Modeling Growth and Decay

**Strategic Advice:** Determining the type of growth represented by the data will help to eliminate half of the choices immediately. Look at what happens to the height from each measurement to the next. From 15 to 18 months, the child's height increases by 2.5 centimeters. The same is true for 18 to 21 months, and for 21 to 24 months, and so on. Since 2.5 centimeters are added each equal time interval, the best model for this data would be linear.

**Getting to the Answer:** Because this growth is linear, eliminate choices (C) and (D) immediately because they represent exponential growth. The remaining two choices differ in both the coefficient of $t$ and the value being added. When linear growth is modeled with the equation $y = mx + b$, $m$ represents the rate of growth and $b$ represents the starting amount. In this case, the starting height is 80 centimeters and the growth rate is 2.5 centimeters every 3 months, or $\frac{5}{6}$ centimeter per month, so choice **(B)** is correct.

## 9. C

**Difficulty:** Hard

**Category:** Rational Expressions and Equations

**Getting to the Answer:** Because the denominators are the same (just written in different forms), multiplying both sides of the equation by $3x - 15$ will immediately clear all the fractions, the result of which is a much easier equation to solve:

$$8x + 2x = 50$$
$$10x = 50$$
$$x = 5$$

Because there are variables in the denominator, you must check the solution to make sure it is not extraneous. When $x = 5$, each of the denominators is equal to 0, and division by 0 is not possible. Therefore, there is no solution to the equation, making **(C)** the correct answer.

## 10. B

**Difficulty:** Hard

**Category:** Rational Expressions and Equations

**Getting to the Answer:** Begin by putting the $x$ terms on one side and the $a$ and $b$ terms on the other for the first equation:

$$6a - 4b = \frac{10}{2x - 3} - \frac{6}{2x - 3} = \frac{10 - 6}{2x - 3} = \frac{4}{2x - 3}$$

Now note that the left side of the equation is $6a - 4b$, which is equivalent to $2(3a - 2b)$. The question states that $3a - 2b = 2$. So $6a - 4b = 2(3a - 2b) = 2(2) = 4$. Substitute 4 for $6a - 4b$, multiply both sides by $2x - 3$ to clear the fractions, and solve for $x$:

$$4 = \frac{4}{2x - 3}$$
$$4(2x - 3) = 4$$
$$2x - 3 = 1$$
$$2x = 4$$
$$x = 2$$

Because "No solution" is an answer choice, make sure that $x = 2$ is not an extraneous solution before selecting choice (B). When $x = 2$, the denominator $2x - 3 \neq 0$. Thus, $x = 2$ is a valid solution, and the answer is **(B)**.

# Exponents

## LEARNING OBJECTIVE

After this lesson, you will be able to:

- Apply exponent rules

## To answer a question like this:

The expression $x\left(x^3 y^2\right)^{-4}$ is equivalent to which of the following?

A) $\dfrac{1}{y^2}$

B) $\dfrac{1}{x^4}$

C) $\dfrac{1}{x^{11} y^8}$

D) $\dfrac{1}{x^{16} y^8}$

## You need to know this:

| Rule | Example |
|---|---|
| When multiplying two terms with the same base, add the exponents. | $a^b \cdot a^c = a^{(b+c)} \rightarrow 4^2 \cdot 4^3 = 4^{2+3} = 4^5$ |
| When dividing two terms with the same base, subtract the exponents. | $\dfrac{a^b}{a^c} = a^{(b-c)} \rightarrow \dfrac{4^3}{4^2} = 4^{3-2} = 4^1$ |
| When raising a power to another power, multiply the exponents. | $(a^b)^c = a^{(bc)} \rightarrow (4^3)^2 = 4^{3 \cdot 2} = 4^6;$ $(2x^2)^3 = 2^3 x^{2 \cdot 3} = 8x^6$ |
| When raising a product to a power, apply the power to all factors in the product. | $(ab)^c = a^c \cdot b^c \rightarrow (2m)^3 = 2^3 \cdot m^3 = 8m^3$ |
| Any non-zero term raised to the zero power equals 1. | $a^0 = 1 \rightarrow 4^0 = 1$ |
| A base raised to a negative exponent can be rewritten as the reciprocal raised to the positive of the original exponent. | $a^{-b} = \dfrac{1}{a^b}; \quad \dfrac{1}{a^{-b}} = a^b \rightarrow 4^{-2} = \dfrac{1}{4^2}; \quad \dfrac{1}{4^{-2}} = 4^2$ |
| A negative number raised to an even exponent will produce a positive result; a negative number raised to an odd exponent will produce a negative result. | $(-2)^4 = 16$, but $(-2)^3 = -8$ |

**You need to do this:**

- Identify the appropriate rule by looking at the operation
- Apply the rule
- Repeat as necessary

SAT exponent questions should be quick points. Make sure you memorize the rules in the table above before test day.

**Explanation:**

You'll need several exponent rules to answer the question at the beginning of this lesson. The order of operations dictates that you start with the negative exponent. When one power is raised to another, multiply the exponents:

$$x\left(x^3y^2\right)^{-4} = x\left(x^{3(-4)}y^{2(-4)}\right) = x\left(x^{-12}y^{-8}\right)$$

The x out front has no exponent, which means it is raised to the power of 1. To do the multiplication, add the exponents:

$$x^1\left(x^{-12}y^{-8}\right) = x^{-11}y^{-8}$$

Finally, because this expression is not among the choices, you'll need the rule for negative exponents: you can write them as the reciprocal of the positive exponent. Like this:

$$x^{-11}y^{-8} = \frac{1}{x^{11}y^8}$$

The correct answer is **(C)**.

If exponents give you trouble, study the rules in the table above and try these Drill questions before completing the Try on Your Own questions that follow. Simplify each expression (without using a calculator). Turn the page to see the answers.

**Drill**

a. $3^4$

b. $(-5)^3$

c. $4^2 \times 2^{-4}$

d. $\dfrac{2^4}{2^3}$

e. $\left(\dfrac{1}{3}\right)^{-2}$

f. $\left(2^2\right)^3$

g. $(7x)^2$

h. $\left(-\dfrac{1}{2}\right)^{-2}$

i. $\left(a^2\right)^5$

j. $\left(b^3\right)^{-6}$

## Try on Your Own

**Directions:** Take as much time as you need on these questions. Work carefully and methodically. There will be an opportunity for timed practice at the end of the chapter.

---

HINT: For Q1, how can you get all three bases to have the same value?

---

1. What is the value of $\dfrac{3^5 \times 27^3}{81^3}$ ?

---

HINT: For Q2, look for common factors in the numerator and denominator.

---

$$\frac{18x^4 + 27x^3 - 36x^2}{9x^2}$$

2. If $x \neq 0$, which of the following is equivalent to the expression above?

   A) $2x^2 + 3x - 4$

   B) $2x^2 + 3x - 6$

   C) $2x^4 + 3x^3 - 4x^2$

   D) $2x^6 + 3x^5 - 4x^4$

3. Human blood contains three primary cell types: red blood cells (RBC), white blood cells (WBC), and platelets. In an adult male, a single microliter $(1 \times 10^{-3}$ milliliters) of blood contains approximately $5.4 \times 10^6$ RBC, $7.5 \times 10^3$ WBC, and $3.5 \times 10^5$ platelets on average. What percentage of an adult male's total blood cell count is comprised of red blood cells?

   A) 1.30%

   B) 6.21%

   C) 60.79%

   D) 93.79%

4. If $n^3 = -8$, what is the value of $\dfrac{\left(n^2\right)^3}{\dfrac{1}{n^2}}$ ?

---

HINT: For Q5, how can you get rid of the fraction on the left side?

---

$$\frac{x^{5r}}{x^{3r-2s}} = x^t$$

5. If $r + s = 6$, what is the value of $t$ in the equation above?

   A) 6

   B) 12

   C) 18

   D) 30

## Radicals

| LEARNING OBJECTIVE |
| --- |
| After this lesson, you will be able to: |
| • Apply radical rules |

### To answer a question like this:

$$\frac{\sqrt[3]{x} \cdot x^{\frac{5}{2}} \cdot x}{\sqrt{x}}$$

If $x^n$ is the simplified form of the expression above, what is the value of $n$ ?

Drill answers:

a. $3^4 = 3 \times 3 \times 3 \times 3 = 81$

b. $(-5)^3 = (-5) \times (-5) \times (-5) = -125$

c. $4^2 \times 2^{-4} = \frac{16}{16} = 1$

d. $\frac{2^4}{2^3} = 2^1 = 2$

e. $\left(\frac{1}{3}\right)^{-2} = \left(\frac{3}{1}\right)^2 = 9$

f. $\left(2^2\right)^3 = 2^{2 \times 3} = 2^6 = 64$

g. $(7x)^2 = 49x^2$

h. $\left(-\frac{1}{2}\right)^{-2} = (-2)^2 = 4$

i. $\left(a^2\right)^5 = a^{10}$

j. $\left(b^3\right)^{-6} = b^{-18} = \frac{1}{b^{18}}$

## You need to know this:

| Rule | Example |
|---|---|
| When a fraction is under a radical, you can rewrite it using two radicals: one containing the numerator and the other containing the denominator. | $\sqrt{\dfrac{a}{b}} = \dfrac{\sqrt{a}}{\sqrt{b}} \rightarrow \sqrt{\dfrac{4}{9}} = \dfrac{\sqrt{4}}{\sqrt{9}} = \dfrac{2}{3}$ |
| Two factors under a single radical can be rewritten as separate radicals multiplied together. | $\sqrt{ab} = \sqrt{a} \times \sqrt{b} \rightarrow \sqrt{75} = \sqrt{25} \times \sqrt{3} = 5\sqrt{3}$ |
| A radical can be written using a fractional exponent. | $\sqrt{a} = a^{\frac{1}{2}} \rightarrow \sqrt{289} = 289^{\frac{1}{2}}$ <br><br> $\sqrt[3]{a} = a^{\frac{1}{3}} \rightarrow \sqrt[3]{729} = 729^{\frac{1}{3}}$ |
| When you have a fractional exponent, the numerator is the power to which the base is raised, and the denominator is the root to be taken. | $a^{\frac{b}{c}} = \sqrt[c]{a^b} \rightarrow 5^{\frac{2}{3}} = \sqrt[3]{5^2}$ |
| When a number is squared, the original number can be positive or negative, but the square root of a number can only be positive. | If $a^2 = 81$, then $a = \pm 9$, BUT $\sqrt{81} = 9$ only. |
| Cube roots of negative numbers are negative. | $\sqrt[3]{-27} = -3$ |

## You need to do this:

- Identify the appropriate rule by looking at the answer choices. What form do you need to get the expression into? What rule do you need to apply to get there?
- Apply the rule
- Repeat as necessary

SAT Radicals questions should be quick points. Make sure you memorize the rules in the table above before test day.

## Explanation:

Write each factor in the expression in exponential form (using fractional exponents for the radicals). Next, use exponent rules to simplify the expression:

$$\frac{\sqrt[3]{x} \cdot x^{\frac{5}{2}} \cdot x}{\sqrt{x}} = \frac{x^{\frac{1}{3}} \cdot x^{\frac{5}{2}} \cdot x^1}{x^{\frac{1}{2}}}$$

Math

Now add the exponents of the factors that are being multiplied and subtract the exponent of the factor that is being divided, find common denominators, and simplify:

$$= x^{\frac{1}{3}+\frac{5}{2}+\frac{1}{1}-\frac{1}{2}} = x^{\frac{2}{6}+\frac{15}{6}+\frac{6}{6}-\frac{3}{6}}$$

$$= x^{\frac{20}{6}} = x^{\frac{10}{3}}$$

The question states that $n$ is the power of $x$, so the value of $n$ is $\frac{10}{3}$.

If radicals give you trouble, study the rules in the table above and try these Drill questions before completing the following Try on Your Own questions. Simplify each expression (without using a calculator). Turn the page to see the answers.

## Drill

a. $\sqrt{\dfrac{121}{9}}$

b. $\sqrt{225}$

c. $\sqrt{\dfrac{16 \times 125}{5}}$

d. $\sqrt{\dfrac{50}{288}}$

e. $\sqrt[3]{-27}$

f. $\dfrac{\sqrt{5}\sqrt{60}}{\sqrt{3}}$

g. $\dfrac{4\sqrt{21} \times 5\sqrt{2}}{10\sqrt{7}}$

h. $9^{\frac{1}{2}} \times \sqrt{4} \times 81^{\frac{1}{4}}$

i. $\dfrac{\sqrt{81x^2}}{\sqrt{64y^4}}$

j. $\sqrt{\dfrac{x^8}{y^{12}}}$

## Try on Your Own

**Directions:** Take as much time as you need on these questions. Work carefully and methodically. There will be an opportunity for timed practice at the end of the chapter.

$$8 + \frac{\sqrt{2x + 29}}{3} = 9$$

6. What do you need to do before squaring both sides?

For what value of $x$ is the equation above true?

A) $-10$

B) $-2$

C) $19$

D) No solution

$$3x = x + 14$$

$$\sqrt{3z^2 - 11} + 2x = 22$$

7. If $z > 0$, what is the value of $z$ ?

A) 1

B) 3

C) 5

D) 8

8. Which of the following expressions is equivalent to $-x^{\frac{1}{4}}$ ?

A) $-\dfrac{1}{4x}$

B) $-\dfrac{1}{x^4}$

C) $-\sqrt[4]{x}$

D) $\dfrac{1}{\sqrt[4]{-x}}$

For Q9, remember that the denominator of the exponent becomes the root, and the numerator remains the exponent.

9. When simplified, $8^{\frac{4}{3}}$ is what number?

HINT: For Q10, which approach is faster for you? Algebra or Backsolving?

$$\sqrt{3a + 16} - 3 = a - 1$$

10. In the equation above, if $a > 0$, which of the following is a possible value of $a$ ?

A) 3

B) 2

C) 1

D) $-4$

# Polynomials

Math

> **LEARNING OBJECTIVE**
>
> After this lesson, you will be able to:
>
> - Add, subtract, multiply, and factor polynomials

## To answer a question like this:

If $-2x^2 + 5x - 8$ is multiplied by $4x - 9$, what is the coefficient of $x$ in the resulting polynomial?

A) $-77$

B) $-45$

C) $-32$

D) $-13$

## You need to know this:

A **polynomial** is an expression composed of variables, exponents, and coefficients. By definition, a polynomial cannot have a variable in a denominator, and all exponents must be integers. Here are some examples of polynomial and non-polynomial expressions:

| Polynomial | $23x^2$ | $\frac{x}{5} - 6$ | $y^{11} - 2y^6 + \frac{2}{3}xy^3 - 4x^2$ | $z + 6$ |
|---|---|---|---|---|
| **NOT a Polynomial** | $\frac{10}{z} + 13$ | $x^3 y^{-6}$ | $x^{\frac{1}{2}}$ | $\frac{4}{y - 3}$ |

Drill answers:

a. $\dfrac{\sqrt{121}}{\sqrt{9}} = \dfrac{11}{3}$

b. $\sqrt{25} \times \sqrt{9} = 5 \times 3 = 15$

c. $\dfrac{4 \times 5\sqrt{5}}{\sqrt{5}} = 20$

d. $\dfrac{5\sqrt{2}}{12\sqrt{2}} = \dfrac{5}{12}$

e. $-3$

f. $\dfrac{\sqrt{5} \times 2\sqrt{3}\sqrt{5}}{\sqrt{3}} = 2 \times 5 = 10$

g. $\dfrac{4\sqrt{3}\sqrt{7} \times 5\sqrt{2}}{10\sqrt{7}} = \dfrac{20\sqrt{6}}{10} = 2\sqrt{6}$

h. $3 \times 2 \times 3 = 18$

i. $\dfrac{9|x|}{8y^2}$

j. $\dfrac{x^4}{y^6}$

**You need to do this:**

To add and subtract polynomials, start by identifying like terms—that is, terms in which the types of variables and their exponents match. For example, $x^2$ and $3x^2$ are like terms; adding them would give $4x^2$ and subtracting them would give $x^2 - 3x^2 = -2x^2$. Note that you cannot add or subtract unlike terms. For example, there is no way to simplify $x^2 + y$. You can, however, multiply unlike terms: $x^2 \cdot y = x^2 y$.

To multiply two polynomials, multiply each term in the first factor by each term in the second factor, then combine like terms.

To factor a polynomial, find a value or variable that divides evenly into each term, for example: $2x^3 + 2x^2 + 2x = 2x(x^2 + x + 1)$. (Factoring quadratics into binomials is discussed in chapter 12.)

**Explanation:**

Multiply each term in the first factor by each term in the second factor, then combine like terms:

$$\left(-2x^2 + 5x - 8\right)(4x - 9)$$
$$= -2x^2(4x - 9) + 5x(4x - 9) - 8(4x - 9)$$
$$= -8x^3 + 18x^2 + 20x^2 - 45x - 32x + 72$$
$$= -8x^3 + 38x^2 - 77x + 72$$

The coefficient of $x$ is $-77$, so **(A)** is correct.

## Try on Your Own

**Directions:** Take as much time as you need on these questions. Work carefully and methodically. There will be an opportunity for timed practice at the end of the chapter.

11. What is the sum of the polynomials $6a^2 - 17a - 9$ and $-5a^2 + 8a - 2$?

    A) $a^2 - 9a - 11$

    B) $a^2 - 25a - 7$

    C) $11a^2 - 9a - 11$

    D) $11a^2 - 25a - 7$

12. What is the difference when $3x^3 + 7x - 5$ is subtracted from $8x^2 + 4x + 10$?

    A) $5x^2 - 3x + 15$

    B) $-3x^3 - 3x + 5$

    C) $3x^3 - 8x^2 + 3x - 15$

    D) $-3x^3 + 8x^2 - 3x + 15$

HINT: For Q13, as you calculate each term, eliminate choices. Stop when there's only one choice left.

13. If $A = 4x^2 + 7x - 1$ and $B = -x^2 - 5x + 3$, then what is $\frac{3}{2}A - 2B$?

    A) $4x^2 + \frac{31}{2}x - \frac{9}{2}$

    B) $4x^2 + \frac{41}{2}x - \frac{15}{2}$

    C) $8x^2 + \frac{31}{2}x - \frac{9}{2}$

    D) $8x^2 + \frac{41}{2}x - \frac{15}{2}$

HINT: Which is more efficient for you? Math or backsolving the choices?

14. If $x^3 - 9x = 9 - x^2$, which of the following CANNOT be the value of $x$?

    A) $-3$

    B) $-1$

    C) $1$

    D) $3$

$$(2x^2 + 3x - 4)(3x + 2) = 6x^3 + ax^2 - 6x - 8$$

15. In the above equation, $a$ is a constant. If the equation is true for all values of $x$, what is the value of $a$?

    A) $4$

    B) $9$

    C) $13$

    D) $16$

# Polynomial Division

**LEARNING OBJECTIVE**

After this lesson, you will be able to:

- Divide polynomials

## To answer a question like this:

Which of the following is equivalent to $\dfrac{x^2 + 3x + 7}{x + 4}$?

A) $\dfrac{3+7}{4}$

B) $x + \dfrac{3}{4}$

C) $3 + \dfrac{7}{x+4}$

D) $x - 1 + \dfrac{11}{x+4}$

## You need to know this:

To divide polynomials, you can use an approach called **polynomial long division**. This process is similar to ordinary long division, except that you use polynomials instead of numbers. In the process described below, the *dividend* is the polynomial to be divided, the *divisor* is the polynomial you are dividing the dividend by, and the *quotient* is the result of the division.

## You need to do this:

- Start with the dividend arranged so that the powers are in descending order, for example: $x^4 + x^3 + x + 1$. If any terms are missing, put in zeros, like this: $x^4 + x^3 + 0x^2 + x + 1$. Write the problem using a long division sign.
- Divide the first term of the dividend by the first term of the divisor to yield the first term of the quotient.
- Multiply the divisor by the first term of the quotient.
- Subtract the product you got in the last step from the dividend, then bring down the next term, just as you would in ordinary long division. Use the result as the new dividend.
- Repeat the process until you arrive at the remainder.

### Explanation:

To divide $x^2 + 3x + 7$ by $x + 4$, set up a long division problem:

$$x + 4 \overline{)\, x^2 + 3x + 7}$$

Start by dividing the first term of the dividend, $x^2$, by the first term of the divisor, $x$. Multiply the entire divisor by $x$ and subtract this product from the dividend:

$$
\begin{array}{r}
x \phantom{{} + 3x + 7} \\
x + 4 \overline{)\, x^2 + 3x + 7} \\
-\left(x^2 + 4x\right) \\
\hline
-x + 7
\end{array}
$$

Next, divide the first term of the result of this subtraction, $-x$, by the first term of the divisor, $x$, to get $-1$. Repeat the process of multiplying and subtracting:

$$
\begin{array}{r}
x - 1 \phantom{x + 7} \\
x + 4 \overline{)\, x^2 + 3x + 7} \\
-\left(x^2 + 4x\right) \\
\hline
-x + 7 \\
-(-x - 4) \\
\hline
+11
\end{array}
$$

You're left with a remainder of 11. Put this over the divisor, $x + 4$, and you're done. The result of the division is $x - 1 + \dfrac{11}{x + 4}$, which is choice **(D)**.

## Try on Your Own

**Directions:** Take as much time as you need on these questions. Work carefully and methodically. There will be an opportunity for timed practice at the end of the chapter.

HINT: For Q16, because $a - 3$ is not a factor of the numerator, you'll have to use polynomial long division.

16. Which of the following is equivalent to $\dfrac{2a^2 - 5a - 1}{a - 3}$?

    A) $2a - 2$

    B) $2a + 1 - \dfrac{2}{a - 3}$

    C) $2a + \dfrac{2}{a - 3}$

    D) $2a + 1 + \dfrac{2}{a - 3}$

HINT: For Q17, if the fraction simplifies to $ax + b$, the denominator divides evenly into the numerator. Does that suggest another approach?

$$\dfrac{6x^2 + 19x + 10}{2x + 5}$$

17. If $ax + b$ represents the simplified form of the expression above, then what is the value of $a + b$?

    A) 2

    B) 3

    C) 5

    D) 6

18. Which of the following is equivalent to $\dfrac{4x^2 - 6x}{2x + 2}$?

    A) $2x - \dfrac{10}{2x + 2}$

    B) $2x - 5 + \dfrac{10}{2x + 2}$

    C) $2x - 3$

    D) $2x + 5 - \dfrac{10}{2x + 2}$

HINT: The quotient (result of division) times the divisor (the denominator) equals the dividend (the numerator.) For Q19, stop as soon as you have the value of $t$.

19. The equation $\dfrac{36x^2 + 16x - 21}{tx - 4} = -9x + 5 - \dfrac{1}{tx - 4}$ is true for all values of $x$ for which $x \ne \dfrac{4}{t}$, where $t$ is a constant. What is the value of $t$?

    A) $-20$

    B) $-4$

    C) 4

    D) 12

20. If the polynomial $f(x)$ is evenly divisible by $x - 5$ and the polynomial $g(x) = f(x) + 4$, what is the value of $g(5)$?

    A) $-4$

    B) 0

    C) 4

    D) 9

# Graphs of Polynomial Functions

**LEARNING OBJECTIVE**

After this lesson, you will be able to:

- Define root, solution, zero, and *x*-intercept and identify them on the graph of a nonlinear function

**To answer a question like this:**

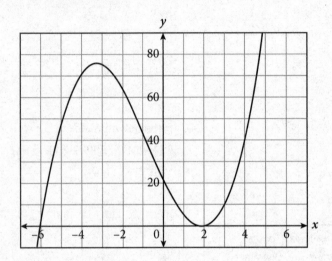

Which of the following could be the function whose graph is shown above?

A) $f(x) = (x - 6)(x + 2)^2$

B) $f(x) = (x + 6)(x - 2)^2$

C) $f(x) = 3x + 23$

D) $f(x) = 6x + 23$

## You need to know this:

When applied to polynomial functions, the words **root**, **solution**, **zero**, and ***x*-intercept** all mean the same thing: the *x*-values on the function's graph where the function touches or crosses the *x*-axis. You can find the roots of a polynomial function by setting each factor of the polynomial equal to zero. For example, the polynomial function $f(x) = x^2 + x$ factors into $f(x) = x(x + 1)$. Set each factor equal to zero to find that $x = 0$ and $x = -1$. These are the function's solutions, also known as zeros. A solution can be represented using the coordinate pair $(x, 0)$.

Note that if a function crosses the *x*-axis, the factor associated with that *x*-intercept will have an odd exponent. If the function touches but does not cross the *x*-axis, the factor associated with that zero will have an even exponent. For example, the function $f(x) = x(x + 1)$ will cross the *x*-axis at $x = 0$ and $x = -1$, while the function $f(x) = x^2(x + 1)$ will cross the *x*-axis at $x = -1$ but only touch the *x*-axis at $x = 0$.

## You need to do this:

- Identify the *x*-values where the function crosses or touches the *x*-axis.
- For each *x*-intercept, change the sign of the *x*-value and add it to the variable *x* to find the associated factor. For example, if the function crosses the *x*-axis at $x = -1$, then the factor associated with that root must be $x + 1$ (since $x + 1 = 0$ will produce the solution $x = -1$).
- Recognize that if the function only touches the *x*-axis without crossing it, the factor must have an even exponent.

## Explanation:

Start by looking at the answer choices. The function is clearly not linear, so rule out (C) and (D). Next, look at the *x*-intercepts on the graph: the function crosses the *x*-axis at $x = -6$ and touches the *x*-axis at $x = 2$. Remember that the *x*-intercepts occur where the factors of the function equal zero. For the *x*-intercepts to be $-6$ and 2, the factors of the function must be $(x + 6)$ and $(x - 2)$. Because the function touches, but does not cross, the *x*-axis at $x = 2$, the $(x - 2)$ factor must have an even exponent. **(B)** is correct.

## Try on Your Own

**Directions:** Take as much time as you need on these questions. Work carefully and methodically. There will be an opportunity for timed practice at the end of the chapter.

---

HINT: For Q21, set each factor equal to 0 and solve for x to find the x-intercepts.

---

21. Which of the following could be the equation of the graph above?

    A) $y = x^2(x + 4)(x - 6)$

    B) $y = x(x + 4)(x - 6)$

    C) $y = x^2(x - 4)(x + 6)$

    D) $y = x(x - 4)(x + 6)$

| x | h(x) |
|----|------|
| −3 | 6 |
| −1 | 0 |
| 0 | −5 |
| 2 | −8 |

22. The function h is defined by a polynomial. The table above gives some of the values of x and h(x). Which of the following must be a factor of h(x) ?

    A) $x - 8$

    B) $x - 1$

    C) $x + 1$

    D) $x + 5$

---

HINT: In Q23, the definition of the *b* function has a variable in the denominator. What does this tell you about the value of *x*?

---

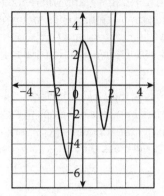

23. The graph of the function $a(x)$ is shown above. If $b(x) = \dfrac{1}{x}$, which of the following is a true statement about $b(a(x))$ ?

    A) $b(a(x))$ is defined for all real numbers.

    B) $b(a(x))$ is undefined for exactly one real value of x.

    C) $b(a(x))$ is undefined for exactly four real values of x.

    D) $b(a(x))$ is undefined for all real numbers.

24. If function *f* has exactly two distinct real zeros, which of the following graphs could be the complete graph of *f*(*x*) ?

A)

B)

C)

D)

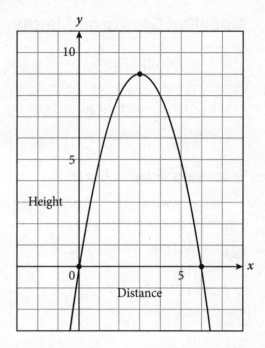

25. The graph of $f(x) = -(x - 3)^2 + 9$ above approximates the trajectory of a water balloon shot from a cannon at ground level. In terms of the trajectory, what information is represented by a root of this function?

A) The maximum height achieved by the balloon.

B) The total horizontal distance traveled by the balloon.

C) The maximum speed of the balloon.

D) The initial acceleration of the balloon.

# Modeling Growth and Decay

## LEARNING OBJECTIVES

After this lesson, you will be able to:

- Determine whether the growth or decay described in a question is linear or exponential
- Apply the linear and exponential equations to answer growth and decay questions

## To answer a question like this:

A certain car costs $20,000. If the car loses 15 percent of its value each year, approximately how much will the car be worth after 5 years?

A) $5,000

B) $8,900

C) $11,200

D) $15,000

## You need to know this:

The terms **growth** and **decay** refer to situations in which some quantity is increased or decreased over time according to a rule.

- If the rule is to add or subtract the same amount each time, then the growth or decay is **linear**. Because the graph of linear growth and decay is a line, you can use the slope-intercept form of a line—$y = mx + b$—to describe it, where $b$ is the starting amount and $m$ is the amount added or subtracted each time.

Linear Growth

Linear Decay

- If the rule is to multiply or divide by the same amount each time, then the growth or decay is **exponential**. The general form of an exponential function is $y = ab^x$, where $a$ is the $y$-intercept and $b$ is the amount multiplied or divided each time. Given that $a > 0$ and $b > 1$, when $x$ is positive, the equation describes exponential growth, and when $x$ is negative, the equation describes exponential decay.

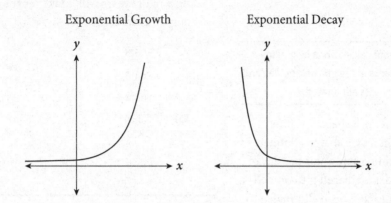

- When an exponential growth or decay question gives you a growth rate over time, you can use a modified version of the exponential function, $f(x) = f(0)(1 + r)^t$, where $f(0)$ is the amount at time $t = 0$ and $r$ is the growth rate (or decay rate, if negative) expressed as a decimal.

## You need to do this:

- First, determine whether the situation described is linear or exponential. If an amount is added or subtracted each time, then the growth is linear; if the original quantity is multiplied or divided by some amount each time, then the growth is exponential.
- Plug the values from the question into the appropriate equation and solve for the missing quantity.
- When the numbers are manageable, you might be able to avoid using the equations by simply carrying out the operations described. For example, if the question says that an amount doubles each day and asks for the amount after three days, then doubling the initial quantity three times will likely be more efficient than plugging the numbers into the exponential growth equation.

## Explanation:

The question says that the car loses value at a certain rate per year, which means the question involves exponential decay. The question gives three pieces of important information: the initial value $f(0) = \$20,000$, the rate $r = -0.15$, and the time $t = 5$. The question asks for the approximate value of the car after 5 years, which is $f(5)$. The rate must be expressed as a decimal, and since the value of the car is decreasing, the rate is also negative. Plug these values into the equation $f(t) = f(0)(1 + r)^t$ and use your calculator to solve:

$$f(t) = 20,000(1 - 0.15)^5$$

$$= 20,000(0.85)^5 \approx \$8,900$$

Choice **(B)** is correct.

## Try on Your Own

**Directions:** Take as much time as you need on these questions. Work carefully and methodically. There will be an opportunity for timed practice at the end of the chapter.

---

HINT: For Q26, keep track of your calculations by making a chart with the number of applicants at the start of the day and the number of applicants eliminated.

---

26. In determining the winner of a speech-writing competition, a panel of judges is able to eliminate one-quarter of the remaining applicants per day of deliberations. If 128 students entered the competition, how many applicants have been eliminated by the end of the third day of deliberations?

27. The manager of a health club determines that the club's membership has increased at a rate of 16 percent per year for the past four years. The club currently has 42 members. If this trend continues, how many years will it take for the club's membership to exceed 100 members?

A)  4 years

B)  5 years

C)  6 years

D)  7 years

---

HINT: For Q28, no original amount is given. What would be a good number to pick for that amount?

---

28. Radioactive carbon dating can determine how long ago an organism lived by measuring how much of the $^{14}C$ in the sample has decayed. $^{14}C$ is an isotope of carbon that has a half-life of 5,600 years. Half-life is the amount of time it takes for half of the original amount to decay. If a sample of a petrified tree contains 6.25 percent of its original $^{14}C$, how long ago did the tree die?

A)  22,400 years

B)  28,000 years

C)  35,000 years

D)  89,600 years

HINT: For Q29, is she saving more, the same, or less each
month? What does that tell you about the function?

29. Penelope receives the same amount of money each
month for her allowance. Each month she spends
half of her allowance and puts the rest in a piggy
bank. On Penelope's 8th birthday, the piggy bank
contains $40. If the piggy bank contains $244 after
2 years, what is her monthly allowance? (Ignore the
dollar sign when gridding your response.)

30. At a certain bank, money held in account X earns
a monthly interest equal to 2 percent of the original investment, while account Y earns a monthly
interest equal to 2 percent of the current value of
the account. If $500 is invested into each account,
what is the positive difference between the value of
account X and account Y after three years? (Round
your answer to the nearest dollar and ignore the
dollar sign when gridding your response.)

# Rational Expressions and Equations

> **LEARNING OBJECTIVES**
>
> After this lesson, you will be able to:
>
> - Simplify a rational expression
> - Isolate a variable in a rational equation

## To answer a question like this:

$$\frac{5y + 7}{(y + 4)^2} - \frac{5}{(y + 4)}$$

If the expression above is equal to $\dfrac{-b}{(y + 4)^2}$, where $b$ is a positive constant and $y \neq -4$, what is the value of $b$?

A)  4

B)  7

C)  13

D)  27

## You need to know this:

A **rational expression** is a ratio expressed as a fraction with a polynomial in the denominator. A **rational equation** is an equation that includes at least one rational expression.

- Factors in a rational expression can be canceled when simplifying, but under no circumstances can you do the same with individual terms. Consider, for instance, the expression $\dfrac{x^2 - x - 6}{x^2 + 5x + 6}$. Some test takers will attempt to cancel the $x^2$, $x$, and 6 terms to give $\dfrac{1 - 1 - 1}{1 + 5 + 1} = \dfrac{-1}{7}$, which is *never* correct. Instead, factor the numerator and denominator: $\dfrac{(x + 2)(x - 3)}{(x + 2)(x + 3)}$. Cancel the $x + 2$ factors to get $\dfrac{x - 3}{x + 3}$.

- If a rational expression has a higher-degree numerator than denominator $\left(\text{e.g.,} \dfrac{x^2 + 3}{1 - x}\right)$, it can be simplified using polynomial long division. If a rational expression has a lower-degree numerator than denominator $\left(\text{e.g.,} \dfrac{1 - x}{x^2 + 3}\right)$, it cannot.

- Because rational expressions have polynomial denominators, they will often be undefined for certain values. For example, the expression $\dfrac{x - 4}{x + 2}$ is defined for all values of $x$ except $-2$. This is because when $x = -2$, the denominator of the expression is 0, which would make the expression undefined.

- Beware of undefined expressions when solving rational equations. Take the equation $\dfrac{1}{x + 4} + \dfrac{1}{x - 4} = \dfrac{8}{(x + 4)(x - 4)}$, for instance. After multiplying both sides by the common denominator $(x + 4)(x - 4)$, you have $(x - 4) + (x + 4) = 8$. Solving for $x$ yields $2x = 8$, which simplifies to $x = 4$. When 4 is substituted for $x$, however, you get 0 in the denominator of both the second and third terms of the equation. Therefore, this equation is said to have no solution. (A value that causes a denominator to equal 0 is called an extraneous solution.)

## You need to do this:

- Find a common denominator
- Multiply each term by the common denominator and simplify
- Make sure you haven't found an extraneous solution

## Explanation:

Start by setting the two expressions equal:

$$\frac{5y+7}{(y+4)^2} - \frac{5}{y+4} = \frac{-b}{(y+4)^2}$$

Next, get rid of the fractions. To do this, multiply both sides of the equation by the common denominator, $(y+4)^2$:

$$\left( \frac{5y+7}{(y+4)^2} - \frac{5}{y+4} = \frac{-b}{(y+4)^2} \right)(y+4)^2$$

$$5y + 7 - 5(y+4) = -b$$

Now all that remains is to solve for $b$:

$$5y + 7 - 5y - 20 = -b$$
$$-13 = -b$$
$$b = 13$$

The correct answer is **(C)**.

## Try on Your Own

**Directions:** Take as much time as you need on these questions. Work carefully and methodically. There will be an opportunity for timed practice at the end of the chapter.

---

HINT: For Q31, multiply both sides by a common denominator or cross-multiply. (They are the same thing.)

---

31. Given the equation $\dfrac{6}{x} = \dfrac{3}{k+2}$ and the constraints $x \neq 0$ and $k \neq -2$, what is $x$ in terms of $k$?

    A) $x = 2k + 4$

    B) $x = 2k + 12$

    C) $x = 2k - \dfrac{1}{4}$

    D) $x = \dfrac{1}{4}k + 12$

---

HINT: For Q32, how do you add fractions with different denominators?

---

$$\dfrac{3a+9}{(a-3)^2} + \dfrac{-9}{3a-9}$$

32. In the expression above, $(a-3)^2 = 6$. What is the value of the expression?

33. If $a > 6$, which of the following is equivalent to
$$\dfrac{\dfrac{2}{a}}{\dfrac{1}{a-2} + \dfrac{1}{a-6}}?$$

    A) $2a^2 - 16a + 24$

    B) $a(2a - 8)$

    C) $\dfrac{a^2 - 8a + 12}{a^2 - 4a}$

    D) $\dfrac{2a - 8}{a^2 - 8a + 12}$

34. If $\dfrac{5}{x+2} = \dfrac{2}{x+1} + \dfrac{1}{2}$ and $x > 1$, what is the value of $x$?

    A) 2

    B) 3

    C) 6

    D) 9

35. If $\dfrac{16}{7x+4} + A$ is equivalent to $\dfrac{49x^2}{7x+4}$, what is $A$ in terms of $x$?

    A) $7x + 4$

    B) $7x - 4$

    C) $49x^2$

    D) $49x^2 + 4$

---

HINT: A common denominator is possible, but messy. Is there another approach to Q36?

---

$$\dfrac{c+5}{6c} + \dfrac{2}{2c-4} = 0$$

36. The equation above is true for all values of $c$ such that $c \neq -6$ and $c \neq 2$. If $c < 0$, what is the value of $c$?

    A) $-20$

    B) $-10$

    C) 1

    D) 10

## On Test Day

Remember that the SAT doesn't ask you to show your work. If you find the algebra in a question challenging, there is often another way to get to the answer.

Try this question first using algebra and then using the Picking Numbers strategy from chapter 3. Which approach do you find easier? There's no right or wrong answer—just remember your preferred approach and try it first if you see a question like this on test day.

37. The expression $\dfrac{3x-1}{x-4}$ is equivalent to which of the following?

   A) $\dfrac{1}{2}$

   B) $3x - \dfrac{1}{x-4}$

   C) $3 - \dfrac{11}{x-4}$

   D) $3 + \dfrac{11}{x-4}$

The correct answer and both ways of solving can be found at the end of this chapter.

## How Much Have You Learned?

**Directions:** For testlike practice, give yourself 18 minutes to complete this question set. Be sure to study the explanations, even for questions you got right. They can be found at the end of this chapter.

38. An object launched upwards at an angle has parabolic motion. The height, $h$, of a projectile at time $t$ is given by the equation $h = \frac{1}{2}at^2 + v_v t + h_0$, where $a$ is the acceleration due to gravity, $v_v$ is the vertical component of the velocity, and $h_0$ is the initial height. Which of the following equations correctly represents the object's acceleration due to gravity in terms of the other variables?

    A) $a = \dfrac{h - v_v t - h_0}{t}$

    B) $a = \dfrac{h - v_v t - h_0}{2t^2}$

    C) $a = \dfrac{2(h - v_v t - h_0)}{t^2}$

    D) $a = t\sqrt{2(h - v_v t - h_0)}$

39. If $\left(16^{3x}\right)\left(32^x\right)\left(8^{3x}\right) = \dfrac{\left(4^{6x}\right)\left(32^{3x}\right)}{4}$, then what is the value of $x$?

    A) $-2$

    B) $-1$

    C) $1$

    D) $2$

40. Given that $\dfrac{y}{\sqrt{x} - 3} = \dfrac{\sqrt{x} + 3}{3}$ and $2x + 42 = 9x - 63$, what is the value of $y$?

$$y = \frac{3x^2 + 7}{x - 3}$$

41. Which of the following expressions is equivalent to $y$?

    A) $3x + 9 - \dfrac{20}{x - 3}$

    B) $3x + 9 + \dfrac{34}{x - 3}$

    C) $3x + 43$

    D) $3x^2 + \dfrac{9}{x - 3}$

$$z = 15x^2 + 10xy - 6x - 4y$$

42. For which of the ordered pairs, $(x, y)$, below is $z \neq 0$?

    A) $(-3, 2)$

    B) $(-2, 3)$

    C) $\left(\dfrac{2}{5}, 0\right)$

    D) $\left(\dfrac{2}{5}, 10\right)$

43. $\sqrt{27^{\frac{2}{3}} + 128^{\frac{4}{7}}} =$

44. Which of the following is equivalent to $\dfrac{4x^2 - 8}{2x + 3}$ ?

    A) $2x - 3 + \dfrac{1}{2x + 3}$

    B) $2x - 2$

    C) $2x + 3 - \dfrac{1}{2x + 3}$

    D) $2x + 4$

$g(x) = \dfrac{2}{2x^3 - 12x^2 - 14x}$

45. For which of the following values of $x$ is the function $g(x)$ defined?

    A) $-1$

    B) $0$

    C) $1$

    D) $7$

$x^3 + 4 = 3x^2 - 7x + 25$

46. For what real value of $x$ is the above equation valid?

    A) 0

    B) 3

    C) 4

    D) 7

47. Which of the following equations has a graph for which all roots are greater than 0 ?

    A) $y = 4|x|$

    B) $y = x^2 - 4$

    C) $y = (x - 2)^2$

    D) $y = x(x - 2)^2$

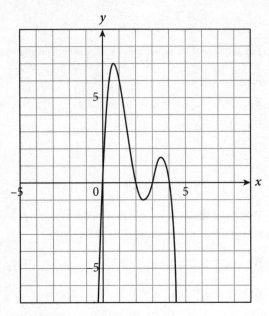

49. A marketing team conducted a study on the use of smartphones. In a certain metropolitan area, there were 1.6 million smartphone users at the end of 2018. The marketing team predicted that the number of smartphone users would increase by 35 percent each year beginning in 2019. If $y$ represents the number of smartphone users in this metropolitan area after $x$ years, then which of the following equations best models the number of smartphone users in this area over time?

A) $y = 1,600,000(1.35)^x$

B) $y = 1,600,000(35)^x$

C) $y = 35x + 1,600,000$

D) $y = 1.35x + 1,600,000$

48. The graph of the function
$f(x) = -x(x - 4)(x - 3)(x - 2)$ is shown above.
If $f(x) = 0$, how many real solutions exist?

A) 0

B) 2

C) 3

D) 4

# Reflect

**Directions:** Take a few minutes to recall what you've learned and what you've been practicing in this chapter. Consider the following questions, jot down your best answer for each one, and then compare your reflections to the expert responses on the following page. Use your level of confidence to determine what to do next.

How do you multiply two polynomials?

_____

_____

_____

What are the zeros of a polynomial function?

_____

_____

_____

Describe the difference between linear and exponential growth.

_____

_____

_____

Name two ways to simplify rational expressions.

_____

_____

_____

## Expert Responses

How do you multiply two polynomials?

*Distribute each term in the first set of parentheses to each term in the second set, then combine like terms.*

What are the zeros of a polynomial function?

*The zeros are the points at which the value of the function (that is, the y-value) is zero. Think of the zeros as the x-intercepts of the function. The words "roots" and "solutions" mean the same thing.*

Describe the difference between linear and exponential growth.

*Linear growth is modeled by a linear function, with the equation $y = mx + b$, such that the slope of the line is positive. You're essentially adding the same amount over and over again. (In linear decay, the slope of the line is negative, and you're subtracting the same amount over and over again.)*

*Exponential growth is modeled by an exponential function in the form $y = ab^x$, where a is the y-intercept and b is the amount multiplied each time, over and over. The slope of an exponential growth function steepens with increasing x-values. (In exponential decay, b is the amount divided by each time, and the slope starts out steeply negative and flattens with increasing x-values.)*

Name two ways to simplify rational expressions.

*One way is to use polynomial long division, though this will work only if the higher-order polynomial is in the numerator. Another way is to cancel factors that appear in both the numerator and denominator.*

## Next Steps

If you answered most questions correctly in the "How Much Have You Learned?" section, and if your responses to the Reflect questions were similar to those of the SAT expert, then consider exponents and polynomial functions an area of strength and move on to the next chapter. Come back to this topic periodically to prevent yourself from getting rusty.

If you don't yet feel confident, review those parts of this chapter that you have not yet mastered. In particular, review the lessons covering Exponents, Modeling Growth and Decay, and Rational Expressions and Equations as these are high-yield topics on the SAT. Then try the questions you missed again. As always, be sure to review the explanations closely.

# Answers and Explanations

**1.  9**

**Difficulty:** Medium

**Getting to the Answer:** You are not allowed to use your calculator on this question, so look for ways to rewrite the larger numbers as the same base. Memorizing the values of small integers up to the fourth or fifth power will help you see these patterns: $27 = 3^3$ and $81 = 3^4$. Now, rewrite the expression as $\dfrac{3^5 \times \left(3^3\right)^3}{\left(3^4\right)^3}$, which becomes $\dfrac{3^5 \times 3^9}{3^{12}} = \dfrac{3^{14}}{3^{12}}$. Subtract the exponents to get $3^2$, which equals **9**, the correct answer.

**2.  A**

**Difficulty:** Easy

**Getting to the Answer:** Find the greatest common factor (GCF) of both the numerator and the denominator, which in this question happens to be the denominator. Factor out the GCF, $9x^2$, from the numerator and denominator and then cancel what you can:

$$\frac{18x^4 + 27x^3 - 36x^2}{9x^2} = \frac{9x^2\left(2x^2 + 3x - 4\right)}{9x^2}$$

$$= 2x^2 + 3x - 4$$

This matches **(A)**. As an alternate method, you could split the expression up and reduce each term, one at a time:

$$\frac{18x^4 + 27x^3 - 36x^2}{9x^2} = \frac{18x^4}{9x^2} + \frac{27x^3}{9x^2} - \frac{36x^2}{9x^2}$$

$$= 2x^2 + 3x - 4$$

**3.  D**

**Difficulty:** Medium

**Getting to the Answer:** Start by setting up a ratio that compares RBC count to total blood cell count. Manipulate the quantities to make all the exponents the same (to convert $7.5 \times 10^3$ to a product of $10^6$ and another number, move the decimal point in 7.5 three places to the left and write "$\times 10^6$" after it), factor out $10^6$, and then add the quantities in parentheses together. Once there, you can use exponent rules to simplify your equation. Divide through and multiply by 100 to get the RBC component as a percentage:

$$RBC = \frac{5.4 \times 10^6}{5.4 \times 10^6 + 7.5 \times 10^3 + 3.5 \times 10^5}$$

$$= \frac{5.4 \times 10^6}{5.4 \times 10^6 + 0.0075 \times 10^6 + 0.35 \times 10^6}$$

$$= \frac{5.4 \times 10^6}{10^6 (5.4 + 0.0075 + 0.35)}$$

$$= \frac{5.4}{5.7575}$$

Note that the answer choices are, for the most part, far apart. Because 5.4 is relatively close to 5.7575, you can conclude with confidence that the correct answer is likely close to 100%. Therefore, **(D)** is the correct answer. If this question is in the calculator section, you can plug the numbers into your calculator to check:

$$\%RBC = \frac{5.4}{5.7575} \times 100 \approx 93.79\%$$

Choice **(D)** is still correct.

**4.  256**

**Difficulty:** Medium

**Getting to the Answer:** If $n^3 = -8$, then $n = -2$. Simplify the given expression via exponent rules and then plug $-2$ in for $n$:

Grid in **256**.

**5.  B**

**Difficulty:** Hard

**Getting to the Answer:** To simplify the division on the left side of the equation, subtract the powers and combine:

$$\frac{x^{5r}}{x^{3r-2s}} = x^{5r-(3r-2s)}$$

$$= x^{5r-3r+2s}$$

$$= x^{2r+2s}$$

Note that in the expression $2r + 2s$, it is possible to factor out a 2. Thus, $x^{2r+2s} = x^{2(r+s)}$. The question indicates that $r + s = 6$, so $x^{2(r+s)} = x^{2(6)} = x^{12}$. This is equal to $x^t$, so $t = 12$. The answer is **(B)**.

**6. A**

**Difficulty:** Medium

**Getting to the Answer:** Solve equations containing radical expressions the same way you solve any other equation: isolate the variable using inverse operations. Start by subtracting 8 from both sides of the equation, and then multiply by 3. Then, square both sides to remove the radical.

$$8 + \frac{\sqrt{2x + 29}}{3} = 9$$
$$\frac{\sqrt{2x + 29}}{3} = 1$$
$$\sqrt{2x + 29} = 3$$
$$2x + 29 = 9$$

Now you have a simple linear equation that you can solve using more inverse operations: subtract 29 and divide by 2 to find that $x = -10$. Be careful—just because the equation started with a radical and the answer is negative, it does not follow that *"No solution"* is the correct answer. If you plug $-10$ into the expression under the radical, the result is a positive number, which means $-10$ is a perfectly valid solution. Therefore, **(A)** is correct.

**7. C**

**Difficulty:** Medium

**Getting to the Answer:** First, solve for $x$ and plug that value into the second equation. Subtract $x$ from both sides of the equation to get $2x = 14$, so $x = 7$. Plugging this into the second equation gives you $\sqrt{3z^2 - 11} + 2(7) = 22$. Thus, $\sqrt{3z^2 - 11} = 8$. Square both sides of this equation and solve for $z$:

$$3z^2 - 11 = 64$$
$$3z^2 = 75$$
$$z^2 = 25$$
$$z = \pm 5$$

Since the question specifies that $z > 0$, **(C)** is correct.

**8. C**

**Difficulty:** Easy

**Getting to the Answer:** Follow the standard order of operations—deal with the exponent first and then attach the negative sign (because a negative in front of an expression means multiplication by $-1$). The variable $x$ is being raised to the $\frac{1}{4}$ power, so rewrite the term as a radical expression with 4 as the degree of the root and 1 as the power to which the radicand, $x$, is being raised:

$$x^{\frac{1}{4}} = \sqrt[4]{x^1} = \sqrt[4]{x}$$

Now attach the negative to arrive at the correct answer, $-\sqrt[4]{x}$, which is **(C)**.

**9. 16**

**Difficulty:** Medium

**Getting to the Answer:** Because this is a no-calculator question, you need to rewrite the exponent in a way that makes it easier to evaluate: use exponent rules to rewrite $\frac{4}{3}$ as a unit fraction raised to a power. Then write the expression in radical form and simplify:

$$8^{\frac{4}{3}} = \left(8^{\frac{1}{3}}\right)^4$$
$$= \left(\sqrt[3]{8}\right)^4$$
$$= 2^4$$
$$= 2 \times 2 \times 2 \times 2$$
$$= 16$$

**10. A**

**Difficulty:** Medium

**Getting to the Answer:** Start by isolating the radical on the left side of the equation by adding 3 to both sides to get $\sqrt{3a + 16} = a + 2$. Now you can square both sides to get rid of the radical: $3a + 16 = (a + 2)^2 = a^2 + 4a + 4$. Since the right side of this equation is a quadratic, set it equal to 0 in order to determine the solutions: $0 = a^2 + 4a + 4 - (3a + 16) = a^2 + a - 12$. Next, factor the quadratic using reverse FOIL. The two factors of $-12$ that add up to 1 are $-3$ and 4, so $(a - 3)(a + 4) = 0$. Thus, $a$ can be either 3 or $-4$, but the question says $a > 0$, so the only permissible value is 3. **(A)** is correct.

## 11. A

**Difficulty:** Easy

**Getting to the Answer:** Add polynomial expressions by combining like terms. Be careful of the signs of each term. It may help to write the sum vertically, lining up the like terms:

$$6a^2 - 17a - 9$$
$$\underline{+ -5a^2 + 8a - 2}$$
$$a^2 - 9a - 11$$

The correct choice is **(A)**.

## 12. D

**Difficulty:** Medium

**Getting to the Answer:** First, write the question as a subtraction problem. Pay careful attention to which expression is being subtracted so that you distribute the negative sign correctly:

$$8x^2 + 4x + 10 - \left(3x^3 + 7x - 5\right)$$
$$= -3x^3 + 8x^2 - 3x + 15$$

This expression matches **(D)**.

## 13. D

**Difficulty:** Medium

**Getting to the Answer:** Multiply each term in the first expression by $\frac{3}{2}$ and each term in the second expression by $-2$. Then add the two polynomials by writing them vertically and combining like terms. You'll have to find a common denominator to combine the $x$-coefficients and to combine the constant terms:

$$\frac{3}{2}A = \frac{3}{2}\left(4x^2 + 7x - 1\right) = 6x^2 + \frac{21}{2}x - \frac{3}{2}$$
$$-2B = -2\left(-x^2 - 5x + 3\right) = 2x^2 + 10x - 6$$

$$6x^2 + \frac{21}{2}x - \frac{3}{2}$$
$$\underline{+ 2x^2 + \frac{20}{2}x - \frac{12}{2}}$$
$$8x^2 + \frac{41}{2}x - \frac{15}{2}$$

This means **(D)** is correct. Notice that if you are simplifying the expression from left to right, after you find the $x^2$ coefficient, you can eliminate (A) and (B). After you find the $x$ coefficient, you can eliminate (C) and stop your work.

## 14. C

**Difficulty:** Hard

**Getting to the Answer:** In order to solve the equation, move all the terms to one side of the equation and set them equal to 0, then factor the expression. Thus, the given equation becomes $x^3 + x^2 - 9x - 9 = 0$. Think of this as two pairs of terms, $(x^3 + x^2)$ and $(-9x - 9)$. The first pair of terms share a common factor of $x^2$, so they can be written as $x^2(x + 1)$. The second pair share the common factor of $-9$, so they are equivalent to $-9(x + 1)$. So, the equation becomes $x^2(x + 1) - 9(x + 1) = 0$. Now, factor out the $(x + 1)$ term: $(x^2 - 9)(x + 1) = 0$.

In order for the product of two terms to be 0, either one or both must be 0. If $x^2 - 9 = 0$, then $x^2 = 9$ and $x = \pm 3$. Eliminate (A) and (D). If $x + 1 = 0$, then $x = -1$. Eliminate (B), so **(C)** is correct. You could also answer the question using Backsolving by plugging in each answer choice until you found the value for $x$ that did *not* satisfy the equation.

## 15. C

**Difficulty:** Medium

**Strategic Advice:** To multiply two polynomials, multiply each term in the first factor by each term in the second factor, then combine like terms.

**Getting to the Answer:** Multiply each part of the trinomial expression by each part of the binomial one piece at a time and then combine like terms:

$$\left(2x^2 + 3x - 4\right)(3x + 2)$$
$$= 2x^2(3x + 2) + 3x(3x + 2) - 4(3x + 2)$$
$$= 6x^3 + 4x^2 + 9x^2 + 6x - 12x - 8$$
$$= 6x^3 + 13x^2 - 6x - 8$$

Because $a$ represents the coefficient of $x^2$, $a = 13$. Hence, **(C)** is correct.

**Math**

## 16. D

**Difficulty:** Medium

**Getting to the Answer:** Use polynomial long division to simplify the expression:

$$
\begin{array}{r}
2a + 1 \\
a - 3 \overline{\smash{\big)}\, 2a^2 - 5a - 1} \\
\underline{-\left(2a^2 - 6a\right)} \\
a - 1 \\
\underline{-(a - 3)} \\
2
\end{array}
$$

The quotient is $2a + 1$ and the remainder is 2, which will be divided by the divisor in the final answer: $2a + 1 + \dfrac{2}{a - 3}$. Thus, **(D)** is correct.

## 17. C

**Difficulty:** Hard

**Getting to the Answer:** A fraction is the same as division, so you can use polynomial long division to simplify the expression:

$$
\begin{array}{r}
3x + 2 \\
2x + 5 \overline{\smash{\big)}\, 6x^2 + 19x + 10} \\
\underline{-\left(6x^2 + 15x\right)} \\
4x + 10 \\
\underline{-(4x + 10)} \\
0
\end{array}
$$

The simplified expression is $3x + 2$, so $a + b = 3 + 2 = 5$, which is **(C)**. As an alternate approach, you could factor the numerator of the expression and cancel common factors:

$$
\frac{6x^2 + 19x + 10}{2x + 5} = \frac{\cancel{(2x + 5)}(3x + 2)}{\cancel{(2x + 5)}} = 3x + 2
$$

## 18. B

**Difficulty:** Medium

**Getting to the Answer:** Use polynomial long division to simplify the expression:

$$
\begin{array}{r}
2x - 5 \\
2x + 2 \overline{\smash{\big)}\, 4x^2 - 6x} \\
\underline{-\left(4x^2 + 4x\right)} \\
-10x \\
\underline{-(-10x - 10)} \\
+10
\end{array}
$$

The quotient is $2x - 5$ and the remainder is 10. Put the remainder over the divisor and add this to the quotient: $2x - 5 + \dfrac{10}{2x + 2}$; **(B)** is correct.

## 19. B

**Difficulty:** Hard

**Getting to the Answer:** The question provides the quotient of $-9x + 5$ of a division problem and asks you to find the coefficient of the first term of the divisor $tx - 4$. Set this up in polynomial long division form to better understand the relationship between $t$ and the other terms:

$$
\begin{array}{r}
-9x + 5 \\
tx - 4 \overline{\smash{\big)}\, 36x^2 + 16x - 21}
\end{array}
$$

Note that, although the quotient of $-9x + 5$ leaves a remainder of $-\dfrac{1}{tx - 4}$, it's not necessary to consider the remainder when determining the value of $t$.

Viewed this way, it becomes apparent that $36x^2 \div tx = -9x$. Multiplying both sides by $tx$ gives you $tx(-9x) = 36x^2$; therefore, $t(-9) = 36$, so $t = -4$. **(B)** is correct.

## 20. C

**Difficulty:** Hard

**Getting to the Answer:** Because $f(x)$ is divisible by $x - 5$, the value $x - 5$ must be a factor of $f(x)$. Therefore, you can define $f(x)$ as $(x - 5)(n)$, where $n$ is some unknown polynomial. Since $g(x)$ is $f(x) + 4$, you can say that $g(x)$ must be $(x - 5)(n) + 4$.

Thus, $g(5)$ will be $(5 - 5)(n) + 4 = 0(n) + 4 = 0 + 4 = 4$. Therefore, **(C)** is correct.

**21. B**

**Difficulty:** Medium

**Getting to the Answer:** The solutions, or $x$-intercepts, of a polynomial are the factors of that polynomial. This polynomial has $x$-intercepts of $-4$, 0, and 6. The factors that generate those solutions are $(x + 4)$, $x$, and $(x - 6)$. Eliminate (C) and (D) because they do not include those three factors. Because the graph *crosses* the $x$-axis at each $x$-intercept (rather than merely touching the $x$-axis), none of the factors can be raised to an even exponent. Therefore, the $x^2$ term in (A) means it is incorrect. **(B)** is correct.

**22. C**

**Difficulty:** Medium

**Getting to the Answer:** To find the solutions to a polynomial function, factor the polynomial and set each factor equal to 0. The solutions of a function are the $x$-intercepts, so $h(x)$ or the $y$-coordinate of the solution must equal 0. From the chart, the only point with $h(x) = 0$ is at $x = -1$. If $x = -1$, the factor that generates that solution is $x + 1 = 0$ because $(-1) + 1 = 0$. **(C)** is correct.

**23. C**

**Difficulty:** Hard

**Getting to the Answer:** Translate the notation: $b(a(x))$ means $b$ of $a(x)$. This tells you to use $a(x)$ as the input for $b(x)$. You can rewrite this as $\dfrac{1}{a(x)}$, which is the reciprocal of $a(x)$. This new function will be undefined anywhere that $a(x) = 0$ because a denominator of 0 is not permitted. Looking at the graph, you can see that $a(x)$ crosses the $x$-axis four times, at which point the value of $a(x)$ is 0. Since division by 0 is undefined, **(C)** is correct.

**24. A**

**Difficulty:** Easy

**Getting to the Answer:** The phrase "exactly 2 distinct real zeros" means that the graph must have exactly two different $x$-intercepts on the graph. An $x$-intercept is indicated any time that the graph either crosses or touches the $x$-axis. (B) and (D) have three distinct zeros, and (C) has two zeros, but because the graph only touches the $x$-axis, they are the same, not distinct. The only graph with exactly 2 distinct zeros is **(A)**.

**25. B**

**Difficulty:** Easy

**Getting to the Answer:** The keyword "root" in the question stem means that you should examine the places at which the graph intersects the $x$-axis. Thus, this graph has roots at $(0, 0)$ and $(6, 0)$. The $x$-axis, according to the graph, represents the distance traveled by the balloon. When $x = 0$, the distance the water balloon has traveled is 0, which is the balloon's starting position. The initial location of the balloon is not an answer choice, so the correct answer must be what the other root represents. When $x = 6$, the balloon's height is 0, which is the end point of the balloon's trajectory. This value, 6, is a root that represents the total horizontal distance traveled. **(B)** is correct.

**26. 74**

**Difficulty:** Easy

**Strategic Advice:** The goal is to find the number of applicants *eliminated* after four days, not the number remaining.

**Getting to the Answer:** The question describes the decay as the result of removing a certain fraction of the remaining applicants each day. The situation involves repeated division, so this is an example of exponential decay. You could use the exponential decay formula for a given rate, but without a calculator, raising a decimal to an exponent might create time-consuming calculations. Instead, determine how many applicants are eliminated each day and tally them up.

After the first day, the judges eliminate one-fourth of 128, or 32 applicants. This leaves $128 - 32 = 96$ applicants. On the second day, one-fourth of 96, or 24 applicants are eliminated, leaving $96 - 24 = 72$. Finally, on the third day, one-fourth are eliminated again; one-fourth of 72 is 18, so there are $72 - 18 = 54$ applicants remaining. If 54 applicants remain, then $128 - 54 = \mathbf{74}$ applicants have been eliminated.

## 27. C

**Difficulty:** Medium

**Strategic Advice:** This question gives you a percent increase per year, so use the exponential growth equation to solve for the number of years. Note that the question provides unnecessary information. It doesn't matter that the trend has been happening for the last four years because the question asks only about the number of years after the present.

**Getting to the Answer:** Use the formula for exponential growth and plug in the values from the question. The rate is 16%, which as a decimal is 0.16. The rate will remain positive because the question asks about increase, or growth; therefore, $r = 0.16$. The current number of members is 42, so this will be $f(0)$. The goal is at least 100 members so that will be the output, or $f(t)$. Put it all together:

$$f(t) = f(0)(1 + r)^t$$
$$100 = 42(1 + 0.16)^2$$
$$100 = 42(1.16)^t$$

At this point, Backsolving is the best approach. Plug in the number of years for $t$. Because the answer choices are in ascending order, try one of the middle options first. You might be able to eliminate more than one choice at a time. Choice (B) is $t = 5$:

$$42(1.16)^5 \approx 88$$

Since (B) is too small, (A) must be as well. Eliminate them both. Unfortunately, 88 is not close enough to 100 to be certain that **(C)** is the correct answer, so test it:

$$42(1.16)^6 \approx 102$$

Six years is enough to put the club over 100 members. **(C)** is correct.

## 28. A

**Difficulty:** Hard

**Strategy Advice:** The term "half-life" signals exponential decay because it implies repeated division by 2. Using the exponential decay formula here would be complicated. Instead, you can use the percentage given in the problem, along with the Picking Numbers strategy, to figure out how many half-lives have elapsed.

**Getting to the Answer:** Instead of providing an actual amount of $^{14}C$, this question tells you what percent is left. For questions involving percentages of unknown values, it is often a good idea to pick 100. So, assume that the amount of $^{14}C$ in the sample when the tree died is 100. (Fortunately, there is no need to worry about the units here.) After one half-life, the amount of $^{14}C$ is halved to 50. A second half-life leaves 25, a third leaves 12.5, and a fourth leaves 6.25, which is 6.25% of 100. So four half-lives have elapsed. Since each half-life is 5,600 years, the tree died $4 \times 5,600$ or 22,400 years ago. Choice **(A)** is correct.

## 29. 17

**Difficulty:** Medium

**Strategic Advice:** The question describes a situation with linear growth since Penelope is adding the same amount of money to her piggy bank each month. Note: the question is asking for her monthly allowance, but she puts in only half that amount each month.

**Getting to the Answer:** Use the linear growth equation $y = mx + b$. The question gives you the starting amount $b$ ($40), the final amount $y$ ($244), and the amount of time $x$ (2 years, which is 24 months). Plug these values into the equation and solve for $m$, which is the slope, or the rate of change—or in this case, how much Penelope puts in her piggy bank each month:

$$y = mx + b$$
$$244 = m(24) + 40$$
$$24m = 204$$
$$m = 8.5$$

Remember that what she puts in the piggy bank is only half of her allowance, so her total monthly allowance is twice $8.50. Grid in **17**.

## 30. 160
**Difficulty:** Hard

**Strategic Advice:** This question describes both types of growth. Account X adds a percentage of the original amount, which never changes, so the same amount of money is added each month. Account X grows linearly. Account Y, however, adds a percentage of the current balance, which grows monthly, so account Y grows exponentially.

**Getting to the Answer:** Account X begins with $500 (the $y$-intercept, or $b$) and adds 2% of $500, or $500 \times 0.02 = $10$ (the rate of change, or $m$), each month for 3 years, which is 36 months (the input, or $x$). Plug these values into the linear growth equation to solve for the final value of the account:

$$y = mx + b$$
$$y = 10(36) + 500$$
$$y = 360 + 500 = \$860$$

Account Y begins with $500 ($f(0)$) and adds 2%, or 0.02, ($r$) each month for 36 months ($t$). Plug these values into the exponential growth equation to solve for the final value of the account:

$$f(t) = f(0)(1 + r)^t$$
$$f(t) = 500(1 + 0.02)^{36}$$
$$f(t) = 500(1.02)^{36} \approx \$1{,}019.94$$

The positive difference between the two accounts is therefore $1,019.94 − $860 = $159.94. Round up, and grid in **160**.

## 31. A
**Difficulty:** Medium

**Getting to the Answer:** There are two variables and only one equation, but because you're asked to solve for one of the variables *in terms of* the other, you solve the same way you would any other equation, by isolating $x$ on one side of the equation. Cross-multiplying is a quick route to the solution:

$$\frac{6}{x} = \frac{3}{k+2}$$
$$6(k + 2) = 3x$$
$$6k + 12 = 3x$$
$$\frac{6k}{3} + \frac{12}{3} = \frac{3x}{3}$$
$$2k + 4 = x$$

Switch $x$ to the left side of the equation and the result matches **(A)**.

## 32. 3
**Difficulty:** Hard

**Getting to the Answer:** Because the expression is adding fractions with different denominators, you'll need to establish a common denominator. Note that the second fraction is divisible by 3, so you can simplify the expression and then create the common denominator:

$$\frac{3a + 9}{(a - 3)^2} + \frac{-3}{a - 3}$$
$$= \frac{3a + 9}{(a - 3)^2} + \frac{-3}{a - 3} \times \frac{a - 3}{a - 3}$$
$$= \frac{3a + 9}{(a - 3)^2} + \frac{-3a + 9}{(a - 3)^2}$$
$$= \frac{18}{(a - 3)^2}$$

The question specifies that $(a - 3)^2 = 6$, so $\frac{18}{(a - 3)^2} = \frac{18}{6} = 3$. Therefore, the expression equals 3. Grid in **3**.

## 33. C

**Difficulty:** Medium

**Getting to the Answer:** The denominator of the expression contains the sum of two fractions that themselves have different denominators, so start by finding a common denominator:

$$\frac{\dfrac{2}{a}}{\dfrac{a-6}{(a-2)(a-6)}+\dfrac{a-2}{(a-2)(a-6)}}=\frac{\dfrac{2}{a}}{\dfrac{2a-8}{a^2-8a+12}}$$

Next, multiply the numerator of the expression by the reciprocal of the denominator and simplify:

$$\frac{2}{a}\times\frac{a^2-8a+12}{2a-8}$$

$$=\frac{2\left(a^2-8a+12\right)}{2a^2-8a}$$

$$=\frac{a^2-8a+12}{a^2-4a}$$

This expression matches **(C)**.

## 34. B

**Difficulty:** Hard

**Getting to the Answer:** First, subtract $\dfrac{2}{x+1}$ from both sides to consolidate the two rational expressions on the same side of the equation. Next, multiply the left side of the equation by $\dfrac{(x+1)(x+2)}{(x+1)(x+2)}$ to establish a common denominator to enable subtraction of fractions. Next, combine like terms and cross-multiply:

$$\frac{5}{x+2}-\frac{2}{x+1}=\frac{1}{2}$$

$$\frac{5x+5}{x^2+3x+2}-\frac{2x+4}{x^2+3x+2}=\frac{1}{2}$$

$$\frac{3x+1}{x^2+3x+2}=\frac{1}{2}$$

$$6x+2=x^2+3x+2$$

Next, set the equation equal to zero by subtracting $6x+2$ from both sides: $0=x^2-3x$. Now, factor the right side to yield $0=x(x-3)$.

Therefore, either $x=0$ or $x=3$. Since the question specifies that $x>1$, $x$ must equal 3, and **(B)** is correct.

Note that, if you wanted to avoid the algebra, you could backsolve this question by plugging in the answer choices to find which works in the original equation.

## 35. B

**Difficulty:** Hard

**Getting to the Answer:** Because the question states that the expressions are equivalent, set up the equation $\dfrac{16}{7x+4}+A=\dfrac{49x^2}{7x+4}$ and solve for $A$. Start by subtracting the first term from both sides of the equation to isolate $A$. Then, simplify if possible (usually by cancelling common factors). The denominators of the rational terms are the same, so they can be combined:

$$\frac{16}{7x+4}+A=\frac{49x^2}{7x+4}$$

$$A=\frac{49x^2}{7x+4}-\frac{16}{7x+4}$$

$$A=\frac{49x^2-16}{7x+4}$$

$$A=\frac{(7x+4)(7x-4)}{7x+4}$$

$$A=7x-4$$

The correct choice is **(B)**.

## 36. B

**Difficulty:** Medium

**Getting to the Answer:** While you might be tempted to establish a common denominator in order to add the fractions together, that would be extremely cumbersome. Instead, move the second fraction over to the other side of the equation by subtracting it from both sides. Then cross-multiply to simplify:

$$\frac{c+5}{6c}=\frac{-2}{2c-4}$$

$$(c+5)(2c-4)=-12c$$

$$2c^2+6c-20=-12c$$

$$2c^2+18c-20=0$$

$$c^2+9c-10=0$$

$$(c+10)(c-1)=0$$

Therefore, either $c=-10$ or $c=1$. The question specifies that $c<0$, so $c$ must equal $-10$. **(B)** is correct.

**37. D**

**Difficulty:** Medium

**Getting to the Answer:** The first thought at seeing this question may be to try to break the expression into two separate fractions or see if some expression can be factored out. Unfortunately, that does not help with simplifying the expression. You'll need polynomial long division if you're going to use algebra:

$$\begin{array}{r} 3 \phantom{xxxx} \\ x-4\overline{)3x-1} \\ \underline{-(3x-12)} \\ 11 \end{array}$$

That results in the expression $3 + \dfrac{11}{x-4}$, so the correct answer is **(D)**.

Another effective alternative for solving this question is to use Picking Numbers. Choose a small, permissible value like $x = 2$ to find a value for the original expression:

$$\frac{3(2)-1}{(2)-4} = \frac{6-1}{-2} = -\frac{5}{2}$$

Now check each answer choice to see which one is equal to $-\dfrac{5}{2}$ when you plug in $x = 2$:

(A): $\dfrac{3-1}{4} = \dfrac{2}{4} = \dfrac{1}{2}$ ..., eliminate.

(B): $3(2) - \dfrac{1}{(2)-4} = 6 - \dfrac{1}{-2} =$

$6 - \left(-\dfrac{1}{2}\right) = 6 + \dfrac{1}{2} = 6\dfrac{1}{2} = \dfrac{13}{2}$ ..., eliminate.

(C): $3 - \dfrac{11}{(2)-4} = 3 - \dfrac{11}{-2} = 3 - \left(-\dfrac{11}{2}\right) = 3 + \dfrac{11}{2} = \dfrac{17}{2}$
..., eliminate.

(D): $3 + \dfrac{11}{(2)-4} = 3 + \dfrac{11}{-2} = 3 + \left(-\dfrac{11}{2}\right) = -\dfrac{5}{2}$

**38. C**

**Difficulty:** Medium

**Category:** Rational Expressions and Equations

**Getting to the Answer:** When solving polynomial equations for one variable, begin by moving all terms that don't contain that variable (in this case $a$) to one side of the equation. Once there, multiply both sides by 2 to eliminate the fraction, and then divide by $t^2$ to isolate $a$:

$$h = \frac{1}{2}at^2 + v_0t + h_0$$

$$h - v_0t - h_0 = \frac{1}{2}at^2$$

$$at^2 = 2(h - v_0t - h_0)$$

$$a = \frac{2(h - v_0t - h_0)}{t^2}$$

Choice **(C)** is the correct answer.

**39. D**

**Difficulty:** Medium

**Category:** Exponents

**Getting to the Answer:** In order to combine terms with exponents by multiplication or division, the terms must all have the same base. All the bases in the given equation are powers of 2, so restate that equation with all the terms in base two: $\left(2^4\right)^{3x}\left(2^5\right)^{x}\left(2^3\right)^{3x} = \dfrac{\left(2^2\right)^{6x}\left(2^5\right)^{3x}}{2^2}$.
When a base with an exponent is raised to a power, multiply the exponents. An exponent in a denominator is equivalent to the same exponent in the numerator with the sign flipped, so $(2^{12x})(2^{5x})(2^{9x}) = (2^{12x})(2^{15x})(2^{-2})$.

When the numbers with exponents and the same base are multiplied, add the exponents. Thus, the equation further simplifies to $2^{12x+5x+9x} = 2^{12x+15x-2}$. Because the base on each side of the equation is the same, the total of the exponents on both sides must be equal. Therefore, $12x + 5x + 9x = 12x + 15x - 2$. This further simplifies to $26x = 27x - 2$, so $x = 2$. **(D)** is correct.

## 40. 2

**Difficulty:** Medium

**Category:** Radicals

**Getting to the Answer:** Conveniently, the conjugate of the denominator, $\sqrt{x} - 3$, is the numerator of the other fraction, $\sqrt{x} + 3$, so cross-multiplying will rationalize the fraction.

Cross-multiplying the first equation yields $(y)(3) = (\sqrt{x} + 3)(\sqrt{x} - 3)$, which simplifies to $3y = x - 9$. (If this is a difficult simplification for you, study FOIL and the classic quadratics in chapter 12.) In the second equation, you are given that $2x + 42 = 9x - 63$, so $7x = 105$, and $x = 15$. Therefore, $3y = 15 - 9 = 6$, and $y = 2$. Grid in **2**.

You could have chosen to solve the second equation for the value of $x$, then substituted the result into the proportion and solved for $y$. Either approach would be equally effective.

## 41. B

**Difficulty:** Medium

**Category:** Polynomial Division

**Getting to the Answer:** Since there's no common factor in the numerator and denominator, you'll need to resort to using polynomial long division. Notice that the numerator does not have an $x$ term, so include $0x$ in the long division so that the fraction can be shown as $x - 3 \overline{)3x^2 + 0x + 7}$. Next, do the long division:

$$
\begin{array}{r}
3x + 9 \\
x - 3 \overline{\smash{)}3x^2 + 0x + 7} \\
\underline{3x^2 - 9x} \\
9x + 7 \\
\underline{9x - 27} \\
34
\end{array}
$$

The result of the long division is $3x + 9$ with a remainder of 34. The remainder is the "leftover" part that hasn't yet been divided by $x - 3$, so it can be expressed as $\frac{34}{x - 3}$.

Thus, **(B)** is correct.

## 42. A

**Difficulty:** Hard

**Category:** Polynomials

**Strategic Advice:** You could plug the $x$- and $y$-values from each choice into the given equation to see which does not equal zero. However, if you factor the polynomial, you'll save time by avoiding extra calculations.

**Getting to the Answer:** Look for common factors in the polynomial by groups. The first two terms, $15x^2$ and $10xy$, share the common factor $5x$. The third and fourth terms share a common factor of $-2$, so you can write the equation as $z = 5x(3x + 2y) - 2(3x + 2y)$. Next, factor out the $(3x + 2y)$ to regroup this as $z = (5x - 2)(3x + 2y)$. Since $z$ is the product of two factors, if either factor equals 0, then $z = 0$.

If $(5x - 2) = 0$, then $x = \frac{2}{5}$. You can immediately eliminate (C) and (D) because, if $x = \frac{2}{5}$, $z = 0$ no matter what the value of $y$ might be. If $(3x + 2y) = 0$, then $x = -\frac{2}{3}y$, as it is in (B). Thus, **(A)** is the only ordered pair for which $z \neq 0$.

## 43. 5

**Difficulty:** Hard

**Category:** Radicals

**Getting to the Answer:** Remember that the rules for combining terms under a radical are different for addition and multiplication. Although $\sqrt{xy}$ can be written as $\sqrt{x} \times \sqrt{y}$, terms that are added under a radical, such as $\sqrt{x + y}$, must be combined before taking the root. Now, find the value of each term in the radical above, add them, and then take the square root of the sum.

The term, $27^{\frac{2}{3}}$, is the square of the cube root of 27. Since $3 \times 3 \times 3 = 27$, the cube root of 27 is 3, which squared is $3^2 = 9$. The denominator of the exponent in $128^{\frac{4}{7}}$ quite likely means that 128 is some number to the seventh power. A good place to start would be to try 2 because it is small and easy to raise to high powers. Indeed, you'll find that $2 \times 2 \times 2 \times 2 \times 2 \times 2 \times 2 = 128$. So $128^{\frac{4}{7}} = \left(2^7\right)^{\frac{4}{7}} = 2^4 = 16$. Thus, $\sqrt{27^{\frac{2}{3}} + 128^{\frac{4}{7}}} = \sqrt{9 + 16} = \sqrt{25} = 5$. Grid in **5**.

## 44. A

**Difficulty:** Medium

**Category:** Rational Expressions and Equations

**Strategic Advice:** Since there is no common factor in the numerator and denominator, you might be tempted to dive into polynomial long division. However, if you noticed that the numerator, $4x^2 - 8$, is very close to being the difference of two squares, $4x^2 - 9$, there is a more efficient way to unravel this fraction.

**Getting to the Answer:** Restate the fraction as $\frac{4x^2 - 9}{2x + 3} + \frac{1}{2x + 3}$. Now factor the numerator and cancel like terms: $\frac{\cancel{(2x + 3)}(2x - 3)}{\cancel{2x + 3}} + \frac{1}{2x + 3}$. **(A)** is correct.

## 45. C

**Difficulty:** Medium

**Category:** Rational Expressions and Equations

**Strategic Advice:** Recall that a denominator equal to zero results in an undefined value for the fraction. To answer this question, determine which of the choices does *not* result in the denominator being equal to zero.

**Getting to the Answer:** You could plug each of the answer choices into the denominator to see which three equal zero, or you could factor the denominator first to simplify the identification of those values. Start by factoring out $2x$ to show the denominator as $2x(x^2 - 6x - 7)$. The denominator is the product of the two factors, so if either one is 0, the denominator will be 0. If $2x = 0$, $x = 0$, so eliminate (B) because $x = 0$ makes $g(x)$ undefined.

Next, you could either plug the remaining choices into $x^2 - 6x - 7$ to see which choice does not produce a result of zero, or you could factor the expression into $(x - 7)(x + 1)$. Thus, either $x = 7$ or $x = -1$ results in the denominator of $g(x)$ equal to zero. Eliminate (A) and (D); **(C)** is correct. For the record, $g(1) = \frac{2}{-24}$.

## 46. B

**Difficulty:** Medium

**Category:** Polynomials

**Getting to the Answer:** In order to solve for possible values of $x$, first group all the terms on one side of the equation and set the other side to 0. Thus, $x^3 + 4 = 3x^2 - 7x + 25$ can be written as $x^3 - 3x^2 + 7x - 21 = 0$. Factor this by grouping the terms into two pairs. The first pair, $x^3 - 3x^2$, contains the common factor $x^2$, so it is equivalent to $x^2(x - 3)$. The second pair, $7x - 21$, factors to $7(x - 3)$. Thus, another form of the entire equation is $x^2(x - 3) + 7(x - 3) = 0$. Factor out $(x - 3)$ to get $\left(x^2 + 7\right)(x - 3) = 0$.

If the product of two factors is zero, one or both of the factors must be zero. If $\left(x^2 + 7\right) = 0$, then $x^2 = -7$. Since the square root of a negative number is not a real number, move on to $x - 3 = 0$. In this case, $x = 3$, so **(B)** is correct.

### 47. C

**Difficulty:** Medium

**Category:** Graphs of Polynomial Functions

**Strategic Advice:** Equations with roots of 0 as well as roots that are less than 0 will be incorrect and can be eliminated. When using elimination, start with the easiest looking choice first, then proceed to the next easiest, and so forth.

**Getting to the Answer:** Roots on a graph are the points at which $y = 0$. Start by plugging in 0 for $y$ in each choice and solving for $x$, and then eliminate those choices for which $x$ could be 0 or less. For (A), you would plug in 0 such that $0 = 4|x|$, which is true only for $x = 0$. Eliminate (A). For (B), plug in 0 for $y$ and solve for $x$:

$$0 = x^2 - 4$$
$$x^2 = 4$$
$$\sqrt{x^2} = \sqrt{4}$$
$$x = \pm 2$$

Since $x$ could equal $-2$, eliminate (B) as well. Choices (C) and (D) are the products of two factors. If the product of 2 factors is 0, then one of the factors must be 0. In (C), the only value for $x$ that would make the equation equal to 0 is 2, which is greater than 0, so **(C)** is correct. On test day, you would move on, but for the record, in choice (D), $x = 0$ is a root, so (D) is incorrect.

### 48. D

**Difficulty:** Medium

**Category:** Graphs of Polynomial Functions

**Getting to the Answer:** The notation $f(x) = 0$ is another way of describing the $x$-axis, so this question is asking how many times the graph intersects or touches the $x$-axis. This graph crosses the $x$-axis four times, once each at $x = 0$, $x = 4$, $x = 3$, and $x = 2$, so **(D)** is correct.

### 49. A

**Difficulty:** Easy

**Category:** Modeling Growth and Decay

**Getting to the Answer:** If the number of smartphone users increases by 35% each year, then the amount of the increase is variable (because it's 35% of a bigger number each time), which means exponential growth. Eliminate (C) and (D). Consider the two remaining equations in terms of the exponential growth function, $f(x) = f(0)(1 + r)^x$. Note that the only difference between the two remaining choices is the $r$ value. Recall that when assembling an exponential growth model, $r$ (the rate) must be in decimal form. Therefore, the number raised to the power of $x$ should be $1 + 0.35$, or 1.35. Choice **(A)** is the only one that fits these criteria.

# Quadratics

# How Much Do You Know?

**Directions:** Try the questions that follow. Show your work so that you can compare your solutions to the ones found in the Check Your Work section immediately after this question set. The "Category" heading in the explanation for each question gives the title of the lesson that covers how to solve it. If you answered the question(s) for a given lesson correctly, and if your scratch-work looks like ours, you may be able to move quickly through that lesson. If you answered incorrectly or used a different approach, you may want to take your time on that lesson.

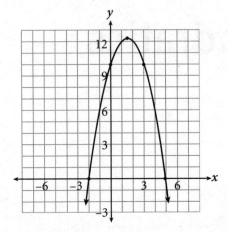

1. Which of the following linear expressions divides evenly into $6x^2 + 7x - 20$ ?

   A)  $3x - 10$

   B)  $3x - 5$

   C)  $3x - 4$

   D)  $3x - 2$

$$x^2 - 10x - 7$$

2. Which of the following expressions is equivalent to the expression above?

   A)  $(x - 5)^2 - 32$

   B)  $(x - 5)^2 + 32$

   C)  $(x + 5)^2 - 32$

   D)  $(x + 5)^2 + 32$

$$3x^2 - 5x = -k$$

3. In the equation above, $k$ is a constant. For which of the following values of $k$ does the equation have at least one real solution?

   A)  2

   B)  3

   C)  4

   D)  5

4. Which of the following could be the equation of the graph shown?

   A)  $y = 2x + 10$

   B)  $y = -x^2 + \dfrac{3}{2}x + 10$

   C)  $y = -(x - 2)(x + 5)$

   D)  $y = -(x + 2)(x - 5)$

5. The $x$-coordinates of the solutions to a system of equations are 3.5 and 6. Which of the following could be the system?

   A)  $\begin{cases} y = x + 3.5 \\ y = x^2 + 6 \end{cases}$

   B)  $\begin{cases} y = 2x - 7 \\ y = -(x - 6)^2 \end{cases}$

   C)  $\begin{cases} y = \dfrac{1}{2}x + 3 \\ y = -(x - 5)^2 + 7 \end{cases}$

   D)  $\begin{cases} y = \dfrac{1}{2}x + 7 \\ y = -(x - 6)^2 + 3.5 \end{cases}$

Answers and explanations are on the next page. ▶ ▶ ▶

# Check Your Work

## 1. C

**Difficulty:** Medium

**Category:** Solving Quadratics by Factoring

**Getting to the Answer:** Understanding that in algebra "divides evenly" means "is a factor" is the key to answering the question. You could use polynomial long division, but in most cases, factoring is quicker. The leading coefficient of the equation is not 1, so you'll need to use grouping to factor the equation. The general form of a quadratic is $ax^2 + bx + c$. To find the factors, multiply $a$ by $c$, $6 \times -20 = -120$, and then look for two factors of that product whose sum is equal to $b$, the coefficient of the middle term. The two factors of $-120$ that add up to 7 are 15 and $-8$:

$$6x^2 + 7x - 20 = 6x^2 + 15x - 8x - 20$$
$$= \left(6x^2 + 15x\right) - (8x + 20)$$
$$= 3x(2x + 5) - 4(2x + 5)$$
$$= (2x + 5)(3x - 4)$$

Therefore, $3x - 4$ divides evenly into the expression, so **(C)** correct.

## 2. A

**Difficulty:** Medium

**Category:** Completing the Square

**Getting to the Answer:** There are no integer factors of $x^2 - 10x - 7$, since no two integers whose product is $-7$ add up to $-10$. Note that the answer choices are stated in vertex format, the same as you would obtain by completing the square of the given expression. Half of the $x$-coefficient, $-10$, is $-5$, so the constant term needed to complete the square is $(-5)^2 = 25$. Thus, you can rewrite and group the given expression as $(x^2 - 10x + 25) - 25 - 7$. This simplifies to $(x - 5)^2 - 32$, which is **(A)**. Noticing that $x^2 - 10x + 25$ is a classic quadratic makes the process of factoring very quick.

## 3. A

**Difficulty:** Medium

**Category:** The Quadratic Formula

**Getting to the Answer:** Restate the equation in "standard" quadratic form, $3x^2 - 5x + k = 0$. Recall that a quadratic equation has two real solutions if the discriminant, $b^2 - 4ac$, is positive. The equation has one real solution if the discriminant is 0. For the given equation, $a = 3$, $b = -5$, and $c = k$, so you can set up the inequality $(-5)^2 - 4(3)k \geq 0$. This simplifies to $25 \geq 12k$. The only choice for which this is true is **(A)**.

If you didn't recall the shortcut about the discriminant, consider the quadratic formula, $x = \dfrac{-b \pm \sqrt{b^2 - 4ac}}{2a}$.

If the term inside the radical, $b^2 - 4ac$, is negative, then there are no real solutions.

## 4. D

**Difficulty:** Easy

**Category:** Graphs of Quadratics

**Getting to the Answer:** The graph is a parabola, so you can eliminate (A) because its equation is linear. The $x$-intercepts of the graph are $-2$ and 5, so the factors of the quadratic are $(x + 2)$ and $(x - 5)$. These factors make $y = 0$ when $x = -2$ and $x = 5$. Eliminate (B) and (C). Only (D) is left, so it must be correct. On test day, you would move on. For the record, the parabola opens downward, so there should be a negative sign in front of the factors. **(D)** is correct.

**5.    C**

**Difficulty:** Hard

**Category:** Systems of Quadratic and Linear Equations

**Getting to the Answer:** You don't actually need to solve each system. Instead, plug 3.5 or 6 into each answer choice and eliminate each one whose $y$-values don't come out the same. (If the same $x$-value produces different $y$-values in two equations, then it is not the $x$-coordinate of the solution to the system.) Because 3.5 is a decimal, doing arithmetic with it is likely to be messy. So start with 6:

(A): $y = 6 + 3.5 = 9.5$

$y = 6^2 + 6 = 36 + 6 = 42$

Different $y$-values; eliminate.

(B): $y = 2(6) - 7 = 12 - 7 = 5$

$y = -(6 - 6)^2 = -(0)^2 = 0$

Different $y$-values; eliminate.

(C): $y = \frac{1}{2}(6) + 3 = 3 + 3 = 6$

$y = -(6 - 5)^2 + 7 = -(1)^2 + 7 = -1 + 7 = 6$

Keep for now. You need to test (D) because it's possible that (D) is the right answer and (C) just happens to work for $x = 6$ (but not for $x = 3.5$).

(D): $y = \frac{1}{2}(6) + 7 = 3 + 7 = 10$

$y = -(6 - 6)^2 + 3.5 = -(0)^2 + 3.5 = 3.5$

Different $y$-values; eliminate.

**(C)** is correct.

Math

# Solving Quadratics by Factoring

## To answer a question like this:

If $x^2 - 7x = 30$ and $x > 0$, what is the value of $x - 5$ ?

A)  5

B)  6

C)  10

D)  25

## You need to know this:

A quadratic expression is a second-degree polynomial—that is, a polynomial containing a squared variable. You can write a quadratic expression as $ax^2 + bx + c$.

The **FOIL** acronym (which stands for First, Outer, Inner, Last) will help you remember how to multiply two binomials: multiply the first terms together ($ac$), then the outer terms ($ad$), then the inner terms ($bc$), and finally the last terms ($bd$):

$$(a + b)(c + d) = ac + ad + bc + bd$$

FOIL can also be done in reverse if you need to go from a quadratic to its factors.

To solve a quadratic equation by factoring, the quadratic must be set equal to 0. For example:

$$x^2 + x - 56 = 0$$
$$(x + 8)(x - 7) = 0$$

From the binomial factors, you can find the **solutions**, also called **roots** or **zeros**, of the equation. For two factors to be multiplied together and produce zero as the result, one or both those factors must be zero. In the example above, either $x + 8 = 0$ or $x - 7 = 0$, which means that $x = -8$ or $x = 7$.

## You need to do this:

Here are the steps for solving a quadratic equation by factoring:

• Set the quadratic equal to zero.
• Factor the squared term. (For factoring, it's easiest when $a$, the coefficient in front of $x^2$, is equal to 1.)
• Make a list of the factors of $c$. Remember to include negatives.
• Find the factor pair that, when added, equals $b$, the coefficient in front of $x$.
• Write the quadratic as the product of two binomials.
• Set each binomial equal to zero and solve.

## Explanation:

Set the equation equal to zero and factor the first term:

$$x^2 - 7x = 30$$
$$x^2 - 7x - 30 = 0$$
$$(x \pm \text{?})(x \pm \text{?}) = 0$$

Next, consider factors of $-30$, keeping in mind that they must sum to $-7$, so *the factor with the greater absolute value must be negative.* The possibilities are: $-30 \times 1$, $-15 \times 2$, $-10 \times 3$, and $-6 \times 5$. The factor pair that sums to $-7$ is $-10 \times 3$. Write that factor pair into your binomials:

$$(x - 10)(x + 3) = 0$$

Set each factor equal to zero and solve:

$$(x - 10) = 0 \qquad (x + 3) = 0$$
$$x = 10 \qquad x = -3$$

The question says that $x > 0$, so $x = 10$. Now that you solved for $x$, you can answer the question, which asks for $x - 5$: $10 - 5 = 5$. **(A)** is correct.

If factoring quadratics gives you trouble, study the steps in the table above and try these Drill questions before completing the following Try on Your Own questions. Factor each quadratic expression (without using a calculator). Turn the page to see the answers.

## Drill

a. $a^2 + 8a + 15$

b. $x^2 + 4x - 21$

c. $b^2 - 7b - 18$

d. $y^2 - 10y + 24$

e. $x^2 + \frac{1}{2}x - \frac{1}{2}$

f. $5x^2 + 10x + 5$

g. $2x^2 + 12x - 54$

h. $3x^2 - 6x + 3$

i. $x^2 + 3xy + 2y^2$

j. $4a^2 + 4ab - 8b^2$

## Try on Your Own

**Directions:** Take as much time as you need on these questions. Work carefully and methodically. There will be an opportunity for timed practice at the end of the chapter.

1. Which of the following is an equivalent form of the expression $(6 - 5x)(15x - 11)$ ?

   A)  $-75x^2 + 35x - 66$

   B)  $-75x^2 + 145x - 66$

   C)  $90x^2 - 141x + 55$

   D)  $90x^2 + 9x + 55$

---

HINT: For Q2, what is the easiest way to factor the denominator?

2. Which of the following is equivalent to $\dfrac{x^2 - 10x + 25}{3x^2 - 75}$ ?

   A)  $\dfrac{3(x - 5)}{(x + 5)}$

   B)  $\dfrac{3(x + 5)}{(x - 5)}$

   C)  $\dfrac{(x - 5)}{3(x + 5)}$

   D)  $\dfrac{(x + 5)}{3(x - 5)}$

---

HINT: For Q3, what value in the denominator would make the fraction undefined?

---

3. For what positive value of $x$ is the equation $\dfrac{3}{2x^2 + 4x - 6} = 0$ undefined?

$$3x^2 + 9x = 54$$

4. What is the sum of the roots of the equation above?

   A)  $-6$

   B)  $-3$

   C)  $3$

   D)  $6$

Drill answers from previous page:

a. $a^2 + 8a + 15 = (a + 3)(a + 5)$

b. $x^2 + 4x - 21 = (x - 3)(x + 7)$

c. $b^2 - 7b - 18 = (b + 2)(b - 9)$

d. $y^2 - 10y + 24 = (y - 4)(y - 6)$

e. $x^2 + \frac{1}{2}x - \frac{1}{2} = (x + 1)\left(x - \frac{1}{2}\right)$

f. $5x^2 + 10x + 5 = 5(x + 1)(x + 1)$

g. $2x^2 + 12x - 54 = 2(x - 3)(x + 9)$

h. $3x^2 - 6x + 3 = 3(x - 1)(x - 1)$

i. $x^2 + 3xy + 2y^2 = (x + y)(x + 2y)$

j. $4a^2 + 4ab - 8b^2 = 4(a - b)(a + 2b)$

$$f(x) = (1.3x - 3.9)^2 - \left(0.69x^2 - 0.14x - 9.79\right)$$

5. Which of the following functions is equivalent to the function above?

A) $f(x) = (x - 5)^2$

B) $f(x) = x^2 + 10.28x + 5.42$

C) $f(x) = 0.61x^2 + 0.14x + 25$

D) $f(x) = 1.3(x - 3)^2 - 0.69x^2 + 0.14x + 9.79$

**Math**

## Classic Quadratics

---

### LEARNING OBJECTIVE

After this lesson, you will be able to:

- Recognize the classic quadratics

---

### To answer a question like this:

Which of the following expressions is equivalent to $25x^2y^4 - 1$ ?

A) $5(x^2y^4 - 1)$

B) $-5(xy^2 + 1)$

C) $(5xy - 1)(5xy + 1)$

D) $(5xy^2 - 1)(5xy^2 + 1)$

### You need to know this:

Memorizing the following classic quadratics will save you time on test day:

- $x^2 - y^2 = (x + y)(x - y)$
- $x^2 + 2xy + y^2 = (x + y)^2$
- $x^2 - 2xy + y^2 = (x - y)^2$

### You need to do this:

When you see a pattern that matches either the left or the right side of one of the above equations, simplify by substituting its equivalent form. For example, say you need to simplify the following:

$$\frac{a^2 - 2ab + b^2}{a - b}$$

You would substitute $(a - b)(a - b)$ for the numerator and cancel to find that the expression simplifies to $a - b$:

$$\frac{a^2 - 2ab + b^2}{a - b} = \frac{(a - b)(a - b)}{a - b} = \frac{a - b}{1} = a - b$$

### Explanation:

The expression $25x^2y^4 - 1$ is a difference of perfect squares. It corresponds to the first of the three classic quadratic patterns above. The square root of $25x^2y^4$ is $5xy^2$ and the square root of 1 is 1, so the correct factors are $\left(5xy^2 - 1\right)\left(5xy^2 + 1\right)$. Choice **(D)** is correct.

## Try on Your Own

**Directions:** Take as much time as you need on these questions. Work carefully and methodically. There will be an opportunity for timed practice at the end of the chapter.

6. For all $a$ and $b$, what is the sum of $(a - b)^2$ and $(a + b)^2$?

   A) $2a^2$

   B) $2a^2 - 2b^2$

   C) $2a^2 + 2b^2$

   D) $2a^2 + 4ab + 2b^2$

---

HINT: For Q7, how can you remove the fraction to make factoring easier?

---

7. What is the positive difference between the roots of the equation $y = \frac{1}{3}x^2 - 2x + 3$?

---

HINT: For Q8, look for a classic quadratic in the denominator.

---

$$f(x) = \frac{3}{(x - 7)^2 + 6(x - 7) + 9}$$

8. For which value of $x$ is the function $f(x)$ undefined?

9. Suppose $a^2 + 2ab + b^2 = c^2$ and $c - b = 4$. Assuming $c > 0$, what is the value of $a$?

$$2x^2 - 28x + 98 = a(x - b)^2$$

10. In the expression above, $a > 1$ and both $a$ and $b$ are constants. Which of the following could be the value of $b$?

    A) $-7$

    B) $7$

    C) $14$

    D) $49$

Math

## Completing the Square

### LEARNING OBJECTIVE

After this lesson, you will be able to:

- Solve a quadratic equation by completing the square

### To answer a question like this:

Which of the following equations has the same solutions as the equation $40 - 6x = x^2 - y$?

A) $y = (x - 6)^2 - 40$

B) $y = (x - 6)^2 + 40$

C) $y = (x + 3)^2 - 49$

D) $y = (x + 3)^2 + 49$

### You need to know this:

For quadratics that do not factor easily, you'll need one of two strategies: completing the square or the quadratic formula (taught in the next lesson). To complete the square, you'll create an equation in the form $(x + h)^2 = k$, where $h$ and $k$ are constants.

As with factoring, completing the square is most convenient when the coefficient in front of the $x^2$ term is 1.

### You need to do this:

Here are the steps for completing the square, demonstrated with a simple example.

| Step | Scratchwork |
|---|---|
| Starting point: | $x^2 + 8x - 8 = 0$ |
| 1. Move the constant to the opposite side. | $x^2 + 8x = 8$ |
| 2. Divide $b$, the $x$-coefficient, by 2 and square the quotient. | $b = 8;\ \left(\dfrac{b}{2}\right)^2 = \left(\dfrac{8}{2}\right)^2 = (4)^2 = 16$ |
| 3. Add the number from the previous step to both sides of the equation and factor. | $x^2 + 8x + 16 = 8 + 16$ <br> $(x + 4)(x + 4) = 24$ <br> $(x + 4)^2 = 24$ |
| 4. Take the square root of both sides. | $\sqrt{(x + 4)^2} = \pm\sqrt{24} \rightarrow x + 4 = \pm\sqrt{24}$ <br> $= \pm\sqrt{4}\sqrt{6}x + 4 = \pm 2\sqrt{6}$ |
| 5. Split the result into two equations and solve each one. | $x + 4 = 2\sqrt{6} \rightarrow x = 2\sqrt{6} - 4$ <br> $x + 4 = -2\sqrt{6} \rightarrow x = -2\sqrt{6} - 4$ |

## Explanation:

First, write the equation in standard form: $y = x^2 + 6x - 40$. Add 40 to both sides and complete the square on the right-hand side. Find $\left(\frac{b}{2}\right)^2 = \left(\frac{6}{2}\right)^2 = 3^2 = 9$, and add the result to both sides of the equation:

$$y = x^2 + 6x - 40$$
$$y + 40 = x^2 + 6x$$
$$y + 40 + 9 = x^2 + 6x + 9$$
$$y + 49 = x^2 + 6x + 9$$

Note that all of the answer choices are in factored form. The right side of the equation is a classic quadratic that factors as follows:

$$y + 49 = (x + 3)(x + 3)$$
$$y + 49 = (x + 3)^2$$

Finally, solve for $y$ to get $y = (x + 3)^2 - 49$, which means **(C)** is correct.

If you find completing the square to be challenging, study the steps in the table above and try these Drill questions before completing the following Try on Your Own questions. Turn the page to see the answers.

## Drill

a.   $x^2 = 10x + 2$

b.   $-9 = 2x^2 + 16x + 3$

c.   $x^2 - x - 11 = 0$

d.   $x^2 + \frac{x}{2} = 4$

e.   $-x^2 + 6ax = 2a^2$

## Try on Your Own

**Directions:** Take as much time as you need on these questions. Work carefully and methodically. There will be an opportunity for timed practice at the end of the chapter.

11. Which of the following is a value of $x$ that satisfies the equation $x^2 + 2x - 5 = 0$ ?

    A)  $-1$

    B)  $1 - \sqrt{6}$

    C)  $1 + \sqrt{6}$

    D)  $-1 - \sqrt{6}$

---

HINT: For Q12, the algebra will be easier if you substitute another variable for $a^2$.

---

$$a^4 - 12a^2 - 72 = 0$$

12. Which of the following is the greatest possible value of $a$ ?

    A)  $\sqrt{6 + \sqrt{3}}$

    B)  $\sqrt{6\left(1 + \sqrt{3}\right)}$

    C)  12

    D)  $6\left(1 + \sqrt{3}\right)$

---

HINT: For Q13, treat the square root in the $b$ term just like any other: divide it by 2, then square it.

---

$$x^2 - \left(6\sqrt{5}\right)x = -40$$

13. What is the sum of the possible values of $x$ given the above equation?

    A)  15

    B)  $5\sqrt{5}$

    C)  $6\sqrt{5}$

    D)  60

$$x^2 + 7x + 1 = 2x^2 - 4x + 3$$

14. Which of the following is a value of $x$ that is valid in the above equation?

    A)  $5.5 - \sqrt{28.25}$

    B)  $\sqrt{5.5}$

    C)  $\sqrt{30.25}$

    D)  $5.5 + \sqrt{30.25}$

Drill answers from previous page:

a. $x = 5 \pm 3\sqrt{3}$

b. $x = -4 \pm \sqrt{10}$

c. $x = \dfrac{1 \pm 3\sqrt{5}}{2}$

d. $x = \dfrac{-1 \pm \sqrt{65}}{4}$

e. $x = 3a \pm a\sqrt{7}$

# The Quadratic Formula

## To answer a question like this:

Which of the following are the real values of $x$ that satisfy the equation $2x^2 - 5x - 2 = 0$ ?

A) 1 and 4

B) $-\dfrac{5}{4} + \dfrac{\sqrt{41}}{4}$ and $-\dfrac{5}{4} - \dfrac{\sqrt{41}}{4}$

C) $\dfrac{5}{4} + \dfrac{\sqrt{41}}{4}$ and $\dfrac{5}{4} - \dfrac{\sqrt{41}}{4}$

D) No real solutions

## You need to know this:

The quadratic formula can be used to solve any quadratic equation. It yields solutions to a quadratic equation that is written in standard form, $ax^2 + bx + c = 0$:

$$x = \frac{-b \pm \sqrt{b^2 - 4ac}}{2a}$$

The $\pm$ sign that follows $-b$ indicates that you will have two solutions, so remember to find both.

The expression under the radical ($b^2 - 4ac$) is called the **discriminant**, and its value determines the *number* of real solutions. If the discriminant is positive, the equation has two distinct real solutions. If the discriminant is equal to 0, there is only one distinct real solution. If the discriminant is negative, there are no real solutions because you cannot take the square root of a negative number.

The arithmetic can get complicated, so reserve the quadratic formula for equations that cannot be solved by factoring and those in which completing the square is difficult because a $\neq$ 1.

## You need to do this:

Get the quadratic equation into the form $ax^2 + bx + c = 0$. Then substitute $a$, $b$, and $c$ into the quadratic formula and simplify.

### Explanation:

In the given equation, $a = 2$, $b = -5$, and $c = -2$. Plug these values into the quadratic formula and simplify:

$$x = \frac{-b \pm \sqrt{b^2 - 4ac}}{2a}$$

$$x = \frac{-(-5) \pm \sqrt{(-5)^2 - 4(2)(-2)}}{2(2)}$$

$$x = \frac{5 \pm \sqrt{25 - (-16)}}{4}$$

$$x = \frac{5 \pm \sqrt{41}}{4}$$

$$x = \frac{5}{4} + \frac{\sqrt{41}}{4} \quad \text{or} \quad x = \frac{5}{4} - \frac{\sqrt{41}}{4}$$

The correct answer is **(C)**.

If you find the quadratic formula to be challenging, study the formula and try these Drill questions before completing the following Try on Your Own questions. Turn the page to see the answers.

### Drill

a. $x^2 - 2x - 20 = 0$

b. $3x^2 - 5x - 2 = 0$

c. $-7x^2 + 14x + 24 = -4$

d. $0.3x^2 + 0.7x - 1 = 0$

e. $\frac{x^2}{2} - x\sqrt{2} - 2 = 0$

## Try on Your Own

**Directions:** Take as much time as you need on these questions. Work carefully and methodically. There will be an opportunity for timed practice at the end of the chapter.

---
HINT: For Q15, use the discriminant.

---

15. Given the equation $2x^2 + 8x + 4 + 2z = 0$, for what value of $z$ is there exactly one solution for $x$?

16. The product of all the solutions to the equation $3v^2 + 4v - 2 = 0$ is $M$. What is the value of $M$?

A) $-3$

B) $-\dfrac{2}{3}$

C) $-\dfrac{1}{3}$

D) $\dfrac{4}{3}$

17. What are the solutions to the equation $4x^2 - 24x + 16 = 0$?

A) $x = 3 \pm \sqrt{5}$

B) $x = 4 \pm \sqrt{6}$

C) $x = 5 \pm \sqrt{3}$

D) $x = 5 \pm 2\sqrt{2}$

$$3x^2 = m(5x + v)$$

18. What are the values of $x$ that satisfy the equation above, where $m$ and $v$ are constants?

A) $x = -\dfrac{5m}{6} \pm \dfrac{\sqrt{25m^2 + 12mv}}{6}$

B) $x = \dfrac{5m}{6} \pm \dfrac{\sqrt{25m^2 + 12mv}}{6}$

C) $x = -\dfrac{5m}{3} \pm \dfrac{\sqrt{12m^2 + 25mv}}{3}$

D) $x = \dfrac{5m}{3} \pm \dfrac{\sqrt{25m^2 + 12mv}}{3}$

---
HINT: For Q19, start with the standard form of a quadratic equation.

---

$$x(dx + 10) = -3$$

19. The equation above, where $d$ is a constant, has no real solutions. The value of $d$ could be which of the following?

A) $-12$

B) $4$

C) $8$

D) $10$

20. Which of the following equations does NOT have any solutions that are real numbers?

A) $x^2 + 8x - 12 = 0$

B) $x^2 - 8x + 12 = 0$

C) $x^2 - 9x + 21 = 0$

D) $x^2 + 100x - 1 = 0$

Math

# Graphs of Quadratics

### LEARNING OBJECTIVE

After this lesson, you will be able to:

- Relate properties of a quadratic function to its graph and vice versa

## To answer a question like this:

Given the equation $y = -(2x - 4)^2 + 7$, which of the following statements is NOT true?

A) The vertex is $(4, 7)$.

B) The $y$-intercept is $(0, -9)$.

C) The parabola opens downward.

D) The graph crosses the $x$-axis at least one time.

## You need to know this:

A quadratic function is a quadratic equation set equal to $y$ or $f(x)$ instead of 0. Remember that the solutions (also called "roots" or "zeros") of any polynomial function are the same as the $x$-intercepts. To solve a quadratic function, substitute 0 for $y$, or $f(x)$, then solve algebraically. Alternatively, you can plug the equation into your graphing calculator and read the $x$-intercepts from the graph.

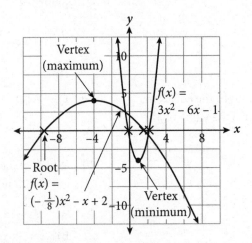

The graph of every quadratic equation (or function) is a **parabola**, which is a symmetric U-shaped graph that opens either upward or downward. To determine which way a parabola will open, examine the value of $a$ in the equation. If $a$ is positive, the parabola will open upward. If $a$ is negative, it will open downward. Take a look at the examples above to see this graphically.

Drill answers:

a. $x = 1 \pm \sqrt{21}$

b. $x = 2, x = -\frac{1}{3}$

c. $1 \pm \sqrt{5}$

d. $x = -\frac{10}{3}, x = 1$

e. $\sqrt{2} \pm \sqrt{6}$

Like quadratic equations, quadratic functions will have zero, one, or two distinct real solutions, corresponding to the number of times the parabola touches or crosses the $x$-axis. Graphing is a powerful way to determine the number of solutions a quadratic function has.

There are three algebraic forms that a quadratic equation can take: standard, factored, and vertex. Each is provided in the following table along with the graphical features that are revealed by writing the equation in that particular form.

| Standard | Factored | Vertex |
|---|---|---|
| $y = ax^2 + bx + c$ | $y = a(x - m)(x - n)$ | $y = a(x - h)^2 + k$ |
| $y$-intercept is $c$ | Solutions are $m$ and $n$ | Vertex is $(h, k)$ |
| In real-world contexts, starting quantity is $c$ | $x$-intercepts are $m$ and $n$ | Minimum/maximum of function is $k$ |
| Format used to solve via quadratic formula | Vertex is halfway between $m$ and $n$ | Axis of symmetry is given by $x = h$ |

You've already seen standard and factored forms earlier in this chapter, but vertex form might be new to you. In vertex form, $a$ is the same as the $a$ in standard form, and $h$ and $k$ are the coordinates of the **vertex** $(h, k)$. If a quadratic function is not in vertex form, you can still find the $x$-coordinate of the vertex by plugging the appropriate values into the equation $h = \dfrac{-b}{2a}$, which is also the equation for the axis of symmetry (see graph that follows). Once you determine $h$, plug this value into the quadratic function and solve for $y$ to determine $k$, the $y$-coordinate of the vertex.

The equation of the **axis of symmetry** of a parabola is $x = h$, where $h$ is the $x$-coordinate of the vertex.

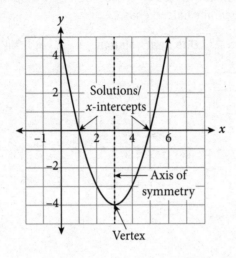

Vertex

## You need to do this:

- To find the vertex of a parabola, get the function into vertex form: $y = a(x - h)^2 + k$ or use the formula $h = \frac{-b}{2a}$.
- To find the $y$-intercept of a quadratic function, plug in 0 for $x$.
- To determine whether a parabola opens upward or downward, look at the coefficient of $a$. If $a$ is positive, the parabola opens upward. If negative, it opens downward.
- To determine the number of $x$-intercepts, set the quadratic function equal to 0 and solve or examine its graph. (Quadratic function questions show up on both the no-calculator and calculator sections of the SAT.)

## Explanation

Be careful—the equation looks like vertex form, $y = a(x - h)^2 + k$, but it's not quite there because of the 2 inside the parentheses. You could rewrite the equation in vertex form, but this would involve squaring the quantity in parentheses and then completing the square, which would take quite a bit of time. Alternatively, you could notice that the greatest possible value for $y$ in this function is 7, which happens when the squared term, $-(2x - 4)^2$, equals zero. To check (A), find the $x$-value when $y = 7$:

$$2x - 4 = 0$$
$$2x = 4$$
$$x = 2$$

For the record:

Choice (B): Substitute 0 for $x$ and simplify to find that the $y$-intercept is indeed $(0, -9)$.

Choice (C): There is a negative in front of the squared term, so the parabola *does* open downward.

Choice (D): Because the parabola opens downward and the vertex is at $y = 7$, above the $x$-axis, the parabola must cross the $x$-axis twice. This statement is true as well, which confirms that **(A)** is correct.

## Try on Your Own

**Directions:** Take as much time as you need on these questions. Work carefully and methodically. There will be an opportunity for timed practice at the end of the chapter.

---
HINT: For Q21, which form of a quadratic equation tells you the *x*-intercepts? Consult the table given earlier if you can't remember.

---

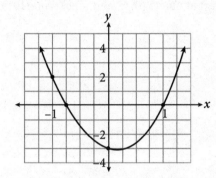

21. The following quadratic equations are all representations of the graph above. Which equation clearly represents the exact values of the *x*-intercepts of the graph?

    A)  $y = 4x^2 - x - 3$
    B)  $y = (4x + 3)(x - 1)$
    C)  $y = 4(x - 0.125)^2 - 3.0625$
    D)  $y + 3.0625 = 4(x - 0.125)^2$

---
HINT: For Q22, through which point on a parabola does the axis of symmetry pass?

---

22. Which equation represents the axis of symmetry for the graph of the quadratic function
    $f(x) = -\frac{11}{3}x^2 + 17x - \frac{43}{13}$ ?

    A)  $x = -\frac{102}{11}$
    B)  $x = -\frac{51}{22}$
    C)  $x = \frac{51}{22}$
    D)  $x = \frac{102}{11}$

23. How many times do the parabolas given by the equations $f(x) = 3x^2 - 24x + 52$ and $g(x) = x^2 + 12x - 110$ intersect?

    A)  Never
    B)  Once
    C)  Twice
    D)  More than twice

24. What is the positive difference between the *x*-intercepts of the parabola given by the equation $g(x) = -2.5x^2 + 10x - 7.5$ ?

---
HINT: For Q25, what does "maximum height" correspond to on the graph of a quadratic equation?

---

25. A toy rocket is fired from ground level. The height of the rocket with respect to time can be represented by a quadratic function. If the toy rocket reaches a maximum height of 34 feet 3 seconds after it was fired, which of the following functions could represent the height, *h*, of the rocket *t* seconds after it was fired?

    A)  $h(t) = -16(t - 3)^2 + 34$
    B)  $h(t) = -16(t + 3)^2 + 34$
    C)  $h(t) = 16(t - 3)^2 + 34$
    D)  $h(t) = 16(t + 3)^2 + 34$

## Systems of Quadratic and Linear Equations

> **LEARNING OBJECTIVE**
>
> After this lesson, you will be able to:
>
> - Solve a system of one quadratic and one linear equation

### To answer a question like this:

In the $xy$-plane, the graph of $y + 3x = 5x^2 + 6$ and $y - 6 = 2x$ intersect at points $(0, 6)$ and $(a, b)$. What is the value of $b$?

### You need to know this:

You can solve a system of one quadratic and one linear equation by substitution, exactly as you would for a system of two linear equations. Alternatively, if the question appears on the calculator section, you can plug the system into your graphing calculator.

### You need to do this:

- Isolate $y$ in both equations
- Set the equations equal to each other
- Put the resulting equation into the form $ax^2 + bx + c = 0$
- Solve this quadratic by factoring, completing the square, or using the quadratic formula. (You are solving for the $x$-values at the points of intersection of the original two equations.)
- Plug the $x$-values you get as solutions into one of the original equations to generate the $y$-values at the points of intersection. (Usually, the linear equation is easier to work with than the quadratic.)

**Explanation:**

Start by isolating $y$ in both equations to get $y = 2x + 6$ and $y = 5x^2 - 3x + 6$. Next, set the right sides of the equations equal and solve for $x$:

$$2x + 6 = 5x^2 - 3x + 6$$
$$5x^2 - 5x = 0$$
$$5x(x - 1) = 0$$
$$x = 0 \text{ or } x = 1$$

The question says that $(0, 6)$ is one point of intersection for the two equations and asks for the $y$-value at the other point of intersection, so plug $x = 1$ into either of the original equations and solve for $y$. Using the linear equation will be faster:

$$y = 2(1) + 6$$
$$y = 8$$

Therefore, the point $(a, b)$ is $(1, 8)$. Grid in **8**.

Math

## Try on Your Own

**Directions**: Take as much time as you need on these questions. Work carefully and methodically. There will be an opportunity for timed practice at the end of the chapter.

---

HINT: For Q26, note that both equations are equal to $a$.

---

$$\begin{cases} a = b^2 + 4b - 12 \\ a = -12 + b \end{cases}$$

26. The ordered pair $(a, b)$ satisfies the system of equations above. What is one possible value of $b$ ?

    A)  $-6$

    B)  $-3$

    C)  $2$

    D)  $3$

27. In the $xy$-coordinate plane, the graph of $y = 5x^2 - 12x$ intersects the graph of $y = -2x$ at points $(0, 0)$ and $(a, b)$. What is the value of $a$ ?

$$\begin{cases} y + 3x = 10 \\ y - x^2 + 7x = 13 \end{cases}$$

28. How many real solutions are there to the system of equations above?

    A)  Exactly 4 real solutions

    B)  Exactly 2 real solutions

    C)  Exactly 1 real solution

    D)  No real solutions

29. The graph of the function $f$, defined by $f(x) = -2(x - 3)^2 - 4$, is shown in the $xy$-plane above. The function $g$ (not shown) is defined by $g(x) = 2x - 10$. If $f(c) = g(c)$, what is one possible value of $c$ ?

    A)  $-6$

    B)  $-4$

    C)  $2$

    D)  $4$

HINT: For Q30, solve for the points of intersection, then use the formula for distance in the coordinate plane.

30. On the $xy$-plane, points $P$ and $Q$ are the two points where the parabola with the equation $y = 3x^2 + \dfrac{14}{3}x - \dfrac{73}{3}$ and the line with the equation $y = -\dfrac{4}{3}x - \dfrac{1}{3}$ meet. What is the distance between point $P$ and point $Q$?

A)   5

B)   8

C)   10

D)   12

## On Test Day

On the SAT, there is often more than one strategy that will get you to the answer. When a question involves a graph of two functions of $x$ intersecting, you can either set the two functions equal to each other and solve for $x$, or you can use the coordinates of an intersection of the functions and set the values of both functions for that point equal to each other.

Try out this question using both approaches. Which approach do you find easier? There's no right or wrong answer—just remember your preferred approach and use it if you see a question like this on test day.

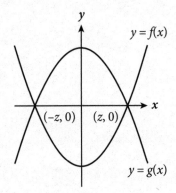

31.  The functions $f(x) = 4x^2 - 25$ and $g(x) = -4x^2 + 25$ are graphed in the $xy$-plane above. The points where the two functions intersect are $(z, 0)$ and $(-z, 0)$. What is the value of $z$?

A)  0.5

B)  1.0

C)  2.5

D)  4.0

The correct answer and both ways of solving can be found at the end of this chapter.

# How Much Have You Learned?

**Directions:** For testlike practice, give yourself 18 minutes to complete this question set. Be sure to study the explanations, even for questions you got right. They can be found at the end of this chapter.

32. The equation $\frac{1}{4}\left(4x^2 - 8x - k\right) = 30$ has two solutions: $x = -5$ and $x = 7$. What is the value of $2k$?

33. The maximum value of the data shown in the scatterplot above occurs at $x = 25$. If the data is modeled using a quadratic regression and the correlation coefficient is 1.0 (the fit is exact), then what is the $y$-value when $x = 35$?

    A)  10
    B)  15
    C)  22
    D)  27

**Questions 34 and 35 refer to the following information.**

The height of a boulder launched from a Roman catapult can be described as a function of time according to the following quadratic equation: $h(t) = -16t^2 + 224t + 240$.

34. What is the maximum height that the boulder attains?

    A)  240
    B)  784
    C)  1,024
    D)  1,696

35. How much time elapses between the moment the boulder is launched and the moment it hits the ground, assuming that the ground is at a height of 0?

    A)  7
    B)  12
    C)  14
    D)  15

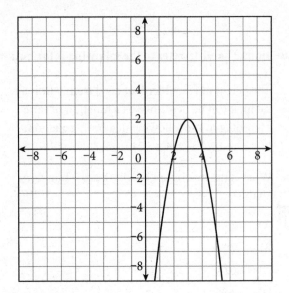

36. If the function shown in the graph is represented by $f(x) = a(x-h)^2 + k$, which of the following statements is NOT true?

   A)   The value of $a$ is negative.

   B)   $f(x)$ is symmetrical across the line $y = 3$.

   C)   The function $g(x) = \dfrac{2x}{3}$ intersects $f(x)$ at its vertex.

   D)   The value of $h$ is positive.

$$\begin{cases} y = 2x \\ 2x^2 + 2y^2 = 240 \end{cases}$$

37. If $(x, y)$ is a solution to the system of equations above, what is the value of $x^2$?

38. What are the $x$-intercepts of the parabolic function $f(x) = x^2 - 7x + 8\dfrac{1}{4}$ ?

   A)   $-1\dfrac{1}{2}$ and $3\dfrac{1}{2}$

   B)   $1$ and $8\dfrac{1}{4}$

   C)   $1\dfrac{1}{4}$ and $5\dfrac{3}{4}$

   D)   $1\dfrac{1}{2}$ and $5\dfrac{1}{2}$

39. If $g(x) = (x-2)^2 - 5$, which of the following statements is true?

   A)   The function $g(x)$ is increasing over the entire domain.

   B)   The function $g(x)$ is decreasing over the entire domain.

   C)   The function $g(x)$ is increasing for $x < 2$ and decreasing for $x > 2$.

   D)   The function $g(x)$ is decreasing for $x < 2$ and increasing for $x > 2$.

40. What is the sum of the solutions of $(6x+5)^2 - (3x-2)^2 = 0$ ?

   A)   $-\dfrac{8}{3}$

   B)   $-\dfrac{1}{6}$

   C)   $\dfrac{7}{3}$

   D)   $3$

$$4x - 12\sqrt{x} + 9 = 16$$

41. If the equation above is true, then what is the positive value of the expression $10\sqrt{x} - 15$ ?

   A)   20

   B)   25

   C)   30

   D)   35

42. In the equation $x - 2 = \dfrac{3}{x-2}$, which of the following is a possible value of $x - 2$?

    A) $\sqrt{3}$

    B) 2

    C) $2 + \sqrt{3}$

    D) 3

43. If $\dfrac{z^{x^2+y^2}}{z^{-2xy}} = \left(z^3\right)^3$, $x$ and $y$ are positive integers, and $x > y$, what is the value of $x - y$?

    A) 1

    B) 2

    C) 3

    D) 8

# Reflect

**Directions:** Take a few minutes to recall what you've learned and what you've been practicing in this chapter. Consider the following questions, jot down your best answer for each one, and then compare your reflections to the expert responses on the following page. Use your level of confidence to determine what to do next.

What features in a quadratic equation should you look for to decide whether to factor, complete the square, or apply the quadratic formula?

_____

_____

_____

Which constant in the vertex form of a quadratic function gives its maximum or minimum?

_____

_____

_____

Which form of a quadratic equation gives its $y$-intercept?

_____

_____

_____

Which form of a quadratic equation gives its $x$-intercepts, assuming the equation has two real roots?

_____

_____

_____

How do you solve a system of one linear and one quadratic equation?

_____

_____

_____

## Expert Responses

What features in a quadratic equation should you look for to decide whether to factor, complete the square, or apply the quadratic formula?

*Get the equation into standard form. If the coefficient in front of the squared term is 1, try factoring, but don't spend longer than about 15 seconds on the attempt. If you can't get the quadratic factored quickly, look at the coefficient on the middle term: if it is even, completing the square will be an efficient approach. Finally, the quadratic formula will work for any quadratic, no matter what the coefficients are.*

Which constant in the vertex form of a quadratic function gives its maximum or minimum?

*The vertex form is $y = a(x - h)^2 + k$. The constant k is the y-value at the vertex, which occurs at the maximum or minimum.*

Which form of a quadratic equation gives its $y$-intercept?

*The standard form, $y = ax^2 + bx + c$. The y-intercept is given by c.*

Which form of a quadratic equation gives its $x$-intercepts, assuming the equation has two real roots?

*The factored form, $y = a(x - m)(x - n)$. The x-intercepts are at $x = m$ and $x = n$.*

How do you solve a system of one linear and one quadratic equation?

*Put the linear equation in the form $y = mx + b$ and the quadratic in the form $y = ax^2 + bx + c$. Set the right sides of the equations equal to each other and solve.*

## Next Steps

If you answered most questions correctly in the "How Much Have You Learned?" section, and if your responses to the Reflect questions were similar to those of the SAT expert, then consider quadratics an area of strength and move on to the next chapter. Come back to this topic periodically to prevent yourself from getting rusty.

If you don't yet feel confident, review those parts of this chapter that you have not yet mastered. In particular, study the table describing the different forms of quadratics in the Graphs of Quadratics lesson. Then try the questions you missed again. As always, be sure to review the explanations closely.

# Answers and Explanations

## Try on Your Own

**1. B**

**Difficulty:** Easy

**Getting to the Answer:** FOIL the binomials $(6 - 5x)(15x - 11)$: First, Outer, Inner, Last. First: $(6)(15x) = 90x$. Outer: $(6)(-11) = -66$. Inner: $(-5x)(15x) = -75x^2$. Last: $(-5x)(-11) = 55x$. Add all the terms together and combine like terms: $90x - 66 - 75x^2 + 55x = -75x^2 + 145x - 66$. The correct answer is **(B)**.

**2. C**

**Difficulty:** Easy

**Getting to the Answer:** First, factor out a 3 in the denominator to make that quadratic a bit simpler. Then factor the numerator and denominator using reverse-FOIL to reveal an $x - 5$ term that will cancel out:

$$\frac{x^2 - 10x + 25}{3x^2 - 75} = \frac{x^2 - 10x + 25}{3(x^2 - 25)}$$

$$= \frac{(x - 5)(x - 5)}{3(x - 5)(x + 5)} = \frac{x - 5}{3(x + 5)}$$

The correct answer is **(C)**.

**3. 1**

**Difficulty:** Medium

**Getting to the Answer:** An expression is undefined when it involves division by 0, so the key to the problem is to recognize that the denominator will be 0 if either of the factors of the quadratic are zero. Factoring 2 out of the denominator leaves a relatively easy-to-factor quadratic:

$$\frac{3}{2x^2 + 4x - 6} = 0$$

$$\frac{3}{2(x^2 + 2x - 3)} = 0$$

$$\frac{3}{2(x + 3)(x - 1)} = 0$$

The denominator will be zero if the value of $x$ is either 1 or $-3$. Because the question asks for a positive value of $x$, grid in **1**.

**4. B**

**Difficulty:** Medium

**Getting to the Answer:** Set the equation equal to zero, then divide through by 3 on both sides to remove the $x^2$-coefficient:

$$3x^2 + 9x - 54 = 0$$

$$x^2 + 3x - 18 = 0$$

$$(x - 3)(x + 6) = 0$$

$$x = 3 \text{ or } -6$$

The question asks for the sum of the roots, which is $3 + (-6) = -3$. The correct answer is **(B)**.

**5. A**

**Difficulty:** Hard

**Strategic Advice:** The question asks for an equivalent expression, so ignore the function notation and focus on manipulating the polynomial into standard form so it matches most of the answer choices.

**Getting to the Answer:** Expand the polynomial and distribute as necessary so that all of the parentheses are eliminated:

$$(1.3x - 3.9)^2 - \left(0.69x^2 - 0.14x - 9.79\right)$$

$$(1.3x - 3.9)(1.3x - 3.9) - 0.69x^2 + 0.14x + 9.79$$

$$1.69x^2 - 10.14x + 15.21 - 0.69x^2 + 0.14x + 9.79$$

Decimals are harder to work with than integers, so multiply by 100. Then combine like terms. Factor 100 back out and check to see if the result matches any of the answer choices:

$$169x^2 - 1,014x + 1,521 - 69x^2 + 14x + 979$$

$$100x^2 - 1,000x + 2,500$$

$$\frac{100x^2 - 1,000x + 2,500}{100}$$

$$x^2 - 10x + 25$$

Factor the polynomial: $x^2 - 10x + 25 = (x - 5)^2$. **(A)** is correct.

**6.   C**

**Difficulty:** Easy

**Getting to the Answer:** Expand both classic quadratics and combine like terms to find the sum:

$$(a - b)^2 + (a + b)^2$$
$$= \left(a^2 - 2ab + b^2\right) + \left(a^2 + 2ab + b^2\right)$$
$$= 2a^2 + 2b^2$$

This matches **(C)**.

**7.   0**

**Difficulty:** Medium

**Getting to the Answer:** To find the roots, set the equation equal to 0, factor it, and then solve. Clear the fraction the same way you do when solving equations and multiply both sides of the equation by the denominator of the fraction:

$$0 = \frac{1}{3}x^2 - 2x + 3$$
$$3(0) = 3\left(\frac{1}{3}x^2 - 2x + 3\right)$$
$$0 = x^2 - 6x + 9$$
$$0 = (x - 3)(x - 3)$$

The equation only has one unique solution ($x = 3$), so the positive difference between the roots is $3 - 3 = $ **0**.

**8.   4**

**Difficulty:** Hard

**Getting to the Answer:** A fraction is undefined when the denominator equals 0. To find the value of $x$ where $f(x)$ is undefined, set the denominator to 0 and solve for $x$.

The equation $(x - 7)^2 + 6(x - 7) + 9 = 0$ is the expansion of the classic quadratic $a^2 + 2ab + b^2 = (a + b)^2$, where $a = (x - 7)$ and $b = 3$, so the denominator will factor as $\left[(x - 7) + 3\right]^2$. That's equivalent to $(x - 4)^2$. Set this expression equal to zero to find that the function is undefined when $x - 4 = 0$, or $x = $ **4**.

**9.   4**

**Difficulty:** Hard

**Strategic Advice:** Look for classic quadratics so you can avoid reverse-FOIL and save time:
$x^2 + 2xy + y^2 = (x + y)^2$

**Getting to the Answer:** Recognize that $a^2 + 2ab + b^2$ is a classic quadratic that simplifies to $(a + b)^2$. Factor the polynomial and take the square root of both sides to simplify the result:

$$(a + b)^2 = c^2$$
$$\sqrt{(a + b)^2} = \sqrt{c^2}$$
$$a + b = \pm c$$

The question says that $c$ is positive. Subtracting $b$ from both sides gives $a = c - b$. Plugging in 4 for $c - b$ gives $a = $ **4**.

**10.   B**

**Difficulty:** Medium

**Strategic Advice:** Recognizing the classic quadratic $(x - y)^2 = x^2 + 2xy + y^2$ will save you time in factoring.

**Getting to the Answer:** In this question, the goal is to manipulate the polynomial so that it matches the factored form given. First, recognize that 2, the coefficient of $x^2$, can be factored out. The resulting expression is then $2\left(x^2 - 14x + 49\right)$. Notice that $\sqrt{49} = 7$ and factor the quadratic to get $2(x - 7)(x - 7) = 2(x - 7)^2$. Now the expression is in the same form as $a(x - b)^2$. Therefore, $b = 7$, so **(B)** is correct.

## 11. D

**Difficulty:** Medium

**Getting to the Answer:** Factoring won't work here because no two factors of $-5$ sum to 2. However, the coefficient of $x^2$ is 1, so try completing the square:

$$x^2 + 2x - 5 = 0$$
$$x^2 + 2x = 5$$
$$\left(\frac{b}{2}\right)^2 = \left(\frac{2}{2}\right)^2 = 1^2 = 1$$
$$x^2 + 2x + 1 = 5 + 1$$
$$(x+1)^2 = 6$$
$$x + 1 = \pm\sqrt{6}$$
$$x = -1 \pm \sqrt{6}$$

**(D)** matches one of the two possible values of $x$, so it's correct.

## 12. B

**Difficulty:** Hard

**Getting to the Answer:** Even though the given equation contains the value $a^4$, this is a quadratic-style question. You can say that $x = a^2$, so $x^2 - 12x - 72 = 0$. To complete the square, restate this as $x^2 - 12x = 72$. One-half of the $x$-coefficient is 6, which, when squared, becomes 36. So, $x^2 - 12x + 36 = 108$. Factor to find that $(x - 6)^2 = 108$ and then take the square root of both sides to get $x - 6 = \pm\sqrt{108}$. Since $108 = 36 \times 3$, the radical simplifies to $6\sqrt{3}$.

Now substitute $a^2$ back in for $x$: $a^2 - 6 = \pm 6\sqrt{3}$ and $a^2 = 6 \pm 6\sqrt{3}$. Since the question asks for the root with the greatest value, you can ignore the root with the minus sign, so $a^2 = 6 + 6\sqrt{3} = 6(1 + \sqrt{3})$. Take the square root of both sides, and ignore the root with the negative sign to get $a = \sqrt{6(1 + \sqrt{3})}$. **(B)** is correct.

## 13. C

**Difficulty:** Hard

**Getting to the Answer:** The radical looks as if it will make the calculation difficult, but it will drop out when you complete the square. The coefficient, $b$, is $6\sqrt{5}$, so $\left(\frac{6\sqrt{5}}{2}\right)^2 = \left(\frac{36 \times 5}{4}\right) = 45$. Adding 45 to both sides of the equation gives you $x^2 - \left(6\sqrt{5}\right)x + 45 = 5$, so the factored form is $\left(x - 3\sqrt{5}\right)^2 = 5$. Take the square root of both sides to get $x - 3\sqrt{5} = \pm\sqrt{5}$. The two possible values of $x$ are $3\sqrt{5} + \sqrt{5} = 4\sqrt{5}$ and $3\sqrt{5} - \sqrt{5} = 2\sqrt{5}$. The question asks for the sum of these values, which is $4\sqrt{5} + 2\sqrt{5} = 6\sqrt{5}$. **(C)** is correct.

## 14. A

**Difficulty:** Hard

**Getting to the Answer:** Subtract the left side of the equation from the right side:
$0 = 2x^2 - x^2 - 4x - 7x + 3 - 1 = x^2 - 11x + 2$.
Combine like-terms to get $x^2 - 11x = -2$. So, $b = -11$, and $\left(\frac{b}{2}\right)^2 = \left(\frac{11}{2}\right)^2 = 30.25$. Thus, completing the square gives you $x^2 - 11x + 30.25 = 28.25$. (This is a calculator-allowed question, so feel free to use the calculator if you need to do so. You could also have used the calculator to backsolve to find the correct choice.) Factor the left side to get $(x - 5.5)^2 = 28.25$ and $x - 5.5 = \pm\sqrt{28.25}$. Therefore, $x$ can be either $5.5 + \sqrt{28.25}$ or $5.5 - \sqrt{28.25}$. The latter solution matches **(A)**.

## 15. 2

**Difficulty:** Hard

**Strategic Advice:** Recall that when the value of the discriminant, $b^2 - 4ac$, is 0, there is exactly one solution to the quadratic equation.

**Getting to the Answer:** The given equation is $2x^2 + 8x + 4 + 2z = 0$, but there is a common factor of 2 in all the terms, so this becomes $x^2 + 4x + 2 + z = 0$. So $a = 1$, $b = 4$, and $c = 2 + z$. Set the discriminant $4^2 - 4(1)(2 + z)$ equal to 0 so that there is only one solution. Expand the equation to $16 - 8 - 4z = 0$. Thus, $8 = 4z$, and $z = 2$. Grid in **2**.

**16. B**

**Difficulty:** Hard

**Getting to the Answer:** The question presents a quadratic equation that cannot be easily factored. Therefore, use the quadratic formula to solve. The quadratic formula states that $x = \dfrac{-b \pm \sqrt{b^2 - 4ac}}{2a}$.

In this case, $a = 3$, $b = 4$, and $c = -2$. Plug in these values to get:

$$x = \dfrac{-4 \pm \sqrt{4^2 - 4(3)(-2)}}{6}$$

$$= \dfrac{-4 \pm \sqrt{16 - (-24)}}{6}$$

$$= \dfrac{-4 \pm \sqrt{40}}{6}$$

Thus, the solutions to the equation are $\dfrac{-4 + \sqrt{40}}{6}$ and $\dfrac{-4 - \sqrt{40}}{6}$. The question asks for their product:

$$\left(\dfrac{-4 + \sqrt{40}}{6}\right)\left(\dfrac{-4 - \sqrt{40}}{6}\right)$$

$$= \dfrac{16 + 4\sqrt{40} - 4\sqrt{40} - 40}{36}$$

$$= \dfrac{-24}{36}$$

$$= -\dfrac{2}{3}$$

**(B)** is correct.

**17. A**

**Difficulty:** Medium

**Strategic Advice:** When all of the coefficients in a quadratic equation are divisible by a common factor, simplify the equation by dividing all terms by that factor before solving.

**Getting to the Answer:** The given equation is $4x^2 - 24x + 16 = 0$, but there is a common factor of 4 in all the terms, so this becomes $x^2 - 6x + 4 = 0$. Therefore, $a = 1$, $b = -6$, and $c = 4$.

The radicals in the answer choices are a strong clue that the quadratic formula is the way to solve this equation.

The quadratic formula is $x = \dfrac{-b \pm \sqrt{b^2 - 4ac}}{2a}$, and after you plug in the coefficients, you get:

$$x = \dfrac{6 \pm \sqrt{-6^2 - 4(1)(4)}}{2(1)}$$

$$= \dfrac{6 \pm \sqrt{36 - 16}}{2}$$

$$= \dfrac{6 \pm \sqrt{20}}{2}$$

This doesn't resemble any of the answer choices, so continue simplifying:

$$\dfrac{6 \pm \sqrt{20}}{2}$$

$$= \dfrac{6 \pm \sqrt{4}\sqrt{5}}{2}$$

$$= \dfrac{6 \pm 2\sqrt{5}}{2}$$

$$= \dfrac{6}{2} \pm \dfrac{2\sqrt{5}}{2}$$

$$= 3 \pm \sqrt{5}$$

Hence, **(A)** is correct.

**18. B**

**Difficulty:** Hard

**Getting to the Answer:** The question presents a variation of a quadratic equation. A glance at the radicals in the answer choices suggests that using the quadratic formula to solve is appropriate. Because there are so many variables, it might help to write down the quadratic formula in your notes as a guide $x = \dfrac{-b \pm \sqrt{b^2 - 4ac}}{2a}$.

Begin by reorganizing the quadratic into the standard form $ax^2 + bx + c = 0$:

$$3x^2 = m(5x + v)$$

$$3x^2 = 5mx + mv$$

$$3x^2 - 5mx - mv = 0$$

In this case, $a = 3$, $b = -5m$, and $c = -mv$. Now solve:

$$x = \dfrac{-(-5m) \pm \sqrt{(-5m)^2 - 4(3)(-mv)}}{6}$$

$$= \dfrac{5m \pm \sqrt{25m^2 - (-12mv)}}{6}$$

$$= \dfrac{5m \pm \sqrt{25m^2 + 12mv}}{6}$$

$$= \dfrac{5m}{6} \pm \dfrac{\sqrt{25m^2 + 12mv}}{6}$$

Therefore, **(B)** is correct.

## 19. D

**Difficulty:** Medium

**Getting to the Answer:** Get the equation $x(dx + 10) = -3$ into the form $ax^2 + bx + c = 0$. Multiply out the left side of the equation $x(dx + 10) = -3$ to get $dx^2 + 10x = -3$. Add 3 to both sides to yield $dx^2 + 10x + 3 = 0$.

When $a$, $b$, and $c$ are all real, the equation $ax^2 + bx + c = 0$ (when $a \neq 0$) does not have real solutions only if the discriminant, which is $b^2 - 4ac$, is negative. In the equation $dx^2 + 10x + 3 = 0$, $a = d$, $b = 10$, and $c = 3$. The discriminant in this question is $10^2 - 4(d)(3) = 100 - 12d$.

Since you're looking for a negative discriminant, that is, $b^2 - 4ac < 0$, you need $100 - 12d < 0$. Solve the inequality $100 - 12d < 0$ for $d$:

$$100 - 12d < 0$$
$$100 < 12d$$
$$\frac{100}{12} < d$$
$$\frac{25}{3} < d$$
$$8\frac{1}{3} < d$$

Among the answer choices, only 10 is greater than $8\frac{1}{3}$, so **(D)** is correct.

## 20. C

**Difficulty:** Medium

**Getting to the Answer:** Recall that when a quadratic equation has no real solutions, its discriminant, which is $b^2 - 4ac$, will be less than 0. Calculate the discriminant of each answer choice and pick the one that's negative. You don't need to actually solve for $x$:

(A) $8^2 - 4(1)(-12) = 64 + 48 > 0$. Eliminate.

(B) $(-8)^2 - 4(1)(12) = 64 - 48 > 0$. Eliminate.

(C) $(-9)^2 - 4(1)(21) = 81 - 84 = -3 < 0$. Pick **(C)** and move on. For the record:

(D) $(100)^2 - 4(1)(-1) = 10,000 + 4 > 0$. Eliminate.

## 21. B

**Difficulty:** Easy

**Getting to the Answer:** Quadratic equations can be written in several different forms that tell various pieces of important information about the equation. For example, the constant $k$ in the vertex form of a quadratic equation, $y = a(x - h)^2 + k$, gives the minimum or maximum value of the function. The standard form, $y = ax^2 + bx + c$, gives the $y$-intercept as $c$. The factored form of a quadratic equation makes it easy to find the solutions to the equation, which graphically represent the $x$-intercepts. Choice **(B)** is the only equation written in factored form and therefore is correct. You can set each factor equal to 0 and quickly solve to find that the $x$-intercepts of the graph are $x = -\frac{3}{4}$ and $x = 1$, which agree with the graph.

## 22. C

**Difficulty:** Medium

**Getting to the Answer:** An axis of symmetry splits a parabola in half and travels through the vertex. Use the formula to find $h$, plug in the correct values from the equation, and simplify:

$$x = -\frac{b}{2a}$$
$$= -\frac{17}{2\left(\frac{-11}{3}\right)}$$
$$= -\frac{17}{\left(\frac{-22}{3}\right)}$$
$$= -17 \cdot \frac{-3}{22}$$
$$= \frac{51}{22}$$

The correct answer is **(C)**.

### 23. B

**Difficulty:** Hard

**Getting to the Answer:** To find where the two functions intersect, set them equal to each other and solve for $x$:

$$f(x) = g(x)$$
$$3x^2 - 24x + 52 = x^2 + 12x - 110$$
$$2x^2 - 36x + 162 = 0$$
$$2(x^2 - 18x + 81) = 0$$
$$x^2 - 18x + 81 = 0$$

Notice that this is a classic quadratic:

$$x^2 - 18x + 81 = 0$$
$$(x - 9)^2 = 0$$
$$x = 9$$

Since there is only one solution for $x$, there must be only one point of intersection. **(B)** is correct.

### 24. 2

**Difficulty:** Medium

**Getting to the Answer:** An $x$-intercept of a function is a point at which the $y$-coordinate equals 0. Set the equation equal to zero, simplify, and factor:

$$g(x) = -2.5x^2 + 10x - 7.5$$
$$0 = -2.5x^2 + 10x - 7.5$$
$$0 = -2.5(x^2 - 4x + 3)$$
$$0 = x^2 - 4x + 3$$
$$0 = (x - 1)(x - 3)$$
$$x = 1 \text{ or } x = 3$$

The question asks for the *difference* between the $x$-intercepts, not for the $x$-intercepts themselves. Thus, $3 - 1 = $ **2**.

### 25. A

**Difficulty:** Hard

**Getting to the Answer:** The answer choices are all similar, so pay special attention to their differences and see if you can eliminate any choices logically. A rocket goes up and then comes down, which means that the graph will be a parabola opening downward. The equation, therefore, should have a negative sign in front. Eliminate (C) and (D).

To evaluate the two remaining choices, recall the *vertex form* of a quadratic, $y = a(x - h)^2 + k$, and what it tells you: the vertex of the graph is $(h, k)$. The $h$ is the $x$-coordinate of the maximum (or minimum) and $k$ is the $y$-coordinate of the maximum (or minimum). In this situation, $x$ has been replaced by $t$, or time, and $y$ is now $h(t)$, or height. The question says that the maximum height occurs at 3 seconds and is 34 feet, so $h$ is 3 and $k$ is 34. Substitute these values into vertex form to find that the correct equation is $y = -16(x - 3)^2 + 34$. The function that matches is **(A)**.

### 26. B

**Difficulty:** Medium

**Strategic Advice:** Because each of the two expressions containing $b$ is equal to $a$, the two expressions must be equal to each other.

**Getting to the Answer:** Set the two expressions equal to each other and then solve for $b$:

$$b^2 + 4b - 12 = -12 + b$$
$$b^2 + 4b = b$$
$$b^2 + 3b = 0$$
$$b(b + 3) = 0$$

If $b(b + 3) = 0$, then $b = 0$ or $b = -3$. Of these two values, only $-3$ is among the answer choices, so **(B)** is correct.

### 27. 2

**Difficulty:** Medium

**Getting to the Answer:** The points of intersection of the graphs are the points at which the equations are equal. Since $(a, b)$ is the label for an $(x, y)$ point, set the two equations equal to each other and solve for the value of $x$ to find the value of $a$:

$$-2x = 5x^2 - 12x$$
$$0 = 5x^2 - 10x$$
$$0 = 5x(x - 2)$$

Thus, $x = 0$ or $x = 2$. The question states that the intersection points are $(0, 0)$ and $(a, b)$, so $a$ must equal 2. Grid in **2**.

## 28. B

**Difficulty:** Medium

**Getting to the Answer:** The solutions to a system of equations are the points at which the equations intersect, which occurs when they are equal. Begin by setting both equations equal to $y$:

$$\begin{cases} y = -3x + 10 \\ y = x^2 - 7x + 13 \end{cases}$$

Because both equations are equal to $y$, they are also equal to each other. Set them equal and solve for $x$:

$$-3x + 10 = x^2 - 7x + 13$$
$$-3x = x^2 - 7x + 3$$
$$0 = x^2 - 4x + 3$$
$$0 = (x - 1)(x - 3)$$

Thus, there are 2 solutions, $x = 1$ and $x = 3$. **(B)** is correct.

Note that you could also use the discriminant, $b^2 - 4ac$, to determine how many solutions there are. If the discriminant is greater than 0, there are two real solutions; if it's equal to 0, there is one real solution; and if it's less than 0, there are no real solutions. In this case, $b^2 - 4ac = (-4)^2 - 4(1 \times 3) = 16 - 12 = 4$. Because $4 > 0$, there are 2 real solutions. **(B)** is correct.

## 29. C

**Difficulty:** Hard

**Getting to the Answer:** Because the question states that $f(c) = g(c)$, set the two functions equal to each other and solve for $x$. To make calculations easier, begin by converting $f(x)$ into standard form:

$$-2(x - 3)^2 - 4$$
$$= -2(x - 3)(x - 3) - 4$$
$$= -2\left(x^2 - 6x + 9\right) - 4$$
$$= -2x^2 + 12x - 18 - 4$$
$$= -2x^2 + 12x - 22$$

Now set the two functions equal:

$$-2x^2 + 12x - 22 = 2x - 10$$

Simplify by dividing all terms by $-2$:

$$x^2 - 6x + 11 = -x + 5$$

Next, combine like terms and solve for $x$:

$$x^2 - 6x + 11 = -x + 5$$
$$x^2 - 5x + 6 = 0$$
$$(x - 2)(x - 3) = 0$$

Therefore, $x = 2$ or $x = 3$, which means that $c$ could also be either 2 or 3. Because 3 is not an answer choice, the answer must be 2. **(C)** is correct.

## 30. C

**Difficulty:** Hard

**Strategic Advice:** When you need to find the points of intersection of two equations, set the equations equal to each other.

**Getting to the Answer:** The question indicates that points $P$ and $Q$ are the points of intersection of the two equations, so set the two equations equal to each other, consolidate terms to get a single quadratic equation equal to 0, and simplify:

$$3x^2 + \frac{14}{3}x - \frac{73}{3} = -\frac{4}{3}x - \frac{1}{3}$$
$$3x^2 + \frac{18}{3}x - \frac{72}{3} = 0$$
$$3x^2 + 6x - 24 = 0$$
$$x^2 + 2x - 8 = 0$$

Factor the equation to find the values of $x$:

$$x^2 + 2x - 8 = 0$$
$$(x + 4)(x - 2) = 0$$
$$x = -4 \text{ or } 2$$

You can plug each value of $x$ into either of the original equations to find the corresponding values of $y$. (The linear equation appears easier to work with.) For $x = -4$:

$$y = -\frac{4}{3}(-4) - \frac{1}{3}$$
$$y = \frac{16}{3} - \frac{1}{3}$$
$$y = \frac{15}{3} = 5$$

Therefore, one of the points of intersection is $(-4, 5)$. Find the other point of intersection by plugging in 2 for $x$ into the linear equation:

$$y = -\frac{4}{3}(2) - \frac{1}{3}$$

$$y = -\frac{8}{3} - \frac{1}{3}$$

$$y = -\frac{9}{3} = -3$$

Thus, the other point of intersection is $(2, -3)$.

The question asks for the distance between these two points. The formula for the distance, $d$, between the points $(x_1, y_1)$ and $(x_2, y_2)$ is $d = \sqrt{(x_2 - x_1)^2 + (y_2 - y_1)^2}$. Thus, find the distance between points $P$ and $Q$:

$$\sqrt{(-4 - 2)^2 + (5 - (-3))^2}$$

$$= \sqrt{(-6)^2 + 8^2}$$

$$= \sqrt{36 + 64}$$

$$= \sqrt{100}$$

$$= 10$$

Therefore, the distance between points $P$ and $Q$ is 10. **(C)** is correct.

### 31. C

**Difficulty:** Medium

**Getting to the Answer:** The first approach is to set $f(x)$ equal to $g(x)$: $4x^2 - 25 = -4x^2 + 25$. Isolate the $x^2$ terms on one side to get $8x^2 = 50$, so $4x^2 = 25$. Take the square root of both sides to see that $2x = \pm 5$, which means that the two intersections of the functions occur where $x = -2.5$ and $x = 2.5$. From the graph, you can see that these are the values of $\pm z$, so $z = 2.5$. **(C)** is correct. (Note that even if you had not been given the $y$-coordinates of the points of intersection, you could have calculated them from knowing their corresponding $x$-coordinates.)

The second approach is to plug in the coordinates of one of the intersections into either function. Using $f(x)$, the $y$-coordinate is 0 and the $x$-coordinate is $z$. So, $0 = 4z^2 - 25$. The math works out exactly the same as the first method: $4z^2 = 25$, so $z = \pm 2.5$, and, from the graph, you can determine that $z = 2.5$.

### 32. 40

**Difficulty:** Medium

**Category:** Graphs of Quadratics

**Getting to the Answer:** Since the given equation is valid for both $x = -5$ or $x = 7$, you can plug in either of those values and solve for $k$. Using 7 as the value of $x$ gives you $\frac{1}{4}\left(4(7)^2 - 8(7) - k\right) = 30$. Multiply both sides by 4 to get $4(49) - 56 - k = 120$. Thus, $-k = 120 - 196 + 56 = -20$, so $k = 20$ and $2k = 40$. Grid in **40**.

### 33. D

**Difficulty:** Hard

**Category:** Graphs of Quadratics

**Getting to the Answer:** Because the quadratic regression is an exact fit of the data, you can treat the data points as a quadratic function.

The graph of a quadratic function is symmetric with respect to its axis of symmetry, which passes through the $x$-value of the vertex, or the maximum (or minimum) of the function. The question tells you the maximum occurs at $x = 25$, which makes it the line of symmetry. Because 35 is $35 - 25 = 10$ units to the right of the axis of symmetry, you know that the $y$-value will be the same as the point that is 10 units to the left of the axis of symmetry, which is $x = 25 - 10 = 15$. Find the corresponding $y$-value in the table: 27. Therefore, **(D)** is correct.

### 34. C

**Difficulty:** Hard

**Category:** Graphs of Quadratics

**Getting to the Answer:** Because the height of the boulder is expressed as a quadratic equation with a negative $t^2$ coefficient, the path of the boulder is a downward-facing parabola. Therefore, the maximum height occurs at the vertex of the parabola. The $t$-coordinate (generally called the $x$-coordinate) of the vertex of a parabola is given by $t = \frac{-b}{2a} = \frac{-224}{2(-16)} = 7$. Plug the result into the function to get the $h$-coordinate: $h(7) = -16(7)^2 + 224(7) + 240 = 1{,}024$. **(C)** is correct.

### 35. D

**Difficulty:** Medium

**Category:** Graphs of Quadratics

**Getting to the Answer:** Set the quadratic expression for the height of the boulder equal to 0 and solve for $t$:

$$-16t^2 + 224t + 240 = 0$$
$$-16\left(t^2 - 14t - 15\right) = 0$$
$$t^2 - 14t - 15 = 0$$
$$(t - 15)(t + 1) = 0$$
$$t = 15 \text{ or } t = -1$$

Because time can't be negative, $t = 15$. **(D)** is correct.

### 36. B

**Difficulty:** Medium

**Category:** Graphs of Quadratics

**Getting to the Answer:** Keep in mind that the question asks for the statement that's false, so eliminate the true choices as you go. The parabola opens downward, so the $a$ term should be negative. Eliminate (A). The parabola's vertex is in quadrant I, so $h$ and $k$ are both positive. That makes choice (D) true as well; eliminate it. The axis of symmetry is $x = h$, so $x = 3$. According to the graph, the vertex is (3, 2). Choice (B), however, claims that the axis of symmetry is $y = 3$. Choice **(B)** is false and is therefore the correct answer.

For the record, (C) is a true statement because the line $g(x) = \frac{2x}{3}$ passes through the point (3, 2), which is indeed the vertex of $f(x)$.

### 37. 24

**Difficulty:** Medium

**Category:** Systems of Quadratic and Linear Equations

**Getting to the Answer:** The question tells you that $y = 2x$, so solving the system using substitution is a good option. Divide the second equation by 2 and plug in $2x$ for $y$:

$$2x^2 + 2y^2 = 240$$
$$x^2 + y^2 = 120$$
$$x^2 + (2x)^2 = 120$$
$$x^2 + 4x^2 = 120$$
$$5x^2 = 120$$
$$x^2 = 24$$

The question asks for the value of $x^2$, not $x$, so stop here. Grid in **24**.

### 38. D

**Difficulty:** Medium

**Category:** Completing the Square

**Getting to the Answer:** The $x$-intercepts of a function are the values of $x$ that make the function equal to 0. Factoring this function would be cumbersome because you would need to determine two numbers whose product is $8\frac{1}{4}$ and whose sum is $-7$. This is a good candidate for completing the square.

Start with $x^2 - 7x + 8\frac{1}{4} = 0$, then subtract $8\frac{1}{4}$ from each side to get $x^2 - 7x = -8\frac{1}{4}$. Half of the $b$ coefficient, $-7$, is $-3\frac{1}{2}$, which, when squared, is $12\frac{1}{4}$. Add that to both sides to get $x^2 - 7x + 12\frac{1}{4} = 4$. So $\left(x - 3\frac{1}{2}\right)^2 = 4$. Take the square root of both sides to get $x - 3\frac{1}{2} = \pm 2$. Therefore, the $x$-intercepts are $3\frac{1}{2} \pm 2$, or $1\frac{1}{2}$ and $5\frac{1}{2}$. **(D)** is correct.

**39. D**

**Difficulty:** Medium

**Category:** Graphs of Quadratics

**Getting to the Answer:** Draw a quick sketch of the equation (or graph it in your graphing calculator):

Based on the equation, the graph is a parabola that opens upward with a vertex of $(2, -5)$. A parabola changes direction at the $x$-coordinate of its vertex. You can immediately eliminate (A) and (B). To the left of 2 on the $x$-axis (or $x < 2$), the parabola is decreasing, and to the right of 2 on the $x$-axis (or $x > 2$), it is increasing. **(D)** is correct.

**40. A**

**Difficulty:** Medium

**Category:** Solving Quadratics by Factoring

**Getting to the Answer:** Rearrange the given equation to read $(6x + 5)^2 = (3x - 2)^2$. Given that the square of a number is the same value as the square of its negative counterpart, you can write that $\pm(6x + 5) = \pm(3x - 2)$. Therefore, either $6x + 5 = 3x - 2$ or $6x + 5 = (-1)(3x - 2) = -3x + 2$.

Solve the first case by subtracting $3x$ and 5 from both sides of the equation: $6x + 5 - 3x - 5 = 3x - 2 - 3x - 5$. Thus, $3x = -7$ and $x = -\frac{7}{3}$. For the alternative equation, add $3x$ to and subtract 5 from both sides: $6x + 5 + 3x - 5 = -3x + 2 + 3x - 5$. Thus, $9x = -3$, so $x = -\frac{1}{3}$.

The question asks for the sum of the two solutions which is $-\frac{7}{3} + \left(-\frac{1}{3}\right) = -\frac{8}{3}$. **(A)** is correct.

**41. A**

**Difficulty:** Hard

**Category:** Classic Quadratics

**Strategic Advice:** Technically, this isn't a quadratic equation because the highest power on the variable isn't 2. However, it is a "quadratic-type" equation because the square of the variable part of the middle term is equal to the variable in the leading term. In other words, squaring $\sqrt{x}$ gives you $x$. You can use factoring techniques you learned for quadratics to answer the question.

**Getting to the Answer:** The presence of 4, 9, and 16—all perfect squares—is a big clue. Note that $4x - 12\sqrt{x} + 9$ is an instance of the classic quadratic $(a - b)^2 = a^2 - 2ab + b^2$. Use this shortcut to factor the equation and see where that leads you:

$$4x - 12\sqrt{x} + 9 = 16$$
$$\left(2\sqrt{x} - 3\right)^2 = 16$$
$$2\sqrt{x} - 3 = \pm 4$$

The question asks for $10\sqrt{x} - 15$, which happens to be 5 times the quantity on the left side of the last equation above, so multiply the positive result, 4, by 5 to get 20. The correct answer is **(A)**.

**42. A**

**Difficulty:** Medium

**Category:** Solving Quadratics by Factoring

**Strategic Advice:** When a question asks for a value of an expression, isolate that expression on one side of the equation, if possible, rather than solving for the variable.

**Getting to the Answer:** Notice that the question asks for a possible value of $x - 2$, not $x$. Isolate $x - 2$ on one side of the equation by multiplying both sides by $x - 2$ and taking the square root of both sides:

$$(x - 2)(x - 2) = \frac{3}{x - 2}(x - 2)$$
$$(x - 2)^2 = 3$$
$$\sqrt{(x - 2)^2} = \sqrt{3}$$
$$x - 2 = \pm\sqrt{3}$$

Thus, **(A)** is correct.

An alternative strategy is to backsolve, plugging each choice in for $x - 2$ to see which results in a true statement.

### 43.  A

**Difficulty:** Hard

**Category:** Classic Quadratics

**Getting to the Answer:** Use exponent rules to simplify the fraction. Since the terms in the numerator and denominator have the same base, $z$, subtract the exponent of the denominator from that of the numerator: $z^{x^2+y^2-(-2xy)} = z^{x^2+2xy+y^2}$. When a value with an exponent is raised to another exponent, multiply the exponents. So, for the term on the right side, $\left(z^3\right)^3 = z^9$. Now the equation is $z^{x^2+2xy+y^2} = z^9$. Since both sides have the common base, $z$, their exponents must be equal and you can write $x^2 + 2xy + y^2 = 9$.

Factor $x^2 + 2xy + y^2$, a classic quadratic, to get $(x + y)^2 = 9$. Thus, $x + y$ must be either 3 or $-3$. However, the question limits $x$ and $y$ to positive integers, so they must be 1 and 2. Furthermore, since $x > y$, $x$ must be 2 and $y$ must be 1. Consequently, $x - y = 2 - 1 = 1$. **(A)** is correct.

# Other Topics in Math

# CHAPTER 13

# Geometry

## LEARNING OBJECTIVES

After completing this chapter, you will be able to:

- Identify similar triangles and apply their properties
- Calculate the length of one side of a right triangle given the lengths of the other two sides
- Recognize the most common Pythagorean triples
- Given one side length of a 45-45-90 or 30-60-90 triangle, calculate the other two
- Interpret and manipulate the equation for a circle
- Calculate the length of an arc or the area of a sector defined by a central angle
- Convert degrees to radians
- Calculate the volume of common solids
- Calculate the surface area of common solids

65/600 SmartPoints®

# How Much Do You Know?

**Directions:** Try the questions that follow. Show your work so that you can compare your solutions to the ones found in the Check Your Work section immediately after this question set. The "Category" heading in the explanation for each question gives the title of the lesson that covers how to solve it. If you answered the question(s) for a given lesson correctly, and if your scratchwork looks like ours, you may be able to move quickly through that lesson. If you answered incorrectly or used a different approach, you may want to take your time on that lesson.

Make use of the formula sheet below as needed; you'll have these same formulas available in your test booklet when you take the real SAT.

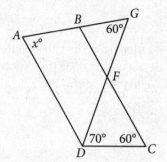

1. In the figure above, line segments *AD* and *BC* are parallel. What is the value of *x* ?

   A) 60

   B) 70

   C) 80

   D) 110

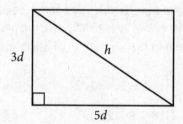

2. In the figure above, the diagonal of the rectangle has length *h*. What is the value of *h* in terms of *d* ?

   A) $d$

   B) $4d$

   C) $\sqrt{34d}$

   D) $d\sqrt{34}$

3. What is the area of the triangle shown in the figure?

   A) $18\sqrt{3}$

   B) $9 + 9\sqrt{3}$

   C) $9 + 18\sqrt{3}$

   D) $18 + 18\sqrt{3}$

4. What is the maximum value of *y* on the circumference of the circle defined by the equation

   $x^2 + y^2 + 6x - 10y - 47 = 0$ ?

   A) 9

   B) 14

   C) 16

   D) 19

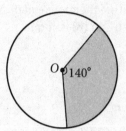

5. If the area of the shaded sector in circle *O* is $14\pi$ square units, what is the radius of the circle?

   A) 6

   B) 8

   C) 9

   D) 12

6. A yogurt factory fills cylindrical containers 80 percent of the way to the top, putting 6 ounces of yogurt in each cup. The containers are 4 inches tall and 2.5 inches wide. What is the approximate volume of one ounce of yogurt in cubic inches?

   A) 2.1

   B) 2.6

   C) 3.3

   D) 4.2

# Check Your Work

**1.   B**

**Difficulty:** Medium

**Category:** Similar Triangles

**Getting to the Answer:** Notice that $\triangle CDF$ and $\triangle BFG$ are similar: they share a 60° angle, and the vertical angles formed at point $F$ are equal, so their third angles must be equal as well. It follows that $\angle FBG = 70°$. Because line segments $AD$ and $BC$ are parallel, $\angle FBG$ and $\angle BAD$ are corresponding angles (and are therefore equal). You can now conclude that $\angle x = 70°$, so **(B)** is correct.

**2.   D**

**Difficulty:** Medium

**Category:** Pythagorean Theorem

**Getting to the Answer:** The sides $3d$, $5d$, and $h$ form a right triangle, so plug these values into the Pythagorean theorem and then solve for $h$. When you square $3d$ and $5d$, be sure to square the coefficient and the variable:

$$a^2 + b^2 = c^2$$
$$(3d)^2 + (5d)^2 = h^2$$
$$9d^2 + 25d^2 = h^2$$
$$34d^2 = h^2$$
$$\sqrt{34d^2} = h$$
$$d\sqrt{34} = h$$

Choice **(D)** is correct.

**3.   B**

**Difficulty:** Hard

**Category:** Special Right Triangles

**Getting to the Answer:** First, find the measure of the missing angle in the triangle: $180° - 105° - 45° = 30°$. Next, draw the height of the triangle up from $B$ to a point, $D$, on side $AC$ to create two right triangles:

Triangle $ABD$ is a 45-45-90 triangle, so its side lengths are in the ratio $x:x:x\sqrt{2}$. Because side $AB$ is the hypotenuse, set up an equation using the ratio of the sides:

$$6 = x\sqrt{2}$$
$$\frac{6}{\sqrt{2}} = x$$
$$\frac{6}{\sqrt{2}}\left(\frac{\sqrt{2}}{\sqrt{2}}\right) = x$$
$$\frac{6\sqrt{2}}{2} = x$$
$$3\sqrt{2} = x$$

This is the length of both $AD$ and $BD$. Triangle $BDC$ is a 30-60-90 triangle, so its side lengths are in the ratio of $x:x\sqrt{3}:2x$. You just found that the length of the shorter leg, $BD$, is $3\sqrt{2}$, so multiply it by $\sqrt{3}$ to find the length of the longer leg $\left(\sqrt{3} \times 3\sqrt{2} = 3\sqrt{6}\right)$. Now, find the length of $AC$, which is the base of triangle $BDC$, by adding lengths $AD$ to $DC$. The result is $3\sqrt{2} + 3\sqrt{6}$. Finally, use the area formula, $A = \frac{1}{2}bh$, to find the area of the whole triangle:

$$A = \frac{1}{2}\left(3\sqrt{2} + 3\sqrt{6}\right)\left(3\sqrt{2}\right)$$
$$= \frac{1}{2}\left(18 + 9\sqrt{12}\right)$$
$$= \frac{1}{2}\left(18 + 9 \cdot 2\sqrt{3}\right)$$
$$= \frac{1}{2}\left(18 + 18\sqrt{3}\right)$$
$$= 9 + 9\sqrt{3}$$

Choice **(B)** is correct.

**4.   B**

**Difficulty:** Medium

**Getting to the Answer:** Complete the square of the given equation to arrange it into the standard format for a circle, $(x - h)^2 + (y - k)^2 = r^2$, to determine the center and the radius. The maximum value of $y$ on the circle will be that of a radius drawn vertically up from the center.

The value $6x$ means that one of the terms in the equation for the circle will be $(x + 3)^2$ because that expands to $x^2 + 6x + 9$. Similarly, $10y$ means that the other term on the left side of the circle equation will be $(y - 5)^2 = y^2 + 10y + 25$.

Rewrite the given equation by adding $9 + 25$ to each side: $x^2 + 6x + 9 + y^2 - 10y + 25 - 47 = 9 + 25$. Next, simplify the $x$ and $y$ terms and add 47 to each side to yield $(x + 3)^2 + (y - 5)^2 = 9 + 25 + 47 = 81$. So, the $y$-coordinate of the center is 5. Since $r^2 = 81$, the radius of the circle is 9. Therefore, the $y$-coordinate of the point straight above the center is $5 + 9 = 14$. **(B)** is correct.

### 5.   A

**Difficulty:** Medium

**Category:** Arc Length and Sectors

**Getting to the Answer:** The question asks for the radius. If you know the area of the circle, you can find the radius. The question gives enough information to find the area of the circle. Use the relationship $\dfrac{\text{area of sector}}{\text{area of circle}} = \dfrac{\text{central angle}}{360°}$:

$$\frac{14\pi}{A} = \frac{140}{360}$$
$$5{,}040\pi = 140A$$
$$36\pi = A$$

Now, solve for $r$ using $A = \pi r^2$:

$$36\pi = \pi r^2$$
$$36 = r^2$$
$$\pm 6 = r$$

The radius can't be negative, so the correct answer is 6, which is **(A)**.

### 6.   B

**Difficulty:** Hard

**Category:** Three-Dimensional Figures

**Getting to the Answer:** Find the volume of the container using the formula for volume of a cylinder, $V = \pi r^2 h$. The question gives you the width, or the diameter, of the container, so divide by 2 to get the radius: one-half of 2.5 is 1.25. Now, solve:

$$V = \pi(1.25)^2(4)$$
$$V = \pi(1.5625)(4)$$
$$V = 6.25\pi$$

The factory fills the cup only 80% of the way up, so multiply the container volume by 0.8 to find that the actual volume of the yogurt is $6.25\pi \times 0.8 = 5\pi$, or about 15.708 cubic inches. Divide this by 6 ounces to determine that 1 ounce takes up approximately 2.6 cubic inches of space, which matches **(B)**.

## Similar Triangles

**To answer a question like this:**

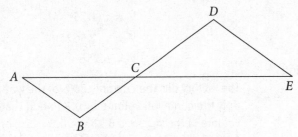

Note: Figure not drawn to scale.

In the figure above, segments *AE* and *BD* intersect at point *C*, and $\angle ABC \cong \angle CDE$. If $BC = DE = 5$ and $AB = 2$, what is the measure of *CD*?

**You need to know this:**

The corresponding angles and side lengths of **congruent triangles** are equal. **Similar triangles** have the same angle measurements and proportional sides. In the figure that follows, the two triangles have the same angle measurements, so the side lengths can be set up as the following proportion: $\frac{A}{D} = \frac{B}{E} = \frac{C}{F}$.

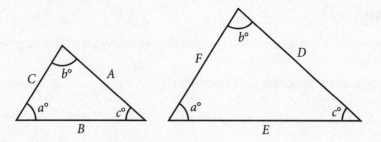

Two triangles are similar if three specific conditions are met:

- Two of their three angles are congruent (**angle-angle**). For example, two triangles that each have one 40° and one 55° angle are similar.

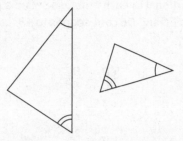

- Two of their three sides are in the same proportion and the intervening angle is congruent (**side-angle-side**). For example, a triangle with sides of 10 and 12 and an intervening angle of 40° and another triangle with sides of 20 and 24 and an intervening angle of 40° are similar.

- Their three sides are in the same proportion (**side-side-side**). For example, a triangle with sides of 5, 6, and 8 and a triangle with sides of 15, 18, and 24 are similar.

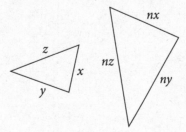

## You need to do this:

- Determine whether two triangles are similar by checking for angle-angle, side-angle-side, or side-side-side relationships
- Find a missing side length by setting up a proportion

## Explanation:

Label the figure with information from the question stem and information you can deduce from geometry principles. These two triangles are similar because they have two sets of congruent angles: one set is the set of vertical angles ($\angle ACB \cong \angle DCE$) and one set is given in the question stem ($\angle ABC \cong \angle CDE$). Corresponding sides in similar triangles are proportional to each other, so set up a proportion to find the missing side length. In this case, $CD$ corresponds to $BC$ and $DE$ corresponds to $AB$. Let the measure of $CD$ be represented by $x$ and solve:

$$\frac{CD}{BC} = \frac{DE}{AB}$$

$$\frac{x}{5} = \frac{5}{2}$$

$$x = \frac{25}{2}$$

Grid in $\frac{25}{2}$ or **12.5**.

## Try on Your Own

**Directions:** Take as much time as you need on these questions. Work carefully and methodically. There will be an opportunity for timed practice at the end of the chapter.

HINT: Triangles with a shared angle and parallel sides are similar. How can you use this fact in Q2?

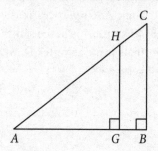

Note: Figure not drawn to scale.

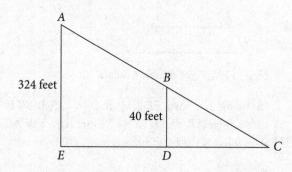

1.   The diagram above shows similar triangles *ACE* and *BCD*. If segment *DC* is 50 percent longer than segment *BD*, how long is segment *DE* ?

2.   Triangle *ABC* above has an area of 150 square units. If lengths $AB = AH = 20$, then what is the length of *HG* ?

A)   5

B)   12

C)   16

D)   20

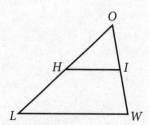

Note: Figure not drawn to scale.

3.   Triangle *LOW* is shown in the figure above, where segment *HI* is the bisector of both segments *LO* and *OW*. Given that $LW = 30$ and $HI = 4x - 1$, what is the value of *x* ?

A)   3.5

B)   4

C)   7.75

D)   8

4. Triangle *DEF* is similar to triangle *ABC*, and both are plotted on a coordinate plane (not shown). The vertices of triangle *DEF* are $D(3, 2)$, $E(3, -1)$, and $F(-1, -1)$. Two of triangle *ABC*'s vertices are $(-8, -3)$ and $(8, -3)$. If vertex *A* is in the same quadrant of the coordinate plane as vertex *D*, what is the *y*-coordinate of vertex *A* ?

HINT: For Q5, translate carefully from English into math and fill in the lengths on the figure.

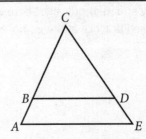

Note: Figure not drawn to scale.

5. In the figure above, $\overline{BD} \parallel \overline{AE}$ and $AB = 5$. If *BC* is three times *AB*, and if *CD* is 2 more than half *AC*, then what is the length of segment *DE* ?

A) 3

B) 4

C) 5

D) 6

# Pythagorean Theorem

## To answer a question like this:

What is the area of the triangle shown?

## You need to know this:

The **Pythagorean theorem** states that in any right triangle (and *only* in right triangles), the square of the hypotenuse (the longest side) is equal to the sum of the squares of the legs (the shorter sides). If you know the lengths of any two sides of a right triangle, you can use the Pythagorean equation, $a^2 + b^2 = c^2$, to find the length of the third. In this equation, $a$ and $b$ are the legs of the triangle and $c$ is the hypotenuse, the side across from the right angle of the triangle.

Consider an example: a right triangle has a leg of length 9 and a hypotenuse of length 14. To find the missing leg, plug the known values into the Pythagorean equation: $9^2 + b^2 = 14^2$. This simplifies to $81 + b^2 = 196$, which becomes $b^2 = 115$. Take the square root of both sides to find that $b = \sqrt{115}$.

Some right triangles have three side lengths that are all integers. These sets of integer side lengths are called **Pythagorean triples**. The two most common Pythagorean triples on the SAT are 3:4:5 and 5:12:13. Look for multiples of these (for example, 6:8:10 and 10:24:26) as well. Memorizing these triples now can save you valuable calculation time on test day.

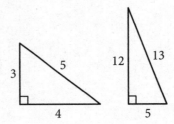

### You need to do this:

- Keep in mind that the Pythagorean theorem applies only to right triangles.
- When you need to find a side length of a right triangle, look first for the common Pythagorean triples or their multiples.
- If you cannot identify any Pythagorean triples, substitute any two known side lengths into the equation $a^2 + b^2 = c^2$, where $c$ represents the hypotenuse, to find the third.

### Explanation:

You could answer this question by applying the Pythagorean equation, but you would have to do a fair amount of algebra. It's much faster if you recognize that this is a 6:8:10 Pythagorean triple. Then it's just a matter of calculating the area, using the legs as the base and height:

$$A = \tfrac{1}{2}bh = \tfrac{1}{2}(8)(6) = 24$$

For the record, here's the solution using the Pythagorean equation:

$$x^2 + (x + 2)^2 = 10^2$$
$$x^2 + x^2 + 4x + 4 = 100$$
$$2x^2 + 4x - 96 = 0$$
$$x^2 + 2x - 48 = 0$$
$$(x + 8)(x - 6) = 0$$
$$x = -8 \quad \text{or} \quad x = 6$$

At this point, you would throw out the negative root because length must be positive, so you would use 6 and $6 + 2 = 8$ as the legs and calculate the area as shown above.

Grid in **24**.

## Try on Your Own

**Directions:** Take as much time as you need on these questions. Work carefully and methodically. There will be an opportunity for timed practice at the end of the chapter.

---

HINT: For Q6, draw the direct path and use it as the hypotenuse of a right triangle.

---

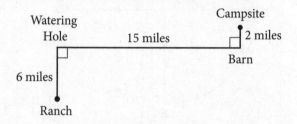

6. A tourist ranch built the horse-riding trail shown in the figure. The trail takes a rider from the ranch to an old watering hole, then to a historic barn, and finally to a campsite where riders can spend the night. If a rider took a horse on a direct path from the ranch to the campsite, how much shorter, in miles, would the trip be?

    A) 6
    B) 8
    C) 17
    D) 23

7. When Ted earned his driver's license, he wanted his first solo drive to be to a friend's house. Previously, Ted had always biked to his friend's house and was able to cut through the yards of neighbors to travel in a straight line. In his car, however, Ted travels a longer distance as he follows the streets. As a result, he travels 6 miles east, 6 miles south, and 2 more miles east by car. How much shorter, in miles, is Ted's bike route than his car route?

| | | / | / | |
|---|---|---|---|---|
| | . | . | . | . |
| | 0 | 0 | 0 | |
| 1 | 1 | 1 | 1 | |
| 2 | 2 | 2 | 2 | |
| 3 | 3 | 3 | 3 | |
| 4 | 4 | 4 | 4 | |
| 5 | 5 | 5 | 5 | |
| 6 | 6 | 6 | 6 | |
| 7 | 7 | 7 | 7 | |
| 8 | 8 | 8 | 8 | |
| 9 | 9 | 9 | 9 | |

8. During a camping trip, Aundria and Annette decide to travel to their campsite using two different routes. Aundria takes the hiking trail that travels 5 miles south, 6 miles east, 7 miles south, and 2 miles west to the campsite; Annette uses the cross-country route that starts at the same point as the hiking trail but goes in a straight line from there to the campsite. About how many miles total will the two travel?

    A) 32.65
    B) 33.42
    C) 34.00
    D) 34.42

9.  The lengths of the legs of a right triangle are $3x$ and $x + 1$. The hypotenuse is $3x + 1$. What is the value of $x$?

HINT: For Q10, use the triangle to find the radius of the semicircle.

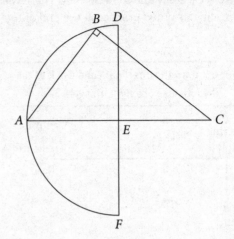

10. In the figure above, $E$ is the center of the semicircle and $AE = EC$. If $AB = 5$ and $BC = 12$, then what is the area of the semicircle?

    A) $13\pi$

    B) $26\pi$

    C) $\dfrac{169}{4}\pi$

    D) $\dfrac{169}{8}\pi$

# Special Right Triangles

## To answer a question like this:

Given triangle *ABC* and triangle *ABD* above, what is the perimeter of triangle *ACD* ?

A) $2\sqrt{6} - 2\sqrt{2}$

B) $4\sqrt{3}$

C) $4 + 2\sqrt{6} + 2\sqrt{2}$

D) $2\sqrt{6} + 6\sqrt{2}$

## You need to know this:

The question above requires you to be able to recognize two **special right triangles**. These triangles are defined by their angles. As a result, the ratios of their side lengths are always the same. If you know the length of any one of the three sides of a special right triangle, you can find the lengths of the other two.

The ratio of the sides of a **45-45-90** triangle is $x:x:x\sqrt{2}$, where $x$ is the length of each leg and $x\sqrt{2}$ is the length of the hypotenuse.

The ratio of the sides of a **30-60-90** triangle is $x:x\sqrt{3}:2x$, where $x$ is the shorter leg, $x\sqrt{3}$ is the longer leg, and $2x$ is the hypotenuse.

These side length ratios are given on the SAT formula sheet, but for the sake of efficiency on test day, we recommend that you memorize them.

## You need to do this:

- Look for hidden special right triangles within other shapes. For example, an equilateral triangle can be bisected (cut in half) to form two congruent 30-60-90 triangles and a square can be divided with a diagonal into two congruent 45-45-90 triangles.
- Use one known side length to deduce the other two. For example, if the shorter leg of a 30-60-90 triangle has a length of 5, then the longer leg has a length of $5\sqrt{3}$, and the hypotenuse has a length of $5(2) = 10$.

## Explanation:

Look for hidden special right triangles and add new information to your diagram as you go. Start by finding $\angle ACD$ from the two given angles: $\angle ACD = 180° - 15° - 30° = 135°$. Because $\angle ACB$ is supplementary to $\angle ACD$, $\angle ACB$ measures 45°. $\triangle ABC$ is a right triangle, so its missing angle ($\angle BAC$) is also 45°, making $\triangle ABC$ a 45-45-90 triangle. Since $\angle ADB$ is 30° and $\angle ABC$ is 90°, $\angle BAD$ is 60° and $\triangle ABD$ is a 30-60-90 triangle.

Knowing that you have two special right triangles will allow you to unlock the unknown side lengths. $AC$ is the hypotenuse of the 45-45-90 triangle (side ratio of $x:x:x\sqrt{2}$), so $AB$ and $BC$ (the two legs) must be $2\sqrt{2}$ (solve the equation $4 = x\sqrt{2}$ to find this). $AB$ is also the shorter leg of the 30-60-90 triangle (side ratio of $x:x\sqrt{3}:2x$), so $BD$ (the longer leg) is $2\sqrt{6}$ and $AD$ (the hypotenuse) is $4\sqrt{2}$. To determine $CD$, take the difference of $BD$ and $BC$: $2\sqrt{6} - 2\sqrt{2}$. With all sides and angles labeled, the figure looks like this:

You now have all three sides of $\triangle ACD$, so add them together for the perimeter:

$$4 + \left(2\sqrt{6} - 2\sqrt{2}\right) + 4\sqrt{2}$$

This simplifies to $4 + 2\sqrt{6} + 2\sqrt{2}$, so **(C)** is correct.

## Try on Your Own

**Directions:** Take as much time as you need on these questions. Work carefully and methodically. There will be an opportunity for timed practice at the end of the chapter.

---

HINT: For Q11, don't rush to use the Pythagorean theorem. Which of the special triangles is triangle *ADB* ?

---

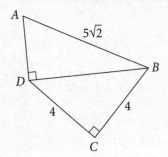

11. What is the area of triangle *DAB* ?

A) $3\sqrt{2}$

B) 8

C) 12

D) $20\sqrt{2}$

12. The distance from point *O* to point *M* of an amusement ride course shown in the figure above is $200\sqrt{3}$ feet. If the angle of ascent is 30°, what is the height, in feet, of the amusement ride at point *M* ?

A) $\frac{20}{3}\sqrt{3}$

B) $100\sqrt{3}$

C) 200

D) 300

13. Jonas plans to paint the top face of three corner shelves, one of which is shown above. If the longest side of one shelf is 10 inches, what is the total surface area, in square inches, Jonas needs to paint?

A) 25

B) 50

C) 75

D) 100

14. A tablet screen has a 12-inch diagonal. If the length of the screen is $\sqrt{3}$ times longer than the width, what is the area, in square inches, of the screen?

A) 12

B) $12\sqrt{3}$

C) 36

D) $36\sqrt{3}$

15. A theater is building a portable ramp to allow equipment and people easy access to the stage, which is 2 meters high. If the ramp is 4 meters long, what is the angle of the incline in degrees?

## Circles

---

### LEARNING OBJECTIVE

After this lesson, you will be able to:

- Interpret and manipulate the equation for a circle

---

### To answer a question like this:

Which of the following points in the *xy*-plane represents the center of the circle defined by the equation $x^2 + y^2 - 4x - 8y - 16 = 0$ ?

A) $(-4, -8)$

B) $(-2, -4)$

C) $(2, 4)$

D) $(4, 8)$

### You need to know this:

The equation of a circle in the coordinate plane is as follows:

$$(x - h)^2 + (y - k)^2 = r^2$$

In this equation, called the **standard form**, $r$ is the radius of the circle, and $h$ and $k$ are the $x$- and $y$-coordinates of the circle's center, respectively: $(h, k)$.

You might also see what is referred to as **general form**:

$$x^2 + y^2 + Cx + Dy + E = 0$$

In the general form, the fact that there are $x^2$ and $y^2$ terms with coefficients of 1 is an indicator that the equation does indeed graph as a circle. To convert to standard form, complete the square for the $x$ terms, then repeat for the $y$ terms. Refer to chapter 12 on quadratics for a review of completing the square if needed.

**You need to do this:**

- Get the circle into standard form
- Determine the center and radius using the standard form equation
- Use the center and/or radius to answer the question

**Explanation:**

The equation given is in general form rather than in standard form, so complete the square for both $x$ and $y$. Start by grouping the $x$ terms together and $y$ terms together:

$$x^2 - 4x + y^2 - 8y = 16$$
$$(x - 4x + ?) + (y - 8y + ?) = 16$$
$$(x - 4x + 4) + (y - 8y + 16) = 16 + 4 + 16$$
$$(x - 2)^2 + (y - 4)^2 = 36$$

With the equation in standard form, it is now easy to see that the center is $(2, 4)$. Choice **(C)** is correct.

## Try on Your Own

**Directions:** Take as much time as you need on these questions. Work carefully and methodically. There will be an opportunity for timed practice at the end of the chapter.

HINT: For Q16, which part of the circle's equation would be the easiest to use to eliminate answer choices? The coordinates of the circle's center? The radius?

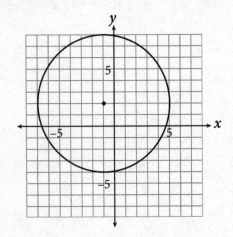

16.   Which of the following represents the equation of the circle shown above?

A)   $(x - 1)^2 + (y + 2)^2 = 6$

B)   $(x + 1)^2 + (y - 2)^2 = 6$

C)   $(x - 1)^2 + (y + 2)^2 = 36$

D)   $(x + 1)^2 + (y - 2)^2 = 36$

HINT: For Q17, complete the square for the $x$ and $y$ terms.

$$x^2 + 6x + y^2 - 8y = 171$$

17.   The equation of a circle in the $xy$-plane is shown above. What is the positive difference between the $x$- and $y$-coordinates of the center of the circle?

$$x^2 + y^2 + 8x - 20y = 28$$

18.   What is the diameter of the circle given by the equation above?

A)   12

B)   24

C)   28

D)   56

19.   A circle in the $xy$-plane is defined by the equation $(x - 4)^2 + (y + 2)^2 = 100$. Which of the following points is located on the circumference of the circle?

A)   $(-3, 5)$

B)   $(0, 9)$

C)   $(4, -2)$

D)   $(4, 8)$

# Arc Length and Sectors

## LEARNING OBJECTIVES

After this lesson, you will be able to:

- Calculate the length of an arc or the area of a sector defined by a central angle
- Convert degrees to radians

## To answer a question like this:

A circle with a diameter of 8 inches is divided into a number of equal sectors such that each sector has an area of $\frac{4\pi}{3}$ square inches. What is the central angle of each sector, in radians?

A) $\frac{\pi}{12}$

B) $\frac{\pi}{6}$

C) $\frac{\pi}{3}$

D) $\frac{2\pi}{3}$

## You need to know this:

The SAT may ask you about the following parts of circles: arcs, central angles, and sectors. The ability to set up ratios and proportions correctly is essential for these questions.

- An **arc** is part of a circle's circumference. If the circumference is divided into exactly two arcs, the smaller one is called the **minor arc** and the larger one is called the **major arc**. If a diameter cuts the circle in half, the two arcs formed are called **semicircles**. An arc length can never be greater than the circle's circumference.

- An angle formed by two radii is called a **central angle**. Because a full circle contains 360°, a central angle measure cannot be greater than this.

- The part of a circle's area defined by a central angle is called a **sector**. The area of a sector cannot be greater than the circle's total area.

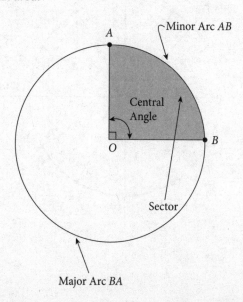

Here's a summary of the ratios formed by these three parts and their whole counterparts:

$$\frac{\text{central angle}}{360°} = \frac{\text{arc length}}{\text{circumference}} = \frac{\text{sector area}}{\text{circle area}}$$

Notice that all of these ratios are equal. Intuitively, this should make sense: when you slice a pizza into four equal slices, each piece should have $\frac{1}{4}$ of the cheese, crust, and sauce. If you slice a circle into four equal pieces, the same principle applies: each piece should have $\frac{1}{4}$ of the degrees, circumference, and area.

An angle whose vertex is on the edge of the circle is called an **inscribed angle**. As this vertex moves along the edge, the measure of the inscribed angle remains constant as long as the minor arc created does not change. When the line segments that create an inscribed angle define the same minor arc that a pair of radii do, a special relationship appears: the central angle measure is twice that of the inscribed angle.

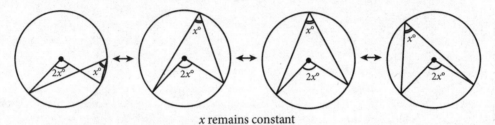

*x* remains constant

Most Geometry questions present angle measures in degrees, but some may present angle measures in radians. To convert between degrees and radians, use this relationship as a conversion factor: $180° = \pi$ radians. For instance, if you're asked to convert 90° into radians: $90° \times \frac{\pi}{180°} = \frac{\pi}{2}$. Note that there isn't a symbol for radians, so $\frac{\pi}{2}$ is read as "$\frac{\pi}{2}$ radians." This conversion works in the opposite direction as well: to convert radians to degrees, multiply by $\frac{180°}{\pi}$.

Most graphing calculators have both degree and radian modes, so make sure you're in the correct mode for the problem you're working on.

Below is a detailed unit circle diagram with common degree and radian measures (and the coordinates of the ends of their respective radii) that you may see on test day:

The coordinates at a particular angle measure translate into the leg lengths of the triangle created when a vertical line is drawn from the end of the radius down (or up if you're in quadrant III or IV) to the *x*-axis. For example, at 60°, the horizontal leg has a length of $\frac{1}{2}$ and the vertical leg has a length of $\frac{\sqrt{3}}{2}$.

## You need to do this:

- To find the length of an arc or the area of a sector, you need to know the angle that defines the arc or sector as well as the radius of the circle. Questions that are especially tricky might not give you those values directly but will instead give you a way of calculating them.

- When converting between degrees and radians, set up the conversion fraction so that the units cancel:

$$\text{degrees} \times \frac{\pi\,\text{radians}}{180\,\text{degrees}} \quad \text{and} \quad \text{radians} \times \frac{180\,\text{degrees}}{\text{radians}}$$

## Explanation:

Use the radius to find the area of the circle and divide the total area by the area of one sector to find the number of sectors. Divide the 360° in the whole circle by the number of sectors to find the central angle of each. Finally, convert to radians.

The question says the diameter of the circle is 8 inches, so the radius is 4 inches. A circle with a radius of 4 inches has an area of $\pi r^2 = 16\pi$. The area of each sector multiplied by the number of sectors will be equal to the total area:

$$\text{area of a sector} \times \text{number of sectors} = \text{total area}$$

$$\text{number of sectors} = \frac{\text{total area}}{\text{area of a sector}} = \frac{16\pi}{\frac{4\pi}{3}}$$

$$= 16\pi \times \frac{3}{4\pi} = 4 \times 3 = 12$$

If there are 12 sectors, the central angle defining each sector must be $\frac{1}{12}$ of 360°, or $\frac{1}{12} \times 2\pi = \frac{\pi}{6}$ radians. Choice **(B)** is correct.

## Try on Your Own

**Directions:** Take as much time as you need on these questions. Work carefully and methodically. There will be an opportunity for timed practice at the end of the chapter.

---

HINT: For Q20, what fraction of the total circumference is arc *AB*? What does that tell you about central angle *AOB*?

---

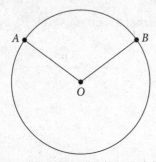

Note: Figure not drawn to scale.

20. In the figure above, circle *O* has a radius of 120 centimeters. If the length of minor arc *AOB* is 200 centimeters, what is the measure of minor angle *AOB*, to the nearest tenth of a degree?

    A)   95.5

    B)   98.2

    C)   102.1

    D)   105.4

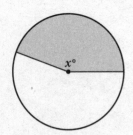

21. In the figure above, the ratio of the shaded area to the non-shaded area is 4 to 5. What is the value of *x*, in degrees?

    A)   135

    B)   145

    C)   160

    D)   170

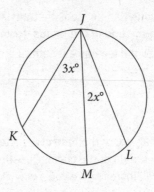

22. In the figure above, points *J*, *K*, *L*, and *M* lie on the circle. If the measure of arc *KML* is 150°, what is the value of *x*?

    A)   12

    B)   15

    C)   30

    D)   60

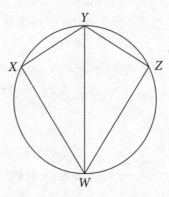

23. In the figure above, points *W*, *X*, *Y*, and *Z* lie on the circle. The measure of arc *YXW* is 180°, and the measure of arcs *XY* and *YZ* each is 60°. If *YZ* = 3, then what is the length of *WX*?

    A)   $\sqrt{3}$

    B)   3

    C)   $3\sqrt{3}$

    D)   6

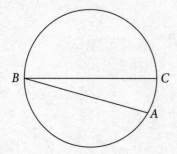

24. In the figure above, *BC* is the diameter of the circle. If the measure of arc *AC* is 30°, then what is the measure of minor arc *BA*, in radians?

   A)  $\dfrac{\pi}{2}$

   B)  $\dfrac{2\pi}{3}$

   C)  $\dfrac{3\pi}{4}$

   D)  $\dfrac{5\pi}{6}$

# Three-Dimensional Figures

### LEARNING OBJECTIVES

After this lesson, you will be able to:

- Calculate the volume of common solids
- Calculate the surface area of common solids

## To answer a question like this:

Marcus's yard has a large square sandbox serving as a cactus bed. The side lengths of the box are 24 feet, and the box is currently one-third full of sand from the bottom up. Marcus purchases 480 cubic feet of sand, which, when added to the box, will completely fill it. How many inches deep is the cactus bed?

A)  10

B)  15

C)  20

D)  25

## You need to know this:

Over the last several sections, you learned about two-dimensional (2-D) shapes and how to tackle SAT questions involving them. Now you'll learn how to do the same for questions containing three-dimensional (3-D) shapes, also called solids. There are several different types of solids that might appear on test day—rectangular solids, cubes, cylinders, prisms, spheres, cones, pyramids—knowing their structures will help you on test day.

The following diagram shows the basic anatomy of a 3-D shape:

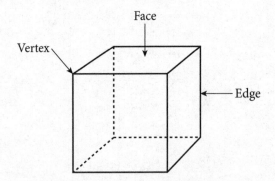

A **face** (or **surface**) is a 2-D shape that acts as one of the sides of the solid. Two faces meet at a line segment called an **edge**, and three faces meet at a single point called a **vertex**.

## Volume

**Volume** is the amount of 3-D space occupied by a solid. Volume is analogous to the area of a 2-D shape. You can find the volume of many 3-D shapes by finding the area of the base and multiplying it by the height. In the table of formulas, the pieces that represent the areas of the bases are enclosed in parentheses.

| Rectangular Solid | Cube | Right Cylinder |
|:---:|:---:|:---:|
| | | |
| $(l \times w) \times h$ | $(s \times s) \times s = s^3$ | $(\pi \times r^2) \times h$ |

The three 3-D shapes shown above are prisms. Almost all prisms on the SAT are right prisms; that is, all faces are perpendicular to those with which they share edges.

Following are some examples of less commonly seen prisms:

| Triangular Prism | Hexagonal Prism | Decagonal Prism |
|:---:|:---:|:---:|
| | | |

Like the rectangular solids, cubes, and cylinders you saw earlier, these right prisms use the same general volume formula ($V = A_{\text{base}} \times h$).

You might not be told explicitly the area of the base of a prism, in which case you'll need to rely on your two-dimensional geometry knowledge to find it before calculating the volume.

More complicated 3-D shapes include the right pyramid, right cone, and sphere. The vertex of a right pyramid or right cone will always be centered above the middle of the base. Their volume formulas are similar to those of prisms, albeit with different coefficients.

Some of these formulas might look daunting, but you won't have to memorize them for test day. They'll be provided on the reference page at the beginning of each Math section.

| Right Rectangular Pyramid | Right Cone | Sphere |
|:---:|:---:|:---:|
| | | |
| $\frac{1}{3} \times (l \times w) \times h$ | $\frac{1}{3} \times \left(\pi \times r^2\right) \times h$ | $\frac{4}{3} \times \pi \times r^3$ |

A right pyramid can have any polygon as its base, but the square variety is the one you're most likely to see on the SAT. Also note that the vertex above the base of a right pyramid or cone is not necessarily formed by an intersection of exactly three faces, as in prisms, but it is still a single point and is still called a vertex.

## Surface Area

**Surface area** is the sum of the areas of all faces of a solid. To calculate the surface area of a solid, simply find the area of each face using your 2-D geometry skills, then add them all together.

You won't be expected to know the surface area formulas for right pyramids, right cones, and spheres. They'll be provided at the beginning of each Math section. However, you could be asked to find the surface area of a prism, in which case you'll be given enough information to find the area of each surface of the solid.

You might think that finding the surface area of a solid with many sides, such as a right hexagonal prism, is a tall order. However, you can save time by noticing a vital trait: this prism has two identical hexagonal faces and six identical rectangular faces. Don't waste time finding the area of each of the eight surfaces. Find the area of one hexagonal face and one rectangular face only. Then multiply the area of the hexagonal face by 2 and the area of the rectangular face by 6, add the products together, and you're done. The same is true for other 3-D shapes such as rectangular solids (including cubes), other right prisms, and certain pyramids.

## You need to do this:

- To answer questions that involve regular solids, look for ways to find the area of the base and the height.
- To answer questions that involve solids that are not regular, look up and apply the appropriate formula.
- To answer questions that involve surface area, look for surfaces that are the same. Calculate the area of each kind of surface once, and then multiply by the number of identical surfaces in the solid.

## Explanation:

One way to approach this question is to find the total volume of the cactus bed first and then use that volume to calculate its depth. If the bed is one-third full, it is two-thirds empty, and according to the question, this empty space is 480 cubic feet. So two-thirds of the total volume is 480:

$$\frac{2}{3} \times V = 480 \text{ ft}^3$$

$$V = 480 \times \frac{3}{2} = 720 \text{ ft}^3$$

The volume of the cactus bed is also equal to the product of its length, width, and height. The question states that the length and width are each 24 feet, so plug these values into the formula and solve for height:

$$V = l \times w \times h$$

$$h = \frac{V}{l \times w}$$

$$= \frac{720}{24 \times 24}$$

$$= \frac{720}{576}$$

$$= 1.25 \text{ feet}$$

The question asks for inches, so do the conversion:

$$1.25 \text{ feet} \times \frac{12 \text{ inches}}{1 \text{ foot}} = 15 \text{ inches}$$

Choice (**B**) is correct.

## Try on Your Own

**Directions:** Take as much time as you need on these questions. Work carefully and methodically. There will be an opportunity for timed practice at the end of the chapter.

---

HINT: For Q25, refer to the formulas at the beginning of the chapter. On test day, they are included at the beginning of each Math section in your test booklet.

---

25. Two ornamental glass spheres have diameters of 6 inches and 12 inches, respectively. What is the positive difference in their volumes?

    A) $36\pi$

    B) $252\pi$

    C) $288\pi$

    D) $2{,}016\pi$

---

HINT: For Q26, when the water is poured into a larger glass, what information about the water does not change?

---

26. Alma pours water into a small cylindrical glass with a height of 6 inches and a diameter of 3 inches. The water fills the glass to the very top, so she decides to pour it into a bigger glass that is 8 inches tall and 4 inches in diameter. Assuming Alma doesn't spill any when she pours, how many inches high will the water reach in the bigger glass?

    A) 1.5

    B) 2.25

    C) 3.375

    D) 6.0

27. If the volume of the pyramid shown in the figure above can be represented by the function $V(x) = x^3 - x$, which of the following expressions represents the pyramid's height?

    A) $x$

    B) $2x$

    C) $x - 1$

    D) $x - 3$

28. A pet store decided to begin selling fish, so the manager purchased 50 of the fish tanks shown above to hold the fish. The staff need to fill the bottom two inches of each tank with sand, which comes only in full-size 40-pound bags. If 1 cubic inch of sand weighs 2 ounces, how many bags of sand does the pet store need to buy? (There are 16 ounces in 1 pound.)

    A) 45

    B) 68

    C) 84

    D) 125

29. In the figure above, a cylindrical candle with a
diameter of 2 inches and height of 8 inches sits
within a rectangular glass box. The box is the same
height as the candle and the area of the base of the
box is 15 square inches. If Felipe wants to fill the
space between the candle and the box with wax,
how many cubic inches of wax does he need?

A) $120 - 8\pi$

B) $120 - 32\pi$

C) $225 - 8\pi$

D) $225 - 32\pi$

## On Test Day

What students often find most challenging about questions involving geometry is not the need to remember or apply formulas but rather the fact that the test maker likes to "hide" the path to the solution. The starting information you need will be given, but you'll need to make deductions from that information to assemble all the facts you need to answer the question.

As you consider the question below, ask yourself what information you need to be able to solve. How can you get that information from what you're given?

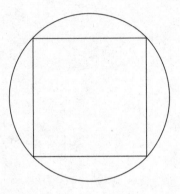

30. In the figure above, a square is inscribed in a circle, and the area of the square is 400 square units. What is the area of the circle in square units?

A) $50\pi$

B) $100\pi$

C) $200\pi$

D) $400\pi$

The explanation appears at the end of this chapter.

## How Much Have You Learned?

**Directions:** For testlike practice, give yourself 22 minutes to complete this question set. Be sure to study the explanations, even for questions you got right. They can be found at the end of this chapter. Note that this question set includes foundational topics in Geometry covered in Math Fundamentals in chapter 2.

Make use of the formula sheet below as needed; you'll have these same formulas available in your test booklet when you take the real SAT.

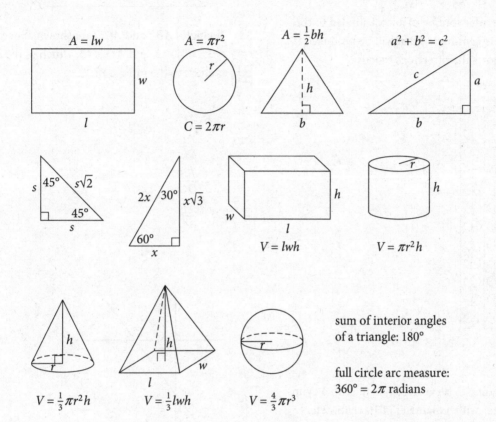

**Questions 31 and 32 refer to the following stimulus.**

Desiree is making apple juice from concentrate. The cylindrical container of concentrate has a diameter of 7 centimeters and a height of 12 centimeters. To make the juice, the concentrate must be diluted with water so that the mix is 75 percent water and 25 percent concentrate.

31. What is the total volume of juice, rounded to the nearest cubic centimeter, that will be produced if Desiree follows the directions exactly?

32. Desiree is going to serve the apple juice in a cylindrical pitcher with a diameter of 10 centimeters. What is the minimum height of the pitcher, rounded to the nearest centimeter, required for it to hold the apple juice that Desiree made?

33. Triangles ABE and ACD are shown above. If AB is 3, DC is 12, and AD is 15, which of the following is equal to the ratio 1:3 ?

A) $\dfrac{EB}{AC}$

B) $\dfrac{AE}{DC}$

C) $\dfrac{EB}{DC}$

D) $\dfrac{AE}{AC}$

34. In the figure above, if $q = 140$, what is the value of $r - p$ ?

A)    0

B)    10

C)    90

D)    130

35. The area of a right triangle is 35 square inches. If the longer leg is 3 inches longer than the shorter leg, what is the length of the hypotenuse, in inches?

    A) 10

    B) $\dfrac{\sqrt{35}}{2}$

    C) $7\sqrt{10}$

    D) $\sqrt{149}$

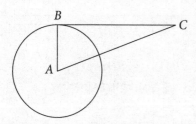

36. Point $A$ is the center of the circle and line segment $BC$ is tangent to the circle. If the measure of $\angle A$ is $(3k + 23)°$ and the measure of $\angle C$ is $(4k - 31)°$, what is the value of $k$?

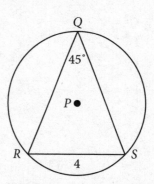

37. A sphere with a diameter of 2 inches is resting on a table. If the distance from the center of the sphere to the edge of the table is 10 inches, what is the distance, in inches, between the point where the sphere contacts the table and the table edge?

    A) $4\sqrt{6}$

    B) $3\sqrt{11}$

    C) 10

    D) $\sqrt{101}$

38. At Wesley's Pizzeria the small pizza is 4 inches smaller in diameter than the large pizza, whose diameter is 16 inches. If each pizza is cut into eight equal slices, one large slice is approximately what percent larger than one small slice?

    A) 44%

    B) 62%

    C) 78%

    D) 84%

Note: Figure not drawn to scale.

39. In circle $P$ above, $RS = 4$ and $\angle RQS$ measures $45°$. What is the circumference of circle $P$?

    A) $4\pi$

    B) $4\pi\sqrt{2}$

    C) $8\pi$

    D) $8\pi\sqrt{2}$

40. An airport instrumentation technician needs to calibrate the air traffic control radar system. An air traffic control radar system display consists of four concentric circles in a coordinate plane. The diameter of the smallest circle is two units, and the diameter of each successive circle is two units larger than that of the previous circle. The diagram above shows the radar system grid before calibration. What is the equation for the smallest dotted circle before the calibration?

A) $(x+3)^2 + (y+4)^2 = 4^2$

B) $(x-3)^2 + (y-4)^2 = 2^2$

C) $(x-3)^2 + (y-4)^2 = 4^2$

D) $(x+3)^2 + (y+4)^2 = 8^2$

| Material | Price per Square Foot |
|---|---|
| Quartz | $75 |
| Stainless steel | $67 |
| Granite | $102 |
| Laminate | $71 |
| Wood | $81 |
| Concrete | $55 |
| Soapstone | $97 |
| Travertine | $72 |

41. An interior designer is trying to determine the best counter material for a kitchen remodel. The designer must cover all of the shaded counter areas in the floor plan above.

What is the area of the counter surface that must be covered, in square feet?

A)    9

B)    46

C)    55

D)   104

42. The family gives the interior designer a $4,500 budget to buy materials for the counter. A list of the available materials and the price per square foot appears in the table above. Which choice provides only options that the interior designer can present to the family that stay within the allotted budget?

    I. Wood

    II. Laminate

    III. Soapstone

    IV. Quartz

    V. Granite

A) I and III

B) II, III, IV

C) I, II, IV

D) III and V

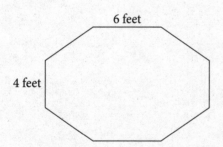

43. A carpenter creates the octagonal dining room table, shown above, by cutting an isosceles right triangle from each corner of the original piece of lumber. If all four isosceles right triangles are congruent and each has an area of $\frac{9}{2}$ square feet, what are the dimensions of the original piece of lumber, in feet?

A) $8 \times 8$

B) $10 \times 12$

C) $12 \times 14$

D) $14 \times 18$

44. Sixty fourth-grade students are making kites that are 18 inches wide and 24 inches tall. Each student uses the vertically symmetrical pattern, shown above, to cut out the kite from an 18- by 24-inch piece of material, such that the height of each kite is parallel to the longer edge of the material. After the students finish making the kites, one of the teachers collects all of the leftover kite material. If all the students successfully make their kites on the first try, how much leftover material will the teacher collect?

A)     1.5 square feet

B)     15 square feet

C)     90 square feet

D)  12,960 square feet

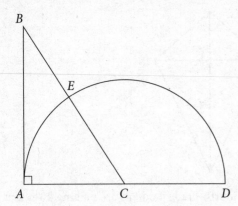

45. In the figure above, *C* is the center of the semicircle and points *A*, *E*, and *D* are on the semicircle. If *CB* equals 12 and the measure of angle *ABC* is 30°, what is the length of *CE*? (Round your answer to the nearest unit.)

# Reflect

**Directions:** Take a few minutes to recall what you've learned and what you've been practicing in this chapter. Consider the following questions, jot down your best answer for each one, and then compare your reflections to the expert responses on the following page. Use your level of confidence to determine what to do next.

How can you tell whether two triangles are similar?

_____

_____

_____

What are the two Pythagorean triples you are most likely to see on test day?

_____

_____

_____

What are the ratios of the side lengths of a 45-45-90 triangle? Of a 30-60-90 triangle?

_____

_____

_____

What is the standard form for the equation of a circle?

_____

_____

_____

What is the relationship of a circle's central angle to the arc and sector the angle defines?

_____

_____

_____

How would you find the surface area of a right triangular prism with equilateral triangles as its bases?

_____

_____

_____

## Expert Responses

How can you tell whether two triangles are similar?

*There are three ways to tell:*

- *Two of their three angles are congruent (angle-angle).*
- *Two of their three sides are in the same proportion and the intervening angle is congruent (side-angle-side).*
- *Their three sides are in the same proportion (side-side-side).*

What are the two Pythagorean triples you are most likely to see on test day?

*The two most common Pythagorean triples on the SAT are 3:4:5 and 5:12:13. You may also see multiples of these, e.g., 6:8:10 or 10:24:26.*

What are the ratios of the side lengths of a 45-45-90 triangle? Of a 30-60-90 triangle?

*The side lengths of a 45-45-90 triangle are always in the ratio of $x:x:x\sqrt{2}$. The side lengths of a 30-60-90 triangle are always in the ratio of $x:x\sqrt{3}:2x$. Remember that the shortest side of any triangle is across from the smallest angle and the longest side is across from the greatest angle.*

What is the standard form for the equation of a circle?

*The equation of a circle in the coordinate plane is $(x - h)^2 + (y - k)^2 = r^2$, where r is the radius of the circle and (h, k) is the ordered pair representing its center.*

What is the relationship of a circle's central angle to the arc and sector the angle defines?

*The central angle, the arc, and the sector are all in proportion to the full circle:*

$$\frac{\text{central angle}}{360°} = \frac{\text{arc length}}{\text{circumference}} = \frac{\text{sector area}}{\text{circle area}}$$

How would you find the surface area of a right triangular prism with equilateral triangles as its bases?

*Calculate the area of one of the equilateral triangles and multiply by 2. Calculate the area of one of the rectangular faces and multiply by 3. Then add the results.*

## Next Steps

If you answered most questions correctly in the "How Much Have You Learned?" section, and if your responses to the Reflect questions were similar to those of the SAT expert, then consider Geometry an area of strength and move on to the next chapter. Come back to this topic periodically to prevent yourself from getting rusty.

If you don't yet feel confident, review those parts of this chapter that you have not yet mastered. In particular, review the lessons on similar triangles, the Pythagorean theorem, and special right triangles, as these are high-yield topics on the SAT. Then try the questions you missed again. As always, be sure to review the explanations closely.

# Answers and Explanations

## 1. 426

**Difficulty:** Medium

**Strategic Advice:** The figure contains a pair of similar triangles. Use the fact that their sides are in proportion to find the required length.

**Getting to the Answer:** The question asks for the length of $DE$. Note that $DC + DE = EC$, which means $DE = EC - DC$. First, find the length of $EC$ by setting up a proportion where $BD$ is related to $AC$ in the same way that $DC$ is related to the unknown $EC$. $AC$ is 324 and $DC$ is 50% longer than segment $BD$, or $1.5 \times 40 = 60$ feet:

$$\frac{BD}{AE} = \frac{DC}{EC}$$
$$\frac{40}{324} = \frac{60}{EC}$$
$$\frac{10}{81} = \frac{60}{EC}$$
$$10x = 4{,}860$$
$$EC = 486$$

Subtract the length of $DC$, 60, from from the length of $EC$, 486, to obtain 426, the length of $DE$. Grid in **426**.

## 2. B

**Difficulty:** Medium

**Getting to the Answer:** Given the area of $\triangle ABC$ and the length of the base $AB$, you can find $BC$, its height:

$$150 = \frac{1}{2}(20)(BC)$$
$$150 = 10(BC)$$
$$15 = BC$$

Because lengths $BC = 15$ and $AB = 20$, $\triangle ABC$ is a 3:4:5 triangle with dimensions scaled up by a factor of 5. The hypotenuse, $AC$, must be $5 \times 5 = 25$. $\triangle ABC$ and $\triangle AGH$ are similar triangles because they share an angle at vertex $A$ and they each have a right angle. Therefore, their corresponding sides must be proportional. The question says that the hypotenuse of $\triangle AGH$, $AH$, is 20, so use this information to create a proportion:

$$\frac{AH}{AC} = \frac{HG}{CB}$$
$$\frac{20}{25} = \frac{HG}{15}$$
$$300 = 25\,HG$$
$$HG = 12$$

Choice **(B)** is the correct answer.

## 3. B

**Difficulty:** Medium

**Getting to the Answer:** The question says that segment $HI$ is the bisector of segments $LO$ and $OW$. This tells you two things: 1) $HI$ divides both $LO$ and $OW$ exactly in half and 2) $HI$ is parallel to $LW$.

Because $HI$ is parallel to $LW$, angles $L$ and $H$ must be congruent (they are corresponding angles) and angles $W$ and $I$ must be congruent (they are also corresponding angles). Angle $O$ is shared by both triangles. The triangles, therefore, are similar. Side lengths of similar triangles are in proportion to one another. Because $I$ is the midpoint of $OW$, $OI$ is half as long as $OW$. (The same is true for the other side: $OH$ is half as long as $OL$.) So the sides are in the ratio 1:2. The question gives the side lengths of $LW$ and $HI$. Use this ratio and these side lengths to set up a proportion and solve for $x$:

$$\frac{1}{2} = \frac{HI}{LW}$$
$$\frac{1}{2} = \frac{4x - 1}{30}$$
$$30 = 2(4x - 1)$$
$$30 = 8x - 2$$
$$32 = 8x$$
$$4 = x$$

The correct answer is **(B)**.

**4. 9**

**Difficulty:** Hard

**Getting to the Answer:** Corresponding sides of similar triangles are proportional. Draw a quick sketch to find as many side lengths as you can, find the ratio of the sides between the two triangles, and use that ratio to find the missing vertex.

Plot all the points given in the question, labeling them as you go so you don't get confused (especially because you won't have graph paper). You know that $D$ and $A$ are in the same quadrant, which means the triangles are both oriented the same way, so make your sketch accordingly:

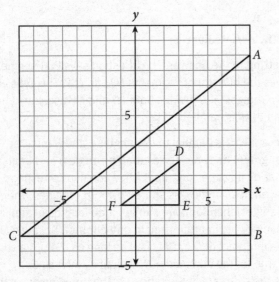

Once you have plotted triangle $DEF$ and the base of triangle $ABC$, you can determine that the ratio of the triangles is 1:4 (the base of $DEF$ has a length of 4 and the base of $ABC$ has a length of 16). To determine where you should put $A$, find the length of side $DE$ and then multiply by 4. The length of the vertical side of triangle $ABC$ is $3 \times 4 = 12$. Because one vertex is at $(8, -3)$, vertex $A$ must be 12 vertical units above that point, or $(8, 9)$. The $y$-coordinate of $A$ is **9**.

**5. B**

**Difficulty:** Hard

**Getting to the Answer:** The figure gives two triangles that look as though they have a lot in common. Analyze them, looking for similarities so you can set up a proportion. Angle $C$ is shared by both triangles. And, because $BD$ is parallel to $AE$, angles $CAE$ and $CBD$ are congruent—they are corresponding angles. Two pairs of congruent angles means that triangles $ACE$ and $BCD$ are similar by

angle-angle. (You could have analyzed angles $CDB$ and $CEA$, but you need only two pairs of congruent angles to conclude that two triangles are similar.)

Set up a proportion using the triangles' side lengths. You'll need to translate from English into math as you go: $AB = 5$ and $BC$ is three times that, or 15. This means $AC = 5 + 15 = 20$. $CD$ is 2 more than half $AC$, $\frac{20}{2} + 2 = 10 + 2 = 12$. Use the three known side lengths to create a proportion and solve for $EC$:

$$\frac{BC}{AC} = \frac{DC}{EC}$$
$$\frac{15}{20} = \frac{12}{EC}$$
$$15EC = 240$$
$$EC = 16$$

The question asks for the length of segment $DE$, which is $EC - CD$, or $16 - 12 = 4$. **(B)** is correct.

**6. A**

**Difficulty:** Medium

**Getting to the Answer:** Start by connecting the ranch to the campsite. Then draw in a horizontal line and a vertical line to form a right triangle.

The length of one leg of the triangle is 15 miles, the distance from the watering hole to the barn. The length of the other leg is $6 + 2 = 8$ miles, the distance from the ranch to the watering hole plus the distance from the barn to the campsite. The two legs of the right triangle are 8 and 15. You might recognize the Pythagorean triple 8:15:17, but if you don't, you can always rely on the Pythagorean theorem:

$$8^2 + 15^2 = c^2$$
$$64 + 225 = c^2$$
$$289 = c^2$$
$$\sqrt{289} = \sqrt{c^2}$$
$$17 = c$$

The actual trail is $6 + 15 + 2 = 23$ miles long. The direct route is 17 miles, so the direct route is $23 - 17 = 6$ miles shorter, so **(A)** is the correct answer.

## 7.  4

**Difficulty:** Medium

**Getting to the Answer:** Start by drawing Ted's car and bike routes to his friend's house and labeling your diagram with the distances you know. To find the distance of Ted's bike route create a right triangle:

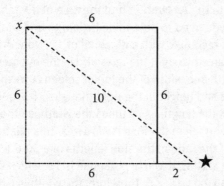

You can use the Pythagorean theorem to find the hypotenuse (bike route), but you'll save time if you recognize that you have a Pythagorean triple (6:8:10, a common multiple of 3:4:5). Thus, Ted's bike route is $6 + 6 + 2 = 14$ miles, and his car route is 10 miles; the difference between the two is **4**.

## 8.  A

**Difficulty:** Medium

**Getting to the Answer:** The question asks for the total distance they traveled. Aundria traveled $5 + 6 + 7 + 2 = 20$ miles. To find the distance Annette traveled, draw and label a diagram of Aundria and Annette's routes and look for a place to sketch in a right triangle so that Annette's direct route is the hypotenuse:

Use the Pythagorean theorem to calculate the distance Annette will travel:

$$c^2 = (5+7)^2 + 4^2$$
$$c^2 = 144 + 16$$
$$c^2 = 160$$
$$c = \sqrt{160}$$

Note that the answers are in decimal form, so convert the root value to a decimal: about 12.65 miles. Add this to Aundria's travel distance to find the total distance: $20 + 12.65 = 32.65$ miles. Choice **(A)** is correct.

## 9.  4

**Difficulty:** Medium

**Getting to the Answer:** Use the Pythagorean equation to solve for $x$:

$$(3x+1)^2 = (3x)^2 + (x+1)^2$$
$$9x^2 + 6x + 1 = 9x^2 + x^2 + 2x + 1$$
$$6x = x^2 + 2x$$
$$4x = x^2$$
$$4 = x$$

(Note that $x$ represents a distance and cannot be negative, so $-4$ is not a viable solution. Moreover, you cannot grid in a negative number.)

Grid in **4**.

## 10.  D

**Difficulty:** Hard

**Getting to the Answer:** To calculate the area of the semicircle, you need to find the length of the radius, which is $AE$. Since $AE = EC$, $AE$ is half of $AC$. Start by solving for the length of $AC$, which is the hypotenuse of right triangle $ABC$. Note that the sides of the triangle are a Pythagorean triple: 5, 12, 13. If you did not recognize the triple, you could have solved for $AC$ using the Pythagorean theorem: $AC = \sqrt{5^2 + 12^2} = 13$. Thus, $AC = 13$ and $AE = \frac{13}{2}$. The area of the semicircle is therefore $\frac{1}{2}\pi r^2 = \frac{1}{2}\pi\left(\frac{13}{2}\right)^2 = \frac{169}{8}$. **(D)** is correct.

## 11. C

**Difficulty:** Medium

**Getting to the Answer:** Triangle *DBC* is an isosceles right triangle, which means that it is a 45-45-90 right triangle with side length ratios of $x:x:x\sqrt{2}$. Because the two legs are each 4 units long, the hypotenuse *DB* is $4\sqrt{2}$. *DB* also acts as one leg of right triangle *DAB*. Since this leg is $4\sqrt{2}$ and the hypotenuse is $5\sqrt{2}$, triangle *DAB* is a 3:4:5 right triangle, and the length of *AD* is $3\sqrt{2}$. The legs of a right triangle are also its base and height, so plug the lengths of the legs into the formula for the area of a triangle, $\frac{1}{2}bh$, to get $\frac{1}{2}\left(4\sqrt{2}\right)\left(3\sqrt{2}\right) = 6 \times 2 = 12$. The correct answer is **(C)**.

## 12. B

**Difficulty:** Easy

**Getting to the Answer:** The height of the amusement ride at point *M* is perpendicular to the ground, and the roller coaster's angle of ascent is 30°, which creates a 30-60-90 triangle. Use the ratio of the sides $x:x\sqrt{3}:2x$ to find the height at point *M*. Because the distance from point *O* to point *M* is $200\sqrt{3}$ and corresponds to the hypotenuse of the triangle, then $200\sqrt{3} = 2x$. Solving for *x* by dividing both sides by 2 gives the length of the side opposite the 30° angle, which corresponds to the height of the amusement ride: $x = 100\sqrt{3}$ feet. **(B)** is correct.

## 13. C

**Difficulty:** Medium

**Getting to the Answer:** The top face of the corner shelf is a 45-45-90 triangle. Define the length of the shorter side, say *s*, and use the ratio of the sides $x:x:x\sqrt{2}$ to solve for it:

$$\frac{1}{\sqrt{2}} = \frac{s}{10}$$
$$s\sqrt{2} = 10$$
$$s = \frac{10}{\sqrt{2}}$$

Next, determine the top face surface area of one corner shelf using $\frac{1}{2}bh$. Note that in a right triangle, the sides that form the 90° angle are the base and height. Thus, the surface area of one corner shelf is $\frac{1}{2}\left(\frac{10}{\sqrt{2}}\right)\left(\frac{10}{\sqrt{2}}\right) = \frac{100}{4} = 25$ square inches. The question asks for the total surface area of three corner shelves, so $3 \times 25 = 75$ square inches. Choice **(C)** is correct.

Alternatively, you could find the altitude perpendicular to the longest side. Note the triangle can be split into two smaller 45-45-90 triangles. Thus, the altitude is the leg of the smaller 45-45-90 triangles, which is half of 10. The top face surface area of one corner shelf is therefore $\frac{1}{2}(10)(5) = 25$ square inches, and the total surface area for the three shelves is $3 \times 25 = 75$ square inches.

## 14. D

**Difficulty:** Hard

**Getting to the Answer:** To find the area of the tablet screen, you need to determine its length and width. Sketch a rectangle with a diagonal of 12. Note the diagonal creates two right triangles and is the hypotenuse. The length and width of the tablet screen correspond to the base and height of the right triangles. The question says that the length is $\sqrt{3}$ times the width, so the ratio of the short leg to the long leg is $1:\sqrt{3}$. This relationship is part of the ratio of the side lengths of a 30-60-90 triangle: $x:x\sqrt{3}:2x$. The hypotenuse is 12, which corresponds to $2x$, so $x = 6$. Therefore, the width is 6, and the length is $\sqrt{3} \times 6 = 6\sqrt{3}$. Use $l \times w$ to calculate the area: $6\sqrt{3} \times 6 = 36\sqrt{3}$ square inches. The correct answer is **(D)**.

## 15. 30

**Difficulty:** Medium

**Getting to the Answer:** Sketch a right triangle with a height of 2 and hypotenuse of 4 to represent the ramp to the stage. The ratio of the short side to the hypotenuse is 2:4, or 1:2. Notice that this matches the ratio of the sides for a 30-60-90 triangle: $x:x\sqrt{3}:2x$. The angle of incline is opposite the short side, which is 30°. Grid in **30**.

## 16. D

**Difficulty:** Easy

**Getting to the Answer:** The standard form of the equation of a circle is $(x - h)^2 + (y - k)^2 = r^2$, where $(h, k)$ is the center of the circle and *r* is the length of the radius.

The answer choices have many similarities, which will make them easy to eliminate piece by piece. Use the graph to find the radius. From the center, you can count horizontally or vertically to the edge of the circle to find that its radius is 6. If $r = 6$, then $r^2 = 36$. Eliminate (A) and (B). Now find the *x*-coordinate of the center of the circle, $-1$. This means the $(x - h)^2$ part of the equation is $(x - (-1))^2 = (x + 1)^2$. Eliminate (C). Only **(D)** is left and is correct. Note that you do not even need to find the $(y - k)^2$ part of the equation, but for the record: because the $y$-coordinate of the center of the circle is 2, then $(y - k)^2$ becomes $(y - 2)^2$, and the full equation is $(x + 1)^2 + (y - 2)^2 = 36$. **(D)** is indeed correct.

## 17. 7

**Difficulty:** Hard

**Getting to the Answer:** Rewrite the given equation for the circle in standard form to find the coordinates of the center. Start by completing the square for each of the variables. Take half of the coefficient and then square it. For the $x$-coefficient, half of 6 is 3, and 3 squared is 9. For the $y$-coefficient, half of 8 is 4, and 4 squared is 16. Add 9 and 16 to both sides and rewrite as two separate squares of binomials:

$$(x - h)^2 + (y - k)^2 = r^2$$
$$x^2 + 6x + y^2 - 8y = 171$$
$$x^2 + 6x + 9 + y^2 - 8y + 16 = 171 + 9 + 16$$
$$(x + 3)^2 + (y - 4)^2 = 196$$

The coordinates of the center of the circle are $(-3, 4)$. The positive difference is $4 - (-3) = 7$. Grid in **7**. If you came up with a negative number, remember that the answer to a Grid-in question cannot be negative.

## 18. B

**Difficulty:** Hard

**Getting to the Answer:** The question asks for the diameter, which is twice the radius. When the equation of a circle is in the form $(x - h)^2 + (y - k)^2 = r^2$, the $r$ represents the length of the radius. The question gives the equation in general form, so you need to complete the square to put the equation into standard form.

You already have an $x^2$ and a $y^2$ in the given equation and the coefficients of $x$ and $y$ are even, so completing the square is fairly straightforward—there are just a lot of steps. Start by grouping the $x$'s and $y$'s together. Then, take the coefficient of the $x$ term and divide it by 2, square it, and add it to the two terms with $x$ variables.

Do the same with the $y$ term. Remember to add these amounts to the other side of the equation as well. Then factor the perfect squares and simplify:

$$x^2 + y^2 + 8x - 20y = 28$$
$$x^2 + 8x + y^2 - 20y = 28$$
$$\left(x^2 + 8x + 16\right) + \left(y^2 - 20y + 100\right) = 28 + 16 + 100$$
$$(x + 4)^2 + (y - 10)^2 = 144$$

The equation tells you that $r^2$ is 144, which means that the radius is 12 and the diameter is twice that, or 24, which is **(B)**.

## 19. D

**Difficulty:** Medium

**Getting to the Answer:** The given equation defines a circle with its center at $(4, -2)$ and a radius of 10. Any point on the circumference of the circle must satisfy that equation. Eliminate (C) because it is the center of the circle. Plug the other choices into the equation to see if they satisfy the given equation:

(A) $(-3 - 4)^2 + (5 + 2)^2 = (-7)^2 + (7)^2 = 49 + 49 = 98$. Since $98 < 100$, this is inside the circle. Eliminate (A).

(B) $(0 - 4)^2 + (9 + 2)^2 = (-4)^2 + (11)^2$. Since the second term alone is greater than 100, this is outside the circle. Eliminate (B).

Only **(D)** is left and is correct. For the record:

(D) $(4 - 4)^2 + (8 + 2)^2 = (0)^2 + (10)^2 = 100$. This point satisfies the equation and is therefore on the circumference. **(D)** is indeed correct.

### 20. A

**Difficulty:** Medium

**Getting to the Answer:** To find a central angle based on a known arc length, use the relationship $\frac{\text{arc length}}{\text{circumference}} = \frac{\text{central angle}}{360°}$. The unknown in the relationship is the central angle, so call it $a$. Before you can fill in the rest of the equation, you need to find the circumference of the circle: $C = 2\pi r = 2\pi(120) = 240\pi$. Now, you're ready to solve for $a$:

$$\frac{\text{arc length}}{\text{circumference}} = \frac{\text{central angle}}{360°}$$

$$\frac{200}{240\pi} = \frac{a}{360°}$$

$$\frac{200(360)}{240\pi} = a$$

$$95.5° \approx a$$

**(A)** is correct. Be careful when you enter this expression into your calculator—you need to put $240\pi$ in parentheses so that the calculator doesn't divide by 240 and then multiply by $\pi$.

### 21. C

**Difficulty:** Medium

**Getting to the Answer:** Because the ratio of the shaded area to the non-shaded area is 4:5, the ratio of the shaded area to the entire circle is $4:(4 + 5) = 4:9$. This ratio is the same as the ratio of the interior angle of the shaded sector to 360°, or $x:360$. Set up a proportion using these ratios:

$$\frac{4}{9} = \frac{x}{360}$$

$$360(4) = 9x$$

$$1,440 = 9x$$

$$160 = x$$

Choice **(C)** is correct.

### 22. B

**Difficulty:** Medium

**Getting to the Answer:** The measure of an arc is directly related to the degree measure of its central angle. The measure of an inscribed angle is half of that of the central angle. Because the measure of arc *KML* is 150°,

the degree measure of the inscribed angle is half of that. The inscribed angle for arc *KML* can be written as $3x + 2x$. Set up an equation to solve for $x$:

$$3x + 2x = \frac{1}{2}(150)$$

$$5x = 75$$

$$x = 15$$

Choice **(B)** is correct.

### 23. C

**Difficulty:** Hard

**Getting to the Answer:** Note that the figure is composed of two triangles inscribed in a circle. If you have enough information about the triangles, you can find the length of *WX*. Arcs *XY* and *YZ* are each 60°. Because an inscribed angle is half of its corresponding arc, the inscribed angles *XWY* and *ZWY* are each 30°. Similarly, the sum of inscribed angles *XYW* and *ZYW* is half of arc *XWZ*: $\frac{1}{2}(360 - (60 + 60)) = 120$. Thus, angles *XYW* and *XWY* are each 60°. Therefore, both triangles are 30-60-90 special right triangles, so use the ratio of the sides $x : x\sqrt{3} : 2x$ to find the length of *WX*. Given $YZ = 3$, *XY* also equals 3 and $\frac{3}{WX} = \frac{1}{\sqrt{3}}$, so $WX = 3\sqrt{3}$. Choice **(C)** is correct.

### 24. D

**Difficulty:** Medium

**Getting to the Answer:** Since *BC* is the diameter, the measure of arc *BAC* is 180°. Therefore, the measure of arc *BA* is the measure of arc *BAC* minus the measure of arc *AC*: $180° - 30° = 150°$. Use $180° = \pi$ to convert to radians: $150° \times \frac{\pi}{180°} = \frac{5\pi}{6}$. Thus, **(D)** is correct.

### 25. B

**Difficulty:** Medium

**Getting to the Answer:** Begin by finding the volume of each sphere using the volume formula for a sphere, remembering to halve the diameters first:

$$V_1 = \frac{4}{3}\pi r^3 = \frac{4}{3}\pi(3)^3 = \frac{4}{3}\pi(27) = 36\pi$$

$$V_2 = \frac{4}{3}\pi r^3 = \frac{4}{3}\pi(6)^3 = \frac{4}{3}\pi(216) = 288\pi$$

The positive difference is $288\pi - 36\pi = 252\pi$, which is **(B)**.

**26. C**

**Difficulty:** Medium

**Getting to the Answer:** After the water is poured into the larger glass, the volume of the water in the glass will be the same as the volume when it was in the smaller glass. Find the volume of the water in the smaller glass, whose height is 6 inches and radius is 3 inches. Then, substitute this volume into a second equation where the height is unknown and the radius is 4 inches (the radius of the larger glass) and solve for $h$. The volume of a cylinder equals the area of its base times its height, or $V = \pi r^2 h$:

$$V = \pi r^2 h$$
$$V = \pi (1.5)^2 (6)$$
$$V = \pi (2.25)(6)$$
$$V = 13.5\pi$$

$$13.5\pi = \pi (2)^2 h$$
$$13.5\pi = 4\pi h$$
$$3.375 = h$$

The water will reach 3.375 inches high in the bigger glass. **(C)** is correct.

**27. C**

**Difficulty:** Medium

**Getting to the Answer:** The formula for finding the volume of a pyramid with a rectangular base is $V = \frac{1}{3} lwh$. Start by substituting what you know into the formula. The volume is represented by $x^3 - x$, the length is $x + 1$, and the width is $3x$:

$$V = \frac{1}{3} lwh$$
$$x^3 - x = \frac{1}{3}(x + 1)(3x)h$$
$$x(x^2 - 1) = (x + 1)xh$$

Notice that if you divide both sides of the equation by $x$, you'll be left with $x^2 - 1$ on the left side and $(x + 1)$ times $h$ on the right side. Note that this is a classic quadratic: the factors of $x^2 - 1$ are $x + 1$ and $x - 1$. So:

$$(x + 1)(x - 1) = (x + 1)h$$
$$x - 1 = h$$

This means the height of the pyramid must be represented by $x - 1$. Therefore, **(C)** is correct.

**28. B**

**Difficulty:** Hard

**Getting to the Answer:** When a question involves many steps, as this one does, plan out the order of your calculations and conversions. In this case, you can go from volume of sand in 1 tank to volume of sand in 50 tanks, to weight of sand in ounces, to weight of sand in pounds, to the number of bags of sand.

The volume of sand in one tank (only 2 inches of the height) will be $V = 24 \times 9 \times 2 = 432$ cubic inches, which means the volume of sand in all 50 tanks will be $50 \times 432 = 21,600$ cubic inches. Each cubic inch of sand weighs 2 ounces, so the weight of all the sand will be $2 \times 21,600 = 43,200$ ounces. There are 16 ounces in one pound, so the weight of the sand in pounds is $43,000$ ounces $\times \dfrac{1\ pound}{16\ ounces} = 2,700$ pounds. Finally, each bag contains 40 pounds of sand, so the pet store needs to buy 2,700 pounds $\times \dfrac{1\ bag}{40\ pounds} = 67.5$ bags. Because the store cannot buy one-half of one 40-pound bag of sand, it will need to buy 68 bags of sand. **(B)** is the correct answer.

**29. A**

**Difficulty:** Medium

**Getting to the Answer:** Determine the volumes of the rectangular box and of the cylindrical candle. Then calculate the difference between the two to find the volume of space between them. The volume of the box is the area of the base times its height: $15 \times 8 = 120$ cubic inches. Eliminate (C) and (D). Next, use $\pi r^2 h$ to calculate the volume of the cylinder. The diameter is 2 inches, so the radius is 1 inch: $\pi (1)^2 (8) = 8\pi$. The difference of the volumes gives you **(A)**. Felipe needs $120 - 8\pi$ cubic inches of wax.

## 30. C

**Difficulty:** Hard

**Category:** Special Right Triangles

**Strategic Advice:** The diagonal of the square divides it into two 45-45-90 triangles. Use this information to find the diagonal of the square, which is also the diameter of the circle. From there, you can calculate the area of the circle.

**Getting to the Answer:** The area of the square is 400, so each side of the square is $\sqrt{400} = 20$. The sides of a 45-45-90 triangle are in the ratio $x:x:x\sqrt{2}$, so the diagonal of the square is $20\sqrt{2}$ and the radius of the circle is half of that, or $10\sqrt{2}$. The area of the circle is then $\pi\left(10\sqrt{2}\right)^2 = \pi(10)^2\left(\sqrt{2}\right)^2 = \pi(100)(2) = 200\pi$.

Choice **(C)** is correct.

## 31. 1,847 centimeter³

**Difficulty:** Medium

**Category:** Three-Dimensional Figures

**Getting to the Answer:** The question asks for the total volume of juice, which is the volume of the cylinder that contains the concentrate plus the amount of water that is added. The height of the can of concentrate is 12 centimeters, and its diameter is 7 centimeters, making the radius 3.5 centimeters. Plug this information into formula for the volume of a cylinder, $V = \pi r^2 h$:
$V_{conc} = \pi \times 3.5^2 \times 12 = 147\pi$ cm³.

The ratio of concentrate to total juice is $V_{conc}:(V_{conc} + V_{water})$ or $25:(25 + 75)$, which simplifies to 1:4. Set up the following ratio to calculate the total volume:

$$\frac{147\pi}{V_{Total}} = \frac{1}{4}$$

Cross-multiply to find the total volume of juice:

$$V_{Total} = (147\pi)(4)$$
$$V_{Total} = 588\pi \approx 1,847.2$$

The value 1,847.2 rounds to 1,847. Grid in **1847**.

## 32. 24

**Difficulty:** Medium

**Category:** Three-Dimensional Figures

**Getting to the Answer:** The diameter of the serving pitcher is given as 10 centimeters, so the radius is 5 centimeters. Use the radius and the total volume of apple juice you found in the last question to find the minimum height of the serving pitcher:

$$V_{Total} = 588\pi = \pi\left(5^2\right)(\text{height})$$
$$588\pi = \pi(25)(\text{height})$$
$$588 = 25(\text{height})$$
$$23.52 = \text{height}$$

The height needs to be rounded up to **24**, which is the correct answer.

## 33. C

**Difficulty:** Medium

**Category:** Similar Triangles; Special Right Triangles

**Strategic Advice:** For questions with right triangles, look for Pythagorean triples and special right triangles.

**Getting to the Answer:** Begin by transferring all of the information in the question stem to the diagram:

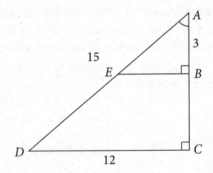

Triangle $ACD$ is a right triangle with side length 12 and a hypotenuse of 15, which means its other side length, $AC$, is 9. These side lengths are the 3:4:5 triple multiplied by 3. Because they share angle $A$ and both have a right angle, the two triangles are similar by way of angle-angle. Therefore, triangle $ABE$ is also a 3:4:5 triangle. Since triangle $ACD$ is three times the size of triangle $ABE$, you can easily create a ratio of 1:3. Look for a side of $ABE$ in the numerator and the corresponding side of $ACD$ in the denominator. Only **(C)** correctly matches up the corresponding sides of $ABE$ and $ACD$.

Another option to solve this question is to plug in the values for all of the sides based on the Pythagorean triples and plug those lengths into the answer choices. The diagram below shows the side lengths of the two triangles:

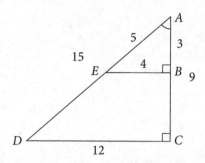

Plugging the lengths into the choices results in:

(A): $\dfrac{EB}{AC} = \dfrac{4}{9}$

(B): $\dfrac{AE}{DC} = \dfrac{5}{12}$

**(C):** $\dfrac{EB}{DC} = \dfrac{4}{12} = \dfrac{1}{3}$

There is no need to check (D) because there will be only one set of lengths that work. **(C)** is indeed correct.

### 34. C

**Difficulty:** Easy

**Category:** Lines and Angles

**Getting to the Answer:** Line *L* forms a right triangle whose right angle is created by the intersection of the *x*- and *y*-axes. The figure shows that *q* and *p* are complementary, as they form a straight line, the *y*-axis, which means $q + p = 180$. The question says that $q = 140$, so $p = 180 - 140 = 40$. One of the interior angles of the triangle, the one created by the *y*-axis and line *L*, is vertical to *p*, so that angle also is 40. Now, find the last angle measure inside the triangle by subtracting: $180 - 90 - 40 = 50$. This angle is supplementary to *r*, so $r = 180 - 50 = 130$. This means that $r - p = 130 - 40 = 90$. **(C)** is the correct.

### 35. D

**Difficulty:** Hard

**Category:** Pythagorean Theorem

**Getting to the Answer:** In a right triangle, one leg is the base and the other is the height. Because the question states that one leg is 3 inches longer than the other, use $x$ and $x + 3$ to represent the lengths of these two legs. Use the formula for the area of a triangle to solve for $x$, the shorter leg:

$$35 = \tfrac{1}{2}(x)(x + 3)$$
$$2(35) = 2\left[\tfrac{1}{2}(x)(x + 3)\right]$$
$$70 = (x)(x + 3)$$
$$70 = x^2 + 3x$$

Next, subtract 70 to make the equation equal 0. Use reverse-FOIL to find that the factors are $(x + 10)$ and $(x - 7)$, which means $x = -10$ and $x = 7$. Lengths cannot be negative, so the shorter leg has a length of 7, and the longer leg has a length of $7 + 3 = 10$. Now, use the Pythagorean theorem to find the length of the hypotenuse:

$$a^2 + b^2 = c^2$$
$$7^2 + 10^2 = c^2$$
$$49 + 100 = c^2$$
$$149 = c^2$$
$$\sqrt{149} = \sqrt{c^2}$$
$$\sqrt{149} = c$$

Choice **(D)** is correct.

### 36. 14

**Difficulty:** Medium

**Category:** Pythagorean Theorem

**Getting to the Answer:** Since a line tangent to a circle is perpendicular to a radius drawn to meet the tangent line, $\triangle ABC$ must be a right triangle. Therefore, the sum of the measures of $\angle A$ and $\angle C$ is $90°$, and you can write the equation $(3k + 23) + (4k - 31) = 90$. This simplifies to $7k - 8 = 90$ and then to $7k = 98$. Divide both sides by 7 to see that $k = 14$. Grid in **14**.

## 37. B

**Difficulty:** Medium

**Category:** Pythagorean Theorem

**Getting to the Answer:** Draw a diagram to visualize the situation. A cross section of the sphere resting on the table is shown. Note that the sphere is tangent to the table and that a right triangle is present:

Plug the values from your diagram into the Pythagorean equation: $1^2 + x^2 = 10^2$. Solving for $x$ results in $x = \sqrt{99} = \sqrt{9 \times 11} = 3\sqrt{11}$, so **(B)** is correct.

## 38. C

**Difficulty:** Medium

**Category:** Arc Length and Sectors

**Strategic Advice:** You can save time solving this question if you recognize that information about 8 slices is unnecessary. The whole large pizza will be the same percent larger than a whole small pizza as a large slice will be compared to a small slice. In other words, if a large slice is 25% larger than a small slice, a large pizza is also 25% larger than a small pizza. That means you need to calculate only the areas of each pizza and plug them into the percent change formula.

**Getting to the Answer:** The radius of the large pizza is one-half of its diameter of 16 inches, or 8 inches. Use the radius to find the area of the large pizza: $\pi r^2 = \pi(8)^2 = 64\pi$ square inches. The question states that the small pizza is 4 inches smaller in diameter than the large pizza, or $16 - 4 = 12$ inches. The radius of the small pizza is one-half of its diameter of 12 inches, or 6 inches, and the small pizza has an area of $\pi(6)^2 = 36\pi$ square inches.

The question asks by what percent is the large pizza larger than the small pizza, which means that the percent change is in terms of the small pizza. Plug the values in:

$$\frac{64\pi - 36\pi}{36\pi} = \frac{28\pi}{36\pi} = \frac{7}{9} \approx 78\%$$

**(C)** is correct.

## 39. B

**Difficulty:** Medium

**Category:** Special Right Triangles

**Getting to the Answer:** Start by drawing in *PR* and *PS* as shown here:

Because the angle formed by *PR* and *PS* defines the same arc as the angle formed by segments *QR* and *QS*, ∠*RPS* must be twice ∠*RQS*, which is $45° \times 2 = 90°$. In addition to being legs of △*PRS*, *PR* and *PS* are radii, so they are congruent, which makes △*PRS* a 45-45-90 triangle. Therefore, the radius of circle *P* is $\frac{4}{\sqrt{2}} = 2\sqrt{2}$, and the circumference is $2\pi \times 2\sqrt{2} = 4\pi\sqrt{2}$, so **(B)** is correct.

## 40. B

**Difficulty:** Medium

**Category:** Circles

**Getting to the Answer:** To find the equation of the smallest dotted circle on the diagram, you need the standard form of the equation of a circle, $(x - h)^2 + (y - k)^2 = r^2$, the coordinates of the center of the circle, and its radius. The center of the circles before calibration is $(3, 4)$. Eliminate (A) and (D). The diameter of the smallest dotted circle is 4 units, which makes its radius 2 units.

Plugging that information into the circle equation results in $(x - 3)^2 + (y - 4)^2 = 2^2$. **(B)** is correct.

**41. C**

**Difficulty:** Medium

**Category:** Quadrilaterals

**Getting to the Answer:** To find the area of the counter surface that needs to be covered, add the area of the L-shaped portion of the counter and the square portion in the middle. Determine the area of the L-shaped portion of the counter by subtracting the area of the smaller 8 foot by 13 foot rectangle from the larger 10 foot by 15 foot rectangle:

$$\text{Area of L-shaped portion} =$$
$$(10 \times 15) - (8 \times 13) = 150 - 104 = 46 \, \text{ft}^2$$

Finally, to find the total area add the area of the 3 foot by 3 foot square in the center, $3 \times 3 = 9 \, \text{ft}^2$, to the $46 \, \text{ft}^2$: $9 + 46 = 55 \, \text{ft}^2$. **(C)** is correct.

**42. C**

**Difficulty:** Medium

**Category:** Quadrilaterals

**Getting to the Answer:** From the answer to the previous question, you already know the area that needs to be covered, 55 square feet. Divide the budget by the area to find the maximum amount that can be spent per square foot:

$$\frac{\$4,500}{55 \text{ square feet}} \approx \$82 \text{ per square foot.}$$

Instead of finding the prices for each of the materials, you can take advantage of how the answer choices are set up to speed up the elimination process. Option III, soapstone, appears in three of the four choices, so check it first. Soapstone is $97 per square foot, which is over budget, so eliminate (A), (B), and (D), which all contain option III. **(C)** is correct.

**43. B**

**Difficulty:** Medium

**Category:** Special Right Triangles

**Getting to the Answer:** Use the area of one isosceles triangle, $\frac{9}{2}$, to solve for the length of the legs of the triangle and add the sum of both legs to the side lengths of the octagonal table given in the diagram. The formula for the area of a triangle is $A = \frac{1}{2}bh$, and since the base and the height are same for an isosceles right triangle, $b = h$, you can simplify the formula: $A = \frac{b^2}{2}$. Plug in $\frac{9}{2}$ for the area and solve for the length of one of the legs:

$$A = \frac{b^2}{2}$$
$$\frac{9}{2} = \frac{b^2}{2}$$
$$b^2 = 9$$
$$b^2 = \pm 3$$

Lengths cannot be negative, so the length of each leg is 3 feet. Adding the side length to both ends of the 6-foot dimension results in $6 + 3 + 3 = 12$ feet. Adding the side length to both ends of the 4-foot dimension results in $4 + 3 + 3 = 10$ feet. The dimensions of the original piece of lumber are 10 by 12. **(B)** is correct.

Another approach is to recognize that if you use the variable $x$ to represent the leg length of the right isosceles triangle, then the dimensions of the original piece of lumber must be $(6 + 2x)$ feet by $(4 + 2x)$ feet. By extension, since the $2x$ is the same in both, the dimensions of the original piece of lumber must only differ by $6 - 4$, or 2, feet. Eliminate (A) and (D) because the dimensions do not differ by 2 inches. Test (B) by setting $(6 + 2x)$ feet $= 12$ feet to find a value for the leg length of the triangle:

$$6 + 2x = 12$$
$$2x = 6$$
$$x = 3$$

Plugging $x = 3$ into area formula results in $\frac{3^2}{2} = \frac{9}{2}$, which confirms **(B)** as the correct answer.

**44. C**

**Difficulty:** Medium

**Category:** Triangles

**Getting to the Answer:** To calculate the amount of leftover material for all 60 students, first calculate the amount of material that will remain when one student cuts out the pattern. Note that while the dimensions of the material are given in inches, the final answer is in square feet. Do the conversion up front: each student starts out with a 1.5 foot by 2 foot piece of material, the area of which is $1.5 \times 2 = 3$ ft$^2$.

How do you find the area of the kite? Since it is symmetrical along the vertical axis, if you fold the pattern in half along the vertical axis, you have two equal triangles with a base of 2 feet and a height of $\frac{1.5}{2} = 0.75$ ft. Plugging those values into the area formula results in:

$$\text{Area of both triangles} = 2\left(\frac{1}{2}\right)(2 \text{ ft})(0.75 \text{ ft}) = 1.5 \text{ ft}^2$$

The difference between the area of the original piece of material and area of the kite, $3 - 1.5 = 1.5$ ft$^2$, is the area of leftover material for one kite. To find the total amount of leftover material, multiply 1.5 ft$^2$ by 60 to get 90 ft$^2$. **(C)** is correct. If you noticed that the area of the kite is exactly half the area of the original rectangle, you can save time and simply calculate the area of the kite and multiply it by 60. If you chose (D), be careful and always make sure to check the units.

**45. 6**

**Difficulty:** Hard

**Category:** Special Right Triangles

**Getting to the Answer:** Since $C$ is the center of the semicircle and points $A$, $E$, and $D$ lie on the circumference, $CA$, $CE$, and $CD$ are each equal to the radius of the semicircle. Note that $CA$ is also the base of triangle $ABC$, which is a 30-60-90 triangle given that angle $ABC$ is 30° and that angle $BAC$ is 90°. You know $CB = 12$, so use the ratio of the sides $x:x\sqrt{3}:2x$ to find $CA$:

$$\frac{CA}{12} = \frac{1}{2}$$
$$CA = \frac{1}{2}(12)$$
$$CA = 6$$

Thus, $CA = 6$ and $CE = \mathbf{6}$. Grid in **6**.

# CHAPTER 14

# Trigonometry

## LEARNING OBJECTIVES

After completing this chapter, you will be able to:

- Calculate side lengths of right triangles using trigonometric ratios and vice versa
- Describe the relationship between the sine and cosine of complementary angles

5/600 SmartPoints®

# How Much Do You Know?

**Directions:** Try the questions that follow. Show your work so that you can compare your solutions to the ones found in the Check Your Work section immediately after this question set. If you answered most of the questions correctly, and if your scratchwork looks like ours, you may be able to move quickly through this chapter. If you answered incorrectly or used a different approach, you may want to take your time on this chapter.

1. If $\tan x = \dfrac{7}{24}$, then what is the value of $\sin x$?

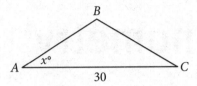

Note: Figure not drawn to scale.

2. If the area of $\triangle ABC$ is 225 and $AB = 17$, then what is the value of $\cos x$?

   A) $\dfrac{8}{17}$

   B) $\dfrac{8}{15}$

   C) $\dfrac{17}{30}$

   D) $\dfrac{15}{17}$

3. In a right triangle, one of the acute angles is $\cos\left(\dfrac{\pi}{3}\right)$, and $\cos\left(\dfrac{\pi}{3}\right) = \sin x$. What is the measure of $x$?

   A) $\dfrac{\pi}{12}$

   B) $\dfrac{\pi}{6}$

   C) $\dfrac{\pi}{3}$

   D) $\dfrac{2\pi}{3}$

4. If the hypotenuse of the triangle shown above has length 24 units, what is the area in square units of the triangle?

   A) $72\sqrt{3}$

   B) $144\sqrt{3}$

   C) $288$

   D) $288\sqrt{3}$

Answers and explanations are on the next page. ▶ ▶ ▶

# Check Your Work

## 1. 7/25 or .28

**Difficulty:** Medium

**Getting to the Answer:** Recall that $\tan x = \frac{\text{opp}}{\text{adj}}$. This means you know the lengths of the two legs of the triangle, but not its hypotenuse. Draw a picture with the given lengths:

Remember that $\sin x = \frac{\text{opp}}{\text{hyp}}$, so use the Pythagorean theorem to calculate the length of the hypotenuse:

$$7^2 + 24^2 = \text{hyp}^2$$
$$49 + 576 = \text{hyp}^2$$
$$\sqrt{625} = \sqrt{\text{hyp}^2}$$
$$25 = \text{hyp}$$

Plug the length of the hypotenuse into the sine ratio: $\sin x = \frac{7}{25}$. Grid in **7/25** or **.28**.

## 2. A

**Difficulty:** Hard

**Getting to the Answer:** Begin by drawing a height in the triangle:

Next, find the length of $BD$ using the triangle area formula:

$$A = \frac{1}{2}bh$$
$$225 = \frac{1}{2} \times 30h$$
$$h = \frac{225}{15} = 15 = BD$$

You now have two sides of a right triangle ($\triangle ABD$)—but not necessarily the two sides you need. To find the value of $\cos x$, you need the side adjacent to $x$ and the hypotenuse. Here, you have the opposite side ($BD$) and

the hypotenuse ($AB$), so you need to find the length of the third side ($AD$). You might recognize $\triangle ABD$ as an 8-15-17 Pythagorean triple, but if you don't, you can use the Pythagorean theorem:

$$AD^2 + 15^2 = 17^2$$
$$AD^2 = 17^2 - 15^2$$
$$AD^2 = 289 - 225$$
$$AD = \sqrt{64} = 8$$

You can now find $\cos x$: $\frac{\text{adj}}{\text{hyp}} = \frac{8}{17}$. **(A)** is correct.

## 3. B

**Difficulty:** Medium

**Getting to the Answer:** The sine and cosine of complementary angles are equal, and the sum of the acute angles in a right triangle is $180° - 90° = 90°$. Convert this to radians to find the measure of the missing angle. The sum of the acute angles in a right triangle, in radians, is $90° \times \frac{\pi}{180°} = \frac{90\pi}{180} = \frac{\pi}{2}$. Subtract the known angle to find the other angle: $\frac{\pi}{2} - \frac{\pi}{3} = \frac{3\pi}{6} - \frac{2\pi}{6} = \frac{\pi}{6}$. **(B)** is correct.

## 4. A

**Difficulty:** Medium

**Getting to the Answer:** When the measure of an angle in a triangle is given in radians, you'll usually want to convert it to degrees because you might be able to find a special right triangle. Use the relationship $180° = \pi$ to convert the angle: $\frac{\cancel{\pi}}{3} \times \frac{180°}{\cancel{\pi}} = 60°$.

Now you know the triangle is a 30-60-90 triangle, which has sides that are in the ratio $x : x\sqrt{3} : 2x$. The hypotenuse is $2x = 24$, so $x = 12$ and $x\sqrt{3} = 12\sqrt{3}$. Therefore, the base and height of the triangle are 12 and $12\sqrt{3}$, and the area of the triangle is $\frac{1}{2}(12\sqrt{3})(12) = 72\sqrt{3}$, so **(A)** is correct. Note that because it is a right triangle, it does not matter which leg you call the base and which the height.

# Sine, Cosine, and Tangent

**LEARNING OBJECTIVES**

After this lesson, you will be able to:

- Calculate side lengths of right triangles using trigonometric ratios and vice versa
- Describe the relationship between the sine and cosine of complementary angles

## To answer a question like this:

One angle in a right triangle measures $y°$ such that $\cos y° = \frac{24}{25}$. What is the measure of $\sin (90° - y°)$ ?

## You need to know this:

The SAT tests three trigonometric functions: **sine, cosine**, and **tangent**. All three are simply the ratios of side lengths within a right triangle. The notation for sine, cosine, and tangent functions always includes a reference angle; for example, $\cos x$ or $\cos \theta$. That's because you'll need to refer to the given angle within a right triangle to determine the appropriate side ratios.

There is a common mnemonic device for the sine, cosine, and tangent ratios: SOHCAHTOA (commonly pronounced: so-kuh-TOE-uh). Here's what it represents: **S**ine is **O**pposite over **H**ypotenuse, **C**osine is **A**djacent over **H**ypotenuse, and **T**angent is **O**pposite over **A**djacent. See the following triangle and the table for a summary of the ratios and what each equals for angle $A$ in triangle $CAB$:

| Sine (sin) | Cosine (cos) | Tangent (tan) |
|:---:|:---:|:---:|
| $\dfrac{\text{opposite}}{\text{hypotenuse}}$ | $\dfrac{\text{adjacent}}{\text{hypotenuse}}$ | $\dfrac{\text{opposite}}{\text{adjacent}}$ |
| $\dfrac{3}{5}$ | $\dfrac{4}{5}$ | $\dfrac{3}{4}$ |

**Complementary angles** have a special relationship relative to sine and cosine:

- $\sin x° = \cos(90° - x°)$
- $\cos x° = \sin(90° - x°)$

In other words, the sine of an acute angle is equal to the cosine of the angle's complement and vice versa. For example, $\cos 30° = \sin 60°$, $\cos 45° = \sin 45°$, and $\cos 60° = \sin 30°$.

### You need to do this:

- Apply the appropriate trigonometric ratio to a right triangle or use the relationship between the sine and cosine of complementary angles.

### Explanation:

There are two ways to approach this question. You might choose to draw the triangle:

To find $\sin(90° - y°)$, put the side opposite the angle labeled $90° - y°$ over the hypotenuse. You'll get $\dfrac{24}{25}$, exactly the same as $\cos y°$.

Alternatively, you could use the property of complementary angles that says that $\cos x° = \sin(90° - x°)$ to find that $\sin(90° - y°) = \dfrac{24}{25}$.

The fraction can't be gridded in because it takes too many spaces, so divide 24 by 25 and grid in the result, **.96**. Although it doesn't apply here, pay attention to any rounding guidelines in the question stem.

## Try on Your Own

**Directions:** Take as much time as you need on these questions. Work carefully and methodically. There will be an opportunity for timed practice at the end of the chapter.

---

HINT: Pythagorean triples frequently appear in trig questions. What is the triangle's missing side length in Q1?

---

1. Based on the figure above, which of the following is true?

A) $\sin 22.6° = \dfrac{5}{12}$

B) $\sin 67.4° = \dfrac{5}{13}$

C) $\cos 22.6° = \dfrac{5}{13}$

D) $\cos 67.4° = \dfrac{5}{13}$

2. The triangle shown above is a cross section of a feeding trough. The triangular cross section is 24 inches deep and 36 inches across the top. If $\cos x = B$, what is the value of $B$?

Note: Figure not drawn to scale.

3. If the area of the triangle shown above is 240 square inches, what is tan $\beta$?

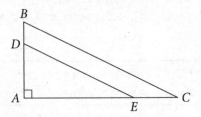

4. In the figure above, $DE$ is parallel to $BC$ and sin $\angle C = 0.6$. Side $AC = 16$ and side $BD = 3$. What is the length of side $AE$?

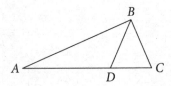

5. If sin $\angle A = \cos \angle C$, what is sin $\angle ABD - \cos \angle DBC$?

A) 0

B) $\dfrac{1}{2}$

C) 1

D) The result of the subtraction cannot be determined without additional information.

## On Test Day

Occasionally, a question will give you more information than you need to determine the correct answer. Think about what information you really need to arrive at the answer before you begin your calculations so that you don't get sidetracked and spend time doing unnecessary work.

As you read through this question, plan your strategy to get the correct value and identify what information you need to carry out that strategy. Note if there is any unnecessary information that you can ignore.

6. Triangle *PQR* is a right triangle with the 90° angle at vertex *Q*. The length of side PQ is 25 and the length of side QR is 60. Triangle *STU* is similar to triangle *PRQ*. The vertices *S*, *T*, and *U* correspond to vertices *P*, *Q*, and *R*, respectively. Each side of triangle *STU* is $\frac{1}{10}$ the length of the corresponding side of triangle *PRQ*. What is the value of cos ∠*U* ?

A) $\frac{5}{13}$

B) $\frac{5}{12}$

C) $\frac{5}{6}$

D) $\frac{12}{13}$

The answer and explanation can be found at the end of this chapter.

# How Much Have You Learned?

**Directions:** For testlike practice, give yourself 7 minutes to complete this question set. Be sure to study the explanations, even for questions you got right. They can be found at the end of this chapter.

7.  If $\sin x = \cos\left(\dfrac{13\pi}{6}\right)$, which of the following could be the value of $x$?

    A) $\dfrac{\pi}{6}$

    B) $\dfrac{\pi}{4}$

    C) $\dfrac{\pi}{3}$

    D) $\dfrac{\pi}{2}$

8.  If $\cos x = \sin y$, then which of the following pairs of angle measures could NOT be the values of $x$ and $y$, respectively?

    A) $\dfrac{\pi}{4}, \dfrac{\pi}{4}$

    B) $\dfrac{\pi}{6}, \dfrac{\pi}{3}$

    C) $\dfrac{\pi}{8}, \dfrac{3\pi}{8}$

    D) $\dfrac{\pi}{2}, \dfrac{\pi}{2}$

9.  Angle $x$ is one of the acute angles in a right triangle. If the measure of angle $x$ is $30°$, what is the value of $(\sin x)^2 + (\cos x)^2$?

    A) $\dfrac{1}{4}$

    B) $\dfrac{1}{2}$

    C) $1$

    D) $2$

10. In a certain triangle, the measures of $\angle A$ and $\angle B$ are $(6k - 8)°$ and $(7k - 45)°$, respectively. If $\dfrac{\sin \angle A}{\cos \angle B} = 1$, what is the value of $k$?

11. In the above triangle, if side $AB = 5$, segment $AD = 3$, and $\tan \angle B = 2.4$, what is the length of segment $BE$?

    A) $3$

    B) $3\dfrac{1}{4}$

    C) $3\dfrac{3}{4}$

    D) $4\dfrac{1}{4}$

# Reflect

**Directions:** Take a few minutes to recall what you've learned and what you've been practicing in this chapter. Consider the following questions, jot down your best answer for each one, and then compare your reflections to the expert responses on the following page. Use your level of confidence to determine what to do next.

What are the definitions of sine, cosine, and tangent?

_____

_____

_____

What is the special relationship of sine to cosine in complementary angles?

_____

_____

_____

## Expert Responses

What are the definitions of sine, cosine, and tangent?

*Sine is defined as opposite over hypotenuse, cosine as adjacent over hypotenuse, and tangent as opposite over adjacent. The acronym SOHCAHTOA can help you remember these definitions.*

What is the special relationship of sine to cosine in complementary angles?

*For two complementary angles, sin $x° = $ cos $(90° - x°)$ and cos $x° = $ sin $(90° - x°)$. In other words, if two angles are complementary (add up to 90 degrees), the sine of one equals the cosine of the other.*

## Next Steps

If you answered most questions correctly in the "How Much Have You Learned?" section, and if your responses to the Reflect questions were similar to those of the SAT expert, then consider trigonometry an area of strength and move on to the next chapter. Come back to this topic in a few days to prevent yourself from getting rusty.

If you don't yet feel confident, review those parts of this chapter that you have not yet mastered, then try the questions you missed again. As always, be sure to review the explanations closely.

# Answers and Explanations

## 1. D

**Difficulty:** Medium

**Getting to the Answer:** Find the unknown leg length and angle measure. The triangle is a right triangle with one leg length of 5 and a hypotenuse of 13, so the other leg is length 12. (If you didn't see the Pythagorean triple 5:12:13, you could have used the Pythagorean theorem to find the missing leg length.) Use the measures of the internal angles find the missing angle:

Sine and cosine both involve the hypotenuse, 13, so you can eliminate (A). Compare the remaining answer choices to the trig ratios given by SOHCAHTOA. Sine is opposite over hypotenuse, but the side opposite the 67.4° angle has length 12 (not 5), so eliminate (B). Cosine is adjacent over hypotenuse, but the side adjacent to the 22.6° angle has length 12 (not 5), so eliminate (C). Only **(D)** is left and must be correct. For the record, the side adjacent to the 67.4° angle has length 5 and the hypotenuse has length 13, so $\cos 67.4° = \frac{5}{13}$.

## 2. 3/5 or .6

**Difficulty:** Hard

**Getting to the Answer:** Because trig functions typically apply to right triangles, draw in an altitude and label what you know. You know the trough is 24 inches deep and 36 inches across the top. Because the given angles have equal measures, $x°$, the triangle is isosceles and the altitude bisects the top. Draw a figure:

You're given that $B = \cos x$, and the cosine of an angle involves the hypotenuse, so you need to find the length of the hypotenuse using the Pythagorean theorem:

$$18^2 + 24^2 = c^2$$
$$324 + 576 = c^2$$
$$\sqrt{900} = \sqrt{c^2}$$
$$30 = c$$

Finally, $\cos x = \frac{adj}{hyp} = \frac{18}{30} = \frac{3}{5}$. Grid in **3/5** or **.6**.

## 3. 12/5 or 2.4

**Difficulty:** Hard

**Getting to the Answer:** Find the height of the triangle using the information given about the area and add it to the figure.

$$A = \frac{1}{2}bh$$
$$240 = \frac{1}{2}(40)h$$
$$240 = 20h$$
$$12 = h$$

After you find the height, you might recognize the 5-12-13 Pythagorean triple, which gives you another side of the triangle that contains $\beta$:

Note: Figure not drawn to scale.

Now use SOHCAHTOA: $\tan \beta = \frac{opp}{adj} = \frac{12}{5}$. Grid in **12/5** or **2.4**.

**4.  12**

**Difficulty:** Hard

**Getting to the Answer:** The fact that $DE$ is parallel to $BC$ means that triangles $ABC$ and $ADE$ are similar. Convert $\sin C$, 0.6, to a fraction, $\frac{3}{5}$. Because sin is $\frac{\text{opposite}}{\text{hypotenuse}}$, both triangles have the side ratio 3:4:5. The question states that $AC = 16$. This is the long leg of a 3:4:5 right triangle, so $AB = 12$ and $BC = 20$.

The other known dimension is $BD = 3$. Since the length of $AB$ is 12, the length of $AD$ is $12 - 3 = 9$. Thus, the ratio of the sides of triangle $ADE$ to those of triangle $ABC$ is $\frac{9}{12} = \frac{3}{4}$. Therefore, AD is $\frac{3}{4}$ of AC, which is $\frac{3}{4} \times 16 = 12$. Grid in **12**.

**5.  A**

**Difficulty:** Hard

**Getting to the Answer:** The sine of an angle is equal to the cosine of its complementary angle, so $\angle A + \angle C = 90°$. Since $\angle B$ is the third interior angle of the triangle $ABC$, $\angle B = 180° - 90° = 90°$. Therefore, the measures of angles $ABD$ and $DBC$ must total $90°$, which means they are complementary angles. Thus, $\sin \angle ABD = \cos \angle DBC$, and $\sin \angle ABD - \cos \angle DBC = 0$. **(A)** is correct.

**6.  D**

**Difficulty:** Medium

**Getting to the Answer:** The question tells you that triangles $PQR$ and $STU$ are similar. Therefore, their corresponding angles are equal and all sides of $STU$ have the same ratio to their corresponding sides in $PQR$, in this case, $\frac{1}{10}$. However, since the angles of both triangles are the same, their trig functions are also the same, so there is no need to calculate the lengths of the sides of triangle $PQR$. Because they are the same ratio, cosine of $U$ will have the same value as the cosine of $R$, so just calculate the cosine of $R$ value using the side lengths of triangle $PQR$.

Since $\angle Q = 90°$, sides $PQ$ and $QR$ are legs of the right triangle and $PR$ is the hypotenuse. (If you have trouble visualizing this, you can draw a very quick sketch.) Thus, $\cos R = \frac{QR}{PR}$. You can calculate the value of $PR$ using the Pythagorean theorem:

$$25^2 + 60^2 = PR^2$$
$$625 + 3{,}600 = PR^2$$
$$\sqrt{4{,}225} = \sqrt{PR^2}$$
$$PR = 65$$

You can save a lot of time calculating, if you recognize that the two legs, 25 and 60, are the legs of a 5:12:13 triangle multiplied by 5. You can calculate $PR$ as $5 \times 13 = 65$, so look for Pythagorean triples. Either way, $\cos U = \cos R = \frac{60}{65} = \frac{12}{13}$. **(D)** is correct.

**7.  C**

**Difficulty:** Hard

**Getting to the Answer:** Dealing with smaller angles usually makes trig questions easier, so start by subtracting $2\pi$ from $\frac{13\pi}{6}$ to get $\frac{13\pi}{6} - 2\pi = \frac{13\pi}{6} - \frac{12\pi}{6} = \frac{\pi}{6}$. (This is permissible because $2\pi$ is once around the unit circle; you are not changing the quadrant of the angle.) The equation in the question stem becomes $\sin x = \cos\left(\frac{\pi}{6}\right)$. Complementary angles have a special relationship relative to trig values—the cosine of an acute angle is equal to the sine of the angle's complement and vice versa. The angle measures are given in radians, so you're looking for an angle that, when added to $\frac{\pi}{6}$, gives $\frac{\pi}{2}$ (because $\frac{\pi}{2} = 90°$). Because $\frac{\pi}{6} + \frac{2\pi}{6} = \frac{3\pi}{6} = \frac{\pi}{2}$, the two angles, $\frac{\pi}{6}$ and $\frac{\pi}{3}$, are complementary angles, which means **(C)** is correct.

**8. D**

**Difficulty:** Medium

**Getting to the Answer:** Use the special relationship that complementary angles have in terms of trig functions: the cosine of an acute angle is equal to the sine of the angle's complement and vice versa.

The question asks for the pair of angles that are *not* complementary. In degrees, complementary angles add up to 90, so in radians they add up to $90° \times \frac{\pi}{180°} = \frac{\pi}{2}$.

The only pair of angles that is not complementary is **(D)**, the correct answer, because they add up to $\frac{\pi}{2} + \frac{\pi}{2} = \frac{2\pi}{2} = \pi$.

**9. C**

**Difficulty:** Medium

**Getting to the Answer:** Use the definitions of the common trig functions to put some context to this question. Substitute $\left(\frac{\text{opposite}}{\text{hypotenuse}}\right)^2 + \left(\frac{\text{adjacent}}{\text{hypotenuse}}\right)^2$ for $(\sin x)^2 + (\cos x)^2$. This simplifies to $\frac{\text{opposite}^2 + \text{adjacent}^2}{\text{hypotenuse}^2}$. The Pythagorean theorem states $a^2 + b^2 = c^2$, which is equivalent to $\text{opposite}^2 + \text{adjacent}^2 = \text{hypotenuse}^2$, so this fraction is actually $\frac{\text{hypotenuse}^2}{\text{hypotenuse}^2} = 1$. **(C)** is correct.

If you prefer to work with actual values, recall that the side ratio of a 30-60-90 triangle is $1:\sqrt{3}:2$. So, $\sin x = \frac{1}{2}$ and $\cos x = \frac{\sqrt{3}}{2}$. The question asks for the sum of the squares of those values: $\left(\frac{1}{2}\right)^2 + \left(\frac{\sqrt{3}}{2}\right)^2 = \frac{1}{4} + \frac{3}{4} = 1$. **(C)** is indeed correct.

**10. 11**

**Difficulty:** Hard

**Getting to the Answer:** If $\frac{\sin A}{\cos B} = 1$, then $\sin A = \cos B$, so $\angle A$ and $\angle B$ are complementary. Therefore, the sum of the measures of $\angle A$ and $\angle B$ is 90°, and you can write the equation $(6k - 8) + (7k - 45) = 90$. This simplifies to $13k - 53 = 90$ and then to $13k = 143$. Divide both sides by 13 to see that $k = 11$. Grid in **11**.

**11. B**

**Difficulty:** Hard

**Getting to the Answer:** Since $BA$ and $ED$ are both perpendicular to $AC$, they are parallel, and triangles $ABC$ and $DEC$ are similar. If $\tan \angle B = \frac{AC}{AB}$, then $2.4 = \frac{AC}{5}$, and $AC = 12$. Triangle $ABC$ is a 5:12:13 right triangle, and the length of $BC$ is 13. (If you didn't recall Pythagorean triple, you could have calculated the hypotenuse using the Pythagorean theorem.) Given that $AD = 3$ and $AC = 12$, it follows that $DC = 12 - 3 = 9$, and the ratio of the side lengths of $\triangle DEC$ to $\triangle ABC$ is 9:12, which simplifies to 3:4. Because this ratio is the same for all sides, $BE$ is $\frac{1}{4}$ the length of $BC$, or $\frac{1}{4}(13) = 3\frac{1}{4}$. **(B)** is correct.

# CHAPTER 15

# Imaginary Numbers

**LEARNING OBJECTIVE**

After completing this chapter, you will be able to:

- Perform arithmetic operations on imaginary and complex numbers

5/600 SmartPoints®

# How Much Do You Know?

**Directions:** Try the questions that follow. Show your work so that you can compare your solutions to the ones found in the Check Your Work section immediately after this question set. If you answered most of the questions correctly, and if your scratchwork looks like ours, you may be able to move quickly through this chapter. If you answered incorrectly or used a different approach, you may want to take your time on this chapter.

1. Which of the following is the correct simplification of the expression $(2i - 3) - (6 + 4i)$, where $i = \sqrt{-1}$ ?

   A)  $-9 - 2i$

   B)  $-9 + 6i$

   C)  $-7 - 4i$

   D)  $3 + 6i$

2. Given that $i = \sqrt{-1}$, which of the following is equivalent to $(6i^2 - 7i) + (3 + 6i)$ ?

   A)  $6i^2 + i + 3$

   B)  $-3 - i$

   C)  $-9 - i$

   D)  $10$

3. Which of the following is equal to $(17 + 7i)(3 - 5i)$ ? (Note: $i = \sqrt{-1}$)

   A)  $16$

   B)  $86$

   C)  $16 - 64i$

   D)  $86 - 64i$

4. If the expression $\dfrac{2 - i}{2 + i}$ is written as the complex number $a + bi$, where $a$ and $b$ are real numbers, then what is the value of $a$ ? (Note: $i = \sqrt{-1}$)

Answers and explanations are on the next page. ▶ ▶ ▶

# Check Your Work

**1.   A**

**Difficulty:** Easy

**Getting to the Answer:** The real and imaginary components of the two binomials aren't in the same order. Distributing the negative sign inside the second set of parentheses produces $2i - 3 - 6 - 4i$. Combine like terms to obtain $-9 - 2i$, which makes **(A)** correct.

**2.   B**

**Difficulty:** Easy

**Getting to the Answer:** Treat $i$ like a variable and simplify the expression by getting rid of the parentheses and combining like terms:

$$\left(6i^2 - 7i\right) + (3 + 6i)$$
$$= 6i^2 - 7i + 3 + 6i$$
$$= 6i^2 - i + 3$$

Notice that the resulting expression almost, but not quite, matches (A), so eliminate (A). Because $i = \sqrt{-1}$, you can square both sides to find that $i^2 = -1$. Plug in $-1$ for $i^2$ and combine like terms:

$$6(-1) - i + 3$$
$$= -i - 3$$

Rewrite in $a + bi$ form: $-3 - i$. **(B)** is correct.

**3.   D**

**Difficulty:** Medium

**Getting to the Answer:** Use FOIL to multiply the binomials and simplify:

$$(17 + 7i)(3 - 5i)$$
$$= (17 \times 3) + (17 \times (-5i)) + (7i \times 3) + (7i \times (-5i))$$
$$= 51 - 85i + 21i - 35i^2$$
$$= 51 - 64i - (35 \times (-1))$$
$$= 86 - 64i$$

Choice **(D)** is correct.

**4.   3/5**

**Difficulty:** Medium

**Getting to the Answer:** The question is really asking you to manipulate this expression out of its fraction form to match the form $a + bi$ and identify the real component $a$. To rationalize the denominator, use the conjugate of the denominator, $2 - i$, to multiply the expression by 1:

$$\left(\frac{2-i}{2+i}\right)\left(\frac{2-i}{2-i}\right)$$
$$= \frac{4 - 2i - 2i + i^2}{4 + 2i - 2i - i^2}$$

Since squaring $\sqrt{-1}$ would result in $-1$, plug in $-1$ for $i^2$ and combine like terms:

$$\frac{4 - 2i - 2i + (-1)}{4 + 2i - 2i - (-1)}$$
$$= \frac{3 - 4i}{5}$$

Splitting the terms so that the expression matches the form $a + bi$ results in $\frac{3}{5} - \frac{4}{5}i$. Grid in **3/5**.

# Arithmetic Operations with Complex Numbers

**LEARNING OBJECTIVE**

After this lesson, you will be able to:

* Perform arithmetic operations on imaginary and complex numbers

## To answer a question like this:

Which of the following complex numbers is equivalent to $\frac{2+i}{3+5i}$ ?

A) $\frac{2}{3} + \frac{i}{5}$

B) $\frac{2}{3} - \frac{i}{5}$

C) $\frac{11}{34} + \frac{7i}{34}$

D) $\frac{11}{34} - \frac{7i}{34}$

## You need to know this:

The square root of a negative number is not a real number but an **imaginary number**.

To take the square root of a negative number, use $i$, which is defined as $i = \sqrt{-1}$. For example, to simplify $\sqrt{-49}$, rewrite $\sqrt{-49}$ as $\sqrt{-1 \times 49}$, take the square root of $-1$ (which is by definition $i$), and then take the square root of 49, which is 7. The end result is $7i$.

The simplification $i^2 = \left(\sqrt{-1}\right)^2 = -1$ is also useful when working with imaginary numbers. For example:

$$\sqrt{-16} \times \sqrt{-25}$$
$$= i\sqrt{16} \times i\sqrt{25}$$
$$= 4i \times 5i$$
$$= 20i^2$$
$$= 20 \times (-1)$$
$$= -20$$

When a number is written in the form $a + bi$, where $a$ is the real component and $b$ is the imaginary component (and $i$ is $\sqrt{-1}$), it is referred to as a **complex number**.

## You need to do this:

You can add, subtract, multiply, and divide complex numbers just as you do real numbers:

- To add (or subtract) complex numbers, simply add (or subtract) the real parts and then add (or subtract) the imaginary parts.
- To multiply complex numbers, treat them as binomials and use FOIL. To simplify the product, use the simplification $i^2 = -1$ and combine like terms.
- To divide complex numbers, write them in fraction form and multiply the numerator and denominator by the **conjugate** of the complex number in the denominator. To form the conjugate, change the sign in the complex number. For example, the conjugate of $2 + i$ is $2 - i$.

## Explanation:

Use the conjugate to simplify complex numbers in the denominator. The conjugate of $3 + 5i$ is $3 - 5i$, so multiply the expression by 1 in the form $\frac{3 - 5i}{3 - 5i}$ and simplify:

$$\frac{2 + i}{3 + 5i} \times \frac{3 - 5i}{3 - 5i} = \frac{6 - 10i + 3i - 5i^2}{(3 + 5i)(3 - 5i)} = \frac{6 - 7i - 5i^2}{9 - 25i^2}$$

You know $i^2 = -1$, so the expression simplifies to $\frac{6 - 7i - 5(-1)}{9 - 25(-1)} = \frac{11 - 7i}{34}$. To separate the complex expression into its real and imaginary components, write each of the terms in the numerator over the denominator in separate fractions, which produces $\frac{11}{34} - \frac{7i}{34}$. Choice **(D)** is correct.

## Try on Your Own

**Directions:** Take as much time as you need on these questions. Work carefully and methodically. There will be an opportunity for timed practice at the end of the chapter.

---

HINT: For Q1, what is the value of $i^2$ ?

---

1. Given that $i = \sqrt{-1}$, what is the sum of the complex numbers $(21i^2 - 12i) + (3 - 5i)$ ?

    A)  7

    B)  $7i$

    C)  $-18 - 17i$

    D)  $24 - 17i$

2. What is the result of the multiplication $(5 - 6i)$ $(3 + 3i)$ ? (Note: $i = \sqrt{-1}$)

    A)  $33 - 3i$

    B)  $23 - 3i$

    C)  $11 - i$

    D)  $-6$

---

HINT: For Q3, multiply the top and bottom of the fraction by the conjugate of the denominator.

---

3. Which of the following is equivalent to $\dfrac{38 + 18i}{4 + 6i}$ ?
    (Note: $i = \sqrt{-1}$)

    A)  $\dfrac{11}{13} - 3i$

    B)  $5 - 3i$

    C)  $\dfrac{19}{2} + 3i$

    D)  $44 + 300i$

$$\frac{7 + i}{8 - i}$$

4. If the expression above is expressed in the form $a + bi$, where $i = \sqrt{-1}$, what is the value of $b$ ?

    A)  $-1$

    B)  $\dfrac{3}{13}$

    C)  $\dfrac{11}{13}$

    D)  $\dfrac{15}{64}$

5. If the expression $\dfrac{-3i^2 + 2i}{2 + i}$ is written in the form $a + bi$, where $a$ and $b$ are real numbers and $i = \sqrt{-1}$, what is the value of $a$ ?

## On Test Day

The SAT tests the same patterns over and over again, but they can be presented in a number of different ways. Before you start doing calculations, look closely at this question and see if you recognize a pattern that will help you simplify it. Once you spot the pattern, this question should take you no more than a few seconds to solve.

$$\frac{25i^2 - 9}{5i + 3}$$

6.  For $i = \sqrt{-1}$, the expression above is equal to which of the following complex numbers?

A)  $5i - 3$

B)  $5i + 3$

C)  $16i - 9$

D)  $80i - 48$

The correct answer and explanation can be found at the end of the chapter.

## How Much Have You Learned?

**Directions:** For testlike practice, give yourself 7 minutes to complete this question set. Be sure to study the explanations, even for questions you got right. They can be found at the end of this chapter.

$$(3 + 4i) - (2 + 3i)$$

7. Given that $i = \sqrt{-1}$, what is the value of the expression above?

   A) $1 - i$

   B) $1 + i$

   C) $1 + 7i$

   D) $5 + 7i$

$$\frac{3i + 2}{-i - 3}$$

8. If the expression above is expressed in the form $a + bi$, where $i = \sqrt{-1}$, what is the value of $b$?

   A) $-0.7$

   B) $0.7$

   C) $-0.9$

   D) $0.9$

$$\frac{5 + 3i}{7 - 3i}$$

9. Which of the following expressions is equivalent to the expression above, assuming that $i = \sqrt{-1}$?

   A) $\dfrac{1}{5}$

   B) $\dfrac{5}{7}$

   C) $\dfrac{13 + 18i}{20}$

   D) $\dfrac{13 + 18i}{29}$

10. If the expression $\dfrac{1 + 2i}{4 + 2i}$ is rewritten as a complex number in the form of $a + bi$, what is the value of $a$? (Note: $i = \sqrt{-1}$)

11. Given that $i = \sqrt{-1}$, what is the product of $\dfrac{2 - 4i + 2i^2}{2}$ and $\dfrac{1}{1 - i}$?

   A) $-1 + i$

   B) $-1 - i$

   C) $1 - i$

   D) $1 + i$

Math

# Reflect

**Directions:** Take a few minutes to recall what you've learned and what you've been practicing in this chapter. Consider the following questions, jot down your best answer for each one, and then compare your reflections to the expert responses on the following page. Use your level of confidence to determine what to do next.

In a complex number in the form $a + bi$, what is the definition of $i$?

_____

_____

_____

What is the procedure for adding, subtracting, or multiplying complex numbers?

_____

_____

_____

What is the procedure for dividing complex numbers?

_____

_____

_____

## Expert Responses

In a complex number in the form $a + bi$, what is the definition of $i$ ?

*In any complex number written as $a + bi$, $i = \sqrt{-1}$.*

What is the procedure for adding, subtracting, or multiplying complex numbers?

*To perform arithmetic operations on complex numbers, treat $i$ as a variable and simplify $i^2$ to $-1$.*

What is the procedure for dividing complex numbers?

*To divide two complex numbers, write the division as a fraction, multiply the numerator and denominator by the conjugate of the denominator, and simplify.*

## Next Steps

If you answered most questions correctly in the "How Much Have You Learned?" section, and if your responses to the Reflect questions were similar to those of the SAT expert, then consider imaginary numbers an area of strength and move on to the next chapter. Come back to this topic periodically to prevent yourself from getting rusty.

If you don't yet feel confident, review those parts of this chapter that you have not yet mastered, then try the questions you missed again. As always, be sure to review the explanations closely.

# Answers and Explanations

**1. C**

**Difficulty:** Easy

**Getting to the Answer:** Plug in $-1$ for $i^2$ and combine like terms. Remember to treat $i$ like a variable:

$$\left(21i^2 - 12i\right) + (3 - 5i)$$
$$= 21(-1) - 12i + 3 - 5i$$
$$= -18 - 17i$$

**(C)** is correct.

**2. A**

**Difficulty:** Medium

**Getting to the Answer:** Treat $i$ as a variable and expand the expression as if it were a binomial. Use FOIL to distribute and then plug in $-1$ for any $i^2$ and combine like terms:

$$(5 - 6i)(3 + 3i)$$
$$= 15 + 15i - 18i - 18i^2$$
$$= 15 - 3i - 18(-1)$$
$$= 33 - 3i$$

**(A)** is correct.

**3. B**

**Difficulty:** Hard

**Getting to the Answer:** Multiply the numerator and denominator by the latter's conjugate and then use FOIL. Combine like terms and reduce fractions as needed:

$$\frac{38 + 18i}{4 + 6i}$$
$$= \frac{38 + 18i}{4 + 6i} \times \frac{4 - 6i}{4 - 6i}$$
$$= \frac{(38 \times 4) + (38 \times -6i) + (18i \times 4) + (18i \times -6i)}{16 - 36i^2}$$
$$= \frac{152 - 228i + 72i - 108i^2}{16 - (-36)}$$
$$= \frac{152 - 156i - (-108)}{52}$$
$$= \frac{260 - 156i}{52}$$
$$= \frac{260}{52} - \frac{156}{52}i$$
$$= 5 - 3i$$

**(B)** is correct.

**4. B**

**Difficulty:** Medium

**Getting to the Answer:** The question asks for the value of $b$ when a certain complex number is in the form $a + bi$. The given expression has a complex number in the denominator, so start by multiplying the top and bottom by the conjugate of the complex number in the denominator:

$$\left(\frac{7 + i}{8 - i}\right)\left(\frac{8 + i}{8 + i}\right)$$
$$= \frac{56 + 7i + 8i + i^2}{64 + 8i - 8i - i^2}$$

Since squaring $\sqrt{-1}$ results in $-1$, plug in $-1$ for $i^2$ and then combine like terms and reduce:

$$\frac{56 + 7i + 8i + (-1)}{64 + 8i - 8i - (-1)}$$
$$= \frac{55 + 15i}{65}$$
$$= \frac{5(11 + 3i)}{5(13)} = \frac{11 + 3i}{13}$$

Next, write each of the terms in the numerator over the denominator in separate fractions so that the expression matches the form $a + bi$: $\frac{11}{13} + \frac{3i}{13}$. Thus, $b = \frac{3}{13}$, so **(B)** is correct.

**5. 8/5 or 1.6**

**Difficulty:** Medium

**Getting to the Answer:** First, notice that the expression simplifies if you plug in $-1$ for $i^2$ in the numerator. Then rationalize the denominator by multiplying the top and bottom by the conjugate of the denominator:

$$\left(\frac{-3(-1) + 2i}{2 + i}\right)\left(\frac{2 - i}{2 - i}\right)$$
$$= \frac{6 + 4i - 3i - 2i^2}{4 + 2i - 2i - i^2}$$

Notice again that plugging in $-1$ for $i^2$ and combining like terms results in more simplification:

$$\frac{6 + 4i - 3i - 2(-1)}{4 + 2i - 2i - (-1)}$$

$$= \frac{8 + i}{5}$$

$$= \frac{8}{5} + \frac{i}{5}$$

Since the question asks for the value of $a$, grid in **8/5** or **1.6**.

### 6.  A

**Difficulty:** Medium

**Strategic Advice:** The expression in the numerator contains a coefficient and a constant that are both perfect squares, with the constant being subtracted. This pattern signals that the numerator is a difference of perfect squares, which can be factored.

**Getting to the Answer:** While you could rationalize the given fraction with the denominator's conjugate, in this case, the difference of perfect squares in the numerator means you can factor it into binomials and then cancel a factor from the numerator and denominator:

$$\frac{25i^2 - 9}{5i + 3}$$

$$= \frac{(5i + 3)(5i - 3)}{5i + 3}$$

$$= \frac{\cancel{(5i + 3)}(5i - 3)}{\cancel{5i + 3}}$$

$$= 5i - 3$$

Thus, **(A)** is correct.

### 7.  B

**Difficulty:** Easy

**Getting to the Answer:** To subtract complex numbers, simply subtract the real parts and then subtract the imaginary parts. Remember to distribute the $-1$ to the both 2 and $3i$ in the second binomial:

$$(3 + 4i) - (2 + 3i)$$

$$= 3 + 4i - 2 - 3i$$

$$= 1 + i$$

**(B)** is correct.

### 8.  A

**Difficulty:** Medium

**Getting to the Answer:** Rewrite the expression so that each complex number is in the standard $a + bi$ form. Then rationalize using the conjugate of the denominator:

$$\left(\frac{3i + 2}{-i - 3}\right) \Rightarrow \left(\frac{2 + 3i}{-3 - i}\right)$$

$$= \left(\frac{2 + 3i}{-3 - i}\right) \times \left(\frac{-3 + i}{-3 + i}\right)$$

$$= \frac{-6 - 9i + 2i + 3i^2}{9 + 3i - 3i - i^2}$$

Combine like terms and plug in $-1$ for $i^2$:

$$\frac{-6 - 7i + 3i^2}{9 - i^2}$$

$$= \frac{-6 - 7i + 3(-1)}{9 - (-1)}$$

$$= \frac{-9 - 7i}{10}$$

$$= -\frac{9}{10} - \frac{7i}{10}$$

Since the question asks for the value of $b$, convert the fraction to a decimal. **(A)** is correct.

## 9.   D

**Difficulty:** Medium

**Strategic Advice:** If part of an answer choice is incorrect, then the whole answer choice is incorrect. Notice that multiplying the numerator by the conjugate of the denominator will result in a complex number in the numerator, so eliminate (A) and (B).

**Getting to the Answer:** Multiply the expression by the conjugate of the denominator to remove the complex number from the denominator. Note that the two remaining answer choices have the same numerator, $13 + 18i$, which means that you need to simplify the denominator only to decide which is correct. For the record, the simplification of the numerator is included:

$$\frac{5 + 3i}{7 - 3i} \times \frac{7 + 3i}{7 + 3i}$$

$$= \frac{35 + 21i + 15i + 9i^2}{49 - 21i + 21i - 9i^2}$$

$$= \frac{35 + 36i + 9i^2}{49 - 9i^2}$$

Next, plug in $-1$ for $i^2$ and combine like terms. The resulting fraction can be reduced by factoring out 2:

$$\frac{35 + 36i + 9(-1)}{49 - 9(-1)}$$

$$= \frac{26 + 36i}{58} = \frac{\cancel{2}(13 + 18i)}{\cancel{2}(29)} = \frac{13 + 18i}{29}$$

**(D)** is correct.

## 10.  8/20 or 4/10 or 2/5 or .4

**Difficulty:** Medium

**Getting to the Answer:** The question wants the expression to be in the form $a + bi$. When there is a complex number in the denominator, multiply the top and bottom of the fraction by the conjugate of the the denominator. Plug in $-1$ for $i^2$ and combine like terms:

$$\frac{1 + 2i}{4 + 2i} \times \frac{4 - 2i}{4 - 2i}$$

$$= \frac{4 + 8i - 2i - 4i^2}{16 - 8i + 8i - 4i^2}$$

$$= \frac{4 + 6i - 4(-1)}{16 - 4(-1)}$$

$$= \frac{8 + 6i}{20}$$

$$= \frac{8}{20} + \frac{6i}{20}$$

Grid in **8/20, 4/10,** or **2/5** or **.4.** Any of these formats is correct.

## 11.  C

**Difficulty:** Hard

**Strategic Advice:** If you factor out the 2, the expression in the numerator of the first  fraction is a classic quadratic $x^2 - 2xy + y^2 = (x - y)^2$. Factor the quadratic and and look for terms that cancel.

**Getting to the Answer:** Multiply the two fractions and factor out a 2. After factoring the classic quadratic, the term $(1 - i)$ cancels out:

$$\left( \frac{2 - 4i + 2i^2}{2} \right)\left( \frac{1}{1 - i} \right) = \frac{2\left(1 - 2i + i^2\right)}{2(1 - i)}$$

$$= \frac{2(1 - i)^2}{2(1 - i)} = \frac{\cancel{2}\,\cancel{(1 - i)}(1 - i)}{\cancel{2}\,\cancel{(1 - i)}} = 1 - i$$

**(C)** is correct.

# CHAPTER 16

# SAT Math: Timing and Section Management Strategies

## LEARNING OBJECTIVES

After completing this chapter, you will be able to:

- Make quick decisions about which questions to spend time on and which to skip
- Attack multi-part questions efficiently

## SAT Math Timing and Triage

The non-calculator section has 20 questions to be completed in 25 minutes, which means you'll have 1 minute and 15 seconds per question; the calculator section has 38 questions to be completed in 55 minutes, which means you'll have a little less than a minute and a half per question. This is an average, though. Some questions will be straightforward, meaning that you can get the correct answer in 30 seconds or less. Others will be more difficult and time consuming. Test takers who start at the beginning of the section, attempt the questions in order, and only move on to the next question when the previous one is complete often find that they get bogged down and don't make it to the end of the section, potentially missing questions that they could have answered correctly. Flexibility can earn you more points.

A better approach would be to make your way through the section with a plan to deal with each question. Each time you read a new question, take a moment to gauge your gut reaction:

- Does this question seem quick and easy? Do it immediately.
- Does this question seem time consuming but manageable? Skip it for now. Put a circle around it and try it on a second pass through the section.
- Does this question look confusing or difficult? Skip it. Don't worry about circling or marking questions like this. You'll approach them only after you have worked on the other questions in the section, and only if you have time.

Try to make this decision quickly. The more you practice, the easier it will be to recognize which questions are easier and which are more challenging for you.

When you approach a section this way, you'll end up taking two or three passes through it. This technique ensures that you'll get all of the easy points first, and that if you run out of time, you'll know that the questions you didn't attempt were the hardest in the section and that it would have been tougher to get those questions right anyway.

Before the end of the section, make sure you have something bubbled in for every question since there is no penalty for guessing. Also, be very careful when bubbling your answers. It's easy to skip a question but forget to skip a line on the grid and bubble your answer to the next question in the wrong place.

The questions in each Math section will be in approximate order of difficulty, with the easiest questions at the beginning of the section and the most difficult questions at the end of the section. There are two exceptions:

- The difficulty resets with the Grid-in questions. That is, the first Grid-in question is much easier than the last multiple-choice question. If the multiple-choice questions start getting too tough, skip to the Grid-ins.

- The individual questions in a two- or three-part question set might be easier or harder than the questions around them. It's a good idea to attempt them in order, since sometimes the work you did for an earlier question will help you with a later question, but you should still be ready to skip questions within one of these sets if they get too tough.

If you tend to finish the Math sections early but find that you are making speed mistakes, you may consider pausing at the confirmation step to check your logic and calculations before bubbling your response to each question.

## Try on Your Own

**Directions:** Use this question set to practice effective question triage. Skip those questions that you feel will take too long; come back to them if you have time. Try to get as many questions correct as you can in 15 minutes. As always, be sure to study the explanations, even for questions you got correct. They can be found at the end of this chapter.

Note: Figure not drawn to scale.

1. Quadrilateral *ABEF* is a rectangle and the length of side *FE* is 9. If quadrilateral *BCDE* is a square, what is its area?

   A)  27

   B)  36

   C)  $27\sqrt{3}$

   D)  81

2. If $\frac{7}{9}x - \frac{1}{6}x = \frac{1}{3} + \frac{1}{2}$, what is the value of *x* ?

   A)  $\frac{15}{14}$

   B)  $\frac{15}{11}$

   C)  $\frac{3}{2}$

   D)  $\frac{25}{14}$

3. If $f(x) = 2x^2 - 5x + 7$, what is the value of $f(8) - f(3)$ ?

4. Anthony recently completed a trip in 3 hours. If his average speed had been 20 percent faster, how long would the same trip have taken?

   A)  2.2 hours

   B)  2.4 hours

   C)  2.5 hours

   D)  2.8 hours

   Note: Figure not drawn to scale.

5. If $\tan \angle B = 1$, and the length of side *BC* is $\frac{6}{\sqrt{2}}$, what is the length of side *AC* ?

   A)  $\frac{3}{\sqrt{2}}$

   B)  3

   C)  $\frac{6}{\sqrt{2}}$

   D)  6

$$x^2 + 12x = -30$$

6. What is the absolute value of the difference between the two solutions for $x$ in the equation above?

   A) $2\sqrt{6}$

   B) 4

   C) $6\sqrt{2}$

   D) 12

$$3x = 4y - 13$$
$$3y = 31 - 2x$$

7. Given the equations above, what is the value of $x + y$?

**Questions 8–10 refer to the following information.**

A diagram of a gambrel roof attic is shown above. Gambrel roofs are common on barns because they allow the maximum space for storage while still having a sloped roof. The steepness of the slope of a roof is called its pitch. Gambrel roofs are unique because they have a pitch break where the pitch changes. In a standard plan, the pitch break is calculated so that the four roof trusses all have the same truss length, $t$. The formula for the length of the base where $t$ is the truss length and $n$ is the number of trusses is as follows:

$$d = \frac{5t}{3 \sin\left(\frac{360}{n}\right)}$$

A cross-section of a typical gambrel roof, which is symmetrical about the vertical axis, is shown in the diagram above.

8. Which of the following expresses truss length in terms of the length of the base and the number of trusses?

   A) $t = \dfrac{5 \sin\left(\frac{360}{n}\right)d}{3}$

   B) $t = \dfrac{3 \sin\left(\frac{360}{n}\right)d}{5}$

   C) $t = \dfrac{3d}{5 \sin\left(\frac{360}{n}\right)}$

   D) $t = \dfrac{5d}{3 \sin\left(\frac{360}{n}\right)}$

9. The Greer family is building a new barn and calculating the dimensions based on how much winter
hay storage space they need in the gambrel roof attic. If $l$ is the length of the barn from front to back,
which one of the following equations can be used to
calculate the volume, $V$, of the attic roof space?

A) $V = l\left(\dfrac{xy + (y+h)(d-2x)}{2}\right)$

B) $V = \dfrac{\left(xy + \dfrac{(y+h)(d-2x)}{2}\right)}{l}$

C) $V = l\left(xy + \dfrac{(y+h)(d-2x)}{2}\right)$

D) $V = l\left(\dfrac{(y+h)(d-2x)}{2}\right)$

10. After completing the volume calculations, the family decides to use a standard plan for the gambrel
roof where the base, $d$, is 30 feet and the length of
the barn from front to back, $l$, is 40 feet. All four
surfaces of the barn roof will need to be shingled
at a rate of $3.17 per square foot. Approximately
how much will the Greer family spend to have the
gambrel roof shingled?

A) $2,300

B) $3,800

C) $9,100

D) $15,200

# Answers and Explanations

## 1. A

**Difficulty:** Easy

**Category:** Geometry (Chapter 13)—Special Right Triangles

**Getting to the Answer:** The fact that the figures are a rectangle and a square means that all the angles other than those formed by the diagonal are 90°, which means that $\triangle BEF$ is a 30-60-90 triangle. If you don't recall the side ratios of such a triangle, you might consider skipping this question even though you can look up the side ratios on the formula sheet. (It's best to memorize the higher-yield information on the formula sheet so you won't have to spend time looking it up on test day.)

The side ratios of the triangle are $x:x\sqrt{3}:2x$. Since the length of the longer leg, $FE$, is 9, $x = \dfrac{9}{\sqrt{3}}$ and the lengths are $\dfrac{9}{\sqrt{3}}:9:\dfrac{18}{\sqrt{3}}$. Thus, the side length of the square, $BE$, is $\dfrac{9}{\sqrt{3}}$, and the area of square $BCDE$ is $s^2 = \left(\dfrac{9}{\sqrt{3}}\right)^2 = \dfrac{81}{3} = 27$. **(A)** is correct.

## 2. B

**Difficulty:** Easy

**Category:** Linear Equations and Graphs (Chapter 4)—Solving Equations

**Getting to the Answer:** If you recall that the way to simplify multiple fractions is to clear the denominators by multiplying all terms by a common denominator, then proceed with this question. The numbers appear manageable, so you probably won't even need to use the calculator.

The lowest common denominator (LCD) of the fractions is 18, so multiply all terms by 18. (If you didn't notice that LCD, you could have multiplied by $9 \times 6 = 54$.)

$$18\left(\frac{7}{9}x\right) - 18\left(\frac{1}{6}x\right) = 18\left(\frac{1}{3}\right) + 18\left(\frac{1}{2}\right)$$
$$14x - 3x = 6 + 9$$
$$11x = 15$$
$$x = \frac{15}{11}$$

**(B)** is correct.

## 3. 85

**Difficulty:** Easy

**Category:** Functions (Chapter 10)—Function Notation

**Getting to the Answer:** Although this is a Grid-in question, the amount of calculations needed to get the answer are minimal since all that is required is to evaluate a single-variable function twice and make one subtraction. Therefore, you would probably choose to answer this question on a first pass. Even though the question permits the use of the calculator, you are certainly not required to use it. Usually, if you are comfortable making the calculations without the calculator, you will save time and avoid keying errors.

Substitute the two values given into the function. Notice that since you will be subtracting $f(3)$ from $f(8)$, the constant term, 7, will cancel out. Therefore, the calculation is $2(8)^2 - 5(8) - [2(3)^2 - 5(3)]$, which is $2(64) - 5(8) - 2(9) + 5(3)$. This simplifies to $128 - 40 - 18 + 15$, which is 85. Grid in **85** and move on.

## 4. C

**Difficulty:** Medium

**Category:** Linear Equations and Graphs (Chapter 4)—Word Problems

**Getting to the Answer:** Your time management decisions often depend on whether you are able to quickly identify the strategy you can use to answer a question. For this question, you will use the formula Distance = rate × time to determine the answer. Since distance is the constant factor and rate and time vary, you'll set rate × time for both scenarios equal to each other. If you don't see this approach fairly quickly, you should move on and mark this question to come back to later.

Set the initial rate to $r$ and the time to make the trip at the new rate to $t$. The distance for the actual trip is $3r$ and the distance if Anthony increases his average speed is $t(1.2r)$. Set these two equal to each other, $3r = t(1.2r)$. The $r$'s cancel out, so you can write that $t = \dfrac{3}{1.2} = 2.5$. **(C)** is correct.

**5. B**

**Difficulty:** Medium

**Category:** Trigonometry (Chapter 14)—Sine, Cosine, and Tangent

**Getting to the Answer:** The key to unraveling this question is recognizing that $\angle B = \angle C = 45°$. That fact enables you to set up a side ratio and solve for the length of side $AC$. If you are unable to make this determination, pass on this question for now and move on.

Given that $\tan = \dfrac{\text{opposite}}{\text{adjacent}}$, $\tan \angle B = 1$ means that the sides opposite and adjacent to vertex $B$ are equal.

Triangle $ABC$ is an isosceles right triangle. The side ratio for a 45-45-90 triangle is $s:s:s\sqrt{2}$, so $s\sqrt{2} = \dfrac{6}{\sqrt{2}}$, and $s = \dfrac{6}{\sqrt{2} \times \sqrt{2}} = \dfrac{6}{2} = 3$. **(B)** is correct.

**6. A**

**Difficulty:** Medium

**Category:** Quadratics (Chapter 12)—The Quadratic Formula

**Getting to the Answer:** Add 30 to each side to get $x^2 + 12x + 30 = 0$. Since there are not any integer factors of 30 that add to 12, you'll have to use either completing the square or the quadratic formula to solve for the possible values of $x$. If you see a question like this on test day and are not comfortable with those techniques or feel that this question could take too much time to answer, come back to it on a second pass.

If you choose to solve via the quadratic equation, $\dfrac{-b \pm \sqrt{b^2 - 4ac}}{2a}$, substitute 1 for $a$, 12 for $b$, and 30 for $c$, to get $x = \dfrac{-12 \pm \sqrt{12^2 - 4(1)(30)}}{2(1)}$. This simplifies to $x = \dfrac{-12 \pm \sqrt{144 - 120}}{2} = \dfrac{-12 \pm \sqrt{24}}{2}$. Since $\sqrt{24} = \sqrt{4} \times \sqrt{6}$, this further simplifies to $x = -6 \pm \sqrt{6}$.

The question asks for the difference between the two solutions which is $\left(-6 + \sqrt{6}\right) - \left(-6 - \sqrt{6}\right) = 2\sqrt{6}$. **(A)** is correct.

To complete the square, add the square of half of 12, or 36, to both sides to get $x^2 + 12x + 36 = (x + 6)^2 = 6$. Take the square root of both sides to get $x + 6 = \pm\sqrt{6}$, so $x = -6 \pm \sqrt{6}$. The absolute difference is twice $\sqrt{6}$, or $2\sqrt{6}$, which confirms that **(A)** is correct. Note that the technique of completing the square takes less calculation than using the quadratic formula.

**7. 12**

**Difficulty:** Hard

**Category:** Systems of Equations (Chapter 5)—Combination

**Getting to the Answer:** Even though you are solving for $x + y$ and you are given equations in terms of $3x$ and $3y$, merely adding the two equations to get $3x + 3y = 4y - 13 + 31 - 2x$ and dividing both sides by 3 does not work. You'll need to solve the system of equations by substitution or combination (elimination) for the values of both variables and add them.

First, put the equations in the same format such as $3x - 4y = -13$ and $2x + 3y = 31$. Using substitution would likely result in working with fractions, so use combination. The $x$-coefficients are smaller values than the $y$-coefficients, so the calculations might be a little easier. Create a common $x$-coefficient of 6 by multiplying the first equation by 2 and the second by 3, then subtracting the second equation from the first:

$$\begin{aligned} 6x - 8y &= -26 \\ -(6x + 9y &= 93) \\ \hline -17y &= -119 \end{aligned}$$

So $y = 7$. You can plug $y = 7$ into either of the original equations to find $x$, but because $x$ is already isolated on one side in the first equation, use it: $3x = 4(7) - 13 = 15$, so $x = 5$. The sum of $x$ and $y$ is thus $7 + 5 = 12$. Grid in **12**.

## 8.  B

**Difficulty:** Medium

**Category:** Linear Equations and Graphs (Chapter 4)—Solving Equations

**Getting to the Answer:** Even when an equation looks complicated, to solve for a specific variable, you only need to move everything else in the equation to the other side of the equal sign. The original equation gives the length of the base, $d$, in terms of the truss length, $t$, and the number of trusses, $n$. To solve for $t$, multiply both sides of the expression by the $3 \sin\left(\frac{360}{n}\right)$ term and divide by 5:

$$d = \frac{5t}{3 \sin\left(\frac{360}{n}\right)}$$

$$3 \sin\left(\frac{360}{n}\right)d = 5t$$

$$\frac{3 \sin\left(\frac{360}{n}\right)d}{5} = t$$

$$t = \frac{3 \sin\left(\frac{360}{n}\right)d}{5}$$

**(B)** is correct. (A), (C), and (D) all contain the incorrect expression in the denominator.

## 9.  C

**Difficulty:** Hard

**Category:** Geometry (Chapter 13)—Three-Dimensional Figures

**Getting to the Answer:** The volume for any 3-D prism can be found by taking the area of the base and multiplying it by the height (or in this case, the length of the barn). You can eliminate (B) immediately because it divides by the length instead of multiplying by it. The cross-section of the barn is not a standard shape, but, since it is symmetrical about the vertical axis, it can be broken up into simpler shapes: two equal right triangles and two equal trapezoids.

Start with the area that is easier to calculate: the area of the two right triangles. The base and height of the two triangles are $x$ and $y$, and plugging those values into the triangle area formula results in $\frac{xy}{2}$. There are *two* equal triangles, so multiply by 2 to get $xy$ as the area of the two triangles. At this point on test day, you could make the strategic leap to eliminate (D) because it does not include the $xy$ term and (A) because it divides the $xy$ term by 2. **(C)** is correct.

If you continue with the calculations, the area formula for a trapezoid is (average of parallel bases) × (height of the trapezoid). Based on the cross-section diagram those values will be:

$$\left(\frac{(y+h)}{2}\right)\left(\frac{(d-2x)}{2}\right)$$

Again, there are two trapezoids, so multiply the expression by 2:

$$\frac{(y+h)(d-2x)}{2}$$

Next, add the area of both triangles and both trapezoids:

$$xy + \left(\frac{(y+h)(d-2x)}{2}\right)$$

**(C)** is the only choice that multiplies this value by $l$, which confirms that it is the correct choice. Recognizing that you are building the volume formula from the area of simple shapes allows for powerful strategic elimination (and fewer calculations!).

**10. C**

**Difficulty:** Medium

**Category:** Linear Equations and Graphs (Chapter 4)—
Solving Equations

**Getting to the Answer:** If the cross-section of the roof
shown in the diagram is stretched over the 40-foot
length of the barn, then the four sections of the roof are
four equal rectangles where one dimension is the length
and the other dimension is the truss length. Find the
truss length by plugging the number of trusses, 4, and
the base length, 30 feet, into the truss length formula
that you solved for in question 8:

$$t = \frac{3 \sin\left(\frac{360}{4}\right)(30)}{5} = \frac{3 \sin(90)(30)}{5} = \frac{3(1)(30)}{5}$$

$$= \frac{90}{5} = 18 \text{ feet}$$

Now that you have the dimension for one section of the
roof, 18 feet by 40 feet, find the area of all four sections:

$$\text{Area of four sections} = 4(18)(40) = 2,880 \text{ ft}^2$$

Finally, the price per square foot needs to be multiplied
by the total area of the roof:

$$\text{Total price} = \left(2,880 \text{ ft}^2\right)\left(\$3.17/\text{ft}^2\right) \approx \$9,100$$

**(C)** is correct.

# PART 3

# SAT Reading

# The Method for SAT Reading Questions

300/600 SmartPoints®

## How to Do SAT Reading

The SAT Reading section is made up of four passages and one set of paired passages, each approximately 500–750 words long and accompanied by 10–11 questions for a total of 52 questions in the section. To tackle all of this effectively in 65 minutes, the most successful test takers

- read the passages strategically to zero in on the text that leads to points, and
- approach the questions with a method that minimizes rereading and leads directly to correct answers.

The key to maximizing correct answers is learning in advance the kinds of questions that the test asks. SAT Reading questions focus more on the author's purpose (*why* she wrote this passage) and the passage's structure (*how* the author makes and supports her points) than on the details or facts of the subject matter (*what* this passage is about).

Knowing that the SAT rewards your attention to *how* and *why* the author wrote the passage or chose to include certain words or examples puts you in the driver's seat. You can read more effectively and answer the questions more quickly and confidently.

In this chapter, we'll give you an overview of how to tackle Reading passages and questions. The other chapters in this unit will help you become a stronger reader and present the five SAT Reading question types, as well as tips for improving your approach for paired passages and literature passages.

Try the passage and questions that follow on your own. Then, compare your approach to our recommendations for how to approach SAT Reading and reflect on how you can become a more efficient test taker.

**Questions 1-10 refer to the following passage.**

This passage describes the varying and changing scientific theories surrounding sunspots.

Astronomers noted more than 150 years ago that sunspots wax and wane in number in an 11-year cycle. Ever since, people have speculated that the solar cycle might exert some influence on
5  the Earth's weather. In this century, for example, scientists have linked the solar cycle to droughts in the American Midwest. Until recently, however, none of these correlations has held up under close scrutiny.
10  One problem is that sunspots themselves have been poorly understood. Observation revealed that the swirly smudges represent areas of intense magnetic activity where the sun's radiative energy has been blocked and that they are considerably
15  cooler than bright regions of the sun. Scientists had not been able, however, to determine just how sunspots are created or what effect they have on the solar constant (a misnomer that refers to the sun's total radiance at any instant).
20  The latter question, at least, seems to have been resolved by data from the *Solar Maximum Mission* satellite, which has monitored the solar constant since 1980, which was the peak of a solar cycle. As the number of sunspots decreased
25  through 1986, the satellite recorded a gradual dimming of the sun. Over the next year, as sunspots proliferated, the sun brightened. These data suggest that the sun is 0.1 percent more luminous at the peak of the solar cycle, when
30  the number of sunspots is greatest, than at its nadir, according to Richard C. Willson of the Jet Propulsion Laboratory and Hugh S. Hudson of the University of California at San Diego.
The data show that sunspots do not
35  themselves make the sun shine brighter. Quite the contrary. When a sunspot appears, it initially causes the sun to dim slightly, but then after a period of weeks or months islands of brilliance called faculas usually emerge near the sunspot
40  and more than compensate for its dimming effect. Willson says faculas may represent regions where energy that initially was blocked beneath a sunspot has finally breached the surface.

Does the subtle fluctuation in the solar
45  constant manifest itself in the Earth's weather? Meteorological reports offer statistical evidence that it does, albeit rather indirectly. The link seems to be mediated by a phenomenon known as the quasi-biennial oscillation (QBO), a 180-degree
50  shift in the direction of stratospheric winds above the Tropics that occurs about every two years.
Karin Labitzke of the Free University of Berlin and Harry van Loon of the National Center for Atmospheric Research in Boulder, Colorado, were
55  the first to uncover the QBO link. They gathered temperature and air-pressure readings from various latitudes and altitudes over the past three solar cycles. They found no correlation between the solar cycle and their data until they sorted the
60  data into two categories: those gathered during the QBO's west phase (when the stratospheric winds blow west) and those gathered during its east phase. A remarkable correlation appeared: temperatures and pressures coincident with the
65  QBO's west phase rose and fell in accordance with the solar cycle.
Building on this finding, Brian A. Tinsley of the National Science Foundation discovered a statistical correlation between the solar cycle and
70  the position of storms in the North Atlantic. The latitude of storms during the west phase of the QBO, Tinsley found, varied with the solar cycle: storms occurring toward the peak of a solar cycle traveled at latitudes about six degrees nearer the
75  Equator than storms during the cycle's nadir.
Labitzke, van Loon, and Tinsley acknowledge that their findings are still rather mysterious. Why does the solar cycle seem to exert more of an influence during the west phase of the QBO
80  than it does during the east phase? How does the 0.1 percent variance in solar radiation trigger the much larger changes—up to six degrees Celsius in polar regions—observed by Labitzke and van Loon? Van Loon says simply, "We can't explain it."
85  John A. Eddy of the National Center for Atmospheric Research, nonetheless, thinks these QBO findings as well as the Solar Maximum

*Mission* data "look like breakthroughs" in
the search for a link between the solar cycle
90  and weather. With further research into how
the oceans damp the effects of solar flux,
for example, these findings may lead to models
that have some predictive value. The next few
years may be particularly rich in solar flux.

1.  Which one of the following best describes the main
    idea of the passage?

    A)  The scientific advances provided by the
        research of Labitzke and van Loon have finally
        cleared up some of the mysteries that long
        plagued the study of sunspots.

    B)  Recent research combining astronomical and
        climate data provides a promising foundation
        for better understanding the relationship
        between sunspots and Earth's weather.

    C)  Despite recent breakthroughs, scientists are
        unlikely to ever fully explain correlations
        between sunspot activity and Earth's weather
        patterns.

    D)  Scientists have used data from the *Solar
        Maximum Mission* satellite to explain how
        sunspots affect Earth's climate during the quasi-
        biennial oscillation's west phase.

2.  The author's point of view can best be described as
    that of

    A)  a meteorologist voicing optimism that the
        findings of recent solar research will improve
        weather forecasting.

    B)  an astronomer presenting a digest of
        current findings to a review board of other
        astronomers.

    C)  a science writer explaining the possible
        influence of a solar phenomenon on terrestrial
        weather patterns.

    D)  a historian listing the contributions to climate
        science made by the *Solar Maximum Mission*.

3.  The passage indicates which of the following about
    the sun's luminosity and the solar cycle?

    A)  Scientists have found no correlation between
        the sun's brightness and the solar cycle.

    B)  The sun is brightest at the nadir of the solar
        cycle.

    C)  The sun is brightest at the peak and again at the
        nadir of the solar cycle.

    D)  The sun is brightest at the peak of the solar
        cycle.

Reading

4.  Which one of the following provides the best evidence for the answer to the previous question?

    A)  Lines 10–11 ("One problem . . . understood")

    B)  Lines 15–18 ("Scientists had . . . constant")

    C)  Lines 20–24 ("The latter . . . cycle")

    D)  Lines 27–31 ("These data . . . nadir")

5.  Based on information in the passage, it can most reasonably be inferred that faculas

    A)  are directly responsible for increased temperatures on Earth.

    B)  have a dimming effect on the sun's luminescence during sunspot activity.

    C)  are mostly likely to appear at the peak of the solar cycle.

    D)  grow in number as the number of sunspots decreases.

6.  Which one of the following provides the best evidence for the answer to the previous question?

    A)  Lines 20–24 ("The latter . . . cycle")

    B)  Lines 34–35 ("The data . . . brighter")

    C)  Lines 36–41 ("When a . . . effect")

    D)  Lines 46–47 ("Meteorological . . . indirectly")

7.  As used in line 45, "manifest" most nearly means

    A)  impact.

    B)  disguise.

    C)  itemize.

    D)  reveal.

8.  According to the passage, Labitzke and van Loon's research on the quasi-biennial oscillation (QBO) shows that

    A)  the QBO's west phase correlates to the solar cycle.

    B)  the QBO's west phase has a longer duration than that of its east phase.

    C)  the QBO shows no correlation with the solar cycle.

    D)  the reasons for the QBO's correlation to the solar cycle are now well understood.

9.  The main purpose of the questions in the second-to-last paragraph (lines 76–84) is to

    A)  emphasize how little scientists know about the solar constant.

    B)  explain more fully the mysterious nature of the scientists' findings.

    C)  question the basis upon which these scientists built their hypotheses.

    D)  express doubts about the scientists' interpretations of their findings.

10. The use of the quoted phrase "look like breakthroughs" in line 88 is primarily meant to convey the idea that

    A)  information about the solar cycle has allowed scientists to predict changes in Earth's complex climate system.

    B)  additional analysis of the link between the solar cycle and Earth's weather may yield useful models.

    C)  despite the associated costs, space missions can lead to important discoveries.

    D)  an alternative interpretation of the data may contradict the initial findings.

## Strategic Reading

The SAT Reading Test is an open-book test; the passage is right there for you to reference. Moreover, the SAT actively tests your skill in looking up details; there are Command of Evidence questions that actually ask you to cite the line numbers for the evidence you used to answer a question. Because of the way the test is constructed, it is in your best interest to read fairly quickly, noting the outline of the passage as you go, marking up the page as you read with margin notes, getting a solid understanding of the main idea, but not taking the time to memorize details.

Be sure to read the prepassage blurb, the short introduction that comes before the passage. Identify any information that helps you to understand the topic of the passage or to anticipate what the author will discuss. For the previous passage, the blurb states the topic (sunspots) and announces that the passage will discuss "varying and changing theories" about them. That's an invitation to keep your eye out for multiple theories as you read.

You'll learn all the skills you need to read strategically in chapter 18, but for now, here's an example of an expert's passage map. Don't worry if yours doesn't look exactly like this (or even anything like this, yet). Follow the expert's thought process in the discussion that follows the passage to see what he was thinking and asking as he read the passage.

Reading

Reading

## Questions 1-10 refer to the following passage.

This passage details the varying and changing scientific theories surrounding sunspots.

**Sunspots Passage Map**

Astronomers noted more than 150 years ago that sunspots wax and wane in number in an 11-year cycle. Ever since, people have speculated that the solar cycle might exert some influence on
5  the Earth's weather. In this century, for example, scientists have linked the solar cycle to droughts in the American Midwest. Until recently, however, none of these correlations has held up under close scrutiny.

    *sunspot cycle & earth weather*

10  One problem is that sunspots themselves have been poorly understood. Observation revealed that the swirly smudges represent areas of intense magnetic activity where the sun's radiative energy has been blocked and that they are considerably
15  cooler than bright regions of the sun. Scientists had not been able, however, to determine just how sunspots are created or what effect they have on the solar constant (a misnomer that refers to the sun's total radiance at any instant).

    *sunspots poorly understood*

20  The latter question, at least, seems to have been resolved by data from the *Solar Maximum Mission* satellite, which has monitored the solar constant since 1980, which was the peak of a solar cycle. As the number of sunspots decreased
25  through 1986, the satellite recorded a gradual dimming of the sun. Over the next year, as sunspots proliferated, the sun brightened. These data suggest that the sun is 0.1 percent more luminous at the peak of the solar cycle, when
30  the number of sunspots is greatest, than at its nadir, according to Richard C. Willson of the Jet Propulsion Laboratory and Hugh S. Hudson of the University of California at San Diego.

    *SMM satellite*

    *Sunspot cycle and sun's brightness*

The data show that sunspots do not
35  themselves make the sun shine brighter. Quite the contrary. When a sunspot appears, it initially causes the sun to dim slightly, but then after a period of weeks or months islands of brilliance called faculas usually emerge near the sunspot
40  and more than compensate for its dimming effect. Willson says faculas may represent regions

    *sunspots dim, but faculas even brighter*

## ANALYSIS

**Pre-passage blurb:** The passage addresses various and changing theories about sunspots. Keep track of the different ideas and how they've evolved.

**¶1:** The author introduces the passage's topic—*sunspots*—and zeroes in on a more specific question: *how do they affect Earth's weather?* People have been investigating this for 150 years, but (note the contrast word "however" in line 7) only recently have they gotten some answers. The author will say more about these answers in coming paragraphs.

**¶2:** The author defines sunspots: areas where magnetic activity blocks some of the sun's energy. However (again, there's a contrast where the author wants to make a point), scientists still have questions: *how are sunspots created and how do they affect the sun's brightness?*

**¶3:** Here's the first recent discovery. The SMM satellite shows that the sun gets brighter with more sunspots (the solar cycle peak) and dimmer with fewer sunspots (the solar cycle nadir). This sets up a question that the author will have to answer: *If sunspots block and cool the sun's energy, how can the sun be brighter with more sunspots?*

**¶4:** The author clears up the paradox from the previous paragraph. Sunspots *initially* block the sun's energy, but (this author loves contrasts) then faculas—super bright hot spots—pop up around the sunspots. Faculas are so bright that they "more than compensate" for the sunspots' dimming effect. That's a lot about sunspots, but the author still needs to tie this to Earth's weather.

where energy that initially was blocked beneath a sunspot has finally breached the surface.

45 Does the subtle fluctuation in the solar constant manifest itself in the Earth's weather? Meteorological reports offer statistical evidence that it does, albeit rather indirectly. The link seems to be mediated by a phenomenon known as the quasi-biennial oscillation (QBO), a 180-degree
50 shift in the direction of stratospheric winds above the Tropics that occurs about every two years.

*indirect weather effects (QBO)*

Karin Labitzke of the Free University of Berlin and Harry van Loon of the National Center for Atmospheric Research in Boulder, Colorado, were
55 the first to uncover the QBO link. They gathered temperature and air-pressure readings from various latitudes and altitudes over the past three solar cycles. They found no correlation between the solar cycle and their data until they sorted the
60 data into two categories: those gathered during the QBO's west phase (when the stratospheric winds blow west) and those gathered during its east phase. A remarkable correlation appeared: temperatures and pressures coincident with the
65 QBO's west phase rose and fell in accordance with the solar cycle.

*sunspot correlation to temp and air pressure*

Building on this finding, Brian A. Tinsley of the National Science Foundation discovered a statistical correlation between the solar cycle and
70 the position of storms in the North Atlantic. The latitude of storms during the west phase of the QBO, Tinsley found, varied with the solar cycle: storms occurring toward the peak of a solar cycle traveled at latitudes about six degrees nearer the
75 Equator than storms during the cycle's nadir.

*link to storm patterns*

Labitzke, van Loon, and Tinsley acknowledge that their findings are still rather mysterious. Why does the solar cycle seem to exert more of an influence during the west phase of the QBO
80 than it does during the east phase? How does the 0.1 percent variance in solar radiation trigger the much larger changes—up to six degrees Celsius in polar regions—observed by Labitzke and van Loon? Van Loon says simply, "We can't explain it."

*scientists can't fully explain links*

85 John A. Eddy of the National Center for Atmospheric Research, nonetheless, thinks these QBO findings as well as the Solar Maximum

**¶5:** Here, the author starts to connect sunspots to the weather. It introduces something called the QBO that makes winds in the atmosphere change direction every two years. The next paragraph has to tie this to sunspots.

**¶6:** This paragraph discusses the research of two scientists, Labitzke and van Loon. They found that when the winds are moving westward, temperatures and air pressure correlate to the solar cycle (the cycle of more and fewer sunspots).

**¶7:** A different scientist—Tinsley—also correlated the sunspot cycle to the position of storms in the Atlantic Ocean. So far, the studies suggest that sunspots do affect the weather, but they don't say how or why.

**¶8:** This is a little disappointing: the scientists still don't know how or why sunspots seem to affect temperature and air pressure or the location of storms.

**¶9:** The author ends by citing one more scientist—Eddy—who is optimistic. He calls the research and the SMM satellite data a breakthrough and thinks we can learn a lot more about sunspots and the weather in the next few years.

Mission data "look like breakthroughs" in the search for a link between the solar cycle and weather. With further research into how the oceans damp the effects of solar flux, for example, these findings may lead to models that have some predictive value. The next few years may be particularly rich in solar flux.

90

break-
throughs,
but more
research
needed

---

### BIG PICTURE

**Main Idea:** Scientists have learned quite a bit about sunspots and Earth's weather recently (faculas, the QBO, and storms are all evidence for that) and hope to learn more soon.

**Author's Purpose:** To outline the recent data and research suggesting that there is a connection between sunspots and the weather (but she doesn't go too far or say that all the mysteries have been solved)

---

> **SAT READING STRATEGY**
>
> A good rule of thumb for summarizing a passage's main idea is to boil down the author's take-away to the reader to a single sentence. If the author had only a few seconds to make her point, what would she like the reader to remember?

Notice that the SAT expert reads actively, consistently summing up and paraphrasing what the author has said, asking what must come next, and never getting too caught up in details. The expert reader is not thrown off by encountering a new or unfamiliar term. He uses context to understand what it must mean and remembers that he can always consult the passage if he needs to remember a name or a definition. Finally, before turning to the questions, the expert takes a few seconds to summarize the "Big Picture," the Main Idea and Author's Purpose. This will help him answer questions about the passage's main idea and the author's purpose or point of view.

## The Method for SAT Reading Questions

The best-prepared SAT test takers know that time is one of the SAT Reading section's biggest challenges. They also know that trying to speed up and cut corners can lead to sloppy mistakes, or worse, to reading a paragraph over and over because it just isn't sinking in. So, after setting themselves up for success with helpful passage notes and clear big picture summary, SAT experts use a simple four-step method to tackle each question quickly and confidently.

For example, take a look at this question from the set above:

The passage indicates which of the following about the sun's luminosity and the solar cycle?

A) Scientists have found no correlation between the sun's brightness and the solar cycle.

B) The sun is brightest at the nadir of the solar cycle.

C) The sun is brightest at the peak and again at the nadir of the solar cycle.

D) The sun is brightest at the peak of the solar cycle.

Because different question types require different strategies, start by *unpacking* the information in the question stem and identifying the question type. You'll learn to name and characterize six SAT Reading question types in chapter 19. The word "indicates" tells you that this is a Detail question, which means that you should be able to find the correct answer in the passage almost verbatim.

Next, based on the type of question, *research* the passage or consult your passage map to get the information you need. For this question, you have a margin note for paragraph 3 that says, "SMM sat data: more sunspots = brighter," so direct your research to paragraph 3. Here's the sentence you need: "These data suggest that the sun is 0.1 percent more luminous at the peak of the solar cycle, when the number of sunspots is greatest, than at its nadir."

Now, with the relevant part of the passage in mind, *predict* what the correct answer will say. In this case, you're looking for an answer choice that says that the sun is either brighter at the peak of the solar cycle or dimmer at its nadir.

Finally, use your prediction to evaluate the choices and *find* the one correct answer. Only choice **(D)** is a match for the prediction based on the research you did: the sun is indeed brightest at the peak of the solar cycle.

Notice that experts don't merely read or look at the answers; they *evaluate* them, knowing that only one of them answers the question correctly and that the other three are demonstrably incorrect in some way. Because SAT experts arm themselves with strong predictions in step 3, they can often zero in on the correct response without wasting time by rereading or hunting around in the passage to check each answer. You'll learn the strategies and tactics that experts use for steps 2–4 in chapter 20.

The steps are shown in the table below:

| Method for SAT Reading Questions | |
|---|---|
| Step 1. | Unpack the question stem |
| Step 2. | Research the answer |
| Step 3. | Predict the answer |
| Step 4. | Find the one correct answer |

Take a look at our expert's application of the SAT Reading Question Method to the questions from the *Sunspots* passage. Look for questions on which your own approach could have been faster and more confident.

| Question | Analysis |
|---|---|
| 1. Which one of the following best describes the main idea of the passage?<br><br>A) The scientific advances provided by researchers such as Labitzke and van Loon have finally cleared up some of the mysteries that long plagued the study of sunspots.<br><br>B) Recent research combining astronomical and climate data provides a promising foundation for better understanding the relationship between sunspots and Earth's weather.<br><br>C) Despite recent breakthroughs, scientists are unlikely to ever fully explain correlations between sunspot activity and Earth's weather patterns.<br><br>D) Scientists have used data from the *Solar Maximum Mission* satellite to explain how sunspots affect Earth's climate during the quasi-biennial oscillation's west phase. | **Step 1: Unpack the question stem.** Questions that ask for the main idea or primary purpose of a passage are Global questions. With a strong big picture summary, these can be answered quickly and confidently.<br><br>**Step 2: Research the answer.** The main idea of this passage was that scientists have learned quite a bit about sunspots and Earth's weather patterns (e.g., faculas, the QBO, and storms) and are optimistic that they will soon be able to provide more answers.<br><br>**Step 3: Predict the correct answer.** The correct answer will match the Main Idea summary.<br><br>**Step 4: Find the one correct answer.** Choice **(B)** is correct; it matches the scope of the passage without being too broad or too narrow. (A) is too narrow (Labitzke and van Loon were only two of the scientists cited in the passage) and distorts the passage by suggesting that they have "cleared up" the mysteries, when they admit, they're still baffled by some of what they've found. (C) presents a pessimistic tone at odds with the optimism that closes the passage. (D) distorts what the passage said about the solar cycle and the QBO; scientists discovered a correlation between the two, but have not yet explained how or why this happens. |

| Question | Analysis |
|---|---|
| 2. The author's point of view can best be described as that of<br><br>A) a meteorologist voicing optimism that the findings of recent solar research will improve weather forecasting.<br><br>B) an astronomer presenting a digest of current findings to a review board of other astronomers.<br><br>C) a science writer explaining the possible influence of a solar phenomenon on terrestrial weather patterns.<br><br>D) a historian listing the contributions to climate science made by the *Solar Maximum Mission*. | **Step 1: Unpack the question stem.** Questions that ask about the passage's main idea or the author's overall purpose or point of view are called Global questions.<br><br>**Step 2: Research the answer.** This question covers the passage as a whole, so the Big Picture summaries will help predict the answer.<br><br>**Step 3: Predict the answer.** The author's purpose is to outline recent developments in sunspot research, and the tone and language suggest a general readership. The correct answer will reflect this.<br><br>**Step 4: Find the one correct answer.** Choice **(C)** matches the prediction. (A) goes outside the scope of the passage; the author focuses on the science behind the discoveries, not on applications like weather forecasting. (B) suggests an expert presentation to an academic peer group; this passage is more journalistic than that. (D) is too narrow; the *Solar Maximum Mission* is mentioned only in the third paragraph. |
| 3. The passage indicates which of the following about the sun's luminosity and the solar cycle?<br><br>A) Scientists have found no correlation between the sun's brightness and the solar cycle.<br><br>B) The sun is brightest at the nadir of the solar cycle.<br><br>C) The sun is brightest at the peak and again at the nadir of the solar cycle.<br><br>D) The sun is brightest at the peak of the solar cycle. | **Step 1: Unpack the question stem.** A question asking what the passage "indicates" is a Detail question. The correct answer will paraphrase something stated explicitly in the passage. Research paragraph 3 where the author discusses the solar cycle.<br><br>**Step 2: Research the answer.** Data gathered by the SMM satellite shows that the sun is brightest at the peak of the solar cycle and dimmest at its nadir.<br><br>**Step 3: Predict the answer.** Your research provides clear-cut criteria for the correct answer: the sun is brightest at the peak of the solar cycle and dimmest at its nadir.<br><br>**Step 4: Find the one correct answer.** Choice **(D)** matches your prediction and is correct. (A) is contradicted by the passage, though this choice may have been tempting if you stopped after paragraph 2, which says that, until relatively recently, scientists did not know how the two were correlated. (B) says the opposite of what the passage says on this subject. (C) misstates the passage by claiming that the sun brightens again at the nadir of the solar cycle. |

Reading

| Question | Analysis |
|---|---|
| 4. Which one of the following provides the best evidence for the answer to the previous question?<br><br>A) Lines 10–11 ("One problem . . . understood")<br><br>B) Lines 15–18 ("Scientists had . . . constant")<br><br>C) Lines 20–24 ("The latter . . . cycle")<br><br>D) Lines 27–31 ("These data . . . nadir") | **Step 1: Unpack the question stem.** This is a Command of Evidence question that asks you to locate a piece of text stated in the passage that supports another statement, most often, as it is in this case, the correct answer to the preceding question.<br><br>**Step 2: Research the answer.** In Command of Evidence questions, the answer choices all designate specific sentences or statements in the passage and indicate their precise locations by line numbers. Use the choices to conduct your research, keeping in mind that the correct answer here must support the correct answer to the preceding question.<br><br>**Step 3: Predict the answer.** The answer to the preceding question came directly from the final sentence in paragraph 3, lines 27–33.<br><br>**Step 4: Find the one correct answer.** Choice **(D)** cites the evidence for the correct answer to the preceding question, making it the correct choice for this Command of Evidence question. (A) summarizes the problems that scientists studying sunspots had in the past. (B) comes from paragraph 2 and describes the questions scientists still had before the SMM satellite data. (C) comes from the beginning of paragraph 3; it describes the source of the data but does not support the answer to the preceding question. |

| Question | Analysis |
|---|---|
| 5. Based on information in the passage, it can most reasonably be inferred that faculas<br><br>A) are directly responsible for increased temperatures on Earth.<br><br>B) have a dimming effect on the sun's luminescence during sunspot activity.<br><br>C) are mostly likely to appear at the peak of the solar cycle.<br><br>D) grow in number as the number of sunspots decreases. | **Step 1: Unpack the question stem.** Questions that ask you for a statement that is "based on" the passage are Inference questions. The correct answer may combine two statements to reach a conclusion.<br><br>**Step 2: Research the answer.** Faculas are discussed in paragraph 4. The passage says they are likely areas where the energy blocked by sunspots breaks through the sun's surface, and that they are probably why the sun is brightest when sunspot activity is high even though sunspots slightly dim the sun.<br><br>**Step 3: Predict the answer.** In most Inference questions, you won't be able to predict the correct answer word-for-word, but you can characterize the correct answer as the only one that will follow directly from the relevant text (in this case, paragraph 4).<br><br>**Step 4: Find the one correct answer.** Choice **(C)** is correct; if faculas are caused by sunspots, there will likely be more of them when there are more sunspots, in other words, at the peak of the solar cycle. (A) is too strong; scientists have found an indirect relationship between sunspot activity and Earth's weather (line 47). (B) is the opposite of what the passage states; faculas are so bright that they "more than compensate" for sunspots' dimming effect. (D) is the direct opposite of the correct answer. |

Reading

| Question | Analysis |
|---|---|
| 6. Which one of the following provides the best evidence for the answer to the previous question?<br><br>A) Lines 20–24 ("The latter . . . cycle")<br><br>B) Lines 34–35 ("The data . . . brighter")<br><br>C) Lines 36–41 ("When a . . . effect")<br><br>D) Lines 46–47 ("Meteorological . . . indirectly") | **Step 1: Unpack the question stem.** This is a Command of Evidence question that asks you to locate a piece of text stated in the passage that supports another statement, most often, as it is in this case, the correct answer to the preceding question.<br><br>**Step 2: Research the answer.** Because the previous question was about faculas, the correct answer to this question supports the fact that sunspots are most likely to appear at the peak of the solar cycle.<br><br>**Step 3: Predict the answer.** For Command of Evidence questions asking for the text that supports the previous answer, use that answer to evaluate the excerpt in each choice.<br><br>**Step 4: Find the one correct answer.** Choice **(C)** is correct; this is the sentence that explains the relationship between sunspots and faculas, and thus supports the correct answer to the previous question. (A) cites text that provides background information about the SMM. (B) contains a sentence that sets up the introduction of faculas but does not support the correct answer from the previous question. (D) is from the paragraph in which the author begins discussing the relationship between the solar cycle and Earth's weather. |
| 7. As used in line 45, "manifest" most nearly means<br><br>A) impact.<br><br>B) disguise.<br><br>C) itemize.<br><br>D) reveal. | **Step 1: Unpack the question stem.** This is a Vocabulary-in-Context question. The correct answer will be a word that could take the place of the word in the question stem without changing the meaning of the sentence.<br><br>**Step 2: Research the answer.** For Vocab-in-Context, read the full sentence containing the word cited in the question stem.<br><br>**Step 3: Predict the answer.** The scientists in the passage are studying whether the influence of sunspots can be seen in Earth's weather, so manifest must mean something like *show* or *display*.<br><br>**Step 4: Find the one correct answer.** The prediction leads to the correct answer, **(D)**. Choice (A) does not fit the context; the solar cycle might impact the weather, but wouldn't impact itself. (B) means the opposite of the correct answer. (C) suggests another meaning of the word manifest, which could also refer to a list of items in a shipment. |

| Question | Analysis |
|---|---|
| 8. According to the passage, Labitzke and van Loon's research on the quasi-biennial oscillation (QBO) shows that<br><br>A) the QBO's west phase correlates to the solar cycle.<br><br>B) the QBO's west phase has a longer duration than that of its east phase.<br><br>C) the QBO shows no correlation with the solar cycle.<br><br>D) the reasons for the QBO's correlation to the solar cycle are now well understood. | **Step 1: Unpack the question stem.** "According to the passage" signals a Detail question. The answer will be contained in the passage text.<br><br>**Step 2: Research the answer.** The QBO is introduced in paragraph 5, and Labitzke and van Loon's research is discussed in detail in paragraph 6.<br><br>**Step 3: Predict the answer.** In a question like this one, it's difficult to predict the exact language of the correct answer choice, but we know it will conform to one of the facts presented in paragraph 6. The researchers tried to correlate temperature and air pressure to the solar cycle. At first, they saw no connection, but when they broke down the QBO into its east and west phases, they found a correlation to the west phase.<br><br>**Step 4: Find the one correct answer.** Choice **(A)** matches the last sentence of paragraph 6 and is correct. (B) contradicts the passage; the shift from east to west and back occurs roughly every two years. (C) misuses a detail from the passage; the two researchers found no correlation *until* they split the QBO into its east and west phases. (D) contradicts paragraph 8, in which the scientists reveal that they still aren't sure why the QBO's west phase correlates to sunspot activity. |

Reading

| Question | Analysis |
|---|---|
| 9. The main purpose of the questions in the second-to-last paragraph (lines 76–84) is to<br><br>A) emphasize how little scientists know about the solar constant.<br><br>B) explain more fully the mysterious nature of the scientists' findings.<br><br>C) question the basis upon which these scientists built their hypotheses.<br><br>D) express doubts about the scientists' interpretations of their findings. | **Step 1: Unpack the question stem.** A question that asks why the author included something in the text is a Function question. The correct answer will explain the author's purpose for including questions in paragraph 8.<br><br>**Step 2: Research the answer.** This question stem leads you directly to paragraph 8. Determine what the author was trying to achieve by including questions there.<br><br>**Step 3: Predict the answer.** The author uses the questions in paragraph 8 to illustrate why the scientists consider some of their findings "rather mysterious": despite all that they've learned to date, there are still several questions they can't answer.<br><br>**Step 4: Find the one correct answer.** The prediction leads to the correct answer, **(B)**; the questions are included to explain why the scientists would consider their finding *mysterious*. (A) doesn't match the context of paragraph 8, which follows several paragraphs about how much scientists have recently learned. (C) runs counter to the author's purpose; the author doesn't try to call the scientist's findings into question. (D) is also out of step with the author's position; the author doesn't say or imply that the scientists have misunderstood the discoveries. |

| Question | Analysis |
|---|---|
| 10. The use of the quoted phrase "look like break-throughs" in line 88 is primarily meant to convey the idea that<br><br>A) information about the solar cycle has allowed scientists to predict changes in Earth's complex climate system.<br><br>B) additional analysis of the link between the solar cycle and Earth's weather may yield useful models.<br><br>C) despite the associated costs, space missions can lead to important discoveries.<br><br>D) an alternative interpretation of the data may contradict the initial findings. | **Step 1: Unpack the question stem.** A question that asks how an author supports a point made in the passage, or that asks why the author included something, is a Function question.<br><br>**Step 2: Research the answer.** This question stem contains a line number. Examine the text immediately before and after the cited line to determine the context of the quote. The quote from the question stem was given by John A. Eddy who believes that the recent findings will lead to additional exciting discoveries about the relationship between sunspots and Earth's weather patterns<br><br>**Step 3: Predict the answer.** The author includes the quote to show optimism about the potential for further research.<br><br>**Step 4: Find the one correct answer.** The prediction matches correct answer **(B)**. Choice (A) is too strong; scientists may create predictive models in the near future, but they haven't yet. (C) appears to refer to the *Solar Maximum Mission*, but Eddy's quote refers to that *and* the subsequent research; the author doesn't include Eddy's quote to make a point just about space missions. (D) runs contrary to Eddy's optimism. |

## Putting It All Together

That's the expert's approach to SAT Reading in action. Take a moment to go over the steps one more time. Imagine applying them to the next question set you'll try. As you use the Method for Reading Questions repeatedly, it will become second nature. You won't have to say "Step 1, step 2, . . . " in your head; you'll just be performing them, and you'll be improving your score in the SAT Reading section as you do.

As you consider the purpose of strategic reading and the steps of the Method for Reading Questions, think back to what you saw the SAT expert accomplish in each step as he tackled the Sunspots passage and its questions.

---

**SAT READING PASSAGE STRATEGY**

- Extract everything you can from the pre-passage blurb
- Read each paragraph actively
- Summarize the passage's big picture

---

- SAT experts never skip the pre-passage blurb. They quickly process any information that it provides for the context of the passage or that helps them anticipate what the author will cover.

- Great test takers read *actively*, asking what the author's purpose is in writing each paragraph. They also anticipate where the passage will go. Experts "*map*" the passage by jotting down summaries for each paragraph. They might also circle or underline keywords that indicate the author's opinion, details she wishes to highlight or emphasize, and the comparisons and contrasts she makes in the text. You will focus on active reading and passage mapping in chapter 18.

- Experts pause for a moment after actively reading the passage to summarize the big picture by noting the passage's main idea and the author's primary purpose in writing it.

| | **SAT Method for Reading Questions** |
|---|---|
| Step 1. | **Unpack the question stem** |
| Step 2. | **Research the answer** |
| Step 3. | **Predict the answer** |
| Step 4. | **Find the one correct answer** |

- **Step 1**. Great test takers determine the kind of question being asked, which indicates the kind of thinking and research the question requires. They also look for clues in the question stem to tell them where in the passage to find the correct answer. In chapter 19, you'll learn the characteristics of six types of questions found in the SAT Reading section and you'll learn to spot the most common research clues.

- **Step 2**. SAT experts never answer a question on a whim. Instead they turn to the passage text or to their summaries of it. Here's where a good passage map becomes invaluable. If you're unsure where in the passage a detail or opinion was mentioned, many SAT Reading questions could lead you to reread all or most of the passage. That's a huge waste of time. With practice, you'll learn to use the research clues from the question stem to zero in on the relevant lines of text or paragraph summary.

- **Step 3**. Before reading the answer choices, top scorers predict (or at least characterize) what the correct answer will say. This allows them to evaluate each choice against the prediction. It's not always possible to predict the correct answer word for word, but you should be able to use your research to establish the criteria for the correct answer.

- **Step 4**. In SAT Reading questions, there is *one* correct answer. The other choices are demonstrably incorrect. Test takers who start reading the answer choices before completing steps 3 (Research) and 4 (Predict) often find themselves rereading portions of the passage after each answer choice, or worse, comparing the answer choices to each other instead of testing them against a strong prediction. If you find yourself struggling with two or more answer choices, stop. Rephrase your prediction to establish what the correct answer must say and evaluate the choices against that prediction.

By reading strategically and using the Method for SAT Reading Questions every time you practice, you'll internalize the steps. By test day, you'll be attacking this section efficiently and accurately without even thinking about it.

In the next section, you'll see another SAT Reading passage accompanied by 11 questions. Map the passage and apply the Method for SAT Reading Questions presented in this lesson to answer the questions as quickly and confidently as possible.

# How Much Have You Learned?

**Directions:** Take 15 minutes to map this passage and answer the questions. Assess your work by comparing it to the expert responses at the end of the chapter.

**Questions 1-11 refer to the following passage.**

This passage is adapted from Carrie Chapman Catt's 1917 "Address to the United States Congress." Catt served as president of the National American Woman Suffrage Association, which advocated giving women the right to vote; the closing arguments from her speech are excerpted below.

Your party platforms have pledged woman suffrage. Then why not be honest, frank friends of our cause, adopt it in reality as your own, make it a party program and "fight with us"? As
5 a party measure—a measure of all parties—why not put the amendment through Congress and the Legislatures? We shall all be better friends, we shall have a happier nation, we women will be free to support loyally the party of our choice,
10 and we shall be far prouder of our history.

"There is one thing mightier than kings and armies"—aye, than Congresses and political parties—"the power of an idea when its time has come to move." The time for woman suffrage has
15 come. The woman's hour has struck. If parties prefer to postpone action longer and thus do battle with this idea, they challenge the inevitable. The idea will not perish; the party which opposes it may. Every delay, every trick, every political
20 dishonesty from now on will antagonize the women of the land more and more, and when the party or parties which have so delayed woman suffrage finally let it come, their sincerity will be doubted and their appeal to the new voters will
25 be met with suspicion. This is the psychology of the situation. Can you afford the risk? Think it over.

We know you will meet opposition. There are a few "woman haters" left, a few "old males
30 of the tribe," as Vance Thompson calls them, whose duty they believe it to be to keep women in the places they have carefully picked out for them. Treitschke, made world famous by war literature, said some years ago: "Germany, which
35 knows all about Germany and France, knows

far better what is good for Alsace-Lorraine than that miserable people can possibly know." A few American Treitschkes we have who know better than women what is good for them.
40 There are women, too. . . . But the world does not wait for such as these, nor does Liberty pause to heed the plaint of men and women with a grouch. She does not wait for those who have a special interest to serve, nor a selfish reason for
45 depriving other people of freedom. Holding her torch aloft, Liberty is pointing the way onward and upward and saying to America, "Come."

To you the supporters of our cause, in Senate and House, and the number is large, the
50 suffragists of the nation express their grateful thanks. This address is not meant for you. We are more truly appreciative of all you have done than any words can express. We ask you to make a last, hard fight for the amendment during the
55 present session. Since last we asked for a vote on this amendment your position has been fortified by the addition to suffrage territory of Great Britain, Canada, and New York.

Some of you have been too indifferent to give
60 more than casual attention to this question. It is worthy of your immediate consideration—a question big enough to engage the attention of our Allies in war time, is too big a question for you to neglect. . . .
65 Gentlemen, we hereby petition you, our only designated representatives, to redress our grievances by the immediate passage of the influence to secure its ratification in your own state, in order that the women of our nation
70 may be endowed with political freedom that our nation may resume its world leadership in democracy.

Woman suffrage is coming—you know it. Will you, Honorable Senators and Members of the
75 House of Representatives, help or hinder it?

1. What was Carrie Chapman Catt's primary purpose in giving this speech?

   A) To assert that women will vote for the party that supports their cause

   B) To demand more women candidates on political party tickets

   C) To persuade lawmakers to pass an amendment ensuring women's right to vote

   D) To rally support for women's equal representation in Congress

2. The stance that Catt takes in her speech is best described as that of

   A) a historian reflecting on historical events.

   B) an official campaigning for political office.

   C) an activist advocating for legislative reform.

   D) a reporter investigating a current controversy.

3. What counterclaim does Catt offer to the argument that some men and women still oppose suffrage?

   A) They are not voicing their opinions in Congress.

   B) They cannot stop the inevitable.

   C) They do have just cause for opposition.

   D) They have no legal basis for their claims.

4. Which choice provides the best evidence for the answer to the previous question?

   A) Lines 7–10 ("We shall all . . . our history")

   B) Lines 48–51 ("To you . . . grateful thanks")

   C) Lines 55–58 ("Since last . . . New York")

   D) Lines 60–64 ("It is worthy . . . to neglect")

5. As used in line 20, "antagonize" most nearly means

   A) dishearten.

   B) embitter.

   C) humiliate.

   D) inhibit.

6. The phrase in lines 21–25 ("when the party . . . with suspicion") implies that

   A) women voters will not support lawmakers who have resisted suffrage.

   B) women will not run for office because they do not trust politicians.

   C) women will vote more women into political office.

   D) women's influence on Congress will be minimal and is not a threat.

7. Catt most likely discusses Treitschke (lines 33–37) for which of the following reasons?

   A) To demonstrate support for women's suffrage in Europe

   B) To remind her audience of what happened to a politician who supported unpopular legislation

   C) To contrast his views on Alsace-Lorraine with the American values of freedom and democracy

   D) To draw an analogy between his views and the views of those who believe they know better than women what is best for women

8. The passage indicates which one of the following about the status of women's suffrage at the time of Catt's speech?

   A) At the time, only a minority of the U.S. population supported women's right to vote.

   B) Women already had the right to vote in at least one state in the United States.

   C) An earlier amendment to grant women the right to vote had been defeated.

   D) The women's suffrage movement was a recent development in American politics.

9. Which choice provides the best evidence for the answer to the previous question?

   A) Lines 14–17 ("The time . . . inevitable")

   B) Lines 28–33 ("There are . . . them")

   C) Lines 55–58 ("Since last . . . New York")

   D) Lines 65–72 ("Gentlemen . . . democracy")

10. As used in line 66, "redress" most nearly means

   A) appeal.

   B) communicate.

   C) implement.

   D) remedy.

11. What can you most reasonably infer from the thoughts expressed in lines 69–72 ("in order that . . . in democracy")?

   A) No citizen in our democracy is free as long as women cannot vote.

   B) Other nations have demanded that our government grant woman suffrage.

   C) A nation needs more women in positions of leadership.

   D) Woman suffrage is essential to true democracy.

# Answers and Explanations

### Carrie Chapman Catt Passage Map

This passage is adapted from Carrie Chapman Catt's 1917 "Address to the United States Congress." Catt served as president of the National American Woman Suffrage Association, which advocated giving women the right to vote; the closing arguments from her speech are excerpted below.

Your party platforms have pledged woman suffrage. Then why not be honest, frank friends of our cause, adopt it in reality as your own, make it a party program and "fight with us"? As
5 a party measure—a measure of all parties—why not put the amendment through Congress and the Legislatures? We shall all be better friends, we shall have a happier nation, we women will be free to support loyally the party of our choice,
10 and we shall be far prouder of our history.
"There is one thing mightier than kings and armies"—aye, than Congresses and political parties—"the power of an idea when its time has come to move." The time for woman suffrage has
15 come. The woman's hour has struck. If parties prefer to postpone action longer and thus do battle with this idea, they challenge the inevitable. The idea will not perish; the party which opposes it may. Every delay, every trick, every political
20 dishonesty from now on will antagonize the women of the land more and more, and when the party or parties which have so delayed woman suffrage finally let it come, their sincerity will be doubted and their appeal to the new voters will
25 be met with suspicion. This is the psychology of the situation. Can you afford the risk? Think it over.
We know you will meet opposition. There are a few "woman haters" left, a few "old males
30 of the tribe," as Vance Thompson calls them, whose duty they believe it to be to keep women in the places they have carefully picked out for them. Treitschke, made world famous by war literature, said some years ago: "Germany, which
35 knows all about Germany and France, knows far better what is good for Alsace-Lorraine than

**Margin notes:** Call for both parties to support women's vote / Time for women's suffrage is NOW / Those who oppose will be suspect in the future / Still have opponents / Examples

## ANALYSIS

**Pre-passage blurb:** You learn a lot here. Catt is speaking to Congress in 1917. She represents an organization pushing for women's suffrage, that is, the right to vote. The passage represents her closing arguments, so you can expect her to offer evidence and reasoning in support of this cause.

**¶1:** Catt reminds the members of Congress that their parties have supported women's suffrage in their platforms and encourages them, as individuals, to support it as well. It will make the U.S. a happier, prouder nation.

**¶2:** Catt asserts that women *will* get the right to vote and, as a warning to congressmen opposing suffrage, she argues that women with the vote will most likely not support the congressmen who tried to delay or undermine their right.

**¶3:** Catt admits that there will still be some who oppose women's suffrage, but argues that their ideas are out-of-date. She is trying to persuade congressmen who might be swayed by a vocal opposition. She uses a moral argument by equating suffrage with liberty.

that miserable people can possibly know." A few American Treitschkes we have who know better than women what is good for them.

40 There are women, too… But the world does not wait for such as these, nor does Liberty pause to heed the plaint of men and women with a grouch. She does not wait for those who have a special interest to serve, nor a selfish reason for

45 depriving other people of freedom. Holding her torch aloft, Liberty is pointing the way onward and upward and saying to America, "Come."

To you the supporters of our cause, in Senate and House, and the number is large, the

50 suffragists of the nation express their grateful thanks. This address is not meant for you. We are more truly appreciative of all you have done than any words can express. We ask you to make a last, hard fight for the amendment during the

55 present session. Since last we asked for a vote on this amendment your position has been fortified by the addition to suffrage territory of Great Britain, Canada, and New York.

Some of you have been too indifferent to give

60 more than casual attention to this question. It is worthy of your immediate consideration—a question big enough to engage the attention of our Allies in war time, is too big a question for you to neglect…

65 Gentlemen, we hereby petition you, our only designated representatives, to redress our grievances by the immediate passage of the influence to secure its ratification in your own state, in order that the women of our nation

70 may be endowed with political freedom that our nation may resume its world leadership in democracy.

Woman suffrage is coming—you know it. Will you, Honorable Senators and Members of the

75 House of Representatives, help or hinder it?

---

**Margin notes:**

BUT— liberty will overcome

Thanks to supporters- Help us fight

Other countries have suffrage

Suffrage— big/immediate issue

Petition to pass suffrage— then U.S. can again lead in freedom

Final appeal to Congress

---

**¶4:** Catt thanks members who already support her cause and encourages them to vote during the present session. She makes this appeal timely by referring to other countries and states that have adopted women's suffrage already.

**¶5:** Catt chastises those who have ignored the debate over suffrage—it's too big an issue—equating it with war.

**¶6:** Catt encourages lawmakers to support the suffrage amendment in their various states. She argues that only by granting suffrage can the U.S. once again be a leader of democracy in the world.

**¶7:** Catt's final appeal is for members of Congress to pick a side: are you with us or against us?

---

## BIG PICTURE

**Main Idea:** Women's suffrage is inevitable; lawmakers should support it now for reasons both moral (making America freer and more democratic) and practical (better political prospects in the future).

**Author's Purpose:** To persuade members of Congress to pass a bill sending a proposed amendment to the Constitution (to grant women the right to vote) to the states

**1.    C**

**Difficulty:** Medium

**Category:** Global

**Strategic Advice:** A question asking for an author's or speaker's primary purpose is a Global question. Consult your big picture summary to predict the correct answer.

**Getting to the Answer:** The pre-passage blurb tells you that Carrie Chapman Catt is speaking to Congress on behalf of the National American Woman Suffrage Association. In the first paragraph, she asks lawmakers to support a constitutional amendment. Additional context provided in the passage makes clear that the amendment would grant women suffrage, making **(C)** correct. While (A) captures a key part of Catt's reasoning, it does not reflect her purpose in giving the speech. (B) distorts the passage; Catt is calling for suffrage, not necessarily for female candidates. Similarly, (D) goes beyond the scope of Catt's speech.

**2.    C**

**Difficulty:** Easy

**Category:** Global

**Strategic Advice:** Some Global questions ask about an author's overall attitude or the perspective from which the passage was written. Use your big picture summary of the main idea and the author's purpose to predict the correct answer.

**Getting to the Answer:** In the passage, Catt gives a speech in which she appeals to legislators to pass a constitutional amendment, or legislative reform, to grant women suffrage. She is speaking as a political activist. **(C)** is correct. The other three answers all distort Catt's purpose and main point.

**3.    B**

**Difficulty:** Medium

**Category:** Detail

**Strategic Advice:** A question calling for a claim the author or speaker makes explicitly in the text is a Detail question. The research clue in the question stem points to paragraph 3.

**Getting to the Answer:** In paragraph 3, Catt acknowledges the opposition to woman suffrage, citing "woman haters" (line 29), "old males of the tribe" (lines 29–30), and "women, too" (line 40). She suggests that the argu-

ments against suffrage are dated and ineffectual, and goes on to state that the world will not slow down and that the cause of liberty will continue. Her underlying message is that suffrage is unavoidable, which echoes her earlier statement in line 17. All of this leads to **(B)** as the correct answer. (A) distorts Catt's response; whether opponents continue to speak out is almost irrelevant in her opinion. (C) is contradicted by Catt's rhetoric; suffrage is just, and it will prevail. (D) distorts Catt's argument; she addresses the moral and sociological reasons for endorsing suffrage.

**4.    C**

**Difficulty:** Medium

**Category:** Command of Evidence

**Strategic Advice:** This is a Command of Evidence question. The correct answer to this question will cite text that provides evidence, either in reasoning or in fact, to support the claim in the answer to the previous question. Each answer choice contains line numbers that help focus your research as you evaluate the choices.

**Getting to the Answer:** The answer to the previous question asserts that woman suffrage is inevitable. Evidence to support this claim would show that suffrage is advancing, as demonstrated by **(C)**. (A) provides practical reasons to support suffrage but does not support a claim of its inevitability. (B) offers thanks to lawmakers who already support suffrage. (D) is an exhortation to immediate action, not evidence of inevitable victory for the women's suffrage movement.

**5.    B**

**Difficulty:** Medium

**Category:** Vocab-in-Context

**Strategic Advice:** The correct answer to a Vocab-in-Context question like this one will reflect the specific meaning of the word in the context of the surrounding sentence and text.

**Getting to the Answer:** The text states, "Every delay, every trick, every political dishonesty from now on will antagonize the women of the land more and more" (lines 19–21). The surrounding text suggests that women will become only more resolved to their purpose as a result of delay, as well as more angry—or bitter—with politicians who forestall them, making **(B)** correct. (A) implies that women will give up; Catt clearly argues the opposite. (C) distorts the meaning of the sentence;

tricks and delays will anger women and encourage them to punish deceitful politicians at the polls. (D) sounds plausible (after all, the delays and tricks are meant to impede suffrage), but it doesn't fit the context of the sentence, which predicts a backlash from these tactics.

## 6.  A

**Difficulty:** Medium

**Category:** Inference

**Strategic Advice:** The word "implies" identifies this as an Inference question. The correct answer will reflect the underlying or implied meaning of the excerpted line within the context of the surrounding text. The research clue points to the second half of paragraph 2.

**Getting to the Answer:** The text cited in the question stem asserts that new voters (the women enfranchised by suffrage) will mistrust political parties whose members have resisted suffrage; this leads to **(A)** as the correct answer. The message of choice (B) runs counter to Catt's argument. (C) goes too far; Catt asserts that women voters will flee the parties who have resisted suffrage, and not that they will vote for female candidates. (D) states the opposite of what Catt implies here.

## 7.  D

**Difficulty:** Hard

**Category:** Function

**Strategic Advice:** A question that asks why an author included a detail or reference in her text is a Function question. Research the referenced detail (in this case, Treitschke) to see the author's purpose for including it in the passage.

**Getting to the Answer:** For Catt, Treitschke is an example of an outsider who thought he knew better than the residents of an area what was best for them. She analogizes that to male politicians who think they know what's best for women. Choice **(D)** describes Catt's use of the analogy. (A) conflates Treitschke with Catt's later statement that women's suffrage had passed in the United Kingdom. (B) misapplies the Treitschke example to a different argument Catt makes in her speech. (C) distorts Catt's point about Treitschke; she used him as an example of someone whose reasoning was misguided reasoning, not as someone who was anti-democratic.

## 8.  B

**Difficulty:** Medium

**Category:** Detail

**Strategic Advice:** The word "indicates" signals a Detail question. The correct answer will clearly restate or paraphrase something stated in the passage.

**Getting to the Answer:** The entire speech is, of course, about women's suffrage, but Catt addresses the current status of women's right to vote explicitly near the end of paragraph 4. There, she tells Congress that suffrage laws have recently been passed in Great Britain, Canada, and New York. That directly supports choice **(B)**. (A) is too extreme; in paragraph 3, Catt admits that suffrage still had opponents, but she does not state that only a minority of voters support it. (C) is not supported anywhere in Catt's speech. (D) is a distortion of Catt's claim that momentum for women's suffrage was on the rise.

## 9.  C

**Difficulty:** Medium

**Category:** Command of Evidence

**Strategic Advice:** This is a Command of Evidence question asking you to locate the line in the passage that supports the correct answer to the preceding question. Use the line references in each answer choice to research the passage text.

**Getting to the Answer:** The correct answer to the preceding question asserted that, at the time of Catt's speech, at least one state in the Union had already granted women the right to vote. That is directly supported by the text cited in choice **(C)**, where Catt encourages suffrage advocates in Congress with the fact that New York recently gave women the right to vote. (A) is Catt's warning to the members of Congress about a potential backlash for their failure to support the suffrage amendment, which is unrelated to the fact that women in New York can vote. (B) cites text in which Catt describes the opponents of women's suffrage; that might have tempted a test taker who chose (A) for the preceding question. (D) contains Catt's call to action in paragraph 6; that does not support the answer to the preceding question.

**10. D**

**Difficulty:** Medium

**Category:** Vocab-in-Context

**Strategic Advice:** This is a Vocab-in-Context question; the correct answer will correctly replace the original word and retain the meaning of the original sentence.

**Getting to the Answer:** The text states that Catt and her supporters want congressional lawmakers to "redress our grievances" (lines 66–67), meaning to set right—or to remedy—the ills committed against women. **(D)** reflects this meaning. None of the other choices fits logically into the sentence.

**11. D**

**Difficulty:** Medium

**Category:** Inference

**Strategic Advice:** The word "implied" signals an Inference question. The correct answer will follow from Catt's statement in the excerpted line. The research clue points you to paragraph 6.

**Getting to the Answer:** The excerpted line states that once women have the political freedom granted by suffrage, then the nation will resume its leadership in democracy. The implication is that the nation is not a leader in democracy as long as it denies women the right to vote. Therefore, **(D)** is correct. (A) is too extreme for the specific statement cited in the question stem. (B) misuses a detail from paragraph 4; other countries have adopted women's suffrage, but Catt doesn't say they've called on the United States to do the same. (C) is too broad; the quoted statement focuses specifically on the right to vote, not on electing women.

# Reflect

**Directions**: Take a few minutes to recall what you've learned and what you've been practicing in this chapter. Consider the following questions, jot down your best answer for each one, and then compare your reflections to the expert responses on the following page. Use your level of confidence to to determine what to do next.

Describe active, or strategic, reading on SAT passages.

_____

What do SAT experts mean by summarizing the big picture of a passage?

_____

How can writing brief "margin notes" help you answer SAT Reading questions more effectively?

_____

What does an SAT expert look for in the question stem of an SAT Reading question?

_____

Why do expert test takers predict or characterize the correct answer to each SAT Reading question before assessing the answer choices?

_____

What will you do differently on future passages and their questions?

_____

## Expert Responses

Describe active, or strategic, reading on SAT passages.

*Because the SAT asks many questions about why an author has written the passage or about how the author makes a point, expert test takers read for the author's purpose and main idea. Noting keywords that indicate a shift or contrast in points of view or that indicate opinions and emphasis help keep SAT experts on point, as they anticipate where the passage will go.*

What do SAT experts mean by summarizing the big picture of a passage?

*To read for the big picture means being able to accurately summarize the main idea of a passage and to note the author's purpose for writing it. The big picture summary helps you answer Global questions and questions that ask about the author's opinion or point of view.*

How can writing brief "margin notes" help you answer SAT Reading questions more effectively?

*Jotting down margin notes provides a reference "map" to the subject or purpose of each paragraph in the passage. It helps locate specific subjects or opinions expressed in the passage when they are called out in the questions.*

What does an SAT expert look for in the question stem of an SAT Reading question?

*Each question stem indicates the type of question and contains clues as to whether the answer will come from researching the passage text or from the big picture summary. Many question stems have specific clues (for example, line numbers or references to details from the passage) that tell you precisely where to research.*

Why do expert test takers predict or characterize the correct answer to each SAT Reading question before assessing the answer choices?

*Predicting or characterizing the correct answer allows you to evaluate each answer choice one time and to avoid rereading for every answer choice. Wrong answers often distort what the passage said or misuse details from the passage, so it's best to research the passage once to know what the correct answer must say before diving into the choices.*

What will you do differently on future passages and their questions?

*There is no one-size-fits-all answer to this question. Each student has his or her own initial strengths and opportunities in the Reading section. What's important here is that you're honestly self-reflective. Take what you need from the expert's examples and strive to apply it to your own performance. Many test takers convince themselves that they'll never get faster or more confident in SAT Reading, but the truth is, many test takers who now routinely ace the Reading section were much slower and more hesitant before they learned to approach this section systematically and strategically.*

## Next Steps

If you answered most questions correctly in the "How Much Have You Learned?" section, and if your responses to the Reflect questions were similar to those of the SAT expert, then consider the Method for SAT Reading Questions an area of strength and move on to the next chapter. Come back to this topic periodically to prevent yourself from getting rusty.

If you don't yet feel confident, review the material in this chapter, then try the questions you missed again. As always, be sure to review the explanations closely.

# CHAPTER 18

# SAT Reading Passage Strategies

## LEARNING OBJECTIVES

After completing this chapter, you will be able to:

- Identify keywords that promote active reading and relate passage text to the questions
- Create short, accurate margin notes that help you research the text efficiently
- Summarize the big picture of the passage

# How Much Do You Know?

**Directions:** In this chapter, you'll learn how SAT experts actively read the passage, take notes, and summarize the main idea to prepare themselves to answer all of the passage's questions quickly and confidently. You saw this kind of reading modeled in the previous chapter. To get ready for the current chapter, take five minutes to actively read the following passage by 1) noting the keywords that indicate the author's point of view and the passage's structure, 2) jotting down a quick description next to each paragraph, and 3) summarizing the big picture (the passage's main idea and the author's purpose for writing it). When you're done, compare your work to the passage map on the following page.

**Questions 1-11 refer to the following passage.**

This passage is adapted from a 2018 article summarizing two different proposals for solving problems with maintaining New York City's mass transit system.

The history of the New York City subway system, quickly told: the first stations opened in 1904, and over the next century, it expanded to 472 stations,
5  more than any other subway system in the world, with 850 miles of track. Operating 24 hours a day seven days a week, with an average weekday ridership of approximately 5.7 million, it is the
10 planet's 7th-busiest rapid transit system. While the system is, on many levels, an amazing achievement, it is also beset by a problem that harms both quality of life and economic activity. Such a
15 large system must inevitably suffer from service interruptions and delays; normal wear and tear combined with the sheer age of the system necessitates regular maintenance. However, there
20 is no consensus as to the best way to accomplish the required repairs.

The current maintenance scheme is designed to minimize service interruptions. A subway line in need
25 of repair will be taken out of service during a comparatively less busy time, such as nights or weekends, while another line is re-routed to cover as many as possible of the missing line's
30 stops. The main advantage to this approach is that trains are not taken out of service during rush hour, when

most subway trips occur; subway service generally remains predictable
35 and commuters are, for the most part, able to use the system to get to their destinations on time.

But critics are quick to point out the disadvantages to this approach. Perhaps
40 most obvious is the confusion caused by trains switching lines. The labyrinthine system is hard enough to navigate at the best of times, especially for tourists. A subway rider on the A train naturally
45 expects the train to make stops on the A line. If, instead, it is diverted temporarily to the F line, the rider may find herself miles from her intended destination.

50 While annoying, the confusion arising from route switching is hardly the most serious problem with the current approach to repairs. Because the system runs 24 hours a
55 day, routine maintenance can generally be done only during the temporary closures on nights and weekends. This means that more serious repair and crucial preventative maintenance is
60 often neglected. Problems that could have been fixed or prevented reasonably expeditiously given a slightly longer closure wind up leading to major breakdowns and service interruptions
65 later on.

On rare occasions, such breakdowns have resulted in entire subway lines being shut down for months or even a year. Beginning in 2019, for
70 example, the L Train connecting lower

Manhattan to parts of Brooklyn was scheduled to close for as much as 15 months for long overdue service and upgrades. In a city fewer than half

75 of whose households own a car, this can have serious economic impacts. Residents of the affected area may face a much longer commute via an alternate subway line if one is available;

80 or, if there is no alternate subway service, they may need to take other, potentially more expensive, modes of transportation, such as taxis or ferries. Moreover, studies indicate that

85 increased stress from the commute to work can lead to lower productivity, and that businesses near the impacted lines may see decreased revenue as potential customers have a harder time getting to

90 them.

One controversial proposal for reducing breakdowns and the resulting transit interruptions is to end the subway's 24-hour service and to shut

95 down for several hours each night. Proponents of this plan argue that this would allow time, on a regular rather than sporadic basis, for more preventative maintenance. This, they

100 claim, would ultimately lead to more consistent service; rather than shutting down entire lines for long periods of a time, there would merely be shorter service outages overnight, when fewer

105 people use the subway system. While this may seem a preferable outcome to the economic consequences of a total shutdown resulting from a breakdown, it has its liabilities as well. While most

110 subway trips may occur during rush hour, not everyone works during the daytime. New York is famously known as the "the city that never sleeps." Doctors, nurses, bartenders, police

115 officers, and firefighters are just a few examples of occupations whose workers

need transportation at all hours of the day and night. Rather than be subjected to a relatively short period

120 of inconvenience, these workers would find their commutes irrevocably altered. One thing, at least, is clear: the city must carefully consider many economic and social factors in designing a subway

125 maintenance plan.

# Check Your Work

**Questions 1-11 refer to the following passage.**

This passage is adapted from a 2018 article summarizing two different proposals for solving problems with maintaining New York City's mass transit system.

The history of the New York City subway system, quickly told: the first stations opened in 1904, and over the next century, it expanded to 472 stations,
5   more than any other subway system in the world, with 850 miles of track. Operating 24 hours a day seven days a week, with an average weekday ridership of approximately 5.7 million, it is the
10  planet's 7th-busiest rapid transit system. (While) the system is, on many levels, an amazing achievement, it is also beset by a problem that harms both quality of life and economic activity. Such a
15  large system must (inevitably suffer) from service interruptions and delays; normal wear and tear combined with the sheer age of the system necessitates regular maintenance. (However,) there
20  is no consensus as to the best way to accomplish the required repairs.

The current maintenance scheme is designed to minimize service interruptions. A subway line in need
25  of repair will be taken out of service during a comparatively less busy time, such as nights or weekends, while another line is re-routed to cover as many as possible of the missing line's
30  stops. The main (advantage) to this approach is that trains are not taken out of service during rush hour, when most subway trips occur; subway service generally remains predictable
35  and commuters are, for the most part, able to use the system to get to their destinations on time.

But critics are quick to point out the disadvantages to this approach. Perhaps

*[margin notes:]*
NYC subway: how to repair? diff. views

Current approach – night and weekend repairs

Critics: line switch confusion

## ANALYSIS

**Pre-passage blurb:** This tells you that the topic of the passage is a debate over the New York City subway system. Expect to see at least two sides in the debate. Note where each different position is discussed.

**SAT Reading Strategy: On the SAT, the blurb almost always contains the title of the book or article from which the passage was adapted. Sometimes the test maker will provide additional context as well. Always take advantage of it.**

**¶1:** The author introduces the New York City subway system by highlighting its age and size. Those two factors are the reason maintenance is such a big issue. The scope of the passage comes at the end of the paragraph: there is no agreement on *how* best to perform upkeep on the massive system.

**¶2:** This paragraph outlines the current maintenance schedule. Repairs happen mostly on nights and weekends. The main advantage is that subway lines are not down during rush hours.

**¶3:** Here comes the opposing view. One disadvantage of the current system is that trains are re-routed causing confusion for riders.

40 most obvious is the confusion caused by
trains switching lines. The labyrinthine
system is hard enough to navigate at the
best of times, especially for tourists. A
subway rider on the A train naturally
45 expects the train to make stops on
the A line. If, instead, it is diverted
temporarily to the F line, the rider may
find herself miles from her intended
destination.
50     While annoying, the confusion
arising from route switching is
hardly the most serious problem
with the current approach to repairs.
Because the system runs 24 hours a
55 day, routine maintenance can generally
be done only during the temporary
closures on nights and weekends. This
means that more serious repair and
crucial preventative maintenance is
60 often neglected. Problems that could
have been fixed or prevented reasonably
expeditiously given a slightly longer
closure wind up leading to major
breakdowns and service interruptions
65 later on.
    On rare occasions, such breakdowns
have resulted in entire subway lines
being shut down for months or
even a year. Beginning in 2019, for
70 example, the L Train connecting lower
Manhattan to parts of Brooklyn was
scheduled to close for as much as 15
months for long overdue service and
upgrades. In a city fewer than half
75 of whose households own a car, this
can have serious economic impacts.
Residents of the affected area may
face a much longer commute via an
alternate subway line if one is available;
80 or, if there is no alternate subway
service, they may need to take other,
potentially more expensive, modes
of transportation, such as taxis or
ferries. Moreover, studies indicate that
85 increased stress from the commute to

*Even worse
– major
breakdowns*

**¶4:** A second, worse problem with the current
system is that it doesn't allow enough time for
preventative maintenance. That leads to big
problems down the line.

**¶5:** These big problems can shut down subway
lines for weeks or months causing grave economic impact to affected riders and businesses.

*Econ. & Soc.
harms of
shutdowns*

work can lead to lower productivity, and
that businesses near the impacted lines
may see decreased revenue as potential
customers have a harder time getting to
90 them.

One controversial proposal for
reducing breakdowns and the resulting
transit interruptions is to end the
subway's 24-hour service and to shut
95 down for several hours each night.
Proponents of this plan argue that
this would allow time, on a regular
rather than sporadic basis, for more
preventative maintenance. This, they
100 claim, would ultimately lead to more
consistent service; rather than shutting
down entire lines for long periods of
a time, there would merely be shorter
service outages overnight, when fewer
105 people use the subway system. While
this may seem a preferable outcome to
the economic consequences of a total
shutdown resulting from a breakdown,
it has its liabilities as well. While most
110 subway trips may occur during rush
hour, not everyone works during the
daytime. New York is famously known
as the "the city that never sleeps."
Doctors, nurses, bartenders, police
115 officers, and firefighters are just a few
examples of occupations whose workers
need transportation at all hours of
the day and night. Rather than be
subjected to a relatively short period
120 of inconvenience, these workers would
find their commutes irrevocably altered.
One thing, at least, is clear: the city
must carefully consider many economic
and social factors in designing a subway
125 maintenance plan.

*Alt proposal – stop 24-hour service*

*Pros*

*Cons*

**¶6:** This paragraph opens with a controversial proposal: stop running the subway
24/7. While this would make more time for
preventative maintenance, it too has a big
disadvantage: many workers need to commute
overnight. The author's conclusion is neutral:
New York City has to weigh both sides to make
the best decision.

---

### BIG PICTURE

**Main Idea:** New York City must weigh different economic and social factors to design an effective subway
maintenance plan.

**Author's Purpose:** To explain advantages and disadvantages in opposing views of how best to maintain the
New York City subway

---

# SAT Reading Strategies—Keywords, Margin Notes, and the Big Picture Summary

## LEARNING OBJECTIVES

After this lesson, you will be able to:

- Identify keywords that promote active reading and relate passage text to the questions
- Create short, accurate margin notes that help you research the text efficiently
- Summarize the big picture of the passage

## To read and map a passage like this:

This passage was adapted from an article titled "Millennials and the Market," written by a money management expert in 2018.

During the Golden Age of American manufacturing, it was expected that after putting in 30 to 40 years of tedious labor in a factory, workers
5  would be able to retire around age 65 and enjoy the benefits of retirement comforted by the thought that a pension and the Social Security system they had financed for decades would
10  cover their expenses. Unfortunately for millennials (people born between the early 1980s and late 1990s), prospects look increasingly bleak that they will get a return on their investment at
15  retirement age, despite continuing to fund programs like Social Security and Medicare. Fewer than a quarter of all Fortune 500 corporations still offer some form of pension plan to new
20  hires, and the move from company-funded pension plans to 401(k) plans and IRAs that began in the 1970s shows no sign of slackening. In this financial environment, it might be expected
25  that investment in the stock market would be at an all-time high. An analysis of the data, however, indicates a complicated and even fraught relationship between young adults and
30  the stock market.

The trauma associated with the Great Recession (which began in December 2007 and ended in June 2009) left many investors wary of stock
35  market volatility, and that hesitancy was exacerbated among young people, who saw a considerable portion of their families' wealth erased in short order. A study by Pfeffer, Danziger,
40  and Schoeni published in 2014 posited that the average American household

lost a third of its wealth, approximately $28,000, during the Great Recession. This was at the exact moment when a
45  great many millennials were making decisions about attending college, pursuing post-graduate studies, or entering the workforce. For a median-income family, those decisions were
50  all directly correlated to household wealth. The ripple effects of the Great Recession left many millennials ascribing blame directly to the stock market for missed opportunities.
55  Even with a full awareness that the stock market has rebounded and far exceeded the highs seen prior to the Great Recession, many millennials still feel trepidation about investing in the
60  stock market, preferring to save a larger percentage of their salaries than their parents and grandparents did.

Another factor that has directly impacted the willingness of millennials to invest in the stock market is the
65  seismic shift in the job market brought about by the "gig economy," in which short-term contracts and freelance work have replaced permanent
70  employment. To a large degree, the gig economy is still in its nascent phase, with many of the largest purveyors of jobs only incorporated in the last decade. Research has not adequately
75  kept track of the trend, with estimates of participation in the gig economy ranging from 4% to 40% in the United States. The ability to pick up work on a contingency basis allows
80  millennials to feel a greater level of control over their finances, something a significant number of them believe they cannot achieve through stock market investment. The increased
85  diversity of available methods for

building future wealth has caused many millennials to adopt an a la carte approach to preparing for retirement. But is it possible that this approach
90 has been clouded by some common misconceptions about wealth building?

One persistent, albeit erroneous, view is that real estate is a better investment instrument than a stock market
95 portfolio. While it is true that home equity is the stepping-stone from which most individuals begin to build their personal wealth, statistics make it clear that stock market investments are a more
100 stable and lucrative source of long-term wealth. A London Business School study found that over the same 90-year period, the average rate of return on a real estate investment was 1.3% compared to the
105 9.8% annualized total return for the S&P stock 500 index. Investing the $5,500 IRS-imposed annual limit in an IRA for 25 years would result in a return of over $600,000 based on the annualized
110 return rate. Stock investment requires a smaller overhead than real estate investment, and the liquid nature of stocks makes them ideal for retirement: stocks allocated to retirement accounts

115 remain tax-free until they are drawn on. Despite these pieces of tangible evidence, though, the stigma regarding stock market investment persists in the minds of many millennials.
120 Regardless of their feelings about the stock market, one thing is self-evident: without preparation for retirement, millennials will be a generation adrift in a society without the social "safety
125 nets" available to current retirees. The benchmark for the amount of savings the average retiree needs to live comfortably after retirement, which remained at $1 million for many years,
130 now continues to rise, and exacerbating factors, such as the cost of medical care, continue to increase. Armed with that knowledge, millennials need to be proactive about financial planning. By
135 taking full advantage of their penchant for a hands-on approach to finances and leveraging the various financial technologies and services that were not available to the previous generation,
140 millennials can amass the wealth necessary to retire comfortably and on their own terms.

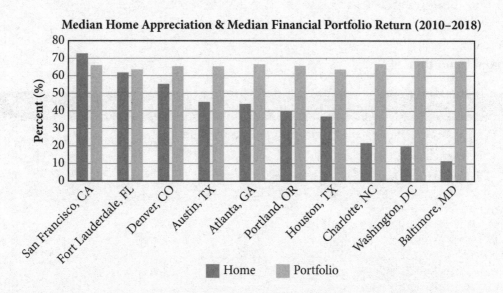

**Median Home Appreciation & Median Financial Portfolio Return (2010–2018)**

Home ■   Portfolio ■

## You need to know this:

- SAT Reading passages are preceded by short blurbs that tell you about the author and source of the passage.
- There are three categories of keywords that reveal an author's purpose and point of view and that unlock the passage's structure:
  - **Opinion and Emphasis**—words that signal that the author finds a detail noteworthy (e.g., *especially*, *crucial*, *important*, *above all*) or has an opinion about it (e.g., *fortunately*, *disappointing*, *I suggest*, *it seems likely*)
  - **Connection and Contrast**—words that suggest that a subsequent detail continues the same point (e.g., *moreover*, *in addition*, *also*, *further*) or that indicate a change in direction or point of difference (e.g., *but*, *yet*, *despite*, *on the other hand*)
    - In some passages, these keywords may show steps in a process or developments over time (e.g., *traditionally*, *in the past*, *recently*, *today*, *first*, *second*, *finally*, *earlier*, *since*)
  - **Evidence and Example**—words that indicate an argument (the use of evidence to support a conclusion), either the author's or someone else's (e.g., *thus*, *therefore*, *because*), or that introduce an example to clarify or support another point (e.g., *for example*, *this shows*, *to illustrate*)
- SAT experts read strategically, jotting down brief, accurate, and useful margin notes next to each paragraph.
- Expert test takers summarize the passage as a whole by paying attention to its big picture:
  - **Main Idea**—the author's primary conclusion or overall takeaway
  - **Purpose**—the author's reason for writing the passage
    - Express this as a verb (e.g., *to explain*, *to evaluate*, *to argue*, *to refute*)

---

### READING PASSAGE AND QUESTION STRATEGY

**Why read the passage before reading the questions?**

Each SAT Reading passage is accompanied by 10 or 11 questions. Two or three of the questions may ask about the passage as a whole. The others will ask about specific paragraphs, details, or arguments within the passage. SAT experts use deliberate Reading strategies to answer all of the questions quickly and accurately, with a minimum of rereading.

---

## You need to do this:

---

### THE SAT READING PASSAGE STRATEGY

- Extract everything you can from the pre-passage blurb
- Read each paragraph actively
- Summarize the passage's big picture

---

### Extract everything you can from the pre-passage blurb

- Quickly prepare for the passage by unpacking the pre-passage blurb:
  - What does the title and date of the original book or article tell you about the author and her purpose for writing?
  - What information can you glean from the source (nonfiction book, novel, academic journal, etc.)?
  - Is there any other information that provides context for the passage?

### Read each paragraph actively

- Note keywords (circling or underlining them may help) and use them to focus your reading on
  - the author's purpose and point of view,
  - the relationships between ideas, and
  - the illustrations or other support provided for passage claims.

---

#### KEYWORDS

**Why pay attention to keywords?**

Keywords indicate opinions and signal structure that make the difference between correct and incorrect answers on SAT questions. Consider this question:

> With which one of the following statements would the author most likely agree?
>
> 1. Coffee beans that grow at high altitudes typically produce dark, mellow coffee when brewed.
>
> 2. Coffee beans that grow at high altitudes typically produce light, acidic coffee when brewed.

To answer that based on an SAT passage, you will need to know whether the author said:

> Type X coffee beans grow at very high altitudes, *and so* produce a dark, mellow coffee when brewed.

That would make choice (1) correct. But if the author instead said:

> Type X coffee beans grow at very high altitudes, *but* produce a *surprisingly* dark, mellow coffee when brewed.

Then choice (2) would be correct. The facts in the statements did not change at all, but the correct answer to the SAT question would be different in each case because of the keywords the author chose to include.

- As you read, jot down brief, accurate margin notes that will help you research questions about specific details, examples, and paragraphs:
  - Paraphrase the text (put it into your own words) as you go
  - Ask "What's the author's point and purpose?" for each paragraph

---

### MARGIN NOTES

**Why jot down notes next to each paragraph?**

SAT Reading is an open-book test. The answer is always in the passage. Margin notes help you zero in on the details and opinions you need to answer questions like these:

> As used in line 38, "erased" most nearly means

> In the context of the passage as a whole, the question in lines 89–91 primarily functions to help the author

> The passage most strongly implies which of the following statements about the Great Recession?

> In the third paragraph (lines 63–91), the most likely purpose of the author's discussion of the "gig economy" is to

---

## Summarize the passage's big picture

- At the end of the passage, pause for a few seconds to summarize the passage's big picture to prepare for Global questions. Ask yourself:
  - "What is the main idea of the entire passage?"
  - "Why did the author write it?"

---

### THE BIG PICTURE

**Why summarize the passage's big picture?**

Summarizing the big picture prepares you to answer Global questions such as the following:

> Which one of the following most accurately expresses the main point of the passage?

> The passage primarily serves to

---

**Reading**

## Explanation:

This passage was adapted from an article titled "Millennials and the Market," written by a money management expert in 2018.

During the Golden Age of American manufacturing, it was expected that after puttingin 30 to 40 years of tedious labor in a factory, workers
5  would be able to retire around age 65 and enjoy the benefits of retirement comforted by the thought that a pension and the Social Security system they had financed for decades would
10  cover their expenses. Unfortunately for millennials (people born between the early 1980s and late 1990s), prospects look increasingly bleak that they will get a return on their investment at
15  retirement age, despite continuing to fund programs like Social Security and Medicare. Fewer than a quarter of all Fortune 500 corporations still offer some form of pension plan to new
20  hires, and the move from company-funded pension plans to 401(k) plans and IRAs that began in the 1970s shows no sign of slackening. In this financial environment, it might be expected
25  that investment in the stock market would be at an all-time high. An analysis of the data, however, indicates a complicated and even fraught relationship between young adults and
30  the stock market.

*Millennials won't have same re-tirement $*

*But they don't like stock mar-ket*

## ANALYSIS

**Pre-passage blurb:** This passage discusses millennials and the stock market. It is written from the perspective of an investment counselor.

**SAT Reading Strategy: On the SAT, the pre-passage blurb will always give the author's name, the title of the book or article from which the passage was adapted, and the year it was published. When necessary, the blurb may also include a context-setting sentence with additional information. Train yourself to unpack the blurb to better anticipate what the passage will cover.**

**¶1:** The first opinion keyword is "[u]nfortunately" (line 10). The author explains that, when they retire, millennials will not have the same kinds of pensions and social "safety net" programs that their parents and grandparents had. Then, the author expresses surprise that despite these challenges, millennials are hesitant to invest in the stock market.

**SAT Reading Strategy: When an author introduces a surprising or confusing event or condition, expect her to offer some explanation in the following paragraph(s).**

The trauma associated with the Great Recession (which began in December 2007 and ended in June 2009) left many investors (wary) of stock

35 market volatility, and that hesitancy was exacerbated among young people, who saw a considerable portion of their families' wealth erased in short order. A study by Pfeffer, Danziger,

40 and Schoeni published in 2014 posited that the average American household lost a third of its wealth, approximately $28,000, during the Great Recession. This was at the exact moment when a

45 great many millennials were making decisions about attending college, pursuing post-graduate studies, or entering the workforce. For a median-income family, those decisions were

50 all directly correlated to household wealth. The ripple effects of the Great Recession left many millennials (ascribing blame) directly to the stock market for missed opportunities.

55 Even with a full awareness that the stock market has rebounded and far exceeded the highs seen prior to the Great Recession, many millennials still feel (trepidation) about investing in the

60 stock market, preferring to save a larger percentage of their salaries than their parents and grandparents did.
(Another factor) that has directly impacted the willingness of millennials

65 to invest in the stockmarket is the seismic shift in the job market brought about by the "gig economy," in which short-term contracts and freelance work have replaced permanent

70 employment. To a large degree, the gig economy is still in its nascent phase, with many of the largest purveyors of jobs only incorporated in the last decade. Research has not adequately

75 kept track of the trend, with estimates of participation in the gig economy

*Reason:*
*07-09*
*recession =*
*millennials*
*blame the*
*market*

*Reason 2:*
*gig economy*
*= diff. ways*
*to make $*

**¶2:** One reason millennials distrust the stock market is that many came of age during the Great Recession. They saw their families' savings wiped out and, right out of high school, they had to make tough decisions about going to college or getting a job.

**¶3:** A second reason millennials avoid stock market investing is the rise of the "gig economy," in which many people have short-term, freelance jobs. This makes millennials open to different ways of managing their money, but maybe they have a mistaken viewpoint.

**SAT Reading Strategy: When the author poses a question, expect her to answer it in the following sentence or paragraph.**

ranging from 4% to 40% in the
United States.The ability to pick up
work on a contingency basis allows
80 millennials to feel a greater level of
control over their finances, something
a significant number of them believe
they cannot achieve through stock
market investment. The increased
85 diversity of available methods for
building future wealth has caused
many millennials to adopt an a la carte
approach to preparing for retirement.
(But) is it possible that this approach
90 has been clouded by some common
misconceptions about wealth building?)
(One persistent, albeit erroneous, view)
is that real estate is a better investment
instrument than a stock market
95 portfolio.(While) it is true that home
equity is the stepping-stone from which
most individuals begin to build their
personal wealth, statistics make it clear
that stock market investments are a more
100 stable and lucrative source of long-term
wealth. A London Business School study
found that over the same 90-year period,
the average rate of return on a real estate
investment was 1.3% compared to the
105 9.8% annualized total return for the S&P
stock 500 index. Investing the $5,500
IRS-imposed annual limit in an IRA
for 25 years would result in a return of
over $600,000 based on the annualized
110 return rate. Stock investment requires
a smaller overhead than real estate
investment, and the liquid nature of
stocks makes them (ideal) for retirement:)
stocks allocated to retirement accounts
115 remain tax-free until they are drawn
on.(Despite) these pieces of tangible
evidence, though, the stigma regarding
stock market investment persists in the
minds of many millennials.
120    (Regardless) of their feelings about the
stockmarket, one thing is self-evident:)
without preparation for retirement,

*Bad think-ing: house > stock mkt*

**¶4:** One mistake millennials make comes from thinking that owning a home is a better investment than the stock market. Studies show that this isn't true. There are also tax advantages to investing in stocks for retirement.

**¶5:** Feelings aside, millennials will need investment to have a retirement income. Money for retirement will get tighter, but if millennials use a variety of investments, they can get the wealth they need.

millennials will be a generation adrift
in a society without the social "safety
125 nets" available to current retirees.
The benchmark for the amount of
savings the average retiree needs to live
comfortably after retirement, which
remained at $1 million for many years,
130 now continues to rise, and exacerbating
factors, such as the cost of medical
care, continue to increase. Armed with
that knowledge, millennials need to be
proactive about financial planning. (By)
135 taking full advantage of their penchant
for a hands-on approach to finances
and leveraging the various financial
technologies and services that were not
available to the previous generation,
140 millennials can amass the wealth
necessary to retire comfortably and on
their own terms.

*Millennials need to adapt their thinking to have re-tirement $*

**Graphic:** The graph shows return on invest-ment for homes and for stock portfolios in 10 cities during the 2010s. This relates back to paragraph 4. The graph shows that stocks outperformed home ownership (sometimes by a lot) in 9 of the 10 cities.

**SAT Reading Strategy: When an SAT Reading passage is accompanied by one or more charts or graphs, ask the following questions as you read them:**

- **What information does the graphic contain?**
- **Why has the author included the graphic?**
- **Which paragraph(s) does this informa-tion relate to?**
- **Does the graphic display any trends or relationships that support a point made in the passage?**

In the Reading section, you will not be asked to perform calculations from the data in graphs. You will be asked how they relate to the passage and which claims or arguments they support or refute.

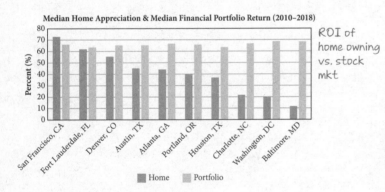

Median Home Appreciation & Median Financial Portfolio Return (2010–2018)

*ROI of home owning vs. stock mkt*

---

## BIG PICTURE

**Main Idea:** Millennials are skeptical of investing in the stock market for multiple reasons but will need a variety of investments to be financially secure at retirement.

**Author's Purpose:** To outline challenges facing millennials in investing for retirement and explain why they are hesitant to invest in the stock market

---

Now, try another passage on your own. Use the SAT Reading strategies and tactics you've been learning to read and map this passage as quickly and accurately as you can.

## Try on Your Own

**Directions:** Actively read and map the following passage by 1) circling or underlining keywords (from the Opinion and Emphasis, Connection and Contrast, or Evidence and Example categories), 2) jotting down brief, accurate margin notes that reflect good paraphrases of each paragraph, and 3) summing up the big picture. When you're done, compare your work to that of an SAT expert in the Expert Responses.

This passage was adapted from an article titled "Quantum Computing: Where Is It Going?" published in a science magazine in 2018. It discusses the background and potential of quantum computing.

Pharmaceutical companies dream of a time when their research and development process shifts from looking for illnesses whose symptoms
5   can be ameliorated by a specific drug to choosing a disease and creating a drug to eradicate it. Quantum computing may be the key to that goal. The powerful modeling potential
10  unlocked by quantum computing may also someday be employed by autonomous vehicles to create a world free of traffic jams. With plausible applications in so many fields, it is
15  worthwhile to learn a bit about how quantum computing works.

Any understanding of quantum computing begins with its most basic element, the qubit. In classical
20  computing, information is processed by the bit, the binary choice of zero or one. Qubits, on the other hand, allow for infinite superpositions between zero and one and thus can
25  store and process exponentially more complicated values. Imagine showing someone where you live on a globe by pointing only to either the North Pole or the South Pole. While you
30  are likely closer to one pole than the other, you need additional information to represent your specific location. If, however, you could provide your home's latitude and longitude, it could
35  be located without any additional information. The power of quantum

computing lies in the ability to express precise information in a single qubit.

Quantum computing may help
40  scientists and engineers overcome another barrier by reducing energy output while increasing computational speed. The positive correlation between energy output
45  and processing speed often causes classical computers to "run hot" while processing overwhelming amounts of data. Along with their ability to store multiple values simultaneously,
50  qubits are able to process those values in parallel instead of serially. How does processing in parallel conserve energy? Suppose you want to set the time on five separate alarm clocks
55  spaced ten feet apart. You'd have to walk to each clock to change its time. However, if the clocks were connected such that changing the time on one immediately adjusted the other four, you
60  would expend less energy and increase processing speed. Therein lies the benefit of the quantum entanglement of qubits.

While quantum computing has moved beyond the realm of the
65  theoretical, significant barriers still stand in the way of its practical application. One barrier is the difficulty of confirming the results of quantum calculations. If quantum computing
70  is used to solve problems that are impossible to solve with classical computing, is there a way to "check" the results? Scientists hope this paradox may soon be resolved. As a graduate
75  student, Urmila Mahadev devoted over a decade to creating a verification

process for quantum computing. The result is an interactive protocol, based on a type of cryptography called
80  Learning With Errors (LWE), that is similar to "blind computing" used in cloud-computing to mask data while still performing calculations. Given current limitations, Mahadev's protocol
85  remains purely theoretical, but rapid progress in quantum computing combined with further refinement of the protocol will likely result in real-world implementation within the next
90  decade or two.

It is unlikely that early pioneers in the field, including Stephen Wiesner, Richard Feynman, and Paul Benioff, could have foreseen the rapid progress
95  that has been made to date. In 1960, when Wiesner first developed conjugate coding with the goal of improving cryptography, his paper on the subject was rejected for publication
100  because it contained logic far ahead of its time. Feynman proposed a basic quantum computing model at the 1981 First Conference on the Physics of Computation. At that same conference,
105  Benioff spoke on the ability of discrete mechanical processes to erase their own history and their application to Turing machines, a natural extension of Wiesner's earlier work. A year later,
110  Benioff more clearly outlined the theoretical framework of a quantum computer.

The dawn of the 21st century brought advancements at an even
115  more impressive pace. The first 5- and 7-qubit nuclear magnetic resonance (NMR) computers were demonstrated in Munich, Germany, and Santa Fe, New Mexico, respectively. In 2006,
120  researchers at Oxford were able to cage a qubit within a "buckyball," a buckminsterfullerene molecule, and

maintain its state for a short time using precise, repeated microwave pulses. The
125  first company dedicated to quantum computing software, 1QB Information Technologies, was founded in 2012, and in 2018, Google announced the development of the 72-qubit Bristlecone
130  chip designed to prove "quantum supremacy," the ability of quantum computers to solve problems beyond the reach of classical computing.

With progress in quantum
135  computing accelerating, it seems inevitable that within a few decades, the general population will be as familiar with quantum computing as they now are with classical computing. At present,
140  quantum computing is limited by the struggle to build a computer large enough to prove quantum supremacy, and the costs associated with quantum computing are prohibitive to all but
145  the world's largest corporations and governmental institutions. Still, classical computing overcame similar problems, so the future of quantum computing looks bright.

# How Much Have You Learned?

**Directions:** Take five minutes to actively read the following passage by 1) noting the keywords, 2) jotting down margin notes next to each paragraph, and 3) summarizing the big picture. When you're done, compare your work to the Answers and Explanations at the end of the chapter.

This passage was adapted from an article entitled "John Snow Knew Something" published in a popular history magazine in 2018.

Few would deny that doctors use critical thinking to solve problems, but most imagine a difference between the practice of medicine and, say,
5 the methods a police detective might use to solve a case. In fact, medical researchers have long used forensic methods of detection and analysis. The case of John Snow, a
10 19th-century anesthesiologist, is often said to have ushered in the modern era of epidemiology, the branch of medicine that tracks the incidence and distribution of diseases and
15 proposes solutions for their control and prevention.

It would not be until 1861 that Louis Pasteur would propose the link between microorganisms and disease,
20 now known as the germ theory. Before Pasteur's breakthrough, the predominant explanation for the cause of most illnesses was the so-called miasma theory, which held that noxious
25 fumes and pollution—quite literally, as the theory's name implies, "bad air"— were responsible for making people sick. Consequently, during the 1854 outbreak of cholera in Westminster,
30 London, doctors and government officials alike blamed "miasmatic particles" released into the air by decaying organic matter in the soil of the River Thames.
35 Despite the widespread acceptance of the miasma theory, there were those, Snow included, who were skeptical of

this view. Snow would not have known, as doctors do today, that cholera
40 is caused by a bacterial infection, *Vibrio cholerae*. Nevertheless, he was convinced that the spread of the disease was caused by some form of matter passed between individuals, likely
45 through contaminated water.

To demonstrate this, Snow targeted a particularly deadly outbreak in the Soho district of Westminster in London. From August 31 to September
50 3, 1854, 127 people in the area died of cholera. Within a week, that number had risen to over 500. Snow took to the streets. Speaking to residents of the area, he found a commonality among
55 them: most of the victims had used a single public water pump located on Broad Street. Though he was unable to find conclusive proof that the pump was the source of the outbreak, his
60 demonstration of a pattern in the cholera cases prompted authorities to disable the pump by removing its handle. The epidemic quickly subsided.

Soon after the Broad Street pump
65 was shut down, Snow's continued investigation provided additional evidence that contaminated water was the source of the outbreak. Snow created a dot map of the cases of cholera in London
70 and demonstrated that they occurred in areas where water was supplied by two companies that obtained their water from wells near the Thames. Investigation of these wells showed that they had been
75 dug three feet from a cesspit that was leaking sewage into the surrounding soil. Snow also discovered that there were no cases of cholera among workers in a

brewery close to the Broad Street pump.
80 These workers were provided a daily
allowance of beer, which they drank
instead of water, and although the beer
was brewed using the contaminated
water, it was boiled during the brewing
85 process. This revelation provided a
practical solution for the prevention of
future outbreaks.

Snow is now hailed as the "father of
modern epidemiology," and the radical
90 nature of his approach—formulating
a new theory, substantiating it with
verifiable evidence, and proposing
preventative action—is fully
appreciated. At the time, however, not
95 all were convinced, at least publicly, of
Snow's findings. As anxiety over the

outbreak flagged, government officials
replaced the handle on the Broad Street
pump and publicly denounced Snow's
100 conclusions. It seems they felt that the
city's residents would be upset and
disgusted to have the unsettling nature
of the well's contamination confirmed.
It wasn't until 1866, more than a decade
105 after Snow's original investigation and
theory—when another cholera outbreak
killed more than 5,500 residents of
London's East End—that officials
working in public health began to
110 accept the link between contaminated
water and certain kinds of illness and
to take appropriate actions to quell such
outbreaks.

# Reflect

**Directions:** Take a few minutes to recall what you've learned and what you've been practicing in this chapter. Consider the following questions, jot down your best answer for each one, and then compare your reflections to the expert responses on the following page. Use your level of confidence to determine what to do next.

Why do SAT experts note keywords as they read?

_____

_____

_____

What are the three categories of keywords? Provide some examples from each category.

- _____

  o Examples: _____

- _____

  o Examples: _____

- _____

  o Examples: _____

Why do SAT experts jot down margin notes next to the text?

_____

_____

_____

What are the elements of a strong big picture summary?

_____

_____

_____

## Expert Responses

Why do SAT experts note keywords as they read?

*Keywords indicate what the author finds important, express his point of view about the subject and details of the passage, and signal key points in the passage structure. Keywords are the pieces of text that help test takers see which parts of the passage are likely to be mentioned in questions and help the test taker to distinguish between correct and incorrect answer choices about those parts of the passage.*

What are the three categories of keywords? Provide some examples from each category.

- *Opinion and Emphasis*
  - Examples: *indeed, quite, masterfully, inadequate*
- *Connection and Contrast*
  - Examples: *furthermore, plus, however, on the contrary*
- *Evidence and Example*
  - Examples: *consequently, since, for instance, such as*

Why do SAT experts jot down margin notes next to the text?

*Margin notes help the test taker research questions that ask about details, examples, and arguments mentioned in the passage by providing a "map" to their location in the text. Margin notes can also help students answer questions about the passage structure and the purpose of a specific paragraph.*

What are the elements of a strong big picture summary?

*A strong big picture summary prepares a test taker to answer any question about the main idea of the passage or the author's primary or overall purpose in writing it. After reading the passage, SAT experts pause to ask, "What's the main point of the passage?" and "Why did the author write it?"*

## Next Steps

If you answered most questions correctly in the "How Much Have You Learned?" section, and if your responses to the Reflect questions were similar to those of the SAT expert, then consider strategic reading and passage mapping an area of strength and move on to the next chapter. Come back to this topic periodically to prevent yourself from getting rusty.

If you don't yet feel confident, review the material in "Reading Passage Strategies," then try the questions you missed again. As always, be sure to review the explanations closely.

# Answers and Explanations

## Try on Your Own

This passage was adapted from an article titled "Quantum Computing: Where Is It Going?" published in a science magazine in 2018. It discusses the background and potential of quantum computing.

Pharmaceutical companies dream of a time when their research and development process shifts from looking for illnesses whose symptoms
5　can be ameliorated by a specific drug to choosing a disease and creating a drug to eradicate it. Quantum computing maybe the(key)to that goal. The(powerful)modeling(potential)
10　unlocked by quantum computing may also someday be employed by autonomous vehicles to create a world free of traffic jams. With plausible applications in so many fields, it is
15　worthwhile to learn a bit about how quantum computing works.

Any understanding of quantum computing begins with its most basic element, the qubit. In classical
20　computing, information is processed by the bit, the binary choice of zero or one. Qubits,(on the other)hand, allow for infinite superpositions between zero and one and thus can
25　store and process(exponentially)more complicated values. Imagine showing someone where you live on a globe by pointing only to either the North Pole or the South Pole. While you
30　are likely closer to one pole than the other, you need additional information to represent your specific location. If, however, you could provide your home's latitude and longitude, it could
35　be located without any additional information. The power of quantum computing lies in the ability to express precise information in a single qubit.

*QC: big potential*

*QC based on qubits – can store more values*

*Qubit > bit, much more data*

### ANALYSIS

**Pre-passage blurb:** Based on the article's title, you can expect to see a discussion of the past and future of quantum computing.

**¶1:** The author claims that quantum computing may help solve two big problems—new pharmaceuticals and traffic management. Because of this potential, she says, it's good to learn about quantum computing. Expect some of that background information in paragraph 2.

**SAT Reading Strategy: Don't panic when confronted with unfamiliar or scientifically advanced subject matter. Pay attention to the author's purpose for discussing it.**

**¶2:** The basis for quantum computing is the qubit, a much more powerful way to store and process information than the bit (which is what we currently use). The author illustrates this with the "globe" example.

**SAT Reading Strategy: When you encounter an example or analogy, always ask, "What does this illustrate or explain?"**

Reading

Quantum computing may help
40  scientists and engineers overcome
another barrier by reducing
energy output while increasing
computational speed. The positive
correlation between energy output
45  and processing speed often causes
classical computers to "run hot" while
processing overwhelming amounts of
data. Along with their ability to store
multiple values simultaneously,
50  qubits are able to process those values
in parallel instead of serially. How
does processing in parallel conserve
energy? Suppose you want to set the
time on five separate alarm clocks
55  spaced ten feet apart. You'd have to
walk to each clock to change its time.
However, if the clocks were connected
such that changing the time on one
immediately adjusted the other four, you
60  would expend less energy and increase
processing speed. Therein lies the benefit
of the quantum entanglement of qubits.
While quantum computing has
moved beyond the realm of the
65  theoretical, significant barriers still
stand in the way of its practical
application. One barrier is the difficulty
of confirming the results of quantum
calculations. If quantum computing
70  is used to solve problems that are
impossible to solve with classical
computing, is there a way to "check"
the results? Scientists hope this paradox
may soon be resolved. As a graduate
75  student, Urmila Mahadev devoted
over a decade to creating a verification
process for quantum computing.
The result is an interactive protocol,
based on a type of cryptography called
80  Learning With Errors (LWE), that is
similar to "blind computing" used in
cloud-computing to mask data while
still performing calculations. Given
current limitations, Mahadev's protocol

*Qubits =
parallel
processing*

*faster AND
cooler*

*One barrier
to QC –
How to
check
results?*

**¶3:** Another advantage: quantum computing is
faster but cooler (current computers overheat).
The reason is parallel processing, illustrated by
the "five clocks" example.

**SAT Reading Strategy: Rhetorical questions
help you focus on the author's point in a paragraph and her reason for writing it.**

**¶4:** Here, the passage shifts to obstacles to
quantum computing. One problem: when they
solve extremely complex problems, regular
computers can't check them. One scientist
is working on a solution, and the author is
optimistic that it will work out in the next 20
years or so.

85  remains purely theoretical, but rapid
    progress in quantum computing
    combined with further refinement of
    the protocol will (likely result) in real-      *probably will*
    world implementation within the next          *get solved*
90  decade or two.

        It is (unlikely) that early pioneers in        **¶5:** The pre-passage blurb indicated that the
    the field, including Stephen Wiesner,        passage would cover quantum computing's
    Richard Feynman, and Paul Benioff,           past, and here it is. The point of this paragraph
    could have foreseen the (rapid)(progress)    is that early developers of quantum computing
95  that has been made to date. In 1960,         (the author names three of them) would be
    when Wiesner first developed conjugate       surprised by how quickly it has developed.
    coding with the goal of improving
    cryptography, his paper on the               *QC pioneers*
    subject was rejected for publication         *- 1960s –*
100 because it contained logic far ahead         *80s*
    of its time. Feynman proposed a basic
    quantum computing model at the 1981
    First Conference on the Physics of
    Computation. At that same conference,
105 Benioff spoke on the ability of discrete
    mechanical processes to erase their
    own history and their application to
    Turing machines, a natural extension
    of Wiesner's earlier work. A year later,
110 Benioff more clearly outlined the
    theoretical framework of a quantum
    computer.

        The dawn of the 21st century                **¶6:** This gives a little more about the past.
    brought advancements at an even              Progress in quantum computing really took off
                                    *QC sped up*  during the 2000s. The author supports that
115 (more impressive) pace. The first 5- and  *in 2000s*   point with examples of companies that have
    7-qubit nuclear magnetic resonance           created and improved quantum computers.
    (NMR) computers were demonstrated
    in Munich, Germany, and Santa Fe,            **SAT Reading Strategy: The SAT doesn't expect**
    New Mexico, respectively. In 2006,           **you to know the definitions of technical terms**
120 researchers at Oxford were able to           **and phrases. The test will ask you why the**
    cage a qubit within a "buckyball," a         **author has included these details or how they**
    buckminsterfullerene molecule, and           **function in the paragraph.**
    maintain its state for a short time using
    precise, repeated microwave pulses. The
125 first company dedicated to quantum
    computing software, 1QB Information
    Technologies, was founded in 2012,
    and in 2018, Google announced the
    development of the 72-qubit Bristlecone
130 chip designed to prove "quantum
    supremacy," the ability of quantum

computers to solve problems beyond the reach of classical computing.

With progress in quantum
135 computing accelerating, it seems (inevitable) that within a few decades, the general population will be as familiar with quantum computing as they now are with classical computing. At present,
140 quantum computing is limited by the struggle to build a computer large enough to prove quantum supremacy, and the costs associated with quantum computing are prohibitive to all but
145 the world's largest corporations and governmental institutions. (Still,) classical computing overcame similar problems, so the future of quantum computing (looks bright.)

*QC still difficult, but bright future*

¶7: The passage ends on a high note: quantum computing will "inevitably" become popular and its future is "bright." The author acknowledges obstacles, but clearly implies that she expects them to be overcome.

---

## BIG PICTURE

**Main Idea:** Quantum computing has many potential uses despite current obstacles.

**Author's Purpose:** To explain some fundamental principles of how quantum computing works to show its enormous potential over classical computing and to give a brief history of its development to anticipate how it can overcome current limitations

---

As with the other passages in this chapter, don't worry about whether you used the exact language found in the expert's map and summary. Instead, focus on how the expert used the skills and strategies outlined here to prepare himself to tackle the question set with speed and confidence.

## How Much Have You Learned?

This passage was adapted from an article entitled "John Snow Knew Something" published in a popular history magazine in 2018.

Few would deny that doctors use critical thinking to solve problems, (but) most imagine a difference between the practice of medicine and, say,
5 the methods a police detective might use to solve a case. In fact, medical researchers have long used forensic methods of detection and analysis. (The case of John Snow,) a
10 19th-century anesthesiologist, is often said to have ushered in the modern era of epidemiology, the branch of medicine that tracks the incidence and distribution of diseases and
15 proposes solutions for their control and prevention.

It would not be until 1861 that Louis Pasteur would propose the link between microorganisms and disease,
20 now known as the germ theory. (Before) Pasteur's breakthrough, the predominant explanation for the cause of most illnesses was the so-called miasma theory, which held that noxious
25 fumes and pollution—quite literally, as the theory's name implies, "bad air"— were responsible for making people sick. (Consequently,) during the 1854 outbreak of cholera in Westminster,
30 London, doctors and government officials alike blamed "miasmatic particles" released into the air by decaying organic matter in the soil of the River Thames.
35 (Despite) the widespread acceptance of the miasma theory, there were those, Snow included, who were skeptical of this view. Snow would not have known, as doctors do today, that cholera

*Snow's work used investigation, changed medicine*

*1854 – didn't know about germs; miasma theory*

**ANALYSIS**

**Pre-passage blurb:** The article is about someone named John Snow, who must be a historical figure of some importance. Beyond that, however, there's not too much to go on in this blurb.

**¶1:** The author provides some background on John Snow. Today, he is known for changing how doctors track and prevent diseases, apparently by using methods often associated with detectives and investigations. The rest of the passage will illustrate why he was so important.

**¶2:** This paragraph sets the stage. At the time of the cholera outbreak in 1854, people did not know that germs and bacteria caused the disease.

**¶3:** The author contrasts (note the keywords "Despite" and "Nevertheless") Snow's theories with the popular ideas of his time. He thought cholera might be passed through contaminated water.

40　is caused by a bacterial infection,
*Vibrio cholerae.* Nevertheless, he was
convinced that the spread of the disease
was caused by some form of matter
passed between individuals, likely

45　through contaminated water.
　　To demonstrate this, Snow targeted
a particularly deadly outbreak in
the Soho district of Westminster in
London. From August 31 to September

50　3, 1854, 127 people in the area died of
cholera. Within a week, that number
had risen to over 500. Snow took to
the streets. Speaking to residents of the
area, he found a commonality among

55　them: most of the victims had used a
single public water pump located on
Broad Street. Though he was unable
to find conclusive proof that the pump
was the source of the outbreak, his

60　demonstration of a pattern in the
cholera cases prompted authorities
to disable the pump by removing its
handle. The epidemic quickly subsided.
　　Soon after the Broad Street pump

65　was shutdown, Snow's continued
investigation provided additional evidence
that contaminated water was the source
of the outbreak. Snow created a dot
map of the cases of cholera in London

70　and demonstrated that they occurred in
areas where water was supplied by two
companies that obtained their water from
wells near the Thames. Investigation of
these wells showed that they had been

75　dug three feet from a cesspit that was
leaking sewage into the surrounding soil.
Snow also discovered that there were no
cases of cholera among workers in a
brewery close to the Broad Street pump.

80　These workers were provided a daily
allowance of beer, which they drank
instead of water, and although the beer
was brewed using the contaminated
water, it was boiled during the brewing

85　process. This revelation provided a

*Snow: cholera from contam. H₂O*

**¶4:** Snow investigated the area and interviewed people. He demonstrated that a specific water pump was "ground zero" for the outbreak and got it turned off.

*Proof from interviews – all used same pump*

**¶5:** Through further investigation, Snow showed that leaking cesspools were the source of contamination and used his observations at a nearby brewery to deduce that boiling water before drinking would prevent the disease.

*Water from contam. wells*

*Boiling first prevented disease*

(practical solution) for the prevention of
future outbreaks.

Snow is (now hailed) as the "father of
modern epidemiology," and the radical
90 nature of his approach—formulating
a new theory, substantiating it with
verifiable evidence, and proposing
preventative action—is fully
appreciated. At the time, (however,) not
95 all were convinced, at least publicly, of
Snow's findings. As anxiety over the
outbreak flagged, government officials
replaced the handle on the Broad Street
pump and publicly denounced Snow's
100 conclusions. It seems they felt that the
city's residents would be upset and
disgusted to have the unsettling nature
of the well's contamination confirmed.
It wasn't until 1866, more than a decade
105 after Snow's original investigation and
theory—when another cholera outbreak
killed more than 5,500 residents of
London's East End—that officials
working in public health began to
110 accept the link between contaminated
water and certain kinds of illness and
to take appropriate actions to quell such
outbreaks.

*Snow not
accepted at
the time*

*1866 –
another
epidemic*

**¶6:** Another contrast: Snow is now seen as a
pioneer but wasn't appreciated at the time. It
took another epidemic for officials to buy in to
his theory.

---

**BIG PICTURE**

**Main Idea:** John Snow's investigative approach to explaining the cholera epidemic of 1854 ushered in the
modern era of epidemiology.

**Author's Purpose:** To demonstrate how Snow's use of interviews, maps, and data altered the way doctors
study the spread and prevention of disease

---

# CHAPTER 19

# SAT Reading Question Types

LEARNING OBJECTIVES

After completing this chapter, you will be able to:

Unpack SAT Reading question stems by

- distinguishing among six SAT Reading question types, and
- determining if the correct answer is best found by researching the passage text or by consulting your big picture summary

# How Much Do You Know?

**Directions:** In this chapter, you'll learn to unpack SAT Reading question stems (Step 1 of the Method for SAT Reading Questions). Unpacking a question stem means identifying your task (as identified by the question type) and noting where the answer will be found (a specific reference within the passage text or in your big picture summary). You first saw the question types defined in chapter 17. For your reference as you complete this quiz, here they are again:

- **Global**—asks about the big picture
- **Detail**—asks about explicitly stated points
- **Inference**—asks about points that are unstated but strongly suggested
- **Command of Evidence**—asks for evidence to support the answer to a previous question
- **Function**—asks why the author wrote specific parts of the text
- **Vocabulary-in-Context**—asks for the meaning of a word as it is used in the passage

For each of the following question stems, identify the question type, cite the language in the stem that helped you identify it, and indicate where you would begin to research this question: either your big picture summary or a specific part of the text.

## Example

The author of the passage would most likely agree with which one of the following statements concerning hydraulic mining?

**Question type:** *Inference*

**Identifying language:** *"would most likely agree"*

**Research where?** *passage, where author discusses hydraulic mining*

1. The passage indicates that non-rush hour commuters

   **Question type:**
   **Identifying language:**
   **Research where?**

2. As used in line 41, "labyrinthine" most nearly means

   **Question type:**
   **Identifying language:**
   **Research where?**

3. According to the passage, which of the following is true of the New York City subway system?

   **Question type:**
   **Identifying language:**
   **Research where?**

4. The fifth paragraph (lines 66–90) serves mainly to

   **Question type:**
   **Identifying language:**
   **Research where?**

5. Which of the following best expresses the primary purpose of the passage?

   **Question type:**
   **Identifying language:**
   **Research where?**

6. Based on the passage, which choice best describes a claim that critics of the current subway maintenance plan would likely make?

   **Question type:**
   **Identifying language:**
   **Research where?**

7. Which choice provides the best evidence for the answer to the previous question?

   **Question type:**
   **Identifying language:**
   **Research where?**

8. With which one of the following statements would the author of the passage be most likely to agree?

   **Question type:**
   **Identifying language:**
   **Research where?**

9. Based on the passage, advocates of the current New York City subway maintenance plan would most likely agree that

   **Question type:**
   **Identifying language:**
   **Research where?**

10. In the third paragraph, the discussion of two specific subway lines (lines 44–49) primarily serves to

    **Question type:**
    **Identifying language:**
    **Research where?**

# Check Your Work

1. The passage indicates that non-rush hour commuters

   **Question type:** Detail
   **Identifying language:** "indicates"
   **Research where?** passage, where author discusses non-rush hour commuters

2. As used in line 41, "labyrinthine" most nearly means

   **Question type:** Vocab-in-Context
   **Identifying language:** "most nearly means"
   **Research where?** passage, line 41

3. According to the passage, which of the following is true of the New York City subway system?

   **Question type:** Detail
   **Identifying language:** "According to the passage"
   **Research where?** passage, where author discusses NYC subway system

4. The fifth paragraph (lines 66–90) serves mainly to

   **Question type:** Function
   **Identifying language:** "serves mainly to"
   **Research where?** passage, fifth paragraph

5. Which of the following best expresses the primary purpose of the passage?

   **Question type:** Global
   **Identifying language:** "primary purpose of the passage"
   **Research where?** big picture summary

6. Based on the passage, which choice best describes a claim that critics of the current subway maintenance plan would likely make?

   **Question type:** Inference
   **Identifying language:** "Based on the passage," "would likely make"
   **Research where?** passage, where author discusses critics' views

7. Which choice provides the best evidence for the answer to the previous question?

   **Question type:** Command of Evidence
   **Identifying language:** "provides the best evidence"
   **Research where?** passage, where you went to answer the previous question

8. With which one of the following statements would the author of the passage be most likely to agree?

   **Question type:** Inference
   **Identifying language:** "most likely to agree"
   **Research where?** big picture summary (no specific clues)

9. Based on the passage, advocates of the current New York City subway maintenance plan would most likely agree that

   **Question type:** Inference
   **Identifying language:** "Based on the passage," "would most likely agree"
   **Research where?** passage, where author discusses advocates' views

10. In the third paragraph, the discussion of two specific subway lines (lines 44–49) primarily serves to

    **Question type:** Function
    **Identifying language:** "primarily serves to"
    **Research where?** passage, third paragraph

# How to Unpack SAT Reading Question Stems

**LEARNING OBJECTIVES**

After this lesson, you will be able to:

● Unpack SAT Reading question stems by

○ distinguishing among six SAT Reading question types, and

○ determining if the correct answer is best found by researching the passage text or by consulting your big picture summary

## To unpack question stems like these:

1. One central idea of the passage is that

2. Which choice best describes the overall structure of the passage?

3. According to the passage, large corporations are

4. As used in line 38, "erased" most nearly means

5. The passage most strongly implies which of the following statements about the Great Recession?

6. Which choice provides the best evidence for the answer to the previous question?

7. In the third paragraph (lines 63–91), the most likely purpose of the author's discussion of the "gig economy" is to

8. In the context of the passage as a whole, the question in lines 89–91 primarily functions to help the author

9. The passage indicates that investing in the stock market

10. Which of the following statements is supported by the graph?

11. Which statement from the passage is most directly reflected by the data presented in the graph?

## You'll need to know this:

- The six kinds of question types, each of which defines a specific task:
  - **Global**—asks about the passage's main idea, the author's primary purpose, or the passage's overall organization

| TYPICAL GLOBAL QUESTION STEMS |
|---|
| The central claim of the passage is that |
| Which choice best summarizes the passage? |
| The main purpose of the passage is to |
| Which choice best describes the developmental pattern of the passage? |
| Which choice best reflects the overall sequence of events in the passage? |

○ **Detail**—asks about something explicitly stated in the passage

### TYPICAL DETAIL QUESTION STEMS

According to the passage, which of the following is true of developmental psychology?

The author indicates that people value solitude because

In the second paragraph (lines 14–27), what does the author claim are key questions the study must answer?

The passage identifies which of the following as a factor that influences economic growth?

○ **Inference**—asks for something that follows from the passage without having been stated explicitly in it

### TYPICAL INFERENCE QUESTION STEMS

Based on the passage, the author's statement "in response, the Federal Reserve will often lower interest rates" (lines 21–22) implies that

Which concept is supported by the passage and by the information in the graph?

Based on information in the passage, it can reasonably be inferred that

The authors of both passages would most likely agree with which of the following statements?

○ **Command of Evidence**—asks you to cite the support offered in the passage for the correct answer to the previous question or for a given statement

### TYPICAL COMMAND OF EVIDENCE QUESTION STEMS

Which choice provides the best evidence for the answer to the previous question?

Which choice best supports the claim that the new policy is unlikely to curtail water pollution?

○ **Function**—asks about the purpose of a piece of text—why the author included it or how the author has used it

### TYPICAL FUNCTION QUESTION STEMS

The sentence in lines 35–37 serves mainly to

The main purpose of the fourth paragraph (lines 42–50) is to

How do the words "must," "necessary," and "imperative" in the third paragraph (lines 35–49) help establish the tone of the paragraph?

The author uses the image of an explorer overlooking a valley (lines 23–28) most likely to

The sentence in lines 74–78 ("After … rest") primarily serves which function in paragraph 7?

o **Vocabulary-in-Context**—asks you to define a word as the author used it in the passage

| TYPICAL VOCABULARY-IN-CONTEXT QUESTION STEMS |
| --- |
| As used in line 55, "platform" most nearly means |
| As used in line 29, "substantial" most nearly means |

- The kinds of research clues found in SAT Reading question stems:

  o **Line Numbers**—Mentions of "line 53" or "lines 37–40," often in parentheses, tend to stand out and give you a clear place to start your research. (In Command of Evidence questions, line numbers are found in the answer choices.)

  o **Paragraph Numbers**—A reference to "paragraph 5," "the third paragraph," or "the last two paragraphs" is not as precise as a line reference but will still give you an idea of where to look. Start with your margin notes for the paragraph.

  o **Quoted Text**—(often accompanied by line numbers)—Check the context of the quoted term or phrase to see what the author meant by it in the passage.

  o **Proper Nouns**—Names like "Professor James," "World War II," and "Baltimore" will likely stand out in question stems due to the capitalization. If a particular proper noun is discussed in only part of the passage, it narrows the range of text you have to research.

  o **Specific Content Clues**—Sometimes a question stem will repeat terminology used in part of the passage like "federalism" or "action potentials." Use your passage map to direct your research to the right part of the passage.

  o **Whole Passage Clues**—If a question lacks specific content clues but refers to the passage as a whole, or to the author in general, you are likely dealing with a Global question or an open-ended Inference question, which should lead you to your big picture summary rather than to rereading parts of the text.

## You need to do this:

| The Method for SAT Reading Questions | |
| --- | --- |
| **Step 1.** | **Unpack the question stem** |
| Step 2. | Research the answer |
| Step 3. | Predict the answer |
| Step 4. | Find the one correct answer |

- Unpack SAT Reading question stems by
  - identifying the question type and anticipating how it will need to be answered, and
  - noting research clues that indicate how best to research the correct answer

---

### QUESTION TYPES

**Why distinguish question types in SAT Reading?**

Unpacking the question stem puts you in control. You'll know exactly what the question is asking, where to find the correct answer, and what form the correct answer will take.

- **Global:** The correct answer must take the entire passage into account. A choice that reflects only part of the passage is incorrect.
- **Detail:** The correct answer must be stated in the passage explicitly. A choice that is not directly stated in the passage is incorrect.
- **Inference:** The correct answer will be a conclusion that can be drawn from the passage. A choice that draws too strong a conclusion from the evidence available in the passage is incorrect.
- **Command of Evidence:** The correct answer must directly support the correct answer to the previous question. A choice about the same subject but providing no direct evidence is not good enough.
- **Function:** The correct answer will say *why* a certain detail is included. Look up the detail, then ask yourself what the author was trying to accomplish by putting it there.
- **Vocab-in-Context:** The correct answer will give the meaning of a word as it is used *in the context of the passage*. Choices that give common meanings of the word are often incorrect.

Correct answers to Reading questions are never random or vague. They are tailored to the precise language of the stem, so being able to distinguish the question types will save you time and eliminate confusion during the test.

---

## Answers and Explanations:

1.  This is a Global question, as is clear from the phrase "central idea of the passage." Your big picture summary will likely have the answer.

---

### GLOBAL STRATEGY

**Start with your big picture summary**

Global questions ask for the big picture of the passage, so always start by reviewing your big picture summary. You should generally avoid rereading passage text when tackling a Global question but, if you get stuck, the first and last paragraphs are usually the best places to look.

---

2.  The mention of the "overall structure of the passage" indicates that this is also a Global question. In addition to your big picture summary, look for structural trends in your marginal notes (particularly for places where the author changes direction or perspective) when answering a Global question about structure.

3.  "According to the passage" is a clear sign of a Detail question. Though this question lacks specific line or paragraph clues, the mention of "large corporations" may help to narrow your research.

---

### DETAIL STRATEGY

**Search for the relevant information**

Don't expect a lot of precise clues such as line numbers with Detail questions. Your task will usually be to extract the stem's specific content clues and then use your passage map to help you locate that content in the text. If you can't find it within about a minute, consider skipping a Detail question and returning to it after you answer the passage's other questions. Researching them may inadvertently lead you to the detail you need.

---

4.  A question stem that begins with a line reference, quotes a term from the passage, and ends in "most nearly means" is always a Vocab-in-Context question.

---

### VOCAB-IN-CONTEXT STRATEGY

**Go back to the context**

At a minimum, go to the line cited in a Vocab-in-Context question and reread the entire sentence that contains the word. If that doesn't give you enough context, look for additional help in the surrounding sentences until you have a clear idea of what the author intended.

---

5.  The word "implies" tells you that this is an Inference question. The proper noun "the Great Recession" gives you something to look for in the passage.

---

### INFERENCE STRATEGY

**What follows from the text?**

Inference questions come in a wider variety of forms than the other question types, but all are united by asking you to identify something that the author only suggests without saying outright. Fortunately for you, these questions are not asking for subtle hints, but for statements that MUST be true given what the author does state. Follow the clues to locate the relevant text, and then ask yourself, "What *must* follow from this?"

6. The vast majority of Command of Evidence questions have this exact wording: "Which choice provides the best evidence for the answer to the previous question?" All Command of Evidence answer choices feature direct quotes with line numbers, which you should use to guide your research.

### COMMAND OF EVIDENCE STRATEGY

**Use your work on the previous question**

The line numbers listed in Command of Evidence answer choices give you four potential locations to look for the correct answer, but preempt this extensive searching by looking first at the lines of text you used to answer the previous question (usually an Inference or Detail). Alternatively, if you're working on a different question and see a Command of Evidence coming up next, you can use the line numbers there to guide your research, increasing your efficiency by answering both questions at once.

7. This is a Function question because it asks for the "most likely purpose" of a specific part of the text. To research it, you should look for mentions of the "gig economy" in the third paragraph.

### FUNCTION STRATEGY

**Why did the author write *that*?**

Most Function questions are *why* questions, asking you to explain what the author intended to accomplish with a particular piece of text, usually singled out with precise clues like line or paragraph numbers. Start researching by looking at the appropriate location on your passage map, reviewing what you described as the author's purpose in that part of the text. If that doesn't help, reread the indicated text and ask yourself, "Why did the author include this?"

8. The use of "primarily functions" gives this away as a Function question. The cited lines tell you where to start researching.

9. This is a Detail question, as can be garnered from "indicates." The other clues in the stem suggest that you'll need to search the passage for a discussion of stock market investment.

10. This is an Inference question because it asks for a statement that "is supported" by part of the passage—in this case, the graph. To research such a question, look for major takeaways from the data presented in the graph.

11. This is a less common variation of Command of Evidence, which would be more obvious after looking at the answer choices (quotes from the text with line references). To research, follow the line references until you come upon a quote that describes a major takeaway from the data in the graph.

## Try on Your Own

**Directions:** Analyze each of the following question stems by 1) identifying the word or phrase that describes your task, 2) naming the question type, and 3) noting how best to research the correct answer (research the text or consult the big picture summary). Answers are found at the end of the chapter.

1. According to the passage, which one of the following is true of Urmila Mahadev's graduate work?

   **Question type:**

   **Identifying language:**

   **Research where?**

2. Which choice provides the best evidence for the answer to the previous question?

   **Question type:**

   **Identifying language:**

   **Research where?**

3. The author's attitude toward the potential success of quantum computing can best be described as

   **Question type:**

   **Identifying language:**

   **Research where?**

4. Which statement best describes the technique the author uses to advance the main point of the third paragraph (lines 39–62)?

   **Question type:**

   **Identifying language:**

   **Research where?**

5. The primary purpose of the passage is to

   **Question type:**

   **Identifying language:**

   **Research where?**

6. Based on the passage, the author would most likely criticize classical computing because it

   **Question type:**

   **Identifying language:**

   **Research where?**

7. The passage indicates that which of the following factors slowed early developments in the theory of quantum computing?

   **Question type:**

   **Identifying language:**

   **Research where?**

8. In the second paragraph, the discussion of locating a person's home on a globe (lines 26–36) primarily serves to

   **Question type:**

   **Identifying language:**

   **Research where?**

9. Which one of the following does the passage imply about the development of quantum computing in the 21st century?

   **Question type:**

   **Identifying language:**

   **Research where?**

10. As used in line 123, "maintain" most nearly means

    **Question type:**

    **Identifying language:**

    **Research where?**

For any question types that you misidentified, return to the definitions and question stem examples before you try the final question set in this chapter.

# How Much Have You Learned?

**Directions:** Now, complete a similar assessment under timed conditions. Take a few minutes to analyze each of the following question stems by 1) identifying the word or phrase that describes your task, 2) naming the question type, and 3) noting how best to research the correct answer (research the text or consult the big picture summary).

11. The passage primarily serves to

    **Question type:**

    **Identifying language:**

    **Research where?**

12. Which of the following is most analogous to John Snow's discovery of the source of the cholera outbreak?

    **Question type:**

    **Identifying language:**

    **Research where?**

13. Which choice provides the best evidence for the answer to the previous question?

    **Question type:**

    **Identifying language:**

    **Research where?**

14. The passage indicates that the main reason government officials rejected Snow's hypothesis was

    **Question type:**

    **Identifying language:**

    **Research where?**

15. The second paragraph serves mainly to

    **Question type:**

    **Identifying language:**

    **Research where?**

16. It can reasonably be inferred from the passage that scientists in 1855 would have found which of the following solutions to be most practical in dealing with future outbreaks of cholera?

    **Question type:**

    **Identifying language:**

    **Research where?**

17. The author of this passage writes from the perspective of a

    **Question type:**

    **Identifying language:**

    **Research where?**

18. Which of the following is cited as the primary reason Snow suspected the Broad Street pump as the source of the epidemic?

    **Question type:**

    **Identifying language:**

    **Research where?**

19. As used in line 97, the word "flagged" most nearly means

    **Question type:**

    **Identifying language:**

    **Research where?**

20. The author uses the final sentence of the passage ("It wasn't ... outbreaks") at least in part to:

    **Question type:**

    **Identifying language:**

    **Research where?**

# Reflect

**Directions:** Take a few minutes to recall what you've learned and what you've been practicing in this chapter. Consider the following questions, jot down your best answer for each one, and then compare your reflections to the expert responses on the following page. Use your level of confidence to determine what to do next.

Why is it important to always unpack the question stem before proceeding?

_____

_____

_____

Can you name the six SAT Reading question types and cite words or phrases that identify each one?

- _____
    - Identifying language: _____

- _____
    - Identifying language: _____

- _____
    - Identifying language: _____

- _____
    - Identifying language: _____

- _____
    - Identifying language: _____

- _____
    - Identifying language: _____

How will you approach SAT Reading question stems differently as you continue to practice and improve your performance in the Reading section? What are the main differences you see between SAT Reading questions and those you're used to from tests in school?

_____

_____

_____

Reading

## Expert Responses

Why is it important to always unpack the question stem before proceeding?

*Knowing the SAT Reading question types makes you a more strategic and efficient reader because the test maker uses the same question types on every test. Fully analyzing each question stem helps you research the text more effectively, predict the correct answer in a way that fits the question stem, and avoid wrong answers made from misreading the question.*

Can you name the six SAT Reading question types and cite words or phrases that identify each one?

- *Global*
  - Identifying language: *main idea of the passage, author's primary purpose*
- *Detail*
  - Identifying language: *according to the passage, identifies, claims*
- *Inference*
  - Identifying language: *implies, can be inferred, based on the passage*
- *Command of Evidence*
  - Identifying language: *provides the best evidence, best supports, the answer to the previous question*
- *Function*
  - Identifying language: *is used to, serves mainly to, functions as*
- *Vocabulary-in-Context*
  - Identifying language: *as used in line [number], most nearly means*

How will you approach SAT Reading question stems differently as you continue to practice and improve your performance in the Reading section? What are the main differences you see between SAT Reading questions and those you're used to from tests in school?

*There is no one-size-fits-all answer here. Reflect on your own strengths and weaknesses as you consider how to best improve your performance in the SAT Reading section. Depending on the kinds of classes and teachers you've had in high school, the skills rewarded on SAT Reading questions may be more or less familiar, but almost every test taker needs to be aware of her own instincts as a reader, and needs to break certain reading habits, to master this section of the test. The more you give yourself an honest self-assessment, the better prepared you'll be to handle all of the SAT Reading question types confidently.*

## Next Steps

If you answered most questions correctly in the "How Much Have You Learned?" section, and if your responses to the Reflect questions were similar to those of the SAT expert, then consider identifying Reading question types an area of strength and move on to the next chapter. Come back to this topic periodically to prevent yourself from getting rusty.

If you don't yet feel confident, review the material in "How to Unpack SAT Reading Question Stems," then try the questions you missed again. As always, be sure to review the explanations closely.

# Answers and Explanations

1. According to the passage, which one of the following is true of Urmila Mahadev's graduate work?

   **Question type:** Detail
   **Identifying language:** "According to the passage"
   **Research where?** passage, where the author discusses Mahadev's work

2. Which choice provides the best evidence for the answer to the previous question?

   **Question type:** Command of Evidence
   **Identifying language:** "provides the best evidence"
   **Research where?** passage, where you answered the previous question

3. The author's attitude toward the potential success of quantum computing can best be described as

   **Question type:** Inference
   **Identifying language:** "can best be described as"
   **Research where?** passage, where author discusses quantum computing success

4. Which statement best describes the technique the author uses to advance the main point of the third paragraph (lines 39–62)?

   **Question type:** Function
   **Identifying language:** "the technique the author uses"
   **Research where?** passage, third paragraph

5. The primary purpose of the passage is to

   **Question type:** Global
   **Identifying language:** "primary purpose of the passage"
   **Research where?** big picture summary

6. Based on the passage, the author would most likely criticize classical computing because it

   **Question type:** Inference
   **Identifying language:** "Based on the passage"
   **Research where?** passage, where author discusses classical computing

7. The passage indicates that which of the following factors slowed early developments in the theory of quantum computing?

   **Question type:** Detail
   **Identifying language:** "indicates"
   **Research where?** passage, where author discusses early developments

8. In the second paragraph, the discussion of locating a person's home on a globe (lines 26–36) primarily serves to

   **Question type:** Function
   **Identifying language:** "primarily serves to"
   **Research where?** passage, second paragraph

9. Which one of the following does the passage imply about the development of quantum computing in the 21st century?

   **Question type:** Inference
   **Identifying language:** "imply"
   **Research where?** passage, where author discusses 21st-century development

10. As used in line 123, "maintain" most nearly means

    **Question type:** Vocab-in-Context
    **Identifying language:** "most nearly means"
    **Research where?** passage, line 123

11. The passage primarily serves to

    **Question type:** Global
    **Identifying language:** "passage primarily serves to"
    **Research where?** big picture summary

12. Which of the following is most analogous to John Snow's discovery of the source of the cholera outbreak?

    **Question type:** Inference
    **Identifying language:** "most analogous"
    **Research where?** passage, where author discusses Snow's discovery

13. Which choice provides the best evidence for the answer to the previous question?

    **Question type:** Command of Evidence
    **Identifying language:** "provides the best evidence"
    **Research where?** passage, where you went to answer the previous question

14. The passage indicates that the main reason government officials rejected Snow's hypothesis was

    **Question type:** Detail
    **Identifying language:** "indicates"
    **Research where?** passage, where author discusses officials' rejection of Snow

15. The second paragraph serves mainly to

    **Question type:** Function
    **Identifying language:** "serves mainly to"
    **Research where?** passage, second paragraph

16. It can reasonably be inferred from the passage that scientists in 1855 would have found which of the following solutions to be most practical in dealing with future outbreaks of cholera?

    **Question type:** Inference
    **Identifying language:** "reasonably be inferred"
    **Research where?** passage, where author discusses cholera outbreak solutions

17. The author of this passage writes from the perspective of a

    **Question type:** Global
    **Identifying language:** "author … writes from the perspective of a"
    **Research where?** big picture summary

18. Which of the following is cited as the primary reason Snow suspected the Broad Street pump as the source of the epidemic?

    **Question type:** Detail
    **Identifying language:** "is cited as"
    **Research where?** passage, where author discusses Broad Street pump

19. As used in line 97, the word "flagged" most nearly means

    **Question type:** Vocab-in-Context
    **Identifying language:** "most nearly means"
    **Research where?** passage, line 97

20. The author uses the final sentence of the passage ("It wasn't … outbreaks") at least in part to:

    **Question type:** Function
    **Identifying language:** "uses … at least in part to"
    **Research where?** passage, final sentence

# CHAPTER 20

# Answering SAT Reading Questions

## LEARNING OBJECTIVES

After completing this chapter, you will be able to:

- Research the answer in the passage or your big picture summary
- Predict the correct answer
- Find the one correct answer choice

# How Much Do You Know?

**Directions:** In this chapter, you'll learn how best to research, predict, and find the correct answers to SAT Reading questions. For this quiz, first take a couple of minutes to refresh your memory of the passage. Then, for each question 1) research the answer in the passage text or from your big picture summary, 2) predict the correct answer in your own words, and 3) identify the one correct answer.

**Questions 1-11 refer to the following passage.**

This passage is adapted from a 2018 article summarizing two different proposals for solving problems with maintaining New York City's mass transit system.

The history of the New York City subway system, quickly told: the first stations opened in 1904, and over the next century, it expanded to 472 stations,
5  more than any other subway system in the world, with 850 miles of track. Operating 24 hours a day seven days a week, with an average weekday ridership of approximately 5.7 million, it is the
10  planet's 7th-busiest rapid transit system. While the system is, on many levels, an amazing achievement, it is also beset by a problem that harms both quality of life and economic activity. Such a
15  large system must inevitably suffer from service interruptions and delays; normal wear and tear combined with the sheer age of the system necessitates regular maintenance. However, there
20  is no consensus as to the best way to accomplish the required repairs.

*NYC subway: how to repair? diff. views*

The current maintenance scheme is designed to minimize service interruptions. A subway line in need
25  of repair will be taken out of service during a comparatively less busy time, such as nights or weekends, while another line is re-routed to cover as many as possible of the missing line's
30  stops. The main advantage to this approach is that trains are not taken out of service during rush hour, when most subway trips occur; subway service generally remains predictable
35  and commuters are, for the most part,

*Current approach – night and weekend repairs*

able to use the system to get to their destinations on time.

But critics are quick to point out the disadvantages to this approach. Perhaps
40  most obvious is the confusion caused by trains switching lines. The labyrinthine system is hard enough to navigate at the best of times, especially for tourists. A subway rider on the A train naturally
45  expects the train to make stops on the A line. If, instead, it is diverted temporarily to the F line, the rider may find herself miles from her intended destination.

*Critics: line switch confusion*

50  While annoying, the confusion arising from route switching is hardly the most serious problem with the current approach to repairs. Because the system runs 24 hours a
55  day, routine maintenance can generally be done only during the temporary closures on nights and weekends. This means that more serious repair and crucial preventative maintenance is
60  often neglected. Problems that could have been fixed or prevented reasonably expeditiously given a slightly longer closure wind up leading to major breakdowns and service interruptions
65  later on.

*Even worse – major breakdowns*

On rare occasions, such breakdowns have resulted in entire subway lines being shut down for months or even a year. Beginning in 2019, for
70  example, the L Train connecting lower Manhattan to parts of Brooklyn was scheduled to close for as much as 15 months for long overdue service and upgrades. In a city fewer than
75  half of whose households own a car,

this can have serious economic impacts.
Residents of the affected area may
face a much longer commute via an
alternate subway line if one is available;
80 or, if there is no alternate subway
service, they may need to take other,
potentially more expensive, modes
of transportation, such as taxis or
ferries. Moreover, studies indicate that
85 increased stress from the commute to
work can lead to lower productivity, and
that businesses near the impacted lines
may see decreased revenue as potential
customers have a harder time getting to
90 them.

One controversial proposal for
reducing breakdowns and the resulting
transit interruptions is to end the
subway's 24-hour service and to shut
95 down for several hours each night.
Proponents of this plan argue that
this would allow time, on a regular
rather than sporadic basis, for more
preventative maintenance. This, they
100 claim, would ultimately lead to more
consistent service; rather than shutting
down entire lines for long periods of
a time, there would merely be shorter
service outages overnight, when fewer
105 people use the subway system. While
this may seem a preferable outcome to
the economic consequences of a total
shutdown resulting from a breakdown,
it has its liabilities as well. While most
110 subway trips may occur during rush
hour, not everyone works during the
daytime. New York is famously known
as the "the city that never sleeps."
Doctors, nurses, bartenders, police
115 officers, and firefighters are just a few
examples of occupations whose workers
need transportation at all hours of
the day and night. Rather than be
subjected to a relatively short period
120 of inconvenience, these workers would
find their commutes irrevocably altered.

One thing, at least, is clear: the city
must carefully consider many economic
and social factors in designing a subway
125 maintenance plan.

*Margin annotations:*

Econ. & Soc. harms of shutdowns

Alt proposal – stop 24-hour service

Pros

Cons

*Side tab:* Reading

1. Which of the following best expresses the primary purpose of the passage?

    A) To argue that the New York City subway system maintenance plan should be altered

    B) To explain the effects of the current New York City subway system maintenance plan and a proposed alternative

    C) To discuss the economic and social importance of the New York City subway system

    D) To show how the history of the New York City subway system has resulted in the current maintenance crisis

2. According to the passage, which of the following is true of the New York City subway system?

    A) It is the oldest subway system in the world.

    B) It is the busiest mass transit system in the world.

    C) It has more stations than any other subway system.

    D) A majority of city residents rely on the subway to get to work.

3. Based on the passage, advocates of the current New York City subway maintenance plan would most likely agree that

    A) given its size, the city's subway system is one of the most well maintained in the world.

    B) avoiding service interruptions during rush hour is a paramount consideration when designing a maintenance schedule.

    C) confusion caused by route switching is a minor inconvenience for commuters and tourists.

    D) operating the subway system 24 hours a day seven days a week is untenable given the wear and tear it causes.

4. Which choice provides the best evidence for the answer to the previous question?

    A) Lines 14–19 ("Such a . . . maintenance")

    B) Lines 30–37 ("The main . . . time")

    C) Lines 50–53 ("While . . . repairs")

    D) Lines 96–99 ("Proponents . . . maintenance")

5. Based on the passage, which choice best describes a claim that critics of the current subway maintenance plan would likely make?

    A) The negative impacts that arise from neglecting preventative maintenance outweigh the benefits of minimizing subway service interruptions.

    B) When devising a subway maintenance plan, no factor is more important than avoiding rush hour service interruptions.

    C) The negative impact from subway line closures is greater on commuters than it is on businesses near the affected lines.

    D) Slightly longer periods of scheduled maintenance would help the subway system minimize rush hour service interruptions.

6. Which choice provides the best evidence for the answer to the previous question?

    A) Lines 24–30 ("A subway . . . stops")

    B) Lines 60–65 ("Problems . . . later on")

    C) Lines 69–74 ("Beginning in . . . upgrades")

    D) Lines 84–90 ("Moreover, studies . . . them")

7. As used in line 41, "labyrinthine" most nearly means

    A) subterranean.

    B) mythological.

    C) meandering.

    D) complicated.

8. In the third paragraph, the discussion of two specific subway lines (lines 44–49) primarily serves to

    A) support the contention that line switching has a negative impact on tourism.

    B) illustrate one problem created by the current subway maintenance plan.

    C) underline the importance of minimizing subway service interruptions.

    D) quantify the social costs that arise from extended subway repair schedules.

9. The fifth paragraph (lines 66–90) serves mainly to

    A) illustrate the impact of the current maintenance plan on one subway line.

    B) advocate for increased funding for subway repair and maintenance.

    C) provide support for a proposal to curtail 24-hour subway service.

    D) outline the negative impacts of extended subway line outages.

10. The passage indicates that non-rush hour commuters

    A) would risk losing public transportation options if 24-hour subway service were suspended.

    B) would face only minor inconveniences if 24-hour subway service were suspended.

    C) work primarily in health care and its related fields.

    D) are among the strongest advocates for a change to the current subway maintenance plan.

11. With which one of the following statements would the author of the passage be most likely to agree?

    A) The controversy surrounding New York City's subway system reflects similar issues for mass transit in many American cities.

    B) Without major changes to its subway maintenance plan, New York City will be unable to provide regular service to its 5.7 million weekly riders.

    C) Any plan for maintaining New York City's subway system will entail advantages and disadvantages for commuters.

    D) The social and economic costs resulting from New York City's current subway maintenance schedule justify an end to 24-hour, seven-day subway service.

Reading

## Check Your Work

**1.    B**

**Difficulty:** Medium

**Category:** Global

**Strategic Advice:** Consult your big picture summary and find the one answer that matches the passage's scope and the author's purpose.

**Getting to the Answer:** Here, the author does not take a side. He lays out advantages and disadvantages to both the current maintenance plan and one proposal offered by critics of the current plan. That matches **(B)**.

(A) distorts the author's position. He doesn't advocate for the critics of the current plan.

(C) is too narrow. It misses the key subject of subway *maintenance*.

(D) is also too narrow. This answer describes only the first paragraph.

**2.    C**

**Difficulty:** Medium

**Category:** Detail

**Strategic Advice:** The correct answer will be something explicitly stated in the passage.

**Getting to the Answer:** Start by checking the answers against paragraph 1 where the author provides general facts about the New York City subway. Doing so will lead you to the correct answer, **(C)**.

(A) is unsupported. You're told that the subway opened in 1904, but not whether other subway systems already existed at that time.

(B) is simply incorrect. New York City's subway system is the seventh busiest in the world.

(D) distorts a fact from the passage. The fifth paragraph states that fewer than half of households in the city own a car, but that doesn't mean that everyone in the majority of households that do not own cars takes the subway.

**3.    B**

**Difficulty:** Hard

**Category:** Inference

**Strategic Advice:** The correct answer will follow from the passage text without having been explicitly stated in the text.

**Getting to the Answer:** The current maintenance plan is outlined in paragraph 3. You're told that its goal is to "minimize service interruptions" and that its main advantage is that trains operate during rush hour. Combining those statements leads to the correct answer, **(B)**.

(A) is too extreme. Everyone seems to agree that maintaining the system is a huge challenge. The debate is over *how* best to implement the necessary repairs.

(C) misuses a detail from the passage. The author says nothing about how serious a problem those who support the current plan consider route switching to be. They might understand that it causes a major inconvenience but still be willing to re-route trains in order to keep the subway open during rush hour.

(D) states a position taken by *critics*, not advocates, of the current plan.

**4.    B**

**Difficulty:** Medium

**Category:** Command of Evidence

**Strategic Advice:** The most common Command of Evidence question stems task you with locating the piece of text that supports the correct answer to the preceding question. Use that answer to direct your research as you evaluate the answer choices.

**Getting to the Answer:** In this case, the correct answer to the preceding question paraphrased the final sentence in paragraph 3. That sentence covers the lines in **(B)** making that the correct answer here.

(A) cites a sentence from paragraph 1. It contains the phrase "wear and tear," which was part of incorrect answer (D) in the preceding question, but doesn't support the correct answer, **(B)**.

(C) comes from the beginning of paragraph 4. It suggests that there are problems with the current system even bigger than the inconvenience caused by line switching. This choice could be tempting if you chose (C) on the preceding question.

(D) provides evidence for the *critics'* proposal to stop running the subway 24/7. That is not the argument made by advocates of the current system who were the subject of the preceding question.

## 5. A

**Difficulty:** Hard

**Category:** Inference

**Strategic Advice:** The phrases "[b]ased on the passage" and "would likely" indicate an Inference question. Note that this question asks specifically for the position of the critics of the current plan. The correct answer will be implied by the passage text.

**Getting to the Answer:** The critics' objections to the current plan are laid out primarily in paragraphs 3 and 4. Quick research shows that they make two arguments. First (paragraph 3), line switching for routine maintenance can be confusing and frustrating for riders. Second (paragraph 4), and worse, the limited time allowed for routine maintenance prevents important preventative maintenance from taking place. That leads to severe service outages that can last for weeks or months. This second criticism accords with the correct answer, **(A)**.

(B) is something that advocates, not opponents, of the current plan might say. See paragraph 2 for this argument.

(C) is an irrelevant comparison. Paragraph 5 lays out the social and economic impacts of extended subway line closures to both riders and businesses, but it doesn't assert that the impacts are worse for one group or the other.

(D) distorts the critics' argument. They contend that slightly longer periods of scheduled maintenance would allow time for preventative maintenance, not that it would reduce rush hour interruptions.

## 6. B

**Difficulty:** Medium

**Category:** Command of Evidence

**Getting to the Answer:** Here, the correct answer to the preceding question paraphrased the critics' argument in paragraph 4. That paragraph's final sentence, represented by **(B)**, provides the support.

(A) is a sentence from paragraph 2. It explains the rationale behind the current maintenance plan and does not support a criticism of that plan.

(C) contains an example of an extended service outage for one subway line. That's an illustration of the kind of problem the critics hope to avoid, but by itself does not support the claim in the correct answer to the preceding question.

(D) cites a line from the end of paragraph 5. It does not support the correct answer to the preceding question, but might be tempting if you chose (C) there.

## 7. D

**Difficulty:** Easy

**Category:** Vocab-in-Context

**Strategic Advice:** Check the sentence in which the word was used to determine the author's intended meaning. The correct answer can be substituted for the word without changing the meaning of the sentence.

**Getting to the Answer:** Here, the author uses *labyrinthine* to describe the New York subway system's complexity. **(D)** fits perfectly.

(A) means *underground*. That is true of the subway system, of course, but it would be redundant for the author to use "labyrinthine" in this way.

(B) plays off the famous labyrinth from Greek mythology, but this definition does not fit the word "labyrinthine" or the context of the sentence.

(C) suggests that the subway system is *random* or *wandering*. While the huge system may be difficult to navigate at times, it isn't random.

## 8. B

**Difficulty:** Hard

**Category:** Function

**Strategic Advice:** The phrase "serves to" tags this as a Function question, asking for the role a specific detail plays in the passage. Research the lines cited in the question stem to see *why* the author has included this example.

**Getting to the Answer:** The third paragraph introduces the first disadvantage cited by critics of the current subway maintenance schedule. The detail referenced in the question stem provides an example. That purpose is accurately described in the correct answer, **(B)**.

(A) misuses a detail from the passage. You're told that line switching—the problem being discussed—is particularly difficult for tourists, but that's not the reason the author included this example.

(C) refers to the rationale provided by supporters of the current maintenance plan in paragraph 2.

In (D), the word "quantify" suggests that the example provides numbers to show the impact of the current maintenance plan. That's something the author never does in this passage.

## 9.  D

**Difficulty:** Easy

**Category:** Function

**Strategic Advice:** In this case, you're asked for the author's purpose for including an entire paragraph. Consult your margin notes to see the role of paragraph 5 in the passage.

**Getting to the Answer:** Paragraph 5 details some of the social and economic harms caused by shutting down subway lines. That matches **(D)**.

(A) distorts the purpose of the paragraph. The specific line—the L train—is given as an example of an extended shutdown, but the harms described in the paragraph apply to all similar extended service outages.

(B) is outside the scope of the passage. The author does not discuss the need for increased funding.

(C) refers to a proposal from paragraph 6. The author does not endorse that proposal and does not use paragraph 5 to support it.

## 10.  A

**Difficulty:** Medium

**Category:** Detail

**Strategic Advice:** The phrase "[t]he passage indicates" shows this to be a Detail question. The correct answer will paraphrase a statement made explicitly in the text.

**Getting to the Answer:** The author discusses non-rush hour commuters in paragraph 5. He lists some examples of these commuters—"doctors, nurses, bartenders, police officers, and firefighters"—and explains that a cessation of 24-hour subway service could permanently alter their commutes. That matches choice **(A)**, the correct answer here.

(B) is the opposite of the what the passage says. The current system creates minor inconveniences for these workers when their subways lines are rerouted or closed for repair, but a suspension of 24-hour service would entail a permanent disruption.

(C) distorts the paragraph. Doctors and nurses are among the non-rush hour commuters, but that doesn't mean they are the majority of them.

(D) is outside the scope of the passage. The author does not discuss which occupations show the strongest support for a change in subway maintenance.

## 11.  C

**Difficulty:** Hard

**Category:** Inference

**Strategic Advice:** For an open-ended Inference question like this one, predict the correct answer based on your big picture summary. Consider also any thesis statement or conclusion that sums up the author's point of view.

**Getting to the Answer:** This author outlines both sides of a debate and discusses the advantages and disadvantages to both the current subway maintenance plan and proposed alternatives. His conclusion at the end of the passage is neutral, encouraging the city to carefully consider all factors without advocating for a specific outcome. This matches up with the correct answer, **(C)**.

(A) strays beyond the scope of the passage. Be careful not to bring in bigger issues if the author has not discussed them in the passage.

(B) is too extreme. To be sure, the author considers subway maintenance a major issue but stops short of dire predictions like the one stated in this answer choice.

(D) matches the position of one side in the debate, but not that of the author, who remains neutral throughout.

# How to Answer SAT Reading Questions

**LEARNING OBJECTIVES**

After this lesson, you will be able to:

- Research the answer in the passage or your big picture summary
- Predict the correct answer
- Find the one correct answer choice

## To answer questions like these:

**Directions:** Choose the best answer choice for the following questions.

**Questions 1-11 refer to the following passage and supplementary material.**

This passage was adapted from an article titled "Millennials and the Market," written by a money management expert in 2018.

During the Golden Age of American manufacturing, it was expected that after putting in 30 to 40 years of tedious labor in a factory, workers
5  would be able to retire around age 65 and enjoy the benefits of retirement comforted by the thought that a pension and the Social Security system they had financed for decades would
10  cover their expenses. Unfortunately for millennials (people born between the early 1980s and late 1990s), prospects look increasingly bleak that they will get a return on their investment at
15  retirement age, despite continuing to fund programs like Social Security and Medicare. Fewer than a quarter of all Fortune 500 corporations still offer some form of pension plan to new
20  hires, and the move from company-funded pension plans to 401(k) plans and IRAs that began in the 1970s shows no sign of slackening. In this financial environment, it might be expected
25  that investment in the stock market would be at an all-time high. An analysis of the data, however, indicates a complicated and even fraught

*Millennials won't have same retirement $*

*But they don't like stock market*

relationship between young adults and
30  the stock market.

The trauma associated with the Great Recession (which began in December 2007 and ended in June 2009) left many investors wary of stock
35  market volatility, and that hesitancy was exacerbated among young people, who saw a considerable portion of their families' wealth erased in short order. A study by Pfeffer, Danziger,
40  and Schoeni published in 2014 posited that the average American household lost a third of its wealth, approximately $28,000, during the Great Recession. This was at the exact moment when a
45  great many millennials were making decisions about attending college, pursuing post-graduate studies, or entering the workforce. For a median-income family, those decisions were
50  all directly correlated to household wealth. The ripple effects of the Great Recession left many millennials ascribing blame directly to the stock market for missed opportunities.
55  Even with a full awareness that the stock market has rebounded and far exceeded the highs seen prior to the Great Recession, many millennials still feel trepidation about investing in the
60  stock market, preferring to save a larger percentage of their salaries than their parents and grandparents did.

*Reason: 07-09 recession = millennials blame the market*

Reading

Another factor that has directly impacted the willingness of millennials to invest in the stock market is the seismic shift in the job market brought about by the "gig economy," in which short-term contracts and freelance work have replaced permanent employment. To a large degree, the gig economy is still in its nascent phase, with many of the largest purveyors of jobs only incorporated in the last decade. Research has not adequately kept track of the trend, with estimates of participation in the gig economy ranging from 4% to 40% in the United States. The ability to pick up work on a contingency basis allows millennials to feel a greater level of control over their finances, something a significant number of them believe they cannot achieve through stock market investment. The increased diversity of available methods for building future wealth has caused many millennials to adopt an a la carte approach to preparing for retirement. But is it possible that this approach has been clouded by some common misconceptions about wealth building?

One persistent, albeit erroneous, view is that real estate is a better investment instrument than a stock market portfolio. While it is true that home equity is the stepping-stone from which most individuals begin to build their personal wealth, statistics make it clear that stock market investments are a more stable and lucrative source of long-term wealth. A London Business School study found that over the same 90-year period, the average rate of return on a real estate investment was 1.3% compared to the 9.8% annualized total return for the S&P stock 500 index. Investing the $5,500 IRS-imposed annual limit in an IRA for 25 years would result in a return of over $600,000 based on the annualized return rate. Stock investment requires a smaller overhead than real estate investment, and the liquid nature of stocks makes them ideal for retirement: stocks allocated to retirement accounts remain tax-free until they are drawn on. Despite these pieces of tangible evidence, though, the stigma regarding stock market investment persists in the minds of many millennials.

Regardless of their feelings about the stock market, one thing is self-evident: without preparation for retirement, millennials will be a generation adrift in a society without the social "safety nets" available to current retirees. The benchmark for the amount of savings the average retiree needs to live comfortably after retirement, which remained at $1 million for many years, now continues to rise, and exacerbating factors, such as the cost of medical care, continue to increase. Armed with that knowledge, millennials need to be proactive about financial planning. By taking full advantage of their penchant for a hands-on approach to finances and leveraging the various financial technologies and services that were not available to the previous generation, millennials can amass the wealth necessary to retire comfortably and on their own terms.

*[Margin annotations:]*
Reason 2: gig economy = diff. ways to make $

Bad thinking: house > stock mkt

Millennials need to adapt their thinking to have retirement $

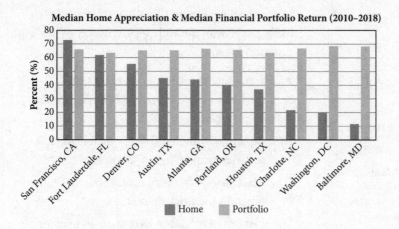

Median Home Appreciation & Median Financial Portfolio Return (2010–2018)

ROI of
home owning
vs. stock
mkt

Home    Portfolio

1. One central idea of the passage is that

A) changes to social "safety net" programs such as Social Security and Medicare will force millennials to retire later in life than their parents did.

B) investing in the stock market is the only money management strategy that will allow millennials to amass savings sufficient to retire comfortably.

C) leveraging opportunities in the "gig economy" has allowed millennials to avoid the risks associated with investing in the stock market.

D) despite their distrust of the stock market, millennials will need a variety of investment tools and strategies to build adequate retirement savings.

2. Which choice best describes the overall structure of the passage?

A) A surprising attitude is introduced, two criticisms of it are offered, an alternative attitude is presented, and data proving the alternative is superior is provided.

B) A surprising attitude is introduced, two reasons for it are described, a mistaken idea associated with it is revealed through data, and its effect on those holding it is assessed.

C) A previously held attitude is presented, reasons for its rejection are offered, new data is presented, and those rejecting the old attitude are endorsed.

D) Two reasons for a previously held attitude are presented, both reasons are rejected, and data is presented to introduce an alternative attitude.

3. According to the passage, large corporations are

A) less likely to offer their employees pension plans than they were in the past.

B) more likely to invest in the stock market than millennial individuals are.

C) opposed to the gig economy because it reduces the number of permanent employees.

D) skeptical that their current employees will receive their full Social Security benefit.

4. As used in line 38, "erased" most nearly means

A) canceled.

B) effaced.

C) laundered.

D) eradicated.

5. The passage most strongly implies which of the following statements about the Great Recession?

A) It could have been avoided by continued funding of Social Security and Medicare.

B) It impacted families with millennial-age children more severely than any other group.

C) It resulted from misconceptions about the stability of stock market investments.

D) It caused at least some millennials to forego their educational and career goals.

6. Which choice provides the best evidence for the answer to the previous question?

A) Lines 10–17 ("Unfortunately . . . Medicare")

B) Lines 39–43 ("A study . . . Recession")

C) Lines 48–54 ("For a . . . opportunities")

D) Lines 89–91 ("But . . . wealth building")

7. In the third paragraph (lines 63–91), the most likely purpose of the author's discussion of the "gig economy" is to

A) argue that short-term contracts and freelance work are preferable to permanent employment.

B) explain why millennials are unable to raise sufficient capital to buy a home.

C) examine one factor in millennials' hesitancy to invest in the stock market.

D) cast doubt on claims that up to 40 percent of workers hold short-term and freelance jobs.

8. In the context of the passage as a whole, the question in lines 89–91 ("But is . . . wealth building") primarily functions to help the author

A) establish that millennials are mismanaging their retirement investments.

B) show how professional money managers diversify their investments to avoid market volatility.

C) introduce data that reveals a flaw in the premises that influence millennials' investment choices.

D) call into question opposing opinions about the effects of the gig economy.

9. The passage indicates that investing in the stock market

A) is the stepping stone from which most individuals begin to build personal wealth.

B) remains less stable and lucrative than home ownership as a source of wealth.

C) has tax implications well suited to retirement planning.

D) is limited by IRS rules to a $5,500 annual maximum.

10. Which of the following statements about the period from 2010 to 2018 is supported by the graph?

    A) Investment in the stock market generated more wealth than home ownership in every market listed in the graph.

    B) The value of a home appreciated by a greater percentage in Portland, Oregon, than in Charlotte, North Carolina.

    C) The return on a median financial portfolio outperformed the value of home ownership by a greater margin in each subsequent year.

    D) Austin, Texas, saw a greater disparity between home value appreciation and return on financial portfolios than Atlanta, Georgia, saw.

11. Which statement from the passage is most directly reflected by the data presented in the graph?

    A) Lines 48–51 ("For a . . . wealth")

    B) Lines 74–78 ("Research . . . United States")

    C) Lines 98–101 ("statistics . . . wealth")

    D) Lines 110–115 ("Stock . . . drawn on")

## You need to know this:

- Use clues to direct your research to a specific portion of the passage or to your big picture summary:
  - **Line Numbers**—Reread the indicated text and possibly the lines before and after; look for keywords indicating why the referenced text has been included or how it's used.
  - **Paragraph Numbers**—Consult your margin notes to see the paragraph's purpose and scope before rereading the text. Sometimes your passage map alone is enough to find an answer.
  - **Quoted Text**—Go back to the passage to read the entire quote if the stem or answer choices use ellipses (. . .). Then check the surrounding context of the quoted term or phrase to see what the author meant by it in the passage.
  - **Proper Nouns**—Use your passage map or look for capital letters in the text to find the term and then check the context to see why the author included it in the passage; note whether the author had a positive, negative, or neutral evaluation of it.
  - **Specific Content Clues**—Use your margin notes to help you search the passage for terms or ideas mentioned in the question stem; these clues will usually refer to something the author offered an opinion about or emphasized.
  - **Whole Passage Clues**—Begin by reviewing your big picture summary, and only go back to the passage if you can't find the information you need. If you do get stuck, the first and last paragraphs are typically the best places to go for global takeaways.
- Predicting what you're looking for in the correct answer saves time and reduces confusion as you read each choice.
- SAT Reading questions always have one correct answer and three incorrect answers:
  - The correct answer will match what the passage says in a way that responds to the task set out in the question stem.
  - Wrong answers often fall into one of five categories. Not every incorrect choice matches one of these types exactly, but learning to spot them can help you eliminate some wrong answers more quickly.
    - **Out of Scope**—contains a statement that is too broad, too narrow, or beyond the purview of the passage
    - **Extreme**—contains language that is too strong (*all*, *never*, *every*, *none*) to be supported by the passage
    - **Distortion**—based on details or ideas from the passage but distorts or misstates what the author says or implies
    - **Opposite**—directly contradicts what the correct answer must say
    - **Misused Detail**—accurately states something from the passage but in a manner that incorrectly answers the question

**You need to do this:**

| The SAT Reading Question Method | |
|---|---|
| Step 1. | Unpack the question stem |
| **Step 2.** | **Research the answer** |
| **Step 3.** | **Predict the answer** |
| **Step 4.** | **Find the one correct answer** |

- Research the answer:
  - When clues point to a specific part of the passage (line or paragraph numbers, quotations, content discussed only in particular paragraphs), begin by rereading the specified text and immediate context.
    - If the immediate context does not provide enough info to answer the question, gradually expand outward, rereading sentences that come before and after.
  - With whole passage clues or questions that seem to lack clear content clues, begin by reviewing your big picture summary.
  - If you can't figure out where to research the question and your big picture summary doesn't help either, consider using process of elimination, skipping the question and coming back to it later, or just making a guess.
- Predict or characterize what the correct answer will say or suggest:
  - Don't worry about phrasing your prediction as a complete sentence or about repeating exactly the language used in the passage. Just try to answer the question posed in your own words based on your research.
  - If you struggle to predict, use your active reading of the passage to characterize the correct answer, setting expectations about characteristics it must possess.
    - For example, if the author has a negative view of a topic in the question, expect a correct answer with negative language and eliminate choices that suggest a positive or neutral view.
- Find the one correct answer:
  - Identify the choice that matches your prediction, if possible.
    - Don't expect a word-for-word match, but look for a correspondence of ideas. For example, if you predict that the function of a detail is to "provide support for the main idea," an answer choice that says it "supplies evidence for the author's thesis" would likely be correct.

- If there is no clear match, use process of elimination:
  - Eliminate any choice that contradicts your prediction or that clearly falls into one of the five wrong answer categories.
    - Choose the only answer remaining or guess among those you were unable to eliminate.

---

### FINDING THE CORRECT ANSWER

**One Correct Choice—Three *Demonstrably* Incorrect Choices**

Great SAT test takers know that there is always one correct answer, written to match the meaning of the passage, and three *demonstrably* incorrect ones. The word "demonstrably" underscores that the wrong answers aren't merely worse than the credited choice; they fail, for one or more reasons, to accurately answer the question. SAT experts don't compare answer choices to one another; they evaluate the choices based on the passage. They never ask themselves, "Do I like (B) or (C) more?" Instead, they ask, "Does the second paragraph imply (B)? Why or why not?"

# Answers and Explanations

| Question | Analysis |
|---|---|

1. One central idea of the passage is that

   A) changes to social "safety net" programs such as Social Security and Medicare will force millennials to retire later in life than their parents did.

   B) investing in the stock market is the only money management strategy that will allow millennials to amass savings sufficient to retire comfortably.

   C) leveraging opportunities in the "gig economy" has allowed millennials to avoid the risks associated with investing in the stock market.

   D) despite their distrust of the stock market, millennials will need a variety of investment tools and strategies to build adequate retirement savings.

**Answer: D**

**Difficulty:** Easy

**Category:** Global

**Strategic Advice:** Answer Global questions based on your big picture summary. Sometimes, the author has already "boiled down" the central idea and summarized it in a sentence, usually near the beginning of or end of the passage.

**Getting to the Answer:** The big picture summary captured the author's main point as it is expressed near the end of the passage: "Millennials are skeptical of investing in the stock market for several reasons, but they'll need a variety of investments to be financially secure at retirement." That matches **(D)** perfectly.

(A) distorts the author's point. The author doesn't compare millennials' potential retirement *age* with that of their parents' generation.

(B) is extreme. The author thinks millennials are too hesitant to use stock market investments, but concludes that their financial stability will come from a variety of financial technologies and services, not from the stock market alone.

(C) is too narrow (the gig economy is discussed only in paragraph 3) and misstates the author's point about the gig economy, which is that it has encouraged millennials to "feel a greater level of control over their finances."

| Question | Analysis |
|---|---|

2. Which choice best describes the overall structure of the passage?

A) A surprising attitude is introduced, two criticisms of it are offered, an alternative attitude is presented, and data proving the alternative is superior is provided.

B) A surprising attitude is introduced, two reasons for it are described, a mistaken idea associated with it is revealed through data, and its effect on those holding it is assessed.

C) A previously held attitude is presented, reasons for its rejection are offered, new data is presented, and those rejecting the old attitude are endorsed.

D) Two reasons for a previously held attitude are presented, both reasons are rejected, and data is presented to introduce an alternative attitude.

**Answer: B**

**Difficulty:** Medium

**Category:** Global

**Strategic Advice:** Occasionally, a Global question will ask you to outline the overall structure of the passage. To answer a question like this, consult your big picture summary and review the notes you've jotted down next to each paragraph.

**Getting to the Answer:** In this passage, the author introduces a surprising opinion (millennials distrust the stock market), gives two reasons for their opinion (the Great Recession and the "gig economy"), points out an oversight in this opinion (the stock market is usually a better investment than home ownership), and concludes with an assessment of how that opinion needs to balance with other considerations (millennials will need a variety of investment strategies). That outline matches up nicely with the correct answer, **(B)**.

(A) starts off well but runs into trouble with "two criticisms of [the attitude] are offered." Paragraphs 2 and 3 explain *why* millennials distrust the market; those paragraphs don't criticize millennials for their point of view. The end of choice (A) is also problematic. The author offers data to show why millennials' attitudes toward the market are mistaken, not to prove an alternative opinion.

The beginning of choice (C) may be tempting because the author does provide background on older generations' expectations upon retirement, but the remainder of this choice wanders far from the structure of the passage.

(D) goes off course right from the start. This passage does not open with reasons for rejecting an older point of view on investing.

| Question | Analysis |
|---|---|
| 3. According to the passage, large corporations are<br><br>A) less likely to offer their employees pension plans than they were in the past.<br><br>B) more likely to invest in the stock market than millennial individuals are.<br><br>C) opposed to the gig economy because it reduces the number of permanent employees.<br><br>D) skeptical that their current employees will receive their full Social Security benefit. | **Answer: A**<br><br>**Difficulty:** Easy<br><br>**Category:** Detail<br><br>**Strategic Advice:** "According to the passage" at the beginning of a question stem signals a Detail question. The correct answer will paraphrase something stated explicitly in the passage.<br><br>**Getting to the Answer:** The author discusses large corporations in paragraph 1. She says that two-thirds of large corporations no longer offer pension plans and indicates that this trend is likely to continue. That supports **(A)**, the correct answer.<br><br>(B) is an irrelevant comparison; the author never discusses how large corporations invest.<br><br>(C) presents a misused detail; in paragraph 3, the author states that the gig economy has replaced permanent employment with short-term contracts and freelance work, but she does not mention corporate opposition to the gig economy.<br><br>(D) distorts the passage; the author expresses concern that individuals will not have enough income at retirement despite their investments in Social Security and Medicare, but she does not ascribe this concern to corporations. |

| Question | Analysis |
|---|---|

4. As used in line 38, "erased" most nearly means

    A) canceled.

    B) effaced.

    C) laundered.

    D) eradicated.

**Answer: D**

**Difficulty:** Medium

**Category:** Vocab-in-Context

**Strategic Advice:** To answer a Vocab-in-Context question, examine the sentence in which the word was used for clues about how the author used the word. You can substitute the correct answer into the sentence without changing the sentence's meaning.

**Getting to the Answer:** Here, the author uses "erased" to mean *lost* or *destroyed*. **(D)**, *eradicated*, is the best fit for the sentence.

(A), *canceled*, carries with it the implication that there was a plan or expected event that was deleted from the calendar before it ever took place. The wealth "erased" by the Great Recession already existed; it wasn't canceled before it was created.

(B), *effaced*, usually refers to removing a sign or indication of something. That doesn't fit the context of money in a savings account or investment.

(C), *laundered*, may bring to mind the financial crime of "money laundering," but that has no logical connection to the sentence in the passage.

| Question | Analysis |
|---|---|

5. The passage most strongly implies which of the following statements about the Great Recession?

A) It could have been avoided by continued funding of Social Security and Medicare.

B) It impacted families with millennial-age children more severely than any other group.

C) It resulted from misconceptions about the stability of stock market investments.

D) It caused at least some millennials to forego their educational and career goals.

**Answer: D**

**Difficulty:** Medium

**Category:** Inference

**Strategic Advice:** The phrase "most strongly implies" marks this as an Inference question. The correct answer will follow from the passage without having been explicitly stated in the passage. The reference in the question stem to the "Great Recession" points you to paragraph 2.

**Getting to the Answer:** Paragraph 2 provides one reason that millennials distrust the stock market. Many millennials were considering college and career options when the market crashed in 2007, leading to the Great Recession. As a result, many of these young people blamed the market for "missed opportunities." This directly supports **(D)**.

(A) is outside the scope; the author does not draw a connection between the Great Recession and the two social programs named here.

(B) distorts the passage; while the author cites the damage that the Great Recession did to the "average American family," she doesn't compare the effect on families with millennial-age children to that on other groups of people.

(C) is outside the scope; the author does not discuss any causes of the Great Recession.

| Question | Analysis |
|---|---|
| 6. Which choice provides the best evidence for the answer to the previous question?<br><br>A) Lines 10–17 ("Unfortunately . . . Medicare")<br><br>B) Lines 39–43 ("A study . . . Recession")<br><br>C) Lines 48–54 ("For a . . . opportunities")<br><br>D) Lines 89–91 ("But . . . wealth building") | **Answer: C**<br><br>**Difficulty:** Medium<br><br>**Category:** Command of Evidence<br><br>**Strategic Advice:** Use the answer from the previous question to evaluate the answer choices here.<br><br>**Getting to the Answer:** The correct answer to the preceding question focused on how the Great Recession curtailed educational and employment opportunities for young people. That is substantiated by the text in **(C)**.<br><br>(A) comes from paragraph 1 and cannot be used to support the answer to the preceding question. This choice may have been tempting to test takers who thought (A) was the correct answer to the previous question.<br><br>(B) cites a study that quantified the harm done by the Great Recession, but that does not directly support the correct answer to the preceding question, which focused on missed opportunities for young adults at the time.<br><br>(D) contains the rhetorical question at the end of paragraph 3; that's outside the scope of the previous question's correct answer. |

| Question | Analysis |
|---|---|
| 7. In the third paragraph (lines 63–91), the most likely purpose of the author's discussion of the "gig economy" is to<br><br>A) argue that short-term contracts and freelance work are preferable to permanent employment.<br><br>B) explain why millennials are unable to raise sufficient capital to buy a home.<br><br>C) examine one factor in millennials' hesitancy to invest in the stock market.<br><br>D) cast doubt on claims that up to 40 percent of workers hold short-term and freelance jobs. | **Answer: C**<br><br>**Difficulty:** Medium<br><br>**Category:** Function<br><br>**Strategic Advice:** Function questions ask you *why* an author included a specific piece of text or *how* she uses it in the passage. In this question stem, the identifying language is "most likely purpose." The research clue sends you back to paragraph 3.<br><br>**Getting to the Answer:** Paragraph 3 opens with a clear-cut topic sentence: this paragraph will examine "[a]nother factor" that leads millennials to distrust the stock market. That factor is the rise of the gig economy and its effects on millennial attitudes toward money management. That leads right to the correct answer, **(C)**.<br><br>(A) distorts the passage; the author expresses no preference for one kind of work or another.<br><br>(B) misuses a detail from paragraph 4; one reason the author gives for considering stock market investment is its lower capital requirements. The author does not explain why millennials would have difficulty raising capital for down payment on a home.<br><br>(D) misuses a detail within paragraph 3; the author cites studies showing a range of gig economy participation, but her purpose is not to cast doubt on the high end of those claims. |

Reading

| Question | Analysis |
|---|---|

8. In the context of the passage as a whole, the question in lines 89–91 ("But is . . . wealth building") primarily functions to help the author

A) establish that millennials are mismanaging their retirement investments.

B) show how professional money managers diversify their investments to avoid market volatility.

C) introduce data that reveals a flaw in the premises that influence millennials' investment choices.

D) call into question opposing opinions about the effects of the gig economy.

**Answer: C**

**Difficulty:** Hard

**Category:** Function

**Strategic Advice:** Most Function questions use "serves to," but occasionally, they'll be as direct as this question stem, asking what a piece of text "functions to" do. The research clue in this stem points to the final sentence in paragraph 3.

**Getting to the Answer:** By ending a paragraph with a rhetorical question, the author signals that the following paragraph will provide the answer. Paragraph 4 discusses the flaw in assuming that home ownership is a more stable or profitable investment than the stock market is. The question at the end of paragraph 3 helps the author set up this discussion, so **(C)** is the correct answer.

(A) is extreme; the author questions one assumption underlying millennials' "a la carte" investment approach, but she doesn't accuse them of overall mismanagement.

(B) is outside the scope. The pre-passage blurb suggests that this author is an investment strategist, but nothing in the passage claims to demonstrate professional approaches to reducing risk.

(D) is outside the scope; the author doesn't present or contradict any opposing views in this paragraph.

| Question | Analysis |
|---|---|
| 9. The passage indicates that investing in the stock market<br><br>A) is the stepping stone from which most individuals begin to build personal wealth.<br><br>B) remains less stable and lucrative than home ownership as a source of wealth.<br><br>C) has tax implications well suited to retirement planning.<br><br>D) is limited by IRS rules to a $5,500 annual maximum. | **Answer: C**<br><br>**Difficulty:** Medium<br><br>**Category:** Detail<br><br>**Strategic Advice:** A question asking for something that the "passage indicates" is a Detail question. The correct answer will paraphrase a fact, opinion, or claim made explicitly in the passage. Broadly speaking, the entire passage is about "investing in the stock market," but the author provides her most detailed analysis in paragraph 4, making it the best place to target your research.<br><br>**Getting to the Answer:** The bulk of paragraph 4 compares investment in the market favorably to home ownership. The author demonstrates the large return on a modest investment and then points out other reasons why they are well suited to retirement income. One of those reasons is the investments' tax-free status (lines 112–115); that matches the correct answer, **(C)**.<br><br>(A) is a misused detail; this answer choice virtually quotes the passage, but the piece of text it cites refers to home ownership, not to stock market investments.<br><br>(B) says the opposite of what's in the passage; the author demonstrates that the stock market is more stable and lucrative than home ownership is.<br><br>(D) misuses a detail contained in paragraph 4; the $5,500 annual cap applies to IRA contributions, not to stock market investments in general. |

Reading

| Question | Analysis |
|---|---|

10. Which of the following statements about the period from 2010 to 2018 is supported by the graph?

A) Investment in the stock market generated more wealth than home ownership in every market listed in the graph.

B) The value of a home appreciated by a greater percentage in Portland, Oregon, than in Charlotte, North Carolina.

C) The return on a median financial portfolio outperformed the value of home ownership by a greater margin in each subsequent year.

D) Austin, Texas, saw a greater disparity between home value appreciation and return on financial portfolios than Atlanta, Georgia, saw.

**Answer: B**

**Difficulty:** Medium

**Category:** Inference

**Strategic Advice:** When a question stem says that the correct answer is "supported by" something in the passage, you're looking at an Inference question. It's no different when the support comes from a graph or chart at the end of the passage. Use the information in the graph to evaluate the answer choices.

**Getting to the Answer:** To see what is implied by a graph or chart accompanying an SAT Reading passage, make sure you understand what is being represented and look for trends. Here, the *x*-axis shows 10 different cities. For each one, the percent increase in value of a median-priced home and a median-size stock portfolio are given on the *y*-axis. Only in San Francisco did the value of a home outperform the value of a portfolio of investments. Note that, along the *x*-axis, the cities are arranged from greatest increase in home value to least. The increases in stock portfolios, while all similar, are not in a particular order. Testing the answers against the graph reveals **(B)** as the correct choice. Charlotte is to the right of Portland on the graph, and you know that means its home values appreciated less than those in Portland.

(A) is contradicted by the case of San Francisco, the one market in which home ownership outperformed stock market investments.

(C) is not supported; the graph does not show year-over-year changes in value. This choice might be tempting to a test taker who glanced at the graph and made the unwarranted assumption that the *x*-axis represents different years instead of different locations.

(D) can be eliminated by comparing the two named locations. Stock portfolios outperformed home ownership in both cities, but the gap is a little smaller for Austin than it is for Atlanta.

| Question | Analysis |
| --- | --- |

11. Which statement from the passage is most directly reflected by the data presented in the graph?

A) Lines 48–51 ("For a . . . wealth")

B) Lines 74–78 ("Research . . . United States")

C) Lines 98–101 ("statistics . . . wealth")

D) Lines 110–115 ("Stock . . . drawn on")

**Answer: C**

**Difficulty:** Hard

**Category:** Command of Evidence

**Strategic Advice:** This question stem is relatively rare. It is a variation on the Command of Evidence question type. Here, instead of asking you to find the text supporting a previous answer choice, the question provides you with the evidence—in this case, it is the graph at the end of the passage—and asks you to find the text it supports.

**Getting to the Answer:** The graph compares the value of home ownership to stock market investment. The author made the same comparison in paragraph 4. Only **(C)** and (D) contain statements from paragraph 4, and a quick check shows that it is the text in **(C)** that follows from the data shown in the graph.

(A) comes from paragraph 2, which discusses the impact on millennials of the Great Recession. Don't get tripped up by the word "median" here; the sentence from paragraph 2 mentions median-income families, while the graph represents median-value homes and median-sized portfolios.

(B) comes from paragraph 3, which discusses the gig economy. Always check the full reference in the answer choice; a hurried or sloppy test taker might see the words "[r]esearch" and "United States" and think that's enough to connect this answer to the graph.

(D) comes from the correct paragraph, but from a point at which the author has moved on from comparing home ownership and is now discussing other advantages of stock market investments as a source of retirement income.

## Try on Your Own

**Directions:** Put the expert question strategies to work on the following passage. First, take a few minutes to refresh your memory of the passage (which you first saw in chapter 18). Then, for each question 1) identify the question type, 2) note where/how you will research the answer, 3) jot down your prediction of the correct answer, and 4) find the one correct answer.

### PREDICTIONS

On the real test, you won't have time to write down your full prediction in complete sentences. If you feel the need to write something to help you hold on to your prediction, keep it very brief: a word or two, or even better, a single abbreviation. For example, if you predict that an author is including a detail as support for a broader point, you might just write "suppt" next to the choices.

**Directions:** Choose the best answer choice for the following questions.

**Questions 1-11 refer to the following passage.**

This passage was adapted from an article titled "Quantum Computing: Where Is It Going?" published in a science magazine in 2018. It discusses the background and potential of quantum computing.

Pharmaceutical companies dream of a time when their research and development process shifts from looking for illnesses whose symptoms
5 can be ameliorated by a specific drug to choosing a disease and creating a drug to eradicate it. Quantum computing may be the (key) to that goal. The (powerful) modeling (potential)
10 unlocked by quantum computing may also someday be employed by autonomous vehicles to create a world free of traffic jams. With plausible applications in so many fields, it is
15 worthwhile to learn a bit about how quantum computing works.

Any understanding of quantum computing begins with its most basic element, the qubit. In classical
20 computing, information is processed by the bit, the binary choice of zero or one. Qubits, (on the other) hand, allow for infinite superpositions between zero and one and thus can
25 store and process (exponentially) more

*QC: big potential*

*QC based on qubits – can store more values*

complicated values. Imagine showing someone where you live on a globe by pointing only to either the North Pole or the South Pole. While you
30 are likely closer to one pole than the other, you need additional information to represent your specific location. If, however, you could provide your home's latitude and longitude, it could
35 be located without any additional information. The power of quantum computing lies in the ability to express precise information in a single qubit.

Quantum computing may help
40 scientists and engineers overcome another barrier by reducing energy output while increasing computational speed. The positive correlation between energy output
45 and processing speed often causes classical computers to "run hot" while processing overwhelming amounts of data. Along with their ability to store multiple values simultaneously,
50 qubits are able to process those values in parallel (instead of) serially. How does processing in parallel conserve energy? Suppose you want to set the time on five separate alarm clocks
55 spaced ten feet apart. You'd have to walk to each clock to change its time.

*Qubit > bit, much more data*

*Qubits = parallel processing*

However, if the clocks were connected such that changing the time on one immediately adjusted the other four, you 60 would expend less energy and increase processing speed. Therein lies the (benefit) *faster AND cooler* of the quantum entanglement of qubits.

While quantum computing has moved beyond the realm of the 65 theoretical, (significant barriers) still stand in the way of its practical application. One barrier is the difficulty of confirming the results of quantum calculations. If quantum computing *One barrier to QC – How to check results?* 70 is used to solve problems that are impossible to solve with classical computing, is there a way to "check" the results? Scientists hope this paradox may soon be resolved. As a graduate 75 student, Urmila Mahadev devoted over a decade to creating a verification process for quantum computing. The result is an interactive protocol, based on a type of cryptography called 80 Learning With Errors (LWE), that is similar to "blind computing" used in cloud-computing to mask data while still performing calculations. Given current limitations, Mahadev's protocol 85 remains purely theoretical, but rapid progress in quantum computing combined with further refinement of the protocol will (likely result) in real- *probably will get solved* world implementation within the next 90 decade or two.

It is (unlikely) that early pioneers in the field, including Stephen Wiesner, Richard Feynman, and Paul Benioff, could have foreseen the (rapid progress) 95 that has been made to date. In 1960, when Wiesner first developed conjugate coding with the goal of improving cryptography, his paper on the subject was rejected for publication *QC pioneers – 1960s – 80s* 100 because it contained logic far ahead of its time. Feynman proposed a basic quantum computing model at the 1981 First Conference on the Physics of

Computation. At that same conference, 105 Benioff spoke on the ability of discrete mechanical processes to erase their own history and their application to Turing machines, a natural extension of Wiesner's earlier work. A year later, 110 Benioff more clearly outlined the theoretical framework of a quantum computer.

The dawn of the 21st century brought advancements at an even *QC sped up in 2000s* 115 (more impressive) pace. The first 5- and 7-qubit nuclear magnetic resonance (NMR) computers were demonstrated in Munich, Germany, and Santa Fe, New Mexico, respectively. In 2006, 120 researchers at Oxford were able to cage a qubit within a "buckyball," a buckminsterfullerene molecule, and maintain its state for a short time using precise, repeated microwave pulses. The 125 first company dedicated to quantum computing software, 1QB Information Technologies, was founded in 2012, and in 2018, Google announced the development of the 72-qubit Bristlecone 130 chip designed to prove "quantum supremacy," the ability of quantum computers to solve problems beyond the reach of classical computing.

With progress in quantum computing accelerating, it seems 135 (inevitable) that within a few decades, the general population will be as familiar with quantum computing as they now are with classical computing. At present, 140 quantum computing is limited by the struggle to build a computer large enough to prove quantum supremacy, and the costs associated with quantum computing are prohibitive to all but *QC pioneers* 145 the world's largest corporations and governmental institutions. (Still,) classical *QC still difficult, but bright future* computing overcame similar problems, so the future of quantum computing (looks bright.)

1. The primary purpose of the passage is to

   A) argue that quantum computing will provide the solution to pressing societal problems.

   B) compare the speed and efficiency of quantum computing to that of classical computing.

   C) explain the progress and potential of quantum computing despite current obstacles.

   D) refute those who argue that quantum computing is too impractical and expensive to succeed.

2. According to the passage, which one of the following is true of Urmila Mahadev's graduate work?

   A) It was focused on ways to improve "cloud computing."

   B) Its results cannot be confirmed by classical computing techniques.

   C) It will likely have applications for the pharmaceutical industry.

   D) It may lead to verification of quantum computing calculations.

3. Which choice provides the best evidence for the answer to the previous question?

   A) Lines 1–9 ("Pharmaceutical . . . goal")

   B) Lines 67–73 ("One barrier . . . results")

   C) Lines 78–83 ("The result . . . calculations")

   D) Lines 84–90 ("Given . . . two")

4. In the second paragraph, the discussion of locating a person's home on a globe (lines 26–36) primarily serves to

   A) contrast the processing power of quantum computing to that of classical computing.

   B) illustrate the rapid progress of research in quantum computing.

   C) argue that quantum computing will allow for exponentially more complicated mapping software.

   D) support the claim that quantum computing will enable autonomous vehicles to navigate.

5. Based on the passage, the author would most likely criticize classical computing because it

   A) has developed more slowly than quantum computing in recent years.

   B) lacks any application for autonomous vehicles.

   C) employs serial processing.

   D) cannot verify quantum computing calculations.

6. Which statement best describes the technique the author uses to advance the main point of the third paragraph (lines 39–62)?

   A) She describes research done by leading scientists and engineers.

   B) She proposes a laboratory experiment that would prove a hypothesis.

   C) She offers a hypothetical example to illustrate a complex comparison.

   D) She cites data demonstrating the superior efficiency of one technique.

7. The passage indicates that which of the following factors slowed early developments in the theory of quantum computing?

   A) Feynman and Benioff were discouraged that their computing models were rejected.

   B) At least one academic journal was reluctant to publish papers containing advanced logic.

   C) Quantum computing was too expensive for colleges and universities to support effectively during the 1980s.

   D) A focus on cryptology in the early 1960s drew the most talented researchers away from quantum computing.

8. Which one of the following does the passage imply about the development of quantum computing in the 21st century?

   A) At least some companies anticipate commercial viability for quantum computing in the future.

   B) Recent advancements in hardware have demonstrated "quantum superiority."

   C) Research into quantum computing led to the discovery of the "buckyball."

   D) It has stalled due to reluctance of major corporations and governments to fund such expensive research.

9. Which choice provides the best evidence for the answer to the previous question?

   A) Lines 115–119 ("The first . . . respectively")

   B) Lines 119–124 ("In 2006 . . . pulses")

   C) Lines 124–133 ("The first . . . computing")

   D) Lines 139–142 ("At present . . . supremacy")

10. As used in line 123, "maintain" most nearly means

    A) sustain.

    B) repair.

    C) resupply.

    D) nurture.

11. The author's attitude toward the potential success of quantum computing can best be described as

    A) skeptical.

    B) resigned.

    C) incredulous.

    D) optimistic.

Reading

# How Much Have You Learned?

**Directions:** Take 13 minutes to read the passage and answer the associated questions. Try to use the various SAT Reading question strategies you learned in this chapter.

**Questions 12-22 refer to the following passage.**

This passage was adapted from an article entitled "John Snow Knew Something" published in a popular history magazine in 2018.

Few would deny that doctors use critical thinking to solve problems, but most imagine a difference between the practice of medicine and, say,

5  the methods a police detective might use to solve a case. In fact, medical researchers have long used forensic methods of detection and analysis. The case of John Snow, a

10  19th-century anesthesiologist, is often said to have ushered in the modern era of epidemiology, the branch of medicine that tracks the incidence and distribution of diseases and

15  proposes solutions for their control and prevention.

It would not be until 1861 that Louis Pasteur would propose the link between microorganisms and disease,

20  now known as the germ theory. Before Pasteur's breakthrough, the predominant explanation for the cause of most illnesses was the so-called miasma theory, which held that noxious

25  fumes and pollution—quite literally, as the theory's name implies, "bad air"— were responsible for making people sick. Consequently, during the 1854 outbreak of cholera in Westminster,

30  London, doctors and government officials alike blamed "miasmatic particles" released into the air by decaying organic matter in the soil of the River Thames.

35  Despite the widespread acceptance of the miasma theory, there were those, Snow included, who were skeptical of

*Snow's work used investigation, changed medicine*

*1854 – didn't know about germs; miasma theory*

this view. Snow would not have known, as doctors do today, that cholera

40  is caused by a bacterial infection, *Vibrio cholerae.* Nevertheless, he was convinced that the spread of the disease was caused by some form of matter passed between individuals, likely

45  through contaminated water.

To demonstrate this, Snow targeted a particularly deadly outbreak in the Soho district of Westminster in London. From August 31 to September

50  3, 1854, 127 people in the area died of cholera. Within a week, that number had risen to over 500. Snow took to the streets. Speaking to residents of the area, he found a commonality among

55  them: most of the victims had used a single public water pump located on Broad Street. Though he was unable to find conclusive proof that the pump was the source of the outbreak, his

60  demonstration of a pattern in the cholera cases prompted authorities to disable the pump by removing its handle. The epidemic quickly subsided.

Soon after the Broad Street pump

65  was shut down, Snow's continued investigation provided additional evidence that contaminated water was the source of the outbreak. Snow created a dot map of the cases of cholera in London

70  and demonstrated that they occurred in areas where water was supplied by two companies that obtained their water from wells near the Thames. Investigation of these wells showed that they had been

75  dug three feet from a cesspit that was leaking sewage into the surrounding soil. Snow also discovered that there were no cases of cholera among workers in a brewery close to the Broad Street pump.

*Snow: cholera from contam. $H_2O$*

*Proof from interviews – all used same pump*

*Water from contam. wells*

80  These workers were provided a daily
allowance of beer, which they drank
instead of water, and although the beer
was brewed using the contaminated
water, it was boiled during the brewing

*Boiling first prevented disease*

85  process. This revelation provided a
(practical solution) for the prevention of
future outbreaks.

Snow is (now hailed) as the "father of
modern epidemiology," and the radical

90  nature of his approach—formulating
a new theory, substantiating it with
verifiable evidence, and proposing
preventative action—is fully
appreciated. At the time, (however,) not

95  all were convinced, at least publicly, of
Snow's findings. As anxiety over the
outbreak flagged, government officials
replaced the handle on the Broad Street
pump and publicly denounced Snow's

*Snow not accepted at the time*

100  conclusions. It seems they felt that the
city's residents would be upset and
disgusted to have the unsettling nature
of the well's contamination confirmed.
It wasn't until 1866, more than a decade

105  after Snow's original investigation and
theory—when another cholera outbreak
killed more than 5,500 residents of
London's East End—that officials
working in public health began to

*1866 – another epidemic*

110  accept the link between contaminated
water and certain kinds of illness and
to take appropriate actions to quell such
outbreaks.

*Reading*

12. The passage primarily serves to

    A) summarize the history of research into the causes and prevention of cholera.

    B) critique government officials for failing to consider evidence that could have prevented further loss of life.

    C) chronicle an episode in the history of medicine that changed the way in which research is conducted.

    D) demonstrate similarities in the methods used by medical researchers and by police detectives.

13. The author of this passage writes from the perspective of

    A) a public health official advocating for improved disease prevention measures.

    B) a journalist narrating medical history to lay readers.

    C) an editorial opinion writer critiquing the actions of local officials.

    D) a medical school professor explaining the techniques of epidemiological research.

14. The second paragraph serves mainly to

    A) suggest a reasonable alternative to a hypothesis presented later.

    B) outline the scientific and historical context for a problem that required a novel solution.

    C) summarize the conditions that led to a recurring public health issue.

    D) criticize the stubbornness of physicians and politicians against considering new evidence.

15. Which of the following is most analogous to John Snow's theory that contaminated water caused the cholera outbreak?

    A) Gregor Mendel described the principles of biological heredity years before the discovery of genes and DNA.

    B) Robert Koch used Louis Pasteur's experiments to develop the postulates of the germ theory of disease.

    C) Rosalind Franklin produced x-ray diffraction images of DNA, which were used by Watson and Crick to describe its structure.

    D) Galileo Galilei promoted a sun-centered model of the solar system but was put on trial because his views conflicted with those of the Spanish Inquisition.

16. Which choice provides the best evidence for the answer to the previous question?

    A) Lines 17–20 ("It would . . . theory")

    B) Lines 38–45 ("Snow would . . . water")

    C) Lines 57–63 ("Though he . . . subsided")

    D) Lines 85–87 ("This revelation . . . outbreaks")

17. The passage indicates that the main reason government officials rejected Snow's hypothesis was

    A) a lack of concrete scientific proof.

    B) a fear of public backlash.

    C) mistrust of Snow's methods.

    D) financial ties to the city's water suppliers.

18. Which choice provides the best evidence for the answer to the previous question?

    A) Lines 35–38 ("Despite the . . . view")

    B) Lines 57–63 ("Though he . . . subsided")

    C) Lines 68–73 ("Snow created . . . Thames")

    D) Lines 100–103 ("It seems . . . confirmed")

19. Which of the following is cited as the primary reason Snow suspected the Broad Street pump as the source of the epidemic?

    A) The discovery of decaying organic matter in soil near the Thames releasing gases into the air

    B) The decline of cases of the disease following the removal of the pump handle

    C) A pattern in the geographical location of cases of the disease

    D) A lack of cases of the disease among those working in a brewery near the pump

20. It can be reasonably inferred from the passage that scientists in 1855 would have found which of the following solutions to be most practical in dealing with future outbreaks of cholera?

    A) Using alcoholic beverages in place of water for all applications

    B) Removing the handles from all water pumps in the affected area

    C) Vaccinating the public against the disease using inactive *V. cholerae* bacteria

    D) Advising the public to boil all water from municipal sources before use

21. As used in line 97, the word "flagged" most nearly means

    A) subsided.

    B) indicated.

    C) penalized.

    D) peaked.

22. The author uses the final sentence of the passage ("It wasn't . . . outbreaks") at least in part to

    A) underscore the assertion that Snow's explanation of the cause of the epidemic was ultimately correct.

    B) demonstrate that an explanation of a phenomenon will not be accepted until after the mechanism behind it is fully detailed.

    C) suggest that there is often a significant delay between medical discovery and its application.

    D) lament the loss of life caused by failing to act on medical recommendations that are reasonably supported by evidence.

Reading

# Reflect

**Directions:** Take a few minutes to recall what you've learned and what you've been practicing in this chapter. Consider the following questions, jot down your best answer for each one, and then compare your reflections to the expert responses on the following page. Use your level of confidence to determine what to do next.

Why do SAT experts research and predict the correct answer to Reading questions before reading the answer choices?

_____

_____

_____

What are the types of research clues contained in SAT Reading question stems?

_____

_____

_____

What are the five common wrong answer types associated with SAT Reading questions?

- _____
- _____
- _____
- _____
- _____

How will you approach the process of answering SAT Reading questions more strategically going forward? Are there any specific habits you will practice to make your approach to SAT Reading more effective and efficient?

_____

_____

_____

## Expert Responses

Why do SAT experts research and predict the correct answer to Reading questions before reading the answer choices?

*Expert test takers know that the correct answer to each SAT Reading question is based on the text of the passage. They research to avoid answering based on memory or on a whim. Predicting the correct answer before reading the choices increases accuracy and speed by helping the test taker avoid rereading, confusion, and comparing answer choices to one another.*

What are the types of research clues contained in SAT Reading question stems?

*Line numbers, paragraph numbers, proper nouns, quoted text, specific content clues, and whole passage clues*

What are the five common wrong answer types associated with SAT Reading questions?

- *Out of scope*
- *Opposite*
- *Distortion*
- *Extreme*
- *Misused detail*

How will you approach the process of answering SAT Reading questions more strategically going forward? Are there any specific habits you will practice to make your approach to SAT Reading more effective and efficient?

*There is no one-size-fits-all answer here. Reflect on your own habits in answering SAT Reading questions and give yourself an honest assessment of your strengths and weaknesses. Consider the strategies you've seen experts use in this chapter, and put them to work in your own practice to increase your accuracy, speed, and confidence.*

## Next Steps

If you answered most questions correctly in the "How Much Have You Learned?" section, and if your responses to the Reflect questions were similar to those of the SAT expert, then consider answering Reading questions an area of strength and move on to the next chapter. Come back to this topic periodically to prevent yourself from getting rusty.

If you don't yet feel confident, review the material in "How to Answer SAT Reading Questions," and then try the questions you missed again. As always, be sure to review the explanations closely.

# Answers and Explanations

**1. C**

**Difficulty:** Easy

**Category:** Global

**Strategic Advice:** "[P]rimary purpose" indicates a Global question. Consult your big picture summary to predict the correct answer.

**Getting to the Answer:** The author is convinced that quantum computing has enormous potential despite current obstacles. She explains the basis of quantum computing, outlines its rapid progress, and describes efforts to make it practicable. **(C)** summarizes all of this and is correct.

(A) is too narrow and too strong. The passage opens with examples of problems that quantum computing may *help* solve, but this isn't the author's main point.

(B) is too narrow. The discussion of processing speed and energy output is included in paragraph 3 as one potential advantage of quantum computing.

(D) misstates the author's purpose. The passage was not written to *refute* an opposing point of view, nor does the author contend that anyone else is mistaken in their criticism of quantum computing.

**2. D**

**Difficulty:** Medium

**Category:** Detail

**Strategic Advice:** "According to the passage" indicates a Detail question. The correct answer is something stated explicitly in the passage. The research clue, Urmila Mahadev, leads you straight to paragraph 4.

**Getting to the Answer:** Paragraph 4 is about an obstacle to quantum computing: the paradox that arises from the fact that classical computing cannot be used to verify the results of quantum computing. How does Mahadev figure in here? Mahadev dedicated her graduate studies to trying to resolve this paradox. She has come up with a theoretical solution that the author concludes will likely have real-world application in the coming years. That final statement matches **(D)**, making it the correct answer.

(A) is a faulty use of detail. Part of Mahadev's protocol is similar to techniques used in cloud computing, but nothing indicates that she was trying to improve cloud computing.

(B) distorts the paragraph. It is the results of quantum computing that cannot be confirmed by classical computing, not the results of Mahadev's graduate work.

(C) brings in a detail from paragraph 1; pharmaceutical research is irrelevant to Mahadev's graduate studies.

**3. D**

**Difficulty:** Medium

**Category:** Command of Evidence

**Strategic Advice:** Questions that ask you to locate the evidence for the preceding question's correct answer are Command of Evidence questions. Use your research for the preceding question to put your finger on the relevant support from the passage and match that to the correct answer choice here.

**Getting to the Answer:** The correct answer to the preceding question said that Mahadev's graduate work would likely lead to verification of quantum computing results. That was from the end of paragraph 4, matching **(D)**.

(A) refers back to paragraph 1; this is irrelevant to Mahadev's work, but matches up with choice (C) in the preceding question.

(B) quotes the statement of the problem that Mahadev's work is trying to solve, but doesn't match the correct answer to the preceding question, which stated that her protocol will likely work.

(C) cites the description of Mahadev's protocol; this answer could be tempting if you incorrectly chose (A) on the preceding question.

**4. A**

**Difficulty:** Medium

**Category:** Function

**Strategic Advice:** The phrase "serves to" identifies this as a Function question. Check the context of the example cited in the question stem and identify *how* the author uses it.

**Getting to the Answer:** The second paragraph outlines why qubits (the basis for quantum computing) are so much more powerful than bits (the building blocks of classical computing). The hypothetical case of pinpointing one's house on a globe illustrates this contrast. Thus, **(A)** is correct.

(B) is off topic. The progress of quantum computing research is discussed in the fifth and sixth paragraphs.

(C) contains a distracting reference to "mapping software," which may remind you of a globe, but the author doesn't discuss software applications at all in this paragraph. Another potentially distracting phrase here is "exponentially more complicated," an exact quote from earlier in the paragraph. When evaluating answer choices in SAT Reading, look for the answer that matches the meaning of your correct-answer prediction, not simply for a choice with familiar words.

(D) inappropriately drags in an example—autonomous vehicles—from the first paragraph. The author does not connect that to the globe analogy in any way.

**5.    C**

**Difficulty:** Hard

**Category:** Inference

**Strategic advice:** "Based on the passage" introduces an Inference question. The correct answer will follow from the passage without having been explicitly stated in the passage. Use the research clues in the question stem to narrow down your search and then consider the implications of what is stated at that point in the passage.

**Getting to the Answer:** The author compares classical computing unfavorably to quantum computing in paragraphs 2 (quantum computing can handle exponentially more complicated values) and 3 (quantum computing uses parallel processing to run faster with less energy output). Paragraph 3 directly supports the correct answer, **(C)**. Because parallel processing gives quantum computing its advantage, serial processing is the reason classical computing is inferior.

(A) distorts the author's point of view. She describes quantum computing's rapid advancement, but doesn't compare that to classical computing's development.

(B) is extreme. The author doesn't say that classical computing has *no value* for driverless cars, but rather that quantum computing may have great value for this technology in the future.

(C) is a faulty use of detail. This answer choice is true according to paragraph 4, but the author doesn't claim that this is a shortcoming of classical computing.

**6.    C**

**Difficulty:** Hard

**Category:** Function

**Strategic Advice:** On occasion, the SAT will ask you to describe the way in which the author has made or supported a point in the passage. Research a question like this from the clues in the question stem. Be prepared for somewhat abstract language in the answer choices as they will be worded to describe the author's technique, not to recount the details in the paragraph.

**Getting to the Answer:** In paragraph 3, the author describes a potential advantage of quantum computing by comparing parallel processing in quantum computing to serial processing in classical computing. She illustrates this with the simple thought experiment about the five clocks. That matches the "complex comparison" and "hypothetical example" described in **(C)**.

(A) distorts the paragraph. Quantum computing, you're told, may help scientists and engineers, but doesn't mention any research by people in those occupations.

(B) distorts the author's example. She doesn't suggest that someone set up the five clocks in a laboratory and test them for efficiency.

(D) misses the paragraph entirely; the author doesn't cite any data here.

**7.    B**

**Difficulty:** Medium

**Category:** Detail

**Strategic Advice:** The word "indicates" signals a Detail question. The correct answer will be something explicitly stated in the text. The research clue "early developments" should send you to paragraph 5 to research.

**Getting to the Answer:** Most of the details in paragraph 5 are positive and speak to a slow but consistent advancement in theorizing and modeling quantum computing. The one setback that is mentioned is the rejection of Wiesner's paper by an academic journal hesitant to publish logic that was "ahead of its time." That's described in the correct answer, **(B)**.

(A) distorts the paragraph, which does not suggest that Feynman's and Benioff's models were rejected.

(C) misapplies a detail from paragraph 7; the expense of quantum computing limits research today. You're told nothing about whether schools funded this research in the 1980s.

(D) contradicts the passage; Wiesner's interest in cryptology appears to have promoted his work leading to early quantum computing models.

**8. A**

**Difficulty:** Medium

**Category:** Inference

**Strategic Advice:** The word "imply" marks this as an Inference question. The correct answer will be supported by something in the passage's discussion of quantum computing's development in the 21st century.

**Getting to the Answer:** The passage focuses on the 21st century development of quantum computing in paragraph 6, which contains three main details: the demonstration of MNR computers, the Oxford research that caged a qubit, and the emergence of commercial interest in quantum computing. The last of those, as exemplified in the passage by 1QB Information Technologies and Google, supports choice **(A)** as the correct answer.

(B) distorts the paragraph; Google's *Bristlecone* chip is intended to prove quantum superiority, but the passage does not say that it has been used successfully.

(C) distorts what the passage says about the Oxford research; there, researchers used a "buckyball," but you're not told who discovered the molecule or when it was discovered.

(D) misuses a claim from paragraph 7; while it's true that quantum computing is very expensive, the last sentence of paragraph 6 contradicts the statement made in this answer choice.

**9. C**

**Difficulty:** Medium

**Category:** Command of Evidence

**Strategic Advice:** This is a standard Command of Evidence question asking you to locate the text that supports the correct answer to the preceding question. Use that answer to guide your research.

**Getting to the Answer:** The final sentence of paragraph 6 demonstrates that companies are pursuing quantum computing research. That matches **(C)**.

(A) comes from paragraph 6 but doesn't support the correct answer to the preceding question.

(B) describes the Oxford research; it might be tempting to a test taker who mistakenly chose (C) on the preceding question.

(D) comes from paragraph 7; it cites a hurdle that quantum computing must overcome.

**10. A**

**Difficulty:** Medium

**Category:** Vocab-in-Context

**Strategic Advice:** For Vocab-in-Context questions, check the sentence in which the word from the question stem is used to paraphrase its meaning in context. The correct answer could be substituted into the sentence without changing the meaning of the sentence at all.

**Getting to the Answer:** In the sentence at line 123, scientists have been able to maintain the state of qubit using an oddly named molecule. You don't need to understand the details of the process to get the gist of the sentence. The scientists are keeping the qubit in a constant, or stable, state. That matches the correct answer, **(A)**.

(B) doesn't work here because nothing suggests that the qubit was "broken" in the process.

(C) implies that the qubit loses something and needs to be refreshed or made whole; that doesn't fit the context.

(D) means to care for the development of, which would add information not implied by the sentence.

**11. D**

**Difficulty:** Medium

**Category:** Inference

**Strategic Advice:** A question about the author's attitude is a variety of Inference question. The correct answer follows from the author's opinions and points of view as they are expressed in the passage.

**Getting to the Answer:** The author concludes the passage on a high note. While acknowledging ongoing difficulties that quantum computing still needs to overcome, she finds it "inevitable" that it will one day be familiar to most people and explicitly states that the field's future "looks bright." Thus, **(D)** is correct.

(A) is too negative to describe this author's point of view.

(B) is also negative; a "resigned" attitude would indicate an author who has accepted an unfortunate result and has stopped fighting against it.

(C) means "unbelieving." If the author were incredulous, she would deny that quantum computing could actually happen.

## 12. C

**Difficulty:** Easy

**Category:** Global

**Strategic Advice:** The phrase "primarily serves to" marks this as a Global question. Consult your big picture summary to predict the correct answer.

**Getting to the Answer:** For this passage, you can summarize the author's purpose as something like: "Narrate the story of how Snow's cholera research changed doctors' understanding and prevention of disease." That leads to the correct answer, **(C)**. The phrase "chronicle an episode" contains a verb that accurately describes the author's journalistic tone and focuses on the correct scope, a single event.

(A) is too broad; the passage does not attempt to sum up the entire history of cholera research.

(B) is too narrow; officials' rejection of Snow's findings the decade after the 1854 cholera outbreak is an unfortunate coda to the story, not the main point of the passage.

(D) is too narrow; the author mentions forensic evidence and investigation in the introduction to familiarize the reader with techniques that will be discussed.

## 13. B

**Difficulty:** Medium

**Category:** Global

**Strategic Advice:** This is a relatively rare variation on Global questions that asks you to describe the author's perspective. Consider your big picture summary, especially the author's purpose, to determine the role this author most likely fills.

**Getting to the Answer:** This passage centers on the story of Snow's cholera research to explain its importance for medical research. The author compares epidemiology to criminal investigation to provide context for the general reader. This leads to **(B)** as the correct answer.

(A) suggests a passage that would likely focus on a current problem and would use language intended to persuade the reader to adopt new policies.

(C) describes an article primarily focused on the mistakes of present-day politicians and bureaucrats.

(D) portrays an expert communicating scientific and technical details to an expert reader.

## 14. B

**Difficulty:** Medium

**Category:** Function

**Strategic Advice:** When a Function question ("serves . . . to") asks about the role of a paragraph, check your margin notes to see why the author wrote the paragraph and how it fits into the rest of the passage.

**Getting to the Answer:** Your note for paragraph 2 should indicate that this is where the author laid out the state of medical knowledge in 1854: doctors didn't know about germs; people still believed the miasma theory of disease. The author included this to show how innovative Snow's hypothesis and investigation were. That analysis leads to the correct answer, **(B)**.

(A) states the opposite of what the author intended; the beliefs outlined in paragraph 2 were unreasonable and soon rejected.

(C) distorts the passage; the conditions that led to the outbreak, such as wells dug too near cesspits, are discussed later in the passage.

(D) describes details the author introduces in paragraph 6, not paragraph 2.

## 15.  A

**Difficulty:** Hard

**Category:** Inference

**Strategic Advice:** A question asking you to select a scenario "analogous to" one described in the passage is an Inference question. The correct answer follows from the passage without having been stated explicitly in the passage.

**Getting to the Answer:** The passage says that Snow hypothesized that cholera was spread by contaminated water even though he and his contemporaries were unaware of germs as the cause of diseases. Among the answer choices, the most appropriate analogy is the one described in **(A)**; Mendel described the workings of heredity even though he didn't know about its underlying structures, genes and DNA.

(B) may be tempting because it mentions Louis Pasteur—a scientist also mentioned in the passage—but it gets the analogy backwards; the situation described in this answer choice involves a scientist building on information already discovered.

(C) describes a situation in which a technological breakthrough (x-ray diffraction images) led to the refinement of a scientific theory; that doesn't match Snow's investigation, performed without the aid of technology.

(D) recounts a case in which social pressure was used in an attempt to silence a scientist; after Snow's discovery, some officials ignored his findings, but the passage does not imply that he was persecuted.

## 16.  B

**Difficulty:** Medium

**Category:** Command of Evidence

**Strategic Advice:** This is a standard Command of Evidence question. Your job is to locate the passage text that directly supports the correct answer to the preceding question.

**Getting to the Answer:** The correct answer to the question immediately before this one suggested that an important aspect of Snow's theory was that he formulated the theory before scientists had discovered the biological mechanism explaining it. The author said this explicitly in the sentence quoted in choice **(B)**.

The sentence quoted in choice (A) discusses the germ theory of disease but does not directly discuss the fact that Snow would not have known about it.

The sentence quoted in (C) focuses on how Snow pinpointed the physical source of the cholera outbreak, not on how he formulated his initial hypothesis.

The text quoted in (D) explains how Snow's research helped find a way to prevent the spread of cholera; the question preceding this one focused on his theory of its cause, not prevention.

## 17.  B

**Difficulty:** Medium

**Category:** Detail

**Strategic Advice:** The word "indicates" signals a Detail question. The correct answer will paraphrase something explicitly stated in the passage. Target paragraph 6 where the author discussed government officials' rejection of Snow's findings.

**Getting to the Answer:** The question stem asks for the *reason* officials ignored Snow's hypothesis. This is discussed in lines 94–103. The officials feared public outcry ("upset and disgusted") upon finding out that sewage had leaked into their water supply, a concern that **(B)** sums up succinctly.

(A) misuses a detail from paragraph 4: Snow persuaded officials to remove the pump handle despite a lack of "conclusive proof."

(C) distorts the passage; the author says that officials publicly rejected Snow's findings for political reasons but doesn't say that they doubted his methods.

(D) is outside the scope; nothing in the passage suggests that corruption played a role in the officials' decisions.

## 18.  D

**Difficulty:** Medium

**Category:** Command of Evidence

**Strategic Advice:** This is a standard Command of Evidence question. Your job is to locate the passage text that directly supports the correct answer to the preceding question.

**Getting to the Answer:** The preceding question focused on why officials rejected Snow's findings. That is directly explained by the sentence quoted in choice **(D)**.

(A) quotes the first sentence of paragraph 3; this addresses Snow's rejection of the miasma theory, not officials' rejection of Snow's theory.

(B) quotes the end of paragraph 4 where the author explained that removal of the pump handle curtailed the cholera outbreak. Because this excerpt contains the phrase "unable to find conclusive proof," it may tempt test takers who mistakenly chose (A) in the preceding question.

(C) quotes a sentence from paragraph 5 that details further steps in Snow's research; it is unrelated to the officials' reactions to his findings.

**19.  C**

**Difficulty:** Hard

**Category:** Detail

**Strategic Advice:** This is a Detail question asking for something "cited" in the passage. Direct your research to paragraph 4, where the author explains how Snow narrowed his search for the cause of the cholera outbreak to the Broad Street pump.

**Getting to the Answer:** According to the passage, Snow interviewed "residents of the area" and discovered that "most of the victims had used a single pump." That is summed up nicely in the correct answer, **(C)**.

(A) restates what those who still held the miasma theory of disease, not Snow, believed to be the outbreak's source.

(B) gets the order of events backwards; Snow's suspicions about the Broad Street pump *led* to the removal of its handle.

(D) also describes a situation Snow discovered *after* the pump handle was removed.

**20.  D**

**Difficulty:** Hard

**Category:** Inference

**Strategic Advice:** The phrase "reasonably inferred" indicates an Inference question. The correct answer will follow from the passage without having been explicitly stated in the passage.

**Getting to the Answer:** At the end of paragraph 5, the passage states that Snow's "revelation"—that workers at the brewery near Broad Street pump boiled the water before using it to make beer—provided a way to prevent future outbreaks. Thus, **(D)** is the correct answer.

(A) is extreme; while the brewery employees were fortunate to avoid contamination, the passage does not imply that drinks containing alcohol could be universally substituted for water.

(B) is extreme; the result of this recommendation would be that no one in the city would have water, which would be untenable.

(C) might be a reasonable suggestion today, but the passage tells you that the bacteria was unknown in 1855.

**21.  A**

**Difficulty:** Medium

**Category:** Vocab-in-Context

**Strategic Advice:** To answer a Vocab-in-Context question, check the sentence in which the word was used for clues about its meaning. The correct answer can be substituted for the word in the question stem without changing the meaning of the sentence.

**Getting to the Answer:** If you know that one meaning of "flag," used as a verb, is *decrease* or *lessen*, this question is straightforward. If you are unfamiliar with this definition, the logic of the sentence still leads to **(A)** as the correct answer. Officials would have replaced the pump handle at the point when public anxiety went down.

(B), *indicated*, suggests a use of "flagged" that would be appropriate in a sentence like, "The teacher flagged the error with a sticky note." In the context of the passage, it does not make sense to say that "public anxiety" was flagged in this way.

(C), *penalized*, might remind you of the way "flagged" is used to describe a referee's actions in a sporting event, but it is not appropriate for this sentence in the passage.

(D), *peaked*, meaning "arriving at the highest point," is opposite of the correct meaning; officials certainly would not replace the pump handle at the height of public anxiety.

## 22. A

**Difficulty:** Hard

**Category:** Function

**Strategic Advice:** A question asking how the author uses a piece of text—in this case, a specific sentence—is a Function question. Research the sentence in the context of the paragraph.

**Getting to the Answer:** The final paragraph of the passage opens with a statement of how Snow is now appreciated as an innovator. The heart of the paragraph then explains how political expediency led to a temporary rejection of his findings. The paragraph's final sentence brings you back to Snow's ultimate vindication, despite an intervening tragedy. **(A)** accurately describes the final sentence's purpose in the paragraph.

(B) distorts the passage; Snow's explanation was accepted because it was effective in preventing cholera, not because he fully explained the bacteria causing the disease.

(C) contradicts the passage; Snow's discovery was applied immediately when officials removed the handle of Broad Street pump.

(D) refers to the 1866 epidemic for the wrong reason; the author mentions this detail to explain what finally motivated acceptance of Snow's ideas, not to criticize the officials' actions.

# CHAPTER 21

# Paired Passages and Primary Source Passages

**LEARNING OBJECTIVES**

After completing this chapter, you will be able to:

- Apply unique strategies to effectively read SAT Reading paired passages in preparation for their question sets

- Apply unique strategies to effectively read SAT Reading passages based on primary sources in preparation for their question sets

- Identify the variations on common SAT Reading questions as they are used in paired passages

# How Much Do You Know?

**Directions:** In this chapter, you'll learn to apply the SAT Reading strategies you learned in earlier chapters to paired passages and passages based on primary sources. Take a few minutes to read the following paired passages and answer the five accompanying questions. When you're finished, compare your work to the explanations on the following pages. Identify ways in which the expert reads these paired passages differently than she would a standard science or social studies passage.

**Questions 1-5 refer to the following passages.**

Passage 1 is adapted from a speech given by Senator Robert Y. Hayne in 1830. Passage 2 is adapted from a speech given in response by Senator Daniel Webster on the following day.

## Passage 1

If I could, by a mere act of my will, put at the disposal of the Federal Government any amount of treasure which I might think proper to name, I should limit the amount to the
5    means necessary for the legitimate purpose of Government. Sir, an immense national treasuring would be a fund for corruption. It would enable Congress and the Executive to exercise a control over States, as well as over
10   great interests in the country, nay even over corporations and individuals—utterly destructive of the purity, and fatal to the duration of our institutions. It would be equally fatal to the sovereignty and independence of the States. Sir,
15   I am one of those who believe that the very life of our system is the independence of the States, and there is no evil more to be deprecated than the consolidation of this Government. It is only by a strict adherence to the limitations imposed
20   by the constitution on the Federal Government, that this system works well, and can answer the great ends for which it was instituted. I am opposed, therefore, in any shape, to all unnecessary extension of the powers, or the
25   influence of the Legislature or Executive of the Union over the States, or the people of the States; and, most of all, I am opposed to

those partial distributions of favors, whether by legislation or appropriation, which has a direct
30   and powerful tendency to spread corruption through the land; to create an abject spirit of dependence; to sow the seeds of dissolution; to produce jealousy among the different portions of the Union, and finally to sap the very
35   foundations of the Government itself.

## Passage 2

As a reason for wishing to get rid of the public lands as soon as we could, and as we might, the honorable gentleman said, he wanted no permanent sources of income. He wished to
40   see the time when the Government should not possess a shilling of permanent revenue. If he could speak a magical word, and by that word convert the whole capital into gold, the word should not be spoken. The administration of a
45   fixed revenue, [he said] only consolidates the Government, and corrupts the people! Sir, I confess I heard these sentiments uttered on this floor with deep regret and pain.

I am aware that these, and similar opinions,
50   are espoused by certain persons out of the capitol, and out of this Government; but I did not expect so soon to find them here. Consolidation!—that perpetual cry, both of terror and delusion— consolidation! Sir, when gentlemen speak of the
55   effects of a common fund, belonging to all the States, as having a tendency to consolidation, what do they mean? Do they mean, or can they mean, anything more than that the Union of the States will be strengthened, by whatever
60   continues or furnishes inducements to the people of the States to hold together? If they mean merely this, then, no doubt, the public lands as well as everything else in which we have a common interest, tends to consolidation; and to
65   this idea of consolidation every true American ought to be attached; it is neither more nor less than strengthening the Union itself. This is the sense in which the framers of the constitution use

the word consolidation; and in which sense I adopt
70 and cherish it. . . .

This, sir, is General Washington's consolidation. This is the true constitutional consolidation. I wish to see no new powers drawn to the General Government; but I confess I rejoice in whatever
75 tends to strengthen the bond that unites us, and encourages the hope that our Union may be perpetual. And, therefore, I cannot but feel regret at the expression of such opinions as the gentleman has avowed; because I think their obvious tendency
80 is to weaken the bond of our connection.

1. In passage 2, Webster most likely refers to General Washington in order to

   A) make a colorful analogy.

   B) emphasize the precedent for his position.

   C) compare himself to Washington in order to seem more credible.

   D) emphasize the honesty of his position.

2. Which choice best characterizes how Webster responds to Hayne?

   A) He challenges Hayne's understanding of economics.

   B) He cites historical examples to show that Hayne's predictions will not come true.

   C) He finds a neutral path between his position and Hayne's.

   D) He attempts to turn a key word that Hayne uses against him.

3. Based on the ideas expressed in Passage 1, Hayne would most likely rebut Webster's claim in lines 61–67 ("If they mean . . . strengthening the Union itself") by stating that

   A) he (Hayne) does not wish the Union to have more money.

   B) it was a mistake to form a Union.

   C) the Union would weaken if the states were less independent.

   D) the Union will be more corrupt if the Legislative and Executive branches consolidate into one.

4. Which choice provides the best evidence for the answer to the previous question?

   A) Lines 1–6 ("If I could . . . of Government")

   B) Lines 6–7 ("Sir . . . corruption")

   C) Lines 22–24 ("am opposed . . . powers")

   D) Lines 32–35 ("to sow . . . itself")

5. On which of the following points do the writers of the passages express agreement?

   A) The Federal Government should not acquire new powers.

   B) The Constitution alone may not adequately address the current situation.

   C) Money can be a corrupting influence.

   D) The Federal Government is spending more than it can afford.

## Check Your Work

Suggested passage notes:

**Passage 1**

> ¶1: (lines 1–14): Limit money of gov't
>
> ¶1: (lines 15–35): Gov't control of states = bad

**Passage 2**

> ¶1: Hayne would not allow gov't perm. income
>
> ¶2: Common fund, Consolidation = Strength of Union
>
> ¶3: Consolid. goes with Constitution, Washington

**1. B**

**Difficulty:** Easy

**Category:** Function

**Strategic Advice:** Function questions ask you why the author included a given detail. Research the detail to help make a prediction, and if necessary, read any surrounding text to help put it in context.

**Getting to the Answer:** The reference to George Washington comes in the third paragraph. Both before and after the reference, Webster mentions the Constitution, and how he wishes to abide by it. Thus, he intends for his ideas to be in the spirit of Washington and the Founders. (Keep in mind that appeals to documents and authorities are common in primary source passages.) Webster is using Washington as a precedent, or established guide, making **(B)** correct.

Washington is neither part of an analogy, nor is he compared to Webster, so eliminate (A) and (C). While you may have a sense of Washington as an "honest" figure, there is nothing in the passage that mentions his honesty, so eliminate (D).

**2. D**

**Difficulty:** Medium

**Category:** Inference

**Strategic Advice:** You need to draw an inference about how Webster "responds to Hayne," so this is an Inference question. Expect the answer to relate to Webster's main point and consult your passage map for help.

**Getting to the Answer:** In the the first paragraph, Webster characterizes Hayne's position, explaining that it makes him feel "deep regret and pain." Primary source passages are explicit about their main ideas, so after reading this, predict that Webster will soon explain *why*

it makes him feel pain. He does so in the second paragraph, focusing on the term *consolidation*. He explains that, no matter how much his opponents claim to fear it, it means "strengthening the Union itself." This matches **(D)**.

You could also get to the correct answer by process of elimination. Although Webster notes with humor that Hayne would not "convert the whole capital into gold" given the chance, he does not discuss Hayne's understanding of economics, so (A) is incorrect. While he mentions George Washington, he never uses historical examples to refute any predictions, so (B) is incorrect. Webster states his position quite strongly; this is no "neutral path," so (C) is incorrect as well.

**3. C**

**Difficulty:** Hard

**Category:** Inference

**Strategic Advice:** For Inference questions asking how one author would respond to a claim made by the other, start by reading the claim. Then, look for clues in the other passage that indicate how its author would respond. The latter step is especially useful when the next question is a Command of Evidence.

**Getting to the Answer:** The claim is that consolidation—in this case, indicating a "common fund" for the government—will keep the people of the states together and "[strengthen] the Union." Go back to Hayne's passage for evidence of how he would respond to this. When discussing consolidation, Hayne valorizes "independence of the States," noting that "there is no evil more to be deprecated than the consolidation of this Government." Hayne would contend that consolidation would weaken the States' independence, and he concludes that this in turn would "sow the seeds of dissolution; produce jealousy among the different portions of the Union, and sap the very foundations of the Government itself." This fits **(C)**.

Choice (A) is incorrect because although Hayne wishes to limit the government's permanent revenue, this does not specifically refute Webster's claim about strengthening the Union. (B) is too extreme; while Hayne may wish to limit the federal government's power, he never indicates that the Union should never have existed. (D) distorts the passage. "Consolidation" in this context has nothing to do with the Legislative and Executive branches becoming one.

**4.   D**

**Difficulty:** Hard

**Category:** Command of Evidence

**Strategic Advice:** Look back at your research for the previous question and determine what portion of text you used to support your answer.

**Getting to the Answer:** Your previous answer was supported with the phrase "sow the seeds of dissolution; produce jealousy among the different portions of the Union, and sap the very foundations of the Government itself." **(D)** is correct.

**5.   A**

**Difficulty:** Hard

**Category:** Detail

**Getting to the Answer:** Hayne's main point is that the federal government should be limited to preserve States' independence. As much as Webster disagrees with Hayne, he actually concedes this point in his final paragraph: "I wish to see no new powers drawn to the General Government." **(A)** is correct.

Both writers would seem to disagree with (B), since they both regard the Constitution as an authority. While Hayne worries about the corrupting influence of money, Webster does not, so (C) is incorrect. You might be tempted by (D), since Hayne wishes to curtail the federal government's activities and Webster believes that it requires permanent income. However, there is not enough information in the passage to determine that the federal government is already spending more than it can afford.

# How to Approach SAT Paired Passages and Primary Sources

**LEARNING OBJECTIVES**

After completing this chapter, you will be able to:

- Apply unique strategies to effectively read SAT Reading paired passages in preparation for their question sets
- Apply unique strategies to effectively read SAT Reading passages based on primary sources in preparation for their question sets
- Identify the variations on common SAT Reading questions as they are used in paired passages

## What are paired passages?

In every SAT Reading section, there is always exactly one pair of shorter passages that takes the place of a single longer passage. The two passages share the same topic (although they'll each have their own take on the subject matter). The combined length of the paired passages is approximately the length of most single passages, so you don't have much, if any, extra reading to do. In this chapter, you'll learn to read paired passages a little differently than you read single passages, and you'll see how the test uses variations of standard SAT Reading questions to test your comprehension of both passages.

## What are primary source passages?

In every SAT Reading section, exactly one of the passages (or paired passage sets) is one in which the text is a primary source—a text written or recorded at the time of an event by people with first-hand knowledge of it (for example, laws, speeches, newspaper accounts, and essays). SAT experts expect the language in these passages to reflect an older and more formal style. In many cases, the documents express the strongly articulated position of its author or speaker.

## Why learn paired passages and primary sources together?

The one set of paired passages in a Reading section often contain primary sources as their texts. While it is possible that you could see science material in a paired passage set, it's more likely that this is where the primary sources will appear, so it makes sense to practice the skills that apply to both categories of passages together.

**To read passages like these and to answer their questions:**

**Directions:** Choose the best answer choice for the following questions.

**Questions 1-2 refer to the following passages.**

Passage 1 is adapted from a speech (1852) by writer, reformer, and ex-slave Frederick Douglass. It was presented at an event commemorating the signing of the Declaration of Independence. Passage 2 is adapted from an essay (1836) by political activist Angelina Emily Grimké. Both writers were active in the abolitionist, or anti-slavery, movement.

**Passage 1**

O! had I the ability, and could I reach the nation's ear, I would, to-day, pour out a fiery stream of biting ridicule, blasting reproach, withering sarcasm, and stern rebuke. For it is
5 not light that is needed, but fire; it is not the gentle shower, but thunder. We need the storm, the whirlwind, and the earthquake. The feeling of the nation must be quickened; the conscience of the nation must be roused; the propriety of
10 the nation must be startled; the hypocrisy of the nation must be exposed; and its crimes against God and man must be proclaimed and denounced.

What, to the American slave, is your 4th
15 of July? I answer: a day that reveals to him, more than all other days in the year, the gross injustice and cruelty to which he is the constant victim. To him, your celebration is a sham; your boasted liberty, an unholy license;
20 your national greatness, swelling vanity; your sounds of rejoicing are empty and heartless; your denunciations of tyrants, brass fronted impudence; your shouts of liberty and equality, hollow mockery; your prayers and hymns,
25 your sermons and thanksgivings, with all your religious parade, and solemnity, are, to him, mere bombast, fraud, deception, impiety, and hypocrisy—a thin veil to cover up crimes which would disgrace a nation of savages. There is not
30 a nation on the earth guilty of practices, more

shocking and bloody, than are the people of these United States, at this very hour.

Go where you may, search where you will, roam through all the monarchies and despotisms
35 of the old world, travel through South America, search out every abuse, and when you have found the last, lay your facts by the side of the everyday practices of this nation, and you will say with me, that, for revolting barbarity and shameless
40 hypocrisy, America reigns without a rival.

**Passage 2**

The women of the South can overthrow this horrible system of oppression and cruelty, licentiousness and wrong. Such appeals to your legislatures would be irresistible, for there is
45 something in the heart of man which will bend under moral suasion. There is a swift witness for truth in his bosom, which will respond to truth when it is uttered with calmness and dignity. If you could obtain but six signatures
50 to such a petition in only one state, I would say, send up that petition, and be not in the least discouraged by the scoffs, and jeers of the heartless, or the resolution of the house to lay it on the table. It will be a great thing if the subject
55 can be introduced into your legislatures in any way, even by women, and they will be the most likely to introduce it there in the best possible manner, as a matter of morals and religion, not of expediency or politics. You may petition, too, the
60 different ecclesiastical bodies of the slave states. Slavery must be attacked with the whole power of truth and the sword of the spirit.

1.  Which best describes the overall relationship between the two passages?

    A)  Passage 2 provides a restatement of Passage 1's central claims.

    B)  Passage 2 describes specific steps that could address a problem described in Passage 1.

    C)  Passage 2 contests the point of view expressed in Passage 1.

    D)  Passage 2 contains additional evidence that could support the claims made in Passage 1.

2.  Based on Passage 2, Grimké would most likely offer which of the following responses to Douglass's statement in lines 7–13 ("The feeling . . . denounced")?

    A)  Women will be the most effective agents of Douglass's call to action.

    B)  The nation's conscience is too hardened to embrace Douglass's rhetoric.

    C)  The most effective way to communicate Douglass's message is to highlight the plight of female slaves.

    D)  Douglass's critique of the United States is too political to be delivered by women.

## You'll need to know this:

### About paired passages

- Paired passages always address the same topic but will likely have different purposes and may reflect different opinions. Common relationships between the passages include:
  - (Passage 1) One side in a debate over a policy, a moral or ethical issue, or the role of government and (Passage 2) the other side of that debate
  - (Passage 1) A law or a policy proposal and (Passage 2) a commentary on or evaluation of the law or proposal (especially from a person affected by the law or policy)
  - (Passage 1) A report on an event or conflict and (Passage 2) a speech or document from a person involved in the event or conflict
  - (Passage 1) Commentary on an issue as reflected through one social context and (Passage 2) commentary on the same issue reflected through a different context
- The authors of paired passages may disagree with each other but do not have to.
- When paired passages refer to the same detail, each author may have a different reason for including the detail and a different point of view toward it.

### About Primary Source Passages

- The SAT always identifies the author(s)/speaker(s) and the date(s) of primary source texts in the blurb introducing the passage(s).
- The main point (thesis or conclusion) of the author/speaker is usually explicitly stated in a primary source text.
- Authors/speakers in primary source texts often support their positions with appeals to broad, abstract concepts (e.g., divine law, natural law, human rights, the common good, dignity, or progress).
- The test never asks if an author's or speaker's opinion is correct (or, in the case of paired passages with primary source texts, which author's position or argument is better).

### About Paired Passage Questions

- The question set accompanying paired passages addresses the passages in order: roughly, the first third of the questions are about Passage 1, the next third are about Passage 2, and the final third are about the relationships between the two passages.
- The questions that address single passages are just like those from standard science and social science passages.
- Some questions that address the relationships between the passages are variations on standard SAT Reading question types. For example:
  - **Global**
    - "The primary purpose of each passage is to"
  - **Detail**
    - "Both passages discuss the role of the judiciary in relationship to"

- ○ **Inference**
  - "Based on the passages, both authors would agree with which of the following claims?"
  - "Both authors would most likely agree that the expansion of enfranchisement reflects"
- ○ **Function**
  - "In the context of each passage as a whole, the examples in lines 30–34 of Passage 1 and lines 60–63 of Passage 2 primarily function to help each speaker"
- Other questions are intentionally written to test how accurately you can compare or contrast the two passages or their authors. For example:
  - ○ **Global**
    - "Which choice best states the relationship between the two passages?"
    - "Which choice identifies a central tension between the two passages?"
  - ○ **Inference**
    - "How would the authors of Passage 1 most likely respond to the points made in the final paragraph of Passage 2?"
    - "Madison in Passage 1 would most likely characterize the position taken by Hancock in lines 71–79 in Passage 2 ("Manners, by which . . . memory") as"
    - "Stanton would most likely have reacted to lines 69–72 ("Therefore . . . without fail") of Passage 2 with"

## You'll need to do this:

### To Actively Read Paired Passages

- Unpack the blurb to discover all that you can about each passage and author; anticipate the possible relationships between the passages.
- Manage your active reading and the question set strategically:
  - ○ Actively read Passage 1 as you would a standard passage—note keywords, jot down the purpose of each paragraph, and summarize the big picture.
  - ○ Answer the questions associated exclusively with Passage 1 (roughly, the first third of the question set).
  - ○ Actively read Passage 2 as you would a standard passage—note keywords, jot down the purpose of each paragraph, and summarize the big picture.
  - ○ Answer the questions associated exclusively with Passage 2 (roughly, the next third in the question set).
  - ○ Answer the questions that ask about both passages in relationship to each other (the final third in the question set).

### To Actively Read Primary Source Passages

- Unpack the opening blurb to identify the author(s) and historical time period of the passage(s).
- If you know something about the author(s), issue, or historical period, use that knowledge to anticipate what the passage(s) will say. However:
  - ○ Be careful *not* to answer questions based on your outside knowledge.
  - ○ The correct answers *must* be supported by the passage text.

- Actively read the passage as you would a standard social science passage, keeping the following in mind:

  o Don't be discouraged if a primary source text contains antiquated or formal language; define unfamiliar words from context.

  o Locate the author's/speaker's main point (it may be a thesis statement near the beginning of the passage or a concluding summary near the end); if you could boil down the author's position to a single sentence, which one would it be?

  o Note where and how the author/speaker supports the main point.

**To Strategically Answer Paired Passages Questions**

- Research, predict, and answer questions exclusively addressing one of the passages as you would any standard SAT Reading question.

- To predict and answer Global questions comparing or contrasting both passages, consider your big picture summaries.

- To research, predict, and answer Inference questions comparing or contrasting both passages:

  1. Locate the piece of text at issue in the question stem.

  2. Consider the other author's likely reaction to or opinion of that piece of text.

  3. Especially if the Inference question is followed by a Command of Evidence question, locate the piece of text that supplies the "other author's" likely response. For example, consider this question stem: "Madison in Passage 1 would most likely characterize the position taken by Hancock in lines 71–79 in Passage 2 ("Manners, by which . . . memory") as"

     - First, research the Hancock text from Passage 2 quoted in the question stem. What does it mean? What is Hancock's point?

     - Second, consider what you know about Madison's likely response. Would he agree or disagree with Hancock's point? Why or why not?

     - Third, put your finger on the text in Passage 1 that supports Madison's likely response.

## Explanation:

**Question 1.** This Global question asks you to determine the "overall relationship" between the passages. Consult your passage notes to determine how the passages relate. As you might expect, given the blurb, each writer expresses a strong anti-slavery sentiment. However, while the first passage deals more with the injustices of slavery in the United States, the second focuses more on specific plans to change relevant law ("If you could obtain but six signatures to such a petition. . ."). Therefore, it's accurate to say that Passage 2 "describes specific steps that could address a problem described in Passage 1," **(B)**.

**Question 2.** This Inference question asks you for the choice that captures Grimké's likely response to Douglass's call to arouse the nation's consciousness in paragraph 1 of Passage 1. The thesis of Grimké's passage is that women can overthrow slavery and, she says, "they will be the most likely to introduce [anti-slavery petitions] in the best possible manner" (lines 56–58). Thus, she seems to believe that women are the most effective messengers for the kinds of critiques Douglass recommends. That matches choice **(A)**.

Choice (B) contradicts Grimké's hopeful attitude toward change. (C) distorts Grimké's suggestion; she thinks women should be the ones to call for an end to slavery, not that focusing on female slaves is the best way to do so. (D) distorts Grimké's point in lines 58–59; she says that, coming from women, the anti-slavery message will be seen as moral and religious rather than political, but her comment does not imply a critique of Douglass's clearly moral message as being political in nature.

## Try on Your Own

**Directions:** Actively read these paired primary source passages and answer their accompanying questions. Try to employ the unique reading strategies experts use for paired passages and primary source texts. Take note of any question stems that are specifically tailored to fit paired passages so that you can research, predict, and answer them strategically.

### Questions 1-10 refer to the following passages.

Passage 1 is adapted from Federalist Paper No. 64 (1788), by John Jay, in which he discusses the powers of the President and the Senate to form treaties under Article II of the Constitution. Passage 2 is adapted from Federalist Paper No. 75 (1788), by Alexander Hamilton, on the same subject.

### Passage 1

The second section gives power to the President, "*by and with the advice and consent of the Senate, to make treaties, provided two thirds of the Senators present concur . . .*"

5 Some are displeased with it, not on account of any errors or defects in it, but because they say the treaties will have the force of laws, and thus should be made only by the legislature. These gentlemen seem not

10 to consider that the judgement of our courts, and the commissions constitutionally given by our governor, are as valid and as binding on all persons whom they concern as the laws passed by our legislature. All constitutional

15 acts of power, whether in the executive or in the judicial department, have as much legal validity and obligation as if they proceeded from the legislature. It surely does not follow that because the people have given the power

20 of making laws to the legislature, they should therefore likewise give the legislature the power to do every other act of government by which the citizens are to be bound and affected.

### Passage 2

The President is to have power, "by and

25 with the advice and consent of the Senate, to make treaties, provided two thirds of the senators present concur." . . .

Though several writers on the subject of government place the power of making

30 treaties in the class of executive authorities, this is evidently an arbitrary classification; for if we attend carefully to its operation, it will be found to partake more of the legislative than of the executive character, though it does

35 not seem strictly to fall within the definition of either of them. The essence of the legislative branch is to enact laws, or, in other words, to prescribe rules for the regulation of the society; while the execution of the laws, and

40 the employment of the common strength, either for this purpose or for the common defense, seem to comprise all the functions of the executive branch. The power of making treaties is, plainly, neither the one nor the

45 other. It relates neither to the execution of the existing laws, nor to the creation of new ones; and still less to an exertion of the common strength. Its objects are CONTRACTS with foreign nations, which have the force of law,

50 but derive it from the obligations of good faith. They are not rules prescribed by the government of the citizen, but agreements between two governments. The power in question seems therefore to form a distinct

55 department, and to belong, properly, neither to the legislative nor to the executive branch. The qualities elsewhere detailed as indispensable in the management of foreign negotiations point to the Executive as the best agent in

60 those transactions; while the vast importance of the trust, and the operation of treaties as laws, plead strongly for the participation of the whole or a portion of the legislative body in the office of making them.

1. Jay includes the reasoning of those who are displeased with the president's treaty-making power (lines 5–9) in order to

   A) provide an opposing conclusion that gives context for his own argument.

   B) acknowledge flaws and defects in Article II of the Constitution.

   C) explain the importance of the legislature in creating laws that impact citizens.

   D) support his own opinions about judicial and executive authority.

2. What does Passage 1 suggest about Jay's opponents' opinion of the second section of Article II of the Constitution?

   A) Jay's opponents' criticisms of the second section would be legitimate if the second section contained errors and defects.

   B) Jay's opponents think anything having the same force as a law is, in effect, a law.

   C) Jay's opponents perceive the legislature as the only branch that should act in ways that legally bind citizens.

   D) Jay's opponents agree with Jay that the legislature should be empowered to enact all duties of government.

3. Which choice provides the best evidence for the answer to the previous question?

   A) Lines 5–9 ("Some are . . . legislature")

   B) Lines 9–14 ("These gentlemen . . . legislature")

   C) Lines 14–18 ("All constitutional . . . legislature")

   D) Lines 17–24 ("It surely . . . affected")

4. Based on Passage 2, it can be inferred that Hamilton would agree with which of the following statements?

   A) Most writers on the subject of government fail to provide evidence sufficient to support their conclusions.

   B) Citizens should not be bound by agreements between one government and another.

   C) Any power that is not properly described as judicial or legislative must be an executive power.

   D) At least some writers on the subject of government reach unsubstantiated conclusions about the scope of executive authority.

5. Which choice provides the best evidence for the answer to the previous question?

   A) Lines 27–31 ("Though several . . . classification")

   B) Lines 36–39 ("The essence . . . society")

   C) Lines 48–51 ("Its objects . . . faith")

   D) Lines 60–64 ("While the . . . them")

6. As used in line 33, "partakes" most nearly means

   A) consumes.

   B) shares.

   C) receives.

   D) savor.

7. As used in line 64, "office" most nearly means

   A) bureaucracy.

   B) workplace.

   C) commission.

   D) situation.

8. Which choice best states the relationship between the two passages?

   A) Both passages refute different points using different evidence but reach the same conclusion.

   B) Passage 2 and Passage 1 examine different but related propositions.

   C) Passage 2 questions assumptions made by the author of Passage 1.

   D) Passages 1 and 2 use different examples to illustrate the same reasoning.

9. Based on Passage 2, how would Hamilton most likely respond to Jay's statement that the decisions of the judicial and executive branches "are as valid and as binding on all persons whom they concern as the laws passed by our legislature" (lines 12–14)?

   A) Hamilton would agree that all non-legislative rules are legitimately binding, and he would agree about the source of that power.

   B) Hamilton would disagree that treaties are as valid as laws passed by the legislature because treaties are contracts.

   C) Hamilton would agree that at least some rules prescribed by the executive branch are just as valid as those issued from the legislature.

   D) Hamilton would disagree with Jay's contention that judicial decisions are as valid as laws passed by the legislature.

10. In Passage 1, Jay's statement at lines 7–9 ("they say . . . legislature") and in Passage 2, Hamilton's statement at lines 36–39 ("The essence . . . society") both serve to help the authors

   A) argue that the power to make treaties should reside exclusively with the legislature.

   B) critique those who place in the power to make treaties in the class of executive authorities.

   C) define the widely accepted role of the legislative branch to make laws.

   D) support the contention that treaties carry the same legal authority as laws.

# How Much Have You Learned?

**Directions:** Now, complete a similar assessment under timed conditions. Take 12 minutes to read the passage and answer the accompanying questions

**Questions 11-21 refer to the following passages.**

Passage 1 is adapted from an 1823 speech by President James Monroe, in which he discusses European colonialism in the Americas. The position expressed in this speech would eventually become known as the Monroe Doctrine. Passage 2 is adapted from a 1905 speech by President Theodore Roosevelt. His position would become known as the Roosevelt Corollary to the Monroe Doctrine.

## Passage 1

The American continents, by the free
and independent condition which they have
assumed and maintain, are hence forth
not to be considered as subjects for future
5  colonization by any European powers.

The citizens of the United States cherish
friendly sentiments in favor of the liberty
and happiness of their fellow men on the
European side of the Atlantic. In the wars of
10  the European powers in matters relating to
themselves we have never taken any part, nor
does it comport with our policy to do so.

It is only when our rights are invaded or
seriously menaced that we resent injuries
15  or make preparation for our defense. With
the movements in our own hemisphere we
are more immediately connected, by causes
which must be obvious to all enlightened and
impartial observers.

20  We owe it, therefore, to candor and to
the amicable relations existing between the
United States and European nations to declare
that we should consider any attempt on their
part to extend their system of government to
25  any portion of this hemisphere as dangerous
to our peace and safety. With the existing
colonies or dependencies of any European
power we have not interfered and shall
not interfere. However, we could not view

30  any meddling with those former European
colonies who have declared their independence
and maintained it, and whose independence
we have, on great consideration and on just
principles, acknowledged, in any other light
35  than as the manifestation of an unfriendly
disposition toward the United States.

## Passage 2

It is not true that the United States feels
any land hunger or entertains any projects
regarding the other nations of the Western
40  Hemisphere except for their welfare. All that
this country desires is to see our neighboring
countries stable, orderly, and prosperous. Any
country whose people conduct themselves
well can count upon our hearty friendship.
45  If a nation shows that it knows how to act
with reasonable efficiency and decency in
social and political matters, if it keeps order
and pays its obligations, it need not fear
interference from the United States. However,
50  chronic wrongdoing, or an impotence
which results in a general loosening of the
ties of civilized society, may in America, as
elsewhere, ultimately require intervention. . . .
In the Western Hemisphere, the adherence of
55  the United States to the Monroe Doctrine may
force the United States, however reluctantly,
in flagrant cases of such wrongdoing or
impotence, to the exercise of an international
police power. If every country washed by
60  the Caribbean Sea would show the progress
in stable and just civilization which Cuba
has shown since our troops left the island,
and which so many of the republics in both
Americas are constantly and brilliantly
65  showing, all question of interference by this
Nation with their affairs would be at an
end. Our interests and those of our southern
neighbors are in reality identical. They have
great natural riches, and if within their
70  borders the reign of law and justice obtains,
prosperity is sure to come to them. While

Reading

they thus obey the primary laws of civilized
society, they may rest assured that they will be
treated by us in a spirit of cordial and helpful
75 sympathy. We would interfere with them only
in the last resort, and then only if it became
evident that their inability or unwillingness to
do justice at home and abroad had violated the
rights of the United States or had invited foreign
80 aggression to the detriment of the entire body
of American nations. Every nation, whether
in America or anywhere else, which desires
to maintain its freedom and independence
must ultimately realize that the right of such
85 independence can not be separated from the
responsibility of making good use of it.

11. The primary purpose of the statement in lines 6–9
    ("The citizens . . . of the Atlantic") is to

    A) respond to critics of the United States.

    B) mislead the audience regarding Monroe's intent.

    C) recommend that people adopt a certain
       attitude.

    D) balance the overall tone of the message.

12. When discussing his views on foreign policy in
    Passage 1, Monroe indicates that the United States
    does not intend to

    A) prevent further European colonization in the
       Americas.

    B) intervene in conflicts that exist solely between
       European powers.

    C) maintain a friendly relationship with European
       powers.

    D) allow European powers to keep their existing
       colonies in the Americas.

13. Which choice provides the best evidence for the
    answer to the previous question?

    A) Lines 9–12 ("In the . . . do so")

    B) Lines 15–19 ("With the . . . observers")

    C) Lines 20–26 ("We owe . . . safety")

    D) Lines 29–36 ("However . . . States")

14. According to Roosevelt in Passage 2, what circum-
    stance must exist before the United States may justi-
    fiably interfere with the affairs of another nation in
    the Western Hemisphere?

    A) The other nation must have been invaded by a
       foreign power.

    B) The other nation must have invaded a foreign
       power.

    C) The other nation must have harmed the
       United States.

    D) The other nation must have committed human
       rights abuses.

15. Which choice provides the best evidence for the answer to the previous question?

    A) Lines 42–44 ("Any country . . . friendship")

    B) Lines 59–67 ("If every . . . end")

    C) Lines 68–71 ("They have . . . them")

    D) Lines 75–81 ("We would . . . nations")

16. As used in line 59, "washed" most nearly means

    A) cleaned.

    B) overwhelmed.

    C) touched.

    D) bathed.

17. As used in line 70, "obtains" most nearly means

    A) gathers.

    B) seizes.

    C) collects.

    D) prevails.

18. Which of the following best describes the relationship between the passages?

    A) Passage 2 expands an idea that was mentioned briefly in Passage 1.

    B) Passage 2 disputes the primary argument advanced in Passage 1.

    C) Passage 2 provides examples to support a central claim made in Passage 1.

    D) Passage 2 offers a justification for the main opinion asserted in Passage 1.

19. Based on the information contained in the passages, it is likely that Monroe and Roosevelt were each motivated at least in part by

    A) a lack of political stability in the Western Hemisphere.

    B) threatened or potential aggression by foreign powers.

    C) ongoing criticism from their political opponents.

    D) a strong commitment to pacifism.

20. Based on the ideas expressed in Passage 1, Monroe would most likely characterize Roosevelt's claim in lines 67–68 ("Our interests . . . identical") as

    A) an appropriate understanding of the relationship between countries in the Americas.

    B) an unfair characterization of an opinion expressed in the Monroe Doctrine.

    C) an unwarranted exaggeration of the actual state of affairs in the Western Hemisphere.

    D) an example of a phenomenon mentioned in the Monroe Doctrine.

21. Which of the following statements can be supported by Passage 2 but not by Passage 1?

    A) The United States intends to maintain friendly relationships with other nations.

    B) European powers should refrain from intervening in matters affecting only North and South America.

    C) At least one nation in the Americas other than the United States has achieved political stability.

    D) The United States should adopt a position of neutrality regarding all conflicts between foreign powers.

# Reflect

**Directions:** Take a few minutes to recall what you've learned and what you've been practicing in this chapter. Consider the following questions, jot down your best answer for each one, and then compare your reflections to the expert responses on the following page. Use your level of confidence to determine what to do next.

What are SAT Reading paired passages? How do expert test takers adjust their active reading to tackle paired passages most effectively?

_____

_____

_____

How are the question sets that accompany paired passages different from those accompanying standard single passages?

_____

_____

_____

What are SAT Reading primary source passages? How do expert test takers adjust their active reading to tackle primary source passages most effectively?

_____

_____

_____

How confident do you feel with paired passages and primary source texts? What can you do in practice to improve your performance and gain even more confidence with these types of passages?

_____

_____

_____

## Expert Responses

What are SAT Reading paired passages? How do expert test takers adjust their active reading to tackle paired passages most effectively?

*On each SAT test, one Reading stimulus is a pair of shorter passages instead of a single, long passage. Expert test takers actively read each passage and answer the questions exclusively associated with each. Then, experts compare and contrast the passages' big pictures and details and answer questions associated with both.*

How are the question sets that accompany paired passages different from those accompanying standard single passages?

*Roughly, the first third of the question set exclusively addresses Passage 1; the next third exclusively addresses Passage 2; and the final third addresses comparisons and contrasts between the passages. The compare/contrast-both-passage question stems are uniquely worded to reward students who accurately summarize the big picture of each passage, and who can determine how one author would likely respond to something argued or proposed by the other author.*

What are SAT Reading primary source passages? How do expert test takers adjust their active reading to tackle primary source passages most effectively?

*On each SAT, one passage (or often, the paired passage set) comes from primary sources, first hand accounts of historical events or issues. Expert readers use what they know about the authors and events to help anticipate the passages. They actively read for the author's main point and note where and how the author supports that point.*

How confident do you feel with paired passages and primary source texts? What can you do in practice to improve your performance and gain even more confidence with these types of passages?

*There is no one-size-fits-all answer for this question. Give yourself honest self-assessment. If you feel that paired passages or primary sources are a strength, congratulations! Continue to practice them so that you'll be able to rack up the points associated with these passages on test day. If you feel less confident about either the paired passage format or primary source content, review the strategies in this chapter and try to consistently apply the expert approaches outlined here whenever you practice passages in this format.*

## Next Steps

If you answered most questions correctly in the "How Much Have You Learned?" section, and if your responses to the Reflect questions were similar to those of the SAT expert, then consider paired and primary source passages an area of strength and move on to the next chapter. Come back to this topic periodically to prevent yourself from getting rusty.

If you don't yet feel confident, review the material in "How to Deal with Paired Passages," then try the questions you missed again. As always, be sure to review the explanations closely.

# Answers and Explanations

Suggested Passage 1 notes:

> Lines 1–4: president + 2/3 senate can make treaties
> Lines 5–9: objection
> Lines 9–18: Jay's response
> Lines 18–23: Jay's conclusion

Suggested Passage 2 notes:

> Lines 24–36: treaties not purely legislative or executive, but legis. better
> Lines 36–39: responsibilities of legislative
> Lines 39–43: responsibilities of executive
> Lines 43–56: treaties = contracts w/foreign nations, don't fit either branch
> Lines 56–60: reasons to assign to executive
> Lines 61–64: reasons to assign to legislative

## 1.   A

**Difficulty:** Medium

**Category:** Function

**Strategic Advice:** When a question asks about the purpose of some part of the passage, consider the author's intentions. What is the author trying *to do* with this paragraph, sentence, phrase, word, or in this case, punctuation? Imagine taking away the selected part of the passage and think about how the meaning of the remaining text changes.

**Getting to the Answer:** Here, if you take away the quotations about what Jay's opponents think (lines 5–9), the beginning of paragraph 2 becomes less clear because there would be no point against which Jay is arguing, so his conclusions would lack context. Thus, your prediction should be that Jay brings up an opposing opinion so he can knock it down to bolster his own conclusion. That matches **(A)**.

Eliminate (B) because it contradicts Jay, who explicitly says that there are no errors or defects in the treaties clause of the Constitution. (C) misuses a detail; the ability of the legislature to create laws that impact citizens' lives is important, but that is not why Jay included the critique of the president's treaty-making authority in the passage. (D) distorts Jay's purpose in mentioning these critics; he goes on to point out what they have overlooked, not to use their criticism to support his own views.

## 2.   C

**Difficulty:** Medium

**Category:** Inference

**Strategic Advice:** Use the main idea of the passage to make a general prediction. Review what was explicitly said in the passage based on your passage map. Then, evaluate each answer choice.

**Getting to the Answer:** The first paragraph of Passage 1 addresses Jay's opponents' opinions. These opponents are displeased because they believe that only the legislature should make laws, so this should be the basis of your prediction. **(C)** provides the best match and is correct.

(A) is incorrect because Jay acknowledges that his opponents' arguments are not based on any errors in the Constitution, and there's no way to know whether Jay would agree with them if there were flaws. (B) is incorrect because it misuses a detail; Jay's opponents are not upset about the loose definition of a law, but rather who has the authority to create rules and bind citizens to those rules. (D) contradicts the passage; Jay disagrees with his opponents.

## 3.   A

**Difficulty:** Easy

**Category:** Command of Evidence

**Strategic Advice:** Look for an answer that cites text supporting the previous answer. Consider keywords in the quotations to spot those that refer to the topic in question.

**Getting to the Answer:** Look back to your answer for question 2; how did you arrive there? The second and third sentences of Passage 1 provide the only direct references to Jay's opponents' opinions. **(A)** is correct because it suggests the viewpoint of Jay's opponents: that laws should be made exclusively by the legislature.

Eliminate (B) because it explains Jay's response to his opponents, not his opponents' opinion. Eliminate (C) because it is part of the evidence Jay uses in his response to the argument of his opponents. (D) is Jay's clarification of his own point, not the opinion of his opponents.

**4. D**

**Difficulty:** Hard

**Category:** Inference

**Strategic Advice:** It may be difficult to make a specific prediction for open-ended Inference questions like this one, but the correct answer must follow from the passage. Review your passage map as needed to evaluate each answer choice.

**Getting to the Answer:** To test the choices for an open-ended Inference question, keep in mind that the correct answer will follow from the passage text. Evaluate each choice by asking: "Is this true based on on the passage?" (A) fails this test because it is too broad; Hamilton passes no judgment on "most" writers. (B) falls outside the scope; Hamilton opines on the power to make treaties, but not on their authority over citizens. (C) is extreme; Hamilton does not claim that *any* power that is neither legislative nor judicial is executive. This leaves **(D)**, the correct answer, which is supported in the text by lines 28–31 ("Though several . . . classification"). If Hamilton thinks this classification is arbitrary, then it must not be adequately substantiated.

**5. A**

**Difficulty:** Medium

**Category:** Command of Evidence

**Strategic Advice:** For a Command of Evidence question, use the line number references in each answer choice to research the passage. If you spotted specific text to support the answer to the preceding question, you can check the answer choices to see if it is cited in one of the Command of Evidence question's choices.

**Getting to the Answer:** The opening lines of Passage 2 address those who incorrectly think treaty power is strictly executive, so predict that your answer can be found here. The correct answer, **(A)**, directly supports the correct answer to question 6; you may have remembered it from your research on that question.

(B) defines legislative power; (C) defines the object of treaty making; and (D) states an argument for legislative involvement in treaty making. None of these choices is related to the correct answer to the preceding question.

**6. B**

**Difficulty:** Medium

**Category:** Vocab-in-Context

**Strategic Advice:** On Vocab-in-Context questions, the correct answer can replace the word cited in the question stem without changing the meaning of the sentence. Predict what the correct answer means as well as you can before evaluating the choices.

**Getting to the Answer:** Historical passages can contain archaic language, so use context clues. The relevant text says that the treaty power "partakes more of the legislative than of the executive character." Hamilton is suggesting that the treaty power *has more in common* with the responsibilities of the legislature than of the executive. **(B)** is correct; *sharing* more characteristics equates to having more in common.

(A) is incorrect; *consume*, or *eat*, doesn't fit into this sentence. (C) would distort the meaning of the sentence. (D) is simply a more evocative form of "consume."

**7. C**

**Difficulty:** Hard

**Category:** Vocab-in-Context

**Strategic Advice:** On Vocab-in-Context questions, the correct answer can replace the word cited in the question stem without changing the meaning of the sentence. Predict what the correct answer means as well as you can before evaluating the choices.

**Getting to the Answer:** "[O]ffice" appears in the sentence at the very end of Passage 2, where it is used in a somewhat dated fashion. A good paraphrase of the sentence in which "office" appears would be: "The fact that treaties are in some ways like laws is a reason the legislative branch should have a role in the job/task of making them." The correct answer will be the one that could mean *job* or *task*, making **(C)** the correct answer. "Commission," in this case, means an official assignment or a task for which one is committed or responsible.

(A) distorts the sentence by implying that the legislature should be part of an administrative system. (B) uses a common definition of office (the physical place where people work) that doesn't fit this sentence at all. (D) offers too vague a word to maintain the meaning of the sentence.

**8.   A**

**Difficulty:** Hard

**Category:** Global

**Strategic Advice:** This question is a variation on the Global question type adapted to fit paired passages. To answer a question like this one efficiently, identify the central goal of each passage, and describe them in relation to one another.

**Getting to the Answer:** Begin by comparing the two passages' main points. Passage 1 supports the way the second section of Article II of the Constitution divides the treaty power between the executive and legislative branches by refuting those who think it should reside solely with the legislature. Passage 2's author also endorses a treaty power shared by the executive and legislative branches, in this case, by refuting those who think treaty powers are an exclusively executive power. **(A)** correctly states that the passages reach the same conclusion through different lines of reasoning.

(B) is incorrect because both passages deal with the same proposition: how treaty power should be allocated between the branches of government. (C) distorts the relationship between passages because Passage 2 does not question any assumptions in Passage 1; the authors generally agree. (D) may sound plausible, but neither passage uses examples to illustrate reasoning.

**9.   C**

**Difficulty:** Medium

**Category:** Inference

**Strategic Advice:** This Inference question asks you to deduce what one author would likely say about the other; the answer will be firmly rooted in the main ideas of both passages.

**Getting to the Answer:** Make sure you're clear on what the question is asking. While the two authors disagree on some points, such as whether treaty power is primarily an executive or legislative power, they agree that the power to legally bind citizens is not exclusively held by the legislative branch. Jay states that all three branches can issue legally binding rules, and Hamilton argues that treaties created by the executive branch are binding. **(C)** states that at least some executive rules are binding under the powers granted in the Constitution, which makes it the correct answer.

(A) is too broad; the only type of non-legislative rules discussed by Hamilton are treaties, so there's no way to know what he would think of other non-legislative rules. (B) contradicts Hamilton's view that treaties are legally binding. (D) falls outside the scope of Passage 2, as Hamilton does not express any opinion regarding the judiciary.

**10.   C**

**Difficulty:** Medium

**Category:** Function

**Strategic Advice:** The phrase "both serve to" signals a Function question that applies to both passages. Check the quoted text in each passage to identify why each author included the phrase.

**Getting to the Answer:** In this case, each of the excerpts noted in the question stem offers a definition of typical legislative powers, the authority to make laws. That function is accurately describe in choice **(C)**.

(A) does not match either author's conclusion, which is that the power to make treaties is appropriately shared between the executive and legislative branches. (B) applies only to Passage 2. (D) is something both authors do, but not by way of the text quoted in the question stem.

Suggested passage notes:

**Passage 1**

¶1: No more European colonization in Americas
¶2: US friends w/Eur; US neutral in Eur conflicts
¶3: US will act only if threatened; Eur activities in own hemisphere = threat
¶4: US conditions: 1) no new colonies, 2) old colonies OK, 3) no interference w/former colonies

**Passage 2**

Lines 37–49: US wants order in W hemisphere
Lines 49–59: If disorder, US will intervene
Lines 59–86: R's explanation

**11. D**

**Difficulty:** Medium

**Category:** Function

**Strategic Advice:** Function questions ask you to determine the purpose of a specific detail or paragraph in the passage. This question wants you to determine the purpose of a statement in the second paragraph, so you should go back to the lines indicated and look for clues that will help you make a prediction. Sometimes, you will need to read before or after the lines indicated to have enough information to answer the question.

**Getting to the Answer:** In lines 6–9, Monroe states that the people of the United States "cherish" their friendship with Europeans. But why does he mention this, when the primary purpose of the passage is to put European powers on notice that the United States will no longer tolerate their interference in the Americas? Monroe reminds Europeans of their friendship with the United States in order to soften his message. Without this reminder, the overall tone of the passage would be more aggressive and would be less likely to be well-received by a European audience. This prediction matches **(D)** perfectly.

There is no indication that Monroe is responding to critics, so you can eliminate (A). (B) can be eliminated because Monroe's tone is very direct; there is nothing in the passage to indicate that he is trying to trick the European powers into thinking his position is something other than what he says. Finally, (C) is incorrect because Monroe is commenting on an existing attitude, not recommending that people adopt one.

**12. B**

**Difficulty:** Easy

**Category:** Detail

**Strategic Advice:** The keyword "indicates" signals that this is a Detail question, which means you are looking for a specific fact mentioned in the passage. Refer back to the passage to find what Monroe says the United States does not intend to do. Keep your finger on those lines, since your next task will be a Command of Evidence question that asks you where you found the answer to this question.

**Getting to the Answer:** In the second paragraph, Monroe states that it is not, and never has been, the policy of the United States to get involved in European matters if they are "relating to themselves" (lines 9–12). In doing so, Monroe indicates that the United States will not intervene in wars that affect only European powers. This prediction matches **(B)**, which is correct.

(A) is the opposite of Monroe's primary message, which is that the United States will not tolerate further European colonization of the Americas (lines 20–26). (C) is also inconsistent with the passage, which states that Americans "cherish" their friendship with Europeans and that the United States enjoys "amicable" relationships with European powers. Finally, (D) contradicts a statement Monroe makes in the final paragraph, where he indicates that the United States will not interfere with existing European colonies.

**13. A**

**Difficulty:** Easy

**Category:** Command of Evidence

**Strategic Advice:** Command of Evidence questions ask you to identify the support for the previous answer. If you see one of these coming, you can keep your finger on the relevant text when you do your research for the previous question, giving you a quick prediction.

**Getting to the Answer:** The previous question drew its correct answer from the second paragraph, specifically the second sentence in lines 9–12. Thus, **(A)** is correct.

## 14. C

**Difficulty:** Hard

**Category:** Detail

**Strategic Advice:** As with other Detail questions, go back to the passage and look up the required information. Keep your finger on the appropriate lines of text so that you can answer the upcoming Command of Evidence question more quickly.

**Getting to the Answer:** Because the question asks for what circumstance "must" exist, look for forceful language in the passage that indicates a necessary requirement that must be met before the United States may act. You'll find such language in lines 75–81, where Roosevelt says that the United States would intervene "only in the last resort." In this sentence, Roosevelt says that only two circumstances would justify intervention: if a nation were to violate the rights of the United States, or if a nation were to put every other country in the Americas at risk by inciting European aggression. Either circumstance would require causing harm to the United States as a prerequisite for intervention, either individually or as part of the collective group of nations in the Americas. Thus, **(C)** is correct.

Regarding the other choices, (A) and (B) are incorrect because Roosevelt does not say that invasion is required to justify intervention. Although invasion may be sufficient to warrant involvement by the United States, there are likely other ways that a country might violate the rights of the United States or invite European aggression. (D) is incorrect because Roosevelt never mentions human rights abuses.

## 15. D

**Difficulty:** Medium

**Category:** Command of Evidence

**Strategic Advice:** Look back at your research for the previous question and determine what portion of text you used to support your answer.

**Getting to the Answer:** The answer to the previous question was found in lines 75–81, so **(D)** is correct.

## 16. C

**Difficulty:** Easy

**Category:** Vocab-in-Context

**Strategic Advice:** For Vocab-in-Context questions, return to the passage, and look for context clues that will reveal something about the meaning of the word in question. To make a prediction, pretend the word is a blank in the sentence and propose a different word to take its place that maintains the original meaning.

**Getting to the Answer:** In lines 59–60, Roosevelt uses the phrase "washed by the Caribbean Sea" to refer to Cuba and other countries located in and around the Caribbean. The word "washed" in this context means "flowed over the shores of." This is a way of saying that these countries are adjacent to, or "touched," by the Caribbean, making **(C)** correct.

Beware the more common and literal meanings of "washed" such as "cleaned" and "bathed." They don't make sense in the context of this passage, so (A) and (D) are incorrect. (B) is incorrect because to be overwhelmed is to be "awash" in something, rather than "washed."

## 17. D

**Difficulty:** Hard

**Category:** Vocab-in-Context

**Strategic Advice:** For Vocab-in-Context questions, go back to the passage and look for context clues. Make a prediction by pretending that the indicated word is a blank and finding a different word to take its place without changing the meaning of the sentence.

**Getting to the Answer:** In line 70, Roosevelt says that countries rich in natural resources will prosper if "the reign of law and justice obtains" in them. In other words, countries that achieve political and legal stability will succeed. In this sense, "obtains" is similar to "becomes a reality," or *prevails*, making **(D)** correct. Generally, you want to avoid the more common meanings of a word in a Vocab-in-Context question, which means the more familiar uses of "obtains" such as *gathers*, *seizes*, and *collects* are likely incorrect. None of them fits the context of this sentence, ruling out (A), (B), and (C).

## 18. A

**Difficulty:** Hard

**Category:** Global

**Strategic Advice:** This is a Global question asking you to describe the relationship between the passages. Refer back to your passage maps. You should also review the pre-passage blurb for any useful information about the relationship between the passages.

**Getting to the Answer:** The passages are generally compatible with one another, and the characterization of Passage 2 as a "corollary" to Passage 1 confirms this impression. (A corollary is a claim that follows from another, preexisting claim.) Passage 1 is primarily concerned with informing European powers about a policy decision made by the United States: moving forward, the United States will view European intervention or colonization in the Americas as a form of aggression against the United States. As part of the justification for his stance, Monroe asserts that the United States is "more immediately connected" (line 17) with events in the Americas than are European powers. However, Monroe never expressly indicates what role the United States should play in policing the affairs of other countries within the Americas. In Passage 2, however, Roosevelt fills in the gap by offering a set of criteria to determine when the United States may intervene in the affairs of other nations. Thus, **(A)** is correct because Roosevelt is expanding on the idea mentioned briefly by Monroe in lines 16–17.

(B) can be eliminated because Passage 2 does not "dispute" Passage 1; their relationship is compatible, not contradictory. (C) is incorrect because Passage 2 provides only one example (a reference to Cuba in lines 59–67), and that example does not support any of the claims made by Monroe in Passage 1. (D) is incorrect because the main opinion in Passage 1 is that European powers should not get involved in disputes between countries in the Americas, but Roosevelt is offering a justification for the different (but related) opinion of when the United States should get involved.

## 19. B

**Difficulty:** Medium

**Category:** Inference

**Strategic Advice:** This question asks you to identify a motivation shared by both authors, so the correct choice must be supported by each passage separately. Because this is an Inference question, the supporting information in one or both of the passages may be implicit rather than explicit.

**Getting to the Answer:** In Passage 1, Monroe is primarily motivated by concerns about European powers intervening in the Americas, via colonization or some other form of aggression. In Passage 2, Roosevelt's references to the Monroe Doctrine (line 55) and "foreign aggression" (lines 79–80) indicate that he also shares this concern. Thus, **(B)** is correct.

(A) describes a circumstance that motivated Roosevelt's argument in Passage 2, but Passage 1 does not indicate any concerns about political instability in the Americas. (C) is incorrect because there is no indication in either passage that the authors are responding to their political opponents. Finally, (D) is incorrect because neither passage refers to nonviolence or pacifism; additionally, Passage 2 advocates for "policing" other nations and implies that military intervention is appropriate in at least some cases.

## 20. A

**Difficulty:** Medium

**Category:** Inference

**Strategic Advice:** For Inference questions that ask you how one author would respond to a claim made by the other, start by reading the claim. Then, look for clues in the other passage that indicate how its author would respond.

**Getting to the Answer:** Roosevelt's claim in lines 67–68 is that the United States and its neighbors in the Americas have the same interests. Looking back at Passage 1, Monroe says in lines 15–18 that the United States is "more connected" with other nations in the Americas. Thus, Monroe would agree with Roosevelt's statement, making **(A)** correct.

(B) and (C) are incorrect because they mischaracterize the relationship between Roosevelt's statement in lines 67–68 and Monroe's opinion; Monroe would generally agree with Roosevelt's statement, so he would not call it an "unfair characterization" or an "unwarranted exaggeration." Lastly, (D) is incorrect because Roosevelt's statement is not an "example" of anything.

## 21. C

**Difficulty:** Medium

**Category:** Inference

**Strategic Advice:** Because this is a "which of the following" Inference question, it is most efficient to work through the answer choices by process of elimination.

**Getting to the Answer:** (A) is incorrect because both Monroe (lines 6–9) and Roosevelt (lines 42–44) mention their intent to maintain friendly relationships with other countries. Likewise, (B) is incorrect because it is a statement that is supported by both passages; the correct choice will be supported only by Passage 2. **(C)** is correct because Passage 2 mentions Cuba (lines 59–67) as an example of another stable country in the Americas, but Passage 1 offers no such examples. (D) is incorrect because it contradicts Passage 2, which advocates for intervention by the United States in at least some circumstances.

# Literature Passages

# How Much Do You Know?

**Directions:** In this chapter, you'll learn to apply the SAT Reading strategies you've learned to Literature passages. Take 10 minutes to actively read this passage and answer the five accompanying questions. Pay close attention to the relationships between characters as you read. When you're finished, compare your work to the explanations on the following pages.

**Questions 1-5 refer to the following passage.**

This passage is from Amy Tan, *The Joy Luck Club*. ©1989 by G. P. Putnam's Sons. The narrator recalls her mother's death and the history of the Joy Luck Club.

My father has asked me to be the fourth corner at the Joy Luck Club. I am to replace my mother, whose seat at the mah jong table has been empty since she died two months
5 ago. My father thinks she was killed by her own thoughts.

"She had a new idea inside her head," said my father. "But before it could come out of her mouth, the thought grew too big and burst. It
10 must have been a very bad idea."

The doctor said she died of a cerebral aneurysm. And her friends at the Joy Luck Club said she died just like a rabbit: quickly and with unfinished business left behind. My
15 mother was supposed to host the next meeting of the Joy Luck Club.

The week before she died, she called me, full of pride, full of life: "Auntie Lin cooked red bean soup for Joy Luck. I'm going to cook
20 black sesame-seed soup."

"Don't show off," I said.

"It's not showoff." She said the two soups were almost the same, *chabudwo*. Or maybe she said *butong*, not the same thing at all. It
25 was one of those Chinese expressions that means the better half of mixed intentions. I can never remember things I didn't understand in the first place.

My mother started the San Francisco
30 version of the Joy Luck Club in 1949, two years before I was born. This was the year my mother and father left China with one

stiff leather trunk filled only with fancy silk dresses. There was no time to pack anything
35 else, my mother had explained to my father after they boarded the boat. Still his hands swam frantically between the slippery silks, looking for his cotton shirts and wool pants.

40 When they arrived in San Francisco, my father made her hide those shiny clothes. She wore the same brown-checked Chinese dress until the Refugee Welcome Society gave her two hand-me-down dresses, all
45 too large in sizes for American women. The society was composed of a group of white-haired American missionary ladies from the First Chinese Baptist Church. And because of their gifts, my parents could not refuse
50 their invitation to join the church. Nor could they ignore the old ladies' practical advice to improve their English through Bible study class on Wednesday nights and, later, through choir practice on Saturday mornings. This was
55 how my parents met the Hsus, the Jongs, and the St. Clairs. My mother could sense that the women of these families also had unspeakable tragedies they had left behind in China and hopes they couldn't begin to express in
60 their fragile English. Or at least, my mother recognized the numbness in these women's faces. And she saw how quickly their eyes moved when she told them her idea for the Joy Luck Club.

65 Joy Luck was an idea my mother remembered from the days of her first marriage in Kweilin, before the Japanese came. That's why I think of Joy Luck as her Kweilin story. It was the story she would always tell me
70 when she was bored, when there was nothing to do, when every bowl had been washed and the Formica table had been wiped down twice, when my father sat reading the newspaper and smoking one Pall Mall cigarette after
75 another, a warning not to disturb him. This is when my mother would take out a box of

old ski sweaters sent to us by unseen relatives from Vancouver. She would snip the bottom of a sweater and pull out a kinky thread of yarn, anchoring it to a piece of cardboard. And as she

80 began to roll with one sweeping rhythm, she would start her story. Over the years, she told me the same story, except for the ending, which grew darker, casting long shadows into her life, and

85 eventually into mine.

1. Over the course of the passage, the main focus shifts from

   A) an analysis of a game of mah jong to a general portrayal of the Chinese community in San Francisco.

   B) a metaphor for unfinished business to a depiction of Kweilin.

   C) a detailed description of the Joy Luck Club to an examination of the narrators' parents' reasons for leaving China.

   D) the recounting of a sudden death to the backdrop for a tale told by the deceased before her death.

2. The main purpose of lines 12–18 ("And her . . . full of life") is to

   A) introduce the characters who have meant the most to the narrator.

   B) underscore the swift and unexpected nature of the narrator's mother's death.

   C) illuminate the relationship between the narrator's parents.

   D) establish a negative dynamic between the narrator and her mother.

3. When discussing the food her mother cooked for the Joy Luck Club, the narrator indicates that she

   A) could not remember the types of dishes her mother prepared.

   B) understood her mother's mixed intentions better than her mother understood them herself.

   C) could not understand why her mother wanted to show off by cooking black sesame-seed soup.

   D) could not clearly remember which Chinese expression her mother used to compare the two soups.

4. With which of the following statements about her parents would the narrator most likely agree?

   A) They were married in Kweilin and lived there until they left China.

   B) They felt a sense of obligation to the Refugee Welcome Society.

   C) They disagreed about whether or not they should join the First Chinese Baptist Church.

   D) They never disagreed about anything and found strength in overcoming obstacles.

5. Which choice provides the best evidence for the answer to the previous question?

   A) Lines 34–36 ("There was . . . boat")

   B) Lines 42–45 ("She wore . . . women")

   C) Lines 48–50 ("And because . . . church")

   D) Lines 54–56 ("This was . . . St. Clairs")

# Check Your Work

Suggested passage notes:

¶1: Narrator to replace Mom in JLC

¶2–3: Mom's death according to Dad, others

¶4–6: Narrator confusion over lang

¶7: Mom & Dad leave China

¶8: Arrive in SF; RWC; join church

¶9: Story of JLC idea

**1. D**

**Difficulty:** Medium

**Category:** Function

**Strategic Advice:** Function questions ask you why the writer included a certain detail.

**Getting to the Answer:** To determine how the focus shifts, review your passage map, particularly the first and last few paragraphs. The author describes the circumstances of her mother's death, then goes on to explain her parents' experience as new residents of San Francisco. Finally, she recounts a story her mother told her many times. Thus, the main focus shifts from the death of the author's mother to a story the mother told to the author. **(D)** is a solid match for this prediction and is correct.

Choice (A) is unsupported since there is no analysis of mah jong. (B) is also unsupported because the "metaphor for unfinished business" is a detail, never the main focus, nor is there any depiction of Kweilin. (C) is unsupported since there isn't any detailed description of the Joy Luck Club or an examination of the parents' reasons for leaving China.

**2. B**

**Difficulty:** Medium

**Category:** Function

**Strategic Advice:** Function questions ask about the purpose of a specific element of the passage. Think about the author's larger purpose for including the cited element; ask yourself, "Why is this here and what does it accomplish?"

**Getting to the Answer:** The author points out that her mother died "quickly and with unfinished business," and that the week before, she was full of life. Therefore, it's logical to conclude that the author's purpose is to point out the sudden and unexpected nature of her mother's death. **(B)** is correct.

While it's true that the narrator's mother is introduced and that she meant a lot to the narrator, the purpose of the cited lines is not merely to introduce important characters, so (A) can be eliminated. There is no discussion in these lines of the narrator's parents' relationship, so (B) is incorrect as well. Finally, there is nothing in this portion of text that indicates a "negative dynamic" between the narrator and her mother, so you can eliminate (D).

**3. D**

**Difficulty:** Medium

**Category:** Detail

**Strategic Advice:** Detail questions ask about a specific point or fact in the passage. Look up the answer in the passage and be aware that the correct answer will be directly stated there.

**Getting to the Answer:** In the paragraph starting in line 22, the narrator mentions two different Chinese terms her mother may have used to compare the two soups; she indicates that she can't remember which of the two terms her mother used. This closely matches **(D)**, the correct answer.

The narrator mentions the specific soup her mother made, so (A) can be eliminated. There is no comparison made between the narrator's understanding and her mother's, so (B) is incorrect as well. Finally, the narrator didn't indicate that she couldn't understand her mother's desire to show off, so you can eliminate (C).

**4. B**

**Difficulty:** Medium

**Category:** Inference

**Strategic Advice:** The keywords "the author . . . would . . . most likely agree" indicate an Inference question. It may not be possible to make a clear and specific prediction for a "which of the following" Inference question, so check each choice against the text and eliminate those that are unsupported.

**Getting to the Answer:** (A): the text states that the mother's first marriage was in Kweilin, so the implication is that her husband at the time was a previous husband and not the author's father. Furthermore, there is nothing in the text to suggest that the author's parents lived in Kweilin until they left China. Eliminate (A).

(B): The text states that, the gifts from the American missionary ladies from the First Chinese Baptist Church put the narrator's parents into a position where they couldn't refuse the invitation to join the church. Her parents felt obligated to join, so **(B)** is correct.

(C): Nothing in the text suggests the parents disagreed about joining the church. Eliminate (C).

(D): There is little in the text to determine whether the parents had disagreements; therefore, the words "never" and "anything" in this choice signal an extreme answer. Eliminate (D).

**5. C**

**Difficulty:** Medium

**Category:** Command of Evidence

**Strategic Advice:** The keywords "provides the best evidence for the answer to the previous question" indicate a Command of Evidence question. Scan the question set for these and be aware of where they are. When you see one of them coming, keep your finger on the lines you used to answer the preceding question.

**Getting to the Answer:** Refer to the evidence in the text that you used to answer the previous question; lines 48–50 indicate the parents' feeling of obligation to join the church. Thus, **(C)** is correct.

# How to Read Literature for the SAT

## LEARNING OBJECTIVES

After this lesson, you will be able to:

- Draw inferences about characters' motivations and relationships
- Identify the tone of a partial or full Literature passage

Exactly one passage in each SAT Reading section is a Literature passage: an excerpt from a novel or short story. The Literature passage is typically the first passage in the section, but that doesn't mean you have to tackle it first. Some test takers may find fiction engaging and feel comfortable reading dialogue and interpreting an author's descriptions of characters and settings. Others may find their strengths lie in more concrete, nonfiction passages on science and social studies. Don't make a snap judgment based on how you feel now, though. Practice all of the passage types to give yourself an honest, informed assessment. You'll find more tips and strategies on how best to approach the section in the chapter on SAT Reading section management.

## To answer a question like this:

The following passage is an excerpt from English novelist Anne Brontë's *The Tenant of Wildfell Hall*, published in 1848. The excerpt is part of a letter the narrator, Gilbert, has written.

My father, as you know, was a sort of gentleman farmer in —shire; and I, by his express desire, succeeded him in the same quiet occupation, not very willingly, for ambition
5   urged me to higher aims, and self-conceit assured me that, in disregarding its voice, I was burying my talent in the earth, and hiding my light under a bushel. My mother had done her utmost to persuade me that I was capable of
10  great achievements; but my father, who thought ambition was the surest road to ruin, and change but another word for destruction, would listen to no scheme for bettering either my own condition, or that of my fellow mortals. He assured me it
15  was all rubbish, and exhorted me, with his dying breath, to continue in the good old way, to follow his steps, and those of his father before him, and let my highest ambition be, to walk honestly through the world, looking neither to the right
20  hand nor to the left, and to transmit the paternal acres to my children in, at least, as flourishing a condition as he left them to me.

"Well!—an honest and industrious farmer is one of the most useful members of society; and
25  if I devote my talents to the cultivation of my farm, and the improvement of agriculture in general, I shall thereby benefit, not only my own immediate connections and dependents, but in some degree, mankind at large:—hence I shall
30  not have lived in vain." With such reflections as these, I was endeavouring to console myself, as I plodded home from the fields, one cold, damp, cloudy evening towards the close of October. But the gleam of a bright red fire through the parlour
35  window, had more effect in cheering my spirits, and rebuking my thankless repinings, than all the sage reflections and good resolutions I had

forced my mind to frame;—for I was young then, remember—only four and twenty—and had not
40  acquired half the rule over my own spirit, that I now possess—trifling as that may be.

1.  The narrator's attitude about becoming a farmer, as expressed in lines 23–38 ("Well!—an honest . . . mind to frame"), seems to be one of

    A)  bitter resentment.

    B)  detached reflection.

    C)  forced optimism.

    D)  hearty good cheer.

## You need to know this:

The SAT does not generally test symbolism, but it does test your ability to draw inferences about characters' relationships and attitudes and to recognize how the author creates a specific tone or effect.

### Unpack the Pre-Passage "Blurb" Effectively

Be sure to read the little blurb that precedes an SAT Reading passage; this can be especially helpful on Literature passages. The blurb will always give you the author's name, the title of the book or short story from which the passage was adapted, and the original publication date. When necessary, it may provide information about the main characters and setting.

**The author.** If you happen to know the author, great, but don't expect to. If the name rings a bell that helps you identify the time frame or setting of the passage, take advantage of that, but otherwise, let it go. No questions will ask about the author's identity or biographical information.

**Title.** A book's title may help you identify its genre—tragedy, romance, coming-of-age stories, etc. It may also give you clues about the setting or theme of the passage.

**Publication date.** The SAT has used Literature passages drawn from various time periods over the last 200 years or so. Obviously, language use and references will be different in passages from the 1850s than those from the 1950s, and you can use that information to provide context about social conditions and historical events, or even about unusual vocabulary.

**Characters and setting.** When the test adds any information beyond author, title, and date, pay close attention. The people writing the test questions felt this information was essential for test takers to know, and it will always give you a head start in interpreting the passage and anticipating where the story is likely to go. Knowing, for example, that the main character is an adolescent or a mother, or knowing that a story takes place in a coal-mining town or an aristocratic palace, will change your understanding of the passage from the outset.

### Tune In to the Narrator's "Voice"

Within the first few lines, you will be able to distinguish a passage written in first person (the narrator as the main character, knowing only what that character knows) from one written in third person (the narrator is separate from the characters and has an omniscient point of view). Keeping this in mind as you read will help you spot the purpose of each paragraph and will help you later with Inference questions ("With which of the following would the narrator/character most likely agree?").

In addition, take note of language that indicates the narrator's or a character's point of view. In a standard science or social studies passage, Opinion and Emphasis keywords help you keep track of an author's ideas about a topic. In Literature passages, the author may put these ideas in the mind or the mouth of a character or in the way a scene or object is described. Take note of the passage's tone (e.g., joyful, nostalgic, anxious, angry, hopeful, ironic, or satirical, etc.), especially if an event or conversation brings about a change in tone. Typically, one or more of the questions will reward your attention to the passage's tone and characters' points of view.

### Track What Happens and the Main Character's Reaction or Response

In a standard SAT Reading passage on science or social studies, you can use an author's purpose to anticipate where the passage will go. When the author says there is a debate over a recent theory, you expect the next couple of paragraphs to lay out one side and then the other. If the author introduces a new idea, there will probably be an example to illustrate it. Literature passages unfold a little differently, but if you are reading actively, you can still anticipate and track the development of the story. Use what you know about a character to anticipate the action and to interpret the character's reactions. If an older worker who is concerned about having enough money for retirement has a conversation with her boss, you can understand what she's after, even if she is using language that talks around the subject. If a studious young man absorbed in a book is interrupted by a boisterous group of revelers, you can expect some annoyance or judgment in his reaction, even if he doesn't say anything to the newcomers. Keeping track of these things will help you jot down good paragraph summaries, just as you would in nonfiction passages.

When a character's reaction or response to an event surprises you, consider whether this signals a change in the tone of the passage or indicates that you've glossed over or misunderstood something about the character or situation. In either case, it's always valuable to track not only the plot but also the character's reactions to and interpretations of what is happening.

**Use What You Already Know about SAT Reading Strategies and Question Types**

While Literature passages have a distinct look and feel, the questions that accompany them are of the same types as those that follow standard science and social studies passages. Thus, while the best test takers apply a few unique reading strategies tailored to Literature, their overall approach remains similar to what they use for all passages. In every case, SAT experts read actively to prepare themselves for the question set. To do that, they read for the big picture, for the author's (or in this case, narrator's or characters') opinions and point of view, and for the passage's structure by noting the purpose and main idea of each paragraph.

For the most part, the questions that accompany Literature passages are worded similarly to those for Science or Social Studies passages. However, in Literature passages, you may also see questions that ask the following:

- For the passage's theme (which corresponds to its main idea)
- About a shift in the narrator's focus
- How the author creates a certain effect
- What is going on in a character's mind

As long as you read actively for tone and characters' motivations, you'll be ready for questions like these.

## You need to do this:

- Use the pre-passage blurb to identify all that you can about the following:
  - The author's identity
  - The time frame and location
  - The passage's main character or characters.
- Quickly recognize whether the passage is in first person or third person
- Focus on the main character's defining characteristics: demographics (such as age, social position, occupation, race, and gender) and mental traits (attitudes, opinions, desires, and conflicts)
- Anticipate the character's responses to events or interactions with other characters
- Note the purpose of each paragraph as you read

### Explanation:

This is an Inference question: you need to infer the narrator's attitude from clues in the text. The narrator says explicitly in line 4 that he became a farmer "not very willingly," and that he had the "ambition" to pursue "higher aims." This earlier context is important for understanding the tone of lines 23–38; without it, the second paragraph sounds very positive, even cheerful. Against the backdrop of the narrator's unwillingness to become a farmer, however, the second paragraph sounds as if he were trying to talk himself into cheerfully accepting his occupation. Then, in line 31, the narrator states that he is "endeavouring to console [himself]." This is equivalent to "forced optimism." Choice **(C)** is correct.

## Try on Your Own

**Directions**: Actively read this Literature passage and answer the questions. Remember to note the tone of the story as you read and pay close attention to characters' attitudes and relationships.

**Questions 1-7 refer to the following passage.**

This passage is adapted from Hortense Calisher's short story "A Box of Ginger," first published in 1948. The nine-year-old protagonist, Kinny, witnesses the events of the morning of his uncle's funeral.

Five stories below, the hot white pavements sent the air shimmering upward. From the false dusk of the awning, Kinny, leaning out to watch the iridescent black top of the funeral
5   car, smelled the indeterminate summer smell of freshly ironed linen and dust. Below, he could see his father help the aunts into the car and stumble in after them, and the car roll away to join the others at the cemetery. The winter
10  before, at the funeral of his father's other brother, everything had left from here, hearse and all. The house had been crowded with people who had entered without ringing and had seated themselves soundlessly in the parlor,
15  greeting each other with a nod or a sidewise shake of the head, and for days there had been a straggling procession of long-faced callers, who had clasped hands with his father and mother and had been conducted, after a decent
20  interval, to his grandmother's rooms, where she lived somewhat apart from the rest of the family. They had all come out clucking, "She's a wonderful woman, a won-der-ful old woman!," had been given coffee, and had gone away.
25  Today, there was no one, and the wide glaring street was blank with light.

"Kinny, where are you?"

"I'm in the parlor."

"How many times have I told you to say
30  'living room?' Parlor!" His mother clicked her tongue as she came into the room. "Why didn't you go to the Park?" She walked toward him and looked at him squarely, something he had noticed grown people almost never seemed to
35  have time to do.

"Listen Kinny!" Her voice had the conspiratorial tone that made him uncomfortable. "You're not to let on to Grandma anything—anything about the
40  funeral. It's a terrible thing to grow to a great age and see your children go before you." Her gaze had already shifted back to normal, slightly to the right of him and just above his head. "Don't lean so far out the window!"
45  She turned and went into the kitchen to help Josie, the maid. His family never sat down to a dinner just themselves; there were always the aunts, or the innumerable cousins, who came to pay their short devoirs to Grandma and stayed
50  interminably at her daughter-in-law's table.

"Kinny! Grandma wants you!" From the sitting room down the hall he heard the familiar clankclank of the gadrooned brass handles on the sideboard. Grandma would
55  be standing stiffly with the yellow box of preserved ginger, uglily lettered in black, clutched in one knuckled hand, waiting for the small afternoon ceremony that had been her only apparent notice of him for as long as he
60  could remember. Reluctantly, he opened the door and went down the hall.

She stood there just as he had known she would, a dainty death's head no taller than he, in the black silk uniform of age, one hand
65  wavering on her cane, the other tight on the yellow box. The sparse hair, dressed so closely on the skull, enlarged the effect of the ears and the high nose with its long nostrils; the mouth, a mere boundary line for tributary wrinkles,
70  firmed itself now and again. She was neat as old vellum, and though time had shrunk her to waxwork, it had left her free of the warts and hairs and pendulous dewlaps he saw on other old people. Her admitted age was ninety-
75  three, but the family was of the opinion that she had concealed a few years, out of vanity.

"Here I am, Grandma." He moved toward her.

"Come here, child." Steadying her hand
80  with his, she fumblingly placed in his palm a few tawny sugared slices of ginger. Under her

Reading

waiting gaze, he placed a slice in his mouth and chewed. There was a small, acrid explosion in his throat; his eyes pinkened, but he swallowed
85 obediently, knowing that she thought she was giving him a confection of which he was fond.

1. Which of the following best describes a main theme of the passage?

   A) The buoyant resilience of a young child

   B) The mundane banality of winter funerals

   C) The redeeming power of enduring social connections

   D) The disruptive effect of a family death

2. Over the course of the passage, the main focus shifts from a

   A) description of important events to a depiction of the relationship between a grandmother and grandson.

   B) discussion of appropriate behavior to the events that occur when proper behavior is ignored.

   C) portrayal of a son's relationship with his father to the effects of that relationship on his grandmother.

   D) general discussion of funeral customs to an examination of the impact of the loss of a child on an aged mother.

3. As used in line 17, "callers" most nearly means

   A) customers.

   B) visitors.

   C) suitors.

   D) shouters.

4. The passage most clearly implies that the family is keeping which of the following secrets from Kinny's grandmother?

   A) The fact that they know her true age

   B) Kinny's fondness for ginger

   C) The death of Kinny's uncle

   D) The regular presence of extended family at their dinner table

5. Which choice provides the best evidence for the answer to the previous question?

   A) Lines 22–24 ("They had . . . away")

   B) Lines 36–41 ("'Listen . . . you'")

   C) Lines 51–54 ("Kinny . . . sideboard")

   D) Lines 81–86 ("Under . . . fond")

6. The author uses the phrase "they had all come out clucking" (line 22) to suggest

   A) a tendency to offer expected sympathy.

   B) grave concern for Kinny's grandmother's health.

   C) fierce independence in forming opinions.

   D) an inability to protect oneself from harm.

7. Kinny believes that adults don't look directly at him because they are

   A) visiting him after a family member has died.

   B) scolding him for misbehaving.

   C) asking him to note carefully what is being said to him.

   D) too busy to pay attention to him.

# How Much Have You Learned?

**Directions:** Now try a full-length Literature passage and question set under timed conditions. Take 13 minutes to read the passage and answer the accompanying questions.

**Questions 8-17 refer to the following passage.**

The following passage is adapted from Jules Verne, *Around the World in Eighty Days,* first published in 1873.

Phileas Fogg, having shut the door of his house at half-past eleven, and having put his right foot before his left five hundred and seventy-five times, and his left foot before
5 his right five hundred and seventy-six times, reached the Reform Club. He repaired at once to the dining-room and took his place at the habitual table, the cover of which had already been laid for him. A flunkey handed him
10 an uncut *Times*, which he proceeded to cut with a skill which betrayed familiarity with this delicate operation. The perusal of this paper absorbed Phileas Fogg until a quarter before four, whilst the *Standard*, his next task,
15 occupied him till the dinner hour. Dinner passed as breakfast had done, and Mr. Fogg re-appeared in the reading-room and sat down to the *Pall Mall*[1] at twenty minutes before six. Half an hour later several members of the
20 Reform came in and drew up to the fireplace. They were Mr. Fogg's usual partners at whist:[2] Andrew Stuart, an engineer; John Sullivan and Samuel Fallentin, bankers; Thomas Flanagan, a brewer; and Gauthier Ralph, one of the
25 Directors of the Bank of England.

"Well, Ralph," said Thomas Flanagan, "what about that robbery?"

"Oh," replied Stuart, "the Bank will lose the money."

30 "On the contrary," broke in Ralph, "I hope we may put our hands on the robber. Skillful detectives have been sent to all the principal ports of America and the Continent, and he'll be a clever fellow if he slips through their
35 fingers."

"But have you got the robber's description?" asked Stuart.

"In the first place, he is no robber at all," returned Ralph, positively.

40 "What! a fellow who makes off with fifty-five thousand pounds, no robber?"

"No."

"Perhaps he's a manufacturer, then."

"The *Daily Telegraph* says that he is a
45 gentleman."

It was Phileas Fogg, whose head now emerged from behind his newspapers, who made this remark. A package of banknotes, to the value of fifty-five thousand pounds, had
50 been taken from the principal cashier's table, that functionary being at the moment engaged in registering the receipt of three shillings and sixpence. Let it be observed that the Bank of England reposes a touching confidence in the
55 honesty of the public. There are neither guards nor gratings to protect its treasures; gold, silver, banknotes are freely exposed, at the mercy of the first comer. A keen observer of English customs relates that, being in one of the rooms
60 of the Bank one day, he had the curiosity to examine a gold ingot weighing some seven or eight pounds. He took it up, scrutinized it, passed it to his neighbour, he to the next man, and so on until the ingot, going from hand
65 to hand, was transferred to the end of a dark entry; nor did it return to its place for half an hour. Meanwhile, the cashier had not so much as raised his head. But in the present instance things had not gone so smoothly. The package
70 of notes not being found when five o'clock sounded from the ponderous clock in the "drawing office," the amount was passed to the account of profit and loss.

[1] *Pall Mall*: an evening newspaper (the *Pall Mall Gazette*) founded in London in 1865

[2] whist: a trick-taking card game; modern derivatives include hearts and spades

There were real grounds for supposing, as
75  the *Daily Telegraph* said, that the thief did
not belong to a professional band. On the day
of the robbery a well-dressed gentleman of
polished manners, and with a well-to-do air,
had been observed going to and fro in the
80  paying room where the crime was committed.
A description of him was easily procured and
sent to the detectives; and some hopeful spirits,
of whom Ralph was one, did not despair of
his apprehension. The papers and clubs were
85  full of the affair, and everywhere people were
discussing the probabilities of a successful
pursuit; and the Reform Club was especially
agitated, several of its members being Bank
officials.

90      Ralph would not concede that the work of
the detectives was likely to be in vain, for he
thought that the prize offered would greatly
stimulate their zeal and activity. But Stuart
was far from sharing this confidence; and, as
95  they placed themselves at the whist-table, they
continued to argue the matter. "I maintain,"
said Stuart, "that the chances are in favour of
the thief, who must be a shrewd fellow."

    "Well, but where can he fly to?" asked Ralph.
100  "No country is safe for him."

    "Pshaw!"

    "Where could he go, then?"

    "Oh, I don't know that. The world is big
enough."

105    "It was once," said Phileas Fogg, in a low
tone.

8.   What is the primary purpose of the passage?

   A)  To illustrate the problems with theft at the
Bank of England

   B)  To examine the lives of wealthy men in
England

   C)  To introduce Phileas Fogg and his social
circle at the Reform Club

   D)  To parody the social customs of the upper
class

9.   The passage suggests that Phileas Fogg is a man
who

   A)  focuses on cultural activities.

   B)  lives beyond his means.

   C)  enjoys routine.

   D)  keeps to himself.

10.  Which choice provides the best evidence for the
answer to the previous question?

   A)  Lines 6–9 ("He repaired . . . for him")

   B)  Lines 9–12 ("A flunkey . . . operation")

   C)  Lines 15–19 ("Dinner . . . six")

   D)  Lines 31–35 ("Skillful . . . fingers")

11.  As used in line 6, "repaired" most nearly means

   A)  fixed.

   B)  returned.

   C)  stormed.

   D)  proceeded.

12.  One impression created by the narrator's description of Phileas Fogg in the first paragraph is that he

   A)  keeps abreast of current events.

   B)  is a political reformer.

   C)  has strong opinions about crime.

   D)  makes his living as a banker.

13. Which choice provides the best evidence for the answer to the previous question?

    A) Lines 9–12 ("A flunkey . . . operation")

    B) Lines 19–20 ("Half . . . fireplace")

    C) Lines 31–35 ("Skillful . . . fingers")

    D) Lines 44–48 ("The *Daily* . . . remark")

14. As used in line 51, "functionary" most nearly means

    A) official.

    B) money.

    C) servant.

    D) criminal.

15. According to the passage, which statement about the Bank of England is true?

    A) The public has faith in the integrity of the Bank.

    B) The Bank has taken few precautions to guard against theft.

    C) The Bank has a history of money being stolen.

    D) The Bank has carefully managed public relations.

16. The passage suggests that the thief was not part of a professional crime ring because

    A) the suspect acted alone.

    B) the Bank had never been burglarized before.

    C) the suspect was described as a gentleman.

    D) the Bank carefully screens its customers.

17. The purpose of lines 105–106 ("'It was once,' . . . a low tone") is to

    A) create an ominous atmosphere at the table.

    B) foreshadow Fogg's ideas about the world.

    C) illustrate Fogg's proper demeanor and social skills.

    D) introduce the conflict of the plot.

# Reflect

**Directions:** Take a few minutes to recall what you've learned and what you've been practicing in this chapter. Consider the following questions, jot down your best answer for each one, and then compare your reflections to the expert responses on the following page. Use your level of confidence to determine what to do next.

What are SAT Reading Literature passages? How do expert test takers adjust their active reading to tackle Literature passages most effectively?

_____

_____

_____

How are the questions that accompany Literature passages different than those accompanying standard Science and Social Studies passages?

_____

_____

_____

How confident do you feel with Literature passages? What can you do in practice to improve your performance and gain even more confidence with these types of passages?

_____

_____

_____

## Expert Responses

What are SAT Reading Literature passages? How do expert test takers adjust their active reading to tackle Literature passages most effectively?

*On each SAT test, one reading stimulus is taken from a work of fiction such as a novel or short story. Expert test takers actively read Literature passages by paying attention to what happens to the main character and how he or she responds to these events.*

How are the questions that accompany Literature passages different than those accompanying standard Science and Social Studies passages?

*For the most part, questions accompanying Literature passages are similar to those from standard nonfiction passages, but in literature, you may see 1) Global questions that focus on a change in the passage's tone, 2) Inference questions that ask what the passage's narrator (as opposed to its author) would agree with, or 3) Function questions that ask how or why a character (as opposed to the author) used a detail or reference from the text.*

How confident do you feel with Literature passages? What can you do in practice to improve your performance and gain even more confidence with these types of passages?

*There is no one-size-fits-all answer for this question. Give yourself honest self-assessment. If you feel that Literature passages are a strength, that's great. Continue to practice them so that you'll be able to rack up the points associated with these passages on test day. If you feel less confident about Literature passages, review the strategies in this chapter and try to consistently apply the expert approaches outlined here whenever you practice passages in this format.*

## Next Steps

If you answered most questions correctly in the "How Much Have You Learned?" section, and if your responses to the Reflect questions were similar to those of the SAT expert, then consider Literature passages an area of strength and move on to the next chapter. Come back to this topic periodically to prevent yourself from getting rusty.

If you don't yet feel confident, review the instructional text in this chapter, especially the sections on characters' responses and points of view. Then try the questions you missed again. As always, be sure to review the explanations closely.

# Answers and Explanations

Suggested passage notes:

¶1: Last uncle's funeral vs. this uncle's funeral

¶2–5: Mom to K: Don't tell G uncle died

¶6: K & G daily ritual

¶7: G old, neat, dressed in black silk

¶8–9: K eats candy he doesn't like for G

## 1.    D

**Difficulty:** Medium

**Category:** Global

**Getting to the Answer:** Look back at your notes on the passage and describe the author's intention in your own words. The passage opens with the description of a funeral and then describes the family's reaction: the fear of the effect the death will have on the grandmother causes the family to hide the death from her. **(D)** matches the prediction and is correct.

(A) is incorrect because, although the passage focuses on Kinny, his resilience in the face of the death of his uncle is not discussed. (B) is incorrect because, even though the passage does describe the day of a funeral, the author's interest lies in the effect the death has on the other characters, not in the funeral itself. (C) is incorrect because there is no sense of "the redeeming power" of the social connections between the family and the mourners or of the connection between Kinny and his grandmother.

## 2.    A

**Difficulty:** Hard

**Category:** Global

**Getting to the Answer:** Review the sequence of events in your passage notes and predict an answer. The first paragraph describes the two funerals of Kinny's uncles: one today, when no one visited his grandmother, and one in the past, when many guests were received in Kinny's home. The next section is an exchange between Kinny and his mother, during which his mother explains to Kinny that they are keeping his uncle's death a secret from his grandmother. The next lines contain a description of Kinny's grandmother: she's very old and formal. The final lines introduce the relationship between Kinny and his grandmother. She calls for him daily to give him a treat of candied ginger, which he accepts and eats but doesn't actually like.

Choice **(A)** matches this sequence of events and is correct. The funerals are the important events that are described, and the interaction of Kinny and his grandmother with the daily treat introduce their relationship. (B) is half-right, half-wrong. Kinny's mother does correct his behavior, but the passage does not go on to describe Kinny behaving badly. (C) is a distortion. Kinny's relationship with his mother is described, not his relationship with his father. (D) is a distortion of the information in the first part of the excerpt. Although some funeral customs are described, the focus of the passage is not on these customs, but rather on why the two funerals were different: the family is trying to hide the death of Kinny's uncle from his grandmother. In addition, the impact of his uncle's death on his grandmother is mentioned, but not "examined" or explained.

## 3.    B

**Difficulty:** Easy

**Category:** Vocab-in-Context

**Getting to the Answer:** Reread the sentence containing "callers" that begins in line 12. Predict another word that could be substituted for "callers" and give the sentence the same meaning as the original one. People are quietly entering the home, holding the hands of family members, speaking with them, drinking coffee, and departing. "Guests" would be a good prediction. **(B)** is a match and is correct.

There is no mention of buying or selling, so the "callers" are not "customers," and (A) is incorrect. In other contexts, "callers" could be suitors or those who shout, but that is not how the passage describes them, so (C) and (D) are incorrect as well.

**4. C**

**Difficulty:** Medium

**Category:** Inference

**Strategic Advice:** Notice that the next question after this one is a Command of Evidence question. When you find the correct answer for this question, keep your finger on the part of the passage where you found it so you'll be able to use it for the Command of Evidence question that follows.

**Getting to the Answer:** In lines 37 and 38, the strong emotional connotations of "conspiratorial" and "uncomfortable" signal that something important is going to be discussed. Kinny's mother is "conspiring" with him to keep his uncle's death a secret from his grandmother. **(C)** is correct.

(A) is a distortion of information in the passage. Although the family suspects that Kinny's grandmother is older than she says, the passage does not state that they actually know her true age. (B) is the opposite of what the passage says. Kinny does not like the ginger. (D) is incorrect because the fact that extended family frequently eat at Kinny's home (lines 46–50) is not a secret kept from his grandmother.

**5. B**

**Difficulty:** Medium

**Category:** Command of Evidence

**Getting to the Answer:** Keep your finger on the lines where you found the answer to the previous question, lines 36–40, and match that section of the passage to the choices. **(B)** is correct.

(A) contains the visitors' comments, not a secret kept from Kinny's grandmother. (C) describes Kinny's summons by his grandmother; no secret is mentioned. (D) depicts Kinny's reaction to the ginger, which is not directly related to the secret of his uncle's death.

**6. A**

**Difficulty:** Medium

**Category:** Function

**Getting to the Answer:** Read a little above and a little below line 22 and predict what the author intended when she used the phrase. The people who "had all come out clucking" had just visited the grandmother after the death of her son and were saying how "wonderful" she was in the face of this tragedy. They

were all saying the same nice things. **(A)** is correct. (B) is incorrect because although Kinny's mother is concerned for the health of his grandmother, the visitors do not mention it. (C) and (D) are incorrect because they are not discussed by the visitors and are in fact not mentioned in the text at all.

**7. D**

**Difficulty:** Hard

**Category:** Detail

**Getting to the Answer:** Find the relevant text in the passage: "Kinny believes that adults don't look directly at him." The idea is found in line 33 where his mother "looked at him squarely." In the following lines, 33–35, the passage states, "something he had noticed grown people never seemed to have time to do." Kinny believes adults are too preoccupied to look at him directly; **(D)** is a perfect match.

(A) is a correct detail from the passage; lines 14–17 describe the guests as silent and "long-faced," but this is not the reason Kinny thinks they don't look directly at him. Similarly, although his mother is scolding him, this isn't why Kinny thinks adults don't look squarely at him, so (B) is incorrect. (C) is the opposite of what the passage says. Kinny's mother is likely looking directly at him in order to impress upon him how important her request is, but the question is asking why Kinny thinks adults do *not* look directly at him.

Suggested passage notes:

¶1: F's daily routine
¶1: cont: F's friends
¶2–10: recent robbery
¶11: lack of security at bank
¶12: thief not a professional robber
¶13–19: disagree whether thief will be caught

**8. C**

**Difficulty:** Hard

**Category:** Global

**Getting to the Answer:** Think about the passage as a whole and use one sentence to predict the purpose of this passage. Make sure the tone of the answer choice matches the tone of the passage. The excerpt provides a brief character sketch of Phileas Fogg and establishes the dynamics of his friendships at the Reform Club. **(C)** is correct; it accurately identifies the purpose of the excerpt.

Choice (A) addresses only a narrow aspect of the passage and ignores the author's careful and extended description of Phileas Fogg. (B) is too broad: the passage describes the life of Fogg, not wealthy English men in general. (D) is extreme. The passage has a neutral tone; there is no evidence of parody.

## 9. C

**Difficulty:** Medium

**Category:** Inference

**Getting to the Answer:** Review the descriptions of Phileas Fogg and his actions in your passage map. Summarize what the beginning of the passage says about Fogg. Paragraph 1 describes Fogg counting out his steps on his way to the club. Upon arriving at the club, Fogg goes to his "habitual table" (line 8) and performs a routine series of actions. Choice **(C)** is correct, as the details in paragraph 1 depict a man who likes to keep to a set routine.

Choice (A) is incorrect because no cultural activities are described in the passage. (B) is incorrect because although the club, with its servants, fireplace, and dining room, may seem to be luxurious, there is no evidence in the passage that Fogg cannot comfortably pay for these services. (D) is contradicted in the passage starting in line 21 where Fogg's card-playing partners are introduced, and in line 44 where Fogg inserts himself into his friends' conversation. People who keep to themselves do not play cards or enter others' conversations.

## 10. A

**Difficulty:** Medium

**Category:** Command of Evidence

**Getting to the Answer:** Review your answer to the previous question. Locate the answer choice that directly supports the conclusion you drew. **(A)** is correct. It provides the best support for the idea that Phileas Fogg is a man of habit and routine. The word "habitual" (line 8) and the fact that his table was prepared ahead of time for him suggest that Fogg followed this routine regularly.

None of the incorrect choices addresses Fogg's fondness for routine. Choice (B) supports the idea that Fogg is skilled in cutting open his newspaper, not that he enjoys routine. (C) describes the routine passing of the time but does not mention Fogg. (D) describes the bank robber and does not mention Fogg at all.

## 11. D

**Difficulty:** Medium

**Category:** Vocab-in-Context

**Getting to the Answer:** Locate context clues to help determine the meaning of the word. Predict a meaning for the word and then match it to the closest answer choice. The sentence describes Fogg arriving at the club and going to his usual table. A good prediction is simply the word "went." Look for the nearest match in the answers. **(D)** fits the tone and context of the sentence and is correct.

Choice (A) is a common definition for "repaired" but does not make sense in the context. You cannot *fixed* to the dining-room. (B) subtly changes the meaning of the sentence. Although you may think Fogg is returning to his table since it's his "habitual" table, the text is describing events as they occur and not referring to what may have happened earlier. (C) is not supported by the passage; there is no evidence that Fogg is moving with great force or anger.

## 12. A

**Difficulty:** Medium

**Category:** Inference

**Getting to the Answer:** Review the first paragraph of the passage before choosing an answer. Fogg is very methodical, he walks to the club, reads two newspapers, has dinner, reads another newspaper, and is joined by the men with whom he plays cards. **(A)** is correct because not only does Fogg read three newspapers daily, but he also later chimes in with a comment on the robbery the other men are discussing based on the information he learned in the paper.

There is no mention of politics, so (B) is incorrect. Although Fogg does comment on the bank robbery, his comment is a neutral observation about the description of the perpetrator, not a "strong opinion about crime," so (C) is incorrect. (D) is incorrect because Fogg's occupation is not mentioned in the excerpt.

## 13. D

**Difficulty:** Easy

**Category:** Command of Evidence

**Getting to the Answer:** Review your answer to the previous question. Decide which lines of text show Fogg's knowledge of current events. **(D)** is correct. In these lines, Fogg interjects with additional information from the newspaper about a crime that is a current event.

Choice (A) simply describes Fogg receiving and preparing one of his papers. (B) describes his partners gathering in the reading room and says nothing about Fogg himself. (C) is describing the bank robber, not Fogg.

## 14. A

**Difficulty:** Easy

**Category:** Vocab-in-Context

**Getting to the Answer:** Find context clues in the target sentence. Predict the meaning of the word and look for a match among the answer choices. "Functionary" (line 51) refers back to the "principal cashier" (line 50) mentioned earlier in the sentence. When you see two related answer choices, such as *official* and *servant*, pay attention to the tone and specific context clues to help you choose. **(A)** is correct; if substituted back into the sentence, the meaning of the sentence is unchanged.

Choice (B) is incorrect because you cannot refer to a "cashier" as *money*. (C), *servant*, is incorrect because it implies a hierarchy that is not present in the passage. Similarly, there is no evidence in the passage that the "cashier" is a *criminal*, so (D) is incorrect.

## 15. B

**Difficulty:** Medium

**Category:** Detail

**Getting to the Answer:** Locate the portion of the text that discusses the bank. Your passage map for paragraph 11 should note a lack of security at the bank. This paragraph describes the lack of security measures at the bank that led to a theft in broad daylight; lines 55–58 note a lack of guards or protective gratings. **(B)** is correct.

Choice (A) is a distortion of information in the excerpt. Lines 53–55 state that the bank had faith in its customers, not that the customers have faith in the bank. (C) and (D) are not mentioned in the passage at all.

## 16. C

**Difficulty:** Medium

**Category:** Inference

**Getting to the Answer:** Find the part of the passage that describes the thief. Locate sentences that focus on a description of the suspect. Summarize the details in a one-sentence description. Lines 76–80 ("On the day . . . crime was committed") describe the suspect as a gentleman. **(C)** is correct because the passage suggests that the police do not believe the man to be a professional thief due to the description of his appearance and demeanor.

Choice (A) may be true but is not presented as a reason the thief was not professional. (B) and (D) are not mentioned in the passage at all.

## 17. B

**Difficulty:** Medium

**Category:** Function

**Getting to the Answer:** Reread the cited line. Concentrate on how the sentence affects the text surrounding it. Examining the surrounding text shows that this comment occurs during a discussion about the thief being on the run. Fogg has silently listened to the conversation to this point, but now quietly interjects. This suggests that Fogg will have more to say about the topic; **(B)** is correct.

(A) is extreme. "Ominous" foreshadows a bad or unpleasant event, and the text simply provides Fogg's view without any negative connotations. (C) is a misused detail. The passage does describe Fogg's demeanor, but the statement in the line reference for the question does not. (D) may be tempting if you're familiar with the plot of the book from which this excerpt is drawn, but remember, your answers on the SAT must be based only on the given passage. Since the line reference is the last line in the passage, it cannot be introducing the conflict of the plot of this excerpt.

# CHAPTER 23

# SAT Reading: Timing and Section Management Strategies

## Timing

You have 65 minutes to complete 5 passages with 52 questions each, so you need to complete each passage and its accompanying questions in an average of 13 minutes to finish on time. (Note that passages are not all the same length or difficulty, so some will take longer than others.) After $32\frac{1}{2}$ minutes, you should be halfway done with the section. When the proctor informs you that there are 5 minutes remaining, you should ideally be working on the last few questions.

Note that this is a brisk pace. Reading for structure can help, as can triaging questions and skipping those that you can see at a glance will be time-consuming. Your real task is not actually to attempt all the questions in 65 minutes but to get as many points from the section as you can.

## Section Management

You may want to triage entire passages on the Reading section, not just questions. Some test takers have a hard time with literature, or primary source passages, or science; if you have distinct preferences about subject matter, you might consider leaving a particular passage type for last. For example, the section typically opens with the Literature passage. If that's the passage you feel least confident about, it makes sense to skip it and do it last. (Just be careful with your bubbling.)

Remember that you probably won't spend the same amount of time on each question for a passage. Every question counts for the same number of points, so be sure to complete the questions you find easiest to answer first. Also be aware that the questions are usually arranged with Globals at the beginning of the set and increasing line number references, and that you will typically see 2 Command of Evidence questions per passage. Approached correctly, these questions should be quick: when you research the Detail or Inference question that immediately precedes the Command of Evidence question, leave your finger on the support you find for the correct answer, then look for that support among the answer choices for the Command of Evidence question.

Finally, moving efficiently through this section is important, but that does not mean that you should skip over any text. Reading all of the text in the passage is essential to answering questions efficiently and accurately.

When considering the structure of the entire test, keep in mind that you will have a break after you complete this section. If you start to feel tired, remind yourself that you'll have a break soon. The more focused you can remain, the easier it will be for you to determine each correct answer.

There is a full Reading section in the "How Much Have You Learned?" part of this chapter. Use it to practice timing: skip questions you find too time-consuming and return to them if you have time and keep an eye on the clock. When you are finished, check your work—and reflect on how well you managed the section.

# How Much Have You Learned?

**Questions 1–10 refer to the following passage.**

The passage is adapted from Wilkie Collins, *The Woman in White*, first published in 1859. It is considered one of the first novels of the mystery genre.

Pesca's face and manner, on the evening when we confronted each other at my mother's gate, were more than sufficient to inform me that something extraordinary had happened.
5  It was quite useless, however, to ask him for an immediate explanation. I could only conjecture, while he was dragging me in by both hands, that, knowing my habits, he had come to the cottage to make sure of meeting
10  me that night and that he had some news to tell of an unusually agreeable kind.

We both bounced into the parlor in a highly abrupt and undignified manner. My mother sat by the open window laughing and
15  fanning herself. Pesca was one of her especial favorites, and his wildest eccentricities were always pardonable in her eyes. From the first moment she found out that the little Professor was deeply and gratefully attached to her son,
20  she opened her heart to him unreservedly and took all his puzzling foreign peculiarities for granted, without so much as attempting to understand any one of them.

My sister Sarah, with all the advantages of
25  youth, was, strangely enough, less pliable. She did full justice to Pesca's excellent qualities of heart, but she could not accept him implicitly, as my mother accepted him, for my sake. Her insular notions of propriety rose in perpetual
30  revolt against Pesca's constitutional contempt for appearances, and she was always more or less undisguisedly astonished at her mother's familiarity with the eccentric little foreigner. I have observed, not only in my sister's case,
35  but in the instances of others, that we of the young generation are nowhere near as hearty and impulsive as some of our elders. I constantly see old people flushed and excited by the prospect of some anticipated pleasure

40  which altogether fails to ruffle the tranquility of their serene grandchildren. Are we, I wonder, quite such genuine boys and girls now as our seniors were in their time? Has the great advance in education taken rather
45  too long a stride, and are we in these modern days just the least trifle in the world too well brought up?

Without attempting to answer those questions decisively, I may at least record that
50  I never saw my mother and my sister together in Pesca's society without finding my mother much the younger woman of the two. On this occasion, for example, while the old lady was laughing heartily over the boyish manner in
55  which we tumbled into the parlor, Sarah was perturbedly picking up the broken pieces of a teacup, which the Professor had knocked off the table in his precipitate advance to meet me at the door.

60  "I don't know what would have happened, Walter," said my mother, "if you had delayed much longer. Pesca has been half mad with impatience, and I have been half mad with curiosity. The Professor has brought some
65  wonderful news with him, in which he says you are concerned, and he has cruelly refused to give us the smallest hint of it till his friend Walter appeared."

"Very provoking: it spoils the set,"
70  murmured Sarah to herself, mournfully absorbed over the ruins of the broken cup.

While these words were being spoken, Pesca, happily and fussily unconscious of the irreparable wrong which the crockery had
75  suffered at his hands, was dragging a large arm-chair to the opposite end of the room, so as to command us all three, in the character of a public speaker addressing an audience. Having turned the chair with its back towards
80  us, he jumped into it on his knees and excitedly addressed his small congregation of three from an impromptu pulpit.

"Now, my good dears," began Pesca, "listen
to me. The time has come—I recite my good
85  news—I speak at last."

"Hear, hear," said my mother, humoring the
joke.

"The next thing he will break, Mamma,"
whispered Sarah, "will be the back of the best
90  arm-chair."

"Among the fine London Houses where I
teach the language of my native country," said
Pesca, "is one, mighty fine, in the big place
called Portland. The golden Papa there, the
95  mighty merchant, says 'I have got a letter from
my friend, and he wants a recommend from
me, of a drawing-master, to go down to his
house in the country. Perhaps you know of a
drawing-master that I can recommend?'

100  "I address myself to the mighty merchant,
and I say, 'Dear sir, I have the man! The first
and foremost drawing-master of the world!'"

1.  The narrator's stance is best described as that of

A)  a writer learning about a possible teaching
    job.

B)  a social historian chronicling generational
    changes produced by evolving social
    conventions.

C)  a young man eager to set out on his own,
    free of the strictures of his family.

D)  a careful observer describing the natures of
    three characters he knows well.

2.  The central purpose of the first paragraph is to

A)  provide insight into the narrator's habits.

B)  demonstrate Pesca's disregard for the
    narrator's feelings.

C)  introduce the tone and setting of the
    passage.

D)  build suspense regarding the nature of the
    news Pesca has brought.

3.  The description of Pesca and the narrator in
    lines 12–13 ("We both . . . manner") is primarily
    meant to

A)  illustrate the personalities of the narrator
    and Pesca.

B)  suggest that their disruptive behavior was
    in fact combative.

C)  portray Pesca as a bad influence on the
    narrator.

D)  provide a humorous contrast to the
    seriousness of the narrator's mother.

4.  The narrator's mother's attitude toward Pesca is
    best described as

A)  confusion about his enthusiastic manner.

B)  disapproving of his unkempt appearance.

C)  amusement at his wild schemes.

D)  appreciative of his relationship with
    her son.

5.  Which choice provides the best evidence for the answer to the previous question?

    A)  Lines 17–23 ("From . . . them")

    B)  Lines 25–28 ("She . . . implicitly")

    C)  Lines 28–31 ("Her . . . appearances")

    D)  Lines 60–62 ("I don't . . . longer")

6.  The questions in lines 41–47 ("Are we . . . brought up?") most nearly imply that

    A)  the narrator and his sister received a poor education.

    B)  some young people may behave too maturely for their age.

    C)  some older people are too childish in their behavior

    D)  some children were raised inappropriately by their parents

7.  According to the passage, the narrator's sister is upset about the broken teacup because

    A)  it makes the tea set incomplete.

    B)  she does not have the money to replace it.

    C)  it was important to her mother.

    D)  Pesca deliberately knocked it off the table.

8.  The attitude of Pesca toward the narrator's sister is best described as

    A)  disrespectful and dismissive of her opinions.

    B)  enthusiastic in furthering her education.

    C)  unfazed by her concern for his behavior.

    D)  disappointed by her disregard for his feelings.

9.  Which choice provides the best evidence for the answer to the previous question?

    A)  Lines 48–52 ("Without . . . two")

    B)  Lines 72–75 ("While . . . his hands")

    C)  Lines 79–82 ("Having . . . pulpit")

    D)  Lines 91–94 ("Among . . . Portland")

10. As used in line 77, "command" most nearly means

    A)  order.

    B)  engage.

    C)  lead.

    D)  bully.

**Questions 11-20 refer to the following passage.**

This is an excerpt from a speech by William Lloyd Garrison, one of the most prominent opponents of slavery in the United States. It was delivered in 1854.

Let me define my positions, and at the same time challenge anyone to show wherein they are untenable.

I am a believer in that portion of the
5   Declaration of American Independence in which it is set forth, as among self-evident truths, "that all men are created equal; that they are endowed by their Creator with certain inalienable rights; that among these
10  are life, liberty, and the pursuit of happiness." Hence, I am an abolitionist. Hence, I cannot but regard oppression in every form—and most of all, that which turns a man into a thing—with indignation and abhorrence. Not
15  to cherish these feelings would be recreancy to principle. They who desire me to be dumb on the subject of slavery, unless I will open my mouth in its defense, ask me to give the lie to my professions, to degrade my manhood,
20  and to stain my soul. I will not be a liar, a poltroon, or a hypocrite, to accommodate any party, to gratify any sect, to escape any odium or peril, to save any interest, or to promote any object. Convince me that one man may
25  rightfully make another man his slave, and I will no longer subscribe to the Declaration of Independence. Convince me that liberty is not the inalienable birthright of every human being, of whatever complexion or clime, and
30  I will give that instrument to the consuming fire. I do not know how to espouse freedom and slavery together. . . .

These are solemn times. It is not a struggle for national salvation; for the nation, as such,
35  seems doomed beyond recovery. The reason why the South rules, and the North falls prostrate in servile terror, is simply this: with the South, the preservation of slavery is paramount to all other considerations—
40  above party success, denominational unity, pecuniary interest, legal integrity, and

constitutional obligation. With the North, the preservation of the Union is placed above all other things—above honor, justice, freedom,
45  integrity of soul. . . . All these she is ready to discard for the union. Her devotion to it is the latest and most terrible form of idolatry. . . . If, at any time, she grows restive under the yoke, and shrinks back aghast at the new atrocity
50  contemplated, it is only necessary for that power to crack the whip of disunion over her head, as it has done again and again, and she will cower and obey like a plantation slave— for has she not sworn that she will sacrifice
55  everything in heaven and on earth, rather than the Union?

What then is to be done? Friends of the slave, the question is not whether by our efforts we can abolish slavery . . . but whether
60  we will go with the multitude to do evil, sell our birthright for a mess of pottage, cease to cry aloud and spare not. . . . Let us stand in our lot, "and having done all, to stand." At least, a remnant shall be saved. Living
65  or dying, defeated or victorious, be it ours to exclaim, "No compromise with slavery! Liberty for each, for all, forever! Man above all institutions!"

11. The primary purpose of the passage is to

    A) compare and contrast the justifications for slavery offered by the North and the South.

    B) encourage abolitionists to continue their efforts against slavery.

    C) invite critiques of the author's position.

    D) outline the reasons justifying slavery in order to argue against them.

12. One central idea of the passage is that

    A) the abolition of slavery will save the nation.

    B) the South is primarily responsible for the national tragedy of slavery.

    C) the ideals of the Declaration of Independence and the institution of slavery are mutually exclusive.

    D) the North should uphold the unity of the nation above all other considerations.

13. The main purpose of the second paragraph is to

    A) argue that a practice is inconsistent with a principle.

    B) describe needed changes to a social system.

    C) discuss the underlying ideas in an important document.

    D) suggest a way to resolve a difficult political issue.

14. Based on the passage, Garrison would be most likely to agree with which claim about the relationships of the North and the South to the institution of slavery?

    A) The South will agree to the abolition of slavery only through an amendment to the Constitution.

    B) Slavery will become an issue of ancillary importance as the industry of the South becomes more mechanized.

    C) The North has been complicit in the growth and continuation of slavery.

    D) Because slavery is incompatible with the Declaration of Independence, the North demands abolition.

15. Which choice provides the best evidence for the answer to the previous question?

    A) Lines 4–11 ("I am . . . abolitionist")

    B) Lines 38–42 ("with . . . obligation")

    C) Lines 42–46 ("With . . . union")

    D) Lines 64–68 ("Living . . . institutions")

16. As used in line 30, "instrument" most nearly means

    A) tool.

    B) document.

    C) expedient.

    D) mechanism.

17. The primary function of the third paragraph is to

    A) contrast the South's use of slavery with the North's opposition to slavery.

    B) describe reasons the South opposes, and the North supports, Garrison's view.

    C) identify the reasons both the North and the South oppose Garrison's view.

    D) outline the requirements for the abolition of slavery.

18. Which choice provides the best evidence for the claim that Garrison believes a personal decision to oppose slavery is paramount, whether or not the abolitionist movement is successful?

    A) Lines 31–32 ("I . . . together")

    B) Lines 46–47 ("Her . . . idolatry")

    C) Lines 57–60 ("Friends . . . evil")

    D) Lines 66–68 ("No compromise . . . institutions")

19. In the third paragraph, Garrison implies the most important reason the North tolerates slavery is that

    A) abolition would cause the South to secede from the Union.

    B) goods from the South would become prohibitively expensive without the use of slave labor.

    C) the Declaration of Independence does not prohibit slavery.

    D) the North will not meddle in the social policies of the South.

20. The passage most strongly suggests that the author believes which of the following regarding the abolition of slavery?

   A) Although the abolitionists may fail, they must continue to fight against slavery.

   B) Because the North and the South both have compelling reasons to tolerate slavery, the abolitionists will fail.

   C) With enough Northern support, slavery will eventually be abolished.

   D) Thanks to the efforts of Garrison's followers, the abolition of slavery is imminent.

**Questions 21–30 refer to the following passage.**

This passage describes some research applications of a bioluminescent jellyfish protein.

Electron excitation is the process by which an electron within an atom is transferred to a higher energy state. Electron excitation is typically followed by the release of a photon
5 when the electron falls back to its normal state. The initial transfer to the higher energy state can be accomplished by absorbing a photon, but it can happen in a variety of other ways as well. For example, the element
10 phosphorus spontaneously combines with oxygen when exposed to air, producing a transfer of energy to the phosphorus electrons. The subsequent release of photons as the electrons fall back to lower energy states is an
15 example of what is termed chemiluminescence, the emission of light as a result of a chemical reaction.

In a related effect called bioluminescence, light is produced by chemical reactions
20 associated with biological activity. Bioluminescence occurs in a variety of life forms and is more common in marine organisms than in terrestrial or freshwater life. Examples of species that exhibit
25 bioluminescence include certain bacteria, jellyfish, clams, fungi, worms, ants, and fireflies. There is considerable diversity in how light is produced, but most processes involve the reaction of a light-emitting
30 molecule with oxygen, catalyzed by an enzyme. The light-emitting molecule varies from one organism to another, but all are grouped under the generic name luciferin. The enzymes catalyzing the reaction fall into
35 two groups: photoproteins and luciferases. As the biochemistry of bioluminescence becomes better understood, researchers are harnessing this biological process in recombinant genetics experiments.
40 In 2008, Osamu Shimomura, Martin Chalfie, and Roger Tsien won the Nobel Prize in chemistry for their work in discovering specific bioluminescent proteins and

employing them to study cellular chemistry.
45 Shimomura laid the foundation through his work on a bioluminescent jellyfish, *Aequorea victoria*. In 1962, he and a colleague isolated three key molecules that produce *A. victoria*'s bioluminescence: coelenterazine, a
50 luciferin; aequorin, a photoprotein; and green fluorescent protein (GFP). The coelenterazine, when combined with aequorin, produces blue light that is then transduced to green light by GFP. Interestingly, GFP does not require any
55 cofactor or substrate besides oxygen; it simply emits a green glow when exposed to blue or ultraviolet light. This means that GFP can be used, by itself, as a marker for the expression of other proteins in a cell. This innovation was
60 Chalfie's contribution, via a paper published in 1992. Roger Tsien's research expanded on this application: he created variants of GFP with stronger fluorescence and in different colors. The result of the collective work of
65 Shimomura, Chalfie, and Tsien is that it is nowadays possible to track a variety of cellular processes using bioluminescent proteins.

One example of this work is the study of cancer using zebrafish that have had
70 the gene for GFP inserted into their DNA immediately next to a gene that codes for certain cancer processes. The result of this genetic manipulation is the ability to see the location of tumor cells. Zebrafish are
75 translucent, so fluorescent tumor cells can be readily identified using a light microscope. A 2003 study of leukemia using this animal model revealed that tumor cells initially arose in the thymus and then spread to muscles and
80 abdominal organs.

Another example is the discovery that bisphenol A (BPA), a common component of plastics, is an endocrine disrupter— specifically, that it has estrogenic activity.
85 In a study conducted in 2002, cells in tissue culture were genetically engineered to express GFP when an estrogen receptor on the cells was stimulated. When exposed to estrogen, the cells glowed fluorescent green. Researchers

90 found that they could cause the cells to
exhibit the same fluorescence by exposing
them to BPA. However, the concentration
of BPA required to induce fluorescence was
100,000 times higher, so it appears that BPA
95 is only weakly estrogenic. Repeating the
same experiment with polychlorinated BPA,
the researchers found it to have stronger
estrogenic activity than ordinary BPA. Because
polychlorinated BPA is not easily biodegraded
100 and tends to persist in the environment, they
concluded that polychlorinated BPA may
function as a worse endocrine disrupter
than BPA.

        The research applications of GFP are
105 endless, and while a great deal remains to be
discovered about bioluminescence in the many
species that exhibit it, the discovery of this
one jellyfish protein has already produced a
variety of useful results.

21. The passage evolves from an explanation of a
natural biochemical process to

   A) a description of research made possible
through extensions of the natural process.

   B) an explanation of how the natural process
developed through evolutionary pressure.

   C) a discussion of efforts by scientists to
reverse the effects of the natural process.

   D) an explanation why research based on this
process will have no practical results.

22. The function of the first paragraph is to

   A) introduce the main idea of the passage.

   B) identify a point of view with which the
author disagrees.

   C) provide evidence for the author's opinion.

   D) discuss a scientific phenomenon similar to
the main topic of the passage.

23. According to the passage, bioluminescence is
most often found

   A) with oxygen when exposed to the air.

   B) among terrestrial creatures.

   C) in marine life.

   D) in light given off by hot objects.

24. Which of the following provides the best evidence for the answer to the previous question?

   A) Lines 9–12 ("For example . . . electrons")

   B) Lines 18–20 ("In . . . activity")

   C) Lines 21–24 ("Bioluminescence . . . life")

   D) Lines 34–35 ("The enzymes . . . luciferase")

25. The passage suggests that the jellyfish *Aequorea victoria*

    A) would emit green light without the presence of aequorin.

    B) would emit blue light without the presence of aequorin.

    C) would emit no light without the presence of GFP.

    D) would emit blue light without the presence of GFP.

26. Which of the following provides the best evidence for the answer to the previous question?

    A) Lines 24–27 ("Examples . . . fireflies")

    B) Lines 47–51 ("In 1962 . . . (GFP)")

    C) Lines 51–54 ("The coelenterazine . . . GFP")

    D) Lines 61–64 ("Roger . . . colors")

27. Based on the passage, it can be inferred that aequorin, part of *A. victoria*'s bioluminescence machinery, is

    A) a bacterium.

    B) a light-emitting molecule.

    C) a luciferase.

    D) an enzyme.

28. As used in line 45, "foundation" most nearly means

    A) basis.

    B) charity.

    C) organization.

    D) innovation.

29. According to the passage, which of the following has NOT been the subject of GFP-based research?

    A) Leukemia

    B) Electron excitation

    C) Endocrine disrupters

    D) Tumor cells

30. In the experiment in which it was concluded that ordinary BPA is only weakly estrogenic, the researchers are assuming that

    A) whether or not GFP illuminates depends in part on the level of estrogenic activity.

    B) the intensity of the illumination in the GFP is directly correlated with the level of estrogenic activity.

    C) polychlorinated BPA has higher levels of estrogenic activity than does ordinary BPA.

    D) the level of endocrine disruption caused by BPA is correlated with the level of estrogenic activity.

**Questions 31-41 refer to the following passage.**

The following passage explores the history and impact of public higher education in the United States.

Every year, hundreds of thousands of students graduate from U.S. public universities. Many of the largest and most elite schools in the nation fall into the
5  category of public, or state, institutions. Unlike private universities, which generally operate independently from any government influence, public higher education was established through government legislation
10  and is sustained through state and federal involvement in various ways. A look into the history of U.S. public higher education can shed light on the changing ideals of the American story over the past century and
15  a half.

America's earliest higher-education institutions, like Harvard, were initially developed by and for clergy, or church workers. For 17th-century Puritans in
20  America, church leadership was of utmost importance. At that time, clergy was the main profession for which college degrees were offered. Later, during the 18th and 19th centuries, paralleling the onset of secular
25  (and increasingly scientifically inclined) modern thought, the nation and government acknowledged the need for broader higher education opportunities. Philosophers and politicians alike were aware that well-educated
30  citizens were a vital element of a functional democracy. A better-informed voting population could secure a better political future. Moreover, with aims to advance the fields of technology and agriculture through
35  higher education, legislators anticipated potential economic improvements nationwide as well. It was in the nation's best interest to make college more accessible.

In 1862, President Lincoln signed the Morill
40  Land-Grant Act. This was, in many ways, the force behind the public university system. The Morill Act ensured that public land would be

set aside for the establishment of universities across the country. The coming decades saw a
45  massive increase in the opening of universities in the nation. Hundreds of U.S. public universities began to operate. These schools received federal and state support, offered practical, accessible education, and sought,
50  originally, to advance the fields of agriculture and mechanics. Soon these schools offered wide varieties of subjects and specialties. These universities would be operated by their respective states, but all would adhere to
55  certain broad federal regulations.

At the time, the government was seeking to mend racial injustices through legislation. To this effect, a second land act was passed in 1890 in hopes of inhibiting discrimination
60  in public universities. While at the time this did not accomplish the intended openness and diversity, it paved the way for the culture of diversity the American university system enjoys today. Many public universities are
65  now richly diverse, with regulations in place to accept students of any race, ethnicity, or socioeconomic status. In a similar vein, women, who were once a minority in colleges, increasingly gained a strong presence in U.S.
70  universities over the past 150 years. Women actually surpassed men in overall U.S. college attendance around the turn of the 21st century.

Since the legislation of the 19th century,
75  public universities have undergone momentous growth. The system has evolved to address and accommodate the nuances of 20th- and 21st-century American culture and development. Offering in-state students some
80  of the most affordable degree programs in higher education, these schools have now graduated millions of undergraduate and graduate students. Public universities also manage the majority of the nation's
85  government-funded academic research initiatives. Featuring some of the most competitive athletic programs in the world, as well as elite scholarship and arts programs,

the U.S. public universities's accomplishments
90 seem boundless. With schools in Alaska,
Hawaii, and even U.S. territories like Puerto
Rico and Guam, public university impact
reaches the farthest corners and populations of
the nation. The state school system has been
95 formative for American culture, philosophy,
economics, medicine, politics, and much more.

The eminence of the U.S. public university
network stretches beyond the United States.
Students travel from across the globe to study
100 at top programs. Cutting-edge schools like the
University of Virginia (UVA) and University
of California at Los Angeles (UCLA) receive
continual international attention for their
accomplishments in scholarship and research.
105 Programs, faculty, and students from these
schools participate in the global conversation
in significant ways, working toward a better
future for the planet.

Given those early visions for a more
110 robustly educated voting population, the
enormity of the system that the Morill
Act launched is remarkable. U.S. public
universities have both shaped and employed
many of America's greatest thinkers.
115 Considering their timeline and their
accomplishments, these schools seem to reflect
the post–Civil War history of diversity, liberty,
creativity, and equal opportunity that in many
ways distinguishes the American cultural
120 identity.

31. The passage's primary purpose is to

A) summarize the accomplishments of U.S.
public universities since the 19th century.

B) explain the historical influence of religion
on the development of the university
system.

C) discuss the relationship between U.S.
higher education and the cultural values of
the nation.

D) summarize the historical effect of the
Morill Land-Grant Act on U.S. public
universities.

32. Which of the following pieces of evidence would
most strengthen the author's line of reasoning
throughout the passage?

A) Information about the ways in which
private and public universities differ in
paragraph 1

B) An example of how the 17th-century
clergy benefited from higher education in
paragraph 2

C) Statistics showing increased enrollment
numbers of minority students in paragraph 4

D) An example of a competitive public
university athletic program in paragraph 5

33. In the second paragraph, the author uses the
idea that educated citizens are necessary for a
functioning democracy to

A) show why an educated workforce increased
agricultural production.

B) demonstrate the continued role of the
clergy in American public life.

C) explain why the government was playing a
larger role in public education.

D) emphasize the importance of technological
innovation for the economy.

34. Which choice provides the best evidence for the answer to the previous question?

    A) Lines 21–23 ("At that time . . . offered")

    B) Lines 23–28 ("Later . . . opportunities")

    C) Lines 31–33 ("A better-informed . . . future")

    D) Lines 33–37 ("Moreover . . . well")

35. The purpose of the third paragraph is to

    A) highlight an example of the government increasing access to public education.

    B) discuss initial technological advances in agriculture and mechanics.

    C) outline the effects of the Morill Land-Grant Act on the U.S. economy.

    D) explain the relationship between federal and state control of public universities.

36. In line 49, the author's use of the word "accessible" implies that

    A) public universities would expand course offerings to encompass a range of subjects.

    B) the likelihood that people with limited means could attend a university was increasing.

    C) agriculture and mechanics would receive the most federal and state support.

    D) President Lincoln supported passage of the Morill Land-Grant Act to expand education.

37. As used in line 54, "adhere" most nearly means

    A) resist.

    B) notice.

    C) acquiesce.

    D) comply.

38. In the fourth paragraph, the author uses the fact that more women than men now attend college to

    A) contrast the advances of women's rights with racial injustice in public universities.

    B) provide an example of how the land acts initially failed to stop discrimination.

    C) show that public universities have grown increasingly diverse over time.

    D) illustrate the challenges many people still face to attend public universities.

39. Which choice provides the best evidence for the answer to the previous question?

    A) Lines 58–60 ("To this effect . . . universities")

    B) Lines 60–64 ("While . . . today")

    C) Lines 64–67 ("Many . . . status")

    D) Lines 67–70 ("In a similar . . . years")

40. As used in line 77, "nuances" most nearly means

    A) eras.

    B) categories.

    C) circumstances.

    D) variations.

41. The fifth paragraph supports the central idea of the passage by

    A) discussing how public university athletic programs have grown increasingly competitive.

    B) providing evidence of the success of federal legislation meant to invest in public universities.

    C) explaining that in-state tuition rates have increased enrollment in U.S. public universities.

    D) noting that the U.S. public university system has expanded into U.S. territories.

**Questions 42–52 refer to the following passages.**

Passage 1 discusses the possibility of panspermia, the idea that life on Earth is of extraterrestrial origin. Passage 2 is a response to Passage 1.

**Passage 1**

Panspermia, the hypothesis that life on Earth originated in outer space, has had a number of supporters since the nineteenth century—some of them quite distinguished—
5 but it has never won general acceptance among biologists. However, recent research has found possible support for panspermia.

Most of the meteorites that strike Earth originated in the lifeless wastes of the asteroid
10 belt. A few, though, have been identified as fragments that were torn from the Moon and Mars by comets and asteroids and eventually drifted to Earth. The Moon and Mars are lifeless, but there is reason to believe that,
15 billions of years ago, Mars was warmer and moister than it is now and capable of supporting life. Indeed, Mars may have been more conducive to the development of life than Earth was during the early history of the
20 solar system. It is feasible that life developed on Mars first and was carried to Earth on space-borne debris.

But could living organisms have survived the journey through space? The effects of cosmic
25 rays on the known Martian meteorites indicate that they took from 700,000 to 15,000,000 years to reach Earth. It seems inconceivable that any life forms could have survived such conditions for so long. However, computer simulations
30 suggest that fragments hurled into space from a collision on Mars would begin reaching Earth in only 16,000 years. Moreover, it is therefore conceivable that an improbable stroke of luck allowed a meteor to carry living things from
35 Mars to Earth—and the Tanpopo experiment has shown that certain bacteria, when clustered together to inhibit damage by ultraviolet rays, can survive in space for at least one year. Panspermia can thus no longer be dismissed
40 as science fiction or the fanciful speculation

of unscientific minds: it is becoming an increasingly viable, even promising, field of research within the field of astrobiology.

**Passage 2**

While absence of evidence is not evidence
45 of absence, the panspermia hypothesis will remain nothing more than a tantalizing idea until incontrovertible evidence is found that interplanetary transfer of microbes is not only possible, but also historical fact. Finding such
50 evidence is absurdly challenging, the more so because alternative explanations abound for the presence of bacteria on objects in space.

Take the recent discovery of marine and land bacteria similar to species found on Earth
55 (they belong to the genera *Mycobacterium* and *Delftia*) in cosmic dust present on the exterior of the International Space Station (ISS). Even if the discovery is genuine and not the result of cross-contamination of the samples at
60 any stage between their collection and their analysis in a laboratory on Earth, it by no means indicates that the bacteria arrived at the ISS from an extraterrestrial source. It is far more likely that they are ordinary Earth
65 bacteria that were transported to the ISS on the surfaces of supplies or other objects as part of routine restocking, as is known to have occurred in the past. It is also possible, though less likely, that they are ordinary
70 Earth bacteria that were hurled into the outer atmosphere by storm systems. Either way, their discovery on ISS surfaces does not demonstrate their extraterrestrial origin—and the issue of indeterminate origin will hamper
75 any similar type of study. It follows that very carefully designed, novel experiments will be required to conclusively demonstrate or refute the panspermia hypothesis, and while multiple researchers are working on this problem, it
80 will be years, and more probably decades, before we can draw plausible and meaningful inferences.

42. The author of Passage 1 would be most likely to agree with which of the following statements about the solar system?

    A) The Moon used to be more capable of supporting life than it currently is.

    B) It is possible that there was a time when Mars had conditions more suitable to life than Earth did.

    C) It is likely that a fragment from the Moon carried life to Earth.

    D) The life found on Mars billions of years ago could have originated from the asteroid belt.

43. Which choice provides the best evidence for the answer to the previous question?

    A) Lines 8–10 ("Most . . . belt")

    B) Lines 10–13 ("A few . . . Earth")

    C) Lines 17–22 ("Indeed . . . debris")

    D) Lines 29–32 ("However . . . years")

44. As used in line 9, the word "wastes" is closest in meaning to

    A) wilderness.

    B) barren zones.

    C) by-products.

    D) fragments.

45. The main purpose of lines 32–38 ("Moreover . . . year") is to

    A) counter an objection to a hypothesis.

    B) indicate the need for further study.

    C) provide the answer to a question.

    D) describe an event that is likely to have occurred many times.

46. According to the author of Passage 2, which of the following best summarizes the reasons to be skeptical of discoveries of bacteria on extraterrestrial objects as evidence for panspermia?

    A) Scientists cannot avoid bias when examining evidence for hypotheses they believe to be true.

    B) A large number of highly improbable events would need to have occurred at precisely the same time.

    C) It is very unlikely that such bacteria would have survived the lengthy journey from Mars to Earth.

    D) There is high probability that the bacteria came from some terrestrial source.

47. Based on the discussion of the bacteria found on the exterior of the International Space Station, the author of Passage 2 would be most likely to agree with which of the following?

    A) It is easier for bacteria to be carried into Earth's outer atmosphere from its surface than from elsewhere in the solar system.

    B) It is not possible that bacteria from an extraterrestrial source could have survived a journey through space.

    C) The time required to create experiments that will determine the origin of the bacteria makes the process of doing so impractical.

    D) The dust on the ISS that the bacteria are found in likely came from rocks that originated on Earth.

48. Which choice provides the best evidence for the answer to the previous question?

    A) Lines 44–49 ("While . . . fact")

    B) Lines 53–57 ("Take . . . (ISS)")

    C) Lines 63–68 ("It is . . . past")

    D) Lines 75–82 ("It follows . . . inferences")

49. In using the phrase "absence of evidence is not evidence of absence . . ." (lines 44–45), the author is

    A) pointing out a logical flaw in critics' arguments.

    B) condemning the lack of research conducted into the panspermia hypothesis.

    C) laying a logical foundation for an argument made later.

    D) acknowledging that a lack of evidence does not disprove a hypothesis.

50. The author of Passage 2 would be most likely to respond to the evidence presented in lines 14–20 by

    A) dismissing the evidence as completely irrelevant to the topic at hand.

    B) conceding that the evidence does, in fact, lend substantial support to the panspermia hypothesis.

    C) asserting that such evidence is insufficient to support the hypothesis of panspermia and therefore inconclusive.

    D) shifting to a position of provisional acceptance of panspermia dependent upon the results of future experiments.

51. The authors of both passages provide an answer to which of the following questions?

    A) What would be required for the panspermia hypothesis to gain widespread acceptance?

    B) How does the panspermia hypothesis compare to other potential explanations of the origins of terrestrial life?

    C) What conditions would have had to exist to allow microorganisms of extraterrestrial origin to have reached Earth?

    D) Is the panspermia hypothesis currently worth serious consideration as an explanation for the origins of life on Earth?

52. Which choice best states the relationship between the two passages?

    A) Passage 2 directly refutes the evidence presented in Passage 1.

    B) Passage 2 challenges the primary argument of Passage 1.

    C) Passage 2 provides a broader context for the ideas discussed in Passage 1.

    D) Passage 2 considers additional evidence to further the goals of Passage 1.

# Answers and Explanations

Suggested passage notes:

¶1: Description of P; good news

¶2: Mom likes P

¶3: Sister doesn't like P b/c too improper; young gen. more stuffy than old

¶4: Mom's reaction to P vs. sister's reaction to P

¶5–6: Mom excited for news; sister upset over cup

¶7–8: P actions

¶9–10: Mom and sister's reactions to P

¶11–12: P's announcement

## 1.  D

**Difficulty:** Medium

**Category:** Inference

**Strategic Advice:** Focus on how the narrator sees the characters and events.

**Getting to the Answer:** Literature passages tend to focus on the relationships among main characters. Here, the main characters are the narrator, his mother, his sister, and Pesca. The narrator focuses on the reaction that each woman has to Pesca's actions. Predict that the author wants to create a sketch of each woman by using those different responses. **(D)** is correct.

(A) is incorrect because, even though a job is mentioned at the end, it is for a "drawing-master," not a writer. And this is just a small point at the end, which ignores everything else that precedes it in the passage. (B) is incorrect because there's no indication of the narrator being a historian, let alone one who is studying generational changes or social conventions. (C) is incorrect because there is no indication that the narrator is looking to leave his family.

## 2.  C

**Difficulty:** Medium

**Category:** Function

**Strategic Advice:** Consult your passage map to identify the function of the first paragraph.

**Getting to the Answer:** This paragraph provides context for the rest of the passage. The narrator describes Pesca's expressive nature, his understanding of Pesca, and the reason for the subsequent events in the passage. Predict that this paragraph sets the stage for

understanding how Pesca's character will impact the rest of the story. **(C)** matches that prediction.

(A) is incorrect because the paragraph describes Pesca's behavior, not the narrator's. Even though the narrator's habits are mentioned in one sentence, the paragraph is still about Pesca using that information. (B) is incorrect because Pesca is just excited. He's not said to be dismissive of the narrator's feelings. (D) is incorrect because Pesca's news is not really important to the story. It's more about people's reaction to Pesca's excitement.

## 3.  A

**Difficulty:** Medium

**Category:** Function

**Strategic Advice:** To understand why a narrator chooses a particular phrase, focus on the author's intention in the surrounding text. The cited section will work to accomplish that intention.

**Getting to the Answer:** Throughout the paragraph, the narrator describes why his mother finds Pesca so pleasing. This introductory wording sets the stage by describing Pesca as undignified. This feature of his personality is a great match for **(A)**.

(B) is incorrect because the word "bouncing" implies good humor, not aggression. (C) is incorrect because the mother appreciates the bond between the narrator and Pesca. There is no suggestion of Pesca being a bad influence. (D) is incorrect because it is the narrator's sister who is more serious, not his mother.

## 4.  D

**Difficulty:** Medium

**Category:** Inference

**Strategic Advice:** Note that the next question is a Command of Evidence question, so make a mark next to any sentences that support the answer to this question. Doing so could come in handy for the next question.

**Getting to the Answer:** The strongest indication of the mother's attitude comes in the second paragraph. She laughs as Pesca excitedly enters the room. But, more tellingly, she is described as accepting his peculiar behavior because he is "deeply and greatly attached to her son." This is echoed in **(D)**.

(A) is incorrect because, if anything, the mother is said to merely accept any of Pesca's peculiarities without even trying to understand them. That doesn't mean she's confused. Even if she were to find those peculiarities a little confusing, it doesn't follow that she's confused by his enthusiasm. (B) is incorrect because it describes the sister's attitude, not the mother's. (C) is incorrect because there is no indication of any wild schemes.

### 5.  A

**Difficulty:** Medium

**Category:** Command of Evidence

**Strategic Advice:** Be sure to use any information used in the previous question to save time on this question.

**Getting to the Answer:** The support for the previous question came primarily from the second paragraph. That includes lines 17–23, which describe how the mother has opened her heart to Pesca because of his attachment to her son. **(A)** is correct.

(B) and (C) are incorrect because they refer to the sister's attitude, not the mother's. (D) is incorrect because, although the mother is speaking, she is not indicating any attitude toward Pesca at that moment.

### 6.  B

**Difficulty:** Medium

**Category:** Inference

**Strategic Advice:** When given a line reference, consider the context of the surrounding text.

**Getting to the Answer:** This question refers to some thoughts the narrator presents at the end of the third paragraph. In that paragraph, the narrator is talking about his sister, who is rather serious compared to her mother. The narrator then describes how this is typical of young people, who don't seem as excitable or impulsive as their elders. The narrator's questions at the end hint that younger people are perhaps *too* serious these days. That matches **(B)**.

(A) is incorrect because it misuses the word "education." The author is actually suggesting that young people are so *well* educated that they forget how to have a little fun. (C) is incorrect because the author seems to regret the serious behavior of young people, not the excitable behavior of older people. (D) is incorrect because there is no questioning of how parents are raising their children.

### 7.  A

**Difficulty:** Medium

**Category:** Detail

**Strategic Advice:** The phrase "According to the passage" means that the correct answer will be spotted directly in the text. Don't rely on memory. Find the detail and literally put your finger on it.

**Getting to the Answer:** The cause of the sister's disappointment is found in the sixth paragraph, in which she mourns the broken teacup and claims that "it spoils the set." This matches **(A)**.

(B) is incorrect because there's no mention of its cost or how much money the sister has. (C) is incorrect because the mother seems unconcerned with the broken teacup. (D) is incorrect because Pesca is said to have knocked it over upon excitedly entering the room. It's presented as an accident, not a deliberate act.

### 8.  C

**Difficulty:** Medium

**Category:** Inference

**Strategic Advice:** A quick glance ahead shows that the next question is a Command of Evidence question. It is worth taking note of any lines that support the answer to this question, as those may be useful for the next question.

**Getting to the Answer:** The passage provides a lot of information about the attitude of the narrator's sister toward Pesca: she has contempt for his appearance and is bothered by his behavior, which resulted in a broken teacup. However, there are few hints about Pesca's attitude. The only clue is in the seventh paragraph, where Pesca is said to be unaware of the broken teacup, suggesting that Pesca is oblivious to the sister's unhappiness. That matches **(C)**.

(A) is incorrect because it's too strong. Pesca is just excited and unaware of the narrator's sister's bad mood; he is not purposely being rude or dismissing her. (B) is incorrect because Pesca's enthusiasm is more about his news, not for any desire to educate the sister. (D) is incorrect because, while the sister is unhappy with Pesca, he does not seem to notice or be disappointed in any way.

**9.  B**

**Difficulty:** Medium

**Category:** Command of Evidence

**Strategic Advice:** Consider the purpose of each given quote to make sure it matches the ideas expressed in the previous question.

**Getting to the Answer:** The previous question asked about Pesca's attitude toward the narrator's sister. As Pesca never addresses the sister directly, the only suggestion of attitude comes from lines 72–75, in which Pesca is seen as oblivious to the sister's concern about her broken teacup. Those are the lines cited in correct answer **(B)**.

(A) is incorrect because those lines indicate more the sister's attitude toward Pesca, not the other way around. (C) is incorrect because it shows Pesca's excitement in sharing his news with everyone in the room, not his attitude toward the sister in particular. (D) is incorrect because it's Pesca talking about himself, without expressing any attitude toward the sister or anyone else.

**10.  B**

**Difficulty:** Hard

**Category:** Vocab-in-Context

**Strategic Advice:** For Vocab-in-Context questions, read the entire sentence for meaning. Be ready to eliminate choices that give a common definition for the word.

**Getting to the Answer:** In line 78, the author is describing how Pesca grabbed a chair so that he could be like "a public speaker addressing an audience." In that sense, commanding an audience means seeking their undivided attention, or keeping them engaged. That makes **(B)** the correct answer.

(A), (C), and (D) are incorrect because they all refer to a different concept of commanding that is not consistent with this passage. Pesca is not giving orders or leading or bullying anyone.

Suggested passage notes:

> ¶1: challenge to find flaw in G's position
> ¶2: slavery incompatible w/ Dec of Independence
> ¶3: South's & North's reasons for slavery
> ¶4: G's opinion—abolitionists can't end slavery, but can oppose it

**11.  B**

**Difficulty:** Medium

**Category:** Global

**Strategic Advice:** Always ask yourself, "Why did the author write this passage?" after you read the passage, and before you start on the questions.

**Getting to the Answer:** Garrison ends the passage by answering the question in line 57, "What then is to be done?" He goes on to state in the final paragraph that abolitionists should continue their efforts to abolish slavery whether or not they are successful. **(B)** is correct.

(A) and (D) are distortions of information presented in the third paragraph. Garrison outlines the reasons the North and the South use to justify slavery, but dismisses them as erroneous without arguing against them (D) or comparing them (A). (C) is too narrow. While, in the first paragraph, Garrison does invite his opponents to criticize his views, this is not mentioned in any of the later parts of the text and is therefore not the central goal of the passage.

**12.  C**

**Difficulty:** Medium

**Category:** Global

**Strategic Advice:** Use your passage map to predict the answer to a Global question.

**Getting to the Answer:** Review the passage map to refresh your memory of the central ideas. **(C)** is found in the summary of paragraph 2 and is the correct answer.

(A) is a distortion of information in the passage. Although the author believes slavery must be abolished, lines 33–35 state his view that the nation may already be beyond saving. (B) is extreme; Garrison believes that both the North and the South are responsible for the institution of slavery, not that the South is "primarily responsible." (D) is the opposite of what the passage says. As stated in lines 42–26, Garrison believes that the North is putting the Union first, but then he goes on to harshly criticize this view, calling it "the latest and most terrible form of idolatry" in lines 46–47.

**13. A**

**Difficulty:** Hard

**Category:** Function

**Strategic Advice:** Function questions ask how or why the author used a feature in the passage. Keep the overall purpose of the passage in mind and answer the question, "Why did the author write the second paragraph?"

**Getting to the Answer:** The passage map notes that slavery is incompatible with the Declaration of Independence, so **(A)** is the correct answer. The practice mentioned in the choice is slavery, and it is inconsistent with the principle that "all men are created equal" in the Declaration of Independence.

(B) is incorrect because although Garrison believes slavery should be abolished, he does not describe what this entails or how it should be done. (C) is incorrect because Garrison states the principle of freedom in the Declaration of Independence and then goes on to discuss how this principle affects his views; he does not discuss the idea of freedom itself. (D) is incorrect because, although Garrison clearly states that slavery should be abolished, he does not propose any way to resolve the conflict that would arise with those who believe slavery should be maintained.

**14. C**

**Difficulty:** Medium

**Category:** Inference

**Strategic Advice:** Research the answer to an Inference question in the passage. The passage must directly support the answer.

**Getting to the Answer:** The relationships of the South and the North with slavery are discussed in the third paragraph. Lines 38–39 state that the South considers the continuation of slavery the "paramount" issue; nothing is more important to the South. The North tolerates slavery because that toleration keeps the nation together. Lines 42–44 state that preservation of the union is the North's top priority. Compare these ideas to the choices, and **(C)** is the match. By putting the unity of the nation first, Garrison would argue the North has allowed slavery to continue and to spread.

(A) is incorrect because it is the opposite of what the passage says. Lines 38–42 state that the South will put the preservation of slavery above "constitutional obligation." (B) is incorrect because it is not mentioned in the

passage at all. (D) is incorrect because while the author does believe that slavery is incompatible with the Declaration of Independence, this view is not also attributed to the North. Also, the text never describes the North as demanding abolition.

**15. C**

**Difficulty:** Medium

**Category:** Command of Evidence

**Strategic Advice:** Put your finger on the lines where you found the answer to the previous question.

**Getting to the Answer:** If you leave your finger on the line in the passage where you found the previous answer, you can answer Command of Evidence questions quickly. The reason the North tolerated slavery was found in lines 42–44, which matches **(C)**.

(A) and (D) are Garrison's views, not those of either the North or the South. (B) describes the South's view, but the answer to the previous question was the North's toleration of slavery, so the correct evidence will support the North's point of view.

**16. B**

**Difficulty:** Medium

**Category:** Vocabulary-in-Context

**Strategic Advice:** Look back in the passage and determine how the author used the word given in a Vocab-in-Context question.

**Getting to the Answer:** Use the line reference to locate the word "instrument," then read above and below that line to determine how the author is using that word. Since "instrument" is preceded by the pronoun "that" in the sentence, determine what "that" is and use the pronoun's antecedent as your prediction. The sentence in line 30 begins in line 27, so "that" must be the noun closest to the start of the sentence—the Declaration of Independence. The Declaration of Independence is a document, so **(B)** is correct.

The remaining answers are incorrect because none of them properly refers to the Declaration of Independence.

## 17. C

**Difficulty:** Hard

**Category:** Function

**Strategic Advice:** Think of the author's purpose in writing the passage and then ask yourself, "How or why did the author use the third paragraph?"

**Getting to the Answer:** The correct answer will describe why the author included the third paragraph, or how the third paragraph contributed to the author's point of view. Review the passage map and predict "to describe the reasons both the North and the South accept slavery in the South." **(C)** is correct.

(A) is incorrect because the third paragraph outlines the justifications for slavery offered by both the South and the North. (B) is incorrect because Garrison's view is that slavery should be abolished, and the third paragraph gives the reasons both the South and the North will allow slavery to continue. (D) is incorrect because the author argues for an absolute and immediate end to slavery, and does not list any requirements for this change.

## 18. C

**Difficulty:** Hard

**Category:** Command of Evidence

**Strategic Advice:** Be sure your choice, on its own, supports the idea in the question.

**Getting to the Answer:** For Command of Evidence questions, the excerpt from the passage in the choice must answer the question. **(C)** is the only choice that addresses both the effort to abolish slavery ("the question is not whether by our efforts we can abolish slavery") and the personal decision to oppose slavery ("but whether we will go with the multitude to do evil").

(A), (B), and (D) all provide evidence that Garrison opposes slavery, but do not connect that opposition to the success (or lack of success) of the abolitionist movement.

## 19. A

**Difficulty:** Easy

**Category:** Inference

**Strategic Advice:** Research the answer in the third paragraph, looking for a statement that must be true based on the passage.

**Getting to the Answer:** The emphasis keywords in the question, "most important," mean the passage must be equally emphatic. In lines 42–44, Garrison states that "above all other things," the North wants "the preservation of the Union." In other words, the North allows slavery to continue because of the fear that, if the North does not, the South will leave the Union. **(A)** is correct.

You may believe (B) to be true if you've studied U.S. history, but this is not mentioned in the text, so it is incorrect. (C) is incorrect because it is the opposite of what the passage says. Garrison argues in the second paragraph that slavery and the Declaration of Independence are incompatible. (D) is incorrect because it is not mentioned in the passage at all.

## 20. A

**Difficulty:** Medium

**Category:** Inference

**Getting to the Answer:** Use your understanding of the main idea to eliminate choices and then match the remaining choices to the passage. Garrison's main idea is that abolitionists must continue to fight slavery, even though they may not be successful (lines 57–60.) **(A)** is correct.

(B) is a distortion of information in the third paragraph. While Garrison did outline the reasons the North and South were both willing to tolerate slavery, Garrison did not consider either view "compelling." Rather, he argued that these were the reasons "the nation seems . . . doomed beyond recovery" (lines 34–35.) (C) and (D) similarly distort information in the passage. While Garrison is arguing for the abolition of slavery, he argues, in lines 57–60, that efforts for abolition must continue regardless of their success. Garrison does not state slavery will eventually (C), or soon (D), be abolished.

Suggested passage notes:

¶1: chemiluminescence can be caused by electron excitation. ex: phosphorus + oxygen = light

¶2: bioluminescence: light from animals; description of general chemical process

¶3: biolum. in jellyfish; GFP is important molecule

¶4: cancer research based on GFP

¶5: toxic plastics research based on GFP

¶6: GFP research is promising; much is unknown but many results already

## 21. A

**Difficulty:** Medium

**Category:** Global

**Getting to the Answer:** Use the passage map to see how the passage proceeds. After the discussion of the natural bioluminescence through paragraph 3, the passage moves on to a discussion of research based on this process. Paragraphs 4 and 5 discuss how jellyfish proteins involved in bioluminescence have helped scientists research topics such as cancer and potentially harmful components in plastic. **(A)** describes this part of the passage perfectly and is correct.

Choice (B) is incorrect because there's no discussion in the passage of how bioluminescence evolved. (C) can be eliminated because the research is not intended to reverse the effects of bioluminescence; it's using those effects in an attempt to make new discoveries. (D) is contradicted by the last line of the passage, which says that the research has already produced "useful results."

## 22. D

**Difficulty:** Medium

**Category:** Function

**Getting to the Answer:** When asked for the function of a paragraph, consider how it relates to the overall purpose of the passage. The purpose of the passage as a whole is to discuss bioluminescence and its research applications. The first paragraph describes chemiluminescence, and the first line of paragraph 2 says that bioluminescence is a "related effect." Therefore, you can predict that the first passage is something that is similar to the main idea but which itself is not the main idea. **(D)** matches this prediction perfectly and is correct.

(A) is incorrect because the first paragraph does not actually discuss the main idea, merely a related topic.

(B) and (C) both imply that the author expresses an opinion; they are both incorrect because the author expresses no opinions in this neutral, explanatory passage.

## 23. C

**Difficulty:** Easy

**Category:** Detail

**Strategic Advice:** Answer Detail questions by reading around the cited text until you find the information that answers the question.

**Getting to the Answer:** Paragraph 2 contains general information about bioluminescence. Read around the cited lines to find the detail you need: "Bioluminescence occurs in a variety of life forms and is more common in marine organisms than in terrestrial or freshwater life" (lines 21–24). This matches **(C)**, which is correct.

According to the first paragraph, phosphorus does emit light when combined with oxygen, but this is an example of chemiluminescence, not bioluminescence, so (A) is incorrect. (B) is directly contradicted by the lines you found in your research, so it can be eliminated. (D) is not mentioned anywhere in the passage, so it is also incorrect.

## 24. C

**Difficulty:** Easy

**Category:** Command of Evidence

**Getting to the Answer:** While researching the previous question, you found that lines 21–24 supported the correct answer. Thus, **(C)** is correct. (A) describes the reaction between phosphorus and oxygen, not bioluminescence. (B) describes bioluminescence in general, but it doesn't establish that it's most common in marine life. (D) merely describes the two types of enzymes that might be involved in a bioluminescent reaction, so it can be eliminated.

## 25. D

**Difficulty:** Medium

**Category:** Inference

**Getting to the Answer:** Paragraph 3 is where this jelly-fish is discussed, so direct your research there. There are a lot of facts in the paragraph, but what it tells you about the *A. victoria* is fairly straightforward: coelenter-azine and aequorin interact to emit blue light, which is transformed into green light by GFP. Look for an answer that lines up with this information.

**(D)** is correct. GFP's function is to turn the blue light into green light, so if it wasn't there, the light would be blue. Since aequorin is described as being part of the light-producing process, there would be no biolumines-cence without it, which means (A) and (B) can be elim-inated. (C) is incorrect because the GFP is not directly involved in producing light; it merely changes the color.

## 26. C

**Difficulty:** Medium

**Category:** Command of Evidence

**Getting to the Answer:** Use your research for the previ-ous question to point you to the correct answer here. The correct answer to the previous question depended on knowing how the *A. victoria* produced light; this is described in lines 51–54, so **(C)** is correct.

(A) cites lines that merely give examples of biolumines-cent creatures, so it can be eliminated. (B) may seem tempting, because lines 47–51 describe the chemicals involved in *A. victoria*'s bioluminescence. However, it doesn't actually provide any information on how they interact to produce light, so it's incorrect. (D) can be eliminated because it describes further research done on GFP, not how GFP works in *A. victoria*.

## 27. D

**Difficulty:** Hard

**Category:** Inference

**Getting to the Answer:** *A. victoria* is the biolumines-cent jellyfish that, according to the passage map, is discussed in paragraph 3, so start your research there. Aequorin is described as a photoprotein that interacts with a luciferin, which then produces light. However, the passage map indicates that the chemical process of bioluminescence is described in paragraph 2 as

well. Photoproteins are mentioned there as a class of enzymes; therefore, aequorin is an enzyme, so **(D)** is correct.

(A) is incorrect because bacteria are mentioned as an example of an organism that could exhibit biolumines-cence itself. (B) may be tempting since aequorin is part of the light-emitting process. However, according to the passage, it's the luciferin that is the light-emitting molecule; the photoproteins merely start the reaction. According to paragraph 2, luciferase is another class of enzyme, distinct from photoproteins, that could be involved in a bioluminescent reaction, so (C) can be eliminated.

## 28. A

**Difficulty:** Easy

**Category:** Vocab-in-Context

**Getting to the Answer:** Check out the context in which "foundation" is used. It's used in paragraph 3 in the discussion of how three scientists won a Nobel Prize; the passage says that one of the scientists "laid the foundation" with research on a bioluminescent jellyfish. Thus, you can predict that here, "foundation" is used to mean something like *groundwork*. **(A)**, *basis*, matches this prediction and is correct. While (B), *charity*, and (C), *organization*, can be synonyms for "foundation," they don't fit the context here. (D) can be eliminated because, while the passage does discuss many innova-tions, this isn't one of them.

## 29. B

**Difficulty:** Hard

**Category:** Detail

**Strategic Advice:** This is a Detail question for which the three incorrect answers will be examples of GFP-based research, while the correct answer will not be. You can't predict something that doesn't appear in the passage, but you can use details from the passage to predict the wrong answers.

**Getting to the Answer:** According to the passage map, paragraphs 4 and 5 discuss this research. Paragraph 4 mentions that GFP was used to research tumor cells, with leukemia being given as an example of of one type of cancer that was studied. That means (A) and (D) can be eliminated. Paragraph 5 mentions that GFP was used to determine that BPA, a type of plastic, is an endocrine disrupter, so (C) is incorrect. That leaves **(B)**, electron excitation, as the correct answer. This topic is discussed at the beginning of the passage as a process that can sometimes lead to chemiluminescence, not as a subject of GFB research.

## 30. A

**Difficulty:** Hard

**Category:** Inference

**Getting to the Answer:** This asks for an assumption about estrogen levels in BPA; according to the passage, plastics research is discussed in paragraph 5, so direct your attention there. The researchers concluded that BPA was only weakly estrogenic since more BPA than pure estrogen was needed to trigger the illumination. This means that they must be assuming there's some link between the level of estrogen and whether the GFP illuminates. This is captured perfectly in **(A)**, so it is correct.

(B) is incorrect because there's no indication that the GFP glows more brightly if estrogen levels are higher; the distinction was whether or not the GFP illuminated at all. (C) is a true statement according to the passage, but it's the conclusion of a different study; the question is about ordinary BPA, not polychlorinated BPA, so it is incorrect. (D) can be eliminated since this experiment wasn't intended to test the levels of endocrine disruption; it merely tested whether BPA contained estrogen.

Suggested passage notes:

¶1: 2 types of univ. = pub. & private
¶2: pub univ. goal = ↑ higher ed opportunity
¶3: 1862—gov't gave pub. land for univ.
¶4: history of diversity
¶5: major growth
¶6: US univ. part of global conv.
¶7: univ. reflect diversity, liberty, creativity

## 31. C

**Difficulty:** Hard

**Category:** Global

**Strategic Advice:** Consider what the passage is about overall and what the author wants the reader to learn, rather than an idea that is mentioned only in passing or in support of the passage's purpose. Reviewing your whole passage map can help you focus on the entirety of the passage.

**Getting to the Answer:** The author has written a brief history of public higher education in the United States; in both the introduction and conclusion, the author connects the evolution of the public university system with the evolution of generally accepted ideals and cultural values, such as diversity and liberty. Predict that the author is discussing the connection between public higher education and generally accepted ideals. **(C)** is correct.

## 32. C

**Difficulty:** Hard

**Category:** Inference

**Strategic Advice:** It is difficult to predict the exact answer for this type of question, but concisely stating the author's line of reasoning before reviewing the answer choices will help you eliminate the choices that do not strengthen that theme.

**Getting to the Answer:** Throughout the passage, the author discusses how the expansion of public universities has impacted American culture. In paragraph 4, the author describes how public universities have gradually become more diverse, offering educational opportunities to many people who would not have otherwise had them in previous years. This has had a significant impact on American culture. Consider which of these pieces of evidence best supports that theme; **(C)** is correct.

## 33. C

**Difficulty:** Hard

**Category:** Function

**Getting to the Answer:** The correct answer will reflect a specific position supported in both the second paragraph and the passage as a whole. Predict that the author is citing political and economic reasons to explain why the government "acknowledged the need" (line 27) for educated citizens. **(C)** is correct.

## 34. B

**Difficulty:** Medium

**Category:** Command of Evidence

**Getting to the Answer:** Use your support for the previous question to predict the answer. Consider which choice best shows a clear relationship to your answer. In the previous question, line 27 offered support for your answer; **(B)** is correct because it explicitly states that the government saw the "need for broader higher education opportunities" (lines 27–28).

**35. A**

**Difficulty:** Medium

**Category:** Function

**Getting to the Answer:** Summarize the paragraph and think about what the author would want the reader to know after reading it. Be sure to review your passage map, which should already state important information about the paragraph. Your passage map notes that in 1862, the government gave public land for university development; the paragraph states that the Morill Act was an early example of the federal government's desire to increase enrollment at public universities. Predict that the purpose of the paragraph is to explain how the government supported public higher education. **(A)** is correct.

**36. B**

**Difficulty:** Medium

**Category:** Function

**Getting to the Answer:** The author's choice of words is deliberate. Read the sentence carefully and think about what the author is suggesting when he uses the word "accessible." The passage notes that public universities received federal and state support, which means the universities could then function at a lower cost and could enable more students to attend. Predict that "accessible" was used to describe how higher education was remodeled to be available to more people, especially those with limited means. **(B)** is correct.

**37. D**

**Difficulty:** Easy

**Category:** Vocab-in-Context

**Getting to the Answer:** Use context clues to help you predict the meaning of the word as it is used in the sentence. The last sentence in paragraph 3 contrasts the fact that although universities would be operated by states, they would still need to follow, or comply with, federal regulations because they received federal support. Predict that "adhere" most nearly means *follow* or *comply with*. **(D)** is correct.

**38. C**

**Difficulty:** Medium

**Category:** Function

**Getting to the Answer:** Think about why the author would want to include this fact. The paragraph's central idea is that the student populations of public universities have grown increasingly diverse. Predict that the author is describing an example of how public universities have become more diverse. Look for the answer choice that matches this prediction. **(C)** is correct.

**39. B**

**Difficulty:** Easy

**Category:** Command of Evidence

**Getting to the Answer:** There should be a clear relationship between the correct choice and the previous answer. Since you used the fourth paragraph as a whole to predict the last question, look for the choice that offers support for the specific answer to the previous question. **(B)** clearly states that public universities are diverse today, even though the 1890 land act did not increase diversity when it was passed. This corresponds to the answer to the previous question.

**40. D**

**Difficulty:** Easy

**Category:** Vocab-in-Context

**Getting to the Answer:** Predict the meaning of the word with context clues from the sentence and paragraph. The second sentence of paragraph 5 states that the public university system "has evolved," which implies it has done so in response to changes or variations in American culture over time. Predict that "nuances" most nearly means *changes* or *variations*. Check your answer choice in the sentence to ensure it makes sense. **(D)** is correct.

## 41. B

**Difficulty:** Medium

**Category:** Inference

**Getting to the Answer:** Consider the central idea of the passage that you identified in a previous question and the central idea in the fifth paragraph. The passage is primarily about the way in which U.S. higher education has reflected American cultural identity. The fifth paragraph summarizes the major growth public higher education has undergone. Predict that as the American culture has grown to value public higher education, public higher education has undergone major growth; the fifth paragraph gives an example that supports the central idea. **(B)** is correct.

Suggested Passage 1 notes:

> ¶1: Panspermia not generally accepted but new research may suppt
>
> ¶2: Asteroids from Moon/Mars to Earth; Mars may have once had life
>
> ¶3: Transfer of life possible

Suggested Passage 2 notes:

> ¶1: Panspermia just hypothesis—no evidence
>
> ¶2: Bacteria on ISS likely from Earth. Special experiments needed to confirm or refute panspermia—concl likely years away.

## 42. B

**Difficulty:** Medium

**Category:** Inference

**Strategic Advice:** The correct answer will be the one that logically follows from the statements made in the passage.

**Getting to the Answer:** The keywords in the question, "would be most likely to agree with," identify this as an Inference question. Begin by referring back to the place in the passage where the author discusses elements of the solar system. In paragraph 2, the author states that the Moon and Mars are now lifeless, but that billions of years ago, Mars was warmer and moister and "may have been capable of supporting life." The paragraph further states that Mars may have been more conducive to the development of life than Earth was during the early history of the solar system. **(B)** logically follows from these statements and is the correct answer.

There was no discussion of the Moon being able to support life, so (A) and (C) are incorrect. The author never states that life was actually found on Mars or where such life might have originated, so (D) can be ruled out as well.

## 43. C

**Difficulty:** Medium

**Category:** Command of Evidence

**Getting to the Answer:** While researching the previous question, you found that lines 17–22 supported the answer. Thus, **(C)** is correct. (A) describes the lifeless area of the asteroid belt but does not discuss whether conditions were favorable for life on either Earth or Mars. (B) indicates that a few asteroids may have come from the Moon and Mars but doesn't mention the conditions of life on Earth or Mars. (D) indicates the relatively short time in which asteroids may have reached Earth from Mars but has nothing to do with the conditions for life on either planet.

## 44. B

**Difficulty:** Medium

**Category:** Vocab-in-Context

**Strategic Advice:** Look back in the passage and determine how the author used the word given in a Vocab-in-Context question. Imagine that the word is missing and needs to be filled in; predict a synonym.

**Getting to the Answer:** Use the line reference to locate the word "wastes," then read above and below that line to determine how the author is using that word. Since "wastes" is preceded by the adjective "lifeless" in the sentence, and is being used to describe an area of space, the asteroid belt, you can predict "lifeless area." **(B)** is correct.

The remaining answers are incorrect because, although each of them is an alternative definition of "wastes," none of them makes sense in the context of the sentence.

## 45. A

**Difficulty:** Hard

**Category:** Function

**Strategic Advice:** Think of the author's purpose in writing this paragraph and then ask yourself: "Why did the author include these lines; how do they help advance the purpose?"

**Getting to the Answer:** The paragraph begins with a discussion of the problems with the hypothesis of panspermia: the harsh conditions in space and the great amount of time that seems necessary for objects to travel from Mars to Earth. These are reasons that people object to the hypothesis. The cited lines go on to discuss information that might weaken those objections. Therefore, **(A)** is correct.

(B) is incorrect because there is no discussion of further study in this section of the passage. (C) may be tempting, but the information in the cited lines is not there to definitively answer the question of whether panspermia occurs; it is merely there to give evidence that weakens the objections. (D) is incorrect because the author never hints at how often an event might have occurred.

## 46. D

**Difficulty:** Medium

**Category:** Detail

**Strategic Advice:** Answer Detail questions by reading around the cited text until you find the information that answers the question.

**Getting to the Answer:** Paragraph 2 of Passage 2 contains information about bacteria found on the exterior of the International Space Station. The author then engages in a lengthy discussion describing the likely terrestrial origins of these bacteria. This matches **(D)**, which is correct.

The author never mentions bias among scientists, so (A) is incorrect. While the author might agree with the statements in (B) and (C), neither of these is the reason given for skepticism about the possibility of extraterrestrial origins for the bacteria found on the ISS, so both are incorrect.

## 47. A

**Difficulty:** Hard

**Category:** Inference

**Strategic Advice:** The correct answer to an Inference question will be the one that logically follows from the statements made in the passage.

**Getting to the Answer:** The keywords in the question, "would be most likely to agree with," identifies this as an Inference question. Begin by referring back to the place in the passage where the author discusses the bacteria found on the ISS. The author states that the bacteria are more likely to be from Earth than from an extraterrestrial source—either contamination introduced sometime during the testing process or bacteria that were lofted into the outer atmosphere by storms on Earth. **(A)** logically follows from this information and is the correct answer.

(B) is incorrect because it is too extreme: the author thinks it unlikely that the bacteria have an extraterrestrial origin, but never implies that it is impossible. (C) is incorrect because the author indicates that further "novel experiments" will be needed to make meaningful determinations about the possibility of panspermia and that the process may take decades, but never mentions that such experimentation will take too long to be practical. (D) can be ruled out since the author refers to the dust on the ISS as "cosmic dust," implying that it has a nonterrestrial origin.

## 48. C

**Difficulty:** Easy

**Category:** Command of Evidence

**Getting to the Answer:** While researching the previous question, you determined that the information in lines 63–71 supported the answer. Thus, **(C)** is correct.

Choice (A) merely says that hard evidence for the panspermia hypothesis is needed, so it can be eliminated. Choice (B) indicates that the bacteria are similar to those found on Earth, but doesn't discuss the likely origins of the bacteria. Choice (D) discusses what kind of experiments will be needed in the future, but this does not support the author's assertion that the bacteria on the ISS likely came from Earth.

## 49. D

**Difficulty:** Medium

**Category:** Function

**Strategic Advice:** Think of the author's overall purpose in writing the passage and then ask: "Why did the author include this line; in what way does it function?"

**Getting to the Answer:** Note how the author begins the passage with the cited phrase "While absence of evidence is not evidence of absence" to contrast with what follows: "the panspermia hypothesis will remain nothing more than a tantalizing idea until incontrovertible evidence is found . . ." The author is pointing out that the hypothesis is unsupported by any evidence, but is also conceding that the lack of such evidence is not sufficient to disprove the hypothesis. Therefore, **(D)** is correct.

(A) is incorrect because the cited line is a concession to logic, not a flaw. (B) is incorrect because the author isn't condemning the lack of research, merely stating that there isn't evidence to support the hypothesis. (C) is incorrect because the statement is not a foundation for the author's argument, but an acknowledgment that the lack of evidence is inconclusive.

## 50. C

**Difficulty:** Medium

**Category:** Inference

**Strategic Advice:** Find the answer that logically follows from the information in the passages.

**Getting to the Answer:** The keywords in the question, "would be most likely to respond," indicates an Inference question. Begin by referring back to the cited evidence in Passage 1; it provides evidence to support the idea that Mars may have been suitable for life at an earlier time in the history of the solar system. Next, recall the central claim of Passage 2: there is not adequate evidence to consider panspermia as anything more than a "tantalizing hypothesis" until conclusive evidence is found that shows that the interplanetary transfer of microbial life has actually occurred in the past. Since the evidence presented in the cited lines does not accomplish this goal, it follows that the author of Passage 2 would say that such evidence is inadequate; **(C)** logically follows from these statements and is correct.

(A) is too extreme; there is no reason to believe that the author of Passage 2 would consider the cited evidence "completely irrelevant," only insufficient. Because the author's central position is that evidence for the actual transfer of life from Mars to Earth would be needed to conclude that panspermia is a valid hypothesis, (B) and (D) can both be eliminated.

## 51. D

**Difficulty:** Medium

**Category:** Detail

**Strategic Advice:** You may have a hard time predicting the answer to a "which of the following" question. If so, check each answer choice against information in the passages.

**Getting to the Answer:** (A) is incorrect because, while Passage 1 states that there is recent research that makes panspermia a more viable hypothesis, it never explains what additional evidence would lead to wider acceptance.

Neither author compares the panspermia hypothesis to other hypotheses regarding the origins of terrestrial life, so (B) is incorrect.

(C) is incorrect because, although Passage 1 hints at some of the factors that might make the transfer of life from Mars to Earth possible, Passage 2 never delves into the conditions necessary for microorganisms to have originated from an extraterrestrial source.

**(D)** is correct because Passage 1 concludes that the panspermia hypothesis is worthy of scientific consideration while Passage 2 argues that there is insufficient evidence to consider panspermia an explanation for the origins of life on Earth.

## 52. B

**Difficulty:** Medium

**Category:** Function

**Strategic Advice:** Think about each author's central claim in order to determine the relationship between the two passages.

**Getting to the Answer:** In simplest terms, the author of Passage 1 argues that the panspermia hypothesis is worthy of serious consideration because there is suggestive evidence that life might have once existed on Mars and evidence that life might be able to survive a voyage through space from Mars to Earth. In contrast, the author of Passage 2 argues that there is insufficient evidence to make the case for panspermia anything more than mere speculation. This matches **(B)**, which is the correct choice.

(A) is incorrect because Passage 2 doesn't refute the evidence presented in Passage 1, but rather considers it inadequate. (C) is incorrect because Passage 2 does not provide a broader context for the ideas discussed in Passage 1, but instead refutes them. (D) is incorrect because Passage 2 does not have the purpose of furthering the goals of Passage 1.

# PART 4

# SAT Writing and Language

# CHAPTER 24

# The Method for SAT Writing and Language Questions

---

**LEARNING OBJECTIVE**

After completing this chapter, you will be able to:

- Efficiently apply the SAT Writing and Language Method

---

## How to Do SAT Writing and Language

The Writing and Language section of the SAT tests a limited number of grammar errors and style or logic issues. You should feel empowered in knowing that you can familiarize yourself with these recurring errors and learn to spot them and address them quickly and efficiently. We'll describe the issues that you're likely to see on test day and how to deal with them in the next two chapters. In this chapter, we'll present a simple series of steps for tackling Writing and Language questions.

Take a look at the passage and questions that follow and think about how you would approach them on test day. Then compare your approach to the recommendations presented.

**Questions 1 and 2 refer to the following passage.**

**Child Expenditures**

   A report from the United States Department of Agriculture estimates that the average cost of raising a child born in 2015 until age seventeen is over $230,000. This cost includes housing, food, transportation, health care, child care, and education; the overall cost varies considerably from family to family. **1** Therefore, with the average cost of raising a child set at nearly a quarter million dollars, and with additional children in the family raising that financial expenditure accordingly, it becomes clear that parenthood is a major undertaking. When planning a family, **2** financial considerations should be kept in mind by future parents.

1. A) NO CHANGE
   B) However,
   C) Moreover,
   D) Subsequently,

2. A) NO CHANGE
   B) financial considerations should be at the forefront of parents' thinking.
   C) future parents should keep financial considerations in mind.
   D) future parents should consider financial issues to be of paramount importance in the process of their preparations.

There is no need to read the entire passage before you start to answer questions. Instead, answer them as you read. When you see a number, finish the sentence you are reading and then look at the corresponding question. If you can answer the question based on what you've read so far, do so—this will likely be the case if the question is testing grammar. If you need more information—which may happen if the question is testing organization or relevance—keep reading until you have enough context to answer the question.

Sometimes the issue being tested will be obvious to you when you look at the underlined segment. If it isn't, glance at the answer choices to help you determine what the test maker is after. For instance, in question 1, a transition word plus a comma is underlined. Is the question testing the transition or the punctuation? A quick glance at the choices makes it obvious that it's the former, given that they all include the comma but feature different transition words. **Identifying the issue**, using the choices if necessary, is step 1 of the Writing and Language Method.

To find the correct transition, use the surrounding text. The previous sentence addresses the variability of child expenditures, while the sentence that includes the transition word draws a conclusion from the *average* expenditure, not from the variability. The correct transition must highlight this contrast, so the sentence is incorrect as written, and you can eliminate (A). Among the remaining choices, there is only one contrast word: "However." Of the other choices, "Moreover" conveys continuation and "Subsequently" conveys a sequence in time. Neither fixes the error, so eliminate both and choose **(B)** as the correct answer to question 1. **Eliminating answer choices that do not address the issue** is step 2 of the Writing and Language Method.

Sometimes there will be more than one choice that addresses the issue. When that happens, you'll need to base your final response on three considerations: conciseness, relevance, and the potential of a given choice to introduce a new error. Question 2 is an example of a question in which more than one choice addresses the issue. This question features an underlined segment immediately following an introductory phrase—a signal to check for a modification error. Indeed, it is future parents who would be planning a family, so the phrase "future parents" should be right next to the introductory modifying phrase. That eliminates (A) and (B), but you still have to decide between (C) and (D), both of which fix the misplaced modifier. Both of these choices are grammatically correct and relevant to the surrounding context. However, **(C)** is more concise and is therefore the correct answer for question 2. **Choosing the most concise and relevant response from those that are grammatically correct** is step 3 of the Writing and Language method.

Here are the steps we just illustrated:

| Method for SAT Writing and Language Questions | |
|---|---|
| Step 1. | Identify the issue (use the choices if need be) |
| Step 2. | Eliminate answer choices that do not address the issue |
| Step 3. | Plug in the remaining answer choices and select the most *correct, concise,* and *relevant* one |

**Correct, concise**, and **relevant** means that the answer choice you select:

- Has no grammatical errors
- Is as short as possible while retaining the writer's intended meaning
- Is relevant to the paragraph and the passage as a whole

Correct answers do *not* change the intended meaning of the original sentence, paragraph, or passage, or introduce new grammatical errors.

## Try on Your Own

**Directions:** Take as much time as you need on these questions. Work carefully and methodically. Practice using the steps that you just learned.

**Questions 1-4 refer to the following passage.**

**Bebop Jazz**

For a jazz musician in New York City in the early 1940s, the most interesting place to spend the hours between midnight and dawn was probably a Harlem nightclub called Minton's. After finishing their jobs at other clubs, young musicians like **1** <u>Charlie Parker, Dizzy Gillespie, Kenny Clarke, Thelonious Monk</u> would gather at Minton's and have jam sessions, informal performances featuring lengthy group and solo improvisations. The all-night sessions resulted in the birth of modern jazz as these African American artists together forged a new sound, known as bebop.

Unlike swing, the enormously popular jazz played in the 1930s, bebop was not dance music. It was often blindingly fast, incorporating tricky, irregular rhythms and discordant sounds that jazz audiences had never heard before. Earlier jazz used blue notes but, like much of Western music up to that time, generally stuck to chord tones to create melodies. Bebop, in contrast, relied heavily on chromatic ornamentation and borrowed notes from altered **2** <u>scales. Thereby, it opened up</u> new harmonic opportunities for musicians.

The musicians who pioneered bebop shared two common elements: a vision of the new music's possibilities and astonishing improvisational skill—the ability to play or compose a musical line on the spur

1. A) NO CHANGE
   B) Charlie Parker; Dizzy Gillespie; Kenny Clarke; and Thelonious Monk
   C) Charlie Parker and Dizzy Gillespie, and Kenny Clarke and Thelonious Monk
   D) Charlie Parker, Dizzy Gillespie, Kenny Clarke, and Thelonious Monk

2. Which choice most effectively combines the sentences at the underlined portion?
   A) scales, thereby, it opened up
   B) scales, and thereby opening up
   C) scales, opening up
   D) scales, thereby opening up

of the moment. After all, **3** improvisation, within the context of a group setting, is a hallmark of jazz. Parker, perhaps the greatest instrumental genius jazz has known, was an especially brilliant improviser. He often played double-time, twice as fast as the rest of the band, and his solos were exquisitely shaped, revealing a harmonic imagination that enthralled his listeners.

Like many revolutions, unfortunately, the bebop movement encountered heavy resistance. Opposition came from older jazz musicians initially, but also, later and more lastingly, from a general public alienated by the **4** music's complexity and sophistication. Furthermore, due to the government ban on recording that was in effect during the early years of World War II (records were made of vinyl, a petroleum product that was essential to the war effort), the creative ferment that first produced bebop was poorly documented.

3. A) NO CHANGE

   B) improvisation within the context of a group setting is a hallmark

   C) improvisation within the context of a group setting, is a hallmark

   D) improvisation, within the context of a group setting is a hallmark

4. A) NO CHANGE

   B) musics

   C) musics'

   D) music

# Answers and Explanations

**1. D**

**Difficulty:** Easy

**Category:** Sentence Structure: Commas, Dashes, and Colons

**Getting to the Answer:** Use commas to separate three or more items forming a series or list. This series contains four items. Separate each item with a comma and use a comma with the conjunction "and" to separate the final item from the rest of the series. Choice **(D)** is correct.

**2. C**

**Difficulty:** Hard

**Category:** Organization: Conciseness

**Getting to the Answer:** Consider the relationship between the sentences in order to determine how best to combine them. The second sentence contributes useful information regarding the results of using the "chromatic ornamentation" and "altered scales." Making the second sentence a modifying phrase and connecting it to the first with a comma will eliminate unnecessary words and more clearly and smoothly show the relationship between the ideas. Choice **(C)** is correct. Choice (D) is similar and may be tempting, but since "opening up vast new harmonic opportunities" now directly modifies "altered scales," the word "thereby" is redundant.

**3. B**

**Difficulty:** Medium

**Category:** Sentence Structure: Commas, Dashes, and Colons

**Getting to the Answer:** When you see a phrase set off by commas, always read the sentence without the phrase to determine if the phrase is nonessential. Although the sentence is still grammatically correct without the information that is set off by the commas, an essential part of the meaning is lost. The author is stating that it is the group setting that characterizes the type of improvisation important to jazz. Choice **(B)** properly removes the commas that set off the phrase.

**4. A**

**Difficulty:** Easy

**Category:** Agreement: Modifiers

**Getting to the Answer:** When an underlined section features an apostrophe after a noun, check the noun's number. This sentence is correct as written. Although there are many styles of music, the noun "music" is a collective noun and singular. Choice **(A)** correctly uses the singular possessive.

# CHAPTER 25

# Spotting and Fixing Errors: Sentence Structure, Punctuation, and Agreement

145/300 SmartPoints®

# How Much Do You Know?

**Directions:** Try the following questions. The "Category" heading in the explanation for each question gives the title of the lesson that covers how to answer it. If you answered the question(s) for a given lesson correctly, you may be able to move quickly through that lesson. If you answered incorrectly, you may want to take your time on that lesson.

**Questions 1-6 refer to the following passage.**

### The Hindenburg

Although they are best known today for their peculiar niche as floating commercials over sports **1** arenas, airships, now more commonly called "blimps," widely used as passenger transportation in the early twentieth century. The most infamous was the *Hindenburg*. When the 804-foot *Hindenburg* was launched in 1936, it was the largest airship in the world. Like most airships, and more specifically zeppelins, of the period, **2** a light gas in the *Hindenburg* filled a simple balloon encased by a solid frame—in this case, hydrogen. In an age when airplanes could carry no more than 10 passengers at a time, **3** they could initially carry 50 passengers, a capacity that was later upgraded to 72. Transatlantic journeys in an airship could cut the travel time in half compared to voyages in ocean liners at the time.

Despite these advantages, the *Hindenburg* was hampered by many of the same drawbacks as other airships. Tickets to fly in the *Hindenburg* were not affordable for most people. The massive amount of fuel needed not only to fill the balloon **4** and to power the propellers made this airship very expensive to operate.

1. A) NO CHANGE
   B) arenas; airships, more commonly called "blimps" today, widely used as
   C) arenas, airships, more commonly called "blimps" today, were widely used as
   D) arenas, airships, more commonly called "blimps" today, widely used to

2. A) NO CHANGE
   B) the *Hindenburg*'s simple balloon was filled with a light gas encased by the solid frame
   C) the solid frame of the *Hindenburg* encased a simple balloon filled with a light gas
   D) the *Hindenburg* was built with a solid frame that encased a simple balloon filled with a light gas

3. A) NO CHANGE
   B) it
   C) the *Hindenburg*
   D) each

4. A) NO CHANGE
   B) but also
   C) and also
   D) nor

Worst of all was the safety concern: hydrogen gas is extremely flammable. Any spark or flame that came near the gas could cause a horrific **5** explosion, which is exactly what happened. On May 6, 1937, in Lakehurst, New Jersey, as the *Hindenburg* **6** landed, it suddenly burst into flames, killing 36 of the 97 passengers and crew on board. By the 1940s, commercial airplanes had advanced in development far beyond the airship's capacity. The airship thus became outdated as a mode of passenger service and acquired its modern-day role as an advertising platform.

5. A) NO CHANGE
   B) explosion; which is
   C) explosion: which is
   D) explosion which—is

6. A) NO CHANGE
   B) had landed
   C) would have landed
   D) was landing

## Check Your Work

**1. C**

**Difficulty:** Hard

**Category:** Sentence Structure: The Basics

**Getting to the Answer:** The first sentence is long and grammatically complex. Identify the most important pieces and outline the structure. The sentence begins with the word "although," which means that the first clause, "they are best known," is dependent. The following clause, therefore, needs to be independent for the sentence to have a complete, grammatically correct structure. The second clause as written, "airships . . . widely used as passenger transportation," is not an independent clause—it could not stand alone as its own complete sentence. Eliminate (A). Choice (B) is incorrect because the semicolon does not turn the second clause into an independent clause. Similarly, (D) does not make the second clause independent by replacing "as" with "to." Choice **(C)** is correct because "airships . . . were widely used as passenger transportation" is an independent clause: it has a subject "airships" and a predicate verb "were used."

**2. D**

**Difficulty:** Hard

**Category:** Agreement: Modifiers

**Getting to the Answer:** The phrases that precede the underlined portion are introductory modifiers. The subject of the sentence needs to immediately follow these modifiers. The introductory phrases talk about something that is like most airships; therefore, the subject must be comparable to most other airships. Neither "a light gas," "the *Hindenburg*'s simple balloon," nor the "solid frame" are comparable to "most airships." The *Hindenburg* itself is a specific airship, which can be logically compared to most airships. Only **(D)** correctly places "the *Hindenburg*" immediately after the introductory phrase as the subject of the sentence. Additionally, the underlined portion must end with "a light gas" because the phrase after the dash specifies which gas: hydrogen.

**3. C**

**Difficulty:** Medium

**Category:** Agreement: Pronouns

**Getting to the Answer:** Complex sentences can often benefit from the use of pronouns, reducing wordiness and repetition. That said, make sure that the use of a pronoun will not introduce ambiguity into the sentence. In a complicated sentence including multiple nouns, it is often better to avoid pronouns to preserve the clarity of the author's claims. Choice **(C)** is correct because it avoids any confusion over what the pronoun refers to.

**4. B**

**Difficulty:** Medium

**Category:** Agreement: Idioms

**Getting to the Answer:** Check to see if the underlined section is part of an idiomatic expression, such as *either . . . or*. The sentence contains the first half of the idiomatic combination *not only . . . but also*. The use of "and" in this context is incorrect. Choice **(B)**, "but also," is correct.

**5. A**

**Difficulty:** Medium

**Category:** Sentence Structure: Commas, Dashes, and Colons

**Getting to the Answer:** Commas set off non essential information from the main part of the sentence just as parentheses do. The sentence's concluding phrase "which is exactly what happened" is not necessary for understanding the sentence's main clause, which explains how a spark or flame could ignite the hydrogen and cause an explosion. The use of a semicolon or a colon is not appropriate for setting off non essential information. Eliminate (B) and (C). A dash can replace a comma as a way to emphasize the parenthetical phrase, which would be appropriate here, but (D) misplaces the dash. Choice **(A)** is correct because it uses the necessary punctuation, a comma, in the proper location.

**6. D**

**Difficulty:** Hard

**Category:** Agreement: Verbs

**Getting to the Answer:** The sentence expresses a main action that occurs once, "burst," while another action is in process, "landed." An action that occurs once in the past should be in simple past tense. An action that is in process in the past—signaled by the word "as"—should be in past progressive tense, ending in *-ing*. Eliminate (A). Only **(D)** gives the verb in past progressive and is correct.

# Sentence Structure: The Basics

## LEARNING OBJECTIVES

After this lesson, you will be able to:

- Determine the correct punctuation and/or conjunctions to form a complete sentence
- Identify and correct inappropriate uses of semicolons

## To answer a question like this:

In the late spring of 1953, New Zealand mountaineer Sir Edmund Hillary and Nepalese Sherpa Tenzing Norgay became the first people to walk on the top of the world. After a grueling expedition that spanned several **1** months. They had finally reached the summit of Mount Everest.

A) NO CHANGE
B) months, and they
C) months; they
D) months, they

Writing & Lang

## You need to know this:

### Fragments and run-ons

A complete sentence must have both a subject and a verb and express a complete thought. If any one of these elements is missing, the sentence is a **fragment**. You can recognize a fragment because the sentence will not make sense as written. There are some examples in the table below.

| Missing Element | Example | Corrected Sentence |
|---|---|---|
| Subject | *Ran a marathon.* | *Lola ran a marathon.* |
| Verb | *Lola a marathon.* | |
| Complete thought | *While Lola ran a marathon.* | *While Lola ran a marathon, her friends cheered for her.* |

The fragment "While Lola ran a marathon" is an example of a dependent clause: it has a subject (Lola) and a verb (ran), but it does not express a complete thought because it starts with a subordinating conjunction (while). Notice what the word "while" does to the meaning: While Lola ran a marathon, what happened? To fix this type of fragment, eliminate the subordinating conjunction or join the dependent clause to an independent clause using a comma. Subordinating conjunctions are words and phrases such as *since*, *because*, *therefore*, *unless*, *although*, and *due to*.

Unlike a dependent clause, an independent clause can stand on its own as a complete sentence. If a sentence has more than one independent clause, those clauses must be properly joined. If they are not, the sentence is a **run-on**: *Lucas enjoys hiking, he climbs a new mountain every summer.* There are several ways to correct a run-on, as shown in the table below.

| To Correct a Run-on | Example |
| --- | --- |
| Use a period | *Lucas enjoys hiking. He climbs a new mountain every summer.* |
| Use a semicolon | *Lucas enjoys hiking; he climbs a new mountain every summer.* |
| Use a colon | *Lucas enjoys hiking: he climbs a new mountain every summer.* |
| Make one clause dependent | *Since Lucas enjoys hiking, he climbs a new mountain every summer.* |
| Add a FANBOYS conjunction: For, And, Nor, But, Or, Yet, So | *Lucas enjoys hiking, so he climbs a new mountain every summer.* |
| Use a dash | *Lucas enjoys hiking—he climbs a new mountain every summer.* |

## Semicolons

Semicolons are used in two specific ways:

- A semicolon may join two independent clauses that are not connected by a FANBOYS conjunction (also called a coordinating conjunction), just as you would use a period.
- Semicolons may be used to separate items in a list if those items already include commas.

| Use semicolons to . . . | Example |
| --- | --- |
| Join two independent clauses that are not connected by a comma and FANBOYS conjunction | *Gaby knew that her term paper would take at least four hours to write; she got started in study hall and then finished it at home.* |
| Separate sub lists within a longer list when the sub lists contain commas | *The team needed to bring uniforms, helmets, and gloves; oranges, almonds, and water; and hockey sticks, pucks, and skates.* |

## You need to do this:

To recognize and correct errors involving fragments, run-ons, and semicolons, familiarize yourself with the ways in which they are tested:

- Fragments
  - If a sentence is missing a subject, a verb, or a complete thought, it is a fragment.
  - Correct the fragment by adding the missing element.

- Run-ons
  - If a sentence includes two independent clauses, they must be properly joined.
  - Employ one of the following options to properly punctuate independent clauses:
    - Use a period
    - Insert a semicolon
    - Use a comma and a FANBOYS (for, and, nor, but, or, yet, so) conjunction
    - Use a dash
    - Make one clause dependent by using a subordinating conjunction (since, because, therefore, unless, although, due to, etc.)
- Semicolons
  - A semicolon is used to join two independent clauses that are not connected by a comma and FANBOYS conjunction.
  - Semicolons separate sub lists within a longer list. (The items inside the sub lists are separated by commas.)

## Explanation:

The sentence before the period in the underlined segment is a fragment; it is a dependent clause that does not express a complete thought. Eliminate (A) because, as written, there is an error. Eliminate (B) because you need only one conjunction to join two clauses, not two. In (B), using both "although" and "and" creates an error. Eliminate (C) because it does not correct the original error: the semicolon serves exactly the same function as the period in the original. Choice **(D)** is correct.

If sentence formation or semicolons give you trouble, study the information above and try these Drill questions before completing the following Try on Your Own questions. Answers can be found on the next page.

## Drill

a.  Correct the fragment by adding a subject: Brought snacks to the weekend study session.

b.  Correct the fragment by completing the thought: After getting to the stadium.

c.  Correct the run-on sentence with a punctuation mark: The new arts center just opened it has a crafts room for children under thirteen.

d.  Correct the run-on sentence with a punctuation mark: Herodotus is known as one of the first historians he is even called "The Father of History."

e.  Make one clause dependent to correct the run-on sentence: Herodotus is sometimes accused of making up stories for his histories, he claimed he simply recorded what he had been told.

Writing & Lang

## Try on Your Own

**Directions:** Take as much time as you need on these questions. Work carefully and methodically. There will be an opportunity for timed practice at the end of the chapter.

**Questions 2-6 refer to the following passage.**

**The Sun**

It is perhaps impossible to overestimate the impact of the Sun on our planet Earth. [2] The Sun is situated roughly 100 million miles away from the Earth, the Sun provides essentially all of Earth's heat. Functioning like a great thermonuclear reactor, [3] the Sun's core temperature of nearly 30 million degrees Fahrenheit. The energy sources we use daily to fuel our cars and heat our homes, resources like oil and coal harvested from deep within the Earth's crust, were produced by the power of the Sun acting upon living organisms millions of years ago. The radiant energy of the Sun is the reason the Earth has [4] light, warmth, and other forms of electromagnetic waves; plants, animals, and all metabolic life; weather patterns, atmospheric movement, and many more of the Earth's natural phenomena. Yet, while the Sun's ability to provide heat and light can be easily felt by simply lying out on a beach or gazing up into a brilliant blue sky, closer inspection of the Sun's dynamic surface through special telescopes has revealed activity capable of affecting the Earth in less obvious ways.

2.
A) NO CHANGE
B) However, the Sun
C) Not many know that the Sun
D) Even though the Sun

3.
A) NO CHANGE
B) the Sun has a core temperature
C) the core temperature of the Sun
D) the temperature of the Sun's core

4.
A) NO CHANGE
B) light, warmth, and other forms of electromagnetic waves—plants, animals, and all metabolic life—weather patterns, atmospheric movement, and many more of the Earth's natural phenomena.
C) light, warmth, other forms of electromagnetic waves, plants, animals, all metabolic life, weather patterns, atmospheric movement, and many more of the Earth's natural phenomena.
D) light, warmth, and other forms of electromagnetic waves, plants, animals, and all metabolic life, weather patterns, atmospheric movement, and many more of the Earth's natural phenomena.

Drill answers from previous page:

Note: These are not the only ways to correct the sentences; your answers may differ.

a. **My friend** brought snacks to the weekend study session.

b. After getting to the stadium, **we went looking for our seats.**

c. The new arts center just opened. It has a crafts room for children under thirteen.

d. Herodotus is known as one of the first historians; he is even called "The Father of History."

e. **Although** Herodotus is sometimes accused of making up stories for his histories, he claimed he simply recorded what he had been told.

One of the most curious features of the Sun's violent surface is sunspots, which are dark stormy areas half the temperature of the Sun's surface and as large as 19,000 miles across. They were first viewed by telescope as early as [5] <u>1610 but scientists</u> today know relatively little about them. Scientists have noticed that these spots seem to erupt and fade in 11-year cycles, affecting the Sun's luminosity and, in turn, the Earth's climate. Studies have shown that the charged particles released by solar flares, associated with sunspots, can react with the Earth's magnetic [6] <u>field, the radiation</u> can disrupt satellite communications, radio broadcasts, and even cell phone calls. As scientists continue to carefully observe such occurrences, referred to as "space weather," they gain a greater understanding of the powerful ability of the Sun to impact our lives.

5. A) NO CHANGE
   B) 1610, but scientists
   C) 1610 still scientists
   D) 1610, still scientists

6. A) NO CHANGE
   B) field, however the radiation
   C) field so the radiation
   D) field; the radiation

# Sentence Structure: Commas, Dashes, and Colons

---

**LEARNING OBJECTIVES**

After this lesson, you will be able to:

- Identify and correct inappropriate uses of commas, dashes, and colons
- Use punctuation to set off simple parenthetical elements

---

## To answer a question like this:

But climbing Mount Everest may be easier than answering the question posed by decades of non-climbers: Why? Perhaps Mallory said it best in 1923 before his ill-fated **7** <u>climb; "Because it is there."</u>

A) NO CHANGE

B) climb: "Because it is there."

C) climb. "Because it is there."

D) climb "Because it is there."

## You need to know this:

Answer choices often move punctuation marks around, replace them with other punctuation marks, or remove them altogether. When underlined portions include commas, dashes, or colons, check to make sure the punctuation is used correctly in context.

### Commas

There are two ways in which commas are not interchangeable with any other punctuation: a series of items and introductory words or phrases.

| Use commas to . . . | Comma(s) |
|---|---|
| Set off three or more items in a series | *Jeremiah packed a sleeping bag, a raincoat, and a lantern for his upcoming camping trip.* |
| Separate an introductory word or phrase from the rest of the sentence | *For example, carrots are an excellent source of several vitamins and minerals.* |

## Commas and Dashes

In many cases, either a comma or a dash may be used to punctuate a sentence.

| Use commas or dashes to . . . | Comma(s) | Dash(es) |
| --- | --- | --- |
| Separate independent clauses connected by a FANBOYS conjunction (For, And, Nor, But, Or, Yet, So) | *Jess finished her homework earlier than expected, so she started an assignment that was due the following week.* | *Jess finished her homework earlier than expected—so she started an assignment that was due the following week.* |
| Separate an independent and dependent clause | *Tyson arrived at school a few minutes early, which gave him time to organize his locker before class.* | *Tyson arrived at school a few minutes early—which gave him time to organize his locker before class.* |
| Separate parenthetical elements from the rest of the sentence (use either two commas or two dashes, not one of each) | *Professor Mann, who is the head of the English department, is known for assigning extensive projects.* | *Professor Mann—who is the head of the English department—is known for assigning extensive projects* |

## Colons and Dashes

Colons and dashes are used to include new ideas by introducing or explaining something or by breaking the flow of the sentence. Note that the clause before the colon or dash must be able to stand on its own as a complete sentence.

| Use colons and dashes to . . . | Colon | Dash |
| --- | --- | --- |
| Introduce and/or emphasize a short phrase, quotation, explanation, example, or list | *Sanjay had two important tasks to complete: a science experiment and an expository essay.* | *Sanjay had two important tasks to complete—a science experiment and an expository essay.* |
| Separate two independent clauses when the second clauses explains, illustrates, or expands on the first sentence | *Highway 1 in Australia is one of the longest national highways in the world: it circles the entirety of the continent and connects every mainland state capital.* | *Highway 1 in Australia is one of the longest national highways in the world—it circles the entirety of the continent and connects every mainland state capital.* |

### Unnecessary Punctuation

Knowing when punctuation should not be used is equally important. If an underlined portion includes punctuation, take time to consider if it should be included at all.

| Do NOT use punctuation to... | Incorrect | Correct |
|---|---|---|
| Separate a subject from its verb | *The diligent student council, meets every week.* | *The diligent student council meets every week.* |
| Separate a verb from its object or a preposition from its object | *The diligent student council meets, every week.* | *The diligent student council meets every week.* |
| Set off elements that are essential to a sentence's meaning | *The, diligent student, council meets every week.* | *The diligent student council meets every week.* |
| Separate adjectives that work together to modify a noun | *The diligent, student council meets every week.* | *The diligent student council meets every week.* |

### Parenthetical Elements

Parenthetical elements may appear at the beginning, in the middle, or at the end of a sentence. They must be properly punctuated with parentheses, commas, or dashes for the sentence to be grammatically correct. A phrase such as *the capital of France* is considered parenthetical if the rest of the sentence is grammatically correct when it is removed. Do not mix and match; a parenthetical element must begin and end with the same type of punctuation.

| Parenthetical Element Placement | Parentheses | Comma(s) | Dash(es) |
|---|---|---|---|
| Beginning | *N/A* | *The capital of France, Paris is a popular tourist destination.* | *N/A* |
| Middle | *Paris (the capital of France) is a popular tourist destination.* | *Paris, the capital of France, is a popular tourist destination.* | *Paris—the capital of France—is a popular tourist destination.* |
| End | *A popular tourist destination is Paris (the capital of France).* | *A popular tourist destination is Paris, the capital of France.* | *A popular tourist destination is Paris— the capital of France.* |

### You need to do this:

If the underlined portion includes punctuation, ask yourself:

- Is the punctuation used correctly?

    The punctuation needs to be the correct type (comma, dash, or colon) and in the correct location.

- Is the punctuation is necessary?

    If you cannot identify a reason why the punctuation is included, the punctuation should be removed.

## Explanation:

The underlined segment includes a semicolon that is used incorrectly because it neither joins two independent clauses nor separates items containing commas in a series or list. The underlined segment here is intended to emphasize a short quotation, so a colon or dash would be appropriate. **(B)** is correct.

If commas, dashes, and colons give you trouble, study the information above and try these Drill questions before completing the following Try on Your Own questions. Edit each sentence to correct the punctuation issue. Answers can be found on the next page.

## Drill

a. For my birthday, I asked for my favorite dessert chocolate pecan pie.

b. The story of Emperor Nero playing the fiddle while Rome burned has been debunked by historians but the saying based on it remains popular.

c. Koalas' fingerprints are nearly indistinguishable from human fingerprints which has occasionally led to mistakes at crime scenes.

d. Invented by Sir John Harrington in 1596 the flush toilet actually precedes modern indoor plumbing.

e. Toni Morrison born Chloe Wofford is one of America's most celebrated writers.

## Try on Your Own

**Directions:** Take as much time as you need on these questions. Work carefully and methodically. There will be an opportunity for timed practice at the end of the chapter.

**Questions 8-15 refer to the following passage.**

**Mauritius**

[8] Although, most of the products we buy today are made abroad in places well-known to Americans, such as Mexico and China, a quick check of many clothing labels will reveal the name of a country that might not be so [9] familiar. Mauritius. Named in honor of Prince Maurice of Nassau by the Dutch who colonized it in 1638, this small island in the Indian Ocean has a complicated history influenced by several international powers. Since gaining independence in [10] 1968— Mauritius has emerged as a stable democracy with one of Africa's highest per capita incomes. Mauritius is considered a significant [11] player: in the modern global economy one of the few in the Southern Hemisphere.

Yet, before its hard-won economic and political stability, Mauritius underwent several tumultuous phases. After the Portuguese landed on the island in 1511, they hunted a large, slow-moving, native bird known as the dodo into extinction. The Portuguese

8.  A)  NO CHANGE
    B)  Although most
    C)  Although; most
    D)  Most

9.  A)  NO CHANGE
    B)  familiar and it's Mauritius
    C)  familiar: Mauritius
    D)  familiar which is Mauritius

10. A)  NO CHANGE
    B)  1968; Mauriutius
    C)  1968 as Mauritius
    D)  1968, Mauritius

11. A)  NO CHANGE
    B)  player in the modern global economy, one
    C)  player—in the modern global economy—one
    D)  player in the modern, global economy one

Drill answers from previous page:

Note: These are not the only ways to correct the sentences; your answers may differ.

a. For my birthday, I asked for my favorite dessert: chocolate pecan pie.

b. The story of Emperor Nero playing the fiddle while Rome burned has been debunked by historians, but the saying based on it remains popular.

c. Koalas' fingerprints are nearly indistinguishable from human fingerprints—which has occasionally led to mistakes at crime scenes.

d. Invented by Sir John Harrington in 1596, the flush toilet actually precedes modern indoor plumbing.

e. Toni Morrison, born Chloe Wofford, is one of America's most celebrated writers. OR Toni Morrison—born Chloe Wofford—is one of America's most celebrated writers.

were followed by the Dutch, who brought waves of [12] traders, planters, and slaves; and indentured laborers, merchants, and artisans, whose collective arrival brought international recognition to Mauritius. In 1715, the island again changed hands, this time to the French, and in 1810, with a successful invasion during the Napoleonic Wars, the British became the fourth European power to rule the island. Yet it was during this period of changing [13] colonial powers—Mauritius was traded like a commodity, that the demographics of the island began to experience important changes with great political ramifications.

By the time slavery was abolished in 1835, for example, the growing Indian population, the Creoles who could trace their roots back to island's sugarcane plantations, and the Muslim community originating from present-day Pakistan far outnumbered the remaining Franco-Mauritian elites. And with these demographic changes came political change. The first step toward self-rule came with the legislative elections of [14] 1947 and in March of 1968, an official constitution was adopted. Today, Mauritius peacefully balances the diversity of its multicultural society and flourishes in international [15] trade through its advantageous geographic location and large labor force.

12. A) NO CHANGE
    B) traders, planters and slaves, indentured laborers, merchants and artisans,
    C) traders, planters, slaves, indentured laborers, merchants, artisans,
    D) traders, planters, slaves, indentured laborers, merchants, and artisans,

13. A) NO CHANGE
    B) colonial powers—Mauritius was traded like a commodity that
    C) colonial powers—Mauritius was traded like a commodity—that
    D) colonial powers, Mauritius was traded like a commodity that

14. A) NO CHANGE
    B) 1947, and in March
    C) 1947 and, in March
    D) 1947 and in March,

15. A) NO CHANGE
    B) trade, through
    C) trade through,
    D) trade; through

## Agreement: Verbs

> **LEARNING OBJECTIVE**
>
> After this lesson, you will be able to:
>
> - Identify and correct verb agreement issues

### To answer questions like this:

For example, the editors had their work cut out for them when the part of the book devoted to avalanches and landslides 16 <u>were found</u> to be inaccurate.

A) NO CHANGE

B) was found

C) are found

D) is found

### You need to know this:

**Verb Tense**

Verb tense indicates when an action or state of being took place: in the past, present, or future. The tense of the verb must fit the context of the passage. Each tense can express three different types of action.

| Type of Action | Past | Present | Future |
|---|---|---|---|
| Single action occurring only once | Connor **planted** vegetables in the community garden. | Connor **plants** vegetables in the community garden. | Connor **will plant** vegetables in the community garden. |
| Action that is ongoing at some point in time | Connor **was planting** vegetables in the community garden this morning before noon. | Connor **is planting** vegetables in the community garden this morning before noon. | Connor **will be planting** vegetables in the community garden this morning before noon. |
| Action that is completed before some other action | Connor **had planted** vegetables in the community garden every year until he gave his job to Jasmine. | Connor **has planted** vegetables in the community garden since it started five years ago. | Connor **will have planted** vegetables in the community garden by the time the growing season starts. |

**Subject-Verb Agreement**

A verb must agree with its subject in person and number:

- Person (first, second, or third)
    - First: *I **ask** a question.*
    - Second: *You **ask** a question.*
    - Third: *She **asks** a question.*

- Number (singular or plural)
  - Singular: *The apple **tastes** delicious.*
  - Plural: *Apples **taste** delicious.*

The noun closest to the verb is not always the subject: *The chair with the lion feet is an antique.* The singular verb in this sentence, *is*, is closest to the plural noun *feet*. However, the verb's actual subject is the singular noun *chair*, so the sentence is correct as written.

When a sentence includes two nouns, only the conjunction *and* forms a compound subject requiring a plural verb form:

- Plural: *Saliyah and Taylor **are** in the running club.*
- Singular: *Either Saliyah or Taylor **is** in the running club.*
- Singular: *Neither Saliyah nor Taylor **is** in the running club.*

Collective nouns are nouns that name entities with more than one member, such as *group*, *team*, and *family*. Even though these nouns represent more than one person, they are grammatically singular and require singular verb forms:

- *The collection of paintings **is** one of the most popular art exhibits in recent years.*
- *The team **looks** promising this year.*

### Parallelism

Verbs in a list, a compound, or a comparison must be parallel in form.

| Feature | Example | Parallel Form |
|---|---|---|
| A list | Chloe **formulated** a question, **conducted** background research, and **constructed** a hypothesis before starting the experiment. | 3 simple past verb phrases |
| A compound | **Hunting** and **fishing** were essential to the survival of Midwestern Native American tribes such as the Omaha. | 2 *-ing* verb forms |
| A comparison | Garrett enjoys **sculpting** as much as **painting**. | 2 *-ing* verb forms |

Note that parallelism may be tested using other parts of speech besides verbs. In general, any items in a list, compound, or comparison must be in parallel form. For example, if a list starts with a noun, the other items in the list must also be nouns; if it starts with an adjective, the other items must be adjectives, etc.

| Incorrect | Correct |
|---|---|
| Naomi likes **pumpkin pie and to drink coffee** on chilly weekend afternoons. | Naomi likes **pumpkin pie and coffee** on chilly weekend afternoons.<br><br>*or*<br><br>Naomi likes **to eat pumpkin pie and drink coffee** on chilly weekend afternoons. |
| Which of the dogs is the **most docile and better behaved**? | Which of the dogs is the **most docile and best behaved**?<br><br>*or*<br><br>Which of the dogs is the **more docile and better behaved**? |

## You need to do this:

If the underlined portion includes a verb, check that the verb:

- Reflects the correct tense: does it fit the context?
- Agrees with the subject in person and number
- Is parallel in form with other verbs in a series, list, or compound if there is one in the sentence

## Explanation:

The subject of the verb "were found" is the noun "part," which is singular. The verb is plural, so there is an error. Rule out (A) and (C). (Note that the test makers like to put prepositional phrases or other descriptive phrases, such as the phrase, "devoted to avalanches and landslides," between the subject and verb to make the subject-verb agreement error trickier to spot.)

To decide between (B) and (D), look at the context defined by the other verb tense in the sentence. The editors "*had* their work cut out for them," so the sentence describes past events. Choice **(B)** is also in the past tense and is consistent with this context. It is the correct answer.

If verbs give you trouble, study the information above and try these Drill questions before completing the following Try on Your Own questions. Edit each sentence to correct the verb issue. Turn the page to see the answers.

## Drill

a.   Angel audition for the school play next week.

b.   The song, with its upbeat rhythm and catchy lyrics, were wildly popular.

c.   Either the governor or the lieutenant governor usually present the award.

d.   By the time the last runner completed the marathon, the winner has crossed the finish line hours ago.

e.   Few people know that Stephen Hawking both revolutionized physics and co-written children's books with his daughter.

## Try on Your Own

**Directions:** Take as much time as you need on these questions. Work carefully and methodically. There will be an opportunity for timed practice at the end of the chapter.

**Questions 17-22 refer to the following passage.**

**SMOM**

At 69 Condotti Street in Rome sits what **17** is believed by many to be the smallest country in the world, a country that few have ever heard of. The Sovereign Military and Hospitaller Order of St. John of Jerusalem of Rhodes and of Malta, or SMOM, **18** were an ancient order of knights well known for its humanitarian activities. The order's headquarters in Rome—a mere 6,000 square meters, or about one acre— is considered an independent state by at least 75 nations. How SMOM got to Rome is a story almost a millennium old, spanning as many places as the order's official name suggests.

SMOM began in 1099, during the First Crusade, a large-scale military conflict pitting Christian armies against the Muslim rulers of what is now Israel. The order's task was to protect and defend Christian pilgrims traveling to Jerusalem as well as **19** providing a hospital for their care. Though it began as a religious order, SMOM developed into a military knighthood as a result of the volatile political situation.

First because of the ongoing conflict between Muslims and Christians and, later, Napoleon Bonaparte's expansionist ambitions, the order was forced to move a number of times. After the Muslims had taken Jerusalem in the 1170s, forcing SMOM to relocate first to the Mediterranean island of Cyprus and then to the nearby island of Rhodes, the Ottoman Turks

17. A)   NO CHANGE
    B)   are believed
    C)   is to be believed
    D)   are to be believed

18. A)   NO CHANGE
    B)   was
    C)   are
    D)   is

19. A)   NO CHANGE
    B)   to provide
    C)   providing them
    D)   ensuring availability of

**20** had seized Rhodes in 1522, forcing SMOM to move again, this time to Malta. Then **21** Napoleon drives the order from Malta in 1798, and the island fell into British hands soon after. SMOM wandered from city to city in Italy, finally establishing its current headquarters in 1834.

Today, SMOM **22** will concentrate on providing humanitarian aid to everyone regardless of creed, establishing hospitals and charities in all corners of the world. Its many activities include vaccination programs, refugee relief, and philanthropic works to combat deadly diseases, such as leprosy and malnutrition.

20. A) NO CHANGE
    B) seized
    C) have seized
    D) would have seized

21. A) NO CHANGE
    B) Napoleon drove
    C) Napoleon had driven
    D) Napoleon was driving

22. A) NO CHANGE
    B) will be concentrating
    C) concentrates
    D) concentrates and is concentrating

Drill answers:

Note: These are not the only ways to correct the sentences; your answers may differ.

a. Angel **will** audition for the school play next week.

b. The song, with its upbeat rhythm and catchy lyrics, **was** wildly popular.

c. Either the governor or the lieutenant governor usually **presents** the award.

d. By the time the last runner completed the marathon, the winner **had** crossed the finish line hours ago.

e. Few people know that Stephen Hawking both revolutionized physics and **co-wrote** children's books with his daughter.

# Agreement: Pronouns

## To answer a question like this:

In their search for Ozark cavefish, the researchers were encouraged by the stability of the caves' groundwater as well as by **23** <u>its</u> length and by the presence of bats.

A) NO CHANGE

B) it's

C) their

D) there

## You need to know this:

### Pronoun forms

A pronoun is a word that takes the place of a noun. Pronouns can take three different forms, each of which is used based on the grammatical role it plays in the sentence.

| Form | Pronouns | Example |
|---|---|---|
| **Subjective:** The pronoun is used as the subject. | I, you, she, he, it, we, they, who | *Rivka is the student **who** will lead the presentation.* |
| **Objective:** The pronoun is used as the object of a verb or a preposition. | me, you, her, him, it, us, them, whom | *With **whom** will Rivka present the scientific findings?* |
| **Possessive:** The pronoun expresses ownership. | my, mine, your, yours, his, her, hers, its, our, ours, their, theirs, whose | *Rivka will likely choose a partner **whose** work is excellent.* |

Note that a pronoun in subjective form can, logically, be the subject in a complete sentence. Pronouns that are in objective form cannot.

When there are two pronouns or a noun and a pronoun in a compound structure, drop the other noun or pronoun to tell which form to use. For example: *Leo and me walked into town*. If you were talking about yourself only, you would say, "I walked into town," not "Me walked into town." Therefore, the correct form is subjective, and the original sentence should read: *Leo and I walked into town*.

### Pronoun-Antecedent Agreement

A pronoun's antecedent is the noun it logically represents in a sentence. If the noun is singular, the pronoun must be singular; if the noun is plural, the pronoun must be plural.

| Antecedent | Incorrect | Correct |
|---|---|---|
| selection | The selection of books was placed in **their** designated location. | The selection of books was placed in **its** designated location. |
| Addison | Addison fed the giraffes all of the lettuce **they** had purchased. | Addison fed the giraffes all of the lettuce **she** had purchased. |
| sapling | The sapling, along with dozens of flowers, was relocated to where **they** would thrive. | The sapling, along with dozens of flowers, was relocated to where **it** would thrive. |
| student | If a student is confused, **they** should ask for clarification. | If a student is confused, **he** or **she** should ask for clarification. |

### Ambiguous Pronouns

A pronoun is ambiguous if its antecedent is either missing or unclear. When you see an underlined pronoun, make sure you can identify the noun to which it refers.

| Ambiguous Pronoun Use | Corrected Sentence |
|---|---|
| Anthony walked with Cody to the ice cream shop, and **he** bought a banana split. | Anthony walked with Cody to the ice cream shop, and **Cody** bought a banana split. |

## You need to do this:

If the underlined portion includes a pronoun, *find the logical antecedent*. If there is no clear antecedent, the pronoun is ambiguous and this error must be corrected. Then check that the pronoun:

- Uses the correct form
  - If the pronoun is the subject of the sentence, use a subjective pronoun such as *I, you, she, he, it, we, they,* or *who*.
  - If the pronoun is an object within the sentence, use an objective pronoun such as *me, you, her, him, it, us, they,* or *whom*.
  - If the pronoun indicates possession, use a possessive pronoun such as *my, mine, your, yours, his, her, hers, its, our, ours, their, theirs,* or *whose*.
- Agrees with its antecedent
  - A singular antecedent requires a singular pronoun; a plural antecedent requires a plural pronoun.

## Explanation:

The phrase "its length" logically refers to the caves, not the groundwater. You need the possessive form, but because the word "caves" is plural, you need the plural "their." Choice **(C)** is correct.

If pronouns give you trouble, study the information above and try these Drill questions before completing the following Try on Your Own questions. Edit each sentence to correct the pronoun issue. Answers can be found on the next page.

## Drill

a.    Although the teacher gave the student detention after school, she was not angry.

b.    My uncle likes to go bowling with my sister and I.

c.    The box of nails has been moved from their usual place in the shed.

d.    My favorite singer, who I have wanted to see in person for years, will give a concert a week after my birthday.

e.    The cathedral of Notre Dame, with vast vaulted ceilings and intricate carvings, never fails to amaze their visitors.

## Try on Your Own

**Directions:** Take as much time as you need on these questions. Work carefully and methodically. There will be an opportunity for timed practice at the end of the chapter.

### Questions 24-29 refer to the following passage.

### Akira Kurosawa

What do samurai,[1] cowboys, shogun,[2] gangsters, peasants, and William Shakespeare all have in common? 24 He is just one of the varied influences on the work of Akira Kurosawa (1910–1998), a Japanese film director considered by movie critic Leonard Maltin to be "one of the undisputed giants of cinema." Over his career, Kurosawa's unique blend of Western themes and Eastern settings made 25 them arguably the most important Japanese filmmaker in history.

The most famous example of Kurosawa's style is his 1954 film *Seven Samurai*. Although the setting is medieval Japan, with peasants and samurai, 26 its story is influenced by Western films: a village, terrorized by local bandits, turns to seven down-on-their-luck yet good-hearted samurai for the protection

24.  A)   NO CHANGE
     B)   His is just one
     C)   They are just some
     D)   Theirs are just some

25.  A)   NO CHANGE
     B)   he
     C)   him
     D)   his

26.  A)   NO CHANGE
     B)   their
     C)   the film's
     D)   the setting's

Drill answers from previous page:

Note: These are not the only ways to correct the sentences; your answers may differ.

a. Although the teacher gave the student detention after school, **the student** was not angry.

b. My uncle likes to go bowling with my sister and **me**.

c. The box of nails has been moved from **its** usual place in the shed.

d. My favorite singer, **whom** I have wanted to see in person for years, will give a concert a week after my birthday.

e. The cathedral of Notre Dame, with vast vaulted ceilings and intricate carvings, never fails to amaze **its** visitors.

---

[1] samurai: noble warriors of medieval Japan, similar to European knights
[2] shogun: military dictators of Japan from 1603 to 1868

[27] they need. Like movie cowboys, these samurai are romantic heroes, sure of their morals and battling clear forces of evil. The traditional Japanese version of a samurai was a noble and often distant symbol of Japan's imperial heritage, but Kurosawa considered the main characters differently. To [28] him, the film's samurai were distinctly human characters, each with a conscience and the will to act to correct the wrongs around them.

Although Kurosawa's films enjoy a lofty reputation in the West, many critics and moviegoers in his home country view his films as neither original nor particularly Japanese. His use of Western ideals and themes—even reinterpreting Western authors such as William Shakespeare and Fyodor Dostoyevsky—leads Japanese cinema lovers, many of [29] who see Kurosawa's use of Japanese culture as mere "window dressing" applied to essentially foreign stories, to regard his work with suspicion. Ironically, it was Kurosawa's success that opened the door for other, more "Japanese" directors, such as Yasujiro Ozu and Kenji Mizoguchi, to gain a wider audience.

27. A) NO CHANGE
    B) it needs.
    C) he needs.
    D) you need.

28. A) NO CHANGE
    B) me
    C) you
    D) us

29. A) NO CHANGE
    B) whose
    C) which
    D) whom

## Agreement: Modifiers

> **LEARNING OBJECTIVES**
>
> After this lesson, you will be able to:
>
> - Identify and correct modifier agreement issues
> - Identify and correct inappropriate uses of apostrophes

### To answer a question like this:

**30** Called "Mother of the Universe" by the Tibetan people, the lives of George Mallory and Andrew Irvine had already been claimed by Mount Everest, despite its maternal appellation, before Hillary and Norgay finally conquered its icy peak.

A) NO CHANGE

B) Hillary and Norgay, called "Mother of the Universe" by the Tibetan people, finally conquered the icy peak of Mount Everest, which had already claimed the lives of George Mallory and Andrew Irvine, despite its maternal appellation.

C) The lives of George Mallory and Andrew Irvine, called "Mother of the Universe" by the Tibetan people, had already been claimed by Mount Everest, despite its maternal appellation, before Hillary and Norgay finally conquered its icy peak.

D) Called "Mother of the Universe" by the Tibetan people, Mount Everest had already, despite its maternal appellation, claimed the lives of George Mallory and Andrew Irvine before Hillary and Norgay finally conquered its icy peak.

### You need to know this:

A **modifier** is a word or phrase that describes, clarifies, or provides additional information about another part of the sentence. Modifier questions require you to identify the part of a sentence being modified and use the appropriate modifier in the proper place.

In order to be grammatically correct, the modifier must be placed as close to the word it describes as possible. Use context clues in the passage to identify the correct placement of a modifier; a misplaced modifier can cause confusion and is always incorrect on test day.

Note that a common way the SAT tests modifiers is with modifying phrases at the beginning of a sentence. Just like any other modifier, the modifying phrase grammatically modifies whatever is right next to it in the sentence. For example, consider the sentence, "While walking to the bus stop, the rain drenched Bob." The initial phrase, "While walking to the bus stop," grammatically modifies "the rain," creating a nonsense sentence; the rain can't walk to the bus stop. The writer meant that Bob was walking to the bus stop, so the sentence should read, "While walking to the bus stop, Bob was drenched by the rain."

| Modifier/Modifying Phrase | Incorrect | Correct |
|---|---|---|
| nearly | Andre **nearly** watched the play for four hours. | Andre watched the play for **nearly** four hours. |
| in individual containers | The art teacher handed out paints to students **in individual containers**. | The art teacher handed out paints **in individual containers** to students. |
| A scholar athlete | **A scholar athlete**, maintaining high grades in addition to playing soccer were expected of Maya. | **A scholar athlete**, Maya was expected to maintain high grades in addition to playing soccer. |

## Adjectives and Adverbs

Use adjectives only to modify nouns and pronouns. Use adverbs to modify everything else.

- **Adjectives** are single-word modifiers that describe nouns and pronouns: *Ian conducted an **efficient** lab experiment.*
- **Adverbs** are single-word modifiers that describe verbs, adjectives, or other adverbs: *Ian **efficiently** conducted a lab experiment.*

Note that nouns can sometimes be used as adjectives. For example, in the phrase "the fashion company's autumn line," the word "fashion" functions as an adjective modifying "company," and the word "autumn" functions as an adjective modifying "line."

## Comparative/Superlative

When comparing similar things, use adjectives that match the number of items being compared. When comparing two items or people, use the **comparative** form of the adjective. When comparing three or more items or people, use the **superlative** form.

| Comparative (two items) | Superlative (three or more items) |
|---|---|
| better, more, newer, older, shorter, taller, worse, younger | best, most, newest, oldest, shortest, tallest, worst, youngest |

**Possessive Nouns and Pronouns**

Possessive nouns and pronouns indicate that something that belongs to someone or something. In general, possessive nouns are written with an apostrophe, while possessive pronouns are not.

| To spot errors in possessive noun or pronoun construction, look for . . . | Incorrect | Correct |
|---|---|---|
| Two nouns in a row | The **professors lectures** were both informative and entertaining. | The **professor's lectures** were both informative and entertaining. |
| Pronouns with apostrophes | The book is **her's**. | The book is **hers**. |
| Words that sound alike | The three friends decided to ride **there** bicycles to the park over **they're** where **their** going to enjoy a picnic lunch. | The three friends decided to ride **their** bicycles to the park over **there** where **they're** going to enjoy a picnic lunch. |

**Apostrophes**

| Use an apostrophe to . . . | Example |
|---|---|
| Indicate the possessive form of a single noun | My oldest **sister's** soccer game is on Saturday. |
| Indicate the possessive form of a plural noun | My two older **sisters'** soccer games are on Saturday. |
| Indicate a contraction (e.g., *don't*, *can't*) | **They've** won every soccer match this season. |

Note that plural nouns are formed without an apostrophe.

| Incorrect | Correct |
|---|---|
| Sting **ray's** are cartilaginous fish related to **shark's**. | Sting **rays** are cartilaginous fish related to **sharks**. |
| There are many **carnival's** in this area every summer. | There are many **carnivals** in this area every summer. |

To check whether *it's* is appropriate, replace it in the sentence with *it is* or *it has*. If the sentence no longer makes sense, *it's* is incorrect. The following sentence is correct:

*The tree frog blends perfectly into its surroundings. When it holds still, it's nearly invisible.*

Note that *its'* and *its's* are never correct.

## You need to do this:

If the underlined portion includes a modifier, determine whether the modifier:

- Is placed correctly
  - Is it as near as possible to the word it logically modifies?
  - If it is not in the correct place, where should it be moved?
- Agrees with the word or words it is describing
  - Does the sentence require an adjective or an adverb?
  - Does the noun or pronoun show proper possession?

If the underlined portion includes an apostrophe, make sure it correctly indicates either possession or a contraction. If an apostrophe is missing, select the answer choice that places it in the correct location.

## Explanation:

The phrase "despite its maternal appellation" indicates that it was Mount Everest that was known in Tibetan culture as the "Mother of the Universe." That means "Mount Everest" must be placed immediately next to the phrase, "[c]alled 'Mother of the Universe' by the Tibetan people." This is not the case in the current sentence, so there is a modification error. The only choice that corrects the error is **(D)**.

If modifiers give you trouble, study the information above and try these Drill questions before completing the following Try on Your Own questions. Edit each sentence to correct the modifier or apostrophe issue. Answers can be found on the next page.

## Drill

a. Computers have grown exponential more efficient since their invention.

b. Estella chose to take the route with the most attractively scenery to her destination.

c. The leaf-tailed gecko's amazing natural camouflage enables it to blend perfectly into it's surroundings.

d. Between basketball and baseball, basketball is the most popular sport in the United States.

e. From Edgar Allan Poe to Monty Python, the infamous Spanish Inquisition has provided material for many artists.

## Try on Your Own

**Directions:** Take as much time as you need on these questions. Work carefully and methodically. There will be an opportunity for timed practice at the end of the chapter.

**Questions 31-37 refer to the following passage.**

**Sergei Eisenstein**

Considered the father of the montage, a popular cinematic technique that involves a rapid succession of shots, often superimposed, **31** the modern movie has as one of its principal architects Russian director Sergei Eisenstein. Although his career was not particularly prolific—he completed only seven feature-length films—Eisenstein's work contains a clarity and sharpness of composition that make the depth of his plots and the **32** powerfully complexity of his juxtaposed images easily accessible to most viewers. In fact, few filmmakers were **33** most instrumental in pushing the envelope of the established, conservative nineteenth-century Victorian theatre than Eisenstein, whose films helped to usher in a new era of abstract thought and expression in art.

Eisenstein's feature debut, a film entitled *Statchka* (*Strike* in English) released in 1925, was many **34** moviegoer's first experience of montage on the big screen. Based on the contemporary theory of biomechanics and criticizing the mechanical and

31. A) NO CHANGE
    B) the modern movie has Russian director Sergei Eisenstein to thank as one of its principal architects.
    C) the Russian director Sergei Eisenstein was one of the principal architects of the modern movie.
    D) critics name the Russian director Sergei Eisenstein as one of the principal architects of the modern movie.

32. A) NO CHANGE
    B) powerful
    C) power
    D) power of

33. A) NO CHANGE
    B) more instrumental
    C) the best at being instrumental
    D) better at instrumentally

34. A) NO CHANGE
    B) movie's goer
    C) moviegoers
    D) moviegoers'

Drill answers from previous page:

Note: These are not the only ways to correct the sentences; your answers may differ.

a. Computers have grown **exponentially** more efficient since their invention.

b. Estella chose to take the route with the most **attractive** scenery to her destination.

c. The leaf-tailed gecko's amazing natural camouflage enables it to blend perfectly into **its** surroundings.

d. Between basketball and baseball, basketball is the **more** popular sport in the United States.

e. The infamous Spanish Inquisition has provided material for many artists, **from Edgar Allan Poe to Monty Python**.

repetitive movements required of exploited factory workers, [35] Eisenstein's montage consisted of a powerful sequence of conflicting images that were able to abbreviate time spans in the film while introducing new metaphors and allusions to the storyline. Essentially, Eisenstein sought to use the montage to create a cumulative emotional effect that was greater than the sum of the individual shots.

[36] Enormously, it was with the successful technique of montage that Eisenstein's work caught the eye of the new Communist Party leaders in Moscow, who saw in his cinematic style a film for the "common man." His next two films, *Battleship Potemkin* and *October: Ten Days That Shook the World*, were commissioned by party officials in an attempt to use Eisenstein's mass appeal to disseminate Soviet propaganda. As a result, these achievements have been frequently criticized [37] for they're lack of artistic integrity. Yet, in the end, regardless of politics, Eisenstein's films continue to have an undeniably significant and lasting impact on filmmakers.

35. A) NO CHANGE
    B) Eisenstein arranged a powerful sequence of conflicting images into a montage that was
    C) Eisenstein used conflicting images in a powerful sequence, composing a montage that was
    D) Eisenstein created a montage consisting of a powerful sequence of conflicting images that were

36. A) NO CHANGE
    B) It was enormously with the successful technique of montage that Eisenstein's work caught the eye of the new Communist Party leaders
    C) It was with the enormously successful technique of montage that Eisenstein's work caught the eye of the new Communist Party leaders
    D) It was with the successful technique of montage that Eisenstein's work caught the eye of the enormously new Communist Party leaders

37. A) NO CHANGE
    B) therefore
    C) for their
    D) for there

# Idioms

---

**LEARNING OBJECTIVES**

After this lesson, you will be able to:

- Identify and correct expressions that deviate from idiomatic English
- Determine the appropriate word in frequently confused pairs

---

## To answer a question like this:

**38** The goal of the conference was not only to find ways to reduce carbon emissions but to provide information to communities threatened by sea level rise as well.

A) NO CHANGE

B) Not only was the goal of the conference to find ways to reduce carbon emissions, albeit also to provide information to communities threatened by sea level rise.

C) The goal of the conference was not only to find ways to reduce carbon emissions, and to provide information to communities whom sea level rise threatens.

D) The goal of the conference was not only to find ways to reduce carbon emissions but also to provide information to communities threatened by sea level rise.

## You need to know this:

An **idiom** is a combination of words that must be used together to convey either a figurative or literal meaning. Idioms are tested in three ways:

1.  Proper preposition use in context: the preposition must reflect the writer's intended meaning.

    *She waits **on** customers.*
    *She waits **for** the bus.*
    *She waits **with** her friends.*

2.  Idiomatic expressions: some words or phrases must be used together to be correct.

    *Simone will **either** bike **or** run to the park.*
    ***Neither** the principal **nor** the teachers will tolerate tardiness.*
    *This fall, Shari is playing **not only** soccer **but also** field hockey.*

3.  Implicit double negatives: some words imply a negative and therefore cannot be paired with an explicit negative. The words "barely," "hardly," and "scarcely" fall into this category.

    Correct: *Janie **can hardly** wait for vacation.*
    Incorrect: *Janie **can't hardly** wait for vacation.*

| Frequently Tested Prepositions | Idiomatic Expressions | Words That Can't Pair with Negative Words |
|---|---|---|
| at | as . . . as | barely |
| by | between . . . and | hardly |
| for | both . . . and | scarcely |
| from | either . . . or | |
| of | neither . . . nor | |
| on | just as . . . so too | |
| to | not only . . . but also | |
| with | prefer . . . to | |

## Commonly Confused Words

English contains many pairs of words that sound alike but are spelled differently and have different meanings, such as *accept* (to take or receive something that is offered) and *except* (with the exclusion of).

Other words, such as *among* (in a group of, or surrounded by, multiple things or people) and *between* (distinguishing one thing from one other thing), do not sound alike but have similar meanings that are often confused.

You'll want to familiarize yourself with the following list of commonly misused words so you can spot them on test day.

| | |
|---|---|
| **Accept:** to take or receive something that is offered | *My niece **accepted** her pile of birthday gifts with great enthusiasm.* |
| **Except:** with the exclusion of | *All of the presents are toys **except** for a box containing a popular book series.* |

| | |
|---|---|
| **Affect:** to act on, to have influence on something | *The dreary, rainy weather negatively **affected** Rahul's mood.* |
| **Effect:** something that is produced by a cause; a consequence | *A recent study explored the **effects** of weather on mental well-being.* |

| | |
|---|---|
| **Lay:** to put or place something | *My boss asked me to **lay** the report on her desk before I left for the day.* |
| **Lie:** to rest or recline | *After a long day of work, I just want to **lie** down on the couch.* |

| **Raise:** to build or lift up something; to support the growth of someone | *Many books are dedicated to the topic of **raising** children.* |
|---|---|
| **Rise:** to get up | *Ted likes to **rise** early in the morning to exercise before his children wake up.* |

| **Whose:** a possessive pronoun | ***Whose** uniform shirt is this?* |
|---|---|
| **Who's:** a contraction meaning "who is" | ***Who's** responsible for ordering new uniforms?* |

| **Their:** a possessive pronoun for a plural noun or pronoun | *The college students plan to travel internationally after **their** graduation.* |
|---|---|
| **They're:** a contraction for "they are" | ***They're** going to visit several countries in East Asia.* |
| **There:** at a certain point or place | *The students are excited to experience the foods and cultures **there**.* |
| **There's:** a contraction for "there is" | ***There's** a tour of an ancient palace that they're looking forward to seeing.* |

| **Among:** in a group of, or surrounded by, multiple things or people | *Navya was **among** many doctoral candidates who visited the university.* |
|---|---|
| **Between:** distinguishing one thing from one other thing | *Navya had to decide **between** her top two doctoral program choices.* |

| **Amount:** sum or quantity of multiple things that cannot be counted | *The **amount** of pollution in the ocean is affecting dolphin populations.* |
|---|---|
| **Number:** Sum or quantity of a finite collection that can be counted | *Scientists report that the **number** of dolphins has decreased significantly.* |

| **Less:** a smaller extent or amount of things that cannot be counted | *The common supermarket sign "10 items or **less**" is actually incorrect.* |
|---|---|
| **Fewer:** of a smaller number, referring to things that can be counted | *Since the items can be counted, the sign should read "10 items or **fewer**."* |

| **Much:** great in quantity, referring to things that cannot be counted | *My sister has **much** more patience than I have.* |
|---|---|
| **Many:** great in quantity, referring to things that can be counted | ***Many** of her friends admire her ability to stay calm in difficult situations.* |

| **Good:** satisfactory in quality, quantity, or degree; adjective | *Dakota considered both the **good** and bad effects of wind energy before composing her essay.* |
| --- | --- |
| **Well:** To perform an action in a satisfactory manner; adverb | *Dakota wrote her essay so **well** that her professor used it as an example of excellent persuasive writing.* |

## You need to do this:

- If the underlined portion includes a preposition, a conjunction, or *barely/hardly/scarcely*, look for a common idiom error.
- If the underlined segment includes a commonly misused word, check the context to determine whether it is used properly.

## Explanation:

A sentence that contains the phrase "not only" must also contain the phrase "but also" (and vice versa). The only choice that includes the phrase "but also" is **(D)**, making it the correct answer.

If idioms give you trouble, study the information above and try out these Drill questions before completing the following Try on Your Own questions. Edit each sentence to correct the incorrect idiom. Answers can be found on the next page.

## Drill

a. When Fatima returned home from school, she was unpleasantly surprised to find that her hamster had escaped to its cage again.

b. The surgeon took great pride of her work, saying she was honored to be able to help when her patients thanked her.

c. Neither apples or cherries will grow in the Phillipines due to its hot climate.

d. The day after Kumar tried yoga for the first time, he was so sore he couldn't hardly move.

e. The attorney wanted to except the case but couldn't because his caseload was already full.

## Try on Your Own

**Directions:** Take as much time as you need on these questions. Work carefully and methodically. There will be an opportunity for timed practice at the end of the chapter.

**Questions 39-44 refer to the following passage.**

**The Intriguing Opossum**

Much maligned as a repulsive nuisance, the opossum is actually one of North America's most interesting animals, exhibiting many notable characteristics. For example, opossums boast an incredible array of 50 razor-sharp teeth, the most of any mammal in the world. Also, because opossums are partially or totally immune, [39] <u>neither rabies or snake venom presents much of a danger to them.</u>

While their beady eyes, pointy snouts, and bald tails might make them seem like a cousin of the rat, opossums are actually closely related to the kangaroo and are the only marsupial native to the continent. One of the most primitive animals, existing since the time of the dinosaurs, opossums have survived for millions of years by adapting to diverse habitats—including dense urban areas—and food supplies. [40] <u>There isn't hardly anything that opossums will not eat;</u> included in their possible diet are rodents, birds, frogs, eggs, insects,

39. A) NO CHANGE

    B) neither rabies nor snake venom presents much of a danger to them

    C) not even rabies nor snake venom presents much of a danger to them

    D) not much of a danger is presented by even rabies or snake venom

40. A) NO CHANGE

    B) There is hardly nothing that opossums will not eat;

    C) There is hardly anything that opossums will not eat;

    D) Opossums will not eat hardly anything;

Drill answers from previous page:

Note: These are not the only ways to correct the sentences; your answers may differ.

a. When Fatima returned home from school, she was unpleasantly surprised to find that her hamster had escaped **from** its cage again.

b. The surgeon took great pride **in** her work, saying she was honored to be able to help when her patients thanked her.

c. Neither apples **nor** cherries will grow in the Phillipines due to its hot climate.

d. The day after Kumar tried yoga for the first time, he was so sore he **could hardly** move.

e. The attorney wanted to **accept** the case but couldn't because his caseload was already full.

snails, slugs, earthworms, plants, tree roots, fruits, and grains. Today, many opossums that live in areas densely populated by humans survive on garbage and small mice, even consuming the bones to satisfy their high need for calcium.

Of course, the opossum does have vulnerabilities. Its average three-year life span is not unusual for its size, typically **41** between two or three feet long. What is unusual is that opossums continue growing throughout their lifetimes. Such a state of constant development is linked with metabolic limitations **42** of the amount of food and energy that can be stored within the opossum's body, requiring that ready food sources be available year-round. In addition, opossums are highly susceptible to the cold, making it rather common to see opossums with frostbitten ears and tails.

Nevertheless, opossums have displayed amazing resilience over the years, often surviving attacks from intimidating predators like dogs and even hawks. While the opossum's first reaction when threatened is to begin running to the nearest tree, their primary defense **43** is an affect of the nervous system that, when sensing danger, throws the opossum's body into a catatonic state that dramatically slows its heart rate. The opossum will then **44** lay still, begin to drool, and appear dead, another trait that only adds to the fascinating nature of these animals.

41. A)  NO CHANGE
    B)  either two or three
    C)  at least two or three
    D)  between two and three

42. A)  NO CHANGE
    B)  on
    C)  with
    D)  for

43. A)  NO CHANGE
    B)  is an effect of the nervous system
    C)  effects the nervous system so
    D)  of the nervous system is an affect

44. A)  NO CHANGE
    B)  have laid
    C)  lie
    D)  have lain

# How Much Have You Learned?

**Directions:** For testlike practice, give yourself 9 minutes to complete this question set. Be sure to study the explanations, even for questions you got right. They can be found at the end of this chapter.

**Questions 45-55 refer to the following passage.**
**The Experts of Visual Communication**

When people consider different types of [45] communication often, they think of only verbal or written forms. Few, perhaps, think of art as a [46] mode of communication; however, from early cave paintings and the intricate craftwork of ancient civilizations to contemporary, esoteric, abstract works that challenge traditional notions of aesthetic representation, art has played an essential role in visual communication. In the world of business, the intersection of art and communication is graphic design. [47] The explosion of media brought on by the digital age offered a growing platform for art, through graphic design, to express ideas and messages.

There is almost no detail too small, no space too unimportant to escape the attention of a graphic designer. [48] Their work is nearly ubiquitous in modern commercial life: [49] business logos, billboard advertisements; website layouts, T-shirt designs; and even the decorated cardboard of cereal boxes and coffee cups feature graphic design. In a culture increasingly wired for visual communication, graphic designers wield a powerful influence over the ordinary consumer. They craft the formats, styles, images, and symbols that shape how we perceive products, services, and ideas.

45. A) NO CHANGE
    B) communication often, they think of only verbal
    C) communication, often only they think of verbal
    D) communication, often they think of only verbal

46. A) NO CHANGE
    B) mode of communication; however from early cave paintings
    C) mode of communication, however, from early cave paintings
    D) mode of communication, however from early cave paintings

47. A) NO CHANGE
    B) The explosion of media brings on by the digital age offers
    C) The explosion of media brought on by the digital age offering
    D) The explosion of media brought on by the digital age offers

48. A) NO CHANGE
    B) The work of them
    C) The work of graphic designers
    D) The work of theirs

49. A) NO CHANGE
    B) business logos, billboard advertisements, website layouts, T-shirt designs, and even the decorated cardboard of cereal boxes and coffee cups feature graphic design.
    C) business logos, billboard advertisements, website layouts, T-shirt designs, and, even the decorated cardboard of cereal boxes, and coffee cups feature graphic design.
    D) business logos; billboard advertisements; website layouts; T-shirt designs; and even the decorated cardboard of cereal boxes, and coffee cups feature graphic design.

How do these visual innovators navigate a career path? Most 50 began by studying graphic design and earn a bachelor's degree at a four-year college, where they build skills through interactive class settings to hone expertise. These programs are heavily project-based and provide the sort of experience professional work will require. Students gradually compile design portfolios to showcase their best work. Once students have graduated, these portfolios are essential for the job search because 51 it demonstrates the ability and creative potential of designers.

Competition in the job market for graphic designers is 52 rigorous yet the field offers a variety of professional options. Some work in design studios. There they team with other graphic designers, taking on projects for external clients. Others work "in-house" for businesses that staff their own graphic designers to create media on a more frequent basis. Those with more entrepreneurial inclinations can work as freelance graphic designers, doing their own networking and contracting. Trying to expand their possibilities, 53 many graphic designers are also now applying their knowledge to website and web application design, which continues to be a growing field for tech-minded artists.

54 Although the demand for graphic designers persists the highly competitive job market gives some prospective artists pause. The trope of the "struggling artist" holds true, it seems, even in our highly visually oriented society. Still, most graphic designers find their 55 careers both satisfying and also invigorating. Perhaps, for the dedicated artists who seek a career in graphic design, the thrill and beauty of the work yields enough motivation and inspiration to persevere and succeed.

50. A) NO CHANGE
    B) have begun by studying graphic design and earning
    C) begin by studying graphic design and earning
    D) will begin by studying graphic design and will earn

51. A) NO CHANGE
    B) you demonstrate
    C) they demonstrate
    D) theirs demonstrate

52. A) NO CHANGE
    B) rigorous, although the field offers
    C) rigorous; even though the field offers
    D) rigorous, but the field offers

53. A) NO CHANGE
    B) much graphic design knowledge also now applies to website and web application design, which
    C) many graphic designers' knowledge also now applies to website and web application design, which
    D) website and web application design allows many graphic designers to apply their knowledge, which

54. A) NO CHANGE
    B) Yet the demand for graphic designers persists; the highly competitive job market
    C) While the demand for graphic designers persists, but the highly competitive job market
    D) Even though the demand for graphic designers persists, the highly competitive job market

55. A) NO CHANGE
    B) careers neither satisfying or invigorating
    C) careers both satisfying and invigorating
    D) career not only satisfying but invigorating

# Reflect

**Directions:** Take a few minutes to recall what you've learned and what you've been practicing in this chapter. Consider the following questions, jot down your best answer for each one, and then compare your reflections to the expert responses on the following page. Use your level of confidence to determine what to do next.

Name at least three ways to correct a run-on sentence.

_____

_____

_____

How does the SAT test subject-verb agreement and parallelism?

_____

_____

_____

What are the three different pronoun forms? When do you use each one?

_____

_____

_____

What is the difference between an adjective and an adverb?

_____

_____

_____

What are the three ways that apostrophes are tested on the SAT?

_____

_____

_____

Which commonly confused words do you need to be especially careful to look out for?

_____

_____

## Expert Responses

Name at least three ways to correct a run-on sentence.

*There are a number of ways to fix a run-on sentence on the SAT. The six ways that you are likely to see are: 1) use a period to create two separate sentences, 2) use a semicolon between the two independent clauses, 3) use a colon between the two independent clauses, 4) make one clause dependent, 5) add a FANBOYS conjunction after the comma, or 6) use a dash between the two independent clauses.*

How does the SAT test subject-verb agreement and parallelism?

*A subject and verb must always agree in person (first, second, or third) and number (singular or plural). You will need to be able to spot subject-verb mismatches and correct them. Parallelism requires that all items in a list, a compound, or a comparison are in parallel form. The SAT may test lists or comparisons in which one item is in the wrong form.*

What are the three different pronoun forms? When do you use each one?

*The three forms are subjective (when the pronoun is the subject), objective (when the pronoun is the object of a verb or preposition), and possessive (when the pronoun expresses ownership).*

What is the difference between an adjective and an adverb?

*An adjective is a single word that modifies a noun or a pronoun, while an adverb is a single word that modifies a verb, an adjective, or another adverb.*

What are the three ways that apostrophes are tested on the SAT?

*Apostrophes on the SAT are used to 1) indicate the possessive form of a singular noun ('s), 2) indicate the possessive form of a plural noun (s'), or 3) indicate a contraction (don't = do not).*

Which commonly confused words do you need to be especially careful to look out for?

*The answer to this question is specific to you. If you have concerns about more than half of the words out of the list of 24, consider making flash cards to help you practice. The extra effort will ensure that you do not confuse any of the commonly confused words on test day.*

## Next Steps

If you answered most questions correctly in the "How Much Have You Learned?" section, and if your responses to the Reflect questions were similar to those of the SAT expert, then consider sentence structure, punctuation, and agreement areas of strength and move on to the next chapter. Come back to these topics periodically to prevent yourself from getting rusty.

If you don't yet feel confident, review those parts of this chapter that you have not yet mastered. In particular, review punctuation usage in the Sentence Structure: The Basics and Commas, Dashes, and Colons lessons, as well as how to select the appropriate pronoun or modifier in the Agreement: Pronouns and Agreement: Modifiers lessons. Then try the questions you missed again. As always, be sure to review the explanations closely.

# Answers and Explanations

**1.** Review the Explanation portion of the Sentence Structure: The Basics lesson.

**2. D**

**Difficulty:** Medium

**Getting to the Answer:** The sentence as written is a run-on. Two independent clauses are joined incorrectly by a comma. Eliminate (A). Because the comma is not underlined, you cannot fix the run-on by adding a coordinating conjunction or by replacing the comma with a semicolon. Instead, you need to change one of the independent clauses into a dependent clause. Choice **(D)** is correct because it makes the first clause dependent.

**3. B**

**Difficulty:** Medium

**Getting to the Answer:** In the passage, the sentence has a subject but is missing a verb. In other words, there is no main action that "the Sun's core temperature" is performing. Eliminate (A). The correct answer will add a verb to the underlined portion. Choice **(B)** is correct because it is the only answer choice that includes a verb, "has."

**4. A**

**Difficulty:** Hard

**Getting to the Answer:** The underlined portion lists examples of benefits that the Sun provides for the Earth. The list is long, but it is broken up into three main parts: electromagnetic waves, metabolic life, and the Earth's natural phenomena. Each is a category that has two specific items that precede it. When a list has multiple categories, each with its own members, then commas alone are often not sufficient to express the information clearly. Use semicolons to distinguish the main categories, and use commas to separate the items within each category. Choice **(A)** does exactly this and is correct.

**5. B**

**Difficulty:** Easy

**Getting to the Answer:** When two independent clauses are joined by a coordinating conjunction, such as "but," as is the case in this sentence, the conjunction needs to be preceded by a comma. Eliminate (A) and (C). Also eliminate (D) because "still" is not a FANBOYS conjunction. Choice **(B)** is correct.

**6. D**

**Difficulty:** Medium

**Getting to the Answer:** Two independent clauses are joined incorrectly by a comma, so you need to combine them according to correct grammar. Eliminate (A). There are several ways to combine two independent clauses, but only one answer choice offers an acceptable method: **(D)** uses a semicolon to join the two independent clauses and is correct. (B) does not use a FANBOYS conjunction and (C) erroneously omits the comma.

**7.** Review the Explanation portion of the Sentence Structure: Commas, Dashes, and Colons lesson.

**8. B**

**Difficulty:** Medium

**Getting to the Answer:** When a comma is underlined, check to see if the parts of the sentence before and after the comma need to be separated. In this sentence, the comma separates the subordinating conjunction "although" from the clause it introduces and breaks the link between the dependent clause and the main clause. Choice **(B)** correctly eliminates the unnecessary punctuation.

**9. C**

**Difficulty:** Medium

**Getting to the Answer:** Technically, "Mauritius" is not a complete sentence; there is no verb. Eliminate (A). You need a choice that will either make "Mauritius" a complete sentence or combine it with the first sentence. Choice **(C)** correctly uses a colon to introduce important information. Both (B) and (D) are missing commas after "familiar," making them grammatically incorrect.

**10. D**

**Difficulty:** Hard

**Getting to the Answer:** The beginning of the sentence, "Since gaining independence in 1968," is a short introductory phrase that needs to be set off with a comma. Eliminate (A). Neither a dash nor a semicolon is appropriate in this scenario, so eliminate (B) as well. (C) incorrectly makes the independent clause that begins "Maritius has emerged" dependent. **(D)** correctly uses a comma to separate the introductory phrase from the main clause.

**11. B**

**Difficulty:** Hard

**Getting to the Answer:** When a colon is used to introduce a short phrase, it emphasizes the information in the phrase. A colon that introduces and emphasizes information should be used only if the phrase is not connected to the sentence in another way. In this sentence, the phrase "in the modern global economy" is connected to the main clause with the preposition "in," so the colon is unnecessary. Eliminate (A). Dashes set off unnecessary information, but the phrase "in the modern global economy" is essential to the meaning of the sentence because it describes what kind of player Mauritius is. Eliminate (C). The adjectives "modern" and "global" are cumulative, meaning that their order can change the sense of the phrase. In other words, "modern" describes "global economy," and the phrase "global modern economy" has a different meaning from what is intended. Cumulative adjectives should not have a comma between them, so (D) is incorrect. The sentence's final phrase, "one of the few in the Southern Hemisphere" does need to be set off with a comma because it is a parenthetical phrase that could have been omitted from the sentence. **(B)** is correct.

**12. D**

**Difficulty:** Easy

**Getting to the Answer:** When you have a list of three or more items in a series, separate them with commas, and separate the last two items with a comma and the conjunction "and." This series contains six distinct items. In longer lists, it can be appropriate to use a semicolon to separate the list into logical groups of items. In the underlined portion, however, there is no logical grouping, so a semicolon is unnecessary. Eliminate (A). Choice (B) is incorrect because "and" should appear only between the last and second to last items in the list. (C) is incorrect because it omits "and" altogether. Only **(D)** offers the list correctly.

**13. C**

**Difficulty:** Easy

**Getting to the Answer:** If a dash is used to introduce a break in thought, a second dash must be used to end the parenthetical phrase unless a period ends both the phrase and the sentence. Determine whether the information after the dash is parenthetical by reading the sentence without that information. Although the phrase provides a description of how the "colonial powers" treated Mauritius, the sentence makes logical sense without it. The phrase is therefore parenthetical and must be properly set off. Only choice **(C)** correctly sets off the phrase with both an opening and a closing dash.

**14. B**

**Difficulty:** Easy

**Getting to the Answer:** When two independent clauses are combined with a FANBOYS conjunction, a comma needs to precede the conjunction. Eliminate (A). Only **(B)** places the necessary comma in the appropriate spot.

**15. A**

**Difficulty:** Medium

**Getting to the Answer:** Avoid using unnecessary punctuation. Reread the sentence to determine how its parts are related. This sentence is correct as written because no punctuation is required. The phrase "through its advantageous geographic location and large labor force" completes the thought in the sentence by providing information on how Mauritius "balances" and "flourishes." Choice **(A)** is correct.

**16.** Review the Explanation portion of the Agreement: Verbs lesson.

**17. A**

**Difficulty:** Medium

**Getting to the Answer:** When a verb is underlined, one of your tasks is to identify its subject to ensure that there is proper subject-verb agreement. The sentence construction is a little unusual, "what is believed," but the vague word "what" is indeed the subject for the verb "is believed." The subject, "what," is singular, so eliminate (B) and (D), which use "are," a verb that goes with a plural subject. The writer is referring to what is believed at the moment, not some time in the future; therefore, eliminate (C). Choice **(A)** is correct because "is" is the correct singular form of the verb and in the correct present tense.

## 18. D

**Difficulty:** Medium

**Getting to the Answer:** Determining whether a subject is singular or plural can be difficult sometimes, especially if the subject refers to many things. Here, "SMOM" is a group of knights, but because it is a single entity, the word functions as a singular. The use of the singular possessive pronoun "its" at the end of the sentence confirms that SMOM is singular. Eliminate (A) and (C). When a verb is underlined, also consider the tense. The entire first paragraph is in present tense and it is clear from the context that SMOM, though an "ancient" order, still exists, so maintain the same tense in this sentence. Choice **(D)** is correct because "is" is a singular verb in present tense.

## 19. B

**Difficulty:** Medium

**Getting to the Answer:** When a subject has multiple verbs, known as compound verbs, they must all be in the same form. The sentence begins with two verbs, both in infinitive form, "to protect" and "to defend." The underlined portion includes a third verb, which needs to be in the infinitive form, as well, to maintain parallelism. **(B)** is correct because it matches the form of the verbs earlier in the sentence.

## 20. B

**Difficulty:** Hard

**Getting to the Answer:** The perfect forms of verbs (i.e. have/has, had, and will have + a past participle) present special challenges in interpretation. It is crucial to determine the order of events. Because the sentence is rather long, focus on the underlined verb "had seized" and the verb in the opening phrase, "had overrun." The past perfect tense of "had overrun" signals that the action happened in the past and was completed in the past before some other action. The word "After" that begins the sentence and the dates show that the seizing of Rhodes happened after the overrunning of Jerusalem was completed. The only verb tense that expresses that temporal relationship is simple past tense. **(B)** is correct.

## 21. B

**Difficulty:** Easy

**Getting to the Answer:** The paragraph describes actions that occurred in the past and uses the simple past tense to do so, so the underlined portion should follow suit. Simple past describes a single event that occurred in the past, which is what Napoleon did. **(B)** is correct.

## 22. C

**Difficulty:** Easy

**Getting to the Answer:** The first word of the last paragraph is "Today," which signals a shift from the past tense of the previous paragraphs to present tense. The following sentence's main verb "include" is in present tense and confirms the shift. **(C)** is correct.

23. Review the Explanation portion of the Agreement: Pronouns lesson.

## 24. C

**Difficulty:** Medium

**Getting to the Answer:** When a pronoun is underlined, identify its antecedent. In the passage's first sentence, the writer gives a list, and in the second sentence, you find that these are the varied influences. The pronoun "He" is singular, but it refers to the plural group of "samurai, cowboys, shogun, gangsters, peasants, and William Shakespeare." Eliminate (A). The plural, third-person, subject pronoun "they" is needed to refer to the list. **(C)** is correct.

## 25. C

**Difficulty:** Medium

**Getting to the Answer:** The underlined portion should refer to "the most important Japanese filmmaker" as stated later in the sentence. "Filmmaker" is singular, but "them" is plural, so eliminate (A). In addition to being singular, the pronoun needs to be in the objective form because it is the "themes" and "settings" that are acting on the filmmaker, the object. The singular, objective (and third-person) pronoun is "him." **(C)** is correct.

## 26. C

**Difficulty:** Medium

**Getting to the Answer:** Pronouns can be in the grammatically correct form, but if they lack a clear referent, they need to be replaced with a specific word. The singular pronoun "its" is underlined and several singular nouns precede it, which makes it ambiguous. Eliminate (A). The underlined pronoun "its" is also possessive, so ask yourself, "whose story is the writer referring to?" The logical answer is "the film's story." **(C)** is correct.

**27. B**

**Difficulty:** Hard

**Getting to the Answer:** When a pronoun's antecedent is far away from the pronoun itself, it can be difficult to identify the antecedent. Checking for agreement between a pronoun and its antecedent is also tricky when the noun being replaced is singular in grammar but plural in concept. Both hurdles are present in this question. The entity seeking protection is the "village," which grammatically is singular. The third-person, singular pronoun "it" is required. **(B)** is correct.

**28. A**

**Difficulty:** Medium

**Getting to the Answer:** The pronoun "him" is replacing the third-person noun "Kurosawa." The end of the previous sentence raises the topic of what the samurai (in the film *Seven Samurai*) meant to Kurosawa. Any other change in person would cause an undesired shift in the passage. **(A)** is correct.

**29. D**

**Difficulty:** Hard

**Getting to the Answer:** In the passage, the word "of" means that the pronoun that follows should be in the objective form. However, the next word, "who," is in the subjective form; therefore, eliminate (A). Choice (B) is incorrect because "whose" is a possessive pronoun, but an objective pronoun is needed. Choice (C) is incorrect because "many" refers to people and "which" is for inanimate objects. Only **(D)** has the right pronoun in objective form and is correct.

**30.** Review the Explanation portion of the Agreement: Modifiers lesson.

**31. C**

**Difficulty:** Hard

**Getting to the Answer:** The sentence begins with a modifier, "Considered the father of montage," which means that the subject of the sentence must be the father of montage. Typically, the subject will immediately follow the opening modifying phrase, but in this sentence the next phrase, beginning "a popular cinematic technique," is an additional description, not the main clause. The underlined section is where the main clause begins, and the first words need to be the subject, the father of montage, Sergei Eisentstein. **(C)** is correct.

**32. B**

**Difficulty:** Easy

**Getting to the Answer:** Because the underlined word modifies "complexity," a noun, the underlined word needs to be an adjective. Choice **(B)** is correct.

**33. B**

**Difficulty:** Medium

**Getting to the Answer:** When making a comparison, you should note whether it is between two things or among three or more. In this sentence "few filmmakers" are being compared to Eisenstein. Although "filmmakers" is plural, the logic of the sentence treats them as one thing, so there are two things being compared. The comparative form "more" is needed. Choice **(B)** is correct.

**34. D**

**Difficulty:** Medium

**Getting to the Answer:** The qualifier "many" that precedes the underlined word shows that "moviegoers" is meant to be plural. The plural possessive is constructed by adding an apostrophe after the last "s." Choice **(D)** is correct .

**35. A**

**Difficulty:** Hard

**Getting to the Answer:** The sentence opens with an opening modifying phrase. Whatever that phrase modifies must immediately follow it. Ask yourself what is "[b]ased on the contemporary theory of biomechanics." The answer is Eisenstein's montage, so the underlined segment is correct and no change is needed. Choice **(A)** is correct.

Note that while Eisenstein could be using the montage to make a criticism, it does not make sense to say that Eisenstein is based on the theory of biomechanics. Therefore, the correct answer will not have "Eisenstein" as its subject; eliminate (B), (C), and (D). Choice **(A)** is correct because "Eisenstein's montage" is the subject, and the montage can both criticize and be based on the theory of biomechanics.

**36. C**

**Difficulty:** Medium

**Getting to the Answer:** The only difference among the underlined section and the answer choices is the placement of the word "enormously." The word is an adverb, so it needs to modify a verb, an adjective, or another adverb. Also, modifiers need to be placed near the word or phrase that they modify. Choice **(C)** is correct because it provides the closest placement to "successful," the only word that could be logically modified by "enormously."

**37. C**

**Difficulty:** Medium

**Getting to the Answer:** An apostrophe can signal a contraction, a shortening of two words. The underlined "they're" is a contraction of "they are," which does not make sense in the context of the sentence. Eliminate (A). You need a plural possessive pronoun because it refers back to "achievements." Choice **(C)** is correct.

**38.** Review the Explanation portion of the Idioms lesson.

**39. B**

**Difficulty:** Easy

**Getting to the Answer:** The construction "neither . . . nor" is idiomatic, so a phrase beginning with "neither" must be followed by "nor." Choice **(B)** is correct.

**40. C**

**Difficulty:** Easy

**Getting to the Answer:** The word "hardly" is a negative like "not." Double negatives, like "not hardly," are grammatical mistakes. Eliminate (A). The word "nothing" is another negative, so eliminate (B). Choice **(C)** is correct because it removes the double negative around "hardly."

**41. D**

**Difficulty:** Medium

**Getting to the Answer:** The construction in the underlined section is not idiomatic: "between . . . or" is incorrect. Eliminate (A). The three answer choices are all correct idiomatically, but only one makes logical sense in the sentence. (B) makes it sound as if an opossum cannot be two and a half feet long, which doesn't make sense. Similarly, (C) does not fit in the context of the passage because the word "typically" means that the opossum length given will be authoritative and precise, not a loose estimation as "at least" suggests. **(D)** is correct because it has the appropriate idiomatic phrase "between . . . and."

**42. B**

**Difficulty:** Hard

**Getting to the Answer:** Make sure that the proper prepositions are being used in the passage. As written, "of" implies that the metabolic limitations belong to the amount of food and energy that can be stored, but the intended meaning is that the metabolic limitations belong to the opossum and put a restriction on the amount of food and energy that can be stored. Eliminate (A). The preposition "on" is correct, given the context because there is a restriction *on* the amount of food that can be stored. Choice **(B)** is correct. If idioms are tricky, think of an analogous situation. A computer's limited warranty has limitations *on* the parts of the computer that are covered if something breaks. It doesn't have limitations *of* or *with* or *for* the parts of the computer.

**43. B**

**Difficulty:** Medium

**Getting to the Answer:** It will help to memorize commonly confused words like "affect" and "effect" and know what they mean and how to use them in various contexts. As written, the underlined portion incorrectly uses "affect," which is almost always a verb, as a noun. Eliminate (A). The intended word is "effect," which means some sort of change brought on by some cause (think *cause and effect*). Choice **(B)** is correct. Choice (C) also uses the word "effect" but incorrectly as a verb. "Effect" is almost always a noun, a thing that happens, but when "effect" is a verb, it means to cause or bring about. The nervous system is not an action that can be caused to happen, so (C) is incorrect.

## 44. C

**Difficulty:** Hard

**Getting to the Answer:** The distinction between "lay" and "lie" is mostly lost in everyday speech, but in formal written English, the difference is important. The word "lay" takes an object; the word "lie" does not. In other words, you lay down your book, but you lie down. Because the opossum is doing the action (the opossum is not, for example, laying down some food it had just picked up), "lie" is the appropriate verb. **(C)** is correct. The word "laid" is the past participle of "lay," and "lain" is the past participle of "lie." Neither (B) nor (D) offer verb tenses that make sense in the context of the sentence.

## 45. D

**Difficulty:** Medium

**Category:** Agreement: Modifiers

**Getting to the Answer:** Scan the answer choices to see that the difference is the placement of the words "often" and "only." These two words are modifiers, so they need to be placed as closely as possible to words or phrases that they modify. The word "often" tells the frequency with which people think of verbal or written forms; therefore, it needs to be at the beginning of the phrase. Eliminate (A) and (B), which put "often" before the comma so that it incorrectly modifies the previous phrase. The word "only" describes the limits of which forms of communication people think of, so the word needs to be nearest those forms of communication, "verbal and written." **(D)** is correct. (C) incorrectly places "only" so that it modifies "they."

## 46. A

**Difficulty:** Medium

**Category:** Sentence Structure: The Basics

**Getting to the Answer:** The underlined section is part of a long sentence that has two independent clauses. To join them you need to use a semicolon, a comma and coordinating (i.e., FANBOYS) conjunction, or a dash. The word "however" is not a coordinating conjunction; eliminate (C) and (D). While "however" does help in connecting the ideas of the first and second clauses, the word is not necessary, and should therefore be set off by a comma. **(A)** is correct.

## 47. D

**Difficulty:** Medium

**Category:** Agreement: Verbs

**Getting to the Answer:** Verb tense should stay consistent unless a certain thought requires a shift. In the underlined portion, the main verb is "offered," which is past tense, but the rest of the paragraph is in present tense. Eliminate (A). The correct verb form is present tense. Eliminate (C) because the *-ing*, or progressive, form is not a main verb. The passive voice "brought" is correct because it is the digital age that is bringing on the explosion of media; **(D)** is correct.

## 48. C

**Difficulty:** Medium

**Category:** Agreement: Pronouns

**Getting to the Answer:** Pronouns need to agree with their antecedents. In the underlined portion, the plural pronoun "their" incorrectly refers to the singular "a graphic designer" at the end of the previous sentence. Eliminate (A). Also, eliminate (B) and (D) because the pronouns they use are also plural and incorrectly refer to a singular antecedent. (B) is also incorrect because "them" is not possessive. **(C)** is correct because it replaces the pronoun with the correct plural referent.

## 49. B

**Difficulty:** Medium

**Category:** Sentence Structure: Commas, Dashes, and Colons

**Getting to the Answer:** You can treat the underlined portion after the colon as a long list, but also notice that it is a compound subject. All of the underlined items do the same thing: they feature graphic design. Sometimes, it can be helpful to use semicolons to organize complicated and long lists into groups of items, but in this case, the placement of the semicolons is not logical. There is no obvious reason why website layouts and T-shirt designs should be grouped together, nor why they should belong to a group that is separate from business logos and billboard advertisements. Eliminate (A). Both (C) and (D) are incorrect because the last item in the list is decorated cardboard, not cereal boxes and coffee cups. Placing a comma between "the decorated cardboard of cereal boxes" and "and coffee cups" would mean that the coffee cups are not decorated cardboard. **(B)** is correct because it separates each item in the list with a comma.

## 50. C

**Difficulty:** Medium

**Category:** Agreement: Verbs

**Getting to the Answer:** Verb tense should remain constant unless there is shift in meaning. The second half of the sentence has "they build," which is present tense. The sentence before and the sentence after also have main verbs in present tense, so the main verb of the underlined clause needs to be in present tense, too. **(C)** is correct.

## 51. C

**Difficulty:** Medium

**Category:** Agreement: Pronouns

**Getting to the Answer:** Pronouns need to match the noun that they are replacing. In the underlined portion, the singular pronoun "it" is supposed to replace the plural "portfolios," so eliminate (A) and (B). The word "portfolios" is not a possessive like "theirs," so (D) is also incorrect. Only **(C)** is left and is correct because "they" correctly replaces "portfolios."

## 52. D

**Difficulty:** Medium

**Category:** Sentence Structure: The Basics

**Getting to the Answer:** The sentence as constructed has two independent clauses, so they need to be joined correctly either with a comma and FANBOYS (coordinating) conjunction, or with a semicolon, or with a dash. As written, there is no comma between "rigorous" and "yet," so eliminate (A). Only **(D)** uses a comma and FANBOYS conjunction, so it is correct.

## 53. A

**Difficulty:** Medium

**Category:** Agreement: Modifiers

**Getting to the Answer:** When a sentence begins with a modifying phrase, whatever follows must be the thing that is modified and is the subject of the sentence. Logically, the modifying phrase "Trying to expand their possibilities" can refer only to the graphic designers. The pronoun "their" is plural and so is "graphic designers." **(A)** is correct.

## 54. D

**Difficulty:** Medium

**Category:** Sentence Structure: The Basics

**Getting to the Answer:** The word "Although" in the underlined portion signals that the first clause is a dependent clause and the second clause is independent. A comma is required to separate the two, but the sentence as written has no comma. Eliminate (A). A semicolon is not appropriate for subordinating one clause to another, and "yet" is a coordinating (FANBOYS) conjunction, not a subordinating conjunction. Eliminate (B). Choice (C) is incorrect because "while" makes the first clause dependent, and "but" cannot be used to join a dependent and an independent clause. That leaves **(D)**, which is correct because "Even though" subordinates the first clause and uses a comma to separate it from the second clause.

## 55. C

**Difficulty:** Medium

**Category:** Agreement: Idioms

**Getting to the Answer:** Idiomatic expressions have no logical rules, so they must be memorized. The construction "both . . . and also" is not a valid idiomatic phrase in formal written English. Eliminate (A). The correct construction is "both . . . and," which makes **(C)** correct. (B) is an incorrect form of "neither . . . nor," and it does not make sense in the context of the sentence. The idiom in (D) should be "not only . . . but also," so it is incorrect, too.

# CHAPTER 26

# Spotting and Fixing Issues: Organization, Development, and Graphs

# How Much Do You Know?

**Directions:** Try the questions below. The "Category" heading in the explanation for each question gives the title of the lesson that covers how to answer it. If you answered the question(s) for a given lesson correctly, you may be able to move quickly through that lesson. If you answered incorrectly, you may want to take your time on that lesson.

**Questions 1-11 refer to the following passage.**

**Genetically Modified Organisms**

    Although biotechnology companies and the chronically naïve [1] imagine that there is no danger to be feared from genetically modified foods, they overlook a plethora of evidence indicating that they may be gambling with people's lives by continuing to [2] interfere and tamper with nature to create these "Frankenfoods." Potential problems range from the relatively minor—increased possibilities of allergic reactions to certain foods, for instance—to the potentially devastating—the complete skewing of the balance of an ecosystem. All of these factors should be carefully considered before [3] we choose to risk so much for the possibility of a better tomato.

    [1] [4] For example, the cultivation of insect-resistant plants could lead to the reduction or even destruction of certain insect species that naturally feed on those plants. [2] A change in the insect population could have a disastrous impact on certain bird species that rely on the affected insects as their food source. [3] [5] Ecosystems are relatively stable, and the ripple created by genetically altering one variety of soybean [6] will translate into a shock wave

1. A) NO CHANGE
   B) insist
   C) hope
   D) think

2. A) NO CHANGE
   B) thoughtlessly interfere and casually tamper
   C) interfere by casually tampering
   D) tamper

3. A) NO CHANGE
   B) we as a society
   C) those of us who comprise society
   D) the citizens making up our population

4. Which choice best connects the sentence with the previous paragraph?

   A) NO CHANGE
   B) On the other hand,
   C) Although unlikely,
   D) DELETE the underlined portion and begin the sentence with a capital letter.

5. Which choice most effectively sets up the information that follows?

   A) NO CHANGE
   B) Humans are tightly connected to ecosystems,
   C) Each ecosystem is an independent entity,
   D) An ecosystem is a delicate thing,

6. A) NO CHANGE
   B) must
   C) would
   D) could

of unforeseen repercussions in the long term. [4] And alterations in the balance of the bird population could have further-reaching consequences, all the way up the food chain. [7]

Further, it is likely that there are dangerous impacts on the genetically modified organisms themselves and on those who consume foods produced from genetically modified organisms. [8] Human studies have not been performed, [9] <u>and</u> the possibility that tampering with an organism's genetic structure could cause far-reaching health consequences for the people who eat genetically modified foods must be prioritized in future scientific research.

Arguments about the potential for genetic engineering to end world hunger by maximizing the quantity and quality of food grown around the world are based on an essential fallacy: people do not starve because there is a lack of food. People starve because it is more profitable for businesses to let food go to waste than to distribute it to the world's impoverished and famine-stricken regions. We have plenty of farmland sitting fallow and plenty of food rotting in

7. To make this paragraph most logical, sentence 4 should be placed

A) where it is now.
B) after sentence 1.
C) after sentence 2.
D) DELETED from the paragraph.

8. At this point, the writer is considering adding the following sentence.

> Some studies indicate that certain genetically modified foods have negative effects on the digestive systems and cardiac health of rats that consume those foods in high quantities.

Should the writer make the addition here?

A) Yes, because it provides evidence that helps support the main idea of the paragraph.
B) Yes, because it provides a significant counter-argument to the main claim of the paragraph.
C) No, because it unnecessarily repeats a detail that appears later in the passage.
D) No, because it shifts the focus of the passage away from the writer's primary topic.

9. A) NO CHANGE
B) so
C) or
D) since

warehouses. **10** And shockingly, the governments in some countries that struggle with hunger may actually thwart food supplies from reaching their citizens. Many of the agribusinesses arguing that genetically modified foods can solve world hunger are the same companies that accept government subsidies now to limit their production of crops in order to avoid flooding the market. These companies are primarily concerned with profit, and whatever lip service they pay to global well-being, the driving force behind genetically modified organisms and foods is profit, not people. **11** In conclusion, the benefits and risks of any new technology must be carefully considered before implementing that technology.

10. The writer is considering deleting the underlined sentence. Should the sentence be kept or deleted?

A) Kept, because it provides an alternate explanation for the main claim of the paragraph.

B) Kept, because it explains background information about the topic of the paragraph.

C) Deleted, because it contradicts the writer's main claim in the passage.

D) Deleted, because it interrupts the flow of the writer's argument in the paragraph.

11. Which choice most effectively concludes the paragraph and the passage?

A) NO CHANGE

B) It would be nice if we could trust the very companies that could benefit most from the creation of genetically modified organisms.

C) Unfortunately, those companies affect so many aspects of modern life that we have no choice but to trust them.

D) Why would we trust our own well-being and that of the planet to companies recklessly pursuing money at the risk of Mother Earth?

# Check Your Work

**1. B**

**Difficulty:** Medium

**Category:** Development: Precision

**Getting to the Answer:** Read the sentence to understand the context in which the underlined word, "imagine," is used. The writer uses "imagine" to describe how certain groups portray the risks associated with genetically modified organisms. Because the writer views these groups as the opposition, the word needs to convey a stronger sense of resistance to the truth. As written, this part of the sentence is too benign to match the later references to "gambling with people's lives" and creating "Frankenfoods." Choice **(B)** is correct.

**2. D**

**Difficulty:** Easy

**Category:** Organization: Conciseness

**Getting to the Answer:** "Interfere" and "tamper" have the same meaning and are used to express a single idea about intentionally changing nature. The correct answer will eliminate one of those words. Choice **(D)** is correct.

**3. B**

**Difficulty:** Medium

**Category:** Organization: Conciseness

**Getting to the Answer:** This question tests wordiness, but pure length is not the only consideration in this type of question. The correct answer choice must fully convey the writer's intended meaning. As written, the underlined segment is the shortest answer choice, but it is difficult to determine exactly which group of people the "we" is referring to. Choice **(B)** is correct because it specifies the people included in "we" using the fewest words.

**4. A**

**Difficulty:** Medium

**Category:** Organization: Transitions

**Getting to the Answer:** In order to determine how best to connect two parts of a passage, identify the relationship between those parts. The previous paragraph discusses the potential for various risks from genetically modified foods, while this sentence identifies one particular risk: danger to insect species. Since it presents a specific instance of a general group, an example transition word is needed; **(A)** is correct. There is no contrast relationship, so (B) is incorrect. Choice (C) is incorrect because the writer is concerned about the risks, so downplaying them would contradict the writer's purpose. Choice (D) would remove the needed connection altogether.

**5. D**

**Difficulty:** Medium

**Category:** Development: Relevance

**Getting to the Answer:** The rest of the sentence discusses the possible unforeseen dangers of genetically modified organisms, so the correct answer must introduce the potential for harm. Eliminate (A) and (C) because stability and independence do not effectively set up the idea of potential harm. Choice (B) introduces humans, which are off-topic for the paragraph, so it is also incorrect. Choice **(D)** describes ecosystems as "delicate" and therefore easily damaged, so it effectively sets up the information that follows and is the correct answer.

**6. D**

**Difficulty:** Medium

**Category:** Development: Precision

**Getting to the Answer:** Although the word "will" is underlined, neither it nor any of the verbs in the answer choices change the grammatical functions of the sentence or cause an error. In a question like this, check the context to make sure the underlined word suits the meaning the writer wants to convey. Throughout the paragraph, the writer uses the verb "could" to indicate the possibility that certain things are possible but not certain—"could lead" and "could have." Nothing in the paragraph suggests that the writer has shifted from conjecture (indicated by "could") to either certainty ("will" and "would") or necessity ("must"). Choice **(D)** is correct.

**7. C**

**Difficulty:** Hard

**Category:** Organization: Sentence Placement

**Getting to the Answer:** Sentence 4 discusses how changes to the bird population could have further impacts and begins with the continuation word "And." Logically, it should follow sentence 2, which introduces how changes to the bird population might come about; that way, the paragraph forms a clear logical chain from a change in plants to insects to birds to the larger ecosystem. This also places sentence 3 at the end of the paragraph to sum up with an explanation of the ecology behind the information in the paragraph. The correct answer is **(C)**.

**8. A**

**Difficulty:** Medium

**Category:** Development: Revising Text

**Getting to the Answer:** When deciding whether to add a sentence, consider what it would contribute to the purpose and main idea of the paragraph. The topic sentence states that harm from eating genetically modified organisms is "likely," but the next sentence says that there have not yet been any human studies. The paragraph's main claim is currently not well supported, and the proposed addition would provide better evidence for it; **(A)** is correct.

**9. B**

**Difficulty:** Medium

**Category:** Organization: Transitions

**Getting to the Answer:** This question is about choosing the appropriate transition word to connect two clauses of a sentence. The first clause is about the lack of human studies on the effect of eating genetically modified organisms, and the second clause identifies the need for such studies given the potential health risks. The ideas in the second clause are clearly a result of the information in the first, so a cause-and-effect transition is needed. Eliminate (A) and (C). Choice (D) is a cause-and-effect transition, but it would reverse the cause-and-effect relationship of the clauses, so it is incorrect. Only **(B)** correctly conveys the relationship between the ideas in the sentence.

**10. D**

**Difficulty:** Medium

**Category:** Development: Revising text

**Getting to the Answer:** When a question asks whether to delete a sentence, determine what the main idea of the paragraph is and what the sentence in question contributes to it. In this paragraph, the writer argues that people go hungry not just because of lack of food but because of agribusinesses seeking profit. This sentence offers another reason people go hungry, but that reason is not relevant to the writer's point. In fact, the sentence interrupts the writer's discussion of how agribusiness contributes to hunger. The correct answer is **(D)**.

**11. D**

**Difficulty:** Hard

**Category:** Development: Introductions and Conclusions

**Getting to the Answer:** To effectively conclude a passage, a sentence must align with the writer's purpose both in the passage as a whole and in the final paragraph. The passage as a whole is a strong argument against GMOs, based primarily on the potential dangers they pose. The final paragraph grows more passionate, criticizing the counterargument raised by advocates for genetically modified organisms. The final sentence must match these arguments. Choice **(D)** is correct because it suggests that the stakes for the planet are enormous and our misplaced trust would have dire consequences. Choice (A) is too objective, and choices (B) and (C) are too submissive, to match the writer's critical tone.

# Organization: Conciseness

### LEARNING OBJECTIVE

After this lesson, you will be able to:

- Revise redundant or wordy writing

## To answer a question like this:

As the nineteenth century progressed, nursing became increasingly considered "women's work," until, at the turn of the 20th century, female nurses began to organize, unofficially excluding men. The American Nursing Association was formed in 1917, and men were not officially permitted to join until 1930. One of first goals of the female-dominated nursing community was to have men **1** <u>denied admission to and excluded from</u> military nursing. Traditionally, non-volunteer military nurses had been exclusively male, but in 1901, the United States Army Nurse Corps was formed exclusively for women.

A) NO CHANGE

B) denied to and excluded from

C) excluded from

D) denied and excluded from

## You need to know this:

A concise sentence does not include any unnecessary words. Phrasing that is wordy is considered stylistically incorrect on the SAT and needs to be revised. Each word must contribute to the meaning of the sentence; otherwise, it should be eliminated.

A *redundant* sentence says something twice: "The new policy precipitated a crisis situation." A crisis is a type of situation, so there is no need to include both "crisis" and "situation." The sentence should be rephrased as, "The new policy precipitated a crisis." Redundancy is always incorrect on the SAT.

| Wordy/Redundant Sentence | Concise Sentence |
|---|---|
| *The superb musical score **added enhancement to the experience of** the play's development.* | *The superb musical score **enhanced** the play's development.* |
| *I did not anticipate the **surprising, unexpected plot twist.*** | *I did not anticipate the **plot twist.*** |
| *The students **increased some of their knowledge of** Tuscan architecture.* | *The students **learned about** Tuscan architecture.* |

## You need to do this:

Choose the most concise grammatically correct option that conveys the writer's intended meaning. When answering questions about conciseness:

- Consider selecting the "DELETE the underlined portion" answer choice if there is one, according to the following guidelines:
  ° If the underlined portion is wordy or redundant, delete it.
  ° If the underlined portion does not enhance the intended meaning or clarity of the passage, delete it.
  ° Each of the four answer choices is equally likely, so give this option the same weight as the others.
- Identify the shortest answer choice (it will not always be the correct answer, but it is an efficient place to start).
- Identify words and phrases that have the same meaning (e.g., *thoughtful* and *mindful* or *end result* and *final outcome*). Find a choice that deletes one of the redundant expressions.

## Explanation:

As written, the underlined segment is redundant: "denied admission to" and "excluded from" have the same meaning. Look for a choice that eliminates one of these phrases. Choice **(C)** is correct.

If conciseness gives you trouble, study the information above and try these Drill questions before completing the following Try on Your Own questions. Eliminate word(s) to make the sentences more concise without losing meaning. Turn the page to see the answers.

## Drill

a. It is important to carefully consider and think about what kind of college you wish to attend.

b. Often, a house cat will typically sleep for up to 16 hours per day.

c. The whole team felt a sense of excited anticipation in the seconds before the whistle blew.

d. My sister and I couldn't come to an agreement with each other about what movie we wanted to watch that afternoon.

e. Noctilucent clouds appear approximately 82 kilometers above Earth's surface. This is an altitude more than seven times higher than commercial airlines fly.

# Try on Your Own

**Directions:** Take as much time as you need on these questions. Work carefully and methodically. There will be an opportunity for timed practice at the end of the chapter.

**Questions 2-6 refer to the following passage.**

**Modern Readers**

Judging by the types of novels that typically receive the top rankings on contemporary "best seller" lists, one would be wise to conclude that book consumers today do not enjoy reading ancient mythology. Seemingly, such antiquated stories hold little relevance to the concerns of a member of modern society. It is a literature not for the **2** current-day, distracted reader immersed in his "everyday" cares, but for a more imaginative audience with more universal tastes.

To even begin **3** to understand or comprehend this issue, we must understand what it is that most readers seek out in the works they read. What is it in a book—a novel, for example—that causes them to continue turning the pages? The answer can be a bit slippery. Is it the psychological realism of the characters? Is it the drama of the events they encounter? Is it the modern author's consciousness of her position as author and the relationship—distant or intimate, serious or playful—that she develops with her readers?

The obvious answer is that it is all of these things. The defining features of the modern story are its complexity and ambivalence. Narrators are not always reliable. Loyalties are often fleeting, and even a character's central motives may undergo a transformation before the story is done. There is no neat conclusion, no definitive redemption or damnation, and not always even a clear message. In this confusion

2.  A)  NO CHANGE
    B)  modern,
    C)  presently current,
    D)  DELETE the underlined portion.

3.  A)  NO CHANGE
    B)  to understand or to comprehend
    C)  to understand and comprehend
    D)  to understand

and dislocation, the modern reader sees his own life reflected, complete with all of its **4** complexity and ambivalence.

In a world where the disparate lives of alienated individuals still manage to affect each other on a daily basis, there is a paradoxical credulity extended toward anything murky and unclear. Far from the cosmopolitan savant he would like us to believe he is (to say nothing of the author who writes for him), the modern reader is only able to take comfort in his own confusion. When, for example, **5** George and Jane suddenly find themselves unable to live together after they come to the completion of their fairy-tale courtship, the contemporary pop intellectual will **6** nod his head sagely. He will think about the relationships in his own life that he didn't understand either.

What escapes the minds of the masses is that, taken past a certain point, realism is not art. Neither unsatisfying conclusions, nor irritating characters, nor obscure motives are indications of the literary talents of

4. A) NO CHANGE
   B) ambivalence
   C) complexity
   D) ambivalent complexity

5. A) NO CHANGE
   B) George and Jane finish their fairy-tale courtship and suddenly find themselves unable to live together,
   C) the fairy-tale courtship of George and Jane is at a finish and they suddenly find themselves unable to live together,
   D) with sudden abruptness George and Jane find themselves unable to live together when they finish their fairy-tale courtship,

6. Which choice most effectively combines the sentences at the underlined portion?

   A) nod his head sagely, and he will think about
   B) nod his head sagely; he will think about
   C) nod his head sagely, thinking about
   D) nod his head sagely, be thinking about

Drill answers:

Note: These are not the only ways to correct the sentences; your answers may differ.

a. It is important to carefully consider ~~and think about~~ what kind of college you wish to attend.

b. ~~Often, a~~ **A** house cat will typically sleep for up to 16 hours per day.

c. The whole team felt ~~a sense of~~ **excited** ~~anticipation~~ in the seconds before the whistle blew.

d. My sister and I couldn't ~~come to an~~ **agree**~~ment with each other~~ about what movie we wanted to watch that afternoon.

e. Noctilucent clouds appear approximately 82 kilometers above Earth's surface. ~~This is an altitude,~~ more than seven times higher than commercial airlines fly.

the author. The older, mythic characters may be drawn with a broad brush and may possess a simplicity and singularity of purpose that finds no parallel in day-to-day life, but that simplicity is not a sign of an author lacking in subtlety. Rather, a purposeful author will have purposeful characters. Whether the story is meant to illustrate moral principles, explore character types, or simply entertain, a quality work of art must have a purpose.

## Organization: Transitions

> **LEARNING OBJECTIVE**
>
> After this lesson, you will be able to:
>
> - Determine the appropriate transition word or phrase to establish logical relationships within and between sentences
> - Determine the appropriate transition sentence to establish logical relationships between paragraphs

### To answer a question like this:

I still remember the magic of walking home under the cold, brittle blue sky, watching the sun strike the glittering blanket laid down by that first snowfall. The world dripped with frosting, and everything was pure and silent. I breathed deeply, enjoying the sting of the icy air in my nostrils, and set off through the trees, listening to the muffled crunch of my footsteps and the chirps of the waking birds. Later, the cars and schoolchildren and mundane lives would turn the wonderland back into dingy slush; the hush would be interrupted by horns and shouts. **7** <u>Indeed,</u> for now, the sparkling, cloistered world was mine alone. I smiled, and for a moment, my mind was still.

A) NO CHANGE

B) But

C) Consequently,

D) In fact,

### You need to know this:

Writers use transitions to show relationships such as contrast, cause and effect, continuation, emphasis, and chronology (order of events). Knowing which words indicate which type of transition will help you choose the correct answer on test day.

| Contrast Transitions | Cause-and-Effect Transitions | Continuation Transitions | Emphasis Transitions | Chronology Transitions |
|---|---|---|---|---|
| although, but, despite, even though, however, in contrast, nonetheless, on the other hand, rather than, though, unlike, while, yet | as a result, because, consequently, since, so, therefore, thus | also, furthermore, in addition, moreover | certainly, in fact, indeed, that is | before, after, first (second, etc.), then, finally |

## You need to do this:

If a transition word is underlined, you must determine the writer's intended meaning and find the transition that best conveys this meaning. Use the surrounding text to pinpoint the appropriate word.

## Explanation:

The transition must logically connect the information and ideas in the sentences before and after the underlined portion. In the sentence before the underlined transition, the author acknowledges that the specialness of the day will later wear off. In the sentences following the transition, the author puts aside thoughts of the coming noise and slush to enjoy the first snowfall. So there is a contrast between the idea that the wonder of the day will fade and the perception of that wonder in the present moment. The only contrast transition among the choices is **(B)**, which is thus the correct answer.

If transitions give you trouble, study the information above and try these Drill questions before completing the following Try on Your Own questions. Answers can be found on the next page.

## Drill

a.   The train was delayed; (<u>therefore/in addition</u>), we arrived at our destination two hours late.

b.   (<u>Since/Although</u>) the critics agreed that the movie was terrible, I went to see it anyway.

c.   We need to finish our project (<u>consequently/before</u>) we leave this afternoon.

d.   The hiking trail was difficult to navigate; (<u>finally/indeed</u>), state park guidelines recommend that only experienced hikers attempt the climb.

e.   The morphology of the amoeba is more complex than you might expect; (<u>furthermore/in contrast</u>), the mechanism underlying amoeboid motion is still not fully understood.

Writing & Lang

# Try on Your Own

**Directions:** Take as much time as you need on these questions. Work carefully and methodically. There will be an opportunity for timed practice at the end of the chapter.

**Questions 8-12 refer to the following passage.**

**The Internet and Conversation**

For as long as I can remember, conversation has always struck me as a strange chimera, something that is half two minds exchanging sophisticated ideas and half two dogs barking at each other. I do not find the banalities of small talk comforting, but boring and idiotic. **8** Now I can dispense with it altogether and proceed right to substantive dialogue, it is almost like flying. I can be talking with the closest of friends or a mere acquaintance with a shared interest. Either way, the kinship is there. I don't feel myself included by smiles, pats on the back, or eye contact so much as by the willingness of a partner to share my ideas or gift me with thoughts of his own. There is nothing more ingratiating than intellectual passion.

In part, this has to do with my habit of observing the world from my bedroom. As a child, I was frequently ill and forced to stay inside. Although my health is much better now, **9** I still go out much less than most people. After all, I have everything I need inside. From my room,

8. A) NO CHANGE
   B) When
   C) Later
   D) Where

9. Which choice provides the best transition within the paragraph?

   A) NO CHANGE
   B) I still remember those long afternoons cooped up inside.
   C) I am still careful to eat well and get plenty of rest.
   D) I regret not being able to play outdoors with other children.

Drill answers from previous page:

a. The train was delayed; **therefore**, we arrived at our destination two hours late.

b. **Although** the critics agreed that the movie was terrible, I went to see it anyway.

c. We need to finish our project **before** we leave this afternoon.

d. The hiking trail was difficult to navigate; **indeed**, state park guidelines recommend that only experienced hikers attempt the climb.

e. The morphology of the amoeba is more complex than you might expect; **furthermore**, the mechanism underlying amoeboid motion is still not fully understood.

I have access to people all over the world through online communities. I can talk about medieval literature with a friend in China and later collaborate on a piece of music with a synthesizer virtuoso in Spain. Everyone can be everywhere they want when they want, **10** and every social interaction feels completely comfortable and natural. There is no need for awkward introductions or a graceful exit—people feel free to launch right into what they want to talk about and, when they are done, just sign off with a "TTYL," or "talk to you later." Every exchange is relaxed and succinct.

**11** The Internet facilitates authentic connections among diverse users who share common interests, but empty chatter is far from universal. On certain discussion boards, you can witness opinions stated and arguments debated with an eloquence that people rarely use when speaking, freely sharing knowledge just for the joy of it. I participate in an online Renaissance music discussion group that has a library of original articles that are the product of a master's thesis. The author gained no monetary reward for the information (which he made available for free) and receives little praise for it outside the community that shares his interest. He posts because he is passionate about his **12** subject; nonetheless, his enthusiasm for the music inspires him to share what he knows with anyone who wants to learn.

10. Which choice results in the most effective transition to the information that follows in the paragraph?

A) NO CHANGE

B) and knowledge of useful text acronyms is nearly universal among online conversationalists.

C) and those desiring profound discussion can find one at any time of day or night.

D) DELETE the underlined portion and end the sentence with a period.

11. Which choice best connects the sentence with the previous paragraph?

A) NO CHANGE

B) Though cloistered in a private space, you can now use technology to access virtually any information in the world, but

C) Internet speak is often maligned as vacuous in its reliance on acronyms and abbreviations, but

D) DELETE the underlined portion and begin the sentence with a capital letter.

12. A) NO CHANGE

B) subject; lastly,

C) subject; however,

D) subject; indeed,

# Organization: Sentence Placement

## To answer a question like this:

[1] It is amazing how little the structure of the American public school system has changed since its inception. [2] Students still change classes according to bells, even though the bell system originated during the days of factories. [3] School is still not in session during the summer, although most students will not use that time to work on farms. [4] Although class and school sizes have varied widely and the curriculum has certainly become varied, the actual system remains surprisingly similar to the way it once was. [5] Despite these idiosyncrasies, however, the American public school system continues to educate the children of this country in a fair and equitable fashion. [6] Without the established structure, the chaotic nature of school would severely inhibit learning. **13**

To make this paragraph most logical, sentence 4 should be placed

A) where it is now.

B) before sentence 1.

C) after sentence 1.

D) after sentence 6.

## You need to know this:

Some organization questions will ask you to check and potentially fix the placement of a sentence within a paragraph (or a paragraph within a passage, though this is rare). Others will ask you for the best place to insert a new sentence. Your approach in both cases should be the same.

## You need to do this:

Look for specific clues that indicate the best organization. Common clues include:

- **Chronology:** If the information is presented in order by the time when it occurred, place the sentence within the correct time frame.

- **Explanation of a term or phrase:** If the passage features a term, such as nuclear fusion, the writer will explain what it is (in this case, the joining of two or more nuclei to form a heavier nucleus) before using the term in other contexts.

- **Introduction of a person:** If the passage introduces someone, such as Grace Hopper, the writer will first refer to the person by first and last name before referring to the person by either first name (Grace) or last name (Hopper) only.

- **Examples:** A general statement is often followed by support in the form of examples.

- **Logic:** Transition words such as "however," "also," "furthermore," and "therefore" may signal the logic of the paragraph. For example, the word "therefore" indicates that a conclusion is being drawn from evidence that should logically come before it.

### Explanation:

Sentence 4 argues that the school system has not changed much, so it should precede a sentence that further discusses the unchanged aspects of the school system. If you place sentence 4 after sentence 1, sentences 2 and 3 become examples of specific ways in which the school system has not changed. Moreover, the word "surprising" in sentence 4 echoes the word "amazing" in sentence 1. Sentence 4 also elaborates on sentence 1 by clarifying that the phrase "school system" does not mean only class sizes or curriculum, so sentence 4 fits best after sentence 1 rather than before it. Choice **(C)** is correct.

# Try on Your Own

**Directions:** Take as much time as you need on these questions. Work carefully and methodically. There will be an opportunity for timed practice at the end of the chapter.

**Questions 14-18 refer to the following passage.**

**Earthquakes**

[1]

Devastating earthquakes in China, Haiti, Chile, Mexico, and elsewhere have caused many to wonder if earthquake activity so far in 2010 is unusual.

[2]

Still, earthquake activity has obviously disastrous consequences. As USGS Associate Coordinator for Earthquake Hazards, Dr. Michael Blanpied, explains, "While the number of earthquakes is within the normal range, this does not diminish the fact that there has been extreme devastation and loss of life in heavily populated areas."

[3]

[1] Scientists say 2010 is not showing signs of unusually high earthquake activity. [2] Some years have had as few as six such earthquakes, as in 1986 and 1989, while 1943 had 32, with considerable variability from year to year. [3] Since 1900, an average of 16 magnitude 7 or greater earthquakes—the size that seismologists define as major—have occurred worldwide each year. [4] With six major earthquakes striking in the first four months of this year, 2010 is well within the normal range. [5] From April 15, 2009, to April 14, 2010, there have been 18 major earthquakes, a number also well within the expected variation. **14**

14. To make this paragraph most logical, sentence 2 should be placed

A) where it is now.

B) before sentence 1.

C) after sentence 3.

D) after sentence 4.

[4]

[1] What will happen next in recent earthquake locations? [2] It is unlikely that any of these aftershocks will be stronger than the earthquakes experienced so far, but structures damaged in the previous events could be further damaged and should be treated with caution. [3] Beyond the ongoing aftershock sequences, earthquakes in recent months have not raised the likelihood of future major events; that likelihood has not decreased, either. [4] Aftershocks will continue in the regions around each of this year's major earthquakes sites. [5] Large earthquakes will continue to occur just as they have in the past. **15**

[5]

[1] Though the recent earthquakes are not unusual, they are a stark reminder that earthquakes can produce disasters when they strike populated areas, especially areas where the buildings have not been designed to withstand strong shaking. [2] What can be done to prepare? [3] However, families and communities can improve their safety and reduce their losses by taking actions to make their homes, places of work, schools, and businesses as earthquake-safe as possible. **16**

[6]

[1] The Federal Emergency Management Agency (FEMA) recommends specific earthquake preparedness measures, which are especially vital for those who live in earthquake-prone areas. [2] Most importantly, homeowners should check that their homes meet those building codes that are meant to ensure buildings are structurally solid and safe, such as reinforcing masonry walls and securely installing gas appliances. [3] The

15. To make this paragraph most logical, sentence 4 should be placed

A) where it is now.

B) before sentence 1.

C) after sentence 1.

D) after sentence 2.

16. Where is the most logical place in this paragraph to add the following sentence?

> Scientists cannot predict the timing of specific earthquakes.

A) Before sentence 1

B) After sentence 1

C) After sentence 2

D) After sentence 3

house should be assessed for furniture placement that could be potentially hazardous during an earthquake, such as unsecured cabinets, and, based on each room's layout, every family member should learn the safest place to take cover in every part of the house. [4] While we cannot prevent earthquakes, we must take all possible precautions and heed the predictions of scientists. 17

**Question 18 asks about the previous passage as a whole.**

17. Where is the most logical place in this paragraph to add the following sentence?

> FEMA also advises families to create a plan about what to do if an earthquake were to occur while they were at home.

A) Before sentence 1

B) After sentence 2

C) After sentence 3

D) After sentence 4

**Think about the passage as a whole as you answer question 18.**

18. To make the passage most logical, paragraph 2 should be placed

A) where it is now.

B) after paragraph 3.

C) after paragraph 5.

D) after paragraph 6.

# Development: Precision

---

**LEARNING OBJECTIVE**

After this lesson, you will be able to:

- Identify the word that accomplishes the appropriate purpose

---

## To answer a question like this:

Incredibly, men could not work as military nurses until after the Korean War. Today, depending on the branch of service, anywhere between 35% and 70% of military nurses are men; this is in sharp **19** complement to the civilian world, where an average of 9% of American nurses are men.

A) NO CHANGE

B) completion

C) contour

D) contrast

## You need to know this:

Some questions test your knowledge of the correct word to use in context. You must identify which word(s) best convey the writer's intended meaning.

| Incorrect | Correct |
|---|---|
| The **initial** reason the students gather in the auditorium is that it is the only location large enough for all of them. | The **primary** reason the students gather in the auditorium is that it is the only location large enough for all of them. |
| It is common for children to **perform** the actions of their parents. | It is common for children to **mimic** the actions of their parents. |
| Zeke apologized for **overstepping** when he walked into the crowded conference room. | Zeke apologized for **intruding** when he walked into the crowded conference room. |

## You need to do this:

Read the surrounding text to deduce the author's intended meaning. Then evaluate all four answer choices. Eliminate the answer choices that:

- Create grammatical errors
- Do not make sense in context
- Do not convey the writer's intended meaning

If one or more of the words among the answer choices are unfamiliar, the process of elimination can still help you get to the correct answer. If you recognize any of the options, decide whether to keep or eliminate them. For the words that remain, use roots, prefixes and suffixes, and word charge to make your decision. If all else fails, trust your instincts and guess; never leave a question blank.

## Explanation:

The percentages given are the best clue here: 35–70% of military nurses are men, while only 9% of civilian nurses are men. Those are very different numbers, so the correct word must convey the discrepancy. The only choice that does so is **(D)**.

# Try on Your Own

**Directions:** Take as much time as you need on these questions. Work carefully and methodically. There will be an opportunity for timed practice at the end of the chapter.

**Questions 20-25 refer to the following passage.**

**Batteries Out in the Cold**

Many people have trouble starting their cars on a cold winter morning. In a cold car, the engine turns over more slowly or sometimes does not turn over at all. Car owners may **20** credit their cold engines, but the real problem is a cold battery.

A car's electric starter motor is powered by the car's battery. When the motor is **21** united to a battery in a circuit, electrons move through the circuit, creating a current. The more current there is in the circuit, the more power there is to turn the starter motor. Decreasing the number of electrons moving through the circuit decreases the current, resulting in a **22** reduction in the amount of power available to the starter motor. Conversely, increasing the number of electrons moving boosts the current, which then increases the amount of power available to the motor.

Electrons move through a battery as a result of two chemical reactions that occur within the battery, one at each pole. A typical car battery uses lead and sulfuric acid to create these reactions. At the negative pole, lead reacts with sulfate ions in the acid solution around it to form lead sulfate, giving off electrons. At the positive pole, lead oxide reacts with sulfate ions, hydrogen ions, and electrons in the same solution to also form lead sulfate, taking in electrons. The electrons produced at the negative pole flow through the circuit to the positive pole, **23** providing an electric current in the circuit.

20. A)  NO CHANGE
    B)  critique
    C)  accuse
    D)  blame

21. A)  NO CHANGE
    B)  correlated
    C)  coupled
    D)  assimilated

22. A)  NO CHANGE
    B)  regression
    C)  retraction
    D)  constriction

23. A)  NO CHANGE
    B)  producing
    C)  promulgating
    D)  asserting

Writing & Lang

Temperature affects the speed of chemical reactions in two ways. For a chemical reaction to happen, the molecules of the reactants must collide with enough energy to get the reaction going. As the temperature increases, the motion of the molecules increases. The increased motion of the molecules increases the **24** <u>practicality</u> that they will collide and therefore increases the rate of reaction. The amount of energy in the reactants also increases as temperature increases. These factors make it more likely that the molecules in a battery will collide with enough energy to react, thereby increasing the power in the circuit.

Low temperatures have the opposite effect from high temperatures. The chemicals in the battery react more slowly at low temperatures, due to fewer and less energetic collisions, so fewer electrons move through the circuit. Because of this, a cold battery may not provide enough energy to start a car. A cold car that will not start will need either **25** <u>associative</u> power from a connection to another car's battery or a source of heat to warm up the car's own battery and speed up the chemical reactions within it.

24. A)  NO CHANGE
    B)  process
    C)  confirmation
    D)  probability

25. A)  NO CHANGE
    B)  auxiliary
    C)  optional
    D)  extraordinary

# Development: Relevance

**LEARNING OBJECTIVE**

After this lesson, you will be able to:

● Determine the relevance of a sentence within a passage

## To answer a question like this:

For hundreds of years, the medical community and conventional wisdom held that ulcers were caused by stress. Strong gastric juices would sometimes burn sores through the lining of the stomach or intestines causing widely varied symptoms, including internal bleeding, inflammation, and stomach pain. Doctors reasoned that if patients with ulcers changed their daily habits to reduce the level of tension in their lives, altered their diets to avoid foods that would irritate the stomach, and took medicine to moderate the amount of stomach acid, these ulcers would heal. Although the problem often recurred, no one seriously questioned why. This medical advice remained standard for generations, until Dr. Barry Marshall came along.

Beginning in the 1980s, Marshall, an Australian physician, hypothesized that at least some ulcers were caused by bacteria that often lie dormant in the human stomach. 26 The international medical community was fascinated by rare gastric phenomena. It was common knowledge, or so Marshall's colleagues believed, that no microbes could survive for long in the highly acidic environment of the stomach. At medical conferences, the young, unknown Marshall was regarded as at best, a maverick, and at worst, a quack. Over several years, he and his fellow researcher, Dr. J. Robin Warren, attempted to isolate and identify the bacteria that caused ulcers. As is the case with many medical discoveries, their breakthrough came about partly by accident, when they left a culture growing in the lab longer than intended.

Which choice most effectively sets up other physicians' negative opinion of Marshall as described later in the paragraph?

A) NO CHANGE

B) The international medical community scoffed.

C) Marshall had attended the University of Western Australia School of Medicine, graduating in 1974.

D) The stomach produces hydrochloric acid so that the interior of the stomach is highly acidic.

## You need to know this:

Some questions will ask you to choose the most relevant information to include at a specific point in a passage. In questions like this, all of the answer choices are grammatically and stylistically correct. Given this fact, your task is to determine which option provides information that is most pertinent to the passage. The correct choice will relate directly to the surrounding text and will provide one or more of the following:

- An example
- Support for a point
- A transition to a new idea

Note that when the question has a question stem, you are not being tested on conciseness, even when asked about deleting information. *When you see a question stem, focus on relevance rather than conciseness.*

## You need to do this:

Read a bit of text before and after the underlined portion (at least the entire sentence in which it appears), looking for clues. Eliminate answer choices that:

- Mention information that is beyond the scope of the writer's discussion
- Do not relate to the surrounding text
- Do not help express the purpose of the sentence or paragraph

## Explanation:

The "negative opinion" referred to in the question stem is the statement, later in the paragraph, that Marshall was regarded as "at best, a maverick, and at worst, a quack." The underlined sentence, as currently written, is irrelevant to the passage, which does not define ulcers as "rare gastric phenomena," so eliminate (A) and examine the other choices for a negative opinion. Both (C) and (D) state neutral facts, but the word "scoffed" in (B) indicates that the medical community was unimpressed with, even disdainful of, Marshall. Choice **(B)** directly relates to the idea that Marshall was perceived as "at worst, a quack" and is correct.

# Try on Your Own

**Directions:** Take as much time as you need on these questions. Work carefully and methodically. There will be an opportunity for timed practice at the end of the chapter.

**Questions 27-31 refer to the following passage.**

**James Polk**

For much of his distinguished career, James Knox Polk followed in the footsteps of Andrew Jackson.[1] In fact, "Young Hickory's" policies were very similar to Jackson's: [27] <u>both men favored lower taxes, championed the frontiersmen, farmers, and workers, and neither was afraid to indulge in Tennessee whiskey.</u> Polk, however, did not share Jackson's rather fierce temperament; he was instead known for remaining soft-spoken even as he worked energetically toward his goals. Although history will likely always remember the frontier persona of Andrew Jackson, it was Polk who did much more to shape the course of American history.

The Polk family was poor—James's father had emigrated from Scotland and arrived in the U.S. South penniless. From an early age, Polk suffered ill health that would turn out to be a lifelong affliction. Despite his physical shortcomings, he was an able student and graduated from the University of North Carolina with honors in 1818. Two years later, Polk was admitted to the bar to practice law, and in 1823, [28] <u>he married Sarah Childress, the daughter of a prominent planter and merchant from Murfreesboro.</u> From there, he was elected to the U.S. House of Representatives in 1825, serving until 1839. Polk was also Speaker of the House from 1835 to 1839.

27. A)  NO CHANGE

B)  while they agreed on little regarding taxes or the suffrage of frontiersmen, farmers, and workers, both men were known to indulge in Tennessee whiskey.

C)  both men favored lower taxes; championed the frontiersmen, farmers, and workers; and opposed the controversial Bank of the United States.

D)  both men favored lower taxes; championed the frontiersmen, farmers, and workers; and yet they could not agree on the controversial Bank of the United States.

28. Which choice results in a sentence that best supports the point developed in the paragraph and is consistent with the information in the rest of the passage?

A)  NO CHANGE

B)  he married Sarah Childress.

C)  he was elected as governor of Tennessee.

D)  he was elected to the Tennessee House of Representatives.

---

[1] U.S. president from 1829 to 1837 and War of 1812 hero often referred to as "Old Hickory."

After he left Congress to serve as governor of Tennessee in 1839, it became clear that Polk's political aspirations were high indeed. During the 1844 presidential campaign, [29] a young Abraham Lincoln threw his support behind Whig Henry Clay instead of the Democratic ex-President Martin van Buren. Both men, as part of their platforms, opposed expansionist policies, and neither intended to annex the independent state of Texas or the Oregon Territory. [30] Polk, spurred on by Jackson's advice, recognized that neither candidate had correctly surmised the feelings of the people, so he publicly announced that, as president, he would do his utmost to acquire Texas and Oregon. Polk was the first "dark horse" in American politics, coming out of nowhere to win the Democratic nomination and the election.

As the eleventh President of the United States, Polk pursued an agenda of [31] territorial stability and peace with America's neighbors. First, he reached an agreement with England that divided the Oregon Territory, carving out the present-day states of Washington and Oregon. Polk also quickly annexed Texas and provoked war with Mexico to acquire California and the New Mexico territory. While these achievements were somewhat diminished by controversy from abolitionists who opposed the spread of slavery into new territories, under Polk's leadership the dream of "manifest destiny" became a reality, and the United States fully extended its borders from the Atlantic to the Pacific.

29. Which choice provides the most relevant detail?

A) NO CHANGE

B) the leading Democratic candidate was ex-President Martin van Buren and the Whig candidate was Henry Clay.

C) the issue of slavery's expansion into new territories began its long stint as the most divisive issue to plague national politics.

D) both the leading Democratic candidate, ex-President Martin van Buren, and the Whig candidate, Henry Clay, sought to campaign under the banner of "Manifest Destiny" and territorial expansion.

30. A) NO CHANGE

B) Polk, against Jackson's advice, recognized

C) Polk failed to recognize

D) Polk, against the wishes of his advisors, recognized

31. A) NO CHANGE

B) continued expansion of U.S. territory.

C) an end to slavery in new U.S. territories.

D) pushing the United States into a role on the international stage.

# Development: Revising Text

---

**LEARNING OBJECTIVE**

After this lesson, you will be able to:

- State whether a sentence should be revised, added, or deleted, and provide reasoning

---

## To answer a question like this:

In an effort to demonstrate that ulcers were caused by bacteria, as he and his colleague Warren believed, Dr. Marshall took a bold step. Although the medical community frowns on such potentially dangerous actions, the doctor experimented on himself by deliberately drinking a flask of the bacteria. Over a two-week period, Marshall developed vague, though not disabling, symptoms, and medical tests showed evidence of ulcers and infection. **32**

In 2005, Marshall's bold move earned him and Warren the Nobel Prize in Medicine. Their important advance, like many other scientific discoveries in history, was a combination of experimentation, persistence, and luck.

At this point, the writer is considering adding the following sentence.

> Other researchers' studies later confirmed that Marshall's and Warren's findings apply to about 90% of all ulcers, which can now be cured by a short course of antibiotics instead of being temporarily managed by antacids.

Should the writer make this addition here?

A) Yes, because the new sentence demonstrates that Marshall was not foolish in drinking the flask of bacteria as he could cure himself with antibiotics.

B) Yes, because the new sentence provides conclusive support for Marshall's inference and explains why Marshall and Warren won the Nobel Prize in Medicine.

C) No, because Marshall was a brilliant scientist, and his findings did not need to be confirmed by other researchers.

D) No, because Marshall would not have drunk the flask of bacteria had he believed that doing so would cause ulcers and infection.

## You need to know this:

These questions often ask about deleting an underlined portion or adding new text. Consider what information the selection provides and whether that information 1) matches the writer's focus and 2) helps express the purpose of the sentence or paragraph. Consider what the passage might gain or lose if the proposed revision were made. Read the passage both ways—with and without the proposed change—to see which sounds more cohesive. Be sure to read the sentences before and after the proposed revision to best assess the change in context.

The same principle applies if the question asks whether a sentence should be revised: consider what the passage gains or loses as a result of the revision.

## You need to do this:

- Examine the sentences before and after the proposed revision.
- Think about what is gained or lost, if anything, as a result of the revision. This could be an example, support for an idea, or a better transition.
- Look for the choice that paraphrases your reasoning.

## Explanation:

The big clue for this question comes from the final paragraph, which states that Marshall won the Nobel Prize for Medicine for his discovery that bacteria cause ulcers. The new sentence confirms that this conclusion was correct and reveals that his discovery led to a new treatment for ulcers. This is powerful support for his winning the Nobel Prize for Medicine, so it adds relevant context to the passage. This reasoning matches choice **(B)**, which is the correct answer.

# Try on Your Own

**Directions:** Take as much time as you need on these questions. Work carefully and methodically. There will be an opportunity for timed practice at the end of the chapter.

**Questions 33-37 refer to the following passage.**

**Jupiter**

As the fifth planet from the Sun `33` in our solar system, Jupiter has inspired fascination and scientific study for centuries. In fact, it was the initial discovery of this colossal, gaseous planet that marked the first time most astronomers seriously considered the possibility that the movement of other planets was not centered around the Earth. More specifically, when Italian astronomer Galileo first viewed Jupiter by telescope, he discovered four large moons in orbit around this enormous planet. `34`

The first close look at Jupiter came in 1973, when the unmanned NASA probe *Pioneer 10* completed a successful flyby and collected important data regarding the planet's chemical composition and interior

33. The writer is considering revising the underlined portion of the sentence to read:

> and by far the most massive in our solar system,

Should the writer make this revision here?

A) Yes, because it establishes an important contrast between Jupiter and the Sun.

B) Yes, because it provides an example for a detail that appears later in the sentence.

C) No, because statistics about Jupiter should be placed in a later paragraph.

D) No, because it contains a fact that contradicts the main claim of the passage.

34. At this point, the writer is considering adding the following sentence.

> Because these moons seemed to revolve around a planet other than Earth, their discovery provided important evidence for Galileo's outspoken support of Copernicus's heliocentric theory of planetary movement.

Should the writer make this addition here?

A) Yes, because it explains a detail that was mentioned earlier in the paragraph.

B) Yes, because it adds to the authority of the passage's claim by identifying famous scientists who studied Jupiter.

C) No, because the subject of planetary movement is outside the scope of the passage.

D) No, because it includes information that is on topic, but irrelevant to the paragraph.

structure. **35** <u>After completing its mission to Jupiter, *Pioneer 10* became the first spacecraft to leave the solar system.</u> Designated as one of the gas planets—along with Saturn, Uranus, and Neptune—Jupiter is composed of about 90 percent hydrogen and 10 percent helium and has no solid surface, only varying densities of gas. In fact, very little is known about the interior of Jupiter. When looking at a gas planet like Jupiter, it is really only possible to see the tops of the clouds making up the outermost atmosphere, and probes have been able to penetrate only about 90 miles below this layer. However, after analyzing traces of water and minerals collected from Jupiter's atmosphere, scientists believe that the planet has a core of rocky material amounting to a mass perhaps as much as 15 times that of Earth.

Jupiter's powerful winds are responsible for unique characteristics of the planet. Its high-velocity winds blow in wide bands of latitude, each moving in an alternate direction. Slight chemical and temperature variations result in particular chemical reactions within each band. **36** Measurements taken by a number of probes indicate that the powerful winds moving these bands can reach speeds exceeding 400 miles per hour and likely extend thousands of miles below Jupiter's outer atmosphere. **37** <u>The planet can also rotate on its axis in less than half the time it takes the earth to complete a rotation.</u>

Overall, Jupiter's size and features have intrigued astronomers of the past and continue to invite scientific investigation today.

35. The writer is considering deleting the underlined sentence. Should the writer do this?

A) No, because it adds an interesting detail about the *Pioneer 10* mission.

B) No, because it provides support for the claim that the mission was successful.

C) Yes, because it shifts the focus of the passage from Jupiter to the *Pioneer 10* mission.

D) Yes, because it does not include information about when *Pioneer 10* left the solar system.

36. At this point, the writer is considering adding the following sentence.

These interactions are responsible for creating the array of distinctive, colorful stripes that dominate the planet's appearance.

Should the writer make this addition here?

A) Yes, because it provides support for the claim made in the paragraph's topic sentence.

B) Yes, because it provides a useful transition between ideas in the paragraph.

C) No, because it interrupts the paragraph's discussion of latitude bands on Jupiter's surface.

D) No, because it supplies information that is irrelevant to the main claim of the passage.

37. The writer is considering deleting the underlined sentence. Should the sentence be kept or deleted?

A) Kept, because it provides a relevant detail for the paragraph.

B) Kept, because it effectively links this paragraph with the conclusion paragraph.

C) Deleted, because it does not reflect the topic of the overall passage.

D) Deleted, because it does not support the topic sentence of the paragraph.

# Introductions and Conclusions

## LEARNING OBJECTIVE

After this lesson, you will be able to:

- Provide an introduction or conclusion to a paragraph or passage

## To answer a question like this:

**38** <u>As if malpractice suits and unnecessary bankruptcies were not enough of a problem, lawyers have chosen to increase the burden that they place on society by engineering an excess of increasingly ridiculous product warnings.</u> Why else would a box of sleeping pills be marketed with the cautionary note that consumers may experience drowsiness? Or a cup of coffee be emblazoned with a notice that "THIS PRODUCT MAY BE HOT"? Anyone with common sense will not need to be warned about these possibilities, and anyone without common sense is probably not going to be stopped by a warning label from undertaking a foolish course of action anyway. So honestly, in the long run, the only ones who benefit from these warnings are the lawyers who are paid hundreds of dollars an hour to compose them.

Which choice most effectively establishes the main topic of the paragraph?

A) NO CHANGE

B) Each year, effective product warning labels help countless people avoid serious injuries resulting from their use of consumer products.

C) In recent years, a coalition of lawyers and consumer safety advocates has successfully campaigned to require companies to include safety warnings on product labels.

D) Product safety warnings are necessary to protect consumers who thoughtlessly use products without first thinking about the possible risks involved.

## You need to know this:

Some questions ask you to improve the beginning or ending of a paragraph or passage.

- An introduction should:
  - Explain the topic and purpose of a paragraph/passage
  - Include information discussed later in the paragraph/passage
  - When applicable, provide an appropriate transition for the previous paragraph
- A conclusion should:
  - Summarize the topic and purpose of a paragraph/passage
  - Include information discussed earlier in the paragraph/passage
  - When applicable, provide an appropriate transition for the next paragraph

### You need to do this:

- Determine the writer's intended purpose. This may be stated explicitly in the question stem ("The writer wants to reinforce the earlier claim about mockingbirds...") or may need to be inferred from the passage text.
- Eliminate answer choices that do not reflect this purpose
- Choose the most relevant option

### Explanation:

The author introduces the central idea that lawyers are responsible for an excess of product warnings. In the remainder of the paragraph, the author argues that many product warnings are unnecessary and ineffective for consumers and beneficial only to the lawyers who write them. There is no discrepancy between the opening statement and the evidence for it, so **(A)** is correct.

# Try on Your Own

**Directions:** Take as much time as you need on these questions. Work carefully and methodically. There will be an opportunity for timed practice at the end of the chapter.

**Questions 39-42 refer to the following passage.**

**Human Skin**

Although it likely doesn't immediately come to mind when thinking about body organs, **39** our skin is the organ that most directly interacts with our environment, communicating messages both to our brains and to those around us. An adult's skin comprises between 15 and 20 percent of the total body weight, even though the outer layer, the epidermis, is only 0.07 to 0.12 millimeters thick (the thickness of a piece of paper). Despite its slimness, the skin serves many essential roles for the human body.

First, the skin serves to regulate and protect the body. One square inch of skin contains up to 4.5 meters of blood vessels, which regulate body temperature. Further, skin forms a protective barrier against the action of physical, chemical, and bacterial agents on the deeper tissues. The skin constitutes the body's first line of defense against external threats including dehydration, infection, injuries, and extreme temperatures, **40** and thus the skin requires careful upkeep and care.

**41** The skin serves another essential function in the human body. Whereas our other senses have a definite key organ that can be studied, receptors located at the ends of nerve fibers all over the surface of the body are used to detect external stimuli. These fibers convert tactile stimuli into neural impulses to be sent to the brain through the peripheral and central nervous

39. Which choice provides the most appropriate introduction to the passage?

A) NO CHANGE

B) the skin is not only the human body's largest organ but also crucial for the body's healthy functioning.

C) each square centimeter of human skin has 6 million cells, 5,000 sensory points, and 100 sweat glands.

D) the skin is an interesting organ of the human body and thus highly studied by biologists.

40. Which choice most effectively concludes the sentence and paragraph?

A) NO CHANGE

B) modifying substances that come into contact with the skin's surface.

C) although other organs, such as the liver, detoxify harmful substances with special enzymatic processes.

D) detoxifying harmful substances with many of the same enzymatic processes the liver uses.

41. Which choice is the best introduction to the paragraph?

A) NO CHANGE

B) Another important property of the skin is that it provides our sense of touch.

C) Although scientists disagree about the total number, we most commonly refer to five human senses.

D) The central nervous system communicates messages to our brain about our tactile sensations.

systems. Thus, our skin serves to facilitate our physical interactions with our surroundings.

The most vital function of the skin is to shield the inside of the body; it acts like a "shock absorber." If a body falls, the skin protects all of the internal organs. When the skin is broken, it has its own defense system that immediately goes into repair mode. [42] It is no exaggeration to say that skin is among the most important organs; without it, a body simply cannot continue living.

42. Which choice most effectively concludes the passage?

A) NO CHANGE

B) Since skin covers the body and is easily visible, it is no wonder that its decoration has important cultural meanings.

C) However, more important organs do indeed exist and likely deserve more scientific attention than the skin.

D) Without the skin's properties, most importantly the sense of touch, life would hardly be worth living.

# Graphs

**LEARNING OBJECTIVE**

After this lesson, you will be able to:

● Revise text based on a graph or table

## To answer a question like this:

Yet perhaps the most fascinating characteristic of this planet is the rotational speed of the entire globe of gas itself. While Earth takes 24 hours to make a full rotation, Jupiter completes a full rotation **43** in less time, an amazingly short period of time for a planet with a diameter roughly 11 times the diameter of our planet. How Jupiter is able to rotate so fast is just one of many mysteries that scientists continue to explore in their efforts to understand our largest neighbor.

| Planets in Our Solar System | | | | |
|---|---|---|---|---|
| Planet | Period of Revolution Around the Sun (1 planetary year) | Period of Rotation (1 planetary day) | Mass (kg) | Diameter (miles) |
| Mercury | 87.96 Earth days | 58.7 Earth days | $3.3 \times 10^{23}$ | 3,031 miles |
| Venus | 224.68 Earth days | 243 Earth days | $4.87 \times 10^{24}$ | 7,521 miles |
| Earth | 365.26 days | 24 hours | $5.98 \times 10^{24}$ | 7,926 miles |
| Mars | 686.98 Earth days | 24.6 Earth hours | $6.42 \times 10^{23}$ | 4,222 miles |
| Jupiter | 11.862 Earth years | 9.84 Earth hours | $1.90 \times 10^{27}$ | 88,729 miles |
| Saturn | 29.456 Earth years | 10.2 Earth hours | $5.69 \times 10^{26}$ | 74,600 miles |
| Uranus | 84.07 Earth years | 17.9 Earth hours | $8.68 \times 10^{25}$ | 32,600 miles |
| Neptune | 164.81 Earth years | 19.1 Earth hours | $1.02 \times 10^{26}$ | 30,200 miles |

Which choice most accurately reflects the data in the table?

A) NO CHANGE

B) in half that time,

C) in fewer than 10 Earth hours,

D) in more time than all the other planets,

## You need to know this:

One or more passages on the Writing and Language section may be accompanied by some sort of informational graphic such as a table, bar chart, or pie chart. If a passage is accompanied by a graphic, at least one question will ask you to revise the passage based on the data presented or will ask you to draw an inference based on the data. Search both the question stem and the answer choices for information that will help you pinpoint the specific parts of the table or graph that apply to the question. The correct answer will:

- Be relevant and make sense in context
- Accurately describe data in the table or graph

## You need to do this:

- Use the question stem and surrounding context in the passage to determine what data you need from the graphic

Eliminate choices that:

- Misrepresent information presented in the graphic
- Are irrelevant to the surrounding context

## Explanation:

The sentence to which the underlined portion belongs is comparing Earth's rotational speed to that of Jupiter's. The relevant information is how much faster Jupiter rotates. Look in the third column of the table for that data to find that Jupiter completes one rotation in 9.84 Earth hours. Compare this information to the answer choices; 9.84 is "fewer than 10," so **(C)** is correct.

# Try on Your Own

**Directions:** Take as much time as you need on these questions. Work carefully and methodically. There will be an opportunity for timed practice at the end of the chapter.

**Questions 44-47 refer to the following passage.**

**Child Expenditures**

A report from the United States Department of Agriculture estimates that the average cost of raising a child born in 2015 until age seventeen is over $230,000. This total includes **44** housing, food, transportation, health care, child care, and education; the overall cost varies considerably from family to family. However, with the average cost of raising a child set at nearly a quarter million dollars, and with additional children in the family raising that financial expenditure accordingly, it becomes clear that parenthood is a major undertaking. When planning a family, future parents should keep financial considerations in mind.

Even for families that plan for children, costs may be higher than many first-time parents anticipate. For instance, if one parent chooses to spend the first years of the child's life as a full-time caretaker and homemaker, he or she can lose career momentum and end up making a substantially lower salary than someone with the same background who maintains consistent employment. On the other hand, having both parents in the workforce significantly increases what the family must spend on child care, **45** which constituted an average of 18 percent of the overall costs to raise a child in 2012. While these factors should in no way be construed as a recommendation against having children, they speak to the need

44. The writer wants to provide an accurate and specific description of all the components that are included in the cost of raising a child based on the information in the pie charts. Which choice most effectively accomplishes this goal?

A) NO CHANGE

B) basic necessities and other needs;

C) primary needs such as housing, food, clothing, and health care, in addition to child care, transportation, education, and other assorted costs;

D) child care, health care, clothing, transportation, housing, and food;

45. Which choice completes the sentence with accurate data based on the pie charts?

A) NO CHANGE

B) which, combined with education, averaged nearly a fifth of the overall costs to raise a child in 2012.

C) which, combined with education, costs families considerably more in 2012 than in 1960.

D) which made up the largest portion of a family's average expenditures to raise a child in 2012.

for responsible family planning and financial preparation.

**Expenditures on a Child from Birth Through Age 17: Average Budgetary Component Shares, 1960 versus 2012**

**1960**

**2012**

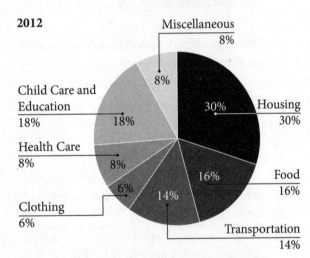

**Questions** 46 **and** 47 **ask about the pie charts.**

46. Which choice offers an accurate interpretation of the data in the pie charts?

    A) In 1960, health care and transportation together accounted for an average of 20 percent of a budget to raise a child.

    B) Households in 1960 spent an average of 31 percent of their total income on housing costs.

    C) The smallest proportion of an average 2012 budget to raise a child was tied between health care and miscellaneous costs.

    D) Households in 2012 spent, on average, less money per child on clothing than did households in 1960.

47. Which claim about the cost of raising children is supported by the two pie charts?

    A) Between 1960 and 2012, the percent of a budget spent on food increased.

    B) Between 1960 and 2012, the percent of a budget spent on health care decreased.

    C) Between 1960 and 2012, the percent of a budget spent on transportation experienced the greatest decrease.

    D) Between 1960 and 2012, the percent of a budget spent on child care and education experienced the greatest increase.

# How Much Have You Learned?

**Directions:** For testlike practice, give yourself 9 minutes to complete this question set. Be sure to study the explanations, even for questions you got right. They can be found at the end of this chapter.

**Questions 48-58 refer to the following passage.**

**Reefs at Risk**

Coral reefs are essential to water and coastal ecosystems, yet they are currently at great risk. **48** A coral reef is formed by a community of very small plants and animals. These plants and animals are known as algae and polyps. The algae use sunlight to produce their own food for energy and growth. The polyps eat other small animals that come to feed on the algae. Polyps also make a hard substance, called limestone, which eventually builds up to form a reef. Many people enjoy snorkeling and fishing near these reefs. **49** Coral reefs contain more than one quarter of all marine life and help reduce storm damage to coastal lands. **50** Ultimately, about 10 percent of the world's coral reefs have already been destroyed, and **51** nearly 60 percent of the remaining reefs face at least a medium level of risk.

48. Which choice most effectively combines the underlined sentences?

A) A coral reef is formed by a community of very small plants and animals; these plants and animals are known as algae and polyps.

B) Very small plants and animals, known as algae and polyps, make up the community that forms a coral reef.

C) A coral reef is formed by a community of very small plants and animals.

D) Known as algae and polyps, the community that is called a coral reef is formed by very small plants and animals.

49. The writer is considering deleting the previous sentence. Should the writer make this change?

A) Yes, because it introduces the writer's own opinion and thus does not match the tone of the passage.

B) Yes, because it contains information that is not related to the main ideas of the paragraph.

C) No, because it adds an interesting detail about the topic of the passage.

D) No, because it provides a specific example of why coral reefs are important.

50. A) NO CHANGE
    B) Unfortunately,
    C) Consequently,
    D) Inevitably,

51. Which choice most accurately represents the information in the chart?

A) NO CHANGE

B) 36 percent of the surviving reefs face overexploitation.

C) more than 6 in 10 reefs have faced threats of some kind or another.

D) scientists have classified 36 percent of the remaining reefs as "High Risk."

**52** Fishing and boating are popular sports near coral reefs. People who fish for a living often use explosives to catch the many fish that are attracted to coral reefs, causing significant damage. Boats also destroy reefs with their anchors, **53** yet tourists who swim in coral reefs often break coral off to keep as a souvenir.

The health of a coral reef depends on having clean water and sunlight, but industrial activities can threaten these **54** simple resources. Oil or chemical spills in the water near the reefs can harm the polyps, and chemical runoff into streams from mines and farms can also destroy the polyps and algae. Further, development along a coast, such as cutting down trees and building roads or parking lots, increases the amount of dirt and sand that washes into the ocean and settles on the bottom. This debris covers the reef and **55** disrupts sunlight from reaching the coral. Without sufficient sunlight, the algae cannot grow, and in turn, the polyps lack the energy needed to produce limestone and build up the reef.

[1] Marine biologists have found that small crabs living in coral reefs can help prevent the damage caused by coastal development. [2] They remove the particles of dirt and sand that settle on the coral and stop sunlight. [3] The crabs also eat some of the polyps, which **56** would probably suggest that the crabs might also be a threat to the coral. [4] The crabs help the coral survive **57** but benefit from the relationship as well. [5] The crabs living on the coral have a steady source of food, and the reef provides the crabs with shelter from

52. Which choice most effectively establishes the paragraph's central idea?

   A) NO CHANGE

   B) People who participate in activities near coral reefs often cause damage.

   C) Boats are dangerous to the health of coral reefs.

   D) Coral reefs are fragile, and people should be careful around them.

53. A) NO CHANGE

   B) and

   C) but

   D) so

54. A) NO CHANGE

   B) elusive

   C) committed

   D) vital

55. A) NO CHANGE

   B) delays

   C) blocks

   D) covers

56. A) NO CHANGE

   B) suggests

   C) maybe suggests

   D) almost certainly suggests

57. Which choice results in a sentence that best supports the central idea of the paragraph?

   A) NO CHANGE

   B) but are one of millions of animals that live in coral reefs.

   C) and can be very large or very small in size.

   D) and are found on coral reefs all over the world.

predators. [6] However, when the biologists removed crabs from sections of coral, less coral survived than in the sections where the crabs remained. [58]

The destruction of coral reefs does not have to continue. Recognizing the part that local animals, such as crabs, can play to reduce the amount of damage will help to slow the loss of coral reefs and may provide better ways to protect them.

58. To make this paragraph most logical, sentence 6 should be placed

A) where it is now.

B) before sentence 1.

C) after sentence 2.

D) after sentence 3.

### The World's Coral Reefs

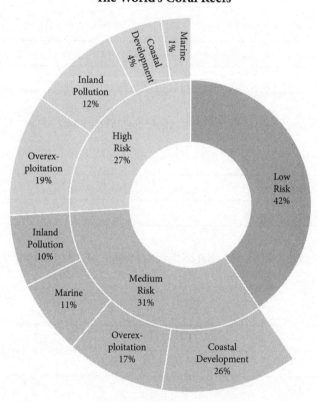

(Citation Adapted from Wheeling Jesuit University/NASA-supported Classroom of the Future, "Exploring the Environment: Coral Reefs.")

# Reflect

**Directions:** Take a few minutes to recall what you've learned and what you've been practicing in this chapter. Consider the following questions, jot down your best answer for each one, and then compare your reflections to the expert responses on the following page. Use your level of confidence to determine what to do next.

When should you consider selecting "DELETE the underlined portion"?

_____

_____

_____

How can transition words help you determine the most logical placement for a sentence?

_____

_____

_____

Why is relevance important in determining whether a sentence should be revised, added, or deleted?

_____

_____

_____

Name one goal of the introduction of a paragraph/passage. Name one goal of the conclusion of a paragraph/passage.

_____

_____

_____

How can you determine what you need from a graph or table on the SAT Writing and Language section?

_____

_____

_____

## Expert Responses

When should you consider selecting "DELETE the underlined portion"?

*If the underlined portion is wordy/redundant, does not enhance the meaning of the sentence, or or does not provide clarity, select "DELETE the underlined portion." Remember that "DELETE the underlined portion" is just as likely as any of the other three choices.*

How can transition words help you determine the most logical placement for a sentence?

*The kind of transition word that a sentence begins with (contrast, cause and effect, continuation, emphasis, chronology) determines the purpose the sentence should serve within the context. If the sentence does serve that purpose within the context, it is logically placed.*

Why is relevance important in determining whether a sentence should be revised, added, or deleted?

*If a sentence is missing relevant information, it needs to be revised. If you are going to add a sentence, it should be relevant to the existing information in the passage. If information is not relevant to the passage, it should be deleted.*

Name one goal of the introduction of a paragraph/passage. Name one goal of the conclusion of a paragraph/passage.

*A good introduction should explain the topic and purpose and include information that will be discussed later in the paragraph/passage. A good conclusion should summarize the topic and purpose and include information that was discussed earlier in the paragraph/passage*

How can you determine what you need from a graph or table on the SAT Writing and Language section?

*The question stem and the context surrounding where the graph or table is mentioned in the passage are the best clues as to what is important. Always read the question stem and take a look at the answer choices before you start to analyze the graph or table.*

## Next Steps

If you answered most questions correctly in the "How Much Have You Learned?" section, and if your responses to the Reflect questions were similar to those of the SAT expert, then consider organization, development, and graphs areas of strength and move on to the next chapter. Come back to these topics periodically to prevent yourself from getting rusty.

If you don't yet feel confident, review those parts of this chapter that you have not yet mastered. In particular, review common transition words and how they are used in the Organization: Transitions lesson and how to determine if information is relevant in the Development: Relevance lesson. Then try the questions you missed again. As always, be sure to review the explanations closely.

# Answers and Explanations

1. Review the Explanation portion of the Organization: Conciseness lesson.

2. **D**

**Difficulty:** Medium

**Getting to the Answer:** Since the previous sentence already identifies that the "distracted reader" is a "member of modern society," repeating a word that means "modern" is redundant. Deleting the underlined phrase is most concise, so choice **(D)** is correct.

3. **D**

**Difficulty:** Easy

**Getting to the Answer:** Using two words with essentially the same meaning in the same sentence is redundant. Because "understand" and "comprehend" have the same meaning, the correct answer will eliminate one of those words. Choice **(D)** is the only answer choice that does so and is correct.

4. **A**

**Difficulty:** Medium

**Getting to the Answer:** "Complexity" and "ambivalence" are not synonyms, so the inclusion of both is not automatically a conciseness issue. Check the surrounding context to see if both words should be included. The purpose of the paragraph is to suggest that the modern story mirrors modern life. In sentence 2, the writer describes the modern story as having "complexity and ambivalence." It is thus appropriate to repeat the phrase to describe the modern reader's life, making choice **(A)** correct. (B) and (C) are incorrect because using only one of the words changes the meaning of the writer's comparison of the modern story and the modern reader's life. (D) changes the intended meaning by using "ambivalent" to describe "complexity" rather than the reader's "life."

5. **B**

**Difficulty:** Medium

**Getting to the Answer:** Choice **(B)** is correct because it most concisely expresses the intended meaning by using "George and Jane" as the subject and "finish . . . and . . . find" as the compound predicate. (A) is incorrect because the phrase "come to the completion" is unnecessarily wordy. (C) is incorrect because it expresses the intended meaning less concisely than **(B)** by including both "George and Jane" and "they" and using the wordy phrase "at a finish." (D) is incorrect because the words "sudden" and "abruptness" are redundant.

6. **C**

**Difficulty:** Hard

**Getting to the Answer:** Questions that require you to combine sentences usually are not testing punctuation, so consider issues such as conciseness. Choice **(C)** most effectively combines the sentences by turning the second sentence into a modifying phrase that provides information about the action in the independent clause. Although (A) and (B) correctly combine the two independent clauses, both are incorrect because repeating the subject ("he") is unnecessary.

7. Review the Explanation portion of the Organization: Transitions lesson.

8. **B**

**Difficulty:** Medium

**Getting to the Answer:** A transition word must correctly convey the relationship between the information or ideas it connects. In the sentence before the underlined transition, the author describes small talk as boring. In the following sentence, he compares a conversation without small talk to flying. Since the sentence suggests that small talk can be dispensed with only occasionally, choice **(B)** is correct. Choices (A) and (C) are incorrect not only because they use inappropriate transition words, but also because they result in run-on sentences.

9. **A**

**Difficulty:** Medium

**Getting to the Answer:** To answer questions about effective transitions within a paragraph, identify the focus of the paragraph both before and after the transition. The first part of the paragraph discusses the reasons the narrator stayed in his room as a child—because he was ill. After the transition, the narrator discusses why he still stays in his room—because he has access to the world through the Internet. The transition needs to show how those ideas are linked. Choice **(A)** provides a logical transition as written.

**10. A**

**Difficulty:** Medium

**Getting to the Answer:** This sentence transitions from a discussion of the geographic freedom offered by Internet communication to one about the ease of Internet communication. To complete the transition, the underlined clause needs to relate to ease of communication. The sentence does this effectively as written, so **(A)** is correct. Choice (D) is incorrect because deleting the underlined portion would remove the transition. Choice (C) is incorrect because it references ideas from a different part of the passage. Choice (B) may be tempting because the sentence following the transition does mention text acronyms, but the writer is focused on ease rather than usefulness or frequency, so (B) is not a correct transition.

**11. C**

**Difficulty:** Medium

**Getting to the Answer:** The end of the previous paragraph describes Internet conversations as "relaxed and succinct;" the remainder of this sentence states that "empty chatter" is not everywhere. The change of opinion from "relaxed and succinct" to "empty chatter" is jarring without a transition, so eliminate (D). The remaining answer choices all contain the contrast word "but," so the underlined portion must contrast with the writer's positive opinion about Internet communication. Choice **(C)** is correct.

**12. D**

**Difficulty:** Easy

**Getting to the Answer:** To determine the correct transition word to use in context, first determine the relationship between the ideas it must connect. The first part of this sentence describes a person as "passionate," and the second part says that "his enthusiasm . . . inspires him." The second part elaborates on how his passion motivates him, so a continuation transition is needed to connect the two clauses. The correct answer is **(D)**.

**13.** Review the Explanation portion of the Organization: Sentence Placement lesson.

**14. C**

**Difficulty:** Hard

**Getting to the Answer:** Sentence 2 includes some unclear references like "some years" and "such earthquakes," while also including very specific information about variations in earthquake frequency in particular years. Sentence 3 defines "some years" (since 1900) and "such earthquakes" (major ones) and establishes the average number of earthquakes per year. Sentence 2 would thus fit best after sentence 3 so that its references are more clear and it can elaborate on the established baseline with more specific information. Additionally, this placement results in a general-to-specific and chronological structure for the paragraph, improving its overall logic. Choice **(C)** is correct.

**15. C**

**Difficulty:** Medium

**Getting to the Answer:** When reordering a sentence within a paragraph, identify the information in the sentence and locate where in the paragraph that information is discussed. The topic of sentence 4 is aftershocks. Aftershocks are also discussed in sentences 2 and 3. However, in sentence 2 the pronoun "these" indicates that aftershocks have been previously discussed in the paragraph, so a sentence about aftershocks prior to sentence 2 is necessary. Thus, the logical place for sentence 4 is before sentence 2. Choice **(C)** is correct.

**16. C**

**Difficulty:** Medium

**Getting to the Answer:** The transition word "However" at the beginning of sentence 3 indicates that it must contrast with the sentence before it. Sentence 3 is about how to prepare for an earthquake, and sentence 2 asks how to prepare. This does not provide a contrast, but inserting the new sentence before sentence 3 would give a contrast between the inability to precisely predict earthquakes and ways to prepare for them anyway. Placing the new sentence anywhere else in the paragraph would not resolve the logical problem in the paragraph, so **(C)** is the correct answer.

**17. B**

**Difficulty:** Medium

**Getting to the Answer:** The word "also" in this sentence shows that the sentence needs to follow something else that FEMA advises. Additionally, the paragraph will likely elaborate on how to make a home earthquake plan, so this sentence must come before that information. The correct answer is **(B)**. Placing the new sentence anywhere before sentence 2 would make the "also" logically inconsistent, since sentence 2 contains the first recommendation from FEMA, and placing it anywhere after sentence 3 would put it after the explanation of the plan it introduces.

**18. B**

**Difficulty:** Hard

**Getting to the Answer:** An effective body paragraph can provide evidence to support the writer's central idea or introduce a change in the focus of the passage. This paragraph begins with the transition word "still" and establishes a contrast between the number of recent earthquakes and the damage that those earthquakes can cause. The passage also shifts focus from a discussion of earthquake frequency to one of earthquake damage. Therefore, placing this paragraph between the two discussions in paragraph 3 and paragraph 4 makes the most sense. Choice **(B)** is correct.

**19.** Review the Explanation portion of the Development: Precision lesson.

**20. D**

**Difficulty:** Medium

**Getting to the Answer:** Establish how the underlined word is used in the sentence; consider the negative or positive tone of the answer choices. The correct word should reflect a negative tone in relation to the problem with the cold engine. "Credit" is a term with a positive connotation, so it's incorrect. "Critique" means to critically evaluate, which is not the correct meaning in this context. "Accuse" means to charge with a crime, which one wouldn't do with a car's engine. "Blame" has the appropriately negative connotation and the correct meaning in this context, so **(D)** is correct.

**21. C**

**Difficulty:** Hard

**Getting to the Answer:** Establish how the underlined word is used in the sentence based on the surrounding context. The correct word should reflect a connection between the battery and the motor. "United" means made into one entity, so it's incorrect in this context. "Correlated" means associated with, not connected, so it's incorrect. "Coupled" means connected and has the correct meaning in this context. "Assimilated" means to absorb into or to have taken on the customs or characteristics of one's surroundings, so it's not correct here. **(C)** is correct.

**22. A**

**Difficulty:** Medium

**Getting to the Answer:** Use the surrounding context to establish how the underlined word is used in the

sentence; the following sentence points out that the converse situation is when more electrons result in an increase in power, so it makes sense that fewer electrons result in a decrease in power. "Reduction" means decrease, so it is correct. "Regression" means moving backwards. "Retraction" means pulling back or pulling in. "Constriction" means squeezing or putting under inward pressure. Therefore, **(A)** is correct.

**23. B**

**Difficulty:** Medium

**Getting to the Answer:** Establish how the underlined word is used in the sentence; the previous lines describe the process by which the battery "makes" electricity. You can predict a similar meaning for the correct choice. "Providing" means giving, not making. "Producing" means making, so it is correct. "Promulgating" means declaring or making known formally, so it doesn't make sense here, and "asserting" means stating confidently, so it also doesn't make sense. Choice **(B)** is correct.

**24. D**

**Difficulty:** Medium

**Getting to the Answer:** Look at how the word is used in the sentence and analyze its meaning. Use context clues to determine which choice is correct. The last sentence of the paragraph says that the molecules will be "more likely" to collide. "Practicality" is a noun meaning feasibility or usefulness and doesn't make sense here. "Confirmation" means verification, which doesn't make sense in this context; "process" means method or way, but that is not what's being described. "Probability" is a noun meaning likelihood, which does make sense in this context. **(D)** is correct.

**25. B**

**Difficulty:** Hard

**Getting to the Answer:** Use context clues to determine which choice is correct. The sentence says that power will need to be added from another car's battery, so predict something like "additional." "Associative" means resulting from association, which is not logical in this context. Auxiliary" means additional or supplementary, and is correct. "Optional" means by choice or not required, which doesn't make sense here. "Extraordinary" means exceptional or remarkable, which also doesn't fit the intended meaning. **(B)** is correct.

**26.** Review the Explanation portion of the Development: Relevance lesson.

**27. C**

**Difficulty:** Medium

**Getting to the Answer:** Pay close attention to long lists of evidence to make sure that each component is in line with the central idea and context of the sentence. Choice **(C)** is correct because it is the only answer choice that both stays focused on matters of policy (as the first part of the sentence mentions) and supports the thesis that Polk and Jackson were in agreement on most points of public policy.

**28. D**

**Difficulty:** Medium

**Getting to the Answer:** Supporting details fit the context of the paragraph and do not contradict details found elsewhere in the passage. They must also logically lead to the information that follows. Select the answer choice that satisfies these guidelines. This paragraph is narrowly concerned with Polk's origins and early political career. Only **(D)** fits the context, does not introduce irrelevant information, and does not contradict later details.

**29. B**

**Difficulty:** Medium

**Getting to the Answer:** Remember that supporting evidence needs to focus on and contribute to the central idea. The author's intent is to introduce the two main candidates in the 1844 election, leading to the following sentence that discusses their opinions of expansionism. Choice **(B)** is correct because it stays focused on the paragraph's topic and contributes to the argument that Polk recognized popular support for expansionism that other candidates overlooked or ignored. All other choices introduce details that are either irrelevant or that contradict information elsewhere in the passage.

**30. A**

**Difficulty:** Medium

**Getting to the Answer:** Examine details and parenthetical asides for relevance to the central idea. The goal is to make sure that no contradictions are being introduced into the narrative. No change is necessary because the underlined section touches on two central themes of the passage: Polk's support for expansionist policies and his close alignment with Jackson's views. All other choices contradict information in other parts of the passage. Choice **(A)** is correct.

**31. B**

**Difficulty:** Medium

**Getting to the Answer:** Examine the paragraph for relevance to the central idea. Be sure that the underlined portion is consistent with the information that follows in the rest of the paragraph. Choice (A) is incorrect because the following sentences describe Polk's expansion of U.S. territory and his provoking a war with Mexico. (B) correctly indicates the idea that Polk's policies expanded U.S. territory. (C) is inconsistent with the information that follows: there's a strong implication that Polk's policies did allow for the expansion of slavery. (D) is incorrect because nothing in the paragraph indicates an expanding international role for the United States. Thus, **(B)** is correct.

**32.** Review the Explanation portion of the Development: Revising Text lesson.

**33. B**

**Difficulty:** Medium

**Getting to the Answer:** In order to decide whether to revise or add information, consider how the change would contribute to the sentence or paragraph. This sentence states that Jupiter interests scientists but does not provide strong reasoning for why. Making the suggested revision would improve the sentence by offering a detail about what makes Jupiter unique that helps to support the sentence's conclusion. Choice **(B)** is correct.

**34. A**

**Difficulty:** Medium

**Getting to the Answer:** When considering whether to add a sentence, examine the paragraph to determine whether the sentence to be added would contribute useful information or ideas to it. Before the place the writer is thinking of inserting this sentence, the passage states that the discovery of Jupiter prompted scientists to consider that other planets might not orbit Earth. It then notes that moons orbiting Jupiter were discovered at the same time as the planet. However, the passage does not explain the connection between these statements or support the first statement. The sentence to be added would accomplish both, so **(A)** is correct.

**35. C**

**Difficulty:** Easy

**Getting to the Answer:** If you have the option to omit a sentence, think carefully about the author's topic. If the underlined portion strays from the topic, omit it. The author's topic is Jupiter. The underlined portion adds information about *Pioneer 10* that is irrelevant to the topic. Choice **(C)** correctly omits the sentence for this reason.

**36. A**

**Difficulty:** High

**Getting to the Answer:** In order to decide whether a sentence should be added, examine the paragraph to see if the sentence supports its purpose. This paragraph is about the winds of Jupiter causing some of its unique features. The sentence in question might not seem related to Jupiter's winds at first glance, but the sentences before and after it make clear that the "stripes" referred to in the new sentence are the result of bands of wind, since it is these bands that isolate the chemical reactions creating individual colors. Additionally, the colorful, distinctive stripes that the sentence describes are among Jupiter's unique features, so this sentence supports the paragraph's topic; **(A)** is correct.

**37. D**

**Difficulty:** Medium

**Getting to the Answer:** When determining whether to delete a sentence, consider whether it supports the main idea of the passage and the paragraph. This sentence is about Jupiter's rotation speed. While the passage is about Jupiter, this paragraph is specifically about the winds of Jupiter, so its rotation speed is off topic for the paragraph. Choice **(D)** is correct because it deletes the sentence for this reason.

**38.** Review the Explanation portion of the Introductions and Conclusions lesson.

**39. B**

**Difficulty:** Medium

**Getting to the Answer:** The underlined portion will need to introduce the passage as a whole in addition to fitting well with the rest of its sentence and paragraph. The primary purpose of the passage is to describe the functions of the skin. Choice **(B)** introduces this topic effectively; the detail about the body's largest organ connects to the sentence via a contrast with people not thinking about skin as an organ and to the paragraph via an emphasis on the skin's size. Choice (A) focuses too narrowly on the skin's communication functions. Choice (C) gives details about the skin's composition rather than an introduction to the passage. Choice (D) is vague and the mention of biologists is off topic.

**40. D**

**Difficulty:** Medium

**Getting to the Answer:** Pick the answer choice that is in line with the writer's central idea. In this paragraph, the writer explains how the skin regulates and protects the body. The final sentence is focused on how the skin protects the body, so the underlined portion must be as well. Only **(D)** correctly centers on the protection the skin offers. Choice (A) is about us protecting our skin rather than vice versa; (B) does not discuss protection; (C) does not discuss the skin.

**41. B**

**Difficulty:** Hard

**Getting to the Answer:** When a question asks for a good introduction sentence, first determine the main idea of the paragraph. This paragraph uses a lot of scientific jargon, but the second sentence refers to "other senses," and nerves on the body's surface that receive "tactile stimuli" must refer to the sense of touch. The only answer choice that focuses on the skin and the sense of touch is **(B)**. Choice (A) is too vague to effectively introduce the paragraph. Choice (C) is too broadly focused on all senses and does not mention the skin. Choice (D) does mention touch but discusses the nervous system rather than the skin.

**42. A**

**Difficulty:** Medium

**Getting to the Answer:** Concluding sentences often reassert or summarize the writer's central idea; therefore, they cannot fundamentally conflict with the writer's assertions. In this passage, the writer has made clear that the skin is a very important organ that protects the body from a variety of illnesses and disorders, as well as from physical harm. Choice **(A)** is correct, as it ties preceding points and details together into a coherent conclusion for the writer's argument.

**43.** Review the Explanation portion of the Graphs lesson.

## 44. C

**Difficulty:** Medium

**Getting to the Answer:** The writer wants a specific, comprehensive list of child care costs as presented in the pie graphs. While (A) seems exhaustive, careful reading shows it lacks the categories of clothing and miscellaneous needs; eliminate it. Choice (D) is similarly missing education and miscellaneous expenses. Only **(B)** includes all of the expense categories in the pie charts, with the added bonus of sorting them by importance for easier comprehension.

## 45. B

**Difficulty:** Hard

**Getting to the Answer:** The sentence brings up "what a family must spend on child care," and the underlined portion must elaborate with accurate information from the pie charts. According to the charts, "Child Care and Education" represented 18 percent of expenditures on a child in 2012. Choice **(B)** includes education with child care and correctly describes their combined cost as "nearly a fifth" of total expenses. Choices (A) and (D) omit education, and (D) incorrectly identifies child care as the largest expenditure (rather than housing). Choice (C) may be tempting, since it also includes education, but it inaccurately represents the data: the pie charts show that the *percent* of total expenditures spent on child care and education has increased, but the charts offer no actual dollar amounts, which makes it impossible to compare those amounts.

## 46. A

**Difficulty:** Medium

**Getting to the Answer:** To answer this type of question, carefully check each answer choice against the information in the graphs until you find the one that is correct. In 1960, health care and transportation represented 6 percent and 14 percent, respectively, of the total and 20 percent together. Choice **(A)** is correct. Choice (B) is incorrect because the pie graphs represent budgets spent on children, not total household income. (C) is incorrect because clothing constituted the smallest percent. (D) is incorrect because the graphs do not offer dollar amounts, just proportions of budgets.

## 47. D

**Difficulty:** Medium

**Getting to the Answer:** When a question is very broad and does not offer clues as to what part of the graph to examine, use the answer choices to determine where to look. All of the answer choices for this question require a comparison of percents between the two years. The percent spent on food decreased; eliminate (A). The percent spent on health care increased; eliminate (B). The percent spent on transportation decreased, but not as much as the percent spent on food; eliminate (C). The percent spent on child care and education increased from 2 percent to 16 percent, a greater increase than any other category; **(D)** is correct.

## 48. B

**Difficulty:** Medium

**Category:** Organization: Conciseness

**Getting to the Answer:** As written, the sentences contain redundant language. Look for the answer choice that retains the meaning of the two original sentences but is less wordy and redundant. Choice **(B)** is the correct answer because it contains the same information as the original sentences but in a more concise manner. While (C) is similar, it omits mention of "algae and polyps"; it also uses passive voice, which you should avoid using on the SAT. Choice (D) also includes the necessary information, but it introduces a modifier error, with "Known as algae and polyps" describing "the community" rather than "very small plants and animals."

## 49. B

**Difficulty:** Medium

**Category:** Development: Revising Text

**Getting to the Answer:** Identify the main idea of the paragraph and then determine whether the sentence supports it. Although sentence 3 is related to the main topic of the paragraph, coral reefs, the information in this sentence does nothing to support the main idea: coral reefs' significance and threatened status. Choice **(B)** is correct.

## 50. B

**Difficulty:** Medium

**Category:** Organization: Transitions

**Getting to the Answer:** Look for a relationship between the ideas in this sentence and the preceding sentences. The previous sentences describe the importance of coral reefs, and this sentence states that they are in danger of disappearing. "Unfortunately" indicates a shift from positive to negative ideas, so it effectively connects these sentences. Choice **(B)** is the correct answer.

**51. A**

**Difficulty:** Medium

**Category:** Graphs

**Getting to the Answer:** Evaluate the data presented in the graphic that accompanies the passage. Read each answer choice and eliminate those not supported by the data in the graph. Choice **(A)** is correct. As the chart shows, almost 60 percent of living reefs are in danger: "Medium Risk" 37% + "High Risk" 21% = 58%.

**52. B**

**Difficulty:** Easy

**Category:** Development: Introductions and Conclusions

**Getting to the Answer:** The correct answer will briefly describe the main idea of the paragraph and will be supported by the details in the paragraph. Be careful of answer choices like (C) that summarize a detail provided in the paragraph rather than the central idea. Choice **(B)** best describes the main idea of the paragraph. All of the details presented in the paragraph are related to how people engaging in activities near coral reefs often cause damage.

**53. B**

**Difficulty:** Easy

**Category:** Organization: Transitions

**Getting to the Answer:** To determine the best transition word to connect ideas, determine the relationship between the ideas. Boat anchors and people taking souvenirs both damage coral reefs, so the correct answer will show that the ideas are similar. Choice **(B)** is correct.

**54. D**

**Difficulty:** Hard

**Category:** Development: Precision

**Getting to the Answer:** Look for the answer that most clearly conveys the writer's meaning. The writer states that the reef "depends on" the resources of clean water and sunlight. These resources are necessary to the coral reefs, so **(D)**, "vital," is the correct answer. While the resources are "simple," as in (A), that is not the writer's intended meaning in this context. Similarly, it is a distortion of the writer's meaning to say that these resources are "elusive," (B); the writer does not suggest that clean water and sunlight are rare but that the reef's access to what it needs is threatened.

**55. C**

**Difficulty:** Medium

**Category:** Development: Precision

**Getting to the Answer:** Look for the answer that creates the clearest idea within the sentence. The word "blocks" most clearly illustrates how the particles that settle on the coral keep sunlight from reaching the coral. Choice **(C)** is correct.

**56. B**

**Difficulty:** Easy

**Category:** Organization: Conciseness

**Getting to the Answer:** Avoid answers that are grammatically correct but wordy or redundant. Since the word "might" appears later in the sentence, another word that indicates doubt, such as "probably," (A), or "maybe," (C), would result in a redundancy. "Suggests" fits grammatically and is the most concise choice, so **(B)** is the correct answer.

**57. A**

**Difficulty:** Medium

**Category:** Development: Relevance

**Getting to the Answer:** Avoid answers that are related to the paragraph topic but do not contribute to the paragraph's purpose. The paragraph explains how crabs and coral reefs help each other. Choice **(A)** is the only one that supports this central idea. The other choices offer details about crabs but not about their mutually beneficial relationship with reefs. The correct answer is **(A)**.

**58. D**

**Difficulty:** Medium

**Category:** Organization: Sentence Placement

**Getting to the Answer:** In order to determine the best place for a sentence, look for clues in the the sentence and the surrounding paragraph. Sentence 6 states that more coral survived with the crabs than without them, implying that the crabs are good for the coral. Additionally, the sentence starts with the contrast word "however," so it must contrast with the sentence before it. Thus, the sentence would effectively follow and refute sentence 3's suggestion that crabs might be damaging the coral; this supports the central idea of the paragraph, that crabs and reefs are good for each other. Choice **(D)** is the correct answer.

# CHAPTER 27

# SAT Writing and Language: Timing and Section Management Strategies

---

**LEARNING OBJECTIVE**

After completing this chapter, you will be able to:

- Move quickly and efficiently through the Writing and Language section so that you have a fair chance at every question

---

## Timing

You have 35 minutes to complete 4 passages with 11 questions each. To finish on time, you need to complete each passage and its accompanying questions in an average of 8 minutes and 45 seconds. This means that after 17.5 minutes, you should be halfway done with the section. When the proctor informs you that there are 5 minutes remaining, you should have a little more than half of a passage to finish.

## Section Management

While you do want to spend approximately the same amount of time on each passage, you definitely do not need to spend the same amount of time on each question. Every question counts for the same number of points, so be sure to complete the questions you find easiest to answer first. If a particular question is challenging, take a guess and come back to it if you have time. The test rewards students for conciseness, so when you guess, choose the shortest option.

Moving efficiently through this section is important, but that does not mean that you should skip over any text. Even if sections of a passage may not be underlined, you need an understanding of the passage as a whole to answer certain questions. Reading all of the text in the passage is essential to answering questions efficiently and accurately.

There is a full Writing and Language section in the "How Much Have You Learned?" part of this chapter. Use it to practice timing: skip questions you find too time-consuming and return to them if you have time and keep an eye on the clock. When you are finished, check your work—and reflect on how well you managed the section.

# How Much Have You Learned?

**Directions:** For testlike practice, give yourself 35 minutes to complete this question set, which is the equivalent of a full Writing and Language section. Be sure to study the explanations, even for questions you got right. They can be found at the end of this chapter.

**Questions 1-11 refer to the following passage.**

**Long History, Short Poem: The Haiku**

[1] Of the many forms poetry can take, triolet, ballad, ode, and epigram, to name a few, none is quite as briefly beautiful as the Japanese haiku. With a [2] complex history and a challenging structure, the haiku is as popular as it is difficult to master. Composed of only three lines and 17 or fewer syllables, haiku have been written by some of the world's most prominent poets.

[3] [1] Pre-Buddhist and early Shinto ceremonies included narrative poems called "uta," or songs. [2] These songs were written about common activities like planting and prayer. [3] The most popular "uta" were "waka," or songs featuring 31 syllables broken into five different lines. [4] Later, the "waka" format was distilled into the 5-7-5-7-7 syllables-per-line format that is still used and recognized today. [5] During the same time period, writers played word games. [6] The syllabic 5-7-5-7-7 structure would remain throughout the work, adhering to the guidelines used in ceremonies and royal court proceedings. [7] They would compose lines of poetry, alternating turns, until long strings of text called "renga" were created. [8] It was not until the 15th and 16th centuries that writers of "renga" broke with tradition and shortened the form, writing "hokku,"

1. A) NO CHANGE
   B) Of the many forms poetry can take—triolet, ballad, ode, and epigram, to name a few—none is quite as briefly beautiful as the Japanese haiku.
   C) Of the many forms poetry can take, triolet, ballad, ode and epigram to name a few—none is quite as briefly beautiful as the Japanese haiku.
   D) Of the many forms poetry can take: triolet, ballad, ode, and epigram to name a few, none is quite as briefly beautiful as the Japanese haiku.

2. A) NO CHANGE
   B) composite
   C) compound
   D) variegated

3. Which choice, if added here, would provide the most appropriate introduction to the topic of the paragraph?
   A) Although the format remained unknown to Americans until the 1950s, haiku dates back as early as the seventh century.
   B) The art of haiku includes specific rules about how lines are to be structured, but these rules are difficult to pin down.
   C) Despite its difficult reputation and the years it takes to master, haiku is highly entertaining.
   D) Haiku is a Japanese poetic art form and many poets enjoy the challenge of writing a poem within its rules.

meaning "first verse." [9] [4] <u>This name changed into "haiku" over time.</u> [5]

[6] <u>Previously,</u> hokku master Matsunaga Teitoku began teaching renga in an attempt to ignite a classical renaissance. He founded a writing school where he taught Matsuo Basho, who is now known as one of Japan's most famous writers. Basho traveled throughout Japan writing about nature and his travels.

It is through Basho's many poems that [7] <u>haiku came to be known as being closely connected with</u> nature and the seasons. [8] Basho influenced many students of verse over the course of his lifetime and was declared the saint of the haiku in the Shinto religion. One of Basho's literary heirs was Fukuda Chiyo-ni, whose popularity during the Edo period, in the eighteenth century, opened opportunities for women poets who followed her.

4. A) NO CHANGE
   B) Nobody is quite sure when it became known as "haiku."
   C) These days, we know this word as "haiku."
   D) DELETE the underlined portion.

5. To make this paragraph most logical, sentence 7 should be placed
   A) where it is now.
   B) after sentence 1.
   C) after sentence 5.
   D) after sentence 8.

6. A) NO CHANGE
   B) However,
   C) In the next century,
   D) As a result,

7. A) NO CHANGE
   B) haiku transformed into a mode of artistic expression that was irreversibly intertwined with the themes of
   C) haiku became popular because it was seen as having something to do with
   D) haiku developed its common association with

8. Which choice, if added here, would provide the most relevant detail?
   A) However, haiku can be used to communicate many other ideas as well, from love to humor.
   B) His words emphasized contentment and solitary contemplation, ideals linked to Japanese religions.
   C) Basho's poetic influence continues to be felt even now in the work of several modern poets.
   D) For example, a Basho haiku might focus on a frog or on the coming of spring.

It was not until 1827 that hokku was renamed haiku by Masaoka Shiki. [9] Shiki was a poet, and he most famously shrank the structure of the haiku to its current format of 5-7-5. His work [10] helped Western writers like e. e. cummings and Ezra Pound, but haiku did not become the easily recognizable, popular type of poetry that it is today until writers like Allen Ginsberg and Jack Kerouac popularized it.

These writers were taken by [11] the brevity of the form, but it provided them a new, challenging form of expression while enabling them to share full ideas in such a short form. Both Japanese and American poets continue to use the haiku structure to create snapshots of beauty and calm.

9. A)   NO CHANGE
   B)   Shiki was a poet who also shrank the structure of the haiku to the current 5-7-5 format.
   C)   Shiki was the poet who shrank the structure of the haiku to its current 5-7-5 format.
   D)   Shiki was the poet who was also known for shrinking the structure of the haiku to its current format of 5-7-5.

10. A)   NO CHANGE
    B)   inspired
    C)   aided
    D)   started

11. A)   NO CHANGE
    B)   the brevity of the form, it
    C)   the brevity of the form, and it
    D)   the brevity of the form, as it

**Questions 12-22 refer to the following passage.**

**Physical Therapy Careers: Health Care in Motion**

Physical therapy is a health care field that is [12] concurrently rated by the U.S. Bureau of Labor Statistics as one of today's best career choices. Featuring considerable variety in work environments, patient relationships, and job activity levels, the work of a physical therapist has the potential to be both highly motivating and satisfying. [13] Current projections indicate that this particular field of physical therapy should grow significantly over the next decade and continue to be one of the more flexible—not to mention enjoyable and fun—jobs in health care.

[14] A license is required to practice as a physical therapist, whether in the United States or elsewhere. After completing a bachelor's degree (and specific science-related prerequisites), students must obtain a Doctor of Physical Therapy (DPT) degree. This program typically lasts three years. All graduates of DPT programs must then pass the National Physical Therapy Examination. After the exam, they must complete any additional requirements for licensure in the state in which they intend to practice. Once licensed by the state, physical therapists (PTs) are equipped to begin their careers.

[15] PTs work with a broad range of patients in a wide variety of settings, such as hospitals or private clinics. Some clientele, for example, are elderly or ill. Other patients include athletes ranging from elite professionals and college sports stars to middle school sports players.

12. A) NO CHANGE
    B) consistently
    C) unusually
    D) finally

13. A) NO CHANGE
    B) And current projections indicate that the field should grow significantly over the next several years and the next decade and remain one of the more flexible—not to mention enjoyable—jobs in health care.
    C) Current projections and predictions by the Bureau of Labor indicate that the field should grow significantly over the next decade and remain one of the more flexible and even enjoyable—jobs in the health care industry.
    D) Current projections indicate that the field should grow significantly over the next decade and remain one of the more flexible and enjoyable jobs in health care.

14. Which choice most effectively establishes the main topic of the second paragraph?
    A) NO CHANGE
    B) Those pursuing careers in physical therapy must undergo the appropriate education and licensure processes.
    C) Requirements vary from state to state to practice physical therapy, just as they do for physicians and physicians' assistants.
    D) Physical therapists must pass a national exam that covers a wide range of material.

15. A) NO CHANGE
    B) PTs work with a broad range of patients, in a wide variety of settings some work in hospitals, while others work in private clinics.
    C) PTs work with a broad range of patients; in a wide variety of settings. Some work in hospitals; others in private clinics.
    D) PTs work with a broad range of patients: the variety of settings, includes hospitals and private clinics.

Writing & Lang

**16** Some kinds of PTs have personal, long-term patient **17** relationships, while others focus on research or testing and interact with patients minimally.

[1] **18** A physical therapist primarily works with patients who have suffered motion loss from illness or injury. The goal is to restore mobility while managing and limiting pain.

16. At this point, the writer is considering adding a sentence to support the main topic of the paragraph. Which choice best supports the main topic of paragraph 3?

A) PTs must demonstrate their willingness to spend long hours on the job.

B) Still others include people who have been injured at work.

C) The clientele pay for their physical therapy services according to their ability, so some PTs earn more than others.

D) No special license is required to work with patients who are professional athletes, but some states may require additional courses to work with students.

17. A) NO CHANGE

B) relationships, while others, who focus on research or testing, interact minimally with patients.

C) relationships; others minimal interact with patients and focus on research or testing.

D) relationships. Others focus on research or testing and interact with patients minimally.

18. Which choice most effectively combines the underlined sentences to provide a smooth flow of ideas?

A) NO CHANGE

B) A physical therapist primarily works with patients. They have suffered motion loss from illness or injury. And the therapist's goal is to restore mobility. While managing and limiting pain.

C) A physical therapist, whose goal is to restore mobility and manage pain primarily works with patients who have suffered motion loss or illness or injury.

D) A physical therapist primarily works with patients who have suffered motion loss from illness or injury to restore mobility while managing and limiting pain.

[2] **19** This job often involves long-term planning, creatively personalized application, and patience, in addition to highly refined medical knowledge. [3] In many cases, physical therapists invite and rely on patients to participate actively in their own recovery. [4] This interpersonal and **20** collaborative aspect of physical therapy is often essential to the medical work itself. [5] For example, recovering athletes must often commit to long-term conditioning programs before returning to their sports. [6] Surgery or medication alone isn't always enough to restore full mobility; many PT patients must relearn their muscle use and work hard to increase flexibility. [7] PTs determine the course of action and coach their patients through the steps to recovery. **21**

[1] The horizon for employment rates in physical therapy is exceptionally bright. [2] The Bureau of Labor Statistics predicts that the coming decade will see a 36% growth in PT jobs. [3] This means that there should be a need for over 70,000 new PTs nationwide. [4] Physical therapist assistants (PTAs) will also be needed. [5] For those willing to commit the time and effort to become experts in physical therapy, the possibilities and quality of the PT work environment are among the most desirable in health care, and considering projected employment rates, such a career seems to be an especially prudent choice. **22**

19. A) NO CHANGE
    B) This job often involves long-term planning, creatively personalized application, patience, and highly refined medical knowledge.
    C) This job often involves long-term planning, creative personalized application and patience, in addition to highly refined medical knowledge.
    D) This job often involves long-term planning, creatively personal application and patience, as well as highly refined medical knowledge.

20. A) NO CHANGE
    B) concentrated
    C) planned
    D) consolidated

21. To make this paragraph most logical, sentence 2 should be placed
    A) before sentence 1.
    B) after sentence 3.
    C) after sentence 5.
    D) after sentence 7.

22. Which sentence should be removed in order to improve the focus of this paragraph?
    A) Sentence 1
    B) Sentence 2
    C) Sentence 3
    D) Sentence 4

**Questions 23-33** refer to the following passage.

**Feeling the Burn of Lactic Acid**

As a person works a muscle excessively or for a long period of time, that person will most likely feel a burning sensation. Coaches and trainers often encourage **23** they're athletes to exercise until they "feel the burn" because that is an indication that the muscle is working hard. Some people **24** bond the burning feeling with "burning" calories, but the burning sensation has nothing to do with the energy released during exercise; **25** first, it is caused by chemicals that form when muscles use more oxygen than they have available.

**26** Blood brings the energy muscles need to move in the form of glucose. The muscles cannot use the glucose directly, however; they can use only adenosine triphosphate (ATP), which is a molecule formed when cells break down glucose. First, the muscle cells break the six-carbon glucose into two three-carbon molecules of pyruvic acid. This makes two ATP molecules available for the muscle cells to use. When enough oxygen is available, the cells **27** then continues to break the pyruvic acid down in a series of steps, each of which produces more ATP. The full cycle releases another 34 ATP molecules, as well as carbon dioxide and water, from one molecule of glucose.

When a cell breaks down glucose without oxygen present, however, it can only accomplish the first step. Even the first step will halt, unless the cell converts the pyruvic acid formed into lactic acid. The longer we exercise without enough oxygen, the more lactic acid we build up in our muscle tissues. You are probably familiar with the discomfort acetic **28** acid found in vinegar, causes when it comes in contact with a cut; lactic acid

23. A) NO CHANGE
    B) their
    C) it's
    D) its

24. A) NO CHANGE
    B) equate
    C) acquaint
    D) observe

25. A) NO CHANGE
    B) instead
    C) although
    D) consequently

26. Which choice most effectively establishes the central idea of this paragraph?
    A) NO CHANGE
    B) Adenosine triphosphate (ATP) is a molecule that is found in all living cells.
    C) Glucose is a carbohydrate that is absorbed into the blood during digestion.
    D) Muscles are made of soft tissue and require an external energy source to move.

27. A) NO CHANGE
    B) did continue
    C) continue
    D) continued

28. A) NO CHANGE
    B) acid, found in vinegar, causes
    C) acid found, in vinegar, causes
    D) acid found in vinegar causes

**29** annoys muscle tissues in a similar way, causing a burning sensation.

**30** [1] Lactic acid does not form during normal daily activities because our muscles have a small store of ATP available, which is easily replenished as it is used. [2] More intense activity, however, quickly uses up that **31** store once the store is used up, and if the level of oxygen needed for the activity is greater than the amount reaching the muscles, lactic acid starts to build up. [3] The buildup of lactic acid occurs most quickly while engaging in so-called power sports, such as sprinting. [4] After we stop exercising, **32** you continue to breathe harder in order to get enough oxygen to convert the lactic acid back to pyruvic acid, to be used in the normal cycle once again. [5] As a result, lactic acid does not return to normal immediately after we stop exercising. **33**

**Concentration of Lactic Acid in Blood Before, During, and After Exercise (5-minute fast run)**

Based on data from Journal of Sport Sciences, 28(9) pp. 975-982.

29. A) NO CHANGE
    B) rubs
    C) hurts
    D) irritates

30. Which choice provides the least support for the central idea of this paragraph?
    A) Sentence 1
    B) Sentence 2
    C) Sentence 3
    D) Sentence 4

31. A) NO CHANGE
    B) store once, the store
    C) store; once the store
    D) store: once the store

32. A) NO CHANGE
    B) we
    C) they
    D) them

33. Based on the information in the graph, which choice, if added here, would provide the most effective conclusion to the passage?
    A) Lactic acid concentration peaks at eight minutes then begins to drop.
    B) At 28 minutes, lactic acid concentration is half of what it is during exercise.
    C) We continue to "feel the burn" for nearly 40 minutes after we stop.
    D) Lactic acid concentration declines steadily when exercise stops.

Writing & Lang

**Questions 34-44 refer to the following passage.**

**Inside Looking Out: Post-Impressionism**

Post-Impressionism was an artistic movement that took place between 1886 and 1892 and [34] produces some of the world's foremost artists. Post-Impressionism emerged as one of the many different artistic styles created in response to the Impressionist movement, which focused on creating realistic representations of human perceptions. [35] Next, Impressionists sought to [36] restate nature in their work. They used small, controlled brush strokes in an effort to capture how the human eye sees light. Post-Impressionism was radically different. Artists of this time focused more on self-discovery than anything else. Instead of looking out on a landscape and [37] attempt to paint exactly what they saw, they turned their eyes inward. They interpreted subjects through their own [38] unique vision, which included their personal experiences and emotions. This change influenced the course of all art created since.

[39] Among the Impressionist artists were Claude Monet, Pierre-Auguste Renoir, Edgar Degas, and Mary Cassatt. Paul Cezanne and Georges Seurat used shape and color to describe their worlds rather than mimic them. Their work acted as a bridge between Impressionist art and the more abstract subcategories of Post-Impressionism. Two such subcategories were Cubism and Abstract Expressionism.

34. A) NO CHANGE
    B) produced
    C) was producing
    D) will produce

35. A) NO CHANGE
    B) For example,
    C) Consequently,
    D) However,

36. A) NO CHANGE
    B) clone
    C) counterfeit
    D) replicate

37. A) NO CHANGE
    B) attempting
    C) was attempted
    D) is attempting

38. A) NO CHANGE
    B) single
    C) cautious
    D) acceptable

39. Which choice most effectively establishes the central idea of the paragraph?
    A) NO CHANGE
    B) Modern artists are well versed in many different kinds of styles thanks to the many artists of the past.
    C) Artists in the Post-Impressionist era employed a wide range of methods when creating their art.
    D) Prior to the Impressionist and Post-Impressionist eras, artists painted in a much more realistic style.

**40** Cubism was created by Spanish painter Pablo Picasso and French painter Georges Braque. It featured geometric shapes used to construct conceptual portraits. Both of these artists rejected traditional views on modeling nature and people, as well as classical techniques. Abstract Expressionism used color instead of geometric figures, and artists like Jackson Pollock and Willem de Kooning covered their canvases with color and indistinct forms. Abstract Expressionists aimed to express deep emotional themes. Paul Gauguin and Vincent van Gogh are also considered Abstract Expressionists, as **41** they both prioritized the depiction of their memories and emotions over observations that could be made with the eye. Helen Frankenthaler, whose body of work evolved over the six decades of her career, began painting within this genre as well, before coming to reject its highly personal perspective. **42** Never before had such an emphasis on individualism taken precedence over classical technique, a change that laid the foundation for art in the 20th century and beyond.

40. Which choice most effectively combines the sentences at the underlined portion?

A) NO CHANGE

B) Created by Spanish painter Pablo Picasso and French painter Georges Braque, Cubism featured geometric shapes used to construct conceptual portraits.

C) Cubism was created by Spanish painter Pablo Picasso and French painter Georges Braque so it featured geometric shapes.

D) Cubism was created by Spanish painter Pablo Picasso and French painter Georges Braque, but it featured geometric shapes.

41. A) NO CHANGE

B) it

C) you

D) we

42. Which choice, if added here, most effectively supports the central idea of the paragraph?

A) Some Impressionist artists, such as Renoir, painted images of children, flowers, and social gatherings.

B) Degas often painted ballet dancers at the barre as well as molding sculptures of them.

C) Art is often viewed as a window into the minds and experiences of artists as they lived their lives.

D) To transfer their emotions to their canvases, Post-Impressionist artists sometimes used violent gestures to apply paint.

[1] These artists worked and created during the same time period and movement. [2] However, they had varying world views and techniques. [3] Today, we can get to know the souls of some of the world's greatest artists by visiting **43** <u>they're</u> Post-Impressionist work in museums around the world. [4] These differences cumulatively succeeded in breaking from the natural guidelines of Impressionism to create something entirely new that dramatically influenced all artists who came after them. [5] In the words of Edvard Munch, another Post-Impressionist painter, "Nature is not only all that is visible to the eye … it also includes the inner pictures of the soul." **44**

43. A) NO CHANGE
    B) their
    C) they are
    D) there

44. To make this paragraph most logical, sentence 3 should be placed
    A) where it is now.
    B) after sentence 1.
    C) before sentence 5.
    D) after sentence 5.

# Answers and Explanations

**1.    B**

**Difficulty:** Medium

**Category:** Sentence Structure: Commas, Dashes, and Colons

**Getting to the Answer:** Read the sentence to determine how the list within it should be formatted. If it is more of an aside than a direct part of the sentence's main structure, the list should be set off by punctuation. As the sentence is written, its many commas are confusing. Because there is a list in the sentence, the commas within that list should remain. However, the list of poetic forms is not directly related to the rest of the sentence, so this should be clarified with punctuation. Dashes are the best way to mark this as a separate thought. Choice **(B)** correctly adds dashes to both the beginning and end of the list.

**2.    A**

**Difficulty:** Medium

**Category:** Development: Precision

**Getting to the Answer:** This sentence is correct as written. The author wants to convey the idea that the history of the haiku is complicated. Choice **(A)**, "complex," accurately conveys this thought. The words (B) "composite" and (C) "compound" both imply that something is made up of numerous smaller parts and do not describe history. Choice (D), "variegated," can mean either multicolored or various, neither of which makes sense as a way to describe history.

**3.    A**

**Difficulty:** Hard

**Category:** Development: Introductions and Conclusions

**Getting to the Answer:** Consider the purpose of the paragraph, then determine which answer choice makes the most sense as an introduction to the paragraph. The purpose of this paragraph, based on its other sentences, is to explain the history of haiku and how its structure has changed over time. Choice **(A)** is the only answer choice related to these ideas. While the other answer choices may briefly mention the structure of haiku or its history, they all focus on other aspects of haiku—its entertainment value, the difficulty of understanding its rules, or the challenge of writing it.

**4.    D**

**Difficulty:** Medium

**Category:** Development: Revising Text

**Getting to the Answer:** The sentence's placement in the passage is not optimal. The next sentence returns the discussion to the hokku form and readers encounter another explanation of the name "haiku" later, in paragraph 5. Choice **(D)** is correct because the sentence should be omitted from paragraph 2.

**5.    C**

**Difficulty:** Medium

**Category:** Organization: Sentence Placement

**Getting to the Answer:** Consider the information presented by the rest of the paragraph to determine the meaning of the phrase "alternating turns." Sentence 7 describes the specifics of different word games introduced in sentence 5, so it makes sense that it would follow sentence 5. Choice **(C)** is correct.

**6.    C**

**Difficulty:** Medium

**Category:** Organization: Transitions

**Getting to the Answer:** Make sure that this sentence clearly and precisely transitions from the topic of the previous paragraph to the topic of this paragraph. As currently written, the first sentence does not make a clear connection to the preceding paragraph. By making the discussion of time more precise, the beginning of this paragraph flows better from the previous one. The reader understands more clearly how the details in each paragraph connect. Choice **(C)** is correct.

**7.    D**

**Difficulty:** Medium

**Category:** Organization: Conciseness

**Getting to the Answer:** The original underlined portion is far wordier than is needed to convey its meaning. Choice **(D)** correctly communicates the information of this sentence without using excess words.

**8. D**

**Difficulty:** Hard

**Category:** Development: Relevance

**Getting to the Answer:** Find the answer choice that clearly supports the topic sentence of the paragraph. The topic sentence of this paragraph emphasizes the themes in Basho's work and how haiku became associated with nature and the seasons. Only **(D)** provides examples of nature-related subjects of Basho haiku and is therefore correct.

**9. C**

**Difficulty:** Hard

**Category:** Organization: Conciseness

**Getting to the Answer:** This sentence uses more words than needed to communicate its point. Combining ideas by making the second clause dependent creates a more concise sentence. Choice **(C)** is correct because it maintains the sentence's meaning while using fewer words. Choices (B) and (D) also make the second clause dependent, but include extra words such as "also."

**10. B**

**Difficulty:** Medium

**Category:** Development: Precision

**Getting to the Answer:** Consider the precise relationship between Shiki and the other poets mentioned. The correct answer choice will describe his effect on them. It seems clear that Shiki's work influenced cummings and Pound. While "helped" and "aided" both generally suggest that his effect on them was positive, "inspired" is more accurate. Shiki had left his mark, and the other poets learned from him. Choice **(B)** is correct.

**11. D**

**Difficulty:** Medium

**Category:** Organization: Transitions

**Getting to the Answer:** Read the sentence and determine whether its thoughts are joined logically. The two parts of the sentence are directly related; the writers are "taken with the brevity of the form" because of what it provides them. The sentence does not express this relationship as written, so eliminate (A). Eliminate (B) and (C) because neither choice correctly relates the two parts of the sentence. Choice **(D)** correctly combines the sentence while maintaining the relationship between the two clauses.

**12. B**

**Difficulty:** Medium

**Category:** Development: Precision

**Getting to the Answer:** Read the entire paragraph to determine if a career in physical therapy is rated as a good career choice by the Bureau of Labor Statistics. "Concurrently" means at the same time and "unusually" means not common. "Finally" implies that physical therapy was not a good career choice in the past. Choice **(B)** is correct because it means with regularity.

**13. D**

**Difficulty:** Medium

**Category:** Organization: Conciseness

**Getting to the Answer:** The sentence as written is unnecessarily wordy and includes a redundancy in the phrase "enjoyable and fun." Eliminate (A). Choices (B) and (C) both correct the redundancy but not the overall wordiness of the sentence, and both introduce new errors. Choice **(D)** is the most concise answer and is therefore correct.

**14. B**

**Difficulty:** Medium

**Category:** Development: Introductions and Conclusions

**Getting to the Answer:** Read the paragraph to identify its focus. The second paragraph discusses the process of becoming a physical therapist, including education and licensing. Choices (A), (C), and (D) each offer only one component of the paragraph, and (A) and (C) bring up off-topic details like foreign countries and requirements to be a physician. Only choice **(B)** effectively establishes the main topic of the second paragraph.

**15. A**

**Difficulty:** Easy

**Category:** Sentence Structure: The Basics

**Getting to the Answer:** When an entire sentence is underlined, check that the sentence is structurally sound. Make sure that any independent clauses, dependent clauses, and phrases are correctly joined. Choice (B) forms a run-on with two independent clauses connected without punctuation. (C) includes phrases connected to the sentence with semicolons rather than commas. (D) misuses both colons (not introducing information or ideas) and commas (separating subject from verb). Only the original sentence contains no punctuation errors, so **(A)** is correct.

**16. B**

**Difficulty:** Hard

**Category:** Development: Relevance

**Getting to the Answer:** Read the paragraph to determine its main topic. The topic sentence describes PTs working with a wide variety of patients, and the following sentences provide examples. Since **(B)** is the only sentence that describes potential patients, it is the correct answer. Choices (C) and (D) may be tempting because they both mention patients, but both discuss patients in the context of other topics—income and licensing, respectively—rather than focusing on the patients themselves.

**17. B**

**Difficulty:** Hard

**Category:** Agreement: Modifiers

**Getting to the Answer:** This sentence is complex, so spotting the error may be difficult. The modifier "minimally" describes the verb "interact" and so needs to be next to it. Choices (A) and (D) do not correct this error; eliminate them. Choice (C) corrects the error but introduces a different one by changing the adverb "minimally" to the adjective "minimal," which cannot modify a verb. Choice **(B)** correctly moves the modifier next to the word it modifies without introducing new errors.

**18. D**

**Difficulty:** Medium

**Category:** Development: Relevance

**Getting to the Answer:** As written, the text uses short, choppy sentences. Their topics are related, so combining them by making one no longer an independent clause will both make the paragraph smoother and show the relationship between ideas more clearly. Choice **(D)** is correct. Choice (C) may be tempting because it also makes the second sentence subordinate, but it introduces a comma error so is incorrect.

**19. B**

**Difficulty:** Hard

**Category:** Organization: Conciseness

**Getting to the Answer:** This sentence lists qualities necessary to being a physical therapist. There is no reason that medical knowledge should be set apart from the other qualities; doing so makes the sentence unnecessarily wordy and complex. Choice **(B)** correctly rearranges the sentence so that the four main ideas are combined in a single list, eliminating the unhelpful phrase "in addition to."

**20. A**

**Difficulty:** Easy

**Category:** Development: Precision

**Getting to the Answer:** Read the sentence and any necessary context to determine the meaning of the word. The sentence refers to "This interpersonal ... aspect" of physical therapy; the previous sentence describes how physical therapists "invite" their patients to be active participants. The underlined word must refer to patients and physical therapists working together. Choice **(A)** is correct.

**21. D**

**Difficulty:** Hard

**Category:** Organization: Sentence Placement

**Getting to the Answer:** When determining where to place a sentence, examine the sentence itself and the paragraph as a whole for clues. Sentence 2 summarizes the qualities a physical therapist needs; the paragraph as a whole describes what a physical therapist does and how those qualities impact their work. This suggests sentence 2 should go at either the beginning or the end of the paragraph. Eliminate (B) and (C). Placing sentence 2 at the beginning of the paragraph would disrupt the transition from the previous paragraph, so (A) is incorrect. Choice **(D)** correctly moves the summative sentence to conclude the paragraph.

## 22. D

**Difficulty:** Medium

**Category:** Development: Relevance

**Getting to the Answer:** Closely read the paragraph to find the central idea. Then, determine which sentence does not match the content. The evidence regarding physical therapy assistants does not connect with the main idea of this paragraph, which centers on the benefits of choosing to become a certified physical therapist. Choice **(D)** is correct.

## 23. B

**Difficulty:** Medium

**Category:** Agreement: Pronouns

**Getting to the Answer:** Consider the function of the underlined word in the sentence. The underlined word should be a plural possessive pronoun that refers to "coaches and trainers." Choice **(B)** is correct.

## 24. B

**Difficulty:** Medium

**Category:** Development: Precision

**Getting to the Answer:** Think about the overall meaning of the sentence. Consider which answer choice most closely matches the writer's intended meaning. The writer explains that some people connect, or equate, the exercise-prompted burning feeling with burning calories. "Equate" is the most precise word to convey this meaning. Choice **(B)** is correct.

## 25. B

**Difficulty:** Medium

**Category:** Organization: Transitions

**Getting to the Answer:** Consider the relationship between the thoughts expressed on either side of the semicolon. The writer presents contrasting ideas in this sentence. The relationship between these ideas is best expressed by inserting the transition word "instead" to indicate the contrast between the thoughts. Choice **(B)** is correct.

## 26. A

**Difficulty:** Hard

**Category:** Development: Introductions and Conclusions

**Getting to the Answer:** The correct answer will include an idea that ties together all the information in the paragraph. Paraphrase the central idea in your own words. This paragraph is primarily about how muscles use glucose to get the energy they need to move. Choice **(A)** is correct because it most effectively states the central idea.

## 27. C

**Difficulty:** Medium

**Category:** Agreement: Verbs

**Getting to the Answer:** Identify the noun in the clause. Determine whether the noun is singular or plural and what verb tense is used elsewhere in the sentence. The noun "cells" in this clause is plural, and the rest of the sentence is written in present tense. Choice **(C)** is correct because it features the plural present tense form of the verb.

## 28. B

**Difficulty:** Medium

**Category:** Sentence Structure: Commas, Dashes, and Colons

**Getting to the Answer:** Determine the function of the phrase "found in vinegar" within the sentence. Remember that nonrestrictive elements must be set off from the rest of the sentence with commas before and after. The phrase "found in vinegar" modifies "acetic acid" and is not essential to the understanding of the sentence. Choice **(B)** is correct.

## 29. D

**Difficulty:** Medium

**Category:** Development: Precision

**Getting to the Answer:** Reread the sentence with each of the answer choices in place of the underlined word. All of the answer choices are similar in meaning, so think about the connotation of each one in relation to the overall meaning of the sentence. In this sentence, the connotation of "irritates" most precisely communicates the meaning of what the writer is trying to convey to the reader: bothers. While "annoys" is similar to this meaning, it is mostly used when referring to people, not inanimate or biological objects like lactic acid. Choice **(D)** is correct.

**30. C**

**Difficulty:** Medium

**Category:** Development: Relevance

**Getting to the Answer:** Identify the central idea of paragraph 4. Think about which sentences are essential to understand the rest of the paragraph. The correct answer could be taken out without changing the meaning or the reader's understanding of the central idea. Although **(C)** is related to the central idea, the details in this sentence provide the least amount of support because they provide an example of a situation in which lactic acid builds up more quickly. The central idea of the paragraph, however, is the buildup and conversion of lactic acid during exercise. Choice **(C)** is correct.

**31. C**

**Difficulty:** Medium

**Category:** Sentence Structure: The Basics

**Getting to the Answer:** Determine whether two complete thoughts are expressed in this sentence. Two complete sentences, each with a subject and predicate, become a run-on without proper punctuation. As written, this is a run-on sentence. Placing a semicolon between the two complete thoughts makes the sentence grammatically correct. Choice **(C)** is correct.

**32. B**

**Difficulty:** Easy

**Category:** Agreement: Pronouns

**Getting to the Answer:** Make sure that related pronouns agree in number and person. In this sentence, the writer is referring to all human beings and uses "we" to do so. The underlined pronoun "you" does not match the use of the first person plural pronoun. Choice **(B)** is correct.

**33. C**

**Difficulty:** Hard

**Category:** Graphs

**Getting to the Answer:** The correct answer will both reflect the information presented in the graph and be an appropriate conclusion for the passage. Avoid answers like (B) that do not strengthen the central idea of the passage. Choice **(C)** is correct because it contains details presented in the graph that are relevant to the central idea of the passage and because it provides an appropriate conclusion to the passage.

**34. B**

**Difficulty:** Easy

**Category:** Agreement: Verbs

**Getting to the Answer:** As currently written, this sentence switches verb tense mid-sentence. The other verbs in the sentence, "was" and "took," indicate that the events happened in the past. The tense of the underlined verb should also be in past tense. Eliminate (A) and (D). The underlined verb forms a compound verb with "took," so their forms need to match. Choice **(B)** is correct because it uses the matching past tense.

**35. B**

**Difficulty:** Medium

**Category:** Organization: Transitions

**Getting to the Answer:** To choose the correct transition, look for the relationship between this sentence and the previous one. The previous sentence states that Impressionists sought to represent human perception. This sentence and the one that follows describe how Impressionists sought to capture how humans saw nature, giving an example of what kind of art the Impressionists were creating. Choice **(B)** shows the correct relationship between the two sentences.

**36. D**

**Difficulty:** Medium

**Category:** Development: Precision

**Getting to the Answer:** The writer wants to convey the idea that the Impressionists tried to paint exactly what they saw in nature. Only **(D)** has the correct connotation and fits within the context of the sentence. To "restate" something, choice (A), means to say it again a second time. Choice (B), "clone," means to make an identical genetic copy of something. Finally, (C), "counterfeit," means to imitate something with the intent to deceive.

**37. B**

**Difficulty:** Medium

**Category:** Agreement: Verbs

**Getting to the Answer:** When a sentence has paired verbs like these, the verbs have to be parallel. The correct answer must be in the same form as the first verb in the sentence, "looking." That means that the verb "attempting" in choice **(B)** is correct.

**38. A**

**Difficulty:** Easy

**Category:** Development: Precision

**Getting to the Answer:** Check each word for its connotations and pick the answer choice that fits the context of the sentence. This sentence describes how Post-Impressionists focused on self-discovery in art by letting their personal experiences and emotions guide their interpretation of their subjects. Therefore, each artist had his or her own distinct, or "unique," vision. The underlined portion is correct as written, so choice **(A)** is correct.

**39. C**

**Difficulty:** Medium

**Category:** Development: Introductions and Conclusions

**Getting to the Answer:** Read the entire paragraph and determine the central idea. The paragraph discusses different ways artists in the Post-Impressionism era painted. Choice **(C)** reflects this summary.

**40. B**

**Difficulty:** Hard

**Category:** Organization: Conciseness

**Getting to the Answer:** Choice **(B)** joins the sentences concisely and correctly by changing the verb tense of the first sentence to make it a dependent clause.

**41. A**

**Difficulty:** Easy

**Category:** Agreement: Pronouns

**Getting to the Answer:** Read the sentence prior to the pronoun to determine whom the pronoun is referencing. The pronoun "they" refers to Paul Gauguin and Vincent van Gogh, so the pronoun needs to be plural and in the third person. Choice **(A)** is correct.

**42. D**

**Difficulty:** Hard

**Category:** Development: Relevance

**Getting to the Answer:** Read the entire paragraph to identify the central idea. Then find the answer choice that provides evidence about this idea. The paragraph concerns the Post-Impressionist period and what kinds of methods Post-Impressionists used to create their art. Choice **(D)** addresses the central idea by providing additional information about these methods.

**43. B**

**Difficulty:** Medium

**Category:** Agreement: Idioms

**Getting to the Answer:** "They're" is a contraction meaning "they are," which does not make sense in the context of the sentence. What is needed here is a possessive plural pronoun to match the antecedent "artists." Choice **(B)** is correct.

**44. D**

**Difficulty:** Hard

**Category:** Organization: Sentence Placement

**Getting to the Answer:** When deciding where to place a sentence, examine both the sentence itself and the surrounding paragraph for clues. Sentence 3 discusses getting to know artists' souls by viewing their artwork. Additionally, it begins with the transition word "Today," which suggests in must come after anything the paragraph discusses from the past. Sentence 4 refers to "these differences." Since sentence 3 does not describe any differences to which this phrase could be referring, the sentence cannot be correct where it is; eliminate (A). Sentence 5 includes a quote about "pictures of the soul" that sentence 3 invokes with its mention of artists' souls. Thus, **(D)** is correct.

# PART 5

# SAT Essay

# CHAPTER 28

# The Method for the SAT Essay

## LEARNING OBJECTIVES

After completing this chapter, you will be able to:

- Make an informed decision about whether you will write the SAT Essay
- Map the prompt for its big picture and identify three specific features (techniques or types of evidence used)
- Recognize rhetorical features in the prompt to use in your essay
- Organize the features you choose into an essay outline
- State what the graders are looking for

## Should I Write the SAT Essay?

### LEARNING OBJECTIVE

After this lesson, you will be able to:

- Make an informed decision about whether you will write the SAT Essay

### Is the SAT Essay Optional?

The first thing most students point out about the SAT Essay is: *it's optional*. This is true, and whether you choose to write it will depend on a number of factors.

But there are colleges and universities that either recommend writing the SAT Essay or out-right require it. (Quite a few Ivy League, Big 10, and other highly rated institutions are among them.) An updated list of those schools can be found at the College Board website.

### Why Is There an SAT Essay?

Every college student is surrounded by opinions, in and out of class. Many are expressed by friends, fellow students, and professors around them. Others appear in books, articles, essays, documentary films, TV news shows, and other media.

Some opinions are casual (for example, "Liver tastes gross") and can be left at that. Other opinions, however, have wide-ranging consequences and need support. The process of backing up opinions ("conclusions") with support ("evidence") is called **argumentation** and will be at the heart of much of your college work. A key role of higher education is to prepare people for careers in which evidence-based decision making is central to success, and thus schools must emphasize reading arguments in a critical way. This means being able to evaluate various types of evidence and rhetorical devices.

The SAT Essay provides you an opportunity to show colleges and universities that you already know how to read arguments critically. The SAT Essay asks you to dig into the structure of an argument. You will need to not only understand the author's position, but also to analyze the building blocks of the argument that allow the author to hold that position.

## Should I Complete the SAT Essay?

Whether you choose to write the SAT essay will depend on these factors:

- *Do any of the colleges you are planning to apply to require the essay?* If yes, you must write it.

- *Do any of the colleges you are planning to apply to recommend the essay?* If yes, try to determine how heavily these schools' admissions boards weigh the essay score and act accordingly.

- *How much time do you have to prepare before test day?* The essay can be surprisingly time-consuming to master, especially if you are not already skilled in rhetorical analysis. If you are pressed for time, you may consider not writing the essay and using the time you have to prepare for the required sections of the SAT. On the other hand, if you have a lot of time between now and test day, preparing for and earning a high score on the essay can give you an advantage in the admissions process, even at colleges that don't require or recommend it.

- *How familiar are you with rhetoric and the structure of arguments?* If these are already areas of strength for you, then you may be able to prepare for the essay fairly quickly. In case you are unsure of the answer to this question, we've included a quick self-assessment below to help you determine how much you already know.

# Rhetorical Analysis Skills Assessment

**Directions:** In the space provided, jot down your responses to the following questions. When you've finished, turn the page and compare your thoughts to ours.

1.  The SAT Essay is based on an argument. What do you understand "argument" to mean in this context?

    _____

    _____

    _____

2.  What are the two explicit components of an argument?

    _____

    _____

    _____

3.  Briefly, what is your working definition of each one of the following:

    a.  Analogy

        _____

        _____

        _____

    b.  Counterexample

        _____

        _____

        _____

    c.  Appeal to Emotion

        _____

        _____

        _____

# Rheotrical Analysis Skills Assessment Responses

1. *The SAT Essay is based on an argument. In this context, what do you understand "argument" to mean?*

An argument, in this context, is *the attempt by a writer or speaker to persuade an audience of a point of view.* Whether a candidate wants your vote or a retail store wants your business, they must come up with an argument in favor of their position.

2. *What are the two explicit components of an argument?*

"Explicit" means "stated." An argument must state its **conclusion,** which is the personal point of view the author wants to persuade you of. It must also provide **evidence,** which is whatever facts, opinions, or statistics the author assembles in order to support the conclusion. You will sometimes hear the words **premises** or **reasons,** each of which means the same thing as "evidence."

Here's something else to remember: when someone talks about **reasoning**, they mean the process by which the author goes from the evidence to a conclusion. It's the "how" of the argument. When you write your SAT Essay, you will be examining the reasoning of the prompt.

3. *Briefly, what is your working definition of each one of the following?*

All three of these terms represent authorial tactics you may notice in your SAT Essay prompt. Each one you notice, and discuss, will make your essay stronger.

a. An **analogy** is a literary device, the assertion that two essentially different things have something significant in common. Here are two examples:

   • "Explaining a joke is like dissecting a frog." Why? Because each takes a lot of time and tedious effort, and by the time you're done, the essence of the original, whether joke or frog, is totally lost.

   • "The latest *Mission: Impossible* sequel is a roller coaster ride." This is true only in the sense that it offers, in someone's opinion, a lot of up-and-down emotional excitement.

b. A **counterexample** is evidence that undercuts—"counters"—someone's argument. The statement "All stars appear white in the night sky" can be disproved if even one star appears blue or red or some other color. Such a star would be a counterexample to the argument that all stars are white. Authors of SAT prompts often cite objections that could be made to their own arguments and then counter those objections. A counterexample is one technique for doing so.

c. An **appeal to emotion** is one kind of rhetoric. It tries to get the listeners to agree with the argument by manipulating their emotions on the topic. "Animals are mistreated every day. Please contribute to our animal rights organization." "Our town's centennial is being featured in the national media—come to the celebration next week and show the nation what we're made of!" "Look at our state's magnificent waterways and wildlife. Now imagine what would happen if we allow oil drilling." These arguments are appealing to empathy/pity, civic pride, and enjoyment of natural wonders, respectively. Are these bad? No. Many successful writers and speakers employ some kind of emotional appeal. But if all the argument has going for it is emotion, then it's not likely to be very persuasive.

   Other common types of appeal are these: *Appeal to Patriotism* (do this because it would help our nation), *Appeal to Authority* (do this because I, an expert, am suggesting it), *Appeal to Idealism* (do this because our best instincts tell us it's right), *Appeal to Urgency* (do this because the time is now and the clock is ticking), *Appeal to Statistics* (do this because the hard, cold numbers support it), and *Appeal to Hope* (do this because you will welcome the positive results).

# Essay Essentials

**LEARNING OBJECTIVES**

After this lesson, you will be able to:

- Map the prompt for its "Big Picture," and identify three specific features (techniques or types of evidence used)
- Given the Kaplan Essay Template, organize the points you'll make in an outline

## The Basics

The **prompt**—the subject of your analysis and writing—is a speech or article by a professional writer or other prominent person. The average length is 700–750 words. That person will be arguing for—that is, trying to persuade readers of—some specific viewpoint. The good news is that the test maker will tell you, flat out, what that viewpoint is; you won't need to deduce it from the article.

Most of the time the writer will be *recommending* a particular social or government policy or a personal behavior. Sometimes the writer will be *recommending against* a policy or behavior. And other times, very occasionally, the argument will be making a *prediction* of what may or may not happen.

Either way, the assignment is the same. In 50 minutes, you need to read the prompt, analyze how it's put together, and write an organized essay explaining how the prompt works. The graders give you scores on each of those tasks—reading, analyzing, and writing.

## The Format of the Prompt

It begins with a standard box of text that reads like this:

> As you read the passage below, consider how [name of author] uses
>
> - evidence, such as facts or examples, to support claims.
> - reasoning to develop ideas and to connect claims and evidence.
> - stylistic or persuasive elements, such as word choice or appeals to emotion, to add power to the ideas expressed.

After the introductory text box, there is a note providing the author, date, and origin of the prompt text, and the text itself. The paragraphs are numbered for your convenience, so you can refer the reader to the locations you desire ("In paragraph 3, he says..."). Most prompts are edited down from longer versions, and an ellipsis (...) is used to indicate where text has been removed. You need only consider the text that's present. Don't worry about anything edited out.

Finally, a text box explains the task. It always spells out exactly what the author's point or conclusion is, and tells you what they want you to do. For instance:

> Write an essay in which you explain how George W. Bush builds an argument to persuade his audience that his temporary worker program should be adopted by Congress. In your essay, analyze how Bush uses one or more of the features listed in the directions that precede the passage (or features of your own choice) to strengthen the logic and persuasiveness of his argument. Be sure that your analysis focuses on the most relevant features of the passage.
>
> Your essay should not explain whether you agree with Bush's claims, but rather explain how Bush builds an argument to persuade his audience.

You may annotate the prompt, or take notes in the margins, or use the last sheet for scratchwork.

**Important note:** The graders have to be able to read your writing. They will not read or consider your scratchwork, only the essay itself. You can write in cursive or block letters, whichever is more legible for you. If graders cannot read what you have written in the essay, then they will have to disregard it, which will most likely hurt your score.

## Suggested Essay Structure

Here's a structure that is an excellent basis for the SAT Essay assignment. If you understand and practice it, you won't waste time deciding how to arrange the paragraphs of your essay. The details of this structure will be discussed later in this chapter.

Paragraph 1—Restate the prompt's purpose, and then list the evidence types/rhetorical strategies you will discuss. (We recommend listing three.)

Paragraph 2—Mention one evidence type/rhetorical strategy, with examples and analysis.

Paragraph 3—Mention a second evidence type/rhetorical strategy, with examples and analysis.

Paragraph 4—Mention a third evidence type/rhetorical strategy, with examples and analysis.

Paragraph 5—Summarize the entire argument, in your own words.

Memorize this structure and use it on your practice essays. If you know the form of your essay beforehand, you just have to fill in the content on test day.

## SAT Essay Timing and Scoring

### Timing

You have 50 minutes to complete the essay. Here are some rough guidelines to get you started:

- Reading: 5 minutes
- Note-taking: 5 minutes
- Analyzing and Outlining: 8 minutes
- Writing: 30 minutes
- Quick Proofreading: 2 minutes

Don't be concerned if you have trouble executing your first couple of attempts in 50 minutes. In fact, in your first couple of practice essays, don't worry about time constraints at all and concentrate completely on the quality of your essay. Do still time yourself on these early practice essays so you have a benchmark for how close you are to 50 minutes. After you've written a few of these, you'll be able to shave off time, especially from the reading and analyzing tasks.

### Scoring

Two different graders will score your essay. Each will award you between 1 and 4 points in the categories of Reading, Analyzing, and Writing, and the two graders' points will be added together in each category. You'll get a Reading score between 2 and 8, an Analyzing score between 2 and 8, and a Writing score between 2 and 8. You'll learn more about what makes for a superior score later in this chapter.

The next lesson will focus on how to get the information you need to write an effective essay from the prompt.

# Dissecting the Prompt

> **LEARNING OBJECTIVES**
>
> After this lesson, you will be able to:
>
> • Recognize rhetorical features in the prompt to use in your essay
> • Organize the features you choose into an essay outline

## The Reading—5 Minutes

Always start with the box of directions *below* the prompt, where they spell out the author's purpose (usually, as we've said, some sort of recommendation). Immediately start thinking of how you'll put that purpose into your own words. Then jump into the prompt.

You may benefit from an initial quick skim, without note-taking. Try to *read with interest*, noting the general outline of the author's argument.

Get a casual sense of the author's tone and motives. It'll ease you into the prompt gently and lay the groundwork for your more important second pass through the material.

## Exercise

Take up to 5 minutes to read this prompt. Remember to start with the directions box below the passage itself.

> As you read the passage below, consider how Barack Obama uses
>
> • evidence, such as facts or examples
> • reasoning to develop ideas and to connect claims and evidence
> • stylistic or persuasive elements, such as word choice or appeals to emotion, to add power to the ideas expressed

**Adapted from U.S. President Barack Obama's address to the first session of Conference of the Parties 21 (COP21), the 2015 Paris Climate Conference, on November 30, 2015.**

1   Our understanding of the ways human beings disrupt the climate advances by the day. Fourteen of the fifteen warmest years on record have occurred since the year 2000— and 2015 is on pace to be the warmest year of all. No nation—large or small, wealthy or poor—is immune to what this means.

2   This summer, I saw the effects of climate change firsthand in our northernmost state, Alaska, where the sea is already swallowing villages and eroding shorelines; where permafrost thaws and the tundra burns; where glaciers are melting at a pace unprecedented in modern times. And it was a preview of one possible future—a glimpse of our children's fate if the climate keeps changing faster than our efforts to address it. Submerged countries. Abandoned cities. Fields that no longer grow. . . .

3   That future is one that we have the power to change. Right here. Right now. But only if we rise to this moment. As one of America's governors has said, "We are the first generation to feel the impact of climate change, and the last generation that can do something about it." . . .

4   Over the last seven years, [the U.S. has] made ambitious investments in clean energy, and ambitious reductions in our carbon emissions. We've multiplied wind power threefold, and solar power more than twentyfold, helping create parts of America where these clean power sources are finally cheaper than dirtier, conventional power. We've invested in energy efficiency in every way imaginable. We've said no to infrastructure that would pull high-carbon fossil fuels from the ground, and we've said yes to the first-ever set of national standards limiting the amount of carbon pollution our power plants can release into the sky. . . .

5   But the good news is this is not an American trend alone. Last year, the global economy grew while global carbon emissions from burning fossil fuels stayed flat. And what this means can't be overstated. We have broken the old arguments for inaction. We have proved that strong economic growth and a safer environment no longer have to conflict with one another; they can work in concert with one another.

6   And that should give us hope. One of the enemies that we'll be fighting at this conference is cynicism, the notion we can't do anything about climate change. Our progress should give us hope during these two weeks—hope that is rooted in collective action. . . .

7   So our task here in Paris is to turn these achievements into an enduring framework for human progress—not a stopgap solution, but a long-term strategy that gives the world confidence in a low-carbon future.

8   Here, in Paris, let's secure an agreement that builds in ambition, where progress paves the way for regularly updated targets—targets that are not set for each of us but by each of us, taking into account the differences that each nation is facing.

9   Here in Paris, let's agree to a strong system of transparency that gives each of us the confidence that all of us are meeting our commitments. . . .

10  Here in Paris, let's reaffirm our commitment that resources will be there for countries willing to do their part to skip the dirty phase of development. . . .

11  And finally, here in Paris, let's show businesses and investors that the global economy is on a firm path towards a low-carbon future. If we put the right rules and incentives in place, we'll unleash the creative power of our best scientists and engineers and entrepreneurs to deploy clean energy technologies and the new jobs and new opportunities that they create all around the world. There are hundreds of billions of dollars ready to deploy to countries around the world if they get the signal that we mean business this time. Let's send that signal. . . .

12   For I believe, in the words of Dr. Martin Luther King, Jr., that there is such a thing as being too late. And when it comes to climate change, that hour is almost upon us. But if we act here, if we act now, if we place our own short-term interests behind the air that our young people will breathe, and the food that they will eat, and the water that they will drink, and the hopes and dreams that sustain their lives, then we won't be too late for them....

13   Let's get to work. Thank you very much.

---

Write an essay in which you explain how President Obama builds an argument to persuade his audience that the Paris conference needs to take timely action on the matter of climate change. In your essay, analyze how he uses one or more of the features in the directions that precede the passage (or features of your own choice) to strengthen the logic and persuasiveness of his argument. Be sure that your analysis focuses on the most relevant features of the passage.

Your essay should not explain whether you agree with Obama's claims, but rather explain how Obama builds an argument to persuade his audience.

---

At the very least, your first pass through the prompt should have netted you the following information. The author's purpose (from the directions box): *to get the Paris conference attendees to take specific and immediate action on climate change.* Author's tone (from the passage itself): *urgently persuasive.* The context (from the bolded blurb at the beginning): *an opening speech at a 2015 conference.* Your job (from the directions box): *Explain how he puts together his argument to get them to take action.*

## The Note-Taking—5 minutes

Once you have an overall sense of the prompt, you're ready to start thinking it through, taking notes as you go.

Pencil in hand, go paragraph by paragraph, asking yourself what each block of text is doing there. Why has the author included it? What does it add to the argument? How does it relate to what came before and to what comes just after? If you can identify some rhetorical devices used, note them.

Here are a couple of things to keep in mind at this stage:

1.   You don't want to think about your essay as a whole. Wait a while. First get a sense of what is happening in each paragraph block. Then you can look for patterns.

2.   You don't need to incorporate every single paragraph, or every single rhetorical device, into your essay. If a paragraph strikes you as filler, or unimportant, or secondary, just skip past it and don't worry about it.

## Exercise

Take up to 5 minutes to analyze Obama's speech paragraph by paragraph and note the main points of each paragraph as well as any rhetorical devices you observe. Remember to stay focused on the *why* of the passage rather than the *what*. When you're done, compare your notes to the sample notes below.

**Adapted from U.S. President Barack Obama's address to the first session of Conference of the Parties 21 (COP21), the 2015 Paris Climate Conference, on November 30, 2015.**

1   Our understanding of the ways human beings disrupt the climate advances by the day. Fourteen of the fifteen warmest years on record have occurred since the year 2000—and 2015 is on pace to be the warmest year of all. No nation—large or small, wealthy or poor—is immune to what this means.

*Scary stat!*

*Affects everyone*

2   This summer, I saw the effects of climate change firsthand in our northernmost state, Alaska, where the sea is already swallowing villages and eroding shorelines; where permafrost thaws and the tundra burns; where glaciers are melting at a pace unprecedented in modern times. And it was a preview of one possible future—a glimpse of our children's fate if the climate keeps changing faster than our efforts to address it. Submerged countries. Abandoned cities. Fields that no longer grow. . . .

*Personal memory*

*Eloquent list of changes*

3   That future is one that we have the power to change. Right here. Right now. But only if we rise to this moment. As one of America's governors has said, "We are the first generation to feel the impact of climate change, and the last generation that can do something about it. . . ."

*Can still prevent disaster: call to action*

4   Over the last seven years, [the U.S. has] made ambitious investments in clean energy, and ambitious reductions in our carbon emissions. We've multiplied wind power threefold, and solar power more than twentyfold, helping create parts of America where these clean power sources are finally cheaper than dirtier, conventional power. We've invested in energy efficiency in every way imaginable. We've said no to infrastructure that would pull high-carbon fossil fuels from the ground, and we've said yes to the first-ever set of national standards limiting the amount of carbon pollution our power plants can release into the sky. . . .

*How US has been doing the right thing*

5   But the good news is this is not an American trend alone. Last year, the global economy grew while global carbon emissions from burning fossil fuels stayed flat. And what this means can't be overstated. We have broken the old arguments for inaction. We have proved that strong economic growth and a safer environment no longer have to conflict with one another; they can work in concert with one another.

*How the world has been doing the right thing. Old view: not enough $ to do it*

6   And that should give us hope. One of the enemies that we'll be fighting at this conference is cynicism, the notion we can't do anything about climate change. Our progress should give us hope during these two weeks—hope that is rooted in collective action. . . .

*Possible objection: nothing to be done
Answer: work together*

7   So our task here in Paris is to turn these achievements into an enduring framework for human progress—not a stopgap solution, but a long-term strategy that gives the world confidence in a low-carbon future.

*Let's go big or go home*

8    Here, in Paris, let's secure an agreement that builds in ambition, where progress paves    Go for big targets
the way for regularly updated targets—targets that are not set for each of us but by
each of us, taking into account the differences that each nation is facing.

9    Here, in Paris, let's agree to a strong system of transparency that gives each of us the    Repetition pounds
confidence that all of us are meeting our commitments. . . .    the call to action
Transparency

10    Here, in Paris, let's reaffirm our commitment that resources will be there for countries    Pool resources
willing to do their part to skip the dirty phase of development. . . .

11    And finally, here in Paris, let's show businesses and investors that the global economy    Must guide global
is on a firm path towards a low-carbon future. If we put the right rules and incentives    economy
in place, we'll unleash the creative power of our best scientists and engineers and
entrepreneurs to deploy clean energy technologies and the new jobs and new
opportunities that they create all around the world. There are hundreds of billions of
dollars ready to deploy to countries around the world if they get the signal that we    We have the means
mean business this time. Let's send that signal. . . .

12    For I believe, in the words of Dr. Martin Luther King, Jr., that there is such a thing as    Invoking Dr. King
being too late. And when it comes to climate change, that hour is almost upon us.    to underscore
But if we act here, if we act now, if we place our own short-term interests behind the    urgency
air that our young people will breathe, and the food that they will eat, and the water
that they will drink, and the hopes and dreams that sustain their lives, then we
we won't be too late for them. . . .

13    Let's get to work. Thank you very much.    Final, strong call
to action

## Expert Assessment of Sample Notes

Here is an assessment of this student's annotations so that you can get the best sense of the process.
Italicized numbers refer to paragraphs.

1    The student notes a "scary" statistic, thus noting an effect that the statistic is intended to have on the
audience. The student further notes that the purpose of the statistic is to let "everyone" at the conference
know that they will be affected by climate change.

2–3    Defines the second paragraph as a personal reminiscence; points out a fancy list of dire outcomes we can
look forward to, and a shift to the call to action.

4–5    Excellent one-phrase summaries of each  of these paragraphs. The student is not stopping to look for
patterns. (Finding  patterns is part of the next step, analyzing and outlining.)

6    Constantly asking "Why is he saying this?" the student notes a possible objection to the action Obama is
recommending—as well as the way to combat that objection, with group commitment.

7    The phrase "go big or go home" encapsulates what the author is implying.

8–11    Notes the repeated phrase and sums up each of the things Obama wants done "here in Paris."

12    "Eloquence plus" is one way to sum up Obama's eloquent phrases ending the speech on a high note. The
President is clearly not relying just on wonky statistics and policy recommendations. He's finding poetry in
the challenge to fix the global climate and deftly uses Dr. King's words for emphasis.

13    Student notes final call to action. Acting quickly, "here in Paris," is a running theme throughout the passage.

## The Analysis and Outline—8 Minutes

Now comes the most important part—and perhaps the trickiest part—for many students just starting to attempt the essay. Now you want to organize your thoughts: to group them together into idea blocks that will demonstrate your command of structure and help you write your essay effectively.

We recommend that you plan on an introduction, a conclusion, and three body paragraphs. Each of those paragraphs should focus on *one* type of evidence or rhetorical appeal that you've located in the prompt. That implies that you should identify three types.

You can make do with only two (and, thus, two body paragraphs). But if you carefully examine the published SAT Essays that the test makers have identified as high-scoring, you will notice that most if not all of them come up with three. And if you practice this a few times, you'll get better and better at it.

The key question to ask yourself is: *As I look at the tactics used and points made, are there three categories I can lump them into?* If you can find 2–3 items to list under each category, you've got all the evidence you need for a very strong essay.

Here are the various features the student noted in the Obama prompt above:

- Statistics and facts showing the bad news (about climate trends) and the good news (about what the U.S. and world have already done)
- A personal reminiscence—a time when the President saw firsthand the devastation of the Alaska wilderness
- A lot of fancy turns of phrase, designed to whip up emotional responses—almost preacher-like
- Specific goals and plans the delegates can focus on
- A lot of direct thrusts; here's what we have to do; the clock is ticking; no half-measures; get moving
- Past objections (it's too big a job; we can't afford it)
- Counterarguments to those objections (the job's not too big if we pull together; there IS enough money if we play our cards right)
- Expansive visions of the future if we are successful at this Conference

There are probably a few more, or other ways to phrase them, but that's already a fairly extensive list. All the student has to do now is pick out three—the three the student feels most confident about, interested in, easy to write on—and decide the order in which to mention them. For instance:

Paragraph 2—How Obama paints a grim picture of the current, and possible future, disasters facing the Earth

Paragraph 3—The good news so far: the U.S. has done its job; the world has too, to a degree; we know what needs to be done

Paragraph 4—Obama's employment of emotional, even church-like language to rev up the crowd

That would be one way to go. Here's another:

Paragraph 2—The emotional appeal: all the impassioned language and turns of phrase, which Obama includes from beginning to end

Paragraph 3—The positive reasons he provides for taking action now

Paragraph 4—The objections that have been or could be raised and how Obama's ideas counter them

Either of those structures would be perfectly fine. (Shortly, we'll share with you a sample essay written to still another paragraph structure.) For now, we would recommend that by the end of that 8 minutes of note-taking and analyzing, you will have decided on your three themes and started to assemble the order of the points you want to make in each paragraph.

### A word about the outline

You should use whatever type of outline makes you feel most comfortable and capable as you practice the essay, but it's unlikely that you'd create a "sentence outline," in which each roman numeral, capitalized, and lowercase point is written as a complete sentence: there just isn't time.

You may find it simpler to create a topic outline. Here, for instance, is a potential outline for a paragraph describing how President Obama paints a grim picture of the situation in 2015:

First body paragraph:

- Starts with scares in ¶1
  - 15 yr. trend
  - all countries
- Alaska
  - strong mental pictures for emotion ¶2
  - children affected
- obstacles to progress
  - cynicism/inaction/lack of will ¶6, ¶11

Alternatively, you may want to skip using an outline and instead label your margin notes. You can number your body paragraphs as I, II, and III (or A, B, and C). Put an A in the margin wherever you have a point to make in your first body paragraph, B for the next one, and so on.

Or you might choose to use an "idea map"—jot down points you want to make and then connect those thoughts with arrows that you can follow as you write.

Experiment with more than one method and go with the one that works best for you on test day.

# What the Graders Want

## Student Response

President Barack Obama's address to the 2015 Climate Conference in Paris comes across as a heartfelt plea for the assembled delegates to turn around what he clearly feels is the number one danger to our planet. He wants to appeal to both the heart and the head, so he employs not just factual evidence, but also personal experience and emotional language to rev up his audience.

The statistical evidence Mr. Obama cites is of two types and serves two different functions. In his very first paragraph he points out what he must feel is a frightening piece of data that will make people sit up, the 15 years since 2000 that show an overwhelming trend toward hotter and hotter temperatures. To make sure every delegate sits up, he reminds them that every country, "large or small, wealthy or poor," will have to live with those consequences. Soon after, however, he takes pains to cite many encouraging statistics. Paragraph 4 lays out some of what the United States has done, including reduce or discourage use of fossil fuel, commit to wind and solar, urge Americans to conserve, and put caps on carbon emissions. The next paragraph emphasizes that the U.S. is far from the only nation that has made positive strides. I sense that he feels that he will energize the crowd better not by harping on the doom and gloom of his opening, but by urging the delegates to stay on the right road that the world is already on. He also anticipates any objection that turning the situation around will be too costly, by directly stating that strong economies and a better environment "can work in concert."

Mr. Obama also wants the delegates to feel the personal pain of what's at stake in climate change, so he describes a trip to Alaska, which many people think of as America's last wilderness. There he witnessed the effects of earth's warming on the population and the geography. He doesn't mention wilderness animals but images of endangered polar bears and seals and such are surely evoked by his "preview" of what could happen if climate change outpaces human efforts to turn it around. Creating unhappy mental images in an audience's mind can make more of an impact than statistics, he seems to realize, especially in the litany of sorry situations with which paragraph 2 ends.

The crisp phrases "Submerged countries" and "Abandoned cities" in paragraph 2 are in line with "Right here. Right now" in paragraph 3. They bring in the kind of rhetorical snap with which Mr. Obama surely wants to hit them between the eyes at the urgency of the situation. "Hundreds of billions of dollars" isn't a statistic, it's a bit of overstatement that implies that if we have the will, we'll have the means. The repeated "Here in Paris" in the calls to four specific actions that the Conference could take, keeps reminding the audience that he is not just interested in making them feel bad, he wants them to act. "Act here...act now" he says in paragraph 12. It comes as no surprise that Dr. Martin Luther King, Jr.'s name is evoked, because Mr. Obama is using the same power of the pulpit Dr. King did, to get the world's sinners, meaning all of us, to mend our ways.

Mr. Obama's speech would probably end with great applause for the soaring list of the long-term issues that are at stake for later generations' air, food, water, and dreams. But he doesn't want applause, he wants results. Probably "Let's get to work" is the snappiest way he could fire up the delegates to get those results.

## Graders' Preferences and Analysis

The graders are trained to understand the College Board's stated criteria in particular ways so as to reduce the possibility of personal bias. By studying many graded essays and graders' comments, we have been able to compile the following list of what the graders tend to reward and what they tend to downgrade:

### Reading

| *Graders Tend to Reward:* | *Graders Tend to Downgrade:* |
| --- | --- |
| Expressing the author's central idea in your own words in the introduction to your essay | Restating the central idea in the author's own words, or presenting the central idea only late in the essay |
| Summarizing the particulars of the author's argument in your own words | Long quotations from the prompt or restating elements of the argument largely using the author's own words |
| Identifying relationships between details and the author's claims | Repeating details without considering their connection to the author's claims |
| Accurately reporting any facts or views that you choose to mention | Factual errors or distortions of authorial views |
| Sorting out the key individual issues involved | Leaving out key issues or blending several key issues together |

### Analyzing

| *Graders Tend to Reward:* | *Graders Tend to Downgrade:* |
| --- | --- |
| Clearly identifying rhetorical features/tactics employed (three seems to be the optimum number) | Failing to mention, or misidentifying, rhetorical features/tactics employed; or mentioning too few of them (choosing 3 seems to be very safe) |
| Identification of specific rhetorical features/tactics (e.g., "contrast," "appeal to . . . .," "analogy," "allusions to . . . .," "metaphor," "causality," "hypothetical") | Reliance on too-generic rhetorical features/tactics (for instance, "reasoning," "facts," "statistics," "word choice," "imagery") |
| Explaining those features' intended effect on readers | Omitting consideration of how and why those features were employed |
| Assessing the strength of the author's use of those features | Omitting consideration of whether the argument's points are effectively presented |
| Speculation as to the author's views or motives | Treating the author as an objective source of information, rather than as a person engaged in persuasion |
| A focus on the *why* and *how* of an argument | A focus on the *what* of an argument |

## Writing

| *Graders Tend to Reward:* | *Graders Tend to Downgrade:* |
|---|---|
| Clear, precise assertions | Unclear or vague assertions |
| Following a logical organizational structure | Meandering structure or stream-of-consciousness organization |
| Each paragraph organized around a single idea or theme | Paragraphs that take on too many disparate elements that don't fit together |
| Appropriately qualified statements | Overstatements or hyperbole |
| Correct grammar | Grammar errors that are noticeable and fixable even within a limited time frame |
| Interesting turns of phrase | Clichés and boring or obvious phrasing |
| A variety of sentence structures | Repetitious sentence structure |
| Complex sentences as appropriate | Run-ons, or overreliance on short, clipped sentences |
| A conclusion separate from the rest | A conclusion buried within the final paragraph |

SAT Essay

Now that you've looked over the criteria, let's go paragraph by paragraph through the student essay, with commentary.

| | |
|---|---|
| ¶1 President Barack Obama's address to the 2015 Climate Conference in Paris comes across as a heartfelt plea for the assembled delegates to turn around what he clearly feels is the number one danger to our planet. He wants to appeal to both the heart and the head, so he employs not just factual evidence, but also personal experience and emotional language to rev up his audience. | *¶1 The first sentence summarizes both the context (the conference) and the purpose (call to action), but in the student's own words. We get the three components that will be discussed, and in that order—facts, personal experience, emotional wording—which tells the reader that the essay will be well organized.* |
| ¶2 The statistical evidence Mr. Obama cites is of two types and serves two different functions. In his very first paragraph he points out what he must feel is a frightening piece of data that will make people sit up, the 15 years since 2000 that show an overwhelming trend toward hotter and hotter temperatures. To make sure every delegate sits up, he reminds them that every country, "large or small, wealthy or poor," will have to live with those consequences. Soon after, however, he takes pains to cite many encouraging statistics. Paragraph 4 lays out some of what the United States has done, including reduce or discourage use of fossil fuel, commit to wind and solar, urge Americans to conserve, and put caps on carbon emissions. The next paragraph emphasizes that the U.S. is far from the only nation that has made positive strides. I sense that he feels that he will energize the crowd better not by harping on the doom and gloom of his opening, but by urging the delegates to stay on the right road that the world is already on. He also anticipates any objection that turning the situation around will be too costly, by directly stating that strong economies and a better environment "can work in concert." | *¶2 Noting the two different types and functions of factual evidence shows that the student has thought through and categorized the text that will be cited in the essay. Overall, this paragraph is an excellent illustration of:*<br><br>• *Putting the author's ideas into your own words (e.g., the 15-year trend)*<br>• *Explaining why something's been mentioned (e.g., it's frightening)*<br>• *Emphasizing the intended effect on the audience (e.g., to make them pay attention and take action)*<br><br>*Note the very selective quotations from the speech. That shows care and thought.*<br><br>*Two side notes about word choice. The repeated "Mr. Obama" shows respect, but simply "Obama" would be acceptable. And it's okay to use the first person pronoun ("I sense that…") when you make a point that you particularly want the reader to realize is your opinion. It would be unfair to say, "He feels that he will energize…," as you can't know that for a fact. If you're uncomfortable with using "I," you could instead say, "He seems to feel that he will energize…" That would have the same effect.* |

¶3 Mr. Obama also wants the delegates to feel the personal pain of what's at stake in climate change, so he describes a trip to Alaska, which many people think of as America's last wilderness. There he witnessed the effects of earth's warming on the population and the geography. He doesn't mention wilderness animals but images of endangered polar bears and seals and such are surely evoked by his "preview" of what could happen if climate change outpaces human efforts to turn it around. Creating unhappy mental images in an audience's mind can make more of an impact than statistics, he seems to realize, especially in the litany of sorry situations with which paragraph 2 ends.

*¶3 Here is the second of the three argument elements, connected to the previous paragraph with the simple transition, "also wants the delegates to…" Obama's second paragraph is carefully put into the writer's own words. The last sentence here shows the student's understanding that a good essay will consider the why of an author's choices, not just the what.*

¶4 The crisp phrases "Submerged countries" and "Abandoned cities" in paragraph 2 are in line with "Right here. Right now" in paragraph 3. They bring in the kind of rhetorical snap with which Mr. Obama surely wants to hit them between the eyes at the urgency of the situation. "Hundreds of billions of dollars" isn't a statistic, it's a bit of overstatement that implies that if we have the will, we'll have the means. The repeated "Here in Paris" in the calls to four specific actions that the Conference could take, keeps reminding the audience that he is not just interested in making them feel bad, he wants them to act. "Act here… act now" he says in paragraph 12. It comes as no surprise that Dr. Martin Luther King, Jr.'s name is evoked, because Mr. Obama is using the same power of the pulpit Dr. King did, to get the world's sinners, meaning all of us, to mend our ways.

*¶4 Here is the analysis of the rhetorical devices used by Obama, carefully arranged in a logical order. Notice that the student has not for a moment forgotten the overall purpose of the speech: to get the delegates to act. It's brought up as often as possible.*

¶5 Mr. Obama's speech would probably end with great applause for the soaring list of the long-term issues that are at stake for later generations' air, food, water, and dreams. But he doesn't want applause, he wants results. Probably "Let's get to work" is the snappiest way he could fire up the delegates to get those results.

*¶5 The conclusion of an SAT Essay should be short. The graders already know what you think of the prompt. Finding a new way to summarize the whole, that doesn't sound redundant or clunky, takes practice and is never easy. This student has noticed that the main theme is encapsulated at the very end in the words "Let's get to work," which fortunately allows for a reminder of the prompt's purpose. Such a reminder is crucial to a good conclusion.*

*This conclusion is solid. But the good news is that if the rest of the essay is strong, a weak or problematic conclusion will likely not make a big difference to your scores.*

## Summary of Graders' Analysis

### Reading

This student manages to put both the central idea in Paragraph 1 (Obama's desire to spur the conference into action), and the summary of the whole argument in Paragraph 5, *into the student's own words,* which is crucial to scoring well in this category. There are no inaccuracies in the reporting, and every reported detail relates to some key point Obama is trying to make. (Example: "Hundreds of billions" in Paragraph 4, is recognized as more of a booster point than a hard statistic.) Finally, the student wisely minimizes direct quotations. The brief phrases quoted are few in number, but always relevant to a point the student is making. (Example: The four two-word phrases mentioned in Paragraph 4 as examples of "rhetorical snap" designed to grab the delegates' attention.)

### Analyzing

The student mentions three broad rhetorical features in Paragraph 1 and is always aware of how they're meant to affect readers. (Example: The Alaska trip is cited as a way to get the listeners emotionally engaged in the scientific dilemma.) The student speculates plausibly on Obama's motives (example: the reasoning as to why Obama keeps repeating "Here in Paris"). The reader leaves with no doubt that the student thinks Obama has argued strongly, which is not the same thing as the forbidden step of taking a side. (One can admire the strength of an argument whether or not one agrees with it.)

### Writing

The overall structure follows the [1. Facts 2. Emotions 3. Rhetoric] structure promised by Paragraph 1. Each paragraph properly takes up one of those, in order. The essay contains no notable grammar errors and the sentence structure is pleasingly varied, with a good mix of simple sentences and complex ones. There are some evocative turns of phrase ("appeal to both the heart and the head"; "rev up his audience"; "the doom and gloom of his opening"; "hit them between the eyes"; "get the world's sinners, meaning all of us, to mend our ways"). Finally, the conclusion, which appropriately summarizes the whole speech in new language, is correctly set apart from the rest of the essay.

### Next Steps

Try the SAT Essay prompt in the "How Much Have You Learned?" section of this chapter.

SAT Essay

# How Much Have You Learned?

We're leaving you with an additional prompt and, to extend your skills, a set of notes and outline that a student prepared from it:

> As you read the passage below, consider how George W. Bush uses
>
> - evidence, such as facts or examples
> - reasoning to develop ideas and to connect claims and evidence
> - stylistic or persuasive elements, such as word choice or appeals to emotion, to add power to the ideas expressed

**Adapted from U.S. president George W. Bush's address from the East Room of the White House on January 7, 2004.**

1   Many of you here today are Americans by choice, and you have followed in the path of millions. And over the generations we have received energetic, ambitious, optimistic people from every part of the world. By tradition and conviction, our country is a welcoming society. America is a stronger and better nation because of the hard work and the faith and entrepreneurial spirit of immigrants.

2   Every generation of immigrants has reaffirmed the wisdom of remaining open to the talents and dreams of the world. And every generation of immigrants has reaffirmed our ability to assimilate newcomers—which is one of the defining strengths of our country. . . .

3   During one great period of immigration—between 1891 and 1920—our nation received some 18 million men, women and children from other nations. The hard work of these immigrants helped make our economy the largest in the world. The children of immigrants put on the uniform and helped to liberate the lands of their ancestors. One of the primary reasons America became a great power in the 20th century is because we welcomed the talent and the character and the patriotism of immigrant families.

4   The contributions of immigrants to America continue. About 14 percent of our nation's civilian workforce is foreign-born. Most begin their working lives in America by taking hard jobs and clocking long hours in important industries. Many immigrants also start businesses, taking the familiar path from hired labor to ownership.

5   As a nation that values immigration, and depends on immigration, we should have immigration laws that work and make us proud. Yet today we do not. Instead, we see many employers turning to the illegal labor market. We see millions of hard-working men and women condemned to fear and insecurity in a massive, undocumented economy. The system is not working. Our nation needs an immigration system that serves the American economy, and reflects the American Dream. . . .

6   Today, I ask the Congress to join me in passing new immigration laws that reflect these principles, that meet America's economic needs, and live up to our highest ideals.

7   I propose a new temporary worker program that will match willing foreign workers with willing American employers, when no Americans can be found to fill the jobs. This program will offer legal status, as temporary workers, to the millions of undocumented men and women now employed in the United States, and to those in foreign countries who seek to participate in the program and have been offered employment here. This new system should be clear and efficient, so employers are able to find workers quickly and simply.

8   This program expects temporary workers to return permanently to their home countries after their period of work in the United States has expired. And there should be financial incentives for them to do so. I will work with foreign governments on a plan to give temporary workers credit, when they enter their own nation's retirement system, for the time they have worked in America. . . .

9   Some temporary workers will make the decision to pursue American citizenship. Those who make this choice will be allowed to apply in the normal way. . . .

10  The citizenship line, however, is too long, and our current limits on legal immigration are too low. Those willing to take the difficult path of citizenship—the path of work, and patience, and assimilation—should be welcome in America, like generations of immigrants before them. . . .

11  This new system will be more compassionate. Decent, hard-working people will now be protected by labor laws, with the right to change jobs, earn fair wages, and enjoy the same working conditions that the law requires for American workers. Temporary workers will be able to establish their identities by obtaining the legal documents we all take for granted. And they will be able to talk openly to authorities, to report crimes when they are harmed, without the fear of being deported.

12  . . . [O]ur country has always benefited from the dreams that others have brought here. By working hard for a better life, immigrants contribute to the life of our nation. The temporary worker program I am proposing today represents the best tradition of our society, a society that honors the law, and welcomes the newcomer. This plan will help return order and fairness to our immigration system, and in so doing we will honor our values, by showing our respect for those who work hard and share in the ideals of America.

---

Write an essay in which you explain how George W. Bush builds an argument to persuade his audience that his temporary worker program should be adopted by Congress. In your essay, analyze how he uses one or more of the features in the directions that precede the passage (or features of your own choice) to strengthen the logic and persuasiveness of his argument. Be sure that your analysis focuses on the most relevant features of the passage.

Your essay should not explain whether you agree with Bush's claims, but rather explain how Bush builds an argument to persuade his audience.

---

After reading through the President Bush prompt, you may want to consult the following notes and outline before writing your essay.

### Student's Three Elements/Devices

1. **Praises past and present contributions to immigrants**

   - Statistics and generalizations
   - Paragraph 3: Long tradition, back when 18 mill were welcomed. Grateful for svc in WWI and WWII (immig. kids)
   - Paragraph 4: Continues today, 14% of workforce. Many start as employees and end up employers.

   <u>Effect:</u> Puts facts behind rhetoric about immigrants – makes their contributions concrete & real

2. **Anticipates and rebuts criticisms**

   - Critics might say too costly, out of control bureauc. Paragraph 7: he wants "clear and efficient"
   - Expects temp workers to go back, but critics might worry about their welfare back home. Paragraph 8: we'll help smooth it out
   - Critics might say "you're not talking about citizenship." Yes he is: there are provisions for those who want to stay (Paragraph 9–10).

   <u>Effect:</u> Note he gets all of those out of the way before going on to list advantages in Paragraph 11. He really wants listeners to accept his plan so polishes off potential objections first.

3. **Uses rhetoric to connect plan to fundamental values**

   - Early as Paragraph 2 – U.S. welcomes immigrants
   - Paragraph 5 details current probs w/system, but a solution, same Paragraph, demanded by "Amer economy & Amer dream"
   - Paragraph 12: conclusion evokes "the best tradition of our society," "honor[ing] the law," & "shar[ing] in the ideals of America."

   <u>Effect:</u> wants to make his reform plan a moral imperative, not just a practical one. Implies whether you're worried about economy or fairness, this plan speaks to your concerns.

## Student's Opening Paragraph

To "sell" his immigration reform plan unveiled in early 2004, President Bush goes beyond the strict, narrow topic of the temporary worker to persuade the audience that immigrants in general need to be congratulated and protected. To do so, he praises their past and present contributions, anticipates and rebuts objections to his plan, and uses rhetoric to connect his plan to fundamental values of the U.S.

# PART 6

# Countdown to Test Day

# CHAPTER 29

# Countdown to Test Day

## The Week Before the Test

- Focus your additional practice on the question types and/or subject areas in which you usually score highest. Now is the time to sharpen your best skills, not cram new information.

- Make sure you are registered for the test. Remember, Kaplan cannot register you. If you missed the registration deadlines, you can request Waitlist Status on the test maker's website, collegeboard.org.

- Confirm the location of your test site. Never been there before? Make a practice run to make sure you know exactly how long it will take to get from your home to your test site. Build in extra time in case you hit traffic or construction on the morning of the test.

- Get a great night's sleep the two days before the test.

## The Day Before the Test

- Review the methods and strategies you learned in this book.

- Put new batteries in your calculator.

- Pack your backpack or bag for test day with the following items:
  - Photo ID
  - Registration slip or printout
  - Directions to your test site location
  - Five or more sharpened no. 2 pencils (no mechanical pencils)
  - Pencil sharpener
  - Eraser
  - Calculator
  - Extra batteries
  - Non-prohibited timepiece
  - Tissues
  - Prepackaged snacks, like granola bars
  - Bottled water, juice, or sports drink
  - Sweatshirt, sweater, or jacket

### The Night Before the Test

- No studying!
- Do something relaxing that will take your mind off the test, such as watching a movie or playing video games with friends.
- Set your alarm to wake up early enough so that you won't feel rushed.
- Go to bed early, but not too much earlier than you usually do. You want to fall asleep quickly, not spend hours tossing and turning.

### The Morning of the Test

- Dress comfortably and in layers. You need to be prepared for any temperature.
- Eat a filling breakfast, but don't stray too far from your usual routine. If you normally aren't a breakfast eater, don't eat a huge meal, but make sure you have something substantial.
- Read something over breakfast. You need to warm up your brain so you don't go into the test cold. Read a few pages of a newspaper, magazine, or favorite novel.
- Get to your test site early. There is likely to be some confusion about where to go and how to sign in, so allow yourself plenty of time, even if you are taking the test at your own school.
- Leave your cell phone at home. Many test sites do not allow them in the building.
- While you're waiting to sign in or be seated, read more of what you read over breakfast to stay in reading mode.

### During the Test

- Be calm and confident. You're ready for this!
- Remember that while the SAT is a three-hour marathon (or four if you opt to do the essay), it is also a series of shorter sections. Focus on the section you're working on at that moment; don't think about previous or upcoming sections.
- Use the methods and strategies you have learned in this book as often as you can. Allow yourself to fall into the good habits you built during your practice.
- Don't linger too long on any one question. Mark it and come back to it later.
- Can't figure out an answer? Try to eliminate some choices and take a strategic guess. Remember, there is no penalty for an incorrect answer, so even if you can't eliminate any choices, you should take a guess.
- There will be plenty of questions you *can* answer, so spend your time on those first.
- Maintain good posture throughout the test. It will help you stay alert.
- If you find yourself losing concentration, getting frustrated, or stressing about the time, stop for 30 seconds. Close your eyes, put your pencil down, take a few deep breaths, and relax your shoulders. You'll be much more productive after taking a few moments to relax.
- Use your breaks effectively. During the five-minute breaks, go to the restroom, eat your snacks, and get your energy up for the next section.

## After the Test

- Congratulate yourself! Then, reward yourself by doing something fun. You've earned it!

- If you got sick during the test or if something else happened that might have negatively affected your score, you can cancel your scores by the Wednesday following your test date. Request a score cancellation form from your test proctor or visit the test maker's website for more information.

- Your scores will be available online approximately two to four weeks after your test. The College Board sends scores to colleges 10 days after they are available to you.

# PART 7

# Practice Tests

# SAT Practice Test 1 Answer Sheet

**You will see an answer sheet like the one below on test day. Review the answer key following the test when finished.**

When testing, start with number 1 for each section. If a section has fewer questions than answer spaces, leave the extra spaces blank.

---

**SECTION 1**

| 1. Ⓐ Ⓑ Ⓒ Ⓓ | 14. Ⓐ Ⓑ Ⓒ Ⓓ | 27. Ⓐ Ⓑ Ⓒ Ⓓ | 40. Ⓐ Ⓑ Ⓒ Ⓓ |
| 2. Ⓐ Ⓑ Ⓒ Ⓓ | 15. Ⓐ Ⓑ Ⓒ Ⓓ | 28. Ⓐ Ⓑ Ⓒ Ⓓ | 41. Ⓐ Ⓑ Ⓒ Ⓓ |
| 3. Ⓐ Ⓑ Ⓒ Ⓓ | 16. Ⓐ Ⓑ Ⓒ Ⓓ | 29. Ⓐ Ⓑ Ⓒ Ⓓ | 42. Ⓐ Ⓑ Ⓒ Ⓓ |
| 4. Ⓐ Ⓑ Ⓒ Ⓓ | 17. Ⓐ Ⓑ Ⓒ Ⓓ | 30. Ⓐ Ⓑ Ⓒ Ⓓ | 43. Ⓐ Ⓑ Ⓒ Ⓓ |
| 5. Ⓐ Ⓑ Ⓒ Ⓓ | 18. Ⓐ Ⓑ Ⓒ Ⓓ | 31. Ⓐ Ⓑ Ⓒ Ⓓ | 44. Ⓐ Ⓑ Ⓒ Ⓓ |
| 6. Ⓐ Ⓑ Ⓒ Ⓓ | 19. Ⓐ Ⓑ Ⓒ Ⓓ | 32. Ⓐ Ⓑ Ⓒ Ⓓ | 45. Ⓐ Ⓑ Ⓒ Ⓓ |
| 7. Ⓐ Ⓑ Ⓒ Ⓓ | 20. Ⓐ Ⓑ Ⓒ Ⓓ | 33. Ⓐ Ⓑ Ⓒ Ⓓ | 46. Ⓐ Ⓑ Ⓒ Ⓓ |
| 8. Ⓐ Ⓑ Ⓒ Ⓓ | 21. Ⓐ Ⓑ Ⓒ Ⓓ | 34. Ⓐ Ⓑ Ⓒ Ⓓ | 47. Ⓐ Ⓑ Ⓒ Ⓓ |
| 9. Ⓐ Ⓑ Ⓒ Ⓓ | 22. Ⓐ Ⓑ Ⓒ Ⓓ | 35. Ⓐ Ⓑ Ⓒ Ⓓ | 48. Ⓐ Ⓑ Ⓒ Ⓓ |
| 10. Ⓐ Ⓑ Ⓒ Ⓓ | 23. Ⓐ Ⓑ Ⓒ Ⓓ | 36. Ⓐ Ⓑ Ⓒ Ⓓ | 49. Ⓐ Ⓑ Ⓒ Ⓓ |
| 11. Ⓐ Ⓑ Ⓒ Ⓓ | 24. Ⓐ Ⓑ Ⓒ Ⓓ | 37. Ⓐ Ⓑ Ⓒ Ⓓ | 50. Ⓐ Ⓑ Ⓒ Ⓓ |
| 12. Ⓐ Ⓑ Ⓒ Ⓓ | 25. Ⓐ Ⓑ Ⓒ Ⓓ | 38. Ⓐ Ⓑ Ⓒ Ⓓ | 51. Ⓐ Ⓑ Ⓒ Ⓓ |
| 13. Ⓐ Ⓑ Ⓒ Ⓓ | 26. Ⓐ Ⓑ Ⓒ Ⓓ | 39. Ⓐ Ⓑ Ⓒ Ⓓ | 52. Ⓐ Ⓑ Ⓒ Ⓓ |

☐ # correct in Section 1

☐ # incorrect in Section 1

**SECTION 2**

| 1. Ⓐ Ⓑ Ⓒ Ⓓ | 12. Ⓐ Ⓑ Ⓒ Ⓓ | 23. Ⓐ Ⓑ Ⓒ Ⓓ | 34. Ⓐ Ⓑ Ⓒ Ⓓ |
| 2. Ⓐ Ⓑ Ⓒ Ⓓ | 13. Ⓐ Ⓑ Ⓒ Ⓓ | 24. Ⓐ Ⓑ Ⓒ Ⓓ | 35. Ⓐ Ⓑ Ⓒ Ⓓ |
| 3. Ⓐ Ⓑ Ⓒ Ⓓ | 14. Ⓐ Ⓑ Ⓒ Ⓓ | 25. Ⓐ Ⓑ Ⓒ Ⓓ | 36. Ⓐ Ⓑ Ⓒ Ⓓ |
| 4. Ⓐ Ⓑ Ⓒ Ⓓ | 15. Ⓐ Ⓑ Ⓒ Ⓓ | 26. Ⓐ Ⓑ Ⓒ Ⓓ | 37. Ⓐ Ⓑ Ⓒ Ⓓ |
| 5. Ⓐ Ⓑ Ⓒ Ⓓ | 16. Ⓐ Ⓑ Ⓒ Ⓓ | 27. Ⓐ Ⓑ Ⓒ Ⓓ | 38. Ⓐ Ⓑ Ⓒ Ⓓ |
| 6. Ⓐ Ⓑ Ⓒ Ⓓ | 17. Ⓐ Ⓑ Ⓒ Ⓓ | 28. Ⓐ Ⓑ Ⓒ Ⓓ | 39. Ⓐ Ⓑ Ⓒ Ⓓ |
| 7. Ⓐ Ⓑ Ⓒ Ⓓ | 18. Ⓐ Ⓑ Ⓒ Ⓓ | 29. Ⓐ Ⓑ Ⓒ Ⓓ | 40. Ⓐ Ⓑ Ⓒ Ⓓ |
| 8. Ⓐ Ⓑ Ⓒ Ⓓ | 19. Ⓐ Ⓑ Ⓒ Ⓓ | 30. Ⓐ Ⓑ Ⓒ Ⓓ | 41. Ⓐ Ⓑ Ⓒ Ⓓ |
| 9. Ⓐ Ⓑ Ⓒ Ⓓ | 20. Ⓐ Ⓑ Ⓒ Ⓓ | 31. Ⓐ Ⓑ Ⓒ Ⓓ | 42. Ⓐ Ⓑ Ⓒ Ⓓ |
| 10. Ⓐ Ⓑ Ⓒ Ⓓ | 21. Ⓐ Ⓑ Ⓒ Ⓓ | 32. Ⓐ Ⓑ Ⓒ Ⓓ | 43. Ⓐ Ⓑ Ⓒ Ⓓ |
| 11. Ⓐ Ⓑ Ⓒ Ⓓ | 22. Ⓐ Ⓑ Ⓒ Ⓓ | 33. Ⓐ Ⓑ Ⓒ Ⓓ | 44. Ⓐ Ⓑ Ⓒ Ⓓ |

☐ # correct in Section 2

☐ # incorrect in Section 2

# Reading Test

## 65 Minutes—52 Questions

This section corresponds to Section 1 of your answer sheet.

**Directions:** Read each passage or pair of passages, then answer the questions that follow. Choose your answers based on what the passage(s) and any accompanying graphics state or imply.

**Questions 1-10 are based on the following passage.**

The following passage is adapted from Leo Tolstoy's 1873 novel, *Anna Karenina* (translated from the original Russian by Constance Garnett). Prior to this excerpt, one of the major characters, Levin, has realized that he is in love with his longtime friend Kitty Shtcherbatsky.

At four o'clock, conscious of his throbbing heart, Levin stepped out of a hired sledge at the Zoological Gardens, and turned along the path to the frozen mounds and the skating ground, knowing that he
5 would certainly find her there, as he had seen the Shtcherbatskys' carriage at the entrance.

It was a bright, frosty day. Rows of carriages, sledges, drivers, and policemen were standing in the approach. Crowds of well-dressed people, with hats
10 bright in the sun, swarmed about the entrance and along the well-swept little paths between the little houses adorned with carving in the Russian style. The old curly birches of the gardens, all their twigs laden with snow, looked as though freshly decked
15 in sacred vestments.

He walked along the path towards the skating-ground, and kept saying to himself—"You mustn't be excited, you must be calm. What's the matter with you? What do you want? Be quiet, stupid,"
20 he conjured his heart. And the more he tried to compose himself, the more breathless he found himself. An acquaintance met him and called him by his name, but Levin did not even recognize him. He went towards the mounds, whence came
25 the clank of the chains of sledges as they slipped down or were dragged up, the rumble of the sliding sledges, and the sounds of merry voices. He walked on a few steps, and the skating-ground lay open before his eyes, and at once, amidst all the skaters,
30 he knew her.

He knew she was there by the rapture and the terror that seized on his heart. She was standing talking to a lady at the opposite end of the ground. There was apparently nothing striking either in
35 her dress or her attitude. But for Levin she was as easy to find in that crowd as a rose among nettles. Everything was made bright by her. She was the smile that shed light on all round her. "Is it possible I can go over there on the ice, go up to her?" he
40 thought. The place where she stood seemed to him a holy shrine, unapproachable, and there was one moment when he was almost retreating, so overwhelmed was he with terror. He had to make an effort to master himself, and to remind himself
45 that people of all sorts were moving about her, and that he too might come there to skate. He walked down, for a long while avoiding looking at her as at the sun, but seeing her, as one does the sun, without looking.

50 On that day of the week and at that time of day people of one set, all acquainted with one another, used to meet on the ice. There were crack skaters there, showing off their skill, and learners clinging to chairs with timid, awkward movements, boys,
55 and elderly people skating with hygienic motives. They seemed to Levin an elect band of blissful beings because they were here, near her. All the skaters, it seemed, with perfect self-possession, skated towards her, skated by her, even spoke to her,
60 and were happy, quite apart from her, enjoying the capital ice and the fine weather.

Nikolay Shtcherbatsky, Kitty's cousin, in a short jacket and tight trousers, was sitting on a garden seat with his skates on. Seeing Levin, he shouted
65 to him:

"Ah, the first skater in Russia! Been here long? First-rate ice—do put your skates on."

GO ON TO THE NEXT PAGE

1. According to the passage, how did Levin first know that Kitty was at the Zoological Gardens?

   A) Kitty's carriage was parked near the entrance.

   B) Nikolay said he had been skating with Kitty earlier.

   C) He saw her talking with another woman near the pond.

   D) Kitty invited him to meet her there at a certain time.

2. As used in line 10, "swarmed" most nearly means

   A) invaded.

   B) gathered.

   C) flew.

   D) obstructed.

3. The passage most strongly suggests that which of the following is true of Levin?

   A) He worries about his appearance.

   B) He wants Kitty to be more enthusiastic.

   C) He is a very passionate person.

   D) He is wary of his surroundings.

4. Which choice provides the best evidence for the answer to the previous question?

   A) Lines 7–12 ("It was a bright, frosty day . . . in the Russian style")

   B) Lines 22–27 ("An acquaintance met him . . . merry voices")

   C) Lines 40–46 ("The place where . . . there to skate")

   D) Lines 50–55 ("On that day . . . hygienic motives")

5. What theme does the passage communicate through the experiences of Levin?

   A) Love is a powerful emotion.

   B) People long to have company.

   C) Life should be filled with joy.

   D) People are meant to work hard.

6. The passage most strongly suggests that which of the following is true of how Levin appears to others?

   A) People think that Levin looks agitated because of the way he is acting.

   B) People think that Levin is sick because he seems to be feverish.

   C) People think that Levin seems normal because he is doing nothing unusual.

   D) People think that Levin is in trouble because he is not protecting himself emotionally.

7. Which choice provides the best evidence for the answer to the previous question?

   A) Lines 1–6 ("At four o'clock . . . at the entrance")

   B) Lines 9–12 ("Crowds . . . the Russian style")

   C) Lines 24–30 ("He went . . . he knew her")

   D) Lines 62–67 ("Nikolay Shtcherbatsky . . . your skates on")

8. As used in line 20, "conjured" most nearly means

   A) begged.

   B) created.

   C) summoned.

   D) tricked.

9. The author's use of the word "throbbing" in line 1 implies that Levin

   A) has cut himself badly.

   B) has a sudden pain in his chest.

   C) is about to collapse.

   D) is in an agitated state.

10. Based on the tone of this passage, what emotion does the author wish the reader to feel about Levin?

    A) Empathy

    B) Cynicism

    C) Hostility

    D) Disgust

GO ON TO THE NEXT PAGE ⟹

**Questions 11-20 are based on the following passage.**

This passage is adapted from a speech delivered by President Franklin Roosevelt on January 6, 1941, to the United States Congress. In the passage, Roosevelt reveals his intention to preserve and spread American ideals around the world.

The Nation takes great satisfaction and much strength from the things which have been done to make its people conscious of their individual stake in the preservation of democratic life in America.

5 Those things have toughened the fibre of our people, have renewed their faith and strengthened their devotion to the institutions we make ready to protect.

Certainly this is no time for any of us to stop
10 thinking about the social and economic problems which are the root cause of the social revolution which is today a supreme factor in the world.

For there is nothing mysterious about the foundations of a healthy and strong democracy. The
15 basic things expected by our people of their political and economic systems are simple. They are:

• Equality of opportunity for youth and for others.

• Jobs for those who can work.

• Security for those who need it.

20 • The ending of special privilege for the few.

• The preservation of civil liberties for all.

• The enjoyment of the fruits of scientific progress in a wider and constantly rising standard of living.

These are the simple, basic things that must never
25 be lost sight of in the turmoil and unbelievable complexity of our modern world. The inner and abiding strength of our economic and political systems is dependent upon the degree to which they fulfill these expectations.

30 Many subjects connected with our social economy call for immediate improvement.

As examples:

• We should bring more citizens under the coverage of old-age pensions and unemployment insurance.

35 • We should widen the opportunities for adequate medical care.

• We should plan a better system by which persons deserving or needing gainful employment may obtain it.

40 I have called for personal sacrifice. I am assured of the willingness of almost all Americans to respond to that call.

A part of the sacrifice means the payment of more money in taxes. In my Budget Message I shall
45 recommend that a greater portion of this great defense program be paid for from taxation than we are paying today. No person should try, or be allowed, to get rich out of this program; and the principle of tax payments in accordance with ability
50 to pay should be constantly before our eyes to guide our legislation.

If the Congress maintains these principles, the voters, putting patriotism ahead of pocketbooks, will give you their applause.

55 In the future days, which we seek to make secure, we look forward to a world founded upon four essential human freedoms.

The first is freedom of speech and expression—everywhere in the world.

60 The second is freedom of every person to worship God in his own way—everywhere in the world.

The third is freedom from want—which, translated into world terms, means economic understandings which will secure to every nation
65 a healthy peacetime life for its inhabitants—everywhere in the world.

The fourth is freedom from fear—which, translated into world terms, means a world-wide reduction of armaments to such a point and in
70 such a thorough fashion that no nation will be in a position to commit an act of physical aggression against any neighbor—anywhere in the world.

That is no vision of a distant millennium. It is a definite basis for a kind of world attainable in our
75 own time and generation. That kind of world is the very antithesis of the so-called new order of tyranny which the dictators seek to create with the crash of a bomb.

To that new order we oppose the greater
80 conception—the moral order. A good society is able to face schemes of world domination and foreign revolutions alike without fear.

GO ON TO THE NEXT PAGE

Since the beginning of our American history, we have been engaged in change—in a perpetual
85 peaceful revolution—a revolution which goes on steadily, quietly adjusting itself to changing conditions—without the concentration camp or the quick-lime in the ditch. The world order which we seek is the cooperation of free countries, working
90 together in a friendly, civilized society.

This nation has placed its destiny in the hands and heads and hearts of its millions of free men and women; and its faith in freedom under the guidance of God. Freedom means the supremacy of human
95 rights everywhere. Our support goes to those who struggle to gain those rights or keep them. Our strength is our unity of purpose. To that high concept there can be no end save victory.

11. The primary purpose of President Roosevelt's speech is to

   A) highlight the individuality inherent in patriotism.

   B) define the basic needs of the country.

   C) request money to support worthy causes.

   D) promote support for essential human rights.

12. Which choice provides the best evidence for the answer to the previous question?

   A) Lines 14–16 ("The basic things . . . are simple")

   B) Lines 30–31 ("Many subjects . . . improvement")

   C) Lines 52–54 ("If the Congress . . . applause")

   D) Lines 55–57 ("In the future days . . . freedoms")

13. As used in line 40, "sacrifice" most nearly means

   A) religious offerings to a deity.

   B) service in the military.

   C) losses of limbs in battle.

   D) surrender of interests to a greater good.

14. The passage most strongly suggests a relationship between which of the following?

   A) Protection of human rights abroad and military service

   B) Spread of freedom abroad and defense of democracy at home

   C) Defeat of tyrants abroad and establishment of democratic government at home

   D) Investment in global democracies abroad and strengthening of patriotism at home

15. Which choice provides the best evidence for the answer to the previous question?

   A) Lines 24–29 ("These are . . . expectations")

   B) Lines 52–54 ("If the Congress . . . applause")

   C) Lines 73–78 ("That is no . . . of a bomb")

   D) Lines 94–97 ("Freedom means . . . unity of purpose")

16. In line 53, "pocketbooks" most nearly refers to

   A) local, state, and national taxes.

   B) war debt accumulated by the nation.

   C) citizens' individual monetary interests.

   D) Americans' personal investment in the defense industry.

17. In lines 73–75 ("That is no . . . generation"), President Roosevelt is most likely responding to what counterclaim to his own argument?

   A) The spread of global democracy is idealistic and unrealistic.

   B) The defeat of tyrannical dictators in Europe is implausible.

   C) The commitment of the American people to the war effort is limited.

   D) The resources of the United States are insufficient to wage war abroad.

GO ON TO THE NEXT PAGE ⟩

18. Which choice offers evidence that the spread of global democracy is achievable?

   A) Lines 47–48 ("No person . . . this program")

   B) Lines 56–57 ("we look forward . . . human freedoms")

   C) Lines 83–84 ("Since the beginning . . . in change")

   D) Line 97 ("Our strength . . . purpose")

19. In lines 62–66 ("The third is . . . world"), President Roosevelt sets a precedent by which he would most likely support which of the following policies?

   A) Military defense of political borders

   B) Investment in overseas business ventures

   C) Aid to nations struggling due to conflict and other causes

   D) Reduction of domestic services to spur job growth

20. The function of the phrase "the so-called new order of tyranny" in line 76 is to

   A) connect the global conflict for human rights to citizens on a personal level.

   B) demonstrate the power of the global opposition to the United States.

   C) present an alternative vision of the world without democracy.

   D) provide examples of the political and social revolutions underway.

**Questions 21-31 are based on the following passage and supplementary material.**

The United States Constitution has been amended 27 times since its ratification. Rights such as freedom of speech, religion, and press, for example, are granted by the First Amendment. This passage focuses on the Nineteenth Amendment, which gave women the right to vote.

The American political landscape is constantly shifting on a myriad of issues, but the voting process itself has changed over the years as well. Electronic ballot casting, for example, provides the

5  public with instantaneous results, and statisticians are more accurate than ever at forecasting our next president. Voting has always been viewed as an intrinsic American right and was one of the major reasons for the nation's secession from Britain's

10  monarchical rule. Unfortunately, although all men were constitutionally deemed "equal," true equality of the sexes was not extended to the voting booth until 1920.

The American women's suffrage movement

15  began in 1848, when Elizabeth Cady Stanton and Lucretia Mott organized the Seneca Falls Convention. The meeting, initially an attempt to have an open dialogue about women's rights, drew a crowd of nearly three hundred women and

20  included several dozen men. Topics ranged from a woman's role in society to law, but the issue of voting remained a contentious one. A freed slave named Frederick Douglass spoke eloquently about the importance of women in politics and swayed

25  the opinion of those in attendance. At the end of the convention, one hundred people signed the Seneca Falls Declaration, which demanded "immediate admission to all the rights and privileges which belong to [women] as citizens of the United States."

30  Stanton and Mott's first victory came thirty years later when a constitutional amendment allowing women to vote was proposed to Congress in 1878. Unfortunately, election practices were already a controversial issue, as unfair laws that diminished

35  the African American vote had been passed during Reconstruction. Questionable literacy tests and a "vote tax" levied against the poor kept minority turnout to a minimum. And while several states

allowed women to vote, federal consensus was
40 hardly as equitable. The rest of the world, however,
was taking note—and women were ready to act.

In 1893, New Zealand allowed women the right
to vote, although women could not run for office
in New Zealand. Other countries began reviewing
45 and ratifying their own laws as well. The United
Kingdom took small steps by allowing married
women to vote in local elections in 1894. By 1902,
all women in Australia could vote in elections, both
local and parliamentary.

50 The suffrage movement in America slowly built
momentum throughout the early twentieth century
and exploded during World War I. President
Woodrow Wilson called the fight abroad a war
for democracy, which many suffragettes viewed as
55 hypocritical. Democracy, after all, was hardly worth
fighting for when half of a nation's population was
disqualified based on gender. Public acts of civil
disobedience, rallies, and marches galvanized pro-
women advocates while undermining defenders
60 of the status quo. Posters read "Kaiser Wilson"
and called into question the authenticity of a free
country with unjust laws. The cry for equality
was impossible to ignore and, in 1919, with the
support of President Wilson, Congress passed the
65 Nineteenth Amendment to the Constitution. It was
ratified one year later by three-quarters of the states,
effectively changing the Constitution. Only one
signatory from the original Seneca Falls Declaration
lived long enough to cast her first ballot in a federal
70 election.

America's election laws were far from equal
for all, as tactics to dissuade or prohibit African
Americans from effectively voting were still
routinely employed. However, the suffrage
75 movement laid the groundwork for future
generations. Laws, like people's minds, could
change over time. The civil rights movement in the
mid- to late-twentieth century brought an end to
segregation and so-called Jim Crow laws that stifled
80 African American advancement. The Voting Rights
Act of 1965 signaled the end of discriminatory
voting laws; what emerged was a free nation guided
by elections in which neither skin color nor gender
mattered, but only the will of all citizens.

**Women's Suffrage in the United States**

1848 ➤ Seneca Falls Convention.

1878 ➤ 19th Amendment submitted; not ratified.

1911 ➤ Several states now grant women suffrage.

1914 ➤ Start of World War I.

1917 ➤ Picketing at the White House.

1918 ➤ Amendment passes in the House but fails in the Senate.

1919 ➤ Both the House and Senate pass the amendment.

1920 ➤ 19th Amendment ratified.

21. The stance the author takes in the passage is best described as that of

A) an advocate of women's suffrage proposing a constitutional amendment.

B) a legislator reviewing the arguments for and against women's suffrage.

C) a scholar evaluating the evolution and impact of the women's suffrage movement.

D) a historian summarizing the motivations of women's suffrage leaders.

22. Lines 71–72 ("America's election laws . . . equal for all") most clearly support which claim?

A) The founders of the Constitution did not provide for free and fair elections.

B) The United States still had work to do to secure equal voting rights for some people.

C) Most women in the United States did not want suffrage and equal rights.

D) The women's suffrage movement perpetuated discriminatory voting laws.

GO ON TO THE NEXT PAGE ⟹

23. Which choice provides the best evidence for the answer to the previous question?

    A) Lines 14–15 ("The American . . . in 1848")

    B) Lines 42–43 ("In 1893 . . . to vote")

    C) Lines 64–65 ("Congress . . . the Constitution")

    D) Lines 80–81 ("The Voting Rights Act . . . voting laws")

24. As used in line 58, "galvanized" most nearly means

    A) displaced.

    B) divided.

    C) excited.

    D) organized.

25. The function of lines 76–77 ("Laws, like . . . could change") is to

    A) connect the success of legislative reform with shifts in public sentiment.

    B) dissuade reformers from focusing on grassroots activity rather than political campaigns.

    C) evaluate the effectiveness of judicial rulings based on popular response to public polls.

    D) reject the need for legal actions and court proceedings to attain social change.

26. The passage most strongly suggests that

    A) the American government adapts to the changing needs and ideas of society.

    B) the best-organized reform movements are most likely to achieve their goals.

    C) the nation is more vulnerable to change during the confusion of wartime.

    D) the civil rights movement would not have happened without women suffragists.

27. Which choice provides the best evidence for the answer to the previous question?

    A) Lines 4–7 ("Electronic ballot casting . . . our next president")

    B) Lines 7–10 ("Voting has . . . monarchical rule")

    C) Lines 17–20 ("The meeting . . . dozen men")

    D) Lines 77–80 ("The civil rights . . . advancement")

28. The graphic most clearly illustrates which idea?

    A) The Nineteenth Amendment happened as a result of World War I.

    B) The states slowed reform of national voting rights laws.

    C) Women's suffrage resulted from a slow evolution of events.

    D) Acts of civil disobedience won support for suffrage in Congress.

29. In line 61, the word "authenticity" most nearly means

    A) reliability.

    B) realism.

    C) legitimacy.

    D) truth.

30. The passage suggests that President Wilson contributed to the success of the women's suffrage movement by

    A) circulating government propaganda in support of women's suffrage.

    B) framing the fight in World War I as a fight for democracy and freedom.

    C) engaging in a foreign war to distract the nation from political debate.

    D) working with legislators to write the Nineteenth Amendment.

Practice Tests

31. The graphic helps support which statement referred to in the passage?

   A) Early women suffragists did not live to vote in national elections.

   B) The Nineteenth Amendment passed within a few years of its introduction.

   C) A majority of state representatives opposed women's suffrage in 1918.

   D) Many state governments approved suffrage before the federal government did.

**Questions 32–42 are based on the following passages and supplementary material.**

Passage 1 is about how scientists use radioisotopes to date artifacts and remains. Passage 2 discusses the varying problems with radioactive contaminants.

**Passage 1**

Archaeologists often rely on measuring the amounts of different atoms present in an item from a site to determine its age. The identity of an atom depends on how many protons it has in its nucleus; for
5 example, all carbon atoms have 6 protons. Each atom of an element, however, can have a different number of neutrons, so there can be several versions, or isotopes, of each element. Scientists name the isotopes by the total number of protons plus neutrons. For example,
10 a carbon atom with 6 neutrons is carbon-12 while a carbon atom with 7 neutrons is carbon-13.

Some combinations of protons and neutrons are not stable and will change over time. For example, carbon-14, which has 6 protons and 8 neutrons, will
15 slowly change into nitrogen-14, with 7 protons and 7 neutrons. Scientists can directly measure the amount of carbon-12 and carbon-14 in a sample or they can use radiation measurements to calculate these amounts. Each atom of carbon-14 that changes to
20 nitrogen-14 emits radiation. Scientists can measure the rate of emission and use that to calculate the total amount of carbon-14 present in a sample.

Carbon-14 atoms are formed in the atmosphere at the same rate at which they decay. Therefore,
25 the ratio of carbon-12 to carbon-14 atoms in the atmosphere is constant. Living plants and animals

have the same ratio of carbon-12 to carbon-14 in their tissues because they are constantly taking in carbon in the form of food or carbon dioxide. After
30 the plant or animal dies, however, it stops taking in carbon and so the amount of carbon-14 atoms in its tissues starts to decrease at a predictable rate.

By measuring the ratio of carbon-12 to carbon-14 in a bone, for example, a scientist can determine
35 how long the animal the bone came from has been dead. To determine an object's age this way is called "carbon-14 dating." Carbon-14 dating can be performed on any material made by a living organism, such as wood or paper from trees or
40 bones and skin from animals. Materials with ages up to about 50,000 years old can be dated. By finding the age of several objects found at different depths at an archeological dig, the archeologists can then make a timeline for the layers of the site. Objects
45 in the same layer will be about the same age. By using carbon dating for a few objects in a layer, archeologists know the age of other objects in that layer, even if the layer itself cannot be carbon dated.

**Passage 2**

Radioactive materials contain unstable atoms that
50 decay, releasing energy in the form of radiation. The radiation can be harmful to living tissue because it can penetrate into cells and damage their DNA. If an explosion or a leak at a nuclear power plant releases large amounts of radioactive materials,
55 the surrounding area could be hazardous until the amount of radioactive material drops back to normal levels. The amount of danger from the radiation and the amount of time until the areas are safe again depends on how fast the materials emit radiation.

60 Scientists use the "half-life" of a material to indicate how quickly it decays. The half-life of a material is the amount of time it takes for half of a sample of that material to decay. A material with a short half-life decays more quickly than a material with a long
65 half-life. For example, iodine-131 and cesium-137 can both be released as a result of an accident at a nuclear power plant. Iodine-131 decays rapidly, with a half-life of 8 days. Cesium-137, however, decays more slowly, with a half-life of 30 years.

GO ON TO THE NEXT PAGE

70    If an accident releases iodine-131, therefore, it is a short-term concern. The amount of radiation emitted will be high but will drop rapidly. After two months, less than one percent of the original iodine-131 will remain. An accidental release of cesium-137,
75  however, is a long-term concern. The amount of radiation emitted at first will be low but will drop slowly. It will take about 200 years for the amount of cesium-137 remaining to drop below one percent. The total amount of radiation emitted in both cases
80  will be the same, for the same amount of initial material. The difference lies in whether the radiation is all released rapidly at high levels in a short time, or is released slowly at low levels, over a long time span.

**Decay of Carbon-14**

This data is from the *Journal of Research of the National Bureau of Standards*, Vol. 64, No. 4, April 1951, pp. 328–333.

32. Based on the information in Passage 1, which of the following could be dated using carbon-14 dating?

A) An iron pot found in a cave

B) A rock at the bottom of a quarry

C) An arrowhead made from bone

D) The remains of a house made from stone

33. Which choice provides the best evidence for the answer to the previous question?

A) Lines 9–11 ("For example . . . carbon-13")

B) Lines 26–29 ("Living plants . . . dioxide")

C) Lines 29–32 ("After the plant . . . rate")

D) Lines 37–40 ("Carbon-14 dating . . . animals")

34. As used in line 24, "decay" most nearly means

A) yield.

B) deteriorate.

C) discharge.

D) circulated.

35. Which statement best describes the relationship between carbon-12 and carbon-14 in living tissue?

A) There is more carbon-14 than carbon-12.

B) There is more carbon-12 than carbon-14.

C) The ratio of carbon-12 to carbon-14 is constant.

D) The ratio of carbon-12 to carbon-14 fluctuates greatly.

36. Which choice provides the best evidence for the answer to the previous question?

A) Lines 12–13 ("Some combinations . . . time")

B) Lines 23–24 ("Carbon-14 atoms . . . decay")

C) Lines 26–29 ("Living plants . . . carbon dioxide")

D) Lines 29–32 ("After the plant . . . rate")

37. In Passage 2, the author refers to an accident that results in the release of iodine-131 as a "short-term concern" (line 71) because the initial amount of radiation released is

A) low but will drop slowly.

B) high but will drop quickly.

C) low and will drop quickly.

D) high and will drop slowly.

38. According to Passage 2, living tissue exposed to radioactive material can

A) be destroyed by high levels of heat caused by the radiation.

B) become radioactive itself and damage surrounding tissue.

C) suffer injury when the cells' components are damaged.

D) be killed by extra protons released by the radioactive material.

39. As used in line 73, "original" most nearly means

   A) earliest.

   B) unique.

   C) unusual.

   D) critical.

40. According to Passage 2, scientists use the half-life of radioactive material to determine the

   A) amount of danger posed by radiation immediately following a nuclear accident.

   B) likelihood of a nuclear accident involving the release of radioactive material at any given location.

   C) amount of radiation contained in a sample of iodine-131 or cesium-137 used in nuclear reactions.

   D) length of time that must pass until an area is safe after the release of radioactive material.

41. Which generalization about the study of physics is supported by both passages?

   A) The study of atomic and nuclear physics can have many applications in a variety of fields.

   B) The study of physics has helped revolutionize how archaeologists study artifacts.

   C) Scientists use physics to keep people and wildlife safe following a nuclear accident.

   D) Scientists use different concepts to date ancient items and assess danger from nuclear accidents.

42. Based on the graph and the information in the passages, which statement is accurate?

   A) Carbon-14 has a half-life of about 5,400 years.

   B) The half-life of carbon-14 is similar to that of cesium-137.

   C) The half-life of iodine-131 is greater than that of cesium-137.

   D) All radioactive materials have a half-life of 30 to 5,400 years.

**Questions 43-52 are based on the following passage and supplementary material.**

The following passage is adapted from an essay about the field of biomimicry, which focuses on the design of materials and systems that are based on biological structures.

In 1948, Swiss chemist George de Mestral was impressed with the clinging power of burrs snagged in his dog's fur and on his pant legs after he returned from a hike. While examining the

5  burrs under a microscope, he observed many hundreds of small fibers that grabbed like hooks. He experimented with replicas of the burrs and eventually invented Velcro®, a synthetic clinging fabric that was first marketed as "the zipperless

10  zipper." In the 1960s, NASA used de Mestral's invention on space suits, and now, of course, we see it everywhere.

You might say that de Mestral was the father of biomimicry, an increasingly essential field that

15  studies nature, looking for efficiencies in materials and systems, and asks the question "How can our homes, our electronics, and our cities work better?" As one biomimetics company puts it: "Nature is the largest laboratory that ever existed and ever will."

20  Architecture is one field that is constantly exploring new ways to incorporate biomimicry. Architects have studied everything from beehives to beaver dams to learn how to best use materials, geometry, and physics in buildings. Termite

25  mounds, for example, very efficiently regulate temperature, humidity, and airflow, so architects in Zimbabwe are working to apply what they've learned from termite mounds to human-made structures.

30  Says Michael Pawlyn, author of *Biomimicry in Architecture*, "If you look beyond the nice shapes in nature and understand the principles behind them, you can find some adaptations that can lead to new, innovative solutions that are radically more

35  resource-efficient. It's the direction we need to take in the coming decades."

Designers in various professional fields are drawing on biomimicry; for example, in optics, scientists have examined the surface of insect eyes

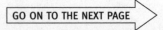

40 in hopes of reducing glare on handheld device screens. Engineers in the field of robotics worked to replicate the property found in a gecko's feet that allows adhesion to smooth surfaces.

45 Sometimes what scientists learn from nature isn't more advanced, but simpler. The abalone shrimp, for example, makes its shell out of calcium carbonate, the same material as soft chalk. It's not a rare or complex substance, but the unique arrangement of the material in the abalone's shell

50 makes it extremely tough. The walls of the shell contain microscopic pieces of calcium carbonate stacked like bricks, which are bound together using proteins just as concrete mortar is used. The result is a shell three thousand times harder than chalk

55 and as tough as Kevlar® (the material used in bullet-proof vests).

Often it is necessary to look at the nanoscale structures of a living material's exceptional properties in order to re-create it synthetically.

60 Andrew Parker, an evolutionary biologist, looked at the skin of the thorny devil (a type of lizard) under a scanning electron microscope, in search of the features that let the animal channel water from its back to its mouth.

65 Examples like this from the animal world abound. Scientists have learned that colorful birds don't always have pigment in their wings but are sometimes completely brown; it's the layers of keratin in their wings that produce color. Different

70 colors, which have varying wavelengths, reflect differently through keratin. The discovery of this phenomenon can be put to use in creating paints and cosmetics that won't fade or chip. At the same time, paint for outdoor surfaces can be made

75 tougher by copying the structures found in antler bone. Hearing aids are being designed to capture sound as well as the ears of the *Ormia* fly do. And why can't we have a self-healing material like our own skin? Researchers at the Beckman Institute at

80 the University of Illinois are creating just that; they call it an "autonomic materials system." A raptor's feathers, a whale's fluke, a mosquito's proboscis—all have functional features we can learn from.

The driving force behind these innovations, aside

85 from improved performance, is often improved energy efficiency. In a world where nonrenewable energy resources are dwindling and carbon emissions threaten the planet's health, efficiency has never been more important. Pawlyn agrees:

90 "For me, biomimicry is one of the best sources of innovation to get to a world of zero waste because those are the rules under which biological life has had to exist."

Biomimicry is a radical field and one whose

95 practitioners need to be radically optimistic, as Pawlyn is when he says, "We could use natural products such as cellulose, or even harvest carbon from the atmosphere to create bio-rock."

*Tiny florets in a sunflower's center are arranged in an interlocking spiral, which inspired engineers in the design of this solar power plant. Mirrors positioned at the same angle as the florets bounce light toward the power plant's central tower.*

Adapted from David Ferris, "Innovate: Solar Designs from Nature." © 2014 by Sierra Club.

43. The central focus of the passage is

    A) the field of biomimicry, which is the study of materials and systems found in nature and replicated in ways that benefit people.

    B) the work of George de Mestral, the Swiss chemist who invented Velcro® after observing burrs under a microscope.

    C) the ways in which architects use termite mounds as models for human-made structures in Zimbabwe.

    D) how scientists are seeking ways to improve energy efficiency as nonrenewable energy sources decline.

44. Which choice provides the best evidence for the answer to the previous question?

    A) Lines 1–6 ("In 1948 . . . hooks")

    B) Lines 13–19 ("You might say . . . ever will'")

    C) Lines 24–29 ("Termite mounds . . . structures")

    D) Lines 84–89 ("The driving . . . more important")

45. The author includes a quote in paragraph 4 in order to

    A) explain why architects are looking to biomimicry for solutions in architecture.

    B) provide an argument for more scientists to study biomimicry.

    C) give an explanation as to why someone might choose a career in architecture.

    D) provide a counterargument to the author's central claim.

46. Based on the information in paragraph 6, how does the shell of an abalone shrimp compare with soft chalk?

    A) The essential building blocks are arranged in a similar manner, but the material that makes up the shell of an abalone shrimp is harder.

    B) Both are made from the same essential building blocks, but the shell of the abalone shrimp is much harder because of the manner in which the materials are arranged.

    C) The essential building blocks of both are the same, but the abalone shrimp shell is harder because the soft chalk lacks a protein binding the materials together.

    D) They are made from different essential building blocks, but they have a similar hardness because the materials are arranged in a similar manner.

47. In paragraph 9, what is the function of the quote from Pawlyn about efficiency?

    A) To convince readers that Pawlyn is an expert in his field

    B) To prove that great strides are being made in creating products that do not generate waste

    C) To demonstrate the limits of what biomimicry can achieve

    D) To support the statement that energy efficiency "has never been more important"

48. In line 32, "principles" most nearly means

    A) sources.

    B) attitudes.

    C) standards.

    D) concepts.

GO ON TO THE NEXT PAGE

49. Of the following, the most reasonable inference from the passage is that

    A) more scientists will utilize solutions developed through biomimicry in the future.

    B) the field of biomimicry will eventually decline as more nonrenewable resources are discovered.

    C) scientists will leave the fields they are currently working in and begin research in biomimicry.

    D) doctors will create a self-healing skin called an "autonomic materials system" using methods based in biomimicry.

50. Which choice provides the best evidence for the answer to the previous question?

    A) Lines 37–41 ("Designers . . . screens")

    B) Lines 57–59 ("Often it is . . . synthetically")

    C) Lines 65–69 ("Examples like . . . color")

    D) Lines 94–98 ("Biomimicry . . . bio-rock")

51. As used in line 92, "radical" most nearly means

    A) pervasive.

    B) drastic.

    C) essential.

    D) revolutionary.

52. The graphic and caption that accompany this passage help illustrate how biomimicry can be used to

    A) make a solar plant more attractive.

    B) increase waste generated by energy sources.

    C) improve the efficiency of existing technologies.

    D) replicate a pattern common in nature.

IF YOU FINISH BEFORE TIME IS CALLED, YOU MAY CHECK YOUR WORK ON THIS SECTION ONLY. DO NOT TURN TO ANY OTHER SECTION IN THE TEST. **STOP**

K 805

# Writing and Language Test

### 35 Minutes—44 Questions

This section corresponds to Section 2 of your answer sheet.

**Directions:** Each passage in this section is followed by several questions. Some questions will reference an underlined portion in the passage; others will ask you to consider a part of a passage or the passage as a whole. For each question, choose the answer that reflects the best use of grammar, punctuation, and style. If a passage or question is accompanied by a graphic, take the graphic into account in choosing your response(s). Some questions will have "NO CHANGE" as a possible response. Choose that answer if you think the best choice is to leave the sentence as written.

**Questions 1-11 are based on the following passage.**

**The Age of the Librarian**

When Kristen Harris **1** is in college, she worked in her university's library and was constantly told, "You really should be studying to be a librarian; this is **2** your home" however Harris was pursuing a bachelor's degree in elementary education at the time. Little did she realize that becoming a school librarian was indeed **3** elective. During the 21st century, the age of information, what could be more necessary than an individual trained to gather, process, and disseminate information? So, after teaching children in the classroom, Harris went back to school to earn her Master of Library Science degree.

Today, Harris is preparing a story time for a group of young students. As it has done with everything else, the technology revolution has elevated the school library to "Library 2.0." Harris's tablet-integrated story time begins when she projects images for *The Very Cranky Bear* onto a projector screen. As a child, Harris got excited whenever a puppet appeared during story time, but now she uses an interactive app (application software) to enhance her own story time and **4** integrate this next generation of children.

1. A) NO CHANGE
   B) has been
   C) was
   D) had been

2. A) NO CHANGE
   B) your home," however Harris
   C) your home."; However Harris
   D) your home." However, Harris

3. A) NO CHANGE
   B) imminent
   C) threatening
   D) optional

4. A) NO CHANGE
   B) enervate
   C) energize
   D) elucidate

GO ON TO THE NEXT PAGE

As she introduces the children to the problem of cheering up a cranky **5** bear, Harris sees Miguel scouring the library shelves for another book by a popular author. **6** Miguel had said asking Harris for a book two weeks earlier "If you have any funny stories, I like those." "It will always be satisfying," reflects Harris, "to find books for students and have them return to say, 'I really liked that one. Are there any more by that author?'"

**7** Harris maintains active profiles on multiple social media networks to connect with her students more effectively. Harris would call herself a media mentor as much as a librarian because she regularly visits her favorite websites for reviews of apps and other digital tools to suggest to students and parents. Librarians have always been an important resource for families in a community, but this importance has grown exponentially because of the advent of technology. Librarians are offering guidance about new media to address the changing information needs in our communities. Furthermore, libraries are becoming increasingly technology driven, for example, **8** enabling access to collections of other libraries, offering remote access to databases, or they house video production studios.

5.  A) NO CHANGE
    B) bear; Harris sees Miguel
    C) bear: Harris sees Miguel
    D) bear Harris sees Miguel

6.  A) NO CHANGE
    B) Miguel had said, "If you have any funny stories, I like those," asking Harris for a book two weeks earlier.
    C) Asking Harris for a book two weeks earlier, Miguel had said, "If you have any funny stories, I like those."
    D) Miguel asked Harris for a book two weeks earlier had said, "If you have any funny stories, I like those."

7.  Which sentence would most effectively establish the main idea of the paragraph?
    A) NO CHANGE
    B) In addition to finding books for students, Harris is expected to meet their digital needs.
    C) Librarians still perform many traditional tasks such as putting great literature in the hands of their students.
    D) In the future, many school libraries are unlikely to have books on the shelves because students prefer electronic media.

8.  A) NO CHANGE
    B) by enabling access to collections of other libraries, offering remote access to databases, or by housing video production studios.
    C) they enable access to collections of other libraries, offering remote access to databases, or they house video production studios.
    D) enabling access to collections of other libraries, offering remote access to databases, or housing video production studios.

**9** <u>Harris sponsors a weekly "Fun Read" book discussion club that is well attended by many of the students at her school.</u> So, in Harris's opinion, librarians must be masters of the digital world.

Harris finishes her story time and heads across the library. A young student stops her and asks, "Ms. Harris, what's new in the library?" **10** <u>She chuckles</u> and thinks about the many collections, services, and programs their school library offers. "Have you seen the Trendy 10 list? You read the books on the list and blog **11** <u>your</u> ideas about them. I'll set you up with a password and username so you can blog," says Harris. In this library full of information, she's the gatekeeper.

9. Which sentence provides evidence that best supports the main idea of the paragraph?

   A) NO CHANGE
   B) Librarians continue to help students and teachers locate the perfect book in the library's collection.
   C) Teachers frequently ask Harris to recommend educational apps to support early literacy for their students.
   D) Many parents are concerned with online safety and digital citizenship due to the proliferation of social media.

10. A) NO CHANGE
    B) He chuckles
    C) Harris chuckles
    D) They chuckle

11. A) NO CHANGE
    B) they're
    C) you're
    D) their

**Questions 12-22 are based on the following passage.**

## Unforeseen Consequences: The Dark Side of the Industrial Revolution

There is no doubt that the Industrial Revolution guided America through the nascent stages of independence **12** and into being a robust economic powerhouse. Inventions like the cotton gin revolutionized the textile industry, and the steam engine ushered in the advent of expeditious cross-country distribution.

The Industrial Revolution marked a shift from an agrarian to an industry-centered society. People eschewed farming in favor of **13** more lucrative enterprises in urban areas which put a strain on existing local resources. Necessary goods such as **14** food crops, vegetables, and meat products also had to be shipped in order to meet the dietary needs of a consolidated population. And because there were fewer people farming, food had to travel farther and in higher quantities to meet demand. Issues like carbon dioxide emissions, therefore, arose not only as by-products of industrial production but also from the delivery of these products. Moreover, booming metropolises needed additional lumber, metal, and coal shipped from rural areas to sustain population and industrial growth.

**15** [1] The negative effects of such expansion on humans were immediately apparent; improper water sanitation led to cholera outbreaks in big cities. [2] Miners suffered from black lung after spending hours harvesting coal in dark caverns. [3] Combusted fossil fuels **16** released unprecedented amounts of human-made carbon dioxide into the air, resulting in

12. A) NO CHANGE
    B) and into the role of a robust economic powerhouse.
    C) and turned into a robust economic power-house.
    D) and then became a robust economic power-house.

13. A) NO CHANGE
    B) more lucrative enterprises in urban areas, which put a strain on
    C) more lucrative enterprises in urban areas; which put a strain on
    D) more lucrative enterprises in urban areas. Which put a strain on

14. A) NO CHANGE
    B) food
    C) food crops
    D) vegetables and meat products

15. To effectively transition from paragraph 2, which sentence should begin paragraph 3?
    A) Sentence 1
    B) Sentence 2
    C) Sentence 3
    D) Sentence 4

16. Which graphic would best support the underlined claim?
    A) A line graph plotting an increase in atmospheric carbon dioxide over time
    B) A pie chart comparing the present percentages of carbon dioxide and other atmospheric gases
    C) A timeline tracking carbon dioxide emissions testing dates
    D) A bar graph showing levels of atmospheric carbon dioxide in different locations

respiratory ailments. [4] The fact remains that smog, now an internationally recognized buzzword, simply did not exist before the factories that produced it.

The critical impact on the environment must also **17** be taken into account. Proper regulations were either not in place or not enforced. Industrial waste was often disposed of in the nearest river or buried in landfills, where it **18** polluted groundwater essential for wildlife to thrive. Deforestation across the United States served the dual purpose of providing inhabitable land and wood, but it also caused animals to migrate or die out completely.

Although the Industrial Revolution heralded an age of consumer ease and excess, it also invited a cyclical process of destruction and reduced resources. **19** Greenhouse gases were released into the atmosphere. Numerous health problems caused by **20** depressing

17. Which choice most effectively combines the sentences at the underlined portion?

   A) be taken into account, and proper regulations

   B) be taken into account since without proper regulations

   C) be taken into account because proper regulations

   D) be taken into account; however, proper regulations

18. A) NO CHANGE

   B) disturbed

   C) drained

   D) enhanced

19. Which choice should be added to the end of the underlined sentence to better support the claim in the preceding sentence?

   A) NO CHANGE

   B) while carbon dioxide–consuming trees were cut down to make way for new living spaces.

   C) and caused an increase in global temperatures as well as a rise in coastal sea levels.

   D) faster than they could be absorbed by the atmosphere's shrinking ozone layer.

20. A) NO CHANGE

   B) urban

   C) substandard

   D) developing

GO ON TO THE NEXT PAGE

working conditions prevented rural emigrants from thriving. And the environment that had cradled humankind since its inception was slowly being **21** degraded. All in the name of progress. **22**

21. A) NO CHANGE
    B) degraded; all
    C) degraded! All
    D) degraded—all

22. Which choice most effectively states the central idea of the essay?

    A) The Industrial Revolution created a new consumer society that replaced the existing farming society.

    B) Politicians and historians today disagree about the true consequences of the Industrial Revolution.

    C) Although some analysts suggest that industrialization had many problems, its immense benefits outweigh these concerns.

    D) Unfortunately, progress came at the expense of environmental and ecological preservation and may well have ruined the future that once looked so bright.

**Questions 23-33 are based on the following passage.**

**Remembering Freud**

Psychology has grown momentously over the past century, largely due to the influence of Sigmund Freud, a pioneer of the field. This Austrian-born neurologist founded the practice of psychoanalysis and 23 began scientific study of the unconscious mind. 24 Since his career which ended in the mid-twentieth century, Freud has remained a common cultural and scientific reference point. 25 Even the abiding popularity of terms such as "id," "ego," and talking about a "Freudian slip" serves to indicate how this psychologist lingers powerfully in Western memory.

As neuroscience has progressed, many early practices and theories, including some of Freud's, have been dismissed as outdated, unscientific, or even harmful. Much of Freud's theory, clinical practice, and even lifestyle are now discredited. But when considered in his historical context, alongside the astounding progress catalyzed by his work, Freud's contribution was significant indeed.

26 Because he is now widely referred to as the Father of Psychoanalysis, Freud was among the first to develop the now-commonplace psychological method of inviting patients to speak freely. For Freud, this was both study and treatment. It helped doctors to

23. A) NO CHANGE
    B) continued
    C) spearheaded
    D) led to

24. A) NO CHANGE
    B) Since his career, which ended in the mid-twentieth century, Freud has remained
    C) Since his career ending in the mid-twentieth century; Freud has remained
    D) Since his career (ending in the mid-twentieth century) Freud has remained

25. A) NO CHANGE
    B) Even the abiding popularity of terms such as the "id," "ego," and a "Freudian slip"
    C) Even the abiding popularity of terms such as talking about an "id," "ego," and "Freudian slip"
    D) Even the abiding popularity of terms such as "id," "ego," and "Freudian slip."

26. A) NO CHANGE
    B) Widely remembered as the Father of Psycho-analysis, Freud was among the first to develop the now-commonplace psychological method of inviting patients to speak freely.
    C) Freud was among the first to develop the now-commonplace psychological method of inviting patients to speak freely, which is why he is now widely remembered as the Father of Psychoanalysis.
    D) Although he is widely remembered as the Father of Psychoanalysis, Freud was among the first to develop the now-commonplace psychological method of inviting patients to speak freely.

GO ON TO THE NEXT PAGE

understand patients, but more importantly it helped patients to understand themselves. Freud employed the classic (now largely outdated) psychiatric style in which the patient lies face-up on a clinical bed, allegedly enabling access to deep **27** parts of the mind. These are better known as the unconscious or subconscious, and they fascinated Freud.

**28** He believed that uncovering repressed memories, was necessary for recovery. For Freud, understanding the activity of the innermost mind was essential. **29** In dealing with the conditions of patients, like neurosis or other psychological trauma, he suspected that there was a great deal going on beneath the "surface" of the psyche. He thought it was possible to reunite external, or conscious, thought with the internal, or unconscious. **30** At the same time that Freud practiced, many people were interested in spiritualism. Moreover, the method of inviting patients to speak and process their thoughts aloud remains central to today's psychological practice.

27. A) NO CHANGE
    B) recesses
    C) places
    D) components

28. A) NO CHANGE
    B) He believed that uncovering repressed memories, being necessary for recovery.
    C) He believed that uncovering repressed memories was necessary for recovery.
    D) He believed that uncovering, repressed memories was necessary for recovery.

29. A) NO CHANGE
    B) In dealing with patients' conditions, like neurosis or other psychological trauma, he suspected that
    C) In dealing with patients like neurosis or other psychological trauma conditions he suspected that
    D) He suspected that, in dealing with patients' conditions like neurosis or other psychological trauma,

30. Which sentence provides the best support for the ideas presented in this section?
    A) NO CHANGE
    B) Freud lived and worked mostly in London although he had originally trained in Austria.
    C) While some of Freud's more unusual practices have been criticized or abandoned, his interest in the unconscious altered the trajectory of the field.
    D) Psychologists today employ many theories, not just those developed by Freud.

Practice Tests

Freud altered the course of twentieth-century medicine by initiating what would become a grand, global conversation about the [31] still vastly mysterious human mind before Freud, medicine had barely scratched the surface in understanding mental health. Patients were met with very few answers, let alone recovery protocols. [32] Through trial and error—scientific method in action—Freud's finding of a method that seemed to work. Since then, decades of ever-sharpening science have used his work as a launching pad. Therefore, as long as occasions arise to celebrate the progress of [33] the field, Sigmund Freud will be remembered for groundbreaking work that enabled countless advances.

31. A) NO CHANGE
    B) still vastly mysterious human mind. Before Freud, medicine
    C) still vastly mysterious human mind, before Freud, medicine
    D) still vastly mysterious human mind before Freud. Medicine

32. A) NO CHANGE
    B) Through trial and error—scientific method in action—Freud's finding a method that seems to work.
    C) Through trial and error—scientific method in action—Freud finds a method that seemed to work.
    D) Through trial and error—scientific method in action—Freud found a method that seemed to work.

33. A) NO CHANGE
    B) the field; Sigmund Freud will be remembered for groundbreaking work that
    C) the field Sigmund Freud will be remembered for groundbreaking work that
    D) the field Sigmund Freud will be remembered for groundbreaking work, and that

GO ON TO THE NEXT PAGE ⟹

**Questions 34-44 are based on the following passage and supplementary material.**

### Success in Montreal

The Montreal Protocol on Substances That Deplete the Ozone Layer is an international treaty that was created to ensure that steps would be taken to reverse damage to Earth's ozone layer and [34] preventing future damage. [35] It was signed in 1987. This document created restrictions on chemicals that were known to be dangerous to the protective barrier that the ozone layer offers Earth. Without the ozone layer, the sun's dangerous UV rays would alter our climate so drastically, life on land and in water would cease to exist.

A hole in Earth's ozone layer was discovered over Antarctica [36] as long as two years prior to the signing of the treaty. The discovery brought the human impact on the environment to the forefront of [37] international conversation, the massive hole was evidence that a global response was necessary and that large-scale action was needed. The Montreal Protocol became effective January 1, 1989, and nearly 100 gases deemed dangerous to the ozone layer have been phased out. As a result, [38] the average size of the ozone hole decreased significantly during the 1990s.

34. A) NO CHANGE
    B) to prevent
    C) prevented
    D) was preventing

35. Which choice most effectively combines the sentences in the underlined portion?
    A) Signed in 1987, this document
    B) Because it was signed in 1987, this document
    C) It was signed in 1987, and this document
    D) It was signed in 1987 so this document

36. A) NO CHANGE
    B) long ago, two years prior.
    C) two years prior.
    D) years prior.

37. A) NO CHANGE
    B) international conversation, yet the massive hole
    C) international conversation. The massive hole
    D) international conversation, so the massive hole

38. Which choice completes the sentence with accurate data based on the graphic?
    A) NO CHANGE
    B) the average size of the ozone hole leveled off beginning in the 1990s.
    C) the average size of the ozone hole decreased beginning in the 2000s.
    D) the average size of the ozone hole increased beginning in the 1980s.

Now that a substantial amount of time has passed since the treaty was put into place, the effects can begin to be [39] looked at. As a part of the treaty, the Montreal Protocol's Scientific Assessment Panel was created to gauge [40] their effect on the hole in the ozone layer. The Panel has since reported the results every four years. The Panel predicts that the ozone layer will return to its former state of health by 2075. [41]

[1] While the treaty is already an obvious success, work continues to ensure that human strides in technology and industry do not reverse the healing process. [2] The Montreal Protocol's Multilateral Fund was established to help developing countries transition away from the consumption and production of harmful chemicals. [3] So far, over $3 billion has been invested by the Fund. [4] The developing countries are referred to as "Article 5 countries." [42]

39. A) NO CHANGE
B) controlled.
C) measured.
D) governed.

40. A) NO CHANGE
B) its
C) it's
D) there

41. Which choice could be added to paragraph 3 to most effectively convey its central idea?

A) It is the Panel's current estimation that the ozone layer is beginning to heal, but the rate of progress is slow.

B) The Panel meets once a year to assess the increase or decrease of each gas that has been identified as dangerous.

C) Of much concern to the Panel was the effect of ultraviolet radiation on the ozone layer.

D) The Panel has recently updated procedures for the nomination and selection of its membership.

42. Which sentence in paragraph 4 provides the least amount of support for the central idea of the paragraph?

A) Sentence 1
B) Sentence 2
C) Sentence 3
D) Sentence 4

GO ON TO THE NEXT PAGE

[1] The Montreal Protocol is a living document. [2] A current amendment proposition has been put forth by the United States, Mexico, and Canada jointly. [3] It aims to cut down on harmful gases that were put into use as an alternative to the gases specified in the original Montreal Protocol treaty. [4] It has been amended four times since its inception. [5] Combating the erosion of our ozone layer will take time and flexibility, but the research is clear: If humans stay conscious of what we emit into the atmosphere, we can not only stall the damage we have done in the past, but we can [43] change it. [44]

43. A) NO CHANGE
    B) switch
    C) invert
    D) reverse

44. For the sake of cohesion of this paragraph, sentence 4 should be placed

    A) where it is now.
    B) before sentence 1.
    C) after sentence 1.
    D) after sentence 2.

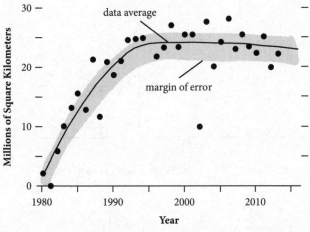

**Size of Ozone Hole**

Adapted from Ozone Hole Watch, NASA Goddard Space Flight Center.

# Math Test

### 25 Minutes—20 Questions

## NO-CALCULATOR SECTION

This section corresponds to Section 3 of your answer sheet.

**Directions:** For this section, solve each problem and decide which is the best of the choices given. Fill in the corresponding oval on the answer sheet. You may use any available space for scratch work.

Notes:

1. Calculator use is NOT permitted.

2. All numbers used are real numbers, and all variables used represent real numbers, unless otherwise indicated.

3. Figures are drawn to scale and lie in a plane unless otherwise indicated.

4. Unless stated otherwise, the domain of any function $f$ is assumed to be the set of all real numbers $x$, for which $f(x)$ is a real number.

Information:

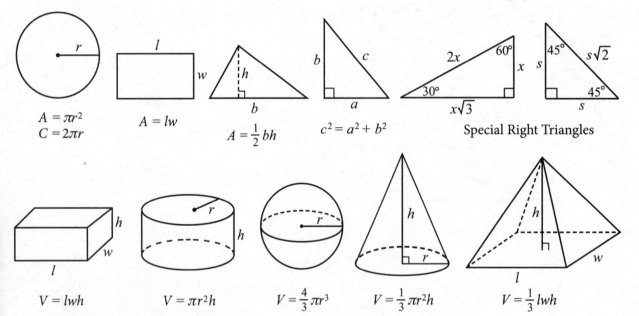

The sum of the degree measures of the angles in a triangle is 180.

The number of degrees of arc in a circle is 360.

The number of radians of arc in a circle is $2\pi$.

GO ON TO THE NEXT PAGE

**Number of Games**

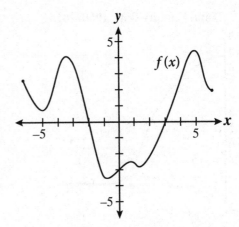

1. The graph above shows the amount that a new, high-tech video arcade charges its customers. What could the $y$-intercept of this graph represent?

   A) The cost of playing 5 games

   B) The cost per game, which is $5

   C) The entrance fee to enter the arcade

   D) The number of games that are played

$$\frac{3x}{x+5} \div \frac{6}{4x+20}$$

2. Which of the following is equivalent to the expression above, given that $x \neq -5$ ?

   A) $2x$

   B) $\dfrac{x}{2}$

   C) $\dfrac{9x}{2}$

   D) $2x + 4$

$$(x+3)^2 + (y+1)^2 = 25$$

3. The graph of the equation above is a circle. What is the area, in square units, of the circle?

   A) $4\pi$

   B) $5\pi$

   C) $16\pi$

   D) $25\pi$

4. The figure above shows the graph of $f(x)$. For which value(s) of $x$ does $f(x)$ equal 0 ?

   A) 3 only

   B) $-3$ only

   C) $-2$ and 3

   D) $-3$, $-2$, and 3

$$\frac{4(d+3)-9}{8} = \frac{10-(2-d)}{6}$$

5. In the equation above, what is the value of $d$ ?

   A) $\dfrac{23}{16}$

   B) $\dfrac{23}{8}$

   C) $\dfrac{25}{8}$

   D) $\dfrac{25}{4}$

**Total Fertility Rate, 1960–2010**

Source: Data from Eurostat.

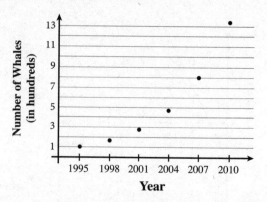

6. One indicator of a declining economy is a continued decline in birth rates. In 2010, birth rates in Europe were at an all-time low, with the average number of children that a woman has in her lifetime at well below two. In the figure above, $f(t)$ represents birth rates for Portugal between 1960 and 2010, and $g(t)$ represents birth rates in Slovakia for the same time period. For which value(s) of $t$ is $f(t) > g(t)$?

A) $1960 < t < 1980$ only

B) $1980 < t < 2000$ only

C) $1960 < t < 1980$ and $1990 < t < 2000$

D) $1960 < t < 1980$ and $2000 < t < 2010$

7. The blue whale is the largest creature in the world and has been found in every ocean in the world. A marine biologist surveyed the blue whale population in Monterey Bay, off the coast of California, every three years between 1995 and 2010. The figure above shows her results. If $w$ is the number of blue whales present in Monterey Bay and $t$ is the number of years since the study began in 1995, which of the following equations best represents the blue whale population of Monterey Bay?

A) $w = 100 + 2t$

B) $w = 100 + \dfrac{t^2}{4}$

C) $w = 100 \times 2^t$

D) $w = 100 \times 2^{\frac{t}{4}}$

GO ON TO THE NEXT PAGE

**Laptop Depreciation**

8. The figure above shows the straight-line depreciation of a laptop computer over the first five years of its use. According to the figure, what is the average rate of change in dollars per year of the value of the computer over the five-year period?

A) −1,100

B) −220

C) −100

D) 100

9. What is the coefficient of $x^2$ when $6x^2 - \frac{2}{5}x + 1$ is multiplied by $10x + \frac{1}{3}$ ?

A) −4

B) −2

C) 2

D) 4

10. The graph above could represent which of the following equations?

A) $-6x - 4y = 5$

B) $-6x - 4y = -5$

C) $-6x + 4y = 5$

D) $-6x + 4y = -5$

$$\begin{cases} \frac{3}{4}x - \frac{1}{2}y = 12 \\ kx - 2y = 22 \end{cases}$$

11. If the system of linear equations above has no solution, and $k$ is a constant, what is the value of $k$ ?

A) $-\frac{4}{3}$

B) $-\frac{3}{4}$

C) 3

D) 4

12. In Delray Beach, Florida, you can take a luxury golf cart ride around downtown. The driver charges $4 for the first $\frac{1}{4}$ mile, plus $1.50 for each additional $\frac{1}{2}$ mile. Which inequality represents the number of miles, $m$, that you could ride and pay no more than $10 ?

A) $3.25 + 1.5m \le 10$

B) $3.25 + 3m \le 10$

C) $4 + 1.5m \le 10$

D) $4 + 3m \le 10$

13. The graph of $g(x)$ is shown in the figure above. If $h(x) = -g(x) + 1$, which of the following statements is true?

    A) The range of $h(x)$ is $-3 \le y \le 3$.

    B) The minimum value of $h(x)$ is $-4$.

    C) The coordinates of point $A$ on the function $h(x)$ are $(2, 4)$.

    D) The graph of $h(x)$ is increasing between $x = -5$ and $x = -2$.

14. If $a + bi$ represents the complex number that results from multiplying $3 + 2i$ times $5 - i$, what is the value of $a$ ?

    A)  2

    B)  13

    C)  15

    D)  17

$$\frac{1}{x} + \frac{4}{x} = \frac{1}{72}$$

15. In order to create safe drinking water, cities and towns use water treatment facilities to remove contaminants from surface water and groundwater. Suppose a town has a treatment plant but decides to build a second, more efficient facility. The new treatment plant can filter the water in the reservoir four times as quickly as the older facility. Working together, the two facilities can filter all the water in the reservoir in 72 hours. The equation above represents the scenario. Which of the following describes what the term $\frac{1}{x}$ represents?

    A) The portion of the water the older treatment plant can filter in 1 hour

    B) The time it takes the older treatment plant to filter the water in the reservoir

    C) The time it takes the older treatment plant to filter $\frac{1}{72}$ of the water in the reservoir

    D) The portion of the water the new treatment plant can filter in 4 hours

 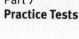
GO ON TO THE NEXT PAGE

**Directions:** For questions 16–20, enter your responses into the appropriate grid on your answer sheet, in accordance with the following:

1.  You will receive credit only if the circles are filled in correctly, but you may write your answers in the boxes above each grid to help you fill in the circles accurately.
2.  Don't mark more than one circle per column.
3.  None of the questions with grid-in responses will have a negative solution.
4.  Only grid in a single answer, even if there is more than one correct answer to a given question.
5.  A **mixed number** must be gridded as a decimal or an improper fraction. For example, you would grid $7\frac{1}{2}$ as 7.5 or 15/2.

    (Were you to grid it as the response shown, this response would be read as $\frac{71}{2}$.)
6.  A **decimal** hat has more digits than there are places on the grid may be either rounded or truncated, but every column in the grid must be filled in to receive credit.

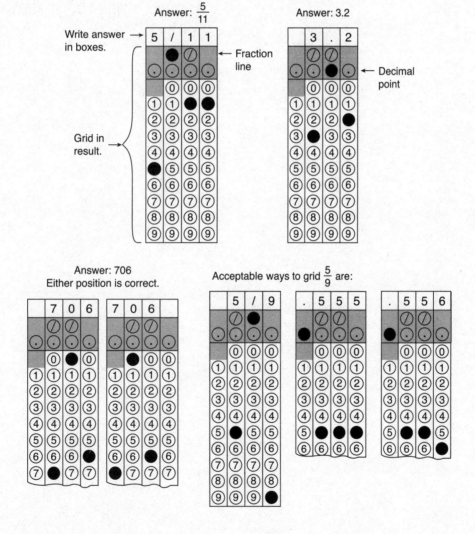

16. If $\frac{1}{4}x = 5 - \frac{1}{2}y$, what is the value of $x + 2y$ ?

$$\begin{cases} x + 3y \le 18 \\ 2x - 3y \le 9 \end{cases}$$

17. If $(a, b)$ is a point in the solution region for the system of inequalities shown above and $a = 6$, what is the minimum possible value for $b$ ?

$$\frac{\sqrt{x} \cdot x^{\frac{5}{6}} \cdot x}{\sqrt[3]{x}}$$

18. If $x^n$ is the simplified form of the expression above, what is the value of $n$ ?

Note: Figure not drawn to scale.

19. In the figure above, the area of the shaded region is 52 square units. What is the height of the larger triangle?

20. If $y = ax^2 + bx + c$ passes through the points $(-3, 10)$, $(0, 1)$, and $(2, 15)$, what is the value of $a + b + c$ ?

IF YOU FINISH BEFORE TIME IS CALLED, YOU MAY CHECK YOUR WORK ON THIS SECTION ONLY.
DO NOT TURN TO ANY OTHER SECTION IN THE TEST.

STOP

824 K

# Math Test

### 55 Minutes—38 Questions

## CALCULATOR SECTION

This section corresponds to Section 4 of your answer sheet.

**Directions:** For this section, solve each problem and decide which is the best of the choices given. Fill in the corresponding oval on the answer sheet. You may use any available space for scratch work.

Notes:

1. Calculator use is permitted.
2. All numbers used are real numbers, and all variables used represent real numbers, unless otherwise indicated.
3. Figures are drawn to scale and lie in a plane unless otherwise indicated.
4. Unless stated otherwise, the domain of any function $f$ is assumed to be the set of all real numbers $x$, for which $f(x)$ is a real number.

Information:

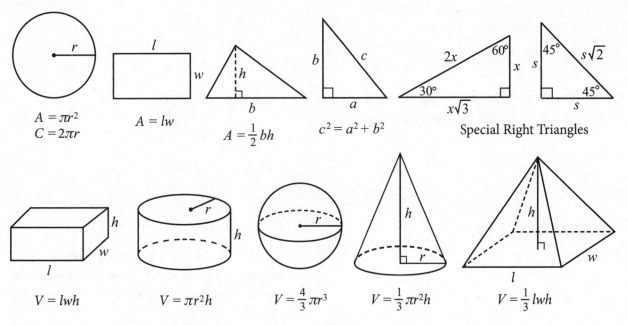

$$A = \pi r^2$$
$$C = 2\pi r$$

$$A = lw$$

$$A = \frac{1}{2}bh$$

$$c^2 = a^2 + b^2$$

Special Right Triangles

$$V = lwh$$

$$V = \pi r^2 h$$

$$V = \frac{4}{3}\pi r^3$$

$$V = \frac{1}{3}\pi r^2 h$$

$$V = \frac{1}{3}lwh$$

The sum of the degree measures of the angles in a triangle is 180.

The number of degrees of arc in a circle is 360.

The number of radians of arc in a circle is $2\pi$.

GO ON TO THE NEXT PAGE

1. Oceans, seas, and bays represent about 96.5 percent of Earth's water, including the water found in our atmosphere. If the volume of the water contained in oceans, seas, and bays is about 321,000,000 cubic miles, which of the following best represents the approximate volume, in cubic miles, of all the world's water?

   A) 308,160,000

   B) 309,765,000

   C) 332,642,000

   D) 334,375,000

2. An electrician charges a one-time site visit fee to evaluate a potential job. If the electrician accepts the job, he charges an hourly rate plus the cost of any materials needed to complete the job. The electrician also charges for tax, but only on the cost of the materials. If the total cost of completing a job that takes $h$ hours is given by the function $C(h) = 45h + 1.06(82.5) + 75$, then the term $1.06(82.5)$ represents

   A) the hourly rate.

   B) the site visit fee.

   C) the cost of the materials, including tax.

   D) the cost of the materials, not including tax.

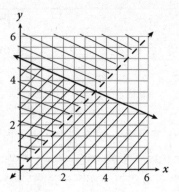

$$\begin{cases} y > x \\ y \le -\dfrac{3}{7}x + 5 \end{cases}$$

3. The figure above shows the solution set for the system of inequalities. Which of the following is not a solution to the system?

   A) (0, 3)

   B) (1, 2)

   C) (2, 4)

   D) (3, 3)

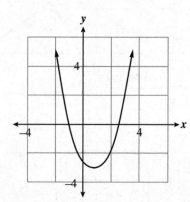

4. Each of the following quadratic equations represents the graph shown above. Which equation reveals the exact values of the $x$-intercepts of the graph?

   A) $y = \dfrac{1}{2}(2x - 5)(x + 1)$

   B) $y = x^2 - \dfrac{3}{2}x - \dfrac{5}{2}$

   C) $y + \dfrac{49}{16} = \left(x - \dfrac{3}{4}\right)^2$

   D) $y = \left(x - \dfrac{3}{4}\right)^2 - \dfrac{49}{16}$

GO ON TO THE NEXT PAGE

**National Government Concerns**

**Average Annual Gas Prices**

Data from U.S. Energy Information Administration.

5. Margo surveyed all the students in the government classes at her school to see what they thought should be the most important concern of a national government. The results of the survey are shown in the figure above. If the ratio of students who answered "Foreign Policy" to those who answered "Environment" was 5:3, what percentage of the students answered "Environment"?

A) 16%

B) 21%

C) 24%

D) 35%

7. The figure above shows the average annual gas prices in the United States from 2003 to 2013. Based on the information shown, which of the following conclusions is valid?

A) A gallon of gas cost more in 2008 than in 2013.

B) The price more than doubled between 2003 and 2013.

C) The drop in price from 2008 to 2009 was more than $1.00 per gallon.

D) The overall change in price was greater between 2003 and 2008 than it was between 2008 and 2013.

6. Which of the following best describes the type of association shown in the scatterplot above?

A) Linear, positive

B) Linear, negative

C) Exponential, positive

D) Exponential, negative

$$\begin{cases} -2x + 5y = 1 \\ 7x - 10y = -11 \end{cases}$$

8. If $(x, y)$ is a solution to the system of equations above, what is the sum of $x$ and $y$ ?

A) $-\dfrac{137}{30}$

B) $-4$

C) $-\dfrac{10}{3}$

D) $-3$

9.  A voltage divider is a simple circuit that converts a large voltage into a smaller one. The figure above shows a voltage divider that consists of two resistors that together have a total resistance of 294 ohms. To produce the desired voltage of 330 volts, $R_2$ must be 6 ohms less than twice $R_1$. Solving which of the following systems of equations gives the individual resistances for $R_1$ and $R_2$?

A) $\begin{cases} R_2 = 2R_1 - 6 \\ R_1 + R_2 = 294 \end{cases}$

B) $\begin{cases} R_1 = 2R_2 + 6 \\ R_1 + R_2 = 294 \end{cases}$

C) $\begin{cases} R_2 = 2R_1 - 6 \\ R_1 + R_2 = \dfrac{294}{330} \end{cases}$

D) $\begin{cases} R_1 = 2R_2 + 6 \\ R_1 + R_2 = 330(294) \end{cases}$

10. If $\dfrac{2}{5}(5x) + 2(x-1) = 4(x+1) - 2$, what is the value of $x$?

A) $x = -2$
B) $x = 2$
C) There is no value of $x$ for which the equation is true.
D) There are infinitely many values of $x$ for which the equation is true.

11. Crude oil is being transferred from a full rectangular storage container with dimensions 4 meters by 9 meters by 10 meters into a cylindrical transportation container that has a diameter of 6 meters. What is the minimum possible length for a transportation container that will hold all of the oil?

A) $40\pi$
B) $\dfrac{40}{\pi}$
C) $60\pi$
D) $\dfrac{120}{\pi}$

12. The percent increase from 5 to 12 is equal to the percent increase from 12 to what number?

A) 16.8
B) 19.0
C) 26.6
D) 28.8

$$b = \frac{L}{4\pi d^2}$$

13. The brightness of a celestial body, like a star, decreases as you move away from it. In contrast, the luminosity of a celestial body is a constant number that represents its intrinsic brightness. The inverse square law, shown above, is used to find the brightness, $b$, of a celestial body when you know its luminosity, $L$, and the distance, $d$, in meters to the body. Which equation shows the distance to a celestial body, given its brightness and luminosity?

A) $d = \dfrac{1}{2}\sqrt{\dfrac{L}{\pi b}}$

B) $d = \sqrt{\dfrac{L}{2\pi b}}$

C) $d = \dfrac{\sqrt{L}}{2\pi b}$

D) $d = \dfrac{L}{2\sqrt{\pi b}}$

GO ON TO THE NEXT PAGE ⟩

**Questions 14 and 15 refer to the following information.**

Each month, the Bureau of Labor Statistics conducts a survey called the Current Population Survey (CPS) to measure unemployment in the United States. Across the country, about 60,000 households are included in the survey sample. These households are grouped by geographic region. A summary of the January 2014 survey results for male respondents in one geographic region is shown in the table below.

| Age Group | Employed | Unemployed | Not in the Labor Force | Total |
|-----------|----------|------------|------------------------|-------|
| 16–19 | 8 | 5 | 10 | 23 |
| 20–24 | 26 | 7 | 23 | 56 |
| 25–34 | 142 | 11 | 28 | 157 |
| 35–44 | 144 | 8 | 32 | 164 |
| 45–54 | 66 | 6 | 26 | 98 |
| Over 54 | 65 | 7 | 36 | 152 |
| Total | 451 | 44 | 155 | 650 |

14. According to the data in the table, for which age group did the smallest percentage of men report that they were unemployed in January 2014?

    A) 20 to 24 years

    B) 35 to 44 years

    C) 45 to 54 years

    D) Over 54 years

15. If one unemployed man from this sample is chosen at random for a follow-up survey, what is the probability that he will be between the ages of 45 and 54?

    A) 6.0%

    B) 13.6%

    C) 15.1%

    D) 44.9%

16. Which of the following are solutions to the quadratic equation $(x-1)^2 = \dfrac{4}{9}$?

    A) $x = -\dfrac{5}{3}, x = \dfrac{5}{3}$

    B) $x = \dfrac{1}{3}, x = \dfrac{5}{3}$

    C) $x = \dfrac{5}{9}, x = \dfrac{13}{9}$

    D) $x = 1 \pm \sqrt{\dfrac{2}{3}}$

17. Damien is throwing darts. He has a total of 6 darts to throw. He gets 5 points for each dart that lands in a blue ring and 10 points for each dart that lands in a red ring. If $x$ of his darts land in a blue ring and the rest land in a red ring, which expression represents his total score?

    A) $10x$

    B) $10x + 5$

    C) $5x + 30$

    D) $60 - 5x$

18. Red tide is a form of harmful algae that releases toxins as it breaks down in the environment. A marine biologist is testing a new spray, composed of clay and water, hoping to kill the red tide that almost completely covers a beach in southern Florida. He applies the spray to a representative sample of 200 square feet of the beach. By the end of the week, 184 square feet of the beach is free of the red tide. Based on these results, and assuming the same general conditions, how many square feet of the 10,000-square-foot beach would still be covered by red tide if the spray had been used on the entire area?

    A) 800

    B) 920

    C) 8,000

    D) 9,200

GO ON TO THE NEXT PAGE

$$\begin{cases} y = \frac{1}{2}x - 2 \\ y = -x^2 + 1 \end{cases}$$

19. If $(a, b)$ is a solution to the system of equations above, which of the following could be the value of $b$?

   A) $-3$
   B) $-2$
   C) $1$
   D) $2$

20. Given the function $g(x) = \frac{2}{3}x + 7$, what domain value corresponds to a range value of 3 ?

   A) $-6$
   B) $-2$
   C) $6$
   D) $9$

21. A landscaper buys a new commercial-grade lawn mower that costs \$2,800. Based on past experience, he expects it to last about 8 years, and then he can sell it for scrap metal with a salvage value of about \$240. Assuming the value of the lawn mower depreciates at a constant rate, which equation could be used to find its approximate value after $x$ years, given that $x < 8$ ?

   A) $y = -8x + 2,560$
   B) $y = -240x + 2,800$
   C) $y = -320x + 2,800$
   D) $y = 240x - 2,560$

22. A microbiologist is studying the effects of a new antibiotic on a culture of 20,000 bacteria. When the antibiotic is added to the culture, the number of bacteria is reduced by half every hour. What kind of function best models the number of bacteria remaining in the culture after the antibiotic is added?

   A) A linear function
   B) A quadratic function
   C) A polynomial function
   D) An exponential function

23. An airline company purchased two new airplanes. One can travel at speeds of up to 600 miles per hour and the other at speeds of up to 720 miles per hour. How many more miles can the faster airplane travel in 12 seconds than the slower airplane?

   A) $\dfrac{1}{30}$
   B) $\dfrac{2}{5}$
   C) $2$
   D) $30$

| State | Minimum Wage per Hour |
|---|---|
| Idaho | \$7.25 |
| Montana | \$7.90 |
| Oregon | \$9.10 |
| Washington | \$9.32 |

24. The table above shows the 2014 minimum wages for several states that share a border. Assuming an average workweek of between 35 and 40 hours, which inequality represents how much more a worker who earns minimum wage can earn per week in Oregon than in Idaho?

   A) $x \geq 1.85$
   B) $7.25 \leq x \leq 9.10$
   C) $64.75 \leq x \leq 74$
   D) $253.75 \leq x \leq 364$

GO ON TO THE NEXT PAGE ⇨

25. In the United States, the maintenance and construction of airports, transit systems, and major roads is largely funded through a federal excise tax on gasoline. Based on the 2011 statistics given below, how much did the average household pay per year in federal gasoline taxes?

    - The federal gasoline tax rate was 18.4 cents per gallon.

    - The average motor vehicle was driven approximately 11,340 miles per year.

    - The national average fuel economy for noncommercial vehicles was 21.4 miles per gallon.

    - The average American household owned 1.75 vehicles.

    A) $55.73

    B) $68.91

    C) $97.52

    D) $170.63

26. Following the catastrophic oil spill in the Gulf of Mexico in April of 2010, more than 900 bottlenose dolphins were found dead or stranded in the oil spill area. The figure above shows the weight of a rescued dolphin during its recovery. Based on the quadratic model fit to the data shown, which of the following is the closest to the average rate of change in the dolphin's weight between week 2 and week 8 of its recovery?

    A) 4 pounds per week

    B) 16 pounds per week

    C) 20 pounds per week

    D) 40 pounds per week

Lifeguard — 60 feet — 30 feet — 40 feet — Swimmer

27. As shown in the figure above, a lifeguard sees a struggling swimmer who is 40 feet from the beach. The lifeguard runs 60 feet along the edge of the water at a speed of 12 feet per second. He pauses for 1 second to locate the swimmer again, and then dives into the water and swims along a diagonal path to the swimmer at a speed of 5 feet per second. How many seconds go by between the time the lifeguard sees the struggling swimmer and the time he reaches the swimmer?

A) 16

B) 22

C) 50

D) 56

28. What was the initial amount of gasoline in a fuel trailer, in gallons, if there are now $x$ gallons, $y$ gallons were pumped into a storage tank, and then 50 gallons were added to the trailer?

A) $x + y + 50$

B) $x + y - 50$

C) $y - x + 50$

D) $x - y - 50$

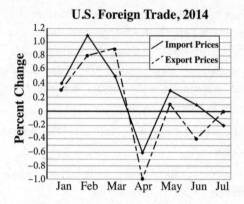

U.S. Foreign Trade, 2014

29. The figure above shows the net change, as a percentage, for U.S. import and export prices from January to July 2014 as reported by the Bureau of Labor Statistics. For example, U.S. import prices declined 0.2 percent in July while export prices remained unchanged for that month. Based on this information, which of the following statements is true for the time period shown in the figure?

A) On average, export prices increased more than import prices.

B) Import prices showed an increase more often than export prices.

C) Import prices showed the greatest change between two consecutive months.

D) From January to July, import prices showed a greater overall decrease than export prices.

GO ON TO THE NEXT PAGE

$$\frac{3.86}{x} + \frac{180.2}{10x} + \frac{42.2}{5x}$$

30. The Ironman Triathlon originated in Hawaii in 1978. The format of the Ironman has not changed since then: it consists of a 3.86-kilometer swim, a 180.2-kilometer bicycle ride, and a 42.2-kilometer run, all raced in that order and without a break. Suppose an athlete bikes 10 times as fast as he swims and runs 5 times as fast as he swims. The variable $x$ in the expression above represents the rate at which the athlete swims, and the whole expression represents the number of hours that it takes him to complete the race. If it takes him 16.2 hours to complete the race, how many kilometers did he swim in 1 hour?

A) 0.85

B) 1.01

C) 1.17

D) 1.87

**Directions:** For questions 31–38, enter your responses into the appropriate grid on your answer sheet, in accordance with the following:

1. You will receive credit only if the circles are filled in correctly, but you may write your answers in the boxes above each grid to help you fill in the circles accurately.

2. Don't mark more than one circle per column.

3. None of the questions with grid-in responses will have a negative solution.

4. Only grid in a single answer, even if there is more than one correct answer to a given question.

5. A **mixed number** must be gridded as a decimal or an improper fraction. For example, you would grid $7\frac{1}{2}$ as 7.5 or 15/2.

   (Were you to grid it as ⌷7⌷1⌷/⌷2⌷, this response would be interpreted as $\frac{71}{2}$.)

6. A **decimal** that has more digits than there are places on the grid may be either rounded or truncated, but every column in the grid must be filled in order to receive credit.

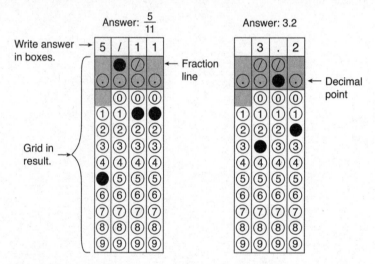

GO ON TO THE NEXT PAGE ⇨

31. What value of $x$ satisfies the equation $\frac{2}{3}(5x + 7) = 8x$ ?

32. Some doctors base the dosage of a drug to be given to a patient on the patient's body surface area ($BSA$). The most commonly used formula for calculating $BSA$ is $BSA = \sqrt{\dfrac{wh}{3,600}}$, where $w$ is the patient's weight (in kilograms), $h$ is the patient's height (in centimeters), and $BSA$ is measured in square meters. How tall (in centimeters) is a patient who weighs 150 kilograms and has a $BSA$ of $2\sqrt{2}$ square meters?

33. A college math professor informs her students that rather than grading the final exam on a curve, she will replace each student's lowest test score with the next to lowest test score, and then re-average the test grades. If Leeza has test scores of 86, 92, 81, 64, and 83, by how many points does her final test average change based on the professor's policy?

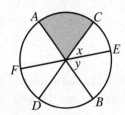

34. In the figure above, $\overline{AB}$, $\overline{CD}$, and $\overline{EF}$ are diameters of the circle. If $y = 2x - 12$, and the shaded area is $\frac{1}{5}$ of the circle, what is the value of $x$ ?

35. If the slope of a line is $-\frac{7}{4}$ and a point on the line is $(4, 7)$, what is the $y$-intercept of the line?

36. Rory left home and drove straight to the airport at an average speed of 45 miles per hour. He returned home along the same route, but traffic slowed him down and he only averaged 30 miles per hour on the return trip. If his total travel time was 2 hours and 30 minutes, how far is it, in miles, from Rory's house to the airport?

**Questions 37 and 38 refer to the following information.**

**Chemical Makeup of One Mole of Chloroform**

| Element | Number of Moles | Mass per Mole (grams) |
|---|---|---|
| Carbon | 1 | 12.011 |
| Hydrogen | 1 | 1.008 |
| Chlorine | 3 | 35.453 |

A chemical solvent is a substance that dissolves another to form a solution. For example, water is a solvent for sugar. Unfortunately, many chemical solvents are hazardous to the environment. One ecofriendly chemical solvent is chloroform, also known as trichloromethane ($CHCl_3$). The table above shows the chemical makeup of one mole of chloroform.

37. Carbon makes up what percent of the mass of one mole of chloroform? Round your answer to the nearest whole percent and ignore the percent sign when entering your answer.

38. If a chemist starts with 1,000 grams of chloroform and uses 522.5 grams, how many moles of chlorine are left?

IF YOU FINISH BEFORE TIME IS CALLED, YOU MAY CHECK YOUR WORK ON THIS SECTION ONLY. DO NOT TURN TO ANY OTHER SECTION IN THE TEST. **STOP**

Practice Tests

K 835

# Essay Test

### 50 Minutes

You will be given a passage to read and asked to write an essay analyzing it. As you write, be sure to show that you have read the passage closely. You will be graded on how well you have understood the passage, how clear your analysis is, and how well you express your ideas.

Your essay must be written on the lines in your answer booklet. Anything you write outside the lined space in your answer booklet will not be read by the essay graders. Be sure to write or print in such a way that it will be legible to readers not familiar with your handwriting. Additionally, be sure to address the passage directly. An off-topic essay will not be graded.

---

As you read the passage, think about the author's use of

- evidence, such as statistics or other facts.

- logic to connect evidence to conclusions and to develop lines of reasoning.

- style, word choice, and appeals to emotion to make the argument more persuasive.

---

**Adapted from Elisabeth Woodbridge Morris's essay "The Tyranny of Things." In this portion, Morris paints a portrait of American consumerism in 1917 and offers a distinct perspective on the joy of freedom from "things, things, things."**

1   Two fifteen-year-old girls stood eyeing one another on first acquaintance. Finally one little girl said, "Which do you like best, people or things?" The other little girl said, "Things." They were friends at once.

2   I suppose we all go through a phase when we like things best; and not only like them, but want to possess them under our hand. The passion for accumulation is upon us. We make "collections," we fill our rooms, our walls, our tables, our desks, with things, things, things.

3   Many people never pass out of this phase. They never see a flower without wanting to pick it and put it in a vase, they never enjoy a book without wanting to own it, nor a picture without wanting to hang it on their walls. They keep photographs of all their friends and Kodak albums of all the places they visit, they save all their theater programmes and dinner cards, they bring home all their alpenstocks.* Their houses are filled with an undigested mass of things, like the terminal moraine where a glacier dumps at length everything it has picked up during its progress through the lands.

4   But to some of us a day comes when we begin to grow weary of things. We realize that we do not possess them; they possess us. Our books are a burden to us, our pictures have destroyed every restful wall-space, our china is a care, our photographs drive us mad, our programmes and alpenstocks fill us with loathing. We feel stifled with the sense of things, and our problem becomes, not how much we can accumulate, but how much we can do without. We send our books to the village library, and our pictures to the college settlement. Such things as we cannot give away, and have not the courage to destroy, we stack in the garret, where they lie huddled in dim and dusty heaps, removed from our sight, to be sure, yet still faintly importunate.

5   Then, as we breathe more freely in the clear space that we have made for ourselves, we grow aware that we must not relax our vigilance, or we shall be once more overwhelmed....

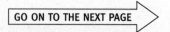

6    It extends to all our doings. For every event there is a "souvenir." We cannot go to luncheon and meet our friends but we must receive a token to carry away. Even our children cannot have a birthday party, and play games, and eat good things, and be happy. The host must receive gifts from every little guest, and provide in return some little remembrance for each to take home. Truly, on all sides we are beset, and we go lumbering along through life like a ship encrusted with barnacles, which can never cut the waves clean and sure and swift until she has been scraped bare again. And there seems little hope for us this side our last port.

7    And to think that there was a time when folk had not even that hope! When a man's possessions were burned with him, so that he might, forsooth, have them all about him in the next world! Suffocating thought! To think one could not even then be clear of things, and make at least a fresh start! That must, indeed, have been in the childhood of the race.

8    Once upon a time, when I was very tired, I chanced to go away to a little house by the sea.... There was nothing in the house to demand care, to claim attention, to cumber my consciousness with its insistent, unchanging companionship. There was nothing but a shelter, and outside, the fields and marshes, the shore and the sea. These did not have to be taken down and put up and arranged and dusted and cared for. They were not things at all, they were powers, presences....

9    If we could but free ourselves once for all, how simple life might become! One of my friends, who, with six young children and only one servant, keeps a spotless house and a soul serene, told me once how she did it. "My dear, once a month I give away every single thing in the house that we do not imperatively need. It sounds wasteful, but I don't believe it really is...."

> Write an essay in which you explain how Morris builds an argument to persuade her audience that possessions are oppressive. In your essay, analyze how Morris uses one or more of the features listed in the box that precedes the passage (or features of your own choice) to strengthen the logic and persuasiveness of her argument. Be sure that your analysis focuses on the most relevant features of the passage.
>
> Your essay should not focus on your own opinion of the author's conclusion, but rather on how the author persuades his readers.

IF YOU FINISH BEFORE TIME IS CALLED, YOU MAY CHECK YOUR WORK ON THIS SECTION ONLY. DO NOT TURN TO ANY OTHER SECTION IN THE TEST.    **STOP**

K    837

# Answer Key
## Reading Test

| | | | |
|---|---|---|---|
| 1. A | 14. B | 27. D | 40. D |
| 2. B | 15. D | 28. C | 41. A |
| 3. C | 16. C | 29. C | 42. A |
| 4. C | 17. A | 30. B | 43. A |
| 5. A | 18. D | 31. D | 44. B |
| 6. C | 19. C | 32. C | 45. A |
| 7. D | 20. C | 33. D | 46. B |
| 8. A | 21. C | 34. B | 47. D |
| 9. D | 22. B | 35. C | 48. D |
| 10. A | 23. D | 36. C | 49. A |
| 11. D | 24. C | 37. B | 50. C |
| 12. D | 25. A | 38. C | 51. D |
| 13. D | 26. A | 39. A | 52. C |

## Writing and Language Test

| | | | |
|---|---|---|---|
| 1. C | 12. B | 23. C | 34. B |
| 2. D | 13. B | 24. B | 35. A |
| 3. B | 14. B | 25. D | 36. C |
| 4. C | 15. A | 26. B | 37. C |
| 5. A | 16. A | 27. B | 38. B |
| 6. C | 17. C | 28. C | 39. C |
| 7. B | 18. A | 29. B | 40. B |
| 8. D | 19. B | 30. C | 41. A |
| 9. C | 20. C | 31. B | 42. D |
| 10. C | 21. D | 32. D | 43. D |
| 11. A | 22. D | 33. A | 44. C |

## Math Test—No-Calculator

| | | | |
|---|---|---|---|
| 1. C | 6. D | 11. C | 16. 20 |
| 2. A | 7. D | 12. B | 17. 1 |
| 3. D | 8. B | 13. A | 18. 2 |
| 4. C | 9. B | 14. D | 19. 14 |
| 5. B | 10. A | 15. A | 20. 6 |

## Math Test—Calculator

| | | | |
|---|---|---|---|
| 1. C | 11. B | 21. C | 31. 1 |
| 2. C | 12. D | 22. D | 32. 192 |
| 3. D | 13. A | 23. B | 33. 3.4 |
| 4. A | 14. D | 24. C | 34. 40 |
| 5. B | 15. B | 25. D | 35. 14 |
| 6. C | 16. B | 26. C | 36. 45 |
| 7. D | 17. D | 27. A | 37. 10 |
| 8. B | 18. A | 28. B | 38. 12 |
| 9. A | 19. A | 29. B | |
| 10. C | 20. A | 30. D | |

# Answers and Explanations

## Reading Test

Suggested passage map notes:

¶1: Levin goes to skating rink to find Kitty

¶2: description of day, people

¶3: walks to skating area; nervous, sees K skating

¶4: knows her right away, still nervous

¶5: lots of happy people skating

¶6: cousin greets him

### 1. A

**Difficulty:** Easy

**Category:** Detail

**Getting to the Answer:** Make sure to read the passage closely so events are clearly understood. The first paragraph explicitly states how Levin knew that Kitty was there: he saw her family's carriage. Choice **(A)** matches the information stated in the passage.

### 2. B

**Difficulty:** Medium

**Category:** Vocab-in-Context

**Getting to the Answer:** Use context clues to help you distinguish the shades of meaning each word has. Two of the answer choices have a somewhat negative connotation. The author is not describing the scene in a negative way. In this passage, the word "swarmed" means "gathered." Therefore, **(B)** is the correct answer. The other words' connotations do not fit with the context of the sentence.

### 3. C

**Difficulty:** Hard

**Category:** Inference

**Getting to the Answer:** Look for clues in the text that suggest what Levin is like. Emotionally charged phrases, such as "the rapture and the terror that seized on his heart" (lines 31–32), help reveal Levin's personality. Choice **(C)** reflects the depiction of Levin as a passionate person.

### 4. C

**Difficulty:** Hard

**Category:** Command of Evidence

**Getting to the Answer:** Eliminate answer choices that don't include a description of Levin. Because the excerpt focuses on Levin's feelings toward Kitty, evidence of the kind of person he is will probably reflect this. Choice **(C)** provides the best evidence.

### 5. A

**Difficulty:** Medium

**Category:** Global

**Getting to the Answer:** The central theme of a passage is the insight about life that the author is trying to get across to the reader. Eliminate any themes that are not revealed by the experiences of Levin. Though you may personally agree with more than one of the themes presented, **(A)** is the only answer choice that is supported by details in the passage. Levin's feelings and actions support this theme.

### 6. C

**Difficulty:** Medium

**Category:** Inference

**Getting to the Answer:** Examine the passage to see what other characters do in response to Levin. The other skaters go about their business. Most take little notice of Levin. Therefore, **(C)** is the correct answer.

### 7. D

**Difficulty:** Medium

**Category:** Command of Evidence

**Getting to the Answer:** Reread each quote in the context of the passage. This will help you decide the correct answer. Of all the answer choices, Nikolay's way of greeting Levin is the strongest evidence that people think Levin seems normal. Choice **(D)** is the correct answer.

**8. A**

**Difficulty:** Medium

**Category:** Vocab-in-Context

**Getting to the Answer:** The context of the passage can help reveal the meaning of the word. Insert each choice in the sentence to see which one makes the most sense. Levin speaks directly to his heart, asking it to behave. Choice **(A)**, "begged," comes closest to meaning the same thing as "conjured" in this context.

**9. D**

**Difficulty:** Medium

**Category:** Function

**Getting to the Answer:** Think about the entire scene described in the passage and decide why the author chose to describe Levin's heart as "throbbing." Choice **(D)** is the correct answer. The author chose this word to capture Levin's agitated state.

**10. A**

**Difficulty:** Hard

**Category:** Inference

**Getting to the Answer:** Eliminate answer choices that are clearly not representative of the author's feelings or attitude about Levin. The author presents Levin's situation as one that is painful. The passage's tone suggests that Levin is worthy of the reader's empathy. Choice **(A)** fits this tone.

Suggested passage map notes:

¶1: U.S. devoted to democracy

¶2: must think about soc. & eco. problems which → soc. revol.

¶3: list of basics of dem.

¶4: must maintain basics

¶5: list of what should be improved

¶6: Americans will personally sacrifice for them

¶7: explain tax changes

¶8: people will be ok with them

¶9: four essential human freedoms

¶10: freedom of speech and expression

¶11: freedom of religion

¶12: freedom from want

¶13: freedom from fear

¶14: are attainable now; against new order of tyranny

¶15: moral order

¶16: change can made done peacefully

¶17: U.S. supports human rights everywhere and will win

**11. D**

**Difficulty:** Hard

**Category:** Global

**Getting to the Answer:** The introduction to the passage states that President Roosevelt intends to preserve and spread democracy. Choice **(D)** makes clear that the president wants to promote human rights, which can be achieved by spreading "American ideals around the world."

**12. D**

**Difficulty:** Hard

**Category:** Command of Evidence

**Getting to the Answer:** Be careful of choices that do not provide direct evidence to support the president's purpose. The correct answer will relate specifically to the stated purpose, or intent, of the passage. President Roosevelt makes clear that his intention is to provide support for global efforts to end tyranny and spread democracy and to garner the support of the American people for these goals. In the previous question, his stated purpose is to "make its people conscious of their individual stake in the preservation of democratic life in America" (lines 3–4). Only **(D)** provides direct evidence for the previous question.

**13. D**

**Difficulty:** Easy

**Category:** Vocab-in-Context

**Getting to the Answer:** All answer choices are alternate meanings of the word "sacrifice." The correct answer will relate directly to the context of the passage. Despite the fact that Roosevelt gave the speech on the eve of America's involvement in World War II, neither (B) nor (C) is the meaning he's after. Choice **(D)**, "surrender of interests to a greater good," is the correct answer.

**14. B**

**Difficulty:** Hard

**Category:** Inference

**Getting to the Answer:** Keep in mind that you're looking for a relationship that is suggested, not stated. To reach the correct answer, you must infer, or make a logical guess, based on information in the passage. The correct answer will provide support for the stated purpose of the passage while demonstrating a logical relationship. Choice **(B)** provides support for the stated goal of winning support among U.S. citizens for the spread of democracy abroad. It does so by suggesting that the security of U.S. democracy depends on the advancement of human rights and freedoms globally.

**15. D**

**Difficulty:** Medium

**Category:** Command of Evidence

**Getting to the Answer:** Avoid answers that provide evidence for incorrect answers to the previous question. The correct answer will use language reflective of the correct answer above to demonstrate a relationship. Principles and ideas such as democracy, freedom, and protection of human rights are used interchangeably throughout Roosevelt's speech. The lines in **(D)** draw the connection between freedom at home and freedom everywhere.

**16. C**

**Difficulty:** Easy

**Category:** Vocab-in-Context

**Getting to the Answer:** Substitute each answer choice for the word in question and decide which one fits the context provided in the passage. In the context of the passage, **(C)** works best. It draws a distinction between individual citizens' monetary interests, or their pocketbooks, and the cause of patriotism, or the greater good.

**17. A**

**Difficulty:** Medium

**Category:** Inference

**Getting to the Answer:** Keep in mind that the correct answer will relate directly to the meaning of the elements in the identified lines. President Roosevelt is arguing against those who would oppose the overarching goal of his speech, namely to garner support for the spread of democracy overseas. Choice **(A)** fits best; Roosevelt asserts that his goals are realistic and attainable, not just idealistic visions, as his opponents might claim.

**18. D**

**Difficulty:** Medium

**Category:** Command of Evidence

**Getting to the Answer:** Be wary of answers like (A) and (B) that seem to offer specific advice or state specific goals relevant to the purpose of the passage without suggesting how those goals might be achieved. The correct answer will offer a tool, a condition, or another asset for achieving the passage's claim—in this case, the spread of democracy. The previous question identifies that President Roosevelt considers the spread of global democracy achievable. This question asks you to identify how the president envisions achieving that purpose. Choice **(D)** matches the intent. In this line, President Roosevelt identifies "our unity of purpose" as an asset that will help achieve his goal.

**19. C**

**Difficulty:** Hard

**Category:** Inference

**Getting to the Answer:** Be careful of answers that cite other policies that the president might support that are not related to the lines quoted. The correct answer will relate directly to the specific lines in question. In this speech, Roosevelt identifies four freedoms that he views the United States as obligated to defend. The freedom from want signifies a commitment to helping struggling populations at home and abroad. Choice **(C)** fits. The president urges economic understandings among nations to help those in need.

## 20. C

**Difficulty:** Medium

**Category:** Function

**Getting to the Answer:** Be careful of answers like (A) that offer other viable uses of rhetoric within the larger passage. The correct answer will relate specifically to the text cited in the question. Roosevelt suggests that the preservation of American freedoms cannot exist without the preservation of human rights on a global scale. To cement this connection, he contrasts democratic movements with tyrannical movements occurring in the world. Choice **(C)** is the correct answer. President Roosevelt references "the so-called new order of tyranny" in order to show what might happen should the United States and the American people not support other nations in their fight against such tyranny.

Suggested passage map notes:

¶1: changes in Am. voting process

¶2: women's voting history; Seneca Falls declaration

¶3: 1878 — amendment proposed, federal gov't not ready

¶4: women voting in New Zealand, Australia, United Kingdom

¶5: WWI → female activism; 19th Amendment passed in 1919, ratified 1920

¶6: elections still not equal b/c Af. Americans often disenfranchised; 1965 Voting Rights Act → voting equality for all

## 21. C

**Difficulty:** Medium

**Category:** Inference

**Getting to the Answer:** Keep in mind that the "stance" of an author refers to his or her perspective or attitude toward the topic. The passage is written by a scholar or a historian who is looking back on the events that led to the adoption of the Nineteenth Amendment. It is not written by a primary source, such as a legislator or an advocate in the midst of the movement's events. For this reason, **(C)** is the correct answer. The author of the passage is clearly a scholar evaluating not just the motivation of women's suffrage leaders but the key events and impact of the movement as a whole.

## 22. B

**Difficulty:** Hard

**Category:** Inference

**Getting to the Answer:** Avoid answers like (A) that refer to related issues not relevant to the passage's purpose and answers like (D) that go too far. The correct answer will identify a claim that is supported by the quotation. In the quote, the author notes that election laws following passage of the Nineteenth Amendment did not secure equal voting rights for all. From this statement, it becomes clear that other groups of people still needed support for their voting rights. Answer **(B)** is correct.

## 23. D

**Difficulty:** Medium

**Category:** Command of Evidence

**Getting to the Answer:** Reread the line quoted in the previous question and notice that it occurs in the passage after ratification of the Nineteenth Amendment. Therefore, the evidence you're looking for will refer to an event that came later. The author suggests that the Nineteenth Amendment did not win equal voting rights for all citizens but that it did serve as an important step on the way to free and fair elections. Choice **(D)** demonstrates that a later event expanded voting rights further, to citizens regardless not only of gender but also of race.

## 24. C

**Difficulty:** Easy

**Category:** Vocab-in-Context

**Getting to the Answer:** Consider the events that are being described in the paragraph in which the word appears. This will help you choose the best answer. It's clear in this paragraph that the women's suffrage movement was gaining momentum at this time. Events and tactics excited those who supported the movement and attracted more supporters. Therefore, **(C)** reflects the correct meaning of "galvanized."

**25. A**

**Difficulty:** Hard

**Category:** Function

**Getting to the Answer:** Carefully review the paragraph in which the line appears before choosing the best answer. Choice **(A)** demonstrates the connection between successfully changing one element (people's minds) in order to change the other (laws).

**26. A**

**Difficulty:** Hard

**Category:** Inference

**Getting to the Answer:** Be wary of answers like (D) that go too far in asserting unsubstantiated causal relationships. The correct answer will reference an idea or a relationship that is supported by the content of the passage. Choice **(A)** expresses the idea implicit in the passage that the American government responds, sometimes slowly, to the changing needs and sentiments of the American people.

**27. D**

**Difficulty:** Hard

**Category:** Command of Evidence

**Getting to the Answer:** Watch for answers like (A) and (C) that cite specific changes or examples but do not provide direct support. The correct answer to the previous question states the idea implicit in the passage that the government responds and adapts to changes in U.S. society. This suggests a gradual change. Choice **(D)** demonstrates the idea that both society and the government have changed over time as the civil rights movement of the late twentieth century overcame social and legal inequalities inherited from earlier in the nation's history.

**28. C**

**Difficulty:** Medium

**Category:** Inference

**Getting to the Answer:** Be careful of answers that aren't backed by sufficient evidence in the graphic. The graphic shows proof that women's suffrage unfolded through a series of events over a long period of time. Choice **(C)** is the correct answer.

**29. C**

**Difficulty:** Medium

**Category:** Vocab-in-Context

**Getting to the Answer:** Read the sentence in which the word appears. The correct answer should be interchangeable with the word. The passage states in lines 60–62 that "Posters . . . called into question the authenticity of a free country with unjust laws." Choice **(C)** is the correct answer as "legitimacy" refers to something that is in accordance with established principles.

**30. B**

**Difficulty:** Medium

**Category:** Inference

**Getting to the Answer:** Be cautious about answers that present accurate facts but that do not directly relate to the content of the question. Choice **(B)** is the correct answer. Wilson's framing of the conflict abroad as a fight for democracy and freedom helped women suffragists draw attention to the fact that the U.S. government was fighting for justice abroad while denying justice at home.

**31. D**

**Difficulty:** Medium

**Category:** Inference

**Getting to the Answer:** A question like this is asking you to compare information provided in the graphic with information provided in the passage text. Consider each answer choice as you make your comparison. Choice **(D)** is the correct answer. Both the graphic and the passage indicate that women's suffrage gained early victories in several states quite a few years before becoming law at the federal level through passage of the Nineteenth Amendment.

Practice Tests

Suggested passage map notes:

Passage 1

>¶1: (central idea): use atoms to date things; isotopes def. & exs.
>¶2: isotopes unstable; measure C-14
>¶3: C-14 decay = predictable
>¶4: C-14 dating; materials; timeline based on layers

Passage 2

>¶1: def. radioactive; why dangerous; danger = radiation rate
>¶2: half-life def. = decay rate; exs.
>¶3: long half-life = long problem

**32. C**

**Difficulty:** Hard

**Category:** Inference

**Getting to the Answer:** Use your passage map to locate the paragraph that explains carbon-14 dating. This paragraph will contain the description of what materials can be dated using this method. In paragraph 4, the author states that carbon-14 dating can be used on materials made by a living organism. An arrowhead made from a bone is constructed of such material, choice **(C)**.

**33. D**

**Difficulty:** Hard

**Category:** Command of Evidence

**Getting to the Answer:** Locate each of the answer choices in the passage. The correct answer should provide direct support for the answer to the previous question: the bone arrowhead can be dated using carbon-14 dating. In paragraph 4, the author describes the process for carbon-14 dating. Choice **(D)** is correct because this sentence provides a direct description of the materials that can be dated using carbon-14 dating.

**34. B**

**Difficulty:** Medium

**Category:** Vocab-in-Context

**Getting to the Answer:** Pretend that the word "decay" is a blank. Reread around the cited word to predict a word that could substitute for "decay" in context.

The previous paragraph discusses how scientists measure the rate of emission to calculate the amount of carbon-14 in a sample. "Emission" means release; therefore, the amount of carbon-14 is becoming smaller if the atoms are releasing it. In this sentence, therefore, predict "decay" means to *decrease*, which matches "deteriorate," choice **(B)**.

**35. C**

**Difficulty:** Easy

**Category:** Detail

**Getting to the Answer:** Look at your notes for paragraph 3. Summarize the ratio of carbon-12 to carbon-14 in living tissue in your own words. Look for the answer choice that most closely matches your prediction. In paragraph 3, the author explains that the ratio of carbon-12 to carbon-14 for living things is the same as the ratio in the atmosphere: constant. Choice **(C)** is correct.

**36. C**

**Difficulty:** Medium

**Category:** Command of Evidence

**Getting to the Answer:** Review what part of the passage you used to predict an answer for the previous question: the ratio is constant for living things. Of the answer choices, only lines 26–29 explain the ratio of carbon-12 to carbon-14 in living things. Choice **(C)** is correct.

**37. B**

**Difficulty:** Medium

**Category:** Detail

**Getting to the Answer:** Read around the cited lines. The author directly states why a release of iodine-131 is not cause for long-term concern. In paragraph 3, the author explains that the initial release of radiation from an accident involving iodine-131 will be high, but the level of radiation will drop quickly (lines 71–72). Choice **(B)** is correct.

**38. C**

**Difficulty:** Medium

**Category:** Detail

**Getting to the Answer:** Use your passage map to find the information about why exposure to radiation is dangerous.

**Getting to the Answer:** In paragraph 1, lines 50–52, the author explains that radiation is harmful to living tissue because it can cause damage to the cells' DNA, which matches choice **(C)**.

**39. A**

**Difficulty:** Easy

**Category:** Vocab-in-Context

**Getting to the Answer:** Pretend that the word "original" is a blank. Reread around the cited word to predict a word that could substitute for "original" in context. The previous paragraph explains how scientists use "half-life" to determine how quickly material decays. If the material is decaying, then predict "original" refers to the *first* material. Choice **(A)** matches your prediction.

**40. D**

**Difficulty:** Medium

**Category:** Detail

**Getting to the Answer:** Review your notes for Passage 2. Try to put into your own words how scientists use half-life calculations of radioactive materials. Look for the answer that most closely matches your idea. In paragraph 1, the author explains that the level of danger posed by radiation released during a nuclear accident depends on how quickly radiation is released (lines 57–59). In paragraph 2, the author discusses how the half-life of radioactive material is used to determine how long a material will emit radiation. Paragraph 3 then explains how different half-lives translate into short-term or long-term radiation concerns. Choice **(D)** is correct because it most clearly paraphrases the information in the passage about how scientists use half-life calculations.

**41. A**

**Difficulty:** Hard

**Category:** Inference

**Getting to the Answer:** The central idea will be supported by all of the evidence presented in both passages. Review the central idea you identified for each passage in your passage maps. Passage 1 discusses the application of atomic and nuclear physics in archaeology, while Passage 2 details how scientists apply atomic and nuclear physics to studies of radioactivity in nuclear power plant accidents. Choice **(A)** is correct.

**42. A**

**Difficulty:** Hard

**Category:** Inference

**Getting to the Answer:** Analyze the graph to see that it describes the decay of carbon-14 over time. Think about how this data relates to the texts. The graph portrays the decay of carbon-14 as described in Passage 1. The definition of "half-life" is given in Passage 2. The half-life of a material is the amount of time it takes for half of that material to decay. The graph shows that about 50 percent of carbon-14 remains after 5,400 years. Choice **(A)** is correct.

Suggested passage map notes:

> ¶1: George de Mestral—invented velcro
> ¶2: biomimicry—study nature to improve people's homes, cities, etc.
> ¶3: used in architecture
> ¶4: Michael Pawlyn—adapt principles behind natural shapes → innovative solutions
> ¶5: used in optics and robotics
> ¶6: some natural stuff not advanced but simple: abalone shell
> ¶7: nanoscale features; Andrew Parker—skin of thorny devil
> ¶8: can learn from animal features
> ¶9: improve energy efficiency
> ¶10: radical, optimistic field

**43. A**

**Difficulty:** Medium

**Category:** Global

**Getting to the Answer:** Look for the answer choice that describes an idea supported throughout the passage rather than a specific detail. The passage cites several examples of biomimicry, the study of how materials and systems found in nature can be replicated to benefit humans. Therefore, **(A)** is the best summary of the central idea of the passage.

**44. B**

**Difficulty:** Medium

**Category:** Command of Evidence

**Getting to the Answer:** Think back to why you chose your answer to the previous question. This will help you pick the correct quote as evidence. Choice **(B)** is the correct answer because it provides evidence for the central idea that the author presents about the field of biomimicry.

**45. A**

**Difficulty:** Hard

**Category:** Function

**Getting to the Answer:** Think about the primary purpose of the quote. Eliminate any answer choices that don't support this purpose. The quote, which is from a book on architecture, explains why architects turn to biomimicry for solutions in their work. Choice **(A)** is the correct answer.

**46. B**

**Difficulty:** Medium

**Category:** Inference

**Getting to the Answer:** Reread the paragraph that the question is asking about. Look for specific details about the abalone shrimp shell and soft chalk. The passage clearly states that the abalone shrimp shell is harder than soft chalk because of the way the basic material composing each is arranged, so **(B)** is the correct answer.

**47. D**

**Difficulty:** Medium

**Category:** Function

**Getting to the Answer:** In order to understand why an author includes a quote from another person, examine the surrounding sentences. This often makes clear the author's reason for including the quotation. The author includes the quote from Pawlyn to support and strengthen his or her own view that energy efficiency "has never been more important." Therefore, **(D)** is the correct answer.

**48. D**

**Difficulty:** Easy

**Category:** Vocab-in-Context

**Getting to the Answer:** Replace the word in question with each of the answer choices. This will help you eliminate the ones that don't make sense in the context. Choice **(D)**, "concepts," is the only answer choice that makes sense in this context because it reflects the foundational reasons behind the structures.

**49. A**

**Difficulty:** Medium

**Category:** Inference

**Getting to the Answer:** Keep in mind that you're being asked to make an inference, a logical guess based on information in the passage. Therefore, the correct answer is not stated in the passage. The variety of examples of biomimicry mentioned in the passage make it reasonable to infer that more scientists will utilize solutions developed through biomimicry in the future. Choice **(A)** is the correct answer.

**50. C**

**Difficulty:** Medium

**Category:** Command of Evidence

**Getting to the Answer:** Reread each quotation in the context of the passage. Consider which one is the best evidence to support the inference made in the previous question. The examples cited in **(C)** provide strong evidence for the inference that more scientists will probably make use of biomimicry in years to come.

**51. D**

**Difficulty:** Medium

**Category:** Vocab-in-Context

**Getting to the Answer:** Eliminate answer choices that are synonyms for the word in question but do not work in the context of the sentence. Because biomimicry is such an innovative approach, it makes sense that the meaning of "radical" in this context is closest to **(D)**, "revolutionary."

**52. C**

**Difficulty:** Hard

**Category:** Inference

**Getting to the Answer:** Remember that a graphic might not refer to something explicitly stated in the passage. Instead, it often provides a visual example of how an important concept discussed in the passage works. The graphic and its caption help illustrate an example of biomimicry not mentioned in the passage: that of a solar power plant designed to mimic the arrangement of petals in a sunflower. This directs more energy toward the power plant's central tower and improves the efficiency of the power plant. Choice **(C)** is the correct answer.

## Writing and Language Test

**1. C**

**Difficulty:** Easy

**Category:** Agreement: Verbs

**Getting to the Answer:** Examine the verb tense in the rest of the sentence. This will help you find the correct answer. As written, the sentence switches verb tense mid-sentence. Other verbs in the sentence, "worked" and "was," indicate that the events happened in the past. Choice **(C)** is the correct choice because it correctly uses the past tense of the target verb.

**2. D**

**Difficulty:** Medium

**Category:** Sentence Structure: The Basics

**Getting to the Answer:** Pay attention to the quotation marks. Reading through the sentence and the answer choices shows that two issues might need correcting. The sentence inside the quotation marks is a complete sentence. The correct answer needs to punctuate that sentence before closing the quote. Additionally, "however" is being used as a connector or transition word and needs to be followed by a comma after beginning the new sentence. Choice **(D)** appropriately uses a period prior to the end quotes and correctly inserts a comma after the transition word "However."

**3. B**

**Difficulty:** Medium

**Category:** Development: Precision

**Getting to the Answer:** Watch out for choices that distort the tone of the passage. The passage suggests that people expected or anticipated that Harris would become a librarian. Evidence for this idea is found in the statement that she was "constantly told" that she "should be studying to be a librarian." Harris was certainly aware that people anticipated this course of study for her, but the presence of the phrase "Little did she realize" tells you that she didn't expect to become one. The correct choice is **(B)**, "imminent," meaning that becoming a librarian was about to occur despite her own expectations.

**4. C**

**Difficulty:** Hard

**Category:** Development: Precision

**Getting to the Answer:** Read the sentence carefully for context clues. Also, think about the tone of what is being described. This will help you choose the best answer. Given the phrasing of the sentence, the answer must be close in meaning to "excited," which is used earlier in the sentence. Therefore, **(C)** is the correct answer.

**5. A**

**Difficulty:** Medium

**Category:** Sentence Structure: The Basics

**Getting to the Answer:** Determine whether a clause is dependent or independent to decide between a comma and a semicolon. Choice **(A)** is the correct answer. The sentence is correctly punctuated as written because it uses a comma at the end of the introductory dependent clause.

**6.    C**

**Difficulty:** Medium

**Category:** Agreement: Modifiers

**Getting to the Answer:** Read the sentence carefully. The sentence sounds clunky and awkward. Look for an answer choice that makes the sentence clear and easy to understand. Notice that the word "asking" is part of a participial phrase that modifies "Miguel." A participial phrase should be placed as close as possible to the noun it modifies. When a participial phrase begins a sentence, it should be set off with a comma. Choice **(C)** is correct. The placement of commas and modifiers makes the content easy to understand, and the sentence is free of grammatical or punctuation errors.

**7.    B**

**Difficulty:** Medium

**Category:** Development: Introductions and Conclusions

**Getting to the Answer:** Read the entire paragraph carefully and predict the main idea. Then, look for a close match with your prediction. The paragraph discusses how the role of librarian has changed due to an increased use of technology. Choice **(B)** is the correct answer as it explicitly addresses the changing role of the librarian.

**8.    D**

**Difficulty:** Medium

**Category:** Agreement: Verbs

**Getting to the Answer:** Read the sentence and note the series of examples. A series should have parallel structure. The sentence is not correct as written. The items in the series switch forms from participial phrases beginning with "enabling" and "offering" to "they house." All of the items need to fit the same pattern or form. Choice **(D)** is correct because it appropriately begins each item in the series with a participle.

**9.    C**

**Difficulty:** Hard

**Category:** Development: Introductions and Conclusions

**Getting to the Answer:** Don't be fooled by answer choices that are true statements but do not directly support the main idea of the paragraph. The paragraph concerns how the role of the librarian has changed due

to an increased use of technology. The correct answer needs to support the idea that librarians work with technology in new ways. Choice **(C)** works best. It offers a specific example of how teachers look to the librarian to be a "media mentor" and illustrates this new role for school librarians.

**10.    C**

**Difficulty:** Easy

**Category:** Agreement: Pronouns

**Getting to the Answer:** Read the sentence prior to the pronoun and determine whom the pronoun is referencing. Pronouns should not be ambiguous and they must match the verb in number. The sentence is ambiguous as written. "She" would presumably refer back to the "young student," but it seems unlikely that the student would be laughing and thinking about the collections in the library after asking the librarian a question. Choice **(C)** is the best choice. It clearly indicates the subject of the sentence (Harris) and avoids ambiguity.

**11.    A**

**Difficulty:** Medium

**Category:** Agreement: Pronouns

**Getting to the Answer:** Figure out whom the pronoun refers to and make sure it matches the antecedent in number. Watch out for confusing contractions and possessives. The pronoun in the sentence needs to indicate who will have the ideas. Harris is talking to a single student, so the sentence will need a singular possessive pronoun. Choice **(A)** is correct. As it is, the sentence correctly uses a singular possessive pronoun.

**12.    B**

**Difficulty:** Medium

**Category:** Agreement: Parallelism

**Getting to the Answer:** Be careful of answers that sound correct when they stand alone but do not conform to the structure of the sentence as a whole. The existing text is incorrect as it does not maintain parallel structure. Choice **(B)** is the correct answer as it maintains the parallel structure of preposition ("into") + noun ("the role").

**13. B**

**Difficulty:** Easy

**Category:** Sentence Structure: The Basics

**Getting to the Answer:** Eliminate answers that confuse the usage of commas and semicolons. Choice **(B)** is correct. Without the comma, the following clause modifies "urban areas" when it should modify the entire preceding clause.

**14. B**

**Difficulty:** Medium

**Category:** Organization: Conciseness

**Getting to the Answer:** Avoid choices that are redundant and imprecise. The correct answer will use the clearest, most concise terminology to communicate the idea. Choice **(B)** is correct. It is the most concise—and clearest—word choice because all of the items listed in the original sentence are simply types of food. The other choices use more words than necessary to convey meaning.

**15. A**

**Difficulty:** Medium

**Category:** Organization: Transitions

**Getting to the Answer:** The first sentence should function as a transition between ideas in the previous paragraph and ideas in the current paragraph. Choice **(A)** makes sense. This choice connects ideas from the previous paragraph with the content of paragraph 3. The sentences that follow provide details to support that introductory idea.

**16. A**

**Difficulty:** Hard

**Category:** Graphs

**Getting to the Answer:** Eliminate answers like (B) that fail to support the cited sentence directly. The underlined sentence references "unprecedented amounts of human-made carbon dioxide into the air." This suggests an increase in the amount of carbon dioxide in the atmosphere over time. Therefore, **(A)** is the correct answer.

**17. C**

**Difficulty:** Medium

**Category:** Development: Transitions

**Getting to the Answer:** Choose the answer that presents the correct relationship between ideas. Choice **(C)** is correct. It shows the causal relationship without adding verbiage.

**18. A**

**Difficulty:** Easy

**Category:** Development: Precision

**Getting to the Answer:** Plug in the answer choices and select the one that reflects a specific meaning relevant to the sentence. The paragraph focuses on the negative effects of industrialization and waste production. Therefore, **(A)** is the correct answer.

**19. B**

**Difficulty:** Hard

**Category:** Relevance

**Getting to the Answer:** Be careful of choices that relate to the underlined portion of the text without showing clearly how the underlined portion supports the full implications of the preceding sentence. The paragraph explains that industrialization resulted in the destruction of resources. The correct answer, **(B)**, serves as clear evidence of the "process of destruction and reduced resources."

**20. C**

**Difficulty:** Medium

**Category:** Development: Precision

**Getting to the Answer:** Be careful of answers that make sense but do not fully support the meaning of the content. The correct answer will not only flow logically but will also reflect the precise purpose and meaning of the larger sentence and paragraph. Choice **(C)** is the correct answer. "Substandard" communicates clearly that the working conditions were the cause of the health problems.

**21. D**

**Difficulty:** Medium

**Category:** Sentence Structure: The Basics

**Getting to the Answer:** Eliminate choices that result in sentence fragments or fragmented clauses. The correct answer will maintain appropriate syntax without misusing punctuation. Choice **(D)** is correct. It sets off the dependent clause without using incorrect punctuation to signal a hard break before an independent clause or second complete sentence.

**22. D**

**Difficulty:** Hard

**Category:** Development: Introductions and Conclusions

**Getting to the Answer:** Avoid answers that draw on similar ideas but combine those ideas in a way that communicates a proposition not supported by the essay as a whole. The correct answer will make sense within the larger context of the essay. The central idea of the entire essay is that industrialization and progress came at a cost that made the promise of a bright future difficult to fulfill. Choice **(D)** is the correct answer.

**23. C**

**Difficulty:** Hard

**Category:** Development: Precision

**Getting to the Answer:** Consider the fact that there may be a choice that helps make the meaning of the sentence very precise. Choice **(C)** most accurately indicates that Freud led a whole movement.

**24. B**

**Difficulty:** Medium

**Category:** Sentence Structure: Commas, Dashes, and Colons

**Getting to the Answer:** Plug in each answer choice and select the one that seems most correct. Choice **(B)** makes it clear to the reader that this is extra information modifying the word "career."

**25. D**

**Difficulty:** Medium

**Category:** Agreement: Parallelism

**Getting to the Answer:** Remember that in a list, all things listed should be presented with the same grammatical structure. "Id," "ego," and "Freudian slip" are all nouns. Choice **(D)** is the correct answer because it uses a parallel structure for all three nouns.

**26. B**

**Difficulty:** Hard

**Category:** Development: Introductions and Conclusions

**Getting to the Answer:** Notice that the underlined sentence is the first sentence in the paragraph. Think about which choice would make the best topic sentence, given the content of the rest of the paragraph. Choice **(B)** correctly makes the free-speaking technique the focus of the paragraph's topic sentence, while suggesting that the technique was radical enough to earn Freud his title.

**27. B**

**Difficulty:** Medium

**Category:** Development: Precision

**Getting to the Answer:** Eliminate any choices that don't seem as precise as others. Choice **(B)** is correct. The word "recesses" is more precise; it connotes smaller parts of the brain and a sense of being hidden.

**28. C**

**Difficulty:** Easy

**Category:** Sentence Structure: The Basics

**Getting to the Answer:** Think about how the sentence sounds when read aloud. This often helps you get a good sense of whether or not a comma is needed. Choice **(C)** would fit here. The sentence eliminates the unneeded comma.

**29. B**

**Difficulty:** Hard

**Category:** Agreement: Modifiers

**Getting to the Answer:** Remember that a modifier should be adjacent to the noun it is modifying and set off by punctuation. Choice **(B)** is correct. The modifier "like neurosis or other psychological trauma" should come directly after "conditions."

**30. C**

**Difficulty:** Hard

**Category:** Development: Relevance

**Getting to the Answer:** Consider how this sentence relates to the one before it and the one that follows it. Does it offer strong support of the connecting ideas? This section discussed the development and lasting influence of Freud's ideas. The best supporting sentence will provide details connecting these concepts. Choice **(C)** is correct. It emphasizes that Freud developed new ideas that have had a lasting influence on psychological practices.

**31. B**

**Difficulty:** Medium

**Category:** Sentence Structure: The Basics

**Getting to the Answer:** Notice that you are dealing with a run-on sentence. Identify the point in the run-on where it appears two sentences have been fused together. Choice **(B)** is correct. This choice splits the run-on sentence into two separate, grammatically correct sentences.

**32. D**

**Difficulty:** Easy

**Category:** Agreement: Verbs

**Getting to the Answer:** Eliminate answer choices that are not complete sentences or do not maintain the correct verb tense. Choice **(D)** correctly changes the phrase "Freud's finding of a method" to "Freud found a method," making the sentence complete. It also corrects the verb tense.

**33. A**

**Difficulty:** Hard

**Category:** Sentence Structure: Commas, Dashes, and Colons

**Getting to the Answer:** Recall that when a dependent clause precedes an independent clause, it should be set off with a comma. Choice **(A)** is the best choice. Although lengthy, the dependent clause in the sentence ("as long as occasions arise . . .") is correctly combined with its independent clause ("Sigmund Freud will be remembered . . .") by use of a comma.

**34. B**

**Difficulty:** Easy

**Category:** Agreement: Verbs

**Getting to the Answer:** Always check whether two or more verbs that serve the same function have a parallel structure. Choice **(B)** is correct. "To prevent" is in the infinitive form like the earlier verb in the sentence, "to reverse."

**35. A**

**Difficulty:** Hard

**Category:** Organization: Transitions

**Getting to the Answer:** Look for the choice that most concisely and correctly joins the two sentences. Choice **(A)** is the best fit. This option joins the sentences concisely and correctly.

**36. C**

**Difficulty:** Medium

**Category:** Organization: Conciseness

**Getting to the Answer:** Remember that the best answer is the most concise and effective way of stating the information while ensuring that the information is complete. Choice **(C)** works best here. It uses the fewest necessary words to convey the complete information.

**37. C**

**Difficulty:** Medium

**Category:** Organization: Transitions

**Getting to the Answer:** Eliminate any choices that use transition words inappropriately. Two complete thoughts should be separated into two different sentences. Therefore, **(C)** is the best choice.

**38. B**

**Difficulty:** Hard

**Category:** Graphs

**Getting to the Answer:** Examine the graphic for details that suggest which answer is correct. Choice **(B)** accurately reflects the information in the graphic. Beginning in the 1990s, the size of the ozone hole began to level off.

**39. C**

**Difficulty:** Medium

**Category:** Development: Precision

**Getting to the Answer:** Check each word to see how it fits with the context of the sentence. While all of the words have similar meanings, only one fits the context of the paragraph. Choice **(C)**, "measured," has a connotation that corresponds to "gauge" in the following sentence.

**40. B**

**Difficulty:** Easy

**Category:** Agreement: Pronouns

**Getting to the Answer:** Remember that the possessive form must agree with its antecedent. The correct answer will reflect the gender and number of its antecedent; in this case, the word "treaty." Therefore, **(B)** is correct.

**41. A**

**Difficulty:** Hard

**Category:** Development: Relevance

**Getting to the Answer:** To find the central idea of a paragraph, identify important details and then summarize them in a sentence or two. Then, find the choice that is the closest to your summary. Choice **(A)** most clearly states the paragraph's central idea, that the ozone layer is beginning to return to normal.

**42. D**

**Difficulty:** Medium

**Category:** Development: Relevance

**Getting to the Answer:** To find the correct answer, first determine the central idea of the paragraph. Choice **(D)** is the least essential sentence in the paragraph, so it is the correct answer.

**43. D**

**Difficulty:** Medium

**Category:** Development: Precision

**Getting to the Answer:** Context clues indicate which word is appropriate in the sentence. Check to see which word fits best in the sentence. The word "reverse," **(D)**, fits with the context of the sentence and connotes a more precise action than does "change."

**44. C**

**Difficulty:** Hard

**Category:** Organization: Sentence Placement

**Getting to the Answer:** Examine the entire paragraph. Decide whether the sentence provides more information about a topic mentioned in one of the other sentences. This sentence provides more information related to sentence 1, "The Montreal Protocol is a living document"; it describes how the document is "living." Choice **(C)** is the correct answer.

# Math Test—No-Calculator

**1. C**

**Difficulty:** Easy

**Category:** Heart of Algebra/Linear Equations

**Getting to the Answer:** To determine what the $y$-intercept could mean in the context of a word problem, examine the labels on the graph and note what each axis represents. According to the labels, the $y$-axis represents cost and the $x$-axis represents the number of games played. The $y$-intercept, $(0, 5)$, has an $x$-value of 0, which means 0 games were played, yet there is still a cost of $5. The cost must represent a flat fee that is charged before any games are played, such as an entrance fee to enter the arcade. **(C)** is correct.

**2. A**

**Difficulty:** Easy

**Category:** Passport to Advanced Math/Exponents

**Getting to the Answer:** To divide one rational expression by another, multiply the first expression by the reciprocal (the flip) of the second expression. Rewrite the division as multiplication, factor any factorable expressions, and then simplify if possible:

$$\frac{3x}{x+5} \div \frac{6}{4x+20} = \frac{3x}{x+5} \cdot \frac{4x+20}{6}$$

$$= \frac{3x}{x+5} \cdot \frac{4(x+5)}{6}$$

$$= \frac{12x}{6}$$

$$= 2x$$

Note that the question also states that $x \neq -5$. This doesn't affect your answer—it is simply stated because the denominators of rational expressions cannot equal 0. Choice **(A)** is correct.

**3. D**

**Difficulty:** Easy

**Category:** Additional Topics in Math/Geometry

**Getting to the Answer:** When the equation of a circle is written in the form $(x - h)^2 + (y - k)^2 = r^2$, the point $(h, k)$ represents the center of the circle on a coordinate plane and $r$ represents the length of the radius. To find the area of a circle, use the formula $A = \pi r^2$. In the equation given in the question, $r^2$ is the constant on the right-hand side (25)—you don't even need to solve for $r$ because the area formula involves $r^2$, not $r$. Therefore, the area is $\pi(25)$, or $25\pi$, which matches **(D)**.

**4. C**

**Difficulty:** Easy

**Category:** Passport to Advanced Math/Functions

**Getting to the Answer:** When using function notation, $f(x)$ is simply another way of saying $y$, so this question is asking you to find the values of $x$ for which $y = 0$, or in other words, where the graph crosses the $x$-axis. The graph crosses the $x$-axis at the points $(-2, 0)$ and $(3, 0)$, so the values of $x$ for which $f(x) = 0$ are $-2$ and $3$, which matches choice **(C)**.

**5. B**

**Difficulty:** Medium

**Category:** Heart of Algebra/Linear Equations

**Getting to the Answer:** Choose the best strategy to answer the question. You could start by cross-multiplying to get rid of the denominators, but simplifying the numerators first will make the calculations easier:

$$\frac{4(d + 3) - 9}{8} = \frac{10 - (2 - d)}{6}$$

$$\frac{4d + 12 - 9}{8} = \frac{10 - 2 + d}{6}$$

$$\frac{4d + 3}{8} = \frac{8 + d}{6}$$

$$6(4d + 3) = 8(8 + d)$$

$$24d + 18 = 64 + 8d$$

$$16d = 46$$

$$d = \frac{46}{16} = \frac{23}{8}$$

Choice **(B)** is correct.

**6. D**

**Difficulty:** Medium

**Category:** Passport to Advanced Math/Functions

**Getting to the Answer:** This is a crossover question, so quickly skim the first couple of sentences. Then, look for the relevant information in the last couple of sentences. It may also help to circle the portions of the graph that meet the given requirement.

Because *greater* means *higher* on a graph, the statement $f(t) > g(t)$ translates to "Where is $f(t)$ above $g(t)$?" The solid curve represents $f$ and the dashed curve represents $g$, so $f > g$ between the years 1960 and 1980 and again between the years 2000 and 2010. Look for these time intervals in the answer choices: $1960 < t < 1980$ and $2000 < t < 2010$. This matches **(D)**.

**7. D**

**Difficulty:** Medium

**Category:** Passport to Advanced Math/Scatterplots

**Getting to the Answer:** Use the shape of the data to predict the type of equation that might be used as a model. Then, use specific values from the graph to choose the correct equation. According to the graph, the population of the whales grew slowly at first and then more quickly. This means that an exponential model is probably the best fit, so you can eliminate (A) (linear) and (B) (quadratic). The remaining equations are both exponential, so choose a data point and see which equation is the closest fit.

Be careful—the vertical axis represents *hundreds* of whales, and the question states that $t$ represents the number of years since the study began, so $t = 0$ for 1995, $t = 3$ for 1998, and so on. If you use the data for 1995, which is the point $(0, 100)$, the results are the same for both equations, so choose a different point. Using the data for 2007, $t = 2007 - 1995 = 12$, and the number of whales was 800. Substitute these values into (C) and (D) to see which one is true. Choice (C) is not true because $800 \neq 100 \times 2^{12}$. Choice **(D)** is correct because:

$$800 = 100 \times 2^{\frac{12}{4}} = 100 \times 2^3 = 100 \times 8$$

**8. B**

**Difficulty:** Medium

**Category:** Heart of Algebra/Linear Equations

**Getting to the Answer:** To find the average rate of change over the 5-year period, find the slope between the starting point (0, 1,200) and the ending point (5, 100):

$$m = \frac{y_2 - y_1}{x_2 - x_1} = \frac{100 - 1,200}{5 - 0} = \frac{-1,100}{5} = -220$$

Choice **(B)** is correct. (The average rate of change is negative because the laptop decreases in value over time.)

Note: Because the question involves *straight-line* depreciation, you could have used any two points on the graph to find the slope. As a general rule, however, you should use the endpoints of the given time interval.

**9. B**

**Difficulty:** Medium

**Category:** Passport to Advanced Math/Exponents

**Getting to the Answer:** When multiplying polynomials, carefully multiply each term in the first factor by each term in the second factor. This question doesn't ask for the entire product, so check to make sure you answered the correct question (the coefficient of $x^2$). Set up an equation and solve:

$$\left(6x^2 - \frac{2}{5}x + 1\right)\left(10x + \frac{1}{3}\right)$$
$$= 6x^2\left(10x + \frac{1}{3}\right) - \frac{2}{5}x\left(10x + \frac{1}{3}\right) + 1\left(10x + \frac{1}{3}\right)$$
$$= 60x^3 \underline{+ 2x^2 - 4x^2} - \frac{2}{15}x + 10x + \frac{1}{3}$$

The coefficient of $x^2$ is $2 + (-4) = -2$, which is **(B)**.

**10. A**

**Difficulty:** Medium

**Category:** Heart of Algebra/Linear Equations

**Getting to the Answer:** The line is decreasing, so the slope ($m$) is negative. The line crosses the $y$-axis below 0, so the $y$-intercept ($b$) is also negative. Put each answer choice in slope-intercept form, one at a time, and examine the signs of $m$ and $b$. Begin with (A):

$$-6x - 4y = 5$$
$$-4y = 6x + 5$$
$$y = \frac{6x}{-4} + \frac{5}{-4}$$
$$y = -\frac{3}{2}x - \frac{5}{4}$$

You don't need to check any of the other equations. Choice **(A)** has a negative slope and a negative $y$-intercept, so it is the correct equation.

**11. C**

**Difficulty:** Hard

**Category:** Heart of Algebra/Systems of Linear Equations

**Getting to the Answer:** Graphically, a system of linear equations that has no solution indicates two parallel lines or, in other words, two lines that have the same slope. So, write each of the equations in slope-intercept form ($y = mx + b$) and set their slopes ($m$) equal to each other to solve for $k$. Before finding the slopes, multiply the top equation by 4 to make it easier to manipulate:

$$4\left(\frac{3}{4}x - \frac{1}{2}y = 12\right) \rightarrow 3x - 2y = 48 \rightarrow y = \frac{3}{2}x - 24$$
$$kx - 2y = 22 \rightarrow -2y = -kx + 22 \rightarrow y = \frac{k}{2}x - 11$$

The slope of the first line is $\frac{3}{2}$, and the slope of the second line is $\frac{k}{2}$. Set them equal and solve for $k$:

$$\frac{3}{2} = \frac{k}{2}$$
$$2(3) = 2(k)$$
$$6 = 2k$$
$$3 = k$$

Choice **(C)** is correct.

**12. B**

**Difficulty:** Hard

**Category:** Heart of Algebra/Inequalities

**Getting to the Answer:** Before you write the inequality, you need to find the per-mile rate for the remaining miles. The driver charges $4.00 for the first $\frac{1}{4}$ mile, which is a flat fee, so write 4. The additional charge is $1.50 per $\frac{1}{2}$ mile, or $1.50 \times 2 = \$3.00$ per mile. The number of miles after the first $\frac{1}{4}$ mile is $m - \frac{1}{4}$, so the cost of the trip, not including the first $\frac{1}{4}$ mile, is $3\left(m - \frac{1}{4}\right)$. This means the cost of the whole trip is $4 + 3\left(m - \frac{1}{4}\right)$. The clue "no more than $10" means that much or less, so use the symbol $\leq$. The inequality is $4 + 3\left(m - \frac{1}{4}\right) \leq 10$, which simplifies to $3.25 + 3m \leq 10$. This matches **(B)**.

**13. A**

**Difficulty:** Hard

**Category:** Passport to Advanced Math/Functions

**Getting to the Answer:** Based on the equation, the graph of $h(x) = -g(x) + 1$ is a vertical reflection of $g(x)$, over the $x$-axis, that is then shifted up 1 unit. The graph looks like the dashed line in the following graph:

Now, compare the dashed line to each of the answer choices: the range of $h(x)$ is the set of $y$-values from lowest to highest (based on the dashed line). The lowest point occurs at point $B'$ and has a $y$-value of $-3$; the highest value occurs at both ends of the graph and is 3,

so the range is $-3 \leq y \leq 3$. This means **(A)** is correct and you can move on to the next question. Don't waste valuable time checking the other answer choices unless you are not sure about the range. (Choice (B): The minimum value of $h(x)$ is $-3$, not $-4$. Choice (C): The coordinates of point $A$ on $h(x)$ are $(-2, -2)$, not $(2, 4)$. Choice (D): the graph of $h(x)$ is decreasing, not increasing, between $x = -5$ and $x = -2$.)

**14. D**

**Difficulty:** Medium

**Category:** Additional Topics in Math/Imaginary Numbers

**Getting to the Answer:** Multiply the two complex numbers just as you would two binomials (using FOIL). Then, combine like terms and use the definition $i^2 = -1$ to simplify the result:

$$
\begin{aligned}
(3 + 2i)(5 - i) &= 3(5 - i) + 2i(5 - i) \\
&= 15 - 3i + 10i - 2i^2 \\
&= 15 + 7i - 2(-1) \\
&= 15 + 7i + 2 \\
&= 17 + 7i
\end{aligned}
$$

The question asks for $a$ in $a + bi$, so the correct answer is 17, **(D)**.

**15. A**

**Difficulty:** Hard

**Category:** Exponents

**Getting to the Answer:** Think of the rate given in the question in terms of the constant term you see on the right-hand side of the equation. Working together, the two treatment plants can filter the water in 72 hours. This is equivalent to saying that they can filter $\frac{1}{72}$ of the water in 1 hour. If $\frac{1}{72}$ is the portion of the water the two treatment plants can filter *together*, then each term on the left side of the equation represents the portion that each plant can filter *individually* in 1 hour. Because the new facility is 4 times as fast as the older facility, $\frac{4}{x}$ represents the portion of the water the new plant can filter in 1 hour, and $\frac{1}{x}$ represents the portion of the water the older plant can filter in 1 hour. This matches **(A)**.

## 16. 20

**Difficulty:** Medium

**Category:** Heart of Algebra/Linear Equations

**Getting to the Answer:** Only one equation is given and it has two variables. This means that you don't have enough information to solve for either variable. Instead, look for the relationship between the variable terms in the equation and those in the expression that you are trying to find, $x + 2y$. First, move the $y$-term to the left side of the equation to make it look more like the expression you are trying to find. The expression doesn't have fractions, so clear the fractions in the equation by multiplying both sides by 4. This yields the expression that you are looking for, $x + 2y$, so no further work is required—just read the value on the right-hand side of the equation:

$$\frac{1}{4}x = 5 - \frac{1}{2}y$$

$$\frac{1}{4}x + y\frac{1}{2} = 5$$

$$4\left(\frac{1}{4}x + \frac{1}{2}y\right) = 4(5)$$

$$x + 2y = 20$$

The answer is **20**.

## 17. 1

**Difficulty:** Medium

**Category:** Heart of Algebra/Inequalities

**Getting to the Answer:** This question is extremely difficult to answer unless you draw a sketch. It doesn't have to be perfect—you just need to get an idea of where the solution region is. Don't forget to flip the inequality symbol when you graph the second equation.

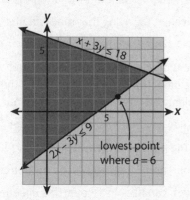

If $(a, b)$ is a solution to the system, then $a$ is the $x$-coordinate of any point in the darkest shaded region and $b$ is the corresponding $y$-coordinate. When

$a = 6$, the minimum possible value for $b$ lies on the lower boundary line, $2x - 3y \leq 9$. It looks like the $y$-coordinate is 1, but to be sure, substitute $x = 6$ into the equation and solve for $y$. You can use $=$ in the equation, instead of the inequality symbol, because you are finding a point on the boundary line:

$$2x - 3y = 9$$

$$2(6) - 3y = 9$$

$$12 - 3y = 9$$

$$-3y = -3$$

$$y = 1$$

## 18. 2

**Difficulty:** Hard

**Category:** Passport to Advanced Math/Exponents

**Getting to the Answer:** Write each factor in the expression in exponential form: $\sqrt{x} = x^{\frac{1}{2}}$ and $\sqrt[3]{x} = x^{\frac{1}{3}}$. Then, use the rules of exponents to simplify the expression. Add the exponents of the factors that are being multiplied and subtract the exponent of the factor that is being divided:

$$\frac{\sqrt{x} \cdot x^{\frac{5}{6}} \cdot x}{\sqrt[3]{x}} = \frac{x^{\frac{1}{2}} \cdot x^{\frac{5}{6}} \cdot x^1}{x^{\frac{1}{3}}}$$

$$= x^{\frac{1}{2} + \frac{5}{6} + 1 - \frac{1}{3}} = x^{\frac{3}{6} + \frac{5}{6} + \frac{6}{6} - \frac{2}{6}}$$

$$= x^{\frac{12}{6}} = x^2$$

Because $n$ is the power of $x$, the value of $n$ is **2**.

## 19. 14

**Difficulty:** Hard

**Category:** Additional Topics in Math/Geometry

**Getting to the Answer:** The shaded region is the area of the larger triangle minus the area of the smaller triangle. Set up and solve an equation using the information from the figure. You don't know the height of the smaller triangle, so call it $h$. You do know the area of the shaded region—it's 52 square units.

Larger triangle: base $= 12$; height $= h + 3 + 3$

Smaller triangle: base $= 8$; height $= h$

Shaded area $=$ large area $-$ small area

The question asks for the height of the *larger* triangle, so the correct answer is $8 + 3 + 3 = $ **14**.

**20. 6**

**Difficulty:** Hard

**Category:** Passport to Advanced Math/Quadratics

**Getting to the Answer:** The highest power of $x$ in the equation is 2, so the function is quadratic. Writing quadratic equations can be tricky and time-consuming. If you know the roots, you can use factors to write the equation. If you don't know the roots, you need to create a system of equations to find the coefficients of the variable terms. You don't know the roots of this equation, so start with the point that has the easiest values to work with, $(0, 1)$, and substitute them into the equation $y = ax^2 + bx + c$:

$$1 = a(0)^2 + b(0) + c$$
$$1 = c$$

Now your equation looks like $y = ax^2 + bx + 1$. Next, use the other two points to create a system of two equations in two variables:

$$(-3, 10) \rightarrow 10 = a(-3)^2 + b(-3) + 1 \rightarrow 9 = 9a - 3b$$
$$(2, 15) \rightarrow 15 = a(2)^2 + b(2) + 1 \rightarrow 14 = 4a + 2b$$

You now have a system of equations to solve. None of the variables has a coefficient of 1, so use elimination to solve the system. If you multiply the top equation by 2 and the bottom equation by 3, the $b$ terms will eliminate each other:

$$2[9a - 3b = 9] \rightarrow 18a - 6b = 18$$
$$3[4a + 2b = 14] \rightarrow \underline{12a + 6b = 42}$$
$$30a = 60$$
$$a = 2$$

Now, find $b$ by substituting $a = 2$ into either of the original equations. Using the top equation, you get:

$$9(2) - 3b = 9$$
$$18 - 3b = 9$$
$$-3b = -9$$
$$b = 3$$

The value of $a + b + c$ is $2 + 3 + 1 = $ **6**.

## Math Test—Calculator

**1. C**

**Difficulty:** Easy

**Category:** Problem Solving and Data Analysis/Rates, Ratios, Proportions, and Percentages

**Getting to the Answer:** You can use the formula $\text{Percent} = \frac{\text{part}}{\text{whole}} \times 100\%$ whenever you know two out of the three quantities. The clue "all" tells you that the "whole" is what you don't know. The percent is 96.5, and the part is 321,000,000:

$$96.5 = \frac{321,000,000}{w} \times 100\%$$
$$96.5w = 32,100,000,000$$
$$w = \frac{32,100,000,000}{96.5}$$
$$w = 332,642,487$$

The answer choices are rounded to the nearest thousand, so the answer is 332,642,000, **(C)**.

**2. C**

**Difficulty:** Easy

**Category:** Heart of Algebra/Linear Equations

**Getting to the Answer:** The total cost consists of the one-time site visit fee (a constant), an hourly cost (which depends on the number of hours), and the cost of the materials (which are taxed). The constant in the equation is 75 and is therefore the site visit fee; 45 is being multiplied by $h$ (the number of hours), so $45 must be the hourly rate. That leaves the remaining term, $1.06(82.5)$, which must be the cost of the materials ($82.50) plus a 6% tax. This matches **(C)**.

**3. D**

**Difficulty:** Easy

**Category:** Heart of Algebra/Inequalities

**Getting to the Answer:** The intersection (overlap) of the two shaded regions is the solution to the system of inequalities. Check each point to see whether it lies in the region with the darkest shading. Don't forget to check that you answered the right question—you are looking for the point that is *not* a solution to the system. Each of the first three points clearly lies in the overlap. The point (3, 3) looks like it lies on the dashed line, which means it is *not* included in the solution. To check this, plug (3, 3) into the easier inequality: $3 \not> 3$ (3 is equal to itself, not greater than itself), so **(D)** is correct.

**4. A**

**Difficulty:** Easy

**Category:** Passport to Advanced Math/Quadratics

**Getting to the Answer:** Quadratic equations can be written in several forms, each of which reveals something special about the graph. The factored form of a quadratic equation reveals the solutions to the equation, which graphically represent the *x*-intercepts. Choice **(A)** is the only equation written in this form and therefore must be correct. You can set each factor equal to 0 and solve to find that the *x*-intercepts of the graph are $x = \frac{5}{2}$ and $x = -1$.

**5. B**

**Difficulty:** Easy

**Category:** Problem Solving and Data Analysis/Rates, Ratios, Proportions, and Percentages

**Getting to the Answer:** Break the question into steps. Before you can use the ratio, you need to find the percent of the students who answered either "Foreign Policy" or "Environment." The ratio given in the question is 5:3, so write this as 5 parts "Foreign Policy" and 3 parts "Environment." You don't know how big a *part* is, so call it *x*. This means that $5x + 3x$ equals the percent of the students who answered either "Foreign Policy" or "Environment," which is 100% minus all the other answers:

$$100 - (16 + 14 + 9 + 5) = 100 - 44 = 56$$
$$5x + 3x = 56$$
$$8x = 56$$
$$x = 7$$

Each part has a value of 7, and 3 parts answered "Environment," so the correct percentage is $3(7) = 21\%$. **(B)** is the correct answer.

**6. C**

**Difficulty:** Easy

**Category:** Problem Solving and Data Analysis/ Scatterplots

**Getting to the Answer:** A data set that has a linear association follows the path of a straight line; a data set that is exponential follows a path that is similar to linear data, but with a curve to it because the rate of increase (or decrease) changes over time. This data set has a curve to it, so "exponential" describes the association better than "linear." This means you can eliminate (A) and (B). A positive association between two variables is one in which higher values of one variable correspond to higher values of the other variable, and vice versa. In other words, as the *x*-values of the data points go up, so do the *y*-values. This is indeed the case for this data set, so **(C)** is correct.

**7. D**

**Difficulty:** Easy

**Category:** Problem Solving and Data Analysis/Statistics and Probability

**Getting to the Answer:** Your only choice for this question is to compare each statement to the figure. Don't waste time trying to figure out the exact value for each bar—an estimate is good enough to determine whether each statement is true. Choice (A) is incorrect because the price in 2008 was slightly less (not more) than $3.50, while the price in 2013 was right around $3.50. Choice (B) is incorrect because the price in 2003 was more than $2.00, and the price in 2013 was not more than twice that ($4.00). Choice (C) is incorrect because the price in 2008 was about $3.25 and the price in 2009 was about $2.75—this is not a difference of more than $1.00. This means **(D)** must be correct. You don't have to check it—just move on. (Between 2003 and 2008, the change in price was about $3.40 - $2.30 = $1.10; between 2008 and 2013, the change in price was only about $3.50 - $3.40 = $0.10; the change in price was greater between 2003 and 2008.)

Practice Tests

## 8. B

**Difficulty:** Medium

**Category:** Heart of Algebra/Systems of Linear Equations

**Getting to the Answer:** Because none of the variable terms has a coefficient of 1, solve the system of equations using elimination (combining the equations). Before you choose an answer, check that you answered the right question (the sum of $x$ and $y$). Multiply the top equation by 2 to eliminate the terms that have $y$'s in them:

$$2[-2x + 5y = 1] \rightarrow -4x + 10y = 2$$
$$7x - 10y = -11 \rightarrow \underline{7x - 10y = -11}$$
$$3x = -9$$
$$x = -3$$

Now, substitute the result into either of the original equations and simplify to find $y$:

$$-2x + 5y = 1$$
$$-2(-3) + 5y = 1$$
$$6 + 5y = 1$$
$$5y = -5$$
$$y = -1$$

The question asks for the *sum*, so add $x$ and $y$ to get $-3 + (-1) = -4$, which is **(B)**.

## 9. A

**Difficulty:** Medium

**Category:** Heart of Algebra/Systems of Linear Equations

**Getting to the Answer:** Take a quick peek at the answers just to see what variables are being used, but don't study the equations. Instead, write your own system using the same variables as given in the answer choices. One of the equations in the system needs to represent the sum of the two resistors $(R_1 + R_2)$, which is equal to 294. This means you can eliminate (C) and (D). The second equation needs to satisfy the condition that $R_2$ is 6 less than twice $R_1$, or $R_2 = 2R_1 - 6$. This means **(A)** is correct.

## 10. C

**Difficulty:** Medium

**Category:** Heart of Algebra/Linear Equations

**Getting to the Answer:** Use the distributive property to simplify each of the terms that contains parentheses. Then, use inverse operations to solve for $x$:

$$\frac{2}{3}\left(3x\right) + 2(x - 1) = 4(x + 1) - 2$$
$$2x + 2x - 2 = 4x + 4 - 2$$
$$4x - 2 = 4x + 2$$
$$-2 \neq 2$$

All of the variable terms cancel out, and the resulting numerical statement is false (because negative 2 does not equal positive 2), so there is no solution to the equation. Put another way, there is no value of $x$ for which the equation is true. **(C)** is correct.

## 11. B

**Difficulty:** Medium

**Category:** Additional Topics in Math/Geometry

**Getting to the Answer:** Think about this question logically before you start writing things down—after it's transferred, the volume of the oil in the cylindrical container will be the same volume as the rectangular container, so you need to set the two volumes equal and solve for $h$. The volume of the rectangular container is $4 \times 9 \times 10$, or 360 cubic meters. The volume of a cylinder equals the area of its base times its height, or $\pi r^2 h$. Because the diameter is 6 meters, the radius, $r$, is half that, or 3 meters. Now, you're ready to set up an equation and solve for $h$ (which is the height of the cylinder or, in this case, the length of the transportation container):

Volume of oil = Volume of rectangular container
$$\pi(3)^2 h = 360$$
$$9\pi h = 360$$
$$h = \frac{360}{9\pi} = \frac{40}{\pi}$$

Choice **(B)** is correct.

## 12. D

**Difficulty:** Medium

**Category:** Problem Solving and Data Analysis/Rates, Ratios, Proportions, and Percentages

**Getting to the Answer:** Even though this question uses the word *percent*, you are never asked to find the actual percent itself. Set this question up as a proportion to get the answer more quickly. Remember, percent change equals amount of change divided by the original amount:

$$\frac{12 - 5}{5} = \frac{x - 12}{12}$$

$$\frac{7}{5} = \frac{x - 12}{12}$$

$$12(7) = 5(x - 12)$$

$$84 = 5x - 60$$

$$144 = 5x$$

$$28.8 = x$$

Choice **(D)** is correct.

## 13. A

**Difficulty:** Medium

**Category:** Passport to Advanced Math/Exponents

**Getting to the Answer:** Focus on the question at the very end—it's just asking you to solve the equation for $d$. First, cross-multiply to get rid of the denominator. Then, divide both sides of the equation by $4\pi b$ to isolate $d^2$. Finally, take the square root of both sides to find $d$:

$$b(4\pi d^2) = L$$

$$\frac{b(4\pi d^2)}{4\pi b} = \frac{L}{4\pi b}$$

$$d^2 = \frac{L}{4\pi b}$$

$$\sqrt{d^2} = \sqrt{\frac{L}{4\pi b}}$$

$$d = \sqrt{\frac{L}{4\pi b}}$$

Unfortunately, this is not one of the answer choices, so you'll need to simplify further. You can take the square root of 4 (it's 2), but be careful—it's in the denominator of the fraction, so it comes out of the square root as $\frac{1}{2}$.

The simplified equation is $d = \frac{1}{2}\sqrt{\frac{L}{\pi b}}$. This matches **(A)**.

## 14. D

**Difficulty:** Easy

**Category:** Problem Solving and Data Analysis/Statistics and Probability

**Getting to the Answer:** To calculate the percentage of men in each age group who reported being unemployed in January 2014, divide the number in *that* age group who were unemployed by the total number in *that* age group. There are six age groups but only four answer choices, so don't waste time on the age groups that aren't represented. Choice **(D)** is correct because $7 \div 152 \approx 0.046 = 4.6\%$, which is a lower percentage than that for any other age group (20 to 24 = 12.5%; 35 to 44 = 4.9%; 45 to 54 = 6.1%).

## 15. B

**Difficulty:** Medium

**Category:** Problem Solving and Data Analysis/Statistics and Probability

**Getting to the Answer:** The follow-up survey targets only those respondents who said they were unemployed, so focus on that column in the table. There were 6 respondents out of 44 unemployed males who were between the ages of 45 and 54, so the probability is $\frac{6}{44} = 0.13\overline{6}$, or about 13.6%, **(B)**.

## 16. B

**Difficulty:** Medium

**Category:** Passport to Advanced Math/Quadratics

**Getting to the Answer:** Taking the square root is the inverse operation of squaring, and both sides of the equation are already perfect squares, so take their square roots. Then, solve the resulting equations. Remember, there will be two equations to solve. Set up and solve:

$$(x - 1)^2 = \frac{4}{9}$$

$$\sqrt{(x - 1)^2} = \sqrt{\frac{4}{9}}$$

$$x - 1 = \pm\frac{\sqrt{4}}{\sqrt{9}}$$

$$x = 1 \pm \frac{2}{3}$$

Now, simplify each equation: $x = 1 + \frac{2}{3} = \frac{3}{3} + \frac{2}{3} = \frac{5}{3}$ and $x = 1 - \frac{2}{3} = \frac{3}{3} - \frac{2}{3} = \frac{1}{3}$. Choice **(B)** is correct.

## 17. D

**Difficulty:** Medium

**Category:** Heart of Algebra/Linear Equations

**Getting to the Answer:** Write the expression in words first: points per blue ring (5) times number of darts in blue ring ($x$), plus points per red ring (10) times number of darts in red ring ($6 - x$). Now, translate the words into numbers, variables, and operations: $5x + 10(6 - x)$. This is not one of the answer choices, so simplify the expression by distributing the 10 and then combining like terms: $5x + 10(6 - x) = 5x + 60 - 10x = 60 - 5x$. This matches **(D)**.

## 18. A

**Difficulty:** Medium

**Category:** Problem Solving and Data Analysis/Statistics and Probability

**Getting to the Answer:** This is a science crossover question. Read the first two sentences quickly—they are simply describing the context of the question. The last two sentences pose the question, so read those more carefully. In the sample, 184 out of 200 square feet were free of red tide after applying the spray. This is $\frac{184}{200} = 0.92 = 92\%$ of the area. For the whole beach, $0.92(10,000) = 9,200$ square feet should be free of the red tide. Be careful—this is *not* the answer. The question asks how much of the beach would still be covered by red tide, so subtract to get $10,000 - 9,200 = 800$ square feet, **(A)**.

## 19. A

**Difficulty:** Medium

**Category:** Passport to Advanced Math/Quadratics

**Getting to the Answer:** The solution to a system of equations is the point(s) where their graphs intersect. You can solve the system algebraically by setting the equations equal to each other or you can solve it graphically using your calculator. Both equations are given in calculator-friendly format ($y = \ldots$), so graphing them is probably the more efficient approach. The graph looks like the following:

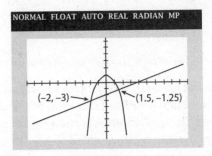

The solution point in the question is given as $(a, b)$, so $b$ represents the $y$-coordinate of the solution. The $y$-coordinates of the points of intersection are $-3$ and $-1.25$, so choice **(A)** is correct.

## 20. A

**Difficulty:** Medium

**Category:** Passport to Advanced Math/Functions

**Getting to the Answer:** The given range value is an output value, so substitute 3 for $g(x)$ and use inverse operations to solve for $x$, which is the corresponding domain value:

$$g(x) = \frac{2}{3}x + 7$$
$$3 = \frac{2}{3}x + 7$$
$$-4 = \frac{2}{3}x$$
$$-12 = 2x$$
$$-6 = x$$

Choice **(A)** is correct. Note that you could also graph the function and find the value of $x$ (the domain value) for which the value of $y$ (the range value) is 3. The point on the graph is $(-6, 3)$.

## 21. C

**Difficulty:** Medium

**Category:** Heart of Algebra/Linear Equations

**Getting to the Answer:** Write your own equation using the initial cost and the rate of change in the value of the lawn mower. Remember: when something changes at a constant rate, it can be represented by a linear equation. When a linear equation in the form $y = mx + b$ is used to model a real-world scenario, $m$ represents the constant rate of change and $b$ represents the starting amount. Here, the starting amount is easy—it's the purchase price, $2,800. To find the rate of change, think of the initial cost as the value at 0 years, or the point $(0, 2800)$, and the salvage amount as the value at 8 years, or the point $(8, 240)$. Substitute these points into the slope formula:

$$m = \frac{y_2 - y_1}{x_2 - x_1} = \frac{240 - 2,800}{8 - 0} = \frac{-2,560}{8} = -320$$

The correct equation is $y = -320x + 2,800$. This matches **(C)**.

## 22. D

**Difficulty:** Medium

**Category:** Problem Solving and Data Analysis/Functions

**Getting to the Answer:** Determine whether the change in the number of bacteria is a common difference (linear function) or a common ratio (exponential function) or if the number of bacteria changes direction (quadratic or polynomial function). The question tells you that the number of bacteria is reduced by half every hour after the antibiotic is applied. The microbiologist started with 20,000, so after one hour, there are 10,000 left, or $20,000 \times \frac{1}{2}$. After 2 hours, there are 5,000 left, or $20,000 \times \frac{1}{2} \times \frac{1}{2}$, and so on. The change in the number of bacteria is a common ratio $\left(\frac{1}{2}\right)$, so the best model is an exponential function, **(D)**, of the form $y = a\left(\frac{1}{2}\right)^x$. In this scenario, $a$ is 20,000.

## 23. B

**Difficulty:** Medium

**Category:** Problem Solving and Data Analysis/Rates, Ratios, Proportions, and Percentages

**Getting to the Answer:** Let the units in this question guide you to the solution. The speeds of the airplanes are given in miles per hour, but the question asks about the number of miles each airplane can travel in 12 seconds, so convert miles per hour to miles per second and multiply by 12 seconds:

*Slower airplane:*

$$\frac{600 \text{ miles}}{\text{hour}} \times \frac{1 \text{ hour}}{60 \text{ min}} \times \frac{1 \text{ min}}{60 \text{ sec}} \times 12 \text{ sec} = 2 \text{ miles}$$

*Faster airplane:*

$$\frac{720 \text{ miles}}{\text{hour}} \times \frac{1 \text{ hour}}{60 \text{ min}} \times \frac{1 \text{ min}}{60 \text{ sec}} \times 12 \text{ sec} = 2.4 \text{ miles}$$

The faster plane can travel $2.4 - 2 = 0.4$ miles farther, which is the same as $\frac{2}{5}$ miles. **(B)** is correct.

## 24. C

**Difficulty:** Medium

**Category:** Heart of Algebra/Inequalities

**Getting to the Answer:** Based on the data in the table, a worker would earn $9.10 - $7.25 = $1.85 more for 1 hour of work in Oregon than in Idaho. If he worked 35 hours per week, he would earn $35(1.85) = $64.75 more. If he worked 40 hours per week, he would earn $40(1.85) = $74 more. So, the worker would earn somewhere between $64.75 and $74 more per week, which can be expressed as the compound inequality $64.75 \leq x \leq 74$. This matches **(C)**.

## 25. D

**Difficulty:** Medium

**Category:** Problem Solving and Data Analysis/Rates, Ratios, Proportions, and Percentages

**Getting to the Answer:** This is another question where the units can help you find the answer. Use the number of vehicles owned to find the total number of miles driven to find the total number of gallons of gas used to find the total tax paid:

$$1.75 \text{ vehicles} \times \frac{11{,}340 \text{ miles}}{\text{vehicle}} = 19{,}845 \text{ miles}$$

$$19{,}845 \text{ miles} \times \frac{1 \text{ gallon of gas}}{21.4 \text{ miles}} = 927.336 \text{ gallons}$$

$$927.336 \text{ gallons} \times \frac{\$0.184}{\text{gallon}} = \$170.63$$

Choice **(D)** is correct.

## 26. C

**Difficulty:** Medium

**Category:** Problem Solving and Data Analysis/ Scatterplots

**Getting to the Answer:** The average rate of change of a function over a given interval, from $a$ to $b$, compares the change in the outputs, $f(b) - f(a)$, to the change in the inputs, $b - a$. In other words, it is the slope of the line that connects the endpoints of the interval, so you can use the slope formula. Look at the quadratic model, not the data points, to find that the endpoints of the given interval, week 2 to week 8, are (2, 280) and (8, 400). The average rate of change is $\frac{400 - 280}{8 - 2} = \frac{120}{6} = 20$, so the dolphin's weight increased by about 20 pounds per week, which matches **(C)**.

## 27. A

**Difficulty:** Hard

**Category:** Additional Topics in Math/Geometry

**Getting to the Answer:** In this question, information is given in both the diagram and the text. You need to relate the text to the diagram, one piece of information at a time, to calculate how long the lifeguard ran along the beach and how long he swam. Before you find the swim time, you need to know how *far* he swam. Whenever you see a right triangle symbol in a diagram, you should think Pythagorean theorem or,

in this question, special right triangles. All multiples of 3-4-5 triangles are right triangles, so the length of the lifeguard's swim is the hypotenuse of a 30-40-50 triangle, or 50 feet. Add this number to the diagram. Now, calculate the times using the distances and the speeds given. Don't forget the 1 second that the lifeguard paused.

Run time $= 60 \text{ feet} \times \frac{1 \text{ second}}{12 \text{ feet}} = \frac{60}{12} = 5$ seconds

Pause time $= 1$ second

Swim time $= 50 \text{ feet} \times \frac{1 \text{ second}}{5 \text{ feet}} = \frac{50}{5} = 10$ seconds

Total time $= 5 + 1 + 10 = 16$ seconds. Choice **(A)** is correct.

## 28. B

**Difficulty:** Hard

**Category:** Heart of Algebra/Linear Equations

**Getting to the Answer:** Call the initial amount $A$. After you've written your equation, solve for $A$.

Amount now ($x$) = Initial amount ($A$) minus $y$, plus 50:

$$x = A - y + 50$$
$$x + y - 50 = A$$

The initial amount was $x + y - 50$ gallons, **(B)**. Note that you could also use Picking Numbers to answer this question.

## 29. B

**Difficulty:** Hard

**Category:** Problem Solving and Data Analysis/Statistics and Probability

**Getting to the Answer:** When a question involves reading data from a graph, it is sometimes better to skip an answer choice if it involves long calculations. Skim the answer choices for this question—(A) involves finding two averages, each of which is composed of 7 data values. Skip this choice for now. Start with (B). Be careful—you are not looking for places where the line segments are increasing. The $y$-axis already represents the change in prices, so you are simply counting the number of positive values for the imports (5) and for the exports (4). There are more for the imports, so **(B)** is correct and you don't need to check any of the other statements. Move on to the next question.

## 30. D

**Difficulty:** Hard

**Category:** Passport to Advanced Math/Exponents

**Getting to the Answer:** The key to answering this question is deciding what you're trying to find. The question tells you that $x$ represents the athlete's swim rate, and you are looking for the number of kilometers he swam in one hour—these are the same thing. If you find $x$ (in kilometers per hour), you will know how many kilometers he swam in one hour. Set the equation equal to the total time, 16.2, and solve for $x$. To do this, write the variable terms over a common denominator, $10x$, and combine them into a single term. Then, cross-multiply and go from there:

$$16.2 = \frac{10}{10}\left(\frac{3.86}{x}\right) + \frac{180.2}{10x} + \frac{2}{2}\left(\frac{42.2}{5x}\right)$$

$$16.2 = \frac{38.6}{10x} + \frac{180.2}{10x} + \frac{84.4}{10x}$$

$$16.2 = \frac{303.2}{10x}$$

$$10x(16.2) = 303.2$$

$$162x = 303.2$$

$$x = \frac{303.2}{162} \approx 1.87$$

Choice **(D)** is correct.

## 31. 1

**Difficulty:** Easy

**Category:** Heart of Algebra/Linear Equations

**Getting to the Answer:** Choose the best strategy to answer the question. If you distribute the $\frac{2}{3}$, it creates messy calculations. Instead, clear the fraction by multiplying both sides of the equation by 3. Then, use the distributive property and inverse operations to solve for $x$:

$$\frac{2}{3}(5x + 7) = 8x$$

$$\cancel{3} \cdot \frac{2}{\cancel{3}}(5x + 7) = 3 \cdot 8x$$

$$2(5x + 7) = 24x$$

$$10x + 14 = 24x$$

$$14 = 14x$$

$$\mathbf{1} = x$$

## 32. 192

**Difficulty:** Medium

**Category:** Passport to Advanced Math/Exponents

**Getting to the Answer:** Before you start substituting values, quickly check that the units given match the units required to use the equation—they do, so proceed. The patient's weight ($w$) is 150 and the patient's BSA is $2\sqrt{2}$, so the equation becomes $2\sqrt{2} = \sqrt{\dfrac{150h}{3,600}}$. The only variable left in the equation is $h$, and you are trying to find the patient's height, so you're ready to solve the equation. To do this, square both sides of the equation and then continue using inverse operations. Be careful when you square the left side—you must square both the 2 and the root 2:

$$2\sqrt{2} = \sqrt{\frac{150h}{3,600}}$$

$$\left(2\sqrt{2}\right)^2 = \left(\sqrt{\frac{150h}{3,600}}\right)^2$$

$$2^2\left(\sqrt{2}\right)^2 = \frac{150h}{3,600}$$

$$4(2) = \frac{150h}{3,600}$$

$$28,800 = 150h$$

$$\mathbf{192} = h$$

## 33. 3.4

**Difficulty:** Medium

**Category:** Problem Solving and Data Analysis/Statistics and Probability

**Getting to the Answer:** The test average is the same as the mean of the data. The *mean* is the sum of all the values divided by the number of values. Break the question into short steps to keep your calculations organized. Before gridding in your answer, make sure you answered the correct question (how much the final test average changes).

*Step 1*: Find the original test average:

$$\frac{86 + 92 + 81 + 64 + 83}{5} = \frac{406}{5} = 81.2$$

*Step 2*: Find the average of the tests after replacing the lowest score (64) with the next to lowest score (81):

$$\frac{86 + 92 + 81 + 81 + 83}{5} = \frac{423}{5} = 84.6$$

*Step 3*: Subtract the original average from the new average: $84.6 - 81.2 = \mathbf{3.4}$.

**34. 40**

**Difficulty:** Hard

**Category:** Additional Topics in Math/Geometry

**Getting to the Answer:** Because $\overline{AB}$, $\overline{CD}$, and $\overline{EF}$ are diameters, the sum of $x$, $y$, and the interior angle of the shaded region is 180 degrees. The question tells you that the shaded region is $\frac{1}{5}$ of the circle, so the interior angle must equal $\frac{1}{5}$ of the degrees in the whole circle, or $\frac{1}{5}$ of 360. Use what you know about $y$ (that it is equal to $2x - 12$) and what you know about the shaded region (that it is $\frac{1}{5}$ of 360 degrees) to write and solve an equation:

$$x + y + \frac{1}{5}(360) = 180$$
$$x + (2x - 12) + 72 = 180$$
$$3x + 60 = 180$$
$$3x = 120$$
$$x = \mathbf{40}$$

**35. 14**

**Difficulty:** Hard

**Category:** Heart of Algebra/Linear Equations

**Getting to the Answer:** When you know the slope and one point on a line, you can use $y = mx + b$ to write the equation. The slope is given as $-\frac{7}{4}$, so substitute this for $m$. The point is given as $(4, 7)$, so $x = 4$ and $y = 7$. Now, find $b$:

$$y = mx + b$$
$$7 = -\frac{7}{\cancel{4}}(\cancel{4}) + b$$
$$7 = -7 + b$$
$$14 = b$$

The $y$-intercept of the line is **14**.

You could also very carefully graph the line using the given point and the slope. Start at $(4, 7)$ and move toward the $y$-axis by rising 7 and running *to the left* 4 (because the slope is negative). You should land at the point $(0, 14)$.

**36. 45**

**Difficulty:** Hard

**Category:** Problem Solving and Data Analysis/Rates, Ratios, Proportions, and Percentages

**Getting to the Answer:** Make a chart that represents rate, time, and distance and fill in what you know.

|              | Rate   | Time    | Distance |
|--------------|--------|---------|----------|
| **To airport**  | 45 mph | $t$     | $d$      |
| **Back to home** | 30 mph | $2.5 - t$ | $d$      |

Now, use the formula $d = r \times t$ for both parts of the trip: $d = 45t$ and $d = 30(2.5 - t)$. Because both are equal to $d$, you can set them equal to each other and solve for $t$:

$$45t = 30(2.5 - t)$$
$$45t = 75 - 30t$$
$$75t = 75$$
$$t = 1$$

Now, plug the value of $t$ back in to solve for $d$:

$$d = 45t$$
$$d = 45(1)$$
$$d = \mathbf{45}$$

**37. 10**

**Difficulty:** Medium

**Category:** Problem Solving and Data Analysis/Rates, Ratios, Proportions, and Percentages

**Getting to the Answer:** You don't need to know chemistry to answer this question. All the information you need is in the table. Use the formula $\text{Percent} = \frac{\text{part}}{\text{whole}} \times 100\%$. To use the formula, find the part of the mass represented by the carbon; there is 1 mole of carbon and it has a mass of 12.011 grams. Next, find the whole mass of the mole of chloroform: 1 mole carbon (12.011 g) + 1 mole hydrogen (1.008 g) + 3 moles chlorine ($3 \times 35.453 = 106.359$ g) $= 12.011 + 1.008 + 106.359 = 119.378$. Now, use the formula:

$$\text{Percent} = \frac{12.011}{119.378} \times 100\%$$
$$= 0.10053 \times 100\%$$
$$= 10.053\%$$

Before you grid in your answer, make sure you follow the directions—round to the nearest whole percent, which is **10**.

**38. 12**

**Difficulty:** Hard

**Category:** Problem Solving and Data Analysis/Rates, Ratios, Proportions, and Percentages

**Getting to the Answer:** Think about the units given in the question and how you can use what you know to find what you need. Start with grams of chloroform; the chemist starts with 1,000 and uses 522.5, so there are $1{,}000 - 522.5 = 477.5$ grams left. From the previous question, you know that 1 mole of chloroform has a mass of 119.378 grams, so there are $477.5 \div 119.378 = 3.999$, or about 4 moles of chloroform left. Be careful—you're not finished yet. The question asks for the number of moles of *chlorine*, not chloroform. According to the table, each mole of chloroform contains 3 moles of chlorine, so there are $4 \times 3 = \mathbf{12}$ moles of chlorine left.

# Essay Test Rubric

## The Essay Demonstrates...

| 4—Advanced | • **(Reading)** A strong ability to comprehend the source text, including its central ideas and important details and how they interrelate, and effectively use evidence (quotations, paraphrases, or both) from the source text. |
|---|---|
| | • **(Analysis)** A strong ability to evaluate the author's use of evidence, reasoning, and/or stylistic and persuasive elements and/or other features of the student's own choosing; make good use of relevant, sufficient, and strategically chosen support for the claims or points made in the student's essay; and focus consistently on features of the source text that are most relevant to addressing the task. |
| | • **(Writing)** A strong ability to provide a precise central claim; create an effective organization that includes an introduction and conclusion, as well as a clear progression of ideas; successfully employ a variety of sentence structures; use precise word choice; maintain a formal style and objective tone; and show command of the conventions of standard written English so that the essay is free of errors. |
| 3—Proficient | • **(Reading)** Satisfactory ability to comprehend the source text, including its central ideas and important details and how they interrelate, and use evidence (quotations, paraphrases, or both) from the source text. |
| | • **(Analysis)** Satisfactory ability to evaluate the author's use of evidence, reasoning, and/or stylistic and persuasive elements and/or other features of the student's own choosing; make use of relevant and sufficient support for the claims or points made in the student's essay; and focus primarily on features of the source text that are most relevant to addressing the task. |
| | • **(Writing)** Satisfactory ability to provide a central claim; create an organization that includes an introduction and conclusion, as well as a clear progression of ideas; employ a variety of sentence structures; use precise word choice; maintain an appropriate formal style and objective tone; and show control of the conventions of standard written English so that the essay is free of significant errors. |
| 2—Partial | • **(Reading)** Limited ability to comprehend the source text, including its central ideas and important details and how they interrelate, and use evidence (quotations, paraphrases, or both) from the source text. |
| | • **(Analysis)** Limited ability to evaluate the author's use of evidence, reasoning, and/or stylistic and persuasive elements and/or other features of the student's own choosing; make use of support for the claims or points made in the student's essay; and focus on relevant features of the source text. |
| | • **(Writing)** Limited ability to provide a central claim, create an effective organization for ideas, employ a variety of sentence structures, use precise word choice, maintain an appropriate style and tone, or show control of the conventions of standard written English, resulting in certain errors that detract from the quality of the writing. |

| 1—Inadequate | • **(Reading)** Little or no ability to comprehend the source text or use evidence from the source text. |
| --- | --- |
| | • **(Analysis)** Little or no ability to evaluate the author's use of evidence, reasoning, and/or stylistic and persuasive elements; choose support for claims or points; or focus on relevant features of the source text. |
| | • **(Writing)** Little or no ability to provide a central claim, organization, or progression of ideas; employ a variety of sentence structures; use precise word choice; maintain an appropriate style and tone; or show control of the conventions of standard written English, resulting in numerous errors that undermine the quality of the writing. |

## Sample Essay Response #1 (Advanced Score)

As anyone knows who has had to help their family move house, find a textbook in a cluttered room, or even just clean a crowded apartment, possessions can have a huge amount of power over people. Far from being simply objects that we enjoy or that bring us pleasure, it can sometimes feel that our possessions oppress us. This is the point Morris eloquently makes in her essay "The Tyranny of Things." By using anecdotes, examples, reasoning, and powerful imagery, Morris argues that the very things we cherish are nearly crushing the life out of us.

The author begins by relating an anecdote about two teenagers becoming fast friends over their love of things. It is a touching moment, one to which readers can easily relate; even Morris herself says that we all probably go through this phase. This helps establish her credibility with readers, because her examples make sense to them. Gradually, however, Morris makes it clear that this touching moment has a sinister side—the love of things will only result in resentment.

Morris reasons that while it's natural to go through a phase of wanting objects, it is unhealthy to remain in this state. "Many people never pass out of this phase," she writes ominously. "They never see a flower without wanting to pick it … they bring home all their alpenstocks." It begins to sound obsessive, this need to control things. Morris goes on to develop her argument by suggesting that possessions are metaphorically suffocating us. She makes the idea of too many possessions sound repulsive by describing them as "an undigested mass of things." The things almost take on a kind of life force, according to Morris: "they possess us." They "have destroyed" our empty spaces and we feel "stifled."

Another way Morris supports her argument is by giving examples of the unnecessary "tokens" associated with social occasions. She describes how at events, luncheons, and parties, gifts are given and received. She then uses powerful negative imagery to describe the effects of these gifts, comparing the recipient to a "ship encrusted with barnacles" that needs to be "scraped bare again." This language suggests that the gifts are burdensome and even harmful.

By contrast, the imagery Morris uses to describe a simple life filled with fewer things is imagery of ease and relaxation. "We breathe more freely in the clear space that we have made for ourselves," she writes. It is not just that we have literally regained control from our possessions and are now acting rather than being acted upon; it is that we are physically more at ease.

In her conclusion, Morris longs for a day when we can live more simply, with fewer possessions. She describes a "house by the sea" that was simple and empty; it did not "demand care" or "claim attention" or otherwise act upon her. Her wish is that "we could but free ourselves" from the tyranny of things that she feels is draining us of our freedom. And at this point, it is likely the reader's wish, too.

## Sample Essay Response #2 (Proficient Score)

Although as people we like to think of ourselves as owners of things, in fact it can sometimes feel like the things we own end up owning us. At least this is what Morris argues in her essay "The Tyranny of Things." Through her use of evidence, reasoning, and word choice, she makes a strong argument that we should own fewer things if we ever want to be truly happy.

Morris tells a story about two teenage girls who instantly know they will be friends because they both like things. They are not happy just to be. They have to own things. It's like their own experiences aren't enough for them. But Morris says that this is bad for people, because they will end up feeling like their possessions own them.

Morris's reasoning is that we can basically get control back over our own lives if we stop needing things so much. If we have too many things, "they possess us." So we have to get rid of things, and then we can feel better. At least these days we aren't buried with our things anymore, like they were in the olden days.

The word choices in the essay are interesting. She talks about the way things become a problem for us: "our books are a burden to us, our pictures have destroyed every restful wall-space, our china is a care." By using a lot of repetition, it shows how powerful things are.

Morris's essay encourages people to free themselves from their things. If they do so, they will be happier. Through her personal anecdotes, reasoning, and repetitive word choices, she makes her essay very powerful.

# SAT Practice Test 2 Answer Sheet

**You will see an answer sheet like the one below on test day. Review the answer key following the test when finished.**

When testing, start with number 1 for each section. If a section has fewer questions than answer spaces, leave the extra spaces blank.

**SECTION 1**

1. Ⓐ Ⓑ Ⓒ Ⓓ
2. Ⓐ Ⓑ Ⓒ Ⓓ
3. Ⓐ Ⓑ Ⓒ Ⓓ
4. Ⓐ Ⓑ Ⓒ Ⓓ
5. Ⓐ Ⓑ Ⓒ Ⓓ
6. Ⓐ Ⓑ Ⓒ Ⓓ
7. Ⓐ Ⓑ Ⓒ Ⓓ
8. Ⓐ Ⓑ Ⓒ Ⓓ
9. Ⓐ Ⓑ Ⓒ Ⓓ
10. Ⓐ Ⓑ Ⓒ Ⓓ
11. Ⓐ Ⓑ Ⓒ Ⓓ
12. Ⓐ Ⓑ Ⓒ Ⓓ
13. Ⓐ Ⓑ Ⓒ Ⓓ

14. Ⓐ Ⓑ Ⓒ Ⓓ
15. Ⓐ Ⓑ Ⓒ Ⓓ
16. Ⓐ Ⓑ Ⓒ Ⓓ
17. Ⓐ Ⓑ Ⓒ Ⓓ
18. Ⓐ Ⓑ Ⓒ Ⓓ
19. Ⓐ Ⓑ Ⓒ Ⓓ
20. Ⓐ Ⓑ Ⓒ Ⓓ
21. Ⓐ Ⓑ Ⓒ Ⓓ
22. Ⓐ Ⓑ Ⓒ Ⓓ
23. Ⓐ Ⓑ Ⓒ Ⓓ
24. Ⓐ Ⓑ Ⓒ Ⓓ
25. Ⓐ Ⓑ Ⓒ Ⓓ
26. Ⓐ Ⓑ Ⓒ Ⓓ

27. Ⓐ Ⓑ Ⓒ Ⓓ
28. Ⓐ Ⓑ Ⓒ Ⓓ
29. Ⓐ Ⓑ Ⓒ Ⓓ
30. Ⓐ Ⓑ Ⓒ Ⓓ
31. Ⓐ Ⓑ Ⓒ Ⓓ
32. Ⓐ Ⓑ Ⓒ Ⓓ
33. Ⓐ Ⓑ Ⓒ Ⓓ
34. Ⓐ Ⓑ Ⓒ Ⓓ
35. Ⓐ Ⓑ Ⓒ Ⓓ
36. Ⓐ Ⓑ Ⓒ Ⓓ
37. Ⓐ Ⓑ Ⓒ Ⓓ
38. Ⓐ Ⓑ Ⓒ Ⓓ
39. Ⓐ Ⓑ Ⓒ Ⓓ

40. Ⓐ Ⓑ Ⓒ Ⓓ
41. Ⓐ Ⓑ Ⓒ Ⓓ
42. Ⓐ Ⓑ Ⓒ Ⓓ
43. Ⓐ Ⓑ Ⓒ Ⓓ
44. Ⓐ Ⓑ Ⓒ Ⓓ
45. Ⓐ Ⓑ Ⓒ Ⓓ
46. Ⓐ Ⓑ Ⓒ Ⓓ
47. Ⓐ Ⓑ Ⓒ Ⓓ
48. Ⓐ Ⓑ Ⓒ Ⓓ
49. Ⓐ Ⓑ Ⓒ Ⓓ
50. Ⓐ Ⓑ Ⓒ Ⓓ
51. Ⓐ Ⓑ Ⓒ Ⓓ
52. Ⓐ Ⓑ Ⓒ Ⓓ

☐ # correct in Section 1

☐ # incorrect in Section 1

**SECTION 2**

1. Ⓐ Ⓑ Ⓒ Ⓓ
2. Ⓐ Ⓑ Ⓒ Ⓓ
3. Ⓐ Ⓑ Ⓒ Ⓓ
4. Ⓐ Ⓑ Ⓒ Ⓓ
5. Ⓐ Ⓑ Ⓒ Ⓓ
6. Ⓐ Ⓑ Ⓒ Ⓓ
7. Ⓐ Ⓑ Ⓒ Ⓓ
8. Ⓐ Ⓑ Ⓒ Ⓓ
9. Ⓐ Ⓑ Ⓒ Ⓓ
10. Ⓐ Ⓑ Ⓒ Ⓓ
11. Ⓐ Ⓑ Ⓒ Ⓓ

12. Ⓐ Ⓑ Ⓒ Ⓓ
13. Ⓐ Ⓑ Ⓒ Ⓓ
14. Ⓐ Ⓑ Ⓒ Ⓓ
15. Ⓐ Ⓑ Ⓒ Ⓓ
16. Ⓐ Ⓑ Ⓒ Ⓓ
17. Ⓐ Ⓑ Ⓒ Ⓓ
18. Ⓐ Ⓑ Ⓒ Ⓓ
19. Ⓐ Ⓑ Ⓒ Ⓓ
20. Ⓐ Ⓑ Ⓒ Ⓓ
21. Ⓐ Ⓑ Ⓒ Ⓓ
22. Ⓐ Ⓑ Ⓒ Ⓓ

23. Ⓐ Ⓑ Ⓒ Ⓓ
24. Ⓐ Ⓑ Ⓒ Ⓓ
25. Ⓐ Ⓑ Ⓒ Ⓓ
26. Ⓐ Ⓑ Ⓒ Ⓓ
27. Ⓐ Ⓑ Ⓒ Ⓓ
28. Ⓐ Ⓑ Ⓒ Ⓓ
29. Ⓐ Ⓑ Ⓒ Ⓓ
30. Ⓐ Ⓑ Ⓒ Ⓓ
31. Ⓐ Ⓑ Ⓒ Ⓓ
32. Ⓐ Ⓑ Ⓒ Ⓓ
33. Ⓐ Ⓑ Ⓒ Ⓓ

34. Ⓐ Ⓑ Ⓒ Ⓓ
35. Ⓐ Ⓑ Ⓒ Ⓓ
36. Ⓐ Ⓑ Ⓒ Ⓓ
37. Ⓐ Ⓑ Ⓒ Ⓓ
38. Ⓐ Ⓑ Ⓒ Ⓓ
39. Ⓐ Ⓑ Ⓒ Ⓓ
40. Ⓐ Ⓑ Ⓒ Ⓓ
41. Ⓐ Ⓑ Ⓒ Ⓓ
42. Ⓐ Ⓑ Ⓒ Ⓓ
43. Ⓐ Ⓑ Ⓒ Ⓓ
44. Ⓐ Ⓑ Ⓒ Ⓓ

☐ # correct in Section 2

☐ # incorrect in Section 2

Practice Tests

**SECTION 3**

1. Ⓐ Ⓑ Ⓒ Ⓓ    5. Ⓐ Ⓑ Ⓒ Ⓓ    9. Ⓐ Ⓑ Ⓒ Ⓓ    13. Ⓐ Ⓑ Ⓒ Ⓓ

2. Ⓐ Ⓑ Ⓒ Ⓓ    6. Ⓐ Ⓑ Ⓒ Ⓓ    10. Ⓐ Ⓑ Ⓒ Ⓓ    14. Ⓐ Ⓑ Ⓒ Ⓓ

3. Ⓐ Ⓑ Ⓒ Ⓓ    7. Ⓐ Ⓑ Ⓒ Ⓓ    11. Ⓐ Ⓑ Ⓒ Ⓓ    15. Ⓐ Ⓑ Ⓒ Ⓓ

4. Ⓐ Ⓑ Ⓒ Ⓓ    8. Ⓐ Ⓑ Ⓒ Ⓓ    12. Ⓐ Ⓑ Ⓒ Ⓓ

# correct in Section 3

# incorrect in Section 3

16. 17. 18. 19. 20.

**SECTION 4**

1. Ⓐ Ⓑ Ⓒ Ⓓ    9. Ⓐ Ⓑ Ⓒ Ⓓ    17. Ⓐ Ⓑ Ⓒ Ⓓ    25. Ⓐ Ⓑ Ⓒ Ⓓ

2. Ⓐ Ⓑ Ⓒ Ⓓ    10. Ⓐ Ⓑ Ⓒ Ⓓ    18. Ⓐ Ⓑ Ⓒ Ⓓ    26. Ⓐ Ⓑ Ⓒ Ⓓ

3. Ⓐ Ⓑ Ⓒ Ⓓ    11. Ⓐ Ⓑ Ⓒ Ⓓ    19. Ⓐ Ⓑ Ⓒ Ⓓ    27. Ⓐ Ⓑ Ⓒ Ⓓ

4. Ⓐ Ⓑ Ⓒ Ⓓ    12. Ⓐ Ⓑ Ⓒ Ⓓ    20. Ⓐ Ⓑ Ⓒ Ⓓ    28. Ⓐ Ⓑ Ⓒ Ⓓ

5. Ⓐ Ⓑ Ⓒ Ⓓ    13. Ⓐ Ⓑ Ⓒ Ⓓ    21. Ⓐ Ⓑ Ⓒ Ⓓ    29. Ⓐ Ⓑ Ⓒ Ⓓ

6. Ⓐ Ⓑ Ⓒ Ⓓ    14. Ⓐ Ⓑ Ⓒ Ⓓ    22. Ⓐ Ⓑ Ⓒ Ⓓ    30. Ⓐ Ⓑ Ⓒ Ⓓ

7. Ⓐ Ⓑ Ⓒ Ⓓ    15. Ⓐ Ⓑ Ⓒ Ⓓ    23. Ⓐ Ⓑ Ⓒ Ⓓ

8. Ⓐ Ⓑ Ⓒ Ⓓ    16. Ⓐ Ⓑ Ⓒ Ⓓ    24. Ⓐ Ⓑ Ⓒ Ⓓ

# correct in Section 4

# incorrect in Section 4

31. 32. 33. 34.

35. 36. 37. 38.

# Reading Test

## 65 Minutes—52 Questions

This section corresponds to Section 1 of your answer sheet.

**Directions:** Read each passage or pair of passages, then answer the questions that follow. Choose your answers based on what the passage(s) and any accompanying graphics state or imply.

**Questions 1-10 are based on the following passage.**

This passage is adapted from *A Study in Scarlet*, Sir Arthur Conan Doyle's first story in his acclaimed Sherlock Holmes series. In this excerpt, the narrator, Dr. Watson, observes Mr. Holmes, with whom he has recently entered into a shared housing arrangement, although he knows very little about this new roommate as of yet.

As the weeks went by, my interest in him and my curiosity as to his aims in life gradually deepened and increased. His very person and appearance were such as to strike the attention of the most
5   casual observer. In height he was rather over six feet, and so excessively lean that he seemed to be considerably taller. His eyes were sharp and piercing, save during those intervals of torpor to which I have alluded; and his thin, hawk-like nose gave his
10   whole expression an air of alertness and decision. His chin, too, had the prominence and squareness which mark the man of determination. His hands were invariably blotted with ink and stained with chemicals, yet he was possessed of extraordinary
15   delicacy of touch, as I frequently had occasion to observe when I watched him manipulating his fragile philosophical instruments....

He was not studying medicine. He had himself, in reply to a question, confirmed Stamford's[1]
20   opinion upon that point. Neither did he appear to have pursued any course of reading which might fit him for a degree in science or any other recognized portal which would give him an entrance into the learned world. Yet his zeal for certain studies

25   was remarkable, and within eccentric limits his knowledge was so extraordinarily ample and minute that his observations have fairly astounded me. Surely no man would work so hard or attain such precise information unless he had some
30   definite end in view. Desultory readers are seldom remarkable for the exactness of their learning. No man burdens his mind with small matters unless he has some very good reason for doing so.

His ignorance was as remarkable as his knowledge.
35   Of contemporary literature, philosophy and politics he appeared to know next to nothing. Upon my quoting Thomas Carlyle,[2] he inquired in the naïvest way who he might be and what he had done. My surprise reached a climax, however, when I found
40   incidentally that he was ignorant of the Copernican Theory and of the composition of the solar system. That any civilized human being in this nineteenth century should not be aware that the earth travelled round the sun appeared to be to me such an
45   extraordinary fact that I could hardly realize it.

"You appear to be astonished," he said, smiling at my expression of surprise. "Now that I do know it I shall do my best to forget it."

"To forget it!"

50   "You see," he explained, "I consider that a man's brain originally is like a little empty attic, and you have to stock it with such furniture as you choose. A fool takes in all the lumber of every sort that he comes across, so that the knowledge which might
55   be useful to him gets crowded out, or at best is jumbled up with a lot of other things so that he

---

[1]Stamford is the mutual acquaintance who introduced Dr. Watson to Mr. Holmes. In a previous scene, he told Watson that Holmes was not a medical student.

[2]Thomas Carlyle was an influential writer and philosopher whose work was well known at the time of this novel's publication.

has a difficulty in laying his hands upon it. Now the skillful workman is very careful indeed as to what he takes into his brain-attic. He will have
60 nothing but the tools which may help him in doing his work, but of these he has a large assortment, and all in the most perfect order. It is a mistake to think that that little room has elastic walls and can distend to any extent. Depend upon it there comes
65 a time when for every addition of knowledge you forget something that you knew before. It is of the highest importance, therefore, not to have useless facts elbowing out the useful ones."

"But the solar system!" I protested.
70 "What the deuce is it to me?"

1. According to the passage, as time passes, Watson finds Holmes

   A) increasingly intriguing.

   B) frequently irritating.

   C) somewhat snobby.

   D) occasionally generous.

2. As used in line 5, "casual" most nearly means

   A) impulsive.

   B) comfortable.

   C) relaxed.

   D) occasional.

3. As presented in the passage, Sherlock Holmes is best described as

   A) very secretive and hard to understand.

   B) an excellent companion to Watson.

   C) highly regarded by his peers.

   D) an unusual and extraordinary man.

4. As used in line 8, "torpor" most nearly means

   A) agitation.

   B) sluggishness.

   C) alertness.

   D) illness.

5. The passage most strongly suggests that which of the following is true of Holmes?

   A) He tried, but failed, to become a doctor.

   B) He was an excellent student at the university.

   C) He studies things he is passionate about.

   D) He is considered an expert in philosophy.

6. Which choice provides the best evidence for the answer to the previous question?

   A) Lines 12–17 ("His hands were… instruments")

   B) Lines 18–20 ("He was not…that point")

   C) Lines 24–28 ("Yet his…astounded me")

   D) Lines 28–30 ("Surely no man…in view")

7. The passage most strongly suggests that Holmes believes which of the following about learning?

   A) People should study broadly to know something about everything.

   B) Philosophy is not a valid field of study to pursue.

   C) The brain is limited in capacity, so you should prioritize what you learn.

   D) The Copernican Theory is unfounded and therefore should not be studied.

8. Which choice provides the best evidence for the answer to the previous question?

   A) Line 34 ("His ignorance…his knowledge")

   B) Lines 35–36 ("Of contemporary…nothing")

   C) Lines 42–45 ("That any…realize it")

   D) Lines 66–68 ("It is…useful ones")

9. The comparison of the brain to an attic mainly serves to

   A) demonstrate Holmes's unique views on how a person should make use of knowledge.

   B) illustrate Watson's combative nature.

   C) provide an alternate explanation for why Holmes doesn't know about Copernicus.

   D) resolve the conflict between Watson and Holmes.

GO ON TO THE NEXT PAGE ⟹

10. The decision to tell the story from Watson's point of view suggests that the author

    A) wants the reader to dislike Holmes.

    B) needed a sympathetic narrator.

    C) will focus the rest of the story on Watson's actions.

    D) hopes the reader will share Watson's curiosity about Holmes.

**Questions 11-20 are based on the following passage.**

This passage is adapted from a speech given by President Woodrow Wilson to Congress on January 8, 1918. Here Wilson proposes a 14-point program for world peace. These 14 points became the basis for peace negotiations at the end of World War I.

It will be our wish and purpose that the processes of peace, when they are begun, shall be absolutely open and that they shall involve and permit henceforth no secret understandings of any

5　kind. The day of conquest and aggrandizement is gone by; so is also the day of secret covenants entered into in the interest of particular governments and likely at some unlooked-for moment to upset the peace of the world. It is this happy fact,

10　now clear to the view of every public man whose thoughts do not still linger in an age that is dead and gone, which makes it possible for every nation whose purposes are consistent with justice and the peace of the world to avow now or at any other

15　time the objects it has in view.

　　We entered this war because violations of right had occurred which touched us to the quick and made the life of our own people impossible unless they were corrected.... What we demand in this

20　war, therefore, is nothing peculiar to ourselves. It is that the world be made fit and safe to live in; and particularly that it be made safe for every peace-loving nation which, like our own, wishes to live its own life, determine its own institutions, be assured

25　of justice and fair dealing by the other peoples of the world.... The programme of the world's peace, therefore, is our programme; and that programme, the only possible programme, as we see it, is this:

　　I.　Open covenants of peace...with no private

30　international understandings of any kind but diplomacy shall proceed always frankly and in the public view.

　　II.　Absolute freedom of navigation upon the seas...alike in peace and in war, except as

35　the seas may be closed in whole or in part by international action for the enforcement of international covenants.

　　III.　The removal, so far as possible, of all economic barriers and the establishment of

40　an equality of trade conditions among all the nations consenting....

　　IV.　Adequate guarantees given and taken that national armaments will be reduced to the lowest point consistent with domestic safety.

45　　V.　A free, open-minded, and absolutely impartial adjustment of all colonial claims....

　　VI.　The evacuation of all Russian territory and such a settlement of all questions affecting Russia as will secure the best and freest

50　cooperation of the other nations of the world.

　　VII.　Belgium...must be evacuated and restored, without any attempt to limit the sovereignty which she enjoys in common with all other free nations....

55　　VIII.　All French territory should be freed and the invaded portions restored....

　　IX.　A readjustment of the frontiers of Italy should be effected along clearly recognizable lines of nationality.

60　　X.　The peoples of Austria-Hungary...should be accorded the freest opportunity to autonomous development.

　　XI.　Rumania, Serbia, and Montenegro should be evacuated; occupied territories restored;

65　and Serbia accorded free and secure access to the sea....

　　XII.　The Turkish portion of the present Ottoman Empire should be assured a secure sovereignty, but the other nationalities

70　which are now under Turkish rule should be assured an undoubted security of life....

　　XIII.　An independent Polish state should be erected which should include the territories inhabited by indisputably Polish populations.

75 ...[The state] should be assured a free and secure access to the sea....

XIV. A general association of nations must be formed under specific covenants for the purpose of affording mutual guarantees

80 of political independence and territorial integrity to great and small states alike.

11. Based on the first two paragraphs, which choice best identifies Wilson's purpose in making this speech?

A) To build an international military and political alliance

B) To declare the sovereignty and independence of the United States

C) To outline ways to maintain peaceful relations in the world

D) To reform governments in aggressor nations bent on conquest

12. Which choice provides the best evidence for the answer to the previous question?

A) Lines 1–5 ("It will be...of any kind")

B) Lines 5–6 ("The day of...is gone by")

C) Lines 16–17 ("We entered...occurred")

D) Lines 26–27 ("The programme...is our programme")

13. As used in line 31, "frankly" most nearly means

A) in an honest manner.

B) in a blunt manner.

C) in an abrupt manner.

D) in an outspoken manner.

14. Based on the information in the passage, it can reasonably be inferred that in the past,

A) the United States avoided alliances.

B) some nations formed private pacts with one another.

C) wars usually involved only two nations.

D) the borders of France and Italy were not well-defined.

15. Which choice provides the best evidence for the answer to the previous question?

A) Lines 1–5 ("It will be...of any kind")

B) Lines 16–19 ("We entered...corrected")

C) Lines 55–59 ("All French...of nationality")

D) Lines 77–81 ("A general...states alike")

16. As used in line 44, "consistent" most nearly means

A) dependable.

B) continuing.

C) agreeable.

D) rigid.

17. In lines 45–46 ("A free...colonial claims"), Wilson argues that to preserve peace, nations must

A) engage in free, open, and fair trade with colonies.

B) give up all aspirations for territorial and economic expansion.

C) provide constitutional protections for colonies.

D) work to resolve conflicts originating from imperial conquests.

18. Points VI through VIII serve as evidence to support which claim made by Wilson throughout the speech?

A) Democratic nations ought to sign pacts of economic and political cooperation.

B) During the war, aggressors damaged property that they should be required to repair.

C) In the past, nations violated one another's territorial sovereignty.

D) Current colonies are entitled to establish free and democratic governments.

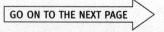

19. Which of the following approaches to international relations is most similar to Wilson's approach?

    A) Economic sanctions against ideological enemies

    B) Joint efforts to mediate conflict among nations

    C) Nongovernmental organizations to regulate trade

    D) Unilateral military action against unfriendly regimes

20. Which choice best describes the developmental pattern of Wilson's argument?

    A) A statement and restatement of the argument

    B) A statement of the argument followed by specific examples

    C) Initial claims followed by counterclaims

    D) Specific examples leading to a concluding argument

**Questions 21-31 are based on the following passages and supplementary material.**

The following passages are concerned with meditation, particularly the practice of mindfulness. Passage 1 provides an overview of meditation, while Passage 2 focuses on a particular practitioner, U.S. Representative Tim Ryan.

**Passage 1**

Meditation has been around for thousands of years, starting as a religious practice. Hindu scripture from around 1500 b.c.e. describes meditating on the divine, and art from this time period shows
5  people sitting cross-legged and solitary in a garden. In China and India around the fifth century b.c.e., other forms of meditation developed. Several religions, including Taoism, Buddhism, Islam, and Christianity, have meditative rites. In 20th-century
10  Europe and America, secular forms of meditation arrived from India. Rather than focusing on spiritual growth, secular meditation emphasizes stress reduction, relaxation, and self-improvement.

Although it still isn't exactly mainstream,
15  many people practice meditation. Mindfulness meditation, in particular, has become more popular in recent years. The practice involves sitting comfortably, focusing on one's breathing, and bringing the mind's attention to the present.
20  Concerns about the past or future are let go of. An individual can picture worries popping like a bubble or flitting away like a butterfly.

Mindfulness is about increasing awareness and practicing acceptance. To be present is to
25  have sharpened attention, or to be in a state of heightened consciousness. Practitioners of mindfulness report having a better quality of experience, deeper engagement, and greater measure of fulfillment.
30    There are also health benefits. According to the Mayo Clinic, "Meditation can give you a sense of calm, peace and balance that benefits your emotional well-being." Among the emotional benefits are reducing negative emotions, increased
35  self-awareness, and stress management skills. Asthma, depression, and sleep disorders are all conditions worsened by stress. Several studies have shown that patients with these conditions benefit from meditation.
40    Dr. Robert Schneider, director of the Institute for Natural Medicine and Prevention, says, "I have been researching effects of meditation on health for thirty years and have found it has compelling benefits. The benefits of meditation are coming to
45  be widely accepted by health professionals, business leaders, and the media. It is now time for the medical profession to catch up."

**Passage 2**

U.S. Representative Tim Ryan took a weekend retreat where he first practiced mindfulness meditation.
50  "I came out of it," he says, "with a whole new way of relating with what was going on in the world." Now Ryan is an advocate for the benefits of meditation on health, performance, and social awareness. In the busy and aggressive world of Washington
55  politics, he's a voice for calm consideration.

Every week Ryan, a Democrat representing the 13th congressional district of Ohio, hosts a meditation session for his staff and any other members of Congress who want to join.
60  Despite the fact that Republicans and Democrats are considered politically opposed, Ryan believes that the

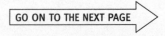

benefits of meditation ought to appeal to members of both parties. Meditation promotes self-reliance and fiscal conservation because it's a
65 health practice that can be self-sustained and doesn't require costly memberships or equipment.

In 2010, Ryan wrote the book *A Mindful Nation: How a Simple Practice Can Help Us Reduce Stress,*
70 *Improve Performance, and Recapture the American Spirit,* in which he advocates increased mindful-ness in many disciplines and professions. After its publication, kindergarten classes in his Ohio district started using deep-breathing techniques;
75 now teachers rave about their students' improved behavior. "Mental discipline, focus, self-reliance, deep listening—these are fundamental skills that are essential to kids' education," Ryan says. "We yell at kids to pay attention, but we never teach them
80 *how* to pay attention."

Word seems to be spreading around Capitol Hill. "I've had members of Congress approach me and say, 'I want to learn more about this,'" Ryan says. "Between the fundraising, being away from fam-
85 ily, (and) the environment of hyperpartisanship, Washington is really stressing people out."

Ryan supports legislation that puts meditation to good use for everyone. Among other bills, he has sponsored one to increase the holistic-medicine
90 offerings of the Department of Veterans Affairs. "And I haven't met anyone in the country that isn't feeling a high level of anxiety right now, given the economy and what's going on in the world. So mindfulness is for everyone."
95 Mr. Ryan is quick to point out that mindfulness is not a religious practice, but rather a secular mental technique that can be effective regardless of spiritual beliefs. He compares it to his grandparents' praying and to athletes' working out until they feel
100 "in the zone."

"Your mind and body sync up into a flow state, without a lot of mental chatter," Mr. Ryan says.

**Improvements after Employee Meditation Program**

After the third year of its employee meditation program, a Detroit chemical plant reported these improvements.

21. The central idea of Passage 1 is that meditation and mindfulness

A) were first practiced as religious rites.

B) are becoming more accepted because of their benefits.

C) are valuable tools for psychologists.

D) help practitioners focus on their inner lives.

22. Passage 1 most strongly suggests that which of the following is true?

A) Individuals who practice meditation are more likely to develop illness.

B) Meditation helps people advance in their careers.

C) Not many studies have been done on the results of daily meditation.

D) Many medical professionals embrace the benefits of meditation.

23. Which choice provides the best evidence for the answer to the previous question?

A) Lines 2–5 ("Hindu scripture…in a garden")

B) Lines 15–17 ("Mindfulness meditation…in recent years")

C) Lines 24–26 ("To be present…consciousness")

D) Lines 30–33 ("According to…well-being'")

GO ON TO THE NEXT PAGE ⟶

24. As used in line 43, "compelling" most nearly means

    A) creative.

    B) judicial.

    C) persuasive.

    D) adaptable.

25. In Passage 2, what can be inferred about the author's point of view on meditation?

    A) The author is uncertain about its value.

    B) The author likes it but acknowledges its limits.

    C) The author appreciates its value.

    D) The author is devoted to it.

26. Passage 2 most strongly suggests that which of the following is true of Mr. Ryan?

    A) He acts on his beliefs.

    B) He is afraid to try new things.

    C) He likes to try new things.

    D) He is concerned about bipartisanship.

27. Which choice provides the best evidence for the answer to the previous question?

    A) Lines 48–49 ("In 2008…mindfulness meditation")

    B) Lines 63–67 ("Meditation promotes…or equipment")

    C) Lines 88–90 ("Among other bills…Affairs")

    D) Lines 95–98 ("Mr. Ryan…spiritual beliefs")

28. As used in line 96, "secular" most nearly means

    A) nonreligious.

    B) serious.

    C) impersonal.

    D) pristine.

29. In Passage 2, the author's use of the word "chatter" (line 102) implies that

    A) having an inner dialogue is a useful tool.

    B) people enjoy imagining themselves in various situations.

    C) meditation supporters talk about its surprises.

    D) much of what people think is relatively unimportant.

30. Both passages support which generalization about mindfulness meditation?

    A) It has become an acceptable way to show spirituality.

    B) It is making inroads into U.S. culture.

    C) It should be utilized in public institutions.

    D) It will soon be embraced by the American public.

31. Data in the graph provide most direct support for which claim from the passages?

    A) Meditation improves a person's focus and discipline.

    B) Children benefit from learning deep-breathing techniques.

    C) Meditation makes a person more generous.

    D) Health professionals are open to the idea of meditation being healthful.

**Questions 32-42 are based on the following passage.**

The following passage describes possible causes
and impacts of colony collapse disorder, the
mysterious disappearance of honeybee colonies.

Colony collapse disorder, sometimes referred
to as CCD, is a phenomenon that has garnered
much attention over the past few years from both
the scientific community and the media alike. The
5 disorder, which causes entire honeybee colonies
to mysteriously disappear, is a major threat to both
the environment and the economy. Honeybees are
the world's natural pollinators and are responsible
for the production of about one-third of everything
10 we eat. Without honeybees, produce that we're
used to having in our diets, like apples, blueberries,
strawberries, and nuts, would no longer be
available. Honeybees also have an effect on the
meat industry in the United States. They pollinate
15 the various types of feed used by beef and dairy
farmers. The services of the honeybee population
are invaluable, and the survival of many different
species depends on their well-being.

When colony collapse disorder was first
20 recognized, beekeepers and scientists assumed that
a pathogen was to blame. For example, there are
several known viruses and pests that can kill off
entire hives of honeybees quickly and be extremely
hard to prevent. Mites, fungus, and bacterial
25 infections are all common killers. Because of how
often they're seen in hives, farmers assumed that
these common plights were responsible for colony
collapse disorder. However, as time passed and the
disorder was studied, researchers noticed some-
30 thing odd. In many cases, there were simply no
dead bees to discover. While common killers of the
honeybee left telltale signs, colony collapse disorder left nothing behind but empty hives.

Scientists attributed the rapid disappearance of
35 the bees to a form of altruistic behavior. When a
bee gets sick, it flies away from the hive so as not
to spread its illness to the other bees. It naturally
prioritizes the overall health of the hive over its
own. Although this behavior explained the bees'
40 disappearing act, the cause of the disorder is yet to
be understood and the list of possible explanations
just keeps getting longer.

One team of researchers hypothesized that
fluctuations in the Earth's magnetic field might
45 be doing damage to the magnetoreceptors, or
built-in homing devices, that bees use to find
their way home to their hives after flying all day.
Honeybees, as well as birds and fish, use the Earth's
magnetic field to identify their location. Sunspots,
50 which cause the strength of the Earth's magnetic
field to fluctuate, might be damaging the
honeybee's biological tools.

While solar activity is outside the control of
humans, another theory about the cause of colony
55 collapse disorder points to the human invention
of pesticides. Pesticides, which are chemicals used
to prevent pest infestation of crops on a large scale
around the world, are often picked up by honeybees
during their foraging and pollination flights.
60 Scientists have found that more than one pesticide
can be found in the honey of one hive. They are
currently studying the interaction of two or more
pesticides, which travel into the hives and are stored
by the bees in the pollen they use for protein.

65 While the presence of one pesticide in a hive would
certainly limit the life spans of bees and impair their
navigational skills, it could be that it is the interaction
of two or more pesticides that cause the entire colony
to collapse. There are many ingredients in pesticides
70 that are not regulated by world governments, and
this leaves a lot of ground for bee scientists to cover
when doing their research.

Research over time usually helps to narrow down
the field of possible causes of a disorder, but in the
75 case of colony collapse disorder, scientists feel farther
away than ever from finding the root cause and a
cure. Many people around the world are taking up
the cause of keeping honeybees alive by keeping
bees in their backyards or on their roofs. Some
80 cities and towns have relaxed regulations on beekeeping in response to the honeybee population crisis.
Hopefully, community initiatives and research can
both help to save the world's honeybee population.

GO ON TO THE NEXT PAGE ⟶

32. The primary purpose of the passage is to

    A) show that honeybees require certain conditions in order to live.

    B) instruct the reader on how to increase the number of honeybees.

    C) explain the relationship between sunspots and colony collapse disorder.

    D) alert the reader to the impending crisis of decreasing numbers of honeybees.

33. The author's point of view is most similar to that of

    A) an advocate for honeybee survival.

    B) an environmentalist concerned about toxic materials.

    C) a naturalist who researches changes in animal populations.

    D) a concerned citizen who hopes to raise honeybees.

34. The author uses the word "mysteriously" (line 6) to emphasize

    A) that fluctuations of the Earth's magnetic field are uncontrollable.

    B) how little is known about why colony collapse occurs.

    C) that the reason a bee leaves its hive when it is sick is unknown.

    D) why researchers are studying the effect of pesticides on honeybees.

35. As used in line 27, "plights" most nearly means

    A) causes.

    B) promises.

    C) intentions.

    D) troubles.

36. The author uses the fact that no bees are found in a hive after a colony collapses to

    A) examine the extent of damage to the honeybee population that has occurred.

    B) emphasize the ways in which honeybees relate to human beings.

    C) refute the possibility that pathogens are the reason for the collapse.

    D) show that pesticides are not to blame for the decrease in the honeybee population.

37. Which choice provides the best evidence for the answer to the previous question?

    A) Lines 4–7 ("The disorder…the economy")

    B) Lines 21–24 ("For example…to prevent")

    C) Lines 31–33 ("While common…empty hives")

    D) Lines 37–39 ("It naturally . . . its own")

38. As used in line 59, "foraging" most nearly means

    A) rejecting.

    B) offering.

    C) watching.

    D) searching.

39. The passage most strongly suggests that

    A) the author is cautiously optimistic about the future existence of the honeybee.

    B) the author thinks that scientists have not tried hard enough to find the reason for colony collapse.

    C) one team of scientists believes that they will have an answer to the problem of colony collapse very soon.

    D) scientists have ruled out the theory that pesticides are at fault for colony collapse.

40. Which choice provides the best evidence for the answer to the previous question?

    A) Lines 7–10 ("Honeybees…eat")

    B) Lines 25–28 ("Because of how…disorder")

    C) Lines 53–56 ("While solar…pesticides")

    D) Lines 82–83 ("Hopefully…population")

Practice Tests

41. According to the passage, which of the following events has occurred in response to colony collapse disorder?

    A) Concerned citizens have fought to ban certain pesticides.

    B) Some towns have relaxed their regulations on beekeeping.

    C) Farmers have resorted to other means of pollinating their feed.

    D) Scientists are working to control the use of electromagnetic devices.

42. Based on information in the passage, which statement best describes the relationship between honeybees and human beings?

    A) Human beings depend on honeybees to keep the environment and economy healthy.

    B) Human beings depend on honeybees to keep the effects of sunspots to a minimum.

    C) Honeybees depend on human beings to provide them with food.

    D) Honeybees depend on human beings to protect them from solar flares.

**Questions 43-52 are based on the following passage and supplementary material.**

The following passage describes the potential problems caused by debris that humans have left behind in space.

In the first days of space exploration, one concern was the possibility that astronauts or spacecraft might be hit by meteoroids. Scientists calculated that this possibility was extremely
5  small because meteoroids are rare. Astronauts and spacecraft, on the other hand, wouldalmost certainly encounter micrometeorites, which are about the size of grains of dust and much more common.

However, in the 60 years since the beginning of
10  space exploration, large quantities of human-made orbital debris have accumulated. Much of the debris consists of satellites that have stopped functioning or rocket booster sections that separated from the main spacecraft during a mission. Some of
15  the debris consists of items lost by astronauts, such

as tools or space suit parts. Still, more of the debris is the result of collisions, such as when one satellite collides with another or with a large piece of debris.

NASA estimates there are millions of debris
20  particles that are too small to be tracked. These circle Earth at speeds up to 17,500 miles per hour, making even the smallest particles dangerous. One scientist calculated that a chip of paint hitting the window of a spacecraft at orbital speeds will hit
25  with the same amount of force as a bowling ball traveling at 60 mph. Such an impact occurred on the space shuttle *Challenger*'s second flight, chipping the windows and causing minor damage to the protective tiles on the spacecraft. While the damage
30  was not immediately dangerous, it led to the fear that any craft in orbit for long periods of time could accumulate enough damage to cease functioning.

Larger objects are even more dangerous, but they can be monitored and avoided. NASA tracks
35  about 500,000 pieces of debris larger than a marble, about 20,000 of which are larger than a softball. When NASA was still flying shuttle missions, it would often have to direct the shuttle to maneuver to avoid collisions with the larger debris. This could
40  usually be planned and accomplished in a few hours, but moving the International Space Station to avoid a collision takes up to 30 hours of advance notice.

Many satellites have the ability to adjust their
45  course slightly and can be remotely directed to avoid collisions with larger objects that would damage or destroy the satellites. NASA and the European Space Agency (ESA) have departments of scientists and engineers dedicated to cataloging,
50  modeling, and predicting the movements of space debris.

Some debris falls back to Earth, and most of it is burned up in the atmosphere. However, a large piece will survive long enough to get through
55  the atmosphere and crash. In 1979, the obsolete Skylab fell out of orbit, and much of it withstood the trip through the atmosphere, crashing in the Australian outback. Space agencies also monitor debris to predict if and when any particular piece
60  might fall. Although they can issue warnings, there

GO ON TO THE NEXT PAGE ⇒

is currently nothing that can be done about pieces that might get through the atmosphere.

To avoid adding to the aggregation of debris, future satellites may need to be able to take
65 themselves out of orbit as their usefulness comes to an end. Until a way to remove these remains is implemented, however, those 500,000 pieces of large fragments, along with the millions of smaller pieces, will continue to orbit Earth.

**Debris in Space**

Adapted from NASA: U.S. Satellite Catalog.

43. The passage is primarily concerned with the

A) unintended consequences of space exploration.

B) composition of the space debris that orbits Earth.

C) dangers posed by space debris created by humans.

D) causes and consequences of collisions in space.

44. Which choice provides the best evidence for the answer to the previous question?

A) Lines 3–8 ("Scientists calculated…common")

B) Lines 20–22 ("These circle…dangerous")

C) Lines 33–34 ("Larger objects…avoided")

D) Lines 44–47 ("Many satellites…satellites")

45. The second paragraph helps support the central idea of the passage by providing

A) an explanation of why space debris left by humans is more dangerous than meteors.

B) a summary of problems caused by old satellites and discarded equipment.

C) a description of the types of human-made space debris that are causing problems.

D) an argument for better tracking of the space debris that is orbiting Earth.

46. According to the passage, why does space debris created by humans pose a greater threat than meteoroids?

A) Meteoroids are rare, while there are large quantities of space debris.

B) Meteoroids are much smaller than most pieces of space debris.

C) Space debris cannot be tracked and monitored, but meteoroids can.

D) Space debris is only found in a narrow band around Earth.

47. Which of the following pieces of evidence most strengthens the author's central claim?

A) An explanation of early concerns about space collisions in paragraph 1

B) Information about how space debris is tracked in paragraph 5

C) An example of space debris falling to Earth in paragraph 6

D) The suggestion that obsolete satellites take themselves out of orbit in paragraph 7

48. As used in line 55, "obsolete" most nearly means

A) displaced.

B) redundant.

C) excessive.

D) outdated.

49. Based on information in the passage, which con-clusion can reasonably be inferred?

A) One way to prevent space debris from causing injuries on Earth is to warn people to avoid the predicted impact site.

B) The smallest pieces of space debris can be removed by astronauts while they are working in space.

C) Most space debris is not dangerous to space travelers because of its small size and rela-tively low speed.

D) Pieces of space debris will become more of a problem as spacecraft travel farther into outer space.

50. Which choice provides the best evidence for the answer to the previous question?

A) Lines 19–22 ("NASA estimates…dangerous")

B) Lines 33–34 ("Larger objects…avoided")

C) Lines 34–36 ("NASA tracks…softball")

D) Lines 60–62 ("Although…atmosphere")

51. As used in line 67, "implemented" most nearly means

A) employed.

B) investigated.

C) prevented.

D) appointed.

52. Based on the passage and the graphic, if NASA were to place a new satellite into orbit, which alti-tude range would pose the greatest danger?

A) 500–700 kilometers

B) 700–900 kilometers

C) 1,400–1,600 kilometers

D) 1,800–2,000 kilometers

# WRITING AND LANGUAGE TEST

## 35 Minutes—44 Questions

This section corresponds to Section 2 of your answer sheet.

**Directions:** Each passage in this section is followed by several questions. Some questions will reference an underlined portion in the passage; others will ask you to consider a part of a passage or the passage as a whole. For each question, choose the answer that reflects the best use of grammar, punctuation, and style. If a passage or question is accompanied by a graphic, take the graphic into account in choosing your response(s). Some questions will have "NO CHANGE" as a possible response. Choose that answer if you think the best choice is to leave the sentence as written.

**Questions 1-11 are based on the following passage.**

**A Sweet Discovery**

[1] Like most chemists, a laboratory was where Constantin Fahlberg worked on his research. However, the discovery for which he is famous occurred not in the laboratory, but at supper.

[2] Chemical compounds are derived from coal tar, which is what Fahlberg began working on as a research chemist in a laboratory at Johns Hopkins University in early 1878. Coal tar was a by-product of steel manufacturing, and compounds derived [3] from them had been used as medicines and in dye formulations. Fahlberg, and others in the laboratory, were studying ways to add different chemicals to molecules found in coal tar to see if the new compounds formed had other useful properties.

1. A) NO CHANGE
   B) Like most chemists, Constantin Fahlberg worked on his research in a laboratory.
   C) Constantin Fahlberg worked on his research, like most chemists, in a laboratory.
   D) A laboratory, like most chemists, is where Constantin Fahlberg worked on his research.

2. A) NO CHANGE
   B) Johns Hopkins University is where Fahlberg began working as a research chemist in a laboratory, making chemical compounds derived from coal tar in early 1878.
   C) Coal tar creates chemical compounds. This is what Fahlberg began working on as a research chemist in a laboratory at Johns Hopkins University in early 1878.
   D) In early 1878, Fahlberg began working as a research chemist in a laboratory at Johns Hopkins University, making chemical compounds derived from coal tar.

3. A) NO CHANGE
   B) from it
   C) from these
   D) from him

GO ON TO THE NEXT PAGE

One night in June, Fahlberg finished a long day of work; he had been so [4] demanding in his research that he forgot to eat lunch, so he hurried to his supper without stopping to wash his hands. He might have considered handwashing unnecessary because he had not handled any toxic chemicals that day, or he might have just been so hungry he did not think about it. [5]

The bread tasted so sweet that Fahlberg thought he might have picked up some cake by mistake. He rinsed out his mouth with water and then patted his mustache dry with a napkin. He was surprised to find that the napkin tasted sweet as well. He took another sip of water and realized that the water now tasted sweet. [6] The bread, napkin, and glass of water had something in common. He then tasted his thumb, and it tasted sweeter than any candy he had ever had.

[1] Fahlberg rushed back into the lab and began to taste the contents of every beaker he had used that day. [2] Fortunately, he had not worked with anything poisonous or corrosive, or the story [7] may have a different ending.

4. A) NO CHANGE
   B) delayed
   C) engrossed
   D) excited

5. At this point, the writer wants to create an ideal transition to the next paragraph. Which choice most effectively accomplishes this goal?
   A) Later, hand washing would become a critical protocol in the laboratory.
   B) Thankfully, he didn't, or he never would have discovered what came next.
   C) Fahlberg had not eaten any cake, or indeed anything sweet, that day.
   D) Either way, he picked up his bread in his unwashed hands and took a bite.

6. A) NO CHANGE
   B) Was there something that the bread, napkin, and glass of water had in common, he wondered?
   C) In fact, everything Fahlberg touched seemed to taste sweeter than usual, which intrigued his scientific mind.
   D) Fahlberg quickly realized that the one thing the bread, napkin, and glass of water had in common was that they had all touched his fingers.

7 A) NO CHANGE
   B) would have had
   C) might have
   D) could have had

GO ON TO THE NEXT PAGE

[3] 8 He had discovered saccharin, which he named for its intense sweetness. [4] He found a sweet-tasting mixture of chemicals and worked for weeks to isolate the sweet substance from the rest and to determine its chemical composition. [5] Although it is many times more sweet tasting than sugar, it cannot be used for energy by the body and therefore does not contribute to calories consumed or energy use. [6] Soon after Fahlberg started 9 making saccharin commercially in 1886, it became popular with people who needed to lose weight and with diabetic patients who needed to avoid sugar. 10 11

8. Which choice most clearly and effectively conveys the central idea of the paragraph?

   A) NO CHANGE

   B) The substance was saccharin, and it became known as an artificial sweetener.

   C) Instead, the substance was a harmless sweetener called saccharin.

   D) Interestingly, the substance was extremely sweet and would later be known as saccharin.

9. A) NO CHANGE

   B) inventing

   C) creating

   D) producing

10. To make this paragraph most logical, sentence 4 should be placed

    A) where it is now.

    B) before sentence 1.

    C) before sentence 3.

    D) before sentence 6.

11. Which of the following sentences would provide the best conclusion for the passage?

    A) Clearly, Constantin Fahlberg's legacy of research, along with his accidental discovery, continues to have lasting effects on society even today.

    B) If Fahlberg had stopped to wash his hands that day, he might have continued his experiments on coal tar derivatives, never knowing that an important substance sat at the bottom of one of his laboratory beakers.

    C) In addition to his discovery of saccharin, his work on coal tar proved that Constantin Fahlberg was a talented scientist whose work has applications in the present day, even though a number of new artificial sweeteners have been developed.

    D) Fahlberg's discovery of saccharin is just one of the many examples of times when science was advanced through what some might call "a happy accident."

 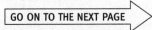

Practice Tests

**Questions 12-22 are based on the following passage.**

**René Descartes: The Father of Modern Philosophy**

Throughout history, philosophy has shaped culture in pivotal ways. From the ancients to the postmoderns, great philosophers have spoken powerfully within [12] there respective contexts. For modern Western culture, one philosopher's formative impact surpassed his contemporaries: France's René Descartes. Called "the father of modern philosophy," Descartes crucially influenced Western perspectives on knowledge and rationality.

This 17th-century philosopher ushered Western thought through an era of great public doubt and upheaval and into the age of self-reliant rationalism. Political and religious tradition and authority— the [13] obvious premodern sources of truth and knowledge—were being questioned and rejected as new ideas identified potential inconsistencies. [14] Because foundations of truth seemed to be crumbling, Descartes's writings proposed an alternative foundation: individual reason.

[15] An expert in many fields, Descartes's work would on many levels serve to establish foundations for modern culture and science.

12. A) NO CHANGE
    B) their
    C) its
    D) it's

13. A) NO CHANGE
    B) makeshift
    C) innovative
    D) reigning

14. A) NO CHANGE
    B) In a time when foundations of truth seemed to be crumbling, Descartes's writings proposed an alternative foundation: individual reason.
    C) Despite the fact that foundations of truth seemed to be crumbling, Descartes's writings proposed an alternative foundation: individual reason.
    D) Before foundations of truth seemed to be crumbling, Descartes's writings proposed an alternative foundation: individual reason.

15. A) NO CHANGE
    B) Expertise in many fields, Descartes created work that
    C) An expert in many fields, Descartes would create work that
    D) With his expertise in many fields, Descartes's work

GO ON TO THE NEXT PAGE ⟹

[16] This emphasis on reason, as opposed to traditional or authoritative bases for certainty, would become the modern mechanism for determining truth and knowledge.

[17] Modern culture would come to cherish this as an intellectual ideal. In his most famous project, Descartes sought certainty by mentally stripping away every layer of knowledge that was remotely possible to doubt. Descartes arrived at his memorable [18] conclusion, "I think, therefore I am," he could only be certain of the fact that he was thinking.

16. At this point, the writer wants to add specific information that supports the central claim of the paragraph. Which choice provides the strongest support?

A) Even so, his most impressive contribution was his advocacy for the individual's rationality.

B) Unlike Descartes, other philosophers argued that reason alone could not provide the basis for knowledge.

C) The idea known as "Cartesian dualism" posited that in the world there exists only mind and matter.

D) His work on philosophy has proven to have more importance than his ideas about anatomy, many of which have since been disproven.

17. Which sentence should be added in front of sentence 1 to clarify the topic of the paragraph?

A) Descartes's contributions to philosophy were seen as threatening to religion.

B) Descartes focused his work on the pursuit of fact-based certainty.

C) The foundation for the ideas of many other philosophers is Descartes's work.

D) Descartes's ideas were rooted in his Jesuit training.

18. A) NO CHANGE

B) conclusion "I think, therefore I am," he could only be certain of the fact that he was thinking.

C) conclusion, "I think, therefore I am" he could only be certain of the fact that he was thinking.

D) conclusion, "I think, therefore I am." He could only be certain of the fact that he was thinking.

[19] Building from there, he could work toward rational certainty in other areas of knowledge.

Emphasizing the importance of building knowledge on certain evidence, Descartes modeled a reversal of the reigning scientific processes (which typically worked backward from observation to explanation). Descartes founded the modern scientific method, in which research and study could be reliably conducted based on certain evidence. Scientific method, and the emphasis on human reason, would become standard elements of modern thought. Though reimagined by ensuing culture and philosophy, [20] these changes propelled by Descartes's initial contributions to that conversation.

[21] Some people may argue that it is impossible to separate what Descartes accomplished from the things his contemporaries did. Certainly, most scientists and philosophers influence and build on each other's work. But Descartes was the crucial voice in early modern dialogue. His expertise drew trusted readership, and his well-read ideas pointed culture down the road to modern understanding—a road paved with reason, modernism's great intellectual virtue. Shifts [22] begun by Descartes's work would influence the very structure of ideas and systems in the modern world, from research methods to public processes like government and health systems.

19. Which choice most logically follows the previous sentence and sets up the information that follows?

A) This revelation came as a shock to many people.

B) However, he believed that this certainty offered evidence to confirm his existence.

C) Still, it was a place to start.

D) This was a radical new way to think about thinking.

20. A) NO CHANGE

B) these changes being propelled by

C) these changes having been propelled by

D) these changes were propelled by

21. A) NO CHANGE

B) Some may argue that it is impossible to separate Descartes's accomplishments from those of his contemporaries.

C) Some people may argue that it is impossible to separate Descartes from his contemporaries.

D) Some may argue that what Descartes accomplished is no different from what his contemporaries did.

22. A) NO CHANGE

B) foreseen

C) initiated

D) evolved

GO ON TO THE NEXT PAGE

## Questions 23-33 are based on the following passage.

### The Novel: Introspection to Escapism

Art is never **23** <u>immovable</u>, nor is it meant to be. A poem written today looks and sounds vastly different from a poem by Shakespeare, and a modern symphony no longer resembles one by Beethoven. So it is with the novel, that still relatively young member of the literary family (many consider *Don Quixote*, published in 1605, to be the first). The novel is evolving to reflect the **24** <u>changing world; for better</u> or for worse.

**25** <u>The novel, while well regarded, would never match the poem as the ideal form for conveying the struggles of humanity.</u> A few quotations from acclaimed novelists of the past illustrate how **26** <u>loftily</u> the form was once regarded. G. K. Chesterton said, "A good novel tells us the truth about its hero; but a bad novel tells us the truth about its author." English writer Ford Madox Ford believed the novelist played an important role as a recorder of history. **27** <u>Ford said of his friend Joseph Conrad,</u> "We agreed that the novel is absolutely the only vehicle for the thought of our day."

23. A) NO CHANGE
    B) sluggish
    C) static
    D) stationary

24. A) NO CHANGE
    B) changing world—for better
    C) changing world: for better
    D) changing world for better

25. Which choice most effectively establishes the main topic of the paragraph?
    A) NO CHANGE
    B) The novel was once sacred ground, meant to capture and reveal universal truths, to depict society and all its ills, to explore and expound upon the human condition.
    C) Both poetry and novels enjoyed a resurgence of popularity in the early 1900s due to the notoriety of many of the prominent authors of the day.
    D) By the early 1900s, novels had evolved into something entirely different from the form Cervantes pioneered with *Don Quixote*.

26. A) NO CHANGE
    B) broadly
    C) haughtily
    D) pretentiously

27. Which choice best improves the sentence?
    A) Ford said of his friend, the novelist Joseph Conrad,
    B) Ford said of his great friend, Joseph Conrad,
    C) Ford said of Joseph Conrad,
    D) Ford said of his friend, Joseph Conrad, a Pole who moved to Britain,

It's not that over centuries writers of novels have shed these ambitions; novels today still address complexities and intricate social dynamics. [28] However, in recent decades, popular novels and their film adaptations have driven the novel market in a broader direction. [29] Novels are considered just another entertainment medium, which are now available on digital devices, one that ought to enthrall its passive reader and relieve him or her of the stress and tedium of life. The difficulties, challenges, and triumphs of real life are [30] less often the subject of popular novels; instead, escapist tales of fantastical lands and escapades are more popular. [31]

28. A) NO CHANGE
    B) However: in recent decades,
    C) However in recent decades,
    D) In recent decades however;

29. A) NO CHANGE
    B) Novels, which are now available on digital devices, are considered just another entertainment medium,
    C) Novels are considered just another entertainment medium, now available on digital devices,
    D) Novels, just another entertainment medium which are now available on digital devices

30. A) NO CHANGE
    B) less often the subject of popular novels instead, escapist tales of fantastical lands and escapades are more popular.
    C) less often the subject of popular novels, instead, escapist tales of fantastical lands and escapades are more popular.
    D) less often the subject of popular novels: instead, escapist tales of fantastical lands and escapades, are more popular.

31. At this point, the writer wants to add specific information that supports the ideas presented in the paragraph. Which choice provides the most relevant detail?

    A) Novels exploring deep social issues remain the most heavily decorated books come literary award season.
    B) Director James Cameron remarked recently about the "inherent difficulty" of adapting novels with fantasy themes.
    C) Writing in the *New Yorker* magazine in 2014, critic James Woods stated that readers now want novels that, like popcorn, are "easy to consume."
    D) The "slice of life" novel remains tremendously popular among books targeting younger readers.

GO ON TO THE NEXT PAGE →

It is rare today for a novelist to attempt to ask, "What does it mean?" Instead, [32] we strive to provide the reader with an answer to the question, "What happens next?"

"Publishers, readers, booksellers, even critics," critic James Woods wrote, "acclaim the novel that one can deliciously sink into, forget oneself in, the novel that returns us to the innocence of childhood or the dream of the cartoon, the novel of a thousand confections and no unwanted significance. What becomes harder to find, and lonelier to defend, is the idea of [33] the novel as—in Ford Madox Ford's words—a 'medium of profoundly serious investigation into the human case.' "

32. A) NO CHANGE
    B) they strive
    C) it strives
    D) he or she strives

33. A) NO CHANGE
    B) the novel as, in Ford Madox Ford's words—a 'medium of profoundly serious investigation into the human case.'"
    C) the novel as, in Ford Madox Ford's words: a 'medium of profoundly serious investigation into the human case.'"
    D) the novel as, in Ford Madox Ford's words; a 'medium of profoundly serious investigation into the human case.'"

**Questions 34-44 are based on the following passage and supplementary material.**

**Interning: A Bridge Between Classes and Careers**

Kelli Blake, a chemical engineering major, recently **34** excepted a summer internship with BP, an international energy company, to gain career experience. Some argue against the value of internships, claiming they pay very little and can involve performing **35** boring tasks, yet Kelli feels her internship is critical to helping her discover whether engineering is right for her.

Kelli wants a real-world perspective on information she has gained in her classes. Her internship with a corporate leader is affording her the opportunity to apply her conceptual knowledge to tasks inside a major oil company. **36** During this internship, for example, Kelli is working on a glycol dehydration project; she will be using the classroom skills she learned from thermodynamics, organic chemistry, and more. She can later add this project to her résumé and portfolio, giving her an edge over other college graduates.

**37** Offshore engineers have many rules and regulations. Helicopter underwater egress safety training is required of employees traveling to offshore facilities, so she will **38** stand out from other applicants by already being safety certified. "I have a new appreciation for the protocols followed by engineers at refineries," she states. Kelli believes that gaining new skills and showing she can apply her classroom knowledge to real situations will give her an advantage over her competition should she decide to join BP.

34. A) NO CHANGE
    B) accepted
    C) adopted
    D) adapted

35. A) NO CHANGE
    B) skilled
    C) menial
    D) challenging

36. Which choice best supports the central idea of the paragraph?

    A) NO CHANGE
    B) Kelli can use the materials from her internship in a professional-quality presentation; she can then deliver the presentation to her classmates when she returns to college after her internship.
    C) In addition, Kelli is designing the next internship proposal for her classmates after she completes her own and graduates.
    D) Kelli is hoping to formulate her project results as a professional published document to sell to BP.

37. Which choice provides the most appropriate introduction to the paragraph?

    A) NO CHANGE
    B) Kelli admires the engineers who administer the safety training.
    C) The skills Kelli acquires can be applied to existing knowledge.
    D) Kelli will also earn an underwater safety training certificate.

38. A) NO CHANGE
    B) stand down
    C) stand up
    D) stand alone

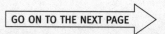

Everyone has [39] their own reason for wanting to become an intern. Kelli has several other reasons behind her decision. [40] For example, Kelli wants to meet people to learn about the variety of careers available, from entry level to senior engineer. She will accomplish all of her intern goals [41] by working on technical projects, attend "lunch and learn" meetings, watching webinars, and shadow coworkers.

What are some further benefits of internships? Besides gaining exposure in the field, Kelli is networking. The most important person to her now is her mentor, Dan, a senior engineer who can help her grow professionally by answering her questions. Gaining valuable contacts and [42] good role model. These are other reasons she has pursued this internship.

Kelli is now an acting member of a corporate team. She realizes she will be learning a lot about the industry and will benefit from adopting an entirely new vocabulary. She views her internship as an adventure, one in which engineering teams worldwide must work collaboratively and efficiently.

39. A) NO CHANGE
    B) your
    C) its
    D) his or her

40. A) NO CHANGE
    B) For example; Kelli wants to meet people to learn about the variety of careers available, from entry level to senior engineer.
    C) For example, Kelli wants to meet people—to learn about the variety of careers available, from entry level, to senior engineer.
    D) For example, Kelli wants to meet people to learn about the variety of careers available; from entry level to senior engineer.

41. A) NO CHANGE
    B) by working on technical projects, attending "lunch and learn" meetings, watching webinars, and shadowing coworkers.
    C) by working on technical projects, attend "lunch and learn" meetings, watch webinars, and shadow coworkers.
    D) by working on technical projects, attending "lunch and learn" meetings, watch webinars, and shadowing coworkers.

42. A) NO CHANGE
    B) a good role model, these are other reasons
    C) a good role model; are other reasons
    D) a good role model are other reasons

**43** It is worth it to give up her summer, Kelli argues, because though she is losing her summer she is doing the job of an actual engineer through her internship. Moreover, she views the experience as one of the best ways to learn about her field and industry, which typically offers around **44** 35 internships per 1,000 hires.

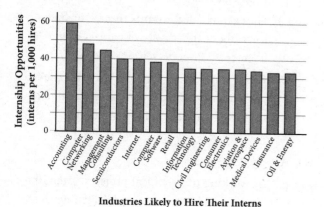

**Industries Likely to Hire Their Interns**

Adapted from Kurt Wagner, "Which Internships Really Pay Off?" ©2014 by Revere Digital LLC.

43. A) NO CHANGE

    B) It is worth giving up, Kelli argues, because though she is losing her summer, she is doing the job of an actual engineer through her internship.

    C) It is worth it to give up her summer, Kelli argues, because she is doing the job of an actual engineer through her internship.

    D) It is worth it to Kelli to give up her summer, because though summers are usually a time to relax, she argues, she is doing the job of an actual engineer through her internship.

44. Which choice most accurately and effectively represents the information in the graph and the passage?

    A) NO CHANGE

    B) 32 internships per 1,000 hires.

    C) 35 internships per 60 hires.

    D) 32 internships per 60 hires.

IF YOU FINISH BEFORE TIME IS CALLED, YOU MAY CHECK YOUR WORK ON THIS SECTION ONLY.
DO NOT TURN TO ANY OTHER SECTION IN THE TEST.

STOP

**898** K

# MATH TEST

### 25 Minutes—20 Questions

## NO-CALCULATOR SECTION

This section corresponds to Section 3 of your answer sheet.

**Directions:** For this section, solve each problem and decide which is the best of the choices given. Fill in the corresponding oval on the answer sheet. You may use any available space for scratch work.

Notes:

1. Calculator use is NOT permitted.

2. All numbers used are real numbers, and all variables used represent real numbers, unless otherwise indicated.

3. Figures are drawn to scale and lie in a plane unless otherwise indicated.

4. Unless stated otherwise, the domain of any function $f$ is assumed to be the set of all real numbers $x$, for which $f(x)$ is a real number.

Information:

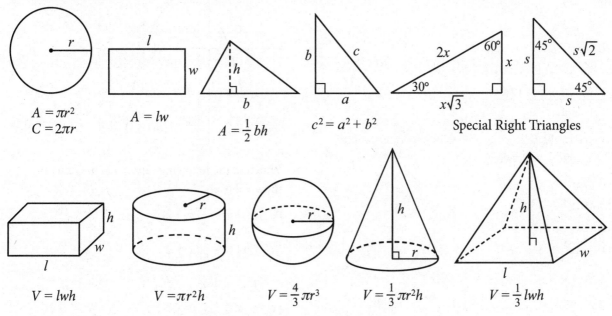

$A = \pi r^2$
$C = 2\pi r$

$A = lw$

$A = \frac{1}{2}bh$

$c^2 = a^2 + b^2$

Special Right Triangles

$V = lwh$

$V = \pi r^2 h$

$V = \frac{4}{3}\pi r^3$

$V = \frac{1}{3}\pi r^2 h$

$V = \frac{1}{3}lwh$

The sum of the degree measures of the angles in a triangle is 180.

The number of degrees of arc in a circle is 360.

The number of radians of arc in a circle is $2\pi$.

GO ON TO THE NEXT PAGE

**Fence Installation**

1. The above graph shows the cost of installing a vinyl privacy fence. The company charges a flat installation fee plus a cost per linear foot of fencing. Based on the graph, how much does one linear foot of this particular vinyl fence cost?

   A)  $5

   B)  $15

   C)  $75

   D) $150

$$\frac{24x^4 + 36x^3 - 12x^2}{12x^2}$$

2. Which of the following expressions is equivalent to the expression shown above?

   A) $2x^2 + 3x$

   B) $24x^4 + 36x^3$

   C) $2x^2 + 3x - 1$

   D) $24x^4 + 36x^3 - 1$

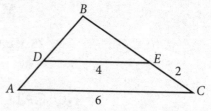

Note: Figure not drawn to scale.

3. In the figure shown, $\triangle ABC \sim \triangle DBE$. What is the length of $\overline{BE}$ ?

   A)  3.5

   B)  3.75

   C)  4

   D)  4.5

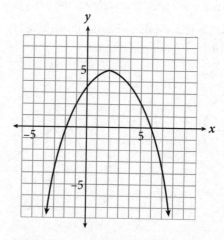

4. Which of the following represents the function shown above?

   A) $f(x) = -\frac{1}{3}(x - 2)^2 + 5$

   B) $f(x) = -\frac{1}{3}(x + 2)^2 + 5$

   C) $f(x) = \frac{1}{3}(x + 2)^2 + 5$

   D) $f(x) = 3(x - 2)^2 + 5$

GO ON TO THE NEXT PAGE ⟹

Practice Tests

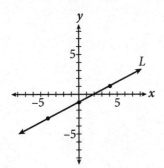

5. If line $L$ shown above is reflected over the $x$-axis, what is the slope of the new line?

A) $-2$

B) $-\dfrac{1}{2}$

C) $\dfrac{1}{2}$

D) $2$

6. If $p = 4x^3 + x - 2$, $q = x^2 - 1$, and $r = 3x - 5$, then what is $2p - (q + r)$ ?

A) $7x^3 - x + 2$

B) $8x^3 - x^2 - x + 2$

C) $8x^3 - x^2 - x - 10$

D) $8x^3 - x^2 + 5x - 8$

7. Which of the following are the roots of the equation $2x^2 + 4x - 3 = 0$ ?

A) $\dfrac{-2 \pm \sqrt{10}}{2}$

B) $-2 \pm \sqrt{5}$

C) $-1 \pm \sqrt{10}$

D) $-1 \pm 2\sqrt{10}$

8. If $g(x) = 3x - 5$ and $h(x) = \dfrac{7x + 10}{4}$, at what point does the graph of $g(x)$ intersect the graph of $h(x)$ ?

A) $(-2, -11)$

B) $(-2, 1)$

C) $(3, 4)$

D) $(6, 13)$

9. If $x = k^{-\frac{1}{3}}$, where $x > 0$ and $k > 0$, which of the following equations gives $k$ in terms of $x$ ?

A) $k = \dfrac{1}{x^3}$

B) $k = \dfrac{1}{\sqrt[3]{x}}$

C) $k = -\sqrt[3]{x}$

D) $k = -x^3$

$$4x - (10 - 2x) = c(3x - 5)$$

10. If the equation shown above has infinitely many solutions, and $c$ is a constant, what is the value of $c$ ?

A) $-2$

B) $-\dfrac{2}{3}$

C) $\dfrac{2}{3}$

D) $2$

11. If $0 < 1 - \dfrac{a}{3} \le \dfrac{1}{2}$, which of the following is not a possible value of $a$ ?

A) $1.5$

B) $2$

C) $2.5$

D) $3$

$$\begin{cases} y - \dfrac{2}{k}x \le 0 \\ \dfrac{1}{k}x - \dfrac{1}{2}y \le -1 \end{cases}$$

12. If the system of inequalities shown above has no solution, what is the value of $k$ ?

A) $1$

B) $2$

C) There is no value of $k$ that results in no solution.

D) There are infinitely many values of $k$ that result in no solution.

$$\frac{4x}{x-7} + \frac{2x}{2x-14} = \frac{70}{2(x-7)}$$

13. What value(s) of $x$ satisfy the equation above?

    A) 0

    B) 7

    C) No solution

    D) Any value such that $x \neq 7$

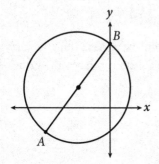

14. The circle shown above is given by the equation $x^2 + y^2 + 6x - 4y = 12$. What is the shortest distance from $A$ to $B$?

    A) 5

    B) 10

    C) $4\sqrt{3}$

    D) 24

15. If $g$ is a function defined over the set of all real numbers and $g(x-1) = 3x^2 + 5x - 7$, then which of the following defines $g(x)$?

    A) $g(x) = 3x^2 - x - 9$

    B) $g(x) = 3x^2 + 5x + 1$

    C) $g(x) = 3x^2 + 11x + 1$

    D) $g(x) = 3x^2 + 11x - 6$

GO ON TO THE NEXT PAGE

**Directions:** For questions 16-20, enter your responses into the appropriate grid on your answer sheet, in accordance with the following:

1. You will receive credit only if the circles are filled in correctly, but you may write your answers in the boxes above each grid to help you fill in the circles accurately.

2. Don't mark more than one circle per column.

3. None of the questions with grid-in responses will have a negative solution.

4. Only grid in a single answer, even if there is more than one correct answer to a given question.

5. A **mixed number** must be gridded as a decimal or an improper fraction. For example, you would grid $7\frac{1}{2}$ as 7.5 or 15/2. (Were you to grid it as [7 1 / 2], this response would be read as $\frac{71}{2}$.)

6. A **decimal** that has more digits than there are places on the grid may be either rounded or truncated, but every column in the grid must be filled in order to receive credit.

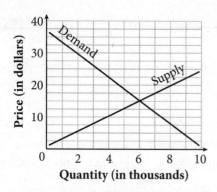

16. Retail businesses strive to price their products so that they sell as many as possible without losing money. Economic equilibrium is the price point at which the supply for a product is equal to the demand for that product. The graph above models this scenario. According to the graph, at what price in dollars will supply equal demand for this particular product?

17. Once an insect reaches its larval stage, its mass increases linearly for a short period of time and then slows down as it prepares to enter pupation. Suppose the larva of a certain species has an initial mass of 10 grams and grows linearly from $t = 0$ to $t = 48$ hours of its larval stage. If after 48 hours the mass of the larva is 14 grams, what was its mass in grams at $t = 6$ hours?

| $x$ | $f(x)$ |
|-----|--------|
| $-1$ | $-2$ |
| 0 | 0 |
| 1 | 2 |
| 2 | 4 |
| 3 | 6 |

| $x$ | $g(x)$ |
|-----|--------|
| $-2$ | 3 |
| $-1$ | 2 |
| 0 | 1 |
| 1 | $-1$ |
| 2 | $-2$ |

18. Several values for the functions $f(x)$ and $g(x)$ are shown in the tables above. What is the value of $f(g(-1))$ ?

19. If $(4 + 3i)(1 - 2i) = a + bi$, then what is the value of $a$ ? (Note that $i = \sqrt{-1}$.)

20. The maximum value of the data shown in the scatterplot above occurs at $x = 56.25$. If the data is modeled using a quadratic regression and the model is an exact fit, then what is the $y$-value when $x = 90$ ?

IF YOU FINISH BEFORE TIME IS CALLED, YOU MAY CHECK YOUR WORK ON THIS SECTION ONLY.
DO NOT TURN TO ANY OTHER SECTION IN THE TEST.

**STOP**

**904** K

# Math Test

### 55 Minutes—38 Questions

## CALCULATOR SECTION

This section corresponds to Section 4 of your answer sheet.

**Directions:** For this section, solve each problem and decide which is the best of the choices given. Fill in the corresponding oval on the answer sheet. You may use any available space for scratch work.

Notes:

1. Calculator use is permitted.
2. All numbers used are real numbers, and all variables used represent real numbers, unless otherwise indicated.
3. Figures are drawn to scale and lie in a plane unless otherwise indicated.
4. Unless stated otherwise, the domain of any function $f$ is assumed to be the set of all real numbers $x$, for which $f(x)$ is a real number.

Information:

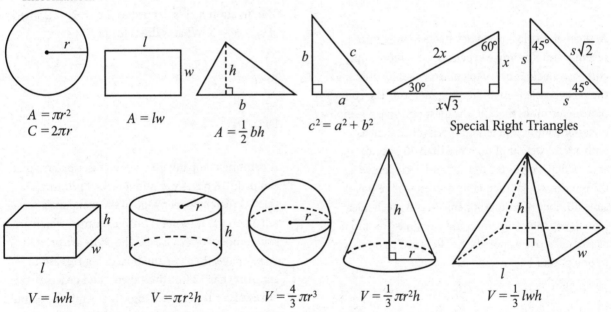

$A = \pi r^2$
$C = 2\pi r$

$A = lw$

$A = \frac{1}{2}bh$

$c^2 = a^2 + b^2$

Special Right Triangles

$V = lwh$

$V = \pi r^2 h$

$V = \frac{4}{3}\pi r^3$

$V = \frac{1}{3}\pi r^2 h$

$V = \frac{1}{3}lwh$

The sum of the degree measures of the angles in a triangle is 180.

The number of degrees of arc in a circle is 360.

The number of radians of arc in a circle is $2\pi$.

1. The U.S. Centers for Disease Control recommends that adults engage in 2.5 hours per week of vigorous exercise. A local health society conducts a survey to see if people are meeting this goal. They ask 100 people with gym memberships how many minutes of exercise they engage in per week. After analyzing the data, the health society finds that the average respondent exercises 142 minutes per week, but the margin of error was approximately 36 minutes. The society wants to lower this margin of error. Using which of the following samples instead would do so?

   A) 50 people with gym memberships

   B) 50 people randomly selected from the entire adult population

   C) 100 people with gym memberships, but from a variety of gyms

   D) 200 people randomly selected from the entire adult population

2. As a general rule, businesses strive to maximize revenue and minimize expenses. An office supply company decides to try to cut expenses by utilizing the most cost-effective shipping method. The company determines that the cheapest option is to ship boxes of ballpoint pens and mechanical pencils with a total weight of no more than 20 pounds. If each pencil weighs 0.2 ounces and each pen weighs 0.3 ounces, which inequality represents the possible number of ballpoint pens, $b$, and mechanical pencils, $m$, the company could ship in a box and be as cost-effective as possible? (There are 16 ounces in one pound.)

   A) $0.3b + 0.2m < 20 \times 16$

   B) $0.3b + 0.2m \leq 20 \times 16$

   C) $\dfrac{b}{0.3} + \dfrac{m}{0.2} < 20 \times 16$

   D) $\dfrac{b}{0.3} + \dfrac{m}{0.2} \leq 20 \times 16$

3. Where will line $Q$ shown in the graph above intersect the $x$-axis?

   A) 13

   B) 14

   C) 15

   D) 16

4. The function $f(x)$ is defined as $f(x) = 2g(x)$, where $g(x) = x + 5$. What is the value of $f(3)$ ?

   A) $-4$

   B) 6

   C) 8

   D) 16

5. A printing company uses a color laser printer that can print 18 pages per minute when printing on thick cardstock paper. One of the company's best sellers on the Internet is business cards, which are sold in boxes of 225 cards. The cards are printed 10 per page, then cut and boxed. If a real estate company has 12 full-time agents and orders two boxes of cards per agent, how many minutes should it take to print the cards, assuming the printer runs continuously?

   A) 15

   B) 20

   C) 30

   D) 45

GO ON TO THE NEXT PAGE

6. If $0.002 \le x \le 0.2$ and $5 \le y \le 25$, what is the maximum value of $\dfrac{x}{y}$ ?

   A) 0.04

   B) 0.4

   C) 4

   D) 40

7. Following a study of children in the United States under three years old, the American Academy of Pediatrics stated that there is a positive correlation between the amount of time spent watching television and the likelihood of developing an attention deficit disorder. Which of the following is an appropriate conclusion to draw from this statement?

   A) There is an association between television time and attention disorders for American children under three years old.

   B) There is an association between television time and attention disorders for all children under three years old.

   C) An increase in attention disorders is caused by an increase in television time for American children under three years old.

   D) An increase in attention disorders is caused by an increase in television time for all children under three years old.

8. A bicyclist is training for the Liège-Bastogne-Liège, one of Europe's oldest road bicycle races. The line graph above shows the number of miles she biked each week for eight weeks. According to the graph, what was the greatest change (in absolute value) in the weekly number of miles she biked between two consecutive weeks?

   A) 7

   B) 8

   C) 9

   D) 10

9. If a line that passes through the coordinates $(a - 1, 2a)$ and $(a, 6)$ has a slope of 5, what is the value of $a$ ?

   A) $-2$

   B) $-\dfrac{1}{2}$

   C) $\dfrac{1}{2}$

   D) $2$

GO ON TO THE NEXT PAGE

Practice Tests

10. An occupational health organization published a study showing an increase in the number of injuries that resulted from elderly people falling in the bathtub. In response to this increase, a medical supply company decided to drop its price on bathtub lifts from $450 to $375, hoping to still break even on the lifts. The company breaks even when its total revenue (income from selling $n$ bathtub lifts) is equal to its total cost of producing the lifts. If the cost, $C$, in dollars, of producing the lifts is $C = 225n + 3,150$, how many more of the lifts does the company need to sell at the new price to break even than at the old price?

A) 7

B) 12

C) 14

D) 21

**Questions 11 and 12 refer to the following information.**

A zoo is building a penguin exhibit. It will consist of an underwater area and a land area. The land area is made of thick sheets of ice. An outline of the total space covered by the ice is shown below. A pipe 2 feet in diameter runs the full length of the exhibit under the ice. A substance known as ice-cold glycol continuously runs through the pipe to keep the ice frozen.

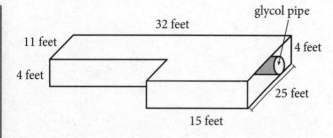

11. About how many cubic feet of water are needed to create the ice portion of the exhibit?

A) 1,850

B) 2,150

C) 2,450

D) 3,100

12. The zoo is planning to hire a company to fill the space with water. The company plans to use two 4-inch hoses that can each pump 60 gallons of water per minute. About how long should it take to fill the space? (There are 7.48 gallons of water in 1 cubic foot of ice.)

A) 1 hour

B) 1 hour, 30 minutes

C) 1 hour, 55 minutes

D) 2 hours, 15 minutes

13. Which of the following quadratic equations has no solution?

A) $0 = -2(x - 5)^2 + 3$

B) $0 = -2(x - 5)(x + 3)$

C) $0 = 2(x - 5)^2 + 3$

D) $0 = 2(x + 5)(x + 3)$

**Questions 14 and 15 refer to the following information.**

Three airplanes depart from three different airports at 8:30 a.m., all traveling to Chicago O'Hare International Airport (ORD). The distances the planes must travel are recorded in the following table. (Note: Assume all times provided are in Eastern Standard Time.)

| From | Distance to Chicago |
|---|---|
| Kansas City (MCI) | 402 |
| Boston (BOS) | 864 |
| Miami (MIA) | 1,200 |

14. The plane traveling from Boston traveled at an average speed of 360 miles per hour. The plane traveling from Kansas City arrived at 10:34 a.m. How many minutes before the plane from Boston arrived did the plane from Kansas City arrive?

A) 20

B) 28

C) 42

D) 144

GO ON TO THE NEXT PAGE

15. For the first $\frac{1}{4}$ of the trip, the plane from Miami flew through heavy winds and dense cloud cover at an average speed of 200 miles per hour. For the remaining portion of the trip, the weather was ideal, and the plane flew at an average speed of 450 miles per hour. Due to a backlog of planes at ORD, it was forced to circle overhead in a holding pattern for 25 minutes before landing. At what time did the plane from Miami land in Chicago?

    A) 12:00 p.m.

    B) 12:25 p.m.

    C) 12:50 p.m.

    D) 1:15 p.m.

16. If $h(t) = \sqrt{t^2 + 9}$ for all real values of $t$, which of the following is not in the range of $h(t)$ ?

    A) 1

    B) 3

    C) 9

    D) 10

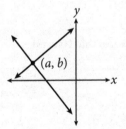

17. If $(a, b)$ represents the solution to the system of equations shown in the graph and $a = -3b$, then which of the following could be the value of $a + b$ ?

    A) $-9$

    B) 0

    C) 3

    D) 6

**Thermostat A**

**Thermostat B**

18. A car manufacturer tested two types of thermostats to determine which one it wanted to use in a new model of car. The more consistently the thermostat engages the engine's cooling fan, the better the cooling system performs over the long run. The double dot plot above shows the test results, given the following conditions:

    - Zero indicates that the cooling fan engaged at exactly the temperature at which the thermostat was set (the target temperature).

    - Negative numbers indicate that the fan engaged below the target temperature.

    - Positive numbers indicate that the fan engaged above the target temperature.

    - The safe range for the fan to engage is 10 degrees above or below the target temperature.

Which of the following best states which thermostat the car manufacturer is likely to choose and why?

A) Thermostat A because the median of the data is 0, and the range is greater than that of thermostat B

B) Thermostat B because the median of the data is 0, and the range is less than that of thermostat A

C) Thermostat A because the mode of the data is 0, which indicates a more consistent thermostat

D) Thermostat B because the data is bimodal (has two modes), which indicates a more consistent thermostat

GO ON TO THE NEXT PAGE

19. If $p$ and $q$ represent the zeros of a quadratic function and $p + q = -3$, which of the following could be the factored form of the function?

A) $f(x) = (x - 3)(x + 3)$

B) $f(x) = (x - 4)(x + 1)$

C) $f(x) = (x - 1)(x + 4)$

D) $f(x) = (x - 6)(x + 3)$

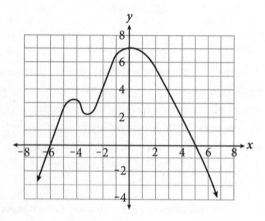

20. The figure above shows the graph of $p(x) - 4$. What is the value of $p(0)$ ?

A) 3

B) 4

C) 7

D) 11

21. Geraldine is making a simple AC electric generator for a science project using copper wire, cardboard, a nail, and magnets. The first step in building the generator is wrapping the wire around a rectangular prism made from the cardboard and connecting it to a small light bulb, as shown in the figure. If Geraldine has 18 feet of wire and needs to leave 3 inches on each end to connect to the light bulb, how many times can she wrap the wire around the cardboard prism? (Note: 1 foot = 12 inches.)

A) 21

B) 28

C) 35

D) 42

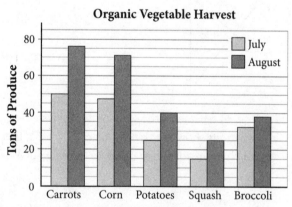

**Organic Vegetable Harvest**

22. The bar graph above shows the vegetable harvest, in tons, at an organic produce farm during July and August. Of the following, which best approximates the percent increase in the harvest of squash at this farm from July to August?

A) 67%

B) 60%

C) 53%

D) 40%

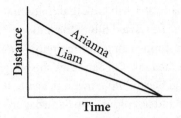

| | Unemployed | Employed | Totals |
|---|---|---|---|
| **Female Degree** | 12 | 188 | 200 |
| **Female No Degree** | 44 | 156 | 200 |
| **Male Degree** | 23 | 177 | 200 |
| **Male No Degree** | 41 | 159 | 200 |
| **Totals** | 120 | 680 | 800 |

23. Arianna and her brother Liam both walk home from school each day, but they go to different schools. The figure shows their trip home on Monday. Based on the graph, which of the following statements is true?

A) It took Liam longer to walk home because his school is farther away.

B) It took Arianna longer to walk home because her school is farther away.

C) Arianna and Liam walked home at the same rate.

D) Arianna walked home at a faster rate than Liam.

24. If line $L$ passes through the points $(-4, -8)$ and $(8, 1)$, which of the following points does line $L$ not pass through?

A) $(0, -5)$

B) $(4, -1)$

C) $(12, 4)$

D) $(16, 7)$

25. The table above shows the results of a sociological study identifying the number of males and females with and without college degrees who were unemployed or employed at the time of the study. If one person from the study is chosen at random, what is the probability that that person is an employed person with a college degree?

A) $\dfrac{73}{160}$

B) $\dfrac{10}{17}$

C) $\dfrac{17}{20}$

D) $\dfrac{73}{80}$

**Infected Patient**

26. Typically, when people contract an infectious disease, their immune system immediately begins to produce extra white blood cells to fight the disease. The scatterplot shows the white blood cells reproducing in an infected patient, along with several values found when modeling the data using a graphing calculator. According to this model, how many white blood cells per microliter of blood did the patient have before he contracted the disease?

   A) 3,400

   B) 8,500

   C) 10,000

   D) 13,600

27. A rodeo is building a circular arena. The arena will have a total area of $64\pi$ square yards and can either be left open for rodeo competitions or divided into 12 equal sections through the center for auctions. When holding auctions, the rodeo has an average of 4 bulls and 8 horses for sale. A bull cannot be placed in a section directly beside another section containing a bull, and all edges of these sections must be reinforced with strong steel to keep the bulls from getting out. Which of the following represents how much steel in yards the rodeo will need to reinforce the 4 bull sections?

   A) $32\pi$

   B) $64\pi$

   C) $32 + \dfrac{16\pi}{3}$

   D) $64 + \dfrac{16\pi}{3}$

28. Lena bought a saltwater fish tank that holds 400 gallons of water. She started filling the tank on Friday, but then stopped after putting only 70 gallons of water in the tank. On Saturday, she bought a bigger hose and began filling the tank again. It took her 1 hour and 50 minutes on Saturday to completely fill the tank. Which equation represents the number of gallons of water in the fish tank on Saturday, given the amount of time in minutes that Lena spent filling the tank?

   A) $y = 3x + 70$

   B) $y = 3x + 330$

   C) $y = 70x + 330$

   D) $y = 110x + 70$

29. A self-storage company has three sizes of storage units. The ratio of small to medium units is 3:5. The ratio of medium to large units is 3:2. The company analyzes its business model and current consumer demand and determines that it can benefit from utilizing larger economies of scale. In other words, it decides to grow its business based on current economic conditions and plans to build a second, larger self-storage building. The company's research indicates that the new market would benefit from having only two sizes of storage units, small and large, in the same ratio as its current facility. What ratio of small to large units should it use?

   A) 1:1

   B) 3:2

   C) 5:3

   D) 9:10

GO ON TO THE NEXT PAGE ⟹

$$\frac{1}{x} + \frac{3}{x} = \frac{1}{7}$$

30. The equation shown above represents the following scenario: A chemical laboratory uses two air purifiers to clean the air of contaminants emitted while working with hazardous materials. One is an older model, and the other is a new model that is considerably more energy efficient. The new model can clean the air of contaminants three times as quickly as the older model. Working together, the two air purifiers can clean the air in the lab in 7 hours. Which of the following describes what the term $\frac{1}{x}$ in the equation represents?

A) The portion of the air the older model can clean in 1 hour

B) The portion of the air the new model can clean in 1 hour

C) The time it takes the older model to clean the air by itself

D) The time it takes the older model to clean $\frac{1}{7}$ of the air by itself

GO ON TO THE NEXT PAGE

**Directions:** For questions 31-38, enter your responses into the appropriate grid on your answer sheet, in accordance with the following:

1. You will receive credit only if the circles are filled in correctly, but you may write your answers in the boxes above each grid to help you fill in the circles accurately.

2. Don't mark more than one circle per column.

3. None of the questions with grid-in responses will have a negative solution.

4. Only grid in a single answer, even if there is more than one correct answer to a given question.

5. A **mixed number** must be gridded as a decimal or an improper fraction. For example, you would grid $7\frac{1}{2}$ as 7.5 or 15/2.

   (Were you to grid it as | 7 | 1 | / | 2 |, this response would be interpreted as $\frac{71}{2}$.)

6. A **decimal** that has more digits than there are places on the grid may be either rounded or truncated, but every column in the grid must be filled in order to receive credit.

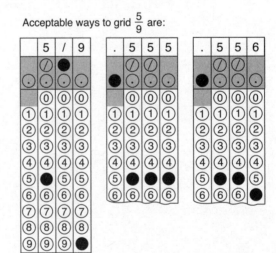

GO ON TO THE NEXT PAGE

$$\frac{1}{3}(90x - 12) = \frac{1}{2}(8x + 10)$$

31. What is the solution to the equation shown above?

32. If $n^{\frac{5}{2}} = 32$, what is the value of $n$ ?

33. When a thrift store gets used furniture in good condition to sell, it researches the original price and then marks the used piece down by 40 percent of that price. On the first day of each of the following months, the price is marked down an additional 15 percent until it is sold or it reaches 30 percent of its original price. Suppose the store gets a piece of used furniture on January 15th. If the piece of furniture costs $1,848 new and it is sold on March 10th of the same year, what is the final selling price, not including tax? Round your answer to the nearest whole dollar.

Note: Figure not drawn to scale.

34. Many sailboat manufacturers sell kits that include instructions and all the materials needed to build a simple sailboat. The figure shows the finished dimensions of a sailboat from such a kit. The instructions indicate that cos $x° = b$, but do not give the value of $b$. What is the value of $b$ ?

35. In the figure shown above, line $B$ (not shown) is parallel to $\overline{CD}$ and passes through the point $(0, -1)$. If line $B$ also passes through the point $(2, y)$, what is the value of $y$ ?

36. Recycling of certain metals has been a common practice dating back to preindustrial times. For example, there is evidence of scrap bronze and silver being collected and melted down for reuse in a number of European countries. Today, there are recycling companies and even curbside collection bins for recycling. As a general rule, recycling companies pay for metals by weight. Suppose a person brings in 3 pounds of copper and receives $8.64, and 24 ounces of nickel and receives $10.08. If another person brings in equal weights of copper and nickel, what fractional portion of the money would he receive from the copper? (Note: There are 16 ounces in 1 pound.)

**Questions 37 and 38 refer to the following information.**

Body mass index, or BMI, is one of several measures used by doctors to determine a person's health as indicated by weight and height. Low-density lipoprotein, or LDL cholesterol, known as the "bad" cholesterol, is another health indicator and consists of fat proteins that clog arteries. Following are the results of a study showing the relationship between BMI and LDL for 12 individuals and the line of best fit for the data.

**Body Mass Index (BMI)**

37. How many of the 12 people have an actual LDL that differs by 10 or more milligrams per deciliter from the LDL predicted by the line of best fit?

38. According to the line of best fit, what is the closest whole number BMI approximation for a person that has an estimated LDL level of 140 milligrams per deciliter?

**IF YOU FINISH BEFORE TIME IS CALLED, YOU MAY CHECK YOUR WORK ON THIS SECTION ONLY.
DO NOT TURN TO ANY OTHER SECTION IN THE TEST.**    STOP

916  K

# Essay Test

### 50 Minutes

You will be given a passage to read and asked to write an essay analyzing it. As you write, be sure to show that you have read the passage closely. You will be graded on how well you have understood the passage, how clear your analysis is, and how well you express your ideas.

Your essay must be written on the lines in your answer booklet. Anything you write outside the lined space in your answer booklet will not be read by the essay graders. Be sure to write or print in such a way that it will be legible to readers not familiar with your handwriting. Additionally, be sure to address the passage directly. An off-topic essay will not be graded.

---

As you read the passage, think about the author's use of

- evidence, such as statistics or other facts.

- logic to connect evidence to conclusions and to develop lines of reasoning.

- style, word choice, and appeals to emotion to make the argument more persuasive.

---

**This passage deals with the issue of compensation for college athletes.**

1   In the world of college sports, there is growing debate about whether student athletes should be awarded monetary compensation for their contribution to teams that garner millions of dollars for universities. Presently, the National Collegiate Athletics Association (NCAA), the governing body of college sports, doesn't allow it. Some hold this law as sacrosanct, saying it keeps college sports from becoming commercial and corrupting the experience of student athletes, who are in school, after all, for an education. But the reality is that we are past that point: college sports are big business, and the system that caps student salaries at zero is tantamount to wage fixing and collusion. If such practices happened in the investment market, universities would be fined by the FTC.

2   In a labor market, they'd be shut down. Student athletes are being defrauded and taken advantage of.

3   So how much money is at stake? Basketball and football are the two main sports in question. Every year, the month of March becomes synonymous with a weeks-long basketball bracket that winnows down 64 teams to the single best. In football, a season of stadium-filling regular season games culminates in half a dozen lucrative "bowl games" sponsored by some of the biggest corporations in the world: FedEx, AT&T, and Mobil Oil.

4   For television networks, advertisers, universities, and local businesses where the events are held, these games are every bit as big as the NFL's Super Bowl and the NBA playoffs. In 2011, ESPN and Fox signed television rights deals worth $3 billion to the Pacific-12 conference. *Forbes* magazine reported that CBS and Turner Broadcasting make more than one billion dollars off the March Madness broadcasts, "thanks in part to a $700,000 advertising rate for a 30-second spot during the Final Four." One study put the value of a Texas A&M home game at $86 million for businesses in Brazos County, where A&M is located.

5   The dollar figures are indeed vast, and universities get their share. Here are two examples from schools with top football teams. According to the most recent federal data, the University of Texas football team netted a profit of $77.9 million in 2011–2012. Michigan made $61.6 million from football and $85.2 million in revenue.

6  Coaches, too, are a big part of the equation. Average salaries for major college football coaches have jumped more than 70 percent since 2006, to $1.64 million, according to *USA Today*. Nick Saban, head coach for Alabama, makes $7.3 million a year.

7  And yet, players take home no money. None. How can this be? Because, like unscrupulous tycoons from a Dickens novel, college presidents, athletic directors, and conference commissioners set their players' wages as low as they can get them—zero.

8  According to a recent study, if college football operated under the same revenue-sharing model as the NFL, each player on the Texas A&M squad would see a paycheck of about $225,000 per year.

9  All this talk of money might have you thinking that we should go back to square one and take the money out of college sports. But money is in college sports' DNA. It was conceived that way. It all grew out of the Morrill Land-Grant College Act of 1862. "As large public institutions spread into sparsely populated states, the competition for students grew fierce," says Allen Sack, a business professor at the University of New Haven. Football happened to be invented around that time, and schools took it up as a tool to draw students, and spectators, to campuses. The 1894 Harvard-Yale football game, for example, generated $119,000, according to the *New York Times*. That's nearly $3 million in today's dollars.

10  The historic justification for not paying players is that they are amateur student-athletes, and the value of their scholarships is payment enough. But the NCAA's own study shows that its scholarship limit leaves so-called "full" scholarship athletes with $3,000 to $5,000 in out-of-pocket expenses each year. The average shortfall is $3,200. Furthermore, most scholarships are revokable, so if an athlete doesn't perform well on the field, or is injured, he can, in a sense, lose that compensation. A student athlete devotes 40 hours a week on average toward sport; that's equivalent to a full-time job. Zero pay and immediate termination with no recourse? Those are labor conditions that any sensible workforce would unionize to change. But students are powerless to change. They are up against the NCAA, the Big 10 commission, university boards, and the almighty corporate dollar. Someone needs to become their advocate and get student athletes the compensation they deserve.

> Write an essay that analyzes the author's approach in persuading her readers that possessions are oppressive. Focus on specific features, such as the ones listed in the box above the passage, and explain how these features strengthen the author's argument. Your essay should discuss the most important rhetorical features of the passage.
>
> Your essay should not focus on your own opinion of the author's conclusion, but rather on how the author persuades his readers.

IF YOU FINISH BEFORE TIME IS CALLED, YOU MAY CHECK YOUR WORK ON THIS SECTION ONLY.
DO NOT TURN TO ANY OTHER SECTION IN THE TEST.    **STOP**

918    K

# Answer Key

## Reading Test

| | | | |
|---|---|---|---|
| 1. A | 14. B | 27. C | 40. D |
| 2. D | 15. A | 28. A | 41. B |
| 3. D | 16. C | 29. D | 42. A |
| 4. B | 17. D | 30. B | 43. C |
| 5. C | 18. C | 31. A | 44. B |
| 6. C | 19. B | 32. D | 45. C |
| 7. C | 20. B | 33. A | 46. A |
| 8. D | 21. B | 34. B | 47. C |
| 9. A | 22. D | 35. D | 48. D |
| 10. D | 23. D | 36. C | 49. A |
| 11. C | 24. C | 37. C | 50. D |
| 12. D | 25. C | 38. D | 51. A |
| 13. A | 26. A | 39. A | 52. B |

## Writing and Language Test

| | | | |
|---|---|---|---|
| 1. B | 12. B | 23. C | 34. B |
| 2. D | 13. D | 24. B | 35. C |
| 3. B | 14. B | 25. B | 36. A |
| 4. C | 15. C | 26. A | 37. D |
| 5. D | 16. A | 27. A | 38. A |
| 6. D | 17. B | 28. A | 39. D |
| 7. B | 18. D | 29. B | 40. A |
| 8. A | 19. B | 30. A | 41. B |
| 9. D | 20. D | 31. C | 42. D |
| 10. C | 21. B | 32. D | 43. C |
| 11. B | 22. C | 33. A | 44. B |

## Math Test—No-Calculator

| | | | |
|---|---|---|---|
| 1. B | 6. B | 11. D | 16. 15 |
| 2. C | 7. A | 12. D | 17. 10.5 or 21/2 |
| 3. C | 8. D | 13. C | 18. 4 |
| 4. A | 9. A | 14. B | 19. 10 |
| 5. B | 10. D | 15. C | 20. 50.5 |

## Math Test—Calculator

| | | | |
|---|---|---|---|
| 1. D | 11. B | 21. A | 31. 9/26 or .346 |
| 2. B | 12. D | 22. A | 32. 4 |
| 3. C | 13. C | 23. D | 33. 801 |
| 4. D | 14. A | 24. B | 34. 2/3 or .666 or .667 |
| 5. C | 15. B | 25. A | 35. 3.5 or 7/2 |
| 6. A | 16. A | 26. B | 36. 3/10 |
| 7. A | 17. A | 27. D | 37. 3 |
| 8. D | 18. B | 28. A | 38. 24 |
| 9. C | 19. C | 29. D | |
| 10. A | 20. D | 30. A | |

# Answers and Explanations

## Reading Test

Suggested passage map notes:

¶1: W describes H

¶2: W stunned by H's deep knowledge of some subjects

¶3: W astonished by what H doesn't know

¶4: H: brain has only so much room, isn't interested in "useless facts"

**1.   A**

**Difficulty:** Easy

**Category:** Detail

**Getting to the Answer:** Eliminate answers that go against your understanding of the characters in the passage. The first paragraph explicitly states that Watson's curiosity about Holmes "gradually deepened and increased" (lines 2–3). Choice **(A)** is the correct answer.

**2.   D**

**Difficulty:** Medium

**Category:** Vocab-in-Context

**Getting to the Answer:** Predict a word that could be substituted for "casual" in context. Watson is explaining that Holmes's appearance is noticeable even to someone who hasn't seen him very often; therefore, occasional, **(D)** is correct.

**3.   D**

**Difficulty:** Easy

**Category:** Inference

**Getting to the Answer:** The central idea in this passage should reflect the overall picture the author paints of Sherlock Holmes. The passage develops Holmes as an unusual and eccentric character. Watson marvels at Holmes's failure to pursue a typical path for an intelligent person, for example, and describes in detail how Holmes's behavior and knowledge deviate from the ordinary. Choice **(D)** is the only answer choice that is directly supported by details in the passage.

**4.   B**

**Difficulty:** Medium

**Category:** Vocab-in-Context

**Getting to the Answer:** Use context clues to help you predict the meaning of the word as it is used in the sentence. In this sentence, the context clues provide a contrast to the target word. Watson says Holmes is usually "sharp" and "hawk-like" with great "alertness" except when he is in a period of "torpor" (lines 7–10). You can predict that the meaning of "torpor" will be something close to *the opposite of sharp and alert*. Choice **(B)** is the correct answer.

**5.   C**

**Difficulty:** Easy

**Category:** Inference

**Getting to the Answer:** Look for clues in the passage about how and why Holmes studies and learns. Watson notes that Holmes has not studied anything "which might fit him for a degree" (lines 21–22). This suggests that his learning is not motivated by something external, like a degree, but by his personal interests. Likewise, he has a "zeal" for particular subjects (line 24). Choice **(C)** reflects Holmes's motives for studying.

**6.   C**

**Difficulty:** Medium

**Category:** Command of Evidence

**Getting to the Answer:** Eliminate answer choices that don't explain why Holmes studies. A correct answer will allow you to make a logical guess as to Holmes's motives for studying. Choice **(C)** provides the best evidence by illustrating that Holmes pursues topics that he is passionate about rather than studying for external motivations.

Practice Tests

**7. C**

**Difficulty:** Medium

**Category:** Inference

**Getting to the Answer:** Closely read Holmes's own statements for clues about his views. Holmes clearly suggests that the brain can only hold a limited amount of information, so one should prioritize the things that are most important. Therefore, **(C)** is the correct answer.

**8. D**

**Difficulty:** Easy

**Category:** Command of Evidence

**Getting to the Answer:** Reread each quote in the context of the passage. Find the one that supports the previous answer by giving evidence of Holmes's own ideas about learning. Of all the answer choices, Holmes's own statement about the necessity of prioritizing useful facts most directly supports the previous answer. Choice **(D)** is the correct answer.

**9. A**

**Difficulty:** Medium

**Category:** Function

**Getting to the Answer:** Consider what this figurative use of "attic" helps reveal about the character of Holmes. The author has Holmes compare the human brain to an attic to help illustrate Holmes's beliefs about useful facts versus those not worth learning. Choice **(A)** is the correct answer.

**10. D**

**Difficulty:** Medium

**Category:** Inference

**Getting to the Answer:** Think about what insights the reader gains by having Watson narrate the story. The author is able to establish Holmes as an intriguing character by showing Watson's thoughts and reactions to Holmes. Presumably, readers will want to find out more about Holmes because the narrator depicts him as a fascinating person. Choice **(D)** fits this situation.

Suggested passage map notes:

¶1: should be no secrets in peace process
¶2: war fought for justice; 14 pts for world peace
¶3: no secrets
¶4: freedom on the seas
¶5: equal trade
¶6: fewer weapons and armies worldwide
¶7: fair colonial land claims
¶8: Russia develop own gov't, Germans leave Russia
¶9: Germans leave Belgium, Belgium independent
¶10: France regain all territory
¶11: reestablish Italian borders
¶12: Austria–Hungary indep.
¶13: Serbia, Montenegro, Romania evacuated and indep.
¶14: Turkish people have own country
¶15: indep. Polish state
¶16: form League of Nations to protect indep.

**11. C**

**Difficulty:** Easy

**Category:** Inference

**Getting to the Answer:** Examine the first two paragraphs. Try to paraphrase the reason Wilson gives for making the speech. In the first two paragraphs, Wilson anticipates the end of the war and alludes to the "processes of peace" (line 2). Although he refers to national sovereignty and conquest, he states that his purpose is to lay out a program for peace in the world, making **(C)** the correct answer.

**12. D**

**Difficulty:** Medium

**Category:** Command of Evidence

**Getting to the Answer:** Remember that the correct answer will provide information that directly relates to the answer to the previous question. The correct answer to the previous question concerns Wilson's plan to maintain peaceful relations in the world. Lines 26–27 read, "The programme of the world's peace, therefore, is our programme," making **(D)** the correct answer.

**13. A**

**Difficulty:** Medium

**Category:** Vocab-in-Context

**Getting to the Answer:** Predict a word that could substitute for "frankly" in context. In the list of points he presents, Wilson is defining actions and policies that will promote peace and open communication among nations. In this context, "frankly" suggests honesty, which makes **(A)** the correct answer.

**14. B**

**Difficulty:** Medium

**Category:** Inference

**Getting to the Answer:** Eliminate answer choices that cannot be inferred by the information provided in the passage. Calling for an end to "private international understandings" is one of Wilson's 14 points (lines 29–30). Therefore, it can be inferred that in the past, certain nations did indeed form "secret covenants" (line 6), or pacts, with one another. Choice **(B)** is correct.

**15. A**

**Difficulty:** Medium

**Category:** Command of Evidence

**Getting to the Answer:** The correct answer will reference a detail that provides evidence for the answer to the previous question. In the first paragraph of his speech, Wilson refers to "secret understandings" (line 4) that cannot exist anymore if there is to be peace among nations. Therefore, **(A)** is correct.

**16. C**

**Difficulty:** Medium

**Category:** Vocab-in-Context

**Getting to the Answer:** Pretend the word is a blank in the sentence. Next, predict what word could be substituted for the blank. The sentence states that "national armaments will be reduced to the lowest point consistent with domestic safety" (lines 43–44). In this sense, Wilson aims to assure nations that they will still be able to protect themselves. Predict that armaments will be reduced to an extent agreeable with maintaining their own safety. **(C)** is the correct choice.

**17. D**

**Difficulty:** Hard

**Category:** Inference

**Getting to the Answer:** Though the question is asking you about a specific line, it makes sense to choose an answer that is compatible with the broader context of the passage. In the excerpted line, Wilson identifies the "adjustment of all colonial claims" (line 46) as an item in his program for world peace. If his goal is to safeguard world peace, this must mean he believes conflicts resulting from colonization, itself an imperial pursuit, must be addressed. Choice **(D)** is correct.

**18. C**

**Difficulty:** Hard

**Category:** Inference

**Getting to the Answer:** Locate the three points to which the question refers. Do not confuse them with other numbered points in the speech. Points VI through VIII refer to territorial sovereignty, evacuation of occupied lands, and restoration of lands. These points align with the claim that nations have violated one another's territorial sovereignty through invasion and occupation. This makes **(C)** the correct answer.

**19. B**

**Difficulty:** Hard

**Category:** Inference

**Getting to the Answer:** Be sure that the answer you choose reflects the ideology and positions expressed by Wilson in his speech. In the passage, Wilson expresses that he is in favor of international cooperation to promote and sustain global peace. Choice **(B)** is the correct answer because it describes an approach to international relations that is analogous to Wilson's.

**20. B**

**Difficulty:** Medium

**Category:** Global

**Getting to the Answer:** When asked a question involving the structure of a passage, consider the text as a whole. Often, the structure is visually noticeable. Wilson begins by stating his argument that countries must work together toward peace. He then follows up with specific examples (the 14 points) of how his ideas should be carried out. Choice **(B)** is the correct answer.

Suggested passage map notes:

Passage 1

> ¶1: history of meditation; secular meditation
>
> ¶2: describe mindfulness meditation
>
> ¶3: mindfulness → more fulfillment
>
> ¶4: health benefits
>
> ¶5: Dr. S — meditation good, drs should use it

Passage 2

> ¶1: Ryan uses mindfulness and sees many benefits
>
> ¶2: holds weekly bipartisan meditation sessions
>
> ¶3: wrote book on mindfulness; improved attention
>
> ¶4: members of Congress getting interested
>
> ¶5: R supports legislation encouraging meditation
>
> ¶6: Ryan — not religious but secular

**21. B**

**Difficulty:** Medium

**Category:** Global

**Getting to the Answer:** Focus on the big picture rather than supporting details. Choice **(B)** correctly identifies the central idea in the passage. Choice (A) is a detail found in paragraph 1; (C) is not actually stated in the passage; and (D) distorts information mentioned in paragraphs 3 and 4.

**22. D**

**Difficulty:** Hard

**Category:** Inference

**Getting to the Answer:** Keep the central idea of the passage in mind as you look for information in the passage about each of the choices. Determine which one can be inferred as true. The last two paragraphs of Passage 1 discuss "health benefits" of meditation (line 30), studies showing positive results of meditation, and a quote from a professional about meditation's advantages. This matches choice **(D)**.

**23. D**

**Difficulty:** Medium

**Category:** Command of Evidence

**Getting to the Answer:** Avoid choices that do not provide direct evidence to support your answer to the previous question. Choice **(D)** supports the inference that some medical professionals accept meditation as beneficial.

**24. C**

**Difficulty:** Easy

**Category:** Vocab-in-Context

**Getting to the Answer:** Predict a word that could substitute for "compelling" in context. The context of the sentence suggests that meditation has great or convincing benefits, which is another way of saying "persuasive." Therefore, **(C)** is correct.

**25. C**

**Difficulty:** Easy

**Category:** Inference

**Getting to the Answer:** Remember that you're analyzing the author's point of view on meditation, not Tim Ryan's view. Since the author makes statements such as calling Ryan a "voice for calm consideration" (line 55), the author must hold a positive view of meditation. However, there is little evidence that the author is devoted to meditation. Choice **(C)** correctly reflects the author's point of view.

**26. A**

**Difficulty:** Easy

**Category:** Inference

**Getting to the Answer:** Determine what can be inferred about Ryan's personality from what is stated in the passage. The passage contains numerous examples of Ryan putting his belief in the value of mindfulness into action. For instance, he hosts meditation sessions for his staff and supports legislation promoting meditation. Choice **(A)** is the correct answer.

**27. C**

**Difficulty:** Medium

**Category:** Command of Evidence

**Getting to the Answer:** Be careful of choices that do not provide direct evidence to support the inference about Ryan from the previous question. Choice **(C)** is correct. Mr. Ryan shows that he acts on what he believes by supporting legislation that encourages meditation, such as the bill supporting the increase in holistic medicine offered by the Department of Veterans Affairs.

**28. A**

**Difficulty:** Easy

**Category:** Vocab-in-Context

**Getting to the Answer:** Predict a word that is a synonym for "secular" in context. In the context of the sentence, "but rather" indicates that "secular" means the opposite of "religious," which would be "nonreligious," so **(A)** is the correct answer.

**29. D**

**Difficulty:** Easy

**Category:** Inference

**Getting to the Answer:** Reread the sentence to determine what connotative meaning the author suggests through the use of "chatter." Since "chatter" in this sentence is contrasted with the "mind and body" syncing together, the word has a negative connotation that suggests background noise or frequent talk. Only **(D)** fits with this meaning.

**30. B**

**Difficulty:** Medium

**Category:** Inference

**Getting to the Answer:** Look for an answer that fits with the purposes of both passages. Avoid choices that are suggested by only one of the passages. Both passages discuss changing attitudes regarding the efficacy of mindfulness meditation: Passage 1 states it is becoming "more popular" (lines 16–17) and "widely accepted by health professionals" (line 45), while Passage 2 describes the impact of a politician who is promoting meditation. Only **(B)** reflects this.

**31. A**

**Difficulty:** Medium

**Category:** Inference

**Getting to the Answer:** Examine the graphic and the two passages to figure out which answer choice is supported by all three. The passages both discussed benefits of meditation. The graphic shows that workers were more productive and had fewer injuries after being in a meditation program. Choice **(A)** is the only one that relates to the information in the graphic.

Suggested passage map notes:

¶1: CCD—all bees disappear; bees perform invaluable services

¶2: pathogens aren't the cause

¶3: altruism explains disappearance but doesn't explain cause

¶4: may be used by fluctuation in Earth's magnetic field

¶5: may be cause by pesticides

¶6: may be caused by pesticide combos

¶7: need more research; encourage more beekeeping, relax city rules

**32. D**

**Difficulty:** Hard

**Category:** Global

**Getting to the Answer:** Think of what the author wants the reader to learn about bees. This will help you figure out the passage's purpose. Choice **(D)** is the primary purpose of the passage. The author most wants the reader to know about colony collapse disorder.

**33. A**

**Difficulty:** Hard

**Category:** Inference

**Getting to the Answer:** Think back to the author's purpose that you explored in question 32. Consider what this purpose suggests about the author's point of view. The author seems knowledgeable about honeybees and very concerned about their loss. The author points out the many losses humans would have if honey bees were to disappear. Therefore, **(A)** is the correct answer.

**34. B**

**Difficulty:** Hard

**Category:** Function

**Getting to the Answer:** Notice that the word "mysteriously" appears toward the beginning of the passage, when the author is first introducing the topic. As the author introduces the topic of colony collapse disorder in the first paragraph, the word "mysterious" helps emphasize how puzzling the disorder truly is. Choice **(B)** is the correct answer.

## 35. D

**Difficulty:** Medium

**Category:** Vocab-in-Context

**Getting to the Answer:** Predict a word that is a synonym for "plights" in context. In the sentence, "common plights" refers to pests such as mites, fungus, and bacteria, which farmers commonly see in beehives. Predict a negative word. In this context, **(D)**, "troubles," is the correct answer.

## 36. C

**Difficulty:** Hard

**Category:** Function

**Getting to the Answer:** Examine the part of the passage that discusses the lack of bees after a collapse. The author wants to stress the fact that research has shown that pathogens are not the reason for colony collapse. Choice **(C)** is the correct answer.

## 37. C

**Difficulty:** Medium

**Category:** Command of Evidence

**Getting to the Answer:** Be careful of choices that do not directly support your answer to the previous question. In the context of its paragraph, lines 31–33 provide evidence to support the inference that the cause of colony collapse is not pathogens, since "common killers" such as pathogens would leave "telltale signs." Choice **(C)** is the correct answer.

## 38. D

**Difficulty:** Easy

**Category:** Vocab-in-Context

**Getting to the Answer:** Predict a word that could substitute for "foraging" in context. Predict an action that bees might perform during their "pollination flights," such as searching for flowers. The context of the sentence rules out all but **(D)**, the correct answer.

## 39. A

**Difficulty:** Hard

**Category:** Inference

**Getting to the Answer:** Review your passage map and use the passage's central idea as a general prediction. Choice **(A)** is correct. Though the author laments the disappearance of honeybees and says how challenging it is to solve the problem, the last paragraph ends the passage on a cautiously optimistic note, particularly with the use of the word "hopefully" (line 82).

## 40. D

**Difficulty:** Medium

**Category:** Command of Evidence

**Getting to the Answer:** Be careful of choices that might support an incorrect answer in the previous question. Choice **(D)** is evidence that the author is cautiously optimistic about the future of the honeybee.

## 41. B

**Difficulty:** Medium

**Category:** Detail

**Getting to the Answer:** Watch out for answer choices that might sound plausible but are not explicitly stated in the passage. Choice **(B)** is correct; the last paragraph states that some towns and cities are relaxing their regulations about beekeeping "in response to the honeybee population crisis" (line 81).

## 42. A

**Difficulty:** Medium

**Category:** Inference

**Getting to the Answer:** Look for information in the passage that tells what honeybees and human beings do for each other. Paragraph 1 states that if honeybees disappear, people will not have certain foods; even the beef industry will be affected. Therefore, humans depend on the honey bees to keep the environment and economy healthy. Choice **(A)** is correct.

Suggested passage map notes:

> ¶1: concern that spacecraft could be hit by micro-meteorites
>
> ¶2: human-made debris in space; more likely than meteorites to hit spacecraft
>
> ¶3: small pieces are dangerous
>
> ¶4: larger pieces dangerous, but can be avoided
>
> ¶5: satellites can adjust course to avoid collision
>
> ¶6: some debris falls to Earth; sci. can't stop it
>
> ¶7: in future, maybe spacecraft leave orbit when not used anymore

## 43. C

**Difficulty:** Medium

**Category:** Global

**Getting to the Answer:** Think about the idea that is developed throughout the passage. Avoid answers that refer only to supporting details. Choice **(C)** is the correct answer because all the information in the passage relates to the dangers posed by space debris created by humans.

## 44. B

**Difficulty:** Medium

**Category:** Command of Evidence

**Getting to the Answer:** Look at each quote from the passage and decide which most clearly supports the central idea. In paragraph 3, the author describes how space debris created by humans is dangerous to spacecraft and the people inside of them. Choice **(B)** is the correct answer.

## 45. C

**Difficulty:** Medium

**Category:** Function

**Getting to the Answer:** Consider the central idea that you identified in question 43. Identify the central idea of paragraph 2. The passage is mostly about the dangers associated with human-made space debris. Paragraph 2 contains details about the types of human-made space debris orbiting Earth, thus providing support for the central idea. Choice **(C)** is the correct answer.

## 46. A

**Difficulty:** Medium

**Category:** Detail

**Getting to the Answer:** Reread the information about meteoroids at the beginning of the passage. Think about how this compares with the descriptions of space debris in the following paragraphs. The author states that although there were concerns about meteoroids in the early days of space travel, scientists concluded that the risk was small because meteoroids were rare. The author goes on to explain that space debris created by humans is a greater concern because it is so plentiful. Choice **(A)** is the correct answer.

## 47. C

**Difficulty:** Hard

**Category:** Inference

**Getting to the Answer:** The author's central claim in the passage is that space debris left by humans is dangerous. Think about which of the answer choices most directly supports that claim. In paragraph 6, the author describes how Skylab fell to Earth. This example strengthens the claim, illustrating that the debris left in space can be dangerous even on Earth. Therefore, **(C)** is the correct answer.

## 48. D

**Difficulty:** Medium

**Category:** Vocab-in-Context

**Getting to the Answer:** Eliminate answers that are synonyms for "obsolete" but do not make sense in context. Since it was debris that fell out of space, Skylab was no longer in use. In this context, "obsolete" means "outdated," so **(D)** is the correct answer.

**49. A**

**Difficulty:** Hard

**Category:** Inference

**Getting to the Answer:** Eliminate answer choices that cannot be supported with information found in the passage. In paragraph 6, the author describes how space debris can be dangerous on Earth if a large enough piece gets through the atmosphere without burning up. It is logical, then, that **(A)** is the correct answer; warnings could help people avoid areas where impacts are predicted, thereby decreasing the chance of injury. The author explicitly states that agencies monitor debris to make predictions and issue warnings (lines 58–62).

**50. D**

**Difficulty:** Medium

**Category:** Command of Evidence

**Getting to the Answer:** Avoid answer choices that provide evidence for incorrect answers to the previous question. Choice **(D)** is the correct answer, because in lines 60–62, the author states that there is nothing to be done about space debris falling to Earth except to issue warnings.

**51. A**

**Difficulty:** Medium

**Category:** Vocab-in-Context

**Getting to the Answer:** Predict a word that is a synonym for "implemented" in context. Since the debris will remain in space unless a method of removal is "implemented," predict the word that means employed. In this context, **(A)** is the correct answer.

**52. B**

**Difficulty:** Hard

**Category:** Inference

**Getting to the Answer:** Make sure you understand the units and labels in the graphic before choosing an answer. The graphic shows that the highest density of space debris occurs at an altitude just under 800 kilometers, posing the greatest risk of the dangers discussed in the passage. It is reasonable to conclude, therefore, that if NASA were to place a new satellite into orbit, the agency should choose to avoid the altitude range of 700–900 kilometers. Choice **(B)** is the correct answer.

# Writing and Language Test

**1. B**

**Difficulty:** Medium

**Category:** Sentence Structure: The Basics

**Getting to the Answer:** Determine the noun to which the modifier in this sentence is referring. Then, check the noun's placement to make sure it is as close as possible to the modifier. The modifier is "like most chemists." Therefore, the noun it modifies should be a person. Choice **(B)** correctly rearranges the sentence so that "chemists" clearly refers to "Constantin Fahlberg."

**2. D**

**Difficulty:** Medium

**Category:** Development: Introductions and Conclusions

**Getting to the Answer:** This is the topic sentence of the paragraph. Make sure that it focuses on the correct subject. The purpose of this sentence is to discuss Fahlberg and the circumstances in which he was working. Choice **(D)** correctly focuses the sentence on Fahlberg and flows well into the next sentence, which discusses the specifics of coal tar.

**3. B**

**Difficulty:** Easy

**Category:** Agreement: Pronouns

**Getting to the Answer:** The pronoun should agree with the noun to which it refers. Identify this noun to determine the correct pronoun. The antecedent of the pronoun here is "coal tar," a singular, impersonal noun. Choice **(B)**, "from it," is therefore the correct answer.

**4. C**

**Difficulty:** Easy

**Category:** Development: Precision

**Getting to the Answer:** Predict what meaning the correct word should convey before choosing an answer. The sentence suggests that while working, Fahlberg was so "___" that he forgot to eat lunch. A word that means *focused on* or *preoccupied with* would be most appropriate. Choice **(C)**, "engrossed," conveys this meaning successfully.

**5. D**

**Difficulty:** Hard

**Category:** Organization: Transitions

**Getting to the Answer:** The passage is telling a story. Choose the answer that most effectively makes the transition between the paragraphs while maintaining a consistent tone with the rest of the story. The correct answer will relate to the sentences both before and after it. While answer (B) may intrigue readers, its tone is out of place when compared with that of the rest of the passage. Choice **(D)** is the correct answer. It provides a transition from the previous sentence and tells the next logical step in the story.

**6. D**

**Difficulty:** Hard

**Category:** Organization: Transitions

**Getting to the Answer:** The correct answer will clearly present the central idea of the paragraph. Identify the answer choice that presents the most important point about the scene being described. To be effective as a central idea, the sentence needs to sum up the supporting details in the paragraph and convey their meaning. Only **(D)** both explains what happened and describes why it was significant, which is the central idea of the paragraph.

**7. B**

**Difficulty:** Hard

**Category:** Agreement: Verbs

**Getting to the Answer:** Examine the context of the sentence. Notice that it's describing a potentially disastrous outcome if conditions had been different. Fortunately, he had not worked with anything poisonous or corrosive or the story would have had a different ending. If Fahlberg had been working with poisonous or corrosive materials, there is no doubt that "the story" would have had a different—and terrible—ending. The word "might" is too conditional for this situation; therefore, **(B)**, which includes the word "would," is the correct answer.

**8. A**

**Difficulty:** Hard

**Category:** Development: Introductions and Conclusions

**Getting to the Answer:** Determine which option clearly states the most important information in this paragraph. The most important fact in this paragraph is that Fahlberg discovered a new substance accidentally. The rest of this paragraph provides details about this discovery. Therefore, the correct answer choice will state that Fahlberg made a discovery. Choice **(A)** makes this idea clear.

**9. D**

**Difficulty:** Easy

**Category:** Development: Precision

**Getting to the Answer:** Look for clues in the rest of the sentence to determine which verb fits with the exact meaning of the sentence. The sentence states that Fahlberg is making the saccharin "commercially," or as part of a business. Choice **(D)**, "producing," is correct, as it emphasizes the business nature of his work.

**10. C**

**Difficulty:** Medium

**Category:** Organization: Sentence Placement

**Getting to the Answer:** Try each answer choice. What information seems confusing when not presented in the correct order? Logically, Fahlberg should find the mixture of chemicals and work to isolate it before he names it and understands its significance. Therefore, **(C)** is the most logical place for sentence 4 and is the correct answer.

**11. B**

**Difficulty:** Hard

**Category:** Organization: Introductions and Conclusions

**Getting to the Answer:** Specifically state in your own words what the passage is about. Then, read the answer choices to see what fits best. The passage focuses on the specific moment of Fahlberg's discovery, including the significance of the discovery itself and its applications. Only **(B)** convincingly ties the sentence to the main ideas of the passage.

**12. B**

**Difficulty:** Easy

**Category:** Agreement: Pronouns

**Getting to the Answer:** A modifier should match its antecedent in number and gender. Also, be wary of words that sound alike but have different meanings and uses. As it stands, the sentence incorrectly uses the adverb "there." Since it refers to "great philosophers," the correct word is the possessive pronoun "their," which is often confused with "there." Choice **(B)** is the correct answer.

**13. D**

**Difficulty:** Hard

**Category:** Development: Precision

**Getting to the Answer:** Read carefully to identify the context of the underlined word. Then, choose the word that best fits the context of the sentence. The underlined word modifies "premodern sources of truth and knowledge," which in turn refers to "political and religious tradition and authority." The context of the sentence indicates that these were powerful ideas that were being challenged by newer ideas. Choice **(D)**, "reigning," conveys the idea that "political and religious tradition and authority" had monarch-like, or ruling, levels of power in people's lives.

**14. B**

**Difficulty:** Easy

**Category:** Organization: Transitions

**Getting to the Answer:** Determine the relationship between the two parts of the underlined sentence, and then think about which answer choice best conveys this relationship. The sentence states that "foundations of truth seemed to be crumbling" and "Descartes's writings proposed an alternative foundation." The two ideas are connected to each other: Descartes's writings were a response to this "crumbling." Choice **(B)** is the answer that identifies this relationship.

**15. C**

**Difficulty:** Hard

**Category:** Agreement: Modifiers

**Getting to the Answer:** Determine whether the modifying phrase in this sentence references the correct noun. If the modifier in this sentence is describing a person, then the noun that is described by the modifier should also be a person. Choice **(C)** correctly matches the modifier (beginning with "an expert") to the noun "Descartes," rather than the noun "work."

**16. A**

**Difficulty:** Hard

**Category:** Development: Relevance

**Getting to the Answer:** Determine the central claim in the paragraph and then come back to the question. The central claim of the paragraph is that Descartes's work established the foundation for many modern ideas. The statement found in (A) provides information that best supports this claim and logically transitions to the following sentence. Choice **(A)** is correct.

**17. B**

**Difficulty:** Medium

**Category:** Development: Introductions and Conclusions

**Getting to the Answer:** In your own words, identify what idea ties together the ideas presented in the rest of the paragraph. Sentence 1 states that "modern culture would come to cherish this." The question is, what is "this"? The rest of the paragraph goes into detail about Descartes's philosophical methods. Choice **(B)** identifies Descartes's general philosophical focus and is, therefore, the correct answer.

**18. D**

**Difficulty:** Medium

**Category:** Sentence Structure: The Basics

**Getting to the Answer:** Identify whether the sentence consists of two independent clauses or an independent and a dependent clause. This will provide guidance for punctuating it. The sentence consists of two independent clauses ("Descartes arrived . . ." and "he could only be . . ."). Separating the independent clauses into two sentences is the best way to punctuate them. Choice **(D)** is the correct answer.

**19. B**

**Difficulty:** Hard

**Category:** Development: Relevance

**Getting to the Answer:** Look for the answer choice that most clearly helps to develop the ideas in the surrounding sentences. The inserted sentence comes after a discussion of Descartes's only certainty—that he was thinking. The sentence that follows it explains that from this, he could build additional knowledge. The correct answer will develop the idea of certainty and how it can be used to acquire more knowledge. Choice **(B)** best conveys this information and therefore is the correct choice.

**20. D**

**Difficulty:** Medium

**Category:** Agreement: Verbs

**Getting to the Answer:** A grammatically correct sentence will include a verb whose form makes the sentence an independent clause. "Propelled by" needs the addition of an auxiliary verb for this sentence to stand alone. Inserting "were" before this phrase makes the sentence grammatically complete. Choice **(D)** is the correct answer.

**21. B**

**Difficulty:** Medium

**Category:** Agreement: Verbs

**Getting to the Answer:** Determine whether there is a way to make the sentence less wordy without changing its intended meaning. The sentence, especially in the context of the paragraph, seems to be saying that it's difficult to determine exactly what Descartes did versus what other people at the time did. Both answer choices (C) and (D) change the meaning of the sentence slightly to say either that Descartes himself could not be separated from his contemporaries or that what they did was identical. Choice **(B)** is correct because it eliminates the wordiness of the sentence while maintaining its meaning.

**22. C**

**Difficulty:** Medium

**Category:** Development: Precision

**Getting to the Answer:** Determine what role this verb has in the sentence. What is the precise nature of the action it is describing? The sentence is about how Descartes's work brought about shifts in thinking that critically influenced other developments. However, the word "begun," (A), does not precisely convey the power with which this occurred. Choice **(C)**, "initiated," conveys this meaning and is the correct answer.

**23. C**

**Difficulty:** Medium

**Category:** Development: Precision

**Getting to the Answer:** Reread the surrounding sentences to look for context clues. Then, review the answer choices, paying attention to the meaning and nuance of each word. The passage states that art is constantly evolving and changing. The correct answer will represent the opposite of this meaning. The word "static" means that something does not change, so **(C)** is the correct answer.

**24. B**

**Difficulty:** Medium

**Category:** Sentence Structure: Commas, Dashes, and Colons

**Getting to the Answer:** Read the sentence and determine whether the parts of the sentence on either side of the semicolon are independent clauses. If they are not, identify their function and choose the appropriate punctuation. "For better or worse" is not an independent clause; rather, it is a parenthetical element that adds an opinion to the main thrust of the sentence. Choice **(B)** is correct. It uses a dash to set off this additional information in the sentence.

**25. B**

**Difficulty:** Medium

**Category:** Development: Introductions and Conclusions

**Getting to the Answer:** To determine the main topic of a paragraph, identify important details and then summarize them in a sentence or two. Find a choice that matches your prediction. Avoid choices like (A) and (C), which include details about poetry that are not in the paragraph. The details in this paragraph are about how the writers of the past viewed the novel as a vital way to record and comment on the human experience. Choice **(B)** captures this main topic.

**26. A**

**Difficulty:** Medium

**Category:** Development: Precision

**Getting to the Answer:** Read the surrounding sentences to get a sense of what the underlined word is meant to convey. Then, review the answer choices to find the one that is closest to this meaning. The passage suggests that the novel was held in high regard. The correct answer needs to indicate high regard with a positive connotation. The word "loftily," **(A)**, connotes both high regard and a positive view of the novel as a literary form.

**27. A**

**Difficulty:** Medium

**Category:** Development: Relevance

**Getting to the Answer:** Look for the answer choice that improves the sentence by adding important, relevant information. The paragraph is about the opinions of acclaimed novelists. Choice **(A)** adds the information that Joseph Conrad was also a novelist.

**28. A**

**Difficulty:** Medium

**Category:** Sentence Structure: Commas, Dashes, and Colons

**Getting to the Answer:** Identify the role of the underlined phrase; then, use this information to determine the necessary punctuation. "However" is an introductory adverbial element that modifies the rest of the sentence. It should be followed by a comma. Choice **(A)** is correct.

**29. B**

**Difficulty:** Medium

**Category:** Agreement: Modifiers

**Getting to the Answer:** Check the placement of dependent clauses set off by commas. A dependent clause that modifies a noun in a sentence should be adjacent to or as close as possible to the noun it is modifying. The dependent clause "which are now available on digital devices" modifies "novels," not "entertainment medium." It should be as close as possible to "novels," making **(B)** the correct answer.

**30. A**

**Difficulty:** Medium

**Category:** Sentence Structure: The Basics

**Getting to the Answer:** A compound sentence should be combined with a semicolon or a comma with a conjunction. Choice **(A)** is correct. This keeps the semicolon, which appropriately separates two related independent clauses.

**31. C**

**Difficulty:** Hard

**Category:** Development: Relevance

**Getting to the Answer:** Evaluate the paragraph for the central idea. Next, review the answer choices to find the one that directly supports that idea. This paragraph discusses the change from novels that tackle serious social issues to books that are meant as light entertainment for mass consumption. Choice **(C)** is correct. It emphasizes that readers want novels to be "fun," providing a means of escape from their lives.

**32. D**

**Difficulty:** Medium

**Category:** Agreement: Pronouns

**Getting to the Answer:** A pronoun needs to match its antecedent. Locate the antecedent of the pronoun and then predict an answer. The correct answer will match the antecedent in gender and number. The antecedent is "novelist," so the answer must be singular. Choice **(D)** is correct, as it matches the antecedent in number and appropriately identifies both gender options, since the antecedent did not specify gender.

**33. A**

**Difficulty:** Hard

**Category:** Sentence Structure: Commas, Dashes, and Colons

**Getting to the Answer:** Remember that dashes and parentheses act in similar ways. If the phrase is offering additional information before you get back to the main thrust of the sentence, then a dash is appropriate. A dash is an appropriate way to punctuate the phrase, so **(A)** is the correct choice.

**34. B**

**Difficulty:** Easy

**Category:** Development: Precision

**Getting to the Answer:** Read the entire paragraph to understand the context in which the underlined word appears. Be careful to distinguish between commonly confused words. The paragraph makes it clear that Kelli has started working at BP as a summer intern. The correct answer will convey this meaning. Choice (A), "excepted," meaning "excluded from a group," is a word that is commonly confused with "accepted," which means "to have taken or received something." In this case, Kelli has taken the job offer with BP, making **(B)** the correct choice.

**35. C**

**Difficulty:** Medium

**Category:** Development: Precision

**Getting to the Answer:** Read the entire sentence to determine the context of the underlined word. The context implies that the tasks assigned to interns are low level and meaningless. Choices (B), "skilled," and (D), "challenging," suggest that the tasks are important, which does not match the context. Only **(C)** fits the tone and context of the paragraph and is more precise than "boring."

**36. A**

**Difficulty:** Hard

**Category:** Development: Relevance

**Getting to the Answer:** Identify the central idea and then review the answer choices to find the one that best supports it. The paragraph is about the importance of gaining a real-world perspective on classroom knowledge. Choice **(A)** supports this central idea by showing how Kelli's internship will allow her to apply her classroom knowledge to the real world.

**37. D**

**Difficulty:** Hard

**Category:** Development: Introductions and Conclusions

**Getting to the Answer:** Skim the paragraph to determine what content the sentences have in common. The paragraph discusses the safety training Kelli is required to complete and explains how this training will offer her an advantage over other job applicants. Choice **(D)** most effectively establishes the main topic of the paragraph; it introduces the type of certification Kelli will earn.

**38. A**

**Difficulty:** Medium

**Category:** Development: Precision

**Getting to the Answer:** Analyze the sentence to determine which phrase best fits the context. Choice **(A)** is the correct answer. "Stand out" means that Kelli will clearly be noticed when compared with other applicants.

**39. D**

**Difficulty:** Medium

**Category:** Agreement: Pronouns

**Getting to the Answer:** Examine the structure of the sentence and identify the pronoun or pronouns that match the antecedent. Use the word "everyone" in a simple sentence to determine if it's singular or plural: for example, "Everyone goes." "Everyone" is a singular pronoun referring to a person, so it requires a singular possessive pronoun. Using the plural "their" is accepted only in informal usage. Choice **(D)** is the correct answer because it correctly matches the antecedent in number and appropriately identifies both gender options, since the antecedent did not specify a gender.

**40. A**

**Difficulty:** Medium

**Category:** Sentence Structure: Commas, Dashes, and Colons

**Getting to the Answer:** Determine the need for punctuation within the sentence. "For" and "from" are both prepositions, a clue that both phrases are correctly set off with commas. Because both phrases are dependent on the remainder of the sentence, they are correctly connected with commas. Choice **(A)** is correct.

## 41. B

**Difficulty:** Easy

**Category:** Agreement: Verbs

**Getting to the Answer:** In a sentence with a series of actions, make sure all verbs or verb forms are parallel. Focusing on the action verbs, it becomes clear that they should all end in "*-ing*." Inconsistencies in this pattern result in a lack of parallel structure. Choice **(B)** is correct, as it uses the gerund form (nouns formed by adding "*-ing*" to verbs) of all four action verbs.

## 42. D

**Difficulty:** Medium

**Category:** Sentence Structure: The Basics

**Getting to the Answer:** Identify the subject and predicate of each sentence to determine if it is a complete sentence or a fragment. As the sentences are written in (A), the first one is an incomplete sentence, or fragment. Only **(D)** correctly and concisely combines the two to eliminate the fragment.

## 43. C

**Difficulty:** Medium

**Category:** Organization: Conciseness

**Getting to the Answer:** Often, when a sentence is long, it's a good idea to see if there are ways to edit out certain words or phrases to make the sentence more concise. Choice **(C)** is correct. By leaving out the phrase "though she is losing her summer," this answer choice conveys the intended meaning of the sentence with logical and concise language.

## 44. B

**Difficulty:** Medium

**Category:** Graphs

**Getting to the Answer:** Make sure you understand the information conveyed by the graphic's labels before you attempt to choose the correct answer. The passage informs you that Kelli's chosen field is oil and energy, represented by the bar on the far right of the graphic. Choice **(B)** is the correct answer as it matches the number of oil and energy interns per 1,000 hires noted on the *y*-axis.

# Math Test—No-Calculator

## 1. B

**Difficulty:** Easy

**Category:** Heart of Algebra/Linear Equations

**Getting to the Answer:** In a real-world scenario, the slope of a line represents a unit rate and the *y*-intercept represents a flat fee or a starting amount. The cost of one linear foot is the same as the unit rate (the cost per linear foot), which is represented by the slope of the line. Use the grid lines and the axis labels to count the rise and the run from the *y*-intercept of the line (0, 150) to the next point that hits an intersection of two grid lines. Pay careful attention to how the grid lines are marked (by 5s on the *x*-axis and by 25s on the *y*-axis). The line rises 75 units and runs 5 units, so the slope is $\frac{75}{5} = 15$ dollars per linear foot of fence, which is **(B)**. Note that you could also use the slope formula and two points from the graph to find the unit rate.

## 2. C

**Difficulty:** Easy

**Category:** Passport to Advanced Math/Rational Expressions

**Getting to the Answer:** Don't be tempted—you can't simply cancel one term when a polynomial is divided by a monomial. Instead, find the greatest common factor of *both* the numerator and the denominator. Factor out the greatest common factor from the numerator and from the denominator, and then you can cancel it. The GCF is $12x^2$. Here is the math:

$$\frac{24x^4 + 36x^3 - 12x^2}{12x^2}$$
$$= \frac{12x^2 \left(2x^2 + 3x - 1\right)}{12x^2}$$
$$= 2x^2 + 3x - 1$$

This matches **(C)**.

**3. C**

**Difficulty:** Easy

**Category:** Additional Topics in Math/Geometry

**Getting to the Answer:** Corresponding sides of similar triangles are proportional, so write a proportion (paying careful attention to the order of the sides) using the sides that you know and the side that you're looking for. Then, solve the proportion for the missing side.

Call the missing side $x$. Write a proportion using words first, and then fill in the lengths of the sides that you know:

$$\frac{\text{right side small}\,\triangle}{\text{base of small}\,\triangle} = \frac{\text{right side large}\,\triangle}{\text{base of large}\,\triangle}$$

$$\frac{x}{4} = \frac{2+x}{6}$$

$$6x = 4(2+x)$$

$$6x = 8+4x$$

$$2x = 8$$

$$x = 4$$

The length of $\overline{BE}$ is 4, so **(C)** is correct.

**4. A**

**Difficulty:** Easy

**Category:** Passport to Advanced Math/Quadratics

**Getting to the Answer:** Recognizing the different forms of a quadratic equation can save valuable time on test day. Each of the answer choices is given in vertex form, so start by matching the vertex of the parabola in the graph to the correct equation.

When a quadratic equation is written in vertex form, $y = a(x - h)^2 + k$, the vertex is $(h, k)$. The vertex of the parabola in the graph is $(2, 5)$; therefore, the equation should look like $y = a(x - 2)^2 + 5$. This means you can eliminate (B) and (C). To choose between (A) and (D), consider the value of $a$. The parabola in the graph opens downward, so $a$ must be negative. This means **(A)** is correct.

**5. B**

**Difficulty:** Medium

**Category:** Heart of Algebra/Linear Equations

**Getting to the Answer:** You can approach this question conceptually or concretely. Drawing a quick sketch is most likely the safest approach. Line $L$ shown in the graph rises from left to right, so it has a positive slope. Once reflected over the $x$-axis, it will fall from left to right, so the new line will have a negative slope. This means you can eliminate (C) and (D). Now, draw a quick sketch like the one below of the reflected line on the coordinate plane in your test booklet and count the rise (or fall) and the run from one point to the next:

The reflected line falls 2 units and runs 4 units, so the slope is $-\frac{2}{4}$, which reduces to $-\frac{1}{2}$. Thus, **(B)** is the correct choice.

**6. B**

**Difficulty:** Medium

**Category:** Passport to Advanced Math/Polynomials

**Getting to the Answer:** To answer this question, you need to combine like terms, being careful to distribute negative signs where appropriate. Break the calculation into steps: find $2p$, find $q + r$, and then subtract the results. Arranging the terms in descending order will help keep them organized:

$$2p = 2\left(4x^3 + x - 2\right) = 8x^3 + 2x - 4$$

$$q + r = x^2 - 1 + 3x - 5 = x^2 + 3x - 6$$

$$2p - (q + r) = 8x^3 + 2x - 4 - \left(x^2 + 3x - 6\right)$$

$$= 8x^3 + 2x - 4 - x^2 - 3x + 6$$

$$= 8x^3 - x^2 + 2x - 3x - 4 + 6$$

$$= 8x^3 - x^2 - x + 2$$

This matches **(B)**.

## 7. A

**Difficulty:** Medium

**Category:** Passport to Advanced Math/Quadratics

**Getting to the Answer:** The roots of an equation are the same as its solutions. The answer choices contain radicals, which tells you that the equation can't be factored. Instead, either complete the square or solve the equation using the quadratic formula, whichever you are most comfortable using. The equation is already written in the form $y = ax^2 + bx + c$ and the coefficients are fairly small, so using the quadratic formula is probably the quickest method. Jot down the values that you'll need: $a = 2$, $b = 4$, and $c = -3$. Then, substitute these values into the quadratic formula and simplify:

$$x = \frac{-b \pm \sqrt{b^2 - 4ac}}{2a}$$

$$= \frac{-(4) \pm \sqrt{(4)^2 - 4(2)(-3)}}{2(2)}$$

$$= \frac{-4 \pm \sqrt{16 + 24}}{4}$$

$$= \frac{-4 \pm \sqrt{40}}{4}$$

This is not one of the answer choices, so simplify the radical. To do this, look for a perfect square that divides into 40 and take its square root:

$$x = \frac{-4 \pm \sqrt{4 \times 10}}{4}$$

$$= \frac{-4 \pm 2\sqrt{10}}{4}$$

$$= \frac{-2 \pm \sqrt{10}}{2}$$

Be careful—you can't simplify the answer any further because you cannot divide the square root of 10 by 2, so **(A)** is correct.

## 8. D

**Difficulty:** Medium

**Category:** Heart of Algebra/Systems of Linear Equations

**Getting to the Answer:** Although this question asks where the *graphs* of the functions intersect, it is not necessary to actually graph them. Two graphs intersect at the point where they have the same $x$-value and the same $y$-value. The notations $g(x)$ and $h(x)$ can both be interpreted as "the $y$-value at a given value of $x$," so set $g(x)$ equal to $h(x)$ and solve for $x$. Then, if needed, plug this value into either function to find the corresponding $y$-value. Don't let the fraction intimidate you—you can write $g(x)$ as a fraction over 1 and use cross-multiplication:

$$\frac{3x - 5}{1} = \frac{7x + 10}{4}$$

$$4(3x - 5) = 7x + 10$$

$$12x - 20 = 7x + 10$$

$$5x = 30$$

$$x = 6$$

There is only one answer choice for which the $x$-coordinate is 6, **(D)**, so the graphs of the functions will intersect at $(6, 13)$.

## 9. A

**Difficulty:** Medium

**Category:** Passport to Advanced Math/Exponents

**Getting to the Answer:** When you write an equation *in terms of* a specific variable, you are simply solving the equation for that variable. In this question, you'll need to relate fractional exponents to radicals and understand how to use negative exponents. Be careful—you're not just rewriting the equation, you're solving it for $k$.

Raising a quantity to the one-third power is the same as taking its cube root. Applying a negative exponent to a quantity is the same as writing its reciprocal. Rewrite the equation using these properties and then solve for $k$ using inverse operations. Note that the inverse of taking a cube root of a quantity is cubing the quantity:

$$x = k^{-\frac{1}{3}}$$

$$x = \frac{1}{\sqrt[3]{k}}$$

$$(x)^3 = \left(\frac{1}{\sqrt[3]{k}}\right)^3$$

$$x^3 = \frac{1}{k}$$

$$kx^3 = 1$$

$$k = \frac{1}{x^3}$$

Choice **(A)** is correct.

### 10. D

**Difficulty:** Medium

**Category:** Heart of Algebra/Linear Equations

**Getting to the Answer:** There are two variables and only one equation, so you can't actually solve the equation for *c*. Instead, recall that an equation has infinitely many solutions when the left side is identical to the right side. When this happens, everything cancels out and you get the equation $0 = 0$, which is always true.

Start by simplifying the left side of the equation. Don't forget to distribute the negative sign to both terms inside the parentheses:

$$4x - (10 - 2x) = c(3x - 5)$$
$$4x - 10 + 2x = c(3x - 5)$$
$$6x - 10 = c(3x - 5)$$

Next, quickly compare the left side of the equation to the right side. Rather than distributing the *c*, notice that if *c* were 2, then both sides of the equation would equal $6x - 10$, and it would have infinitely many solutions. Therefore, *c* is 2, which is **(D)**.

### 11. D

**Difficulty:** Medium

**Category:** Heart of Algebra/Inequalities

**Getting to the Answer:** You don't need to separate this compound inequality into pieces. Just remember, whatever you do to one piece, you must do to all three pieces. Don't forget to flip the inequality symbols if you multiply or divide by a negative number. Here, the fractions make it look more complicated than it really is, so start by clearing the fractions by multiplying everything by the least common denominator, 6:

$$0 < 1 - \frac{a}{3} \le \frac{1}{2}$$
$$6(0) < 6\left(1 - \frac{a}{3}\right) \le 6\left(\frac{1}{2}\right)$$
$$0 < 6 - 2a \le 3$$
$$-6 < -2a \le -3$$
$$3 > a \ge \frac{3}{2}$$
$$1.5 \le a < 3$$

Now, read the inequality symbols carefully. The value of *a* is between 1.5 and 3, including 1.5, but *not* including 3, so **(D)** is the correct answer.

### 12. D

**Difficulty:** Hard

**Category:** Heart of Algebra/Inequalities

**Getting to the Answer:** The only way a system of inequalities can have no solution is if the graph consists of two parallel lines with shading in opposite directions so that there is no overlap.

Start by writing each equation in slope-intercept form to help you envision what the graphs will look like. You'll need to multiply the second equation by $-2$, so don't forget to flip the inequality symbol:

$$y - \frac{2}{k}x \le 0 \rightarrow y \le \frac{2}{k}x$$

$$\frac{1}{k}x - \frac{1}{2}y \le -1 \rightarrow -\frac{1}{2}y \le -\frac{1}{k}x - 1 \rightarrow y \ge \frac{2}{k}x + 2$$

Now, think about the graphs. The first equation has a slope of $\frac{2}{k}$, a *y*-intercept of 0, and is shaded below the line. The second equation also has a slope of $\frac{2}{k}$, but it has a *y*-intercept of 2 and is shaded above the line. This means that no matter what value of *k* is used (other than 0), the two lines are parallel and shaded in opposite directions, and thus there are infinitely many values of *k* that result in a system with no solution, **(D)**.

## 13. C

**Difficulty:** Hard

**Category:** Passport to Advanced Math/Exponents

**Getting to the Answer:** When solving a rational equation, start by getting a common denominator. Then, you can set the numerators equal and solve for the variable. Don't forget, however: if the answer produces zero in any denominator, then it is not a valid answer. The denominators are almost the same already; you just need to multiply the top and bottom of the first term by 2, factor the denominator of the second term, and you'll be ready to solve the equation:

$$\frac{2}{2}\left(\frac{4x}{x-7}\right) + \frac{2x}{2x-14} = \frac{70}{2(x-7)}$$

$$\frac{8x}{2(x-7)} + \frac{2x}{2(x-7)} = \frac{70}{2(x-7)}$$

Now that the denominators are all the same, you can solve the equation represented by the numerators:

$$8x + 2x = 70$$
$$10x = 70$$
$$x = 7$$

Be careful—this isn't the correct answer. Because there are variables in the denominator, you must check the solution to make sure it isn't extraneous, or in other words, doesn't cause a zero in the denominator of any term. Here, if $x = 7$, then all of the denominators are zero (and division by zero is not possible), so the equation has no solution, **(C)**.

## 14. B

**Difficulty:** Hard

**Category:** Additional Topics in Math/Geometry

**Getting to the Answer:** The shortest distance from $A$ to $B$ is through the center of the circle, along the diameter, which is twice the radius. When the equation of a circle is written in the form $(x-h)^2 + (y-k)^2 = r^2$, you can easily find the center and the radius of the circle. To find $r$, complete the square for the $x$ terms and for the $y$ terms. Start by reordering the terms. Then, take the coefficient of the $x$ term and divide it by 2, square it, and add the result to the two terms with $x$ variables. Do the same with the $y$ term. Remember, you must also add

these amounts to the other side of the equation. This creates a perfect square of $x$ terms and $y$ terms, and the equation will look more like a circle:

$$x^2 + y^2 + 6x - 4y = 12$$
$$x^2 + 6x + y^2 - 4y = 12$$
$$\left(x^2 + 6x + 9\right) + \left(y^2 - 4y + 4\right) = 12 + 9 + 4$$
$$(x+3)^2 + (y-2)^2 = 25$$

This means that the radius of the circle is $\sqrt{25} = 5$, so the diameter is 10, which is also the distance from $A$ to $B$, making **(B)** correct. Note that you can do a quick check of your work by looking at the center; according to the equation, the center is $(-3, 2)$, which appears to match the location of the center on the graph.

## 15. C

**Difficulty:** Hard

**Category:** Passport to Advanced Math/Functions

**Getting to the Answer:** The key to answering this question is in having a conceptual understanding of function notation. Here, the input $(x-1)$ has already been substituted and simplified in the given function. Your job is to determine what the function would have looked like had $x$ been the input.

To keep things organized, let $u = x - 1$, the old input. This means $x = u + 1$. Substitute this into $g$ and simplify:

$$g(x-1) = 3x^2 + 5x - 7$$
$$g(u) = 3(u+1)^2 + 5(u+1) - 7$$
$$= 3\left(u^2 + 2u + 1\right) + 5u + 5 - 7$$
$$= 3u^2 + 6u + 3 + 5u + 5 - 7$$
$$= 3u^2 + 11u + 1$$

This means $g(u) = 3u^2 + 11u + 1$. When working with function notation, you evaluate the function by substituting a given input value for the variable in the parentheses. Here, if the input value is $x$, then $g(x) = 3x^2 + 11x + 1$, which matches **(C)**.

## 16. 15

**Difficulty:** Easy

**Category:** Heart of Algebra/Systems of Linear Equations

**Getting to the Answer:** The equilibrium price occurs when the supply and demand are equal. Graphically, this means where the two lines intersect. The lines intersect at the point (6, 15). You can see from the axis labels that price is plotted along the $y$-axis, so the equilibrium price is **$15**.

## 17. 10.5 or 21/2

**Difficulty:** Medium

**Category:** Heart of Algebra/Linear Equations

**Getting to the Answer:** The key word in this question is *linear*. In a real-world scenario that involves a constant rate, you almost always need to find the slope and the initial amount so you can write an equation. The question states that the initial mass of the larva was 10 grams, so all you need to do is find the slope.

Write the information given in the question as ordered pairs (time, mass) so you can find the slope. At $t = 0$, the larva has a mass of 10 grams, so one pair is (0, 10). After 48 hours, the larva has a mass of 14 grams, so a second pair is (48, 14). Now, use the slope formula:

$$m = \frac{y_2 - y_1}{x_2 - x_1}$$
$$= \frac{14 - 10}{48 - 0}$$
$$= \frac{4}{48} = \frac{1}{12}$$

The equation is $y = \frac{1}{12}x + 10$, where $y$ represents the mass of the larva after $x$ hours. Substitute 6 for $x$ to find the mass after 6 hours: $\frac{1}{12}(6) + 10 = \frac{6}{12} + 10 = $ **10.5 grams**.

## 18. 4

**Difficulty:** Medium

**Category:** Passport to Advanced Math/Functions

**Getting to the Answer:** The notation $f(g(x))$ indicates a composition of two functions, which is read "$f$ of $g$ of $x$." It means that the output when $x$ is substituted in $g(x)$ becomes the input for $f(x)$. Use the second table to find that $g(-1)$ is 2. This is your new input. Now, use the first table to find $f(2)$, which is **4**.

## 19. 10

**Difficulty:** Medium

**Category:** Additional Topics in Math/Imaginary Numbers

**Getting to the Answer:** Multiply the two complex numbers just as you would two binomials (using FOIL). Then, combine like terms. The question tells you that $i = \sqrt{-1}$. If you square both sides of the equation, this is the same as $i^2 = -1$, which is a more useful fact. Now, solve:

$$(4 + 3i)(1 - 2i) = 4(1 - 2i) + 3i(1 - 2i)$$
$$= 4 - 8i + 3i - 6i^2$$
$$= 4 - 5i - 6(-1)$$
$$= 4 - 5i + 6$$
$$= 10 - 5i$$

The question asks for $a$ in $a + bi$, so the correct answer is **10**.

## 20. 50.5

**Difficulty:** Hard

**Category:** Passport to Advanced Math/Scatterplots

**Getting to the Answer:** This question requires a conceptual understanding of modeling data and properties of quadratic functions. Because the regression model fits the data exactly, you can use what you know about quadratic functions to answer the question.

The graph of a quadratic function is symmetric with respect to its axis of symmetry. The axis of symmetry occurs at the $x$-value of the vertex, which also happens to be where the maximum (or minimum) of the function occurs. The question tells you this value—it's $x = 56.25$. Because $x = 90$ is 33.75 (because $90 - 56.25 = 33.75$) units to the right of the axis of symmetry, you know that the $y$-value will be the same as the point that is 33.75 units to the left of the axis of symmetry. This occurs at $x = 56.25 - 33.75 = 22.5$. Read the $y$-value from the graphing calculator screenshot to find the answer, which is **50.5**.

## Math Test—Calculator

### 1. D

**Difficulty:** Easy

**Category:** Problem Solving and Data Analysis/Statistics and Probability

**Getting to the Answer:** To reduce the margin of error, the society should use a larger sample size selected from a better representation of the population. The target population is *all* adults, not just those that have gym memberships. Using only adults with gym memberships is likely to skew the results because these respondents probably exercise considerably more than people who do not have gym memberships. This means **(D)** is correct.

### 2. B

**Difficulty:** Easy

**Category:** Heart of Algebra/Inequalities

**Getting to the Answer:** Think about this question conceptually. If the box cannot weigh *more than* 20 pounds (or 20 × 16 ounces), this means it can weigh *that much or less*, so the right half of the inequality you are looking for is $\leq 20 \times 16$. This means you can eliminate (A) and (C) based on the inequality symbol. A box is made up of ballpoint pens, $b$, and mechanical pencils, $m$. Each pen weighs 0.3 ounces, and each pencil weighs 0.2 ounces. The total weight of the box would be the number of pens, $b$, multiplied by their weight, 0.3, added to the number of pencils, $m$, multiplied by their weight, 0.2. So the inequality is $0.3b + 0.2m \leq 20 \times 16$, which matches **(B)**.

### 3. C

**Difficulty:** Easy

**Category:** Heart of Algebra/Linear Equations

**Getting to the Answer:** Finding an $x$-intercept is easy when you know the equation of the line—it's the value of $x$ when $y$ is 0. Everything you need to write the equation is shown on the graph. The $y$-intercept is 5 and the line falls 1 unit and runs 3 units from one point to the next, so the slope is $-\frac{1}{3}$. This means the equation of the line, in slope-intercept form, is $y = -\frac{1}{3}x + 5$. Now, set the equation equal to zero and solve for $x$:

$$0 = -\frac{1}{3}x + 5$$

$$\frac{1}{3}x = 5$$

$$x = 15$$

Line $Q$ will intercept the $x$-axis at 15, which is **(C)**.

### 4. D

**Difficulty:** Easy

**Category:** Passport to Advanced Math/Functions

**Getting to the Answer:** When you see an expression such as $f(x)$, it means to substitute the given value for $x$ in the function's equation. When there is more than one function involved, pay careful attention to which function should be evaluated first. You are looking for the value of $f(x)$ at $x = 3$. Because $f(x)$ is defined in terms of $g(x)$, evaluate $g(3)$ first by substituting 3 for $x$ in the expression $x + 5$:

$$g(3) = 3 + 5 = 8$$
$$f(3) = 2g(3) = 2(8) = 16$$

Choice **(D)** is correct.

### 5. C

**Difficulty:** Easy

**Category:** Problem Solving and Data Analysis/Rates, Ratios, Proportions, and Percentages

**Getting to the Answer:** Pay careful attention to the units. As you read the question, decide how and when you will need to convert units. In this problem, work backward—you need to know how many pages of cards will be printed. To find this number, you first need to know how many cards will be printed. So, start with the number of agents (which tells you the number of boxes) and multiply by the number of cards per box:

$$12 \text{ agents} \times \frac{2 \text{ boxes}}{1 \text{ agent}} \times \frac{225 \text{ cards}}{1 \text{ box}} = 5,400 \text{ cards}$$

Next, use the information about *pages* to finish the calculations:

$$5,400 \text{ cards} \times \frac{1 \text{ page}}{10 \text{ cards}} \times \frac{1 \text{ minute}}{18 \text{ pages}} = 30 \text{ minutes}$$

This means **(C)** is correct.

**6. A**

**Difficulty:** Medium

**Category:** Heart of Algebra/Inequalities

**Getting to the Answer:** The question is asking about $\frac{x}{y}$, so think about how fractions work. Larger numerators result in larger values $\left(\frac{3}{2}\text{, for example, is greater than }\frac{1}{2}\right)$, and smaller denominators result in larger values $\left(\frac{1}{2}\text{, for example, is greater than }\frac{1}{4}\right)$. The largest possible value of $\frac{x}{y}$ is found by choosing the largest possible value for $x$ and the smallest possible value for $y$, which gives $\frac{0.2}{5} = 0.04$, or **(A)**.

**7. A**

**Difficulty:** Medium

**Category:** Problem Solving and Data Analysis/
Statistics and Probability

**Getting to the Answer:** Results from a study can only be generalized to the population from which the sample was taken. Also, keep in mind that positive correlations do not prove causation. The study was conducted by the American Academy of Pediatrics on children in the United States under three, so the sample is American children under three, which means conclusions can only be drawn about *this* population. Also, because correlations do not prove causation, the only conclusion that can be drawn is that there is an association between television time and attention disorders for American children under three years old, **(A)**.

**8. D**

**Difficulty:** Medium

**Category:** Problem Solving and Data Analysis/
Statistics and Probability

**Getting to the Answer:** The greatest change (in absolute value) in miles ridden per week could be an increase or a decrease. You don't have to worry about whether the change is positive or negative, so to keep things simple, always subtract the smaller number from the larger number. Make a list to show the changes in miles ridden per week between each pair of consecutive weeks.

Save yourself some time by skipping weeks that clearly have smaller changes, such as between weeks 1 and 2 and between weeks 3 and 4. Your list would look like this:

Weeks 2–3: $72 - 64 = 8$
Weeks 4–5: $78 - 70 = 8$
Weeks 5–6: $85 - 78 = 7$
**Weeks 6–7: $85 - 75 = 10$**
Weeks 7–8: $82 - 75 = 7$

Of the differences, the greatest is from week 6 to week 7, which is a change of 10 miles, making **(D)** correct.

**9. C**

**Difficulty:** Medium

**Category:** Heart of Algebra/Linear Equations

**Getting to the Answer:** Given two points (even when the coordinates are variables), the slope of the line is $\frac{y_2 - y_1}{x_2 - x_1}$. You are given a numerical value for the slope and a pair of coordinate points with variables. To find the value of $a$, plug the points into the slope formula, and then solve for $a$:

$$\text{Slope} = \frac{y_2 - y_1}{x_2 - x_1}$$
$$5 = \frac{6 - 2a}{a - (a - 1)}$$
$$5 = \frac{6 - 2a}{1}$$
$$5 = 6 - 2a$$
$$-1 = -2a$$
$$\frac{1}{2} = a$$

Choice **(C)** is correct.

**10. A**

**Difficulty:** Hard

**Category:** Heart of Algebra/Systems of Linear Equations

**Getting to the Answer:** Questions about breaking even usually involve creating a system of equations (one for cost and one for revenue), setting the equations equal to each other, and solving for the variable. Create a system of equations at each price point using $n$ for the number of bathtub lifts. Then solve each system. Note that the cost equation will be the same for both systems, and it is already given to you in the question.

$$\text{Old price: } C = 225n + 3{,}150; R = 450n$$
$$C = R$$
$$225n + 3{,}150 = 450n$$
$$3{,}150 = 225n$$
$$14 = n$$

$$\text{New price: } C = 225n + 3{,}150; R = 375n$$
$$C = R$$
$$225n + 3{,}150 = 375n$$
$$3{,}150 = 150n$$
$$21 = n$$

At the old price, the company needed to sell 14 lifts to break even. At the new price, it needs to sell 21 lifts, so it needs to sell $21 - 14 = 7$ more lifts at the new price to break even, which is **(A)**.

**11. B**

**Difficulty:** Medium

**Category:** Additional Topics in Math/Geometry

**Getting to the Answer:** The amount of water needed to create the ice portion of the exhibit is another way of saying the *volume* of the ice. So, you need to find the volume of the entire space and then subtract the volume of the cylinder that runs through the ice. The volume of a rectangular prism is given by $V = l \times w \times h$, and the volume of a cylinder equals the area of its base times its height, or $\pi r^2 h$. To determine the volume of the ice, start by decomposing the figure into two rectangular prisms and adding their volumes. You can decompose

the figure left to right or front to back. Front to back, it looks like the following figure:

The prism in the back has a volume of $32 \times 11 \times 4 = 1{,}408$ cubic feet. The prism in the front has a length of 15 feet and a height of 4 feet, but the width is missing. Find the missing width by subtracting 11 from 25, which is 14 feet. So, the volume of the prism in the front is $15 \times 14 \times 4 = 840$ cubic feet. The total volume of the prisms is $1{,}408 + 840 = 2{,}248$ cubic feet. Be careful—that's not the answer. You still need to find the amount of space taken up by the glycol pipe and subtract it. The diameter of the pipe is 2 feet, so its radius is 1 foot, and the height (or the length in this question) is 32 feet, so the volume is $\pi(1)^2(32) \approx 100.53$ cubic feet. This means the amount of ice needed is $2{,}248 - 100.53 = 2{,}147.47$, or about 2,150 cubic feet, **(B)**.

**12. D**

**Difficulty:** Medium

**Category:** Problem Solving and Data Analysis/Rates, Ratios, Proportions, and Percentages

**Getting to the Answer:** Let the units in this question guide you to the answer. You'll also need to use the answer you found in the previous question. The company will use two hoses, each of which pumps at a rate of 60 gallons per minute, so the rate is actually 120 gallons per minute. Convert the volume you found earlier from cubic feet to gallons, and then use the rate to find the time:

$$2{,}150 \ \cancel{ft^3} \times \frac{7.48 \ \cancel{gal}}{1 \ \cancel{ft^3}} \times \frac{1 \ min}{120 \ \cancel{gal}} = 134 \text{ minutes}$$

The answers are given in hours and minutes, so write 134 minutes as 2 hours and 14 minutes, or about 2 hours and 15 minutes, which is **(D)**.

## 13. C

**Difficulty:** Medium

**Category:** Passport to Advanced Math/Quadratics

**Getting to the Answer:** The graph of every quadratic equation is a parabola, which may or may not cross the x-axis, depending on where its vertex is and which way it opens. Don't forget: if the equation is written in vertex form, $y = a(x - h)^2 + k$, then the vertex is $(h, k)$, and the value of $a$ tells you which way the parabola opens.

The graph of an equation that has *no solution* does not cross the x-axis, so try to envision the graph of each of the answer choices. When a quadratic is written in factored form, the factors tell you the x-intercepts, which means every quadratic equation that can be written in factored form (over the set of real numbers) must have solutions. This means you can eliminate (B) and (D). Now, imagine the graph of the equation in (A): the vertex is (5, 3) and $a$ is negative, so the parabola opens downward and consequently must cross the x-axis. This means you can eliminate (A), and (C) must be correct. The graph of the equation in **(C)** has a vertex of (5, 3) and opens *up*, so it does not cross the x-axis and, therefore, has no solution.

You could also graph each of the answer choices in your graphing calculator, but this is not the most time-efficient way to answer the question.

## 14. A

**Difficulty:** Medium

**Category:** Problem Solving and Data Analysis/Rates, Ratios, Proportions, and Percentages

**Getting to the Answer:** Questions that involve distance, rate, and time can almost always be solved using the formula Distance = rate × time. Use the speed, or rate, of the plane from Boston, 360 miles per hour, and its distance from Chicago, 864 miles, to determine when it arrived. You don't know the time, so call it $t$:

$$\text{Distance} = \text{rate} \times \text{time}$$
$$864 = 360t$$
$$2.4 = t$$

This means it took 2.4 hours for the plane to arrive. This is more than 2 full hours, so multiply 2.4 by 60 to find the number of minutes it took: $60 \times 2.4 = 144$ minutes. Now, determine how long it took the plane from Kansas City. It left at 8:30 a.m. and arrived at 10:34 a.m., so it took 2 hours and 4 minutes, or 124 minutes. This means the plane from Kansas City arrived $144 - 124 = 20$ minutes before the plane from Boston, **(A)**.

## 15. B

**Difficulty:** Hard

**Category:** Problem Solving and Data Analysis/Rates, Ratios, Proportions, and Percentages

**Getting to the Answer:** Break the question into short steps (first part of trip, second part of trip, circling overhead). To get started, you'll need to find the distance for each part of the trip—the question only tells you the total distance. Then, use the formula Distance = rate × time to find how long the plane flew at 200 miles per hour and then how long it flew at 450 miles per hour:

$$\text{First part of trip:} \quad \frac{1}{4} \times 1,200 = 300 \text{ miles}$$
$$300 = 200t$$
$$t = \frac{300}{200} = 1.5 \text{ hours}$$
$$1.5 \times 60 = 90 \text{ minutes}$$

$$\text{Second part of trip:} \quad \frac{3}{4} \times 1,200 = 900 \text{ miles}$$
$$900 = 450t$$
$$t = \frac{900}{450} = 2 \text{ hours}$$
$$2 \times 60 = 120 \text{ minutes}$$

This means the plane flew for a total of $90 + 120 = 210$ minutes. Next, add the time the plane circled overhead: $210 + 25 = 235$ minutes. The total trip took 235 minutes (3 hours and 55 minutes), which means the plane landed at $8:30 + 3$ hours $= 11:30 + 55$ minutes $= 12:25$ p.m., **(B)**.

**16. A**

**Difficulty:** Medium

**Category:** Passport to Advanced Math/Functions

**Getting to the Answer:** The range of a function is the set of possible outputs, or *y*-values, on a graph. For all real values of any number $t$, the value of $t^2$ cannot be negative. This means the smallest possible value of $t^2$ is 0 and, consequently, the smallest possible value of $h(t)$ is $h(0) = \sqrt{0^2 + 9} = \sqrt{9} = 3$. Thus, the number 1 is not in the range of the function, making **(A)** correct.

You could also graph the function in your graphing calculator and examine the possible *y*-values. The graph follows here:

NORMAL FLOAT AUTO REAL RADIAN MP

Notice that the lowest point on the graph is (0, 3), which tells you that the range of the function is $h(t) \geq 3$.

**17. A**

**Difficulty:** Medium

**Category:** Heart of Algebra/Systems of Linear Equations

**Getting to the Answer:** Graphically, the solution to a system of equations is the point or points where the graphs intersect. Whenever a graph with no grid lines or axis labels is shown, you are usually interested primarily in the sign of the coordinates of a point, not the actual values. The graphs intersect in Quadrant 2 of the coordinate plane, so the *x*-value of the point of intersection (or *a*) is negative, and the *y*-value (or *b*) is positive. The question states that $a = -3b$, so you can eliminate (B) right away—the coordinates would have to be equal if their sum was 0. Now try Picking Numbers. Let $b = 1$, which means $a = -3$ and the sum of $a + b$ is $-2$, which is not one of the answer choices. Try another pair: if $b = 2$, then $a = -6$, and the sum is $-4$. This is still not one of the answer choices, but you should see a pattern—the *x*-coordinate will always overpower the *y*-coordinate, resulting in a negative sum, so the correct answer must be **(A)**.

**18. B**

**Difficulty:** Medium

**Category:** Problem Solving and Data Analysis/Statistics and Probability

**Getting to the Answer:** When comparing two data sets for consistency, consider both the data center (mean or median) and the spread (standard deviation or range). Each set of data has a median of 0, and thermostat A also has a mode of 0. Both of these measures indicate good test results. However, thermostat A has a greater range of data. If the company chooses this thermostat, the cooling fan is likely to engage anywhere from −9 degrees below the target temperature to 10 degrees above the target temperature. Although this is within the safe temperature range, it is not as consistent as thermostat B, which engaged the fan within 6 degrees on either side of the target temperature. This means **(B)** is correct.

**19. C**

**Difficulty:** Medium

**Category:** Passport to Advanced Math/Quadratics

**Getting to the Answer:** When a quadratic function is written in factored form, you can find its zeros by setting each factor equal to 0 and solving for the variable. Each of the answer choices is written in factored form, so mentally solve each one by asking yourself what number would make each factor equal to 0. Then find the sum of the results:

Choice (A): $3 + (-3) \neq -3$. Eliminate.
Choice (B): $4 + (-1) \neq -3$. Eliminate.
Choice (C): $1 + (-4) = -3$, so **(C)** is correct.
Choice (D): $6 + (-3) \neq -3$. Eliminate.

**20. D**

**Difficulty:** Hard

**Category:** Passport to Advanced Math/Functions

**Getting to the Answer:** A constant added or subtracted inside a function will shift the function left or right, while a constant added or subtracted from the outside will shift the function up or down. You're looking for the value of $p(0)$, but the graph shows $p(x) - 4$, which means the original graph has been shifted down 4 units. You'll need to find the *y*-value of the graph when $x = 0$, then add 4 to get back up to the original function. The graph passes through the point $(0, 7)$, so $p(0) - 4 = 7$. Add 4 to both sides of the equation to get $p(0) = 7 + 4 = 11$, which is **(D)**.

## 21. A

**Difficulty:** Medium

**Category:** Heart of Algebra/Linear Equations

**Getting to the Answer:** Sometimes writing an equation is the quickest route to answering a question. Assign a variable to the unknown, write the equation in words, and then translate from English into math. The unknown in this question is the number of times Geraldine can wrap the wire around the prism. Call this $n$. Now, write an equation in words: total amount of wire equals distance around the prism times the number of wraps plus the extra on the ends. To fill in the numbers, you'll need to make a few calculations. Because the dimensions of the prism are given in inches, convert the amount of wire to inches as well: 18 feet is equal to $18 \times 12 = 216$ inches. Next, figure out the distance around the prism using the picture. Don't forget, you have to go all the way around: $1.5 + 3.5 + 1.5 + 3.5 = 10$ inches. Finally, read the question again to determine that the *extra on the ends* is $3 + 3 = 6$ inches. Now, you're ready to translate from English into math to write your equation and then solve it:

$$216 = 10n + 6$$
$$210 = 10n$$
$$21 = n$$

Geraldine can wrap the wire around the prism 21 times, which matches **(A)**.

## 22. A

**Difficulty:** Medium

**Category:** Problem Solving and Data Analysis/Statistics and Probability

**Getting to the Answer:** To find a percent change (increase or decrease), use the percent change formula:

$$\text{Percent change} = \frac{\text{new amount} - \text{original amount}}{\text{original amount}} \times 100\%$$

The question asks about the increase *from* July *to* August, so the original amount is the July harvest of squash and the new amount is the August harvest. Read the graph's key and the axis labels carefully. Each grid line represents 5 tons, so the July squash harvest was 15 tons and the August harvest was 25 tons. Substitute these numbers into the percent change formula and simplify:

$$\text{Percent change} = \frac{\text{new amount} - \text{original amount}}{\text{original amount}} \times 100\%$$

$$= \frac{25 - 15}{15} = \frac{10}{15} \approx 0.667 = 67\%$$

The percent increase is about 67 percent, which matches **(A)**.

## 23. D

**Difficulty:** Medium

**Category:** Problem Solving and Data Analysis/Rates, Ratios, Proportions, and Percentages

**Getting to the Answer:** Add reasonable numbers to the graph to help you answer the question. An example follows:

Use the numbers to help you evaluate each statement. It took Liam and Arianna each 30 minutes to walk home, so (A) and (B) are incorrect. Arianna walked 3 miles in 30 minutes, while Liam only walked 2 miles in 30 minutes; their rates are not the same, so (C) is also incorrect. This means **(D)** must be true. Arianna started out farther away than Liam, so she must have walked at a faster rate to arrive at home in the same amount of time.

## 24. B

**Difficulty:** Medium

**Category:** Heart of Algebra/Linear Equations

**Getting to the Answer:** The slopes between sets of points that lie on the same line are equal. You can find the slope between points using the slope formula or by looking for patterns. Before immediately jumping to the slope formula, take a peek at the answer choices—all the x-coordinates of the points are multiples of 4, so looking for a pattern is the quickest way to answer this question. It may help to put all the points in a table (including those given in the question stem), with the x-coordinates arranged from smallest to largest, and then see which point doesn't fit the pattern.

| x | y |
|---|---|
| −4 | −8 |
| 0 | −5 |
| 4 | −1 |
| 8 | 1 |
| 12 | 4 |
| 16 | 7 |

Notice that all the x-coordinates increase by 4, while most of the y-coordinates increase by 3. For the slope between each pair of points to be equal, the y-coordinate at $x = 4$ would need to be −2, not −1, so the point given in **(B)** does not lie on the line.

## 25. A

**Difficulty:** Medium

**Category:** Problem Solving and Data Analysis/Statistics and Probability

**Getting to the Answer:** Identify which pieces of information from the table you need. The question asks for the probability that a randomly chosen person from the study is employed and has a college degree, so you need the total of both females and males with college degrees who are employed compared to all the participants in the study. There are 188 employed females with a college degree and 177 employed males with a college degree for a total of 365 employed people with a college degree out of 800 participants, so the probability is $\frac{365}{800}$, which reduces to $\frac{73}{160}$. **(A)** is correct.

## 26. B

**Difficulty:** Medium

**Category:** Problem Solving and Data Analysis/Scatterplots

**Getting to the Answer:** Translate from English into math. The number of cells in the original sample means the value of the function at 0 hours, or $f(0)$. The first x-value on the graph is 4, not 0, so you'll need to use the values shown in the calculator screenshot to write an equation for the model. Notice that the y-values in the calculator screenshot double as the x-values increase by 1. This means that the model is an exponential growth function of the form $f(x) = f(0) \cdot 2^x$. Choose a point from the calculator screenshot such as (4, 136), substitute the values into the function, and solve for $f(0)$:

$$136 = f(0) \cdot (2)^4$$
$$136 = f(0) \cdot 16$$
$$\frac{136}{16} = f(0)$$
$$8.5 = f(0)$$

The y-axis title tells you that the numbers are given in thousands, so there were 8,500 white blood cells per microliter in the original sample. **(B)** is correct.

You could also work backward from the calculator screenshot by dividing by 2 four times (from 4 hours to 3 hours, 3 hours to 2 hours, 2 hours to 1 hour, and 1 hour to before the patient contracted the disease). The result is $136 \div 2^4 = 136 \div 16 = 8.5$, which in thousands is 8,500, again matching choice **(B)**.

## 27. D

**Difficulty:** Hard

**Category:** Additional Topics in Math/Geometry

**Getting to the Answer:** Drawing a sketch is the key to answering this question. Your sketch might look like the one below:

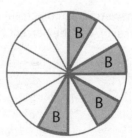

Notice that two radii and an arc form each section, so the amount of steel needed for one section is the length of the radius times 2, plus the length of the outer arc. Once you know this, you can simply multiply by 4.

You are given the total area, which means you can find the radius by substituting $64\pi$ for $A$ in the area formula, $A = \pi r^2$:

$$64\pi = \pi r^2$$
$$64 = r^2$$
$$8 = r$$

For auctions, the arena is divided into 12 equal sections through the center, so divide 360 by 12 to find that the central angle measure for each section is 30 degrees. Now, use the arc length formula:

$$\frac{n°}{360°} \times 2\pi r = \frac{30°}{360°} \times 2\pi(8)$$
$$= \frac{1}{12} \times 16\pi$$
$$= \frac{4\pi}{3}$$

The amount of steel needed for one section is $8 + 8 + \frac{4\pi}{3} = 16 + \frac{4\pi}{3}$, so the amount needed for all four sections is $4\left(16 + \frac{4\pi}{3}\right) = 64 + \frac{16\pi}{3}$, which is **(D)**.

### 28. A
**Difficulty:** Hard

**Category:** Heart of Algebra/Linear Equations

**Getting to the Answer:** To write the equation of a line, you need two things—the starting amount ($y$-intercept) and the rate of change (slope). Substitute these values into slope-intercept form of a line ($y = mx + b$), and you have your equation.

The initial amount of water in the tank on Saturday is 70 gallons, so you already know $b$. To find $m$, you'll need to use the information given in the question to write two data points.

The amount of water in the tank *depends* on how long Lena has been filling it, so the number of gallons is the dependent variable and time is the independent variable. This tells you that the data points should be written in the form (time, gallons). At time = 0 on Saturday, the number of gallons is 70, so the data point is (0, 70). After 1 hour and 50 minutes, which is $60 + 50 = 110$ minutes, the tank is full (400 gallons), so another data point is (110, 400). Now, use the slope formula to find

that the rate of change is $\frac{400 - 70}{110 - 0} = \frac{330}{110} = 3$ gallons per minute. Substituting $m$ and $b$ into slope-intercept form results in the equation $y = 3x + 70$, so **(A)** is correct.

### 29. D
**Difficulty:** Hard

**Category:** Problem Solving and Data Analysis/Rates, Ratios, Proportions, and Percentages

**Getting to the Answer:** You need to find the ratio of small units to large units. You're given two ratios: small to medium and medium to large. Both of the given ratios contain medium size units, but the medium amounts (5 and 3) are not identical. To directly compare them, find a common multiple (15). Multiply each ratio by the factor that will make the number of medium units equal to 15:

small to medium: $(3:5) \times (3:3) = 9:15$
medium to large: $(3:2) \times (5:5) = 15:10$

Now that the number of medium units needed is the same in both ratios, you can merge the two ratios to compare small to large directly: 9:15:10. Therefore, the proper ratio of small units to large units is 9:10, which is **(D)**.

### 30. A
**Difficulty:** Hard

**Category:** Problem Solving and Data Analysis/Rates, Ratios, Proportions, and Percentages

**Getting to the Answer:** Think of the rate given in the question in terms of the constant term you see on the right-hand side of the equation. Working together, the two air purifiers can clean the air in 7 hours. This is equivalent to saying that they can clean $\frac{1}{7}$ of the air in 1 hour. If $\frac{1}{7}$ is the portion of the air the two purifiers can clean *together* in 1 hour, then each term on the left side of the equation represents the portion that each purifier can clean *individually* in 1 hour. Because the new model is 3 times as fast as the older model, $\frac{3}{x}$ represents the portion of the air the new model can clean in 1 hour, and $\frac{1}{x}$ represents the portion of the air the older model can clean in 1 hour, which is **(A)**.

**31. 9/26 or .346**

**Difficulty:** Easy

**Category:** Heart of Algebra/Linear Equations

**Getting to the Answer:** Distribute the fractions because the numbers inside each set of parentheses are evenly divisible by the denominators of the fractions by which they are being multiplied:

$$\frac{1}{3}(90x - 12) = \frac{1}{2}(8x + 10)$$
$$30x - 4 = 4x + 5$$
$$26x = 9$$
$$x = \frac{9}{26}$$

**32. 4**

**Difficulty:** Medium

**Category:** Passport to Advanced Math/Exponents

**Getting to the Answer:** When solving any type of equation, you should always think of inverse operations. The inverse of raising a quantity to the $\frac{5}{2}$ power is raising it to the $\frac{2}{5}$ power. Eliminate the exponent using inverse operations and then go from there:

$$n^{\frac{5}{2}} = 32$$
$$\left(n^{\frac{5}{2}}\right)^{\frac{2}{5}} = (32)^{\frac{2}{5}}$$
$$n = 32^{\frac{2}{5}}$$

Now, you have two choices—you can enter this value into your calculator as 32^(2/5) or you can evaluate the number using rules of exponents:

$$32^{\frac{2}{5}} = \left(\sqrt[5]{32}\right)^2 = 2^2 = 4$$

**33. 801**

**Difficulty:** Hard

**Category:** Problem Solving and Data Analysis/Rates, Ratios, Proportions, and Percentages

**Getting to the Answer:** Draw a chart or diagram detailing the various price reductions for each 30-day period. You'll need to make several calculations, so don't round until the final answer.

| Date | Percent of Most Recent Price | Resulting Price |
|---|---|---|
| Jan. 15 | $100 - 40\% = 60\%$ | $\$1{,}848 \times 0.6 = \$1{,}108.80$ |
| Feb. 1 | $100 - 15\% = 85\%$ | $\$1{,}108.80 \times 0.85 = \$942.48$ |
| March 1 | $100 - 15\% = 85\%$ | $\$942.48 \times 0.85 = \$801.108$ |

You can stop here because the item was sold on March 10th. Before gridding in your answer, check that $801 is not less than 30% of the original price: $0.30 \times \$1{,}848 = \$554.40$. It's not, so the final selling price, rounded to the nearest whole dollar, was **$801**.

**34. 2/3 or .666 or .667**

**Difficulty:** Hard

**Category:** Additional Topics in Math/Trigonometry

**Getting to the Answer:** Two angles of the triangle have equal measures, so the triangle is isosceles, which means that drawing an altitude from the top to the base will bisect the base, resulting in two smaller right triangles as shown here:

Now, use $\cos x° = \dfrac{\text{adjacent}}{\text{hypotenuse}}$ to find that $b = \dfrac{8}{12}$, which can be simplified to $\dfrac{2}{3}$.

**35. 3.5 or 7/2**

**Difficulty:** Hard

**Category:** Heart of Algebra/Linear Equations

**Getting to the Answer:** Remember that parallel lines have the same slope. Use the slope formula $m = \frac{y_2 - y_1}{x_2 - x_1}$ to find the slope of $\overline{CD}$. Because $\overline{CD}$ passes through the points $(0, 0)$ and $(2, 4.5)$, its slope is $\frac{4.5 - 0}{2 - 0} = 2.25$. Line $B$ has the same slope and passes through $(0, -1)$, so you can use the slope formula again to find the $y$-coordinate of the given point, $(2, y)$:

$$2.25 = \frac{y - (-1)}{2 - 0}$$
$$2.25 = \frac{y + 1}{2}$$
$$4.5 = y + 1$$
$$3.5 = y$$

The $y$-coordinate of the point is **3.5**.

**36. 3/10**

**Difficulty:** Hard

**Category:** Problem Solving and Data Analysis/Rates, Ratios, Proportions, and Percentages

**Getting to the Answer:** Whenever rates are given in different units, start by converting to the same units. In most cases, converting to the smaller unit avoids fractions and decimals. Start with nickel because the weight is already in ounces: $10.08 \div 24 = \$0.42$ per ounce. Now, find the per-ounce rate for copper. There are 16 ounces in one pound, so three pounds is 48 ounces: $\$8.64 \div 48 = \$0.18$ per ounce. So, if a person were to bring in equal amounts of each, he would receive $0.18 per ounce of copper and $0.42 per ounce of nickel. To find the fractional portion he would receive from the copper, set up a comparison between the amount received for copper and the total amount received, $\$0.18 + \$0.42 = \$0.60$. The portion of the total amount he receives from copper would be $\frac{0.18}{0.60}$, which reduces to $\frac{3}{10}$.

**37. 3**

**Difficulty:** Easy

**Category:** Problem Solving and Data Analysis/ Scatterplots

**Getting to the Answer:** Each grid line along the vertical axis represents 5 units, so look for points that are at least two grid lines away from the line of best fit. The people who have BMIs of 20, 25, and 28 have LDLs that are 10 or more milligrams per deciliter greater than the LDLs predicted by the line of best fit. This represents **3** people.

**38. 24**

**Difficulty:** Medium

**Category:** Problem Solving and Data Analysis/ Scatterplots

**Getting to the Answer:** A line of best fit serves as an approximation of data from which you can estimate an output for a given input (or vice versa). The key is in reading the axis labels carefully. To determine the requested BMI, find the LDL level of 140 (which is already reported in milligrams per deciliter) on the vertical axis. The question says "Based on the line of best fit," so trace over to the line (*not* to the closest data point) and then down to the corresponding value on the horizontal axis, which represents BMI. You should end up just slightly to the right of the 24 line. Be sure to follow directions. The closest whole number approximation is **24**.

# Essay Test Rubric

## The Essay Demonstrates...

| 4—Advanced | • **(Reading)** A strong ability to comprehend the source text, including its central ideas and important details and how they interrelate, and effectively use evidence (quotations, paraphrases, or both) from the source text.<br><br>• **(Analysis)** A strong ability to evaluate the author's use of evidence, reasoning, and/or stylistic and persuasive elements and/or other features of the student's own choosing; make good use of relevant, sufficient, and strategically chosen support for the claims or points made in the student's essay; and focus consistently on features of the source text that are most relevant to addressing the task.<br><br>• **(Writing)** A strong ability to provide a precise central claim; create an effective organization that includes an introduction and conclusion, as well as a clear progression of ideas; successfully employ a variety of sentence structures; use precise word choice; maintain a formal style and objective tone; and show command of the conventions of standard written English so that the essay is free of errors. |
|---|---|
| 3—Proficient | • **(Reading)** Satisfactory ability to comprehend the source text, including its central ideas and important details and how they interrelate, and use evidence (quotations, paraphrases, or both) from the source text.<br><br>• **(Analysis)** Satisfactory ability to evaluate the author's use of evidence, reasoning, and/or stylistic and persuasive elements and/or other features of the student's own choosing; make use of relevant and sufficient support for the claims or points made in the student's essay; and focus primarily on features of the source text that are most relevant to addressing the task.<br><br>• **(Writing)** Satisfactory ability to provide a central claim; create an organization that includes an introduction and conclusion, as well as a clear progression of ideas; employ a variety of sentence structures; use precise word choice; maintain an appropriate formal style and objective tone; and show control of the conventions of standard written English so that the essay is free of significant errors. |
| 2—Partial | • **(Reading)** Limited ability to comprehend the source text, including its central ideas and important details and how they interrelate, and use evidence (quotations, paraphrases, or both) from the source text.<br><br>• **(Analysis)** Limited ability to evaluate the author's use of evidence, reasoning, and/or stylistic and persuasive elements and/or other features of the student's own choosing; make use of support for the claims or points made in the student's essay; and focus on relevant features of the source text.<br><br>• **(Writing)** Limited ability to provide a central claim, create an effective organization for ideas, employ a variety of sentence structures, use precise word choice, maintain an appropriate style and tone, or show control of the conventions of standard written English, resulting in certain errors that detract from the quality of the writing. |

| 1—Inadequate | • **(Reading)** Little or no ability to comprehend the source text or use evidence from the source text. |
| | • **(Analysis)** Little or no ability to evaluate the author's use of evidence, reasoning, and/or stylistic and persuasive elements; choose support for claims or points; or focus on relevant features of the source text. |
| | • **(Writing)** Little or no ability to provide a central claim, organization, or progression of ideas; employ a variety of sentence structures; use precise word choice; maintain an appropriate style and tone; or show control of the conventions of standard written English, resulting in numerous errors that undermine the quality of the writing. |

## Sample Essay Response #1 (Advanced Score)

Anyone who watches NFL football every Sunday is most likely aware that the athletes on the field make a significant amount of money for their efforts. The NFL generates a lot of income from television contracts, corporate sponsors, and advertisers, and the teams themselves benefit from ticket and merchandise sales. The players in turn are paid market-appropriate salaries. Anyone who watches college football games on Saturday will see similar, if slightly younger athletes, yet how much are those players making? The author of this article correctly notes these players don't earn a salary, and that's something he would like to correct. His argument? College athletes deserve compensation for their work just like any other employee.

The author begins by detailing how much money corporations, athletic conferences, and universities make from advertising and sponsor revenue. The Pacific-12 conference, for example, "signed television rights deals worth $3 billion." Speaking of television, CBS and Turner Broadcasting made a lot of money as well—thirty seconds of commercial advertising during the Final Four cost $700,000. Schools with successful programs also do well. The article points out that the University of Texas football program netted $77.9 million in 2011–2012.

The author uses this evidence to portray corporations, athletic conferences, and universities as the "unscrupulous tycoons from a Dickens novel." Those familiar with Dickens can picture more than one wealthy character who doesn't care for the working poor left eking out miserable lives in relative poverty. And who are these working poor? Student athletes, of course! The author uses the Dickens metaphor to convince the reader that corporations, athletic conferences, and universities do not have the student athletes' interests at heart. He then pivots to how much the athletes make for their efforts on behalf of the "unscrupulous tycoons"—absolutely nothing.

How much is the average student scholarship worth? According to the author, most leave a few thousand dollars in yearly out-of-pocket expenses to the student in spite of an average "forty hours a week" dedicated to their sport. And if an athlete is unable to play due to injury, even that scholarship money can be revoked. The author uses this information to compare a student athlete with an employee who benefits from federal and state labor laws. The comparison is painfully clear and made even more so when the author points out that student athletes do not have the right to unionize.

Throughout his essay, the author has effectively painted a Dickensian picture in which student athletes literally sweat, strain, and toil under the watchful eye of their universities, while those in power rake in millions of dollars. The evidence presented convincingly leads the reader to one conclusion: that student athletes deserve to be compensated.

## Sample Essay Response #2 (Proficient Score)

Anyone who watches NFL football Sunday knows that those players make a lot of money. They make so much money because the teams and the league make money from television and advertising. But what about college football players or other college athletes? They don't make any money at all. The author thinks that isn't right. He argues that student athletes should get paid for their work just like anyone else.

The author talks about how much money schools, conferences, and corporations make off of college sports. It's a lot of money. For example, a television deal was worth $3 billion for the Pacific-12 conference, and it cost $700,000 for a television commercial during the Final Four basketball tournament. The author includes this to make the point that other people make a lot of money, but student athletes don't. This helps the reader feel some sympathy for the players and supports the author's argument that they should be paid.

The author then turns to a comparison of student athletes and employees. Student athletes don't earn salaries. They do get a scholarship, but that still leaves many of them short of money to pay the bills. They work forty hours a week. If they are hurt, then they may lose their scholarship because they can't play. The author talks about this to compare how student athletes earn money with how typical employees earn money. Employees have legal rights, but student athletes don't really have any. This is a good comparison, and it makes the reader believe that student athletes should be paid like employees, which is the author's concluding point.